# DOSTOEVSKY

The bust of Dostoevsky on his grave

# DOSTOEVSKY

## The Mantle of the Prophet

### 1871–1881

JOSEPH FRANK

PRINCETON UNIVERSITY PRESS
PRINCETON
AND OXFORD

Copyright © 2002 by Princeton University Press
Published by Princeton University Press,
41 William Street, Princeton, New Jersey 08540
In the United Kingdom:
Princeton University Press, 3 Market Place,
Woodstock, Oxfordshire OX20 1SY

Library of Congress Cataloging-in-Publication Data
Frank, Joseph (1918–)
Dostoevsky: the mantle of the prophet, 1871–1881 / Joseph Frank.
p.  cm.
Includes bibliographical references and index.
ISBN 0-691-08665-6 (cloth : alk. paper)
1. Dostoyevsky, Fyodor, 1821–1881.
2. Novelists, Russian—19th century—Biography.
3. Russia—Intellectual life—1801–1917.
I. Title: Mantle of the prophet, 1871–1881.  II. Title.
PG3328 .F678 2002
891.73′3—dc21
[B]          2001038749

British Library Catalogining-in-Publication Data is available

This book has been composed in Adobe Utopia
Designed by Jan Lilly

Printed on acid-free paper. ∞

www.pup.princeton.edu

Printed in the United States of America

3 5 7 9 10 8 6 4 2

This final volume, like my first,
is dedicated to my wife,
Marguerite, my lifelong companion,
critic, and inspiration.

And to our
daughters Claudine and Isabelle,
and grandchildren Sophie and Henrik.

# CONTENTS

CONTENTS

# LIST OF ILLUSTRATIONS

Unless otherwise noted, all illustrations are from *Feodor Mikhailovich Dostoevsky v Portretakh, illyustratsiyakh, dokumentakh,* ed. V. S. Nechaeva (Moscow, 1972).

This is the fifth and final volume of my series of books on Dostoevsky. It marks the end of a long journey, and if someone, many years ago, had told me that I should someday embark on it, I would certainly have replied that nothing was more unlikely. Before undertaking the present work I had been primarily interested in contemporary literature, and had published a volume of essays (*The Widening Gyre*) that included "Spatial Form in Modern Literature," still recognized as an important contribution to the aesthetics of the modern novel. I saw myself primarily as a literary critic, not as a biographer or cultural historian, though I had no objection to using whatever information was relevant to the better understanding of a work of art. My original project was thus to undertake a single, reasonably sized volume on Dostoevsky, devoted mainly to his novels. But by the time I came to write a first draft, the very nature of my approach made it almost inevitable that my initial intention would grow in size and scope. Indeed, it continued to do so even after I was well under way; and on completing my second volume, I realized that what had become a four-volume project would have to be extended to five.

My concern with Dostoevsky, as I explained in the preface to my first volume, had grown out of my interest in French Existentialism. For Sartre and Camus, a work such as *Notes from Underground*, and characters such as Raskolnikov (in *Crime and Punishment*) and Kirillov (in *The Devils*), had become essential landmarks to which they referred in defining their own points of view. (And of course it was not only for French Existentialists that Dostoevsky was important; his picture hung in Heidegger's study throughout his lifetime.) But the more I read him, the more dissatisfied I became with the usual interpretations I encountered. Either he was viewed largely in purely personal, psychological terms, or he was discussed in relation to the general philosophical and theological issues raised in his novels; and these were frequently, as in the case of Existentialism, linked to one or another contemporary philosophical movement, beginning with the Nietzschean vogue of the late nineteenth century.

It is impossible to read Dostoevsky, however, without becoming aware that his major characters are deeply involved in the social-political ideologies and problems of their time; but his own so-called political ideas seemed so eccentric that hardly anyone took them seriously. Indeed, it was felt necessary to get them out of the way if one were to do him justice as a novelist. I still recall an article by Philip Rahv on *The*

*Devils* many years ago, in which, while praising Dostoevsky's prophetic insight into the dangers of Russian radicalism, the critic carefully explained that he had known nothing about Socialism. But if he could read the future of Socialism in Russia with such clairvoyance, how could he have been so ignorant of what its doctrines really represented?

Questions such as these arose for me regarding other works as well, and I found highly unsatisfactory the general notion that, since Dostoevsky's involvement with the ideologies of his time seemed so unsympathetic, it was best either to forget about them or to expatiate on the vast difference between literary creativity and social-political sobriety. Moreover, the more I learned about the actual social-cultural context from which his writings had emerged, the more I began to feel that the usual opinion should be entirely reversed, and that it was necessary to study their ideological background very carefully. To be sure, this analysis had been undertaken very conscientiously in contemporary Russian criticism and scholarship of the last half-century, and I have drawn freely and gratefully on its results. But, as I also became aware, these scholars were forced to adopt a view of Russian cultural history that placed severe constraints on how they could interpret the role played by Dostoevsky in their own past. There thus seemed to be room for a study unhampered by such limitations, one that probed his point of departure with as much objectivity and impartiality as possible.

Of course, Dostoevsky's genius raised the problems he was dramatizing to moral-philosophical heights involving the most crucial questions of Judeo-Christian thought and experience. My aim was certainly not to remove them from this empyrean realm; but these questions had been posed for him in the Russian terms of his own time and place, and if we are to follow the trajectory by which they were elevated to a level rivaling that of great poetic tragedy, it seemed to me necessary to grasp their point of origin as accurately as could be done.

My own attempt along these lines began with *Notes from Underground.* It was in grappling with this text that I began to understand the complexity of the relations in his writings between psychology and ideology, and how important it was for a proper comprehension of the first to identify its roots in the social-cultural context of the second. Once launched, I continued to investigate other works from the same point of view, and finally to study his creative career as a whole. But I thought it essential, as a literary critic, not only to explore this context but also to show how it could be applied to offer fresher views of Dostoevsky's artistic aims and accomplishments.

Each of my previous books has thus been dominated by the ideology of the period in which Dostoevsky was creating, and in this final one I focus on the relatively unexplored relation of his novels of the 1870s to the doctrines of Russian Populism. Since I was, however, writing for American readers who had only the haziest knowledge (if any at all) of Russian cultural history, this meant filling in the background at some length. It was this necessity that ultimately compelled me, as the pages piled up, to abandon my one-volume idea and to settle down for the long haul.

In a colloquium held at Stanford University in 1989, devoted to the writings of Ian Watt and myself, I was asked whether it was really essential to devote so many volumes to a single author (three had been published by then). As I recall, I replied that if I were writing about him only as an individual, so many volumes might not be necessary; but since in fact I was also writing a condensed history of nineteenth-century Russian culture, with Dostoevsky at the center, I felt that my voluminosity was not unjustified. Indeed, he had focused all the problems of that culture in his great novels—not on the level in which they ordinarily appeared to his contemporaries, but transforming them in terms of his own eschatological and messianic vision. And the rapturous response which this vision evoked in its own time makes it all the more important to clarify it for our own.

OVER the years, I have noted in my various volumes all the people to whom I felt grateful for their aid and support. It would take too long to list here all their names again, but I can see them with my mind's eye, and I should like to invoke their united presences once more as the work(s) they helped to foster and encourage is brought to an end.

My thanks also go to the members of my department at Stanford, who have spurred me on by their appreciation of my past books and their eagerness to see the next. I am especially grateful to my chairman, Grigory Freidin, whose conversations about Russian culture, whether nineteenth- or twentieth-century, are always enormously stimulating, and who has done everything in his power from a practical point of view to aid my work.

Two Slavist colleagues and friends from other universities have also placed me very deeply in their debt. Both Gary Saul Morson of Northwestern and Caryl Emerson of Princeton have been kind enough to go over my original manuscript with a fine-tooth comb, and have helped me to improve it considerably in response to their suggestions. I cannot thank them enough for their devoted labor of friendship.

This particular volume, for various reasons, proved to be very difficult to write, and I should like once more to express my gratitude to my copyeditor at Princeton University Press, Gretchen Oberfranc, with whose patience and skill I had long been familiar. But now her advice proved of importance as well as I went from one version to another;

and she generously approved of my doing so even though this increased the burden of her own work.

In addition, I feel it incumbent to express my gratitude to the cohort of Russian scholars and critics who toiled for so many years over the splendid Academy edition of Dostoevsky's works in thirty volumes, sometimes at the cost of advancement in their own careers. Dostoevsky was not a politically correct writer for the Soviet establishment, and those who devoted their labors to him did so at some risk. Time and again I have thanked such scholars in my thoughts as I benefited from their labors, which produced a gold mine of material not only on Dostoevsky but on the whole cultural, literary, and political world in which he lived. Here, I should like to express these thanks publicly to a whole list of names with which I am very familiar but have never met.

For more personal reasons, my gratitude also goes out to the many friends in Princeton, Paris, and Stanford who have provided emotional sustenance and support during the many years when this series of books was being written, and who have all been mentioned in earlier volumes. Among these I should like to single out here Jacques Catteau, my friend and fellow Dostoevskian, who did me the great honor of sponsoring the award of the honorary doctorate that I received from the Sorbonne in 1999, and whose generous *éloge* of my work spurred me on to its completion.

Each of my volumes has included a tribute to my wife, Marguerite, who has always taken time off from her own work as a mathematician to give me the benefit of her rigorous mind and linguistic and literary sensitivity. This has often led to major revisions both of structure and style, and in the case of the present volume her aid was more vital than ever. I submitted a first draft of the manuscript to the press about which I had some doubts myself; and these were confirmed by her criticisms (especially of the handling of the *Diary of a Writer*) and suggestions of how it might be reorganized. I thus decided to withdraw the manuscript and rewrite it in large part, and during every step of the way there were very few occasions when I did not follow her editorial and stylistic recommendations. Nothing I can say will adequately express what every one of my books, and this one in particular, owes to her participation.

Last but by no means least, I should like to thank a foundation, which wishes to remain anonymous, for the generosity of its unsolicited support of my work.

The problem of transliteration is always a difficult one, and I have opted for the simplest solution. For all Russian words, names, or otherwise, I use System I in the transliteration chart contained in J. Thomas Shaw, *The Transliteration of Modern Russian for English Language Publications* (Madison, Milwaukee, and London, 1967), 8–9. I have, however, occasionally inserted a "y" to indicate a soft sound where this would not be the natural pronunciation of the transliterated word in English, even though System I does not pay any attention to this feature of Russian. And I have always used English forms, rather than transliteration, where such exist and have become customary (Alexander rather than Aleksandr, for example).

Citations to Dostoevsky's texts and correspondence are made to the volumes of the great Academy of Sciences edition: F. M. Dostoevsky, *Polnoe Sobranie Sochinenii*, 30 vols. (Leningrad, 1972–1980). For the other texts cited here, I have used the excellent new translation of the *Diary of a Writer* by Kenneth Lantz. *A Raw Youth* has been translated both by Constance Garnett and Andrew McAndrew, and I have consulted both. For *The Brothers Karamazov*, I have used mainly the translation of Constance Garnett revised by Ralph Matlaw, but supplemented with the versions of Richard Pevear and Larissa Volokhonsky, as well as that of Ignat Avsey. Dostoevsky's letters have been cited mainly from the complete translation by Donald Lowe but also from the selection translated by Andrew McAndrew.

All citations have been checked with the Russian text and alterations made whenever necessary.

PART I

# A New Beginning

Parched with the spirit's thirst, I crossed
An endless desert sunk in gloom,
And a six-winged seraph came
Where the tracks met and I stood lost.
Fingers light as dream he laid
Upon my lids; I opened wide
My eagle eyes, and gazed around.
He laid his fingers on my ears
And they were filled with roaring sound:
I heard the music of the spheres,
The flight of angels through the skies,
The beasts that crept beneath the sea,
The heady uprush of the vine;
And, like a lover kissing me,
He rooted out this tongue of mine
Fluent in lies and vanity;
He tore my fainting lips apart
And, with his right hand steeped in blood,
He armed me with a serpent's dart;
With his bright sword he split my breast;
My heart leapt to him with a bound;
A glowing livid coal he pressed
Into the hollow of the wound.
There in the desert I lay dead,
And God called out to me and said:
"Rise, prophet, rise, and hear, and see,
And let my works be seen and heard
By all who turn aside from me,
And burn them with my fiery word."

A. S. Pushkin, "The Prophet"
(trans. D. M. Thomas)

## CHAPTER 1

# Introduction

The last ten years of Dostoevsky's life, the subject of the present volume, mark the end of an extraordinary literary career and of a life that touched both the heights and depths of Russian society. It became customary during these years, even among people who disagreed (and sometimes quite violently) with Dostoevsky on social-political issues, to regard him with a certain reverence, and to feel that his words incarnated a prophetic vision illuminating Russia and its destiny. One of his favorite poems, which he often read aloud, was Pushkin's powerfully evocative "The Prophet"; and each time he did so, his mesmerized listeners invariably felt that he was assuming this function himself. The unprecedented stature he attained astonished even his friends and admirers, and transcended all personal and political boundaries. In the eyes of the vast majority of the literate public, he became a living symbol of all the suffering that history had imposed on the Russian people, as well as of all their longing for an ideal world of (Christian) brotherly love and harmony.

A number of factors contributed to the unique status that Dostoevsky enjoyed during the 1870s. His now little-read *Diary of a Writer*, a monthly periodical written entirely by himself for two years, commented on the passing scene with passion, verve, and eloquence, and also included literary reminiscences, short stories, and sketches. This personal periodical was an enormous success, reaching a larger audience than any previous journal of comparable intellectual seriousness; and although many of its ideas do not represent Dostoevsky at his best, they elicited a wide response that made him the most important public voice of the time. It was the *Diary of a Writer*, in combination with his appearances on the platform as reader and speaker, that helped to create his "prophetic" status. Moreover, during the last two years of his life he held all of literate Russia spellbound with the monthly installments of his greatest novel, *The Brothers Karamazov*. Its gripping theme placed the murder of a father in a vast religious and moral-philosophical context; and no Russian reader of the time could avoid associating its deeply probing pages with the increasingly frequent attempts then being made to assassinate the Tsar.

Nor was Dostoevsky averse to assuming such a prophetic role, one that he could well have felt had been accorded to him by destiny itself. His life had placed him in an extraordinary position from which to understand the problems of Russian society, and his artistic-ideological evolution embodies and expresses all the conflicts and contradictions that made up the panorama of Russian social-cultural life. Moreover, at no moment was Russian opinion more ready to seek guidance than in the crisis period the country was then living through. This stormy and unsettled time reached its climax, just a month after Dostoevsky's own death, with the assassination of Alexander II, the Tsar-Liberator whom he revered.

To place Dostoevsky's triumphal apotheosis in a proper perspective, let us glance briefly at his life up to this point. Born in 1821, he belonged to a family legally classified as nobility according to the table of ranks established by Peter the Great. But this was simply a civil service ranking and did not provide his family with a social status equal to that of the established gentry class of landowners from whom, for example, Turgenev and Tolstoy—Dostoevsky's most important literary contemporaries—were descended. Mikhail Andreevich, Dostoevsky's father, was an army doctor who had risen through the ranks, and his parents had belonged to the provincial clergy, a group in Russia whose prestige was far from elevated. The family of his mother was of the merchant class, and though it had acquired a certain degree of cultivation, this origin still placed it on the lower rungs of the Russian social ladder. Dostoevsky's own position in the Russian hierarchy was thus ambiguous. He was legally, but not socially, equal to the scions of the gentry; and from remarks in a letter about Turgenev, we know how greatly he resented the superficial amiability of his typically aristocratic manners. The intensity of Dostoevsky's feeling for the theme of humiliation thus very probably sprang from the anomalies of his own situation.

Whatever the personal moral defects of Dostoevsky's father, which have been amply explored elsewhere, Mikhail Andreevich conscientiously looked after his family and provided his sons with the best possible education. He sent them to private schools to shield them from corporal punishment, and tutors came to the house to give instruction in French and religion. Dostoevsky recalled having learned to read from a religious primer, and he also remembered the annual pilgrimages with his pious mother to the monastery of the Trinity and Saint Sergei, about sixty versts from Moscow, as well as the visits to the many cathedrals within the city itself. He was thus taught to revere the Russian religious tradition, and attributed a decisive influence on his later development to these early impressions. This religious aspect of his education again sets him off from the usual pattern of the gentry class (though not all, to be sure, since the devout Slavophils were of the same stock). But for the most part, religious faith among the upper class had been undermined by Voltaire and eighteenth-century French thought, and gentry children received very little, if any, instruction in religion, whose precepts of self-sacrifice and reverence for martyrdom they absorbed mainly from their servants.

Dostoevsky's father had destined his two older sons, Mikhail and Feodor, for military careers, and Feodor succeeded in passing the examination for entrance into the Academy for Military Engineers in St. Petersburg. He thus received the education of an officer and a gentleman, though he had no interest whatever in military engineering and apparently no talent for it either. Luckily, the academy also included courses in Russian and French literature, and he emerged with both a genuine appreciation of French Classicism (he particularly admired Racine), as well as an increased knowledge of the very latest productions of socially progressive writers like George Sand and Victor Hugo, with whom he was already partially familiar. Literature had been his passion ever since learning to read, and he had long ago decided that he wanted to become a writer like his idol, Pushkin; he said that if he were not already wearing mourning for his mother, who died in 1837, he would have worn it when Pushkin was killed in a duel in the same year. One of Dostoevsky's greatest public triumphs, just a year before his death in 1881, was the speech he made at the ceremonies accompanying the dedication of a monument to Pushkin in Moscow.

Long believed, according to local rumor, to have been murdered by his serfs, though officially reported as being overcome by an apoplectic stroke, Dostoevsky's father went to his grave in 1839. Some recent investigation has cast doubt on the murder story, based entirely on hearsay and rejected by a judicial investigation at the time; but it has been extremely popular since Freud's famous article on "Dostoevsky and Parricide." It cannot be established whether Dostoevsky himself believed the rumors, well known to the family, that his father had been murdered. A small income from the estate allowed him to resign his army commission in 1844, primarily, no doubt, to devote himself to literature, but also because one of his official duties—the supervision of the disciplinary punishment of flogging—had revolted him to the core. He had begun to write seriously years before, and two of his poetic tragedies, the most prestigious literary genre of the time, have regrettably been lost. He was soon swept up, however, in the new literary movement sponsored by the fiery critic Vissarion Belinsky, who had become converted to Utopian Socialism. Belinsky urged the members of the new Russian literary generation to turn their attention to the world around them, and particularly to follow the lead of the Gogol of *The Overcoat* and *Dead Souls* in revealing the glaring injustices of Russian society. Gogol was very far from being a progressive (quite the contrary!), and his intention was satirical and comic rather than subversive; but his sharp eye for the incongruities of Russian society objectively exposed all of its morally abhorrent reality.

The young writers who grouped themselves around Belinsky's program came to be known as the Natural School, and they included many of the important creators of the nineteenth-century Russian novel—Turgenev and Goncharov as well as Dostoevsky, not to mention the "civic" poet Nekrasov. Dostoevsky's first novel, *Poor Folk* (1845), was hailed by Belinsky as the most important work so far produced under his inspiration, and it immediately brought the young author into the forefront of the Russian literary scene. His personal acquaintance with Belinsky—a vibrantly powerful personality, who left an indelible impression both on his friends and on his time—was to prove of the utmost importance for shaping his own moral-spiritual and ideological evolution. The *Diary of a Writer* abounds in references to Belinsky, and one article in particular, recording a conversation with the great critic some thirty years earlier, contains the nucleus of what was to become the Legend of the Grand Inquisitor.

*Poor Folk* already exemplifies certain features that were to continue to distinguish Dostoevsky's literary artistry. Written in the form of an exchange of letters, it illustrates his preference for a poetics of subjectivity in which his characters directly express their innermost thoughts and feelings; and he will continue to favor dramatic monologues or dialogues, rather than third-person expository narration, in all of his later novels. Even when he uses a third-person narrator, as in his next work, *The Double*, this narrator is never a purely objective, detached observer; he blends with the character's consciousness in a manner anticipating later developments of the stream-of-consciousness technique. *The Double* was not a success, however, being roundly pummeled by Belinsky for centering on an atypical "psychopathic" character—a criticism that continued to be leveled against him throughout his life. Between 1845 and 1849 he tried his hand at various types of stories, but these did not succeed in raising a reputation badly damaged by Belinsky's strictures. They failed primarily because they no longer provided the obvious social pathos so movingly expressed in *Poor Folk*; but Dostoevsky had not lost interest in the social issues then agitating the Russian intelligentsia. He was, rather, experimenting with artistic modes that expressed them more indirectly through their effect on character and personality.

In 1847 he began to frequent the meetings of the Petrashevsky circle, a group of young men who gathered once a week for conviviality and conversation, and who were known as disciples of one or another school of Utopian Socialism (the theories of Charles Fourier predominated).

Dostoevsky did not become a convert to any of these schools and shared the opinion of his friend, the young literary critic Valerian Maikov, that each placed too many constraints on the freedom of the individual to be completely acceptable. (This concern for the freedom of the individual was later to become one of the dominating leitmotifs of Dostoevsky's work.) Nonetheless, he received a thorough schooling in Socialist thought, and this indoctrination left a permanent impress on his ideas and values. The notion of a utopian transformation of earthly life into what would be, in effect, a realization of the Christian ideal of Paradise as a realm of mutual love never ceased to haunt his imagination—though it is very far from clear to what extent he literally believed this might be possible.

The somewhat desultory discussions at the Petrashevsky gatherings became much more animated as a result of the European revolutions of 1848, and the wave of uprisings that swept over Europe did not fail to lap, though feebly, at the shores of Russia. The Petrashevsky, to be sure, were dedicated to peaceful persuasion; but Nikolay Speshnev, probably the prototype of the character of Stavrogin in *The Devils*—and whom Dostoevsky at this time called his "Mephistopheles"—formed a small, secret society inside the larger circle. The purpose of this underground group was to circulate propaganda among the peasantry aimed at stirring up a revolution against serfdom. Dostoevsky rarely participated in the theoretical public discussions of the larger gatherings; but on the few occasions when he did speak, it was to castigate, with passionate indignation, the intolerable injustice of this keystone of the Russian social order. It is thus not surprising that he joined Speshnev's revolutionary group and tried to recruit others to the cause.

In 1849 the Petrashevsky were rounded up by the secret police of Nicholas I, who had decided, in view of the revolutionary groundswell sweeping over Europe, not to tolerate any longer even the discussion of such subversive ideas. However, the existence of the genuinely revolutionary organization in their midst, though suspected, was not discovered in the investigation that ensued, and only uncovered in 1922; indeed, it was not until 1956 that the names of all the seven members came to light. Dostoevsky lived all his life with the knowledge that he had once himself been a revolutionary, who had not recoiled at the idea of bloodshed; and his profound understanding of the psychology of characters attracted to radical ideas may surely be attributed to such a history.

His arrest and its aftermath unquestionably became one of the defining moments (perhaps *the* defining moment) of his life. He was submitted—along with all the others—to the ordeal of a mock execution, and he stood in the second row of those presumably to be shot. He was convinced that his life was shortly to be snuffed out; but though the terror of the moment is communicated in *The Idiot*, it is clear, from the recollections of a fellow Petrashevist, that he also believed in some form of afterlife. To the convinced atheist Speshnev, he said, "We shall be with Christ." But the latter only replied ironically, pointing to the ground, "A handful of dust." This confrontation with eternity marked the transition between the Dostoevsky of the 1840s—a Christian, to be sure, but one essentially focused on the problems of earthly life—and the later Dostoevsky, for whom the origins of the world and of human existence, as he wrote in *The Brothers Karamazov*, lay in other, unearthly realms. The religious-metaphysical Dostoevsky of the great novels emerged from this sadistic charade staged by Nicholas I, though its effects would take a long while to be assimilated and mastered for artistic purposes.

The next four years are of equal importance, but on a different level. Dostoevsky was sent to Siberia and lived in a prison camp, mainly with peasant convicts, many of whom had committed murder. Dostoevsky was thus placed in a situation that few other members of his class had ever been forced to endure, and he always attributed the greatest importance to this exposure—on the basis of a status of equality if not inferiority—to the grim realities of Russian peasant life. He felt that he had acquired a special insight into the Russian folk character as a result of his travails, and that his Calvary, as he later wrote in the *Diary of a Writer*, had led to "the regeneration of [his] convictions."

Dostoevsky had assumed that members of the upper-class intelligentsia could lead the social revolution that he and the Speshnev group had been planning. Through bitter personal experience, he now discovered that the cultural and spiritual gap between the classes was so enormous that no genuine understanding between them was possible; and he became convinced that no tolerable Russian future could begin until this gap was bridged. On a more personal level, his intuition of the importance for the human personality of a sense of its own freedom, already present in his rejection of Socialist blueprints, was immensely broadened and deepened. His observations of his fellow convicts revealed that freedom of the will was not only a social desiderata, not only a religious postulate, but a primordial need of the human personality. Acts that might seem senseless or irrational to a superficial observer sprang irresistibly, among the imprisoned convicts guarded night and day, from "the poignant hysterical craving for self-expression, the unconscious yearning for [one]self, the desire . . . to assert [a] crushed personality, a desire which suddenly takes possession of [someone] and reaches the pitch of fury, of spite, of mental aberration" (4: 66–67). Dostoevsky compared this uncontrollable fury to the reaction of a man buried alive and hopelessly beating on the lid of his coffin; the certain knowledge of futility would not restrain his visceral desperation. From that time on, the notion that rationality or reasonableness could be counted on as a controlling and dominant force in human life seemed to him the height of folly.

At first appalled by the barbarities of his peasant fellow prisoners, Dostoevsky's attitude toward them gradually changed. He came to understand that many of their crimes had been provoked by, and were a revolt against, the pitiless cruelties they had been forced to endure; and he began to detect (or believed he could detect), underneath the brutalities of their surface behavior, the kindness and gentleness he had encountered long ago among the peasants on his father's small estate. In a revelatory sketch, "The Peasant Marey," Dostoevsky depicts his revulsion at the spectacle of the drunkenly carousing peasant convicts on a feast day; but then he recalled the tenderness of Marey, his father's serf, who had calmed and blessed him as a frightened child. Were not all these roisterous savages so many Mareys, if one could look into their hearts? All the more so because, whatever their crimes, they always recognized them as such, and "when [at Easter], with the chalice in his hands, the priest read the words 'accept me, O Lord, even as the thief,' almost all of them bowed down to the ground with the clanking of chains" (4: 177). Dostoevsky's faith in the innately Christian virtues of the Russian peasantry, which he felt he could discern even under the repellent exteriors of hardened peasant criminals, was never shaken in the future and became a crucial—if highly questionable—cornerstone of his later ideology.

On returning to Russia in 1860, after serving for six years as a common soldier and an officer in the Russian Army, Dostoevsky found the social-cultural atmosphere entirely changed. He belonged to the generation of the 1840s, which had been inspired by a French Utopian Socialism imbued with a veneration for Christ, and whose philosophical ideas had been absorbed from the spacious metaphysical horizons of the German Idealism of Hegel, Schelling, and Schiller. A new generation, that of the 1860s, now dominated Russian cultural life; and its leaders, Nikolay Chernyshevsky and N. A. Dobrolyubov, were the sons of priestly families. Educated in religious seminaries but disillusioned with the church, they had been converted to social-political radicalism and sought their philosophical nurture in the atheism of Feuerbach, the materialism and rationalism of eighteenth-century French thought, and the English Utilitarianism of Jeremy Bentham. Russian radicalism thus acquired a new ideological basis, which was formulated by Chernyshevsky as a doctrine of "rational egoism."

At the same time, the social-political climate of the country was also undergoing a momentous change. The new Tsar, Alexander II, had decided to abolish serfdom, and this great event, which took place relatively peacefully in 1861, made a profound impression on Dostoevsky. He had been sent to Siberia because of his hatred of this detestable enslavement of the vast majority of the population, and it had been eliminated by "the hand of the Tsar"—without the bloody revolutions that had been required to improve the conditions of the lower classes in Europe (not to mention the Civil War then raging in the United States). Dostoevsky was thus confirmed even more strongly in his conviction, which he had expressed as early as his Petrashevsky days, that Russia need not look to Europe for the solution to its indigenous social problems. Moreover, he had long since become convinced that the Russian people (the peasants) would not respond to revolutionary agitators from the intelligentsia propagating essentially European panaceas. What he feared most was that such agitation would slow down or obstruct the reforms that the Tsar-Liberator was pursuing, not only with regard to the serfs but also in the army, the court system, and other areas of government.

Dostoevsky returned to the literary life of the early 1860s as the editor of two journals, *Vremya* (*Time*) and *Epokha* (*Epoch*), which advocated a doctrine called *pochvennichestvo* (from *pochva*, native soil). It urged the Europeanized Russian intelligentsia, and the upper class in general, to return to the values of their native soil. In their turn, the intelligentsia would bring home from their European education the presumably civilizing benefits of their cultivation; but this latter aspect of the program became less and less significant as time went on. For Dostoevsky, the alienated intelligentsia were obligated to take the first step toward bridging the abyss by assimilating the beliefs and psychology of the people, rooted in their traditional religious faith. The radicals, on the other hand, having become dissatisfied with the economic terms under which the serfs had been liberated, were attempting to stir up trouble; and Dostoevsky opposed their agitations because they were provoking the reaction that he feared. More important, though, the doctrine of "rational egoism" clashed sharply and profoundly with the reshaping of his convictions that had resulted from his arrest and prison camp years. To believe that all the needs and desires of the human personality could be satisfied by reason was for him the most short-sighted naïveté; and to take egoism as the basis of a moral philosophy was not simply self-contradictory but could justify the worst abuses. After Siberia, Dostoevsky had come to regard the Christian values of love and self-sacrifice as an ineradicable possession of the Russian moral-social psyche, and as the sole ray of light shining in the midst of the surrounding moral darkness.

*House of the Dead*, a semifictional autobiography of his prison camp experiences, was hailed unanimously and restored Dostoevsky's literary reputation. Written in a style totally different from the psychological explorations of his novels, it also reveals the versatility of his talent; and this sharply observed and objectively written memoir was greatly admired by Tolstoy, who was quite critical of certain features of the better-known fiction. No one before had ever exposed this secluded world of the prison camps, or exhibited so much understanding and sympathy for its inhabitants. Dostoevsky's next important work, his novella *Notes from Underground*, went largely unnoticed, but is now rightly considered a highly original creation. The predecessor of a whole line of modern portraits of cynical and atrabilious characters, it is also the prelude to Dostoevsky's own great creative period.

Here he launches a full-scale attack against the premises of radical ideology by dramatizing its consequences on the personality of his now-famous underground man. He penetratingly depicts a character filled with repressed resentment and rage against both himself and others, and traces all his malignant traits to the acceptance of certain radical ideas. No other writer equals Dostoevsky in his ability to portray this relation between ideas and their effects on the human personality. What would it really mean for human behavior if one *accepted*, as does the underground man, Chernyshevsky's denial of the reality of freedom of the will? Part 1 of this work, the most influential, portrays the underground man's struggle as a human being to reconcile himself emotionally to all the real-life implications of such a doctrine (though it does so in such a tortuous and involuted fashion that this ideological source can be easily overlooked). Nonetheless, this discovery of the relation between ideology and psychology, or rather, Dostoevsky's genius for portraying all the subtle intricacies of their involvement, became the hallmark of his particular talent and opened the way for his great novelistic creations.

The three novels he wrote between 1865 and 1871 all follow in the path first trodden by *Notes from Underground. Crime and Punishment* takes its point of departure from the Utilitarian component of radical ideology—"one death and a hundred lives in exchange, it's simple arithmetic"—combined with the ideas of another influential radical, Dimitry Pisarev, who had sketched the outlines of a new proto-Nietzschean hero, an embryonic Superman, for whom good and evil, including murder, is only a matter of taste and personal inclination. Raskolnikov had thus imagined himself as "a great man" dedicated to improving the lot of humanity; but he discovers that a true great man cares nothing for others, and that he cannot become one precisely because he is psychically unable to eliminate the moral component of his personality.

Caught in this treacherous dialectic of radical ideas, Raskolnikov finds it impossible to suppress his inherited Christian conscience; and the portrayal of his inner struggle has no equal this side of *Macbeth.*

In *The Idiot,* Dostoevsky attempts to depict his own ideal as "a perfectly beautiful man," the Christ-figure of Prince Myshkin, whose radiance inspires others but who himself comes to grief because the universality of his Christian compassion proves incompatible with the limitations of his earthly nature as a human being. In the only direct statement he ever made of his religious convictions, jotted in a notebook while keeping a vigil at the bier of his first wife, Dostoevsky wrote: "To love man like *oneself,* according to the commandment of Christ, is impossible. The law of personality on earth shackles one. The *Ego* stands in the way. . . . [B]ut Christ was a perpetual eternal ideal to which man strives and, according to the law of nature [presumably human nature], should strive" (20: 172). These melancholy reflections are dramatized in the history of Prince Myshkin, certainly the most poignant Christian hero in all of modern literature, whose psychology is shaped by Dostoevsky's own ponderings over the meaning of Christ's incarnation for human life.

*The Idiot* was written during Dostoevsky's four-year sojourn abroad (1867–1871), originally planned as a short vacation trip but prolonged for fear of being thrown into debtor's prison on return. These were years of genteel poverty and isolation, relieved only by the companionship of Anna Grigoryevna, his staunchly loyal, devoted, and much younger second wife, who became his amanuensis as well. It was also the period of his gambling fever, a sporadic indulgence given far too much attention by biographers searching for the key to his work in some pathological aspect of his personality. One might keep in mind that in these years he wrote *The Idiot* under extremely difficult practical circumstances, as well as two brilliant novellas, *The Gambler* and *The Eternal Husband.* He also sketched out notes for a never-written major work in several volumes, *The Life of a Great Sinner,* on which he drew for both *The Devils* and *The Brothers Karamazov.*

He began to write *The Devils* while still abroad, and with this coruscating creation, probably the greatest novel ever written about political conspiracy, he returned to the attack on radical ideology initiated earlier. In *Crime and Punishment,* Dostoevsky had only *imagined* that radical ideas could lead to murder, but now an underground group led by Sergey Nechaev had assassinated one of its own members, presumably through fear of betrayal. Dostoevsky seized on this event as a confirmation of his own worst fears about the morally dangerous effects of radical principles, which during his years of exile he had come to regard as an infection of European society now spread to the Russian body politic. Intending at first to dash off a quick "political pamphlet" about the Nechaev affair, he found the work growing in scope and complexity; and it took much longer to complete than he had planned.

Ultimately, it became in part a reworking of the conflict-of-generations theme so impressively handled by Turgenev in *Fathers and Children*, but grasped at a later stage. The weak-willed, ridiculous but charming, and fundamentally humane Liberal Idealist Stepan Trofimovich Verkhovensky personifies the generation of the 1840s; the totally cynical and ruthless machinations of his son Peter (who applies Nechaev's pitilessly Machiavellian ideas and provokes the murder) represent the disastrous culmination of the "rational egoism" of the generation of the 1860s. This theme is combined with that of Stavrogin, a character taken over from *The Life of a Great Sinner*—a glamorous Byronic dandy à la Eugene Onegin, who has lost his religious faith and futilely seeks for a cause to which he can devote his strength. *The Devils* is the most intellectually rich of the great novels, practically an encyclopedia of Russian nineteenth-century culture filtered through a witheringly derisive and often grotesquely funny perspective. No other novel so amply displays Dostoevsky's underestimated talents as a satirist.

Dostoevsky returned to Russia in 1871 with *The Devils* only half written, and its completion in 1872 began a new phase in his artistic-ideological career. For he discovered that Russian radicalism had now developed views that, at least partially, were far closer to his own than in the past. Notably, the radicals were now willing to accept the validity of Christian moral values (though not the religion itself). These were the very values previously scorned and discarded, and which Dostoevsky had defended and propagated in his works all through the 1860s. His writings during the 1870s would thus be strongly affected by this mutation in radical ideology, and even lead to a temporary alliance with the left-wing Populists, in whose journal *Otechestvenniye Zapiski* (*Notes of the Fatherland*) he published his next novel. The prophetic status that Dostoevsky now attained may be attributed in part to this alteration in the radical point of view, whose adherents would no longer automatically reject out of hand any utterances couched in terms of Christian morality. But this brings us to the beginning of the present volume, and to these astonishing last ten years of Dostoevsky's life, which culminated, not only in personal triumph, but in *The Brothers Karamazov*, his artistic response of genius to all their tormenting agitations.

## CHAPTER 2

# A Quiet Return

On July 8, 1871, Dostoevsky and his family returned to Russia after a four-year period of living abroad, making as unobtrusive a reentry as possible into the St. Petersburg he had quit presumably only for a summer vacation. Eleven years earlier, in 1860, he had come back to European Russia after an even longer absence—the ten years he had spent in Siberia, four in a prison camp serving a sentence of hard labor, and six as a soldier and then an officer in the Russian Army. His return at that time had been equally unremarked, but for different reasons. Dostoevsky's artistic reputation had suffered a steep decline by the time of his arrest in 1849, and he was generally considered to have been a literary flash in the pan who had failed to live up to his earlier promise.

Since then, however, Dostoevsky's literary stature had changed drastically; in 1871 he was unanimously recognized as a worthy rival to both Turgenev and Tolstoy. His fame had been reestablished by his first post-Siberian novel, *The Insulted and Injured*, and particularly by his unprecedented semidocumentary prison camp memoirs, *House of the Dead*. Even though his *Notes from Underground* had gone largely unremarked, *Crime and Punishment* had been a great success; and although *The Idiot* had received a mixed reception, it was treated with great respect even by such a social-political opponent as the great satirist Mikhail E. Saltykov-Shchedrin. By the summer of 1871, Dostoevsky had already published all of Part I and two chapters of Part II of his latest novel, *The Devils*, whose plot made spine-chilling use of the most spectacular event of the moment, the murder of a young student by members of the radical Nechaev group. Indeed, the public trial of the Nechaevtsy was taking place at the very moment of Dostoevsky's arrival in the capital, and some of the essential documents, including the cold-bloodedly Machiavellian *Catechism of a Revolutionary* (written by either Mikhail Bakunin or Sergey Nechaev, and perhaps both) were placed in evidence and made publicly available on the very day that Dostoevsky stepped off the train.

Dostoevsky's reappearance would thus certainly have attracted more attention if he had let his plans become known in advance, but he had carefully kept them concealed. He had left Russia saddled with the financial debts of his brother Mikhail, which he had assumed after the latter's sudden death in 1864, and he had been threatened with imprisonment because of them. Indeed, only by quitting the country had he escaped being thrown into debtor's prison; and he stayed away as long as he did because he feared that otherwise the threat would be carried out. The obscurity of his homecoming was thus a protection against a swarm of creditors immediately appearing and clamoring to be paid—a situation that he knew would disturb the tranquillity he needed to continue work on the unfinished novel that was his sole source of income. Only his immediate relatives and a few close friends were informed in advance that he would be in Petersburg again—as well as the editors of the *Russian Messenger*, the journal in which *The Devils* was being published. He thus managed to conceal his presence in his homeland for two months, until his whereabouts became known in September through mention in a newspaper.

2
———

The first problem facing the Dostoevskys was to find suitable lodgings and settle down as quickly as possible. They stayed in a hotel for two days and then rented two furnished rooms near Yusupov Park, where their daughter Lyubov could gambol amidst the cooling greenery during the stifling summer heat. Assailed by visits from relatives and friends, as Dostoevsky complains in a letter to his favorite niece, Sofya Ivanova, "there was hardly any time to sleep."[1] In the midst of this overwhelming conviviality, Anna Grigoryevna suddenly felt labor pains at dinner and gave birth to a son, Feodor, on July 16, happily without suffering the severe contractions of her earlier pregnancies. Dostoevsky was overjoyed and hastened to convey the good news to Anna's mother (then temporarily abroad) and to his family in Moscow. In his letter to Sofya Ivanova, he also informed her that he was planning to travel to Moscow for a visit with Mikhail Katkov, the powerful editor of the *Russian Messenger*, about business matters. For despite this whirlwind of family events, it was necessary for him to carry on with the serialization of *The Devils*. "I am sitting down to work now," he tells his niece on July 18, "although my head isn't clear and I fully expect an attack [of epilepsy]. Everything here is chaos, the servant is awful, and I am constantly running errands."[2]

A week later, at the end of July, Dostoevsky was in Moscow to straighten out his accounts with Katkov, receiving payment for the chapters he had supplied in recent months. The new supply of funds, skimpy though it was, enabled the Dostoevskys to envisage moving from their furnished flat, which "was very expensive, full of comings and goings, and owned by nasty Yids."[3] The very practical Anna Grigoryevna, who had made a quick recovery after the birth of Feodor, immediately tackled the problem. Since they had no furniture and not enough funds to buy any outright, Anna struck a deal with a merchant who agreed to provide what was needed (though of very inferior quality) in return for installment payments that allowed him to retain ownership until the price had been paid in full. (This fortuitous arrangement turned out to be very advantageous for the Dostoevskys in the short run.) Once assured of the furniture, Anna began to hunt for an apartment and was considerably put out when Dostoevsky's stepson, Pasha (Pavel), suggested one with eight rooms that he had managed to turn up.

Pasha had lived with his stepfather previously. Indeed, one of the reasons they had initially planned to vacation abroad was Anna's determination to break the hold he had managed to obtain over her husband—a hold that, she had become convinced, posed a serious threat to her marriage. Even though now married himself, Pasha seemed to assume he could resume his old status as a *prizhivalchik*, a sponger or hanger-on. But Anna, who had been reduced to tears by Pasha's reproaches four years earlier in the first days of her marriage, was now in full command of the situation. In no uncertain terms, she explained that setting up a common household was out of the question. An appeal to Dostoevsky was enough to convince Pasha that the old days would never return: he was told curtly that his stepfather "had turned over the entire household management to [Anna]" and that "however she decides, that's the way it will be."[4]

Pasha, however, still persisted in applying to his stepfather for financial aid, and Dostoevsky continued not only to help him when temporary shortfalls occurred but also to assist him in obtaining employment through mutual friends. Several notes written shortly after his return document such recommendations; but the feckless Pasha never stayed long in any employment, much to his stepfather's exasperation, and continually offered one excuse after another for his repeated dissatisfactions with his posts.

If Pasha still clung to Dostoevsky's coattails in this way, the situation was greatly improved, from Anna's point of view, regarding the family of his late brother Mikhail. Not only had Dostoevsky assumed his brother's debts, but he had also felt responsible for supporting the surviving family as much as he could. Even during the darkest days of his penury in Europe, he had driven Anna into a repressed fury (indignantly confided only to her notebooks) by assigning them a small portion of whatever income he earned. Mikhail's children, however, were now all fully grown and self-supporting; and, as Anna notes with relief, their mother, Emilya Feodorovna, "had become accustomed to the idea that Feodor Mikhailovich, having a family of his own, could help her out only in special cases."[5]

Anna soon turned up a very suitable four-room dwelling and rented it in her own name. Presumably, she did so to spare Dostoevsky the bother of the legal formalities; but once again her assumption of ownership, perhaps more calculated than she admits, would work to ward off the greatest threat to his peace of mind. Although forced to buy furniture, Anna believed she could retrieve the dinnerware and kitchen utensils, as well as the winter clothing, left in the care of relatives and friends four years earlier. But all had been lost—through careless reshufflings, the clumsiness of servants who had broken precious porcelain and glassware, or what seemed like outright dishonesty in the failure to pay insurance premiums sent from abroad. Worst of all was the loss of Dostoevsky's library, which had been left in the care of Pasha on condition that he preserve it intact; but it had been sold piecemeal and irretrievably scattered. Anna mentions as of particular value the books inscribed by other writers, "serious works on history and on the sect of Old Believers [*raskolniki*], in which [my husband] took an intense interest."[6] This remark confirms Dostoevsky's fascination, quite evident in his work, with the messianic religiosity of the Old Believers, whom he had come more and more to regard as the genuine repository of Old Russian values. A small consolation in the midst of general disappointment was the discovery of a basket in the attic of Anna's relatives containing the notebooks for *Crime and Punishment*, a good deal of correspondence, and the account books of Dostoevsky's journals.

At the end of September, he filed suit against the publisher Feodor Stellovsky, who had clearly violated a contract by publishing a new edition of *Crime and Punishment* without any payment to the author. But it would take several years before Dostoevsky would succeed in obtaining a penny from the rapacious publisher for whom he had been forced to write *The Gambler* in a month. Just about the same time, news of his return was published, and the expected did not fail to occur: creditors immediately began to hammer at his door. One of the most importunate was the widow of a certain G. Hinterlach, who had been involved in dealings with Mikhail Dostoevsky at the time the latter had owned a tobacco factory. She sent a threatening letter; and when Dostoevsky visited her to ask for an extension of a few months, by which time he expected to receive additional payment from Katkov, he was turned away unceremoniously. He returned home in despair, fearing that Frau Hinterlach would attach his property and, if this proved insufficient, send him to languish in prison.

Returning to plead again for payment by installments, he was answered, according to Anna, with the boast that "a little German merchant" like Hinterlach could put "a prominent Russian author" in jail—and would do so unless promptly paid! "This was just after the [German] victory in the Franco-Prussian War," Anna comments, "when all the Germans grew arrogant and haughty." By this time she had decided to take matters into her own hands and, without informing her husband, paid a visit herself to the implacable lady. Instead of pleading, she advised her that the household furnishings and the Dostoevsky apartment were both in Anna's name, which meant that neither could be assigned for a debt owed by her husband. Moreover, if Dostoevsky were put in debtor's prison, Anna would insist that he remain there until the entire debt was canceled. Besides not obtaining a cent, Frau Hinterlach would also have to foot the cost of the prisoner's upkeep (as the law required of creditors using such a recourse). Anna also threatened to air the whole matter in an article for a journal: "Let everybody see what the honest Germans are capable of!"[7] Realizing that Anna was made of sterner stuff than the nervous and distraught Dostoevsky, the creditor hastened to accept the installment arrangement. After this experience, Anna decided to take over all the debt negotiations; and, meeting the threats with the same arguments, she succeeded in stalling off demands for payment on the spot.

Dostoevsky was busily at work on *The Devils* all this while; but he was also eager to renew relations with old friends and to make up for the cultural isolation from which he had suffered during his European sojourn. The poet Apollon Maikov, his staunchest friend and most faithful correspondent during his years abroad, introduced Dostoevsky to a literary-political circle that had gathered around Prince V. P. Meshchersky, who had founded a new publication, *Grazhdanin* (*The Citizen*), to counter the influence of the liberal and progressive press (though Meshchersky's opinion of what was "liberal" and "progressive" included journals that the radical intelligentsia regarded as pillars of reaction). Prince Meshchersky was little known except as the scion of an ancient aristocratic family, the grandson of Nikolay M. Karamzin, the famous early-nineteenth-century writer and historian, whose works the youthful Dostoevsky had read with admiration; but he soon achieved some notoriety as the author of novels and plays about high-society life in St. Petersburg. He was also a close friend of the heir to the Russian throne, Tsarevich Alexander, whom he had known since boyhood, and he moved freely and easily in the very highest court circles.*

* Prince Meshchersky was an influential and powerful personage who played an important and—according to many who were far from being anti-Tsarist—an unfortunate role in Russian political life. It was, however, only during the reigns of Alexander III and Nicholas II (after Dostoevsky's death) that he reached the height of his power. His reputation was shadowed by his homosexuality, which apparently caused a good bit of scandalous gossip. One supposes that such tale-telling would have reached Dostoevsky's ears, but there is no direct evidence that it did. See W. E. Mosse, "Imperial Favourite: V. P. Meshchersky and the *Grazhdanin*," *Slavonic and East European Review*, 52 (October 1981), 529–549. For the information about charges of homosexuality having been brought against him, but not given any publicity, see p. 534 n.38.

If we are to believe his memoirs, Meshchersky's decision to found a weekly journal that would support the monarchy was met with indifference, if not outright disapproval, by those he wished to champion. The Tsar referred disdainfully to the prince's desire to become "a scribbler" (*pisaka*), and only the Tsarevich encouraged his journalistic ambition.[8] Nonetheless, he gathered around him a small literary circle that included Maikov, the great poet Feodor I. Tyutchev, Nikolay Strakhov (the former chief critic of Dostoevsky's journals), Dostoevsky himself, and the tutor of the Tsarevich, Konstantin P. Pobedonostsev. Pobedonostsev later acquired a sinister reputation when his former pupil succeeded to the throne as Alexander III, and the ex-tutor became known as the malevolent *éminence grise* of his oppressive régime. But in 1871 he was regarded primarily as a legal scholar and highly placed government official with a liberal past (in the Russian sense), who had supported the cause of judicial reform and the abolition of serfdom. He was also extremely cultivated, had read widely in English, French, and German literature, and had published a translation of Thomas à Kempis in 1869. This was the literary-political environment in which Dostoevsky was to be immersed during the next three years.

## 3

At the beginning of the New Year, Dostoevsky made another trip to Moscow, again to meet Katkov and to obtain, if possible, an additional advance; but he was also concerned about the fate of two recent chapters he had submitted, entitled either "At Tikhon's" or, more familiarly, "Stavrogin's Confession." These contained a description of how Stavrogin, a central character in *The Devils*, had seduced a twelve-year-old girl and then, realizing that she was going to commit suicide, had not only failed to intervene but even listened with perversely sadistic anticipation to the sounds of her preparation and death agony. There was some question, for reasons that are quite understandable, whether these chapters were not too scabrous to be published; but Dostoevsky did not receive a definitive answer about them until nine months later. Meanwhile, a letter to his wife from Moscow leaves in doubt whether he was able to obtain any more funds. He mentions only learning that "my accounts are in a big mess" and that "apparently there must be 1,300 rubles that I owe" (advances not yet repaid by his manuscript). Despite visiting relatives for the New Year's celebration and renewing acquaintance both with the playwright Dimitry V. Averkiev (whose current play he attended) and the Slavophil publicist Ivan Aksakov, he remarks that "all in all, I'm miserable here, and the main thing is the complete uncertainty." Dostoevsky's letters to Anna from this time on

1. Konstantin P. Pobedonostsev

are always filled with anxious concern about her and the children, and he inquires constantly after their health and well-being, interspersing his queries with practical advice: "How is Fedya? Is he well? Is it warm there? Stoke the fire, darling, if it is the least bit cold there." Or again: "Feed them well, Anya. Don't skimp on beef."[9]

No information is offered about the final results of Dostoevsky's conversations with Katkov, though he felt encouraged by one incident. Katkov's relation to him and his work was obviously of the first importance for his financial future, and he took as a very promising sign that "I told Katkov, tête-à-tête, the plot of my next novel and I have heard from Averkiev that he had already told two people of the plot."[10] Whether this "next novel" has anything to do with *A Raw Youth* remains unclear; ideas for novels were always piling up in Dostoevsky's notebooks, many of them to remain unwritten, and Dostoevsky may well have spoken of some of these. Katkov, however, clearly wished to retain him as a future collaborator; but Dostoevsky also discovered to his distress that the financial side of the journal had been turned over to a certain Pavel Leontiyev, a scholar of Latin, Greek, and ancient history, "to whom Katkov himself voluntarily yielded despotic power in the matter [of payment to authors]. Thus, everything depends on Leontiyev's consent, and I cannot be certain of that man's favor."[11]

In early February, however, Dostoevsky wrote happily to Sofya Ivanova that, "thanks to a certain occurrence, my affairs have improved. . . . I have gotten some money and satisfied the most impatient creditors."[12] His discretion about this "certain occurrence" can be explained by a letter published for the first time only in the most recent edition of his correspondence. Addressed to A. A. Romanov, the Tsarevich, it also refers to an earlier letter, so far undiscovered, to the same august personage. The published document expresses Dostoevsky's embarrassment "at the boldness I exhibited," and one can only assume that (probably on the advice and with the help of the good offices of both Prince Meshchersky and Pobedonostsev) he had been urged to explain all the difficulties of his circumstances to the Tsarevich, and that the heir to the throne had come to his aid with a grant of money. Dostoevsky thanked the Tsarevich above all "for the priceless attention . . . paid to my request. It is dearer to me than anything else, dearer than the very help that You gave me and which saved me from a great calamity."[13] He had appealed once before to the throne, in 1859, when he was serving as a common soldier and wished promotion to the rank of officer. As a loyal subject, he had felt no hesitation or reluctance then; nor, presumably, did he feel any now. But the request for aid did not prevent him from composing the scathingly hilarious indictment of the incompetence of Governor-General von Lembke, along with his entire administration, in chapters of *The Devils* that are bitingly satirical of the reigning authorities.

One result of this sudden and welcome access of funds was that Dostoevsky could at last pay off a debt to an old friend, Dr. Stepan D. Yanovsky. During a difficult period for the couple in Geneva, the prosperous Yanovsky had responded to a plea for help by sending one hundred rubles; he was now in poor health and had written in January asking for repayment of this old loan. Dostoevsky replied with the dispatch of the money, accompanied by an extremely cordial letter evoking their forty-year friendship and bringing Yanovsky up to date on more recent events. "I spent four years abroad," he wrote, "in Switzerland, Germany, and Italy, and I finally got terribly fed up with it. I began to notice with horror that I was getting out of touch with Russia." Dostoevsky remarks that he hopes to finish his new novel by summer (it would not be completed until the winter of 1872) and mentions an old plan of "going to the East (Constantinople, the Greek Archipelago, Athos, Jerusalem) and writing a book" about the trip. Of great interest is a reference to the 1840s, when Yanovsky had been Dostoevsky's personal physician. "You loved me and put up with me," the ex-patient recalls gratefully, "a person suffering from a mental illness (after all, I recognize that now), before my journey to Siberia, where I was cured."[14] Dostoevsky thus makes a clear separation, in his own mind, between his "mental illness" of the 1840s, which some biographers—as well as Freud—tend to see as the first syndromes of his epilepsy, and the epilepsy itself: the latter had *begun* in his Siberian prison camp, while in fact the symptoms of his former nervous troubles had vanished there for good and all.

Hard at work on *The Devils*, Dostoevsky pleaded lack of time in refusing an invitation to become a contributor to a new publication, *Beseda* (*Conversation*), even though he was flatteringly assured that the editor was a great admirer of his own long defunct journals and intended to carry on in their spirit. But the pressure of labor on his novel did not prevent him from regularly attending the dinners offered every Wednesday evening by Prince Meshchersky; and he began to lead once again something closer to a normal social life. The husband of his niece, Professor M. S. Vladislavlev, who had once been a contributor to Dostoevsky's journals, now taught philosophy at the University of St. Petersburg, and he frequently invited his eminent uncle-in-law to meet some of the luminaries of the learned world. He also began to entertain, and for a party on February 17, the day assigned in the Russian calendar to Saint Feodor Tiron (hence Dostoevsky's name day, which Russians celebrate as a birthday), he sent invitations to close friends. Learning that Nikolay G. Danilevsky, the author of *Russia and Europe*, was then passing through Petersburg, he asked Strakhov, whom he assumed could locate him, to bring Danilevsky along. They had known each other in the faraway days of the Petrashevsky circle during the 1840s, when Danilevsky had earned the reputation of being the most thorough connoisseur of the Utopian Socialist doctrines of Charles Fourier. Since then, he had become a naturalist as well as a speculative historian of culture and had developed a theory of world civilization with a strong Slavophil tendency. Although not agreeing with Danilevsky in every respect, Dostoevsky greatly admired his efforts to prove that Russian culture would soon create a new, independent phase of world history; and he employed some of these ideas for the impassionedly nationalistic speeches of Shatov in *The Devils*.

Parts I and II of this novel had been published by the end of 1871, and the first reactions to these sections of the book were beginning to appear. Dostoevsky, who had initially thought of the work as "a pamphlet," had anticipated that it would be met with fierce hostility by the radical critics who had already attacked *Crime and Punishment* as a slander on the young student generation. And although the novel eventually became what Dostoevsky called "a poem" rather than "a pamphlet"—the political Nechaev theme being interwoven with Stavrogin's tragic efforts to erase from his heart the distinction between good and evil—enough aspects of the pamphlet remained to make the book anathema to those who, without necessarily approving of Nechaev's methods, sympathized with his revolutionary aims. A typical early review, printed in the *Birzhevie Vedomosti* (*Stock Exchange News*), denounced Dostoevsky's lurid portrayal of the radicals as having "surpassed all of the rivals who had embarked on this road in the *Russian Messenger* and other journals of the same ilk which we have already forgotten." In one of the most often quoted passage in the book, a radical theoretician named Shigalev explains that, while he had begun his reflections with the idea of total freedom, he had discovered, to his dismay, that he had ended with that of total despotism. And he insists that the only logical answer to the social problem is to reduce all but one-tenth of humanity to the level of an organic, "physiological" equality like a herd of cattle. The critic compares such notions to the madness of Poprischin in Gogol's "Memoirs of a Madman." The novel, in his view, evokes "a hospital" filled with mental patients "supposedly making up . . . a gathering of contemporary people."[15] One of the commonest charges that continued to be leveled against Dostoevsky was that his characters were too mentally pathological to be taken as serious social commentary. An implicit subtext of such criticism was that the author himself, known to be epileptic, suffered from the same abnormality that filled his pages.

Dostoevsky's immediate entourage, of course, took quite a different view of his new novel, and nothing could have given him more pleasure than a letter he received from Strakhov in April 1871, just before leaving Europe for his return. "It is obvious," wrote the critic, whose literary acumen Dostoevsky valued very highly, "that as regards substance, as regards the quantity and variety of ideas, you are first among us, and even Tolstoy compared to you is more monotonous." Such praise from a great admirer of Tolstoy, with whose achievements he now saw himself to be in competition, could not have been more welcome; but Strakhov then goes on to complain, as he had done in the past, that Dostoevsky packed too much into his novels and thus confused the average reader.[16] Modestly responding that Strakhov ranks him too highly in placing him above Tolstoy, he admits the imputed fault of superabundance: "Many separate novels and stories squeeze themselves suddenly into one for me," he explains, "so that there is neither measure nor harmony." But while conceding a tendency to be "carried away by poetic inspiration" and thus to "undertak[e] to express an artistic idea beyond my capacities," he nonetheless clearly does not underestimate his own artistic stature. In the very next sentence he notes that Victor Hugo and even Pushkin suffered from somewhat the same disability.[17]

Even though quite prepared to bear the brunt of the antagonism that he knew *The Devils* would encounter, Dostoevsky must certainly have been consoled by the testimonies he was receiving that his novels had already assured him a secure place in Russian literature. One such came in a letter from Princess V. D. Obolenskaya, the literary daughter of an important government official and a contributor to various periodicals specializing in the Russian historical past. As she informed the author, *Crime and Punishment* was for her "the finest work in Russian literature," and it had become her "cherished dream" to turn it into a play for the Imperial Theatre. Dostoevsky gave her the permission she requested because he had "taken it as a rule never to hinder such attempts"; but he was not sure that such an adaptation from one form to another was feasible, or at least he knew that it posed considerable difficulties.[18]

His reflections on this problem are of the greatest interest because of the numerous attempts that have been made to turn his novels into plays and, more recently, into films. "There is some secret of art," he continues, "on the basis of which the epic form can never find a correspondence for itself in the dramatic form. I believe that for various forms of art there exists a series of poetic ideas corresponding to them as well, so that a certain idea can never be expressed in another form, one that does not correspond to it." Despite the well-known "dramatic" quality of his novels and stories, which rely more on scenic encounters and dialogic exchanges than on description or exposition, Dostoevsky thus did not assume that it would be a relatively simple matter to turn them into plays. On the contrary, he was willing to envisage, and even to approve, the dramatist taking the greatest liberties with the original text. After remarking that previous attempts of this kind had turned out "rather badly," he goes on: "It will be another matter if you redo the novel as much as possible and change it, saving from it just one episode or another, for reworking into a play, or, taking the original idea, will you completely alter the plot?"[19]

Another welcome evidence of Dostoevsky's stature came in a letter from Pavel M. Tretyakov, the owner of an important art gallery in Moscow, who had commissioned the celebrated artist V. G. Perov to furnish his collection with portraits of the most eminent living figures in Russian culture. He accepted the honor of sitting for Perov with a great deal of satisfaction, joining a group of notables that included Turgenev, the playwright Alexander N. Ostrovsky, the poet Apollon Maikov (at Dostoevsky's suggestion), and the short story writer and lexicographer V. I.

Dal. Perov arrived from Moscow in the spring of 1872 to begin his work, but it was his custom, before putting brush to canvas, to become better acquainted with his subjects. He thus visited Dostoevsky every day for a week and chatted with him for two hours so as to observe him in various moods and attitudes. Even though Dostoevsky was often reticent and even uncivil in the presence of strangers, no such problem arose in the case of Perov; the two men took to each other immediately. Anna Grigoryevna notes that "Perov was an intelligent and pleasant person, and Feodor Mikhailovich loved talking with him."[20]

2. *Dostoevsky in 1872*, by V. G. Perov

Of course, the flattering situation itself was enough to put Dostoevsky at his ease, and one assumes that Perov would have been on his best behavior as he observed Dostoevsky's expressions and gestures. There were probably also other and less immediate reasons why the two men should have sympathized both personally and as artists. As the illegitimate son of a Russian-German baron serving in the Tobolsk district of Siberia, Perov would certainly have admired the intense social pathos of the author's work and his compassion for all those who suffered humiliation because of their lowly origin. Similarly, Dostoevsky would have had no ideological animus against Perov, whose early canvases in the 1860s had exhibited a marked "social" tendency, but who then turned more and more to genre studies and portraiture; most recently, he had favored religious and historical themes.

The portrait is one of Perov's greatest achievements, and Anna comments on how well the artist captured "the Dostoevskian creative impulse," the moment "when he was absorbed in thought about his work."[21] The picture was highly praised in all quarters (it even won the approval of Turgenev), and another important painter, I. N. Kramskoy, wrote: "This portrait is not only Perov's best portrait but one of the best of the Russian school in general. It clearly displays all of his strongest sides as an artist: character, power of expression, strength of relief. . . . The decisiveness of shading and, as it were, something harsh and energetic in the contours, always present in his pictures, in this portrait is softened by the remarkable coloring and harmony of the tones."[22] The friendship between the two artists was renewed in the fall of 1872, when Dostoevsky visited Moscow to make the final arrangements for the publication of *The Devils.* At that time he and Perov visited the Tretyakov gallery, where the picture was on display to the general admiration of the public.

4

---

Despite the pleasures and the stimulus provided by the active social life that he was now once again enjoying, Dostoevsky knew that he needed solitude to work most effectively and that the demands of conviviality were a hindrance to the concentration needed to complete *The Devils.* "In general," he wrote Dr. Yanovsky, "my life is now full of work. It's hard to write and I write at night. But it's impossible to live in seclusion here, even for a working person."[23] On the same day, he tells his niece Sofya that "the obligation of going to parties in the evening somewhat distracts me here. I want to lock myself away completely." He thus planned "to leave Petersburg at the very beginning of the spring," in the expectation that a summer in the country would both relieve him from social pressures and benefit the health of his daughter Lyubov.[24]

At first, the Dostoevskys thought of renting a dacha adjoining the family property at Darovoe, where his sister Vera Ivanova and her family would be staying; but this plan fell through. As an alternate, Dostoevsky remembered that his nephew-in-law, Professor Vladislavlev, had praised the amenities of Staraya Russa, a small watering place some hundreds of versts south of Petersburg at the confluence of several rivers, and which could also boast of salt baths supposedly good for scrofula. Moreover, he could rent "a house with furniture, even with kitchen wares," and, as he wrote to his sister Vera, the town also contained "a station [*voksal*] with newspapers, magazines, etc."[25] Vladislavlev rented a house for the Dostoevskys from a local priest, Father Rumyantsev, and the family lived there from mid-May 1872 to the beginning of September.

To reach Staraya Russa, the most convenient route was to take a train in St. Petersburg, transfer at a local station for Novgorod, and then board a boat for the trip across Lake Ilmen. Anna never forgot the view of Novgorod that greeted the admiring eyes of herself and her husband in the early morning as they watched the city glide by. "It was a glorious spring morning. The sun shone bright on the river's far shore from which the crenellated walls of its kremlin rose up, the gilded cupolas of the Cathedral of St. Sophia were ablaze, and in the chilly air the bells were loudly calling to matins. Feodor Mikhailovich, who loved and understood nature, was in a tender mood, which I unconsciously absorbed."[26] On arriving at Staraya Russa, however, they discovered the inconveniences of the locality. The river level was sometimes too low for the boat to approach the shore in safety, and passengers might be

3. The country house of the Dostoevskys in Staraya Russa

obliged to wait as long as two or three days before disembarking or boarding. In the seventh chapter of Part III of *The Devils*, which recounts the last journey of Stepan Trofimovich Verkhovensky with gently satirical poignancy, his wanderings take him to a riverside inn where passengers wait for the arrival of a boat delayed by such an ebb and are roundly fleeced by the proprietors of their miserable accommodations. Dostoevsky was evidently transferring some of the impressions gathered from his own trips to and from Staraya Russa directly to the pages of his novel.

During his first stay there in 1872, these trips turned out to be far more frequent than he could possibly have anticipated. Just a few weeks before the family had planned to leave Petersburg, little Lyubov fell and injured her right wrist. The doctor diagnosed a dislocation, straightened the joint, and reassured the worried parents that no permanent harm had been done. They soon noticed that a strange, discolored bump had appeared above the palm and were told that it was a normal part of the swelling; but when the bandage was removed in Staraya Russa, they saw to their dismay that the wrist had begun to heal crookedly. Local doctors, including a quite tipsy one from the army, explained that the accident had not been a simple dislocation but a fracture of the bone and that the hand might be deformed if the wrist were not broken again and reset. It was impossible to think of entrusting such an operation to the local doctors; but to return the family to stifling and unhealthy Petersburg would mean incurring extra expenses they could ill afford. Dostoevsky, in Anna's words, was "beside himself with misery and worry, [and] paced rapidly back and forth on the garden terrace, tearing his hair at the temples—always a sign of extraordinary agitation in him; while I waited from minute to minute for him to have a seizure."[27]

A solution to their dilemma was offered by the benevolent Father Rumyantsev, who suggested that little Fedya could be left in the care of himself and his wife, aided by a nanny, while the parents accompanied Lyubov to Petersburg. Once the operation had been performed, Anna could remain for whatever time was necessary for recovery, but Dostoevsky could return immediately to resume the novel that the *Russian Messenger* impatiently awaited. This salutary offer was gratefully accepted, and, returning to the city, they consulted a Dr. Barch, an old friend and chief surgeon at the Maximilian Hospital. Having been warned by the doctors in Staraya Russa that the use of chloroform was dangerous for children, the parents agonized over the pain that poor Lyubov would have to endure; but Dr. Barch, smiling tolerantly, assured them that no such danger existed and that the surgery would be painless. When he ordered the agitated couple out of the operating room, Dostoevsky suggested to Anna that they pray together: "We got down on our knees and prayed as fervently during those moments as perhaps we had ever prayed in our lives before."[28] The operation was successful, and Lyubov suffered no ill effects from the chloroform. But because the healing process would take at least three weeks, Anna remained in Petersburg with their daughter while Dostoevsky hastened back the next day to Staraya Russa, Fedya, and his manuscript.

His letters to Anna from Staraya Russa are those of a terribly worried husband and father, upset by the disruption of his family routine and tormented by the fear that something might yet go awry with Lyubov. "Be careful walking out in the streets with her," he cautions Anna. "People shove so much in Petersburg, there are so many drunks . . . in the crowd her arm will likely be broken again." As for Fedya (who, he reports, dirties his diapers with healthy regularity), he worried about various spots on his face and body but had been reassured by the army doctor that, since the boy is "cheerful, eating, and walking well, [and] there's no fever," there was nothing to be concerned about.[29] His mood, however, was extremely irritable and querulous, and his observations on the local social scene reflect all the intemperance that so often overcame him when his nerves were frayed. "The crowd here is obviously very formal, high-toned, constantly trying to resemble high society, with the vilest French. The ladies all try to shine with their outfits, although they all must be trashy women. . . . The waters are terribly wretched, and I definitely don't like the park. And in general, this whole Staraya Russa is terrible trash."[30] Such a reaction, however, reveals only a momentary flare-up of irascibility; the Dostoevskys eventually bought a house in Staraya Russa, which became their permanent summer residence.

Matters were not improved by a stretch of terrible weather; days of uninterrupted rain turned the streets into such a quagmire of mud that it was impossible even to walk to the post office. "There's nothing more unbearable," he writes disconsolately, "than greenery and wooden houses during a rain and with such a horrible sky." Worst of all, with Anna absent, "you can't help me with stenography, and I would like to send material to the *Russian Messenger.*" Dostoevsky tried to work as best he could, but he complains: "If you only knew what misery to me life is. Writing is fine when the writing is going well, but I keep having a hard time of it. And besides, I don't have any desire at all [to write]. There's also nothing to read."[31] A few days later, his words become bitter: "I'm having a horrible time writing. When will we achieve at least a month of calm, so that I wouldn't have to be worried with all my heart and could be entirely at work. Otherwise I can't earn money and live without cursing. What a gypsy life, painful, most gloomy, without the least joy, and all there is to do is worry and worry!"[32]

Meanwhile in Petersburg, Anna was burdened with the same anxieties as her husband about Lyubov and was apprehensive not only about Fedya's well-being but also about Dostoevsky's suffering an epileptic attack in her absence. As if all these worries were not enough, she was also looking after her mother in Petersburg, bedridden because of an accident to her foot. Anna's sister, the mother of four children, had recently died very unexpectedly in Rome, but the family had decided to keep the news from Mme Snitkina for the moment; Anna was planning to break it to her only when she came to Staraya Russa to convalesce and would be, presumably, better able to absorb the shock.

This decision led to a very interesting exchange of views with her husband, who was vehemently opposed to any such concealment, arguing that "if you tell your mother now, half her grief will be expended on compassion for them [the bereaved husband and motherless children] *and willingly or not* will subside because they have lost more than she has, not less, especially the children. Her grief will have to humble itself before their grief."[33] For Dostoevsky, an effective consolation for one's own grief was to become aware that others have suffered even more and to identify with *their* suffering—a view that illustrates one of the foundations of his own sense of moral values.

Another remark is equally revelatory of an additional trait of Dostoevskian psychology. "You write that you probably miss me more than I do you. I'll only say in reply: I don't know who misses whom more, but I'm so miserable that—would you believe it?—I'm irritated that I haven't had an attack. If I'd at least hurt myself somehow in an attack, that would at least be some sort of diversion."[34] One should not take such a statement at face value, though Dostoevsky often portrays characters who, finding a prolonged state of nervous incertitude impossible to endure, will take any action—even one injurious or self-destructive—to cut short the torment of indeterminate anxiety. When, a day later, he suffered a severe epileptic attack, he sadly reports that "it's still dark in my head and my arms and leg ache. That has interrupted my work even more, so that I don't even know what I am going to do about the *Russian Messenger* and what they think of me there."[35]

Anna and Lyubov returned to Staraya Russa after a four-week absence, and life settled into its normal routine once again—but not for very long. Indeed, Anna recalled these spring and summer months of 1872 as perhaps the most racking in her entire life. She caught a severe chill, developed an abscess in her throat, and ran a very high fever. The doctor treating her warned Dostoevsky that her life was in danger, and "Feodor Mikhailovich fell into utter despair," retreating into another room "to put his face in his hands and sob uncontrollably." Anna believed herself to be dying and, not able to speak, "made signs first to

Feodor Mikhailovich and then to the children to come over to me. I kissed them, blessed them, and wrote down for my husband my instructions as to what he was to do in the event of my death."[36] Happily, the abscess broke that very night, and Anna began to recover, though it was weeks before she regained her full strength. At the beginning of September 1872, the sorely tried family limped back to Petersburg, scarcely having obtained the unruffled months of rustic quietude they had so much hoped for on their departure.

5

The indefatigable Anna had done a bit of apartment hunting in Petersburg during her stay there with Lyubov, and the Dostoevskys moved into a five-room flat, owned by a general of the Izmailovsky Regiment. Dostoevsky's immediate preoccupation, of course, was the fate of his novel, on which he had been working steadily but whose future publication date still remained disturbingly vague. No new installments had appeared after November 1871, when the editors had expressed objections to the shocking details contained in Stavrogin's confession. To help meet their complaints, as Anna explains in an appendix to her *Reminiscences*, he appealed for advice to his literary intimates in the Meshchersky circle. "This chapter," writes Anna, "Katkov indeed refused, and asked the author to revise it. Feodor Mikhailovich was distressed by this refusal, and, wishing to test the accuracy of Katkov's impression, read the chapter to his friends K. P. Pobedonostsev, A. N. Maikov, N. N. Strakhov and others . . . asking for their opinion and, as it were, judgment on himself." They all agreed that it was "far too realistic," and Dostoevsky thus began to think of variants. One involved a story he had heard about a governess who had brought her young female charge to a bathhouse for a rendezvous with her seducer. The Meshchersky circle rejected this alternative on the ground that he might fall afoul of "the woman question" and be accused of insulting governesses, just as, "having depicted a murder by the student Raskolnikov, he had in this way accused our young generation of similar crimes."[37]

Finally discarding the idea of a different episode, he wrote to Sofya Ivanova in early February 1872, "while leaving the essence of the matter, I altered the text enough to satisfy the journal's chastity. And in this sense I'll send them an ultimatum. If they don't agree, then I don't know what I'll do."[38] No such ultimatum has been found among Dostoevsky's papers. Instead we have a letter to N. A. Lyubimov, the assistant editor, declaring that "I think that what I've sent you [the revised chapters] can be printed now. Everything very obscene has been thrown out." Dostoevsky continues by explaining that Stavrogin is "a complete social type (in my opinion), *our* type, a Russian . . . a person who has lost touch with everything native, and, most importantly, faith." Clearly, he is attempting to divert attention from the sordid nature of Stavrogin's deed to the moral-spiritual meaning that he wishes the character to convey; and he describes Stavrogin as "a degenerate out of ennui, but a person with a conscience who undertakes a sufferingly convulsive effort to be renewed and begin believing again. Together with the nihilists, this is a serious phenomenon."[39]

Dostoevsky had hoped that publication would resume with the April 1872 issue but was brusquely informed that the journal wished to have a substantial portion of the remaining manuscript before going ahead. The editors had been badly burned by *The Idiot*, and he was told quite frankly that "we do not wish to begin publication now, and as before await from week to week the dispatch of small sections."[40] He worried that the printing might begin in late spring and end during the summer months, in his view the worst period for installments of a serious novel to appear. Agreement was presumably reached to begin printing in August, if enough manuscript were available, and he dispatched five chapters in the first half of July despite the turmoil of the Staraya Russa months. Ordinarily, this would have been enough; but the question of Stavrogin's confession was still left hanging, and no further parts of the novel appeared in August.

In late September, Dostoevsky wrote to relatives in Moscow, asking them to inquire about Katkov. Had he returned from a voyage abroad, and, if not, when was he expected? He knew that only Katkov in person could make the final decision about the disputed chapter and that a trip to Moscow would probably be necessary to settle its fate once and for all. He arrived there in early October, saw Lyubimov, and wrote Anna that "everything seems to be fixed up . . . they'll be printing in November and December, but they're surprised and frowning that it isn't finished yet. In addition, he has doubts (since we don't have Katkov yet) regarding the censorship."[41] These words do not refer to the controversial confession chapter, which was never submitted to the official censorship, but to what are now Chapters 1 and 2 of Part III, which describe the riotous fête for needy governesses (they did after all appear in the novel!) and scathingly satirize the incompetence and sheer stupidity of Governor-General von Lembke and his administrative cohorts, as well as (superbly anticipating our own day) the disastrous "radical chic" of his wife. No decision had yet been taken about Stavrogin's confession, and the final word was not received until Katkov returned just before the printing of the November issue. The verdict was definitive and negative: the chapter would not appear! (Indeed, it remained buried among Dostoevsky's papers and came to light only in 1922.)

Meanwhile, he had continued writing on the assumption that this chapter, the keystone of the entire work in its original conception, would be included. He now had only a few weeks to save what he could of his novel with this section missing. In fact, the magazine version contains passages that foreshadow the confession, which Dostoevsky removed only when the novel appeared in book form. Although this is not the place to discuss the variant texts of *The Devils*, there is one last-minute addition of such importance that it cannot go unremarked. It concerns the present Chapter 7 of Part III, "Stepan Trofimovich's Last Wanderings," which originally did not contain the scene in which the expiring Liberal Idealist listens to a reading of the crucial passage from Saint Luke. This passage, also used as an epigraph for the novel, describes a man possessed by devils, which then enter into a herd of swine and are drowned in the sea, while the healed sufferer comes to sit at the feet of Jesus. After hearing this text, and under its influence, the conscience-stricken Stepan Trofimovich chooses to assume the guilt of having infested the Russian body politic with "the devils."

It is quite possible that such an admission of guilt had originally been reserved for Stavrogin; but without the confession chapter, Dostoevsky could well have felt that his character was too psychologically and ideologically undeveloped to make such an admission artistically viable. In any event, the remainder of the novel was printed in the November and December issues of the *Russian Messenger*, arousing a fury of abuse and recrimination in the radical and progressive press. As Anna puts it quite mildly, serenely looking back on the turbulent past, "I must say that *The Devils* had an enormous success with the reading public, but at the same time it brought my husband a great many enemies in the literary world."[42]

6

During all this time, the Dostoevskys had been living from hand to mouth on advances from Katkov, and with the conclusion of *The Devils*, this source of income ceased to exist. Anna thought of contributing to the family funds by taking up her old employment as a stenographer, and she obtained a testimony to her skills from her teacher, Professor Olkhin, who had once recommended her to Dostoevsky. Learning from her brother that a stenographer would be required for some sort of conference in the western provinces, she applied for the temporary post and was accepted; but the plan came to nothing when the question arose of her traveling and living arrangements while away from home.

One of her brother's friends, an impetuous and somewhat uncouth young man known as "the wild Asian" to his comrades (he came from the Caucasus), was also going to the conference and was invited by Anna's brother to provide the Dostoevskys with further information on the event. Dostoevsky, as it turned out, was the literary idol of "the wild Asian," who fervently offered to travel with Anna Grigoryevna, so as to shield her from any possible unpleasantness. Also, in response to an inquiry about suitable hotels, he volunteered to change his plans and reside wherever Anna was living. At this, Dostoevsky pounded his fist on the table with such force that he broke a glass of tea, leaped to his feet, threw his overcoat over his shoulders, and rushed out of the apartment. Anna pursued him, both worried about a possible seizure and also indignant at his jealous rage. She finally succeeded in placating him enough so that he became embarrassed under her reproaches at such an unjustified insult to her own fidelity and to her concern for their family happiness. The evening ended with a pledge on his part never to be jealous again (a pledge he found impossible to keep) and some good-humored chaffing by Anna, who confesses that "I couldn't be angry with him for long." All the same, and whatever Dostoevsky's promise, Anna knew that his emotions could easily fly out of control, and "after this episode I realized that I would have to decline any new work." Not being able to endure her absence, he would inevitably come to fetch her, "there would be a scandalous scene," money would be wasted, and all her earnings would go for nothing.[43]

Anna, however, was not one to abandon an idea, and she was determined to help her husband increase the family income. A new opportunity arose when Dostoevsky turned to publishers for the sale of the rights to *The Devils* as an independent volume. He had hoped to net a considerable sum, but the hail of unfavorable criticism lowered the novel's value in the marketplace, and the offers he received were derisory for an important work by a famous author. He and Anna thus decided to publish the book themselves—at last realizing a long-cherished dream that Dostoevsky had nourished ever since the mid-1840s. He had mentioned such an idea to his elder brother Mikhail at that time, and he and Anna had mulled over the same dream during their years of beggary abroad. It is impossible to imagine, however, that he would have embarked on such an enterprise without Anna's enthusiastic encouragement. The project was financially risky and might have the effect of sinking them even further into debt. Publishing in Russia, as Dostoevsky well knew from sad experience, was a cutthroat affair, and they were warned by friends not to venture recklessly into such dangerous waters. But the rewards were too enticing to resist, and, even more important, he had by this time acquired a healthy respect for Anna's ability and resourcefulness as a businesswoman.

With justifiable pride, Anna describes in her *Reminiscences* how she made presumably innocent and casual inquiries of booksellers and printers about costs, discounts, and so on, carefully concealing her real purposes, and gathered all the necessary information about the secrets of the trade. The Dostoevskys then went ahead to publish *The Devils* on their own, buying the paper, arranging for the printing and binding, and turning out an edition of 3,500 copies. When an advertisement in *Golos* (*The Voice*) apprised the public of their venture, the doorbell of their apartment began to ring incessantly. Anna conducted all the negotiations with the buyers, who immediately tried to beat her down on the amount of the discount to booksellers. But she remained firm at 20 percent, except for a large order from the provinces for which she allowed 30 percent. The Dostoevskys were thus launched as a publishing firm. This was, as Anna writes with satisfaction, "the cornerstone of our joint publishing activity, and, after [Feodor Mikhailovich's] death, of my own work, which continued for thirty-eight years." When their first edition was sold out, they had earned a profit of four thousand rubles—which far exceeded what they had lost because "two or three swindlers took advantage of my publishing inexperience."[44] Dostoevsky was thus no longer, as he had once called himself, "a literary proletarian," entirely dependent for subsistence on his wage slavery to editors and publishers, though he never achieved the total independence of his fellow authors from the gentry.

Long before he became a publisher, however, or even fancied that he could really become one, he had thought of another means of rescuing himself from his humiliating literary subservience. Several times in his correspondence from abroad he had mentioned the idea of a new sort of journalistic publication that he wished to create, and he even worked such a notion into the text of *The Devils*. Liza Drozdova, wishing to be "useful" to her country, tells Shatov about her plan for a yearly almanac that would be a selection of facts about Russia, but all chosen in such a way as to convey "an intention, a thought, illuminating all of the whole, all taken together" (10: 103–104). As far back as 1864–1865, Dostoevsky had also jotted down notes for a biweekly publication to be called a *Notebook* (*Zapisnye Knigi*). This is clearly the origin of what became his *Diary of a Writer* (*Dnevnik Pisatelya*); and his wife tells us that he was toying with the possibility of starting such a publication just at this time. But he was afraid to begin because the economic risks were even greater than those of taking the plunge into publishing.

Dostoevsky's inclusion into the Meshchersky circle, though, had already led him to suggest the publication of a yearly almanac à la Liza

Drozdova as a supplement to *The Citizen*, which would contain contributions by himself as well as others, and an announcement of such a supplement had appeared in October. He also participated in discussions about, and revisions of, articles written by Meshchersky during the Wednesday evening gatherings at the prince's home. In effect, he gradually slipped into becoming a member of the magazine's editorial board; and when an editorial crisis arose in the winter of 1872/1873, it was only natural that he, the famous writer now freed from the burden of his novel, should be the person to whom all turned in their hour of need.

G. K. Gradovsky, the moderately liberal editor whom Prince Meshchersky had engaged for a period of two years, proved to be less pliable than the prince had expected. He became increasingly dissatisfied with the prince's interference in editorial matters and notified him in the fall of 1872 that he would offer his resignation unless entrusted with full charge of the journal. Meshchersky was hardly the man to submit to such an ultimatum, and the question of who might replace Gradovsky became an incessant subject of conversation in the circle all through the following months. Whether the novelist, as Meshchersky affirms, suddenly offered to take over the post himself one evening, or whether, as Anna writes, he finally succumbed to the prince's urgings remains unclear; but on December 17, Maikov mentions in a letter that Dostoevsky was to be the new editor. His salary was set at the modest sum of three thousand rubles a year, although he was also to be paid at space rates for all his own contributions; the meticulous Anna estimates that his income as editor amounted to a yearly five thousand rubles. Thus, for the first time in his literary life, he could count on a regular income; and besides this substantial advantage, he now had the opportunity to experiment with his idea for the *Diary of a Writer*. Moreover, after his long isolation from the Russian literary scene, which he had been able to follow only from afar in Europe, he unquestionably savored the chance to make his voice heard directly once again on all the social-cultural issues confronting his troubled country.

Before assuming the editorship, however, his appointment required the approval of the press authorities. As an ex-convict, Dostoevsky was still under police surveillance, and approval of the Third Section (as the secret police were known) was also required. Prudently replying that "they would not take on themselves the responsibility for the future activity of this personality in the position of an editor," these authorities bowed to the assurances by the Meshchersky circle that "Dostoevsky as a novelist has fully atoned for having been a political criminal in 1848."[45] On December 20 he was confirmed as editor-in-chief of *The Citizen*, which, as he would learn to his cost, meant that he, not Prince Meshchersky, would be held legally responsible for any infraction of the press laws. In the last issue of the journal for 1872, an announcement, spread over two pages and replacing the usual leading article, proclaimed that F. M. Dostoevsky would assume the editorship as of January 1, 1873. A new phase in Dostoevsky's literary activity thus began, whose unexpected ideological twists and turns would surprise both his friends and his enemies during the seven years still remaining to his life.

# CHAPTER 3

# *Grazhdanin: The Citizen*

Dostoevsky's assumption of the editorship of *The Citizen* unquestionably gave him a great deal of satisfaction both practically and personally. But his duties turned out to be far more demanding than he had anticipated, partly because of his own exigent literary standards and partly because the editorial interference of Prince Meshchersky plagued him as much as it had Gradovsky. In the memoirs he wrote late in life, the prince declared that he had never encountered "such a staunch and total conservative as Dostoevsky."[1] Although this characterization may have been true of his relation to the Russian monarchy, which he saw as sacrosanct and immutable because so deeply rooted in the sentiments of the people, it was certainly not true of all the current issues of social life on which *The Citizen* took a stand from week to week.

Meshchersky was sarcastically known in radical circles as Prince Full Stop (*tochek*, a period at the end of a sentence) after having flatly declared in one of his articles that "it is necessary to bring the fundamental reforms [initiated by Alexander II with the liberation of the serfs in 1861] to a full stop."[2] Dostoevsky, however, had been, and still was, a strong supporter of such reforms, which he believed crucial for maintaining Russian internal stability whatever their deficiencies in practice. A clash of views between him and the prince thus became inevitable. Moreover, he soon discovered that he was not, as he had probably been led to believe, in full charge of the journal, and his task as editor was complicated by the difficulty of meeting deadlines when galley proofs of every article had to be approved by Meshchersky as well as by himself.

Besides the constant irritations inherent in such a situation, which agitated his easily irascible temperament, it is clear that he had seriously underestimated the amount of time and energy required to edit a weekly journal (his previous experience had been with a monthly). The sheer physical and nervous strain turned out to be far greater than he had anticipated, and he found himself dashing off even the articles of his column, the *Diary of a Writer*, at the very last moment while at work in the printing plant reading the galleys of the issue in which it was to be included. Exhausting though it was, however, his stint as an editor placed him once again in firsthand contact with the problems assailing

Russian society, and gave him a new insight into the young intelligent-sia of the 1870s, who were modifying the views of the previous genera-tion in ways that he found unexpectedly sympathetic.

## 2

Dostoevsky's appearance in the editorial offices of *The Citizen* to take over his new functions is recorded in the best memoir written about him. Twenty-three-year-old Varvara V. Timofeyeva, a young woman who had literary ambitions herself, was then writing a column about social-cultural events in the radical journal *Iskra* (*The Spark*) and worked as a proofreader in the printing plant producing *The Citizen* to supplement her very scanty income. Later in life she published novels and stories, one of which earned a favorable mention from Tolstoy, and she set down her recollections, based on notebook entries, in 1904. Her portrait is particularly valuable for the intelligence and sensitivity of her observations and because, in the course of their work together, a per-sonal and intellectual intimacy developed between them that allowed the usually taciturn and secretive Dostoevsky to speak freely in a quite unusually self-revealing fashion. Timofeyeva thus gives us a striking pic-ture of him, not only as a personality, but also in terms of what may be called his ideological physiognomy at this time of his life; and her own comments help to define the social-cultural climate to which he was then reacting and responding.

Word had spread in the printing plant that Dostoevsky was to be the next editor of *The Citizen*, and Timofeyeva—for whom, despite *The Dev-ils*, he was still the literary idol who had written *The Insulted and In-jured* and *House of the Dead*—could hardly contain her excitement. The idea that she would soon be in his presence filled her with rapture and awe: "At this moment, there would arrive here the famous author of *Poor Folk* and *House of the Dead*, the creator of Raskolnikov and *The Idiot*—he would arrive, and something extraordinary, new would hap-pen to me . . . *afterward*, nothing would be at all like now." Her first glimpse of her idol, however, proved that "my own imagination had painted for me a totally different picture not at all resembling the real one before me." What she saw was a middle-aged man who was "very pale—with a sallow, unhealthy paleness—and who seemed very tired and perhaps ill." He stood there "with a gloomy, exhausted face, cov-ered like a net with some sort of unusually expressive shadings caused by a tightly restrained movement of the muscles. As if every muscle on this face with sunken cheeks and a broad, high forehead was alive with feeling and thought. And these feelings and thoughts were irresistibly pushing to come to the surface, but not allowed to do so by the iron will of this frail and yet at the same time thick-set, quiet and gloomy man with broad shoulders."[3]

If Dostoevsky's appearance failed to conform to Timofeyeva's preconceived image, neither at first did his behavior. On that first morning, the creator of works filled with sympathy and compassion for others politely shook hands with his proofreader, bowing slightly, after a formal introduction. "His hand was cold, dry, and as it were lifeless. Indeed, everything about him that day seemed lifeless: limp, as if without movement, with a barely audible voice and lackluster eyes that fastened on me like two immovable dots." He sat silently at his table, reading proof for an hour without uttering a single word; even his pen moved silently over the proof sheets as he made corrections. Timofeyeva, reading proof as well, was subconsciously disturbed by this impassive presence: "Perhaps, because of this deathly stillness, I suddenly felt some unnatural timidity weighing me down."[4]

Dostoevsky produced a very similar impression on Mikhail A. Alexandrov, the foreman in charge of typesetting at the printing plant. His recollections published in 1892, are of special interest because they convey the impressions of a highly skilled and literate workman, but not someone with a higher education and thus an inferior in the Russian social hierarchy. Alexandrov writes that "under the influence of first impressions, I found that Feodor Mikhailovich was a *mistrustful* and suspicious person. I noticed, for example, that in speaking with me he looked scrutinizingly straight into my eyes, or in general at my face; not at all avoiding the meeting of our eyes, he did not hasten to turn away his look or direct it onto something else; one became uneasy under the effect of this quietly inquisitive regard."[5] Later, when he became more familiar with Alexandrov (as well as with Timofeyeva), he no longer employed this searching, upsetting stare.

Alexandrov also makes a shrewd attempt to analyze this stare as more than simply a personal trait. Not being a member of the intelligentsia himself, Alexandrov is able to intuit a more general sense of how Dostoevsky might be perceived (or thought he might be perceived) by those who knew nothing about him except through hearsay. Remarking that he was "particularly mistrustful in relation to *ordinary* people he did not know," Alexandrov explains this attitude partly by his fear of being looked on only as an ex-convict and thus of being treated with disrespect (italics added). "As a result," Alexandrov continues, "Feodor Mikhailovich considered it necessary to be of a serious strictness in his relations with those whose mode of thought was totally unknown, and only later, when he was fully convinced of the absence of any vulgar prejudice against him, would he begin to trust those whom he examined in this way, the degree of which, however, varied."[6] Even though

Dostoevsky was well known and ill famed for the prickliness of his character, only aggravated after Siberia by the shattering effects of epilepsy on his nerves, Alexandrov's remarks quite plausibly add a social-psychological dimension to what is usually considered only a personal characteristic.

If such extremely wary behavior with "ordinary people" was the result of uncertainty, his reserve with members of the young intelligentsia like Timofeyeva stemmed from quite the opposite cause. After the denunciations of *The Devils* in the radical and progressive press, he could be practically certain that he would be looked on, if not with outright hostility, then certainly with distaste and repulsion as a renegade from the radical ranks. Someone like the young Timofeyeva, he could be sure, would share some of the sentiments expressed in all the personally wounding words that had been uttered against him; and she herself bears out such a view of his suspicions. "In liberal literary circles," she writes, "and among the student youth, with whom I had some familiarity, he was unceremoniously called someone 'off his rocker,' or—more delicately—a 'mystic,' or 'abnormal' (which, as understood in those days, meant the same thing). This was the time just after the din had died down of the Nechaev trial and the publication of *The Devils* in the *Russian Messenger*. We, the young people, had read the speeches of the noted trial lawyers in *The Voice* and the *St. Petersburg News*, and Dostoevsky's novel seemed to us then a monstrous caricature, a nightmare of mystical ecstasies and psychopathology. . . . And after the author of *The Devils* assumed the editorship of *The Citizen*, many of his friends and admirers turned against him once and for all."[7]

Even aside from such ideological undercurrents, Dostoevsky proved to be a stern and exacting taskmaster as an editor, and he did very little (in fact, quite the opposite) to win over his subordinates. Indeed, he made it abundantly clear that he wished his orders to be obeyed without question, even when, as sometimes proved to be the case, they were unreasonable or impossible to carry out. During the first weeks, when he and Timofeyeva had as yet exchanged just a few remarks about editorial matters, she was once bold enough to point out an infraction of Russian grammar in his text. He angrily snapped back: "Every author has his own style, and therefore his own grammar! I don't care at all about someone else's rule!"[8] He became so irritable over such trifles that Timofeyeva decided to leave well enough alone, once letting pass Dostoevsky's mistaken reference to a novel by Herzen when he obviously intended to cite one by Chernyshevsky. When he criticized her "oversight," she explained disingenuously that she had been afraid to make a change because of his insistence that "everything must remain as found in his proof sheets." "Feodor Mikhailovich looked at me suspiciously without uttering a word. Perhaps he understood from this that for me the very spirit of his *Diary* was alien and antipathetic. And he was partly right."[9] The slip, instantly noted by the hostile columnists who pored over Dostoevsky's every word with a magnifying glass, was taken as another instance of his mental debility.

Both Timofeyeva and Alexandrov found it difficult at first to adjust to the severity and imperiousness of Dostoevsky's demands and his manner. For Timofeyeva especially, accustomed to the free-and-easy camaraderie of the radical journalistic milieu, his domineering behavior was an unpleasant and disillusioning surprise. "Neither his peremptory tone, to which I was totally unaccustomed, nor his peevishly dissatisfied remarks and exasperated anxieties over a wrongly placed comma, fitted in with my image of the writer as *man*, the writer as *sufferer*, the writer as *seer of the human heart*."[10] Indeed, Timofeyeva was deeply shocked one day by an episode involving Alexandrov (he also records it, but in a milder form). It was this incident, she remarks, that led the German supervisor of the plant to comment scornfully that the great writer was no less arrogant than Prince Meshchersky, ill famed among the workers for his vociferous abusiveness.

The incident involved a last-minute change in proof that Dostoevsky asked for as the journal was going to press. A dispatch had arrived that he thought would liven up the article, and so, cutting a few lines, he instructed Alexandrov to replace them with the insert. Alexandrov replied that he could not do so without resetting eight pages, and this extra work might hold up the printing schedule. Flying into a rage at this reasonable response, he shouted at Alexandrov "like a landowner" (*pro-barski*) to make the change one way or the other. "'Whether on the wall or the ceiling, I want [this] printed,'" he shrieked, according to Timofeyeva, "his face turning dead-white, his lips twitching spasmodically." Alexandrov answered that he was not capable of such miracles; and at this ironic retort, which could be considered insolent, Dostoevsky thundered that he needed people who would carry out his instructions to the letter "with doglike devotion." (Timofeyeva was outraged by this phrase.) If Alexandrov would not comply with his orders, he would find someone else more obliging. He scribbled off a note on the spot— handing it to the silent and stony-faced Timofeyeva for transmission— demanding that Alexandrov be dismissed immediately. But the insertion was dropped, the note was never passed on, and nothing more was heard about firing Alexandrov.[11]

Dostoevsky was given to such sudden explosions of uncontrollable rage, during which he could not master his behavior or his words, and he was known in the plant as the *serdityi*, the irate or angry one. But there was still something about him, as Alexandrov explains, different from the usual upper-class superciliousness that someone like himself invariably encountered while exercising "my modest profession." And so, despite Dostoevsky's rudeness, Alexandrov was "inspired with the courage to ask him for a favor." *The Devils* had just been published as a book, and copies were kept in the office of the printing plant to be sold to subscribers of *The Citizen* at a discount. Alexandrov was curious about the work, which, as he had heard, "poured scorn on everything that was then called Russian liberalism," but he could not afford to buy a copy. His favor was to ask permission to borrow one from stock. Dostoevsky listened to his request quietly and, probably feeling some remorse, without a moment's hesitation told him to take a copy as a gift.[12] Some months later Alexandrov brought him an article he had written about his schooldays, as a contribution to the never-ending discussion then being carried on about how best to educate the people—a discussion greatly stimulated by Tolstoy's views and the example furnished by his school for peasant children founded at Yasnaya Polyana in 1862. A day later, Dostoevsky told Alexandrov that his article would be published in *The Citizen* and urged him to continue to write. From that time on, he always addressed Alexandrov, both jestingly and flatteringly, as a fellow author. When in 1875 he was making preparations to publish his *Diary of a Writer* as an independent publication, he took great pains to place Alexandrov in charge of its production.

3
———

Varvara Timofeyeva's relations with Dostoevsky were much more complicated, and she only gradually overcame her hostility to his chilling reserve and her own oscillations between past reverence and present disappointment. The ice was broken very late one evening when they were sitting together, almost alone in the deserted printing plant, going over the proofs of an article in his *Diary*. It was devoted to an art exhibition in Petersburg (we shall return to this article in Chapter 5), and Timofeyeva was struck by the analysis of one painting in particular, a work of the well-known artist N. N. Ge called *A Mysterious Evening*. It referred in fact to the Last Supper; but this momentous event was painted as if it had taken place in the Petersburg of the present, and the work was a favorite of the radicals precisely for this reason. Timofeyeva gives their point of view when she speaks of "all the apostles in the picture [being shown] as if they were present-day 'Socialists,' Christ—as we see him—'a good, simple man with an ecstatic temperament,' and Judas—the most ordinary spy or *agent provocateur* receiving payment for a denunciation."[13]

4. *A Mysterious Evening*, by N. N. Ge

Dostoevsky's article criticized this reduction of the great Christian theme to a day in the life of a Russian radical, and Timofeyeva quotes him, not quite literally, as writing: "Where can we find the eighteen centuries of Christianity here? Where is the idea, inspiring so many people, so many minds and hearts? Where is the Messiah, the Savior promised to the world—where is Christ?"[14] Like most of the younger radicals of the 1870s, Timofeyeva had become responsive to the moral values of Christianity, and she was swept away by the passion of Dostoevsky's eloquence, which aroused memories of the reverence for Christ imbibed during childhood from her mother, "a woman of burning faith, sometimes suffering from my 'disbelief.'" "Suddenly," she recalls, "without knowing why myself, I was irresistibly drawn to look at him.... Feodor Mikhailovich looked at me intently and point-blank, with an expression that seemed to indicate he had been observing me for some time and waiting for me to turn my glance toward him."[15] The young woman's face must have shown Dostoevsky that she had been moved, though neither uttered a word; and when, long after midnight, she came to say good-bye, he stood up, clasped her hands, and spoke to her tenderly, almost like a father, as he led her to the door. "You wore yourself out today," he said solicitously. "Hurry home and sleep well.

44

Christ be with you! Be sure to take a cab, don't walk. Some drunken lout might insult you."[16] Timofeyeva did walk home that night all the same, filled with joyful exuberance at having at last encountered what she felt to be the *real* Dostoevsky, the one whose books had moved her so intensely, and by seeing him at last illuminated by the power of his thought and the depth of his feeling.

Dostoevsky's attitude toward his proofreader changed from that time on; and though he was always subject to sudden shifts of mood, when he would retreat broodingly into himself, his relations with Timofeyeva became more relaxed, open, and friendly. He began to take a personal interest in her and once asked what she wanted to do with her life. Why was she in Petersburg at all? Why was she working in the plant? She replied that she wished to study and learn, that she spent all her available time at the public library, and that, eventually, she hoped to become a writer. He asked whether she considered this to be an easy task, and when she gave a negative answer, he went on to say: "Of women writers in the world there is only one worthy of the name—George Sand. Will you be able to become somebody like George Sand?" Paralyzed by this challenge, the poor girl could only stammer: "I want to write! I feel the need. . . . I live only for that!" At these impassioned words, he responded "seriously" that she should certainly pursue her goal; and he gave her some advice only partially borne out by his own practice: "Never invent a story or intrigue. Take what life itself gives you. Life is always richer than all our fabrications."[17]

Dostoevsky returned quite often to such literary topics in conversation with Timofeyeva. Once he warned her against following the younger Populist writers in overusing dialect words or expressions; on another occasion they quarreled about the past. Although the Populists no longer accepted the Utilitarian morality of the 1860s, they nonetheless continued to revere those who had once upheld the banner of revolution in its name. When he launched into a scathing criticism of a poem by Nikolay Dobrolyubov, accusing it of being the typical product of a "seminarian," filled with falsity and empty rhetoric, he could see that he was trampling on someone enshrined in Timofeyeva's pantheon. " 'But, sorry'—he added sarcastically, glancing at me in passing—'it seems that I have just now offended your feelings . . . well, what's to be done! There is no way for me to think of him otherwise!' " Timofeyeva comments that "in the tone and words of Dostoevsky I heard for the first time something *personal*, as if the faraway echo of his quarrels with the enemy camp."[18]

Such altercations with his foes from the 1860s still rankled, but his attitude toward his own generation of the 1840s was more ambivalent. This contrast is clear in *The Devils*, where the lovable reprobate Stepan

Trofimovich Verkhovensky is treated much more kindly than his coldly ruthless son Peter. Dostoevsky never rejected the heritage of the 1840s entirely. Once, as he and Timofeyeva were reading the proofs of an article by Nikolay N. Strakhov on Edward Zeller's history of German philosophy, he suddenly turned to her and said: "Do you wish to be a genuinely cultivated woman?" Upon her enthusiastically positive reply, he instructed her to "go to the public library and ask for the *Notes of the Fatherland* for the years 1840–1845. There you will find a series of essays on the history of the study of nature—by Herzen. Although later, when he became a materialist, he renounced this book, it is the best of his things. It's the best philosophy, not only in Russia—in Europe as well."[19] Alexander Herzen's *Letters on the Study of Nature* (1845), written before he went into exile in Europe, constitutes a brief Left Hegelian history of modern thought, which is set in the context of the rise of science and its effect on such thinkers as Francis Bacon and René Descartes. Herzen called for a synthesis between materialism (empiricism) and idealism because the increasing dominance of materialism from the Renaissance to the Enlightenment had led to "a growing assertion of the self . . . [to] social atomization or even the disintegration of personality."[20] The author of *Notes from Underground* and *Crime and Punishment* still continued to pay tribute to the penetrating insight of such observations, which accord so well with the problems dramatized by his own characters.

Dostoevsky's increasing fondness for his sympathetic and impressionable (but by no means entirely submissive) proofreader from the Populist camp, whose sincerity, literary ambition, and moral idealism he came to admire, is indicated by another conversation. When she "spoke to him of my dreams and hopes, of my efforts to create for myself an independent activity that I loved, to reach my cherished goal— and of how hard this was for a woman," he listened attentively and then said he would pay her a compliment—the compliment of comparing her with his first wife, Marya Dimitrievna. He had once called her, in a letter written long ago, "a knight in female clothing," and more recently he had immortalized her in the imperious and unforgettably moving Katerina Ivanovna Marmeladova of *Crime and Punishment.* "She was," he told his enraptured listener, "a woman with a lofty and fiery soul. She consumed herself, you might say, in the flame of this fieriness, in her striving for the ideal. She was an idealist in the full sense of the word—yes!!—and pure-hearted, and sometimes as naïve as a child."[21] Once he had begun to see Timofeyeva in such a light, it is little wonder that he allowed himself a freedom of utterance with her that provides some rare and unusual glimpses of impulsive self-revelation.

One such is her depiction of him coming across her reading a copy of Goethe's *Torquato Tasso.* Suddenly he began to reel off by heart one of the monologues of the poet-hero in the play and declaimed in lofty tones, "There is nowhere on earth in which I would debase myself / where I could bear insult peacefully."[22] On another occasion, just as his editorship of *The Citizen* was running out, he began to reminisce about his past and recited some favorite verses from the poetry of the noted radical Nikolay Ogarev—verses in which the poet, opening the Bible at random, hopes "That would come to me by the will of fate / The life, and grief, and death of a prophet." Timofeyeva continues: "Feodor Mikhailovich then got up, stepped into the middle of the room, and with flashing eyes and inspired gestures—exactly like a priest before an invisible sacrificial altar—recited for us [another person was present] *The Prophet* of Pushkin, then of Lermontov."* For Timofeyeva, it seemed that the poems "were by neither Byron nor Lermontov but were Dostoevsky's own confession. To this day I still hear how he twice repeated: 'I know only—that I can endure / . . . And can endure!—'"[23]

To Timofeyeva as well, in the course of an impromptu attack on the danger to Russia of absorbing European influences, he rejected bitterly the radical view of the Russian people as "savage and ignorant" compared with European populations (an opinion that by this time was quite out of date among the Populists). "Yes," he said, "our people are holy in comparison with those over there. . . . in Rome, in Naples, on the streets I was made the most shameful offers—youths, almost children. Disgusting, unnatural vices—and openly, before everybody, and no one even bothered about it. Try to do that amongst us! All our people would condemn it, because for *our* people that's a deadly sin, but there—it's in the customs, a simple habit, nothing more." When Timofeyeva objected that it was not *this* aspect that admirers of the West wished to emulate, he rancorously replied that "there is no other," that "Rome went to pieces because they began to transplant Greece among themselves; beginning with luxuries, fashions, and various sciences and arts, it ends with sodomy and general corruption." Timofeyeva then asked whether peoples should build Chinese walls against each other, and Dostoevsky, looking at her wrathfully, snapped back: "You don't understand anything as yet!" He remained silent the remainder of their time together; but the next day "he once again confided his thoughts to me. Obviously he suffered from his spiritual isolation, his sense of not being understood and misinterpreted, and unburdened his heart to me because he never doubted that, no matter what he said, he could count on my sympathy."[24]

---

* The poem of Mikhail Lermontov that Timofeyeva refers to is a translation of Byron's "Farewell," first published by Lermontov in 1859 and then appearing in a collection of translations of Byron by Russian poets in 1864. Dostoevsky cites the original version of Lermontov's translation. See *DVS*, 2: 517.

If Timofeyeva objected to the extremity of Dostoevsky's anti-Western-ism, though probably sharing his dislike of the once-popular denigra-tion of the Russian people in Nihilist thought, she found it even more difficult to accept his literal predictions of apocalyptic doom triggered by recent political events. Lifting up his head from the proofs of an article dealing with Prussia, Bismarck, and the papacy, he declared: "They [presumably Timofeyeva's radical friends] do not suspect that soon everything will come to an end—all their 'progress' and chatter! They have no inkling that the Antichrist has been born . . . and is *com-ing*—." Dostoevsky, she says, "pronounced this with an expression in his face and voice as if announcing to me a terrible and grandiose se-cret." When she gingerly expressed some skepticism, he struck the table with his fist and "proclaimed like a mullah in his minaret: 'The Anti-christ is coming! It is coming! And the end of the world is closer—closer than they think!'" Timofeyeva confesses, with some retrospective em-barrassment, that she could not help recalling the opinion about him accepted by her Populist comrades: "ravings, epileptic hallucinations . . . the mania of one idea . . . an obsession."[25] But, she writes discern-ingly, who knows whether it was not perhaps at such moments that he caught a glimpse of his wonderful *Dream of a Ridiculous Man* or his superb Legend of the Grand Inquisitor? Just how literally Dostoevsky believed in the Antichrist can only remain a matter for speculation; but Timofeyeva rightly saw that his greatest works originated in the eschato-logical imagination that could view the world in the looming shadow of such a possibility.

Timofeyeva had no such negative reaction to another of their dia-logues on religious matters, which followed hard on his compliment to her as resembling his first wife, the *idealistika*. He then said:

"Well, you still haven't told me what is your ideal? . . . "

"There is just a single ideal . . . for anyone who knows the Gospels."

"And you know them?" he asked suspiciously.

"As a child I was very religious, and read them constantly."

"But since then, of course, you have grown up, become wiser, and having received an education from science and art. . . . " On the corners of his lips appeared the "crooked" smile so well known to me.

"Then," I continued in the same tone, "under the influence of science, this religiosity began to take another form, but I have al-ways thought and still think, that we have nothing better and finer than the Gospels."

"But how do you understand the Gospels? They are interpreted in different ways. In your opinion, what is their essential substance?"

The question he posed made me think about the matter for the first time.

But immediately—like some far-off voice from the depths of my memory—the answer came: "The realization of the teachings of Christ on earth, in our life, in our conscience. . . ."

"And that's all?"—he said slowly in a tone of disillusionment.

This seemed little indeed even to me. "No, there's still . . . Not everything finishes here, on earth. . . . All this life on earth is only a step . . . to another existence."

"To other worlds!" he exclaimed triumphantly, throwing up his arm to the wide-open window, through which could be seen a beautiful, bright, and luminous June sky.

This revelatory exchange focuses the crux of Dostoevsky's ideological-artistic preoccupations during the 1870s—the conflict between a worldly (Utopian Socialist and Populist) acceptance of Christian morality and one grounded in divine transcendence. It is then followed by some poignant words: "'And what a wonderful though tragic task this is—to tell this to the people—' he continued, momentarily hiding his eyes with his hands—'wonderful and tragic because there is so much suffering here. So much suffering, but then—so much grandeur! . . . absolutely incomparable! . . . It's impossible to compare it with any well-being in the world!'"[26] Nowhere else in the Dostoevsky canon do we find another passage expressing so simply and spontaneously his conception of his own creative task and the core values of his theodicy.

4

These intimate conversations with Varvara Timofeyeva, combined with the more public expressions of Populist ideas that we shall examine in the next chapter, certainly influenced Dostoevsky's opinion of the new radical generation and led to a softening of the harsh judgment expressed in *The Devils*. Through her reactions he could see that there was no longer any *irreconcilable* opposition between the Christian moral values he had defended all through the 1860s and those of the Populists (no matter how much they might differ as to what such values led to in practice, and whether these beliefs had a divine or exclusively human origin). He could still, he became aware, evoke some responsiveness in the new generation; and this ability was additionally confirmed by a letter from Vsevolod Solovyev (a son of the famous historian, S. M. Solovyev), who wrote Dostoevsky the moment he learned that the novelist was again in Petersburg.

5. Vsevolod Solovyev, a young
writer and friend of Dostoevsky's

Vsevolod Solovyev had just embarked on a career as a journalist, and he was later to become a well-known historical novelist. He told Dostoevsky how much his novels had helped to shape and support his own religious convictions, upheld in arguments with school comrades mouthing the more fashionable doctrines of Nihilist atheism. Moreover, despite such differences of opinion, he assured him that the friends with whom he disputed "consider you among the best Russian writers, and regard *Crime and Punishment* as one of the best works—yes, but all the same, the recognition of your talent still lies ahead. Russian society still does not understand you as it should, it is not yet mature enough for such an understanding, and listens to your words, which amply open its eyes, with confusion and dismay."[27] Dostoevsky was so moved by this tribute that, instead of replying, he called on his young admirer a few days later and left his card. Returning the visit, Solovyev soon became Dostoevsky's friend and literary protégé, and no one in the future would support him more staunchly and more consistently in the Russian press. Like Timofeyeva, he helped to relieve Dostoevsky's fear that he had become isolated from the Russian younger generation, whom he felt it so important to reach and whom he hoped to dissuade from embarking on the self-destructive path (as he knew only too well) of social revolution.

Dostoevsky also exchanged letters with Vsevolod's younger brother Vladimir, destined to become the most important Russian philosopher of the turn of the century. A poet as well as a philosopher, Vladimir was a capricious, eccentric, quite engaging personality, with a whimsical sense of humor. He might be considered a highly intellectualized and spiritualized type of the holy fool (*yurodivi*), which in Russian culture always implies some relation to the religious and the sacred. From Moscow, Vladimir had sent an article to *The Citizen* in 1873, with an accompanying letter that spoke admiringly of the tendency of the journal and of Dostoevsky's initial columns in his *Diary of a Writer*. They had refused, he wrote approvingly, to accept "the superstitious reverence" displayed in Russian literature for "the anti-Christian foundations of civilization," a reverence that made any "free judgment of these foundations" impossible.[28] Dostoevsky rejected Vladimir's first article but accepted another a year later after receiving a copy of Vladimir's master's thesis, *The Crisis in Western Philosophy*. This talented work had caused a considerable stir for its brilliant style, its deep erudition, and its attack on the reigning acceptance of a semiscientific positivism inconsistently mingled with the profession of secularized Christian moral values.

Vladimir Solovyev's work had been strongly influenced by the Slavophilism of Ivan Kireyevsky and Aleksey Khomiakov, whom Dostoevsky also admired, as well as by the religious philosophy of the later Friedrich Schelling. He argued, as all these thinkers had done, that Western rationalism was now bankrupt, and he brought matters up to date by claiming that the most recent developments of Western thought—Arthur

6. Vladimir Solovyev, younger brother of Vsevolod, also a friend of Dostoevsky's and an important Russian philosopher

Schopenhauer and the then-fashionable Eduard Hartmann's *Philosophy of the Unconscious*—were moving in the direction of a fusion with the truths preserved in the religions of the East, specifically in Eastern Orthodox Christianity. Dostoevsky could well have seen the book as a grandiose philosophical elaboration of what he had advocated long ago in his journalism as the program of *pochvennichestvo*, the return of the Europeanized intelligentsia to their native soil and its religious roots.

Like his older brother Vsevolod, Vladimir had gone through an acute radical period under the influence of reading Pisarev, and he confesses that "between the ages of fourteen and eighteen I passed through various phases of theoretical and practical negation."[29] Dostoevsky's novels had certainly been one of the most effective remedies that aided both brothers to overcome their adolescent Nihilism. Vladimir once remarked that among the pages he most admired were certain passages in *The Devils*; and among them would certainly have been those in which Kirillov traverses the deadly dialectic of attempting to replace the God-man with the man-god. Indeed, Dostoevsky's unmasking of the mortal dangers of an unrestrained egoism was decisive for Solovyev's thought, which constantly stresses the importance of attaining a new reconciliation between the atomistic ego, released from the religious bonds of the past, and a revitalized source of absolute moral values.

Dostoevsky, according to his wife, was very much taken with his young philosopher-admirer, who became a frequent visitor to their home in 1873. He reminded her husband, Anna tells us, of a friend of his youth, the restless, innerly tormented, and tempestuous poet and God-seeker Ivan Nikolaevich Shidlovsky,* who had played an important role in his own artistic-spiritual formation. "You resemble him to such a degree in appearance and character," he once told Vladimir, "that at certain moments I feel his soul to be living in you."[30] Solovyev's pale, gaunt, and angular face, with large, black eyes fixed in a distant stare, was framed by locks of hair falling to his stooping shoulders. His image has been compared with the Christ figure appearing in some Russian icons, and peasants, often taking him for a priest, would kneel down to obtain his blessing. Preferring a comparison with Italian Renaissance art, Dostoevsky was reminded of the Christ image in one of his favorite pictures from the Dresden gallery, *The Head of the Young Christ* by Annibale Carracci.

Solovyev left Russia in June 1875 to study abroad, and there he pored over the theosophic and kabbalistic writings in the British Museum. Presumably under their inspiration, he abruptly embarked on a voyage

---

* For more information on Shidlovsky, see my first volume, *Dostoevsky: The Seeds of Revolt, 1821–1849* (Princeton, 1976), chap. 7.

to Egypt. A mysterious revelation, vouchsafed to him in a vision, had assured him that in this land of ancient mystery he would encounter the Divine Sophia, the feminine incarnation of Eternal Wisdom. Learning one day about a tribe in the desert who supposedly had preserved ancient kabbalistic lore, he decided to walk to their camp wearing his usual black-hued European clothes. The local Bedouins took him for some sort of evil spirit, and the story goes that he barely escaped with his life. Solovyev returned unscathed to Russia in July 1876, and became particularly close to Dostoevsky during the very last years of the novelist's life.

## 5

Dostoevsky quickly realized that he had perhaps been overly tempted both by the prospect of financial security and by his desire to participate actively again in Russian literary life. No later than the end of his first month as editor, he confesses to his niece Sofya that he was sadly aware he might have made a mistake. "My time has now shaped up so awfully," he remarks in an apology for not have written more promptly, "that I can only curse myself for the resolve with which I suddenly took upon myself the editorship of the journal."[31]

Soliciting a contribution from the veteran conservative and nationalist historian Mikhail Pogodin, Dostoevsky complains that the weekly, as he discovered to his dismay, had no secretary to take care of routine business matters, and he planned to acquire one as soon as possible. But even so, "I know all the same from experience that it is essential for me to speak in person to the authors of pieces, to those who bring me new ones, and to read through these pieces (and that's horrible). Reading through these articles takes an enormous amount of time and undermines my health, because I sense that time is taken away from my actual employment. Then, having the piece and often deciding to publish it—to correct it from beginning to end, which often has to be done." Even more, "my main source of distress is the mountain of topics on which I would like to write myself." Dostoevsky describes how he often begins an article of his own, realizes that he will not be able to make the deadline, and so starts a new and shorter one, "often late at night on Thursday" because he had promised the prince a piece for that issue and it had to be ready by Friday night (the weekly appeared every Monday). "All of this, I repeat, has a morbid effect on me."[32]

Pogodin, though not a close friend, was an old acquaintance whose staunchly patriotic writings and devotion to Old Russian culture Dostoevsky much admired. Thus, in addition to complaints about the tribulations of his new post, his letter contains a valuable statement of his ideological ambitions as editor. "Much needs to be said," he continues, "for which reason I first joined the journal." As he tells Pogodin, "here is my goal and thought: Socialism, consciously, and both in the most absurdly unconscious way, and in a military dress-coat fashion, in the form of baseness, has corroded an entire generation. . . . We need to fight, because everything has been infected. *My idea is that Socialism and Christianity are antitheses*. That is what I would like to show in a whole series of pieces, but meanwhile I haven't even started" (italics added).[33] Much of the *Diary of a Writer* during 1873 was the fulfillment of this purpose; but here we need only remark on the acuity of Dostoevsky's sense of how the ideological winds had been shifting. It would have been absurd during the 1860s to have wished to *demonstrate* the antithesis of Socialism and Christianity because this was so much taken for granted. The Socialism of Chernyshevsky, Dobrolyubov, and Pisarev, however these three may have differed otherwise, not only advocated atheism but also ridiculed the Christian morality of love and self-sacrifice as the product of an outdated superstition. But times had changed; Socialism was once again being taken, as we have seen in the words of Timofeyeva, much as it had been understood during the days of Dostoevsky's youth in the 1840s—as the realization of the ideals of Christ on earth.

His problems as editor were compounded by the debonair carelessness of Prince Meshchersky about the various rules and regulations governing the Russian press; perhaps he believed that his connections with court circles guaranteed him a certain immunity. If so, as Dostoevsky discovered to his cost, the prince was sadly mistaken. At the end of January 1873, *The Citizen* published an article by the prince describing the reception of a delegation of Kirghiz deputies by the Tsar, and the prince directly quoted some words of Alexander II (he asked the head of the delegation whether he spoke Russian). Unhappily, it was strictly forbidden to cite such august utterances without special permission from the ministry in charge of court affairs, and the nonchalant prince, accustomed to chatting with royalty, had neglected to abide by this formality. *The Citizen* was thus found guilty of violating statute No. 1024 of the rules regulating press behavior. Legal responsibility fell not on the author but on the editor of the publication, F. M. Dostoevsky, who was condemned to pay a fine of twenty-five rubles and spend two days in the guardhouse. His lawyer told him to plead not guilty, and he later commented ironically on the legal advice he was given (and followed) when the violation of the law was perfectly obvious. (The sentence was later served at his convenience in late March 1874, thanks to the good offices of the powerful legal official A. F. Koni.)

What irritated Dostoevsky most was Meshchersky's offhand reaction at having placed his editor in this predicament. Writing to Anna in July 1873, after installing the family in Staraya Russa for the summer, he remarks: "I received quite a nice letter from Meshchersky, who apologizes for my having to go to jail for him (he was probably told by Filippov, to whom I said in my turn that Meshchersky was treating me casually, not even expressing regret that I would be going to jail for him)." Meshchersky's letter, which pleaded ignorance of what had occurred, seemed to satisfy his editor, though it is difficult to comprehend how the matter would not have come to the prince's attention immediately. Dostoevsky also complains to Anna about money matters, the amount supplied by Meshchersky not being sufficient to meet the expenses of paying contributors. "I don't even want to think about the future: my head spins and I fear an attack," he gloomily informs her.[34]

Despite Meshchersky's apology on this occasion, his peremptory tone with an editor whom he considered to be at his beck and call could not help but irritate Dostoevsky's considerable—and, after all, quite justified—sense of self-esteem. The fashionable prince, just then making his début as a writer and eighteen years younger, apparently could not refrain from exercising his authority without giving affront. Just after Dostoevsky returned to Petersburg from a three-day visit to Staraya Russa (he would make the exhausting journey, whenever possible, to spend some time with his family), he writes: "This morning I received at once a telegram and two letters from the prince about publishing his article [concerning a rumor of the engagement of a Russian grand duchess to Prince Alfred of Britain]. His letters struck me as extremely rude: he complains that the issues of the journal cost too much, and that he cannot pay more than 130 rubles per issue and so on. To hell with him! I never wrote that I needed more than 130 rubles and that I lacked money. I'll answer him today sharply enough so that he'll lose the urge to read me a lesson (though, to be sure, his letter also contains very friendly phrases and expressions)."[35] His rankling resentment, as well as his gratitude for Meshchersky's minimal attempt to soothe his feelings, are quite perceptible.

It was, of course, taken for granted that whatever the prince chose to write would be published, and this also caused some friction. One notorious incident occurred when the great Romantic poet Feodor Tyutchev died on July 15, 1873. He had been a member of the Meshchersky circle, and Dostoevsky thus knew him personally, though there is no evidence of any particular intimacy; more important is that Dostoevsky was an enthusiastic admirer of Tyutchev's poetry. Indeed, no contemporary in Russian literature comes closer than Tyutchev to sharing some of the essential features of Dostoevsky's own *Weltanschauung*: his apocalyptic intuitions of impending cosmic chaos, his religious irrationalism, his mystical nationalism. It was Tyutchev who wrote the famous quatrain that might be inscribed on the portals giving entrance to Dostoevsky's creative universe:

> Russia cannot be understood by reason,
> Nor measured by a common rule
> It has its own configuration—
> You can only take Russia on faith.[36]

And in a poem that Dostoevsky would paraphrase in his famous Pushkin speech in 1880, Tyutchev had poignantly depicted Christ in the guise of a Russian peasant pilgrim, humble and ragged, wandering through a Russian land whose lowly *izbas* (peasant huts) were the appropriate setting for His kenotic abasement. The notice announcing Tyutchev's death in *The Citizen*, probably written by Dostoevsky, spoke of him as "our powerful and profound Russian poet, one of the most remarkable and original continuators of the Pushkin era."[37] He had begun to write an article about Tyutchev; but, as he tells Anna, "because of my illness and because of an article about Tyutchev that Meshchersky sent, I gave up on the piece I had started."[38] One can only regret this loss to Russian criticism.

Even worse, however, was that he had to waste his time slaving over Meshchersky's text. He complains bitterly to Anna about the piece: "so illiterate that it was incomprehensible, and with such blunders that he would have been laughed at in satirical columns for ten years. I worked at fixing it for twenty-four hours, without a break, and touched up all the weak spots. I'm going to write him and tell him right out that he puts me in an impossible position. Meanwhile, I need to start a different piece, a political one, for the next issue. I've never written such pieces."[39] He had promised Meshchersky that, in addition to his other obligations, he would supply the weekly with a column of political commentary. He complains in another letter that "I have to read through newspapers by the dozens" in order to write such political articles. No wonder he says to Anna that "horribly depressing thoughts and . . . dejection . . . [have] overcome me almost to the point of illness at the thought that I have tied myself down to all this hard labor at *The Citizen* for at least another year."[40]

The summer of 1873 was a particularly difficult time for Dostoevsky, not only because of his problems with *The Citizen*, but also because his editorial duties required him to remain in Petersburg separated from his family in Staraya Russa. His letters are filled with laments about his sadness and loneliness, his (sometimes frightening) dreams about his children, his concern over Anna's health, and the difficulties of making arrangements so he could spend a few days in the country. As he explains at the end of July, "I have to get terribly much done so as to be able to come to see you, so, for instance, I need to have two-thirds of an issue completed in advance so as to venture to be away for four days." He reports that "I am now absolutely alone. Even Strakhov is gone." In the same letter, after recounting a nightmare in which his son Fedya falls from a fourth-floor windowsill, he instructs Anna: "Write me as soon as possible about whether anything happened to Fedya. . . . I believe in second sight, the more so as it is factual, and I won't calm down until I get your letter."[41]

Dostoevsky also complained about the summertime inconveniences of their apartment, located on a street leading to the railway and thus filled, from morning to night, with the noise of goods being transported for shipment. Even more upsetting were the antics of their despotic landlord, whom he describes as "a crazy person (I seriously think that!)." There is a lengthy depiction of the landlord's various eccentricities, one being picturesque enough to report. *The Citizen* employed a messenger who was dispatched on various errands, and, at Prince Meshchersky's insistence, he sported a full beard and was dressed in a well-tailored version of the Russian national costume instead of in European clothes. One day he arrived with a letter from the prince in his hands; but before he could ring the bell, he was collared by the landlord. "How dare you use the front stairway!" he thundered. "You're a peasant! People wearing peasant dress don't use this stairway! Off you go to the back entrance!"[42] Dostoevsky was afraid that if word of this little contretemps got back to the prince, he would be greatly offended. Very eager to change quarters, he not only visited other available apartments but even included in a letter a floor plan of one that he thought suitable. Despite his efforts and urging, however, Anna probably decided that they could not afford more expensive accommodations.

Although now provided with an income for his own expenses, Dostoevsky was still constantly in economic straits when the time came to meet the installments for the debts of his deceased brother Mikhail. A due date fell in late July, and since he was unable to collect royalties for the sale of fifty copies of *The Devils* (the bookseller had gone to Moscow without leaving any payment), he was forced to pawn his watch to pay off this obligation. Some consolation, however, was provided by an evening spent with K. P. Pobedonostsev, whose invitation he accepted even though he had felt feverish for about a week. He tells Anna gratefully that his host had been very solicitous: "He wrapped me in a blanket; and since there was no one in the empty apartment except for a maid . . . he himself saw me down three flights of stairs, with a candle in his hand, right out to the street entrance. Vladislavlev [Dostoevsky's professorial nephew-in-law] should have seen me." What gratified him even more than such flattering courtesy on the part of so highly placed a personage was the news that the latter had read *Crime and Punishment* with great appreciation "upon the recommendation of a certain person, an admirer of mine very well known to you, whom he accompanied to England." Pobedonostsev had just returned from vacationing on the Isle of Wight with Tsarevich Alexander, who had been the guest of the British royal family. "Consequently," Dostoevsky writes, "things are not as bad as all that. (Please don't chatter about this, darling Anechka)."[43]

Six months earlier, he had sent the crown prince a copy of *The Devils*, with a letter that had responded to the royal wish, conveyed through Pobedonostsev, for an explanation of how the author himself interpreted the book. "My view," Dostoevsky had written, "is that these phenomena [the Nechaev case] are not an accident of fate, not isolated instances. . . . These phenomena are the direct consequences of the age-old divorce of all Russian enlightenment from the native and distinct principles of Russian life." Russians simply refuse to believe that "we ourselves, in the depths and seeds of the Russian soul, contain within ourselves as Russians the ability, perhaps, to bring new light to the world . . . because of the conditions of the distinctiveness of our development." He knows that "thinking that way among us now and stating such thoughts means condemning oneself to the role of pariah"; but he also knows that "our Belinskys and Granovskys would not believe it if they were told that they were Nechaev's direct fathers. It is precisely this kinship and continuity of thought which evolves from the fathers to the children that I wanted to express in my work."[44]

## 6

Anna Grigoryevna returned to Petersburg with the children at the end of August 1873, and Dostoevsky could once again resume the tranquil routine of family life he had so much longed for in their absence. But the obligations and anxieties of his editorship, and the grueling routine of meeting weekly deadlines, never ceased for a moment. To make matters worse, he was sometimes led into unpleasant exchanges with irate contributors, incensed at the slightest alteration to their creations. One such incident involved a little-known and now-forgotten playwright, Dimitry Kishensky, whose play *Pit do dna—ne vidat dobra* (a Russian proverb: nothing good can come from hard drinking) had been printed in six issues of *The Citizen*. Dostoevsky also devoted an essay in his *Diary of a Writer* to discussing the play, which dealt with the disintegration of the morality of the Russian village and its sacrosanct village commune (*obshchina*) as a result of the liberation of the serfs and the rise of local industry. That article will be discussed in Chapter 6; here we shall look at the quarrel that arose over the prologue to another play by the same author, *Padenie* (*Downfall*), which had also been accepted and published.

On the appearance of the issue containing this text, its author ripped off an extremely abusive letter objecting to some changes that had been made. Dostoevsky replied by citing an earlier letter in which Kishensky had amiably agreed to accept such revisions; and he compares the situation to the famous scene in Alain-René Lesage's picaresque novel *Gil Blas* (a work to which he often refers) in which the Archbishop of Granada asks his servant Gil to give him an impartial criticism of one of his sermons. When the still-naïve Gil takes him at his word and allows himself some uncomplimentary observations, the archbishop flies into a rage; and the *pícaro* Gil once again finds himself in search of employment. Besides illustrating some of Dostoevsky's difficulties with his contributors, the exchange also helps to document his gradually softening attitude toward the radicals of the 1870s. For the play was ferociously antiradical, and in a letter that has been lost he obviously expressed some reservations about the treatment of this theme. Kishensky retorted: "You recognize in them a desire for renewal, I acknowledge in them an ignorance stemming from idleness and a desire to chatter."[45]

Another example of his increasing willingness to recognize a moral inspiration even in the furthest extremes of Nihilist behavior comes from the outlines of a projected epilogue to *The Devils*, written perhaps around this time. "Kirillov," says the notebook entry, "embodies an idea which belongs to the people: to sacrifice oneself for the truth." Even Dimitry Karakozov, who attempted to assassinate Alexander II, "did, at the time, believe in his truth. . . . To sacrifice oneself, to sacrifice everything for the truth—that is the national trait of this generation. For the problem amounts to no more than the question as to what ought to be considered truth. That is why this novel was written."[46] The date of this epilogue is uncertain, but it was probably intended for the publication of the serialized text in book form; if so, it would date from 1873, after he had taken over *The Citizen* and become better acquainted with the ideological mood of the Populist generation of the 1870s. Only now could he begin to identify the impulses animating even the worst excesses of Nihilist radicalism with the "truth" of the Russian people's faith, that is, the Christian morality of love and self-sacrifice.

If Prince Meshchersky had caused trouble for his editor on one occasion because of his carelessness about the press laws, his editorial high-handedness provided a constant and unavoidable source of friction. Much more serious conflicts arose when they clashed on fundamental social-cultural issues. In one instance *The Citizen* became involved in a controversy with the *St. Petersburg News*, and both

Dostoevsky and the prince worked on a reply. For some reason, Mesh-chersky brought up the question of revolutionary proclamations from abroad (Switzerland) circulating in the student milieu; and he suggested that such "distractions" might be circumvented if dormitories were built with dining rooms and libraries where the students could gather and live cheaply and comfortably, rather than huddling in the "dark corners" (shades of Raskolnikov!) where they were forced to seek lodgings.

Dostoevsky had no objection to improving student living conditions, but explains—in a note to the prince—why he unceremoniously struck out seven lines that followed this suggestion: "I quite agree to your *polishing* of the reply to the *St. Petersburg News*," he writes diplomatically. "It's very deft. . . . But I threw out altogether the seven lines about surveillance, or, as you put it, about the *task* of government surveillance." Obviously, Meshchersky had intimated that such an improvement in housing would facilitate the obligation of the authorities to keep an eye on student activities. "I have my reputation as a writer," Dostoevsky goes on, "and in addition I have children. I do not intend to *destroy* myself." The next sentence, inked out in the original text, has been deciphered and reads: "Besides, your idea is deeply opposed to my convictions and fills my heart with indignation."[47] This last sentence, which reveals his true feelings, was obviously too impolitic for the eyes of the rabidly reactionary Prince Full Stop; and indeed, the prince countered that "I presume you are not of the opinion that the students should be *without* surveillance."[48] Although no answer was given to this challenge, the odious seven lines, which would have ruined Dostoevsky's reputation forever as the partisan of a police state, remained unprinted.

His opinions were clearly not tailored to any official government line, and his independence brought on another clash with the censorship, one for which he was solely responsible. A widespread famine afflicted several Russian provinces during 1873–1874, and he allowed himself to print several articles highly critical of the government's handling of the situation, especially in the province of Samaria. No effective central organization had been set up to take charge of the distribution of food, and one article suggested that members of the local *zemstvo*s (district councils that were democratically elected) should be enlisted to participate in such a central consultative body. This article, as well as other reproving remarks in the same issue, brought down the wrath of the guardians of the press. Punishment came in the form of a ban on the sale of individual copies of *The Citizen*. Only subscribers could receive the weekly, and this resulted in a considerable loss of revenue. Dostoevsky wrote a fulsomely supplicating letter to a high press official, asking this dignitary to intercede with the Ministry of Internal Affairs, and the ban was lifted a month later.

From this time on, he took considerable care to tread very carefully with regard to the famines. A letter in January 1874 to Orest Miller, a professor at the University of St. Petersburg and a well-known moderate Slavophil scholar and critic (he was later to write half of the first biography of Dostoevsky), indicates his embarrassment: "To my very great regret, I can no longer now venture to publish your article [on the famines]—and, of course, against my wishes. As an editor I was summoned to the Censorship Committee a few days ago and it was impressed on me that although one may in fact write and publish reported facts about the famine, it must be without tendentiousness in a certain direction and in such a way that there is nothing 'alarming.' I'm informing you of this reprimand in secret."[49] Apparently, he had rashly given Miller his assurance that the article would be printed, and Miller replied stiffly that he had been "stupid" to accept such a promise, even going so far as to spread the word "that *The Citizen* in this way puts all our 'liberals' to shame."[50] No doubt Dostoevsky would dearly have wished *The Citizen* to acquire the reputation of being more critically outspoken than "the liberals."

In March 1874 he finally served the sentence condemning him to two days' detention in a guardhouse. A. F. Koni, an official in the Ministry of Justice who had a special interest in criminal psychology and was an admirer, arranged that the date be set at Dostoevsky's convenience. The guardhouse selected was in the center of Petersburg, and Anna Grigoryevna brought her husband a small suitcase with "overnight necessities." "He asked whether the children missed him, and wanted me to give them some goodies for him and tell them he had gone to Moscow for toys."[51] Anna enlisted Apollon Maikov to visit Dostoevsky the next day, and he in turn contacted Vsevolod Solovyev, who also dropped in. Solovyev found the prisoner sitting at a small table in a spacious and "reasonably clean room, drinking tea, rolling and smoking cigarettes," and perusing a copy of Hugo's *Les Misérables* borrowed from Timofeyeva. The only other inmate was "a young man, badly dressed and with a very nondescript countenance." Dostoevsky had apparently tried to engage him in conversation but with no success. "He's a stick of wood," he told Solovyev, "pay him no heed."[52]

The imprisonment evidently revived memories of his confinement in the Peter-and-Paul Fortress almost a quarter of a century earlier, and these were evoked in the conversation that Solovyev records. The two men had not seen each other recently, and the younger complained of suffering from some sort of apathy. Dostoevsky immediately identified this malaise with the nervous troubles that had plagued him in the 1840s. The best treatment, he insisted, was the one that fate had imposed on him—a sudden change, the shock of new situations and the need to adjust to a new environment. "When I found myself in the fortress, I thought: this is the finish, I thought I wouldn't hold out for three days, and—suddenly I calmed down. . . . Oh, that was a great happiness for me: Siberia and the *katorga* [prison camp]. People say: horror, resentment, they speak of the rightness of some sort of resentment! What awful nonsense! Only there did I have a healthy, happy life, I understood myself there, my dear fellow. . . . I understood Christ. . . . I understood Russian man and felt that I was a Russian myself, that I was one of the Russian people."[53]

Such words certainly cannot be taken as even a remotely adequate account of the reality of Dostoevsky's experiences after his arrest and during his years in prison camp. They convey, rather, the sense of triumph over the hardships he had been forced to endure, and the transformation of his personality and convictions that had resulted from these years. One of the most important events of this period was the mock execution he had undergone, during which he was led to believe, along with all the others awaiting punishment, that he would be shot in a very few moments. He emerged from this ordeal with an ecstatic sense of the infinite value of life, which he expressed in a letter just after returning to his cell; and he recalls this epiphanic movement to Solovyev as their talk continued. "Ah, life is a wonderful thing; ah, how good it is sometimes to live! In every incident, in every object, in every word there is so much happiness!" He then praised *Les Misérables* and advised Solovyev (quite superfluously) to read it without fail; but his visitor replied that *Crime and Punishment* was much superior. Hugo's book, in his view, was occasionally long drawn out and awfully pedantic, but Dostoevsky did not cease "to enthuse and found in the book what was not there."[54] In conclusion, asking his admirer to visit Anna Grigoryevna and assure her that he was in the best of spirits, he cautioned him to speak very softly. If the servants heard that their master was under arrest, they would conclude that he was probably guilty of theft.

7
———

By the beginning of 1874, the strains and stresses of editing *The Citizen* began to wear on Dostoevsky's health, and the decline became quite visible to those who knew him best. "The unhappy Dostoevsky is totally worn out," reported Strakhov to Nikolay Danilevsky in January.[55] As Anna notes sadly, "Feodor Mikhailovich, who had to leave the house in every kind of weather . . . and to sit for hours in an overheated proofreading room before each issue went to press, began to catch frequent colds." No mention is made of the sudden changes in temperature occasioned by his trips to and from Staraya Russa. Consequently, "his slight cough became acute and a shortness of breath appeared"—the beginning of the emphysema that was eventually to cause his death. "Compressed air treatment" was prescribed by his doctor, and "Feodor Mikhailovich would sit under the bell for two hours at a time, three times a week"—which only created further problems. Even though "the treatment was very beneficial," it interfered with his schedule and made the fulfillment of his editorial duties all the more difficult.[56]

Such considerations certainly played their part in Dostoevsky's surrender of the editorship on April 1, 1874. There was as well the steady accumulation of more internal reasons connected with editorial policy that made him glad to relinquish his post. "You ask what I've been doing," he writes to Pogodin in November 1873. "I keep being sick and flying into rages. My hands are somewhat tied. In tackling the editorship a year ago, I imagined that I would be much more independent. Because of that I lack energy for work."[57] Another letter, several months later, reveals all the tensions that had gradually exacerbated the relations between the co-editors. Embroiled in a polemic with the poet Yakov P. Polonsky, Meshchersky had printed a piece by his opponent that contained some remarks Dostoevsky considered offensive to himself as editor. "Don't think I constantly wish to bicker with you and contradict you with regard to the journal," he begins his missive to the prince. "Please just take into consideration both the mood that may develop in me and my personal view, and then you'll realize that I cannot help stating my opinion in a matter that touches so directly on me too."[58]

Even aside from such matters, the impossibility to write anything nonjournalistic proved to be a continual torment. Very early in his editorship he had told Pogodin that "the shapes of stories and novels swarm in my head and take shape in my heart. I think them up, jot them down, add new traits every day to the plan that has been sketched out, and at that point I see that all my time is taken up with the journal, that I cannot write any more—and I am driven to repentance and despair."[59] Adding to his distress was the realization that it was impossible, despite all his best efforts, to overcome the prevailing hostility toward *The Citizen.* "His editorial activity," writes Vsevolod Solovyev, "on which he had placed such hopes at our first meeting, were not really successful, and this might have been foreseen knowing his character and circumstances." All the other journals of the time, Solovyev explains, criticized *The Citizen* harshly and even coarsely. "On the new editor, a stupid and vulgar mockery rained down from all sides. The author of *Crime and Punishment* and *House of the Dead* was called a madman, a maniac, a renegade, a traitor; the public were even invited to visit the show at the Academy of Art and contemplate the portrait of Dostoevsky painted by Perov as prime proof that here was such a madman, whose place was in a home for the feeble-minded."[60] Such allusions will be referred to in his grotesque short story "Bobok," and one can well understand his desire to escape from this unremitting hail of invective.

However, his year-and-a-half term as editor was far from having been entirely negative, and a conversation relayed by Timofeyeva discloses the mutation of sensibility that occurred at this time. Telling her of his intention to resign and to begin work on a new novel, he suggested that she ask her Populist friends from *Notes of the Fatherland* whether they would have room for such a novel next year. For the author of *The Devils* even to *think* of publishing in the most prominent of the left-wing journals of the time certainly indicated an astonishing change of front! When the question was posed by Timofeyeva to G. Z. Eliseev, who had once accused Dostoevsky of slandering Russian students in *Crime and Punishment*, he replied "with the friendliest voice: 'Of course, let him send it along. We'll always find a place for him.'"[61] His next novel, *A Raw Youth* (*Podrostok*), thus was serialized in the pages of *Notes of the Fatherland*—to the astonishment of all and to the dismay of his closest and oldest friends.

It is in this context that we can best interpret another remark in a conversation with Timofeyeva. Speaking to him of *Notes from Underground*, which she had just read, she said: "'I am not able to free myself from its impression. . . . What a frightful thing—the human soul! But also what a terrible truth! . . . ' Feodor Mikhailovich smiled with a clear, open smile: 'Kraevsky told me then that this was my *chef d'oeuvre*, and that I should always write in this mode, but I disagree with him completely. It's much too gloomy. *Es ist ein überwundener Standpunkt!* [It's now an out-of-date point of view.] I now *am able* to write more brightly, more reconcilingly. I am now writing something . . . "[62] This last, unfinished sentence, whether or not it refers to the first notes for what became *A Raw Youth*, reveals his awareness that there is no longer any need to attack the ideology of the 1860s. How this ideology had become *ein überwundener Standpunkt* is explored in the next chapter.

## CHAPTER 4

# *Narodnichestvo*: Russian Populism

To understand what occurred in Dostoevsky's artistic-ideological evolution at this time, nothing is more important than to grasp, more clearly
than has been elucidated so far, the mutation of Russian radicalism itself at the onset of the 1870s. All through the 1860s, Dostoevsky had
attempted to reveal the dangerous moral-social consequences of Russian Nihilist ideas, a purely home-brewed amalgam of Benthamite Utilitarianism, atheism, and Utopian Socialism. The Nihilist aim was not
only to oppose Tsarist despotism but also to substitute a morality based
on "rational egoism" for the ideals inherited from the Gospels and the
teachings of Jesus Christ. As a novelist, Dostoevsky had explored—in
such works as *Notes from Underground, Crime and Punishment,* and
*The Devils*—what he feared and foresaw would be the socially disastrous
and self-destructive human results of any attempt to put such a "new
morality" into practice. During his four years of living abroad between
1865 and 1871, he became more than ever convinced that Russian Nihilism was an artificial transplantation of all the ideological maladies undermining Western civilization.

On becoming editor of *The Citizen,* however, he began once again to
take stock of the passing Russian scene. Much had changed, and a new
mood had begun to manifest itself among the young intelligentsia, a
mood that had crystallized into an ideology known as *narodnichestvo,*
or Russian Populism. Dostoevsky's surprising desire to offer his next
novel to the leading Populist journal, *Notes of the Fatherland*—edited by
the poet Nikolay A. Nekrasov, his former friend, and the deadly satirist
Mikhail Saltykov-Shchedrin, who had mercilessly pilloried him in the
1860s—is a direct outcome of this metamorphosis. A pause at this point
will allow for a closer examination of what should have led Dostoevsky
to take such an unpredictable and, to his closest friends and literary
allies, such a shocking step.

## 2

As already noted, the Dostoevskys returned to Russia on the very day
that those arrested in the Nechaev affair were placed on public trial.
Political criminals were usually tried in secret proceedings, but the

documents uncovered in the investigation of the murder—among them the spine-chilling *Catechism of a Revolutionary*, with its unabashed advocacy of total unscrupulousness against both foe and friend alike—were considered so damning that, in order to destroy the moral credit enjoyed by the Nihilists, the government authorities decided to prosecute the case in public. Consequently, the documents introduced as evidence were allowed to be reprinted in newspapers after appearing in the official *Pravitelstvenny Vestnik* (*Government Messenger*). When Tsar Alexander was informed of this decision and its intended results, he noted laconically on the document, "God willing!"[1]

The aim of the public trial was thus to break the grip of Nihilist ideas and attitudes on the rebellious youth of the empire; but this attempt was an egregious failure. There is ample evidence that, quite to the contrary, the stirring speeches made not only by the defense attorneys but also by some of the defendants in the name of liberty and justice produced exactly the opposite effect on the student youth who flocked to the courtroom and jammed the benches. Indeed, the government succeeded in accomplishing what the Nechaevtsy themselves had signally failed to achieve: to bring their propaganda to the attention of a nationwide audience. For many, as one contemporary wrote, "those being tried appeared as fighters struggling to free the people from the oppression of the government and from being sacrifices to its tyranny. The youth surrendered to the fascination of the battle for the ideas of truth and justice *and tried to find a better path for bringing them into being.*"[2]

The final sentence of this passage discloses that the government had not met with failure all along the line. The publicity of the trial may well have helped to spread the radical faith rather than undermine its influence; but the coverage also revealed the tactics of Nechaev in all their sinister details, which led to a horrified revulsion even among those who sympathized with his aims. The considerable memoir literature left by the survivors of the Populist movement returns again and again to their sense of outrage when they learned the awful truth. Vera Figner, for example, wrote that Nechaev's "theory—that the end justifies the means—repelled us, and the murder of Ivanov filled us with disgust." (Nonetheless, she was later to become a member of the executive committee of the terrorist organization Narodnaya Volya [People's Will], which planned the assassination of Alexander II.) Another then-young radical wrote that "Nechaev's program, the jesuitical system of his organization, the blind subordination of members to some sort of invisible center—all this produced a negative reaction to *Nechaevschina*."[3]

The circles of radical youth that began to form at the beginning of the 1870s took the lessons of Nechaevism very much to heart and carefully avoided any temptation to fall into the trap of disregarding morality in the higher interest of the revolutionary cause. Prince Peter Kropotkin—the scion of an ancient noble family destined for a distinguished career at the imperial court, who became instead both a noted scientist and an anarchist and revolutionary—belonged to one of these circles (the Chaikovsky group) and left a portrait of its dominating ethos. "In 1869," he writes, "Nechaev had tried to start a secret revolutionary organization among the youth imbued with the desire of working among the people, and to secure this end he resorted to the ways of old conspirators, without recoiling even before deceit when he wanted to force his associates to follow his lead. . . . The circle of self-education of which I am speaking was constituted *in opposition to the methods of Nechaev.* The few friends [in the circle] had judged, quite correctly, that a morally developed individuality must be the foundation of every organization, whatever political character it may take afterward, and whatever program of action it may adopt in the course of future events" (italics added).[4] To call the murder of Ivanov "deceit" is of course putting matters very mildly, and it is hardly accurate to picture Nechaev as intending to "work among the people" in the peaceful Populist sense that Kropotkin conveys. But his remarks are valuable because they stress the new moral and ethical dimension that had now come to the fore in radical self-awareness.

The younger generation thus abandoned the Utilitarian morality preached by the dominating ideologists of the Nihilist 1860s, such as Nikolay G. Chernyshevsky and Nikolay Dobrolyubov, and especially reacted against Dimitry Pisarev, the most influential radical writer of them all at the end of the decade. The reigning Pisarevism had encouraged a contemptuous elitism among the intelligentsia toward the people, and envisaged the only hope of progress as lying in the self-cultivation of the educated youth through the study of science. From such study, Pisarev had insisted, enlightenment would gradually spread and transform the backwardness of Russian life through the growth of a class of "thinking realists." "The fate of the people," he had boldly declared, "will not be decided in schools for the people but in the universities."[5] When such ideas were combined with Pisarev's panegyric to the glories of personal self-fulfillment and rampant individualism, the *Pisarevschina* of the late 1860s opened the way for a slackening of the moral idealism that had marked the activities of the intelligentsia so notably in the earlier part of the decade. Franco Venturi is no doubt exaggerating somewhat, but there is still a good bit of truth in his linkage of Pisarevism with "the ideas that were later to find expression in Nechaev's venture."[6]

This complex of ideas and attitudes was sharply attacked in Peter L. Lavrov's *Historical Letters* (1869–1870), which became a major source of inspiration for the *narodnik* (Populist) intelligentsia of the 1870s. Lavrov was an ex-artillery colonel who had taught mathematics at various military academies without making any effort to conceal his progressive sympathies. During the student disorders at the University of St. Petersburg in 1861, he encouraged the rebellious youth by addressing one of their turbulent meetings in full military regalia. Later arrested and stripped of his rank after the 1865 attempt on the life of Alexander II (though not involved in this episode in any way), he was sent to live in a dreary and poverty-stricken village in the northern district of Vologda, though he was eventually allowed to reside in its capital city. There he succeeded in writing his letters and publishing them legally under a pseudonym. He escaped abroad after a few years and continued his career as an important, highly respected scholar and publicist who participated actively in the European radical movement. A good friend of Karl Marx, he became the editor and chief contributor of a radical Russian émigré review *Vpered* (*Forward*), writing both as a commentator on Russian affairs and as a learned historian of social thought.

Even before the appearance of his *Historical Letters*, Lavrov had been a fairly well-known figure in the circles of the Petersburg intelligentsia. Dostoevsky had probably met him socially at the home of the Shtakenshneiders, whose literary and cultural salon both men frequented in the early 1860s. (Andrey Shtakenshneider was a well-known, wealthy, and hospitable Petersburg architect who held open house, and the diary of his highly intelligent and extremely cultivated daughter Elena, crippled by a hunchback, is an important source for the Russian culture of the mid-nineteenth century.) The two men also had met as members of the Literary Fund, known more officially as the Society for Aid to Needy Writers and Scholars. Indeed, Lavrov was responsible for Dostoevsky's resignation from his post as secretary of the administrative committee after the officious progressive had objected to loans accorded by the society to the novelist in 1863 and 1865. Most of the borrowed sums had been repaid by the time Dostoevsky relinquished his office, and the charge against him had been rejected by a vote of the entire membership. But because Lavrov had published a newspaper article criticizing the "illegality" of the loans, he felt morally obliged to surrender both the position to which he had been elected and his place on the committee.

Lavrov's *Historical Letters* were far from being his first work to attract attention. The erudite officer had earlier outlined his social-philosophical views in *Sketches in the Domain of Practical Philosophy*, a work that provoked Chernyshevsky to criticize it, respectfully but firmly, as too "eclectic" and to respond with his own much more famous *Anthropological Principle in Philosophy* (1861). What Chernyshevsky found unacceptable was Lavrov's failure to apply a strict "scientific" monism to every aspect of human life, and Chernyshevsky's attempt to fill this gap then became the radical philosophical gospel of the 1860s. Lavrov had also achieved a certain notoriety by expounding his ideas in a series of lectures (1860) in a hall that was part of a public arcade, and Dostoevsky made a jesting reference to this unusual venue in his broadly satirical, unfinished short story "The Crocodile."

Lavrov's *Historical Letters* compose a sweeping, essayistic survey— calculated to appeal to a wide range of readers—whose theme is the rise of civilization from barbarism. This rise, he argued, is always the work of cultivated minorities who prove capable of advancing beyond the limits of their inherited culture. In the immediate Russian context, his most important and influential idea is contained in his fourth letter, "The Cost of Progress," which attempts to assess the exorbitant price paid in human suffering for the advancement of civilization. He stresses the "debt" that cultivated minorities (that is, the Russian intelligentsia) owe to the suffering millions who have toiled through the centuries (the Russian peasantry) to provide them with the means for their self-cultivation. How can this debt be absolved? "I cannot correct the past," Lavrov writes, "and however high the cost of cultivation, I cannot repudiate it: it constitutes the very ideal which arouses me to action. . . . I shall relieve myself of responsibility for the bloody cost of my own development if I utilize this same development to diminish evil in the present and in the future."[7]

These words produced an electrifying effect on a whole generation of Russian youth, who were dispiritedly groping for some sort of positive moral ideal. N. S. Rusanov, later an important publicist, experienced their galvanizing shock as a young student:

At one time we had been attracted to Pisarev, who told us of the great utility of the natural sciences in making a "thinking realist" out of men. . . . we wished to live in the name of our "cultivated egoism," rejecting all authority and making our goal a free and happy life for ourselves and for those who shared our ideas. And suddenly [Lavrov's] little book tells us that there are other things besides the natural sciences. The anatomy of frogs by itself does not take us very far [an allusion to the medical student Bazarov in Ivan Turgenev's novel *Fathers and Children*, who spends his time dissecting frogs]. . . . There are the people, the hungry masses, worn out by labor, the working people who themselves support the whole edifice of civilization solely to make it possible for us to study frogs. . . . How ashamed we were of our miserable bourgeois plans for a happy personal life! To the devil with "rational egoism" and "thinking realism." . . . Henceforth our lives must belong wholly to the masses, and only by dedicating all our strength to the triumph of social justice could we appear anything but fraudulent bankrupts before our country and before all mankind.[8]

Such was the self-sacrificing mood in which the educated youth "went to the people" in the early 1870s; and what they expected to find in the Russian villages was not only absolution from the sin of their privileges but also a morally superior form of life, a primitive Socialist Arcadia far preferable to the supposedly more advanced countries of the West.

If Lavrov had inspired the educated youth with a sense of guilt about their own advantages, it was another Populist thinker, Nikolay K. Mikhailovsky, who persuaded them that the Russian village and the Russian peasant harbored unsuspected treasures that should not be lightly surrendered to the march of "progress." Mikhailovsky, who enjoyed enormous prestige in the 1870s, was a member of the editorial board and a regular contributor to *Notes of the Fatherland*, and his monthly column on social-cultural matters was eagerly devoured and extremely influential. His credentials with the new generation had been established by a small book, *What Is Progress?*, which appeared shortly after Lavrov's *Letters*. These reflections are a product of that widespread disillusionment with the West, particularly France, produced among Russian progressives by the failure of the revolutions of 1848, the assumption of power by Napoleon III, and the ferocious suppression of the Paris Commune in the aftermath of the Franco-Prussian War. The so-called values of the Third Republic, as he had written in a slashing article, found accurate expression in the salacious frivolity of the operettas of Jacques Offenbach. Taking up a refrain to which Herzen had first given voice after 1848, and which Dostoevsky had echoed in his *Winter Notes on Summer Impressions* in 1863, Mikhailovsky argued that a decadent Western civilization could no longer serve as a lodestar to left-leaning Russians eagerly seeking the way toward a more just social-economic order.

Such disenchantment found eloquent expression in Mikhailovsky's notable critique of "progress" as this concept was understood in Europe. Employing the ideas of Charles Darwin and the then-famous Herbert Spencer, but turning them to his own purposes, Mikhailovsky maintained that progress should not simply be identified with the continuing process of modernization and industrialization based on the increasing division of labor. Progress should be measured in terms of the richness and diversity of human life that it furthered, not solely by the accumulating production of material goods. Understood only in this latter sense, as was the case in Europe, progress could well destroy, with

7. Nikolay K. Mikhailovsky, populist critic and publicist

wanton carelessness, the integrity of individual life still preserved in
less-developed social forms (that is, the Russian village). The so-called
"objective" scientific laws governing society—the laws worked out in
Western social thought—offer no help in choosing between these two
notions of progress, and Mikhailovsky argued that a "subjective"
(moral) criterion must be introduced in favor of the protection of the
individual personality.

Thus Lavrov and Mikhailovsky, each from his own point of view, rejected the worship of "science"—so typical of the Nihilism of the
1860s—as the ultimate basis of human values; they firmly broke with
ideas that left no independent room (at least in theory) for the human
personality and hence for morality. For these thinkers, as much earlier
for Immanuel Kant, science determines the laws of the physical world
but not of human desires and ideals. Lavrov made a direct appeal to
the moral sensibility of the intelligentsia as the basis for his radicalism;
and Mikhailovsky too, in his Slavophil-tinged critique of progress, used
"subjective" moral criteria as the justification for his distaste of its Western avatar. Such aspects of Populist thought were much closer to Dostoevsky's own views than anything he had encountered previously
among the radical ideologues; and just how close may be seen by exam-
ining Populist ideas through the prism of Dostoevsky's polemics with
the Nihilism of the 1860s.

One of the dogmas of radical ideology in the 1860s, expounded most intransigently by Chernyshevsky, was a monistic materialism—supposedly the last word in "scientific" thought—that excluded the possibility of any such entity as "free will." The notion of will or "wanting," Chernyshevsky had firmly declared, "is only the subjective impression that accompanies in our minds the rise of thoughts and actions from preceding thoughts, actions, or external facts."[9] In other words, the notion of a human will has no objective validity and is merely an erroneous interpretation of a rigorously causal process. Nothing infuriated Dostoevsky more than this denial of what he—and, of course, not he alone—considered the source of all moral responsibility, as well as of an individual's sense of his own human dignity. In Dostoevsky's case, such a conviction was not merely an abstract moral-philosophical belief or tenet.

Quite the contrary, it was an indelible lesson he had learned during his years in the prison camp. Indeed, one of his most overwhelming impressions was of the ineradicable need for the human personality to express itself through the exercise of its own free will. Such a need is remarkably depicted in his piercing analyses of what, at first sight, seemed to be the senseless, irrational acts of his fellow convicts. It would have been quite possible for them, as he shows, to have used whatever precious money they could scrape together from their after-hours labor to obtain better food or gain access to women. Instead of satisfying such elementary desires, they invariably squandered their money on orgiastic drinking sprees—for which, in addition, they might incur the most terrible penalties. To Dostoevsky's psychological intuition, such behavior was by no means totally capricious or inexplicable. "The whole meaning of the word 'convict,'" he wrote in *House of the Dead*, "implies a man without a will of his own; when he spends money, however, he is acting from *his own free will*," especially when he spends it on what is forbidden and dangerous. The irresistible urge to express one's will, no matter how self-destructively exhibited, "is nothing more than an anguished, convulsive manifestation of the man's personality . . . his desire to declare himself and his humiliated personality, appearing suddenly and developing into fury, insanity, the eclipse of reason, paroxysm, and convulsion" (4: 66–67).

A few years later, in *Notes from Underground*, Dostoevsky placed this same insight at the heart of his creation of the underground man (especially in Part I of that work). For the underground man *accepts* Chernyshevsky's denial of the existence of free will as an inescapable rational conclusion; but he finds it humanly impossible to reconcile this doctrine with an irrepressible need to assert his personality and to act as a free agent. Firmly convinced that he lacks any free will to act positively, however, he can do so only negatively, out of spite and venomous envy, while castigating himself for being unable to adjust his emotions to his reason. When he imagines living in a perfect world, depicted in terms of the Russian adaptation of the Fourierist phalanstery in Chernyshevsky's novel *What Is To Be Done?*—a world in which all desires would be instantly gratified, and where no exercise of will would be necessary—he is certain that something completely unexpected would inevitably occur. "A gentleman of an ignoble or rather a reactionary and sardonic countenance" would surely "arise amid all that future reign of universal common sense . . . to say to us all, 'Well, gentlemen, what about giving all this common sense a mighty kick and letting it scatter in the dust before our feet simply to send all these logarithms to the devil so that we can again live according to our foolish will?'" (5: 113). There is, the underground man proclaims, "one case, one case only, when man can deliberately and consciously desire something that is injurious, stupid, even outrageously stupid, just because he wants *to have the right* to desire for himself even what is very stupid and not to be bound by an obligation to desire only what is sensible" (5: 115).

For Dostoevsky, it was a moral-psychological *necessity* of the human personality to experience itself as free. This insight was one of the cornerstones of his own most deeply rooted view of the human condition; and he now found in the key Populist texts a decisive affirmation of precisely what he had maintained all along—and what Nihilism had declared to be nonexistent. "I take as my point of departure," affirmed Lavrov, "the fact of the *consciousness of freedom*, and on the foundation of these facts I construct a coherent system of moral process."[10] Similarly, Mikhailovsky wrote that "society obeys certain laws in its development; but no less unquestionable is man's *inherent consciousness of a free choice of action*. At the moment of action I am aware that I give myself a goal freely, completely independent of the influence of historical conditions" (italics added).[11] Human consciousness, with its ineluctable need for freedom and moral responsibility (which of course leaves open the possibility of choosing evil), is thus no longer trapped in the tangled labyrinth so subtly dramatized in *Notes from Underground*.

The Nihilist attempt to construct a new morality based on the supposedly "scientific" foundation of "rational egoism" had equally aroused Dostoevsky's antagonism. Chernyshevsky, strongly influenced by Jeremy Bentham and English Utilitarianism, had argued that "egoism"—the feelings of pleasure and pain—were the root causes of human behavior: "good" was whatever satisfied the desires of the individual, "evil" whatever thwarted or frustrated those desires. However, by a totally unconvincing leap of thought (though it proved persuasive to a whole generation of Russian radicals), he also maintained that, because man is a rational being, he would surely reason himself into acknowledging that his own egoistic interests could best be served by identifying them with those of the majority of his fellows. Dostoevsky's first artistic reaction to this doctrine may be found in the villainous Prince Valkovsky of *The Insulted and Injured*, who demonstrates how simple it would be to turn Chernyshevsky's notion into an apologia of the most unscrupulous egoism.

"I only recognize obligations when I seem to have something to gain by them," the prince cynically declares to the idealistic young narrator (a portrait of Dostoevsky himself in the 1840s). "What can I do if I know for a fact that at the root of all human virtues lies the completest egoism. And the more virtuous anything is, the more egoism there is in it" (3: 365). A similar refusal to identify egoism and virtue can be found in *House of the Dead*, written about the same time, in which Dostoevsky describes a woman named Nastasya Ivanovna (an actual person) who, living in the vicinity of his prison camp, devoted herself to easing the lot of the convicts and took special pains on behalf of the educated prisoners. "Some people say (I have heard it and read it)," he comments, "that the most elevated love of one's neighbor is at one and the same time the greatest egoism. What egoism there could be in this instance I cannot for the life of me imagine" (4: 68).

Like Dostoevsky ten years earlier, the generation of the 1870s now explicitly rejected the incongruous attempt to extract a morality of obligation out of "rational egoism," and no one attacked it more eloquently and incisively than Mikhailovsky. The generation of the 1860s, he wrote in 1870, discovered that "the talk about sacrifice was quite compatible with saving one's skin at any price, with delivering to the army shoes without soles, rotten flour, etc." (allusions to the corruption revealed after the Russian defeat in the Crimean War). As a result, this generation began to investigate "the real base of a whole series of phenomena linked with the ideas of sacrifice and self-denial. The real base turned out to be very simple: man is an egoist. Every step he takes, even seemingly the most noble and self-denying, is entirely for his own profit and enjoyment; sacrifice is a fiction, something not really existing—sheer nonsense" (this last phrase in Russian contains a citation from Chernyshevsky). "Clinging to this formula," Mikhailovsky continues, "we lost sight of the fact that, in the first place, the extension of our personal ego to the point of self-sacrifice, to the possibility of identification with an alien life—is just as real as the crudest egoism. And that, in the second place, the formula that sacrifice is sheer nonsense does not at all cover our own psychic situation, for more than ever before are we ready to make the most extreme sacrifices."[12]

After such a passage, it is no surprise to learn that the critic had read *Crime and Punishment* with great admiration. This revival among the Populists of a sensitivity to the ethics of self-sacrifice, so movingly dramatized in that work, went hand in hand with a renewed respect for Christianity itself. In a speech given in 1872, Mikhailovsky explained that "the ancient world knew nothing of the idea of personality. Man as something beyond fixed castes, layers, and nationalities meant nothing to antiquity. . . . Christianity gave a completely new characteristic to history. It brought forth the thought of the absolute worth of man and human personality . . . henceforth, for all people, in spite of delays, mistakes, and wanderings, there is but one goal: the absolute recognition of man, of human personality, and of its many-sided development."[13] Such a positive view of Christianity by a spokesman for the radicals would have been inconceivable in the 1860s; but now he identifies his own social-cultural ideal—a Populist Socialism based on the supreme value of the human personality—with the emergence of Christianity as a world religion.

Such a revaluation of Christianity was typical of the mood of the entire generation for whom Mikhailovsky had become a spokesman. D. N. Ovsyaniko-Kulikovsky, the great turn-of-the-century historian of the Russian intelligentsia, accordingly stressed that what distinguished the Populists of the 1870s from the previous generation was, above all, their "psychological religiosity." "In place of the one-sided attraction for the physical sciences appeared a lively interest in social, economic, and historical questions—in particular, for the history of the movements of the people, in the *raskol* [the religious dissenters] and the sects. The indifferentism and skepticism in religion, which so sharply marked the 'Pisarevist' tendency, notably declined. Unconcerned with dogmatic religion, with official religion, the new generation displayed an unmistakable interest in the Gospels, in Christian ethics, and in Christ the man."[14]

James Billington, in still the best study of Mikhailovsky, notes the effect on him of Pierre-Joseph Proudhon, some of whose works he translated; and he helped to infuse the Populist mentality with Proudhonian ideas, which translate the messianic hopes of the Christian faith into modern, secularized terms. For Proudhon, the Paraclete of the Gospels, "whose coming was awaited by the apostles," was in effect "the regenerating movement of the modern plebe."[15] N. V. Sokolov, a friend of Mikhailovsky's who was arrested and tried in the mid-1860s for a book called *The Heretics*, declared in open court that "the entire guilt of the heretic Socialists consists in the fact that they seek the Kingdom of God not in the clouds but on earth." "Silence me," he told his judges, "if you find in my words any perversion of the commandment of Christian love of neighbor. I know only that none of you loves Christ more than I."[16] Dostoevsky had accepted a very similar view of Socialism in the 1840s, and a copy of Proudhon's *La Célébration du dimanche* was found in his room at the time of his arrest in 1849. Whether or not he had read statements like those of Sokolov, the spirit they conveyed was familiar from his own past and omnipresent in the Russian culture of the 1870s. He had encountered it face-to-face in his daily conversations with Varvara Timofeyeva.

4

———

*Narodnichestvo* could thus hardly have failed to evoke a sympathetic response from Dostoevsky, who just a few years earlier had spoken pityingly of "our poor little defenseless boys and girls," deluded and misled by Nihilism, who became "Nihilists so purely, so unselfishly, in the name of honor, truth, and genuine usefulness."[17] Their rejection of Nechaevism, and the new moral primacy everywhere in evidence, confirmed his conviction of just how pure and unselfish the Russian radical youth really were. Moreover, the specifically social-political emphases of Russian Populism also came quite close to his now-defunct but still privately cherished ideology of *pochvennichestvo*, which he had advanced in the two periodicals he edited in the early 1860s.

Dostoevsky had advocated the necessity for the alienated Russian intelligentsia, divorced from the values and beliefs of their own people by their Western education, to return to their native roots and rediscover all the treasures still hidden there—treasures that, in his view, had been shamefully ignored. He had involuntarily accomplished such a "return to the native soil" in his Siberian prison camp, and he had experienced firsthand (or so he believed) all the moral-spiritual riches concealed in the outwardly crude, ignorant, and backward Russian people. "The best and most outstanding characteristic of our common people," he had written in *House of the Dead*, "is their sense of justice and their desire for it. . . . One has only to remove the outer, superficial husk and look at the kernel within more attentively, and one will see in the common people things one had no inkling of. There is not much that our men of learning can teach the common people. I would even say the reverse: it is they who should take a few lessons from the common people" (4: 121–122). A year later, in his travel sketches gathered in *Winter Notes*, he contrasted the character of European and Russian man. In the first he found only an all-pervasive egoism; the second, instinctively, was drawn to that *fraternité* (he uses the French word) held up as an aim by the French Revolution and still accepted by the Socialists as their ideal. By implication, he suggests that only in Russia can a society based on such fraternity come into being, for only in Russia would it harmonize with the innate bent of the national character, "despite the centuries-old sufferings, despite the barbarous coarseness and ignorance that have taken root in it, despite the slavery of centuries and the invasion of other peoples" (5: 80).

The democratic radicalism of Herzen and Chernyshevsky, to be sure, had also idealized the Russian people. Herzen in particular, whom Turgenev once accused of bowing down before the Russian sheepskin (worn by peasants) as before an idol, had also envisaged those wearing such garb as capable of reinvigorating a moribund European civilization by leading the way to a Socialist future. But both Herzen and Chernyshevsky had seen the *narod* primarily as unconscious Socialists, still uncorrupted by the bourgeois mentality of the West; once made aware of their true interests, they could serve to provide the dynamism for the transition to a juster society. The existing proto-Socialist institutions of the peasantry, such as the *obshchina* (commune) and the *artel* (a wage-sharing association of workers), were for them only an embryo that would have to be carefully nurtured and developed in a consciously Socialist direction. Like Dostoevsky and the Slavophils, however, the Populists, alarmed at the growth of capitalism in the country, were led to regard the existing social-economic institutions of the peasantry (and hence the way of life and the ethos from which they sprang) as uniquely valuable and precious *in themselves and in their present form*. The most essential task of the Populists as they themselves saw it, particularly in face of the threat posed by the increasing pace of industrialization, was to protect peasant life from the forces leading to the disintegration of the commune.

"The working-class question in Europe," Mikhailovsky had declared in 1872, reversing the whole earlier thrust of Russian radicalism, "is a revolutionary question; over there it demands the *transfer* of the tools of labor into the hands of the worker, the expropriation of the present proprietor. In Russia the working-class question is a conservative question; here only the *preservation* of the means of labor in the hands of the workers is required, a guarantee to the present proprietors [the peasants] of their property. . . . Clearly, this goal cannot be obtained without large-scale government intervention, whose first act should be the strengthening of the *obshchina*."[18] As far back as 1850, Dostoevsky had agreed with the Slavophils that European conceptions of revolution had no relevance to Russian social conditions; and Mikhailovsky was now presumably agreeing with such views, in effect renouncing social-political revolution in favor of safeguarding the economic interests of the peasantry.

Even though the Populists now accepted the Christian virtue of self-sacrifice, which for Dostoevsky lay at the root of the peasant *obshchina* in a socially modified form, they preferred to cast their ideas in more contemporary terms. Mikhailovsky thus worked out his own "sociological" variant of the pervasive myth that peasant life was uniquely valuable in its own right. The criterion of progress, he argued, should be the happiness of the concrete individual, the achievement in human life of the most harmonious and well-rounded personality. From this point of view, although Europe had reached a higher "stage" of social development than Russia, the Russian peasant represented a higher "type" of humanity than his counterpart, the European industrial worker. The Russian peasant, in accomplishing his daily tasks, employed all of his diverse physical and mental capacities and thus remained an integral individual; the European industrial worker, ever more splintered by the refinements of the division of labor, had been literally reduced to a de-humanized cog. *Pochvennichestvo* had looked forward to the European-ized intelligentsia returning to the values embodied in their native soil to create a new and richer synthesis; and the aim of Populism was to safeguard the unique worth embodied in the superior type of life of the Russian peasant, raising it to a higher "stage" without destroying its irreplaceable virtues.

Even though *pochvennichestvo* and *narodnichestvo* cannot simply be equated, the similarity in overall perspective—particularly the quasi-Slavophil disaffection with European civilization—is nonetheless evident. Mikhailovsky had been appalled by Marx's depiction of "primitive accumulation," the process by which the English yeomen had been forced from the land in order to create an industrial proletariat dependent on wage labor. "Reason and moral feeling did not influence the economic development of Europe," he had indignantly declared to advocates of Russia's industrial expansion along European lines.[19] This denunciation was a far cry from Pisarev's indiscriminate embrace of capitalist "progress" in the mid-1860s and comes much closer to Dostoevsky's own condemnation of European civilization in 1862, after he had inspected all the marvels of science and technology displayed in the Crystal Palace of the London World's Fair. For Dostoevsky, these marvels represented the triumph of the flesh-god Baal, the god of a rampant materialism: "This is some sort of biblical illustration, some prophecy of the Apocalypse fulfilled before your very eyes. You felt that one must have perpetual spiritual resistance and negation so as not to surrender, . . . not to bow down before the fact and deify Baal" (5: 69–70). To exorcise this monstrous image of evil, Dostoevsky had appealed to the moral values still preserved at the roots of Russian life; and Mikhailovsky now wrote that "we not only do not scorn Russia, but we see in its past, and still in its present, much on which we can rely to ward off the falsities of European civilization."[20]

Whenever Dostoevsky had tried to express concretely his own alternative to radical ideas of revolutionary upheaval, he had done so by images of individual devotion to the welfare of "the insulted and injured." Mockingly giving some advice to the "superfluous men" portrayed in Russian literature since *Evgeny Onegin*, he had urged them to abandon their disdainful decision to sit with arms folded because they could not walk with "seven-league boots" and take giant strides. Why could they not apply their remarkable capacities to a simple but highly desirable task? "You always said that there was nothing you could do. But just try—can't you find something even now? Teach just one child the alphabet—there's your activity! . . . Sacrifice yourself, oh giants! . . . Sacrifice everything, even your grandeur and great ideas for the general good. . . . Stoop down, stoop down, as low as the level of the child" (18: 68). All through Dostoevsky's writings, universal and grandiose abstractions blind his negative heroes to the elementary obligations of a personal concern with living human beings. In *The Devils*, Shatov advises the most glamorous of these negative heroes, Stavrogin, where to seek the source of that sense of good and evil whose loss is leading him to self-destruction. Go, he says, "to find God through work . . . peasant's work. Go, give up your riches" (10: 203).

With all these convergences as background, the concrete form of the activity of the Populists in the early 1870s could well have seemed to Dostoevsky a more than coincidental response to everything he had been advocating in his books. A classic description of their aims and ideals in the spring of 1874 can be found again in the memoirs of Prince Kropotkin. The primary concern of all, he writes, was to find the answer to one important question:

> In what way could they be useful to the masses? Gradually, they came to the idea that the only way was to settle among the people, and to live the people's life. Young men came to the villages as doctors, doctor's helpers, village scribes, even as agricultural laborers, blacksmiths, woodcutters. . . . Girls passed teacher's examinations, learned midwifery or nursing, and went by the hundreds to the villages, devoting themselves to the poorest part of the population. These people went without any idea of social reconstruction in mind, or any thought of revolution. They simply wanted to teach the mass of the peasants to read, to instruct them in other things, to give them medical help, and in this way to aid in raising them from their darkness and misery, and to learn at the same time what were *their* popular ideals of a better social life.[21]

This picture is a little too idyllic to be entirely accurate, although it can be accepted as a firsthand account of the deeply altruistic mood in which the young Populists went to the people. All certainly wished to help them in every way possible; but this was not their only purpose. Their aim was also to "raise the consciousness" of the people, and to prepare the way for an eventual revolution. Some groups, influenced by Mikhail Bakunin, were convinced that only a spark was necessary to ignite a raging fire of revolt among the descendants of Pugachev and Stenka Razin; and they were sadly disappointed to find the Russian folk so distressingly immune to their incendiary rhetoric. The peasants on the whole would have little truck with these educated youth, who mysteriously appeared in their midst awkwardly garbed in peasant clothes, and they loyally reported them to the police. Dostoevsky had prophesied just such a reaction in the masterly concluding pages of *The Devils*, when his pathetic innocent, Stepan Trofimovich Verkhovensky, also decided to "go to the people" about whom he had been prating all his life.

All of literate Russia was emotionally stirred by this moral crusade, which suddenly, and apparently spontaneously, moved thousands of the finest youth to "give up their riches" (many came from wealthy and highly placed families) and "go to the people." The minister of justice, Count Pahlen, noted in surprise that many respectable families helped their own children and their children's friends to embark on this irresistible outpouring of an effort to realize, in the fullest and most literal sense, the Christian ideal of love, the ideal of aiding and comforting those who suffer. Nor is such a reference to religion only a retrospective interpretation; it was made at the time by those who were among the closest to these events. S. M. Kravchinsky, a participant who was scarcely a sentimentalist (a few years later he would stab to death in broad daylight the head of the Russian secret police), spoke of the movement as hardly anything "that could be called political. It was rather some sort of crusading procession, distinguished by the totally infectious and all-embracing character of *a religious movement*. People sought not only the attainment of a definite practical goal, but at the same time the satisfaction of a deep need for *personal moral purification*" (italics added).[22]

Dostoevsky could well have discerned in what he heard of these events—and all of Russian society was abuzz with rumors about them—the beginning of a realization of his own social-political ideal. For the Populist youth were not only concerned to educate and arouse the people; they also wished to be educated themselves, to assimilate to them, to live their lives, suffer their torments, learn about their values and beliefs. Dostoevsky had always dreamed of such a fusion between the intelligentsia and the people, and he could well have believed, during the mad spring and summer of 1874, that the longed-for day had finally dawned. But if so, a major article of Mikhailovsky's on *The Devils* (1873) revealed the gulf between the radicals and himself that would never be bridged.

5
―――

Dostoevsky's acceptance of the editorship of *The Citizen*, which coincided with the publication of *The Devils* in book form, naturally elicited a good deal of violently hostile comment in the Russian press. Sharply contrasting with all the billingsgate, however, were the views of Mikhailovsky in *Notes of the Fatherland*. Far from belaboring Dostoevsky, he took great pains to treat him with genuine respect as "one of the most talented of our contemporary writers." He even expressed some pity that such a talent had become the editor of so characterless and colorless a publication as *The Citizen*, whose best feature was the column *Diary of a Writer*, "which without question one reads with great interest."[23] Quite appropriately, Mikhailovsky begins by discussing one of these columns before his article broadens out into the best analysis of Dostoevsky since Dobrolyubov's *Downtrodden People* (*Zabytie Liudi*) in 1861.

In one of the first entries in his *Diary of a Writer*, entitled "Old People" ("Starye Liudi"), Dostoevsky had sketched a portrait of Vissarion Belinsky, whom he portrayed both as a committed Utopian Socialist and as a fervent atheist. Socialism was thus linked with the rejection of a belief in a supernatural God; and in reply, Mikhailovsky pointed out, quite accurately, that French Utopian Socialism was far from being atheistic. "One could adduce a thousand citations from Fourier, Saint-Simon, Louis Blanc, etc.," he objected, "in which the existence of God is affirmed in the most explicit and sometimes impassioned terms. So far as Christianity in particular is concerned, almost all the Socialists recognized the highly moral nature of its teachings."[24] In other words, by insisting on the atheistic nature of Socialism, the diarist was not only historically inaccurate; he was also, as Mikhailovsky implies, overlooking that the Populists were once again willing to accept the Christian morality that lay at its original base. Such reverence for Christian values, however, is carefully distinguished by Mikhailovsky from the insistence that these values must be grounded in a religious faith; and the Populist critic offers a penetrating insight into the problematic with which Dostoevsky will wrestle for the remainder of his life.

However respectful his tone, Mikhailovsky's views on Dostoevsky as a writer do not diverge from those of other and more hostile critics. Referring to his "brilliant psychiatric talent," Mikhailovsky wonders, with ironic disingenuousness, why Dostoevsky fails to choose his novelistic subjects from medieval European life. "All those flagellants, demoniacs, lycanthropes, all those *danses macabre*, feasts in time of plague and so forth, all that startling intermixture of egoism with a sense of sin and a thirst for expiation—what a fruitful theme that would be for Mr. Dostoevsky!"[25] Mikhailovsky then separates various types of characters in the novel, praising Stepan Trofimovich Verkhovensky (the Romantic Idealist of the 1840s), Karmazinov (a caricature of Turgenev), and particularly the totally incompetent Governor-General von Lembke and his radically chic wife. These are all characters who might have appeared in other Russian novels as well, though Dostoevsky handles them with inimitable verve. But another type of character is entirely his own, entirely Dostoevskian; the examples—Stavrogin, Shatov, Peter Verkhovensky, Kirillov, Shigalev—could not have been created by any other writer because the author has saddled them with his peculiar "eccentric ideas." Such characters exist "on the boundaries of reason and madness . . . [and] possess the possibility of preaching quite complicated theories."[26] In Mikhailovsky's opinion, these characters are far from successful; but he refuses to dismiss them merely as the unfortunate products of a deranged, psychopathic imagination. With an insight that still continues to elude all too many commentators, he writes keenly that "in the majority of cases he resolves, with the aid of his psychiatric subjects, *some moral problem*, and in most instances gives this resolution a mystical character" (italics added).[27]

Dostoevsky erred, he continues, in linking such a type, his own artistic speciality, with the social-political subject he chose to represent. Does he "have any basis . . . for grouping around the Nechaev affair people soaked through with mysticism? I think not, and even less does he have the right to present them as types of contemporary Russian youth in general." Indeed, as Mikhailovsky saw it, even to select the Nechaev affair as the subject of his novel was a mistake. For if the novelist's vision were not so self-enclosed, "he would become convinced . . . that the Nechaev affair is a monster to such a degree and in so many ways that it cannot serve as a theme for a novel with a more or less broad range. It could serve as material for a criminal novel, narrow and limited, and perhaps it might take a place in a picture of contemporary life, but not otherwise than as a third-rate episode." Mikhailovsky, it should be said, minced no words in his condemnation of the Nechaev affair, which he called "a painful, mistaken, and criminal exception."[28] Two years earlier, covering the trial of Nechaev's followers, he had expressed approval of their conviction and praised the manner in which the prosecution had been conducted.

Beginning as a criticism of Dostoevsky's novel, which Mikhailovsky was incapable of evaluating except in terms of the reigning conventions of social realism, the article broadens out into an extremely insightful and still relevant analysis of the ambiguities of Dostoevsky's ideological position. Referring both to the novel and to several of articles, Mikhailovsky focuses on Dostoevsky's depiction of Russian radicalism as the end product of the disintegrating European influence on Russian culture. The Russian educated class had become detached from the Russian people and simultaneously from the people's religion, and had thus lost the capacity to distinguish between good and evil. Hence they were inevitably doomed to the destruction depicted in *The Devils*. Mikhailovsky significantly objects, however, that it is not necessary to share the religious convictions of the people in order to accept the moral values embodied in their way of life. Dostoevsky, he points out, uses the word "God" in *The Devils* sometimes to mean a Supreme Being (like everyone else) and sometimes as a synonym for "national particularities" and national customs, thus identifying attachment to the Russian people with religious faith. But this theory is "simply impossible," and Mikhailovsky carefully disengages the question of religion from that of the relation between the intelligentsia and the people.

This relation is much more complicated than Dostoevsky is willing to acknowledge. For the novelist, there is only the unequivocal condemnation of the intelligentsia pronounced in *The Devils* or the equally unequivocal and uncritical glorification of the people in the *Diary of a Writer*. Dostoevsky is "a happy man," Mikhailovsky writes enviously. "He knows that whatever happens with the people, in the end it will save itself and us."[29] All those who do not share this faith in the people, with all their customs and beliefs, are called *citoyens* by Dostoevsky, who uses this French word to stress their alienation from their native soil. But whatever may have been the case in the past, Mikhailovsky goes on, it is a serious mistake to overlook the new group of *citoyens* (that is, the Populists), who do not fit into this classification. For these new *citoyens*, while fully sharing his reverence for "the Russian people's truth," nonetheless find the traditions of this "truth" contradictory and confusing; they accept only that part which coincides with the general principles of "humanity" acquired from other sources (namely, the ideals of social justice embodied in Western Socialism). Indeed, as Mikhailovsky penetratingly remarks, Dostoevsky does the very same thing himself in many instances, though refusing to acknowledge that he arbitrarily identifies his own humane values with "the Russian people's truth."

What characterizes these new *citoyens* is precisely their devotion to the Russian people and their feelings of guilt and indebtedness toward those at whose expense their own advantages have been acquired. "We have come to the conclusion that we are the debtors of the people," writes Mikhailovsky in a passage that became famous and echoes

83

Lavrov. "Perhaps this conviction is not in the people's truth, surely it is not, but we place it at the center of our life and activity, though perhaps not always with full awareness." As a result, the *citoyens* for whom Mikhailovsky speaks are willing to forgo agitating for legal and political rights, which would benefit only themselves as members of the educated class, and choose to devote their energies to working for social reforms of immediate benefit to the people. "Giving the preference to social reforms over political ones," Mikhailovsky explains, "we are only renouncing the strengthening of our rights and the development of our freedom as instruments for the oppression of the people and even further sin." The situation of the *citoyens* is thus inherently tragic: the very "progress" they wish to further among the people is itself tainted with the age-old injustice for which they feel repentant. "The expiation of involuntary sin with the aid of means attained by sin—that is the law of the *citoyens*, though I am not of course speaking of all."[30]

Mikhailovsky, as we see, employs Dostoevsky's own Christian vocabulary, and he does so to persuade his interlocutor that the image of the radicals projected in *The Devils* is now woefully out of date. Admonishing him directly, he writes: "If you would stop playing with the word 'God' and become acquainted somewhat more closely with your shameful Socialism, you would be convinced that it coincides with at least some of the elements of the Russian people's truth." Rather than attack those who now share a common reverence for the people and their "truth," he urges Dostoevsky to look around and pay attention to all the new "devils" that have recently emerged to plague the country:

> Russia, that frenzied invalid you have depicted, is being girded with railroads, besprinkled with factories and banks—and in your novel there is not a single indication of this world! You focus your attention on an insignificant handful of madmen and scoundrels! There is no devil of national wealth [industrial expansion at the expense of the welfare of the people] in your novel, the most widespread devil of all and less than all the others knowing the boundaries of good and evil. . . . The devil of service to the people—even if it is a devil, driven out of the ailing body of Russia—thirsts for expiation in one or another form, and this is its entire substance. Better avoid it entirely if you can see only its pathological forms.[31]

6

Hastening to acknowledge the impact of Mikhailovsky's article in the very next issue of *The Citizen*, Dostoevsky calls it "in some sense a new revelation for me." Several months later he returns to it again. "I cannot forget N. M. of *Notes of the Fatherland* and my 'debts' to him," he says adroitly. "I have not had the honor of knowing him personally, and likewise have never had the pleasure of learning anything about him as a private individual. But I am convinced with all my heart that he is one of the most sincere publicists to be found in Petersburg" (21: 156). Dostoevsky was evidently touched by the gravity of Mikhailovsky's tone, with its deeply felt expression of the Populists' desire to sacrifice themselves on behalf of the people; and he would also have been favorably struck by the outright condemnation of Nechaev. In his notebooks he had once remarked scornfully: "no one [among the radicals] dares to express an opinion about Nechaev."[32]

But as he soon makes clear, he had no illusions—nor would Mikhailovsky's article have allowed him to have any—concerning the major point on which he and the Populists would continue to differ. "Mr. N. M. attracted my attention for the first time," he explains, "by his opinions about my opinions concerning Belinsky, Socialism, and atheism, and then about my novel *The Devils*." Lack of time prevents him from replying to the criticism of his novel, though he dearly wished to do so; but he then puts his finger on the crucial bone of contention between him and the Populists, no matter how much their views might otherwise coincide. "But to write and assert that Socialism is not atheistic," he admonishes Mikhailovsky, "that Socialism is not at all the formula for atheism, and that atheism is not its central, fundamental essence—that surprises me extremely in a writer who, apparently, has been so much taken up with this subject" (21: 157).

Dostoevsky knew very well that Mikhailovsky was quite justified in claiming that the fathers of French Utopian Socialism had not been atheistic and had revered the sanctified figure of a vaguely defined but still divine Christ. He also knew, however, that since Ludwig Feuerbach had dethroned religion as being, in Marx's words, "the opiate of the people," Feuerbach's views had been accepted in Russia by Herzen, Bakunin, and Chernyshevsky, among others. Their combined influence ruled out any easy acceptance of religious faith as the natural corollary of Christian moral-social ideals. "Socialism—this is also Christianity," Dostoevsky had jotted down in his notebooks (1872–1875), "but it proposes that it can succeed with reason."[33] Such words indicate his awareness of the Christian inspiration underlying Populist Socialism, but pinpoint what he felt to be its self-contradiction. Moreover, just about this time (1873) the antagonism between radicalism and religious faith had been resoundingly proclaimed by a resolution of the Slavic section of the First International. Under the influence of Bakunin, it had declared itself in favor of "atheism and materialism" and had pledged "to fight against any kind of divine worship, against all official religious confessions and . . . to endeavor to eradicate the idea of divinity in all its manifestations."[34]

Nonetheless, because the Russian Populists no longer linked atheism to a rejection of Christian morality or the teachings of Christ *as such*, there will be a noticeable shift of accent in Dostoevsky's relation to this new brand of radicalism. He will treat it with a mildness of tone in sharp contrast with his polemics of the 1860s, and his artistic focus will no longer be on figures like the underground man (who denies, in Part I, the possibility of *any* kind of morality on Nihilist principles) or like Raskolnikov and Stavrogin, who replace Christian conscience with a Utilitarian calculus or with a proto-Nietzschean theory of amoral indifferentism beyond good and evil. The Populists had now come round to accepting the Christian values of "the Russian people's truth," and so he believed he could appeal to them in terms of a morality they would not automatically reject.

His great ambition had always been to reconcile the refractory and radicalized younger generation, if not to the existing conditions of Russian life, then to the government that, as he was convinced, offered the only possibility of changing such conditions for the better. This new basis for dialogue thus offered him an unrivaled opportunity, which he sought to utilize by publishing his next work in *Notes of the Fatherland*. The weakest link in the Populists' ideology was their willingness to revere the Russian people and "the Russian people's truth" while refusing to accept the root of this "truth" in the people's inherited belief in Christ as the divine God-man. How could the Populists idolize and idealize the people without also adhering to the religious faith from which all the people's moral values sprang and which for Dostoevsky provided their only firm anchorage? The theme of the necessity for religious faith takes on a new importance and intensity in the novels of this last period and is conspicuously placed in the foreground. To be sure, it had always been present, but subordinated to a defense of the Christian ethics of love and self-sacrifice against Nihilist onslaughts.

Dostoevsky and the Populists would continue to diverge on this fateful question of religious faith, although enough points of contact remained for him to acquire a unique status. He was regarded as someone who, despite his loyalty to the Tsar, managed to transcend a narrow factionalism; and he tried to use this eminence, as the 1870s wore on, to ward off the catastrophe that loomed closer and closer for his country as the once-peaceful, apolitical Populists turned to terror out of despair.

# CHAPTER 5

# *The Diary of a Writer,*
## 1873: I

One of the major attractions of *The Citizen* under Dostoevsky's editorship was the regular appearance of his *Diary of a Writer*. He had long
cherished an ambition to create such a unique journal, written entirely
by himself, in which he could comment freely on current events and
express, in a variety of literary forms, his reactions to the deeper moral-
social and religious-philosophical problems that they raised. For the
moment, though, he decided to test its possibilities only as a column, a
feuilleton, appearing irregularly in *The Citizen*.

Dostoevsky's column attracted immediate and favorable attention.
Whether one agreed or not with his views, it was impossible not to appreciate the vigor, ingenuity, and expressiveness of his writing and
his novelist's gift for dramatizing his ideas in the form of thumbnail
sketches and sharply etched dialogic exchanges. These imparted an irresistible freshness and animation to whatever subject he addressed.
Mikhail Bakhtin, who gave so much importance to the role of dialogue
in Dostoevsky's novels, also remarked on this feature of his expository
style. His "manner of developing a thought is everywhere the same: he
develops it dialogically, not in a dry logical dialogue, but by juxtaposing
whole, profoundly individual voices; in his polemical articles he does
not really persuade but rather organizes voices, yokes together semantic
orientations in some form of imagined dialogue."[1]

This observation is quite acute, but the terminology may lead to misunderstanding. It is not only "voices" that he yokes together but full-
blooded people and their attitudes and values—sometimes imaginary
characters and situations invented for purposes of illustration, sometimes people and events taken from his own life. For his articles are also
enlivened by the continual employment of autobiographical material,
brief evocations of a personal event or encounter. The *Diary* thus contains a constant flow of anecdotes and reminiscences that refer to such
great names as Alexander Herzen, Vissarion Belinsky, and Nikolay Chernyshevsky, all of whom Dostoevsky had known personally and who appear in his pages to represent various types of the Russian intelligentsia.

Like Herzen's brilliant autobiography, *My Past and Thoughts*, the *Diary* thus became a living link between Dostoevsky's readers and their own social-cultural past. It also served the function of surrounding him with the aureole of this now-hallowed history, in which, as was well known, he had played an honorable part and, to use a Russian euphemism, "had suffered for his convictions." Indeed, the *Diary* still offers one of the major sources of information about Dostoevsky himself, though it must be used with a great deal of caution. Aside from the slips of memory to which he became increasingly prone in later years—perhaps, as he thought, because of the effects of his epilepsy—the "facts" as he presents them are always colored by the particular ideological context in which he was immersed in the early 1870s.

2

The *Diary* begins with an amusing introduction that announces Dostoevsky's installation as editor and vividly illustrates some of the inventiveness he will use to liven up even so casual and unprepossessing an event as his arrival on the journalistic scene. For he seizes on another event that occurred on the same day—the wedding of the Chinese emperor—to highlight the reigning confusion of the Russian cultural situation. The ceremonial of the Chinese wedding had been "decreed a thousand years ago in nearly two hundred volumes"; but his own appointment had taken place in the very simplest and most unassuming fashion. Matters would have been handled differently in China. There would have been no need for a new editor to think at all about his future duties because "there, everything has been anticipated and planned for a thousand years ahead, while here everything is topsy-turvy for a thousand years." Dostoevsky colorfully makes his point and then narrates an anecdote involving a combat between a pig and a lion (supposedly of Indian origin). The king of beasts, catching one whiff of his antagonist, quits the field hastily; and Dostoevsky thus allegorically indicates that he will not engage in polemics with any opponent of a similar fragrance.

Another little story (actually two) deals with the same issue and brings it closer to home. Once, when he had complimented Herzen on his sparkling series of dialogues, *From the Other Shore*, Herzen responded by recalling a conversation with Belinsky about a dialogue written by the critic. Belinsky had left no doubt that the spokesman representing the ideas that *he* favored had gotten the better of the argument. "But whatever," Herzen continued disingenuously, "made you waste your time talking to a fool like that?" (21: 8). Dostoevsky clearly would not waste his time arguing with fools; but like Herzen, he would presumably marshal the most powerful arguments that could be mustered against his own point of view.

3
———

The entries of Dostoevsky's *Diary* are often linked, not in any overt or explicit fashion but through connections that emerge from the depths of associative memory. The recollection of Herzen's story about Belinsky "put me in mind"—as he writes in his next entry, "Old People"—"of my début in literature" (21: 8). Dostoevsky had long wished to record his memories of Belinsky and had even done so in a lost article written in 1867 while living abroad. His letters from this period contain furious and even scurrilous attacks against Belinsky, and there are equally offensive remarks in the notes for *The Devils*. "That man reviled Christ to me in the foulest language," he wrote indignantly to Strakhov in 1871, labeling the great critic "the most foul-smelling, obtuse, and ignominious phenomenon of Russian life."[2] These words were written at the very height of his rage against the radicals, provoked by the Nechaev affair, which he saw as a product of Belinsky's influence. The young Populists, however, could also be seen as Belinsky's descendants, and Dostoevsky's relation to this key figure, who had been so important for him at the beginning of his literary career, thus became much more ambivalent.

Both Herzen and Belinsky are sketched in Dostoevsky's article. In the first he stresses the internal contradiction between Herzen's professed principles and his personal life, calling him a historical type, someone who did not become an émigré but who, "as a product of our aristocracy," was so to speak born in exile. He represented a class, the Russian gentry, who had broken with the Russian people; and "when they broke with the people, they naturally lost God as well." In their eyes, the Russian people, whom they imagined they loved but really despised, "took the form of the Parisian mob of 1793"; and the same inconsistency ran through every aspect of Herzen's career. As a good Socialist, he had renounced all the principles of the old society in which he lived; but he was "a good husband and father," looked after his inherited wealth very carefully, and incited others to embark on the dangerous path of revolution even though he "loved comfort and family peace." Above all, Herzen was a brilliant thinker, writer, and talker, preeminently an artist, with "a superb capacity for self-reflection." "Self-reflection—the ability to make of his own deepest feelings an object which he could set before him, pay tribute to it with one breath and, in the next, perhaps ridicule it scornfully—was a thing he had developed to the highest degree" (21: 9). Although Dostoevsky himself does not draw this conclusion, such a capacity helps to account for the ironically self-critical quality of Herzen's dialogues that he so much admired.

If Herzen was primarily self-reflective, Belinsky was quite the contrary—"an enthusiast" above all else, who gave way completely to whatever new wave of inspiration swept over him. Dubbed "furious Vissarion" by his intimates, Belinsky was well known for the impetuosity and inflammability of his temperament; and Dostoevsky's portrait agrees with the much more detailed one provided by Herzen in *My Past and Thoughts.* The former had met Belinsky just as the influential critic was moving from an acceptance of deistic French Utopian Socialism, which revered Christ as the divine harbinger of a "new Christianity," to a rejection of Christianity and the adoption of a militant atheism under the influence of such Left Hegelian thinkers as D. F. Strauss and Ludwig Feuerbach. The conversation that he recalls, which took place "in the first months of our acquaintance," dwells on this inner debate but somewhat distorts the historical record. Dostoevsky implies, from Belinsky's example, that Socialism must *necessarily* be atheistic, which he knew very well had not been the case in the mid-1840s; he then states that he himself "had passionately accepted all [Belinsky's] teaching," which misleadingly suggests that Dostoevsky had converted to atheism (21: 12). In fact, another article in the *Diary* unmistakably indicates that he was still under the influence of a deistic Christian Socialism at the time of his arrest four years later in 1849.

Aside from such questions, this portrait of Belinsky touches on what will, a few years later, become one of the central motifs of the Legend of the Grand Inquisitor—the motif of the enormous burden placed on humanity by Christ. Dostoevsky had told Mikhail Pogodin that he wished to drive home in the *Diary* the antithesis between Socialism and Christianity, and he begins to do so in this very first article. "While cherishing reason, science, and realism above all," he writes, "[Belinsky] also understood better than anyone that reason, science, and realism alone could only create an ant-heap and not the social 'harmony' in which man could create a life for himself. He knew that moral principles are the basis of everything." Yet "as a Socialist he first had to dethrone Christianity," and so he rejected "the moral responsibility of the individual" and did not hesitate even to attack "the radiant image of the God-man, its moral unattainability, its marvelous and miraculous beauty" (21: 10).

Belinsky went much farther even than an unbeliever like Ernest Renan, who in his *Life of Jesus* had considered Christ "still the ideal of human beauty, an unattainable type, never to be repeated in the future."[3] Not so Belinsky, who "screeched one evening" that man was too weak to bear the burden of moral responsibility imposed on him by

Christ. "Do you know that man's sins cannot be counted against him and that he cannot be laden down with obligations and with turning the other cheek when society is set up in such a foul fashion that a man cannot help but do wrong; economic factors alone lead him to do wrong, and it is absurd and cruel to demand from a man something which the very laws of nature make it impossible for him to carry out, even if he wanted to." Belinsky then commented, as he scrutinized the visage of the silent Dostoevsky (who does not utter a single word), that "I no sooner mention the name of Christ than his whole face changes, just as if he were going to cry." These words are presumably addressed to two others present; and if Belinsky's words brought Dostoevsky to the verge of tears, it was only because of Belinsky's abusively contemptuous language about Christ.

Belinsky then continues in this vein: "Believe me, that your Christ, were He born in our time, would be the most undistinguished and ordinary of men; He would be utterly eclipsed by today's science, and by those forces that now advance humanity" (21: 11). At this point, one of those present intervened to assert that "if Christ appeared now He would join the Socialist movement and take His place at its head." Despite having just maintained that Christ would have no role to play in the modern world, Belinsky hastened to agree: "He would certainly join the Socialists and follow them." Dostoevsky then lists the names of all those Socialists whom Belinsky admired and of whom Christ would become a follower: George Sand, "the now totally forgotten [Etienne] Cabet," Pierre Leroux, and Pierre-Joseph Proudhon, "who was then only beginning his work" (21: 11). All these writers were deistic French Socialists or, like Proudhon, used the language of religion to express Socialist ideals. In this image of a Christ returning to ally Himself with the Socialists, we can already glimpse the motif of a returning Christ and the problematic of the Legend of the Grand Inquisitor. Would Christ subordinate Himself to the Socialists, or were they in fact falsifying and distorting His message? When the Inquisitor claims to speak in the name of Christ, he does so with words similar to those of the compassionate atheist Belinsky, who sought to relieve mankind from the enormous burden of moral freedom out of pity and love.

Whether as a novelist or a publicist, Dostoevsky was never inclined to argue abstractly or conceptually; he preferred instead to set one dramatic image against another. Here he juxtaposes his depiction of Belinsky with another episode from his own life. On arriving in Siberia, he and the other prisoners in the convoy, pausing at Tobolsk on the way to various camps, had been met and aided by the highly educated and gently nurtured wives of the exiled Decembrists, women who had voluntarily abandoned their privileged lives among the gentry to accompany their husbands into Siberian exile. "They gave up everything: their social position, wealth, connections, relatives, and sacrificed it all for the supreme moral duty, the freest duty that can ever exist. Guilty of nothing, they endured for twenty-five long years everything that their convicted husbands endured." They gave Dostoevsky and the others copies of the New Testament (he does not mention the ten rubles concealed in the bindings); and this gift, the only book prisoners were allowed to possess, "lay under my pillow during the four years of my penal servitude" (21: 12). Nothing more is said; but here was the living refutation of Belinsky's image of a humanity too weak to overcome the pressure of environment, a living testimony to the moral ideals enshrined in the New Testament, a living proof that humankind is *not* too weak to assume the heavy weight of moral obligation demanded by Christ and to accomplish the free self-sacrifice of love.

4

The next article, "Environment" ("Sreda"), arises directly from the conclusion of "Old People." Dostoevsky had recalled that during his prison years he had been surrounded by convicts "who, if we are to believe Belinsky, *were not able* to keep from committing crimes, and who thus were justified and only less fortunate than others." Moreover, it was the custom of the Russian people to call all convicts "unfortunates" (Gogol also had noted the same word), and this usage might be taken as justifying Belinsky's view—that the convicts were only victims of fate, not criminals guilty of a violation of any moral law. "But here we have something different," he explains, "not at all that about which Belinsky spoke, and which is heard now, for example, in some of our juries' verdicts" (21: 12). With these words, he leads into his next article, which deals with the hotly debated issues arising from the recent installation of a jury system in Russia.

Several years before, while Dostoevsky had been abroad, a letter from Apollon Maikov recounted the emotions of reverence he had felt when called to serve on one of the new juries. Dostoevsky responded by exhibiting intense interest in the workings of this innovative (for Russia) legal institution. The jury system was one of the reforms initiated by Alexander II, and while expressing great satisfaction at its establishment, he also manifested uneasiness about the leniency of some of the verdicts. Happy that Russian juries looked on crime "from a Christian point of view" and were thus immensely superior to Western ones, he nonetheless worried that perhaps "in this *humanitarianism* there is much that is bookish, liberal, not really independent."[4] Indeed, the unwillingness of Russian juries to enforce the written law had elicited a good deal of contemporary comment. Writing somewhat later, an impartial and highly qualified observer, the eminent English journalist and diplomat D. W. Mackenzie Wallace, found that the Russian jury system worked fairly well but labored under the handicap of a divergence between the moral standards of the peasantry and the norms of Western justice embodied in the reformed legal code. What peasant jurors considered venial or even permissible was often judged very severely; and the judge had no discretion to mitigate the harshness of a penalty so as to take the sentiments of the jury into account. Many offenders, even where guilt was clearly established, were thus let off lightly or even set scot-free by peasant juries.[5]

Dostoevsky's handling of this question provides a classic example of his technique of conveying his point of view through an interplay of competing voices. He begins by finding it quite comprehensible that "the peasants, just yesterday insulted and injured," should wish to show mercy to the criminals brought before them, many of whom were peasants like themselves. But he finds it anomalous that the "sentimentality" of Russian juries was also in evidence even when these were composed of jurors "of the very highest caliber, noblemen and university professors." How can one explain this strange benevolence of Russian juries, which appears to go beyond class distinctions? He refers to a newspaper article attributing it to the desire, on the part of the population as a whole, to twist the tail of the powers that be—out of "playfulness," as it were—because of all the oppression they had been forced to endure in the past. Finding this theory "not at all bad," Dostoevsky yet cannot accept it as an adequate answer to the question (21: 13).

He then cites a remark often heard, that "the Russian people are merciful." But surely the English people are also merciful, and yet decisions in favor of the guilty are much rarer there than in Russia. "There, the juror understands above all that in his hands lies the banner of all England; that he has already ceased to be a private individual and is obliged to represent the opinion of his country"—which is that "in old England . . . vice is still called vice and villainy—villainy." Another voice questioningly intervenes to object that, even if "your firm foundations (Christian ones, that is) endure and that in truth one must be a citizen above all," how can Russians be changed overnight into "citizens," given the history of their past? Citizenship suddenly fell on them as from a mountain, and they have been crushed by its weight! (21: 14).

A third voice is then heard, expressing opinions that Dostoevsky labels "Slavophil." The Russian people feel unworthy, this voice explains, of the power that has been thrust upon them (which in fact shows how *worthy* they really are to receive such power); and they thus pardon, out of fear of the very authority accorded them as a gift. "We have been frightened," this voice imagines them feeling collectively, "by this dreadful power over human fate, over the fates of our brethren, and until we mature into our citizenship, we will show mercy. . . . We have money and are free from want, but if we happened to be in the same situation, we might have done even worse—so we show mercy." Dostoevsky finds the utterances of this voice to be "consoling," and there can be no doubt, though he does not intervene directly, that he thoroughly agrees with another speculation of this speaker. In the opinion of the Slavophil voice, if these are (as he thinks) the sentiments of the Russian people, then "perhaps this was the gage of such a sublime form of Christianity in the future as the world has not yet known" (21: 15).

But this compassion does not mean, Dostoevsky insists, that criminals escape the consequences of their crimes out of such Christian feelings of mutual sinfulness. Rather, it should lead to the opposite result: Russian jurors should accept the pain of their own guilt, "while speaking the truth and calling evil by its name. . . . if this pain is genuine and powerful, it will purify us and make us better. And becoming better ourselves, we improve the environment and make it better" (21: 15). Otherwise, we reach the point of regarding the criminal as a victim of environment, or even of justifying crime "as an obligation, a noble protest against environment." Such a confusion has been fostered by the trial lawyers of the new system, who invariably—and all too often successfully—plead extenuating circumstances for their clients because of "environment." And this "doctrine of environment is the very opposite of Christianity, which, while accepting the pressure of environment and proclaiming mercy toward sinners, insists nonetheless on the moral obligation of humankind to struggle against environment, insists on the limit at which environment ends and moral obligation begins. By declaring man responsible, Christianity in this way recognizes his freedom" (21: 16).

Dostoevsky's position is clear enough, but he reinforces it by appealing to his own past. "I was in prison, and saw criminals. . . . I saw them lonely and pensive; I saw them in church praying before confession. . . . Oh, believe me, in his heart not one of them considered himself justified." If the Russian people call criminals "unfortunates," this epithet only indicates a feeling of Christian solidarity for the universal guilt of evil and is not a refusal to recognize crime as crime; but nothing is easier than to turn such Christian sentiments into a doctrine of "environment." He even goes so far as to argue that it is better for peasant criminals to be punished; if not, "you only plant cynicism in their hearts, you leave them with a seductive question and with contempt for you yourself" (21: 18–19). Such a sanctimonious plea for more severity on behalf of the convict's own good aroused a storm of quite justified criticism; but nothing terrified him more than the prospect of weakening and undermining the age-old inherited pieties of the Russian people. We can already see here the origins of such a character as Smerdyakov in *The Brothers Karamazov*.

Moreover, much may be forgiven Dostoevsky because of his conclusion to this article, which deals with the trial of a peasant arrested after his wife hanged herself to escape his monstrously sadistic mistreatment. Despite the evidence, he was let off with a light sentence of eight months in prison. Deploying all his literary powers, Dostoevsky details the *terrible reality* of the poor woman's suffering, remarking with bitter irony that "peasant life is without aesthetic pleasures, such as music, theaters, and magazines; it is natural that this void be filled with something." The void here was filled by the perverted pleasure taken in the torments inflicted on the terrified victim, to whose "cries and pleading" the husband "listens with delight—otherwise, what satisfaction should there be in beating her?" (21: 21). If such passages have led to the accusation that Dostoevsky was "a cruel talent," his "cruelty" here is inspired by an outraged pity.

In the midst of the tortures that he details with such sickening exactitude, he suddenly breaks forth: "Do you know, gentlemen, people are born in various circumstances: can you not conceive that this woman in other circumstances might have been some Juliet or Beatrice from Shakespeare, or Gretchen from *Faust*. I'm not saying that she was—but yet there could be the embryo of something very noble in her soul. . . . And so this same Beatrice or Gretchen is beaten and whipped like a dog!" (21: 21). This leap from the vile and ignoble to some of the most radiant female figures of the Western literary tradition, who suddenly merge for an instant with the hapless peasant sufferer, tellingly illustrates the creative process by which Dostoevsky continually elevates his lowly material to the heights of his great creations. But here he performs this feat only in passing, returning to his unhappiness with the trial lawyers by imagining them (no such case existed) defending a mother who, to punish her squalling baby, holds its hand under boiling water for ten minutes. Would they not also plead on this mother's behalf that she was the victim of "the corroding environment"? Suddenly he is swept by sympathy for the poor lawyers, who have such "an unbearable job" and who continually are forced to lie "against [their] own consciences, against [their] convictions, against all morality, against all humanity!" And he concludes: "Enough contortions, gentlemen of the bar. Enough of your environment" (21: 22–23). It is symptomatic of the new social-cultural situation that Nikolay Mikhailovsky, commenting on this piece, agreed that "the doctrine of environment in its extreme form morally lowers people and deprives them of personal responsibility" (21: 387).

5

Dostoevsky thus succeeded in winning some acknowledgment from his Populist opponents for the importance of his "Christian" emphasis on personal moral responsibility; and this evidence of a common moral ground made it all the more imperative for him to erase the stigma of being their implacable enemy. Since 1865, a charge had hung over him, namely, that in his unfinished story *The Crocodile* he had written an allegorical defamation of the revered radical publicist N. G. Chernyshevsky. Shortly after the first part of the story was printed in his journal *Epokha* (*Epoch*), a columnist in *Golos* (*Voice*) advised Dostoevsky not to continue to publish "this tactless story, about which rumors are flying of a kind quite harmful to the reputation of the journal *Epoch* and for Mr. Dostoevsky himself" (21: 395).

Chernyshevsky had been arrested in 1862, sentenced in May 1864 in a public ceremony attended by many of his sympathizers as a demonstration of support, and then sent to Siberia. While in prison he had succeeded in publishing his famous novel *What Is To Be Done?*, which then became the enduring bible of Russian radicalism. These events were still fresh in the minds of everyone when the story was published a year later. *The Crocodile* is a satirical fantasy in which a self-important bureaucrat imbued with "progressive" ideas is accidentally swallowed by a crocodile on display in St. Petersburg and establishes himself comfortably in its belly. From there he proclaims his ideas about the future destinies of mankind, becomes a local celebrity, and is taken in a tank with his crocodile host to fashionable dinner parties. Meanwhile, his pretty and flirtatious wife, while appropriately deploring his absence, enjoys her newfound freedom in the company of an extremely attentive "friend." This fantastic situation was alleged to represent the incarcerated Chernyshevsky and to have cast aspersions on his wife. As Dostoevsky explains in his *Diary* article, he had not protested "this vile slander" at the moment and had failed to do so since; but "it is time to say at least a few words about it, *the more so that it is now apropos*" (21: 24; italics added).

He begins his defense by recalling a conversation with Nikolay Nekrasov, a close friend from his early literary days in the Belinsky *pléiade* and now an editor of *Notes of the Fatherland*. Political differences had separated them, but never to the point of an open personal rupture; and he takes care to express his appreciation, which was quite genuine, of Nekrasov's talent. Although no one, he remarks, looks less like a "suffering" poet than Nekrasov (a suffering, it should be understood, stemming from the unhappy plight of the Russian people), "yet he is one of the most passionate, gloomy and 'suffering' of our poets." The two men had met again in 1866, shortly after the publication of the first part of *Crime and Punishment*, which had been roundly berated in the radical journal *Sovremennik (Contemporary)*, of which Nekrasov was then also an editor. Obviously feeling that some justification was in order for the "dressing-down," Nekrasov explained that it was not because the novel had been judged artistically inferior. Rather, the critic assigned the task, G. Z. Eliseev, had taken *The Crocodile* to heart and believed that he had "stooped to mockery and to a caricature of the poor exiled Chernyshevsky." Dostoevsky could only express astonishment at this effect of "the vilest kind of gossip there can be"; and though seven years had now passed, he decided to set the record straight for reasons left unexplained but which we can now infer (21: 24).

The details of Dostoevsky's past included in this article do not concern us here, only his manifest desire to establish his good faith as an interlocutor who, while speaking frankly from his own position, could still enter into an honest discussion with the radicals on the basis of mutual respect and sympathetic understanding of their ideals. He thus ridicules the notion that he had written an "allegory" and charges that, with enough ingenuity on the part of the interpreter, anything can be given a hidden meaning. "You can bring me whatever you like— 'Memoirs of a Madman' [by Gogol], the ode 'God' [by G. R. Derzhavin], 'Yury Miloslavsky' [a historical novel by M. N. Zagoskin], the poetry of [A. A.] Fet—and I will at once set to proving to you from the first ten lines . . . that here is an allegory of the Franco-Prussian War or a lampoon of the actor Gorbunov." Dostoevsky compares such a search with the attitude of the Russian censorship looking for "allegories" of another kind. Nothing in his life, he declares, indicates that he could resemble such a "malicious, heartless writer of lampoons" or, especially, that "I, a former exile and convict, would rejoice in the exile of some other 'unfortunate'" (21: 29).

Dwelling on his few personal contacts with Chernyshevsky, he emphasizes that, unlike some others, he found the radical not at all antipathetic as a personality. "Herzen told me that Chernyshevsky made an unpleasant impression on him by his appearance and manner. As for me, I liked Chernyshevsky's appearance and manner" (21: 25). And even though the radical publicist had been convicted and exiled for subversive agitation, Dostoevsky—quite courageously, under the circumstances—does everything he can to undermine the basis for such a charge. Revolutionary leaflets had circulated in Petersburg during the turbulent spring of 1862, and Dostoevsky writes: "I fully believed then, and I believe now, that [Chernyshevsky] did not support those who ran around distributing proclamations" (21: 26). There is even a hint that the secrecy surrounding the arrest and conviction leaves some doubt as to its justice. "I was never able to learn anything about his case," he declares. "I know nothing even now." And, Dostoevsky adds: "I sincerely regretted and still regret his misfortune" (21: 26, 29).

The most striking passage comes when he imagines someone assuming that he nurtured "a secret hatred" against Chernyshevsky because their political convictions differed. Why should there be such a hatred, he asks. "Chernyshevsky's convictions never offended me. *One can have a great deal of respect for a man even when one has radically different opinions from him*" (21: 29; italics added). To prove his point, he mentions that he had commissioned an article on *What Is To Be Done?* from Strakhov, the chief critic of his journal *Epoch*, and that a highly respectful consideration of it had appeared under his editorial auspices. In fact, only the first part of Strakhov's article saw the light of day because *Epoch* ceased to publish; the second section, which dealt more concretely with Chernyshevsky's optimistic Utopian Socialist vision of the future, appeared a bit later in another journal. Dostoevsky's slip of memory, however, does not undermine his main point—that Chernyshevsky had been treated by him as editor very seriously and courteously.

Dostoevsky was eager to free himself not only from the cloud hanging over his name because of *The Crocodile*. It was also necessary to do so as regards *The Devils*; and one of the most arresting articles in the *Diary* was aimed at accomplishing this much more difficult task. If read with our present knowledge, this article, "One of Today's Falsehoods," comes quite close to disclosing the secret he kept hidden all through his life— that he had taken part in a genuine revolutionary conspiracy during the 1840s. The immediate aim of the article was to counter some remarks about the Nechaev case by a rival publication, *Russkii Mir* (*Russian World*), which had written that "an idiotic fanatic such as Nechaev could find proselytes only among the idle and underdeveloped and not among young people involved in studies" (21: 126). Such an opinion, uttered at the very moment when the finest of Russia's youth were flocking to the villages, seemed to Dostoevsky the height of obtuseness and incomprehension. He thus springs to their defense, while at the same time implicitly warning them of the lurking dangers of self-betrayal.

Far from finding followers only among the dregs of the student population, agitators like Nechaev, Dostoevsky insists, are much more likely to recruit converts among the best of the student body, those capable of being stirred by the highest ideals and the noblest longings. Dostoevsky never forgot that he had once been drawn to such ideals himself, and had belonged to a secret society pledged to revolution. Sometimes Dostoevsky is talking about the Petrashevsky circle as a whole, the majority of whose members were committed only to peaceful change; sometimes he is covertly talking about his Speshnev group, which he assimilates to Nechaev and Nechaevism. His purpose is to show how easily, as he knew from his own experience, the idealism of the first can lead to the murderousness of the second.

The writer in *Russian World,* and others in what he calls "the pseudo-liberal press," believe that by denigrating the personal character of the young radicals they are defending the honor of Russian youth; but they only obstruct any comprehension of the true problem. For what if it should turn out "that those involved in some *case* or other were by no means underdeveloped rowdies . . . were by no means idlers but . . . were diligent, ardent young people who were in fact studying and who possessed good hearts and who had set off on a wrong tendency?" (21: 128). Dostoevsky ridicules the notion that, by simply completing a course of study, young people become immune to falling under the sway of crafty scoundrels (like Nechaev) who "have thoroughly studied the *magnanimous* aspect of the human soul—and most often the soul of youth—so as to be able to play on it as a musical instrument" (italics added). Indeed, "I myself," he writes, "am an old 'Nechaevist'; I also stood on the scaffold condemned to death, and I assure you that I stood in the company of educated people. Almost the whole company had graduated from the highest institutions of learning." The word "Nechaevist" is here placed in quotation marks to indicate that it should not be taken literally; it merely refers to his membership in the Petrashevsky group devoted to Socialist ideas.

As if anticipating the objection that the Petrashevsky circle should not be identified with the Nechaev conspiracy, Dostoevsky responds with a question: "How do you know that the members of that circle could not have become Nechaevists, i.e., set off on Nechaev's path *in the event that things had taken such a turn?*" (italics added). Narrowing the issue to a purely personal one, he continues: "But let me say one thing about myself alone: a *Nechaev* I probably could never have become, but a *Nechaevist*—well, of that I can't be sure; I could have become one . . . in the days of my youth." Here is the closest Dostoevsky ever came to confessing that *he had been a Nechaevist,* that is, a member of a revolutionary group making preparations to unleash a peasant revolution. He himself had moved from peaceful Christian Socialism to accepting the Nechaevist logic of bloodshed; he knew how easily the transition could be made, and how difficult it was to resist (21: 129).

He then switches back to emphasize Socialism's appeal to the moral idealism of youth. Not one of the people who had stood with him on the scaffold had been "a monster" or "a scoundrel"; but "there were not many among us who could resist the well-known cycle of ideas and concepts that had then taken such a firm hold on young society." These ideas were predominantly those of the then reigning "theoretical" (peaceful and Utopian) Socialism, which Dostoevsky sets off against the "political" (revolutionary) Socialism based on the inevitability of class warfare, which emerged after 1848. The theoretical Socialism of those earlier days, as he rightly stresses, "was being compared—even by some of its ringleaders—with Christianity, and was taken merely as a corrective and improvement of the latter, in accordance with the spirit of the age and civilization. . . . All those new ideas of the time had tremendous appeal to us in Petersburg" and "seemed to be sacred and moral in the highest degree" (21: 130–131). When the condemned Petrashevtsy awaited what they believed was certain death, they did so with no feeling of repentance for their imputed "crimes." "Those ideas and those notions that possessed our spirits, we saw as not only requiring no repentance, but even as purifying us in a martyrdom for which much would be forgiven" (21: 133).

Presenting the Petrashevtsy in terms that would certainly appeal to the radical Populists, he then identifies them with the Nechaevtsy he had portrayed in his most recent book. "In my novel *The Devils*, I attempted to depict those diverse and multifarious motives by which even the purest of hearts and the most innocent of people can be drawn into committing such a monstrous offense. And therein lies the real horror: that in Russia one can commit the foulest and most villainous acts without being in the least a villain!" (21: 131). Here is the real tragedy: the perversion of the genuine moral idealism of Russian youth by false ideas such as those propagated by Nechaev, and implicitly those that had once misled him as well.

Sketching the process of his own gradual recovery, he attributes the "regeneration of his convictions" both to "direct contact with the people, the brotherly union with them in common misfortune," and to the patriotic and Christian education he had received as a child. "Each visit to the Kremlin and the Moscow cathedrals," he writes of himself as a boy, "was a solemn event for me." From where, he asks worriedly, can the educated youth of today draw the values that will enable them to resist the influences that could turn them into villains? Certainly not from their families, imbued with "our natural, age-old stifling in ourselves of any kind of independent thought, in the notion of the high status of a European, unfailingly with the proviso of disrespect for oneself as a Russian!" (21: 134).

This indictment of the Russian failure to inculcate proper respect for their own traditions is combined with an ironic attack on the European intellectual authorities to whom the radical intelligentsia continue to pay homage. "Keep in mind, gentlemen, that all those exalted European leaders of ours—our light and our hope—all these Mills, Darwins, and Strausses, sometimes have a very strange view of the moral obligations of a person of today." Indeed, once their ideas are transplanted onto Russian soil, they acquire what Dostoevsky acutely calls "the Russian aspect of their teachings," namely, "those conclusions drawn from their teachings that take on the form of invincible axioms, conclusions that are drawn only in Russia; in Europe, as people say, the possibility of these conclusions is not even suspected" (21: 132). What Europeans regard as relatively inoffensive theory is immediately transformed by Russians into a blueprint for action and put into practice on the spot, regardless of the human cost.

The Utilitarianism of John Mill, the Darwinian struggle for life, and the atheism stemming from David Strauss had all influenced Russian radical thought; but he chooses to focus attention on the latter for the purposes of his covert argument with the Populists. "People will tell me, perhaps . . . that, for example, even if Strauss does hate Christ and has set himself as his life's goal the mocking of Christianity, he nevertheless worships humanity as a whole and his teaching is as elevated and noble as can be." He is quite willing to admit that Strauss's teaching is elevated and noble, and that "the goals of all today's leaders of progressive European thought are philanthropic and magnificent." But he is also convinced of something else, which he expresses in a powerful peroration that now seems remarkably clairvoyant: "If you were to give all these grand, contemporary teachers full scope to destroy the old society and build it anew, the result would be such obscurity, such chaos, something so crude, blind, and inhuman that the whole structure would collapse to the sound of humanity's curses before it could even be completed. Once having rejected Christ, the human heart can go to amazing lengths. That's an axiom" (21: 132–133).

Even though Dostoevsky's article is nominally directed against *Russian World*, L. M. Rosenblyum has pointed out that he is really answering Mikhailovsky's reflections on *The Devils*. Dostoevsky's notebooks reveal that he jotted down his recollections of standing on the scaffold with his fellow Petrashevtsy as a direct response to Mikhailovsky, and only used them several months later in a different context.[6] Mikhailovsky, it will be recalled, had criticized Dostoevsky for having chosen, as the main subject for his novel, "an isolated instance, with no right to be regarded in relation to the general aim"; but his great insight was to realize how inseparably the two were connected. Nechaevism could be the logical outcome even of the highest ideals of his own generation, and his amalgamation of the Petrashevsky circle with the Nechaevtsy, along with his intimation that he might have become a Nechaevist himself, was meant to establish such a continuity through personal testimony.

Dostoevsky was thus arguing that even those who regarded Socialism as an updating of Christian ideals "in accordance with the spirit of the age and civilization"—as the Populists had now begun to do again— were not immune from the temptations of Nechaevism, even though they had rejected the Utilitarian basis of his tactics. His novel had attempted to portray such a continuity (as he explained to Tsarevich Alexander), and he viewed the generation of the 1840s, represented by the charmingly frivolous and irresponsible Stepan Trofimovich Verkhovensky, as ultimately responsible for the deadly depredations of his son Peter. But this father-son theme in the book is overshadowed by Stavrogin, and no direct contact between father and son exists until Peter arrives on the scene as a grown man. Dostoevsky may well have felt that this aspect of his book had not been sufficiently elaborated and that a more developed treatment was now called for—but one that would highlight the failure of the fathers rather than the devastation wrought by the sons. His next novel, *A Raw Youth*, written for Mikhailovsky's own journal, would focus precisely on this father-son theme and raise the same fundamental question as Dostoevsky's article. From where could the young generation derive the moral ideals they were once again searching for? Meanwhile, he had amply demonstrated, while unobtrusively replying to Mikhailovsky, that he refused to accept any crude denigration of the moral character and values of the young Populists.

## CHAPTER 6

# The Diary of a Writer, 1873: II

In response to Mikhailovsky's provocative remark that the new Populist Socialism was conservative rather than revolutionary, Dostoevsky had countered, with a sly reversal of position, that on the contrary "the countenance of this world" was very far from meeting with *his* approval in all its features. Indeed, as the flow of observations and comments in the *Diary* amply illustrates, his criticism of current Russian affairs was extremely sharp, and a Populist reader could well feel that the author of such pages was much more of an ally than an opponent. Whatever the topic he sets out to treat, he time and again returns to the symptoms of the disintegration of Russian peasant life and the peasant economy, and he traces the nation's overwhelming problems to the same social-economic causes advanced by the Populists themselves. Peter Verkhovensky in *The Devils* had dreamed of bringing on an era of total social chaos in Russia, and Dostoevsky's pages sometimes create the impression that the fictional ravings of his character had turned into stark reality.

## 2

"The economic and moral conditions of the people after their liberation from the yoke of serfdom is dreadful," he declares in the article on Chernyshevsky. A sentence or two later, he writes that "the decline of morality, the fall in prices, the Yid tavern keepers, thievery, banditry in broad daylight—all these facts are indisputable, and they grow more ominous every day" (21: 30). He returns to the same litany the next week: "Dreadful things are told and described in print: drunkenness, banditry, drunken children, drunken mothers, cynicism, destitution, corruption, godlessness" (21: 41). In an article entitled "Dreams and Musings," the same calamitous note is struck: "Mothers drink, children drink, the churches are empty, fathers take to banditry, the bronze arm of Ivan Susanin [a Russian hero of the Time of Troubles in the seventeenth century] is sawed off and brought to the tavern, and the tavern accepts it! Just ask the opinion of medicine: What sort of generation can be born from such drunkards?" (21: 94).

There is surely no conservative complacency here about the present condition of the Russian people; and much of the responsibility for this frightening degeneration is laid squarely at the door of the government. "Nearly half our present budget," Dostoevsky writes, "is provided by [the tax on] vodka—that is, by the current drunkenness of the people—and so by the whole future of our people. We are, so to say, funding our grand budget as a great European power with our own future" (21: 94). One of the standard tenets of Populist ideology was that the interests of the peasantry were being sacrificed to the needs of the state, and he makes exactly the same point in castigating the revenue produced by the sale of vodka, which the authorities clearly had good economic reasons not to discourage. For Dostoevsky, however, the remedy was not to dream of some new Socialist order but to collaborate in the establishment of temperance societies, whose first appearance in Russia he greets with enthusiasm and with the hope that "their development is not hindered because of special considerations." (Every Russian reader, accustomed to Aesopian language, would understand this last phrase to mean government interference and harassment.) He sarcastically concludes by inviting support for them from "all our leading intellects, our literary people, our socialists, our clergy, and by each one who writes, month after month, of how he is fainting beneath the burden of his debt to the people" (21: 95).

He returns again and again to this question of drunkenness and in one article, "Apropos of a New Play," places it within the broader context of the collapse of the old values of Russian life. Russia was living through the "extraordinary economic and moral trauma that followed the wide-ranging reforms of the current reign." Despite the liberation of the serfs, the worst moral aspects of the old order—"egoism, cynicism, slavery, disunity"—have multiplied rather than diminished; and "of the good moral aspects of the old way of life—which certainly existed—scarcely anything remains" (21: 96–97). The mainstay of the traditional peasant way of life was the village commune, the *obshchina*; and both Dostoevsky and the Populists were deeply concerned about its disintegration under the impact of the new social-economic conditions.

The "new play" that is the subject of this article is Dimitry Kishensky's *Strong Drink Every Day Keeps Fortune Away*, which, as already mentioned, ran in three issues of *The Citizen*. It had won first prize in a competition sponsored by the People's Theatre in Moscow, but was considered too inflammatory for the censorship to allow it to be staged. Kishensky depicts the breakdown of moral standards in a village whose peasants have left the land to work in a nearby factory. There they have succumbed to the lure of vodka, dispensed with a liberal hand by the wily factory owner so as to keep them in submission. These peasants have become so completely demoralized that the family of an innocent village girl, coveted by the local capitalist, connive at her rape in a drugged sleep. Dostoevsky outlines the action of the plot with sad revulsion, and his dismay reaches its peak when he speaks of the meeting of the village commune in the third act. "This meeting is the only thing that has remained solid and fundamental in Russian life: it is its main link with the past and its hope for the future." What the play reveals, though, is the total erosion of this precious bulwark of Russian peasant values. The members have been bribed to get rid of the hero of the play, an honest and virtuous young man and the betrothed of the girl who has been raped. In violation of all the time-honored rules against depriving a widow (his mother) of her only son and sole support, he will be sent off as a soldier instead of another young man from a wealthy family with other sons. "And now this meeting already bears the element of decomposition . . . its inner spirit and inner age-old truth are tottering along with the tottering people" (21: 100).

Dostoevsky thus refused to close his eyes to the desperately urgent problems assailing Russian society, whose manifestations, regrettably, led him to the first public expressions of the ugly anti-Semitism that mars his last years. But no matter how hopeless the condition of the people seemed to be, he was saved from despair—or at least, *tried* to save himself from despair—by the same belief in their inherent moral virtues that plays so large a part in the mythology of Populism as well. Nor can it be considered merely coincidental that, in the famous article where he expresses this conviction most forcibly, he symbolizes it through a partial commentary on a poem of his old friend Nikolay Nekrasov, whom the Populists considered their own greatest poet.

In the poem "Vlas," Nekrasov depicts a religious pilgrim of that name who wanders up and down the Russian land gathering "offerings for God's church." Previously, he had been a godless reprobate, who had flogged his wife to death and consorted with thieves and highwaymen; but after falling sick and experiencing a vision of his tortures in Hell, he takes an oath and becomes a pilgrim. Now:

> Filled with grief past consolation,
> Dark of face, erect, and tall,
> He passes on with gait unhurried,
> Through the village, through the town
>
> . . . . . . . . . . . . .
>
> But never a word passed e'en his lips,
> A book, an icon at his side,
> Strong chains of iron round his hips,
> To overcome his sinful pride.

105

Dostoevsky singles out such verses as being "wonderfully said" and praises Nekrasov for the grave reverence with which he portrays such a religious type—even though, when the poet comes to Vlas's vision of Hell, he is not able to resist an irreverent thrust ("Pious pilgrims, clever women / can tell you better tales—"). Nonetheless, Nekrasov was a true poet; and though "an *obshchelovek* [a universal man, a Westernizer] and Russian *gentilhomme*," he could not help being impressed by "the frightening force of Vlas's humility, the urge to save himself, this passionate thirst for suffering . . . [that] has wrung rapture and respect even from [Nekrasov's] ultraliberal soul!" (21: 32).

Such remarks play unerringly on the anomaly of the Populist reverence for the people while refusing to accept their religious faith. And they lead directly into the retelling of a story about another "Vlas." He was a young peasant who had arrived at a monastery to seek a holy man, a *starets*, reputed to have an uncanny penetration into the human heart. This Vlas had been carousing with a group of friends, all of whom were boasting of their daring; and he had surpassed them all in vaunting his readiness to face any danger. Another member of the group challenged this braggadocio and won Vlas's agreement to do whatever was commanded of him. He was then told not to swallow the Eucharist at Holy Communion during Lent, but preserve it for another purpose, namely, as a target for his rifle. The heedless young man, unwilling to back down on his boast, set about doing so; but the moment he loaded his gun and took aim, a vision of the crucified Christ appeared to him, and he collapsed in a dead faint. Since then, he had felt irrevocably damned and had come to express repentance and seek absolution at the feet of the *starets*. Dostoevsky speculates that the monk "probably burdened his soul with some terrible load even beyond human strength, considering that, in this case, the heavier the burden the better. He came crawling in looking for suffering after all" (21: 34).

The origins of this story have been traced to both Russian and Western European folklore, and it is often accompanied by the magic belief that whoever hit such a target would thereafter become an infallible sharpshooter.[1] Dostoevsky, however, uses this traditional tale to provide insight into the Russian national character. What strikes him is that "we have before us two national types that represent with full clarity the Russian people in their entirety" (21: 35). These two types are the tempted peasant who accepts the sacrilegious dare and the tempter, his friend, who concocted such a heinous challenge to everything that the people held sacred. He is startled by the appearance of such a "Russian Mephistopheles" among the people because in the past only the gentry and the intelligentsia had trampled upon Russian pieties. ("Atheism is an aristocratic disease, a disease of cultivation and development," he had written in his notebooks.[2]) He had always depicted atheism through such types (Prince Valkovsky, Raskolnikov, Stavrogin) and would continue to do so in the future, while raising the possibility, through the influence of Ivan Karamazov on Smerdyakov, of the spread of this disease among the lower classes. For the moment, he merely notes, as a Russian trait, "the urge for negation in a person who may be the most inclined toward belief and reverence—the urge to negate everything: those things his heart holds most sacred." On the other hand, "it is with the same force, the same impetuosity, the same urge for self-preservation and repentance that the Russian . . . saves himself . . . when he has nowhere else to go." It is this capacity that suddenly appears in the vision of Christ, which thwarted the desecrating deed; and Dostoevsky sees the Russian effort of self-restoration as "always more serious than the former urge to deny and destroy the self" (21: 35).

For him, this capacity for repentance and regeneration was deeply rooted in the Russian moral-cultural psyche, and he generalizes an observation that has recurred repeatedly in his writings ever since the early 1860s. The difference between Russian and European evildoers, Dostoevsky insists, is that the Russian knows in his heart of hearts that he has sinned; the European on the other hand, at least in his jaundiced view, complacently accepts malfeasance as perfectly justified and not at all immoral. This is the context in which Dostoevsky sets down his famous assertion: "I think that the principal and most basic spiritual need of the Russian people is the need for suffering, incessant and unslakeable suffering, everywhere and in everything. I think the Russian people have been infused with this need from time immemorial. . . . There is always an element of suffering even in the happiness of the Russian people, and without it their happiness is incomplete" (21: 36).

Whatever one thinks of such a characterization—Nietzsche and Freud would consider it as much a denigration as an ennoblement of the Russian people—it is quite clear that the "suffering" Dostoevsky refers to has nothing to do with material hardship, physical deprivation, or sadomasochistic experimentation. The Russian people's imputed "love of suffering" meant a desire for moral and spiritual redemption, which in the end would gain the upper hand over the evils of the present time. There is no doubt that sooner or later "Vlas will come to his senses and will set about doing God's work. . . . He will save himself and us as well, for once more the light and salvation will come radiating from below" (21: 41). Dostoevsky thus once again, like the Populists, bows down to the moral riches concealed in the depths of the spirit of the Russian people, while underlining the link between this subliminal treasure trove and the people's unalterable commitment to their religious faith.

In the article on "Vlas," and also in his comments on Kishensky's play, Dostoevsky uses literary works primarily as illustrations of the cultural and social points he is trying to make; but he naturally throws out observations on their literary qualities as well. Aside from such casual remarks, the *Diary* also contains a discussion of Nikolay Leskov's remarkable new novel, *The Sealed Angel* (*Zaplechatyenni Angel*), and a report on Dostoevsky's visit to a showing of Russian paintings prior to their shipment to Vienna as part of a world exhibition.

He had published Leskov's novella *Lady Macbeth from Mtsensk* in *Epoch* in 1865 and praised the work to its author, but relations between them ceased after the journal vanished. Leskov then printed some bitingly negative remarks about *The Idiot* in 1869. Although Dostoevsky unquestionably admired Leskov's literary talent (particularly his ability to portray the Russian clergy), he nonetheless rejected Leskov's brilliant *Enchanted Wanderer* (*Ocharovannego Strannika*) for publication in *The Citizen*. Even *The Sealed Angel*, which presumably should have appealed to him because of its evocative appreciation of the Russian religious tradition of icon painting, receives only grudging praise; rather than focusing on the novel's merits, Dostoevsky devotes most space to criticizing its dénouement. Leskov's book depicts the adventures of an *artel* of pious Old Believer artisans who always travel accompanied by their most precious and sacred icon, the portrait of an angel. It is in dwelling on the beauties of this icon that Leskov's narrator initiates the reader into the technique of such art, relatively undervalued at the time and which the novel did a good deal to raise in public esteem. Surprisingly, Dostoevsky says not a word about this important feature of the book, though he does laud "Mr. Leskov's lovely story" and remarks that it fully deserves all the attention it is receiving: "The story is marvelously narrated and merits much praise" (21: 36).

What disturbs him is the ending, which the Old Believers naïvely consider to be a supernatural event—one which leads the whole group to return to the Orthodox Church. A wax seal had been placed over the face of their angel by a government official, who had confiscated the icon. From a master painter in this tradition, they order a copy made, seal and all, which they intend to substitute for the original by stealth and remove the disfiguring seal. But just as the Old Believers are secretly substituting the copied icon for the original, the wax seal on the face of the copy suddenly vanishes, and they take this as a miracle. What occurred, as Leskov carefully explains, is that the seal on the copy, attached only by a piece of paper, had slipped off; the "miracle" thus turns out to be a simple accident. Dostoevsky objects to this ending on a number of grounds, including the implausibility of the mass conversion once the Old Believers learned the truth of what had occurred (as they do in the book). Would they not have been outraged rather by the powerlessness of the local Orthodox bishop to prevent their icon from being sealed (and hence desecrated) by the government official whose aim was to force them to buy it back with a bribe?

Aside from such considerations based "on the firmness and purity of [the Old Believers'] former beliefs" (and Leskov depicts the sincerity of their devotion with a sympathetic tenderness), what upsets Dostoevsky is the deeper issue of dissolving the "miracle" into a simple accident. Indeed, he suspects Leskov of kowtowing in this way to the liberal prejudices against the superstitions of the people. It is possible that his dissatisfaction with Leskov exercised some influence on *The Brothers Karamazov*, where this question of miracles is treated much more subtly. They are either depicted as part of the traditions of a remote past, or merely hinted at as possible in the present. Indeed, the insistence on a wonder-working miracle to justify faith is viewed as a temptation of the devil and proof that faith is not yet perfect and secure. What put Dostoevsky off, presumably, was Leskov's dissolution of the mystery of the irrational of religious faith in so prosaically humdrum a fashion.

Leskov's reply appeared in *Russian World*, though he wrote under a pseudonym and without actually responding to the issue raised. Instead, he attacked a remark that Dostoevsky had let fall in his article about the paintings (we shall come to this in a moment), and he also pummeled a story in *The Citizen* that, he charged, displayed such ignorance of Russian religious usages that the editor, Mr. Dostoevsky, should be roundly castigated for allowing it to disgrace his pages. Not deceived for a moment by the pseudonyms, Dostoevsky replied in an article called "The Impersonator," which sharply ridicules the charges and, while maintaining the fiction of answering someone named "Pr. P. Kastorsky," intimates his knowledge of the true identity of his opponent. "For Heaven's sake," he remarks of the story in question, "surely someone can write the word *deacon* without intending to take anything away from Mr. Leskov." A bit later, praising the brevity of the story, he suddenly exclaims: "What is the point of the author dragging you through some four hundred and eighty pages and then suddenly, on page four hundred and eighty-one, inexplicably dropping the narrative in Petersburg or Moscow and dragging you off somewhere to Moldavo-Wallachia for the sole purpose of telling you how a flock of ravens and owls flew off some Moldavo-Wallachian roof?" (21: 83–84). In Leskov's *At Daggers Drawn* (*Na Nozakh*), the scene suddenly shifts in the thirty-sixth chapter to Moldavo-Wallachia, and Dostoevsky takes critical aim as well at Leskov's well-known relish for local-color detail.

Dostoevsky's "Apropos of the Exhibition" proves once again, if proof were necessary, that he had no particular sensitivity to painting as such; he was primarily interested in the thematic content, of which, as might be expected, he was a very keen and perceptive observer. In this case his reflections are shaped in good part by the prospect of these Russian paintings being shown to a European public. This destination allows him to enlarge on a favorite topic, namely, why Europeans are congenitally incapable of understanding Russian culture, while Russians possess an uncanny ability to understand that of Europe with complete penetration. Noting that the translations of Gogol into French, even with the help of Ivan Turgenev (the translator was Louis Viardot, husband of Turgenev's inamorata, the famous diva Pauline Viardot), preserve nothing at all of the original, Dostoevsky concludes that "all that is characteristic, all that is ours and predominantly national (and thus all that is truly artistic) is incomprehensible to Europe. . . . Yet I believe that we understand Dickens in Russia almost as well as the English do." Whether this Russian gift of comprehension "promises much for the future . . . or whether it contains something harmful as well" (21: 68–69), he refuses to decide at the moment; but elsewhere he plays variations on each alternative, depending on his polemical purposes.

Besides this dubious contention, he also comments negatively on an inclination exhibited by some of the artists to paint according to a "tendency," that is, to allow their inspiration to be governed by the radical Utilitarian view of art as primarily a weapon in the battle for social justice. Dostoevsky had disputed this question with Belinsky in the 1840s and with Dobrolyubov in the 1860s; he now renews the fight with Mikhailovsky, who had recently written that "the satisfaction of idle curiosity" was not the task of literature. As an example of the type of writing he favored, Mikhailovsky had produced Thomas Hood's "Song of the Shirt," a poem soaked in social pathos; and although Dostoevsky refers to Mikhailovsky only as "a certain dear critic," he counters by declaring that a "work of art . . . without a preconceived tendency" can do "far more *for his purposes* [the critic's] than all the songs about the shirt . . . (not Hood's, but those of our writers)" (21: 72). Dostoevsky had always maintained that, while literature and art unquestionably have an important social-cultural role to play, their influence could best be exercised by allowing artists total independence to create according to their talents. Otherwise, artists end up wearing "a uniform"; and some recent poems by Nekrasov unhappily indicate that "this humble poet of ours is now certainly wearing a uniform." As an example, he cites one detail of a poem in which ideology triumphs over human feelings. A wife, having come to join her prisoner-husband in Siberia, kisses his chains at their first meeting and embraces him only after this gesture of civic protest has been accomplished (21: 73).

He then goes on to discuss one of the most important canvases in the exhibit, I. E. Repin's *Barge Haulers on the Volga*. The subject could certainly have given rise to a work that would shout at the spectator, "Look how unfortunate I am and how indebted you are to the people!" But Dostoevsky is happy to acknowledge that the artist painted "barge haulers, real barge haulers and nothing more." Precisely for this reason, precisely because Repin did *not* attempt to impose any obvious tendentiousness on his theme, "you can't help but think that you are indebted, truly indebted, to the people." All the same, he notes that Repin and other Russian artists are limited because of their preference for what he calls "genre painting," which he defines as "the art of portraying contemporary, immediate reality that the artist has himself felt personally and seen with his own eyes." He contrasts this with "historical painting," which necessarily involves a departure from the immediate and may even include "the ideal"—but Russian artists now "fear the ideal like some kind of unclean spirit" (21: 76).

As he develops this distinction, Dostoevsky not only illustrates his reaction to the paintings but also illuminates an important feature of his own artistry. Any psychologist will explain, he points out, that if one imagines a past event, it will "be imagined in its completed aspect, that is, with the addition of all its subsequent developments that had not yet occurred at the historical moment in which the artist was trying to depict a person or event." The past thus cannot be grasped as genre but must always include a component embodying its aftermath: "And so the artist is overcome by a superstitious fear of the fact that he will perhaps have to 'idealize' despite himself, which to his mind means to lie." By "idealizing," Dostoevsky seems to mean not some kind of

8. *Barge Haulers on the Volga*, by I. E. Repin

glorifying falsification but simply a larger significance than could be seen in the immediate present of the event. Unfortunately, because of their fear of the "ideal," Russian artists attempt to combine the historical and the immediate, and "from this unnatural combination arises the worst kind of untruth." As an instance, he singles out the canvas by N. N. Ge, about which, as we know from the comments of Varvara Timofeyeva, the radicals were enthusiastic because Christ and his disciples were portrayed as average Russian men and women of the 1860s (21: 76).

A satirical thrust against this painting had been made long ago in *Notes from Underground*, and here he attacks it again in a much more thoroughgoing fashion. "There sits Christ," he writes, "—but is that Christ? It may be a very good young man, deeply hurt by his quarrel with Judas, the latter standing there getting dressed to go off and denounce him, but this is not the Christ we know . . . [and] we must ask the question: Where are the eighteen centuries of Christianity that followed? . . . How is it possible that from such an ordinary quarrel of such ordinary people gathered to have supper . . . there could arise something so colossal?" He considers the picture to fail both as "historical truth" and as "genre" because "everything is false"; the picture is not true either to the past it supposedly portrays or to what that past has come to mean in the present (21: 76–77).

This penetrating analysis helps to clarify what Dostoevsky meant by calling his own approach to art "fantastic realism." For he is always striving to apply to the present the mode of apprehension that he sees as a psychological datum in relation to the past. He looks for the essence of the passing and the contemporary by projecting it into the future and *imagining* its completion (which makes it "fantastic"), but then, with an unflinching moral-social and psychological realism, dramatizing all the consequences of this future, as if it had already occurred or was coming into being.

4

Most of the articles appearing in the *Diary of a Writer* consisted of social-cultural commentary; but other entries reveal Dostoevsky in a more artistic mood and mode. One sketch, "A Half-Letter from 'A Certain Person,'" is an imaginary epistle supposedly sent to him by a correspondent who rather resembles the underground man. (It will be recalled that this gentleman penned, but never posted, a furious letter to a journal denouncing the officer who had insulted him.) "Certain Person," on the contrary, is an underground man determined to be heard by the world; he is consumed by an uncontrollable literary fury and "spends his last kopek on postage stamps and even encloses return postage in his letters, supposing that he will at last achieve his end and manage to begin correspondence on civic matters with various editors" (21: 61). Dostoevsky-as-editor, however, has snipped off the first part of his letter because it was so abusive; but he prints the remainder, which ragingly denounces the manners of columnists in the Russian press who berate each other on any and every occasion. "When I read your columns," writes "Certain Person," expressing a general disgust with the literary scene, "I cannot help but imagine a kind of endless, drunken, senseless carnival, that has gone on in our literature for much too long already. . . . And it all goes on a countless number of times without even the least suspicion that the whole thing has finally made us sick to death" (21: 67–68).

If this entry recalls a detail of *Notes from Underground*, then a group of three "Little Pictures" brings to mind the sketch form Dostoevsky had used at the beginning of his literary career, when he had tried his hand as a St. Petersburg feuilletonist. Here, however, he does not disguise himself as a Baudelairian *flâneur*, savoring the sights and sounds of city life, but speaks in his own name as he provides an image of Petersburg sweltering in the summer heat and devoid of people. Even on the Nevsky Prospect, so dangerous to cross in a midwinter fog at the risk of life and limb, "the street was empty for two hundred yards in either direction; one might even stop to discuss Russian literature with a friend, so little was the danger!" (21: 106). In his columns of the 1840s, he had regarded the bewildering array of architectural styles in the city as an invigorating emblem of Russia's absorption of the taste and ideas of Europe; but now this diversity represents "all the lack of character of the idea and all the negativity of the essence of the Petersburg period from its very beginning to its end." All the imitation of European styles— the Italian palazzi and pseudo-Napoleonic edifices—had culminated in "an enormous, modern hotel." "Here we see the businesslike approach, Americanism, hundreds of rooms, an immense commercial enterprise; one sees immediately that we, too, have railways and we have suddenly found ourselves to be businessmen" (21: 107).

A second sketch shows him seeking a breath of fresh air on a Sunday amid the heat and dust, and wondering "why it is so much more melancholy in Petersburg on Sundays than on weekdays. Is it because of the vodka? The drunkenness?" This question leads to a description of a group of six tipsy workmen who carry on a conversation, each expressing his reaction to what his companions have said solely by the repetition of one noun, "which isn't mentioned in the presence of ladies." Dostoevsky speculates that this foreshortened language resolves a difficulty caused by drunkenness, which slows down speech but also speeds up "the flow of thoughts and sensations"; the problem of inebriated self-expression was thus overcome (21: 108–109).

His final picture dwells on the poor of Petersburg out for a Sunday stroll with their children, and he gives his imagination free rein as he fills in their presumed relatives and family background. "How haggard, pale, sickly, and anemic they are, and what gloomy little faces they have, especially those who are still being carried; those who already walk all have crooked legs, and flounder along rocking from side to side." But all are carefully dressed, and the parents obviously "love their poor and sickly children" whom they are forced to raise in such unhealthy surroundings. He concludes with a series of commonplace incidents, all pointing to the careful watchfulness of parents—and even casual passers-by—for the children's welfare (21: 109–112).

The apparently harmless "Little Pictures" were soon attacked in *Voice*, especially the one dwelling on the use of the "one word not found in the dictionary." Dostoevsky was accused of shamefully employing such off-color material so as to titillate his readers in the absence of anything substantial to say. Taking up the challenge, he replied sharply that the point of his sketch was far from frivolous. It was meant, in fact, to illustrate the purity of the people, who, in using such an obscenity, were not at all concerned with its meaning but rather with the problem of utterance; when sober, they did not use profanity at all. And he contrasts their decency with the masculine society of the upper class, who often turn to "risqué subjects" for amusement and whose talk soon "degenerates into such abominations, such foul language . . . that the imagination of the people could never conceive of the like" (21: 116). Moreover, he also retorts, one of the aims of his "little pictures," provoked by recent public utterances lamenting the moral failings of the people, was to share with readers his "cheering impression" that "there is still a striving for dignity, for genuine self-respect[,] love for the family and children" preserved among the people (21: 113).

Another series of "Little Pictures" at this time were not written directly for his *Diary* but for a collective volume entitled *Skladchina* (which means a pooling together of resources). The famine in the province of Samaria during 1873 had moved the Petersburg literati to organize and publish a volume of their writings, whose proceeds would then be donated to famine relief. Dostoevsky's contribution, "Little Pictures (on the road)," consisted of a group of sketches concerned with railroad and steamboat travel. They are sharply observed, often amusing satirical snapshots of the social tensions and maneuverings created by the obligatory encounters with traveling companions, and they focus on a relatively higher social strata than in the Petersburg pictures. Aside from their local-color interest, these sketches are worth particular attention for two reasons. They contain a figure who foreshadows the devil in *The Brothers Karamazov*, and they led to an exchange of letters between Dostoevsky and Ivan Goncharov that illuminates the poetics of both novelists.

The first sketch describes how the initial embarrassment, reticence, and reserve of strangers thrown together on a train gradually breaks down and leads to conversation. One gentleman in particular is notably loquacious and talks uninhibitedly about his life, his travels, and his acquaintances in high official circles. He has been everywhere, seen everything, amuses the assemblage with his anecdotes, but nobody really takes him at his word. He is cultivated and well mannered, with a graying beard, "not quite of Napoleonic cut but certainly of an aristocratic trim." His clothes are acceptably fashionable but rather worn, and though he has obviously *had* a good tailor, the emphasis is on the past. He disappears unexpectedly "at a completely insignificant station," and his fellow passengers, who have by now decided that his anecdotes were all spurious if nonetheless diverting, conclude that he is "a particular old-gentry type of noble sponger (*prizhivalchik*)," very welcome everywhere to relieve the tedium of life in the depths of the Russian countryside (21: 164–165). Exactly the same type, using the same turns of phrase, will six years later furnish the outlines for Ivan Karamazov's devil, also an amusing and entertaining raconteur.

The portrait of this gentleman is struck off so well that Goncharov, who was editor of the volume, singles it out for praise in his letters; but he expresses some hesitation about accepting another figure, who was finally excised. (The original text, except for a few sentences, has regrettably been lost, and Dostoevsky's letters about the question have also vanished.) From Goncharov's comments we learn that the disputed passages portrayed a clergyman obviously influenced by Nihilist ideas (like the future Rakitin of *The Brothers Karamazov*). He smokes incessantly (which was considered undignified for a clergyman), speaks in favor of civil marriage, and dresses like a fop. Goncharov, who compares him with a "fashionable abbé of the time of the Bourbons," finds him unacceptable, probably fearing the censorship but also advancing the aesthetic argument that he was too exceptional to be considered a type. Dostoevsky had said that "such a type was coming to birth," but Goncharov objects that art could only be created when life, over a long period of time, has given shape to a type, not when such a figure is still in the process of gestation. "You portrayed your priest," he objects, "not *sine ira*; here the artist steps aside for the publicist."[3]

So far as can be gathered, Dostoevsky argued that the priest actually existed and was taken from life, "like a photograph." But this assertion simply gives Goncharov another occasion to repeat that a type is formed only "when it has been repeated many times, or been noticed many times, has become customary and well known to all."[4] Nothing better than this exchange illustrates a fundamental difference between the two writers and accounts for a certain schematism in Goncharov's grasp of character. He regards only the already formed, the immediately perceptible and well known, as suitable material for "an objective art-ist." The febrile Dostoevsky, on the contrary, wishes to grasp the life just coming to birth, with all its dangers, uncertainties, and promises, and with all the fluidity of its characters. This same issue will arise again in his next novel, when the stability of Leo Tolstoy's world will serve as a foil for the moral-social mobility of the new breed of "accidental fami-lies" that he views as coming on the scene.

5

There is only one full-fledged fictional creation in this first incarnation of the *Diary of a Writer*, the fantastic short story *Bobok*, which in recent years has attracted considerable attention. Mikhail Bakhtin views it in terms of his wide-ranging theory that Dostoevsky as a writer is linked to the age-old generic tradition of Greco-Roman Menippean satire, and he even finds in *Bobok* "the classical characteristic features of the genre," which "reveals here its greatest potential, realizes its maxi-mum."[5] Bakhtin's claim involves interesting questions of historical poet-ics, but to discuss them here would take us too far afield. In Dostoev-sky's own context, the immediate occasion for the story, aside from the general clamor raised against him because of *The Devils*, was the re-mark of a columnist in *Voice* who wrote under the pseudonym of "Nil Admirari." "The *Diary of a Writer*," he had declared, "recalls the well-known jotting: 'And yet the Bey of Algiers has a wart on his nose!' [a citation from Gogol's *Memoirs of a Madman*]. One has only to look at the portrait of the author of the *Diary of a Writer*, now on exhibit in the Academy of Fine Arts, to feel for Mr. Dostoevsky the very same 'compas-sion' that he scoffs at so inappropriately in his journal [a jab at the article "Environment"]. This is the portrait of a man worn down by a serious illness."[6]

No criticism was more widespread than the charge that he dealt only with the "abnormal," the "unhinged," the "psychopathic"; and now his portrait is said to resemble someone in the same demented condition as the madman of Gogol's story. In reply, the "Certain Person" who writes *Bobok*—the same who plied *The Citizen* and other journals with indignant letters—now, for the first time, puts pen to paper for other than epistolary purposes. "An artist, by mere accident, painted my por-trait. 'Anyhow,' said he, 'you are a literary man, after all,' he says. So I let him have his way, and he put the portrait on exhibit. And now I read: 'Go and look at this sickly face that seems to border on insanity'" (21: 41–42). With an obvious dig at the repeated charge made against him of violating the standards of verisimilitude, Dostoevsky's narrator comments: "I don't think the artist painted me on account of my literary work; it probably was on account of the two symmetrical warts on my forehead; that's a phenomenon of nature, he says. They don't have any ideas, you see, so now they go on about these phenomena. But what a job he did on the warts in the portrait—they're as good as life! That's what they call realism" (21: 42).

The aim of *Bobok*, however, was not to take such isolated potshots at Dostoevskian targets but to depict, in a brief and concentrated form, the general disintegration and moral corruption of the ruling strata of Russian society. This is accomplished through the strange and revolting half-dream, half-hallucination of the distraught narrator, who wanders into a cemetery quite by chance, dozes on a tombstone, and suddenly begins to hear voices. Amazingly, he finds himself eavesdropping on the conversations of the recent dead, who, it seems, continue to possess consciousness even while decomposing; sometimes they remain alive in this state for as long as six months. At the very end, though, all that remains of the corpse will suddenly "mumble one word—meaningless, of course—about a bean or something: 'Bobok, bobok'" (21: 51). Before that time, however, the dead can express themselves very well; and they reveal a world of complete moral and spiritual perversion to the shocked ears of their unseen listener. The narrator chances to wander among the more expensive gravestones, where the voices belong to erstwhile pillars of society of exalted rank; and they replicate in the netherworld all the injustices, corruption, and dissipation of the lives they had led "up above." Only one voice is even remotely concerned with "higher things," and he turns out to be a misplaced shopkeeper, pretentiously buried by his family among his superiors. To a haughty ex-customer who is offended at her proximity to so low a personage, he humbly murmurs: "We are both in the grave, and, before the tribunal of God, we are equal in our sins." "In our sins," the lady mocks him. "And don't you dare to speak to me again" (21: 45).

At the conclusion, the aristocratic characters have decided to amuse themselves by telling stories of their lives without "shame" or "modesty." The climax is a deafening cacophony of impatient cries urging that all restraint be stripped off. "'Oh, how I long to lose my sense of shame,' exclaimed Avdotya Ivanovna rapturously." But the orgy is interrupted when the spying witness suddenly sneezes: "A real sepulchral silence ensued" (21: 52, 53). Haunted by what he has heard, the narrator cannot reconcile himself to such appalling revelations: "Debauchery in a place like this, debauchery of one's final hopes, debauchery among sagging, decomposing bodies, debauchery that does not even spare the final moments of consciousness!" The poor, unbalanced storyteller is just mad enough to be profoundly revolted by such degeneracy. "No, this I cannot accept. . . . I shall visit other 'categories' in the graveyard and listen everywhere. . . . Perhaps I'll stumble on something to give comfort as well." The story ends with this faint hope, and with the resolution "to bring [his story] to *The Citizen*. One of the editors there has also had his portrait exhibited. Perhaps he'll print this" (21: 54). Indeed he did; and no other work of Dostoevsky's presents so bleak a picture of the irremediable decay of the old ruling class, corrupted through and through with the licentiousness fostered by their European culture, or so chillingly impressive an illustration of his ability to employ "the fantastic" to portray the harshest "realism."

6

Dostoevsky's *Diary of a Writer* formed the most important part of his contributions to *The Citizen*, but he was also saddled for a time with the laborious chore of writing a weekly article on foreign affairs. These contributions cover almost a hundred pages in the Academy of Sciences edition of his works and deal with a number of events then occupying the forefront of European politics. He reports at great length on the negotiations being carried on by the French National Assembly, in the aftermath of the Franco-Prussian War, with one of the pretenders to the throne, the comte de Chambord; on Bismarck's *Kulturkampf* against the Catholic Church in Germany; and on the attempt of Don Carlos of Spain, in the midst of general chaos in that country, to gain the throne by force. Political events for him fell into a pattern controlled primarily by religious beliefs and convictions, and he speculates that if a monarch were now restored to the French throne (though he believes this unlikely), the result would be to strengthen the papacy. He also pays particular attention to the Catholic issue in Germany and the attempt of the pope to intervene on behalf of his flock in that country. This is not the place, however, to enter into detail about his views on European politics, many of which will be recycled when his *Diary* became an independent publication. Of greatest interest here is his expressed conviction that the papacy was at its last gasp and that, if it could not find support among the reigning European powers and their ruling classes, it would turn to the people for the first time in fifteen hundred years. "And believe me," he writes,

Rome will know how to turn to the people, to that very people whom the Roman Church has haughtily repelled, even hiding the Gospels of Christ from them by forbidding its translation. The pope will know how to go to the people, on foot and in rags, poor and naked, with an army of twenty thousand Jesuit warriors skilled in the fishing of souls. Will Karl Marx and Bakunin hold out against this army? Hardly! Catholicism knows how, when necessary, to make concessions, to reconcile everybody. And what will it cost to assure the poor and benighted people that Communism is the same as Christianity, and that Christ really said nothing else? Even now there are intelligent and quick-witted Socialists who are convinced that they are one and the same, and seriously take Antichrist for Christ. (21: 202–203)

Along with the reminiscences of Belinsky already cited, here we find another source for the Legend of the Grand Inquisitor. Roman Catholicism and Socialism are equally deceptive substitutes for a genuinely Christian faith because both rely on temporal power (force and violence) to attain their supposedly Christian aims (explicit in the first and implicit in the second). The fear that they would someday unite continued to haunt Dostoevsky, and would soon find expression in the great synthesis of his Legend.

## CHAPTER 7

# At Bad Ems

In the late spring of 1874, Dostoevsky was once again a free man, once again a novelist, and he returned to literary creation with renewed zest. But, because he no longer had a fixed income, it was again necessary to turn to magazine editors to provide the funds to support himself and his family. Some money was now accruing from the publishing business established by Anna Grigoryevna, which had issued both *The Idiot* and *The Devils* and would soon add *House of the Dead* to its list; but that income was hardly enough to meet household expenses. Dostoevsky had also been advised to take a cure for his emphysema, steadily getting worse, at the German spa Bad Ems; and this trip would require an additional outlay.

No open break with Prince Meshchersky had occurred when he relinquished his editorship of *The Citizen*, but he found it difficult to maintain friendly relations with Apollon Maikov and Nikolay Strakhov once they learned he would publish his next novel in the Populist journal *Notes of the Fatherland*. Preliminary work on the novel, which Dostoevsky had begun to plan while still an editor, continued in Bad Ems and then, on his return, in the peaceful solitude of his rustic residence. The first chapters began to appear at the beginning of 1875.

## 2

Dostoevsky resigned from *The Citizen* in April 1874, and it was shortly afterward that an unexpected event occurred. "One April morning, about lunch time, the maid brought me [Anna Grigoryevna] a visiting card on which I read: Nikolay Alexeyevich Nekrasov." Anna was well aware of the old friendship between her husband and Nekrasov, and of their more recent estrangement because of social-political differences. When he hastened to greet his visitor and invite him into his study, she could thus not resist eavesdropping on their conversation. What she heard was an offer from Nekrasov for Dostoevsky to contribute a new novel to *Notes of the Fatherland* during the next year, at "a payment of two hundred and fifty rubles per folio sheet, while until this time Dostoevsky had only gotten a hundred and fifty."[1] Anna recounts this visit without any explanation, as if Nekrasov had simply dropped in out of the blue to make such an offer; and it is possible that Dostoevsky had not informed her of his talk with Varvara Timofeyeva. Nekrasov's unannounced appearance on their doorstep, however, can only be explained in the light of that conversation.

Dostoevsky did not give his consent immediately, explaining that he felt an obligation to Mikhail Katkov of the *Russian Messenger*, who had supported him so loyally for so long; it would be necessary first to determine whether Katkov wished to acquire his new novel for the coming year. He also told Nekrasov that he would need a considerable advance—to which Nekrasov instantly agreed—and he added, somewhat to Nekrasov's surprise, that it was also necessary to obtain the approval of his wife, to whom he entrusted all his business affairs. When he went to consult her, Anna impetuously told him to accept even before he could pose the question. A final decision remained in abeyance until Dostoevsky went to Moscow at the end of April. Katkov consented to the higher rate per folio sheet (noting that P. I. Melnikov-Pechersky, well known for his stories and novels about Old Believers, had requested the same payment—a remark that Dostoevsky would hardly have found very flattering). Pleading poverty, however, Katkov demurred at a large advance, and Dostoevsky, as he probably desired, was thus released from any obligation.

A Russian specialist, Professor Koshlakov, had advised him that his emphysema could be alleviated by a six-week stay at the spa of Bad Ems, whose mineral waters were famous for their curative powers. At the beginning of June he left Staraya Russa for Petersburg and spent a few days looking after urgent matters before undertaking his journey. One such matter was his court case against Feodor Stellovsky, the slippery publisher who had issued, in clear violation of contract, a new edition of *Crime and Punishment* without paying a cent to the author. Another was a case involving the estate of his late aunt, the very wealthy A. F. Kumanina, who had given Dostoevsky and his brother Mikhail ten thousand rubles each in 1864 and then excluded them from her will. Both Dostoevsky and Mikhail's widow were contesting the exclusion. In a letter a month earlier to his younger brother Nikolay, a trained engineer but a man given to drink and often aided by his older brother, he put pressure on him to sign a statement, as one of the heirs, renouncing any claim to the money given to the brothers. "Otherwise," he writes ominously, "don't bother to have any dealings with me at all."[2] Nikolay promptly complied.

Even though he was disappointed to find that only two copies of *The Idiot* had been sold at the offices of *The Citizen*, which served as a depot for the Dostoevsky publishing firm, he was heartened when, at a bank where he went to obtain funds for his journey, he ran into a publisher named M. P. Nadein. This gentleman helped Dostoevsky to expedite his business by introducing him to a clerk who was "an admirer of mine"; but more important, Nadein made him a very flattering offer on the spot. "Nadein took such terrible pains over me (to the point of incredulity), nearly idolized me, that it was strange, and proposed to me definitely to publish *a complete edition of my works*, settling all the business regarding the financial costs of the edition, and all just for 5 percent, and as soon as he collects it, the whole edition will belong to me." This idea tempted Dostoevsky, who said he would give it some thought; "but what ever you decide," he reassures Anna, "that's how it will be." In Dostoevsky's view, his literary stock had just risen because "the booksellers have gotten somewhat excited by Orest Miller's three [actually two] articles about me in *Nedelya* [*The Week*], in the end very laudatory."[3] These articles form part of a still valuable volume, *Russian Literature since Gogol*, and *The Week* was a journal with both marked Populist and Slavophil sympathies (a combination that had now become possible). Nadein himself was known as a personal friend of some of the leading Populist radicals; and his offer indicates how old ideological lines were now being redrawn. As A. S. Dolinin has remarked, Miller's articles helped to remove some of the onus that had marred Dostoevsky's reputation because of his editorship of *The Citizen*.[4]

If Dostoevsky unperturbedly went his own way and allowed his readers to interpret the idiosyncrasies of his social-political position any way they pleased, his old comrades-in-arms were not so serenely untroubled. He remarks that "Maikov was a little cold somehow" when he met his old friend at the home of Nikolay Strakhov, and the latter, ill-famed as an inveterate gossip, also conveyed the unwelcome news that "Turgenev was to stay in Russia the whole year, write a novel, and bragged that he would describe 'all the reactionaries' (that is, including me). Good luck to him, but in the fall the first order of business has to be repaying him the fifty rubles" (loaned to Dostoevsky in 1865).[5] He was obviously worried that if he were to receive the same treatment as his own deadly caricature of Turgenev in *The Devils*, the ignominy of his unpaid debt could well be used against him. From the draft of an unsent letter, we know he intended to pay immediately upon hearing Strakhov's news; but it was not until a year later that he discharged this obligation. Turgenev, as it turned out, remained in Russia for only two months, and his next novel, *Virgin Soil*, did not contain any caricatures of Dostoevsky or other antiradical intellectuals.

This letter also allows us to catch a glimpse of some of the intimacies of his home life and of the nature of his relations with his wife. He was quite worried about *her* health and strongly counseled, on the advice of their Petersburg physician von Brettsall, that she drink a special mineral water. "Brettsall swears that it will help you," he writes, and then adds: "Don't begrudge the twenty rubles, darling. You'll be better!" This admonition strongly suggests a certain tightfistedness on Anna's part, which may perhaps be attributed to her recollections of Dostoevsky's gambling and their penury in the past. Also, he had become accustomed to a very close-knit family life in the isolation of Staraya Russa, and sadly deplores being separated from its amenities. "My spirits are troubled and lonely," he writes. "I think of you, of dear Fedinka, who blessed me with the sign of the cross, of my angel Lyubochka, and very much of you, Anya." The letter continues, however, with lines that Anna later attempted to obliterate because they obviously place her in a rather unflattering light. "Anya, dear," her husband enjoins her, "please be attentive to them [the children]. I know that you love them. Just don't yell at them and keep them clean." There is an intimation as well that Anna ruled the servants with more of an iron hand than suited Dostoevsky's own inclinations. "And be nice to Nanny," he advises her.[6]

The overnight trip to Berlin was a grueling one, both because of the cold (though it was mid-June) and because rail travel by ordinary coach meant sitting upright without sleep. He arrived in Berlin on a Sunday, when the banks were closed and the doctor he wished to consult was unavailable, so he dropped in at the royal museum to see the celebrated mythological paintings of Wilhelm von Kaulbach in the vestibule. They were, he told Anna, "nothing but cold allegory"; other parts of the collection pleased him more, and he admitted that "you and I, our first time here [in April 1867], were wrong not to have visited there." Very far from being a tolerant tourist, he remarks irritably that "the Germans on Sunday were all out in the streets and in holiday clothing, a coarse, uncouth people."[7]

The next day he went to visit the medical luminary, who "lives in a palace (literally)," and to whom he decided to pay three thalers after learning that another patient in the waiting room would give five (apparently the fee was not fixed). The doctor kept Dostoevsky for two minutes, barely touched his chest with a stethoscope, and then pronounced a single word—"Ems"—accompanied with the address of a doctor there. The remainder of the day he spent shopping for a black shawl at the request of their landlady in Staraya Russa. To while away a few evening hours, he stood in the balcony for Giacomo Meyerbeer's *Robert le Diable*, but "I listened to half of the first act and then ran away from the terrible German singers straight home" because it was time to depart.[8]

From Berlin to Bad Ems was another racking ordeal, and "I didn't sleep at all that night. We sat like herrings in a barrel." But when dawn came up, Dostoevsky could not contain his enthusiasm at the spectacle spread before his admiring eyes:

Anya, dear, I've never seen anything like it in my life! What is Switzerland, what is Wartburg (remember?) compared to that last half of the way to Ems. Everything seductive, tender, fantastic that you can imagine in a landscape, the most enchanting in the world: hills, mountains, castles, cities like Marburg, Limburg, with delightful towers in a wondrous combination of mountains and valleys— never before have I seen anything like that, and that's how we rode clear to Ems that hot, sunny morning.

Although delighted at his first glimpse of Ems, which he found more beautiful than he had anticipated, he also reports "that when it rains or the sky is cloudy, this very location turns into such a gloomy and dreary one that it's capable of producing depression in a healthy person."[9] As he discovered more than once during this first stay, and on two visits later, such a prediction turned out to be all too true.

3
—————

Dostoevsky's first order of business was to find suitable lodgings, and he checked in temporarily at a hotel near the railroad station. He had arrived at the height of the tourist season, and "the prices [were] horrible"; all the careful calculations that he and Anna had made bore no relation to reality. Scouring the town, where most private homes also offered guest accommodations, he succeeded in renting two rooms, one with a balcony, at a reasonable price; and he arranged to take his meals there as well. He hastened to see a doctor—not the one recommended in Berlin, but another suggested by his Petersburg physician—and, after being examined very carefully, was assured that there was no sign of consumption. He suffered from "a temporary catarrh" that interfered with his breathing, and he was ordered to drink water from a different spring than the one mentioned in Petersburg (this rather worried him, and was later changed). Prescribed a diet that included red wine, he complained that the local Ems vintage was terrible, but he could not afford "a bottle of Medoc that costs fifty kopeks at home." His period of treatment was set for four weeks instead of the usual six, though his stay was later lengthened to the standard duration.[10]

What worried him was whether he would be able to work on his novel under these altered conditions of his life. Ordinarily, Dostoevsky wrote in the silence and stillness of the late night hours, but in Ems such a schedule was impossible to maintain, and he was forced to adapt to the routine of his cure. "All of Ems," he explains, "wakes up at 6:00 in the morning (me too), and at 6:30 a couple of thousand patients are already crowding around two springs. It starts usually with a very boring Lutheran hymn to God: I don't know anything more sickly and artificial." Such mass punctuality was prompted by the inflexible closure of the springs at 8:30 A.M., after which no curative water could be obtained. His prescription was to drink one glass at 7:00, walk for an hour, drink a second glass, and then return home for coffee. The taste of the spring water, he remarks queasily, "is sourish-salty, and [it] smells somewhat of rotten eggs."[11]

Moreover, how could a person unaccustomed to writing in the day-time manage to do so "with such magnificence and sunshine all around, when I'm tempted to go walking and the streets are noisy? God grant that I can start the novel and get at least a rough draft done. Starting is half the job."[12] But the outdoors was not always so inviting, as Dostoevsky soon discovered, and a few days later "the weather was horrible and it was raining buckets, so that I borrowed an umbrella from the landlady so as to run here [to the spring]." He tried to work after his morning coffee, but "until now I've just been reading Pushkin and getting intoxicated with delight. Each day I find something new. But on the other hand I haven't been able to put something together for a novel."[13]

Ems was overflowing with people, among whom he often heard the sounds of his native Russian; and though he made no effort to meet his fellow countrymen, his presence did not escape their attention. The poet K. K. Sluchevsky, also a frequent visitor to the salon of Elena Shtakenshneider, singled him out, "and he was glad to renew his acquaintance with me." Dostoevsky found him to be tolerable company on the personal level, but not someone with whom he could establish any genuine intimacy. "He's a Petersburg type, a man of the world like all censors [Sluchevsky's official status], with pretensions to high society, who understands little about anything, rather kindhearted and rather vain. Very decent manners."[14] Familiar with all the Russians in Ems, Sluchevsky pointed them out to Dostoevsky, who accepted an invitation for a walk with a group of his acquaintances. "I was so miserable that I went," he reports resentfully. Another member of the party, a lady who was directress of an institute in Novocherkassk, "got terribly on my nerves. . . . That lady made me so miserable that I'll definitely now flee the Russians. A fool such as the world has never produced. A cosmopolitan and an atheist, who adores the Tsar but despises her native land." She was, he tells Anna, "a chatterer and an arguer. I came right out and told her that she was unbearable and that she didn't understand anything, laughing, of course, and in a society manner, but very seriously. We parted politely, but I'll never see her again."[15]

Nevertheless, Dostoevsky did not shun all the Russians in Ems. He looked up an old acquaintance, Princess Shalikova, when he heard that the lady herself had been trying to distinguish him among the bustling throng. He amusedly relates to Anna that the princess's lady companion, offering her advice on how to spot Dostoevsky in the multitude, had said: "Look carefully, and as soon as you find a person with the most *profound gaze*, such as no one else has, then go up to him boldly, that's him."[16] (Dostoevsky later transcribed this advice into the notes for *A Raw Youth*, possibly to be employed for the character Versilov.) He had first met the princess in 1865 while trapped in Wiesbaden, where he had gambled away all his funds and, unable to pay his hotel bill, was appealing to everyone he knew (including Turgenev and Herzen) for a loan. He had just begun to work on *Crime and Punishment*, and the princess, trying to help him in his predicament, urged him to offer his next novel to her brother-in-law, Mikhail Katkov, editor of the *Russian Messenger*. Dostoevsky had been understandably reluctant to do so because Katkov had rejected his novella *The Village of Stepanchikovo* ten years before, and relations between them had become particularly embittered during the ideological warfare of the 1860s. It was Katkov's polemics that had been largely responsible for the suppression of Dostoevsky's successful journal *Vremya* (*Time*) just a few years earlier. But with his back to the wall, he accepted the princess's advice; and this was the beginning of his long association with the powerful editor, who had supported him with advances all through the intervening years.

The princess herself had published fiction under a pseudonym, and Dostoevsky sketches a very flattering portrait of her for Anna's benefit: "I really like the old princess: simple-heartedness, naïveté, uprightness, and a rare, almost childlike merriness. She is small, gray-haired, dressed very modestly, but of extremely fine tone in the highest sense of the word. She has crisscrossed all of Europe, has been everywhere, all the leading English and French writers are personally acquainted with her. But the main thing is her sensitivity, which is even a source of mockery."[17] Unfortunately, the princess left a few days after this letter was written, and he found the vast majority of his remaining compatriots to be intolerable, especially those whose company he could not avoid. "On Monday the Wiesbaden priest Tachalov, the arrogant lout, comes here, but I put him in his place, and he disappeared right away. He's an intriguer and a scoundrel. He'd sell both Christ and everything in a second."[18]

His first enraptured response to the beauties of Ems soon wore off, and his letters become one protracted litany of complaints. "Everything here is miserable and wretched, the stores are awfully shabby," he gloomily informs Anna. "It's the location that's lovely, but just for a minute, because Ems is a narrow ravine between two chains of mountains, and you can get to know all of it in a minute."[19] The unpredictable climate was also very trying, and he grumbled at having to change his

126

shirt three times a day, just as he had done in Florence in the summer of 1869; but while Florence cooled off pleasantly in the evening, Ems remained damp and chilly. Dostoevsky found his irascibility increasing the longer he stayed, though he was told that the waters often had that effect; the epileptic attacks that he mentions in his letters also contributed to the jangled state of his nerves. "I have come to hate every building here, every bush. . . . I have become so irritable that (especially early in the morning) I view as a personal enemy every person in the slovenly crowd that throngs at the Kranchen [spring] and would perhaps be glad to be on bad terms with them."[20]

The only relief for Dostoevsky's aching misery was the news from Anna Grigoryevna, and he awaited her letters with eager impatience as a balm to his gnawing loneliness. He had asked her to write every five days, and she did so faithfully; but her letters never arrived on time—not, as Dostoevsky bemoaned, because of the inefficiency of the Russian post but because, as Anna learned a year later, they were being read by the secret police. (As an ex-political convict, he was still under covert surveillance, and he would remain so until just a year before his death.) What delighted him most was to hear of the children, about whom he worried incessantly. "News about the children is essential to me," he tells Anna. "I can't look at children even here calmly, and if I hear a child crying, I give way to misery and evil premonitions."[21] The letters also reveal that the marriage, despite the twenty years' difference in age between the partners, had now become solidly rooted (for Dostoevsky at any rate) in a passionate sexual attachment. "I have seductive dreams of you," he confides to Anna. "Do you dream of me? . . . You said that I'd probably start chasing after other women here abroad. My friend, I have come to know by experience that I can't even imagine one other than you. . . . And besides, there's nothing better *in this regard* than my Anechka. . . . I hope you won't show this letter to anyone."[22] From a reference in his next letter, one surmises that Anna too had confessed to having "indecent dreams"; and he replies affectionately with a famous quote from Gogol: "Never mind, never mind—silence!"[23]

Dostoevsky also gave Anna a running account of his efforts to make progress on his next novel, which was coming along, if at all, only at a snail's pace. "Anya, my work is moving slowly, and I'm having trouble with the plan. The richness of the plan is my main flaw. When I look at it in its entirety, I see that four novels have been combined in it. Strakhov has always seen that as my flaw."[24] He had been much impressed, perhaps overly so, by a letter of Strakhov's from April 1871 about *The Devils* (already cited), in which the critic, while praising the book in general, had indicated Dostoevsky's greatest artistic weakness to be that "you write for a selected public, and you overload your novels, make them too complicated. If the canvas of your narratives were simpler, they would have a stronger effect . . . instead of twenty characters and a hundred scenes, stay with one character and ten scenes."[25] Strakhov was quite mistaken in charging that Dostoevsky wrote only for "a selected audience." On the contrary, he employed the devices of popular adventure and mystery-story fiction, designed to appeal to the broadest public, to a far greater extent than his literary rivals; but he managed to turn such conventional tricks of the trade into high tragedy by the depth and seriousness of his thematic motivations.

The failure to make much progress on the plan for his next novel upset him for purely practical, as well as artistic, reasons. "I'm terribly troubled by the daily thought of how we will arrange things for ourselves in the fall and on what funds. (I *cannot* ask Nekrasov again [for another advance], and besides, he probably *wouldn't give* me anything.) He isn't Katkov; he's a person from Yaroslavl."[26] Katkov had always responded generously to Dostoevsky's frequent calls for advances, even when a manuscript was still very far from completion; but he expected no such liberality from his new editors. Moreover, the flow of his inspiration was admittedly being hampered by the problem of writing for a journal in which he hesitated to express himself as freely as he would have wished. "The mere fact that *Notes of the Fatherland* will be afraid to publish certain of my opinions practically cuts off my hands."[27]

As the time allotted for his stay in Bad Ems was nearing its end, Dostoevsky attempts to sum up the results of his cure. A week before returning to Russia, he writes that "although there *really* is an improvement, that is, still and all there is less dry coughing, breathing is easier, and so on, . . . [but] a certain (diseased) place remains, and that diseased place in my chest refuses to heal completely."[28] Nonetheless, "the one thing that's certain is that in everything else I feel incomparably healthier than before: energy, sleep, appetite—all of this is excellent. . . . Shtakenshneider [the brother of Elena Shtakenshneider, a jurist also taking the cure] assures me that he has never seen me with such a fresh face as now."[29]

Dostoevsky thus concluded that, for all the discomfiture it had involved, his stay at Bad Ems had been worth the trouble and expense; but he was not at all certain that the improvement would last. "I've prepared two plans for novels here and don't know on which one to venture . . . at the end of August I'll get down to the writing, and do you know what I'm worried about: whether I'll have the energy and health for such hard work as I've given myself until now. . . . I've finished novels, but nonetheless, *on the whole*, have ruined my health."[30]

Anna Grigoryevna had expected him to go either to Berlin or to Paris before returning home, and she sent him fifty extra rubles for the anticipated voyage; but he had no desire to go to Berlin and decided that Paris would be too expensive. Instead, he left Bad Ems on July 27, and, according to Anna's account, "he was not able to deny himself his deep desire to visit once more the grave of our first daughter, Sonya, whose memory he still cherished in his heart. He went to Geneva and visited the children's cemetery of Plein Palais twice; and from Sonya's grave he brought me a few sprigs of cypress, which in the course of six years had grown thick over our little girl's monument."[31]

## CHAPTER 8

# A Literary Proletarian

Dostoevsky returned to Staraya Russa on August 1 and immediately plunged into work on the scenarios for *A Raw Youth*. By this time, Anna had come to an important decision. Why return to Petersburg for the winter? The couple had decided to live in the country in the spring because life there was healthier for the children; and they could reduce their living expenses considerably by remaining (rent and food were one-third cheaper than in Petersburg). Nor would her husband be distracted by the obligations of Petersburg's social life, where "in winter Feodor Mikhailovich hardly belonged to his family" and Anna herself had to play the burdensome role of social hostess. "I personally," she writes, "found very tempting the chance of living throughout a whole winter that peaceful, serene, and pleasant family existence we had in summer, which we used to recall in the winter with such a happy feeling."[1]

Objecting at first, Dostoevsky insisted that Anna would find life in the country boring and tedious, and that she deserved some distraction and amusement. He assured her that "this winter, God willing, my work will go well, and there will be some money. You'll have pretty dresses made up, you'll go into society—I am firmly decided on that."[2] But Anna insisted that all her desires were satisfied by their tranquil family routine, and, as usual in such practical matters, she got her way. The couple immediately rented the top floor of a villa in town, with a study and separate bedroom for Dostoevsky, and it was agreed that he would go to Petersburg two or three times in the course of the winter to see friends and keep in touch with the literary scene.

## 2

Writing to Victor Putsykovich, who had taken over editorship of *The Citizen*, Dostoevsky announced this decision not to return to the capital, and also reminded him of an offer that had been made. Putsykovich had obligingly "promised to collect material on the trial of Dolgushin and company from the newspapers"; but because he would no longer be able to pick them up himself, could they be given to a friend who would send them on?[3] Dostoevsky was referring here to the public trial of a radical group named after its leader, Alexander Dolgushin. The proceedings, conducted in the Senate between July 9 and 15, 1874, had been amply reported in the press and the incriminating documents reproduced verbatim. Such materials will be partially employed in *A Raw Youth* for the fleeting portrayal of the Dergachev group, although Dostoevsky's notes indicate that he planned to give the Dolgushintsy a more important role than they were eventually assigned.

Why this trial should have particularly attracted his attention is not hard to understand. Many of the Dolgushintsy (thirty in all were arrested, although only five received sentences of any severity) had also been in contact with the Nechaevtsy and jailed in connection with that affair, though they took no part in any of Nechaev's activities. But the ideas of the Dolgushintsy—as revealed in the proclamations they managed to circulate and in their private papers confiscated by the police— distinctly reflect that sea change in the social-cultural climate that has already been described. Some of the Dolgushintsy may have been willing to collaborate with Nechaev for the sake of revolution, but, like the members of the group of five in *The Devils*, they by no means shared his Machiavellian ruthlessness; or if they had once done so, they had now converted to that reverence for a Socialist Christ and for Christian moral ideals so typical of the Populists.

The propaganda of the Dolgushintsy was in large measure drawn from the ideas of V. V. Bervi-Flerovsky, an economist whose *Position of the Working Class in Russia* (1869) was one of the major works, along with those already mentioned by Peter Lavrov and Nikolay Mikhailovsky, that inspired the Populist movement. To cite Andrzej Walicki, Bervi-Flerovsky "painted a vivid picture of the growing destitution of the peasantry following the introduction of capitalist social relations in agriculture; the conclusion he drew was that everything possible should be done to prevent capitalism from making further headway, and to utilize, instead, the possibility of the peasant commune."[4] Dostoevsky was certainly familiar with Bervi-Flerovsky's book, if only because a careful and extensive discussion of its ideas had appeared in *Zarya* (*Dawn*), the journal that had printed *The Eternal Husband* in 1869, and we know that he read this journal assiduously during its brief life span.

Many of the details contained in the Dolgushintsy documents could well have brought back memories of his own early days in the Petrashevsky circle, and especially in the Speshnev group. Among the three proclamations, one was a shortened version of a brochure written especially for them by Bervi-Flerovsky, "Of the Martyr Nikolay and How Mankind Should Live by the Laws of Nature and Justice." As the title indicates, this document was written in a semiliturgical style; another, furnished with an epigraph from Saint Matthew, was even more stylistically adapted to the sacramental language of church services. The Speshnev group also had planned to publish an incitement to revolution couched in the same semireligious style and similarly calculated to appeal to the peasant mentality. The dacha in which the Dolgushintsy had set up a printing press was decorated with an unpainted wooden cross on the wall, above which was written "In the Name of Christ," while its cross beam offered a translation of the French slogan, "liberté, égalité, fraternité." Other slogans in four languages also adorned the walls; one in Latin, a quotation from Hippocrates, had served Friedrich Schiller as the epigraph for a play that Dostoevsky practically knew by heart, *The Robbers* (*Die Räuber*): "Quae medicamenta non sanat, ferrum sanat, quae ferrum non sanat, ignis sanat" (what medicines do not cure, iron cures, what iron does not cure, fire cures).[5] Dostoevsky will use this quotation when depicting the Dergachev group in his new novel, and the Schiller play will be of first importance for *The Brothers Karamazov*.

The proclamations of the Dolgushintsy differed entirely from those inflammatory calls to exterminate the enemy that had marked the Nechaev movement. All were based on a moral appeal, whose character is well defined by the commentator in the Academy of Sciences edition of *A Raw Youth*: "The ethical substance of the 'justice' that the Dolgushintsy desired coincided objectively in its sources—and in a series of its tenets—with the substance of the Christian teachings, even though the Dolgushintsy were opponents of Christianity. The idea of a genuine and deep love of mankind, 'the religion of equality' as the source and goal of their strivings, runs through all of their proclamations." As the same commentator remarks, the records of the trial show how thoroughly these "revolutionaries" had studied the New Testament. Passages in a copy found among their belongings were marked out for use in their propaganda, and these stressed "the inevitability of suffering in the struggle for justice and the necessity of bearing one's misfortunes."[6]

Labors on his novel were broken only by letters from his scapegrace stepson Pavel Isaev, now married and having just become a father for the second time. Dostoevsky congratulated him on the birth in September, but two months later a letter from Pavel's wife to Anna revealed that she had no idea of his whereabouts. Also, she requested Anna's aid in finding a foundling home where she could place their baby daughter. Locating Pavel at last, Dostoevsky sent twenty-five rubles, "because of your harsh situation," but urged him "to try and send it all to Nadezhda Nikolayevna [his wife]. Don't buy yourself cuff links, wallets, and so on."[7]

Dostoevsky's tone, as always with Pavel, was unusually mild in view of the circumstances. But Anna Grigoryevna, who had disliked him intensely from the first, resented her husband's tolerance toward Pavel's claims on their resources; and she did not mince words in expressing her disapproval of his behavior in her reply to his wife. Insulted by her contumely, Pavel sent the twenty-five rubles back to his stepfather and complained that Anna had overstepped "*all the bounds of decency*" in dressing him down. Taking this rebuke to Anna very badly, Dostoevsky upbraided Pavel for his own prickliness while remaining totally oblivious to how his conduct affected others. "It's impossible not to be indignant, if only from the side (and I'm not on the side for you) about how you treat your children. Do you have any notion of what a foundling home is and of the raising of the newborn by a Finnish woman, amid refuse, filth, pinches, and perhaps punches: certain death. . . . After all, I didn't send you, only a stepson, just anywhere to be taught, brought up, made into a shoemaker." He details everything he has done for Pavel, including his petitions to "God only knows what people for you—which for me is sometimes a sharp knife. . . . Meanwhile you, . . . so ticklishly inclined to demand the fulfillment of *duties* regarding you—are yourself very carefree regarding your moral obligations, your human obligations—both regarding your children and regarding your father."[8] In the chapters of *A Raw Youth* written just at this time, the young Arkady Dolgoruky momentarily lays aside his aim "to become a Rothschild" in order to prevent an abandoned baby from being sent to a foundling home. The topos is age-old, but Dostoevsky could well have been reminded of it by the behavior of his stepson.

3
———

It was not Dostoevsky who made the first trip to Petersburg from Staraya Russa that winter but Anna Grigoryevna, who left in mid-December to supervise the publication of *House of the Dead* under the Dostoevsky imprint. He was gloomy about the prospects of any further demand for his prison memoirs, one of the most popular of all his books in Russia, but Anna succeeded in selling or placing on commission seven hundred copies, paying off the debts incurred for publication, and returning home with a small profit. She had left him in charge of the children, aided of course by the servants and the old nanny of whom he was so appreciative, and his letters show him to be a devoted *paterfamilias*, observing his children with pleasure and rejoicing in their amusements and accomplishments. "Yesterday," he writes Anna, "during the cigarettes [Dostoevsky, an inveterate smoker, rolled his own cigarettes], they started dancing, and Fedya invented a new *step*: Lilya would stand at the mirror, Fedya opposite her, and they both would go toward each other in time (moreover, Lilya was very graceful); after coming together (all the while in time), Fedya would kiss Lilya, and after kissing they would go their separate ways."[9]

Although he by this time had sent off the first chapters of *A Raw*

*Youth* to *Notes of the Fatherland*, so far no response to them had been forthcoming. "We need money badly," he anxiously tells Anna, "and for a while I can't even consider my relations with Nekrasov trustworthy."[10] A day later he repeats, "There hasn't been any letter [from Nekrasov], and I doubt there will be. Nekrasov probably just sent it off to be printed, but will he send the proofs?"[11] Two days later, from a story in *The Citizen*, Dostoevsky learned that Mikhail Katkov had purchased *Anna Karenina* at five hundred rubles per folio sheet. "We're not very much appreciated, Anya," he remarks ruefully. "They couldn't immediately resolve to give *me* 250 rubles, but they paid L. Tolstoy 500 with alacrity! No, I'm valued too low, and it's because I live on my work."[12]

Even more than this blow to his literary pride, what bothered him was that "now it's quite possible that Nekrasov will cut me back if there is anything contrary to their orientation; he knows that the *Russian Messenger* won't take me now (that is, for next year) because [it is] swamped with novels. But even if we have to beg for alms, I won't compromise my orientation by so much as a line!"[13] There is some indication, however, that he may have altered his plan for the novel so as not to clash too sharply with his Populist editors, though nothing he wrote can be said to have compromised his convictions. The news about *Anna Karenina*, however, may well have affected the book by sharpening Dostoevsky's sense of rivalry with Tolstoy—a rivalry already evident in his notes for his unwritten work, the *Life of a Great Sinner* (1869), on which he partially draws for *A Raw Youth*. The sting of Dostoevsky's resentment, as we shall see, becomes evident in the epilogue of his new novel.

A month later he went to Petersburg, partly for reasons of health and partly to reassure himself at first hand about his novel, whose first chapters had already been published. Nekrasov had finally written that the next installment was to be put into galleys; but he still had not proferred any opinion about the work, and Dostoevsky had begun to fret that perhaps his depiction of the Dergachev group (Part I, Chapter 2) had met with some hostility. He cheerfully informs Anna, however, that Nekrasov had received him "extremely cordially and heartily" and was "terribly happy with the novel, although he hasn't yet read the second part" (that is, Chapters 6–10 of Part I). But the co-editor, Mikhail Saltykov-Shchedrin, the satirist with whom he had slashingly polemicized in the past, "praises [it] very highly." Despite such approbation, Dostoevsky himself remarks that "in proof I don't much like my novel." The opinion of Saltykov-Shchedrin, if correctly reported, also drastically altered with later installments, which he spoke of as being "almost crazy."[14]

Dostoevsky read part of his proofs at Nekrasov's home and took the remainder back to his hotel; but, feeling the need for company, he called on Prince Meshchersky. Unfortunately, the prince had just left for Paris to attend the funeral of his brother. Dostoevsky, as we see, felt no hesitation in alternately visiting the homes of two figures who stood at the opposite extremes of the Russian social-political spectrum. And this behavior clearly symbolizes the freedom he believed he could enjoy to transcend the apparently irreconcilable oppositions of the Russian culture of his time.

Although he apparently felt that he could allow himself such an unprecedented freedom with impunity, his old friends and comrades from the bruising polemics of the 1860s were by no means inclined to take lightly his flirtation with their old enemies. After dinner on the same day that he had received his proofs, Dostoevsky went to visit the Maikovs and found Strakhov there as well. Maikov "greeted me with apparent heartiness," he writes Anna, "but I saw at once that this contained a strong touch of falsity. . . . Not a word about my novel and obviously because of not wanting to *pain* me. They also talked a little about Tolstoy's novel [*Anna Karenina*], and what they said was ridiculous in its enthusiasm. I started to speak and made the point that, if Tolstoy published in *Notes of the Fatherland*, then why were they criticizing me, but Maikov frowned and broke off the conversation and I didn't insist. In short, I see that something is going on here, and precisely what you and I talked about, that is, Maikov has spread that idea about me." When there was talk of further meetings, Maikov remained significantly silent; and when Dostoevsky set an appointment with Strakhov, who said he would come in Maikov's company, the latter immediately pleaded an earlier engagement.[15]

The "idea about me" mentioned was evidently that the appearance of *A Raw Youth* in Nekrasov's journal could be considered a betrayal of his former beliefs and commitments. Dostoevsky attempted to counter such an inference by mentioning Tolstoy's *On the Education of the People* (*O Narodnom Obrazovanie*), a series of articles published in the same journal a year earlier. No one had seemed to consider Tolstoy's choice of venue a renunciation of the patriotic and nationalist sentiments of the author of *War and Peace*, a book hailed by Strakhov as a mighty literary edifice erected to the greater glory of the Russian state. Tolstoy, however, had never been so directly involved as Dostoevsky with the issues of the day; and, for all his personal antipathy to the radicals of the 1860s, he had not made such enmity a major literary theme. Moreover, the *grand seigneur* Tolstoy was probably regarded as remaining his own man wherever he published, while the same credit was not accorded the wage-earning Dostoevsky.

Even though nothing was said about *A Raw Youth* on this occasion, Strakhov was less reticent when he paid Dostoevsky a reassuring visit two days later. Anna was informed that "Maikov had not been involved in any rumors about me, and [Strakhov] doesn't even know for certain if there are any rumors." As regards the novel, "he doesn't much like *A Raw Youth*. He praises the realism, but finds it unappealing and therefore boring. And in general he told me a lot of extremely sensible and sincere things which, however, doesn't put me out of countenance because in the next parts I hope to prove to them that they are very wrong." Probably as a consolation for such uncomplimentary opinions, Strakhov mentioned an article by the Populist critic A. M. Skabichevsky, who had found the first chapters of *A Raw Youth* to be less "pathological" than was usual for Dostoevsky. The article "doesn't exactly offer praise, but it says that [whereas] until now many people took Dostoevsky's characters to be rather fantastic, it seems to be time to disavow that and admit they are profoundly realistic and so on in that vein."[16]

Dostoevsky read the first installments of *Anna Karenina* during this Petersburg visit "under a bell"—that is, the apparatus placed over his head while taking compressed air treatments for his lungs two hours every day. Tolstoy's novel "is rather boring and so-so," he reports to Anna. "I can't understand what they're all so excited about."[17] He would later express enthusiasm for the book; but whether, except for certain scenes, he genuinely changed his evaluation of it as a whole may well be doubted. He was, in any event, overjoyed when Nekrasov, as he proudly told Anna, dropped in unexpectedly on the fourth day of his stay "to express *his delight* after reading the end of the first part [of *A Raw Youth*]. 'I got so carried away that I stayed up all night reading . . . and at my age and with my health I should not really allow myself to do that. And what freshness you have, my dear fellow . . . that sort of freshness doesn't happen at our age and not a single other writer has it. Lev Tolstoy's latest novel only repeats what I've read in him before, only it was better before' (Nekrasov said this)." Nekrasov also, however, criticized the eighth chapter of Part I for containing too much that was "external," and Dostoevsky admits that "when I reread the proofs I myself disliked the eighth chapter most of all and threw a lot of things out of it."[18]

Besides the balm that such words provided his wounded literary self-esteem, particularly vulnerable just as this moment, Nekrasov offered much more financial assistance than Dostoevsky had anticipated. He proposed an extra advance in case one was necessary; and because Dostoevsky had been advised by Professor Koshlakov to make another trip to Ems in the late spring, this offer could not have been more welcome. Nekrasov also agreed to a new plan for publication. No installment of the novel would appear in March or June, and the second and third parts would be printed in April–May and July–August. "Please don't rush and don't spoil it, he said, because it's begun very well."

In short, "the result is that I'm valued extremely highly at *Notes of the Fatherland*, and Nekrasov wants to initiate quite cordial relations." Meanwhile, "Strakhov knows about my displeasure with Maikov and seems to have told him, because Maikov sent me a letter and is inviting me to dinner at his place today, Tuesday. But I also saw him at Strakhov's last night. It was very friendly, but I don't like the two of them, and most of all I don't like Strakhov; they both are sneaky."[19]

Dostoevsky soon changed his mind about Maikov, but the ill humor concerning Strakhov only increased. At the Maikov dinner, "all of them were very nice, but on the other hand Strakhov was very sneaky." In view of the situation, however, it cannot be said that he behaved very diplomatically himself. "When [Strakhov] started asking me about Nekrasov, and when I told him about Nekrasov's comments [including, of course, the remark about Tolstoy], Maikov made a sad face and Strakhov was quite cold." Fully aware of the Tolstoy-worship of his interlocutors, Dostoevsky was of course only rubbing salt into already-smarting wounds; it is little wonder that the atmosphere then became very stiff and strained. "No, Anya," he finally explodes about Strakhov, "he's only a miserable seminarian and nothing else; he's already left me once before in my life when *Epoch* collapsed, and he only came back after the success of *Crime and Punishment*. Maikov is incomparably superior; he gets angry, and then becomes friendly again, and is altogether a fine fellow, not a seminarian."[20]

Just what had passed between Dostoevsky and Strakhov at the time of the collapse of *Epoch* is not known in detail; but Strakhov himself, who wrote part of the first biography, refers there vaguely to "disagreements about which I will not tell any tales." A sentence or two later, he remarks, "We had to share the general misfortune, and each of us endeavored to make his portion as small as possible"—in other words, each was blaming the other.[21] Clearly, the memory of these difficult days continued to fester on both sides, and Dostoevsky's use of the epithet "seminarian"—a deadly insult in the vocabulary of the period because several of the leading radicals had studied in theological institutions— reveals the depth of his bitterness.

Nor, to be fair, was he an easy person to deal with under any circumstances, and especially in a quarrel. He all too easily lost control of his nerves—as he never hesitated to admit himself—and was quite capable of having insulted Strakhov in a manner that the latter could never forget nor forgive. The temporary estrangement of the two men, however, was soon patched up. A month later, after having read the first part of *A Raw Youth* in its entirety, Strakhov wrote him that "you have chosen an excellent theme, and everyone expects a miracle from its development, at least I expect it."[22]

Besides the letters to Anna, there is another document that reveals the extent of Dostoevsky's perturbation over these personal quarrels and over the accidental competition between his novel and *Anna Karenina*. One of the warmest articles greeting the first chapters of *A Raw Youth* had appeared in the *St. Petersburg Gazette*, written by a critic whose pseudonym, Sine Ira, was that of Vsevolod Solovyev. When Dostoevsky paid him a visit, Solovyev recalls instantly becoming aware that the novelist was "in a highly irritable state and in the gloomiest frame of mind. 'Tell me, tell me honestly—do you think I am envious of Lev Tolstoy?' he blurted out, having greeted me and intently looking me in the eye." The startled Solovyev, hardly knowing how to respond to this "strange question," adroitly replied that, because the two writers were so very different, there was no real rivalry between them; nor could he imagine Dostoevsky being envious of Tolstoy. But then he asked him if anyone had accused him of nurturing such a feeling, and Dostoevsky responded: "Yes, exactly, they accuse me of envy. And who? Old friends, who have known me for twenty years." These could only be Maikov and Strakhov; and when Solovyev asked if this charge had been openly stated, Dostoevsky's words were: "Yes, almost openly. . . . This idea has taken such root in them that they can hardly conceal it—it shows itself in every one of their words." He sank into a chair, but then leaped up and, grasping Solovyev by the hand, broke out into an anguished tirade:

> You know, yes, I am in fact envious, but only not in the way, not at all in the way, that they think. I envy his circumstances, and particularly right now. . . . It's painful for me to work as I do, painful to hurry. . . . God!, and all my life! . . . Look, I recently reread my *Idiot*; I had forgotten it completely, entirely forgotten it, I read it as something strange, as if for the first time. . . . There are excellent chapters . . . good scenes . . . a number of them. . . . For example . . . you remember the meeting between Aglaya and the prince on the bench? . . . But I also saw others, how much was unfinished, hasty. . . . And it's always so—as now, *Notes of the Fatherland* presses, it's necessary to keep up . . . you take advances . . . work them off . . . and again go ahead. . . . And there's no end! . . . And he is materially secure, never has to worry about the next day, he can polish every one of his works, and that's a great thing—when the work is before you all ready and then you read it and make improvements. That's what I envy . . . I really envy . . . my dear fellow![23]

Even though matters were smoothed over on the surface between Dostoevsky and Strakhov, and to all external appearances they remained friends, the rancor generated by these incidents and the earlier ones was never dispelled. An entry in Dostoevsky's notebook for 1876–

9. *Tolstoy in 1877*, by I. N. Kramskoy

1877 reveals the depth of his anger, and also a good deal of contempt. He ridicules him for "beating around the bush" in his critical articles and cultivating a literary career that "gave him four readers, no more I think, and a thirst for glory." Leading a sycophantic, sybaritic life, he "loves to eat turkey, and not his own, at others' tables" (Strakhov dined regularly at the Dostoevskys'), while deriving his self-importance from holding "two public posts"—"a purely seminarian trait," Dostoevsky sneers. Even more, he accuses Strakhov of lacking any sense of "civic feeling or duty," so that "for some gross, coarsely voluptuous filth he is ready to sell everyone and everything . . . [including] the ideal which he does not have, and not because he does not believe in the ideal, but because of the thick layer of fat which prevents him from feeling any-thing."[24] This extremely insulting characterization was never published,

139

but one assumes that Strakhov must have come across it in preparing Dostoevsky's biography.*

The estrangement from his oldest friends made him all the more eager to grasp at the chance of reviving his intimacy with Nekrasov, and perhaps establishing a new friendship with the notoriously bearlike Saltykov-Shchedrin. One of the reasons he gave Anna for delaying his departure from Petersburg for a day was that "Nekrasov wants to take me to see Saltykov on a Saturday (and I very much want to strike up an acquaintance with him)."[25] In fact, the two had met in the 1840s but only very casually, and he may well have forgotten their perfunctory contacts. But he had certainly not forgotten their wounding satirical exchanges of the 1860s, which are reflected in his recently reread novel *The Idiot.* Anna Grigoryevna, for her part, expressed satisfaction at such reestablishing of old ties and later wrote that "after returning to [Staraya] Russa my husband told me about his talks with Nekrasov, and I realized how precious this renewal of warm relations with the friend of his youth was to him." "He had a less favorable reaction," she adds discreetly, "to his encounters at that time with several members of his literary circle."[26]

Fearing that he would not be able to express himself freely in *Notes of the Fatherland*, Dostoevsky had insisted that he would not compromise his own ideas by one iota. Although there is nothing to indicate that he was subject to any direct editorial pressure, a curious passage in an article by Mikhailovsky, published alongside Dostoevsky's first chapters in the January issue, raises some questions. The Populist reading public was, apparently, as much taken aback by his presence in the pages of their favorite journal as was his own literary circle, and Mikhailovsky felt called upon to offer some explanation. A journal, he remarks, cannot assume full responsibility for all the opinions of its contributors; all the same, "the tendency of an author's thought" cannot simply be left out of account. Noting that Dostoevsky's chapters contained a depiction of the Dergachev group, with details easily recognizable as borrowed from the trial of the Dolgushintsy, Mikhailovsky refers to what he calls the novelist's "mania for taking as the theme of his novels the criminal actions of young people immediately after their discovery, investigation, and punishment."[27]

Despite such a "mania," *Notes of the Fatherland* is printing Dostoev-

---

* Strakhov may well have taken revenge on Dostoevsky in the letter that he sent to Tolstoy in 1883, declaring that he wrote Dostoevsky's biography only in a struggle against "my own rising revulsion, trying to suppress that ugly feeling in myself." It is in this letter that he reports having been told that Dostoevsky "had boasted of having . . . a little girl in the bathhouse, delivered over to him by her governess." See Anna Dostoevsky, *Reminiscences*, trans. and ed. Beatrice Stillman (New York, 1973), 371–382.

10. Radical writer Mikhail E.
Saltykov-Shchedrin

sky's new book for reasons that Mikhailovsky sets out to clarify. "First, Dostoevsky is one of our most talented belletrists, and second, . . . the scene at Dergachev's, with all its particularities, has only an episodic character. If the novel were based on this motif [as had been the case with *The Devils*], *Notes of the Fatherland* would be forced to renounce the honor of seeing the creation of Dostoevsky in its pages, even if he were a writer of genius."[28] Just how Mikhailovsky could have known what had not yet been written remains a matter for conjecture; but perhaps Dostoevsky's conversations with Nekrasov at this time influenced the extremely perfunctory treatment of the Dergachev motif. "The question arises," wrote A. S. Dolinin in his classic account of the genesis of *A Raw Youth*, "whether the editors of *Notes of the Fatherland* are not responsible for reducing the trial of the Dolgushintsy to a minor episode."[29] From the amount of space accorded them in Dostoevsky's notes, compared with their ancillary role in the novel, it seems likely that he might have wished to avoid any editorial clash over his final text.

He returned to Staraya Russa after two exhausting weeks. As well as looking after his literary affairs and taking his compressed air treatments, he had dispatched the business of his publishing firm, visited the lawyer handling the litigation over the Kumanina estate as well as the dentist repairing his dentures, and made the rounds of a host of friends and relatives. He hardly had time to sleep, and he had even been forced to change his room at the hotel because one night "I heard laughter, a woman's squealing, a man's bass, and on and on like that for about three hours: a merchant had just arrived with two women and taken a room."[30] To make matters worse, he suddenly received a notice from the police informing him, when he showed up, that he lacked an (internal) passport. On protesting that "there are twenty thousand people without passports in Petersburg, and you're detaining a person everybody knows," he was sternly told that, even though he was "a famous person all over Russia," laws still had to be obeyed.[31] However, he was then promised a certificate of residency in a few days and told not to worry, from which Anna concluded that the reason for the harassment had been an unsuccessful attempt to obtain a bribe.

In his last letter from Petersburg, he writes: "Today I'm riding around and living as though in hell. For the whole two weeks I haven't been to the theater once. I've lived in the most vile manner, running around on errands and sitting in the clinic. Tomorrow there are the devil only knows how many things still to take care of."[32] Dostoevsky was under such pressure that he failed to send his wife some of the advance obtained from Nekrasov, having told her previously to borrow in case of need; but she was obviously reluctant to do so and sent him an urgent letter instead. "You wouldn't believe how you have upset and distressed me with your request for money," he replied. "But is it really so shameful to borrow, Anya! I didn't imagine anything of the sort. After all, we're not thieves and swindlers and we've proven that."[33] It is likely, however, that borrowing money, even from their friend the local priest, recalled all too vividly for the efficient businesswoman Anna had now become the humiliations of their years abroad, and she refused to put herself in the same position again.

4
---

Life in Staraya Russa provided Dostoevsky with a securely placid existence he had never known before, and Anna Grigoryevna's *Reminiscences*, filled with homely household detail, allow us to obtain a good picture of his usual routine. Awakening late in the morning, he would dictate what he had written during the night to his wife, and the couple would lunch together. He then retired to read (she mentions as a favorite text, during the winter of 1874–1875, *The Wanderings of the Monk Parfeny*, which later influenced the style of Father Zosima's recollections in *The Brothers Karamazov*) or write letters until half past three, when he went for a stroll "among Russa's quiet, deserted streets."[34] Invariably, he would stop at Plotnikov's shop to buy small quantities of sweetmeats just arrived from Petersburg; and because he was well known there, he was treated with respectful diligence despite the frugality of his purchases.

Dinner with the children was served at five, preceded by a thimbleful of vodka for the children's nanny, Prokhorovna, and the parents restricted their conversation at table to subjects the children could understand. Dostoevsky spent a half-hour afterward telling them fairy tales or reading from Krylov's fables; then he and Anna, leaving the nanny in charge, would take a stroll together at half past seven. They would stop at the post office to pick up mail and the newspapers, just arrived from Petersburg, and return home to examine what the post had brought. At nine the children were put to bed, and "Feodor Mikhailovich would unfailingly go to them to 'bless them for the approaching sleep' and recite with them the Lord's Prayer, the Hail Mary, and his own favorite prayer, 'All my hope in Thee I do repose, O Mother of God, shelter me beneath Thy Veil.'"[35] Anna would settle down to a game of patience while he read the newspapers in his study, though from time to time he would come to chat about the latest news and give Anna a hand with her card game. At eleven she would retire, and he would withdraw to work until three or four in the morning.

Various incidents, however, disturbed the serenity of their peaceful existence. Anna recounts her fright, on returning from the trip to Petersburg, when she was crossing the icebound Lake Ilmen with a party of troikas and her coachman lost the way in a sudden blizzard. "Luckily, the coachman dropped the reins and the wise animals . . . finally brought us back to the beaten path."[36] Fires were also a frequent occurrence, and "they sometimes burned down whole streets" in the largely wooden-built towns. At the first sound of the church bells ringing a warning of fire, Anna would immediately begin to dress the children and then pack extra clothes into large sheets, even if there was no immediate danger. Special care was taken to look after his notebooks and manuscripts in case the family had to flee. No such emergency ever materialized, but because of Anna's nervousness Dostoevsky was always the first to respond to an alarm in the vicinity and was praised for his promptitude by the house porter. "So you see," he remarked amusedly to Anna, "that I do have some virtues whose existence I didn't even suspect myself.'"[37]

Quite understandably, Anna Grigoryevna says nothing in her memoirs about another of her trips to Petersburg, in early April 1875, this time to deal with a family scandal. The wife of her brother had taken a lover, and she would go off with him from time to time, leaving her husband and children, and then return to the family fold. Anna left to straighten out, if possible, this upsetting situation, and Dostoevsky worried that the spring floods and the condition of the roads would make it difficult for her to return home for Easter. He was also greatly concerned because Anna had become pregnant again, and "I'm afraid you'll fall ill and something will happen . . . to the mystery person."[38]

Such dire forebodings happily proved to be unjustified. He himself returned to Petersburg in mid-May to read proof again and obtain another advance for his second trip to Ems. He tells Anna that he went to visit the Maikovs, without any mention of how he was received, and that he also became entangled in the affairs of the Snitkin *ménage*. It was only after they had left his room at midnight that "I got down to work on my proofs, *literally* scarcely able to stand up." As for that couple, "I can't write anything . . . because it's such a mess . . . that it would be impossible for me to express myself comprehensibly."[39] There had been some talk of the Snitkins moving to Staraya Russa; but this idea was abandoned, no doubt much to the relief of the Dostoevskys, and the troubled pair returned to their country estate.

As he was passing through Petersburg two weeks later on his way to Ems, Prince Meshchersky, troubled by the rift between Dostoevsky and Maikov, attempted to effect a reconciliation between these two mainstays of his literary entourage by inviting both to dinner. But Maikov again pleaded an earlier engagement, and Dostoevsky took this as a sign of intransigent ill will. Signing this letter affectionately as "your eternal, unchanging husband," he adds a tender postscript: "Changed for the better, however."[40] Three days later, reassuring Anna about the impending arrival of their next child, about which she had begun to fret, he wrote from Berlin of his visit to her cousin in Petersburg, a well-known pediatrician: "Mikhail Nikolaevich just smiles at my doubts and yours, and says that according to all the signs you should have an excellent delivery."[41] The next day he was in Ems, after an exhausting journey during which it had been impossible to get sufficient sleep.

His second visit to Ems produced many of the same negative reactions that had marked the first after his initial burst of enthusiasm. His discomfiture this time was increased by an even greater sense of isolation (there were literally *no* Russians he knew or whose acquaintance he might wish to make) and by his worry over having left Anna alone to cope with her anxieties and forebodings. The beauty he had noted a year before now left him indifferent. "[T]he first look at Ems produced the most vile, miserable impressions on me," no doubt, as he adds, because "Ems is terribly disgusting when it's raining."[42] If we can infer from the other letters, rain was much more frequent in May and June

1875 than in the previous spring. His health, however, as he reported to Anna with satisfaction, was judged to have improved, and he attributes this amelioration to the salubrious conditions of life in Staraya Russa.

What he saw of his compatriots at Ems did not please him at all, and he describes sarcastically the behavior of the ladies at the Russian church, "who put on airs, sit down in chairs [one is expected to stand during an Orthodox service], and faint. While I was there at church three fainted (allegedly from incense and closeness), but it's most likely they could dance the night through at a ball and pack in a meal that would be enough for two men. It's disgusting."[43] Noting the arrival at Ems of someone whose name he knew, Dimitry I. Ilyovsky, Dostoevsky recounts a meeting, apparently reported to him, of the Society of Admirers of Russian Literature chaired by this gentleman. After a reading from the first part of *Anna Karenina*—the scene in which Anna and Count Vronsky meet during a train trip—"Ilyovsky declared loudly that they (the admirers) didn't need gloomy novels, even talented ones (that is, mine), but rather something light and playful like Count Tolstoy's. I don't know him by sight, but I don't think he'll want to get acquainted, and I of course won't start in myself."[44] He also remarks that installments of *Anna Karenina* had stopped appearing. "But how do you like that: I at least interrupted my novel with Nekrasov after finishing the second part, while here they're interrupting it right in the middle of the third part."[45]

There are constant laments about the difficulty of continuing to work on the third part of *A Raw Youth* while taking the cure and in the upsetting conditions of Ems. "My darling Anya, I keep being horrified by the obligations that I've taken on myself. I see that, try as I might, there'll be almost no time to write."[46] As if all this were not enough, he had read in a Russian guide to Ems, and had also been told authoritatively by his doctors, that patients should "not give [themselves] over to *any* mental exertion, because otherwise not only will there be no benefit from the treatment, but harm and illness will *definitely* occur."[47] Caught between such warnings and his literary commitments, he decided "to decrease the exertion by half" and requested of Nekrasov, who obligingly agreed, that publication of the third part be resumed in September rather than August.

Dostoevsky thus continued to work on his scenarios, even if not as intensively as he might have desired, and echoes of his preparation for them can be found in his letters. "I'm reading about *Elijah* and *Enoch* (it's superb) and Bessonov's *Our Age*," he tells Anna. He was probably seeking inspiration for his presentation of the figure of Makar Dolgoruky, the Russian peasant wanderer (*strannik*) and the legal father of the raw youth, who makes his appearance in Part III and represents an

145

idealized image of peasant religiosity (Bessonov's book is a collection of Russian historical folk poetry). He also enthuses over another text of the Old Testament, and his words not only give us a glimpse into childhood memories but also look forward to the creation of *The Brothers Karamazov*. "I am reading Job and it puts me into a state of painful ecstasy; I leave off reading and I walk about the room almost crying, and if it weren't for the vile notes of the translator, I would perhaps be happy. That book, dear Anna, it's strange, it was one of the first to impress me in my life. I was still practically an infant!"[48]

Such immersion in the Bible did not prevent him from reading the Russian press, and he complains of not having access to *Voice* because other Russians never left it available in the public reading room. *The Citizen*, however, was sent to him by mail, and he comments on some of its recent issues. "But what has Meshchersky gotten himself into in his *Lord and Apostle*?" he asks Anna. "It's awful. And Poretsky has gone completely off his head with Tolstoy."[49] The title refers to a new novel by the prince then running in the weekly and dealing with the activities of the English evangelist of noble birth, Lord Grenville Radstock, then cutting a wide swath in Petersburg aristocratic circles. Lord Radstock preached a Christianity somewhat related to Lutheranism, in which "good deeds" were considered of little importance in relieving the burden of sin. Salvation could be attained only by the acceptance of Christ, whose blood had already redeemed the sins of all those recognizing Him as their Savior. Meshchersky depicts his fellow aristocrat in quite a favorable light, but Dostoevsky will soon, in the *Diary of a Writer*, refer to Radstock's vogue as a symptom of the alienation of the Russian upper class from their own people and from the people's faith.

Alexander Poretsky, an old friend, had furiously defended *Anna Karenina* against a criticism of the radical publicist Peter Tkachev (writing under a pseudonym), who had asked whether it was worth spending so much time talking about a book with such a foolish and even corrupting theme. Dostoevsky was then himself being manhandled in some journals, and he felt very acutely the lack of any defender against those who were deprecating *him*. "Absolutely everyone in literature has turned against me. . . . I won't go chasing after them," he writes defiantly, referring to some criticism in the French-language *Journal de Pétersbourg*. The critic described the end of the second part of *A Raw Youth* as "limp" and concluded that "il n'y a rien de saillant" (nothing stands out). To which Dostoevsky retorts: "You may say anything you please, I can even be reproached for the same old effects, but you can't say that nothing stands out. I see that the novel is a loss, however; it will be buried with full honors under universal contempt." But he refuses to be discouraged: "I won't lose any energy for the future at all—you just be well, my helpmate, and we'll manage one way or another."[50]

5
_____

All but one of these letters from Ems are written to his wife. The single exception is addressed to Elena Pavlovna Ivanova, to whom Dostoevsky was distantly related by marriage and with whom he had once been very close. During the summer of 1868, he had asked Elena Pavlovna, whose husband was presumably in the last stages of a fatal illness, whether she would consider marrying him on becoming a widow. Now he inquires after the whereabouts of the elusive Pavel Isaev and expresses regret at the hostile rumors circulating about himself because of his claim to a share in the Kumanina estate—rumors that had become even more envenomed since the suit he had filed against collateral claimants. His favorite niece, Sofya Ivanova, with whom he had corresponded regularly while abroad and to whom he had dedicated *The Idiot*, had ceased to write to him for this reason. In his letter to Elena Pavlovna, he encloses one to Sofya (unfortunately lost) and asks Elena to read it herself. Elena Pavlovna answered that, if she were Sofya, she would not like to have received such a letter; and she rebukes him for failing to write earlier so as to explain the situation from his point of view and avoid the misunderstandings that had arisen.[51]

Anna Grigoryevna, during Dostoevsky's absences, was always filled with trepidation that he would be stricken by a severe epileptic attack, leaving him helpless among strangers. One can well imagine her consternation when she unexpectedly received a letter from a friend asking if it were true that Dostoevsky was on the point of expiring at Ems since the *St. Petersburg Gazette* had printed a report that "the prominent writer F. M. Dostoevsky is gravely ill." Frightened to death, Anna sent off a telegram and prepared to travel to Ems herself, despite her pregnancy, once Father Rumyantsev and his wife had promised to look after the children. He replied by telegram that he was "ganz gesund" (perfectly healthy) and wondered why the sudden panic.[52] He left Ems after a little less than five weeks of treatment, having been told by his doctor "that my chest is in excellent condition, everything has healed. But the wheezing and difficulty in breathing are left; he said that may go away all on its own."[53]

On arriving in Petersburg, he was so short of money that it was necessary to borrow some from friends; and he hastens to explain why to Anna. "On the way I met Pisemsky and Pavel Annenkov; they were traveling to Petersburg from Baden-Baden (where Turgenev and Saltykov are). I couldn't restrain myself and paid Annenkov (that is, to be passed on to Turgenev) fifty thalers. That's what did me in. I couldn't *possibly* have done anything else; it's a matter of honor. Both Pisemsky and Annenkov treated me superbly."[54] Relations between Turgenev and Dostoevsky, nonetheless, were seemingly doomed to friction and irritation.

A year later, Turgenev empowered an emissary to obtain an additional fifty thalers from Dostoevsky, probably recalling that he had originally asked him for the loan of a hundred. But Dostoevsky was able to locate the letter in which he thanked Turgenev for the smaller amount, and the matter was finally closed—though no one could blame Dostoevsky if he felt that his honor had been impugned all the same.

## CHAPTER 9

# Notes for *A Raw Youth*

The notebooks that Dostoevsky kept while working on *A Raw Youth* (*Podrostok*) are among the most extensive in the corpus of his work. Indeed, we have more information about the preliminary stages of this weakest of his five major novels than for any of the others. One of the reasons for this bulk is that he was sketching an early version of *The Brothers Karamazov* at the same time. The notes can thus be separated into two groups. In one, Dostoevsky was still groping for a subject; in the other, he definitively fixes on portraying the relations between a rebellious young man, born illegitimately and just emerging from adolescence, and his glamorous and mysterious father, a member of the generation of the 1840s. This father figure is not portrayed satirically, but treated with a certain semitragic dignity. Once he had settled on this thematic situation, the book took shape more or less smoothly, without the abrupt shifts of plan and major rewriting of his other novels of the 1860s.

## 2

Dostoevsky had begun to make notes for a new novel beginning in February 1874, and the first jottings indicate that, as an initial step, he went back to mull over undeveloped sketches for earlier works. The first entries are thus reminiscent of others he had made, but not utilized, for *The Idiot*—notes in which Prince Myshkin would be surrounded by children and become their inspirer and leader. Taking up this motif, he outlines a plan, set down in capital letters, of "a novel about children, solely about children, and about a boy-hero (N.B. they save a suffering child, stratagems, etc.)." A line or two later, there is a reference to "Feodor Petrovich (a man who loves children, and the nurse)." Feodor Petrovich turns out to be a Myshkin-like character who places himself at the service of the group of children and addresses them with great solemnity: "Gentlemen, I have finished." Like Myshkin, "he is himself a grown-up child, only imbued with a very strong, and vivid, and long-suffering feeling of love for children" (16: 5–6). Such notes form part of the group that looks forward to *The Brothers Karamazov* and the band of boys clustering around Alyosha Karamazov.

More important for *A Raw Youth* is the name of Lambert, which appears unexplained amidst the notes for the novel about children. It indicates that Dostoevsky was also drawing on a previous plan, set down between December 1869 and January 1870, to write the *Life of a Great Sinner*.[1] There Lambert is a schoolfellow of "the great sinner," just as he will be of the raw youth. As an epitome of sensuality and immorality, Lambert "finds nothing higher" than sensuality because of "the frivolity of national character" (he is of French origin); but "the emptiness, dirtiness, and absurdity of debauchery unhinges him [the great sinner]" (9: 135). Lambert will play exactly the same role in *A Raw Youth*.

The notes for the *Life of a Great Sinner* thus show up in those for *A Raw Youth* at a very early stage, and he continues for quite some time to draw on this earlier project. As we know, he had not been able to include in *The Devils* his chapter containing Stavrogin's confession; and he now returns to this Stavrogin-type (which he calls "predatory," a term borrowed from his friend, now dead, the poet and critic Apollon Grigoryev), as if feeling that he had not yet exhausted all its possibilities. A number of entries refer to the "predatory type," which is conceived as embodying "the meanest coarseness along with the most refined generosity. . . . Both charming and repulsive (the little red beetle, Stavrogin)" (16: 7). The words in parentheses link this passage to Stavrogin's confession, and particularly to his dream of a Golden Age of human innocence as Dostoevsky had imagined it under the inspiration of one of his favorite paintings, Claude Lorrain's *Acis and Galatea*. The "little red beetle," a symbol of Stavrogin's terrible crime, intrudes into this idyllic vision and provokes the torments of his conscience. This dream will later serve, in a revised version, as one of the culminating moments of *A Raw Youth*.

Several extended notes made in Bad Ems are devoted to developing the traits of the predatory type, who swings uncontrollably from one moral extreme to the other both in deeds and in thought. "I know that it is evil," he quotes his character as saying in a snatch of monologue, "and I feel remorse, but I still do it right along with my noblest transports." This moral-psychological duality, which recalls the ecstasies of the underground man about "the sublime and the beautiful" just as he was indulging in "the most odious dissipation," then evolves into the idea for a work including "two lines of action at one and the same time." In one, the predatory type "is a great, righteous man who . . . lives for the exaltation of his spirit. . . . In his other activities, he is a terrible criminal, a liar, and profligate. . . . But when alone with himself, he views both kinds of activities with arrogance and despondency" (16: 8).

These two lines of action, which emerge from the dualism of a single character, evolve into an idea for two novels—one about children, the other about the predatory type—which are then combined (just as, in the early stages of *Crime and Punishment*, Dostoevsky had fused the story of an idealistic murderer with the sufferings of the family of a drunkard). The predatory type is thus brought into relation with a group of children, and the antinomies of his character receive a more "natural" setting in which they can be displayed. Dostoevsky then delineates some possible interactions between the predatory figure and the children. "The predatory type is a great skeptic. The people around him have some social ideals at which he sneers. He unmercifully demolishes the idols of others (a young boy) and derives pleasure from it" (16: 8). This novel-idea is not kept as such, but it anticipates how *A Raw Youth* will develop. The predatory type, who undermines the "social ideals" of a young boy and obtains satisfaction from doing so, foreshadows the relation of the raw youth and his father.

What distinguishes the predatory type is his arrant selfishness, along with a certain capriciousness and unpredictability that sometimes leads to the opposite behavior. He will tell someone, "I am not going to sacrifice my slightest whim for your sake"; but "sometimes he would sacrifice everything to somebody else's whim." Dostoevsky then deepens such a purely psychological motivation with a religious-ideological one that buttresses his character's egoism. The predatory type, declaring himself to be an atheist, bluntly proclaims: "There is no other life. I am on earth for a brief moment only, so why stand on ceremony?" He is well aware that "certain conditions of community have been established by society as a sort of contract" and that his unabashed egoism, which violates these conditions, "introduces a dissonance into the society of the future." But what does this matter "if the earth will open and swallow it up, and me along with the rest of them, *après moi, le déluge!*" The theme of atheism will continue to motivate the psychology of this type, though in a more muted and self-doubting form. The argument advanced here, however, about the meaninglessness of a life restricted only to earthly immanence will be uttered by the raw youth.

### 3

The predatory type is also developed in other directions, and several of his features will be retained in the novel. There is a melodramatic intrigue involving the romantic proclivities of the predatory type, who is married to (or lives with) one woman, is madly in love with another, and has a stepdaughter (or illegitimate daughter) who meets an unhappy fate. Atheism continues to be "the main essence" of the predatory type (who will evolve into the father of the raw youth, Versilov), but becomes complicated by indications of a nostalgia for religious faith. "He is a preacher of the Christian religion," Dostoevsky writes, "and this is why the princess left her high society and followed him. And then he smashes an icon. . . . I am a depraved man, I am an atheist" (6: 14). These antinomies of Versilov's character recall Stavrogin, who both inspires and undermines religious faith, and also smashes an icon at a climactic moment.

Exploring various ways of situating his predatory type in a concrete social environment, Dostoevsky in one note touches on a motif that will be important for his raw youth. "He is from an obscure family, the son of some kind of government clerk. . . . Perhaps he is ashamed of his obscure lineage, and suffers from it. (N.B. His brother says about him, or to him: 'Admit that you are ashamed of not being an aristocrat.')" (16: 12). Arkady, the raw youth, the illegitimate son of a gentry father (Versilov) and a peasant mother, is filled with shame and resentment at both being and not being an aristocrat. He is also insultingly snubbed by his half-brother, the legal son of Versilov, who refuses even to speak to him.

A good number of notes, along with those devoted to the predatory type, are concerned with his opposite, the leader of the band of children, now called Feodor Feodorovich, who still retains his Myshkin-like features. These character traits are illustrated by several incidents, such as his refusal to accept an estate that he wins in a lawsuit and his return of a winning lottery ticket to the clerk from whom he had purchased it, "though his fiancée and her family are clamoring against his intention to return the ticket" (6: 11, 14). This Myshkin-figure is also depicted as a social radical, who is seen as "inflam[ing] the children with the doctrines of communism." He is called "a socialist and fanatic," though he accepts a secular Christianity similar to that of the Populists. "Regarding Christ, Feodor Feodorovich states that much about him was rational, that he was a democrat, that he had firm convictions, and that some of his articles of truth were correct. But not all" (6: 11, 14, 15).

Feodor Feodorovich is contrasted with the predatory type, the atheist and egoist, who now becomes the older brother of the "socialist and fanatic." There is also a third younger brother, who listens to the arguments of the other two, and Dostoevsky presents their debates in terms anticipating the great theme of the Legend of the Grand Inquisitor. "The elder brother (He)* in the presence of his wife and younger brother proves to Feodor Feodorovich that Christ had founded society on freedom, and there could be no other freedom but in Christ. And that he, the communist Feodor Feodorovich, is founding his on slavery and

* To avoid confusion, it should be understood that the capitalized "He" in Dostoevsky's notes refers to the "predatory type" who will eventually become Versilov.

idiocy. Feodor Feodorovich is put out as far as the arguments are concerned, but not in his feelings: 'All right, then, so let us accept Christ's system,' he says, 'only let's straighten out a few things about it'"—which is exactly the argument of the Grand Inquisitor a few years later (6: 14–15).

Nonetheless, Feodor Feodorovich's Socialist convictions come very close to expressing the Christian ideal of a society founded on mutual love. To shake his views, "he is told that, in the new society, children will have no father, for there will be no family ('family, that's as good as private property')." But this notion does not bother him at all, and he retorts: "All will be fathers and mothers, and then we won't need to have natural fathers, which, by the way, is almost tantamount to monopoly.'" Someone tells Feodor Feodorovich at this point: "Thou art not far from the Kingdom of God. . . . You have gotten Christianity mixed up with Communism. Even now there are many who prepare this incompatible mixture" (16: 15). The possibility of such confusion made it all the more imperative to dramatize just how "incompatible" such a mixture would turn out to be.

4

Dostoevsky now had a plan for a novel about three brothers, and he was tempted by the possibility of writing what could have become *The Brothers Karamazov*. One note contains an outline that would require only a little reshuffling to fit the later work. "And so," he writes, "one brother is an atheist. Despair. The other is a thoroughgoing fanatic. The third represents the new generation, a living force, new people. He [the youngest brother] was able to withstand Lambert. (And the children, as the youngest generation.)" (16: 16). Ivan Karamazov's outraged rejection of his ticket of admission to a world of eternal harmony based on injustice and suffering is foreshadowed in the defiance of the older brother. "If the way of the world is that something disgusting always has to turn up in place of something pure, then let it all come crashing down: 'I refuse to accept such a world.'" This declaration is followed by the authorial comment: "His whole misfortune lies in the fact that He is an atheist and does not believe in resurrection"—which of course will be the case with Ivan as well (16: 15).

Similarly, the issue of Ivan's "Euclidian understanding," his refusal to accept the mysteries of faith, also appears in this context. "Infinite wisdom crushes the mind of man, but he seeks it. Existence must be unquestionably and in every instance superior to the mind of man. The doctrine that the mind of man is the final limit of the universe is as stupid as stupid can be, and even stupider, infinitely stupider, than a

153

game of checkers between two shopkeepers." Versilov's relation to others, and his interpretation of the love ethic of Christ, also anticipates Ivan Karamazov's Grand Inquisitor. "It is impossible to love people the way they are," he declares. "And yet one must love them, for this is what we are ordered to do (by Christ)." But "people are base, they like to love and to adore from fear," and so he believes that "without any doubt, Christ could not have loved them; he suffered them, he forgave them, but of course he also despised them. . . . Love for mankind must be understood as love for a perfected mankind, one that exists so far only as an ideal, and God only knows if it will ever become reality" (16: 156–157). Numerous references scattered throughout allude to the temptations of Christ in the desert, which Dostoevsky also planned to use. "Of the three temptations of the devil" (16: 35).

Besides such moral-philosophical exchanges, these notes contain a jotting that supplies a first version of the plot line of *The Brothers Karamazov*: "In Tobolsk, about twenty years ago, like the Ilyinsky story." D. I. Ilyinsky had been a fellow prisoner with Dostoevsky in Siberia, a young army officer convicted of the murder of his father solely on circumstantial evidence. Based on his impressions of Ilyinsky's character, he found it difficult to believe him capable of cold-blooded murder, and he was proven right ten years later when a common criminal confessed. The "drama in Tobolsk" also involved an innocent man convicted of the murder of his father, in this instance, the elder of two brothers in love with the same girl.

The younger brother had committed the crime but threw the guilt on the elder, who was sent to Siberia. Twelve years later, the murderer visits the prisoner, and "silently they understand each other." Seven years afterward, the by now honored and titled younger brother confesses the crime to his wife, who pleads with the elder brother to keep silent. He agrees: "You've been punished without this," he tells the younger. But when the conscience-stricken younger brother ultimately confesses and is sent into exile, the elder agrees to be the father of his children (17: 5–6). This extended note, along with the recollection of Ilyinsky, is obviously the nucleus of *The Brothers Karamazov* (an innocent older brother sent to Siberia for a crime committed by a younger one, finally unable to endure his guilt), and indicates how close Dostoevsky came to embarking on such a novel at this point.

Indeed, he was very well aware of this possibility and wrote about it in his *Diary of a Writer* for January 1876. "When Nikolay Alekseyevich Nekrasov asked me to write a novel for *Notes of the Fatherland*," he explained, "I almost began my *Fathers and Children*, but I held back, and thank God I did, for I was not ready. In the meantime, I wrote only *A Raw Youth*, this first attempt at my idea. But here the child had already passed his childhood and appeared only as an unprepared person, timidly yet boldly wanting to take his first step in life as quickly as possible. I took a soul that was sinless yet already tainted by the awful possibility of vice, by a premature hatred of its own insignificance and 'accidental' nature" (22: 7–8).

Why Dostoevsky decided to confine himself to this "first attempt" cannot be explained with any pretense of certainty; but one or two speculations may be offered. He was, after all, toiling over a book to be published in *Notes of the Fatherland*, the journal in which the influential Mikhailovsky had scoffingly objected to the misuse of his talent as evidenced by his preference for sensational subject matter (such as murder). In addition, articles in his *Diary of a Writer* for 1873 had shown his preoccupation with the problem of the younger generation and its search for moral values. From where could these young idealists acquire those values when their fathers had become so morally bankrupt themselves? Such reasons could well have persuaded him to reserve his murder motif for a less problematic venue and to focus instead on the non-lethal but no less pernicious sins of the fathers in failing to impart any life-enhancing moral values to their sons.

## 5

In a note of July 23, 1874, Dostoevsky finally decided on the shape that his next novel would take. "The BOY," he tells himself in capital letters, "and not HE [the predatory type] is the HERO. . . . HE, on the other hand, is only an ACCESSORY, but what an ACCESSORY!" On a separate line, he inscribes the title of his new work: *A Raw Youth*. And so it would remain. Demoting his predatory type to a subordinate role, but already foreseeing the artistic problem that this will entail (a problem, in fact, that was never solved satisfactorily), he decided to write a novel whose theme would be: "The story of a boy, how he arrives, whom he happens to meet, under whose care he is put . . . he dreams of the university, also, the idea to get rich" (16: 24). Somewhat later, shortly after reminding himself to insert "A LARGER ROLE FOR THE YOUTH," he outlines an inner development: "How he studies Nihilism and other things, learning what is good and what is evil" (16: 29, 39). Once Dostoevsky decides to make the boy his central figure, the earlier structure of the relations of his characters immediately begins to evolve. In a passage following his choice of the boy as protagonist, that character and his older brother, the predatory type, become stepbrothers. The future novel distinctly looms into view with a notation of August 7: "An idea. Couldn't He be a contemporary father, and the Youth His Son? (*Think it over*)" (16: 41). So he did, and decided to make this father-son relation the theme of his new novel.

Another note sketches an image of the son that will remain largely unchanged: "The young man arrives smarting from an insult, thirsting for revenge. Colossal vanity, a plan (to become) a Rothschild (his secret)" (16: 24). The "insult" here is still a particular (unspecified) event, but it will become the irresponsible treatment of Arkady by his father all through his early life; and his vanity will take the form, which appears frequently throughout Dostoevsky's works, of "wishing to become a Rothschild" (though it had not received such a label previously).* This motif appears among the earliest notes, and there is an amusing reminder to himself, when he wishes the Youth to expatiate on stock transactions, to *"get the details from Anna Grigoryevna"* (16: 30).

Such a thematic motif—the accumulation of riches—is associated in Dostoevsky's work with the influence of one of Pushkin's "little tragedies," *The Covetous Knight*, which also exercises a powerful influence on the fictional Arkady. The covetous knight, though willing to commit any crime to increase his fortune, was not really interested in wealth as such; he amassed it only to gloat over the unlimited sense of power, whether actually exercised or not, that his riches would allow him to enjoy. This psychological use of the wealth motif appears in Dostoevsky's work as early as 1846 (*Mr. Prokharchin*) and reappears throughout his career. It can be seen in the *Life of a Great Sinner* and is taken over for the character of the raw youth as well. Indeed, one of the notes for this unwritten work may be used to define Arkady's infatuation with his "Rothschild idea": "Sometimes it seemed to him again that in case he did not become extraordinary and were completely ordinary, money would give him everything—that is, power and the right to have contempt—" (9: 136).

Many of the notes made in August 1874 are devoted to developing the character of the future Versilov and his relation to his son, who both resents and loves his father while attempting to comprehend his taunting and unfathomable behavior. This attitude of the raw youth is defined in a note apparently made even before he became the central figure, and, interestingly, it is already cast in the first-person form that Dostoevsky will eventually adopt: "What is He [the future Versilov] up to? Was He simply chattering with me? As if He had no one else to chat

* Great wealth as a source of power became associated in Russian culture with the name of Rothschild probably in the 1850s, when Herzen published a section of his memoirs containing a tongue-in-cheek description of the supreme self-assurance of James Rothschild, the banker who had successfully sued the government of Nicholas I on Herzen's behalf. A bit later, in 1864, Dostoevsky's journal *Epoch* published some chapters from Heinrich Heine's scintillating *On the History of Religion and Philosophy in Germany*, one passage of which recounts, with ironic delectation, the regular visits of the papal envoy to the same James Rothschild in order to pay interest on the papal debt. See Alexander Herzen, *My Past and Thoughts*, trans. Constance Garnett, rev. Humphrey Higgins, 4. vols. (New York, 1968), 2: 757–765); Heinrich Heine, *Samtliche Werke*, 10 vols., ed. Oskar Walzel (Leipzig, 1910), 7: 283–284.

with. I noticed that there was something wrong, yet at the same time, there was so much strained and spent suffering about every one of His escapades, no matter how contrived, that I simply couldn't leave Him or remain indifferent to Him. On the contrary, I was becoming more attached to Him every day" (16: 21). Here are the tone and stance of the raw youth's narrative as it will finally emerge.

Although by now Dostoevsky could see the moral-psychological contours of the Youth quite clearly, his image of the father was very far from possessing the same clarity. He thus sketches a vita for him limited to external facts: "A landowner and the son of a landowner . . . studied at Russian and German universities. Married very young (the facts about his first wife are lost). Served in the army during the Crimean campaign, but not very long and saw no action. Resigned his commission, district commissioner in the administration of the agrarian reform of the first call-up, resigned. Traveled aimlessly abroad. Married a widow, a princess. . . . Stockholder and society figure." There is, however, also a social-cultural delineation: "Remembers Herzen, used to know Belinsky" (16: 50). Versilov will thus be a member of the generation of the 1840s, and through him Dostoevsky will provide another remarkable portrait of its idealism and its moral-spiritual vagaries.

The figure of Alexander Herzen is one of the sources for Versilov, whose ideas incorporate Herzen's pessimism about the fate of European culture—a pessimism, of course, that Dostoevsky fully shared. Nikolay Strakhov, in an important series of essays on Herzen, had characterized him as a Russian type with "a universal heartache for everyone," and Dostoevsky picked up this phrase as an essential component of Versilov's worldview.[2] Another prototype was the figure of P. J. Chaadaev (1794–1856), who had created a furor (and been declared a madman) for having called Russia an orphan among nations because of the poverty of its cultural heritage, particularly its lack of the classical culture handed down in the West by Roman Catholicism. The rumors of Versilov's flirtation with Catholicism derive from Chaadaev's notorious indictment of Russia; and so does the odd suicide of the young man Kraft, unable to live with the thought that Russia is a second-rate nation.[3]

As well as ruminating over his two main figures, he also sketched his minor ones along the way. The character of old Prince Sokolsky, who will employ Arkady as a sort of secretary, is grasped full-grown from the very start—perhaps because Dostoevsky had already portrayed such a doddering, amiable, and highly Westernized member of the Russian gentry in his novella *Uncle's Dream* (1859). "An old chatterbox. Used to be a dandy and with the horse guards. . . . Now he likes to come up with an occasional bon mot, and will point out to an unsuspecting party, with childish (however quite innocent, cheerful) vanity, that he has done just that, come up with a bon mot. . . . He is a capitalist, and a shareholder in a number of companies" (16: 25). Dostoevsky had been criticized by Mikhailovsky for failing to include in his work "the devils" of capitalist development, and he did not intend to expose himself to such charges again.

On the next page, this character is also given a deeper motivation, though still on the comic level. "The prince has been listening to various atheists for a long time, and has become an atheist himself"—which of course would be in conformity with his inbred and well-bred Western-ism. One sample of his "witty" conversation on the topic of God will be transcribed directly into the novel: "And, finally, if it is really as you say [his interlocutor is probably Arkady], then prove to me, so I can see it, or as they say, have a sensation of it. All right if He (God) exists in person, and not in the form of an effusion of spirit or something (for I must admit, that is even more difficult for me to understand), then what does He wear? How tall is He? Don't be angry, my dear, naturally I have a right to ask the question, for if He is a God, a personal God, i.e., a person, then how tall is he, *et enfin*, where does he live?" (16: 25–26). Dostoevsky thus juxtaposes a comically fatuous atheist with a serious one like Versilov, emotionally torn by his inability to believe; and he also foreshadows the literal questioning of the supernatural that will be displayed more sarcastically by Feodor Pavlovich Karmazov.

The old Prince Sokolsky is also contrasted with a young prince of the same name, in whom the harmless oddities of the doddering *bon vivant* have deteriorated into vices. "The young prince is a fop, disorganized, the last of the family and a degenerate, a spendthrift and a gambler, secretly a coward. . . . Shoots himself. Exalted and sincere dreams about the essence of being a nobleman, and a nobleman's calling, also about how he is going to marry Liza" (the sister of the raw youth, whom he seduces) (16: 240). The young prince plays out the ignominious role as-signed him here, adding to the misdeeds his denunciation of the Derga-chev group to the authorities and his failure to marry Liza before his suicide.

Many pages in the notes are taken up with conversations about So-cialism among Arkady, Versilov, and Vasin (sometimes also called Vitia), who belongs to the Dergachev circle. Completely absorbed by, and committed to, his "Rothschild idea," Arkady is yet eager to learn about these other ideas of which he knows nothing, and he "asks questions about Socialism: he is particularly impressed by the abolition of private property." His friend Vitia, only meagerly informed himself, "introduces him to somebody like Dolgushin, a gathering of young people who carry on discussions about 'normal man' (they are later arrested). He does not agree with Socialism: it is against nature." But although Versilov can at one moment support the arrest of the group, "he immediately confuses [Arkady] again by pointing out the grandeur of the idea of Socialism. For a while, the Youth is actually carried away," presumably by this ideal (16: 46). It is impossible to determine from the notes how far Dostoevsky intended this temporary commitment of Arkady to go.

In another note, we are given the effect of this influence on Arkady, who now defends the Dergachevtsy when Versilov accuses them of being "another instance of moral disorder." The Youth retorts: "Let them be wrong . . . yet their convictions imply honor and duty, and consequently there can be no talk of disorder in this instance." Versilov then remarks ironically: "Convictions implying honor and duty, and aimed at universal destruction; that's some fine order for you; however I don't want to argue with you" (16: 81). In fact, other notes present the Dergachevtsy as opposed to any such universal destruction. At a meeting of the group, when a young man "gets up and suggests that the moral question rests with the fact that it won't matter at all if even all of France were to perish and that millions of people won't matter either, etc., Dolgushin [Dergachev] and the rest won't agree with him" (16: 65). Another member advocates "setting a fire to all the cities and villages all over the land, make that the beginning," but he turns out to be an *agent provocateur* ("it is the spy who says this; some others argue with him") (16: 80). Dostoevsky knew that the generation of the 1870s was no longer captivated by Nechaevism, and Versilov expresses this new outlook explicitly: "Who are they [the radicals] to negate things? With them, even the negation of religion has been turned into a religion."

Versilov finally counters Arkady's attraction to the Socialist ideal with arguments that develop those (already cited) anticipating the Legend of the Grand Inquisitor. Human life should not be seen exclusively in relation to the ideal of "usefulness" and the satisfaction of man's material needs: "I agree that to feed humanity is at a given moment a great idea also, for it implies a goal. But it is a secondary and subordinate idea, for the moment man is fed, he is certain to ask: 'What am I living for?'" (16: 44–45). The relation to the future Legend is explicit when Versilov repeats elsewhere: "I know that the moment I shall have turned stones into bread and feed mankind, man will immediately ask: 'All right, then, I have satisfied my hunger, what shall we do now?'" (16: 283).

There are also several references to what are called "Genevan ideas," and Versilov explains them to Arkady in the novel. "The 'Genevan ideas' concern the idea of virtue without Christ, dear boy," he says, "the French ideas of the present day—or better—the idea dominating the whole of present-day civilization" (16: 281). In opposition, Versilov's "main desire," we read in the notes, "is to explain to people that vice is not repugnant at all. He hates those Genevan ideas (i.e., a love of man, i.e., virtue without Christ) and refuses to recognize that there is anything natural about virtue. The Youth is taken aback, but his aunts tell him that this is an argument *a contrario*, and that it must be taken in the opposite sense" (16: 35).

But the Youth quite rightly surmises that Versilov's words should not be taken only as a rhetorical strategy. For Versilov then insists, like Ivan Karamazov, that "inasmuch as I am an honest and conscientious man, I sincerely favor (under the conditions of atheism) crime and destruction, nor have I any use for those Genevan ideas" (16: 35–36). It is precisely because Versilov is "honest and conscientious" that he becomes an advocate of vice and crime when atheism wipes out, as it invariably does for Dostoevsky, the basis of all morality. (Though why Versilov employs terms like "honest" and "conscientious" when all morality has ceased to exist remains unexplained; perhaps it indicates the *impossibility* for human consciousness to eliminate moral categories entirely.)* Another reference to "Genevan ideas" illuminates the deceptive similarity between Christianity and Socialism: "Of the relationship between Socialism and Christianity, about the fact that Socialism is trying to conceal, by putting forward a series of Genevan ideas, that its ideal is, in spite of everything, nothing else than material prosperity; on the environment, etc." (16: 164). The "virtue" embodied in "Genevan ideas," their moral-social humanitarianism, masks the true, crudely materialistic aims of Socialism.

Many of the notes cited here are taken from dialogues between the father (Versilov) and his natural son, Arkady, in which Dostoevsky tries to work out the terms of their relationship. At first Versilov resembles characters like Prince Valkovsky in *The Insulted and Injured* or Svidrigailov in *Crime and Punishment*; they are both examples of the predatory type, though the latter is closer to some of Versilov's complexity. Like Rousseau, Versilov, too, "would derive a perverse pleasure from baring his innermost secrets before the Youth, actually corrupting him by his frank revelations" (16: 40). But too much of such behavior would clash with Versilov's genuine claim to a certain amount of spiritual dignity—a claim that the Youth was meant to respond to despite all his indignation and resentments. "BUT WHAT IS MOST IMPORTANT," Dostoevsky reminds himself, "retain throughout the entire narrative a tone of His unchallenged superiority over the Youth and everybody else, all His comical traits and all His weaknesses notwithstanding; let the reader feel all along that, at the end of the novel, He is tormented by a

---

* I should like to thank Gary Saul Morson for having pointed out to me the paradox contained in Versilov's statement, which will apply equally well to Ivan Karamazov.

great idea. And motivate the reality of His suffering" (16: 43). Dostoevsky thus gradually abandoned the original notion of Versilov as a predatory type in order to convey a sense of his moral stature. To motivate the reality of Versilov's suffering, however, he falls back on the distressingly trite plot intrigue of his romantic entanglements.

## 6

From the notes made during August 1874, the characters of both Versilov and the Youth emerge much as they will appear in the final text. The Youth is defined by his "Rothschild idea," though this will be softened by accounts of the pathos of his childhood. "1st, the childhood of the Youth (absolutely)," Dostoevsky writes, "in a number of fragments throughout the novel, cursorily, how they used to beat him at the boarding school. . . . Later, about how the idea of alienation was conceived by him early—when he was dreaming of becoming king of an island known to no one, near the Pole, or in the middle of a lake in Central Africa" (16: 93). Versilov is characterized by both his charm and a fundamental inability to take his own convictions seriously. "Thus, for instance, he is an atheist, yet suddenly he is explaining the Sermon on the Mount, though it comes to no decision. On the advent of communism ('What will save the world?—Beauty.' But always with a sneer)" (16: 43).

If Dostoevsky has grasped his two main characters with more or less clarity, the same cannot be said for his plot structure. Sometime around August 7–8, he attempted to sum up his results: "It turns out that he [Versilov] is involved in some frightfully base actions, very nearly a plot, against the princess (think up something)." The princess will eventually become Katerina Akhmakova, and the parenthetical phrase betrays his uncertainty about just what dastardly deeds will be concocted against her. Unfortunately, he can think of nothing better than the most shopworn devices of the penny dreadful: "The Youth himself, having found the letters [which ask about the possibility of the princess having her father, old Prince Sokolsky, declared mentally incompetent], thinks up a scheme to put the princess in a tight spot, and explains his idea to Lambert. He is scared by the way in which Lambert accepted this idea" (which includes blackmail not only for money but also for sexual favors) (16: 42–43). This is the outline of what will, alas, motivate much of the definitive plot intrigue.

Up through mid-August, the notes contain nothing about narrative technique, and one assumes that he intended to cast the book in the third person, perhaps intermingled with first-person insertions from the diary of the Youth similar to the one already cited. But on August 12, following a few paragraphs sketching the Youth's fascination with his "Rothschild idea" and the inquiries he was making about Socialism, a note appears, beginning with the sentence: "AN IMPORTANT SOLUTION OF THE PROBLEM." The "problem" was how best to present the inner development of the Youth, who had now become his main character. The solution is given in the next sentence: "Write in the first person. Start with the word 'I.'" This injunction is followed by a subtitle, "Confession of a great sinner, for himself," and then by a sample opening of a few sentences in which the I-narrator explains why he is taking pen in hand: "For myself, many years hence (for I shall live a long life), I shall understand all the facts much better, but this manuscript will even then help me to know myself better, etc." A few lines later, he tries a sample sentence that stresses the Youth's lack of literary pretensions ("I am writing without paying attention to style, but just for myself"), and he remarks that "the confession is extraordinarily concise (learn from Pushkin)." Dostoevsky sees the character of the Youth "emerging by itself—through the awkwardness of the narrative"; and "just as in the *Tales of Belkin* it is Belkin himself who matters the most, so here, too, it is the primary objective to delineate the character of the Youth" (16: 47–48).

These words appear to establish a definite choice of a first-person narrator, but numerous other notes continue to weigh the alternatives. Should he use a third-person narrator, who would adhere as closely to the Youth as was done in *Crime and Punishment* for Raskolnikov? Or was the first person preferable? But could the reader tolerate the limited perspective of a twenty-year-old narrator throughout a long novel? Its advantage would be that he could skip "from the main line of the narrative to all kinds of anecdotes and details, proper to his [the Youth's] development and immaturity" (16: 98). Probably the clinching argument against a third-person narrator was the concern that the raw youth would become a secondary figure and "He the most important" (16: 115). To avoid this quagmire, Dostoevsky chose a first-person narrator.

Such a choice, however, raised the additional question of narrative distance. Alternating between three months, four or five years, and one year, he decides that the first would be too short because either the narrative would be confused or "the resulting conscious purpose would lose its naïveté" (16: 128). Four or five years would be too long, perhaps even comic, because the narrator would be "describing with great condescension . . . how foolish he used to be." The distance of a year was best because "the whole impact of a recent shock would still be apparent, and a good many things will still remain unclear, yet at the same time there would be this first line: 'A year, what a tremendous interval of time!'" (16: 144). A year it would remain—a year that would bring about a crucial change in Arkady, indeed, a new maturity, but he would still be close enough to his past so that its reverberations in his sensibility had not yet vanished.

7
———

Even while pondering the question of narrative technique, Dostoevsky also made a major thematic addition—one of such importance that he refers to his previous plans as "an earlier novel," as if he had replaced them by "a new story" (16: 117). A new character suddenly appears, Makar Ivanovich Dolgoruky, who has not been seen before and is the legal peasant father of the Youth. Fitting neatly into the family structure already established, his invention, despite Dostoevsky's annotation, did not require the major alteration that he implies. "Makar Ivanov [his name will soon be altered] an old-time house serf, is dead. He lived a pious life. After February 19, 1861 [the date of the liberation of the serfs] he spent his time collecting funds to build a church [like Nekrasov's Vlas]. He had come back to Petersburg to die at the family residence" (16: 117). Versilov's illegitimate children all legally belong to Makar; their mother is Makar's legal wife, an attractive peasant girl married off to a much older man and whom her master had seduced in time-honored Russian fashion. "The mother," Dostoevsky writes, "a Russian type (a tremendous character). They [the peasant pair] can be downtrodden and humble, and firm, like saints" (16: 121). For the first time, the world of peasant Russia thus enters a Dostoevsky novel, no longer simply as part of the background but as a central thematic component.

Dostoevsky's notebook entries regarding this peasant world range much more widely than the more limited picture in the finished work. In one, he demonstrates his acquaintance with the theology of the Old Believers. "Enoch is the natural law," he writes, "Elias is written law, and John is the law of grace (the doctrine of the *bezpopovtsy)"* (16: 137). The *bezpopovtsy* were Old Believers with no established priesthood, and the doctrine he cites bears a remarkable resemblance to the extraordinarily influential, semiheretical teachings of the Italian abbot Joachim di Fiore in the Western religious tradition.* Other notes contain extensive entries about "stinking Lizaveta," who is much more vividly

---

* Joachim di Fiore developed a view of history based on the Trinity, in which "the first age was that of the Father or the Law; the second age that of the Son or the Gospel; the third age would be the Age of the spirit . . . [one] of love, joy, and freedom, when the knowledge of God would be revealed directly to the hearts of all men." This doctrine exercised an enormous influence and can be seen at work, in various secular forms, in nineteenth-century philosophies of history. See Norman Cohn, *The Pursuit of the Millennium* (New York, 1970), 108–109; also Karl Löwith, *Meaning in History* (Chicago, 1949), 145–159.

developed here than she will be in *The Brothers Karamazov*. Not merely an inarticulate half-wit, she is consumed by the self-immolating fire of a passionate faith. "Stinking Lizaveta. 'Do not send me, the stinking one, to your bright paradise, but send me into utter darkness, so that even there, in fire and in pain, I could raise my voice to Thee: "Holy, holy art Thou," and I have no other love'" (16: 138).

The appearance of Makar and his wife in Dostoevsky's notes—he enjoins himself to write about them "in a sweet scriptural style" (16: 137)—finally allowed him to obtain a more balanced focus on his religious-ideological thematic. Two days later, he sketches out the novel as he now sees it, clarifying the symbolic meaning of each of its components:

> The novel contains all the elements of our society. Civilized and desperate, idle and skeptical, the higher intelligentsia—that's HIM [Versilov]. Ancient Holy Russia—Makar's family. What is holy, good about new Russia—the aunts [these later disappear]. A great family gone to seed, the young prince (a skeptic, etc.). High society—the funny and the abstractly ideal type. The young generation—the Youth, all instinct, knows nothing. Vasin [the Socialist] hopelessly ideal. Lambert—flesh, matter, horror, etc." (16: 28)

Initially, Dostoevsky had seen his novel as dominated by "the idea of disintegration" that was "present everywhere, for everything is falling apart and there are no remaining ties not only in the Russian family, but even simply between people in general. Even children are apart" (16: 16). Much of this sense of dissolution will be kept in the book, whose title he once thought could be *Disorder*; but with the inclusion of Makar and his legal wife, Sofya, the humble, downtrodden pair who would be firm as saints, he at last found a center of moral stability amidst the reigning chaos.

Such a center was essential because of the very nature of his theme: the precipitous growth into maturity of a rebellious adolescent who has been badly bruised by the vicissitudes of his haphazard boyhood and youth as a member of "an accidental family" but who learns to accept himself and to acquire a sense of social responsibility. Just how this transformation was to be motivated remained unclear in the earlier plans, as Arkady oscillates between Versilov, his "Rothschild idea," and the Socialism of the Dergachevtsy. "The Youth has the feeling that [Versilov's] idea is higher, more proud and noble than his own," but Versilov himself refuses to offer any clear direction. He undermines "the Rothschild idea," however, by pointing out that it "contains a rather contemptible element of petty concern with one's own material security" (16: 101). And while the Youth's faith "is shaken by Socialism[,] he wants to retain his 'Rothschild idea' and yet remain a noble human being."

Socialism does not provide the moral inspiration he needs to conquer his ego and surrender it to a higher ideal, an inspiration that could only be offered by religious faith (16: 175). Makar admirably fills this function, and Dostoevsky indicates his source by a line from Nekrasov's poem "Vlas": "dark-visaged, tall, and straight." Dostoevsky thus ingeniously introduces into the pages of Nekrasov's own journal a figure based on Nekrasov's famous creation—a figure that both caters to the reverence for the peasantry nourished by the radical Populists and also strongly accentuates the religious origins of those peasant virtues they so admired.

With the appearance of Makar Ivanovich Dolgoruky, Dostoevsky found the underlying moral-ideological relationship among his characters that he had been searching for, and a note in mid-October contains a summary outline of the book approximating the final text. He also admonishes himself to adhere to two rules of composition. One is "to avoid the mistake, made in *The Idiot* and *The Devils*, of describing many of the secondary events in a fragmentary, insinuated, romancelike manner, and dragging them out over a lengthy extension of the novel both in the narrated action as well as in individual scenes, without giving any explanations at all." The second is to remember that "the Youth is the hero of the novel. Everything else is secondary, even He [Versilov] is secondary" (16: 175). Whether his lack of "explanations" was really an artistic defect may well be questioned; his genius lay in dramatic scenes or self-confessions that explain themselves. As for the second reminder, it refers to a problem of which he had been aware from the very first.

The notebooks continue beyond this point for several hundred pages; but these jottings are all devoted to working out the laborious plot intrigue, which Dostoevsky endlessly alters in his usual fashion, or to filling in details of scenes and conversations. Even though no fundamental changes are made, however, they still provide valuable information about accessory aspects of the text.

## 8

In the 1870s Russia was rapidly being transformed by a wave of rampant industrialism that undermined its formerly peasant-based economy, and Dostoevsky had already examined some of the morally disintegrating effects of this change in his 1873 *Diary*. Mikhailovsky, as we have noted, had also chastised him for neglecting such topics in his novels; and in addition to the portrayal of the old prince, Dostoevsky also drew on a recent criminal case to dramatize this aspect of his theme.

Sometime in early December 1874 (the first chapters of *A Raw Youth* were published in January 1875), the name of Kolosov appears among

the notes. He is a swindler "who has launched some forged stock certificates . . . a liberal of the 1850s, conceited and very sure of himself"
(16: 250). Kolosov is the prototype of the obtrusive and sinisterly jovial
character Stebelkov, and contemporary readers would have had no
trouble recognizing him as one of the accused in a sensational court
case involving the forgery of stock certificates for the Tambovo-Kozlov-
skoi railway line. The stock-forging scheme was prosecuted by Dostoevsky's close friend A. F. Koni, and all of the features of Stebelkov are
taken directly from the trial. These include what may seem Stebelkov's
rather implausible connection with the secret police, which motivates
his questions to Arkady several times about the Dergachev group.

On trial with Kolosov was the scion of an old landowning family, Niki-
tin by name, who held the post of librarian at the army medical academy. His part in the whole affair was a relatively minor one, and it has
been plausibly suggested that Dostoevsky took some details from his
testimony to characterize the young Prince Serge Sokolsky, hopelessly
indebted to Stebelkov and completely in his clutches. Also, just before
quitting *The Citizen*, Dostoevsky wrote Prince Meshchersky, "I . . . terribly much wished to write about Olga Ivanovna [the fiancée of one of
the accused] involved in the trial for the forgery of the Tambovo shares,
as about a representative example of Nihilism in its most disgusting and
fullest form, unconsciously corroding a girl who may never even have
heard of Nihilism, and to point her out as a sign of the time."[4]

The notebooks are also sprinkled with literary references that Dostoevsky threw off along the way as he gradually clarified both his thematic ideas and the novelistic means by which they were to be expressed. References to Pushkin abound, and what most hovered before
Dostoevsky as a goal was the classic concision and limpidity of Pushkin's prose. "Write more tightly," he enjoins himself. "(Imitate Pushkin)"
(16: 172). To reassure himself about his choice of theme, he thinks
of other examples of novels with roughly the same aim: "And all together, the whole novel through the person of the Youth who is seeking
the truth of life (*Gil Blas* and *Don Quixote*) could be most attractive"
(16: 63).

A great reader of Dickens, Dostoevsky refers to *David Copperfield*,
also the story of a hapless young boy struggling to find his way to manhood and maturity; but he contrasts the festering resentment and aggressiveness of his raw youth with the amiable and sweet-tempered
David (16: 234). *The Old Curiosity Shop* appears in the text itself, when
Dostoevsky rewrites the famous scene in which little Nell, awakening in
the morning, walks out into the graveyard of the village church in which
she and her grandfather have at last found peace and tranquillity. A
reworking of an equally famous scene, that of Gretchen's death in *Faust*,

also surfaces in the drunken maunderings of Trishatov, who dreams of composing an opera based on the Faust theme and narrates his ideas at length in the text.

Allusions to numerous other writers, both Russian and European, appear in the notes, but before discussing the most important of all, Tolstoy, a word should be said about the playwright A. S. Griboyedov. Arkady's first encounter with his father at the age of ten occurs as Versilov, about to take part in some amateur theatricals, is resplendently dressed to impersonate a character in Griboyedov's classic comedy *Woe from Wit* (1822). This character, Chatsky, is an early incarnation of an intransigent Westernizer, who, returning to Russia after living abroad, finds provincial life in his homeland intolerable and utters a raging denunciation against its backwardness and immobility. Versilov is identified with this ideological aura of Chatsky from the very start, thus establishing his symbolic "Westernizer" significance.

## 9

The writer mentioned most frequently in Dostoevsky's notes is Tolstoy, and these references are central to his artistic aims. Much of *A Raw Youth* is derived from the *Life of a Great Sinner*, where the boyhood of this character was conceived squarely in opposition to Tolstoy's treatment of the same theme. "A type," he wrote, "entirely contrary to the scion of that noble family of counts, degenerate to the point of swinishness, which Tolstoy had depicted in *Childhood and Boyhood*" (9: 128). Once Dostoevsky had fixed on an adolescent as his hero and began to draw on his notes for the great sinner's early years, he was again writing in direct competition with Tolstoy. His desire to pick up the artistic gauntlet had certainly been strengthened recently by the acclaim accorded to *Anna Karenina*.

Dostoevsky would not have felt challenged by Tolstoy, of course, if he had not held him in the very highest esteem, and several notes indicate an unbiased appreciation of his artistic mannerisms. In one entry, when Arkady impulsively goes to kiss his aunt, Dostoevsky writes: "But the aunt is asleep. Nightcap, drooping lip. (Leo Tolstoy)" (16: 73). Evidently, he wished to capture some of the vividness of Tolstoy's depiction of physical features. Of another scene he remarks: "Absolutely include in the Youth's narrative a description of this rendezvous and its settings, with details à la Leo Tolstoy" (16: 87). Where he differed from Tolstoy, however, was in his desire to depict the instability and chaos of contemporary Russian life. As he had written to Nikolay Strakhov three years earlier, both Turgenev and Tolstoy had created only "gentry-landowner literature. It has said everything that it had to say (superbly by Lev

Tolstoy), . . . but there has not yet been a new word to replace that of the gentry-landowners."[5] He certainly saw himself as endeavoring to supply such a "new word" that would go beyond what the gentry writers had accomplished.

Whether he originally intended to enter into more than a covert rivalry with Tolstoy cannot be determined from his notes. If not, he was certainly goaded into doing so in the course of defending himself against some of the hostile attacks provoked by the publication of his first chapters. One critic accused him of excessive "naturalism"—a naturalism so extreme that it violated the rules of art, as if Dostoevsky wished his readers to feel that they were literally participating in the events being depicted, no matter how menacing or threatening. Two venomous articles in the *Russian Messenger*, where his own earlier novels had been published, accused him of being "immoral" and of fixing "the reader in the stinking atmosphere of the underground, [which] little by little, against the intentions of the author and perhaps in spite of them, blunts his sense of smell and accustoms him to this stinking underground."[6]

He was quite understandably upset by such attacks, and particularly the accusation that he was corrupting his readers. His first impulse, which he confided to his notebooks on March 22, 1875, was to answer such denigrations in a preface to be included with the novel's later publication in book form; and the notes for this preface contain the most illuminating self-definitions that he ever gave of his own artistic mission. As he puts it, his aim was to depict the moral-spiritual consequences of living in a society that "had no foundations," and which in fact "hasn't worked out any rules of life, because there really hasn't been any life either." This society has experienced "a colossal shock—and everything comes to a halt, falls down, and is negated as if it hadn't ever existed. And not just externally, as in the West, but internally, morally." Meanwhile, "our most talented writers [he mentions Tolstoy and Goncharov] have been describing the life of the upper middle class," believing they were "describing the life of the majority." But this was an illusion: the life they portray is that "of exceptions, while mine is the life of the general rule" (16: 329).

Dostoevsky speaks of "the civic feeling" that for a moment had led him to think of joining the Slavophils "with the idea of resurrecting the dreams of my childhood" (which included his reverence for Saints Sergius and Tikhon). But instead, he created the underground man, for whom he is now being insulted. "I am proud," he defiantly proclaims, "to have exposed, for the first time, the real image of the Russian majority . . . its misshapen and tragic aspects. *The tragic lies in one's awareness of being misshapen*" (italics added). Listing characters created by other writers (including Prince Bolkonsky of *War and Peace* and Levin in *Anna Karenina*), he sees their defects as arising solely from "petty self-love," which can be corrected according to the fixed social norms of their still unshaken moral-social order. Only *he* had brought out "the tragedy of the underground, which consists of suffering, self-laceration, an awareness of a better life coupled with the impossibility of attaining it. . . . What can sustain those who do try to improve themselves? A reward, faith? Nobody is offering any reward, and in whom could one have faith? Another step from this position, and you have extreme depravity, crime (murder). A mystery" (16: 329).

For him, the most crucial problem of all was the loss of (religious) faith; and he believed that by his attempts to grapple artistically with the moral-social aftermaths of this deprivation he had probed more deeply into the Russian psyche than the gentry-landowner writers who simply accepted the values of their long-established world, with its precepts for good behavior (16: 329). Far from flinching at the charges made against him, Dostoevsky glories in the validity of his moral-artistic vision: "Underground, underground, poet of the underground, our feuilletonists have been repeating over and over again, as if this were something derogatory to me. Silly fools, it is my glory, for that's where the truth lies" (16: 329).

Quickly abandoning the idea of a preface, he then thought of incorporating his self-defense rather implausibly into one of Versilov's monologues. "My friend," he says to Arkady in this version, "if I were a Russian writer of talent, I would definitely take my heroes from among the Russian hereditary nobility, for it is only among this particular type of Russian people that there is a possibility of finding, if not order, at least a semblance of beautiful order and of that very 'harmonious life' which you and I have been looking for" (16: 414–415). He then juxtaposes this world of established forms of honor and duty with the existence of children "who even in their childhood are hurt by the unseemliness of their fathers and their whole environment. We've got too many such underground people" (16: 416).

The dubious notion of giving such a speech to Versilov was rapidly discarded, and Dostoevsky finally confided his self-defense to an epilogue, written not by Arkady but by a very minor character, Nikolay Semyenovich, Arkady's guardian during his high school years. The manuscript is thus submitted for evaluation to someone standing outside all the intricate entanglements of the plot, a solid and respectable citizen whose unpretentious observations and sympathy with Arkady inspire confidence and respect. Nikolay Semyenovich, all the same, is still part of the novel, and some question has been raised as to whether the opinions expressed in his letter should be accepted as those of Dostoevsky himself.

The notes leave no ambiguity on this point; and they also refer explicitly to Tolstoy, whose name is absent from text. "IN THE FINALE," Dostoevsky writes. "The Youth: 'I let a certain person read my notes, and here is what he told me' (and here, quote the author's opinion [that of Nikolay Semyenovich], *that is, my own*). And instead of the traditional family (the Rostovs), a family springing up, an ephemeral family, new, seeking seemliness, seeking to find its own level and even (new) form" (16: 409–410; italics added). The same opposing and contrasting relation to Tolstoy is expressed succinctly in another note: "A history of the Russian noble family, in the form of a majestic historical canvas (*War and Peace*), which flows into posterity and without which posterity could not carry on. An accidental family—that's a much more difficult task" (16: 435). It was precisely this "much more difficult task" that Dostoevsky chose to undertake.

## CHAPTER 10

# *A Raw Youth*: Dostoevsky's
# Trojan Horse

*A Raw Youth* is a curious hybrid of a novel and represents something of an anomaly among the great creations of Dostoevsky's last period. Written between *The Devils* and *The Brothers Karamazov*, it is far from attaining the artistic stature of these two works, although its severest critics may have considerably exaggerated its defects. *A Raw Youth* unquestionably contains some extremely effective and moving scenes of childhood in Dostoevsky's best "philanthropic" manner; and his inner portrait of a rebellious adolescent is often quite touching and persuasive. The book is also distinguished by his most modulated and sympathetic depiction of a member of the Romantic Idealist generation of the 1840s, a portrait that rises to a visionary height of lyrical pathos. All too much of the text, however, relies on a moth-eaten melodramatic plot that swamps the stretches of genuine feeling and ideological elevation.

Why should *A Raw Youth* slump so markedly when compared with Dostoevsky's other major novels? Writers, even great ones, do not necessarily produce masterpieces each time they put pen to paper; but some answer may perhaps be located in the implicit self-censorship that he here exercised on his creative faculties. He was not working freely, as he had always done in the past, and following his inspiration wherever it might lead. Rather, he was writing under the pressure of his commitment to *Notes of the Fatherland*, the leading Populist organ that was carrying on the social-cultural tradition against which he had fought all through the 1860s.

To be sure, for the reasons already explained, Dostoevsky undertook this commitment quite voluntarily. But such a choice of venue inclined him to adapt his inspiration to the literary and ideological standards of his Populist readers. He therefore reduced the theme of parricide to that of parental irresponsibility and substituted a relatively innocent and boyishly illusory romantic rivalry between father and son for the merciless oedipal clash in *The Brothers Karamazov* that so impressed Freud. In other words, he decided to write a social-psychological novel of relatively limited range rather than dramatize the collision of conflicting moral-spiritual absolutes that invariably inspired his best work.

## 2

*A Raw Youth* combines elements of both the picaresque novel and the *Bildungsroman* (novel of education). The protagonist is a young man, the illegitimate son of a Russian nobleman of ancient lineage and a serf mother, who is thrown for the first time into a worldly milieu and, under the impact of his experiences, acquires maturity and self-knowledge. In both types of novel, extended stretches of time are required for their action to be accomplished. The picaresque hero must come into contact with a wide range of adventures up and down the social scale, and a transition to maturity can be completed only over an extended period. In *A Raw Youth*, however, Dostoevsky treats his subject with his usual *roman-feuilleton* technique. He compresses events into a brief span of time, strives for tightly plotted effects of mystery and surprise, and creates a world in which characters exist in a constant state of heightened emotional tension. This supercharged atmosphere is quite appropriate for Dostoevsky's other major novels, in which his eschatological vision of human life blends with his crime-thriller plotting to create a unity of dramatic suspense, psychological verisimilitude, and moral-philosophical profundity. But when the same treatment is accorded a subject of lesser scope, where the conflicts are hardly of the same magnitude, the tragedy becomes melodrama and the sustained heightening of tone is apt to seem exaggeratedly inflated.

With a central figure whose life involved some supreme moral-metaphysical ambition, it was relatively easy to invent a plot action (or to borrow an existing one, as in *The Devils*) that would be both spectacular and true to character. Where the mainspring of the theme is devoid of any such ambition, it is difficult to invent convincing action that both creates extreme dramatic tension and is psychologically plausible. Dostoevsky, alas, takes the easy way out in *A Raw Youth* and stuffs it with all sorts of hackneyed plot ingredients (concealed letters, lawsuits over disputed inheritances, attempts at blackmail, and so on), which allow him to whip up excitement by means that are purely superficial and external. Moreover, he never succeeded in integrating his main thematic concerns with such shopworn devices. Instead of the deeper motifs emerging naturally from the plot action, as they do elsewhere, they appear as extraneous intrusions in the form of static monologues and inset stories.

If some of the defects of *A Raw Youth* may be ascribed to the decision to write for a Populist journal, this place of publication also gives a special interest to many details of the text. For *A Raw Youth* is Dostoevsky's first artistic response to the challenges posed by the new phase of Russian culture inaugurated by the ideology of Russian Populism. Indeed, while narrating the peripeties by which his youthful hero comes to manhood, he interweaves them with what he felt to be the glaring anomaly at the heart of Populist values—their recognition of the Christian moral ideals of the peasant world they idolized, and yet their refusal to accept the very foundation of this world in the divinity of Christ. *A Raw Youth*, if read in this perspective, thus becomes a kind of Trojan horse introduced into the very journalistic citadel of the former enemy to undermine its last defenses.

## 3

*A Raw Youth* is written as a first-person confessional memoir by the title character, Arkady Dolgoruky, the natural son of Andrey Petrovich Versilov, a once-wealthy aristocrat now down on his luck (he has already run through three fortunes) and a philosophical seeker after truth. Arkady sets out, a year after the events have occurred, to recount the circumstances that have brought about a change in his life and transformed his character. These circumstances all took place in a period of six months after his arrival in Petersburg from Moscow to join his family and are compressed within twelve days, leaping from September and November to December. Through the carefully arranged "disorder" of Arkady's narration (he is constantly apologizing for his lack of literary skill), all of the relevant past is included in so-called digressions. Taking full advantage of the time sequence of the memoir form, which narrates events from a point later than when they occurred, Arkady-as-narrator obviously knows the outcome of the episodes that he recounts; but his naïve determination to stick to "the facts" as they appeared to him *then*, allows Dostoevsky to preserve the suspense element of his story. At the same time, Arkady-as-narrator slips in evaluations of the behavior of Arkady-as-character, and by the end he writes: "I have suddenly become aware that I have reeducated myself through the process of recalling events and writing them down" (13: 417).

The major plot involves Versilov and the nineteen-year-old Arkady, who has just come to live with his family (his unmarried peasant mother, Sofya, and equally illegitimate sister, Liza). Arkady carries a letter entrusted to him and sewn into his jacket that compromises Katerina Akhmakova, the beautiful widow of a general and a princess in her own right. The letter asks for legal advice about committing her

elderly father, Prince Sokolsky, to an institution for the mentally enfee-
bled; and she fears that, if he learns of this document, she will be cut
out of his will. Both Katerina and Versilov are in search of this letter
and rightly suspect that Arkady possesses it or can lead them to its
whereabouts.

Two other subplots also run through the book, each concerning another child of Versilov's. One centers on his legitimate daughter by his
deceased first wife, Anna Andreyevna, who has designs on the addle-
pated Prince Sokolsky. The enormously wealthy prince is an ardent but,
by this time, quite harmless admirer of female pulchritude, and the
helpless prince is eventually kidnapped by the much younger Anna,
who plans to marry him and ensure her future. A second subplot focuses on Arkady's sister, Liza, who has an affair with the *young* Prince
Sokolsky and becomes pregnant by this well-meaning but flighty and
spineless aristocratic scion.

All these plots illustrate the moral chaos of Russian society, especially
of its upper class; each reveals some infraction or violation of the normal family structure or of the moral code governing relations between
the sexes. Also, each subplot is meant to bring out, as is typical for
Dostoevsky, the significance of the main one by modulation and contrast. Arkady, who has become madly infatuated with the ravishing Katerina and is troubled by his sexual stirrings, is tempted to behave like
Anna Andreyevna and to blackmail the haughty Katerina into sexual
submission in exchange for the letter. Versilov and the two Princes Sokolsky are similar in their weakness for the fair sex; but Versilov, for all
his personal failings, is endowed with a moral-philosophical dimension
completely beyond the range of the others. He is also carelessly contemptuous about money, whereas the old prince is on the board of various stock companies and the younger one is in the clutches of the unscrupulous swindler and stock forger Stebelkov.

At the center of the book is Arkady, whose problems have been interpreted by one commentator as arising from a crisis of puberty.[1] Some
justification for this view can be found in Dostoevsky's remark that he
had created his "raw youth" as "tainted also by that breadth of character with which a still chaste soul already consciously allows vice to enter
its thoughts . . . in shameful but bold and tempestuous dreams—and
with all this, left solely to his own devices and its own understanding,
yet also, to be sure, with God" (22: 7–8). Arkady is certainly undergoing
such a crisis, but to view this motif as primary is to substitute our own,
sexually hyperconscious twenty-first-century outlook for that of Dostoevsky. More important, in my view, is that Arkady is left "solely to
[his] own devices" and has nowhere to turn for moral guidance and
support. His sexuality is physically but not thematically primary; it is

the biological manifestation of life's challenge to his sense of values and moral conscience.

With his mixture of justified exasperation and scarcely suppressed rage, his quasi-comical and self-glorifying aspiration toward dominance and power, Arkady is an adolescent (and much less articulate) variation of the underground man. He is a touching and sympathetic figure, not a grotesque *persona* acting out one or another dead end of Russian radical ideology. Determined to live as a self-proclaimed egoist and to isolate himself entirely from society, he hopes to amass a fortune and "to become a Rothschild." Once having scaled such a financial height, he will have gained absolute power over the whole world—or rather, the "consciousness" of such power. These self-glorifying intentions, inspired by Pushkin's *The Covetous Knight*, are nothing but the pitiful, compensatory daydreams of a poor, neglected schoolboy left to fend for himself emotionally and constantly humiliated because of his irregular parentage. Dostoevsky thus grounds Arkady's "underground" impulses and behavior in a "philanthropic" social-psychological context that makes them understandable and forgivable. Arkady's love-hate dialectic with the world is presented as the twisted expression of an essentially candid and high-minded young personality shamefully thrown back on itself.

His youthful innocence is conveyed both by the naïvely enthusiastic and hyperbolic style of his narrative and, more obviously, by numerous revealing incidents. Even while determined to become a Rothschild, he spontaneously uses his savings to look after a baby girl left on the doorstep of his home. Perturbed by budding sexual desires, he participates momentarily in uttering obscenities at defenseless young girls in the street, but ends by protecting one young woman who vigorously slaps his partner in this degrading pastime. Moreover, the "ideological" expression of his egoism also has a magnanimous aspect. Arkady wishes to become a Rothschild not because he values money for its own sake, not because he wishes to wallow in luxury and to indulge his appetites to the fullest, but solely for the sensation of power that his wealth would entail. The unhappy boy then imagines himself donating all this enormous wealth to humankind: "Then, not from ennui, not from aimless weariness, but because I have a boundless desire for what is great, I shall give all my millions away, let society distribute my wealth and I . . . I will mix with nothingness again" (13: 76).*

Dostoevsky also takes care to indicate that Arkady wishes to obtain

---

* Arkady here parallels the underground man in his "sublime and beautiful" phase, when he imagines that "I became a multimillionaire and at once devoted all my wealth to the improvement of the human race . . . and I'd go off, barefoot and hungry, to preach new ideas and inflict another Waterloo on the reactionaries" (5: 133).

his financial goal only by "honorable" means; he would not become a pawnbroker or moneylender in order to gain wealth because "pawnbroking and moneylending are for scum" (13: 69). Instead, he would train his body and mind, subsist only on black bread, tea, and a little soup, and save half of the small allowance he received from his guardians. In this way he submitted himself to something "like the monastic life and [performed] feats of monastic self-discipline" (13: 67). Such self-discipline, even if at first misdirected, can always for Dostoevsky be turned into a genuine desire for self-sacrifice on behalf of a worthier goal. The same combination of idealism and self-centered egoism can also be seen in Arkady's father, Versilov, though these traits manifest themselves differently in the world-weary and highly sophisticated aristocrat than in the turbulent adolescent.

4

Versilov is far and away the most interesting character in the book, and after Part I Dostoevsky is unable to prevent him from taking center stage. Initially, he is presented as a typical member of the generation of the 1840s, an affluent and high-minded gentleman filled with the "humanitarian" ideas of his time, a reader of A. V. Druzhinin's *Polinka Saks* and of D. V. Grigorovich's *Anton Goremyka* (*Anton the Miserable*). The first of these books, influenced by George Sand's *Jacques*, is an indictment of the constraints of a loveless marriage; the second depicts the wretched lot of the peasantry in the days of serfdom. Despite his advanced ideas, however, Versilov did not scruple to seduce a bewildered peasant girl who had been married off to a much older husband with no regard for *her* wishes.

Such affairs, of course, were routine for Russian landowners, but Arkady suggests a deeper motivation than merely a momentary flare-up of passion. Prettier and more compliant peasant girls were readily available; but Versilov and his peasant inamorata were linked by an attachment more profound than the merely sexual, a longing in each for the values embodied in the other—and especially, in the case of Versilov, for the Russian social-religious rootedness that was so naturally a part of Sofya's being. As Arkady comments, his father's conduct "was not only natural but well-nigh inevitable"; yet his preservation of the tie with Sofya was far from ordinary. "But to love someone for life—that was too much. I can't swear he loved her, but he dragged her around with him the rest of his life—that's true enough" (13: 12).

Versilov thus does not abandon her entirely, taking her along as a companion on his European travels so long as she remains attractive;

but this attachment does not prevent him from turning over Arkady's upbringing entirely to strangers and callously leaving Sofya to fend for herself when he becomes infatuated with Katerina Akhmakova in Bad Ems. The poor Russian girl, unable to speak a word of any other language, was rescued by "Auntie" Tatyana Pavlovna, who looks after Arkady's welfare as well and turns up in crucial moments of his life to operate as a sharp-tongued, irascible, but unstintingly devoted *deus ex machina*. Versilov's character always exhibits this same mixture of abstract and lofty high-mindedness with a personal self-centeredness that rides roughshod over all other considerations. Dostoevsky had already affectionately satirized such a type of the 1840s in *The Devils* (Stepan Trofimovich Verkhovensky); but here he avoids caricature and stresses rather the earnestness and sincerity of Versilov's moral-cultural aspirations.

Arkady's attitude toward Versilov in Part I combines secret admiration and hero-worship of his glamorous father with hostile resentment and gnawing envy. Once, taken to a sumptuous Moscow mansion, he catches a glimpse of his father performing the role of Chatsky in some amateur theatricals, his one and only admittance to this elegant, upper-class world during all his years of solitary childhood misery. At first he had idealized this radiant image of his father, enthroned in another and higher realm; but the gossip he hears about him changes his mind entirely. Versilov is rumored to have been guilty of the most dishonorable behavior. While presumably paying court to Katerina, he proposed marriage to her invalid stepdaughter (who subsequently poisoned herself). Slapped in the face by the young Prince Sokolsky as a result of these events, he failed to challenge him to a duel. Arkady is plunged into despair by this destruction of his idol. Initially, the character Arkady had dreamed of going to Petersburg to help Versilov fight such "calumny" with the aid of the letter in his possession unmasking Katerina; but he subsequently abandons any such notion. The narrator Arkady analyzes the reason for this change of heart, which occurs not only because of the character Arkady's disillusionment with his father but also for less honorable reasons. "I must confess that the letter sewed in my pocket did not alone arouse in me the passionate desire to rush to Versilov's aid. . . . I had visions of a woman . . . a proud, aristocratic creature . . . whom I should meet face to face. She would laugh at me, despise me, as though I were a mouse; she would not even suspect her future was in my power. . . . Yes, I hated that woman, but already I loved her as my victim" (13: 63). It is through such self-scrutiny that Arkady will finally come to understand (and forgive) Versilov's similar love-hate relationship with the irresistible Katerina.

The events of Part I are designed to change Arkady's image of his father, who is by no means simply the scoundrelly blackguard he now believes him to be. Although Versilov's conduct reveals his inability ever to escape entirely from a flattering and complacent self-concern, the story about Katerina's stepdaughter actually redounds to his credit. She had become pregnant by the young Prince Sokolsky, and Versilov, who has since been looking after her child, had wished to save her reputation by his offer of marriage. But in making this *beau geste*, he deeply wounded the feelings of Arkady's mother, whose consent he asked for— and obtained! Another incident that places him in a much more favorable light is his renunciation of an inheritance after having won it in a lawsuit because Arkady shows him a letter proving that it had been meant for the young Prince Sokolsky. (This plethora of letters is a sure sign of Dostoevsky's difficulties with his plot!)

Arkady is overcome by this evidence of Versilov's rectitude and contempt for filthy lucre. But the cautious and intelligent Vasin, linked to the Dergachev circle, provides another perspective on his behavior. "There's too much of the 'hero on the pedestal' about it," he tells Arkady critically. "Some part of the inheritance, if not half of it, might well have remained with him even from the most scrupulous standpoint." Such a judgment is supported by Tatyana Pavlovna, who makes clear to Arkady that "she had been awfully vexed that the whole of it [the heritage] had been handed back and not just half" (13: 210). Well she might be, since it is she who is supporting Versilov and his illegitimate family entirely from her personal savings. Such magnanimity, as we see, returns his family to poverty and dependence on the charity of a self-sacrificing family protector. Every deed of Versilov is thus inwardly undermined by the desire always "to be on a pedestal."

Another important episode in Part I sharply accentuates this feature while also thickening the "philanthropic" atmosphere of the book. The young, desperately poor but educated student Olya comes to Petersburg with her mother and is driven to suicide by the indignities to which she is exposed (several efforts to buy her favors or to inveigle her into a brothel). Versilov genuinely sympathizes with her plight and comes to her aid; but when she becomes hysterically deranged and begins to suspect him of betrayal, he neglects to take any steps to quiet her suspicions. Instead, he rushes off to renounce the heritage. Expressing regret at this choice of priorities after her death, he typically draws a self-protective moral: "No, never again will I meddle . . . in 'good works'" (13: 148). Arkady too feels guilty about Olya because, in a moment of embitterment, he had spoken sneeringly about Versilov as having spawned a brood of illegitimate children. "Such words about a father from his son," he acknowledges sorrowfully, "must have confirmed all her suspicions about Versilov and the fact that he had humiliated her." But Arkady's self-condemnation leads to an opposite result: "It doesn't matter, it'll pass," he tells himself consolingly. "I'll get the better of it by doing some good deed!" (13: 162).

All these incidents present the continuously shifting perspective from which Versilov is viewed, which is simply the objective correlative of his own inner uncertainty and moral instability. The strongest sense of Versilov's character is given not in such carefully contrived incidents but during his lengthy conversations with Arkady. If there is one circumstance in which a Dostoevsky character comes to life, it is when he or she is given a monologue; and those of Versilov are among the best passages of the novel. His conversations with Arkady in Part I succeed in communicating the mixture of charm, intelligence, and blasé sensibility that makes him so appealing. But they also reveal an attitude of disillusionment, an ingrained inability to take himself (or anything else) with unqualified seriousness, that underlines his basic lack of moral substance.

Arkady, on closer acquaintance, comments on this crippling inner disposition of his father. "He was positively charming to me," he writes, "and jested with me, but I should have liked quarrels better than jests ... [because] there was a strange irony on his part" (13: 18). A typical example is when Versilov first speaks of the peasant husband of Arkady's mother with great respect, but then makes a risqué allusion to his gray hairs. "Versilov had a very nasty aristocratic trick. After saying (when he could not help it) some particularly clever and fine things, he would all at once intentionally cap them with some stupid saying. . . . To hear him, one would suppose he was speaking quite seriously, and all the time he was posing to himself, or laughing" (13: 109). It is Dostoevsky's ability to convey both the sensitivity of Versilov's insight, as well as the disengaging twist of his self-reflexive irony, that redeems a good many of the scenes of *A Raw Youth*.

The history of Versilov will gradually disclose his hopeless inability to master the passions that lie at the root of his self-debilitating mockery. Although he is a man of "ideas," he always regards them from a certain ironic distance; they do not penetrate his entire personality and become "idea-feelings." He is contrasted in this respect with the young man Kraft, whose suicide is clearly meant to illustrate what occurs when such a powerful "idea-feeling" is undermined. Arkady meets Kraft when he visits the Dergachev group; a few days later, Kraft commits suicide out of a motive that can only be called patriotic despair. He has become convinced that the "Russians are a second-rate people destined . . . not to play an independent part in the history of humanity," and this belief has maimed his will to work for "the common cause" (that is, the propaganda work of the Dergachev group). Other members tried to persuade him that, even without faith in Russia, he could still labor "for the future unknown people that will be formed of all humanity without distinction of race"; but Kraft is too emotionally attached to Russia to find this possible (13: 44–45). The destruction of his faith in a glorious future for his people, like the destruction of Kirillov's faith in Christ as God-man in *The Devils*, leads to a crisis of despair that ends in suicide (though Kirillov believed that his death would have a positive significance).

A discussion between Kraft and Arkady at Dergachev's specifically brings out the importance of values being embedded in an "idea-feeling" pervading the personality to its very core, and the impossibility of replacing such an "idea-feeling" by any abstract notion such as a "future unknown people." Dostoevsky here is evidently transposing his own belief in humankind's need for an irrational faith—specifically, a faith in Christ as God-man and hence a belief in immortality and resurrection—as the sole secure buttress of moral values. And if there were any doubt on this score, he indirectly brings out the religious analogy when Arkady illustrates what it means to speak of an "idea-feeling." He tells the story of a general who lost two beloved daughters very suddenly and a few months later himself died of grief. "What could have saved him?" Arkady asks with a naïveté carefully calculated by Dostoevsky. "The answer is . . . a feeling of equal strength. You'd have had to have dug up those two little girls and given them to him—that's all you could have done, or something of the kind" (13: 46–47). No rational considerations ("we are all mortal") were of any help in assuaging his grief; but "a feeling of equal strength" might have been derived from a hope inspired by a belief in immortality and resurrection. The physical impossibility of digging up the two girls is certainly intended to suggest the possibility of some ultimate reunion rooted in age-old religious faith.

The attack on Kraft by other members of the Dergachev circle also inspires Arkady to spring to his defense with a lengthy and impassioned outburst. For just as Kraft is in the grip of an "idea-feeling" about Russia, so Arkady has his own about becoming a Rothschild; no abstract argument can alter the resentments of his ego, in which this "idea-feeling" has its root. Arkady is searching for a new ideal, a new faith, that can help him to overcome his smoldering need for revenge and power; but he sees in his interlocutors only a demand that he surrender his individuality entirely. His tirade has often been compared with that of the underground man, who expressed a similarly passionate, egoistic self-assertion against a Socialist world that Arkady imagines consisting of "barracks, communistic homes, *stricte nécessaire*, atheism, and communistic wives without children" (13: 50). Arkady's anachronistic attack was probably intended to illustrate his callowness once again, and per-haps to evoke a tolerant smile from the up-to-date readers of *Notes of the Fatherland.*

But Arkady also defends his own egoism with a more relevant argu-ment—one aimed directly at the Populist refusal to acknowledge the "idea-feeling" of religious faith. "Why should it concern me what will happen to this humanity of yours in a thousand years' time, if all you allow me under your rules is no love, no life after death, and no possi-bility of being noble and self-sacrificing?" Returning to the charge a bit later, he invokes the doomsday vision of the earth becoming a cold planet, on which—according to the conclusions of the recently discov-ered and widely popularized second law of thermodynamics—human life will have vanished entirely. "And why should I be bound to love my neighbor, or your future humanity," Arkady cries, "which I shall never see, which will never know anything about me, and which will in its turn disappear and leave no trace (time counts as nothing in this) when the earth in its turn will be changed into an iceberg, and will fly off into the void with an infinite multitude of other similar icebergs?" (13: 48–49). A life without the prospect of eternity thus can cripple the will to be "noble and self-sacrificing" in the present. Here Arkady ad-dresses precisely the dedication to an ideal *without* any hope of this kind. From where would the "idea-feelings" necessary for its support be derived? Dostoevsky's Populist readers were thus being informed that merely secular altruistic values would not prove sufficient to sustain them indefinitely, and that, like Kraft, they might reach the limit of despair.

## 5

The encounters between Arkady and Versilov in Part I are touching and effective because they spring from the basic father-son relationship and are not yet distorted by the complications of the intrigue. The plot be-gins to dominate in the second section, which takes place after a lapse of two months. Arkady, in the interval, has become transformed into a fashionable dandy-about-town, and in a series of picaresque adventures he plunges into the whirl of social life with an eagerness fostered by his previous exclusion. His sponsor in this transformation is the young Prince Sokolsky, in whose apartment he lives and who furnishes him with funds very liberally (and, Arkady believes, out of generosity and friendship).

"Why those old painful lacerations, my solitary and gloomy child-hood, my foolish dreams under my quilt, my vows, my calculations, even my 'idea'?" Arkady asks himself. "I imagined and invented all that, and it turns out that the world's not like that at all" (13: 164). But neither, as it also turns out, is the world as rosy-hued as the dazzled Arkady now believes it to be. In fact, he experiences one disillusioning shock after another, and these become so severe that he is seized by the destructive impulse to set the entire world on fire.

All of Arkady's misadventures in this second part may be viewed as an exposure to what Dostoevsky calls "the common Russian fate" (13: 247). This phrase is used by the young Prince Sokolsky to describe his own character, but in fact it applies to all the other upper-class figures as well. To one degree or another, they all exhibit the prince's hopeless moral impotence, which disintegrates under extreme pressure into a pathological split personality. "No, you don't know my nature," he tells Arkady, "or else there is something I don't know myself, because it seems I have more than one nature." The young prince nourishes the highest conceptions of his obligation to maintain the most rigid standards of personal honor; yet he is guilty of the most contemptible and disloyal conduct, and continually violates his own principles. When Arkady, at the height of his euphoria as a man-of-the world, is accused of dishonesty at a high-toned gambling establishment, his supposed friend refuses even to acknowledge his existence. Arkady learns the secret of their connection when he discovers that Prince Sergey had made his sister Liza pregnant (just as the prince had done with Katerina's invalid stepdaughter). His "friendship" with the prince, whose largesse enables Arkady to satisfy his craving to mix with the highest aristocratic society, could well be perceived as a means of capitalizing on his sister's dishonor; and he breaks down and sobs when he learns of what he has been suspected. The prince, implicated in a stock-forgery scheme with Stebelkov, at last summons up enough courage to write a confession; but while in jail, because of jealousy over Liza, he betrays the Dergachev group to the authorities—a deed that, significantly, everyone else in the book considers the nadir of infamy.

The same "Russian fate" casts its shadow over Katerina, whom Dostoevsky fails to characterize in any memorable fashion. She remains the somewhat indistinct figure of a beautiful society woman longing vaguely for a more meaningful life and unhappily trapped in a web of sordid circumstances. Her interest in Arkady is not *completely* calculating and mercenary; she finds in him a youthful freshness and ingenuity sorely lacking in her worldly milieu. Yet she cannot resist using her charms to try and pry out the whereabouts of the compromising letter from her enraptured admirer. One of her major scenes is a rendezvous with Arkady, which arouses his fervent hopes and leads him to display all the youthful ardor of his infatuation. But, as he learns from Versilov, Katerina had arranged for their meeting to be secretly overheard, and this revelation deals a crushing blow to his amorous pretensions. Nevertheless, Katerina's betrayal of his confidence does not destroy his faith in her moral integrity. Rather, he gains a growing awareness of the complexity of human motivation, a knowledge that he is then honest enough to apply to himself. "Why, I had told her a lie," he reminds himself, referring to his assurance that the compromising letter had been burned. "I had deceived her because that, too, could not be helped, and I had lied innocently against my will" (13: 226). The upshot is that Arkady feels less and less inclined to judge others harshly and peremptorily, and the emotional pressure of his resentments gradually ebbs as he becomes conscious of his own fallibility.

None of these disillusionments is so severe as the one that occurs in relation to Versilov, whose elevation of spirit makes his vulnerability to "the Russian fate" all the more disturbing and unsettling. At the beginning of Part II, he is presented as a propounder of the loftiest ideas, a man profoundly preoccupied with the most crucial problems of his time; but his wisdom and insight are always tinged with a feeling of impotence. Haughtily impugning the "materialism" of the modern world, he predicts to Arkady that society will finally collapse in "general bankruptcy," leading to class warfare between "the beggars" and the "bondholders and creditors." When Arkady inquires anxiously what can be done about this frightening prospect, he only replies that "to do nothing is always best. One's conscience is at rest anyway, knowing that one's had no share in anything" (13: 172).

Similarly, Arkady can derive no positive moral guidance from Versilov's general ideas about human nature and human life, some of which have already been cited in the previous chapter. "To love one's neighbor and not despise him is impossible," he informs his son, adding that "'love for humanity' must be understood as love for that humanity which you have yourself created in your soul (in other words, you have created yourself and your love is for yourself), and which, therefore, will never be reality" (13: 174–175). But such disillusioning words are counterbalanced by another dialogue, in which Versilov tells Arkady that "to turn stones into bread . . . is a great thought," but "it's not the greatest." For "men will be satisfied and forget" and then ask: "Well, I've had enough and what can I do now?" The question of the meaning of life and of the ultimate destiny of mankind transcends the issue of the satisfaction of material needs, but to the question, What shall I do now?, Versilov can provide no answer (13: 174–175). His utterances always contain this mixture of misanthropy and exalted aspiration.

As the intrigue of Part II unfolds, these opposing aspects of Versilov are no longer divulged through moral-philosophical dialogues but presented in dramatic action. His split personality is now depicted in terms of trivial capriciousness (such as his senseless act of challenging the young prince to a duel and then withdrawing the summons an hour later) or as dark connivance against his own son. When the young man confides the secret of his infatuation with Katerina, his father leads him to open his heart completely; but he encourages Arkady's effusions only in the hope of obtaining information about the letter to use against Katerina.

The scene takes place in the same sinister and tawdry atmosphere (a sleazy tavern) that had formerly symbolized the profound moral malaise eating away at Svidrigailov in *Crime and Punishment*. "The surroundings, the limping air from *Lucia*, the waiters in their indecently grubby Russian outfits, the fumes of cheap tobacco, the shouts from the billiard room—all of it's so vulgar and prosaic," as Versilov comments, "that it borders on the fantastic" (13: 222). What was appropriate for the cynical and vicious Svidrigailov, however, seems strained and overblown for the weak but high-minded Versilov. Dostoevsky struggles unsuccessfully to inject some deep significance into this scene, drawing on *Othello* for aid; but the upshot is that, using what he learns from Arkady, Versilov writes Katerina an insulting letter asking her not to "seduce" an innocent lad to gain her sordid ends. Arkady is thus humiliated and betrayed by his father in the eyes of the woman he adores.

Much of Part II is vitiated by similar attempts to inflate the rather paltry material of the plot intrigue by various means (such as the Shakespearean allusions). There are some amusing pages involving the rascally mysterious Stebelkov, who likes to speak in conumdrums, as well as the maunderings of old Prince Sokolsky. Dostoevsky strikes a more impressive note only when Arkady delves back into his boyhood with a dream recalling the sole visit of his peasant mother to his school for young noblemen. Made aware of his lowly social status by brutal mistreatment, the poor, forsaken boy has come to internalize the standards of class snobbishness responsible for his persecution. When his mother arrives, he receives her coldly, ashamed of her humility, awkwardness, and lower-class dress and comportment. Arkady's "education" has dried up the sources of the most natural and instinctive emotions, and he thus cannot respond to his mother's love because of his slavish abasement before his upper-class schoolfellows. It is only six months later, when the memory of her visit abruptly floods back, that Arkady's aching loneliness momentarily triumphs over the barrier of class prejudice. Coming across the faded blue cotton handkerchief in which his mother had wrapped a few coins to leave with him, he suddenly, overwhelmed with grief and contrition, kisses the memento as he lies sobbing in his bed. All the genuine pathos of his human situation is poured into this scene; and by placing it close to the end of Part II, Dostoevsky indicates that Arkady has now begun not only to react bitterly against his past but also to overcome the lesions that it has left on his wounded psyche.

6
———

By the end of Part II, Arkady is ready for the major transformation of his personality that will be the reward for all his sufferings. This transformation is the result of his encounter at last with one of the three positive figures in the book (the other two being Arkady's mother and Tatyana Pavlovna). By far the most important is the "legal" father whose name he bears, the peasant Makar Ivanovich Dolgoruky, the only peasant character of any importance in Dostoevsky's novels (excluding the peasant convicts in the semidocumentary *House of the Dead*). His inclusion can surely be attributed to a desire to make literary capital out of the Populist idealization of the peasantry, as well as, unquestionably, an urge to compete with Tolstoy's Platon Karataev in *War and Peace*. Where Versilov's injunctions to Arkady have been those of a man who, at bottom, entertains no belief in his own convictions, Makar possesses a tranquil certainty that Arkady has never encountered before. The religious "wanderer" is depicted as a person of great dignity and purity of heart, who bears no ill will toward either Versilov or his unfaithful wife. On the contrary, he is filled with a loving concern for her welfare and has taken steps to guarantee Sofya's financial security after his death. Nothing could contrast more strongly with the motives and machinations of the "educated" characters, who are unable to overcome the various egotistical ambitions that color all their conduct. Moreover, the words of the old man, waiting to die with a calm and joyous serenity of spirit and an untroubled faith in Christ's promise, provide Arkady with the moral inspiration he has sought in vain all his life.

In Makar, Arkady finds embodied a secure conviction of the ultimate goodness of God's creation and a profound sense of wonder and awe at the transcendent mystery both of human existence and of life after death. "Whether the tiny bird is singing, or the stars in all their multitudes shine at night in heaven, the mystery is one, ever the same. And the greatest mystery of all is what awaits the soul of man in the world beyond" (13: 287). Makar's ecstatic celebration of the beauty of life, as is usual in Dostoevsky, comes from a consciousness haunted by death; but death for him is not the stabbing anguish of despair depicted in *The Idiot* through such a character as the nonbeliever Ippolit Terentyev. It is, rather, the natural fulfillment of a life devoted to God, a life whose termination it would be "sinful" to protest against and which still keeps its contact with the world of the living. "You may forget me, dear ones," he says, "but I love you from the tomb." It is after this affirmation that the deeply impressed Arkady declares to him: "There is no 'seemliness' in them. . . . I won't follow them. I don't know where I'm going, I'll go with you" (13: 290–291). Both Arkady and Makar are in a feverish and slightly hysterical state during this dialogue, and their weakened condition adds psychological plausibility to their rhapsodic words. Although Arkady's resolution "to follow" Makar and presumably become "a wanderer" is obviously not meant to be taken literally, the impression left by Makar will never be forgotten.

Dostoevsky manages to make Makar a touching and believable figure despite the obvious idealization and despite his manifest aim of illustrating the indestructible connection, in the soul of the Russian peasant, between Christian faith and the virtues that the Populists admired. This aim comes out most clearly when Arkady, as an up-to-date young man, decides to argue with him in favor of the "modern" secular emphasis on "good works." "I drew him a picture of the useful work of the man of science, the doctor, of any friend of humanity, and roused him to real enthusiasm. . . . 'That's so, dear, that's so!' Makar said. 'God bless you, your thoughts are true!'" (13: 311).

Makar is thus wholly on the side of working to alleviate the ills of human society; but he adds that the life of "the desert," the life of a Christian hermit or ascetic inspired by faith, is also necessary. Without such an ideal, even the friends of humanity "will forget their great work and will be absorbed in little things." His words then rise to a vision of the earthly paradise that could be created by the fulfillment of Christ's words: "Go and give all that thou hast to the poor and become the servant of all . . . and there shall be no more sorrow and sighing, nothing but one priceless paradise." Arkady enthusiastically tells him that he is preaching "absolute communism"—a remark illustrating Arkady's simplicity but also allowing Dostoevsky to indicate the similarity of his own social ideals (as expressed through Makar) with those of the radical Populists (13: 311).

Arkady's conversations with Makar run through the first five chapters of Part III and provide a commentary to Versilov's discourses at the beginning of Part II. This is evident from Makar's stories about Pyotr Valerianovich, the educated nobleman who lived in the desert with the monks but could not subdue his "understanding." These stories are meant to illuminate Versilov's inner struggle and also to refer more generally to the moral stirrings among the Russian educated class. "'He was a man of pure life and lofty mind,' the old man pronounced impressively, 'and he was not an infidel. There was a cloud over his mind, and his heart was not at peace. Very many such men have come nowadays from the ranks of the gentry and the learned.'" To which Arkady responds: "I like your Pyotr Valerianovich. He's not a man of straw, anyway, but a real person, rather like a man near and well known to us both" (13: 289).

The scenes depicting Makar's stately descent into a dignified death alternate with the unrolling of the intrigue that presents Arkady with his greatest temptation. Arkady's old schoolfellow Lambert finally makes his appearance to serve as his Mephistopheles. If Dostoevsky manages to make Makar a plausible character of some spiritual depth, the figure of Lambert and his French mistress Alphonsine, who pours out long tirades in French in a histrionic style, are pure caricature. The same is true for Lambert's two accomplices, the scallywags Trishatov and Andreev (the latter nicknamed *le grand dadais*), who are the same type of grotesque as several minor characters in *The Idiot* but lack their rueful cynicism. Dostoevsky endows Trishatov, a young aristocrat gone to seed, with a taste for music and literature; and the cultivated, inwardly penitent reprobate enlivens the scene by pouring out his troubled soul to Arkady with garbled versions of *The Old Curiosity Shop* and *Faust*. Andreev, on the other hand, refuses to wash, "out of despair," thinks that "there's no need to do good or bad for it's one and the same," and finally shoots himself offstage (13: 351). Dostoevsky thus plays variations on his major themes in this comically absurdist key, and these two figures—especially Trishatov, a sort of quasi-double for Arkady—reveal the depths of iniquity and despair to which the raw youth might have sunk.

Trishatov's allusions to *The Old Curiosity Shop* and *Faust*, all the same, introduce a deeper symbolic note that is used to foreshadow the high point of the book, Versilov's final speech. He rewrites the famous scene in which little Nell, awakening in the morning, walks out into the graveyard of the village church in which she and her grandfather had at last found tranquillity; and the simple village church of Dickens becomes "a medieval Gothic cathedral," while the sun is not rising but setting. Nor does little Nell in this version feel any sense of quietude or serenity, as she does in Dickens; rather, "she stands there and watches the sunset with a calm, pensive awareness in her childish soul, in a soul astonished by it as if it were some kind of enigma—the sun as the idea of God and the cathedral as the idea of man" (13: 353). What had been in Dickens merely a consoling tableau becomes for Dostoevsky, as A. S. Dolinin has remarked, a vision of the enigma of God's relation to man, once again anticipating his next novel.[2]

And something of the same anticipation can be seen when, in his drunken maunderings, Trishatov tells of his plan to write an opera on the Faust theme. Mephistopheles is depicted stirring up memories of childhood in the agonizing Gretchen, who has lost her innocence to

Faust; and these torments are transformed into "the song of Satan," sung by a high tenor voice that "goes on rising and penetrates even more deeply and more sharply into her soul, ending with the shout: 'All is over, you are accursed.'" But after Gretchen's brief prayer for forgiveness, she falls into a faint as "the choir thunders forth, in a kind of thunderclap of voices, inspired, triumphant, overwhelming . . . and everything is shaken to its foundation and ends in an ecstatic, exuberant universal shout of 'Hosanna' that resounds, as it were, through the universe and she is carried offstage as the curtain falls" (13: 352–353). Nothing of this sort is found in Goethe; and Gretchen's salvation, which defeats Satan, is turned almost into a cosmogonic event involving the universe in its entirety.

Trishatov's improvisations provide only a momentary respite from the unwinding of the plot. Lambert has always been the epitome of soulless and shameless carnality, and his arrival stirs Arkady's lascivious longings with the plan to blackmail Katerina into sexual submission by means of the letter. This temptation comes to the fore in a feverish dream that represents one of Dostoevsky's rare uses of the subconscious to express sexual desire. "The touch of her hands sent an agonizing thrill through me, and I put my lips to her insolent crimson lips that invited me, quivering with laughter" (13: 306). Torn between "seemliness" and naked lust, Arkady finds himself exposed to the full range of the conflict of opposites that constitutes "the Russian fate."

"It always has been a mystery," he writes from his vantage point as narrator, "and I have marveled a thousand times at that faculty in man (and in the Russian, I believe, more especially) of cherishing in his soul the loftiest ideal side by side with the most abject baseness, and all quite sincerely" (13: 307). Arkady's situation is now very similar, in its inextricable tangle of love-hate feelings for Katerina as goddess and temptress, to that of his father. The recognition of this identity allows him to understand and emotionally to master the events that climax the book in a furious cascade.

7

These final pages contain a lengthy confession speech by Versilov that is the high point of the novel. The death of Makar Ivanovich temporarily transfigures Versilov's personality, and in a sudden surge of genuine sincerity he finally divulges to Arkady the "idea" that has given inspiration to his life. To express this "idea," which is actually a "vision," Dostoevsky reaches back into his unpublished files and utilizes the myth of the Golden Age initially intended for the unpublished chapters of Stavrogin's confession. In this new context, however, it acquires quite a different significance. Stavrogin had dreamed of the Golden Age despite his rational disbelief in any distinction between good and evil; and the dream reveals that he cannot free himself from an overpowering sensation of guilt and self-loathing. Versilov's version is not moral-psychological but historical-philosophical; it illustrates Dostoevsky's own ideas about the future of European civilization and its relation to Russia. Moreover, in the ideological structure of *A Raw Youth*, Versilov's fantasy parallels that of Makar and is intended to supplement it, thus disclosing the essential unity of the Russian spirit. For Versilov projects in terms of European history what Makar expresses in terms of Russian apocalyptic religiosity.

His dream evokes "a corner of the Greek archipelago . . . blue smiling waves, isles and rocks, a flowery shore. . . . Here was the earthly paradise of man." The innocent beauty of this vision, "when the gods came down from the skies and were of one kin with men," filled his heart with "the love of all humanity"; this was "the first day of European civilization"— a civilization whose finest flower was precisely "the love of all humanity" that brings tears of all-embracing tenderness to Versilov's eyes. "Oh, here lived a splendid race! They rose up and lay down to sleep happy and innocent. The woods and meadows were filled with their songs and merry voices. Their wealth of untouched strength was spent on simple-hearted joy and love." But when sleep ends, he is jolted back into the hurly-burly of history: "The first day of European civilization which I had seen in my dream was transformed for me at once on awakening into the setting sun of the last day of civilization! One seemed to hear the death knell ringing over Europe in those days" (13: 375).

What sounded this death knell was the recent Franco-Prussian War, the temporary establishment of the Paris Commune, and the burning of the Tuileries that ensued in the struggle for control of the city. In the midst of general chaos, it was only he, as "a Russian European," who could not reconcile himself to this final collapse. "As the bearer of the highest Russian culture, I could not accept it, for the highest Russian thought is the reconciliation of ideas, and who is there in the whole world who could understand such a thought at that time? . . . Oh, for Russians all those old foreign stones, all the wonders of a divine ancient world, all those relics of holy miracles are precious, and even more precious for us than to those who live there!" In a passage quite daring for its time, when even liberal Russian opinion regarded the destruction of the Tuileries as an abomination, Dostoevsky did not hesitate to give it a partial justification as an understandable consequence of the flagrant injustices of European society. "I alone among all the firebugs," Versilov declares, "could have told them to their faces that setting fire to the Tuileries was a mistake. I alone among all the conservative reactionaries could have told those bent on revenge that what happened at the Tuileries, though a crime, was still logical" (13: 375–376).

Just as Makar Ivanovich had been a wanderer in Russia as a religious pilgrim, so he recalls having been "a solitary wanderer" in Europe. Like Makar, Versilov too was preaching the fulfillment of the reign of love and the advent of the Kingdom of God. "I cannot help respecting my position as a Russian nobleman," he declares. "Among us has been created by the ages a type of the highest culture, never seen before and existing nowhere else in the world—a type of worldwide compassion for all." This type of Russian nobleman is a prototype of "the man of the future," and his role is precisely to transcend destructive national differences: "In France I am a Frenchman, with a German I am a German, with the ancient Greeks I am a Greek, and by that very fact I am most typically Russian" (13: 376–377). The Russian European thus fulfills the injunctions of Christian love on the level of history; the law of his being is to be most himself in total abnegation to others. The Russian peasant-pilgrim Makar and the Russian European Versilov, each inspired by their own form of the Christian promise, are thus united in their service to this vision of a new Christian Golden Age.

What continues to separate the two, however, is captured in Versilov's remarkable evocation of an atheistic world deprived of belief in a divine Christ—a world that is the final outcome of the inexorable European process of self-destruction. "The great idea of old has left them, the great source of strength that till then had nourished and warmed them was vanishing like the majestic setting sun in Claude Lorrain's picture. . . . The great idea of immortality would have vanished, and they would have to fill its place, and all the wealth of love lavished of old upon Him who was immortal would be turned upon the whole of nature, on the world, on man, on every blade of grass." The result would be, in its own way, a Golden Age, but one stemming from profane rather than sacred love. "Men left forlorn would begin to draw together more closely and more lovingly; they would clutch one another's hands, realizing that they were all that was left for one another" (13: 378–379). Versilov can intuit both the beauty and the pathos of this ultimate phase of European civilization because he too has been touched by the virus of atheism and become incapable of returning to the faith of the Russian people.

He thus intuits that the profane Golden Age he envisages, a world without immortality, would be pervaded by an aching sense of sadness and sorrow. "On awakening, they [humankind] would hasten to kiss one another, eager to love, knowing that the days are short and that is all that is left to them. . . . Oh, they would be in haste to love, to stifle the great sorrow in their hearts. . . . Meeting, they would look at one another with deep and thoughtful eyes, and in their eyes would be love and sorrow" (13: 379). If Versilov's character was depicted as torn by irony, self-doubt, and melancholy, Makar's was shown as vitalized by a joyous serenity and childlike gladness even in the face of death. The secret of Makar's tranquillity is his belief in the goodness of God— a belief that he expresses in a manner recalling the Christian pantheism of Saint Francis of Assisi—and his faith in immortality, a life beyond the tomb. This accent placed on the "sorrow" of a world without God— even a world that realizes, on its own terms, the Christian ideal of mutual love—is Dostoevsky's artistic answer to the sublimest secular ideals of Socialism, which by this time he had identified with all of Western civilization.

Versilov finally breaks off his speech, acknowledging that "the whole thing is a fantasy, even one that is quite unbelievable"; but "I couldn't have lived my whole life without it," he adds, "and without thinking about it." He defines himself as a "deist, a philosophical deist," not an atheist, which is perhaps meant to suggest an unsatisfied religious longing that remains an abstraction rather than a vitally active personal relationship with the sacred. But Versilov cannot entirely suppress his need for a faith closer to that of Makar. "The remarkable thing," he confides, "is that I always completed what I envisaged with a vision, as did Heine in his 'Christ on the Baltic.' I . . . could not fail to imagine Him in the last resort among the orphaned people. He would come to them and stretch out his arms to them and say: 'How could you have forgotten Him?' And there and then the scales would fall from their eyes and there would burst forth a great exalted hymn to the new and total resurrection" (13: 379).

## 8

This brilliant and moving portrayal of the Golden Age as a Feuerbachian world, in which mankind, rather than alienating all its love from the earthly to the supernatural, would lavish it on themselves, is one of Dostoevsky's great passages. It equals, in expressive poignancy, Raskolnikov's dream of the plague in *Crime and Punishment*, and it would be hard to find its match elsewhere. What follows is almost embarrassing, as the machinery of the plot is dutifully cranked up to display the vacillations of Versilov on the level of the intrigue.

The death of Makar has led Versilov to imagine that he has now overcome his fatal infatuation with Katerina. He now feels firmly united with Arkady's long-suffering mother and the steadfast world of peasant moral-religious values that she represents—a world that Versilov, for all his wanderings, could never entirely abandon. Arkady is also convinced that his father has triumphed over his love-hate entanglement with Katerina, which he analyzes in terms reminiscent of Prince Myshkin's conflict between compassionate (asexual, Christian) love and a full-blooded attraction leading to marriage. "I thought that he loved mother more, so to say," Arkady writes, "with the humane love one feels for all humankind than with the simple love with which women are loved as a rule, and that as soon as he met a woman whom he began to love with that simple love, he at once turned against that [other] love . . . most probably because that feeling was new to him" (13: 385). With poetic justice, the same pattern recurs between Katerina and Versilov. "I really love you," she tells him, "with the sort of *general* love with which you can love everyone and you're never ashamed to admit it" (13: 416).

The morally healing impact of Makar's death proves to be very short-lived, however, and all the most acute symptoms of the "Russian fate" now assail Versilov. Literally, he becomes two people: one is contrite and remorseful over his eccentric and outrageous behavior, while the other continues to perform the most disgraceful actions under the un-controllable influence of "a second self." "Do you know that I feel as though I were split in two," Versilov says. "He looked around at us all with a terribly serious face and with perfectly genuine candor. 'Yes, I am really split in two mentally, and I'm horribly afraid of it'" (13:408–409). Just after uttering these words, moved by the irresistible destructive force of his "second self," he smashes the icon left him as a heritage and pledge for the future by Makar; and though he shouts, "don't take this as being allegorical, Sonya," he admits the significance a moment later: "All right, so take it as an allegory, that's how it was meant!" (13: 409). The Russian European "wanderer" from the intelligentsia, whatever the elevation of his spirit, is ultimately unable to take up the burden of the Cross—the "allegory" of his reunion with the Russian people. On the more prosaic level of the plot, Versilov never marries Arkady's peasant mother, even though he is now legally free to do so.

The action races on fast and furiously at this point, with a plethora of melodramatic twists and turns. While sitting in a jail cell, Arkady overcomes his temptation to blackmail Katerina into sexual submission and resolves not to seek revenge or any sort of personal advantage. "At such moments," he writes as narrator, "a man's future is determined, his final views on life are forged. 'Truth is there and that's where I must pursue it!' he says to himself" (13: 438). Arkady's single night of incarceration marks his transition to responsible manhood, and it is now his passion-racked father who takes up the dastardly plan that Arkady had rejected. Versilov's demonic "second self" displays its last convulsions in joining Lambert to carry out the scheme of humiliating and black-mailing Katerina.

At the final moment, though, the elegant Versilov is unable to withstand the sight of Lambert threatening Katerina with a pistol, and he leaps out of concealment to gun-whip his erstwhile accomplice. Katerina faints dead away when he springs out of hiding, and he carries her body in his arms, "the way a nurse holds a baby," as he walks up and down the room before depositing her gently on the bed (13: 445). With gun in hand, he presumably intends to die with her in a high-Romantic *Liebestod* that would not have been out of place in his favorite opera, *Lucia di Lammermoor*. But Arkady, another onlooker in hiding, deflects his aim, and the bullet only wounds him in the shoulder. The scene ends with Tatyana Pavlovna rushing in, "screaming at the top of her voice" (all this takes place in her apartment), and with Versilov and Lambert both lying on the floor in pools of blood. Matters are tidied up for public consumption, and the police investigation concludes that one "V***, a family man of around fifty, had suddenly declared his passionate love to a highly respectable lady, who did not happen to reciprocate his feelings, and so, in a moment of exasperation, V*** attempted to shoot himself" (13: 449).

Arkady ventures another interpretation of Versilov's demented behavior, but these reflections are constrained by his intellectual limitations as a narrator—limitations that Dostoevsky was careful not to transgress. It was hardly to be expected that the still callow young man should give any sophisticated analysis of his father's psychological contortions. Seeking for aid in "a medical encyclopedia," he learns that "a 'double' is the first stage of a specific nervous disorder that may lead to a very tragic end," and is provided with a "scientific" rationale for Versilov's outrageous actions; but Arkady himself remains unsatisfied. There was, after all, "the wicked symbolism" of the smashing of the icon, which gave a particular significance to this psychiatric symptom (13: 446). But Arkady cannot draw any definite conclusions, and in refusing to go beyond the immaturity of his narrator, Dostoevsky took the considerable risk of turning Versilov *too obviously* into a pathological case, thus furnishing fuel to the critics who had always charged him with an unhealthy concern for psychic abnormality. *A Raw Youth*, unfortunately, is his only major novel in which such a charge seems partly justified by the text. Elsewhere, psychic disorder is always presented as the result of a profound moral-spiritual crisis, and the attempt to "explain" it in purely psychiatric terms is satirized and ridiculed.

These speculations form part of the epilogue, which has a distinctly Dickensian tonality. "Now, as I write these lines, spring is outside the windows. It is mid-May. My mother is sitting by his [Versilov's] bed. He is stroking her cheeks and her hair and tenderly trying to intercept the gaze of her averted eyes. Oh, this is only half of the former Versilov: this man refuses to be parted from Mother, and I know he'll never leave her again." Versilov, the former man-of-the-world, is now a helpless semi-invalid, entirely dependent on Sofya and Tatyana Pavlovna, and "as sincere and unaffected as a child. . . . His intelligence and his moral standards have remained unchanged, while his striving for an ideal has become even stronger." Nonetheless, the old, capricious Versilov emerges in a scaled-down replay of the superb deathbed scene of Stepan Trofimovich Verkhovensky. Versilov first expresses a desire to observe the Lenten fast of the Orthodox Church, but then, two days later, because "something had irritated him unexpectedly, something he described laughingly as 'an amusing incongruity,'" he abandons his intention. "'I do love God very much, my friends,' he said, 'but I simply have no talent for these things'"; no conversion of "the philosophical deist" to the rites of Orthodoxy takes place (13: 446–447).

As for Arkady himself, it appears that he is in correspondence with Katerina, who is living abroad unmarried; there is even a hint that a certain intimacy has developed between them, but Arkady decorously refuses "to divulge the contents of this correspondence or repeat what we said to each other during our last meeting." All this, as with Raskolnikov and Sonya at the end of *Crime and Punishment,* "is a completely *new* story and, indeed, is still located in the future" (13: 447). Other details of the intrigue are also tidied up, but of most significance is Arkady's recasting of his "Rothschild idea," which he insists he has not abandoned at all. "Well, that new life, the new path I have discovered and am now following *is* precisely my 'idea' . . . but in such a completely different form that it is hardly recognizable." Even though refusing to elaborate, he explains that he is hesitating to go to the university because "I have no right to study when I should work to support Mother and Liza" (and Versilov as well). Presumably, the rigorous, almost monastic self-discipline he had imposed on himself to become a millionaire will now be employed to succor his family. But the generous Tatyana Pavlovna, his good angel in the guise of scolding taskmistress, promises to continue to support everyone until he completes his studies (13: 451).

9
———

Dostoevsky did not conclude his epilogue solely with the remarks of Arkady as narrator. It also contains comments from Arkady's former mentor in Moscow, Nikolay Semyenovich, who is described as a "completely objective and even coldly egotistical man, yet one of undoubted intelligence" (13: 452). By the time he had reached the last stages of the book, it is likely that, in addition to wishing to reply to his critics, Dostoevsky also felt an internal aesthetic need to shift to an outside observer who could transcend Arkady's fumbling and tentative point of view. The observations of Nikolay Semyenovich thus allow him to guide the reader toward a broader social-cultural comprehension of the meaning of his novel.

To begin with, Nikolay Semyenovich extends Arkady's experiences so that they become typical of many more members of his generation. "There are a great many boys like you, whose gifts really do always threaten to develop for the worse either [into] subservience, or a covert desire to overthrow the status quo. But this desire to overthrow the status quo springs more often than not from a covert yearning for order and 'nobility' (I use your terms). Youth is pure because it is youth." In the past, according to Nikolay Semyenovich, such youths with time "ended up as part and parcel of the higher cultural layer in our society, and blended with it into an integral whole"; but "now the situation is different because there is almost nothing to which one can feel an attachment" (13: 453).

If he were a novelist, says this judicious gentleman, he would always make sure that his "heroes came from the Russian hereditary nobility, because it is only among that type of cultivated Russian that an appearance of beauty and refinement in living is possible, something so essential to a novel if it is to leave an elegant impression on the reader" (13: 453). Without mentioning Tolstoy, Dostoevsky's spokesman obliquely refers to him when he affirms that a novelist aiming to leave such an elegant impression "would only write historical novels, since there are no longer beautiful types in our time. . . . Such a novel, written by a great talent, would belong not so much to Russian literature as to Russian history; it would provide an artistically finished picture of a Russian mirage, but one that really existed so long as no one guessed it was a mirage" (13: 454). The reference to *War and Peace* is unmistakable, but for Dostoevsky the beauty of that world was only a mirage based on the slavery of serfdom. This is why, as Nikolay Semyenovich adds, implicitly referring to the character of Levin in *Anna Karenina*, "the grandson of the characters depicted in a picture showing a cultured, upper-class Russian family over three generations in a Russian historical setting— such a descendant could not be portrayed otherwise than as misanthropic, isolated; and a sad sight to behold" (ibid.). Levin, in other words, was trying to carry on the tradition but was now gloomily aware that it had been "a mirage."

If this is true for a descendant of such a noble family, how much more would this be the case for someone like Arkady Dolgoruky, the illegitimate offspring of a peasant mother and a father belonging to the hereditary nobility! "Yes, Arkady Makarovich," he is told by his counselor, "you are *a member of an accidental family*, in complete contrast to all our recent types of legitimate hero who had boyhoods and youths quite unlike yours" (those depicted in Tolstoy's trilogy, *Childhood, Boyhood, Youth*). Various members of Versilov's two families are also characterized, and he himself is described as embodying a chaos of opposites. "He belongs to one of the oldest families of the nobility while at the same time belonging to the Paris Commune. He is a genuine poet, loves Russia, and yet completely denies its value. He has no religion, but he is prepared to die for almost anything vague which he cannot name but in which he can passionately believe, on the example of many, many enlightened Russian Europeanizers of the St. Petersburg period of Russian history" (13: 455). Torn by such contradictions, what traditions and moral-cultural heritage can Versilov transmit to his children? "I confess," confides Nikolay Semyenovich, "I would not want to be a novelist trying to describe a hero from an accidental family! It would be thankless work and one lacking formal beauty. Serious mistakes would be possible, and exaggerations and oversights. . . . But what choice does a writer have who has no wish to write historical novels but is possessed by a longing for the present scene? He has to guess . . . and get it wrong!" (ibid.).

Whether or not Dostoevsky believed he had "gotten it wrong," he was here implicitly answering all those critics—among them, some of his closest friends—who were measuring his world against the far more reassuring one created by Tolstoy. He was perfectly justified, of course, in wishing to be judged by his own artistic aims rather than those of Tolstoy, but even by this standard *A Raw Youth* cannot be said to hold its own against the three novels that had been its predecessors. Indeed, if the defects of *A Raw Youth* prove anything, it is that Dostoevsky could do full justice to his talent only when he allowed his eschatological imagination a free rein; and he would take this artistic lesson to heart three years later in *The Brothers Karamazov*.

# PART II

# A Personal Periodical

## CHAPTER 11

# A New Venture

The last chapters of *A Raw Youth* were published in *Notes of the Fatherland* in the winter of 1875, and Dostoevsky was once again faced with the problem of what to undertake next. Even though no longer living in the hand-to-mouth fashion of his four years in Europe, and the publisher of several of his own works, he still had no regular source of income to provide for his family, recently increased to three children. A new son, Aleksey ("the name of Saint Aleksey, the man of God, was particularly revered by my husband," wrote Anna), had been born to the couple on August 10, 1875.[1] This new arrival placed additional burdens on the family finances, and the Dostoevskys, though comfortable, were anything but affluent. Hanging over them always was the burden of the debts incurred by his brother Mikhail, for which Dostoevsky had assumed responsibility.

In the past, he had begun to think of a new novel even before the final pages of the one he had just written were in print. But now he returned to the idea of publishing a new periodical, his *Diary of a Writer*, which he had begun to experiment with in *The Citizen*. The success of his column had encouraged him to believe that a publication of this kind would be possible, although, as Anna Grigoryevna wrote, "if the *Diary* proved to be a failure, we would be put into a hopeless [financial] position."[2] Nonetheless, a family decision was made to take the plunge. Dostoevsky had long dreamed of such a journal, and he had now come to have complete faith in the business expertise of his wife, who had learned to maneuver amidst the treacherous shoals of the Russian book trade and ran their publishing house with a practiced hand.

## 2

As far back as 1864–1865, Dostoevsky had jotted down some notes for a periodical that would be an intermediary between art and journalism, or would combine the two in a hitherto unprecedented fashion: "Project, *Writer's Notebook*, without subscriptions. About 6 folio pages [each folio containing sixteen printed pages] in two weeks. 3 pages of a *Writer's Notebook*, 3 pages of a novel. . . . The entire book, the first will be 36 folio pages in six months."[3] He mentioned this idea in a letter to Baron

Wrangel in November 1865, calling it "useful and advantageous";[4] but nothing came of it at that time. Two years later, the notebook crops up again in a letter to his niece Sofya Ivanova; and there is an obvious reference to it (already mentioned) in *The Devils*, when Liza Drozdova tries to enlist Shatov to work on her plan for a new publication. The venture is described as a sort of almanac, a collection of facts of all sorts, even including "fires, acts of heroism, every good and evil deed," but not piled together pell-mell; each would be selected and linked with "a certain view, with a direction, with a purpose, with thought that will illuminate the whole, the totality" (21: 372). It is this notion of journalistic facts linked together as a whole, and illuminated by an idea, that would define the difference between the *Writer's Notebook* and an ordinary newspaper or even magazine.

Dostoevsky had never drawn any hard-and-fast line between his purely creative works and journalism, and his novels had been nourished by his close scrutiny of the daily press. Both, as he saw it, dealt with the same material—the human reality of life as it was being lived within the conditions of a particular society, at a particular time and place. The novelist, however, undertook the task of penetrating more deeply into the significance of that human reality than the journalist, who remained on the surface of events and had no time to dwell on their ultimate meanings. Indeed, in defending what he called his "fantastic realism," which often took its point of departure from a newspaper account of some event (or found confirmation of its artistic extrapolation in one that was later reported), he had criticized his fellow writers for neglecting such a precious source of inspiration.

Writing to N. N. Strakhov in March 1869, Dostoevsky had stressed that "I have a particular view of reality (in art)," and this view is integrally linked to the sensational stories appearing in the newspapers. "In any issue of a newspaper you run across an account of actual, most surprising facts. For our writers, they are fantastic; they pay no attention to them, and yet they are reality because they are *facts*. Who notices them, who explains them, and sets them down? They occur all the time and every minute, and are by no means *exceptional*. . . . We just let reality pass by our nose. Who will note the facts and delve into them?"[5] He, of course, had tried to do so in his novels; but he had also long been tempted by a publication that would combine the depth of art and the immediacy of journalism.

Dostoevsky's decision to undertake his *Diary of a Writer* was an adventurous gamble that marked a new stage in his astonishing career. Although the relative obscurity in which he had lived during his European exile had long since ended, and he had once more become a name to be reckoned with on the Russian literary-cultural scene, his fame was still largely confined to intelligentsia circles, whether of the right or the left. With the *Diary of a Writer*, however, he reached out to a much larger and diversified reading public, to whom he spoke eloquently and passionately about matters that were uppermost in the minds of all literate Russians. No one had ever written about such matters so forcefully and vividly, with such directness, simplicity, and intimate personal commitment. It is little wonder that the public reaction was enormous, and that Dostoevsky was deluged with correspondence, both pro and contra, the moment his publication appeared in the kiosks.

One of the salons he frequented in these years was that of the extremely perceptive Elena A. Shtakenshneider, who attracted everyone by her intelligence, sensitivity, and kindness and by the stoic courage with which she bore her disfiguring hunchback. Noting the immense popularity of the *Diary*, she wrote in her own diary: "Dostoevsky's fame was not caused by his prison sentence, not by *House of the Dead*, and not even by his novels—at least not primarily by them—but by the *Diary of a Writer*. It was the *Diary* that made his name known in all of Russia, made him the teacher and idol of the youth, yes, and not only the youth but all those tortured by those questions that Heine called 'accursed.'"[6]

A discussion of the astonishingly wide-ranging contents of the *Diary*, the lengthiest of all his works, is reserved for later chapters; but his life for the next two years was intimately intertwined with its redaction. Indeed, the routine necessitated by its regular appearance (and he was fanatic about keeping to schedule) was so rigorous and exhausting that it left him precious little time for anything else. One wonders if he really was aware that he would be committing himself to such a strenuous regimen. The demands of the *Diary* were equal to, if not more arduous than, his editorship of *The Citizen*; but perhaps his willingness to shoulder his new task can be explained in terms of his own famous distinction in *House of the Dead* between free and forced labor. Even though the forced labor in his prison camp had been, for the majority of the peasant convicts, less physically exhausting than the work they had been accustomed to perform in liberty, they had found it more burdensome precisely because it was imposed. The same might be said of Dostoevsky under Prince Meshchersky; but as sole proprietor and author of his new publication, perhaps he felt his burden to be lighter, even though he worked harder than he had ever done for the prince.

## 3

At the end of 1875, an advertisement appeared in the major Russian newspapers announcing the imminent appearance of a new publication—the *Diary of a Writer*, written and edited by F. M. Dostoevsky—to which the public was invited to subscribe. The publication "will be a diary in the literal meaning of the word, an account of what has been seen, heard, and read about. It may, of course, also include narratives and stories, but mainly about actual events."[7] A few days later, he appeared at the printing plant where Mikhail Alexandrov was now employed and asked to speak to him. The proprietor of the plant, a Prince V. V. Obolensky, whom Alexandrov describes as "a dilettante-enthusiast of the typographical art," was someone Dostoevsky had met previously at the home of Prince Meshchersky. No doubt for this reason a brusque exchange occurred when Obolensky spoke to him as if he were simply another client come to work out the conditions of publication. The answer was a stiff reply that formal agreements between people who knew each other well were by no means necessary. Beating a hasty retreat, the prince explained that he had meant nothing legally formal, merely an exchange of information regarding prices and the method for handling manuscripts.

Dostoevsky, as Alexandrov notes, was in any case less concerned about financial details than about the typographic appearance of his new publication. He had already chosen the typeface—one he had seen in a popular series of translations of European classics into Russian. He specified that his format should be in larger type and that more space be allowed between the lines; he was particularly worried about the chapter headings and asked Alexandrov to select a typeface that would consist of letters "more original, with more character, and not small but more visible, more striking."[8] A sample of Alexandrov's choice satisfied the finicky Dostoevsky, and this typeface remained unchanged throughout the life of the *Diary*. Aside from this detail, he had very little to do with the practical affairs of his journal. "All the business side of the publication," Alexandrov remarks admiringly, "that is, all the transactions with the printing plant, with the paper factory, with the binders, with the booksellers and newspaper distributors and also with the packing and shipping of the publications through the mail, was undertaken by Anna Grigoryevna, who had earlier received an excellent preparation for the activity by supervising the publication of individual works of Feodor Mikhailovich."[9] Alexandrov took evident pride in his own craftsmanship, and he clearly thinks very highly of Anna Grigoryevna's business acumen and mastery of detail, always referring to her with the greatest respect.

The *Diary of a Writer* appeared once a month and consisted of one-and-a-half to two quarto pages, which meant sixteen normal pages, all of it written by Dostoevsky (except advertisements and announcements). It went on the newsstands on the last day of each month early in the morning, and he was extremely anxious to keep to such a schedule without fail. A few years back, his letters had been filled with complaints about the inability of the neo-Slavophil publication *Zarya* (*Dawn*), with whose ideas he sympathized, to publish on time; and he attributed the failure of the journal partly to such negligence. Determined not to make the same mistake, he asked Alexandrov to give his sworn word that the typographer would compensate in the plant for any delay caused by Dostoevsky himself. He promised to send in his copy by the seventeenth or eighteenth of each month and to turn the last pages over no later than three days before printing. But Dostoevsky, as he had anticipated, often found it impossible to meet his own deadline, and so Alexandrov presumably worked overtime to meet the timetable.

Dostoevsky thus subjected himself to a rigid routine, which was further constrained by the self-imposed limitations of space, about which he often complained to his readers. He would sometimes apologize for not being able to develop a topic he had started to discuss; and his difficulties were further increased by the need to clear his texts with the censorship before going to press. Even though, at this time, preliminary censorship was no longer the rule and editors were required only to tailor their texts in conformity with certain general regulations (punishment ensued if these were violated, as had occurred when he was editor of *The Citizen*), permission for the ex-convict Dostoevsky to publish the *Diary* had been granted only on condition that he submit to advance censorship.

What this meant is described by Alexandrov: "It was necessary for the printing plant to have time for the typesetting, the corrections in the proofroom, then the corrections of the author; only after this would Feodor Mikhailovich allow the submission of the corrected proofs to the censors—who, as is well known, could not be relied upon to hurry with the page proofs—and then again the corrections of the author, the corrections of the proofroom, and finally the printing." In 1877 the press authorities of the Ministry of Internal Affairs offered Dostoevsky the possibility of printing without preliminary censorship, but he preferred to remain with the established arrangements because "he valued the peace of mind on which he could fully rely."[10]

A vivid picture of what ensued more than once is conveyed in a letter to Khristina Alchevskaya, a lady active in the cause of educating the people, who also corresponded with and met Turgenev and Tolstoy. A great admirer of the early issues of the *Diary*, Alchevskaya wrote to Dostoevsky and later came from Kharkov with her husband to visit her idol. Dostoevsky had intended to call on the couple with Anna Grigoryevna but explains why the rendezvous at their hotel failed to materialize:

On Saturday we had decided definitely to come to visit you, but I went to bed at seven in the morning and was awakened at eleven—trouble!—165 superfluous lines had to be thrown out or 200 extra lines of original copy had to be added. . . . I leaped up, got dressed, ran off to the printing plant, stayed there until five in the afternoon, waited for the impressions, and finally, by cutting into live flesh, found it possible to throw out 165 lines. I went home, I thought we'd now have dinner and then be off to see you. And then a piece of news— . . . my censor had disappeared, left Petersburg, so now what was to be done? Without having dinner and without having rested, I took the impressions to another censor . . . and did not find him in.

Dostoevsky left a letter with the proofs and hurried back to the printing plant, "every moment calculating how much the publication would suffer from the delay—thank God there is hope that it will come out on Monday." And he adds: "But that's how it always is at the very end of the month."[11]

There may be some exaggeration in this disconsolate statement, but probably not very much. Endless problems had to be straightened out, as we can judge from his numerous letters to Alexandrov as the *Diary* went to press. And Dostoevsky himself confesses, in the same letter, that he remained in constant uncertainty over what to include and what to eliminate. "Would you believe," he admits, "that I still haven't managed to work out for myself the form of the *Diary*, and I don't even know that I'll ever get it put right, so that even if the *Diary* continues, for instance, for two years, it will keep on being an unsuccessful thing."[12] Those close to him were well aware of the exhausting pressure, both physical and mental, imposed by his *Diary*, and Alexandrov remarks that "if the expression is justified of some writers that they *write* their works *with their blood*, then this expression fits no one better than Feodor Mikhailovich Dostoevsky. . . . I do not know if [he] wrote his novels and stories easily, but I know that his articles in the *Diary of a Writer* were written with great strain and in general cost [him] much effort." Indeed, on the evidence of working so closely with him for two years, Alexandrov believes that the *Diary* "shortened his life" and that he "squandered on it his physical health, which was affected by it much more than even by his years in *katorga*."[13]

4

The Dostoevskys had lived in Staraya Russa for most of 1875, but the plan to issue the *Diary* required their residence in St. Petersburg once more, and they returned to the capital in mid-September. Unable to afford luxurious accommodations in newer buildings, the Dostoevskys occupied five rooms in an aging apartment house. Alexandrov was particularly struck by the bareness of the study, which reminded him of a monastic cell. A Turkish couch covered with oilcloth also served as a bed, and there were two tables. One was covered with a pile of carefully arranged magazines and newspapers; the other, larger table was garnished with an inkwell, a pen, and a thick notebook "in which Feodor Mikhailovich noted down individual ideas and facts for his future works." This table also supported a pile of letter paper, a box with tobacco, and another with cigarette paper and wadding. Everything else necessary for writing was contained in a sliding case under the table, an arrangement that Alexandrov labels as rather antiquated. Above the table hung a photograph of Dostoevsky, and before it stood an armchair with no padding or pillow on the seat. One corner contained a small bookcase, and the windows were hung with simple, transparent curtains. There was no mistaking that this was the workplace of a writer, and its very unpretentiousness inspired in Alexandrov "a great respect for it." "I maintain that the strict, almost impoverished simplicity of this furniture reflected the character of its occupier more truly and better than furnishings suitable to all such offices in general."[14]

Alexandrov's intimate working relationship with Dostoevsky at this time allows him to provide a vivid picture of the writer's daily routine. Writing late at night and into the early morning, he slept until two in the afternoon and sometimes later. Once having risen, and donning as an outer garment a loose and lengthy jacket of dark broadcloth rather than a dressing gown or slippers, he went immediately to the samovar awaiting him in the dining room, where he poured himself a cup of very strong and very sweet tea. Returning with his glass to the study, he drank several cups that he poured himself as he read the newspapers and rolled cigarettes out of thick yellow paper. "He smoked quite a bit," Alexandrov notes, "thus increasing the already quite intense activity of his nervous system."[15] After tea he received any visitors who might be waiting, and at three o'clock he ate a light meal in the dining room. Dostoevsky drank a wineglass of vodka with the meal, sipping it as he chewed on a slice of black bread, once explaining to Alexandrov that this was the healthiest way to take vodka. After finishing, he went for a walk, dropping in at the printing plant on his stroll, and returning at six o'clock to dine with the family and put the children to bed before settling down to work.

Such was his normal schedule and behavior, which, if nothing unexpected occurred, went smoothly and equably. But if for some reason his sleep had been disturbed and he was awakened by noise, or if, having worked later than usual, he was unwarily aroused before his accustomed time, he was "despondently serious and silent." No visitors were admitted on such occasions, except for Alexandrov, summoned to report on the *Diary*. "I saw him about two or three times in such a mood," he writes, "and each time his look produced an oppressive impression."[16] It was best at such times not to speak first, Alexandrov learned, and to wait for Dostoevsky to begin the conversation, which he did by sometimes offering tea or a cigarette. When in such a temper, he could flare up suddenly in an outburst of irritability: "He easily got angry, and then spoke harshly," appearing to be "rude and despotic even with those close to him." But Alexandrov hastens to add that, while such harshness and wounding words might seem intolerable to an outside observer, those who knew him best were aware that they represented only a momentarily unsettled state of his nerves.[17] Everyone of course knew of his epilepsy; and although Alexandrov never witnessed a fit, he was told about them, apparently in some detail, by Anna Grigoryevna, who must have explained the sharp shifts of mood as a result of his malady.

During the two years that he published the *Diary*, Dostoevsky was entirely absorbed by its production, and most of the recorded events of his life at this time were tied to the *Diary* or are reflected in its pages. At the end of September, for example, he contributed five rubles to a fund organized by *The Citizen* on behalf of the Herzegovinians, then beginning their revolt against the Turkish Empire. In early October, the Petersburg branch of the Slavic Benevolent Committee elected Dostoevsky, along with three other writers and scholars, to edit an anthology of stories by noted Russian authors, the proceeds of which would be donated to the Balkan Slavic cause. Even though he had earlier expressed some suspicion of the Western Slavs, whose intelligentsia were too much under European influence for his taste and too suspicious of Russian domination, his *Diary* would soon show him to be a passionate partisan of the Pan-Slav nationalism that led to the Russo-Turkish War of 1877–1878.

5

---

Whatever the pressure of his literary commitments, Dostoevsky was always glad to maintain cordial relations with his widespread family. He had suffered all through the latter part of the 1860s (after the failure of *Epoch*) from the enmity of the family of his brother Mikhail, even though he had conscientiously shared his meager resources with them. More recently, he had been saddened by the hostility of his sisters, who looked suspiciously upon his behavior regarding the estate of their wealthy aunt Kumanina. He was thus all the more delighted to renew contact with his youngest brother, Andrey, who wrote to inform him that Andrey's oldest daughter and her husband, Mikhail Rykachev, a physicist in a Petersburg scientific institute (he later became a member of the Imperial Academy of Sciences), wished to pay him a visit. Dostoevsky received the young couple very warmly, and they exchanged visits and remained friends throughout the remainder of his life.

Writing to his brother apologetically for not having replied sooner, he explains that he has been "swamped with work" (he was then reading the proofs of the final chapters of *A Raw Youth*) and expresses his great pleasure at reviving relations with family members. Two nephews, the sons of his sister Vera Ivanova, had been living in Petersburg for some time (one for a year, another for three), but they had never bothered to come to see him. He assures his brother that, contrary to rumors, he bore him no ill will in relation to the Kumanina heritage, of which Andrey had been appointed one of the trustees. On the contrary, he insists to Andrey that, in filing the suit to exclude some collateral relatives of his aunt from any claim to a share, he was "looking after their own interests." After getting the money, he would "immediately divide it up among them and would take for myself only enough to cover the expenses of the proceedings and not a kopek more." Dostoevsky adds that, "by giving up to them [his sisters] what *by law should come to me,*" he was "taking away from my children what was legally theirs."[18] His suit proved unsuccessful, however, because Russian law acknowledged the rights of such collateral relatives.

A month later he dispatched a reply to his stepson, Pavel Isaev, then living in Moscow with his family of two children, who had urgently requested a loan of thirty rubles. The sum was necessary to tide him over the expenses of an illness—which, as Dostoevsky remarks ironically, "you described . . . in such detail that I now assume, of course, that you are already well." Despite his griefs against Pavel, for which there was a good deal of justification, his stepfather provided the thirty rubles, though warning him that this might well be the last time he would come to Pavel's aid. "In sending you the thirty rubles, I am depriving my unfortunate children. I know that I will die soon, and when they are left without me, *not a single soul will offer them a kopek.*"[19] (His prediction turned out to be quite untrue, though he could scarcely have known it at the time.)

This reference to the imminence of his death is by no means the only one in Dostoevsky's letters of this period. A few months later, he writes to Andrey that he wishes "to live at least another seven years" in order to establish a firm foundation for the future of his children. Moreover, "the thought that my children will remember my face after my death would be very pleasant for me."[20] He had long been haunted by the fear of death because of his epilepsy, but the dread of a sudden decease had now been replaced by the conviction that he was slowly succumbing to the undermining effects of his emphysema.

Reminiscences of the past crop up later in 1876 when, congratulating Andrey on the engagement of a second daughter, he gives vent to the elegiac mood induced by the apprehension that "my life is now short-lived." "But how strange all this is, my dear Andrey Mikhailovich," he exclaims. "Was it so long ago that you and I were quite small? I recall very, very well the moment, between four and five in the morning, when Father, joyous, woke our late brother and me . . . and announced to us all that a brother for us, Andryushenka, had been born. . . . Our time has flown like a dream." But Dostoevsky then reaffirms his unquenchable will to live. "Not only do I not want to die, but I feel, on the contrary, as if I were only starting to live. I am not in the least bit tired, and meanwhile, I am already fifty-five years old, phew!"[21]

Many years before, just after returning from the mock execution during which he believed that his life would be snuffed out in a few moments, Dostoevsky had written to his brother Mikhail: "Life is a gift, life is happiness, every minute can be an eternity of happiness."[22] This ecstatic feeling for life as an incomparable gift—one at which he never ceased to marvel and to wonder—remained with him to the very end of his days, and he would soon incorporate it into the rhapsodic celebration by Father Zosima of the wonders of God's world.

6

Several months after beginning to publish his *Diary*, Dostoevsky learned from a letter of Khristina Alchevskaya's that some people (though not she herself) considered that he was wasting his time on such an endeavor. Why was he not continuing to create literary masterpieces, rather than preoccupying himself "with trifles, with a survey of current events, little stories and suchlike"? Apparently having heard much the same reproach from other sources, he took this question very seriously and replied to her: "I have reached the irresistible conclusion that in addition to the original artistic inspiration, a writer of belles lettres must also know the reality portrayed down to the smallest detail (historical and current). Among us I think only one person stands out for that—Count Lev Tolstoy." Far from viewing the *Diary* as a departure from his artistic task, he explained that it was an indispensable preliminary for his future works. "That is why, while preparing to write a very long novel, I in fact planned to immerse myself specifically into the study—not of reality, properly speaking, I know it even as it is—but of the details of contemporary life." Among such details, "one of the most important problems of this contemporaneity for me, for instance, is the younger generation, and with it, the contemporary Russian family."[23]

He continues this self-justification by recalling a recent chance encounter with Ivan Goncharov while taking a stroll. The two writers stopped to chat as they stood watching the tumultuous torrent of the passing crowd, and Dostoevsky, turning to his literary colleague (whose *Oblomov* he had always admired), posed the "sincere question as to whether he [Goncharov] understood everything in current reality, or had he already ceased to understand some things?" As we know from their correspondence two years earlier, Goncharov had expressed the opinion that an "objective artist" (as he considered himself to be) could successfully depict only those types that had been fixed and established by time, while those just beginning to be formed were beyond the artistic grasp of objective presentation. His reply to Dostoevsky's question conformed to this conviction: "My ideals and what I have come to cherish in life are dear to me . . . and I want to spend the few years left to me with them. So studying those people (he pointed to the crowd going by on the Nevsky Prospect) is burdensome to me because my valuable time will be spent on them." Dostoevsky, however, refused to lay down his arms before the challenge of the present, and he saw his *Diary*, far from being a distraction from his creative vocation, as a necessary means of keeping abreast of the passing scene, as a guarantee "that the multitude of impressions" he was continually accumulating "will not be wasted" for future artistic employment.[24]

For him, such impressions were acquired from intense perusal of the daily press, both of the capital and of the provinces, whose information he set down in the notebooks that were the preliminary stage for the articles in the *Diary*. But impressions also came from more personal, firsthand acquaintance with places and people that aroused his interest and about which he wished to write. The very first (January 1876) issue of his new *Diary* was devoted to the theme of children, and as a preparation he asked his legal friend A. F. Koni to arrange a visit to a colony of juvenile criminals. The two men made the journey in late December 1875, and Koni recounted the trip in one of his series of "literary portraits" of prominent writers (Tolstoy, Turgenev, Goncharov, Pisemsky, and others).

Koni mentions Dostoevsky's passionate interest in what he observed, "looking around and listening to everything, asking questions and inquiring into the smallest details in the routine of the fledglings." He was particularly struck by Dostoevsky's ability to enter into personal contact with the hardly docile group of boys, whom he gathered together in one of the larger rooms and engaged in dialogue. "He answered their questions, some searching and some naïve, but little by little this conversation turned into a lesson on his part, profound but fully accessible in its content, and filled with the genuine love of children that shines through every page of his creations." There were some interruptions and objections, but he was listened to very carefully, though his audience was totally unaware of who he was; and the group quickly suppressed anyone attempting to create a disturbance. When the two men left the room to visit the adjoining church, the boys flocked around and continued to speak with him about incidents from their lives and about their reactions to the colony. "One felt that between the author of sorrowful stories about life and [life's] youthful, unconscious victims, a spiritual bond had been created, and that they sensed in him not a *curiosity-seeking* visitor but a grieving *friend.*"[25]

On the journey home, after a long period of silence, he conveyed some of his reactions to Koni, not so much concerning the boys as the church they had visited. It was filled with icons, some very old and confiscated from Old Believers by the police (the patron of the colony, an influential senator, had managed to get them released); others, particularly those of the iconostasis guarding the priestly sanctuary, were painted in a newer, Italianate style. "I don't like that church," he muttered. "It's some sort of museum." The profusion of icons seemed to him a mistake; fewer would have been better. "In order to act on the souls of those entering [the church], one needs only a few images, but severe, even stern ones, just as the belief and duty of a Christian must be severe and stern." Such images should accompany the boys when they fell back into the urban maelstrom from which most of them had come, and recall for them the far-off days of their pure and unsullied village childhood. Even though the newer icons conformed to Orthodox tradition, Dostoevsky disliked their "dressed-up Italianateness"; presumably, they would not have the same elevating effect. He also objected to the practice of addressing the boys with the polite plural pronoun *vy* rather than the more familiar (and presumably demeaning) second-person singular *ty*. They were accustomed to the latter, ordinarily used for social inferiors and children; the polite form was more respectful and civil, but it was "colder, much colder." "What was the point of such pretense in any case? Yes, and they are still free of pretense—both in good and in evil."[26]

Much attention is paid in the *Diary* to criminal trials of one kind or another, which he always regarded as an indispensable barometer of the moral climate of the times. As he had written in 1861, when he ran a series of articles about French murder trials in his journal *Vremya* (*Time*), such crimes of violence "light up dark sides of the human soul that art does not like to approach, or which it approaches only glanc-ingly and in passing" (19: 89). Although he was not in the courtroom of all the cases discussed in his *Diary* (full accounts of them were carried in the Russian press), he was present at some and took an active part in at least one, in which a young mother had been condemned to two years and eight months of penal servitude in Siberia and then to exile there for life.

Her name was Ekaterina Kornilova, and her crime had been to push her six-year-old stepdaughter out of a tenement window. The girl re-markably emerged unhurt, and the stepmother immediately went to the police to denounce herself. At the time of the crime, Kornilova was in an advanced state of pregnancy, and the peculiar circumstances of the case—her instinctive self-denunciation without a moment's hesitation—persuaded Dostoevsky that something more was involved here than a ruthless murderess who, in a fit of rage, had given way to her worst instincts. Ordinarily, as we have seen, he felt that Russian juries, misled by skillful defense attorneys, were too lenient in their decisions; but he argued that in this instance the sentence was unduly severe. The moth-er's pregnancy, he believed, may well have constituted an extenuating circumstance because it created an irresistible, abnormal compulsion over which she had no control, and which led her to give way to a latent hostility toward her stepdaughter (as well as her husband, the father, with whom she had quarreled and who had beaten her that very morning).

It was well known, Dostoevsky argued, that pregnant women some-times behaved in a most peculiar fashion (he refers to a respectable Moscow lady reputed to have become a kleptomaniac when pregnant). On these grounds he raised the possibility of reversing the verdict. Dos-toevsky had brilliantly portrayed Raskolnikov as caught in such a com-pulsion, seeming to act as if in full consciousness, and yet in the grip of what resembled a hypnotic trance induced by "monomania"; perhaps Kornilova had been the victim of something similar. A reader of the *Diary*, a lawyer familiar with the process of obtaining pardons for con-victed criminals, wrote Dostoevsky that he had been persuaded by his analysis. Urging him to visit Kornilova, he suggested advising her to ask for such a pardon and volunteered to help guide the request through the bureaucratic labyrinth.

In reply, Dostoevsky reports that a visit he had made to Kornilova was entirely satisfactory, confirming "that in my piece I had *almost* guessed literally everything." Her words bore out his theory about compulsive behavior; nor could there be any suspicion that the young seamstress, whose mind he describes as "firm and clear, but Russian and simple, even ingenuous,"[27] was not uttering the unvarnished truth. He was also impressed by the testimony of the prison wardress that Kornilova's conduct had changed considerably for the better since she had given birth to her child. Dostoevsky's articles unquestionably played their part in the reversal of her conviction on appeal, and then the dismissal of the case, though the jury was warned not to give too much weight to the opinions of "certain talented writers."[28]

7
———

Visits to a juvenile penal colony and to Kornilova's prison cell were not the only occasions when he felt it necessary to verify personally the "impressions" he was gathering for his *Diary*. One of his most brilliant articles in 1876 concerned the vogue of spiritualism, the belief—then enjoying considerable popularity in Russia—that it was possible to communicate through inspired mediums with the supernatural world in which the dead resided. A fervent advocate of the reality of such parapsychic phenomena was Nikolay Wagner, professor of zoology at the University of St. Petersburg and a summer neighbor of the Dostoevskys in Staraya Russa. The two men had met in the summer of 1875, when Wagner had already become notorious for two essays on spiritualism published in the winter of that year. Wagner was also a writer of fantastic stories and allegorical fairy tales under the pseudonym of Kot Murlyika ("Kitty-cat," duplicating the title of E.T.A. Hoffmann's famous novel, supposedly written by a cat, *Kater Murr*). Anna Grigoryevna describes him as a rather picturesque personality, speaking in a shrill, feminine voice, wearing the straw hat of a shepherd, and carrying a plaid shawl in midsummer. He appealed to Dostoevsky for help in publishing one of his tales; but when the manuscript was obligingly left at Nekrasov's home, it was returned the very next day. "The reason," Dostoevsky explained, "is that some uproar has been raised against you for the piece about spiritualism. . . . It would not be liberal, he [Nekrasov] means to say, if we print you."[29]

A letter to Wagner in 1875 regretfully refuses an invitation to visit him because the children were ill with scarlet fever and Anna herself was down with a sore throat. But Dostoevsky's curiosity about spiritualism had been aroused, and he asks Wagner: "What's happening at Aksakov's?" A. N. Aksakov, a half-brother of the famous Slavophils Konstantin and Ivan, was a journalist and popularizer of the views of the Swedish theosophist Emanuel Swedenborg. He organized séances at his home, inviting famous mediums, particularly English and American, to demonstrate their prowess in making contact with the spirit world. "Will there finally be séances?" he inquired. "I am ready to ask myself (when everyone in my family is well, of course) whether he won't admit me to at least one séance of his. I am against Butlerov's article, and it has tickled my interest even more."[30] A. M. Butlerov, a highly reputed chemist then teaching at the University of Kazan, had written an article attempting to account for spiritistic phenomena as the result of "unconscious cerebration," which then became transformed into physical events. "I absolutely cannot, after all, feel indifferent about spiritualism," Dostoevsky concludes.[31]

Two weeks later, he expressed great interest in the arrival of an English medium, a certain Miss Claire, who Wagner had gullibly told him was "a nonprofessional. A very rich gentlewoman, who had agreed to come here because of the present scientific commission."[32] Public interest in spiritualism had waxed so strongly in Russia that, in the spring of 1875, the Physical Society of the University of St. Petersburg, under the chairmanship of the world-renowned chemist D. I. Mendeleyev, had established a commission to investigate the claims of the spiritualists (preceding by seven years the founding of the English Society for Psychical Research for the same purpose). Believers like Wagner were only too eager to meet the challenge, and on February 2, 1876, Wagner invited Vsevolod Solovyev to a séance at his home, adding that Dostoevsky had promised to be present as well; but whether he attended is not clear. He was undeniably present, however, at a séance organized by A. N. Aksakov on February 14, in the company of other literati, including N. S. Leskov and P. N. Boborykin, along with Butlerov, Wagner, and others. A notebook entry also indicates that Dostoevsky took part in other séances as well. "I myself at Wagner's seven times," he jotted down, "no, I was not won over, I did not join hands."[33]

The Aksakov séance was described in an article that Nikolay Leskov wrote about the occasion. "An accordion (from which the strap had been removed) was lowered under the table by Professor Butlerov and gave forth several sounds. Butlerov held it *with one hand* by the lower keyboard. To press and move the accordion *with one hand is impossible*, just as it is impossible to press down on the valves on the other side with the fingers of another hand. In F. M. Dostoevsky's hand, the accordion made *not a single sound*."[34] How he reacted to these events is expressed in another notebook entry: "When I went to Aksakov's— a strong feeling of not wishing to believe [in spiritualism]. Politeness bothered me. . . . The accordion under the table."[35] As he later wrote in the *Diary*: "After that remarkable séance [with Miss Claire, who was suspected of trickery], I suddenly surmised—or rather, I discovered—not only that I did not believe in spiritualism but that I haven't the least wish to believe in it, so that there is no evidence that will *ever* cause me to change my views." Dostoevsky felt that he had discovered "some special law of human nature" at this point, "common to all and pertaining specifically to faith and disbelief in general."[36] One believed or disbelieved because one *wanted* to, not for any other reason; and this volitional element (what William James called "the will to believe") was stronger than any possible "objective" evidence produced for or against. As he was soon to write of the doubting Apostle Thomas in *The Brothers Karamazov*, "who said that he would not believe until he saw," it was most likely that "he believed solely because he desired to believe and possibly he fully believed in his secret heart even when he said, 'I shall not believe except I see'" (14: 24–25).

Indeed, his attitude toward spiritualism is quite similar to that of William James, who welcomed the efforts of the Society for Psychical Research to evaluate the claims of mediums and advocated the strictest scientific standards in conducting research into all so-called parapsychic events. But while applauding the work of the society in exposing frauds, James found that he could not deny the possibility of the actual existence of what was as yet inexplicable within the accepted scientific framework. Dostoevsky, too, was in favor of showing up quacks, but he also wrote: "I was never able *completely* to reject spiritualistic phenomena, with which I had some acquaintance even before the séance with the medium." Nor could he accept trickery as the *only* possible interpretation.

Aside from his personal sentiments, he learned from others—among them Vsevolod Solovyev, who could not possibly be suspected of subterfuge—that strange happenings were taking place before their very eyes. Solovyev's sixteen-year-old brother-in-law, who had initially been taught Darwinism in school and sneered at spiritualism, had now become a convert, and weekly séances were being held at the Solovyev home. "I sometimes reach the furthest pitch of astonishment," he wrote Dostoevsky in January 1876. "Tables and chairs around me positively do a devil's dance." The young man, chair and all, had been violently shoved from the table by some unknown force; and when he was told to sit with his legs tucked under him, even so "his chair rolled around, not even having casters"[37] We shall return to Dostoevsky's reaction to spiritualism in Chapter 15; but both his suspicious wariness and his partial defense can best be clarified by a sentence from the notebooks: "About spiritualism . . . This is the search for moral comfort after the loss of religion—and that is *where the real depth is*."[38] The *unwillingness* to sympathize with spiritualism that he detected in himself may be traced to this sense that it was a somewhat tawdry substitute for genuine religious faith. But he could not condemn the human need that it expressed or his conviction, which would soon be preached by Father Zosima, that man was indeed linked with other worlds through faith in Christ and God.

## CHAPTER 12

# A Public Figure

If Dostoevsky's *Diary of a Writer* brought him into a new and much more intimate relation with his public, one reason was certainly the quality of its style. He addressed his readers as if he were talking to them personally, as if he were conducting a private conversation rather than expounding a doctrine or developing a thesis. His language was always lucid and expressive, never labored or pedantic, and it produced an unusual sense of familiarity with his readers. A typical response can be found in the memoirs of Khristina Alchevskaya, who had always considered Dostoevsky one of her favorite authors, "but when the *Diary* made its appearance he suddenly became especially dear to me." Previously, she had never thought of attempting to communicate with him, but the *Diary* suddenly transformed him into someone far less remote. "Aside from the gifted author of artistic works, before my eyes arose a man with a sensitive heart, with a responsive soul—a man passionately reacting to all the questions of the day; and I wrote him an impetuous letter."[1] Many other readers, instead of only admiring him from afar, were overcome by the same desire to enter into personal contact with the man who was now speaking to them so directly and so compellingly.

## 2

The felt need to communicate with the author of the *Diary of a Writer* occasionally led to unexpected encounters, such as the one recorded in Dostoevsky's letter to Alchevskaya of April 9, 1876. "Suddenly," he tells her, "the day before yesterday, in the morning, two girls, both about twenty, came to see me. They came in and said they had wished to meet me since Lent. 'Everybody laughed at us and said you wouldn't receive us, and even if you did, you wouldn't talk to us. But we decided to try, and so we have now come.'"[2] One can hardly imagine such an incident occurring earlier, when his public image had been shaped by the fearsome convicts he had portrayed in *House of the Dead*, or by the tormented and guilt-stricken protagonists of his novels. The Dostoevsky of the *Diary*, however, was a friend and counselor, and such impromptu visitors as the two girls, whom he found extremely sympathetic, were

11. Dostoevsky in 1876

no longer a rarity. "They said they were students at the medical academy, that about five hundred women were there now, and that 'they enrolled in the academy so as to obtain a higher education and then do some good.'"

The humanitarian aims of these future doctors were extremely appealing, and Dostoevsky took them as an immensely encouraging sign of a new state of mind among the younger female generation, whom he contrasts very favorably with earlier examples of the "new woman." "I hadn't come across this new type of woman (I knew lots of the old *female nihilists*, knew them personally, and have studied them well). Would you believe that rarely have I spent time better than I did these two hours with these girls. What simplicity, naturalness, freshness of feeling, purity of mind and heart, *the most sincere seriousness*, and the most sincere gaiety."[3] He confesses that he finds it impossible (no doubt because of the censorship) to express publicly everything he feels about this visit; but the next two issues of the *Diary* (May and June) both contain strong affirmations of support for providing women the means to obtain a higher education.

The spontaneity of the young women from the medical academy was by no means duplicated in the behavior of other admirers wishing to make his acquaintance. Khristina Alchevskaya waited to receive two replies to her letters before deciding to accompany her husband, a banker traveling frequently to Petersburg, on one of his business trips. Her own epistles had been filled not only with expressions of admiration and praise but also with information about the opinions of her literary circle in Kharkov, which met regularly to read aloud both the *Diary* and installments of *Anna Karenina*. Describing herself as the descendant of a *moldovanka* (her mother was presumably the granddaughter of a Moldavian ruling prince, a woman of "choleric temperament" who had married beneath her rank), she thus called herself the product of an "accidental family" like Arkady Dolgoruky—an appellation that considerably extends Dostoevsky's own use of this term. Clearly proud of inheriting what she calls all "the negative features" of this patrimony, she speaks of it as having given her an impressionable, excitable, and tempestuous character that "prevent[s] a person from looking at God's world calmly and dispassionately."[4] Alchevskaya kept a diary, and her memoirs include accounts of her visits to Dostoevsky that provide a vivid image of him both physically and spiritually at this time.

Her own emotions before their first encounter may be gauged from the notation that "I had only to think of *this* meeting, and immediately I began to weep." A note she sent him from her hotel could not be delivered until three in the afternoon; and she waited on tenterhooks all through the day for a reply. Dinnertime arrived, and she sat down with her husband and a guest, an old friend, to whom, despite his "bright, lively, and wide-ranging mind," she scarcely said a word. At last a bellboy came to announce that a "Mr. Dostoevsky was asking for her." Like a flash, she rose from the table, flew up the stairs headlong with no concern for propriety, and found herself face-to-face with Dostoevsky at the door of her suite. "Before me stood a man of medium height, thin, dressed somewhat carelessly. I would not call him old; neither bald nor gray-haired, these usual appearances of age were not noticeable; it was even hard to tell how old he was. But looking at his face filled with suffering, at his sunken, lackluster eyes, at the deeply engraved wrinkles as if each had its own biography, one could say with certainty that here was a man who had thought much, suffered much, endured much."[5]

Once seated in her suite, Dostoevsky poured out a stream of remarks that reveal the thematic preoccupations of his *Diary*. He spoke to her of the absence in Russian society of staunch, independent convictions; of the sects existing in Petersburg who met supposedly to elucidate the Gospels (an allusion to the vogue of the aristocratic English evangelist, Lord Radstock); of the stupidity of spiritualism and of intelligentsia circles; of his fear of falling behind the times and ceasing to understand the young generation, which, because he was diametrically opposed to it on some issues, would reject him completely. For the moment, though, he received anonymous letters with the signature "Nihilists," which declared: "It is true that you go astray, that you make blunders and mistakes against us, but all the same we still count you one of us and do not wish to exclude you from our camp."[6] Dostoevsky expressed all these feelings with such an utter lack of pretentiousness, such diffidence and almost shyness, that his worshipful admirer could hardly believe she was in the presence of a famous author, psychologist, and creator. "An incomprehensible and invisible soul" seemed to emanate from his personality, and she felt "a desire to fall on [her] knees before him, to bow down and pray." What prevented her was the piercing stare of his eyes, those of "an anatomist of the soul . . . accustomed to look at people as material useful for study."[7]

Among her other observations, Alchevskaya perceptively stresses that, "most sharply of all remains in my memory the following trait, quite outstanding in Dostoevsky . . . his fear of ceasing to understand the young generation, of breaking with it. Quite simply, this apparently had become his *idée fixe*. In this *idée fixe* there was not at all any fear of ceasing to be a beloved writer or of decreasing the number of his followers and readers; no, he obviously regarded a *disagreement* with the young generation as a human *downfall*, as a moral death. He boldly and honorably defends his intimate convictions; and at the same time somehow fears not fulfilling the mission entrusted to him, and inadvertently losing his way."[8] No more penetrating remark about him at this stage of his career has ever been made. For he *did* feel that a mission had been entrusted to him, the mission of guiding the young generation back to the path of the Russian people's truth—which for him meant primarily the faith of the people in God. And for this reason he considered a definitive severance from younger readers to be the equivalent of a human downfall and a moral death.

When Dostoevsky inquired about Alchevskaya's literary circle in Kharkov, she remarked that anyone "reproving [*Anna Karenina*] seems to me almost a personal enemy." To which he replied: "In that case, I remain silent."[9] A few weeks later, when she returned to the charge, he proved to be more forthcoming. " 'Really, I hesitate to speak,' he said. 'Every character is so stupid, commonplace, and trivial that you positively do not comprehend how Count Tolstoy can direct our attention to them. There are so many vital, substantial questions among us, crying out so threateningly, on which depend either life or death, and suddenly we are asked to devote time to Officer Vronsky's infatuation with a fashionable lady and what ensued as a result. We are so accustomed to stifling in this salon atmosphere, and we encounter banality and mediocrity so incessantly, and then you pick up a novel by our best Russian novelist and encounter the very same thing!' " Tolstoy's admirer objected that novelists had the right to depict the world as they saw it and allow readers to draw their own conclusions; but Dostoevsky rejected this position out of hand. In his view, "if our life were only represented by the Vronskys and the Karenins, it surely would not be worth living." Alchevskaya adds that, for all their vehemence, there was nothing offensive in his words because "you felt that it was not a result of self-conceit but a genuine belief in the ideas he was uttering."[10]

To support her favorable opinion of the novel, she appealed to the character of Levin, who was certainly troubled by the questions then agitating Russian society; but Dostoevsky remained firm in his disapproval. "Levin? In my opinion, he and Kitty are stupider than anybody else in the novel. He is some sort of petty tyrant, absolutely doing nothing in his life, and doing that stupidly. What a fine fellow! Five minutes before his marriage he goes to renounce his bride, and without the slightest reason." He found only one scene to be "fully articulate and truthful—the death of Anna" (though she does not die in this particular scene). "I say death," he explained, "because I consider that she really died, and I do not understand why the novel was *prolonged*. This is the only scene I will take up in my *Diary of a Writer*, and I will praise it to the skies; but to criticize is impossible, much as I would wish to. I am a novelist myself—it would be unseemly!"[11] In fact, when he wrote about *Anna Karenina* a year later, he found much more to praise than merely the one scene of reconciliation during Anna's brush with death; but his feelings always remained much more ambivalent about this book than about *War and Peace*.

Other topics were also broached during these conversations, one of them being the extremely prickly issue of nationalism, a subject on which, as Alchevskaya found, Dostoevsky was highly inflammable, intolerant, and dogmatic. As someone with pro-Ukrainian sympathies, she had praised the Little Russian character for its independence and for its attitude toward women ("they do not look on women as cattle"). Dostoevsky, however, saw only the negative side of such independence, which led to the breakup of the communal family, an institution still prevalent among the Great Russians. Moreover, he insisted that Slavic peoples such as the Serbs and Little Russians were being "positively harmful" in cultivating their own indigenous languages and literatures; such clannishness only impeded the work of universal enlightenment fostered by Great Russian literature, "in which lay all salvation, all hope."

Then at the very height of his nationalistic fervor, he told his silently dissenting listener that only the Great Russian people, who had constructed a mighty state, could further the course of civilization. For "only the Great Russian," he assured her, "magnanimously and honestly looks on all nationalities without any malice and prejudice, while the Little Russian, for example, eternally harbors a grudge and cannot relate to the Great Russian."[12] As far back as 1863, in his travel sketches *Winter Notes*, Dostoevsky had written that the Russian social psyche possessed, as a national trait, the feeling of *fraternité* advanced as one of the great slogans of the French Revolution; it was thus only in Russia that the dream of *fraternité* could become a social reality. This illusory conviction had now developed into the identification of the Great Russian character with his highest value, namely, a completely non-egoistic Christian love; and this illusion allowed him to champion Great Russian imperialism while continuing to believe that he was fostering, rather than betraying, his ideal of universal harmony and reconciliation.

By this time, he had reached such a state of irascibility that the prudent Alchevskaya felt it wiser not to object, and the conversation then shifted to religion. In her view, "Dostoevsky sincerely believed in God— so sincerely that he refused to acknowledge, as it were, a lack of faith as being authentic." In the past, he told her, such a lack of faith "was considered an indication of intellect," but now this was no longer the case; yet such a change of outlook seemed to make no difference, though "perhaps with luck they [the atheists] may stop uttering such stupidities!" Dostoevsky then asked Alchevskaya whether she believed in God, which brought the reply that she had determined never, under any circumstances, to respond to such a question. "That means you don't believe," he retorted after a few minutes. "It's bad. I must have a serious talk with you about this."[13]

3
———

Another feminine writer and pedagogue, L. X. Simonova-Khokhryakova, who probably furnished some traits for Mme Khokhlakova in *The Broth-*

ers *Karamazov*, also dropped in on Dostoevsky about this time and reported her observations and their conversations. "Feodor Mikhailovich," she writes, "was a remarkably impressionable, nervous, terribly irritable person, but kind, pure-hearted, and responsive to every genuine feeling. The sudden transitions from extraordinary tenderness and amicability to explosions of irascibility can be explained by his organism racked with illness (as a result of his prison camp years and the attacks of epilepsy). But if in these moments of irascibility someone appeared who was truly devoted to him, and uttered words of friendliness and sympathy, even though this person stood before Dostoevsky for the first time, it made no difference. Immediately he became a friend, to whom Dostoevsky poured out all the depth of his love for humanity, to whom he expressed all the bitterness that had accumulated in his soul." Such was, evidently, Simonova-Khokhryakova's own experience when she rang his doorbell in April 1876, "with a fiercely beating heart, and a consciousness of all the stupidity of my behavior."[14]

On this occasion he cut short the embarrassed explanations of his unexpected visitor, took her by both hands, and seated her by his side on a divan. The conversation turned immediately to the *Diary*, of which she was an avid reader; and the bitterness she mentions probably refers to his complaint that there were no Russian critics "who approached their task seriously and with impartiality." Instead of reading carefully, he lamented, they raced through what they were supposed to be writing about and then "came forth with their opinions either in the form of a joke, or in that of abuse, concentrating on the personality of the author rather than his work. 'And my novels *The Idiot* and *A Raw Youth* also up to now have not been understood,' he said among many other things."[15]

His interlocutress then turned the conversation to *A Raw Youth*. The monologue of Versilov describing the world after the disappearance of God had affected her profoundly, and she remarked acutely that "the atheists remind one of the most ideal Christians," citing the passage about the love that men and women mutually lavish on each other in the absence of God. To which he replied: "Yes, I would also wish that to be so, but it is a dream. Without God, they will tear apart each other's throats, and nothing more."[16] What strikes one here is both his acceptance of the comparison, which implies a recognition of the moral idealism implicit even in the atheistic "dream," and the note almost of regret with which he speaks of the impossibility of its realization. Without God (and Christ), such idealism, he was persuaded, could not by itself conquer the powerful forces of egoism in the human breast.

Another visit by Simonova-Khokhryakova took place after the appearance of the October 1876 issue of the *Diary*, which contained one of his most famous articles, "The Sentence." The text was presumably a suicide note left behind by an atheist and materialist, who had taken his life out of what may be called metaphysical outrage (much of Ivan Karamazov's tirade against God's inhumanity to man is prefigured in this powerful indictment). Simonova-Khokhryakova remarks, with some exaggeration, that Dostoevsky was the only person paying attention to suicide at that time. On the contrary, the epidemic of suicides then sweeping over Russia was being widely discussed; but while others viewed it only as a grave social problem, he approached it on his own religious-metaphysical terms.[17] Refusing to accept the standard medical verdict that such acts were evidence of mental disorder, he insisted that people perfectly capable of rational thought could well reason themselves into a state of despair leading to suicide. And "The Sentence" presented such persuasive arguments for self-destruction, with very little to counterbalance their effect, that many readers like his visitor were seriously perturbed. Of course, Dostoevsky's aim was to show that, without a belief in God and the immortality of the soul, human life is senseless and could thus well end in a "rational" suicide. But because he had left the necessity for religious belief to be inferred from the suicide letter, rather than expressing it in some overt fashion, a number of readers had written him in some perplexity. He admitted to Simonova-Khokhryakova that he was quite disturbed by this widespread reaction.

Her first question was whether he had invented the suicide note himself or had used as its basis a document left by an actual suicide. He replied without hesitation:

"It's mine, I wrote it myself."
"Are you yourself an atheist?"
"I am a deist, a philosophical deist," he answered and then asked me: "But why?"
"Your 'Sentence' is written in such a way that I thought you were setting forth what you had lived through yourself."

She then spoke of the "terrible impression" that the piece could produce on readers, leading some who might never have thought of suicide to contemplate it, or even to kill others so as to put them out of their misery. He became dreadfully upset at these words, jumped up from his seat, and gave vent to his dismay. "'I am not understood, not understood,' he repeated in despair, then suddenly sat beside me, grasped my hands, and uttered in a rapid whisper: 'I wanted to show that it is impossible to live without Christianity. I put in the little word *ergo*: it meant that without Christianity it is impossible to live. How is it that neither you nor the others noticed this word, and did not understand what it meant?'" He then stood up, straightened himself erect, and pro-

222

nounced in a firm voice: "Now I give my promise that to the end of my days I will atone for the evil caused by my 'Sentence.'"[18]

Simonova-Khokhryakova attributes the pronounced "religious character" of Dostoevsky's last work to this incident; and although she no doubt assigns the episode too much importance, it may well have contributed to his desire to express his own, positive point of view less indirectly than in the past. She was not wrong, however, in surmising that, at least in imagination, he had lived through the process of thought so chillingly unrolled in the fictitious suicide note. Many years before, in *House of the Dead*, he had imagined some fiendish camp commandant assigning the convicts the absolutely senseless task, day after day and with no end in sight, of carrying buckets of sand back and forth from one end of the camp to the other. He had predicted that, under such conditions, "the convict would hang himself in a few days or would commit a thousand crimes, preferring to die rather than to endure such humiliation, shame, and torture" (4: 20). For Dostoevsky, to live in a world without God and immortality was the moral-psychological equivalent of the convicts endlessly transporting sand to no purpose; and he was profoundly persuaded that the human psyche would not endure such meaningless indignity. One can hardly doubt that the writer capable of *imagining* the torments of his fellow convicts persecuted in this fashion must have lived through similarly excruciating feelings himself. It is curious, however, that he calls his own faith "philosophical deism," perhaps thinking of the state of mind in which he had composed "The Sentence." For there is a clear contradiction between his own Christocentrism and a philosophical deism which, historically, had accepted God but whose attitude toward the supernatural Jesus was at best extremely dubious.*

One more visitor to the author of the *Diary* remains to be mentioned, Sofya Lurie. The daughter of a banker in Minsk, all of eighteen years old and studying in St. Petersburg, she hoped to obtain his guidance and advice in pursuing her education. He replied that "it is difficult for

---

* Since Dostoevsky said almost nothing directly about his personal religious convictions, this testimony raises many questions and may justify some speculation. Could Dostoevsky have been talking about the fictional narrator of "The Sentence" and not about himself as a person? He might have meant that, as the author of "The Sentence," he had assumed the position of the narrator, who is certainly a "philosophical deist," at least accepting God as a hypothesis against Whom he protests, but not the promises of the Christian faith. One should also note that Versilov in *A Raw Youth* calls himself "a philosophical deist" (13: 379).

On the other hand, Dostoevsky employs the term "deism" elsewhere with a meaning much broader than customary. In writing of George Sand in his *Diary of a Writer*, he said that she "died a *deiste*, firmly believing in God and in the immortality of the soul" (23: 37). Deism here would thus conform to much of Dostoevsky's own sense of the essence of Christianity.

me to send right off, in a letter, several titles of books," and he suggests that she come to visit him "between three and four in the afternoon. . . . A book should be chosen in line with one's cast of mind, and therefore it's best to get to know each other better."[19]

Dostoevsky not only befriended Sofya Lurie, whose name indicates her Jewish origin, but also wrote about her quite warmly if anonymously in the *Diary*. There he speaks of a young girl who "would come to ask my advice on what to read and what to pay particular attention to. She has been visiting me about once a month, staying no more than ten minutes; she would speak only of her own affairs, but briefly, modestly, almost shyly, showing a remarkable trust in me. Yet I could also see she had a very resolute character." On this occasion, she had come to tell him of her intention to enlist as a nurse to serve in Serbia, obviously seeking his approval. Although sympathizing wholeheartedly with this "pure case of longing for sacrifice, for some noble feat, for some good deed," he tried to warn her of the dangers and hardships she might face. "Might you not faint at the sight of some death, some wound or operation? This happens despite one's will, unconsciously." But "it was impossible to dissuade her," and when Dostoevsky finally gave his blessing, "she went away radiant, and, of course, she will be *there* in a week" (23: 51–53). In fact, Sofya Lurie never went to Serbia because she gave way to the entreaties of her father; but she continued to correspond with Dostoevsky and later furnished him with material essential for his notoriously ambivalent reflections on the Jewish Question.

4
---

In the summer of 1876 he made another trip to Bad Ems, where he drank the waters for a month. Such an absence, of course, involved special problems for the publication of his monthly *Diary*, and he published only a July–August combined issue. The voyage proved much less taxing than earlier such journeys, and although both Russian and German coaches were packed, "the people were bearable." As the train approached the German border, he was "pestered by a Yid," whom he calls "one of the superior Yids," rich and educated, who regaled him "with information about his two professional sons in Petersburg (a lawyer and a doctor), as well as about his own medical problem of hemorrhoids" (from which Dostoevsky also suffered). "Out of politeness," he informs Anna, he had to endure this obstreperous gentleman for four hours. Otherwise, he remarks with some surprise, his German fellow passengers "simply waited on me and regarded me almost with respect." What oppressed him, though, was the general conversation—"all only about business deals and interests and the price of items, of goods, about the merry life with camellias [elegant prostitutes] and officers—and that was all. There was neither education nor any higher interests—nothing! I can't at all understand who can now read, and why the *Diary of a Writer* still has several thousand buyers."[20]

On the portion of the journey from Berlin to Ems, conversing with a Russian and his daughter, he found them to be "the epitome of triteness, banality, and haughtiness among those who knock around abroad, and the daughter a nitwit and a numbskull." Dostoevsky was quite intolerant of Russians who chose to live in Europe, tending to regard them as unwilling to adjust to the transformations of Russian life brought about by the liberation of the serfs. Another incident, recorded for Anna's delectation, recalled for him an illustration by Cham (a famous French caricaturist). During a stopover, while he and others were in the men's room, into their midst "*came running* a well-dressed lady, by all indications an Englishwoman," who was in the middle of the urinals before becoming aware of her mistake. She "suddenly shrieked extremely loudly, or rather squealed," and threw up her hands "with a sweeping motion." Dostoevsky carefully notes the movements of this mortified gentlewoman and even intuits her state of mind. "She suddenly covered her face with both palms, and, after turning around rather slowly (everything was lost, it was all over, there was no reason to rush), her entire figure inclined forward, she left the *room* deliberately, and not without dignity." What struck him was the contrast in national psychology that he observed. "The Germans were all gloomily silent, while in Russia people would surely have laughed and guffawed with delight."[21]

By this time he was a familiar figure in Ems, and "at the post office, and everywhere in all of Ems (shopkeepers, porters, women selling fruit, store owners) everyone recognizes me and everyone greets me with a smile." The shock of strangeness, which earlier he had felt so strongly and unpleasantly, had by now dissipated; but nonetheless, "Ems seemed hideously dull to me." His regular physician, Dr. Orth, whom he now regarded much more kindly, gave a mixed report after a careful initial examination. There had been some improvement in one part of his lungs, a deterioration in another. "Then, in reply to my insistent question, he said that death is still far off and that I would live a long time yet, but that, of course, there's the Petersburg climate—that I need to take precautions, and so on and so forth."[22] Dostoevsky found accommodations in a hotel at which he had stayed before (the Ville d'Alger, with a landlady who spoke French) but complained that his neighbors (a mother and daughter from Greece) never stopped chattering. He finally took a less pleasant flat on a higher floor so that he could read and write undisturbed.

His letters from Ems do not differ essentially from the earlier ones, and contain the same complaints about his aching loneliness and constant anxieties about the health and welfare of Anna and the children. The failure to receive a letter at the expected time threw him into a panic, and he imagined all sorts of catastrophes occurring to his family. The treatments were also affecting him very strongly, more so than in the past, "and I suddenly had something like a fainting fit, but for no longer than a second—and I grabbed hold of a tree. Then heart palpitations set in, which lasted until night, and a great rush of blood to the top of my head." All these symptoms, he reassures Anna, are described in a book about the effects of drinking the Ems waters, and so he was not alarmed; his appetite was good, though he found the food barely palatable. The pressure of the *Diary*, however, was weighing him down: "I don't have any ideas and I don't know when I'll get started, and when I asked about literary activities, Orth absolutely forbade them. I won't obey him, of course, but five days have passed now, and I still haven't got anything done."[23]

Dostoevsky's letters from Ems had always been filled with expressions of his tenderness for Anna, as well as reminders of the physical passion that united the couple. The same continues to be the case; and, on reading them over many years later, Anna Grigoryevna thought it prudent to black out a number of passages that were too explicit for her decorous sensibility. These letters are among the most mutilated in the Dostoevsky canon, though one can still read his avowal that he has fallen in love with her four or five times since their marriage, and that this has now occurred again. "Anechka," he writes, "all I do is think of you. I think of you in all possible sorts of pictures and representations. . . . I love you to the point of torment."[24] This flare-up of passion may perhaps be linked to an episode occurring just before his departure, when he and Anna had quarreled because of a curious incident that she recounts in her memoirs.

A friend of theirs had written a novel that both had read and in which an anonymous letter was sent to one of the characters, informing him that his wife had been unfaithful; the proof could be found in a locket that she wore. Anna decided, as a "joke," to send such a letter to Dostoevsky, assuming he would recognize the imitation of the text and that they both would have a hearty laugh. Instead, he ripped her locket from her neck, drawing blood, and was furious at the so-called "prank." " 'You keep on joking, Anechka,' he said, ' . . . but just think what a terrible thing might have happened. I might have strangled you in my rage!' " Once his fury had subsided, however, the evening "passed in apologies, regrets, and the most loving tenderness"—which one suspects was the aim of the whole escapade.[25] An exchange of letters about

12. Anna Grigoryevna Dostoevskaya in 1878

the reappearance of one of Anna's ex-suitors also indicates that she was again attempting to stimulate his jealousy, possibly as a means of warding off possible attractions abroad.

5

Dostoevsky purchased a guest register of the visitors at Ems but was unable to find the names of anyone he knew among those of rank, and he had no wish to meet the others. They were all "Russian Yids and Germans—bankers and pawnbrokers. Not a single acquaintance." He ran into a Baron Gans, a retired artillery general, whom he had met while taking compressed air treatments in St. Petersburg; and he wrote about him to a mutual acquaintance, a society lady encountered under the same circumstances. The baron confided that he had received a death sentence from a renowned Berlin specialist but that he had then gone to Munich to be treated by someone called the *Wunderfrau* (presumably an unorthodox healer), and "she helped me greatly." Dostoevsky told him that "I was also under sentence and one of the incurables, and we even grieved a little over our fate, and then suddenly broke out laughing." He waxes ironic about the advice of the doctors, who assure him that, if he leads an impossibly tranquil existence, he can increase his longevity. "That has absolutely reassured me, of course," he adds with a touch of sarcasm.[26]

Although he made no effort to seek out other Russians, he met by chance the well-known radical publicist G. Z. Eliseev, who was also taking the cure and with whom he had rubbed elbows in St. Petersburg. Despite their sharply differing opinions on social-political and religious matters, Dostoevsky and the Eliseevs (he was accompanied by his wife) managed to remain on speaking terms, though it was always touch and go after each encounter. An important figure in the radical journalism of the era, Eliseev, like many others, had come from a priestly family and been educated in theological seminaries. In his case, he remained within their walls long enough to become a professor at the Ecclesiastical Academy of Kazan and to gain a reputation by his contributions to church history.

Losing his faith, he quit his teaching post for a journalistic career in Petersburg and became an active figure in the intellectual ferment of the 1860s, writing for Chernyshevsky's *Sovremennik* (*The Contemporary*) before its suppression, the radical satirical journal *Iskra* (*The Spark*), and others of the same tendency. It was he, as noted earlier, who had penned a bitterly hostile review of the first chapters of *Crime and Punishment*, accusing Dostoevsky of maliciously indicting the entire student population as murderers. By the 1870s, however, times had changed, and the antagonists had more in common than might appear at first sight. Eliseev had stood out among the radicals of the 1860s by his very positive attitude toward the indigenous institutions of the Russian people, such as the *obshchina* (commune), which others viewed only as the embryo of a future Socialist order. And he maintained, as Dostoevsky and the Slavophils had always done, that Russian history differed from that of Europe because it had never known feudalism and class warfare. Historians generally agree that Eliseev's ideas and personality exercised an important influence on the younger Nikolay K. Mikhailovsky, and that he was one of the precursors of Russian Populism.[27]

The first impression of Eliseev in Ems was hardly favorable. "At the waters here yesterday I ran into Eliseev. He's here with his wife, is being treated, and came up to me himself. I don't think I am going to get on with him, however; the old 'negator' doesn't believe in anything

... and most importantly, he absolutely has a seminarian's haughty smugness." Dostoevsky thought (mistakenly) that Eliseev's wife came from the same clerical milieu: "she's from the ranks of the new, 'progressive' women, the 'negators.'" Amusingly enough, the unbeliever Eliseev, on hearing of a victory of the Montenegrins in their revolt against the Turks, wished to organize a solemn service of thanksgiving, and he asked Dostoevsky to enlist the services of the local Orthodox priest. Much to Dostoevsky's satisfaction, the priest "sensibly rejected [the idea] on the pretext that the news of the victory had not been sufficiently confirmed (which is true), but I persuaded [him] to sign up the Russians for a financial contribution to the Slavic cause." Both he and the priest gave fifteen marks, and Dostoevsky slyly questioned whether Eliseev would do the same, "because seminarians . . . like demonstrations but they very much dislike donating anything." When he failed to see the Eliseevs the next day, he wondered "whether he wasn't angry for my having given it to the seminarians yesterday. His wife is definitely angry at me: she started arguing with me about the existence of God, and I told her, among other things, that she was just repeating her husband's ideas. That made her very angry."[28]

Despite such altercations, relations were not broken off, though every meeting raised the hackles on both sides. "The trashy vulgar little liberals," he fumes nine days later, "have undone even my nerves. They force themselves on me and greet me constantly, but treat me as though they were being careful 'so as not to get soiled by my reactionaryism.' The vainest creatures, especially her, a banal little book with liberal rules. 'Oh what he says, oh what he defends!' These two think of teaching someone like me." Dostoevsky also met one of their friends, a female writer and publicist active in the women's movement, Elena Likhacheva, who had just returned from Belgrade, "and all she does is talk about humane compassion for the Serbs, but I think she's a gossipmonger." Both Populists and Pan-Slavic nationalists like Dostoevsky were supporting the Slav cause against Turkey; but this union did not lessen his dislike of these new allies. Likhacheva had a sixteen-year-old son whom Dostoevsky found sympathetic, and "I kept him at my place for a quarter of an hour and started instructing him in *non*-liberalism, tossing in the fact that *seminarists* have caused a lot of harm for us, without hinting in the least at Eliseev." This halfhearted stab at discretion was of course unsuccessful, "and that evening when I saw them . . . I saw their coldness, and assume that the boy conveyed my conversation to the mother, and she to them."[29] Nonetheless, just a few days before leaving, he informs Anna that "the Eliseevs have again turned to me, and more cordially than ever. But I don't care." What worried him was that he might be forced to "come back with them in the same train car."[30] Fortunately, he was spared this unpleasantness, and they vanish henceforth from his correspondence—but not from his literary purview. For there is good reason to believe that the cynical Rakitin of the *Brothers Karamazov*, who never takes his eyes off of the main chance, and who, Alyosha predicts, will found a radical journal and acquire a plush house with its proceeds, is based on a caricature of the career of Grigory Eliseev.

6

All through this period Dostoevsky continued to fret over the *Diary* and was haunted by the fear that he would not be able to produce it at all. "The possibility of a seizure frightens me," he wrote Anna in mid-July while at Ems. "What then will happen to the *Diary*, which I have not yet gotten down to work on?" But he doggedly continued to make preparations to write and, in the same letter, informs her that "I have been rereading all the correspondence [from his readers] that I brought here. I signed up at the lending library (a pathetic library), took out Zola because I've terribly neglected European literature in recent years, and just imagine, I can scarcely read it, it's such revolting stuff. And in Russia people carry on about Zola as a celebrity, a leading light of realism."[31] Emile Zola was then writing a regular letter from Paris in the liberal *Vestnik Evropy* (*European Messenger*), having been recommended by his friend Turgenev, and he was hailed as the leading proponent and practitioner of a literary naturalism enjoying a considerable vogue. Several translations of one novel alone—*Le Ventre de Paris* (*The Belly of Paris*), the book he borrowed from the Ems library—had been published in 1873, and there were widespread discussions of Zola's works and theories in the Russian press.

He jotted down his first reactions in his notebooks; and though highly critical, they were by no means imperceptive. Pages and pages of Zola's novel are devoted to describing the flood of produce flowing into the then newly built market area of Les Halles, and Dostoevsky notes: "*Le Ventre de Paris*, p. 30 on cabbage and carrots (forced ecstasy)." One character, an artist, is intoxicated both with the vistas of old Paris streets then being demolished by the minions of Baron Haussmann, and with the shapes and colors piled up in such motley profusion in the market area. Of him Dostoevsky writes: "Painter *Claude*. He is not a man. The eternal ecstasy is ridiculous." He then recalls the characters created by a Russian Romantic dramatist now totally discredited because of his bombast, Nestor Kukolnik: "There are the ecstatic figures in Kukolnik's dramas. . . . Only they spoke of Raphael, these, of cabbage." To Dostoevsky, "all this is incorrect, all this is exaggerated, and for that reason far from *réalité*, and for that reason you cannot (should not) spit on George

Sand," whose "idealism" was often used as a foil against which to high-light the grittier merits of Zola.

Insightfully noting Zola's attempt to create impressionistic effects in his prose, he found the results quite tedious: "He will describe every nail in the heel, a quarter hour later, when the sun rises, he will again describe that nail in a different light. That is not art. Give me a single word (Pushkin), but make it the necessary word. Otherwise it rushes off in all directions and drags in ten thousand words, and still cannot express itself, and this with the most complete self-satisfaction, but spare me." Nor can he accept the morality that Zola contrasted with the purely materialistic ambitions and satisfactions of his shopkeeper and tradesman figures. "*Florent* [an ex-revolutionary returned from prison and exile] dies of hunger and proudly spurned the help of an honest woman. *Zola* considers this a heroic deed, but in his heart there is no brotherhood, what sort of republican is he? Accept her help and render it to others out of the fullness of a noble heart—that will be paradise on earth" (24: 238–239). Little did he know, as he was scribbling these remarks, that ten years later his own novels would help to break the grip of Zola's Naturalism on a new French literary generation.

Amidst constant laments over what to include in the *Diary* ("I'm still only compiling . . . and I still haven't started, and it worries me terribly"), one of the few bright spots is an enthusiastic reaction to Beethoven. "My angel, this morning I heard the overture to Beethoven's *Fidelio*. Nothing more lofty than it has ever been written. It's in a light and graceful vein, but with passion. With Beethoven there's passion and love everywhere. He's the poet of love, happiness, and passionate longing."[32] Dostoevsky had always been a devoted music lover, and he faithfully attended the daily concerts at Ems as one of his few distractions.

His morose mood during these days was considerably lifted by a letter from Vsevolod Solovyev, who also sent a copy of an enthusiastic article he had written about the June issue of the *Diary*. This fascicule contained a heartfelt obituary to George Sand, one of the idols of his youth, as well as a statement, in no uncertain terms, of his exalted conception of Russia's world-historical mission. The task of Russia, he proclaimed, was to bring about the union of all the Slavs and thus resolve the Eastern Question; and this unification would be the prelude to a universal reconciliation of all peoples under the banner of the true Christ preserved only in Russian Orthodoxy. Dostoevsky was very pleased with Solovyev's accolade because he felt that in this issue, for the first time, he had at last dared to allow himself "to take *certain* of my convictions to their conclusions, to say *the last word* . . . of my dreams regarding Russia's role and mission amid humanity, and I expressed the idea that this would not only happen in the near future, but was already beginning to come true." The result had been that "even the newspapers and publications friendly to me straight away started yelling that I heaped paradox on paradox." In thanking Solovyev, he tells him "to judge for yourself whether after this your friendly word on behalf of the June issue is dear to me."[33]

For all of Solovyev's praise, Dostoevsky concludes that perhaps such explicitness had been self-defeating, and he uses a religious example to illustrate the point. "If you say for instance, and suddenly, 'such and such is in fact the *Messiah*,' right out and not in a hint . . . no one will believe you precisely because of your naïveté." He had indeed announced something analogous to declaring Russia to be a world-historical Messiah, and this pronouncement had elicited a great deal of skepticism; but he argues that the same skepticism would greet any open declaration of the ultimate ideals of those who scoff at his Russian-Christian messianism. "If any of the most famous wits, Voltaire, for instance, instead of gibes, hints, bare suggestions, and insinuations, had suddenly ventured to state everything they believed, had shown their whole underpinning all at once, their essence, then, believe me, they wouldn't have obtained even a tenth of the earlier effect. Moreover, people would just have laughed at them."[34] Actually, the unusual candor of Dostoevsky's expression of his views, whether his readers agreed with him or not, impressed them very favorably by its sharp contrast with the usual circumlocutions and evasiveness of the Russian press.

Such responses made him all the more determined to maintain the quality of his *Diary*, and he ends his letter to Solovyev by expressing the fear that this will not be possible from Ems. "I promised an August *Diary* in a double number of signatures, but meanwhile I haven't even started and in addition there's the ennui and such apathy that I regard the upcoming writing with revulsion, as a looming misfortune. I have a premonition that a very bad issue will result."[35] Eight days later he tells Anna that the *Diary* "is turning out to be so rubbishy, so pathetic, while, as luck would have it, it needs to be made as striking as possible, otherwise it's kaput. In short, Anka, I'm in a depression, in a literary depression."[36] Life at Ems was becoming too oppressive for him to endure much longer, and the prospect of a mediocre *Diary*—or no *Diary* at all on the promised date—was one that he refused to tolerate. He thus decided to cut short the period of his cure and to return to the nurturing home environment that had now become indispensable for both his psychic and literary well-being.

Announcing to Anna that he would stay only four weeks at Ems instead of the customary six, he attempts to put as good a face as possible on this curtailment, reassuring her that Dr. Orth "says that I don't need any more." The doctor, of course, knew that his patient had decided to depart in any case. Dostoevsky's letters swing back and forth on this point, responding to Anna's anxieties and seeking to placate her with reports of how much his health had already improved. The truth, however, as he admits, is "that my course of treatment should be six weeks instead of four . . . but because of the *Diary* I cannot possibly spend six weeks here."[37] Just after returning, he told Simonova-Khokhryakova that his health was "bad, very bad. Abroad, it did not improve, rather became even worse."[38] In mid-August he was back in Russia, which left him two weeks to whip the July–August issue of the *Diary* into shape.

## 7

Dostoevsky's *Diary* became the most widely read of all such publications during its two-year life span, and reached audiences not only in the depths of the Russian provinces but also in the very highest court circles. In the fall of 1876, Konstantin P. Pobedonostsev requested that he send a copy regularly to Tsarevich Alexander. "I know," wrote the crown prince's tutor, "that yesterday, in the presence of his brothers, he spoke of several articles and recommended them to their attention."[39] Dostoevsky was of course overjoyed at this display of interest from such an exalted personage; and although Pobedonostsev suggested merely sending copies through the post, or through him if a note were included, he decided that some explanation was in order. He wrote directly to Alexander, to whom he had presented a dedicated copy of *The Devils* three years earlier, clarifying why he had not dispatched copies of the *Diary* from the very start: "I was not yet certain myself that I would not break it off at the very beginning because of a lack of energy and health for work possessing a definite urgency. And therefore I did not venture to offer your Imperial Highness such an as yet uncertain work." Now, however, "the present great energies in Russian history have elevated the spirits and hearts of the Russian people with unimaginable power to a height of understanding of much that was not earlier understood, and have illuminated in our consciousness *the sanctity of the Russian idea* more vividly than ever before. I could not fail to respond, either, with all my heart to everything that has begun and appeared in our land, in our just and wonderful people . . . [and] I have long since thought and dreamed of the happiness of offering my modest work to your Imperial Highness." He then excuses himself for his "boldness," and asks that the crown prince "not condemn one who loves you boundlessly."[40]

Although this letter may seem overly obsequious, one should remember that he had ample reasons to be grateful to the royal house of the Romanovs. Nicholas I had reduced his prison sentence and allowed him to retain his civil rights; Alexander II had granted his request to become an officer; and just three years earlier the Tsarevich had come to his aid with a grant of money that saw him through a difficult period. More-over, the peaceful liberation of the serfs by Alexander II had been for him the miraculous realization of the ideals that had sent him to Siberia; and this event is referred to again and again in the *Diary* as the symbolic basis of his own extravagant glorification of "the sanctity of the Russian idea." It was, for him, the historical proof that Russia could solve its social problems without the violence endemic to the West.

Dostoevsky was perfectly well aware that his own veneration for Tsarism was hardly shared by the most socially conscious members of the younger generation he was trying to influence. Indeed, there were disquieting signs that radical activity was no longer confined to "going to the people." Discouraged by their failure to arouse the countryside, the Populists in 1876 were in the process of rethinking their position and turning to political agitation in the effort to attain their aims. One of the first open manifestations of this change of tactics was a demonstration in the square leading to the Church of Our Lady of Kazan in St. Petersburg. In December 1876 a small group led by G. V. Plekhanov (later the founder of the Russian Communist party and the mentor of Lenin) gathered to listen to a speech by their leader and unfurled a red banner bearing the words "Zemlya i Volya" (Land and Liberty), the name of their new revolutionary organization. The police, as well as local workmen and shopkeepers, charged into the group, and many of the demonstrators were severely beaten before being taken into custody. Among the arrests, that of a presumably innocent passerby named Bogolyubov (God-lover) was to have fateful consequences two years later.

For Dostoevsky, the demonstration was simply another instance of how easily Russian youth could be misled because of the purity of their moral idealism. "The young people on December 6 in Kazan Square," he wrote in the *Diary*, "were doubtless nothing more than a 'herd' driven on by the hands of some crafty scoundrels. . . . Without a doubt there was a good deal of malicious and immoral tomfoolery here, a monkeylike aping of someone else's doings; nonetheless, it would have been possible to bring them together simply by assuring them that they were to gather in the name of something sublime and beautiful, in the name of some remarkable self-sacrifice for the greatest of purposes" (24: 52). One of the aims of Dostoevsky's *Diary* was to encourage such youthful self-sacrifice for what he considered worthier causes than those proclaimed in Kazan Square.

## CHAPTER 13

# Intimations of Mortality

The year 1877 brought no notable change in Dostoevsky's laborious life. The rigorous routine of the *Diary* allowed little time for anything else, and all his energies were completely absorbed in keeping up to schedule and coping with the growing number of readers who turned to him for advice and counsel on every conceivable subject. He could not respond to all such appeals, but it is surprising how many he answered. Meanwhile, his family life proceeded along its usual course—which included the management of what had become a small publishing firm, whose operations continued to increase with the success of the *Diary*. Anna Grigoryevna was in charge of this family business, but Dostoevsky took an active part as well when necessity demanded.

The growing circulation of the *Diary* was thus as much a burden as a blessing, and the strain of keeping to schedule became more and more onerous. His letters refer to a rise in the number and severity of his epileptic attacks, which he directly attributes to the pressure of producing the *Diary*. Not only was the writing itself a formidable labor, but he was continually harassed by battles with the censorship. In addition, a new novel was pecking at his brain like a chicken in an eggshell (to use one of his own images); and the end of the year saw his decision to suspend the *Diary* temporarily (as he optimistically believed) to give himself time to write *The Brothers Karamazov*.

## 2

During 1877, Dostoevsky often went to visit the sickbed of Nikolay Nekrasov. For the last two years of his life (he died early in 1878), he was in constant pain, relieved only by opium and other drugs, and practically immobile. A celebrated painting by I. N. Kramskoy depicts the poet much as Dostoevsky must have seen him, lying on a couch propped up with pillows, his wasted body clad only in a shroudlike nightshirt, looking into the distance while composing his *Last Songs* (*Poslednie Pesni*). A sister who kept a diary during the final stages of the poet's illness records that Nekrasov particularly valued these visits. "Dostoevsky arrived; my brother is linked to him by memories of their youth (they are the same age) and he is fond of him. 'I can't speak but tell him to come

13. The ailing Nikolay A. Nekrasov in 1877, by I. N. Kramskoy

in for a [word missing], it does me good to see him.'"[1] On this occasion, to cheer up the moribund Nekrasov, Dostoevsky told him that, on a recent visit to a prison, he had seen in this unlikely locale a copy of *The Physiology of Petersburg* (an important anthology of sketches of urban life, one of the pioneer works of the Natural School), which the poet had edited in 1845.

The conversations between these two aging and ailing veterans of the Russian culture wars quite naturally often dwelt on the halcyon days of their youth, and these are utilized by Dostoevsky in his January 1877 *Diary* for some of the most touchingly evocative autobiographical pages in all of Russian literature. Nekrasov had spoken nostalgically about the 1840s, when, as Dostoevsky puts it, "something happened so characteristic of youth, and so fresh and fine . . . that [it] remains forever in the hearts of those involved." Nekrasov was then sharing an apartment with another young writer, D. V. Grigorovich, to whom Dostoevsky spoke of having just completed *Poor Folk*. *The Physiology of Petersburg* had already appeared, and Grigorovich knew that Nekrasov was planning to edit a successor composed of stories and sketches. Dostoevsky's novel, perhaps, could make a contribution, and Grigorovich asked for a copy. When he and Nekrasov read it aloud that evening, they were so deeply stirred that, at four in the morning, they rushed to Dostoevsky's flat to congratulate him on a masterpiece. They took the manuscript to Belinsky the next day, proclaiming, "A new Gogol has been born." Initially skeptical, Belinsky soon became equally enthusiastic; and Dostoevsky was thus launched on the road to fame, if not to fortune.[2]

The encounter with the dying Nekrasov thus released a flood of memories dwelling on the exhilarating moments unforgettably linking the two men. But mention is also made that "strange things happen to people; we rarely saw one another and there were misunderstandings between us as well" (25: 28). Just a year after the triumph of *Poor Folk*, Dostoevsky's inordinate vanity and egoism, which he sadly acknowledged in a letter, led to the circulation of a satirical poem by Nekrasov and Turgenev describing him as "a pimple" on the face of Russian literature. Nekrasov himself wrote an unfinished short story entitled "What a Great Man I Am!" which contains a withering portrait of Dostoevsky. Even though this satire remained unpublished until 1905, it was surely read privately to members of Dostoevsky's former literary circle, and rumors about it must have reached his ears.

Later, when Dostoevsky returned from Siberia, Nekrasov, as editor of *Sovremennik* (*The Contemporary*), refused one of his stories and let it be known that he thought his talent was gone for good. A divergence of social-cultural views also drove the two men apart as differences hardened among the Russian intelligentsia of the 1860s, and Nekrasov turned his journal over to spokesmen of the new generation like N. G. Chernyshevsky and Nikolay Dobrolyubov, advocates of the materialism and Utilitarianism that Dostoevsky had come to loathe. All the same, when Nekrasov published a volume of poems in 1863, he presented a copy to his old friend and, pointing to one called "The Unfortunate One" ("Nechastnie"), said: "I thought of you when I wrote this." The poem depicts the sad fate of an educated political prisoner thrown, exactly as Dostoevsky had been, into the midst of the turbulent and unruly mob of common-law criminals in Siberia (25: 31). More recently, the Populism of the 1870s had allowed the old friendship to resume after many years of estrangement.

3
———

These autobiographical pages in the *Diary* provide a precious source of information about Dostoevsky's early life and are of great interest in their own right; but there are other signs that he wished to repossess his past as his fame increased and he became, as it were, a historical figure in his own lifetime. A biographical notice about him had appeared in the 1875 edition of a *Russian Encyclopedic Dictionary*, written by the journalist, playwright, and literary jack-of-all-trades Vladimir Zotov. The article was riddled with inaccuracies; and, to make matters worse, the characterization of his writings was highly unflattering. He thus took the trouble to set matters straight in the very first issue of the *Diary* for 1876. His notes for "A Word apropos of My Biography" contain much harsher comments than he allowed himself in print, and he attributes Zotov's manifest ill will to envy at the great success of *Poor Folk* in 1845. Zotov himself, he comments bitingly, wrote innumerable dramas that "passed without a trace, flowed past like spring waters, although without the usefulness of the latter, for they did not irrigate the scraggy plains of our belles lettres."[3]

In the *Diary*, he restricts his remarks largely to correcting factual errors; but also objects to the vagueness of the reference to himself as a "state criminal," with no explanation specifying the nature of his "crime." Zotov, he notes, had simply said that he "was involved in the Petrashevsky affair, that is, in God knows what sort of affair, since no one is obliged to know and remember the Petrashevsky affair—people might think that I was exiled for robbery." He also takes exception to the statement that he was "deported" to Siberia, which implied being sent into permanent exile as a settler. In fact, he served in the Russian Army after completing his sentence at hard labor and reached the rank of officer. Zotov, moreover, badly scrambled the chronology of Dostoevsky's works and erroneously declared him to have been the editor of a journal called *Russkii Mir* (*Russian World*). All these mistakes are noted, though without going into details that he feared might bore his readers; but he offers to specify the errors more precisely if such information were requested (22: 37–38).

Dostoevsky was concerned not only to correct errors about his own life but also to protect the reputation of his deceased elder brother, Mikhail, who had been co-editor and in charge of the finances of their two journals, *Time* and *Epoch*. A recent obituary of the historian A. P. Shchapov, a contributor to *Time*, intimated that Mikhail had cheated the impoverished Shchapov out of a proper fee for his articles. These had developed an influential theory that the religious *Raskol* of the seventeenth century contained a social-political as well as a theological significance. Dostoevsky was outraged at this slur on his brother's character and vehemently denied the accusation. It was more likely, he said, that Mikhail had given advances for articles never written than cheat a contributor. (There is evidence to support this contention in the account books of both journals.)

He also stressed the incongruity of imputing any such behavior to a man of his brother's culture and attainments. "He was highly educated, a gifted writer, an expert in European literatures, a poet, and a well-known translator of Schiller and Goethe." Most important of all, in the defense of his brother he lifts for a moment the secrecy shrouding his own role in the Petrashevsky circle. Mikhail, a devoted Fourierist, had refused to join the Speshnev activists; but "although he took no part in anything, he still *knew a great deal*," that is, he knew about the revolutionary plans of the Speshnev group but said not a word that might have betrayed them. At this time, Mikhail was already the father of three children and could well have broken down under the possibility of life-long exile. "And now people want to show such a man in collusion with some Jewish tailor to cheat Shchapov . . . and put a few rubles in their pockets! What rubbish!" (22: 132–135). If nothing else, such an episode drove home to Dostoevsky the importance of attempting to set the record straight so far as his own life was concerned.

4
-----

Dostoevsky's offer to furnish more information about himself was taken up in March 1876 by P. V. Bykov, a journalist and writer who had met him fleetingly in the 1860s. As a very young man, Bykov had frequented the circle of contributors around Dostoevsky and his journal *Time*. He desired to obtain a reliable biography and bibliography for a volume of essays on Russian writers that he planned to publish, and Dostoevsky replied very positively a month later to the request. But after thanking Bykov for some kind words about his writings, he confesses: "As for your suggestion that I send you an exact biography, I'll tell you right out that at present I am incapable of that. That will require a lot of time and effort, and it's not as easy for me as you think. As a consequence of my epilepsy . . . I have somewhat lost my memory, and—would you believe—have forgotten (literally forgotten, without the slightest exaggeration) plots of my novels and characters portrayed, even in *Crime and Punishment*. Nonetheless, I do remember the general outlines of my life." He promised Bykov that he would perhaps "put together my biography for you" in Ems, where he planned to spend the summer; and he adds, with an obvious allusion to Zotov, "I'll write it in my own way, not the way they write the biographies of writers in lexicons."[4]

Bykov again wrote in October 1876, reminding him of his quasi commitment, and Dostoevsky replied in January 1877, explaining that he had been unable to keep his word mainly for reasons of health. "The fact is that since the summer and practically right up to the present moment I have been more unwell than ever before. And . . . the further along I go, the more the work involved with the *Diary* (that is, not just with writing it, but with the publishing) turns out to be too much (physically) for me." Moreover, there were internal obstacles as well, which impeded this effort to give some faithful and coherent account of his own life. He had tried to work on it "in fits and snatches," but found it impossible to write about himself in such a fragmentary manner. "I sensed that the piece was calling up too much energy from my soul, was raising too much before me the life I have lived, and required great love from my heart in the carrying out of work still unknown to it." Dostoevsky renewed his promise to write such an autobiography, which had now become for him no longer a chore but an interior necessity. "I will definitely write it," he confides to Bykov, "because now I want to write it for myself, and I feel a need to write it, not just because of the promise, but for myself as well, but when I'll get it written—that I do not know."[5] In an informative volume of memoirs published many years later, Bykov claims that Dostoevsky visited him shortly thereafter and left fragments of a sketch of his life; but no such text has ever come to light.

Even though, so far as can be judged, Dostoevsky never found the time to set down this record of his life, there exists a brief vita dictated to Anna Grigoryevna in response to a request from a French journalist. The date of this document is uncertain. It was first printed in 1906, long after his death, as a preface to the seventh edition of his collected works; but the authoritative Academy of Sciences edition places it shortly after the January 1877 letter to Bykov. The text contains an objective account of his career and the most important events of his life (such as his arrest and sentencing to hard labor in Siberia), interspersed with some interesting side remarks. He stresses, for example, his already mentioned belief that Nicholas I made an exception in his favor by allowing him to serve in the Russian Army and thus to regain his civil rights. *House of the Dead*, as he also explains in the third person, "under assumed names recounts his life in the prison camp and describes his comrade convicts of that time"; there is no mention of a narrator (as in the text) supposedly sentenced for the murder of his wife. He is careful to note as well that "the régime and usages described in *House of the Dead* have long been changed in Russia."[6]

Listing the three novels he wrote in the 1860s—*Crime and Punishment*, *The Idiot*, and *The Devils*—he comments that they "were highly prized by the public, although Dostoevsky, perhaps, provided too harsh a picture in them of contemporary Russian society." Such self-criticism was probably included because, in writing for a French audience, he wished to soften the image of Russia that could be derived from his works by foreign readers. "In general," he concludes about himself, "he was beloved by the Russian public. He merited even from his literary opponents the reputation of being an honorable and sincere writer. His convictions were those of a professed Slavophil, who had very strongly altered his previous Socialist convictions."[7]

## 5

Many people, especially young women, appealed to Dostoevsky for advice and counsel. Two of his letters were addressed to an A. F. Gerasimova, the daughter of a merchant family in Kronstadt who had recently graduated from a *gymnasium*. She wrote him about the stifling confines of her life and her desire to study medicine and be useful to humanity. He discouraged her, however, from rushing off to attend courses at the medical faculty in Petersburg: "They don't give even the slightest education and, moreover, something worse happens." What he probably means is that the medical school was a hotbed of materialism and atheism. Ordinarily so dismissive of Europe, he here declares Russian scientists to be inferior to the Europeans in general cultivation. "The majority of our specialists are all *profoundly uneducated* people," unlike "Humboldt and Claude Bernard and similar people with wide-ranging thought." He calls the famous Russian physiologist Ivan Sechenov an "uneducated man, who knows little outside his own field . . . and therefore is harmful with his scientific conclusions rather than doing good."[8] Sechenov's special area of study was the functions of the brain, and he had exercised a strong influence on the radical intelligentsia by his interpretation of the human psyche purely in terms of nervous and physiological responses. Dostoevsky advises Gerasimova, if she plans to come to Petersburg at all, to enroll in the new courses for women on the university level organized by his friend Anna Pavlovna Filosofova, to whom he had already spoken about her desire for a higher education.

Whether Gerasimova accepted his counsel remains unknown, but the woman he mentioned, Anna Pavlovna Filosofova, deserves some attention. The wife of the highest legal official in the Ministry of War, she was a member of the Diaghilev family and the aunt of Sergey Diaghilev, later famous as the editor of the important journal *Mir Iskusstva* (*The World of Art*) and as the impresario of the Ballets Russes. More important, she was well known both for her philanthropic activities and staunch radical sympathies. He may have first made her acquaintance in the early 1860s, when they both frequented the salon of Elena Shtakenshneider, with whom Filosofova had then been engaged in founding a profit-sharing *artel* for women. A letter in February 1873 invites Dostoevsky and his wife to a dinner at which she was gathering all the friends who sympathized with her efforts (finally successful) to organize higher courses for women. In her own memoirs, she dates the beginning of their friendship to the early 1870s, when she met him at one of the literary evenings organized to raise funds for her charitable endeavors (she also founded a society to provide cheap lodging for the homeless and needy). "How happy I was to see him," she recalls. Evidently, since he called on her the next day, they took to each other immediately; "and since then we often saw each other."[9]

Their political opinions, if not their social sympathies, could not have been farther apart, and Anna Pavlovna was not a person to conceal her views even from the formidable Dostoevsky. "I very often behaved toward him in the most unseemly fashion," she admits. "I shouted at him and battled with him with unseemly anger, and he, the dear man, patiently bore all my sallies. At that time I just couldn't digest his novel *The Devils*. I told him that it was an outright denunciation." Filosofova's active goodness probably overshadowed what he may have considered her political misjudgments; and he not only remained her fast friend but also became her spiritual confidant. "How deeply am I indebted to him, my dear moral confessor," she gratefully acknowledges. "I told him everything, confided to him all my heartfelt secrets, and in the most difficult moments of my life he comforted me and guided me to the true path."[10] Such a path did not include any modification of her passionate commitment to the radical cause; nor did such independence, it would appear, alienate Dostoevsky in the slightest.

He also replied to a seventeen-year-old girl, Olga Antipova, who had failed some of her examinations to enter the *gymnasium* and wrote him five letters. Their desperate tenor evidently led him to fear that she was on the edge of a nervous breakdown and, perhaps, with the suicide of the young so frequent a phenomenon, in danger of taking her own life. "Why such tears and despair," he writes consolingly. "I see that you have simply tormented yourself to death and indecently frazzled your nerves." He gives her fatherly advice to look after her health, to take a vacation in the country, and to carry out a plan she had mentioned of working with children.[11]

Some reminiscences are contained in a letter to Alexander Nalimov, a young man who asked for advice about embarking on a literary career. Dostoevsky admits that he had had doubts of the same kind earlier in life, "but I was somehow certain that sooner or later I would definitely enter on my chosen path, and for that reason (I recall this perfectly) was not very worried . . . in my soul there was a sort of fire in which I also believed, and what would come of it did not trouble me very much." Nor did he feel at that time—or so he claims, surely exaggerating for the benefit of his correspondent—any internal conflict between his literary ambitions, his studies as a military engineer, and his service in the army after graduation. In reality, the moment he felt financially able to do so he resigned his army commission to devote himself entirely to literature. But he advises Nalimov, "if, for instance, employment in the service will not hinder your literary pursuits, why then should you not take a position?"[12] Alexander Nalimov later enjoyed a successful, if not particularly outstanding, career as a literary journalist.

6
———

As a member of the Slavic Benevolent Society, an organization in the forefront of support for the Balkan Slavs, Dostoevsky zealously participated in its activities. On April 20, 1877, he complained to Vladimir Lamansky, a close friend and professor of Slavic history and civilization at the University of St. Petersburg, that he had failed to receive a notice of the society's previous meeting. At the same time, he rejects Lamansky's invitation to write a "greeting" to the Tsar on behalf of the society, hailing Russia's declaration of war against Turkey ten days earlier. He is overwhelmed with work on the *Diary*; and besides, because he would be "writing for many people," he could not uninhibitedly express his views. Others "would be dissatisfied, could start criticizing without fail, correcting—and my time would have been lost." Lamansky himself had suggested some ideas for such a greeting, and in a postscript Dostoevsky adds that "the outline of what you laid out for me . . . shows that you will be the first to write it ten times better than many other people."[13]

Many articles written for the *Diary* in 1877 deal with the Russo-Turkish War, whose advent he had looked forward to eagerly as the inauguration of the new Russian epoch of world history that he had so often proclaimed and prophesied. The announcement of the declaration of war had caught the Dostoevskys driving along the Nevsky Prospect on their way to a bank. Joining the crowds clustered around the kiosks of news vendors, they stopped to read the imperial manifesto. He then ordered the cabman to proceed immediately to the Cathedral of Kazan, where a continuous service was being held before the icon of the Virgin of Kazan. Slipping away into the congregation, when Anna Grigoryevna saw him again a half hour later, he was "so absorbed in his rapt and prayerful mood that he did not recognize me for the first moment."[14]

A month later he went to the meeting of another society, the Lovers of Spiritual Enlightenment. It was to take place at the home of Aleksey Suvorin, a well-known journalist and editor of the newspaper *Novoye Vremya* (*New Time*), who had evolved from a liberal to a firmly progovernmental position and supported intervention in the Balkans. He was a lively and skillful writer, whose talent Dostoevsky admired while (in the privacy of his notebooks) accusing him of opportunism and dishonesty—"reviling every one of his columns and terribly fond of reading them." In the belief that a meeting had been scheduled for three o'clock on a Sunday afternoon, he called at Suvorin's home at the appointed time. Instead, he had awakened Suvorin and was properly penitent. "I myself sleep until two when I'm working," he wrote in apology, "and I understand how irritating it is when one is disturbed."[15] His reception, obviously, had been far from hospitable.

Indeed, the visit was cut so short that it left him no time to communicate an opinion about a recent article of Suvorin's that perhaps might have placated the disgruntled sleeper. A week earlier, Suvorin had written of *Anna Karenina* that "the true artist [Tolstoy] has been faithful to the laws of passion and, stripping it of its poetic aureole, has presented it in its true form. Whether it was worth proving this is another question; but the 'social' significance of *Anna Karenina* is indisputable." Whatever his own reservations about the novel, Dostoevsky was pleased, as he wrote Suvorin, that "in our troubled times you proclaim the importance of a literary event as a social fact, without fearing the grandeur of war and so on."[16] Suvorin was in effect defending the importance of literature, which radical critics tended to denigrate or deny unless it spoke for some salient social cause.

In mid-May 1877, Dostoevsky left St. Petersburg for the spring and summer months; but he was not going, as usual, to Staraya Russa or on another excursion to Bad Ems. The family had decided to spend these months at Maly Prikol, the country estate of Anna Grigoryevna's brother Ivan Snitkin, located in the more southerly province of Kursk. Anna's health had begun to flag under her combined responsibilities as mother, homemaker, and business manager; and Dostoevsky insisted that she take a complete rest during the summer. Moreover, his last visit to Bad Ems had not, in his view, brought much benefit, and he was quite content to avoid the fatigues of the voyage, the loneliness, and the problems for the schedule of the *Diary*.

A stay at Maly Prikol would also allow Anna to take the children on a visit to Kiev, the cradle of Old Russian civilization, a pilgrimage on which she had long wished to embark. Since the *Diary* would require him to return to Petersburg during the summer months, he planned to stop over in Moscow and from there to travel to Darovoe, the country property of his parents, unvisited since childhood. The journey to Maly Prikol was impeded by the troop trains occupying the railway lines, and Anna recalls the long delays at various stations, "where our train had to stand for hours because of the movements of the troops being sent off to war. At every stop Feodor Mikhailovich would go to the buffet and buy large quantities of rolls, honey cakes, cigarettes, and matches, and take them into the cars where he would give them out to the soldiers and have long talks with them."[17]

## 7

At the end of June, the family departed together from Maly Prikol and separated at the railroad junction that took Anna and the two older children to Kiev and Dostoevsky to Petersburg. While in the capital, he received only one letter from his wife (from Kiev) in a two-week period and became frantic for lack of news. The four letters he wrote are also filled with exasperation at the problems encountered with issuing the *Diary* on time (publication was in fact delayed), as well as in supervising its printing, binding, and mailing to various distributors. The censor had gone on vacation, and he thus spent a good deal of time shuttling between the printing plant, where he was reading proof, and the censorship office, where a substitute was filling in. Anna's sister, left in charge of business matters, was also behaving unpleasantly. When he asked for an accounting, she replied curtly that a full report had already been sent to his wife. The indispensable Alexandrov had fallen ill, and if he remained away from work, nothing could be done. At the same time, Dostoevsky was carrying on an epic struggle against the cockroaches in their apartment, using "store-bought powder" and keeping Anna informed of the regrettably indecisive results.[18]

The personal origin of some of his most haunting scenes is illuminated in a passage describing the effects of a severe epileptic attack. "At 6:30 this morning," he informs Anna, "on coming to after a seizure [they usually occurred in these early morning hours], I headed off *to your room* and suddenly Prokhorovna [the household servant] told me in the parlor that the mistress wasn't home. 'Where is she?' 'Why, she's in the country at a summer house.' 'How can that be? She should be here. When did she leave?' Prokhorovna persuaded me that I had only arrived the day before yesterday myself."[19] Dostoevsky's remarkable capacity to depict such states of semiawareness and semiconsciousness, when a character, losing cognizance of his actual surroundings, behaves according to subliminal drives and impulses while still seeming to be lucid, evidently derives from such episodes in his own life. He wrote his younger brother Nikolay that the seizure "has shattered me," and he asked Nikolay, whom he saw very rarely under ordinary circumstances, to come for a visit. His friend Pobedonostsev, worried because the May–June issue was not on schedule, had written from Oranienbaum, the royal family's resort on the Gulf of Finland, to inquire whether Dostoevsky had been taken ill. "I'll write to him," he tells Anna, "but I doubt whether I'll go to visit him myself—there's no time."[20]

The torment of not receiving any reply to his almost daily missives was more than he could endure (Anna had in fact written two letters that were delayed in delivery), and he sent off two telegrams to Maly Prikol inquiring about her whereabouts and well-being. When a letter finally arrived on July 16, he wrote the next day to justify his harassed behavior. "I haven't been able to sleep, I worry, sort through the chances [of an accident] pace around the room, have visions of the children, worry about you, my heart pounds (I've had palpitations of the heart start up these last three days). . . . It finally begins to dawn, and I sob, pace around the room and cry, with a sort of shaking (I don't understand it myself, it's never happened before) and I just try not to let the old woman [Prokhorovna] hear it." This passage can stand for many others in which he describes losing control of his nerves as his fertile imagination conjures up every disaster that might befall his family, especially the children.[21]

Despite his overwhelming desire to bask once again in the sheltering warmth of the family circle, Dostoevsky felt it imperative to make his intended journey to Darovoe. "The damned trip to Darovoe," he writes. "How I should like not to go! But I can't: if I deny myself these impressions, how can I be a writer after that, and what is the writer to write about!"[22] He did, in fact, spend forty-eight hours in Darovoe, now occupied by the family of his sister Varvara Ivanova, who had inherited the property. In her memoirs, Anna writes that "his family told me later that during his stay my husband had revisited all the different places in the park and the outskirts dear to him in his memory, and even walked to the grove he had loved as a child, Chermashnaya, about two versts away from the estate." (He would later bestow that name on a grove in *The Brothers Karamazov.*) Many of the peasants, who remembered him as a boy, "were very happy to see him, and regaled him with tea."[23]

He referred to this trip in his July–August 1877 *Diary*, where he reports on a conversation with "one of my old Moscow acquaintances" (probably the noted Slavophil Ivan Aksakov). "This little, unremarkable spot," he told his friend, "had left a deep and strong impression on me for my whole life . . . and everything there was filled with the most cherished memories for me." Dostoevsky emphasizes the importance for children to store up "sacred memories" (a point he will illustrate through Alyosha Karamazov), and writes that "a person cannot even live without something sacred and precious from childhood to carry into life" (25: 172). Much of the article is devoted to lamenting the plight of present-day Russian children, especially those of "accidental families," whose fathers neglect to pass on anything morally sustaining or, even worse, have undermined what little of moral substance remained in their environment. Such children will find it difficult, if not impossible, to accumulate any of the "sacred memories" that will enable them to navigate later amidst the dangerous shoals of life's temptations.

Dostoevsky's visit had unquestionably brought back recollections of his own father, who, even if not the monster depicted in some biographies, had still been a stern, harsh, and exactingly censorious taskmaster, quite unforgiving of any human weakness and error. A serf owner to boot, he had, after the death of his wife, taken a serf girl as his mistress and may have been murdered by his peasants. Whatever his failings, though, Mikhail Andreyevich Dostoevsky had been a deeply religious man, unstintingly devoted to the welfare of his children. He had never raised a finger to punish them, had sent them to the best possible schools, and continued until his death to concern himself about their welfare. All these traits give particular significance to a passage in Dostoevsky's text that can well be read as a confession of how he may have judged (and pardoned) his own progenitor.

"Today's fathers," he writes, do not possess any "great idea" that they pass on to their children, and "in their hearts" they have no great faith in such an idea. Yet,

> It is only a great faith of this kind that is capable of giving birth to *something beautiful* in the memories of children, and indeed it can, even despite the harshest childhood environment, poverty, and even despite that same moral filth that surrounded their cradles. Oh, there are cases where even one of the most fallen of fathers, who still managed to preserve in his soul perhaps only an obscure image of his former great idea and his great faith in it, has been able to transplant the seed of this great idea and great feeling into the impressionable and eager souls of his pitiable children, *and has later been wholeheartedly forgiven by them* because of this good deed alone, despite other things." (25: 180–181; italics added)

Dostoevsky often uses the expression "great idea" to mean the idea of the Christian morality of love and the Christian promise of eternity. He could well have felt, after the visit to Darovoe, that his own far from blameless father had nevertheless succeeded in planting these seeds in the hearts of his children.

## 8

During the fall and winter months of 1877 Dostoevsky continued to toil away at the *Diary*, even though, as he wrote Anna Filosofova, he "was sick this month [November] and *was sick in bed* for two weeks with a fever." His note was a reply to the information that she had been dangerously ill, and "he promised to try to get away to see you just as soon as I see the chance to drop the galleys and page proofs."[24] In October 1877, he informed readers of the *Diary* that he intended to terminate its publication at the end of the year. As he told his stepson, Pavel Isaev, who was again imploring him for financial aid, "you could not have appealed to me for money at a more inopportune time . . . than now [early December]. I am just discontinuing my publication and the liquidation of this business has required much more money than I had expected." Dostoevsky lectures Pavel about his insouciant attitude toward retaining his employment (he planned to quit his job in Moscow and move to Petersburg) and tells him that, as someone now over thirty with a wife and two children, it behooved him to exhibit more responsibility. Not only does he turn down the request for money, but also declares that he will never again debase himself, as he had often done in the past, by appealing to influential friends to find Pasha a post.[25]

An old confidant, Dr. Stepan Yanovsky, wrote from Vevey in Switzerland, expressing gratitude on behalf of the Russian circle there for the patriotic support given their homeland in the *Diary*. Dostoevsky replied with great warmth to this companion of his youth, who had also been his medical consultant, and he fondly recalls Yanovsky "as one of those few people who loved me and forgave me, and to whom I was devoted frankly and simply, with all my heart and without any ulterior thought." Like many others, Yanovsky expressed regret at the cessation of the *Diary*, and Dostoevsky explains that, aside from the worsening of his epilepsy, he had decided to suspend publication because "there is a novel in my head and my heart, and it's begging to be written." Moreover, in the future "I want to try a new publication into which the *Diary* will enter as a part."[26] He had sketched a plan for such a new monthly, one no longer written exclusively by himself, in early 1878. A proposed table of contents includes more literary material (stories and novels), critical essays on past and present writers, and a running commentary on events that would incorporate the *Diary* (26: 175).

Far from regretting his work during these past two years, Dostoevsky writes buoyantly to Yanovsky about the many other correspondents who had urged him to continue publication. "You wouldn't believe to what an extent I have enjoyed the sympathy of Russians during these two years of publication," he exultantly informs the doctor. He had been enormously heartened to find that "here in Russia there have turned out to be incomparably more genuinely Russian people, not those with a corrupted Petersburg intelligentsia view, . . . than I had thought two years ago." All these letters "testify to a thirst for a new, right life, a profound belief in an imminent change in the mode of thought of our intelligentsia, which has lost touch with the people and does not even understand them at all." Yanovsky had spoken disparagingly of Andrey

Kraevsky's newspaper, *Voice*, which had become highly critical of the Russo-Turkish War, and Dostoevsky snaps, "These gentlemen will in fact disappear." "Those who do not understand the people will now undoubtedly have to join the stockbrokers and the Yids, and that's the end of the representatives of our 'progressive' thought."[27] The "Yids" are thus automatically associated with all those non-Jewish Russians who remain skeptical about the war, and whose motives for doing so, in his extremely jaundiced eyes, can only be grossly and sordidly material.

His plan to recast the *Diary* indicates how seriously he was thinking about his literary future. On the reverse of the notebook page containing the plan for his new publication, he had earlier scribbled another note:

1. Write a Russian Candide.
2. Write a book about Jesus Christ.
3. Write my memoirs.
4. Write a work [*poema*] on the *sorokovina* [the celebration of a memorial mass forty days after death] NB. (All this, besides my final novel and the proposed publication of the *Diary*, i.e., ten years of work at a minimum, and I am now fifty-six years old. (17: 14)

Dostoevsky did not live to complete any of these projects, although one of the short stories included in the *Diary*, *The Dream of a Ridiculous Man*, can well be viewed as his version of a Russian Candide. So too, as L. P. Grossman has argued, can *The Brothers Karamazov*, with its numerous references to Voltaire and one to *Candide* itself, and its theme of the impotence of reason to come to terms with the injustices and iniquities of God's world. The book about Jesus Christ may be linked to His appearance in the Legend of the Grand Inquisitor, and many of the autobiographical pages in the *Diary* serve as a substitute for the unwritten memoirs.

The *sorokovina* goes back to a project in the summer of 1875 for "a book of wanderings" (presumably in the afterlife) describing a series of "ordeals 1 (2, 3, 4, 5, 6 etc.)." One of the most important of these ordeals would have been a conversation between a young man and Satan, which anticipates that between Ivan Karamazov and his devil (17: 6). This idea of a series of "ordeals" was taken over for the chapter titles of Book 9 of *The Brothers Karamazov*, where Dimitry is depicted as undergoing "the torments of a soul," listed as the first, second, and third, during the course of the "preliminary investigation" of his supposed crime. This reference to the *sorokovina*, as well as being a literary idea, very probably possessed a more personal significance as well. Death was very much on his mind, and his regular visits to the suffering Nekrasov constantly brought it before his eyes.

To Dimitry Averkiev, a conservative playwright who had sought Dostoevsky's aid to publish in *Notes of the Fatherland*, he wrote: "Nekrasov is keeping to his bed and looks like a corpse, who speaks now and then and will soon die, but takes an interest in *Notes of the Fatherland*."[28] Nekrasov died a month later, in December 1877, and Dostoevsky attended the services, although Anna persuaded him to forgo the two-hour walk following the coffin through the city. He and Anna left the overflowing and overheated church services at the Novodeichy convent and walked out into the cemetery for a breath of fresh air. The hush of the surroundings, exercising a calming influence on him, inevitably suggested intimations of his own mortality, and he turned to Anna with a request not "to bury me in the writer's section of the Volkov cemetery. I don't want to lie among my enemies—I suffered enough from them while I was alive!" Such talk was naturally painful for Anna, who tried to lighten his mood by "weaving a fantasy about the future funeral while beseeching him to live as long as possible." If he kept his part of the bargain, she promised, he would be buried next to the poet V. A. Zhukovsky in the Nevsky Lavra, and "not only the huge crowd of young people will follow your coffin but all Petersburg," while the choir and the church services would be even more lavish and splendid. At this, Dostoevsky "smiled and said: 'All right, I'll try to live a little while longer.'"[29] Anna Grigoryevna's "fantasy," alas, as she sadly comments, became reality only three years later.

## 9

The burial of Nekrasov turned out to be in effect a radical demonstration. Hordes of students and admirers came to pay their last respects to the poet who had given poignant expression to the social-humanitarian themes of the 1840s, and later had written so movingly of the limitless sorrows of Russian peasant life in his great cycle of poems, *Who Is Happy in Russia?* Several people spoke at the graveside, among them Dostoevsky, who improvised some remarks on the spur of the moment in response to a request from "the surrounding crowd of young people."[30] The December *Diary* contains a lengthy obituary that enlarges on his impromptu reflections. Here we shall touch on only one incident, which occurred while he was speaking and left its traces in the annals of Russian literature.

In the course of his tribute, Dostoevsky said that Nekrasov "was the last of that series of poets who came to us with their 'new word,'" and that "among such poets he should stand directly after Pushkin and Lermontov." At this, a dissenting "voice from the crowd cried out that Nekrasov was *greater* than Pushkin and Lermontov and that the latter were only 'Byronists'" (26: 112–113). Several voices then took up the refrain and shouted: "Yes, greater!" These voices came from a small group led by G. V. Plekhanov, who was attending the funeral with a few members of the underground revolutionary organization Zemlya i Volya (Land and Liberty). If we accept Plekhanov's account, written thirty years later, Dostoevsky was surprised and upset by this unexpected intervention, but refused to give way. "Placing Nekrasov on the same level as Push- kin," Plekhanov comments, "was the farthest limit of his concession to the 'young generation.' 'Not higher, but not lower than Pushkin,' he answered with some irritation, turning to us, and then continued de- spite reiterated shouts of 'higher, higher.'"[31] The Populist critic A. M. Skabichevsky, who was not present, wrote that a "thousand-voiced chorus" shouted back against him, but this account was denied by Dos- toevsky and by a more impartial observer, the young V. G. Korolenko, later an important Populist writer.[32]

This small episode, in which the radicals publicly raised their voices to elevate a writer who had expressed their own anguish about Russian life, may stand as a symbolic indication of the growing aggressiveness of the hitherto peaceful Populists. During 1877 the government brought three groups of them to trial: those who had demonstrated before the Cathedral of Kazan and two groups arrested for having "gone to the people" three years earlier. The second trial, known as that of "the fifty," produced a particularly deep and lasting impression on the radical in- telligentsia. The accused testified with great dignity about the intolera- ble conditions they had been forced to endure, and brought the more humane and educated members of the public face to face with the grim realities of a repressive régime. This public was shocked by the uncon- scionable length of time these young people had been imprisoned be- fore being brought to trial, and by the severe sentences meted out for their perfectly peaceable and often charitable "crimes."

There are numerous contemporary accounts of the religiously charged atmosphere that surrounded the trial of "the fifty," during which, ac- cording to the Populist radical writer S. M. Stepniak-Kravchinsky, the word "saints" was often heard uttered about the defendants by those in the courtroom.[33] Another radical observer, Andrey Mikhailov—later one of the key organizers of Narodnaya Volya (People's Will), the group that carried out the assassination of Alexander II—wrote that "the trial of 'the fifty' had an even greater influence on society than the one for the demonstration in Kazan Square. In it were people who could be com- pared to the early Christian martyrs; they were propagandists of pure Socialism, teachers of love, equality, and fraternity, the fundamental principles of the Christian *obshchina* [commune]. But the government did not spare them."[34]

A vivid depiction of the impact of this trial on the educated public is given in the still-indispensable *History of the Russian Intelligentsia* by the liberal academic D. N. Ovsyaniko-Kulikovsky. He was still close enough to these events to communicate how they affected the sensibility of decent and kindhearted observers.

> Not all, perhaps, but very many of those who went to the people were inspired—some consciously, some unconsciously—by the evangelical ideal of loving one's neighbor, and of sacrificing one's worldly goods and personal happiness. When the so-called "trial of the fifty" disclosed the activity of young women self-sacrificingly carrying the "good news" of Socialism, motifs from the Gospel, parallels with the Sermon on the Mount, involuntarily came to mind. These young women could look forward in life to happiness and satisfaction, among them were some with considerable wealth, all were educated, well brought up, all had not only external but an inner moral right to occupy an important place in society. But they preferred to this the life of a saint, they exchanged their happiness for a heroic deed, and sacrificed themselves for a high ideal, which seemed to them only a new expression of this very same evangelical ideal.[35]

At the trial, in a speech that quickly became famous, one of the accused, Sophia Bardini, declared: "As regards religion [whose precepts she had been accused of violating], I may say only that I have always remained faithful to its existing principles, in that pure form in which it was preached by the founder of Christianity."[36]

One of the last poems that Nekrasov wrote on his deathbed was inspired by this trial, and others felt the same urge. The poet Ya. P. Polonsky, a friend of Dostoevsky's who was very far from nourishing any radical velleities, wrote a poem called "The Prisoner" ("Uznitsa"), which begins:

> What is she to me?—not wife, nor mistress
> And not a daughter of my blood,
> So why does her cursed fate
> Never leave me night and day?[37]

Nothing similar can be found in Dostoevsky, but there is good reason to believe that the saintly Christian aura surrounding this trial of "the fifty" echoed in his work as well.

Just a year later, he began to draft *The Brothers Karamazov*; and when he came to describe his young hero, Alyosha, whose life would constitute the second (never written) volume, he wrote: "if he had decided that God and immortality did not exist, he would at once have become an atheist and Socialist (for Socialism is not merely the labor question or the so-called fourth estate, it is before all things the atheistic question, the question of the form taken by atheism today, the question of the Tower of Babel built without God, not to mount to Heaven from earth but to set up Heaven on earth" (14: 25). The Socialists, at least in their Russian incarnation, are thus inspired by the same ideal as Alyosha, whose innate goodness and craving for justice led him to become a novice in a monastery once he had decided in favor of God and immortality. Both he and the Socialists look forward to the reign of goodness and charitable love; they differ only on whether it should be attained under the guidance of a secular or a supernatural Christ. And Dostoevsky's supreme ambition, in these last years of his life, was to influence the young Populists, who so often evoked comparisons with the early Christian martyrs, to follow the way of Alyosha instead of their own.

It was not only through his next novel, however, that he hoped to exercise an influence on the young radicals inspired by this revolutionary Socialist ideal. For over two years he had attempted to do so from month to month in the *Diary of a Writer*. Let us now turn back for a closer look at this massive publication, which it is no exaggeration to say dominated Russian public opinion as no such journal had ever done before.

## CHAPTER 14

# The Diary of a Writer,
## 1876–1877

The appearance of the *Diary of a Writer* in its new form as an independent publication marked an important moment not only in Dostoevsky's literary career but also in the history of Russian journalism. No similar publication had ever been launched in Russia, although magazines written by a single person—in imitation of such a precursor as Joseph Addison's *The Spectator*—were by no means unknown. One, in fact, was authored by no less a personage than Catherine the Great herself. These had consisted of articles, familiar essays, and satirical portraits in the polite eighteenth-century manner designed to amuse and enlighten rather than to provide serious commentary on important moral and social issues. Dostoevsky's *Diary*, on the other hand, took up all the crucial social-political topics of the day, and he threw himself into each one with a hitherto unexampled intensity and gravity.

A good general description of the *Diary* is given by the commentator in the authoritative Academy of Sciences edition of Dostoevsky's works:

> Its pages gave expression to the impressions of a writer's personal life from the end of 1875 through [1876–1877], his reminiscences of earlier years, an account of his literary projects, and reflections on all the important topics concerning Russia of that epoch—literary, cultural, social-political—that were agitating Dostoevsky. . . . Conversing with his readers, the author constantly slides from one current theme to another, and the transition to each of them carries with it a stream of reminiscences and associations. . . . But amidst all these variegated themes and episodes, dissimilar to one another and constantly changing, the author directs his own glance and that of the reader to the same "accursed questions"—those that form the philosophical and artistic contents, a kind of basic nervously sensitive cluster, of the author's thoughts. These questions are those of the relations in Russia between those on "top" and on "bottom," the educated class and the people, of the deep crisis being lived through, each in its own way, both by contemporary Russia and Europe, of their past, present, and future.[1]

Such words accurately capture both the multifariousness of the *Diary* and the unity of the author's personality, which binds all the entries together into a unique expression of Dostoevsky's preoccupations.*

Original to the *Diary* as well was the dialogue that he carried on with his readers, who deluged him with letters to which he often responded both personally and in its pages. To engage in such a conversation was again unheard-of; and the letters that poured in may be attributed not only to the provocation of his ideas but also to a quality of style that was distinctly intimate and personal. One reader, a provincial librarian, eloquently explained that she loved the *Diary* because, as she tells its author:

> You write directly, without any literary form of propriety or cere-
> mony, as if addressing a letter to a friend. You write what you
> think—and that is rare, that is fine. . . . You become visible yourself
> in your sentences; we know you, as it were, we become acquainted
> with you in reading the *Diary*. And besides, you quite simply, and
> without the appearance of being learned, go right to the most pro-
> found questions, to those that are painful for each one of us, and
> treat these questions directly, candidly, without a trace of affecta-
> tion or "scholarliness."[2]

Not only was the content of the articles extremely variegated, with continual changes of subject matter and shifts of perspective, but he also aimed to provide the reading public with more than contemporary commentary. Stories and sketches were included in his pages, offering readers the equivalent of a Russian "thick journal" (which invariably included installments of a novel) in a reduced format. Two of his smaller masterpieces, *A Gentle Creature* and *The Dream of a Ridiculous Man*, first appeared in the *Diary*, along with a number of slighter sketches; and even the harshest critics of his views greeted them with unanimous praise.

The *Diary of a Writer* was remarkable also because it managed to occupy a totally independent position in the sharply partisan world of Russian journalism. The publication of *A Raw Youth* in the Populist *Notes of the Fatherland* had already signaled that Dostoevsky was not one to adhere strictly to party lines. Besides continuing along such a nonconformist path, the *Diary* was also inspired by his ambition to serve as a rallying point for people of good will adrift among the clash-ing antagonisms tearing Russian life apart. Some recent valuable

---

* The *Diary of a Writer* will be discussed here primarily in relation to its substantive and ideological content. For an original and fascinating attempt to view it in aesthetic terms, as an effort to create a new literary form combining divergent aspects of Dos-toevsky's world view, see Gary Saul Morson, *The Boundaries of Genre* (Austin, Texas, 1981).

research in the archives of the *Diary* has thrown new light on the complexities of Dostoevsky's social-political position as seen through the eyes of his first readers. Although his "positive" program has usually been considered "reactionary" because of its support for Tsarism, the correspondence he received reveals that such support, combined with his harsh denunciations of existing social evils, was by no means felt to be as politically subservient as it has appeared to posterity.

Just fifteen years earlier, Alexander II had initiated a sweeping series of reforms inaugurating a new era in Russian history. Dostoevsky assumed, to quote I. L. Volgin, "not only that the Tsarist régime was very far from having exhausted its reformist ideas," but also that this continuing program of "radical historical transformation" could be carried out, as had been the peaceful liberation of the serfs, "within the boundaries of a *nonrevolutionary* endeavor." Such a position proved to be quite attractive to the more educated segment of the population, who longed for change in a liberal direction but had no appetite for violent revolution. In the 1870s, to cite Volgin again, the "government that had brought about the abolition of serfdom, as well as the legal, urban, and military reforms, had not yet lost a certain credit of trust," although this trust ran out in the closing years of the decade.[3]

The publication of *The Devils*, and Dostoevsky's stint as editor of *The Citizen*, had seemed to ally him irrevocably with those opposed to the agitations and hopes of the radical intelligentsia. Yet there is ample evidence that members of this group were also among his most avid readers, and found, expressed in his pages, many of their own ideals and aspirations (though couched in terms that aimed to undermine their revolutionary implications). How could this anomaly—noted by all commentators at the time—have come about? Part of the answer can be found in the remarkable ingenuity with which he played on the reverence for "the people" that he shared with the radical Populists, and which, in fact, transcended ordinary social-political party lines.

The popularity of the *Diary* among the radical youth has been persuasively explained in these terms by D. N. Ovsyaniko-Kulikovsky. Although, as he writes, Dostoevsky's "Slavophil point of view, the conclusions of his 'program' [the abandonment of all revolutionary intentions] could not . . . be accepted by the progressive intelligentsia," they were incapable of resisting his "dogma about the exalted qualities of the Russian people and their sublime mission in the future regeneration of mankind." It was upon this belief that "they based . . . the possibility of their efforts to propagandize Socialist ideas among the people. . . . [And] this dogma was expressed by Dostoevsky with such deep faith, with a sincerity infused with such force, that his preachment unwittingly threw oil on the fire." For while rejecting European Socialism, he "energetically

. . . encouraged among the youth that system of ideas and feelings that was the psychological foundation of the revolutionary illusions of our Socialists."[4]

The *Diary of a Writer* is such a huge farrago of disparate material that it is difficult to give some tolerable notion of its contents. The ideas of the *Diary*, properly so-called, were already familiar from his earlier journalism, as well as from the ideological flights of his novels. But they are given new life and color by the constant parade of fresh examples and illustrations drawn from his omnivorous reading of the current press, from his wide knowledge of history and literature both Russian and European, and, very frequently, from the events of his own life. Such autobiographical revelations were certainly one of the main attractions of the *Diary* and contributed greatly to its appeal; readers felt that they were truly being admitted into the intimacy of one of their great men. This constant interplay between the personal and the public—the incessant shift of level between the social problems of the day, the "accursed questions" that have always plagued human life, and the glimpses into the recesses of Dostoevsky's own private life and sensibility—proved an irresistible combination that gave the *Diary* its unique literary cachet.

In addition, the *Diary* served as a stimulus not only for the shorter stories and sketches already mentioned but also, as he had anticipated from the very first, for the major novel he was planning to write. Time and again motifs appear that will soon be utilized in *The Brothers Karamazov*, and one of the fascinations of this vast journalistic corpus, especially for present-day readers, is to observe the crystallization of such motifs as they emerge spontaneously in the course of dealing with one or another topic. Even if not literally a notebook, the *Diary* lives up to this name in the exact sense of the word. It is genuinely the working tool of a writer in the early stages of creation—a writer who searches for (and finds) the inspiration for his work as, pen in hand, he surveys the passing scene and attempts to cope with its deeper import.

In this chapter, we shall summarize the main social-political theses of the *Diary*. The following will deal with the articles on religious and legal issues that foreshadow *The Brothers Karamazov*, with Dostoevsky's view of the Jewish Question, with the *Diary's* literary commentaries, and, finally, with its sketches and short stories.

## THE RUSSIAN PEOPLE

For all his adoration of the Russian people, the picture he paints of them is very far from being idyllic or sentimentalized. He had already harshly criticized the vices of the people in his 1873 *Diary*, nor had he scrupled to give an unblinkered portrayal of them in *House of the Dead*. Indeed, in the very first issue of the *Diary of a Writer* (January 1876) he wrote that "the Russian people are coarse and ignorant, devoted to darkness and depravity, 'barbarians awaiting the light'" (22: 42–43). His depiction of them, however, was always dominated by what may be called the Vlas paradigm. Just as Vlas, after committing the most heinous crimes, underwent a religious conversion with the same passion that he had displayed in his criminal misdeeds, so the Russian people possessed a religious faith that would not only rescue them from disaster but enable them to lead the way into a new Christian era of regenerated humanity.

Well aware that he could be accused of deprecating the people at the same time that he was offering his Slavophil-Populist tribute to their unique virtues, he tried to cope with this problem in February 1876. In an article published posthumously, the Slavophil Konstantin Aksakov had written that the Russian people had long been "enlightened and educated," and Dostoevsky remarks that, "to my astonishment, others think that these two notions [his own highly critical one and that of Aksakov] are irreconcilable." But he saw no contradiction between them at all, and nothing was easier to reconcile. "One must know how to segregate the beauty in the Russian peasant from the layers of barbarity that have accumulated over it. Through the circumstances of nearly the whole of Russian history, our people have been so given over to depravity, and so corrupted, led astray and continually tormented, that it is a wonder they have survived preserving their human image at all, never mind preserving their beauty." One should look at the people, he insisted, in the light of the historical ideals to which they have clung, ideals embodied in their saints—"Sergey, Theodosius of Pechersk, even Tikhon of Zadonsk . . . and you will be astonished at the beautiful things you would learn" (22: 43).

Indeed, Dostoevsky maintains that he is very far from being alone in having perceived this inner spiritual beauty of the Russian people, which has already been enshrined in Russian literature. All the "nasty types" one finds there have been borrowed from Europe, but "everything in it of true beauty has been taken from the people," beginning with "the meek and simple type, Belkin, created by Pushkin," and continuing through Goncharov's *Oblomov* and Turgenev's *A Nest of Gentlefolk*. These writers, even though not portraying the people as such, "borrowed the people's simplicity, purity, meekness, breadth of outlook, and lack of malice, as opposed to all that was twisted, false, extrinsic, and slavishly borrowed" (22: 43–44). Elsewhere, drawing on his own life, he recalls how his peasant nanny had impulsively offered his family

her life savings when they were in difficulties. He also recounts an illus-
trative episode from Sergey Aksakov's *Family Chronicle*, in which the
peasants took their mistress, in response to her pleas, across the dangerously melting ice of the Volga to visit her sick child. "And when it
was over, the peasants did not even accept any money, realizing that
they had done it all for a mother's tears and for the sake of Christ and
our God. And this happened in the very darkest period of serfdom!"
(22: 112–113).*

Dostoevsky was thus convinced that the inherited Christianity of the
Russian peasants had soaked into their souls, and that the people instinctively possessed all the Christian virtues taught them by their faith.
The contrast between this belief and the ordinary behavior of the people was so glaring, however, that it prompted one critic to ask if it might
not be preferable for the Russian people to have less exalted ideals and
better behavior. And how, in any case, could their inner essence, as
Dostoevsky perceived it, become "public knowledge." As Dostoevsky
frames the criticism: "[W]ho has the gift of prophecy or the knowledge
of the human heart to penetrate and decipher them if the reality contra-
dicts and is unworthy of these ideals?" To the first objection, he responds that "without ideals—that is, without at least some partially defined hope for something better—our reality will never be better." To
the second, he has no direct reply, simply stating that "no matter how
much Mr. Gamma [the pseudonym of his critic] and I were to discuss
this topic, we will never come to an agreement" (22: 74). The sensibility
of a Mr. Gamma, in other words, would be incapable of penetrating
beneath the surface to the riches of the Russian character concealed
under its unedifying exterior.

Even though skeptical voices were raised against what some thought
were his exaggerations of the people's virtues, the social-cultural mood
did not, for the most part, encourage any direct attack on the veracity
of such views. One of the few was made by an intransigent Westernizer,
the novelist, critic, and playwright V. G. Avseyenko, whom Dostoevsky
had ample personal reasons for disliking. Avseyenko had published
harsh criticisms of both *The Devils* and *A Raw Youth*, and now, writing
in Katkov's *Russian Messenger*, he had questioned the injunction to bow

---

*Dostoevsky frequently rearranged the passages he cited to suit his purposes. In
this instance, he referred to the wrong book (the anecdote was not in *The Family
Chronicle* but in Aksakov's *Reminiscences*), though since both were bound together
in the copy he used the error is quite explicable. However, he also altered some
important details. The river in question was not the broad Volga but a smaller one,
and the peasants accepted five rubles each as recompense though refusing a much
larger sum. As Robert Belknap remarks, "each of these changes amplifies the risk or
the nobility of the peasants, supporting Dostoevsky's arguments." See Robert L. Belknap, *The Genesis of The Brothers Karamazov* (Evanston, Ill., 1990), 97–98.

down before the wisdom of the people and to learn to revere their (Christian) ideals. While acknowledging that the people "have preserved the purity of the Christian ideal for us, displaying heroism that is both lofty and humble in its grandeur," Avseyenko could not discern in them "any ideal of a dynamic personality." They live, he wrote, "on the level of elemental being," sunk in "a way of life of passive existence"; and if an "active, energetic personality" emerges in their midst, he "assumes the unattractive form of the bloodsucker, the kulak, the stupid and petty tyrant" (22: 103–104). To speak of the Russian people in this way was to desecrate Dostoevsky's holy of holies, and he turns on Avseyenko in April 1876 with a rare vehemence.

To begin, he points out the self-contradiction of Avseyenko's argument, which praises the people for having supported Russia's "historic mission" on their shoulders while accusing them at the same time of inactivity and passivity. Did they do *nothing* through all those centuries? And he follows with a more telling rebuttal: the definitive enserfment of the Russian peasantry had been installed by Peter the Great, who opened the floodgates of Western culture for the upper class; and such enslavement was an economic precondition for the welfare of that class, whose comfortable existence was based on serf labor. "Can it really be that our people, who were enserfed specifically for the sake of your culture . . . now, after more than two hundred years of slavery, deserve from you . . . only this coarse insult about kulaks and cheats instead of gratitude and compassion?" (22: 104). Such words could well have been written by Peter Lavrov to illustrate the "duty" that the educated class owed to the peasantry, the duty of working to alleviate their lot. Treating Avseyenko's disparaging view of the people with withering contempt, Dostoevsky assures his readers that he would not have bothered to discuss such nonsense at all except that "as a writer [Avseyenko] represents a minor cultural type which . . . has a certain wider meaning" (22: 105).

He then launches into a devastating satirical discussion of Avseyenko as a writer, whose recent novel "suddenly clarified for me the whole nature of Avseyenko as a 'writer-type.'" "What the novel shows," he writes caustically, "is that Mr. Avseyenko . . . represents a figure who has lost his presence of mind in the worship of high society. To put it briefly, he has prostrated himself and is worshiping the gloves, carriages, perfumes, pomades, silk dresses (especially the moment when a lady takes her seat in an armchair and her dress rustles around her feet and body), and finally, the servants who greet their mistress when she returns from the Italian opera. He writes about all this constantly, reverently, piously, devotedly, in short, it is as if he were celebrating some kind of Mass" (22: 107). Avseyenko, the critic of the people, thus "sees the whole point of our culture—its whole achievement, the whole culmination of the two-hundred-year period of our debauchery and our suffering—in carriages, and pomade . . . and he admires these things without a hint of mockery" (22: 107).

Dostoevsky scathingly plays on such infatuation with the fashionable accoutrements of Western civilization affected by the Russian upper class. "I heard (perhaps it was said in fun)," he offers as an aside, "that [Avseyenko] began the novel with the aim of correcting Leo Tolstoy, who depicted high society too objectively [meaning critically] in his *Anna Karenina*" (22: 107). Such a rumor was indeed making the rounds, and Dostoevsky probably gathered it from the same source, Nikolay Strakhov, who had reported it to Tolstoy (22: 376). For all his sarcasm, though, he insists that "one must not regard this only from a comic point of view," that the issue is much more serious: "this debility, this mania for the charms of high society . . . has given rise to a special sort of confirmed advocate of serfdom among those who never owned a serf in their lives." Such worship of the external trappings of Western high society leads to the same contempt for the people that had existed in the days of serfdom, and those sharing Avseyenko's infatuation "can spit on the people quite openly and with the air of the fullest cultural right" (22: 108).

If he could brilliantly sweep aside such denigration of the people, which criticized not only their obvious vices and shortcomings but also the very essence of their moral-spiritual nature, it was still difficult for him to produce evidence to support his own absolutely contrary intuitions. In this respect, the declaration of war by Serbia and Montenegro against Turkey in mid-June 1876 proved to be a godsend. The Russian volunteer movement, organized to support the Slavs in their struggle, led to a mass outpouring not only of material aid but also of men volunteering to join the Serbian Army and women to serve as nurses (as Sofya Lurie had intended to do). More will soon be said about Dostoevsky's articles on the Balkan Question; for the moment, we may focus on his enthusiasm at the response that these events had aroused among the Russian people.

"We had thought," he said, "that the people had already forgotten their spiritual principles and were no longer preserving them in their hearts," but the rise of the volunteer movement had swept away such despairing doubts. The people had embarked on "a new crusade" because they had heard that "their Slav brethren were being tortured and oppressed." Nothing of the kind had been expected of this "supposedly homogeneous and torpid mass." It certified for Dostoevsky that the Russian people still valued the virtue of self-sacrifice and continued to admire someone "who continually works for God's cause, who loves the truth, and who, when it is necessary, rises up to serve that truth, leaving

his home and his family and sacrificing his life." The volunteer movement providentially provided him with, as he saw it, the living proof of
his sublime image of the Russian people; and this is why, as he informs
his readers, "we can joyously allow ourselves to hope anew, our horizon
has cleared, and our new sun rises with dazzling brilliance" (23: 161–162).

The final stage in Dostoevsky's apotheosis of the Russian people came
after the Russian declaration of war against Turkey in April 1877. Now he
argues that the Russian people possess not only all the virtues already
attributed to them but also the capacity to create a new Christian world
order in the future. Indeed, this was the basis on which Dostoevsky
believed that the people and the educated class could finally be united.
All educated Russians believe—and he cites himself as an example—"in
a common humanity . . . [and] that at some time the national barriers
and prejudices that until now have prevented the free communion of
nations through the egoism of national aspirations will someday fall
before the light of reason and consciousness, and . . . then will people
begin to live in a single spirit and in accord, as brothers, rationally and
lovingly striving for general harmony." This is the ultimate aim of the
"cosmopolitanism" on which the educated class prides itself and which
it flaunts to justify its sense of superiority toward the people. Such a
faith, according to Dostoevsky, hardly exists any longer in Europe, or if
so, only as "a metaphysical perception," something purely academic
and not a deep-seated and widespread sentiment. But lo and behold!
Such a conviction flourishes in Russia, not only as "a belief in the world
of intellectuals," but—even more important—"*as a living instinctual
feeling among the common people, whom religion commands to believe
this very thing*" (25: 19–20; italics added).

Just as the philosophical Russian "wanderer" in Europe, Versilov, and
the peasant "wanderer," Makar Ivanovich, in *A Raw Youth* were subliminally united in the same quest for a Golden Age of loving fraternity, so
the Europeanized Russian intellectuals and the people are united, with
no awareness of their agreement, in the same faith. And this is the faith
that Russia "will pronounce the greatest word that the world has heard,"
and that this word will be the mandate for the unity of all humanity in
a spirit transcending "personal egoism" and "the struggle for existence"
that "now unites people and nations artificially and unnaturally" (25:
19–20). That Dostoevsky believed all this, there is no reason to doubt;
but because he made no distinction between the Russian state and the
Russian people, such lofty pronouncements also served to provide a
morally attractive façade for Russian imperialism in the Balkans and
Central Asia. It was, as Josef Bohatec has called it, an "imperialism of
love,"[5] but it was imperialism all the same. Dostoevsky was well aware
that his rapturous vision of such a future world order would be greeted

with incredulity, and he wistfully asks in conclusion, "could I truly have thought to convince anyone? . . . Maybe some 'raw youth,' some member of the new generation will read this" (25: 23). Many of them did; and whether or not they shared his exalted dreams, his words could not fail to encourage their devotion to the Russian people.

## THE INTELLIGENTSIA
## AND THE PEOPLE

No issue in Russian culture was more important for Dostoevsky than the relationship between the intelligentsia and the people. Since the reforms of Peter the Great, an enormous gap had split Russian society into two differing worlds. On one side was the Western-educated upper class, who had absorbed the languages, tastes, manners, and ideas of modern European culture; on the other was the peasantry, rooted in their traditional, religiously oriented way of life and largely untouched by the secularizing influences of modernity. Dostoevsky was very far from being the only Russian writer concerned with this issue, but for him this gap was more than merely a theoretical concern. He had become agonizingly aware of it as a burning personal experience during his prison camp years in Siberia. In the 1860s, his journals had advanced a doctrine advocating the return of the intelligentsia to their own native soil, to a new respect for their own culture and its moral-religious roots and values. The intelligentsia, for its part, would bring with them all the richness of the Western culture they had acquired; and from their fusion with the people, a new and revitalized synthesis of Russian social-cultural life would emerge. This conception of the ideal relation between the intelligentsia and the people forms the background for the treatment of this question in the *Diary*.

The relation of the intelligentsia both to their native culture and to their European formation, as Dostoevsky saw it, was extremely complex and ambiguous. Long ago he had decided that the Russian national character resisted (or at least resented) being reshaped according to a foreign model. An entry in the June 1876 issue entitled "My Paradox" adroitly focuses on the peculiar fact that the most ardent Russian Westernizers—those most in favor of reshaping Russia according to some European model—are also the very same people who aligned themselves theoretically (like Belinsky) or practically (like Herzen and Bakunin, though they are not named) with the extreme European left. In other words, these Russian Westernizers joined the Europeans who were rejecting *their own* institutions and culture, and who wished to destroy the basis (private property) on which Western civilization had been founded. Dostoevsky interprets this anomaly as an instinctive Russian revolt against the European culture that had been so brutally imposed by Peter the Great. As far back as 1863, he had argued that the veneer of European culture and manners remained very superficial; even ardent Westernizers, such as the playwright Denis Fonvizin, had harbored a scarcely concealed antagonism against the social-cultural exemplars they presumably admired and wished to emulate. Taking up the same point again, Dostoevsky now sees these Russian Westernizers as exhibiting their very Russianness by joining those Europeans bent on destroying their own social world. The Russians were manifesting their primordial opposition to an alien European culture and thus proving themselves to be in fact patriots and even Russian conservatives.

Their (or his) paradox, Dostoevsky argues cleverly, arises because they had confused Russia with Europe, "and by rejecting Europe and her order they thought to apply the rejection to Russia." But Russia was not Europe, and "all the things the Westernizers wanted in Europe [a more just and equable social-economic order] already long existed in Russia, in embryo or potentially at least." He is here referring to the proto-Socialist institutions of the Russian peasantry, whose existence he attributed to the effect of Christian moral ideals on the character of the people. Such a potentiality thus exists in Russia's essence, "not in a revolutionary sense but with the sense in which notions of universal human renewal should appear: in the sense of divine Truth, the Truth of Christ, which, God grant, will someday be realized on earth, and which is preserved in its entirety in Orthodoxy" (23: 40–41). In returning to their native soil, Russian Westernizers would thus presumably be correcting their error in confusing Russia with Europe, but without surrendering the ideals which, they had mistakenly believed, could only be realized in European terms.

One example of such a mistake, according to Dostoevsky, was the notion that he cites from Avseyenko, who had written that "this bowing down to popular ideals was a product of the European culture we assimilated, and that without it the peasant would have remained to this day a dog and a scoundrel" (22: 114). Avseyenko was quite right in attributing the romanticization of "the people" to the influence of European culture, but Dostoevsky was enraged at the presumption that "one had to go to Paris to comprehend the ideals of our people, or at least to some second-rate farce at the Mikhailovsky Theatre" (22: 117). He points to the Slavophils, "already fully at home in European civilization," whose ideas nonetheless emerged "from the inexhaustible, ceaseless educative work of the people's principles on [their] individual development" (22: 116). It was the people's (Christian) example, not European culture, which led the Slavophils to reassess positively the virtues of Russian peasant life.

In the February 1876 entry dealing with Konstantin Aksakov, Dostoevsky restates the key idea of *pochvennichestvo*. Putting the question bluntly, he asks: "Who is better, we [the intelligentsia] or the people?" And he answers: "we must bow down before the people's truth and acknowledge it as the truth, even in the awful event that some of it comes from the *Lives of the Saints.*" Following this command, however, he adds a qualification: "we should bow down on only one condition, and that is a *sine qua non*: the people must accept much of what we bring with us. We cannot utterly annihilate ourselves before them and their truth, whatever that truth might be." Dostoevsky even declares that, as a member of the intelligentsia, he "will not give up [the values of his class] for anything on earth, even, at the very worst, for the joy of unity with the people" (22: 44–45). But some doubt soon arises as to whether he really believes these values of the intelligentsia to be of such inestimable merit.

At first, he appears to agree that "we, compared to the people, have developed morally and spiritually, have become humanized and humane, and in so doing, to our credit, we have become quite distinct from the people." But after such a concession, he immediately undermines its significance: what had been learned from Europe was not any "humanizing and humane influence," but solely the acquisition of "science" (which itself becomes simply the skills necessary for technical development, for example, shipbuilding). Why did Russia not develop its own "science" earlier? With a jab at Turgenev, who in *Smoke* had dishonored "the people by sneering that the Russians had invented nothing but the samovar," Dostoevsky appeals to "well-known laws of nature and history" for an explanation of "the cause for our scant contribution to science and industry." While Europe was acquiring science, the Russians were building a great nation and fighting off "cruel enemies who would have fallen on Europe if it had not been for the Russians." And while Russia was struggling, and succeeding, in creating "a kingdom and a political entity without parallel in the world," science emerged in Europe "under different political and geographical circumstances," which were, by implication, partly a result of Russian protection. But what have been the results of "science" in Europe? According to Dostoevsky, "as science developed, the mind and political health of Europe weakened almost everywhere." And so the question is not about science and industry, but about something quite different: "In what way did we, the cultured people, become *morally and essentially* superior to the people when we returned from Europe?" (22: 110). The answer that he gives is unequivocal: in no way at all, and in fact, quite the contrary.

The same point is made when he discusses the example of Foma Danilov in the January 1877 issue. This Russian soldier, captured in Turkestan, had refused under torture to convert to Islam (Smerdyakov, in *The Brothers Karamazov*, thinks he was a fool). A pension had recently been awarded his impoverished family by the Tsar, and for Dostoevsky he becomes "what amounts to the portrait, the complete picture of the Russian people." It is time for the intelligentsia to ask themselves whether there is anything they can teach such a people. Of course, "technology and mathematical knowledge" come to mind, though "these can be taught by Germans brought in to do it if we do not." But is there "something moral, something sublime to pass on to them, to explain to them, and thus to bring light to their dark souls?" Not at all. The people already possess self-respect, a sense of their own dignity, and a respect for the convictions of others (while the intelligentsia are torn apart by internal struggles). "The people have Foma Danilovs by the thousands, while we have no faith at all in Russian strength" (25: 12–17).

One would look in vain in the *Diary* for any recognition that the intelligentsia, having become "humanized and humane," helped to develop the people in such a direction. In June 1876, however, an entry entitled "The Utopian Conception of History" assigns a positive value to the influence of the intelligentsia on the people, though only in the very broadest and vaguest historical terms. Prior to Peter the Great, Dostoevsky explains, Russia had instinctively guarded itself from contact with other countries because it was "charged with preserving the truth of Christ, which had been obscured in all the other religions and in all other nations." With the arrival of Peter, Russia broke out of its isolation and embarked on "an enormous broadening of outlook"; this is "a precious gift . . . we [the intelligentsia] . . . are bringing to the people after our century-and-a-half absence from Russia." This gift is a *sine qua non* that the people must accept, just as the intelligentsia must accept the people's religious truth. For this "broadening of outlook" brought to the people the capacity to develop "our almost brotherly love for other nations" and to become "the servant of all in the service of universal reconciliation." Here is Russia's messianic historical mission, though Dostoevsky adds: "This is how I understand Russia's destiny *in its ideal form*." The italicized phrase at least appears to recognize that its real form—which in this instance comes down to "the uniting of all of Slavdom, so to say, under the wing of Russia," with Constantinople as the capital of this new union—might be viewed by others in somewhat less honorific terms (23: 46–47). He feared, as he wrote to Vsevolod Solovyev in July 1876 (in a letter quoted in Chapter 12), that this outburst of nationalistic exaltation might provoke a considerable outcry—which it did.

## THE STATE OF RUSSIAN SOCIETY

During the 1870s, Russian society experienced a period of transition from what had been essentially a peasant-based economy to one in which industrial expansion began to play a leading role. Dostoevsky had already commented in his 1873 *Diary* on the destructive moral-social effects that this development was bringing in its wake; and he takes up the same theme again three years later.

Not that he wishes to paint any Slavophil-tinged pastoral image of the Russian society of the past. A vivid autobiographical passage in the January 1876 issue recalls the trip he made to Petersburg with his father and older brother in the spring of 1837. During a stopover he saw a government courier arrive and depart, routinely beating his young peasant driver on the back of his neck as they left. The driver, in turn, beat his horses to the rhythm of the blows he was receiving (the article was nominally devoted to an anniversary of the Society for the Protection of Animals). "This disgusting scene," he writes, "has stayed in my memory all my life"; and it became emblematic of the customary cruelty and brutality of the Russian social order. "At the end of the 1840s, in the era of my most selfless and passionate dreams, I suddenly had a notion that if I should ever found a philanthropic society, I would certainly have this troika engraved on the society's seal as an emblem and admonition" (22: 27–29). Dostoevsky's readers would know that "philanthropic society" was a code expression for circles like the Utopian Socialist Petrashevsky group, with which he became affiliated precisely at the end of the 1840s.

Although this type of abuse is no longer tolerated ("couriers do not beat the people"), other evils have now taken its place. One is "demon-vodka" (already denounced in 1873), which leads to endless crimes and is undermining not only the health of the people but also their moral fiber. "A fire broke out in a village; there was a church in the village, but the tavern keeper came out and shouted that if the villagers abandoned the church and saved his tavern, he would stand them a barrel of vodka. The church burned down, but the tavern was saved" (22: 29). In addition to this traditional Russian vice, Dostoevsky now discerns a new one unmistakably linked to the changes taking place in the Russian economy. "An unprecedented distortion of ideas has begun among the people, along with a general worship of materialism . . . what I mean by materialism is the people's adoration of money and the power of the bag of gold." As a result, "the people had begun to believe that a bag of gold is now everything . . . and that everything their fathers have told them and taught them hitherto [the Christian ethic of love and mutual benevolence] is all nonsense" (22: 30).

And not only the people have become infected with the virus of materialism, which dissolves all the ties of mutual solidarity that Dostoevsky associates with the Christian faith. In March 1876 he speaks of the present day as an era of "universal dissociation," in which "everybody sets aside all those things that used to be common to our thoughts and feelings and begins with his own thoughts and feelings" (22: 80). Once before, in his epilogue to *Crime and Punishment*, he had painted a nightmare image of such a dissolution of all social bonds by an untrammeled individualism; and he now sees such a process at work undermining the unity of the Russian spirit. Nor can such unity be replaced artificially, as some Westernizers think, by "the banks, societies, and associations [that] are coming on the scene," and whose mention indicates the modernizing tendencies that are the source of Dostoevsky's apprehension. He then cites an article sent by a reader arguing that the relative paucity of such institutions in Russia should be seen as an advantage rather than a lack; their infrequency demonstrates that "the feeling of unity, without which human society cannot exist, is still effective among us" (22: 81–82).

Dostoevsky returns to an extensive discussion of "materialism" in October 1876, when he takes up the question of who should be considered the "best people" in Russian society—the people deserving of the most respect—and sketches a brief history of the changes that have occurred in this designation. In the past, such people were always those who, in one way or another, served the state and hence, presumably, the common good. Later, they were the educated class, who at least established "the virtual *obligation* to acquire some education." But then, with the liberation of the serfs ("one of the most colossal revolutions Russia had ever experienced"), "everything changed profoundly" (23: 155). The former millionaire-merchant, whose wealth had never entitled him to any influential rank in Russian society, now could pretend to take his place among the leaders of society. "The main thing is that he [the Russian millionaire-merchant] has suddenly found himself in one of the highest places in society, the very place in which the whole of Europe—officially and quite genuinely—has assigned to the millionaire." As a result, "the moneybag is now seen by a *terrible* majority to be the best thing of all . . . but never in Russia until now was the moneybag regarded as the worthiest thing on earth" (23: 157).

While such tendencies were making headway, and he was warning against their accelerating advance, his aim was also to reassure his readers that the situation was very far from hopeless. Russian society was still firm enough in its moral principles to resist the temptations of "dissociation" that accompany "today's itch for debauchery" and "the popular tendency of today: gratuitous gain" (22: 31). For Russia is still united, and Dostoevsky insists that even the quarrels that seem to break out are not irreconcilable. One of his bedrock convictions was that, "with the abolition of serfdom, the reforms of Peter I have been completed"; Russia has entered a new phase of history in which the old antagonisms have become irrelevant (22: 40). He had maintained much the same belief in the early 1860s, without notable success, but the rise of Populism had convinced him more than ever that he had seen quite accurately into the future. "And now we have the Slavophils and Westernizers suddenly in agreement on the same idea: that one must expect everything from the people . . . and that they and they only will utter our ultimate word." The two sides, even though agreeing in principle, nonetheless continue to fight over all the practical problems that have suddenly arisen. Russians have had no experience in dealing with such problems for the past two hundred years, and Dostoevsky compares their disputes to the quarrels of children, "who fight precisely at an age when they haven't yet learned to express their ideas." Despite all the feuding, "there exists everywhere among us an honest and radiant expectation of good—a longing for the common cause and the common good, and this takes precedence over any egoism" (22: 41).

Such a conciliatory image of Russian society is then enlarged into the belief that, if his readers will look carefully, they will observe that "first of all we place our faith in an idea, in an ideal, while the personal, earthly benefits only come later." Of course, "nasty people . . . manage even among us to get their business done," but "these useless people never shape our public opinion, and are not our leaders." In this respect, the Russian educated upper class resembles the people, who "are weighed down by vice" but, as Dostoevsky asserts time and again, always "knew that there was something far better than their misdeeds" and never tried to justify their wrongdoings. The same idealism exists among "our young people," who "want to do heroic deeds and make sacrifices." Now, they may believe in the "naïvest kind of paradox" (presumably that the Russian people are instinctive Socialists waiting to be enlightened), but one day "the paradoxes will disappear." What will remain is "the purity of heart. . . . The desire for sacrifices and heroic deeds that now burns so radiantly in [them] will not die out" (22: 41–42). Dostoevsky thus offers this consoling picture of a society fundamentally united by the same idealistic values, one whose divisions are based on temporary misunderstandings. No doubt he dearly wished to believe that these sanguine images conformed to reality; and one of the aims of the *Diary* was certainly to encourage their widespread acceptance.

## THE SOCIAL QUESTION

Such a starry-eyed image of Russian society was crucial if Dostoevsky were to convince his readers that their homeland would escape the dire fate he ritually predicted for Western Europe. The social question in Russia was certainly troubling, but nothing compared to that confronting the vaunted civilizations of the West. There, particularly in France, the process of "dissociation" and therefore of social disintegration had already reached its furthest limits.

Compared with France, Russia was still a haven of stability. Indeed, Dostoevsky consoles his readers with the thought that, while society may seem to be as disunited at home as in Europe, this is not really the case. In France, the birthplace of revolution and Socialism, disintegration has now reached the point of no return. He regards the recent establishment of a French republic, which many observers took as a guarantee of peace, rather as the prelude to what might well be a new and even more ferocious class war. He sees the republic as having been installed, after the crushing of the Paris Commune, solely for the purpose of making war "against a rival and enemy of all Europe: communism." Sketching in the background of the French Revolution, Dostoevsky writes—much like the Socialists he had read long ago—that the outcome had been the creation of a large class of property owners, the bourgeoisie, who "paralyzed democratic aspirations for years and years," and who were "the prime enemy of the demos" (22: 84–85).

As a result, "the dissociation of political parties has reached the point where the entire organism of the state has been completely ruined, so that there is no longer even the possibility of restoring it." He mentions in passing some "dreamer-socialists" and "dreamer-positivists" who believe that "science" will "provide a new sense of unity in the social organism"; but science is not as yet (will it ever be? he asks) capable of undertaking such a task. Instead, "a most cruel and inhuman tendency" has appeared that is clearly the wave of the future: "millions of the demos . . . have as their primary aim and principal aspiration the plunder of the property owners." Nor does he blame them for this ambition: "the oligarchs" have kept them in such ignorance that "all of these millions of unhappy and blind people" believe "that this is the whole content of the social ideas which their leaders preach to them" (22: 84–87).

Invoking his old obsession with Roman Catholicism, he reiterates that the Church, "having lost the kings as its allies . . . will surely rush to the demos." Socialism is for him merely a secularized version of the Catholic claim to universal earthly domination, which had recently (1870) been reasserted in the proclamation of papal infallibility as an obligatory dogma. Now he imagines a horde of Catholic propagandists preaching to the working masses, in the name of the pope, that while "formerly the main force of religion lay in humility," that time has passed. "Christ Himself commanded you all to be brothers [and] if your elder brothers do not want to accept you, then take up sticks and go into their homes and compel them by force to be your brothers" (22: 89). The purely material aims of the Socialist leaders of the demos would thus receive a moral sanction, and the masses "are once more given a faith, and thereby the hearts of many are set at rest, for too many of them are heartsick without God" (22: 90).

The social question in Europe could thus be resolved only by force and violence, by a ruthless class war, which Dostoevsky saw as inevitable and, one also suspects, anticipated with a certain admixture of *Schadenfreude* (malicious joy). Nothing of the kind would occur in Russia because the pattern of a solution to the social question had already been established. Why, he asks, were the Russian peasants liberated peacefully and with a parcel of land by the ruling class, while "liberation in Europe came not from the owners, the barons, and the landlords, but from uprising and rebellion, fire and sword, and rivers of blood?" (22: 117–118). European civilization, he had long believed, would be destroyed by its inveterate class warfare, while Russia would escape such a fate owing to the Christian principles still alive even among the ruling class. The comparatively tranquil liberation of the serfs with land seemed to him a triumphant confirmation of this belief, and he invokes it to buttress his optimistic predictions. It is "a fact . . . still so little understood among us as a measure of the manifestation of Russian spiritual strength" (25: 197).

Moreover, "if anyone in Europe was liberated without rivers of blood, then it was always done on proletarian principles, so that the newly liberated became absolute slaves." Without land, they were entirely dependent on wage labor and at the mercy of their employers. Dostoevsky, to be sure, overlooked the real situation of the liberated Russian peasant, whose land was usually not sufficient for subsistence, and who was also burdened with heavy taxes to compensate the landowners; but the moral superiority of Russia over Europe seemed to him irrefutably proven nonetheless. The people were liberated with land "because we saw ourselves as Russians, with the Tsar at our head, exactly as the landowner Pushkin dreamed forty years ago, when . . . he cursed his

European upbringing and turned to the principles of the people."* These principles prevailed "not because Europe taught us . . . on the contrary, it was precisely because we suddenly, for the first time, resolved to bow down before the people's truth"—and this, Dostoevsky adds, "was a prophetic moment in Russian life" (22: 117–119).

"Our demos is content," he announces with astonishing complacency, "and the farther we go, the more satisfied it will become, for everything is moving toward that end via the common mood, or, to put it better, the general consensus" (22: 122). Dostoevsky was firmly persuaded, or at least wished to persuade himself and his readers, that the social question in Russia was well on its way to a peaceful solution for the same reason that the peasants had been freed with land— because the governing class would continue to act in the name of the people's own supposedly Christian ideals. When many readers vociferously objected that the Russian demos was very far from being satisfied, he took their criticisms only as additional proof of the good will of the educated class and further corroboration of his point of view.

This liberation of the peasants with land thus became emblematic of the concern of educated Russian society for the people's welfare, and Dostoevsky insisted that such solicitude would also be displayed in the future. "I even believe," he declares, "that the kingdom of thought and light is possible to achieve here, in our Russia, even sooner, perhaps, than anywhere else, for even now no one here will stand up for the idea that we must bestialize one group of people for the welfare of another group that represents civilization, *such as is the case all over Europe*" (22: 31; italics added). Long ago, in his series of travel sketches, *Winter Notes*, Dostoevsky had argued that the French revolutionary ideal of *fraternité*, or brotherhood, existed as an innate moral-psychological instinct of the Russian people. It was only necessary to return this ideal to its original Christian significance, preserved among the Russian people, for the Kingdom of God (or its social equivalent) to be attained in Russia without the bloody class warfare that would inevitably destroy the vaunted edifice of European civilization.

## THE BALKAN QUESTION

The most important political event affecting the *Diary of a Writer* was the outbreak of a revolt against Turkish rule in the Slavic province of

* The commentator of the Academy edition, searching for some basis for Dostoevsky's startling assertion, could only find a quotation from a letter of Pushkin written in 1824. While living in the country, the poet describes his activities during the day, and remarks that in the evening he listens to peasant tales (*skazki*). "With these," he

Herzegovina during the summer of 1875. At the beginning of July 1876, the the independent Slav principalities of Serbia and Montenegro also declared war against Turkey. Eventually, in April 1877, Russia joined the conflict in the Russo-Turkish War of 1877–1878, whose immediate cause was the Turkish refusal to agree to Russian demands to accord more rights to Balkan Christians living under Turkish rule. Dostoevsky was a member of the Slavic Benevolent Society, which had been in the fore-front of Pan-Slavic agitation, and a fervent support of both the rebellion and the war. More and more of the articles in the *Diary*, especially in 1877, were devoted to proclaiming the momentous moral-spiritual con-sequences, not only for Russia but also for world history, of what seemed to others merely another struggle for territory and power. These articles are the least palatable portion of the *Diary* for a modern reader and, as Gary Saul Morson has remarked, are "eminently forgettable."[6] Their inflammatory appeal, justifying the war on the highest moral-religious principles, nonetheless helped to stir up patriotic fervor and evoked a widespread response.

Dostoevsky's first reaction to the Balkan crisis, in the April 1876 issue, was written amidst rumors of an impending war between Russia and the European powers—England and Austria-Hungary—that supported Turkey. "Russia will prove to be stronger than anyone else in Europe," he declared confidently. The great European countries, despite appear-ances, will ultimately falter for a very simple reason: they will be ren-dered impotent and undermined by the unsatisfied democratic aspira-tions of their lower-class citizens—their proletariat and their paupers (22: 122). In the same issue of the *Diary*, he also introduces a dialogue between himself as author and an interlocutor, who turns out to uphold and to praise the virtues of war. This "paradoxicalist," also characterized as a *dreamer*, is described as "a civilian and the most peaceful, affable person you could find on earth"—which of course makes his saber rat-tling all the more piquant (22: 122). Some question has been raised as to whether this character expresses Dostoevsky's own point of view; but since he merely restates, in a livelier and more elaborated fashion, much that can be read in Dostoevsky's letters to his niece Sofya Ivanova during the Franco-Prussian War, there can hardly be any doubt on this score.[7]

To be sure, the diarist pretends to take the opposite, "Christian" side in deploring the cruelty and bloodshed that war inevitably entails, but he argues so weakly that no true dialogue takes place (unlike what

---

says, "I make up for the shortcomings of my damned education." One wonders how much importance should be given to this last remark; but if this is Dostoevsky's source, we see that he took it very seriously indeed (22: 380).

occurs in Herzen's *From the Other Shore*, to which the "dialogic" pages of the *Diary* are often compared). The paradoxicalist, however, to give him credit, is immitigably opposed to one sort of war, which he regards as always pernicious: "a civil, fratricidal war." Such a war "paralyzes and shatters the state . . . and brutalizes the people for centuries on end. But a political, international war brings only benefit in every respect, and thus it is absolutely essential" (22: 123). He knows that his advocacy of war will cause him to be considered "a beast" and "a reactionary," but he stoutly defends his controversial view.

War, according to this inoffensive and quite pacific gentleman, arises not because people wish to kill each other but from a more exalted impulse. They act primarily out of a "noble idea": "they set out to sacrifice their own lives; that must be uppermost in their minds." Nor could humanity "live without noble ideas, and I even suspect that humanity loves war precisely in order to be part of some noble idea." A lengthy period of unbroken peace inevitably leads to social decay because "the social balance always shifts to the side of all that is stupid and coarse in humanity, principally toward wealth and capital." Peace thus encourages all the vices, and it is only because of war that the arts recover from the "ultrarefinement of the feelings" that develops during a prolonged period of peace. "All the best ideas of art are provided by war and struggle. Think of tragedy, look at the statues; there is Corneille's *Horace*; there is the Apollo Belvedere overpowering a monster." When the diarist protests feebly in the name of "the Madonnas" and "Christianity," the paradoxicalist answers: "Christianity itself recognizes the fact of war and prophesies that the sword shall not pass away until the end of the world" (22: 122–124).

Far from accepting the commonplace that war fosters greater enmity between peoples, the paradoxicalist maintains that it creates "a spirit of chivalry" between them (as supposedly occurred during the Crimean campaign). From these hardly convincing claims, Dostoevsky turns to what is unquestionably a social-psychological argument in favor of war much closer to his heart. War has "the finest and most sublime consequences" for the people themselves, because, in a world ruled by money and power, the people cannot help being overcome "by some oppressive feeling of moral inequality . . . that is extremely painful for the common person to live with." War is a remedy for this feeling of moral inferiority: "it makes everyone equal in time of battle and reconciles the master and the slave in the most sublime manifestation of human dignity—the sacrifice of life for the common cause. The landowner and the peasant were closer to each other on the battlefield of 1812 than when living on some peaceful estate in the country" (22: 125–126). War thus brings about that union of classes which Dostoevsky saw as the only hope for solving Russia's social ills; and the prospect of such a union arising (and having in fact arisen) through Russia's support for the Balkan Slavs became a leitmotif in his articles on this topic.

With the possibility looming that his country will be drawn into the conflict, he speculates in June 1876 on the role that Russia will play if, as he assumes, the "sick man" of Europe, the Turkish Empire, should collapse into ruins. Giving free rein to his most extravagant illusions about the noble rectitude of his native land, he unabashedly proclaims that Russia's behavior on the world-political scene has always been governed by the highest moral principles. He is well aware that such a claim will be greeted with incredulity by those too corrupt to believe that any country can behave selflessly and only for the general good. "Russia," he insists, "will act *honorably*—that is the entire answer" to those questioning its intentions. In fact, throughout "the whole Petersburg period of history did she more often than not unselfishly serve the interests of others?" (23: 44–45).

Launching into a discussion of Russia's role in the modern world, he outlines a staggeringly sublime image of his country's messianic destiny. Even when he envisages the first step of Russia's new policy as the unification of "all of Slavdom . . . under the wing of Russia," he specifies that this union is "not for seizing territory . . . nor for crushing the other Slavic personalities under the Russian colossus." No, its sole purpose is the restoration of these long-suffering Slavs to their place in humanity, thus "enabling them to contribute their own mite to the treasury of the human spirit." Sooner or later, he boldly asserts, Constantinople (which he also calls Tsargrad) will inevitably fall into Russian hands and become the capital city of a united Slavdom. Invoking the "Third Rome" ideology of Russian nationalism—which saw Russia as the God-appointed and -anointed successor to the Byzantine Empire (the second Rome), and the inheritor of the toga of Christian world leadership—Dostoevsky argues, with incredible assurance, that Russia's "moral right" to Constantinople would be "clear and inoffensive" to other Slavs, and even to the Greeks (23: 49).

In his January 1877 issue, even before Russia entered the conflict, he viewed the events in the Balkans in apocalyptic terms. "It is evident," he writes, "that the time is at hand for the fulfillment of something eternal, something millenarian, something that has been in preparation since the very beginning of civilization" (25: 6). And he describes this climax of world history as a struggle among the three dominating ideas contending for mastery over the destiny of the world. One was "the Catholic idea," embodied now in France and still at the heart of French Socialism. "For French Socialism is nothing other than the *compulsory* unity of humanity, an idea that derived from ancient Rome and that was subsequently preserved in Catholicism." Contesting this Catholic-Socialist claim to hegemony is "the age-old Protestantism, protesting for nineteen centuries now against Rome and her idea, . . . protesting since the time of Arminius and the Teutoburger Wald." The Protestant idea, essentially the embodiment of the German spirit, appeared long before Luther and has acquired new strength and power since the unification of Germany in 1870. Like the Slavophils, Dostoevsky views German Protestantism as fundamentally a *protest* against Latin Catholic civilization, hence containing nothing positive of its own and ultimately leading to atheism and nihilism (25: 5–9).

Until recently, these two world ideas had struggled for domination, but now a third has dawned on the horizon: "the Slavic idea" contained in Eastern Orthodoxy and incarnating the true image of Christ. What will emerge from the clash of these three world ideas nobody yet knows, "though there is no doubt that it brings with it the end of all the previous histories of European humanity, the beginning of the resolution of their eventual destinies, which lie in the hands of God and which humans can scarcely foresee, even though they may have forebodings." One such prescient observer was obviously Dostoevsky; and to the mocking criticism that he anticipated—and which did not fail to arrive—he replied in advance that "ideas of such dimensions [cannot] be subordinated to petty, Yiddifying, third-rate considerations." Russia, he pronounced, had "two awesome powers that are worth all the others in the world—the intactness and spiritual indivisibility of the millions of our people, and their intimate link with the monarch." All those doubting these two incontestable truths "not only do not understand the people's ideas, they do not even want to understand them" (25: 9).

By October 1876 the Serbian Army, led by the swashbuckling Russian General Chernayev, had been defeated, and Chernayev, who had distinguished himself earlier in Central Asia, came under harsh criticism for rashness and incompetence. The Russian volunteers, though they fought bravely, were ordered to leave the country, having aroused the ire of the Serbs they had come to aid by their swaggering, overbearing, and offensive behavior. Immediately springing to the defense of his countrymen, Dostoevsky praised Chernayev for having placed himself at the head of the great Slavic cause with no thought for personal risk (23: 151). Moreover, he believed the general had been betrayed because he "somehow offended the vanity of Serbian officials," and because the Serbians were afraid (mistakenly, of course) of being annexed by Russia instead of helped to establish their own Slavic kingdom (23: 152).

But no matter—all these misfortunes were the result of the intrigues of the Serbian upper class! Dostoevsky was convinced that "the Serbia of the people . . . considers the Russians alone as their saviors and brethren, and the Russian Tsar as their sun." In looking back over the past year, he also takes heart from the attitude he believed had been displayed by the Russian people themselves, in effect endowing Russia with the halo of a Christ among the nations. For he regards the movement to help the southern Slavs as one "which in its self-sacrificing nature and disinterestedness, in its pious religious thirst *to suffer for a righteous cause*, is almost without precedent among other nations" (23: 150). The annals of nationalism are of course filled with similar adulatory claims for the supreme virtues of one or another people (see Fichte on the Germans and Michelet on the French).

Dostoevsky was especially bitter about the European nations, particularly England, that supported Turkey out of fear of Russian expansionism. He mentions being told about an eight-year-old southern Slav girl who suffered fainting spells because she had seen her father flayed alive before her eyes. Such barbarism is what Russia was attempting to combat, though thwarted by those European countries supposedly representing the values of "civilization." "Oh, civilization!" he exclaims. "Oh, Europe, whose interests would suffer so, were she actually to forbid the Turks to flay the skin from fathers while their children watch! These higher interests of European civilization are, of course, trade, maritime navigation, markets, factories; what can be higher than these things in European eyes?" But "let these interests of civilization, and may civilization itself, be damned," Dostoevsky cries out, "if its preservation demands the stripping of skins from living people" (25: 44).

Once Russia entered the war, Dostoevsky heaps scorn on "the wise men"—those Russians who doubted the wisdom of joining such a conflict—and accuses them of the traditional contempt for the Russian people inspired by their European ideas. All of them "have overlooked the entire Russian people as a living force and . . . one colossal fact: the union of the Tsar with the people." In a letter written ten years earlier to Apollon Maikov, he had affirmed that his recognition of this union had been a major factor in converting him to Tsarism.[8] Nothing like such unity, he was firmly convinced, existed in Europe, "which completely depends on the stock markets of the bourgeoisie and on the 'placidity of the proletariat,'" which will hardly continue for very long. Russia cannot "be conquered by all the Yids of Europe taken together, nor by the millions of their gold, nor by the millions of their armies" (25: 97–98). Dostoevsky's fanaticism has reached such a pitch that Europe as a whole has now become "Yiddish"—ruled only by grossly material considerations—just as have all those Russian liberals and Westernizers, writing in several leading newspapers, who expressed any doubts about the sagacity of Russia's course.

The Russian Army advanced rapidly in the early days of the campaign, but was unexpectedly delayed for four months during the siege of the northern Bulgarian city of Plevna, where it sustained very heavy losses. In the July–August 1877 issue, he describes an incident at a railroad stopover, when he heard someone shouting that "seventeen thousand of our men have been killed" that day. He felt compelled to intervene and say "that it was all nonsense, silly rumors" (though it may have been a garbled version of the news that more than seven thousand had been killed the day before). He notes suspiciously "that Russia this summer has produced a great many fabricators of false and of course malicious rumors about defeats and misfortunes," and he even suggests that "they have a definite aim in mind" (25: 176–177). Three months later, as Russian losses mounted, he draws on his own education as a military engineer to explain that the Turks were equipped with new rifles, whose increased firepower gave the defenders a hitherto unknown advantage against the Russian tactic of a massed frontal assault. Even the Germans, so Dostoevsky reassured his readers, would have been stopped in their tracks. He thus does everything in his power to keep up the spirits of his countrymen, and insists that "the Russian people (I mean the people) all, as one man, want to achieve the great aim of the war for Christianity" (26: 44).

Dostoevsky's lucubrations on the Balkan Question are among the most tedious and deplorable of his pages, and merely repeat the same nationalistic self-panegyrics in differing contexts. From time to time, however, a flash of the novelist relieves the dreariness of the propagandist. Responding to a remark of Disraeli, who had implied that the Russian volunteers flocking to Serbia were mainly radicals and revolutionaries determined to stir up trouble, Dostoevsky brushes in his own affectionate portrait. "And all those captains and majors of ours, old veterans of Sevastopol and the Caucasus, in their rumpled, worn old frock coats with white crosses in their buttonholes . . . all these are socialists! There are some among them who will take a drink, of course; we've heard about that. . . . But it is certainly not socialism. . . . And this old warrior with a family of sons—does he really want to burn down the Tuileries? These old soldiers, these Cossacks of the Don, these parties of Russians who come with medical detachments and field chapels, do they really sleep dreaming only of shooting an archbishop . . . are they all our destructive elements that are to make Europe shake in its boots?" (23: 111).

Another passage about Disraeli depicts him attempting to forget about the atrocities committed by the Turks against the Bulgarians, which had been amply reported in the European and Russian press. Beside himself with fury, Dostoevsky accuses Disraeli of being directly responsible for the slaughter: "It was something he permitted, after all—and not just permitted—he plotted it himself; he is a novelist and this is his *chef d'oeuvre*" (23: 110). With bitter sarcasm, he imagines Disraeli suddenly being disturbed by the image of one of these crimes—the crucifixion of two priests, mercilessly tortured and left hanging on their crosses—just at the moment "when Beaconsfield is preparing for slumber in his richly appointed bedroom, smiling brightly as he recalls the brilliant evening he has just spent, the ball, and all the charming witty things he said to this gentleman and that lady." But "the blackened corpses" suddenly intrude on the statesman's complacency, and Disraeli palliates his discomfort with the thought that "the state is not a private individual," and also with less weighty considerations. "It's their fault for turning up there, in any case, they ought to have hidden somewhere . . . under a sofa" (23: 111).

Once Plevna had been captured, the Russian Army resumed its advance and was soon within sight of Constantinople. But when the Turks sued for peace, the war-weary Alexander II accepted. The initial treaty of San Stefano awarded the Russians a considerable amount of territory and influence in southeast Europe—so much, indeed, that the united European powers demanded (and obtained) a revision of the treaty that deprived Russia of much of the fruits of victory. The war thus ended for Russia in a general sense of disappointment and frustration, and the new era of world history that Dostoevsky had prophesied turned out to be a mirage.

## CODA

No literary figure is mentioned more often in the *Diary* than Don Quixote, who became associated in Dostoevsky's mind with Russia itself in the presumed purity and unselfishness of its foreign policy, and its constant striving to embody an ideal of righteousness on the world scene. Dostoevsky also saw himself as the prophet of a Russian-Christian ideal of world harmony that was often denounced as deluded and deranged by his contemporaries; and he could easily identify himself with the much-abused Knight of the Rueful Countenance. One of the finest entries in the September 1877 *Diary*, written while the battle for Plevna was still raging, contains some reflections on *Don Quixote* that not only interpret the book but add a scene to it wholly of Dostoevsky's own devising.* The poignantly perceptive comments of this article, "A Lie Is

---

* Although difficult to believe, it was only in 1953 that a Spanish scholar, Maldonado de Guevara, pointed out that this episode is not included in *Don Quixote*. See *PSS*, 26: 363–364.

Saved by a Lie," may well be read, considering the time of its composition, as a secret self-questioning about the glorious Russian historical future he was so stridently proclaiming.

"A Lie Is Saved by a Lie" refers to a problem that suddenly assailed the puzzled Don as he contemplated the illustrious deeds recorded in the romances of chivalry. Their heroes, the wandering knights who served as his models, were said to be capable of annihilating "entire armies of even a hundred thousand warriors sent forth against them by some evil power." The more Don Quixote pondered, the less was he able to understand how a single knight, no matter how valiant, could dispose of such a huge mass of enemies. Yet the veracity of "these absolutely truthful books" could not be gainsaid, and so the ingenious Don—in a conversation with Sancho Panza supposedly quoted from the novel—expounds his own solution to the riddle. The answer is quite simple: these armies were made up of men "whose bodies were unlike our own but were more akin to those of slugs, worms, and spiders for example." Hence it was possible to cut through them in the twinkling of an eye, and huge numbers could be disposed of in a manner consonant with the marvelous exploits recorded in the famous romances.

No such conversation appears in Cervantes's masterpiece, but it is entirely faithful to the spirit of the text. Don Quixote uses exactly the same type of reasoning to safeguard his illusion about the incomparable beauty of Dulcinea. And in this unceasing human effort to overcome the discrepancy between some sort of ideal and its disconfirmation by the real, Dostoevsky perceives "one of the most profound and mysterious aspects of the human spirit," an aspect brought to light by Cervantes, "the great poet and seer of the human heart." No books containing such wisdom are being written now, and in his opinion "only one such book is sent to humanity in several hundred years." The fact that Sancho, with all his down-to-earth cunning and common sense, should himself be enraptured by the fantasies of his master, while seeing through them at the same time, is only another instance of Cervantes's profound penetration into the limitless depths of the human psyche. He professes ignorance of "what is now being taught in courses of literature," but believes that "a knowledge of this most splendid and sad of all books created by human genius would certainly elevate the soul of a young person with a great idea . . . and work toward diverting his mind from worship of the eternal and foolish idol of mediocrity, self-satisfied conceit, and cheap prudence."

*Don Quixote* unhappily reveals how "humanity's most sublime beauty, its most sublime purity, chastity, forthrightness, gentleness, courage, and, finally, its most sublime intellect—all these often (alas, all too often) come to naught, pass without benefit to humanity." The reason is that "genius" is lacking "to put all this power to work . . . along a path of action that is truthful, not fantastic and insane." While envisaging the possibility of such success, at the same time he acknowledges its rarity: "Genius, alas, is given out to tribes and peoples . . . in small quantities and so rarely." In most instances, one sees rather "the malicious irony of fate" at work, which all too often "dooms the efforts of some of the noblest and the most ardent friends of humanity to scorn and laughter and to the casting of stones." Such examples, he writes, "may reduce a friend of humanity to despair, evoke not laughter but bitter tears and sour his heart, hitherto pure and believing, with doubt" (26: 24–27).

It is at this point that he returns to Don Quixote's resolution of his doubts about the romances of chivalry. Far from abandoning his ideal, itself a preposterous delusion, he rescues it by an even more absurd notion: a lie is saved by a lie. The first lie was so beautiful that to abandon it "would have been the equivalent of betraying his ideal, his duty, his love for Dulcinea, and for humanity." Dostoevsky then turns to his readers and asks whether they have undergone a similar experience in their own lives. Had they not also cherished "a certain dream, an idea, a theory, or conviction . . . or, at least, a woman who has enchanted you?" And had they not also been troubled by the fear that their ideal might be "a lie, a *delusion*, something that you yourself exaggerated and distorted?" And "didn't you yourself invent some dream, a new lie . . . one that you were quick to embrace lovingly only because it resolved your initial doubt?" (26: 24–27). If this can be true for Dostoevsky's readers, it might be equally true for himself. It is impossible not to wonder whether here, in these pensively melancholy reflections, Dostoevsky was not also giving voice to some inner uncertainty about his own most cherished convictions concerning the Russian people and the future glorious role they were to play in world history. Would not he, who understood so well the human capacity for self-deception, sometimes also have felt that his grandiose predictions were a means of rescuing *himself* from despair as he contemplated his Russian Dulcinea?

## CHAPTER 15

# Toward *The Brothers Karamazov*

One of the most outstanding qualities of Dostoevsky as a novelist is his ability not only to depict characters with a scrupulous social and psychological realism but also to link their conflicts and dilemmas with an exploration of the ultimate problems of human existence—the "accursed questions" that have been traditionally posed (and answered) by religion. This same unique combination can be found in the *Diary of a Writer*. While dealing with the social-political topics of the passing scene, it constantly places them in a moral-religious perspective. Dostoevsky, as we know, considered his *Diary* a preparation for his next novel, and it is in the entries touching on such "accursed questions" that the thematic outlines of *The Brothers Karamazov* begin to emerge.

## 2

Far from beginning his *Diary* with any statement of political principle, the issue of January 1876 opens, as if in the midst of a conversation, with remarks about the spate of suicides among young people then disquieting Russian opinion. What upsets him, besides the suicides themselves, is the apparent triviality of their causes: one young man shot himself because he lacked money to acquire a mistress. "And there is not a moment," Dostoevsky comments sadly, "of Hamlet's pondering 'that dread of something after death . . . '" (22: 6). Indirectly, therefore, the question of immortality is broached, uniting in this way, as will be typical, an eternal "accursed question" with the dispiriting news on which he reports.

Nor, as he goes on to explain, is it a matter of the spread of atheism: "our suicide doesn't even have a shadow of a suspicion that he is called *I* and is an immortal being." Atheism, after all, suggests the existence of such awareness. "Remember the atheists of time gone by: when they lost their faith in one thing, they at once began to believe passionately in something else. Remember the passionate faith of Diderot, Voltaire." Or that of Goethe's Werther, "who regrets, in the last lines he left, that he will never again see 'the beautiful constellation of the Great Bear,' and bids it farewell." Werther feels so deeply about the constellations because "every time he contemplated them he realized he was no mere atom or nonentity before them, and that the whole infinitude of divine, mysterious wonders was by no means beyond his thoughts nor beyond his consciousness, nor beyond the ideal of beauty that lay in his soul." Werther may have killed himself, but not stupidly and ignobly, and he did not destroy "*his image as a human being*" (22: 6). Alyosha Karamazov will soon be saved from despair over the rapid decay of Father Zosima's body when he, like Werther, contemplates the night sky, and "it was as though threads from all of God's countless worlds had converged in his soul, and it quivered in contact with these distant worlds" (14: 328).

Dostoevsky returned to the theme of suicide in October 1876, prompted by a letter from a supposedly unknown reader (actually K. P. Pobedonostsev), who had sent some information about the recent suicide of the seventeen-year-old daughter of "one very well-known Russian émigré." Alexander Herzen's daughter Elizaveta Alexandrovna (Liza) had taken her life in December 1875, and Dostoevsky cited her suicide note, written in French, which displayed a certain adolescent bravura. The note requested that, if her suicide did not succeed, her family and friends should gather "to celebrate my resurrection with Clicquot" (a champagne). Otherwise, she asked that her death be carefully ascertained before burial, "because it is most unpleasant to awake in the coffin underground. *That would not be chic at all.*" Dostoevsky had left similar instructions about himself as a young man when he suffered from lethargic sleep, and he had imagined, in *House of the Dead*, the horror of such a nightmarish awakening. Without comment here, however, he contrasts such words with those of a second suicide, a poor, young St. Petersburg seamstress who "jumped and fell to the ground, *holding an icon in her hands*. This icon in the hands is a strange and unprecedented feature in suicides" (23: 144–146).

Both these deaths haunted his imagination, and the second inspired one of his most beautiful short stories, *A Gentle Creature*. The suicide of Liza Herzen, whom he mistakenly thought he had met in 1863 with her father (it was in fact her older sister, Olga),* led to the composition of an imaginary suicide note, which, as we have already seen, caused Dostoevsky considerable embarrassment and distress. Devoting a few paragraphs to Liza Herzen, he compassionately senses, underneath the strained flippancy of her tone, a protest against the "stupidity" of mankind's appearance on earth, the nonsensical casualness of such a creation, and the oppressive tyranny of a meaningless causality to which humankind, once having reached a certain level of self-consciousness,

---

* For Dostoevsky's encounter with the Herzen family on a boat trip from Naples to Livorno, see my *Dostoevsky: The Stir of Liberation, 1860–1865* (Princeton, N.J., 1986), 276–279.

can never become reconciled. Without, presumably, any conscious awareness of such matters, the young girl had nonetheless been affected by the "linearity" of the ideas "conveyed to her since childhood in her father's house" (23: 145). These ideas—obviously those of atheism and materialism—ultimately impelled her to take her own life. To express their disastrous effect in its most powerful form, Dostoevsky then prints the fictive suicide note entitled "The Sentence," which supposedly contains the reflections "of a suicide *out of tedium*—of course, [written by] a materialist" (23: 146).

The writer refuses to accept, in the name of some hypothetical paradisal bliss, the suffering necessarily imposed by the fact of being born a conscious human being who, as an atheist, does not believe in immortality. A key passage of this text reads: "Nature tells me that—even though I know full well that I neither can nor ever shall participate in this 'harmony of the whole,' and besides that I shall never even comprehend what it means—that nonetheless I must submit to this message, abase myself, accept suffering because of the harmony of the whole and consent to live." He flatly refuses to survive for such an incomprehensible purpose; nor can he accept life because of the prospect of a much more perfect order in the future. "All right, if I were to die but mankind, instead of me, were to persist forever, then, perhaps, I might nevertheless be consoled. . . . [But] no matter how rationally, happily, righteously, and sacredly mankind might humanize life on earth—tomorrow all this would be equal to . . . zero" (presumably because of the inevitable cooling of the universe, according to the second law of thermodynamics, already evoked in *A Raw Youth*). This inconsolable thought impels the writer to see in the creation of human beings, and particularly of himself, "some sort of most profound disrespect for mankind, which, to me, is profoundly insulting, and all the more unbearable as here there is no one who is guilty" (23: 146–147). Rather than endure the humiliation of existing in a senseless universe, where mankind is merely the plaything of a cruel and sadistic Nature, he chooses suicide as the only honorable protest against the indignity of having been born.

The effect of this article anticipates much of the later history of Dostoevsky interpretation. So powerfully had he presented the point of view he was opposing, so penetratingly had he entered into a consciousness whose dangers he wished to expose, that he was immediately accused of supporting what he was striving to combat. "The moment my article was printed," he wrote in December 1876, "I was swamped—by letters and personal callers—with inquiries as to the meaning of 'The Sentence.' 'What do you mean to say, and is it possible that you are justifying suicide?' " A face-to-face encounter on this issue already has been related from the memoirs of Mme Simonova-Khokhryakova. Taking up the question publicly, Dostoevsky admits that he "had some qualms" about not having added an explicit moral to his original article. But, in words that his interpreters would do well to ponder, he explains that "somehow I was ashamed to write it, I felt ashamed to presume, even in a very naïve reader, so much simplicity that he wouldn't guess the *underlying motive* of the article, its object, its moral. I supposed it to be equally clear to everybody. I was proved wrong" (24: 45–46).

He now leaves no doubt that he had tried to express "the formula of a logical suicide"—the only possible conclusion about life as a whole that, in his view, could be drawn by an atheist and materialist. "I have expressed this 'last word of science' in brief terms, clearly and popularly, with the sole purpose of refuting it—*not by reasoning or logic, since it cannot be refuted by logic* . . . but by faith, by the deduction of the necessity of faith in the immortality of the soul" (24: 53; italics added). Employing his usual artistic method of combating dangerous and noxious ideas, he shows the disastrous consequences in action to which the absence of faith may lead.

Laboriously going over the ground again, he now explicitly underlines his positive aim, making one point, however, much more forcibly. It is impossible to give life a meaning by substituting beneficent social action for religious faith. For he insists that, where religious faith is lacking, a true "love of mankind" not only is impossible but runs the risk of being transformed into its opposite. The thought of all the unredeemed suffering that mankind has endured, and the impossibility of alleviating that suffering, cannot help but turn the initial love into hate. To illustrate this point, he offers a vivid example of his genius for finding moral-psychological equivalents to dramatize abstract religious-philosophical ideas. He compares the situation of a compassionate atheist, contemplating both his desire to aid suffering humanity and his inability to do so, with the heart-wrenching situation of parents forced to watch the hopeless suffering of their starving children. The love of such parents has been known to turn into hate "precisely because of the *intolerableness* of their suffering. . . . I assert that the realization of one's utter impotence to help, to render service, or to bring alleviations to suffering mankind, coupled with one's complete conviction of the existence of that suffering, can even *transform the love for humanity in your heart into hatred for humanity*" (24: 49).

Dostoevsky was aiming such words directly at the Populists' commitment to this very combination of a moral idealism unsupported by any religious faith. In another passage, he addresses them directly: "Those who, having deprived man of his faith in immortality, are seeking to substitute for it—as life's loftiest aim—'love of mankind,' those, I maintain are lifting their arms against themselves, since in lieu of love of mankind they are planting in the heart of him who has lost his faith seeds of the hatred of mankind" (24: 49). Ivan Karamazov is exactly this type of despairing idealist who has developed the love-hate relation to mankind that Dostoevsky describes.

3

Still another article on suicide introduces another gestatory stage of his next novel. Speculating on what caused a young woman, struggling to make ends meet, to take her life, he laments the narrow, utilitarian horizon of her ideas, her belief, as he puts it, in "the main prejudice of her whole life—'that these stones be made bread'" (23: 25). Questioned by a correspondent about the significance of this last phrase, Dostoevsky replied with a long, personal letter (not included in the *Diary*) prefiguring the Legend of the Grand Inquisitor both thematically and stylistically. After first informing his correspondent that "the stones and bread . . . symbolize the present-day social question, the environment," he shifts into the liturgical tone of the Legend itself. Christ here is directly addressed by the tempting Devil: "Rather than to go to the ravaged poor, who from hunger and oppression look more like beasts than men, rather than to go and start preaching to the hungry about abstention from sin, humility, chastity, is it not better first to feed them? You are the Son of God—therefore you can do everything. . . . You have only to command and the stones will be turned into bread." Returning then to his own epistolary style, he continues: "Here is the first idea that the evil spirit proposed to Christ," the ideal of contemporary Socialism, which "declares that the cause of all man's miseries is poverty alone, struggle for existence, 'the environment has gone bad.'" To this, Dostoevsky opposes the declaration of Christ: "Not by bread alone does man live."[1]

Such a temptation, he argues, would be irresistible only to a "man-brute." But "if . . . there were no spiritual life, no ideal of beauty, then man would fall into anguish, would die, would go out of his mind, would kill himself, or would indulge in pagan fantasies." Hence Christ decided that "it is better to inspire man's soul with the ideal of beauty; possessing it in their souls, all will become brothers to one another, and then, of course, working for one another, they will also be rich." The question still remains, however, of why God should not have given man "Beauty and Bread together?" The answer is: "then man would be deprived of *labor, individuality, self-sacrifice of one's own good for one's neighbor*—in a word, deprived of all life, the ideal of life."[2] It is thus only the imperfections of God's world that provide the incentive for the moral activity and moral autonomy of the self. Just as Dostoevsky had

always believed that mankind would refuse to accept the artificial Socialist utopias of the 1840s, which allowed no room for the freedom and
initiative of the self, so now he maintains that God, in His infinite wisdom, would know better than to create a world in which the same humanly intolerable loss of the freedom of personality would occur.

4
———

One of the qualities of Dostoevsky's genius was his ability to transpose
his themes from one register or key to another, to treat the same material sometimes as tragedy and sometimes as comedy. The conflict between reason and faith, for example, will be presented in *The Brothers
Karamazov* both with the deepest reverence in the Legend of the Grand
Inquisitor and with dazzlingly satirical ironic jocularity in Ivan's conversation with his devil. Something similar occurs as we turn from the letter just cited to the playful and high-spirited article in the January 1876
*Diary* devoted to spiritualism. Introduced as "a very amusing and fashionable topic," it is also one with which Dostoevsky has had some personal experience.

He begins by good-humoredly outlining some of the extraordinary
phenomena that have recently been reported (including a reference to
the American mediums Horace and William Eddy, whose Vermont
farmhouse had been the site of unusual goings-on detailed by N. P.
Wagner). Dostoevsky solemnly reports that "Gogol writes to Moscow
from the next world and states positively that devils exist. I read the
letter, and the style is his." But clergymen were thundering against spiritualism, and even scientists were being warned against investigating it
too zealously; but perhaps, he adds reassuringly, the Mendeleyev Committee of Inquiry will settle the issue of whether devils really exist or are
only "some new manifestation of universal energy." If the latter, then
people will just say, "how boring," and "go back to their business as
usual." The trouble, though, is that no member of the Mendeleyev Committee really believes in devils, and so "the question is beyond the committee's competence." As it turns out, he has his own problem, which
"is that I simply cannot believe in devils myself," and yet "I have developed a very clear and astonishing theory of spiritualism wholly founded
on the existence of devils" (22: 32–33).

This theory, expounded in the same jocular fashion, is clearly another
of the sources for his next novel. The journalist A. S. Suvorin, in one of
his popular *feuilletons*, had ridiculed the mediocre messages supposedly being conveyed by the spirits, and declared that he had no desire
to spend an eternity in the company of such dimwits; but the manifest obtuseness of the devils, according to Dostoevsky, is a carefully

calculated strategy. What if, instead of violating the rules of Russian grammar in their communications, offering "silly answers" to the questions posed to them, and never uttering "a new idea or pass[ing] on a new discovery," the devils had showered mankind with all possible material blessings? What if they had shown mankind how "to walk or fly through the air, covering immense distances ten times faster than they do by railway?" What if "they would extract fabulous harvests from the earth, create new organisms through chemistry—and there would be beef enough to supply three pounds per person just as our specialists dream. Would this lead to a world in which, at last, everyone would 'become beautiful and righteous . . . and everyone [would] occupy himself with sublime, profound thoughts and with universal concerns'?" (22: 33–34).

Long ago, in *Notes from Underground*, Dostoevsky had imagined such a world in which the human species "had such prosperity bestowed on [it]" that there was "nothing else to do but sleep, eat cakes, and only worry about keeping world history going" (5: 116). The result, alas, would inevitably be boredom and a moral disintegration leading to the worst sensual excesses. For Dostoevsky, the historical symbol for such a world had always been the late Roman Empire (the world in which Christ had appeared), in which Cleopatra had reigned supreme. To quote the underground man again: "They say that Cleopatra (pardon this instance from Roman history), loved to stick golden pins into the breasts of her slave girls and enjoyed their screams and contortions" (5: 112). Cleopatra does not show up in the *Diary*, but if the devils had been imprudent enough to reveal all the mysteries of nature, thus bringing universal prosperity, the result would have been the same desire for perverse and unnatural sensations, followed by despair. For a brief period of rapture (perhaps one generation), voices would rise in a common hymn: "Who can be likened to this beast? Praise to him who has brought fire down from the heavens!" (These are citations from the Apocalypse that will be used in the Legend.) But then, "humanity would begin to decay; people would be covered with sores and begin to bite their tongues in torment, seeing that their lives had been taken away for the sake of bread, for stones turned into bread. . . . People would suddenly see that they had no more life left, that they had no freedom of spirit or will, no personality." And an epidemic of suicide would occur: "Masses of people would gather together, seizing one another's hands and suddenly destroying themselves by the thousands through some new method that they discovered along with all their other discoveries" (22: 33–34).

The situation of mankind would thus become unendurable, "and then, perhaps, those who remained would cry out to God: 'Thou art right, O Lord, man does not live by bread alone!'" Mankind would then "rise up against the devils and abandon witchery"; but the devils were too cunning to run such a risk. Instead, by their tomfoolery, they spread discord and dissension among mankind in accordance with the age-old adage of wily politicians: divide and rule! Dostoevsky instances the split between Catholics and Protestants as an example of such deviltry (it had recently flared up again in Bismarck's attempt to subordinate the German Catholic clergy to the authority of the state). "They [the German Protestants] protested even last year, and what a protest—they took on the pope himself." Another example of such discord is the fight between the supporters of spiritualism and their opponents on the Mendeleyev Committee; neither side can possibly convince the other. What he fears most is that the quarrel will lead to persecution, "and mystical ideas love persecution"; nothing gives them more strength (he probably had the Russian *Raskol* in mind). However that may be, he finally admits that "I have been most definitely joking and having fun from the first word to the last." But he hopes that "the free study of the question" will "eradicate the nasty spirit that is spreading about," and which "is the beginning of intolerance and persecution" (22: 34–37).

5
———

Long convinced, like the Slavophils, that the only genuine Christianity was to be found in Russian Orthodoxy, Dostoevsky welcomed any evidence corroborating this view and illustrating the decline of faith in the West. Although France might be going to pieces politically, England appeared immutably secure, rock-solid in its inner coherence and stability. But "things are the same there as everywhere else in Europe: there is a passionate desire to live and a loss of a higher purpose." As evidence, he produces a passage from a now-forgotten English writer, Sidney Dobell, who had remarked that although Protestantism "is narrow, ugly, impudent, unreasonable, and inconsistent," it is still "educational" and thus should be defended and preserved. Dostoevsky objects to such "a utilitarian outlook" on this question, though he finds Dobell's view to contain "a deep sincerity—but isn't it true that this sincerity seems to border on despair?" Such despair is illustrated in a document, given to him by K. P. Pobedonostsev describing the ritual of an English "Church of Atheists" (22: 95–96).

All the ceremonies in this church are performed with deep solemnity, "the Bible is read, and everyone approaches and kisses the sacred book with tears and love." But "all those praying do not believe in God; their absolute dogma and absolute condition for joining is atheism. They revere the Bible, however, because it has meant so much to humanity during the centuries" and "because once they have rejected God, they have begun to worship Humanity." Dostoevsky is struck, as well he might have been, by the resemblance between this "Church of the Atheists" and his own depiction in *A Raw Youth* of a world in which belief in God has vanished. This is the world of Versilov's vision, the reverie of someone who "also has utterly lost his faith and also worships humanity 'as befits a Russian progressive person.'" He then cites the passage from his novel describing the sorrowful world of mutual love that would exist after faith in God and immortality has been lost. Omitting the novel's concluding reference to Heine's poem and the reappearance of Christ, Dostoevsky asks: "Isn't it true that this fantasy [his own] already exists in the 'Church of the Atheists'?" (22: 96–98). Indeed, if there was such a church, he was perfectly justified in taking credit for having anticipated its mood of reverential melancholy.

After touching on this religious theme, he devotes a few paragraphs in March 1876 to Lord Radstock. The English evangelist had visited Russia again in 1875 and was attracting a considerable following—another instance for Dostoevsky of the "dissociation" everywhere at work in modern culture, and in Russia especially among the educated classes. "It turns out that we, that is, the intelligentsia of our society, now comprise some sort of little foreign nation of our own—a very small, insignificant one, but still having its own customs and its own prejudices that are taken for originality." Far from being hostile to Radstock, he comments that he moves many "to seek out the poor so as to do good deeds for them and almost reach the point of giving away their possessions." But he regrets the appeal of a new sect, which only illustrates "our lamentable dissociation from one another, our ignorance of our own people, our rupture with nationality . . . our weak, barely perceptible knowledge of Orthodoxy" (22: 98).

Although deploring the rise of such sects, Dostoevsky also exhibits his own fascination with these heretical movements. He refers to a whole range of such groups existing in Russia and elsewhere—"the Jumpers, the Shakers, the Convulsionaries, the Quakers awaiting the millennium, and finally, the Flagellants, a universal and very ancient sect." Nor is there anything demeaning in his comparison of Lord Radstock and his aristocratic followers with such plebeian groups and movements. On the contrary, "these Shakers and Flagellants sometimes contain remarkably profound and powerful ideas"—ideas that obviously made a strong appeal to his own eschatological temperament. One such sect met in the Mikhailovsky Castle in the 1820s, where he had resided twenty years later while studying to become a military engineer, and he had heard accounts of their séances. Evoking such gatherings now, he writes that highly placed government officials "used to twirl and speak prophecies along with the enserfed servants. So that there must have been some power of thought and feeling if such an 'unnatural' [classless] union of believers could be created." The overcoming of barriers between the classes was one of his own most cherished social-political aims, and he sought to encourage every possible means (even a foreign war) to bring it about.

6
————

Dostoevsky had begun to analyze court cases in his 1873 *Diary*, and he continued the practice in the *Diary of a Writer*. Indeed, such articles, a regular rubric, were one of the journals' most popular features, and aroused wide comment in the press. They also served as first drafts for the legal pleadings so brilliantly rendered in the last part of *The Brothers Karamazov*. The February 1876 issue contains the first of the five court cases that were treated at length, not so much to illustrate points of law as to criticize existing deficiencies in the Russian legal code and particularly to examine the moral implications of the arguments used by lawyers (especially for the defense) on behalf of their clients. No objection was made to any of the verdicts, only to the unrestrained efforts among lawyers to manipulate the truth in pleading their cases. "So tell me," he remarks to avoid misunderstanding, "am I trying to discredit the legal profession and the new courts? God forbid; I would only like us all to become a little better than we are" (22: 73).

In the first case, an educated Polish gentleman named Kroneberg (he had studied in Brussels and Warsaw universities) freely admitted to having severely beaten his seven-year-old daughter with a heavy bundle of rowan-wood sticks. "I beat her for a long time, I was besides myself, unaware of what I was doing, with whatever was at hand" (22: 66). Such cruelty to a child revolted Dostoevsky when he read the newspaper account, and he rushed to the home of A. S. Suvorin at ten o'clock in the evening to ask for more details. Learning from him that the defendant had been acquitted, he nonetheless found so much of interest in the case that he decided to write an article all the same. For one thing, the complaint had been filed by the family's former maid and the wife of the house porter, who were unable to endure the little girl's screams and imploring outcries (they had come to know her though she spoke only French). Dostoevsky himself remarks on "how averse the common people are to law courts, and how afraid they are to become involved with them" (22: 62). Also, V. D. Spasovich, the attorney assigned by the court to defend the father, enjoyed a reputation as a liberal, having resigned his professorship at the University of St. Petersburg in 1861 in protest against the repression of student unrest. Finally, one of the medical experts called to testify was a person with whom Dostoevsky had once been on the friendliest of terms, Dr. Nadezhda Suslova, the first Russian woman to obtain a medical degree and the sister of his ex-mistress Apollinaria Suslova.

Despite his abhorrence of Kroneberg's viciousness, he approved of the acquittal because, if convicted of the charge ("torture"), the father would have been sent to Siberia and the family destroyed. What aroused his ire was not the verdict but the arguments used to bring it about. He agrees that Spasovich's final speech was "a masterpiece of art"; nevertheless, "it left a foul taste in my mouth" (22: 565). For the "remarkably talented lawyer" undertook not only to prove that no "torture" had taken place, but really nothing at all: "a father [was] being tried for beating his child a little too hard." Spasovich "denied it all: the 'spitzrutens,' the bruises, the blows, the blood, the honesty of the prosecution's witnesses—absolutely everything" (22: 57). Picking apart the speech in detail, Dostoevsky illustrates all the twists and turns of the rhetoric, the hints, suggestions, and shifts of terminology that made the evidence vanish into thin air. This exercise stood him in very good stead when he came to compose the defense speech of the famous attorney Fetyukovich, presumably based in part on Spasovich, in *The Brothers Karamazov.*

While admiring the defense attorney's skill, which Dostoevsky agreed had saved his client from an unjust sentence, he nonetheless insisted that the lawyer had gone beyond the bounds of the morally permissible. He was outraged that the little girl had been put on the stand to confess to the naughty behavior that had provoked her father, and that an attempt was made to minimize the physical evidence of the beating. (Dostoevsky invokes his own observations of convicts who had been cruelly flogged in prison camp to discredit this effort.) What infuriated him was that Spasovich had not been content to argue that no "torture" had taken place, according to its legal definition; "he wants to prove that there was no torture at all, either legal or illegal, and no suffering, none at all." It was this latter aim, not really necessary to absolve Kroneberg, that Dostoevsky denounces. "The whole tactic is to destroy your sympathy for [the little girl]. . . . Mr. Spasovich fears your compassion more than anything . . . when you take pity on her, you might put the blame on the father" (22: 61).

No one could think that the liberal lawyer entertained any sympathy for his client, thus leading Dostoevsky to conclude with "a most absurd paradox . . . that a lawyer can never act according to his conscience . . . that he is doomed to be dishonest" (22: 53–54). He thus attributes the "artistry" of Spasovich's defense simply to the irresistible desire on the part of all gifted people (Dostoevsky lists a whole array of writers) to display their talents. But in failing to restrain his exhibitionism, Spasovich was himself guilty of a crime—that of undermining the tenderness toward children that everyone should feel: "they humanize our souls by their mere presence in our midst. And so we ought to treat them and their angelic images with respect" (22: 68–69). In conclusion, he enjoins Spasovich to "leave us, at least, our pity for this infant. . . . This pity is our treasure and it is a terrible thing to tear it out of our society. When a society ceases to pity its weak and oppressed, it will itself be afflicted; it will grow callous and wither; it will become depraved and sterile" (22: 71). The Populist critic A. M. Skabichevsky, who criticized other articles in the *Diary* very severely, wrote that, although the case itself would soon be forgotten, Dostoevsky's words would immortalize it for the edification of posterity (22: 299).

In the May 1876 issue, he reviewed the case of a woman named Anastasia Kairova. The wife of the man with whom she had been living reappeared one day, moved into their *dacha*, and displaced his paramour. Kairova showed up one night while the couple was in bed, flourished a razor, and a struggle ensued, during which she slashed her rival a few times without inflicting any mortal wound. She had been acquitted on grounds of insanity because her family history revealed a pattern of psychic abnormality.

Dostoevsky once again indicates that he is quite satisfied with the jury's decision, "even though I don't for a moment believe she is insane, despite the views of some experts." Indeed, he expresses more pity for her precisely because, not being insane, "how will she be able to go off bearing such a burden of torment?" He imagines her state of mind when the lawful wife returned after a long absence, "her resentment that grew stronger every hour . . . and finally, this last hour before the 'deed' at night, on the stairs, holding the razor that she had bought the day before—say what you will, but this is all difficult to bear, especially for such a disorderly and unstable soul as Kairova!" (23: 7–8).

What Dostoevsky objects to in this case is her "acquittal," which implies that she had not been guilty of *anything* because not fully responsible. Such a ruling yields too much, in his opinion, to the doctrine of material (in this case, psycho-physiological) determinism. Nor had such a verdict really been necessary. The indictment had charged her with *premeditated* murder, and no jury, as Dostoevsky saw it, could possibly have convicted her on such a charge. "One can only give an affirmative answer to a question posed in that way if one has supernatural, divine omniscience." It is impossible to say whether Kairova intended to murder when she bought the razor, or whether she had any precise notion of what she would do. He even argues that during the attack she might have deliberately decided not to kill (23: 9). If the jury had found her guilty of premeditation, "she would have been ruined, condemned to forced labor. How can a jury take such a burden on their conscience?"

(23: 8–9). Dostoevsky would have preferred conviction on a lesser charge with a lighter sentence; but as the indictment was worded, he agreed with the jury's decision. The psychology of indecisiveness sketched here, the erroneousness of assuming premeditation, is exactly how Dostoevsky will soon portray Dimitry Karamazov.

Again, he criticizes the defense attorney, E. I. Utin—a liberal journalist as well as a lawyer—of going too far in his arguments. The overblown fustian that he employed turned a sordid adulterous relationship into a high-flown romantic tragedy, and Utin *"almost sang praises to the crime"* in defending his client. "Everything about her is ideal, her every step is extraordinary, noble, gracious, while her love is something burning, a poem of epic proportions." Dostoevsky particularly objects to the argument that only a woman with a heart of stone would not have felt the same raging jealousy and behaved in the same fashion. "Just think, sir," he interjects, "that . . . you are, as it were, refusing to admit any . . . more noble and magnanimous outcome," and "if someone had thrown away the razor, you would have called her not a woman but a stone. . . . And so you did almost sing praises to the crime, as I said before" (23: 13–15). Expressing his sympathy for Kairova, he cites one of his favorite passages from Saint John about the woman taken in adultery and forgiven by Christ (he had used it as far back as his early, unfinished novel *Netotchka Nezvanova*). But he reminds Utin that Christ had also said, "Go, and sin no more." "That means that He still called a sin a sin: He forgave it, but did not justify it." Evil, Dostoevsky insists, "must still be called evil, despite any humane feelings, and must not be raised to the level of a heroic deed" (23: 16).

He also rejected Utin's effort to blacken the wife and to "deny . . . even her status as a victim of a crime." Berating the liberal and humane defender, he accuses him of insensitivity in overlooking the suffering of the wife, who awoke to find herself facing imminent death. "She endured several minutes (far too many minutes) of *mortal fear*. Do you know what *mortal fear* is?" And here Dostoevsky speaks out of his own past: "It's almost the same as a death sentence being read to one tied to a stake for execution while they pull the hood over his head" (23: 18–19). Dostoevsky had heard the death sentence read to *him*, and he had never forgotten the mortal fear of that moment.

Utin himself had cited the Gospels, and Dostoevsky found offensive his use of the passage from Saint Luke about a woman accused of adultery: "her sins, which are many, are forgiven; for she loved much." By quoting this text with reference to Kairova, the lawyer was grossly distorting the meaning of the New Testament. "Mr. Utin knows very well that Christ did not have *that kind of love* in mind when he forgave the woman taken in adultery. I think it is a sacrilege to refer here to that great and touching place in the Gospels." (Feodor Pavlovich Karamazov, incidentally, uses the same citation and gives it the same sense as Utin.) Recalling his own days as a military cadet, Dostoevsky remarks on how many "raw youths . . . had truly been instilled with the notion from their schooldays that Christ forgave the woman for that kind of love, that is, precisely . . . for her excess of physical passion" (23: 20). But while there are obvious "physiological" reasons for the popularity of this reading among healthy Russian boys, he professes himself puzzled as to why Mr. Utin, who presumably knew better, should have dragged it in for Anastasia Kairova. Dostoevsky himself, it should be recalled, had very carefully distinguished between these two kinds of love, the carnal and the Christian, in *The Idiot*.

7

---

In the case of Elizaveta Kornilova, which has already been discussed in Chapter 11, Dostoevsky's remarks on the question of "environment" indicate a certain flexibility. Even though an implacable opponent of the idea "that crime . . . is only an illness caused by the abnormal state of society," he was by no means a fanatic when other types of abnormality were involved. He was quite willing to concede "that in *some* instances and in some certain categories" the notion that moral responsibility could be mitigated "is dazzling." But when this idea is taken as a general law and applied unthinkingly (as has all too often occurred in recent court decisions), the result is to deprive "people of their very selfhood and reduce them to the level of a tiny bit of fluff whose fate hangs on the first breath of wind" (23: 137–138). Kornilova's pregnancy had temporarily unbalanced her emotionally, and here "surely an error on the side of mercy is better than on the side of punishment" (23: 139). He was also worried that, after her first conviction had been reversed, she might be tried again and found guilty. And here he once more recalls the agony of his own past, comparing this possibility with the situation of a man reprieved from execution ("he sees the sun again"), only to be "tied to the post five minutes later." Thanks largely to Dostoevsky's intervention, Kornilova was spared the torture that he was so well able to revive in his own sensibility (24: 42).

Although his efforts on behalf of Kornilova met with general approval, in December 1877 he responded to a quite insulting rebuke made eight months earlier. The Kornilova case, according to his critic, was simply another instance of child abuse, all too frequent in Russia, where beating was so much taken for granted. He could find no reason for acquittal on the grounds of temporary derangement because of pregnancy. "Mr. Dostoevsky is too impressionable," he wrote sneeringly, "and besides, 'the pathological manifestations of the will' are right in his line as the author of *The Devils*, *The Idiot*, and so on; he may be excused for having a weakness for such things." The effect of his influence, however, would be to reduce the possibility of obtaining convictions in the very few cases of such abuse that were ever brought to court (26: 94–95).

Dostoevsky retorts strongly that his critic's description of the facts is deliberately distorted and false, and that his assumption of premeditation on the part of Kornilova is totally unwarranted. The critic had also pitied the poor little girl who would be returned to the care of such a stepmother, but she was in fact living in a children's home from which she regularly visited her parents during the holidays (26: 105). Turning to the personal attack, he strikes back: "The entire article was written directly to prove that because of my predilections for 'the pathological manifestations of the will,' my common sense has been so distorted that I would rather take pity on the torturer of a child, the bestial stepmother and murderess, than on the tortured victim—the weak, pitiful little girl who was beaten, abused, and, finally, nearly murdered. I find that offensive." Was he really "condoning the physical abuse of children—a terrible accusation!" Even leaving out of account "the past thirty years of my literary work," he adduces all the instances in the *Diary* where he had sprung to the defense of children. Had his critic ever uttered a word about *these* cases? As for "his weakness for pathological manifestations of the will . . . I will say merely that it seems I actually did sometimes manage, in my novels and stories, to *reveal* certain people who considered themselves healthy, and to prove to them that they were ill," or that "their excessive confidence in their own normalcy infects them with a terrible conceit, a shameless narcissism that sometimes reaches the point of a virtual conviction of their own infallibility" (26: 107).

Continuing with his examination of the new Russian judicial system in July–August 1877, he singles out a family named Dzhunkovsky, a well-to-do couple accused, and acquitted, of mistreating three of their children. He brings up the case in the context of his trip to his childhood home, Darovoe, and the importance for children of acquiring precious and beautiful memories of childhood to sustain them in later life. A copious citation is given from the indictment, which charged the parents with physically neglecting the children, failing to provide them with "housing, clothing, beds, and meals," locking them up in a toilet in punishment for trivial offenses (a detail used in *The Brothers Karamazov*), and beating them unmercifully (25: 182).

Dostoevsky was not surprised that the couple was acquitted because "nowhere in the written law is there any article that makes a father's laziness, incompetence, and heartlessness in raising his children a criminal offense." If there were such a law, he comments sarcastically, "we would have to condemn half of Russia—a lot more than half in fact." What disturbs him, recalling the Kroneberg case, is that the definitions of cruelty and brutality set down in the new laws "were themselves so cruel that they positively resembled the bashibazouks' torture of the Bulgarians." (The bashibazouks were Turkish troops known for their cruelty.) Unless horrific acts similar to theirs were committed, no crime had taken place at all. "They [the children] were beaten with birch rods. . . . Well, who doesn't beat children with birch rods? Nine-tenths of Russia does" (25: 183–184).

In this instance, the abusive treatment of the children resulted from negligence rather than deliberate cruelty—the mother's refusal to be bothered and the father's anger at the children's conduct, about which he complained bitterly to the court. Noting that the children had been standing next to the father in the courtroom and were very restrained in their testimony, Dostoevsky is shocked that the father spoke "with no regard for the future and for the kind of feelings this day will leave in the hearts of these children, not even suspecting what they will take into their hearts from this day" (25: 186). He then offers a long analysis of the possible psychology of the children, arguing that something that may seem "shocking and odious" to the parents more often than not is "only a childish prank and, specifically, childish 'fantasizing,'" which comes "from a child's imagination, not from a depraved heart" (25: 186–187).

No criticism is made of the defense lawyers, but he imagines how the presiding judge, in dismissing the charges, might address the parents. He could tell them that, though acquitted, "there is another court—the court of your conscience," before which they stand condemned; and it is the judgment of this court—not a legal but a moral one—that the judge is now handing down. Before *this* court they stand convicted, because the cruel punishments they inflicted only succeeded in making "the child [become] embittered," which meant that "the most fantastic, distorted, and cynical thoughts might pass through his head." He will have lost his love for his parents because "you place no value at all on his feelings and his human dignity, while a child, even the smallest child, also has a completely formed sense of human dignity—that you must keep in mind." The judge, as Dostoevsky imagines the scene, continues his admonitory lecture by stressing that the very future of Russia is involved in what seems only a matter of private, familial behavior. "What will happen to Russia if Russian fathers shy away from their civic duty and begin seeking . . . a secession, lazy and cynical, from society, from their people, and their most basic duties toward them?" It was, the judge concludes, "for the children and their little golden heads that the

Savior promised to shorten 'the times and seasons' for us. For their sake, the torments of the regeneration of human society into a more perfect one shall be shortened" (25: 188–193).

A final case in October 1877 involved a General Hartung, who shot himself in the courtroom immediately after hearing that he had been convicted of embezzlement. The event created a sensation and led to an outcry against the verdict as having been too harsh. Hartung maintained throughout that he had not acted dishonestly, that he had become unwittingly entangled in a series of dubious actions without any intention to swindle or defraud. The unwary general had agreed, as a friend, to become the executor of the estate of "a former tailor, subsequently a moneylender and a discounter," and then found himself trapped in a dispute among the heirs. He had favored one of the parties, acted in a manner technically illegal without realizing it, and then faced the humiliation of a trial. On his body was found a suicide note swearing by God Almighty that "he has not stolen anything in the affair and that he forgave his enemies" (26: 45).

Without dwelling on the facts, Dostoevsky attempts to discern the conditions of Russian life that had brought an honorable man to such a pass. "Everyone is guilty here: the mores and habits of our educated society; the characters that have been formed and created in that; and finally, the mores and habits of our young courts that we have borrowed and not sufficiently Russified" (26: 46). "The majority of decent Russian people," he asserts, suffer from complacency, a well-known trait of the Russian character. They are not scoundrels at all, but in them "there prevails specifically this quickness to yield, the need to concede, to come to terms" (26: 46–47). Hartung probably became the executor of the estate under pressure from his unsavory friend. There is also another Russian type: those who may "enter life with the paltry remnants of former estates" and "are innocent, virtual Schillers," whose unawareness of "baseness" is touching. These people have a strong sense of honor and will commit suicide if they think this honor has been impugned. Dostoevsky concludes that "there was no mistake . . . no miscarriage of justice. It was fate; here was a tragedy; a blind force for some reason picked out Hartung alone to punish him for the vices that are so widespread in society" (26: 50).

All the same, he does not spare his habitual criticism of the manner in which cases are tried in the Russian courts, whose deficiencies he attributes to an uncritical adoption of the European model. What upsets him is the evident willingness of both prosecution and defense to say *anything*—to utter the most exaggerated accusations on one side or the other—to make their case. He thus pens a series of amusing parodies of an imaginary charge of arson. A prosecutor declares that "I'm in no way making any *direct* accusation of arson" against the defendant, but a few sentences later he asks the jury to convict "this arsonist, this inveterate, confirmed arsonist" of the crime. The defense lawyer, for his part, insists, "with the most absolute politeness, of course," that "the prosecutor is stupid, foolish, rather despicable," and that if anyone was guilty of arson it was the prosecutor himself because he happened to be at a name-day party in the same neighborhood at the very hour of the blaze (26: 51–52).

Jesting for several pages more, he once again lays the fault for much of what unhappily occurs in the courtroom to the vanity of the lawyers, who love to put on a spectacle that the audience thoroughly enjoys. This audience should "depart with a lofty, powerful, edifying impression"; but instead, "they all sit there and see that the whole thing is based on a kind of lie"—a lie deriving from "certain practices borrowed from Europe with an exuberant lack of discrimination, and which have taken root in those responsible for the defense and prosecution." He hopes that "the Russian nationality, the Russian spirit, will some day . . . eliminate the falsity," and that both sides will unite in the search for truth. Could this ever really happen? "All such utopias," he replies disabusedly, "will be possible, maybe, only when we grow wings and are transformed into angels. But then there won't be any law courts either" (26: 53–54). Here we catch Dostoevsky in his Sancho Panza mood, when his utopian visions are sobered by the down-to-earth realities of human existence. And surely one reason he so often appeals to *Don Quixote* is because of the eternal seesaw between utopia and irony so omnipresent in his own work and so superbly exemplified in Cervantes's creation.

So let us conclude with another passage about Cervantes in the *Diary* for March 1876, this time commenting on a genuine episode in the book. "It was Heine, wasn't it," Dostoevsky asks, "who told of how, when reading *Don Quixote* as a child, he burst into tears on reaching the place where the hero was overcome by the wretched and commonsensical barber Samson Carrasco. There is nothing deeper and more powerful in the whole world than this piece of *fiction*. It is still the final and greatest expression of human thought, the most bitter irony that man is capable of expressing, and if the world came to an end and people were asked somewhere *there*: 'Well, did you understand anything from your life on earth, and draw any conclusion from it?,' a person could silently hand over *Don Quixote*: 'Here is my conclusion about life; can you condemn me for it?'" "I don't claim," Dostoevsky goes on, "that a person would be right in saying that, but . . . " (22: 92).

Many years earlier, in a notebook entry made while sitting at the bier of his first wife, he had written that it was impossible for any individual to realize the ideal of Christ on earth because the human ego stood in the way; yet this was the ideal toward which mankind should eternally strive (20: 172). The unhappy fate of Prince Myshkin in *The Idiot*, who is compared to Don Quixote by Aglaya Epanchina among others, would lead one to believe that, at least in certain moments, he was very close to accepting Cervantes's "conclusion" as final. In *The Brothers Karamazov*, however, Dostoevsky would soon portray, on a grandiose scale, the power of the human personality to break free from the bonds of egoism and to transform itself, if not the world, into a personal realization of Christ's law of love.

## CHAPTER 16

# The Jewish Question

The *Diary of a Writer* contains both the most appealing and the most objectionable aspects of Dostoevsky. Its short stories express, in their purest form, his genuine idealism and his heartache over the sufferings of the human condition. But the *Diary* also is distressingly marred by his deep-rooted xenophobia, which extended to every people not of Great Russian origin and is most obvious here in relation to the Jews. Time and again Dostoevsky hurls the direst accusations against them as ruthless exploiters of the misery of others, motivated by a greedy lust for gain, and deploying their international influence against the interests of the Russian state.

Many of Dostoevsky's Jewish readers had thought to find, in the doctrine of love, forgiveness, and reconciliation that he so eloquently preached, an answer to their own deepest yearnings concerning their place in Russian society, and they were deeply disturbed by his anti-Jewish outpourings. Letters arrived carrying their complaints and rejoinders; and he felt called upon to answer them in a special article of the March 1877 *Diary* devoted to "The Jewish Question." The majority of the social-political issues that Dostoevsky takes up in the *Diary* have lost all contemporary interest, but the Jewish Question is certainly not one of them.

## 2

The occasional references to Jews in Dostoevsky's early writings, though exhibiting the prejudices that prevailed in Russian society, are quite incidental and not particularly abusive if judged by the standards of his time and place. In the early 1840s, he had worked on a play to be called *The Jew Yankel*, though it is not clear how much of this was ever written. A Jew with the same cognomen appears in Gogol's *Taras Bulba* and set the pattern for how this grotesquely comic type would be portrayed in Russian literature for a long time to come. Gogol's Jew is ludicrous, treacherous, and obsequious; but in one scene, when asked to aid a Cossack who had saved his life and now has a price on his head, his face flushes red "at his own cupidity, and he struggled to stifle in his heart the eternal obsession with money that, like a worm, gnaws at the soul of a Jew."[1]

In *House of the Dead*, fifteen years later, he portrayed a Jewish convict among his fellow prisoners who is taunted by the others and made the butt of their cruelly insulting jests. Although he is endowed with unpleasant caricatural traits, and is compared with Gogol's Jew Yankel, Dostoevsky does not treat him with any sort of hostility. On the contrary—as even David Goldstein, the severest critic of Dostoevsky's anti-Semitism, has written—"it is with sympathy, if not affection, that he evokes 'the blissful countenance of my prison comrade and barracks mate, the unforgettable Isay Fomich.'"[2] As another commentator has noted, Isay Fomich is the first Jewish figure in the Russian novel to be given a personal name (rather than a typological one like "Yankel") and depicted as an individual with marked distinctive features.[3]

Just at the time (1861–1862) that installments of *House of the Dead* were being published, Dostoevsky's journal *Vremya* (*Time*) became involved in a controversy with the Slavophil journal *Den* (*Day*) concerning the Jews. This was the period, just after the liberation of the serfs in 1861, when reforms were affecting all aspects of Russian life, and a decree was promulgated stipulating that Jews with university degrees were eligible for posts in all branches of the civil service. When *Day* objected to opening administrative positions to individuals "thoroughly denying Christian teachings, Christian ideals and ethics," *Time* replied: "It is not this spirit, it seems to us, that inspired the teachings of Him in whose name *Day* is apparently speaking. The teachings of peace, love, and concord should have prompted other thoughts and other words." Whether Dostoevsky wrote this article has not been established, but as editor he certainly approved it for publication; and while he was in the habit of appending footnotes to articles with which he disagreed, no such addendum appears here. Moreover, to another article in *Day* attacking the Talmud, *Time* printed a reply by a Jewish journalist, Pyotr Lyakub. It should also be noted that in a monthly feature of *Time*, the chronicle of internal affairs, the Jews were consistently defended.[4]

A few years later, in *Crime and Punishment*, the villain Svidrigailov shoots himself before the frightened eyes of a Jewish fireman incongruously wearing "an Achilles helmet." This character not only speaks a garbled Russian, but his face "bore the eternal expression of resentful affliction which is so sharply etched in every Jewish face without exception" (6: 394–395). A good deal has been made of this juxtaposition and this remark, but they hardly seem to justify the weight of attention they have received. The fireman is dignified by performing a civic duty, and his presence and momentary evocation add a touch of grotesquerie to Svidrigailov's sinister end.

In *The Idiot* and *A Raw Youth*, drawing on both Herzen and Heine, Dostoevsky refers to "the Rothschild idea" that embodies the power of money traditionally associated with Jewry; but neither of the characters possessed by this idea is Jewish. Lyamshin in *The Devils*, a member of the conspiratorial group of five organized by Peter Verkhovensky, is labeled a Jew, but there is nothing in his speech, dress, or comportment that marks him out as such. He is tolerated in society, even though he is depicted as a sneak, a coward, and a moneylender, because he has a gift for amusing improvisations on the piano. He is suspected of having desecrated a sacred icon in the company of a Christian peasant ex-convict; but he is not present at the murder and breaks down hysterically when he arrives on the scene. He is the first to confess—which might be considered a positive act under the circumstances—but does so in such a self-demeaning fashion compared to the others, even offering to turn informer, that his treacherousness and duplicity strongly come to the fore. Despite his superficial assimilation to Russian life, Lyamshin continues to embody the distasteful traits unfailingly attributed to the Jewish character in Russian literature until the last quarter of the nineteenth century.[5]

By the 1870s, the liberation of the serfs had led to a period of economic transformation in which the capital of Jewish financiers played an increasingly important role, especially in the intensive spate of railway construction. It is then that Dostoevsky began belaboring the Jews in his *Diary* in the most insulting language, holding them responsible for (or at least, shamelessly profiting from) the growing industrialization and commercialization of Russia and Russian life that he abhorred with every fiber of his being. He now never missed a chance to berate "the crowd of triumphant Jews and kikes that has thrown itself on Russia ... kikes ... both of the Hebraic and Orthodox persuasion" to suck the lifeblood of the liberated but hopelessly indebted peasantry (22: 81). It is all too clear that he was inclined to accept the age-old demonization of the Jews both as ruthless batteners on the misery of others and as concealed masters and manipulators of world politics.

Nonetheless, he did not consider himself to be anti-Semitic out of religious animosity or unreasoning prejudice, and he attempted to justify his rampant hostility to his Jewish readers. Nor had the Dostoevsky who defended the extension of rights to the Jews in 1861 vanished entirely; there are still some traces of an effort to reconcile his version of the Christian ideal of love both with his deep-rooted xenophobia and with his intense hatred of the new shape that Russian society was assuming in these very last years of his life.

3
———

Dostoevsky's article on the Jewish Question contains citations from two letters by Jewish correspondents (the only two to whom he replied). One, from Sofya Lurie, has already been referred to, and we shall return to it later. The other is from a missive sent from Butyurki prison in Moscow on January 26, 1877, by a prisoner named Arkady Kovner. Two days later another letter arrived from the same unlikely location, and Dostoevsky responded to both on February 14. "I have rarely," he wrote, "read anything more intelligent than your first letter to me (your second letter is a special case)."[6] In his first letter, Kovner had taken up the vilification of the Jews; in the second, he dealt with the conviction that, without belief in the immortality of the soul, no morality is possible and human life is deprived of ultimate meaning.

Who was this correspondent-convict whose first letter impressed Dostoevsky so favorably? He was a Jewish journalist, born in Vilna, who had initially received a traditional Hebrew education. At first writing in Hebrew, he published two books attacking the narrowness and provinciality of contemporary Hebrew learning and literature, and calling for both to open themselves to the modern world. Following his own advice, he mastered Russian, moved to St. Petersburg, and contributed to various liberal and progressive journals. He conducted a regular column in *Voice*, "Literary and Social Curiosities," which provided a running commentary on the social-cultural scene; and many of the nastiest digs against *The Devils*, as well as about Dostoevsky's assumption of the editorship of *The Citizen*, have been attributed to his pen. As Kovner remarks in his letter, "I formerly was one of those publicists whom you despised, who hot-temperedly and maliciously cursed you (that is, your articles)." Admitting that he had done his "utmost to enter into a personal polemic with you, to challenge you to battle," he acknowledges failure, because "you silently ignored all my outbursts and did not gratify my egotism."[7]

Journalism, however, was a very ill-paid profession, and Kovner took a job in the St. Petersburg Discount and Loan Bank. Kept at starvation wages and unable to obtain any advancement, he decided on the misstep that led to his imprisonment. As he wrote Dostoevsky, after "carefully observing the bank's operations over two years, I decided that all banks are based on principles of delusion and swindle. Seeing how people acquire millions, I was tempted and decided to steal that amount of money which constitutes 3 percent of the annual profits of the shareholders of the richest bank in Russia. This 3 percent came to 168,000 rubles. . . . With this 3 percent, I would have provided for my aging parents, my large destitute family, the young children from my first wife [he had been married off as an adolescent against his will], my loving sweetheart, her family, and still many others of 'the insulted and injured,' virtually without harming anyone. These were the actual motives of my crime."[8]

Dostoevsky surely recognized in these words the impact of his own work on the young man when he invokes the plight of "the insulted and injured" (the emblematic title of his first post-Siberian novel) to defend his crime. As Leonid Grossman puts it in his indispensable book about Kovner, "the clever casuistry of Raskolnikov," who argues that an even more serious crime (murder) can be justified on humanitarian grounds, "had captured [Kovner's] soul."[9] Kovner's swindle was detected, and he was arrested before he could flee to the United States with his sweetheart, whom he married in an impromptu ceremony at a railroad stopover.

In his reply, Dostoevsky wrote: "You expressed yourself so clearly and comprehensibly (at least for me) about your crime that I, who did not know your case *in detail* view it the same way as you judge it."[10] He thus accepted Kovner's rationale: his crime had been inspired by a meritorious aim, and the prisoner was absolved from any sordid, exclusively criminal, onus. But he took exception to Kovner's declaration that "I . . . boldly declare even to you that I did not then, and do not now, feel any pangs of conscience in regard to this crime. Mine was only a step taken against theoretical and social morality."[11]

To this Dostoevsky answered: "I do not at all like the two lines in your letter when you say that you don't feel any repentance for the deed done by you at the bank. There is something higher than the conclusions of intellect and all the possible circumstances feeding into it— something to which everyone is obliged to submit (that is, again to something like a *standard*)." He evidently feels that Kovner is letting himself off too easily, though he advances this notion very carefully and takes precautions to spare the sensibilities of someone who will be reading his words behind prison bars. "Perhaps you are intelligent enough," he writes, "not to be insulted by the candor and *gratuitousness* of my remark. First, I am no better than you or anyone else (and that is not all false humility, and besides, what would be the point of it for me?), and second, even if *I* do in fact acquit you in my heart in my own way (as I invite you to acquit me too), then it is better, still and all, if I acquit you than if *you* acquit yourself."[12]

Dostoevsky illustrates the point by comparing "a complete, higher, ideal" Christian who says, "I must share my possessions with my brother and serve him in every way," with a communard who says, "You must share your possessions with me, a similar person and a beggar, and you must serve me."[13] The first, inspired by Christian love, would be right; the second, inspired by envy and revenge, would be wrong. He implies that Kovner's self-justification is really that of the communard, who wishes to take revenge on society while claiming to appeal to higher goals.

Aside from information about his personal situation, Kovner's letter also contains comments about his reactions to Dostoevsky's works. He selects as his favorite *The Idiot*, the most intimately autobiographical of Dostoevsky's novels; and the author responds that "everyone who speaks of [*The Idiot*] as my best work has had something special in his mental makeup that has always surprised and pleased me. And if you too have such a mental makeup, then that's so much the better *for me*."[14] Kovner also speaks of Dostoevsky's ability "to keep the reader (that is, me), in a state of constant tension and expectation," rather than going "into petty details in describing the external appearance of characters"; and he praises him for not flaunting "your gift for describing nature as do our aristocratic novelists, beginning with Turgenev, Goncharov, Tolstoy, and ending with Boborykin, who carries these matters to disgusting lengths."[15] Nothing could have pleased Dostoevsky more than such a comparison and such a compliment.

While in prison Kovner had written a novel that had been approved by the censorship and a five-act comedy that had won second place in a competition. He asked for help in placing these works, and Dostoevsky promised to take them to *Notes of the Fatherland*, though without holding out much hope of success (nothing by Kovner appeared in the journal). He also promised to inform Nekrasov and Saltykov that, when *he* had been editor of *Time*, a manuscript arriving from prison would have been accepted if it "suited the journal's orientation the slightest bit."[16]

Kovner's first letter also includes a bitter extract from his own diary—written after reading *A Gentle Creature* in the November 1876 issue of the *Diary*—which Dostoevsky could well have taken as a personal challenge. "I am sure," Kovner wrote, "that the great novelists-psychologists who depict the truest types of flaws and base instincts, who analyze all of their characters' deeds, movements of the soul, who find in them the divine spark, who sympathize with them and desire their rebirth, who elevate them to the level of the Evangelical Prodigal Son—that these very same great writers, were they to meet an actual live criminal in prison, would turn away from him, were such a type to ask for help, advice, consolation, even though he was not an inveterate criminal of the type depicted in many of these writers' works."[17] After reading of Dostoevsky's visit to Kornilova, however, Kovner expresses regret in his second letter for having included this passage.[18]

## 4

If Kovner's remarks about Dostoevsky's works pleased and impressed their author, the same cannot be said about his hard-hitting attack on Dostoevsky's anti-Semitism. Kovner bluntly states that he does not share many of the views advanced in the *Diary* on "patriotism, nationalism in general, the spirit of the Russian people in particular, Slavophilism, and Christianity"; but he refrains from advancing any arguments against them. However, there is "one question that I absolutely cannot explain to myself. That is your hatred of the *zhid*, which appears in almost every issue of your *Diary*."[19] Kovner simply cannot understand how such "a sincere person" and "an absolutely honest man" could exhibit an intense humanitarianism in so many circumstances and, at the same time, heap such abuse on a downtrodden minority within the Russian Empire. "I, no less than you," he writes, "cannot tolerate the prejudices of my people. I have suffered more than a little as a result of them. But I will never concede that unscrupulous exploitation is in the bloodstream of the Jewish people."[20]

Kovner accuses Dostoevsky of refusing "to come to terms with the basic law of all social life," namely, that all citizens in a country should have the same rights and obligations. And he asks whether "the Russian Orthodox *kulak*, peasant exploiter, innkeeper, or bloodsucker" is any better "than similar types among the Jews." He is particularly incensed because such a blanket condemnation takes in "the entire terribly destitute mass of Russia's three million Jews, of whom two million nine hundred thousand are engaged in a desperate struggle for existence, and who are morally purer, not only than other nationalities, but than the Russian people idolized by you." Nor does Dostoevsky take into account the Jews who have received a higher education, "and who are distinguished in every walk of Russian life" (he lists some names, including a Goldstein who died a hero's death as a volunteer in Serbia). Dostoevsky's denunciations will endanger "an enormous multitude of poor people," while influential Jews have nothing to fear either from the press or from "the impotent wrath of the exploited."[21]

In replying to these charges, Dostoevsky already exhibits the oscillations that will be noticeable in his article. On the one hand, he declares unequivocally: "I am not at all an enemy of the Jews and never have been one." He speaks of having "Jewish acquaintances" (though, except for Sofya Lurie, no others are known) "who come to see me for advice on various matters . . . and although they are sensitive, as all Jews are about Judaism, they are not my enemies."[22] Since Dostoevsky did not wish to consider himself an irrationally biased anti-Semite, he seeks some rationale to buttress his attacks on Jews as an undermining force in Russian life. Kovner had remarked on the four-thousand-year-old history of the Jewish people, and Dostoevsky agrees "that this [tribe] has an extraordinarily strong life force"; but he immediately seizes on such longevity to argue that this life force "has then naturally formulated itself in various *status in statu* [state within a state]. . . . And if that is so, then how can [the Jews] not prove to be, at least *partly*, at odds with the root of the nation, the Russian tribe."

The use of the term *status in statu* reveals the influence of an infamous work, *The Book of the Kahal*, written by Yakob Brafman, a Jewish convert to Orthodoxy who was an instructor in Hebrew in an Orthodox seminary. Brafman's book reproduced some of the official minutes of the Minsk *kahal* (the legal organization approved by the government to administer the internal affairs of Jewish communities), accompanied with a hair-raising commentary. He insisted that the *kahal*s, which had been officially abolished in 1844, had never ceased to exist, and he claimed that, to quote Simon Dubnow, the great historian of Russian-Polish Jewry, they "constituted a secret, uncanny sort of organization which wielded despotic power over the communities... incited the Jewish masses against the state, the government, and the Christian religion, and fostered in these masses fanaticism and dangerous national separation."[23] The Russian authorities were very much impressed with Brafman's book, distributing it to all government offices dealing with Jewish affairs. Dostoevsky's library contained three editions, one carrying a dedication from the author "as a token of profound esteem."[24]

Continuing his argument, Dostoevsky observes that "in all my fifty years of life I've seen that Jews, good and wicked, will refuse even to sit down at a table with Russians, while a Russian won't disdain to sit down with them. Just who hates whom? Who is intolerant toward whom?" Even the assimilated Jewish intelligentsia, of whom Kovner himself is a fine example, continue to hate the Russian people; and he finds evidence for this charge in some patronizing words from Kovner's second letter, alleging that sixty million of the eighty million Russians lack any true knowledge of God or Christ. Dostoevsky turns these deprecating words back on their author: "You hate Russians, and *only because you are a Jew*." Moreover, Kovner should realize that "in the question of the degree to which the Russian common person is a Christian—you are not competent in the least to judge. I would never say about the Jews what you do about the Russians." He then proceeds even to deny that the Jews are an "insulted and demeaned nation" and insists that "it's the Russians who are demeaned in all regards vis-à-vis the Jews." The Jews enjoy "almost complete legal equality" (which was very far from true), while "in addition they have their own law, their own religion, and their own status quo, which the Russian laws in fact protect."[25]

Looking beyond anti-Semitism and toward theology, Kovner had stated frankly that he did not agree with Dostoevsky's insistence on the importance of the immortality of the soul. For he finds it impossible to accept the notion of a God who *personally* intervenes in human affairs. Still, he was not an atheist but some sort of deist. "I fully recognize," he writes, "that some kind of 'power' exists (call it God, if you like) which created the universe, which *eternally* creates and which *never* can be grasped by the human mind." But Kovner refuses to believe that this "power" concerns itself with "the life and actions of its creations and *consciously* guides them, whoever and whatever these creations may be."[26]

Such evidence of religious sensitivity, piercing through a tirade of scientific data, could well have reminded Dostoevsky of a letter he had written long ago. There he called himself "a child of the century, a child of disbelief and doubt," but one who thirsted for faith as "the parched grass" thirsts for water.[27] It is perhaps not incidental that, in replying to Kovner, he should have evoked these earlier years of his own struggle with faith. "I won't even talk to you," he writes, "about your ideas about God and immortality. *I swear to you that I knew all these objections (that is, all of yours) at the age of twenty already!* Don't be angry: they surprised me by their elementariness" (italics added). But he encourages Kovner "to elevate your spirit and formulate your ideal. After all, have you been searching for it until now or not?"[28]

In a third letter, after receiving this unexpected reply to the first two, Kovner apologizes for the bluntness and asperity of some of his remarks. He expresses immense gratitude for Dostoevsky's willingness to accept his own explanation for his crime, which meant that, "I am not morally corrupt." Others, even where he was personally known as a journalist, had spoken of him as an unmitigated scoundrel. Dostoevsky's encouragement and willingness to help was much more than he had anticipated, and he excuses himself, "with pangs of conscience," for disturbing him in the midst of his more important obligations. Indeed, he finds it "blasphemous" for him to have said that "he is no better than [Kovner] or anyone else," since as a writer Dostoevsky has "always had before his eyes the highest ideals (whether a real or fantastic one is another problem)."[29]

This overflowing thankfulness, however, did not impede Kovner from continuing to express his disagreements with outspoken frankness. Referring to the comparison between a Christian and a Communist position on the social question, he says that he fully understands the point; but because "the ideal of the one as well as the other has just as little chance ever to be realized, it is completely unimportant which of these is right or wrong." He also informs Dostoevsky that "you greatly exaggerate the Jewish *status in statu*. It hardly exists any longer, and if some traces of it can be found here and there, this is only the result of [the Jews'] involuntarily being packed together in one spot and their despairing struggle for an impoverished existence." Nor does Kovner, as he assures Dostoevsky, hate the Russian people at all. He even goes so far as to say: "I love the much-beaten careworn mass of the Russian people incomparably more than the Jewish." His reference to the "sixty million" was inspired not by hate but by pity, because "such a huge mass . . . is kept in such ignorance . . . and has not the faintest conception of the doctrine of Christ and of true Christianity"—which Kovner claims he is quite capable of grasping as well as anyone else.[30]

It is uncertain when Dostoevsky decided to write on the Jewish Question, but probably one incentive for doing so was these letters. Less than a month after receiving Kovner's third letter, he replied to Sofya Lurie and particularly thanked her for having sent him information about the funeral of a beloved German Protestant doctor in Minsk, an obstetrician named Hindenburg, who had served the Jewish community with the same devotion he had lavished on all the other nationalities. After reading her account—which, as we shall see, allows Dostoevsky to offer a "Christian" answer to the Jewish Question—he wrote her: "I'll definitely use your Dr. Hindenburg and your letter . . . for the *Diary*. I have some things to say on that point."[31]

5
———

Those who read Dostoevsky's works are accustomed to characters who, under the influence of "advanced" ideas, commit dreadful crimes (like Raskolnikov) or sink to the lowest depths of degradation (like Stavrogin). Invariably, however, at a certain point in their tormented lives they encounter or experience the vision of a possible redemption through the morally purifying effects of Christian love. In reading Dostoevsky's article on "The Jewish Question," it is impossible not to be reminded of this inner structural law of his artistic universe. For while the first several sections contain a distressing display of his anti-Semitic prejudices, the finale, without withdrawing or softening any of these accusations, still holds out the hope of a resolution of the Jewish Question deriving from the example of an overflowing charity and benevolence.

There has been a good deal of argument over whether to accept this last section of the article as expressing Dostoevsky's genuine view; and there is no infallible way to resolve this problem. But since this moving conclusion fits so well with the invariable composition of Dostoevsky's work, let us assume it is genuine, and that it may perhaps suggest an inner division within himself—a conflict between the baser passions of egoism (in this case the egoism of national-religious identity, with all its inherited exclusiveness) and the more elevated universally altruistic strivings of the Christian love that he believed was indigenous to the Russian national character. It would certainly not be inconsistent with his grasp of human nature to believe that he felt both these alternatives—if not with equal strength, then at least with enough tension to trouble his sensibility.

As a prelude, Dostoevsky explains that he has no intention of discussing the Jewish problem in all its ramifications: "This question is beyond my limits." But he wishes to answer his Jewish correspondents, who "reproach me severely and bitterly for 'attacking' them and for 'hating the Yids,' hating them not for their flaws, 'not as an exploiter,' but specifically as a race, supposedly because 'Judas betrayed Christ'" (25: 74). No such charge had been made in Kovner's letter, though perhaps it was leveled by others, and Dostoevsky rejects it as totally unfounded and unjustified. Ironically, he remarks that it was made by "educated" Jews, who confided that they no longer participated in the religious rites of their faith "because this is beneath the level of 'their enlightenment.'" Such an attitude was hardly a means of ingratiating oneself with Dostoevsky, and he comments that "a Jew without God is somehow unthinkable; one can't even imagine a Jew without God." He decides, however, that "this is one of those immense topics" that he would do better to drop, and shifts to express his "surprise" that "he could be placed among the haters of the Jews as a people" (25: 75).

His correspondents refuse "to permit me . . . to condemn the Jew for some of his flaws and for being an exploiter," and this is his only charge against them. Another ground for accusation has been his use of the word "Yid" (zhid), "which I never thought . . . so offensive," though he immediately reveals quite the opposite. For he denies using the word for individuals, reserving it only "to denote a well-known idea: 'Yid,' 'Yiddism,' 'the Kingdom of the Yids,' etc. These designated only a well-known concept, a tendency, a characteristic of the age." If the term was so inoffensive, why restrict its usage in this way? And was Dostoevsky really so oblivious to the baneful consequences of identifying the Jews *as a whole* with everything that he found abhorrent in the present age? So he pretends, at least for the moment, and he attributes the criticisms made against him solely to Jewish vulnerability: "It is difficult to find anything more irritable and punctilious than an educated Jew and more ready to take offense—as a Jew" (25: 75).

He continues with several passages from Kovner's letter, interspersed with his own comments. In answer to the charge that he blames only "the Yid and not . . . the exploiter in general," Dostoevsky replies: "We do not boast about our kulaks . . . we agree completely that both types are bad." Denunciations of Russian kulaks in the *Diary*, however, are invariably set off against paeans to the great mass of the instinctively virtuous Russian people, whereas Jewish exploiters are not the exception but the rule. He also cites the passage in which Kovner accuses him of maligning "the terribly impoverished mass of the three million Jewish population . . . who are morally purer . . . than the Russian people whom you deify," and of failing to mention "the honorable number of Jews who have served the Russian state" (25: 76).

Dostoevsky makes no direct reply to this charge, but now assumes the role of the injured party. Nothing he has written in the *Diary*, he avers, could warrant "an attack of such vehemence," and he asks his readers to "note the intemperance of the attack and the degree of touchiness" (25: 76). Apparently, his continual assaults on the Jews should have been accepted by them with placid equanimity! With a little more justification, he points out that "his honorable correspondent, when he touches on the Russian people . . . could not restrain himself and could not resist treating this poor Russian people with rather excessive contempt." From this behavior he concludes that, "when it comes to motives for our alienation from the Jew, it is, perhaps, not only the Russian people who are at fault." Such motives, Dostoevsky continues, "have accumulated, naturally, on both sides, and one still does not know which side has more of them" (25: 77). Despite this pretense of evenhandedness, it very quickly becomes clear that the Russians are much more justified to feel alienated than the Jews.

"No other people in the whole world," Dostoevsky asserts about the Jews, "have complained so much about their fate . . . about their oppression, their suffering, their martyrdom." In fact, he finds all this lamentation quite misplaced. "One would think it is not they who rule in Europe, not they who at least control the stock exchanges there, and accordingly, the policy, the internal affairs, and the morality of the states. The noble Goldstein may die for the Slavic idea. But still, were the Jewish idea not so powerful in the world, that same 'Slavic' Question . . . might well have been solved long ago in favor of the Slavs, not the Turks" (25: 77). Disraeli, a descendant of "Spanish Yids," had conducted English foreign policy *in part* from the viewpoint of a Yid; and Russia's great mission had been thwarted by the rampant commercialism that now dominated the "morality" of European states. There can be no doubt that the frustrations and failures encountered by Russia in the Balkans contributed considerably to fan the flames of Dostoevsky's anti-Semitism.

As for the Jews in Russia, he finds their protestations to be greatly exaggerated. He accuses them of having ruthlessly exploited the Russian peasants in the western provinces even under serfdom, and at the moment of liberation they "were the first who fell upon [the freed serfs] as a victim. Who was foremost in taking advantage of their weakness? Who, in their eternal pursuit of gold, set about swindling them?" (25: 78). He refers sarcastically to Kovner's charge of being ignorant of the "forty centuries of history of these immaculate angels who are 'incomparably morally purer' not only than other nationalities but even purer than 'the Russian people whom I deify.'" Obviously ulcerated by these words, Dostoevsky hits back with extended references to various articles he has recently read, culled from newspapers with anti-Semitic tendencies, about Jewish moneylenders taking advantage of the recently freed slaves in the United States and about similar situations occurring among the Lithuanian population (25: 78–79).

Dostoevsky had earlier disclaimed any preconceived hatred of the Jew on religious grounds, and he now extends this tolerance to the Russian people as a whole—they too have no "preconceived, a priori obtuse religious hatred of the Jew." To illustrate, he draws on his own experiences in the prison camp and as a common soldier. The Russians accepted and respected Jewish peculiarities, which separated them from the others, as part of their religion; "and having understood this great reason," the Russian people forgave the Jew with all their heart (25: 80). Drawing on the picture he had provided in *House of the Dead* of inmates peacefully gathering to watch the spectacle of Isay Fomich saying his prayers in a dramatically agitated fashion, Dostoevsky wonders whether, if the situation were reversed, Jews would behave as tolerantly as the Russian people. The answer is all too obvious: "Would they not massacre them altogether, exterminate them completely, as they did more than once with alien peoples in times of old?" (25: 80). Dostoevsky was determined, at any cost, to vindicate the moral superiority of the Russians against Kovner's denigration, and to demonstrate that "it is not the native people but the Jew himself who is responsible" if a strong antipathy exists in certain parts of Russia.

In the third section of the article, "*Status in statu*," he allows his eschatological imagination full sway to magnify this notion into a terrible indictment of Jewry throughout its four-thousand-year history. Basing himself largely on Brafman's tendentious exploitations of passages from the Old Testament, Dostoevsky attributes the astonishing and mysterious survival of the Jews, which surpasses that "even of the world's greatest civilizations," to the power of the idea embedded in their *status in statu*. What is this idea? "Alienation and estrangement on the level of religious dogma; no intermingling; a belief that there exists but one national individuality in the world—the Jews," who are commanded to "have faith in their victory over the world, have faith that all will submit to them" (25: 81). Using the liturgical accents he will soon employ for the Legend of the Grand Inquisitor, he presents this supposed Jewish claim to world domination in the same biblical style as the Pope's claim to temporal power over earthly kingdoms. Both were the imaginary rivals to Dostoevsky's vision of a new era of world history to be inaugurated by Russia.

Dismissing the explanation that the Jews' *status in statu* had arisen because of their persecution throughout the centuries, he sees it rather as an expression of the religious idea by which they are inspired. "That their Providence, under the former, original name of Jehovah, with his ideal and his covenant continues to lead his people to a fixed goal—that is certainly beyond doubt." And this goal is no less than that "the Messiah will gather them together in Jerusalem once more and will use his sword to bring down all the other peoples to sit at their feet." This vision of apocalyptic menace is then buttressed by a citation from the Romantic dramatist Nestor Kukolnik (long fallen out of fashion because of his bombast), in which the daughter of a wealthy Jewish merchant several centuries back evokes in a song the return to Palestine bearing "the cymbal, flute, and tambourine / The silver, gold, and holy shrine" (25: 82).

Jews thus cling immutably, and by the very essence of their religion, to their *status in statu*; and Dostoevsky uses this premise with sophistical skill to argue that granting Jews equality of rights would in effect give them *more* than the Russian population possesses. Referring once again to the western provinces, he speaks of the "mercilessness" of the Jews toward the native population, which is only a consequence of their imputed "disrespect for every tribe and nation and for every human creature who is not a Jew." Retreating slightly from this implacable condemnation, he acknowledges that "human beings always and at all times idolized materialism and tended to see and understand freedom only as safeguarding one's wealth. But never before have these strivings been elevated so openly and held as a higher principle than in the nineteenth century." Christianity has declined in Europe; and while Dostoevsky cannot condemn the Jews on this score, such weakening nonetheless has opened the way for the victory of what they represent. "What lies ahead . . . is materialism, a blind, carnivorous lust for *personal* material security, a lust for personal accumulation of money by any means—and it is this, and not the Christian idea of salvation only through the closest moral and brotherly unity of people, that is acknowledged as a higher goal, as something rational, representing freedom" (25: 84–85).

All of European culture has thus surrendered to the flesh-god Baal, whom Dostoevsky had denounced in 1863 when writing of the London World's Fair. What has triumphed is the materialism that the Jews embody (and "one cannot help but conclude that the Jews have also exerted their influence"). To be sure, he recognizes that "only the very top level of the Jews are wealthy—the bankers and the kings of the stock market—while almost nine-tenths of the rest . . . are, literally, beggars who rush about looking for a crust of bread." Overlooking the vast number of Jewish craftsmen of every kind, he cruelly attributes their poverty to a punishment by God Himself for trading on the labor of others. Nor is Dostoevsky concerned with whether or not Jews are good or bad people. He is sure there are good people among them, but: "Oh! Heavens, is this really the point? . . . We are talking about the whole and the idea; we are talking about *Yiddism* and about *the idea* of the *Yids*, which is creeping over the whole world in place of 'unsuccessful' Christianity" (25: 85). By this time, all individual and historical reality has dissolved in Dostoevsky's nightmare fantasies about Jewish-European materialism taking over the world, just as all national and political reality dissolves when he envisions the cloud-capped vistas of "the Christian idea of salvation," under the aegis of Holy Russia, leading to a new world-historical era of brotherly love and reconciliation.

In the final section, "But Long Live Brotherhood!" Dostoevsky suddenly interrupts himself, as if he had been subconsciously carried away in this anti-Jewish diatribe. "But what am I talking about, and why? Or am I, too, an enemy of the Jews?" He again denies this accusation, while immediately renewing all his previous charges. He affirms that, "despite all the considerations I have already set forth, in the end I still stand for the full extension of rights to the Jews in formal legislation and, if such is possible, also for the fullest equality of rights with the native population." But he continues to insist that "in some instances" the Jews already have rights, "or have more *possibility to exercise them* than the native population." And then he draws a "fanciful picture" of what might happen if the Russian commune (*obshchina*) were to collapse and "the Jews should descend like a horde" on the poor, innocent Russian peasant "who is so little able to restrain himself from temptation." All his possessions would pass into the hands of the Jews, "and an era would begin that could not be compared with serfdom, or even with the Tartar yoke" (25: 86).

Nonetheless, despite this "fanciful picture"—another example of Dostoevsky's eschatological imagination, so brilliantly employed for worthier purposes in his fiction—he insists that "I still stand for complete and conclusive equality of rights—because this is Christ's law, because this is a Christian principle." "But if that is so," Dostoevsky asks, "then why on earth did I fill so many pages with writing, and what point did I want to make if I *contradicted myself* in such fashion?" He wished to prove to his Jewish readers, he explains, that the Russians are far less to blame than the Jews themselves for their misfortunes. Just as he has continually castigated the Russian upper class for looking down contemptuously on "the people," so now he includes the Jews, on the basis of Kovner's letters, as indulging in the same patronizing disparagement. "Oh, they shout that they love the Russian people; one of them even wrote to me along these lines, saying that he was grieved that the Russian people were without religion and understood nothing of their own Christianity." These words of Kovner's festered and rankled; and

Dostoevsky refers to "self-importance and arrogance" as being "traits of the Jewish character that are very painful for us Russians." Nor do the Jews take into account "the many centuries of oppression and persecution that the Russian people have endured," though Kovner had expressed sympathy because of the centuries of tribulation that had held them in ignorance (25: 88–89).

This section concludes with the same infuriating oscillation between advocacy and attack. Dostoevsky asserts his desire for "a complete and spiritual union between the tribes and no disparity of rights"; but then he insinuates that perhaps "the resentful affliction" of the Jews against the Russians may lie *buried among some far deeper mysteries of their law and makeup*" that cannot be eradicated. If there are no such "deeper mysteries," then "may we all join together in a single spirit, in complete brotherhood, for mutual help and for the great cause of service to our land, our state, our fatherland." But the pro and contra continues as he again qualifies this call for brotherly unity by approving of the extension of rights to Jews only "so far as possible . . . so far as the Jewish people themselves demonstrate their capacity to accept and use these rights without damaging the interests of the native population" (25: 87–88). Considering what already has been said, one wonders how such a "demonstration" would ever be possible. He thus ends with what is perhaps an inner indecision to choose between his anti-Semitism and his desire to bring about "a complete and spiritual union between the tribes."

6
———

Some of the most hostile critics of the *Diary of a Writer* as it was appearing from month to month drew a firm distinction between Dostoevsky the publicist and Dostoevsky the novelist, much preferring the latter to the former. And it is the artist, with his intense empathy for the poor and the humble, and his faith in the redemptive power of the Christian morality of love, who now takes over from the benighted publicist. This concluding chapter of "The Jewish Question" contains a long citation from Sofya Lurie's letter, which, as Dostoevsky explains to the reader, "fits in with the whole chapter on the Jews that I have written," but "shows, as it were, an entirely different and quite opposite side of the question, *and even something that might hint at a solution*" (italics added). He emphasizes, in addition, that "I did not want to conceal the fact that this was written by a Jew and that these feelings are the feelings of a Jew"—and they are quite different from the sentiments he has attributed to Jews up to this point (25: 89).

Sofya Lurie describes the overflowing sense of gratitude, shared by the whole community, for the lifelong devotion of the good doctor to the poor of all faiths, whom he helped not only with his services as an obstetrician but also with money and gifts whenever he was confronted with naked destitution. Minsk had a large Jewish population, and "in particular," Lurie wrote, "the poor Jewish women whom he helped so much wept and prayed for him to go straight to heaven." She recounts several instances of his aid to impoverished Jewish families. In one, "he saw that [the expectant mother] had nothing with which to clothe the child and took off his outer shirt and handkerchief (he wore a handkerchief tied round his head), tore them up and gave them to the woman." To the family of a poor Jewish woodcutter, who had sold their goat to pay him a fee of four rubles, he sent back a much more expensive cow with the explanation that goat's milk was unhealthy. A choir of Jewish boys sang psalms at his funeral, though "it is forbidden to sing such psalms at the funeral of a non-Jew." Jewish musicians asked his son for the honor of playing at the burial. "All the poor people donated something—five kopeks or ten—while the wealthy Jews provided a magnificent, enormous wreath of fresh flowers. . . . Prayers were said for his soul in all the synagogues, and the bells of *all* the churches were rung continuously during the procession." Both the pastor and a rabbi spoke at his graveside, and both wept along with all the others (25: 89–90).

Dostoevsky comments on this letter in the next section, "An Isolated Case," which pokes gentle fun at what he calls Dr. Hindenburg's German *Witz* in the episode of the cow. (Dr. Hindenburg certainly sat for the portrait of Dr. Herzenstube in *The Brothers Karamazov*.) But the story of Dr. Hindenburg also brought to his mind a controversy then raging in Petersburg over realism and idealism in art, a controversy stirred up by a vision of Nero's burning of Rome painted with elaborate detail by G. I. Semiradsky. In conversation, "a mighty poet and refined artist" (probably Apollon Maikov, many of whose poems deal with ancient Rome) had criticized Semiradsky's canvas for lacking "a moral center." With Dr. Hindenburg in mind, Dostoevsky imagines a picture painted from *his* life that would certainly have "a moral center."

The setting would be "the absolute, incredible, stinking misery of a poor Jewish hut," and the artist could do a good deal simply by "reassigning the roles of all those wretched objects and household articles in the poor hut" so that "he can touch your heart deeply at once."* A

---

* Dostoevsky uses the word "humor" to characterize the effect of this household reshuffling, but he can hardly mean comic humor, defining this term rather as "the wit of deep feeling." He may have had in mind the pathetic-grotesque, something similar to the magnificent scene in *Crime and Punishment* in which Katerina Marmeladova forces her weeping children to sing French songs to show their aristocratic breeding while begging in the streets.

special effect of lighting could also be attained with "a guttering tallow candle . . . burning out on a crooked table, while through a tiny, single window covered with ice and hoarfrost, there glimmers the light of a new day, a new day of toil for poor people." He suggests that "the eighty-year-old torso of the doctor, naked and shivering from the morning damp, could take up a prominent place, as well as . . . the face of the worn-out young mother who is looking at her newborn and what the doctor is doing with it." With his novelist's eye, he also visualizes "a tired, ragged old Jewish woman, the mother of the one who gave birth . . . fussing at the stove. A Jew who has gone out for a bundle of kindling opens the door to the hut, and a cloud of frozen vapor bursts into the room for a moment. Two little boys are asleep on the floor in a felt blanket." The picture should try to express the thoughts that Dostoevsky attributes to the doctor, and which might, at least at this moment, be his own as well.

At the center of the canvas would be "the righteous old man," who "has taken off his own wretched, worn uniform coat, has taken off his own shirt, and is tearing it up to make swaddling clothes. . . . The poor, newborn little Jewish baby is squirming on the bed before him; the Christian takes the little Jew in his arms and wraps him with the shirt taken off from his own back. The solution to the Jewish problem, gentlemen!" Dostoevsky then places himself in the consciousness of Dr. Hindenburg as he does with so many of his characters. "Christ sees all this on high, and the doctor knows it: 'This poor little Yid will grow up and, perhaps, he himself may take the shirt from his back and give it to a Christian when he recalls the story of his birth,' thinks the old man to himself with noble and naïve faith. Will this come to pass? Most likely it will not, yet it could come to pass; and on earth we can do nothing finer than to believe that this *can* and *will* come to pass" (25: 90–92). A month later, in his April 1877 issue, Dostoevsky published his masterly story, *The Dream of a Ridiculous Man*, in which a disillusioned progressive, after glimpsing an ideal society of love during a dream, devotes the remainder of his days to communicating his vision to a scornful and mocking world. One hears the accents of this ridiculous man already sounding in the words about Dr. Hindenburg and his Jewish patients.

Overly mawkish though they may be, these passages at least express a certain sympathy with Jewish misery; and it is difficult to reconcile the admirer of the saintly Dr. Hindenburg with the writer who regards the Jews only as exploiters and bloodsuckers engaged in a hidden conspiracy against the Russian-Christian population and, on a world scale, against Russia itself. Must one see him only as a Machiavellian manipulator of Christian sentiment to conceal his ingrained antipathy to the Jews? David Goldstein, justifiably indignant at the regurgitation of one anti-Semitic slander after another, considers this last-minute appeal as hypocritical duplicity for public consumption.[32] Or shall we view Dostoevsky as inwardly caught between the Christian-philanthropic ideals that had always nourished his work and his need to find a scapegoat for the disappointments, frustrations, and social-economic upheavals that had plunged Russian life into turmoil since the liberation of the serfs—a liberation he had longed for with all his heart and been sent to Siberia for plotting to bring about? All one can say is that, for one moment, in the imaginary picture of Dr. Hindenburg, Christian sentiment triumphed over bigoted enmity.

Alas, it is difficult not to question the sincerity even of this solitary flicker of fellow-feeling because it turns out to be so short-lived. Dostoevsky's correspondence reveals that his anti-Jewish venom increased rather than abated, and he was even willing to accept the infamous blood-libel charge brought against Jews (the murder of Christian children to obtain their blood). But let me offer the last word to Arkady Kovner, who was directly involved, and who wrote to Dostoevsky on June 3, 1877, after reading the issue of the *Diary* devoted to his letters. His main purpose was again to ask for help in publishing his writings, but he refused to curry favor by concealing his objections.

> I am naturally not completely in agreement with you; most of all, you are too harsh in your supposition that if in Russia (or anywhere else) there were eighty million Jews and only three million Christians, the Jews would, in the most literal sense of the word, fleece them alive. . . . In my opinion, it is much worse to express such a view (or, better, conviction) publicly about a people, than to assert that the great mass of the Russian people are, up to the present day, idolatrous and pagan. . . . How can the Russian people not hate the Jews when its best representatives speak of them publicly as wild beasts? May you be forgiven, much-esteemed Feodor Mikhailovich, for this thoughtless paradox. I say "thoughtless" because you are, at bottom, the kindest of men (as you have proved for the thousandth time in your superb chapter on "The Universal Man" in the same number of your *Diary*).[33]

Dostoevsky never responded to this letter from Siberia, so impressive in its dignity and generosity, but we rescue it from oblivion as a worthy response to his tortuous efforts to come to terms with himself about "The Jewish Question."

## CHAPTER 17

# Turgenev, Tolstoy, and Others

Dostoevsky's *Diary of a Writer* contains a veritable treasure trove of material about his own literary past and about the social-cultural atmosphere of the 1840s and the 1860s, not to mention the 1870s during which it was being written. So far as literary criticism is concerned, however, the issues for 1876 are notably different from those of 1877. In the first year, one finds scattered literary remarks in articles devoted to other topics; but later, he addresses himself more directly to recent works. He does so, however, not "in a purely literary or critical sense," but apropos of what they disclose about the present state of Russian society (25: 51).

As a novelist himself, he felt ill at ease in criticizing his competitors for public attention, and he explains that he tried "to say as little as possible about current things in Russian literature." If he did permit himself "a few words on this topic now and then, they are expressed exclusively in a rapturously laudatory tone" (whose genuineness, judging from his choice of words, is seriously in doubt). In 1877, however, he found this voluntary renunciation to be weighing on him very heavily. "I am a writer," he remarks ruefully, "and I put out a *Diary of a Writer*, and indeed, I, more than anyone else, took an interest through the course of this year in the things that appeared in literature; so how, then, can I conceal what may be my most powerful impressions?" (25: 51). He therefore resolved to speak his mind about such works despite his scruples. The 1877 *Diary* thus contains a good deal of what may be considered literary criticism in this broad sense, not only reflections on the most recent productions, such as Turgenev's *Virgin Soil* and Tolstoy's *Anna Karenina*, but also a brilliant and penetrating portrait of Nekrasov (25: 51).

## 2

Before turning to the 1877 *Diary*, however, notice should be taken of some cogent literary observations inspired by Dostoevsky's polemic with V. G. Avseyenko. Several years earlier, in an article on the plays of Aleksey F. Pisemsky, the critic had spoken disapprovingly of Russian literature for having fallen too exclusively under the influence of Gogol and his followers. Russian writers of the 1840s (a group that would include Dostoevsky) lacked "inner content" and relied "too heavily on the artistic element alone." Dostoevsky can scarcely contain himself at such an idea. "Never in my life," he writes, "did I expect to hear such news." As for the notion that *Dead Souls* lacked "inner content," he just explodes: "Why the man could have said anything else, even the first thing that came into his head, and it would still have made much more sense than this!" What of Turgenev's *A Sportsman's Sketches*, Goncharov's *Oblomov*, and Ostrovsky's plays? (22: 105–106). (He could well have added his own *Poor Folk* to this list.)

Avseyenko also objects to the preference of writers like Ostrovsky for lower-class figures and for "the mere imitation of the savage manners of coarse, offensive characters and types." In *The Insulted and Injured*, a similar objection is made by the villainous Prince Valkovsky, who urges the narrator (an obvious stand-in for the author) to move "in higher circles" because "in novels we have counts and princes and boudoirs" (3: 355). For Dostoevsky, Avseyenko's snobbish scorn for lower-class types and subjects was a direct attack on his own work, and he lashes back vigorously. In his opinion, the "coarse, unclean" characters of Ostrovsky are far purer morally than the denizens of the French farces that Avseyenko was holding up as models of literary elegance, and which Dostoevsky, like Herzen, had ridiculed in the early 1860s (22: 10).

Moreover, he refuses to accept Avseyenko's distinction between "inner content" on the one hand and "artistry" on the other. In remarks that illuminate his own poetics, he insists that inner content and artistry go hand in hand, that "artistically rendered characters" are the "richest in inner content." By "artistically rendered," he means an internal consistency in presentation; a character should not simply become a mouthpiece for the author. If a character only expresses the *author's own ideas*—Dostoevsky's example is the figure of Chatsky in Griboyedov's *Woe from Wit*—then the author "at once sinks to a most unenviable level" (22: 106).* Dostoevsky allows his characters to express *their own* ideas, to maintain their internal consistency, and in so doing attains his own type of dramatized self-expression through portraying the consequences that such ideas have on his characters' lives.

---

* Dostoevsky here is probably following a letter of Pushkin, who wrote in 1825: "In the comedy *Woe from Wit* [*Gore ut Uma*] who is the intelligent personage? Answer: Griboyedov. And do you know who Chatsky is? A fiery, noble, fine fellow who has spent some time with a very intelligent man (namely, Griboyedov), and who has become steeped in his ideas, witticisms, satirical observations." A. S. Pushkin, *Sobranie Sochinenii*, ed I. Semenko, 10 vols. (Moscow, 1977), 126–127. I should like to thank Caryl Emerson for calling my attention to this letter.

### 3

The *Diary* for January 1877 contains Dostoevsky's observations about *Virgin Soil*, preceded by a shrewd comment on Russian literature cited from the French critic Ferdinand Brunetière. In a review of Chernyshevsky's *What Is to Be Done?*, Brunetière had noted that "Russian satire seems to be frightened of finding a good deed in Russian society." For his own part, Dostoevsky remarks with ironic amusement that, ever since he had begun his literary career forty years ago, he had heard nothing but the perennial complaint that Russian literature had never been in a worse condition. Yet these years had produced Pushkin, Gogol, Lermontov, Ostrovsky, Turgenev, and Goncharov (not to mention Tolstoy and himself, names he omits). With considerable justification, he observes that "one can positively state that scarcely in any other literature, over such a short space of time, have so many talented writers appeared as among us" (25: 26–27).

So far as *Virgin Soil* is concerned, he touches only on the published first part of the novel. His personal relations with Turgenev were very strained, especially after his ferocious caricature of him as the famous (and fatuous) author Karmazinov in *The Devils*; but such sentiments did not prevent him from recognizing that "the artistic worth of Turgenev's creations is beyond doubt." Nonetheless, he picks out a comment by the author on a character named Solomin, "which seems to express the author's whole view of his subject. Unfortunately, this view is entirely mistaken, and I am in deep disagreement with it" (25: 27–28).

Solomin is a young man from a lowly priestly family who refuses to continue the family tradition and enter a seminary. Instead, he studied mathematics and, working in England for several years, learned the benefits of industry and efficiency. Returning to Russia, he becomes the manager of a very profitable factory in the area where the novel is set. Here Solomin makes the acquaintance of the Populist characters, who arrive to undertake the task of stimulating the supposed revolutionary consciousness of the local peasantry. The passage that Dostoevsky objected to reads: "It appeared that Solomin did not believe in the imminent approach of a revolution in Russia; but, not wishing to force his opinion on others, he did not prevent their making the effort, and he looked on, not from afar, but from one side. He was well acquainted with the Petersburg revolutionaries—and to a certain extent, sympathized with them—for he himself was one of the people; but he understood the involuntary absence of that same people, without which 'you will not be able to do anything.' . . . Hence, he held himself aloof, not as a crafty man or a shuffler, but as a young fellow with sense, who does not wish to ruin himself or others for nothing."[1]

One might expect that Dostoevsky, firmly opposed to revolution, would have expressed some approval of Solomin, especially since the latter had also established a school and hospital for the benefit of the factory hands; but the very opposite occurs. Although friendly with the revolutionaries, Solomin refused to compromise himself by aiding them; convinced of the futility of their activities, he neither said nor did anything that might save them from inevitable catastrophe. Solomin was neither "hot nor cold," and exhibited the very opposite of that passionate commitment which Dostoevsky so much admired in the young generation. Moreover, Solomin was the ideal of the inveterate Westernizer Turgenev, and exhibited the uninspiring bourgeois virtues that this semi-expatriate considered necessary if Russia were to make any progress. For Dostoevsky, Turgenev's obvious admiration for Solomin was only another instance of his recent lamentable failure to appreciate the moral sublimity of the Russian folk soul, whose beauty he had once celebrated so lyrically in *A Sportsman's Sketches*. Dostoevsky himself felt far more sympathy for the Populists, who were at least attempting to come closer to the beliefs of the Russian people, even though nourishing totally misguided expectations about their revolutionary potential.

Dostoevsky not only discusses the work of other writers but also takes up some of the problems of his own in remarks on his early novella, *The Double*. He refers to it first by claiming that it introduced a new word into the Russian literary language, *stushevatsia*, which means "to disappear, to perish, to be reduced to *naught*, so to say." He uses it to describe the character of Mr. Golyadkin in this work, which was severely criticized by Belinsky. Dostoevsky now acknowledges that "this tale of mine did not turn out too well, but the idea behind it was clear and logical, and I never expressed anything in my writing more serious than this idea. But I did not succeed at all with the form of the tale." Even after revising it fifteen years later, he "came to the conclusion that the thing was a total failure; and if I now were to take up the idea and elaborate it once more, I would choose an entirely different form" (26: 65). He never explained what was faulty in his "form," but one may speculate that it was the treatment of the double *both* as an emanation of Golyadkin's subconscious, a manifestation of his suppressed desires, and also as an actually existing person whose reality is confirmed by others.

Despite his dissatisfaction, however, Dostoevsky also felt that he had never contributed anything more "serious" to Russian literature, and traces of this work can be found all through his later writings. The consciousness of Mr. Golyadkin in *The Double* becomes, as it were, a sounding board for the influence of other characters on his personality; and the appearance of the double reveals all the hidden ambitions that constitute a timid revolt against the injustices of the social order by which he is confined. It was in *The Double* that Dostoevsky discovered that interpenetration of the consciousness of his characters so well defined by Mikhail Bakhtin. Every figure that Raskolnikov encounters, Bakhtin observed, becomes "for him instantly an embodied solution to his own personal question, a solution different from the one at which he himself had arrived; therefore every person touches a sore spot in him and assumes a firm role in his inner speech."[2] Characters in a Dostoevsky novel are united not only by participating in a common action but also through reflecting subliminal aspects of each others' personalities, much as concealed aspects of Golyadkin come to the fore through his double. Each character exists independently, as a clearly defined individual, yet together they all function as "quasi doubles," linked internally through this sort of mutual illumination. A more internal double appears to Stavrogin in *The Devils*, but this motif was eliminated from the final text. In *The Brothers Karamazov*, begun one year later, the dialogue between Ivan Karamazov and *his* double (the devil) will do superb justice to the "form" he felt he had once so badly botched.

4

References to Tolstoy turn up in the *Diary* in articles pertaining to other subjects, and there are two important pieces entirely devoted to *Anna Karenina*. An appreciative passage on *Childhood and Boyhood* in the January 1877 issue is evoked by the suicide of a schoolboy, twelve or thirteen years old, who killed himself in a classroom after being detained for failing to complete his lessons for the day—a day of particular importance in his life. It was his saint's day, the equivalent of a birthday in Russia, which he had been planning to celebrate that evening with his father. Dostoevsky compares the behavior of this ill-fated lad with that of a young boy in Tolstoy's story, the scion of a noble family, who is locked in a storeroom as punishment for some minor offense. During this incarceration, he indulges in daydreams of military glory, surmises that he must be a foundling because his family treats him so harshly, and finally becomes ill with fever and delirium. "It is," Dostoevsky writes, "a remarkably important psychological study of the soul of a child, beautifully written" (25: 32).

Despite his torments, Tolstoy's young boy did not take his own life in despair, and Dostoevsky explains his will to live in the social-cultural terms already familiar from *A Raw Youth*. "Count Leo Tolstoy . . . appeared just at the time [the 1850s] when the former structures of the Russian nobility, established on the basis of old landowners' ways, had arrived at some new, still unknown but radical crisis." All the same,

Tolstoy's aristocratic stripling "might dream of killing himself, but only *dream*: the strict order of the historically configured noble family would . . . not have allowed his *dream* to become an *actuality*." But now this "upper-middle level of our nobility . . . is already an insignificant and 'dissociated' corner of Russian life generally," and what has replaced it is, literally, moral chaos. Even an artist of "Shakespearean proportions," would not be able to "find a normative law and a guiding thread." And he poses the question: "Who will be the *historian* of these other corners [of Russian life]?" (25: 35). As we know, Dostoevsky saw himself as having undertaken this unenviable artistic task, and his search for "a guiding thread" would shortly lead him to Father Zosima.

Turning to *Anna Karenina*, he reports that he has just read the most recent installment "in amazement." But before responding to the text in question—a conversation between Stiva Oblonsky, Anna's brother, and the young landowner Levin, a seeker after truth and justice—Dostoevsky offers some critical comments on earlier portions of the book. Although "at first it made a very good impression on me," he confesses that he found it less interesting as the story unfolded. "I kept thinking I had read this somewhere before"—and of course he had, namely, in Tolstoy's earlier works, "and in these works it was even fresher." Dostoevsky does not conceal his tedium with Vronsky and his social peers, "who can only speak to one another on the topic of horses." He suggests that "the love affair of this 'stallion in uniform' should perhaps have been depicted ironically"; but Tolstoy took Vronsky "seriously and without irony," and when the author began "to allow me entry into the inner world of his hero, I found it even rather boring" (25: 52).

Nonetheless, he admits that all his "prejudices" were suddenly shattered when he reached the deathbed scene involving Anna (though in fact she did not die), in which the deceived husband and the repentant lover gather at the bedside of the unfaithful wife. And his comments on this encounter sharply illuminate the contrast between the poetics of the two great rivals. Suddenly, Tolstoy's tranquilly epic and unhurried rhythm was replaced by a climactic scene of transformation and regeneration much closer to Dostoevsky's own preference for dramatic moral confrontations. Here at last, it seemed to him, "these petty, insignificant, and dishonest creatures suddenly became genuine and truthful, worthy of the name of human beings—solely through the power of natural law, the law of human mortality." All the petty and artificial conventions of social life were swept away, and in their place "appeared only a love of humanity. Each one forgave and supported the other." Tolstoy had thus shown, much as Dostoevsky had always tried to do, that such moments are "the truth of life," in the face of which everything else immediately is reduced to "the petty, fantastic scramble of life that falls away and vanishes without a struggle." Dostoevsky was grateful to Tolstoy for revealing to Russian readers that "this truth exists in actual fact, not only as a matter of faith, not only as an ideal, but . . . in plain view" (25: 52–53). Or, in effect, that the truth of life could pierce through even in a world as artificial and corrupted as that of Tolstoy's characters.

This scene at Anna's bedside continued to be the high point of the novel for Dostoevsky until the publication of the sixth installment. Here he found another encounter that jolted him out of what was, at best, a tepid tolerance for Tolstoy's characters. Indeed, without this new dialogue, for him "the novel would have had an indeterminate aim that would be far from corresponding to immediate and substantive Russian interests; a certain little corner of life would have been portrayed, with deliberate disregard of what is most important and disturbing in it." But he immediately checks himself here, "because it seems that I am entering specifically into literary criticism." So he turns to the conversation between Oblonsky and Levin, in which "the burning issue of the day" in Russia finally comes to the fore amidst the banalities of upper-class amours and intrigues (25: 53).

What is this "burning issue"? Nothing less than the justice of the entire Russian social order, which these two "hereditary noblemen and dyed-in-the-wool landowners" discuss with a remarkable freedom of judgment. Each represents a special type of the Russian educated class. Oblonsky is "an egoist, an urbane Epicurean," a pleasant, affable, and relatively harmless personage who wishes only to enjoy life to the full and does so without any thought for the future of his wife and children. As an impoverished landowner, no longer able to pay for his pleasures after the liberation of the serfs, he obsequiously courts the favor of the new class of financiers and finds nothing wrong in doing so. Levin, on the other hand, who lives off the proceeds of an inherited estate that he manages himself, considers Oblonsky's shameless toadying to the railway magnates and stockjobbers, with "their scheming, their quick profits, their wheedling of railway concessions, and their speculation," to be personally demeaning as well as socially ignoble (25: 53–54).

The two men have been spending the night in a peasant barn while on a hunting trip, and Oblonsky defends himself against Levin's strictures by acknowledging the injustice of the present system; but he refuses to allow such an admission to spoil his enjoyment of its privileges. Why, he asks, does Levin not simply give his estate to his peasants if he feels that the income he derives from it is terribly unfair? Levin has no answer, but expresses distress at his own bewilderment. Oblonsky tells him bluntly that he must choose between alternatives: "Either regard the present order of society as just, and insist on your rights; or admit that you are enjoying privileges that are unjust, *as I do, and take real pleasure in them.*" For Levin, however, such enjoyment is excluded: *"For me, what is most important is to feel that I am not to blame"* (25: 54–55).

Dostoevsky finds it remarkable that such a conversation could be carried on by two ordinary Russian landowners, by no means "professors or specialists," who discuss "such highly idealistic poppycock" as the justice or injustice of a social order based on the right of private property. As he notes: "Some forty years ago all these ideas were barely beginning even in Europe; even there, only a few people knew anything about Saint-Simon and Fourier, the original 'idealistic' exponents of such ideas." But he considers it now "one of the most characteristic peculiarities of the present Russian state of mind" that such considerations should preoccupy people like Oblonsky and Levin, who question the moral foundations of the very social order in which they live—Oblonsky with a blithe insouciance, Levin with a brooding sense of guilt and shame. The Oblonskys of this world express for Dostoevsky all "the cynicism we've seen over these last twenty years," as people have changed their convictions from one day to the next for the sake of some personal advantage. It is on the Levins of Russia that he bases his hopes for the future (25: 55–56).

No Russian reader would have failed to sense the connection between Levin's troubled moral self-questioning and the young Populists' "going to the people." Dostoevsky surely had this linkage in mind when he affirmed that "there is a multitude of these new people today, of this new core of the Russian people who *must have the truth*, and who, in order to obtain it, will give up everything they have." He is convinced that the Levins will ultimately behave like Nekrasov's Vlas, "whose heart melted in a fit of great awe and who gave away his money. . . . And if he does not gather alms for building a church, then he will do something on the same scale and with the same zeal." But Dostoevsky singles out as "the most Russian trait" of Levin the fact that "*he does not know how to resolve the question troubling him*" because, as a Russian nobleman, he can envisage the problem only within the European perspective provided by his education (25: 56–57).

To illustrate this point, he sketches a brief history of European social development in terms already amply familiar from his political articles: it was nothing but a history of relentless class warfare (25: 57–58). The Europeans have lost sight of any *moral* solution to the problem of social justice, and Levin, like all upper-class Russians steeped in European ideas, is puzzled by his own quandary. For Dostoevsky, however, there is "the Russian solution to the problem . . . the moral one, the Christian approach," which is no longer viable for a Europe doomed to destruction by its own sins. This Christian approach is again symbolized by the conversion of the former reprobate Vlas, who "All the might of his great soul / Devoted to his Godly cause." But it is not necessary to become a Vlas literally, only figuratively: "It is not the giving away of your property and the donning of a peasant coat that is obligatory." What is necessary "is *merely your determination to do all for the sake of active love*, all that you possibly can, all that you yourself sincerely believe is possible for you to do."

The existence of people such as Levin proves that "the pure in heart" like Vlas can be found not only among the peasantry. They "are rising up in our milieu as well," and this is the augury of a future when "the blame" of social injustice that oppresses all of Russian society will be eradicated totally and voluntarily, just as the serfs had been liberated, to quote a famous line of Pushkin's, "by the hand of the Tsar." He knows that he will be accused of having been beguiled by a fantasy and of preaching the advent of "the Kingdom of Heaven"; but he is convinced that he is more "realistic" than those who level such criticisms. Vlases actually exist in Russia "among all our social classes . . . but Europe's 'man of the future' we have never yet seen anywhere, and he himself has vowed to come only after wading through rivers of blood." It was the genius of Tolstoy to have understood this moral fermentation taking place in Russian society, though Dostoevsky carefully distances himself from advocating any doctrine of literal "simplification" on the part of the educated class. "You are too 'complex,'" he tells his readers, "to simplify yourself. . . . You would do better to elevate the peasant to your level of 'complexity'" (25: 59–63).

## 5

If Dostoevsky's reaction to the sixth installment of *Anna Karenina* was warmly favorable, his response to the eighth was bitterly hostile. Like Stavrogin's "confession" in *The Devils*, which had been rejected by Katkov as immoral, this section had been turned down by the editor because he disagreed with Tolstoy's disparaging view of the Russian volunteers who went off to fight in Serbia (Count Vronsky among them). The impoverished Dostoevsky had been forced to submit to such editorial dictates, but the affluent landowner Tolstoy published the contested pages as a brochure. Fully sharing Katkov's antipathy for Tolstoy's denigration of the Russian volunteers, Dostoevsky reaffirms his own position very strongly. But he is clearly troubled at being forced to retract, or at least to modify, his previously glowing eulogy of Levin. Dostoevsky admits that he is now placed "in a painful quandary," which he tries to resolve by separating Tolstoy as author from the now distasteful opinions of Levin as a character. Nonetheless, he confesses that "I still did not expect this from such an author" (25: 193–194).

His stinging attack is preceded—perhaps to cushion the shock of the onslaught—with a grandiose encomium of the main theme of *Anna Karenina*. He begins by recounting a chance conversation with "a dear novelist" whom he is always happy to meet while taking a stroll. "I enjoy showing him, among other things, that I think he is quite wrong in saying that he has become old-fashioned and will write nothing more." The novelist was Ivan Goncharov, who was not, as Dostoevsky notes, "a man of strong enthusiasms"; but he had spoken of *Anna Karenina* with unaccustomed fervor. No Russian writer could equal it, he said, "and neither could anything in European literature of the recent past and even much earlier." Dostoevsky expresses his wholehearted agreement with this judgment and carries it even further: the novel becomes a gauge of the Russian capacity to create "something of its own," something he sees as presaging "the new word" that Russia would ultimately announce to the world. This "new word" had been anticipated by Pushkin, and Dostoevsky launches into a foreshadowing of his famous Pushkin speech by stressing the poet's "universality," his artistic intuition of Russia's "future mission, to comprehend and to unify all the diverse nationalities and to eliminate all their contradictions." By "turning to the people," Pushkin had pointed the way for later writers to see "in the people and in the people alone . . . our whole Russian genius and our consciousness of its mission" (25: 198–200).

*Anna Karenina* is a product of this Pushkinian inspiration, and Dostoevsky regards "the novel's idea" as "something truly our own . . . something which constitutes our 'new word,' or at least its beginnings." The novel deals with "human guilt and transgression," and portrays characters "living under abnormal conditions" and "caught in a world of falsities." The theme is an age-old one in European literature, which has always treated it in one of two ways: by absolute condemnation of the sinners, because "good and evil have been defined and weighed" once and for all; or, more recently, by blaming society instead of individuals and declaring that "crime at present does not exist," because flagrant injustices reign. The defenders of the existing state of affairs demand blind obedience despite all the cruelty that such submission brings in its wake; those who blame society abolish personal guilt entirely and look forward to a new order, based on "science," in which guilt will no longer exist. In his view, which, needless to say, hardly does justice to the rich nuances of European moral reflection, "the world of western Europe offers no other solutions for guilt and human transgression" (25: 200–202).

But just as there was a "Russian solution" to the blood-soaked inevitability of European class warfare, so *Anna Karenina* provides a Russian solution to this problem of personal sin and guilt. Dostoevsky first deals with partisans of the second European alternative, who believe there is no human guilt because the fault lies with defective social arrangements. In reply, he strikes off one of his most often quoted passages:

> It is clear and intelligible to the point of obviousness that evil lies deeper in human beings than our socialist-physicians suppose; that no social structure will eliminate evil; that the human soul will remain as it has always been; that abnormality and sin arise from that soul itself; and, finally, that the laws of the human soul are still so little known, so obscure to science, so undefined, and so mysterious, that there are not and cannot be either physicians or *final* judges.

It is not only the "socialist-physicians" who are taken to task here, but also all those who believe that the *final* word has been spoken about the mystery of human guilt and transgression, a word set down for all time and to be found in the moral-social norms established "historically by humanity's wise men." But only "He who says: 'Vengeance is mine, I will repay'"—only "He alone knows *all* the mystery of this world and the final destiny of man. Humans themselves still cannot venture to decide anything with pride in infallibility" (25: 201–202).

Humans thus have no warrant for arrogating the right to make any final pronouncements, for in so doing they assume the role of God. The human judge must know that he too is a sinner and thus "turn to the only solution—to Mercy and Love." Dostoevsky once again refers to the scene involving Anna's illness, in which "the transgressors and enemies are suddenly transformed into higher beings, into brothers who have forgiven one another everything, into beings who, through mutual forgiveness, have cast off lies, guilt, and crime." Even though the remainder of the novel provides a "gloomy and terrible picture of a full degeneration of a human spirit . . . in this picture there is such a profound lesson for the human judge—that he will naturally exclaim in fear and perplexity: 'No, vengeance is not always mine, and it is not always for me to repay.' . . . He will not, at least, cling to the letter of the law." Dostoevsky concludes by taking the achievements of Russian literature, reaffirmed so impressively in Tolstoy's novel, as a prophecy that Russia will someday assert its creativity in other domains as well. Russians will "*eventually* have *our own science*, and our own economic and social solutions. . . . It would be absurd to suppose that nature has endowed us only with literary talents" (25: 202).

Only after penning such an accolade to *Anna Karenina* as a whole can Dostoevsky, with some embarrassment, criticize both Levin and his creator very harshly. No question at this time agitated him more viscerally than the movement to liberate the Balkan Slavs, and he vehemently attacks Tolstoy—already showing traces of his future pacifism and doctrine of nonresistance to evil—for having denigrated the Russian volunteer movement. Levin ridicules this military initiative as artificial and insincere, whipped up by propaganda rather than inspired by any true, spontaneous feelings of sympathy with brother Slavs. Dostoevsky took such words, with good reason, as a direct challenge to the views he had so passionately expressed in his *Diary*. And he thus mercilessly rips apart this new aspect of Levin, who is now revealed to be, despite his own claim, not really one of "the people" at all. Hence he cannot genuinely understand and sympathize with the national impulse that had arisen spontaneously to aid the Balkan Slavs.

Levin is "the principal hero of the novel" and is meant to express "the positive element" in Tolstoy's portrayal of Russian life. The reader is invited to accept him as a seeker after "truth," who finally discovers it when, instructed by the casual remarks of a peasant, he suddenly realizes that he has been misled all his life by his educated ratiocinations. It is only a direct, instinctive faith in Christ's law of love that has brought him any spiritual peace, and Levin thus believes that he has finally found faith and become one with "the people." But Dostoevsky, using almost the same words that Shatov had addressed to Stavrogin in *The Devils*, writes: "Men such as Levin can hardly possess final faith. Levin likes to call himself 'the people,' but he is a nobleman's son, a Moscow nobleman's son, of the middle upper-class stratum, whose historian Count Tolstoy preeminently has been." No matter how fervently such men try to assimilate to the people—and here he is manifestly talking about Tolstoy himself—"it's not enough simply to think oneself one of the people or to try to become so through an act of will, and a very eccentric will at that." Indeed, he amusingly portrays the process—parodying Tolstoy's didacticism—through which Levin will in the future lose his faith.

> Kitty started to walk and stumbled. Now, why did she stumble? If she stumbled this means that she should not have stumbled for such and such a reason. It is clear that in this case everything depended upon laws which may be strictly ascertained. And if this is so, this means that science governs everything. Where, then, is Providence? What is its role? What is man's responsibility? And if there is no Providence, how can I believe in God? Take a straight line and extend it to infinity. (25: 205–206)

All these barbs, however, are merely preludes to the blistering main offensive aimed at Levin's declaration that the Russian volunteers were the usual bunch of adventurers and freebooters "who are always ready to join a Pugachev gang." In fact, Levin declares that among the Russian people "such an immediate sentiment for the oppression of the Slavs does not and cannot exist." Such words, in Dostoevsky's eyes, are proof of Levin's total alienation from the Russian people, his incapacity to understand their long history of concern for Christ's cause and for their suffering Slavic brothers (25: 213).

He was particularly incensed by the argument that the Russian people, ignorant of both history and geography, could not possibly have any opinion about events in the Balkans. Such notions betrayed the usual contempt for the people among the Westernized upper class and the usual total ignorance of their ideals. The imagination of the people, on the contrary, was filled with stories from the lives of the saints about the Holy Land, and they knew very well that it was now in the hands of the infidel. One of the "historical traits" of the Russian people was precisely their passion for setting off on pilgrimages to such holy places as an "act of contrition"; and Dostoevsky links the upsurge of sentiment for their fellow Christians to this ingrained search for salvation (25: 214–217).

What the people had experienced in recent years—that is, since the liberation of the serfs—was, as he was honest enough to acknowledge, hardly inspiring or encouraging. "Among other things they have seen the spread of drunkenness, the increasing number of solidly established kulaks, misery all around them, and often, the stamp of bestiality on themselves. Many—oh, very many perhaps—have been afflicted at heart by a kind of anguish, a penitent anguish, an anguish of self-accusation, and a quest for something better, something sacred." This quest was given a goal when they heard about the tortures being inflicted on fellow Christians by the hereditary Muslim enemy of Russia, and they took up the cause "*as an appeal to repentance, to preparation for a sacrament*" (25: 215–216). None of these sentiments could be understood by Levin or the old prince, his father-in-law, who refer to the volunteer movement with amused and aristocratic scorn.

Dostoevsky was outraged at Levin's declaration that he himself possessed "no immediate feeling for the oppression of the Slavs." Livid with indignation, Dostoevsky unrolls a horrifying panorama of Turkish atrocities in the Balkans, where "people are being exterminated by the thousands and tens of thousands" and "children are tossed in the air and caught on the point of a bayonet while their mothers watch," a detail close to one used in *The Brothers Karamazov*. Levin's seeming "humaneness," which recoils before the prospect of killing Turks to put an end to such barbarities, is in reality a callous indifference for everything except his own personal interests and narrowly egoistic concerns. Let us imagine Levin, he writes, reading about "a wholesale massacre, about children with crushed heads crawling around their assaulted, murdered

mothers with their breasts cut off . . . and there he stands and medi-
tates: 'Kitty is cheerful; today she ate with an appetite; the boy was
bathed in the tub and he begins to recognize me: What do I care about
the things that are transpiring in another hemisphere?—*No immediate
sentiment for the oppression of the Slavs exists or can exist*—because I
feel *nothing.*'" Dostoevsky cannot understand how Tolstoy could expect
his readers to continue to take Levin "as an example of a righteous and
honorable man." People like the author of *Anna Karenina*, he concludes
sadly, "are the teachers of our society. . . . So what is it, then, that they
are teaching us?" (25: 218–223).

## 6

The very last issue of the *Diary* includes a chapter on Nekrasov that has
already been cited in recounting the incident at the poet's graveside
(Chapter 13). Because of the hullabaloo over this event, Dostoevsky explains, he wished to elucidate more carefully what he had meant in
comparing Nekrasov with Pushkin and Lermontov. He had not been
speaking in purely literary terms, or trying to rank poets in any order of
merit. He had been talking about the line of poets who had uttered a
"new word" in Russian literature, and Nekrasov was the last of that line.
A great poet like Fyodor Tyutchev, "who was broader and more artistic
than Nekrasov," did not belong in this group and would thus, in his
view, not be given the "prominent and memorable place in our literature" that the future would accord to Nekrasov (26: 112). It was thus not
of "art" that Dostoevsky had been speaking; it was of the relation of art
(in this case literature) to the deepest problems that confronted Russian
society in the nineteenth century.

He rebukes those who, in raising their voices against him, had used
"the word 'Byronist' as a term of abuse." Byronism, he retorts, had been
a momentous spiritual event, appearing at a time "when people were
suffering terrible anguish, disillusionment, and almost despair." It had
been a response offered "in the wake of the frenzied raptures of the
new faith and the new ideas proclaimed at the end of the last century
in France"—raptures that had ended in defeat and despair. Byron had
given voice to "the anguish of the people at the time, their gloomy disenchantment with their mission, their betrayed ideals." The spirit of
Byronism had thus swept over all of humanity, and it was inevitable
that "such a great, brilliant, and guiding mind as Pushkin" should feel
its influence as well—though not, Dostoevsky hastens to add, in order
to imitate European fashions, but because Russia too was faced "with
so many new, unsolved, and tormenting questions" (26: 113–114).

Once again he embarks on a dithyrambic celebration of Pushkin that anticipates his sensational speech two years later, and which has little or nothing to do with the actual Pushkin known from historical sources. Pushkin, as Dostoevsky sees him, found in "nationality" (*narodnost*) an answer to the problems assailing Russia, "turning to the people and *bowing down to the truth of the Russian people.*" In this highly personal interpretation, Pushkin's works "testified to the universality and the all-embracing nature of the Russian spirit, thereby divining the future mission of the Russian genius within humanity as a whole as an all-unifying, all-reconciling, and all-regenerating principle." Here Dostoevsky attributes his own ideal to Pushkin—an ideal that supposedly led the poet to accept the Russian people with an all-embracing love, a love such as no one had manifested before. Pushkin loved the people, not with the sentimental pity of "a humane and enlightened" nobleman, but "*for themselves,*" that is, by loving what they loved and cherishing what they cherished. "In no other way will [the people] ever acknowledge you as one of their own, no matter how many tears you may shed for them" (26: 115).

It is only in this sense that he spoke of Nekrasov as coming after Pushkin and Lermontov and uttering "in part the same new word" as theirs. Nekrasov was perhaps even more remarkable in this respect, because "all his life he was under the influence of people who, though they may have loved the people, still never recognized the people's truth and always placed their European enlightenment immeasurably higher than the reality of the people's spirit." Nonetheless, his love of the people enabled Nekrasov, in his best poetry, to overcome his conscious opinions and "to comprehend the beauty of the people, their power, their intellect, their suffering humility." Dostoevsky does not conceal his own social-political differences with Nekrasov, and he observes that the solution offered for the people's problems by Nekrasov "might be a highly mistaken and even fatal one." But the poet is hardly to blame since "political sense is a real rarity among us." Despite the errors of his mind, "his heart's great intuition suggested a sense of the people's sorrows," and it is this empathy which pervades—and saves—his best poetry (26: 118–119). And it is this same love for the people that also saved Nekrasov as a man, or at least should redeem him from being judged too harshly on the personal level.

Nekrasov's private reputation in his own day was not a very edifying one, and there were widespread rumors of his unscrupulous handling of financial affairs. Dostoevsky refuses to discuss such rumors on the "anecdotal" level, though he considers at least "three-quarters" of such stories to be "lies, nonsense, and gossip." Enough remained, however, to require explanation, and he provides a moral-psychological interpretation of Nekrasov by citing an autobiographical poem. The impoverished young poet arrives in Petersburg with "My worldly goods—a traveler's staff / An empty bundle at its end / . . . And fifteen kopeks left to spend." The concluding lines tell a different story: "But in forty years I made my fame: / I've a million in my pocket now." As Dostoevsky comments: "A million—that was Nekrasov's dream!" He thus does not shirk the charges against the poet, but interprets them in terms of the psychology of avarice he had used since the 1840s. The accumulation of wealth is not an end in itself but a bulwark against an undermining sense of insecurity. "His was the demon of pride," he writes of Nekrasov, "a longing for security, a need to isolate himself from others behind a solid wall and look calmly out at them and their threats" (26: 121–123).

All these failings were true of Nekrasov the man; but his poetry is filled with remorse and repentance over his own weaknesses, filled with "those groans, those cries, those tears, those admissions that he has 'fallen,' that passionate confession before the shade of his mother." How was one to take all this? Were these anguished utterances the indications of a genuine repentance, or did Nekrasov console himself "in the beauty of his poetry and nothing more"? Dostoevsky suggests that the first explanation is the truer one. Even though Nekrasov was never able to conquer his "demon," it is only from his poetry that we know of his failings, and "the poet wept, perhaps, over such of his deeds as would not give a moment's pause had we committed them." But the question still remains: did Nekrasov's poems enable him to come to terms with himself too easily and "to gain the peace of mind that allowed him once more to undertake his 'practical dealings' with a light heart"?

Squarely posing the question of the "sincerity" of Nekrasov's public confessions of guilt, Dostoevsky acknowledges how difficult it is to resolve such an issue. But there is one aspect of his work, his worship of the people, that can serve as an objective testimony to the genuineness of his moral torments. The "love of the people in Nekrasov," Dostoevsky writes, "was *an outlet for his own grief for himself.*" Once this idea is accepted, the question of his sincerity can be resolved. For "when he was overcome by disgust for that life to which he succumbed in moments of weakness and wickedness, he broke away . . . and went off to those who were dishonored and also suffered, to the simple-hearted and the humiliated; he went and battered himself against the stone floor of his own poor village church, and he was restored. He would not have chosen such an outlet *had he not believed in it.*" Nekrasov's lifelong reverence for the people and their truth bears witness "to an anguish that never ceased. . . . And who are we to judge him for that? And if we are judges, we are not accusers" (26: 123–125). Nekrasov's personal fallibility is both acknowledged and poetically transcended, and no loftier tribute to him exists in the Russian critical canon.

Dostoevsky's *Diary* not only contains this affecting tribute to the friend and literary comrade of his youth, but also includes an obituary of a writer who had inspired them both. George Sand had played a major role in Dostoevsky's—and Russia's—literary and social-political development. Indeed, as Mikhail Saltykov-Shchedrin wrote in a famous essay, the Russian writers of the generation of the 1840s lived only physically in Russia. Spiritually they existed in France—"the France of Saint-Simon, Cabet, Fourier, Louis Blanc, and particularly George Sand. From there, the belief in humanity came to us; from there, the certainty burst upon us that 'the golden age' lay not behind, but before us."[3] Dostoevsky's eulogy to George Sand in June 1876 thus provides an extremely instructive glimpse into his own formation, as well as into the ideas and values of the literary generation to which he belonged. It also provides a welcome relief from the anti-Europeanism of his political rantings. For in expressing his love and admiration for such European writers as Sand and Friedrich Schiller, he offers a much more historically accurate image of the debt owed by Russian culture to the moral-spiritual inspiration of such literary mentors. "We Russians have two homelands, our own Russia and Europe," he now concedes, "even if we call ourselves Slavophils (and I hope the Slavophils won't be angry at me for saying so)." To be sure, there is no contradiction here because the essence of being Russian for him is precisely a capacity for "universality," a capacity that is "the most important personal characteristic and purpose of the Russian." Hence the extremely questionable boast that "every European poet, thinker, and humanitarian is more clearly and more intimately understood and received in Russia than . . . in any country of the world except his own" (23: 30–31).

In his eloquent appraisal of Sand, who died in May 1875, Dostoevsky rightly points out that her novels had been one of the main sources through which, despite the censorship, Socialists ideas had filtered into Russia in the 1830s and 1840s. It was in the pages of such "Venetian" novels as *L'Uscoque* and *La dernière Aldini*, which he read at the age of sixteen, that Dostoevsky himself had been initiated into the world of "advanced" European ideas. George Sand, he writes, was one of the "brightest, most consistent, and most upright representatives" of the movement that began in reaction to the world established after the fall of Napoleon. "It was precisely at that epoch," he continues, "that suddenly a new word had been uttered and new hopes had arisen; men boldly proclaimed that the cause [the French Revolution] had been interrupted in vain and unjustly, that nothing had been accomplished by the political shift of conquerors . . . that the renovation of humanity must be radical and social." As usual, he views the aftermath of the French Revolution in exactly the same terms as the early Socialists, and he values Sand for having represented the "new word," namely, that "the renovation of humanity" had not stopped with the bourgeoisie but must become more "radical and social" (23: 34).

Despite the charges of immorality so often lodged against Sand's heroines, he celebrates their behavior in words that certainly struck an echoing chord in the breasts of his female Populist readers. Young women had been very prominent in the "going to the people" movement a few years earlier; and now, trained as nurses, they were flocking to the Balkans. Dostoevsky points out how, in Sand's female characters, "the necessity of magnanimous sacrifice (presumably especially from her) startles the youthful girl's heart; and unhesitatingly, without sparing herself, disinterestedly, self-sacrificingly, and fearlessly, she suddenly takes the most perilous and fatal step" (23: 36). Such are the young women in Sand's novels whom he holds up for admiration while sidestepping the sexual theme entirely and remarking cautiously that Sand "was by no means preaching only about women and never invented any notion of a 'free wife.'" Thus "women all over the world should put on mourning in her memory because one of the most elevated and beautiful of their representatives has died" (23: 35).

Drawing on Russian press accounts of Sand's last days, Dostoevsky stresses her unshakable faith in "a happier future awaiting humanity," and he attributes such a radiant vision to her religious faith. "George Sand died a *déiste*, firmly believing in God and her own immortal life, but it is not enough to say only that of her—she was, perhaps, the most Christian of all her contemporaries," despite her rejection of Catholicism (which for Dostoevsky was not true Christianity). "She based her socialism . . . on the human moral sense, on humanity's spiritual thirst, on its striving for perfection and purity, and not on the 'necessity' of the ant-heap. . . . She believed unconditionally in the human personality (even to the point of its immortality). . . . Thus her thoughts and feelings coincided with one of the most basic ideas of Christianity." Even though remarking, not quite justly, that she portrayed mostly upper-class characters, not "the pliant, the eccentric, and the downtrodden, such as we meet in almost every novel of the great Christian Dickens," he considered this only a venial sin that could easily be pardoned and did not weaken the moral stature of her abundant creations (23: 37). Socialism, Christianity, and the immortality of the soul are thus brought together in this tribute, which Dostoevsky certainly hoped would persuade his Populists readers of their ineluctable interpenetration.

## CHAPTER 18

# Stories and Sketches

The sketches and short stories in the *Diary of a Writer* were among its most popular features. They are also some of the purest and most moving expressions of Dostoevsky's genius, happily free from the dubious elements of his ideology so often marring his articles. Even those critics and readers who sharply disagreed with one or another of his strongly held—and just as strongly asserted—opinions were unanimously warm in their praise of such masterpieces as *A Gentle Creature* (*Krotkaya*) and *The Dream of a Ridiculous Man* (*Son Smeshnogo Cheloveka*). Shortly after the publication of the first of these stories, Mikhail Saltykov-Shchedrin invited Dostoevsky to contribute a story of similar length to *Notes of the Fatherland*. As he wrote to a friend: "You simply feel like crying as you read; there are very few such jewels in all of European literature."[1] These stories indeed contain, in concentrated form, the essence of the most sympathetic aspects of Dostoevsky's vision—his acute identification with human suffering, both material and spiritual, and his unswerving commitment to an ideal of human felicity attained through fulfilling the Christian commandment of mutual love.

Dostoevsky's creative work had always been nourished by his indefatigable perusal of the newspapers, whose daily diet of crime reporting he had long viewed as an invaluable and much-neglected repository of the conflicts and dilemmas racking his society. Time and again, in his letters and notebooks, he links the origins of his novels to items he had come across in the press, though by the time his imagination had transformed them, they only remotely resembled their original source. In the *Diary*, however, especially in the sketches, we can observe the process by which he moves from the journalistic context into that of fictional creation. Even in the longer short stories, where the connection is more distant than in the sketches, a linkage can be traced to topics treated in the *Diary*. And this context allows us to follow, more closely here than elsewhere, both the relation of journalism to his fiction and the metamorphoses of the one into the other.

## 2

The very first issue of the *Diary* contains a brief, extremely touching sketch—"A Little Boy at Christ's Christmas Party" ("Malchik u Christa na Elke")—that could not illustrate more clearly the organic relation between his journalism and his art. Just a month before, on December 26, 1875, Dostoevsky had taken his daughter to the annual Christmas ball for children at the Artists' Club in Petersburg, an event famous for the size of the Christmas tree in the ballroom and for the lavishness of its decorations. The next day he paid his visit, already described, to the colony for juvenile delinquents. While going to and fro in the Petersburg streets, and pondering over what to include in his first fascicule, he noticed a little boy begging for alms. These impressions, he wrote Vsevolod Solovyev a few weeks later, solved his problem; he decided to devote a good part of the January issue "to children—children in general, children with fathers, children without fathers . . . under Christmas trees, without Christmas trees, criminal children."[2] And so he begins with the Christmas ball and ends with the visit to the colony for delinquents; between them he inserts his fictional sketch.

The first mention of the sketch in his notebooks, dated December 30, reads: "The Christmas tree. The small boy in Rückert. Christ, ask Vladimir Rafaelovich Zotov" (22: 322). Vladimir Zotov, mentioned earlier in connection with an article he wrote on Dostoevsky's biography, was also a translator with a wide knowledge of European literatures. Dostoevsky obviously thought of him in connection with the other name mentioned, Friedrich Rückert, a minor German poet who had composed a prose poem, *The Orphaned Child's Holy Christ* (*Des Fremden Kindes Heiliger Christ*). The poem had never been translated into Russian, but Dostoevsky had lived in Germany, where its recital was a standard feature of Christmas festivities (much like Dickens's *A Christmas Carol* in English-speaking lands). He no doubt hoped that Zotov would help him locate a copy of the text.

The notebooks containing this jotting were not published until 1935, and no one paid any attention to Rückert until G. M. Fridlender picked up the clue thirty years later and pointed out the thematic similarity of Dostoevsky's story and the poem.[3] An orphaned child wanders through the streets at Christmas, peering dismally into the brightly lit windows of houses where happy children, unlike himself, have Christmas trees. "The heart of the child became unbearably heavy." He knocks on the doors, gates, and windows of the houses, hoping that someone will take pity on his lonely misery; but all remains silent. Overcome with grief, he breaks into tears and calls on Christ to rescue him from his desolation; suddenly another child appears, carrying a torch and dressed in white. It is the Christ-child Himself, who points to a huge Christmas tree shining among the stars more brightly than any in the houses. It has been lit for all the orphans of the world, and, as if in a dream, angels descend from the glittering tree. The orphan is carried up to the light, and in heavenly eternity he forgets all the travails of his life on earth (22: 322–323).

Rückert's quite sentimental and edifying poem touchingly dissolves the miseries of the poor orphan into an eternity of heavenly bliss. Dostoevsky, as one might expect, gives the same theme a much more somber treatment and penetrates far more deeply into the wretchedness of his little beggar-boy. The very placement of the sketch in the *Diary* brings out the pathos of his loneliness by contrast; and because it is set between descriptions of events that actually occurred, a semblance of verisimilitude is imparted to the miraculous intervention of the Christ-child. Indeed, Dostoevsky plays very effectively on the ambiguous status of the sketch as "art" and "invention," but an invention resembling "reality" so closely that it is difficult to tell the difference. "But I am a novelist," the sketch begins, "and it seems that one 'story' I did invent myself. Why did I say 'it seems,' since I know for certain that I actually did invent it; yet I keep fancying that this happened somewhere, sometime, precisely on Christmas Eve, in *a certain* huge city during a terrible frost" (22: 14).

The general absence of specificity in the background detail extends the anecdote into a sort of parable. We find ourselves in an archetypal Dostoevskian milieu, characteristic of almost every work since his very first—a dark, freezing, miserable Petersburg hovel, a dying woman lying neglected and alone on a bare bed, a hungry, shivering little boy dressed in rags, uncomprehendingly watching her death agony. "How did she happen to be here?—She may have come with her little boy from some faraway town, and then suddenly had fallen ill." Everything is left in this atmosphere of vagueness and conjecture, and the situation thus takes on the universal quality of a mythical exemplar. This is not an individual woman dying but one whose fate symbolizes that of thousands. By contrast, as the little boy shiveringly and futilely looks around the room for something to eat, there is a keen acuity of sensuous detail that throws the awfulness of the situation into high relief. "For a moment he stood still, resting his hand on the shoulder of the dead woman. Then he began to breathe on his tiny fingers in an attempt to warm them, and, suddenly, coming upon his little cap that lay on the bedstead, he groped along cautiously and quietly made his way out of the basement" (22: 14–15).

The remainder of the tale records the little boy's reactions as he wanders through the streets of the looming city at night, gazing into houses filled with happy children clustering around sumptuous Christmas trees (this is closest of all to Rückert), and pauses with fascination and delight before mechanical toys in a shop window. Frightened by some older, unruly urchins, he takes refuge in a yard behind a pile of wood (a familiar Dostoevskian setting). There he falls asleep, and his frozen body is found the next morning. But before his pitiful demise, he has dreamed a wonderful dream: "Where is he now? Everything sparkles and glitters and shines, and scattered all over are tiny dolls—no, they are little boys and girls, only they are so luminous, and they all fly around him." These are the children at the party of Christ's Christmas Tree, a party for all the child-victims of human sin and social injustice. Some of these children

> had frozen to death in those baskets in which they had been left at the doors of Petersburg officials; others had perished in miserable hospital wards; still others had died at the dried-up breasts of their famine-stricken mothers (during the Samara famine); these, again, had choked to death from stench in third-class railroad cars. Now they are all here, all like little angels, and they are all with Christ, and He is in their midst holding out His hands to them and to their sinful mothers. . . . Down below, the next morning the porters found the tiny body of the runaway boy who had frozen to death behind the woodpile; they found his mother as well. . . . She had frozen to death even before him; they met in God's Heaven." (22: 16–17)

In the concluding paragraph, Dostoevsky shifts back to himself as narrator and to the "imaginary" aspect of his narrative. "But the point is that I keep fancying that all this could actually have happened—I mean, the things which happened in the basement and behind the piles of kindling wood. Well, and as regards Christ's Christmas Tree—I really don't know what to tell you, and I don't know whether or not this could have happened" (22: 17). Whether or not any of these events could or did happen, the aim of his sketch is manifestly to make something approximating Christ's Christmas party happen on earth.

3
———

A sketch in the March 1876 *Diary*, even shorter than the Christmas piece, also takes on added significance when read in its wider context. Just a month earlier, in his long article devoted to the Kroneberg case, Dostoevsky had dwelt on the disappearance among the upper classes of any feeling for the sanctity of the family; but in the article preceding this sketch, he vigorously defends the reality and existence of high moral ideals among the people. It is in this framework that, without any further explanation, he depicts the peaceful demise of an old woman—the chapter is entitled "The Centenarian," and she is 104 years old—who is first seen toiling her way laboriously through the Petersburg streets to visit her granddaughter on a sunny day. Despite her age and infirmities, she is still vital, still taking a lively interest in other people, and cheerily responding to the friendly questioning of a passer-by. "And she kept on laughing and looking at me," reports her interlocutor. "Her eyes were dim, almost lifeless, and yet a warm ray, as it were, radiated from them" (22: 76).

This real-life encounter is supposed to have been told to Dostoevsky by a lady among his acquaintances, but in fact he heard it from Anna Grigoryevna; and the remainder of the story is his own fictional vision of the old woman's arrival at her destination. Her granddaughter is married to an independent craftsman, a barber by trade, who wears "a suit as greasy as a pancake—is it because of the pomade?—and, like all barbers, a coat collar as white as if rolled in flour." The family warmly greets the new arrival, children come flocking to see "grandmother," a guest teases her affectionately, and her granddaughter immediately launches into the fine points of a new coat just acquired for the older boy. The scene is one of security, serenity, family warmth and stability; and it is in the midst of this comforting group that the old lady—mortally exhausted by the exertions of her walk—peacefully passes away, her hand resting lovingly on the shoulder of her young grand-nephew (22: 78–79).

Such a death is neither frightening nor disquieting, Dostoevsky writes; on the contrary, there is about it something "calm, even solemn and pacifying." "Of course, over such a one no tears are shed. A hundred and four years—'and she passed away painlessly and unashamed.'" The granddaughter immediately sends to the neighbors for help, and the neighbor women come running in haste, listening almost with pleasure to the account of the event, sighing and wailing—"God bless the lives and deaths of simple, kind folk!" He apologizes to his readers for having provided them with such an "inconsequential little scene without a story" rather than writing about "something with a bit of interest in it" (22: 72). But the scene, of course, is as timely as it can be in offering a reassuring contrast with the symptoms of moral dissolution so amply displayed elsewhere in the *Diary*.

## 4

If "The Centenarian" was aimed to counter the dismal image of the Russian people found so frequently in the *Diary*, another sketch, "The Peasant Marey," serves the same purpose in an entirely different setting. In the early pages of the February issue, Dostoevsky has been exalting the Russian people, arguing that everything of value in Russian literature originates in the assimilation by Russian writers of the people's

Christian ideals. Expressing a certain weariness, however, with all these "*professions de foi,*" he decides to relate a reminiscence that, "for some reason, I am quite eager to recount precisely here and now, in conclusion of our treatise on the people" (22: 46). This reminiscence is "The Peasant Marey," and its significance far transcends its immediate purpose in the *Diary*. On one level, it is a supplement—and an extremely valuable one—to *House of the Dead*; on another, it is the only direct evocation of his childhood coming from his pen.

This sketch is also of first importance as a clue to Dostoevsky's ideological evolution during his Siberian years, that is, his transformation from a philanthropic radical with strong Christian Socialist leanings, though uncommitted to any particular Socialist panacea, into a resolute believer in the Russian people as the unique national embodiment of the moral ideals he had found so appealing in Utopian Socialism. One may well wonder why he did not include these pages in *House of the Dead*, why he waited seventeen years before committing them to print. A possible answer is that they are *too* directly autobiographical and confessional to have suited his semi-fictionalized Siberian memoirs, whose narrator, in addition, was not supposed to be Dostoevsky himself. His artistic aim there was to depict the world of the prison camp and of his fellow convicts, and the episode would have stood out too prominently. It is only indirectly that he portrays the evolution of his attitude toward his companions in misery, which began with repulsion and modulated into a much more positive appreciation of their human qualities.[4] The Marey episode depicts this shift, but in terms of a personal encounter that would have clashed with the dominating objectivity of *House of the Dead*.

The episode begins with a sharp and swift evocation of the Easter week celebration in the Siberian stockade—a "celebration" during which the prisoners could drink, carouse, and quarrel to their hearts' content. Dostoevsky looked on, with a feeling of deep loathing, at the raucous turbulence and brutality of the spectacle unrolling before his eyes. "Never," he confesses, "could I stand without disgust drunken popular rakishness, and particularly in this place." Another political criminal, a cultivated Polish patriot, expressed what seemed to be their common reaction when the two met outside the barracks, where they had gone to escape the brawling and the bedlam. "He looked at me gloomily, his eyes flashing; his lips began to tremble: '*Je hais ces brigands!*'—he told me in a low voice, grinding his teeth, and passed by" (22: 46). The use of French, of course, set the two men apart from the uneducated Russian peasant convicts.

Dostoevsky then lies down on the wooden boards where all the convicts slept and begins—as he continually did for consolation—to conjure up his past in memory. And he suddenly recalls how once, at the age of nine, he had been happily exploring the forest on his family's property during a summer vacation. The one or two sentences devoted to the forest are so full of feeling, and so unusual, that they are worth quoting as evidence of a sensibility rarely displayed elsewhere: "And in all my life nothing have I loved so much as the forest, with its mushrooms and wild berries, its insects and birds and little hedgehogs and squirrels; its damp odor of dead leaves, which I so adored" (22: 47). He had been warned by his mother that wolves were in the vicinity, and suddenly, in the midst of his bucolic foraging, he heard distinctly (though it later turned out to be an auditory hallucination) the cry that a wolf had been spotted. Terrified, the boy ran to a peasant plowing in a nearby field.

"This was our peasant Marey. . . . He was almost fifty years old, stocky, pretty tall, with much gray hair in his bushy, flaxen beard." The peasant comforts the little boy, and blesses him. "He extended his hand and stroked me on the cheek. 'Do stop fearing! Christ be with thee. Cross thyself'" (22: 48). The consoling words of the kindly peasant calmed the agitated young Dostoevsky and convinced him that there had been no wolf. The incident had vanished from his memory for twenty years, but lay dormant there, like a seed planted in the soil, ready to blossom and flower at the moment when its reappearance would take on the nature of a revelation. Here, in this childhood experience, in one symbolic and never-to-be-forgotten instant, Dostoevsky had glimpsed all the spiritual beauty contained in the Russian peasant character. "He was our peasant serf, while I was his master's little boy; no one would learn of his kindness to me and no one would reward him. . . . The meeting was a solitary one, in a vacant field, and only God, maybe, perceived from above what a profound and enlightened human sentiment, what delicate, almost womanly tenderness may fill the heart of some coarse, bestially ignorant Russian peasant serf, who, in those days, had even had no intimations about his freedom" (22: 49).

The resurrection of this long-faded childhood incident brought about a complete transformation in Dostoevsky's whole relation to his previously abhorrent surroundings. No longer does he see the drunken and rowdy convicts as coarse and callous brutes, completely incapable of harboring any humane and generous feelings; they now have all become potential Mareys, whose natural purity of soul had been overlaid by the harshness and hopeless oppression of their lives. "I went along, gazing attentively at the faces which I encountered. This intoxicated, shaven and branded peasant, with marks on his face, brawling his hoarse, drunken song—why, he may be the very same Marey; for I have no way of peering into his heart" (22: 49–50). This incident furnishes a valuable paradigm for grasping how Dostoevsky persuaded himself of the validity of his own beliefs about the Russian people. And it illustrates once more his genius for taking an isolated and commonplace personal incident and endowing it with a wide-ranging social and symbolic significance.

## 5

A much more ambitious work, *A Gentle Creature* (*Krotkaya*), took up the entire issue for November 1876. The short story was inspired by a newspaper account at the beginning of October, already mentioned, of a young woman who had jumped to her death while holding a holy icon of the Virgin Mary, the Mother of God. This event was included in the notebook jottings for the article about Liza Herzen, which stressed the contrast between the two. "But what two different beings they are," as he wrote in the article, "as if from two different planets! And how different the two deaths!" (23: 146). The image of what Dostoevsky's notes call "the humble [*smirennoe*] suicide" continued to haunt his imagination, and in late October he decided to use it as the subject for a story. "Look over the old material of subjects for stories . . . ," he admonishes himself. "The girl with the icon" (24: 381).

At first he thought of making "the girl with the icon" an episode, somewhat like the story of Olya in *A Raw Youth*, in a novel (never written) called *The Dreamer* (*Mechtatel*). Some features of this early draft were retained in the final story, among them, the monologue form and a main character who had refused to fight a duel and was convinced that he was seeking the naked truth. Work on the *Diary*, however, left no time to develop this novel project. Deciding that the theme was rich enough to deserve independent treatment, however, he turned again to his old notes. What he found there was his long-standing fascination with the figure of a "usurer"—the base epitome of an egoistic selfishness excluding any concern for others.

Like all Dostoevsky characters, however, even a usurer is capable of displaying unexpected human qualities. Notes for such a figure appear in a plan for a novel in the early 1860s, and were taken up again in 1869 as an idea for a story after the completion of *The Idiot*. The character here is described as "a genuine underground type; has been insulted. Becomes embittered. Immeasurable vanity. . . . His wife cannot fail to notice that he is cultivated, but then realized, not very much; every gibe (and he takes everything as a gibe) angers him, he is suspicious. . . . For a time he endeavors to establish a loving relationship with his wife. But he had broken her heart" (24: 382). This situation already contains an outline of the later story.

Another plan for a story, set down at the same time but never written, gives a more extended description of the psychology associated with the usurer.

> A miser, avenger, usurer, and suddenly rumors entirely the opposite [of these]. . . . A rumor about cowardice. . . . In general, this is a *type*. Most important trait—a misanthrope, but from the underground. This is the essence, but most important trait: a need to confide himself [to others], which peeps out from the terrible misanthropy and the ironically insulting mistrust. . . . This need is convulsive and uncontrollable, so that with frightening naïveté (a bitter, even touching naïveté, worthy of pity) he throws himself suddenly on people and, of course, receives a rebuff, but, once receiving a rebuff, he does not forgive, forgets nothing, suffers, turns it into a tragedy. (24: 382)

These are the contours of the character whose voice will be heard as the narrator of *A Gentle Creature*.

The moral-psychological traits of Dostoevsky's characters are always reinforced by literary and cultural reminiscences, and *A Gentle Creature* is no exception. It contains allusions to Goethe's *Faust*, a remark of John Stuart Mill about women, and an approving reference to one of Dostoevsky's favorite books, Alain-René Lesage's picaresque novel *Gil Blas*. The notes also reveal the influence of a little-known novel, *Pugachevtsi*, by the extremely prolific Russian woman of letters Countess E. A. Salias de Tournemire, whose noble heroine also commits suicide but not before exhibiting the same indifference to her tyrannical husband as does the gentle creature. The most important influence of all, however, is that of Victor Hugo, whose novella *Le dernier jour d'un condamné* Dostoevsky knew by heart, and which had entered his own life at one of its most pivotal moments. In the short span of time during which he thought he would be next in line to face a firing squad, it was a passage from this work of Hugo's that came to his mind.[5]

Hugo's story is the imaginary diary of a man awaiting death by the guillotine, who sets down his thoughts and feelings up to the very moment when he mounts the gallows. In the authorial preface to his own story, Dostoevsky notes that there is something "fantastic" in the assumption that a condemned man would be able to keep a diary under such circumstances; but this infraction of verisimilitude by no means lessens the stunning impact of Hugo's little masterpiece, one of the most powerful indictments of capital punishment ever written. Dostoevsky subtitles his own text "A Fantastic Story" because he reproduces the solitary monologue of the suicide's husband at her bier, using a partial stream-of-consciousness technique; and this equally strains credibility. Who recorded the words? He asks his reader to assume that the monologue of the bewildered and bereaved husband was taken down in shorthand by a stenographer and delivered to him (as author) for some editing. "It is this suggestion . . . that I consider the fantastic element of this story," he writes. But as he remarks of Hugo, if "he had not adopted this fanciful way of telling the story, his novel—one of the most realistic and most truthful he ever wrote—would not have existed" (24: 6). The evaluation applies to his own story as well, which serves as another illustration of Dostoevsky's unalterable conviction that the "truth" of reality could not be conveyed without some admixture of "the fantastic," whether formally (as in this instance) or thematically in some visionary glimpse of a transcendent ideal.

Although the idea for *A Gentle Creature* first emerged in Dostoevsky's thoughts about "the girl with the icon," by the time the story took final shape she had receded into the background. Instead, her husband is the narrator—a variant of the underground man consumed by bitterness and resentment against the world and bent upon oppressing and crushing others because he feels oppressed and crushed himself. What gives this type a special stamp here is the character of his inner self-image. He sees himself as some sort of misunderstood and neglected hero, whose life is a personal protest against an unjust society; and this self-image sustains him emotionally and motivates his behavior. It is what has made life possible for him since—in a rather stock situation in the repertoire of Russian Romanticism—he was expelled from his regiment for having failed to defend its honor on some public occasion.

Before we learn the details of his past, however, the narrator is shown simply as the proprietor of a pawnshop; and this role again strikes a familiar Dostoevskian note. A preoccupation with money is usually—as with Ganya Ivolgin in *The Idiot*, or young Arkady—the symptom of a lust for power stemming from a desire to compensate for a status of inferiority and subordination. So it is here again; but the situation is complicated by the character's need to persuade himself, at the same time, of his own rectitude and virtue. "You say 'pawnbroker'—everybody says it. And what of it? This means that there must, indeed, have been reasons why one of the most magnanimous of all men became a pawnbroker" (24: 16). The narrator thus refuses to view himself as he knows he is regarded by others—and even, naggingly, by some part of himself that he cannot totally suppress. This discrepancy is the source of the tragedy recounted in the story, which arises from the narrator's pitiless attempt, in a hopeless search for love and understanding, to impose his own self-conception on another. But because he seeks love without being willing to love himself (until it is too late), because he wishes to obtain love by a species of psychic rape through the domination of another consciousness, the result is the very opposite of what he desires. "But here," he thinks, looking at the corpse of his dead wife, "there was something I forgot or failed to see. There was something I mismanaged badly. But enough, enough!" (24: 17).

The story traces the course of the unhappy relationship that led the child-bride (she was barely sixteen!) to her final, despairing plunge. What attracts the narrator to the girl, when she first comes to pawn her meager belongings, is the combination of her pride and her poverty, her intelligence and her indigence. He himself is the son of a hereditary nobleman, "a retired staff captain in a brilliant regiment" (24: 10), whereas she, whose dead father had obtained noble rank in the civil service (like Dostoevsky's own), has been reduced to the Petersburg lower depths. The death of her parents threw her back on two aunts for whom the word "disorderly" was rather a compliment, and they had turned her into a virtual slave. But she is, all the same, someone of independent character, who has placed advertisements in journals in search of a position (to no avail), and has absorbed some of the culture and humanitarian ideals of her generation. She is by no means a person ready to play a completely subordinate and subservient role.

The narrator rescues her from being, in effect, sold to a much older suitor. His unexpected proposal of marriage is carefully designed to cast him in the role of a Romantic savior; but his motive is neither genuine magnanimity nor even sexual attraction (though the latter is not entirely absent). Rather, he desperately yearns for someone to recognize his outwardly demeaning life as inspired by an "idea," someone to acknowledge the inherent righteousness and dignity of the path he has chosen, someone to look beyond his ignominious profession and dishonored past into the torments of his wounded soul. "Admitting her to my house, I desired full respect. I wished that she should look at me worshipfully for all my suffering—and I deserved it! I was always proud, and I always sought either everything or nothing" (24: 14).

This overwhelming pride determines the baneful course he adopts after the marriage. Any sign of tenderness or affection on his part might be interpreted as a humiliating appeal, as an indication of remorse or self-doubt. And so the young girl's natural warmth of feeling, spontaneously expressed in the first days of their marriage, is systematically stifled by his policy of coldness and seeming indifference. "The main thing was that from the very beginning, much as she tried to restrain herself, she threw herself at me with love. . . . But at once I threw cold water on all this ecstasy. Precisely therein was my idea. I reacted to these transports with silence—benevolent, of course. . . . " (12: 13).

This treatment leads to the reverse of what the narrator had anticipated. Rather than her accepting the inner sublimity (as he sees it) of her husband's way of life, and bowing down before him in worshipful admiration, they become locked in a secret struggle of wills. "At first she argued—how hotly!—but later she left off speaking, and, finally, she grew quite silent; only, when listening, she would open her eyes awfully wide—such big, big eyes, so attentive. . . . And . . . and, besides, suddenly I noticed a smile—a distrustful, silent, wicked, smile. Well, it was with that smile that I brought her into my house" (12: 14). The supposedly "gentle creature" suddenly erupts into outright rebellion, and we catch a glimpse of *her* values in her efforts, quickly repressed, to behave charitably toward some of the customers in the pawnshop. Moreover, out of hatred and rage at her oppressor, she arranges a rendezvous with an officer of his former regiment and learns the disreputable secret of his past. With the inevitable touch of Dostoevskian melodrama, her husband eavesdrops on the encounter and is overcome with admiration at his wife's manifest purity and goodness when she repulses the advances of the informer with contempt. The irony of the situation, of course, is that these very qualities, which impelled him to choose her as his wife, make it impossible to bend her completely to his will.

The climax of the secret battle occurs just after he has broken in on the meeting, thereby revealing his knowledge of her indiscretion. Waking from sleep, but giving no sign of consciousness, he sees her standing over him with a loaded pistol that he has taught her how to use; and he waits in agony for her to pull the trigger, wondering whether she had seen him momentarily open his eyes. Despite her hatred, though, she is finally unable to take his life—her final and irreparable defeat. By later revealing his awareness of this incident, he can, at one stroke, remove the cloud hanging over his name because of the imputation of cowardice and also reverse the moral situation. No longer will *he* be the person surreptitiously seeking pardon; now he will himself be the kindhearted, great-souled pardoner. But the private joy of this future triumph is so great that he purposely puts off its arrival. He wishes to savor the broken mortification of his wife, who falls ill with "brain fever" after the incident with the pistol and never fully recovers her health. "Yes, at that time there occurred to me something strange and peculiar—I don't know how to call it otherwise. I grew triumphant, and the very knowledge of it proved sufficient to me. This winter passed. Oh, I was content as never before—and this, all winter" (24: 23).

The dénouement occurs in the spring, after a winter spent silently sharing the same apartment but no longer a conjugal bed and totally estranged from each other. "Of course, it was strange that not once," says the husband, "did the thought occur to me that while I liked to look stealthily at her, never throughout the whole winter did I catch even a single glance of hers at me! I thought that this was timidity on her part" (24: 25). Far from timidity, it was a deep and unconquerable aversion—as he discovers when, suddenly seized by pity for her and possessed by his own overwhelming need for love, he finally throws himself at her feet. "She shivered and shook herself away from me in great fear, looking into my face. But, suddenly, her eyes expressed *stern surprise* . . . 'So you are also after love?'—such was the question in that astonishment of hers, even though she remained silent" (24: 28). The uncontrollable fervor of the narrator, who now pours out pell-mell all the psychic torment he had been suppressing in himself and concealing from others for so many years, simply throws the unhappy girl into hysterical convulsions.

The sudden breakdown and reversal of the situation precipitates the catastrophe. The narrator is now ready to abandon everything, to give up his pawnshop and his revenge on society, if only he can recapture the love that was once within his grasp. But it is too late to undo the past. The sweet and gentle spirit of his wife has been irremediably estranged, and she is now consumed by guilt at her *own* incapacity to respond, except with profound pity, to his entreaties to begin a new life of full and truehearted love. All that is left is the leap from the window, clutching to her breast the icon of the Mother of God, the symbol of the promise of eternal love. Nothing that Dostoevsky ever wrote is more poignant than the narrator's cry of despair at the end, walking up and down beside the bier of "the gentle creature," at a moment when the entire world has become for him an image of his desolation. "Oh, nature! Man on earth is alone—this is the calamity! . . . Everything is dead, and everywhere—nothing but corpses. Only men, and, around them, silence—such is earth. 'Love each other!'—Who said this? Whose covenant is this?" (24: 35).

Such are among the final words of one of the finest and purest creations that ever came from Dostoevsky's pen. The subtlety and delicacy of the rendering of the narrator's consciousness (with its blend of shock, guilt, incredulity, and some last, lingering shreds of self-justification), the brilliant portrayal of the wife *through* the eyes of the narrator struggling to understand easily overcomes the all-too-familiar plot ingredients and the touch of melodrama. *A Gentle Creature* is also Dostoevsky's best-rounded and most finely modulated portrait of his "underground man" character type. Nowhere else is he presented so fully as a sensitive and suffering human being, whose inhumanity derives from a need for love that has become perverted and distorted by egoism and vanity. What was presented only embryonically in the final episode of *Notes from Underground*, when the underground man egotistically rejects the offer of love tendered him by the suffering young prostitute Liza, is here developed with a mastery that fully justifies Saltykov-Shchedrin's enthusiastic accolade.

*The Dream of a Ridiculous Man* also emerges from Dostoevsky's preoccupation with the theme of suicide. Indeed, the story can best be seen as the second panel of a diptych, whose first is the imaginary suicide letter, "The Sentence." These two works not only echo but also answer each other: starting from the same point of no return as the letter, this story ends, not in despair and suicide, but in an ecstatic affirmation of the will to live. This affirmation stems from Dostoevsky's own belief in the possibility of an apocalyptic transfiguration of mankind, a moral regeneration of humanity as a whole, which first enters his work in the 1860s. The image of a Golden Age of human happiness, which goes back in Western literature to Hesiod, crops up continuously in his notes for his novels, even though it rarely appears as such (except in *The Devils*, where the chapter containing it was suppressed, and *A Raw Youth*).

No such image, to be sure, can be found in *Notes from Underground*, but even there the underground man defies his scornful reader to furnish him with a more exalted ideal than a Utilitarian Crystal Palace. "Show me something more attractive," he challenges. "Give me another ideal" (5: 120). In the notes for *Crime and Punishment*, Raskolnikov exclaims: "Oh, why is not everyone happy? Picture of the Golden Age. It is carried in the minds and hearts. How can it fail to come to pass?" (7: 280). And reference is made in the notes for *The Idiot* to "an inspired speech by the Prince (Don Quixote and the acorn)," in which Myshkin would presumably have improvised on the Don's vision of a Golden Age, when "those living at that time were ignorant of the words: *thine* and *mine* (25: 404). The Golden Age is evoked again in *The Devils*, with imagery inspired by Claude Lorrain's *Acis and Galatea*, and the dream of this world of primordial innocence and bliss provokes a crisis of moral conscience in Stavrogin. The same imagery recurs in *A Raw Youth*, crowned by the appearance of Christ.

The Golden Age also appears, half-jestingly, in the first number of the *Diary*, when Dostoevsky depicts the guests at the Christmas ball laboriously struggling to enjoy themselves. They do not know "how beautiful [they] are," and that, "if only [they] would so desire, [they] could at once make everybody . . . happy . . . and captivate everybody. And this power is within each of you [his readers], but it is so deeply hidden that long ago it began to appear incredible. And is it really possible that the Golden Age exists only on porcelain cups?" (22: 13). He did not believe so; and in *The Dream of a Ridiculous Man* he expresses both the moral inspiration provided by the radiant image of the Golden Age, and the loss of the instinctive human harmony that was the source of its felicity. But he also believed—or hoped—that such an instinctive harmony might perhaps be restored, even if only partially, through the inspiration of Christian compassion and love for suffering humanity.

This story also bears the subtitle "fantastic," and it is much more obviously so than the history of the "gentle creature." There, it was the narrative technique that justified the term; here it is the content itself, a dream voyage to another earth, where the ridiculous man encounters a society living in a true Golden Age, before the Fall and the existence of sin. The story is a *conte philosophique*, based on "fantasy" in the literal meaning of the word, and has often been compared to Voltaire's *Micromegas*. But the fantasy is framed by a setting taken straight from the iconography of urban shoddiness and misery favored by the Natural School of Russian writers in the 1840s. The central figure is one of those isolated and misanthropic characters estranged from everyone who, if his isolation degenerates into bitterness and resentment, becomes an "underground man." But although the "ridiculous man" suffers because of his "strangeness," Dostoevsky does not ground him in psychology; the horizon of the ridiculous man is much wider and encompasses a metaphysical-religious dimension. "I suddenly felt that it made no difference to me whether the world existed or whether nothing existed anywhere at all. . . . Little by little I became convinced that there would be nothing in the future either. . . . It was then that I suddenly ceased to be angry with people and almost stopped noticing them" (25: 105).

This conviction induces a total sense of apathy and indifference toward the entire outside world. The ridiculous man lives in the midst of seedy St. Petersburg squalor, but pays no attention to his quarrelsome and disreputable neighbors. He is, on the contrary, obsessed by the thought of suicide, and one evening—on a particularly wet, gloomy, and depressing day, when even the rain seemed "full of obvious animosity toward men" (25: 105)—he decides to put a bullet through his head. On the way home to carry out this resolution, he is stopped by a little girl desperately appealing to him to aid her dying mother. With, it would seem, complete unconcern for her plight, he stamps and shouts at her to leave him in peace; but sitting in his room later, with the pistol lying ready on the table, he is troubled and upset by a new sensation. Theoretically, he should have felt nothing at all shameful about having driven away the little girl; it was totally inconsistent for a man on the brink of suicide, to whom everything in the world had become meaningless, to feel pity. And yet, as with the underground man, his heart and his head refuse to act in unison. "I recall that I felt a great pity for her—to the point of some strange pain, which was quite incredible in my situation" (25: 107).

This inconsistency irritates the ridiculous man to the point of anger; and while pondering this disturbing lapse in the conclusions he has drawn about life, he suddenly falls asleep and dreams. "In a word, that little girl saved me, since, because of the questions, I postponed the shot" (25: 108). But the little girl also saves the ridiculous man in a deeper sense: the feelings stirred in him by this encounter are then projected into his dream, and, on waking, he finds that he has been forever freed from the temptation of suicide. "It would seem," Dostoevsky surmises, "that dreams are generated not by the intellect but by desires, not by the brain but by the heart" (25: 108). In his dream, the ridiculous man reveals the desires of a heart that conjures up the panorama of the Golden Age; and in Dostoevsky's story, this opposition between head and heart, between reason and feeling, itself becomes the center of the entire spiritual history of humanity.

The dream begins with the thought of suicide; but there is a significant difference in one detail stressed in the dream. Initially, the narrator had intended to put a bullet through his head, but in the dream he shoots himself through the heart, as if trying to suppress the faculty that had persisted in feeling pity despite all the conclusions of his mind. But then he is plucked from the tomb and transported to another planet, which, in every respect except its inhabitants, is a replica of the earth. The physical setting of this Paradise is the same as those paradises depicted in Stavrogin's daydream and in *A Raw Youth*, but there are some important variations of accent.

Once again Dostoevsky visualizes an island in the Greek archipelago, radiant with a sunlit, Mediterranean beauty; but never before has he struck this particular note of an all-embracing harmony between man and nature. "The calm, emerald sea gently splashed against the shore embracing it with manifest, apparent, almost conscious love. Tall, beautiful trees stood there in the full luxury of their bloom, and their countless leaves—I am sure of it—welcomed me with their gentle, kind murmur, uttering, as it were, words of love. . . . Little birds, in flocks, flew through the air, and, unafraid of me, alighted on my shoulders and hands, joyfully beating at me with their dear little trepidating wings" (25: 112). This last detail irresistibly recalls the legends about Saint Francis or the Russian tradition of saints and hermits (which will soon be evoked by Father Zosima) whose spirit of Christian love shone forth with such strength that it tamed even the wild beasts of the forest.

The same spirit of love radiates from the inhabitants of this Paradise, the innocent and beautiful denizens of the Garden of Eden. "These men, laughing joyously, crowded around and caressed me. They took me to their homes, and each one sought to comfort me" (25: 112). Love was the natural medium in which they existed, or at least the aspect of their lives that was most accessible to the comprehension of an earthling like the ridiculous man. For he realized that it was impossible for him—"a contemporaneous, progressive, and hideous Petersburg resident" (25: 113)—really to understand them because they lived completely on the level of an intuitive feeling that was also a higher form of knowledge. Though having nothing comparable to what on earth is called science—the acme and epitome of reason—"yet their knowledge was deeper and higher than that of our science, since the latter seeks to explain what life is. . . . They, however, knew how to live even without science, and this I understand; but I was unable to comprehend their knowledge" (25: 113). That higher knowledge is, presumably, their totally selfless and loving communion with each other and with everything.

The lives of these fortunate denizens of the Golden Age were thus completely lacking in any sort of self-consciousness, untroubled by any manifestation of egoism or vanity. They lived together like a great, united, and harmonious family, free from any sort of dissension or disunion. "They were endowed with love and children were born to them, but never did I observe in them those impulses of *cruel* voluptuousness which affect virtually everybody on our earth—everybody—and which are the sole source of almost all sin in our human race." They had no specific religion or religious doctrines about God and eternal life, but they greeted death serenely, and "one could imagine that they continued to communicate with their dead even after death, and that the earthly communion between them was not interrupted by death." They composed songs of praise for each other and lived in "a sort of mutual complete and universal enamoredness." To this condition of unalloyed love, which images the world before the Fall of humankind into sin, the ridiculous man compares his own twisted love-hate feelings for his fellow human beings, which arose from the clash between his egoism and his longing for communion (25: 113–114).

7

What next occurs is that, in some mysterious fashion, the ridiculous man introduces this same principle of reflexive self-consciousness and self-awareness—the ultimate psychological root of egoism—into the innocent Paradise of the Golden Age. The catastrophic result is the corruption and fall of its inhabitants. The somber tableau that Dostoevsky sketches here recalls Raskolnikov's terrible dream in the epilogue to *Crime and Punishment*, and he uses the same imagery of the spread of some infectious disease. "Like a horrible trichina, like the germ of the plague infecting whole kingdoms, so did I infect with myself all that happy earth which knew no sin before me" (25: 115). But the emphasis is no longer on the self-destructive horror of a world lacking any instinctive ties of mutuality between human and human; it is, rather, on the dialectical movement by which self-awareness engenders egoism and egoism gives rise to a world whose institutions express the loss in reality of what man becomes aware of in thought. The first step is for consciousness no longer to *live* in a loving harmony with others but to withdraw itself in a manner splitting the unconscious and instinctive acceptance and identification with the other. "They have learned to lie, they became fond of the lie, and they perceived its beauty." From this withdrawal arises an awareness of the ego as opposed to the other; and the psychological and sexual struggle begins. "Shortly after that, voluptuousness was born; voluptuousness generated jealousy, jealousy—cruelty" (25: 115–116).

The process that started on the personal level continued inexorably to infect group and social life as well. "Unions appeared, but unions against one another. . . . They became cognizant of shame, which they extolled as a virtue. The conception of honor was born, and each union hoisted its own banner. . . . A struggle for self-isolation began—for disjunction, for individuality, for 'mine and thine.'" The result was a growing awareness of what had been lost and the attempt to re-create it artificially by self-conscious means. "When they became wicked, they started speaking about brotherhood and humaneness and grasped the meaning of these ideas. When they grew criminal, they invented justice and enacted for themselves codes for its maintenance, and for the enforcement of their codes they used the guillotine" (25: 116).

There is no need to rehearse every detail in the catalogue of evils that arise in this way, and which compose a litany of all the ills of civilization. Slavery, the martyrdom of holy men, fratricidal warfare, the cult and doctrine of power—all came from the belief that "science will give . . . wisdom; wisdom will reveal the laws . . . and the knowledge of the laws of happiness is superior to happiness." But the situation, as might have been expected, continues to go from bad to worse, and culminates in the growth of a cult of suffering. It is somewhat surprising to find "suffering"—one of Dostoevsky's own key values—listed among the symptoms of mankind's downfall; but the suffering in question does not arise from any sort of inner conflict or feeling of repentance and remorse. Instead, it is the perverse enjoyment of suffering as an aesthetic pleasure or as the indication of some sort of intellectual superiority: "Then they proclaimed that suffering was beauty, because only in suffering was there thought" (25: 116–117). The glorification of suffering for its own sake, divorced from any relation with pity, compassion, or self-examination, is for Dostoevsky one of the ultimate corruptions of the human personality.

Very different is the suffering of the ridiculous man at the terrible spectacle he is forced to witness and for which he feels responsible.

"Alas, I always loved grief and sorrow, *but only for myself, for myself, while I went pitying them*" (italics added). Overwhelmed by his sense of guilt, he tries to introduce his perverted innocents to Christianity and its values of self-sacrifice and suffering for others ("I implored them to crucify me; I taught them how to make the cross"). But all to no avail—they simply laughed at what they could not understand. "Finally, they announced to me that I was beginning to be dangerous to them and that they would place me in an asylum if I shouldn't keep silent." This outcome so afflicts and oppresses the ridiculous man, his heart is filled with so much sorrow and sadness, that at this point his sensations become too strong to be endured—and he awakens! (25: 117).

This extraordinary dream is a revelation, and his life becomes transformed from that moment on. Gone are all thoughts of suicide—"ecstasy, immeasurable ecstasy lifted my whole being"—and he instantly decides, like Vlas, if not to become a wanderer and collect money to build churches, then to become an itinerant preacher of the Truth vouchsafed in his dream. "The reason is that I saw the Truth and I know that men can be beautiful and happy without losing their faculty of living on earth. I refuse and am unable to believe that evil is a normal condition for men." What the ridiculous man will preach is a very old Truth, but he has faith in it because he has *seen* and felt all the beauty of the world in which such Truth had once reigned supreme. "The main thing is—love thy neighbors as thyself." And he has also seen and felt the power of the enemy. "The consciousness of life is higher than life; knowledge of the laws of happiness is higher than happiness—this is what we have to fight against!" In the world to which he has returned, everyone scoffs and sneers at his words and considers him mad, just as in the final phase of his dream; but his faith now can never be shaken or confounded, because "I saw, saw it (Truth), and its *live image* filled my soul forever." His first move on his new path is to search for the little girl he had swept aside so callously: "And—I did find that little girl. . . . And I shall go on! I shall go on!" (25: 117–118).

8
———

It has often been noted in Russian criticism that many of the details in Dostoevsky's vision of the Golden Age, aside from its location in the Classical past, resemble those in the French Socialist utopias of the 1840s. And this similarity has given rise to the question of whether Dostoevsky had ever really broken with these enchantments of his youth, for which, it would appear, he still harbored a lingering affection. The answer is that he had always continued to sympathize with the *moral aims* of the Utopian Socialists, though later believing that, if these aims were ever to be realized, it could only be under the inspiration of the God-man Christ, whose teachings had become incorporated in the Russian people. Even though, as N. I. Prutskov has remarked, one can find similarities in *The Dream of a Ridiculous Man* to Cabet's *Voyage to Icaria* and Victor Considérant's *La Destinée sociale* (not to mention others), the "method of collecting parallels between isolated words and phrases, images and motifs" tells us little about "the ideological roots" of the story. In fact, Dostoevsky's version was written *as an answer* to the rational utopias of the Socialists. Dostoevsky's story is thus not anti-utopian; rather, as Prutskov rightly says, "its foundation is *anti-Enlightenment* (the primacy of feelings of the heart and their opposition to truths of the head, the precedence of moral actions prompted by conscience in opposition to those actions motivated by convictions)."[6]

If we are to search anywhere for a "source," we need go no further than the little-known notes for an unwritten article on "Socialism and Christianity" that Dostoevsky set down sometime after completing *Notes from Underground*, and which have been surprisingly overlooked in this connection. Here he outlines the course of human history as beginning from the period "when man lives in masses (in the primitive patriarchal communities about which legends have been left)—then man lives spontaneously." The Golden Age was manifestly such a period, which is then replaced by "civilization," meaning "the development of personal consciousness and the negation of spontaneous ideas and laws." As a result, "man *always* lost faith in God" and "feels bad, is sad, loses the source of living life, doesn't know spontaneous sensations and is conscious of everything." Clearly, the ridiculous man has reached this stage of personal disintegration resulting from individualism and, "being conscious of everything," has lost faith in God and decides to end his life. But the advent of Christ on earth, according to Dostoevsky, provided humans with a new ideal, which consists of "the return to spontaneity, to the masses, but freely . . . in the highest degree willfully and consciously—and this higher willfulness is . . . a higher renunciation of the will" (20: 189–194). The ridiculous man thus devotes himself, on awakening from his dream, to preaching this return to a "higher spontaneity" through the realization on earth of the Christian law of love. *The Dream of a Ridiculous Man* gives superb artistic expression to this historical schema, which is condensed in the extraordinary trajectory of the ridiculous man's personal and public life.

It has been mentioned earlier that this story may also be brought into relation with another idea of Dostoevsky's, jotted down five months after completing the story, namely, that of creating "a Russian Candide." Such a story was never written, but we may wonder whether he had not in fact composed it—or a first version of it—in the one now being discussed. Voltaire's Candide is an incorrigible optimist who is taught by sad experience that life on earth is very far from being the best of all possible worlds; and having lost all faith and hope, he retires from the fray to cultivate his garden. Dostoevsky's Candide would surely have been someone like the ridiculous man, who begins where Voltaire's Candide ends and emerges on the other side of despair. He would continue to remain an optimist but, as it were, a tragic, Russian one, preaching to an incredulous and mocking world that he has *seen* the glories of the Golden Age and that they can be made real once again through Christ. However that may be, *The Dream of a Ridiculous Man* contains Dostoevsky's most vibrant and touching depiction of his positive moral-religious ideal, expressed far more convincingly in this rhapsodic and "fantastic" form than anywhere else in his work.

# PART III

# "With Words to Sear the Hearts of Men"

## CHAPTER 19

# Resurrection and Rebellion

The *Diary of a Writer* for October 1877 contained the following announcement: "On account of illness, which prevents me from publishing the *Diary* on strictly determined dates, I have decided to suspend its publication for two years" (26: 34). Indeed, hardly a letter at this time does not refer to Dostoevsky's ailments, which of course included his congenital epilepsy. When this decision brought a flood of letters pleading with him to continue, even if on a reduced schedule, he felt obliged to offer another justification. In his final (December) issue, he told his readers that "in the forthcoming year of rest from *periodical* publication, I expect, indeed, to engage in belletristic work, which imperceptibly and involuntarily has been taking shape within me during the two years of the publication of the *Diary*" (26: 126). Both reasons certainly played their part, but perhaps the irresistible call of artistic creation was the stronger.

For the next three years, Dostoevsky was thus absorbed primarily by the task of preparing and writing *The Brothers Karamazov*, whose first installment appeared in the *Russian Messenger* at the beginning of 1879. But despite the unremitting pressure of creation, he never was busier or more socially active. He had, to be sure, known a brief period of early celebrity in the 1840s; but most of his life after Siberia had been relatively lonely, relieved only by his immediate family, a few close friends, the literary circle that formed around his journals *Time* and *Epoch*, and the occasional attention elicited by a successful novel such as *Crime and Punishment*. All this was changed, however, by the remarkable success of the *Diary of a Writer*, which provided a decisive stimulus for the public reverence he was accorded in these closing years of his life.

## 2

Testimonies to the significance of the *Diary* abound in the memoir literature of the period. Some idea of its importance may be gathered from the initiative of one subscriber who wished to start a special fund that might encourage Dostoevsky to continue publication. He sent one ruble to a periodical called *Niva* (*The Field*) with a letter asking other subscribers to do the same, "so that the respected, famous, and hardworking [Dostoevsky] does not disregard our wishes and will give us this year, not specifying any particular date, the promise of at least one issue of the *Diary* sent to all previous addresses."[1] No public support was given to this unprecedented proposal, and Dostoevsky was spared the problem of coping with such a flattering testimony. This subscriber, however, spoke for many others, and Dostoevsky received more than a hundred letters regretting his decision. As Anna Grigoryevna notes, they supported his conviction that "there were people who shared his views, and that society valued his objective voice and trusted him."[2]

Dostoevsky's life thus took on the features of what we now call a cult figure, someone regarded with awe and unstinting admiration. One symbolic indication of this new status was his election in 1878 to membership in the Imperial Academy of Sciences, Division of Russian Language and Literature, an honor marked by the receipt of an impressive diploma in Latin. He was very pleased with such official recognition, though remarking to his wife that, compared with some of his contemporaries, his thirty-three years of literary activity made the distinction rather belated.[3]

Another testimony to his growing reputation was an invitation from the Society of French Writers (Société des Gens de Lettres de France) to take part as a delegate to an international congress in Paris presided over by Victor Hugo. The aim of the congress was to establish international copyright laws, and he replied in April with a provisional acceptance. "There is," he wrote, "a quite special attraction for me in this great literary occasion that is to open under the presidency of Victor Hugo, the great poet whose genius has exercised such a powerful influence on me ever since my childhood." But he added that "I must allow for the possibility that my health may create difficulties for me."[4] Another trip to Bad Ems was in the offing, and he could not guarantee his presence. Whether he seriously considered attending is quite unlikely, and the sudden death of his son Alyosha on May 16, 1878, ruled it out entirely.

His reply to this invitation was written in French, and, although he spoke the language fluently, he was wary about his ability to write it correctly. In fact, the letter was written by Anna Jaclard (formerly Korvin-Krukovskaya), whom he had met at a gathering at Anna Filosofova's shortly after receiving the invitation. Dostoevsky had printed stories by Anna Korvin-Krukovskaya in his journal *Epoch* in 1864 and had courted her assiduously when she came to Petersburg, very soon proposing marriage. His offer was amiably refused, and the two remained on good terms until their lives diverged.[5] Well on the way to becoming an impassioned radical by the time she met Dostoevsky, Anna married a French

medical student, Charles Victor Jaclard, and they both became very active in French radical Socialist circles. Jaclard eventually commanded a
brigade of Communards in the Paris uprising that took place after the
French defeat in the Franco-Prussian War—the uprising that so horrified Dostoevsky, as well as many others, because of the destruction
wreaked on the city that had become the symbol of Western civilization.
Anna organized classes for women during the brief life of the self-
proclaimed Paris Commune, served as a nurse, and was an editor and
one of the chief contributors to the best newspaper published while the
Commune was in power.[6]

The Jaclards managed to escape the ruthless repression that followed
the uprising with the help of Anna's father, General Korvin-Krukovsky,
who traveled to Paris for this purpose. When Anna reached London, she
was also aided by another friend, Karl Marx (parts of whose *Das Kapital*
she had translated into French); he sheltered her and arranged for her
travel to Heidelberg. Later, the Jaclards returned to Russia under the protection of Anna's wealthy and influential family. Charles Victor obtained
a post as a teacher of French language and literature in a *gymnasium* for
women, and contributed articles regularly on French and foreign affairs
to the radical journal *Slovo* (*The Word*). Anna Jaclard's command of
French was perfect, and as an old friend Dostoevsky asked her to write
his reply on the basis of a rough draft. This incident marked a renewal
of friendly relations between Dostoevsky and his erstwhile fiancée, and
indeed, of a friendship between the two families that, if nothing else,
illustrates his capacity to overlook social-political differences when
moved by personal sympathy. Discussions of politics were probably
kept in the background, but it is still quite intriguing to picture him
hobnobbing on the friendliest terms with ex-Communards and personal friends of Karl Marx. Versilov, in *A Raw Youth*, had said that he
could understand why the Communards had burned down the Tuileries
even though he was personally opposed to such destruction, and perhaps Dostoevsky was speaking more directly through his fictional character than might have been suspected.

## 3

The period between the cessation of the *Diary* and intensive work on
the novel allowed Dostoevsky to catch up with some of the correspondence from his readers. He disliked writing letters, as he says time and
again, because misunderstandings of what he meant were so likely to
occur, and it was not possible, as in a face-to-face conversation, to clear
up such confusions immediately. As he confides to one well-wisher, "if
I land in hell, then, of course, for my sins I'll be condemned to write a

dozen letters a day, no fewer."[7] Despite this frequently asserted disinclination, he continued to reply to readers all the same, and seemed to find sustenance in doing so.

One enthusiastic subscriber, Lyudmilla Alexandrovna Ozhighina, lived in Kharkov and had written Dostoevsky in October 1877 to express her appreciation. One of her return addresses was that of an old friend of his from the 1840s, Nikolay N. Beketov, now professor of chemistry at the University of Kharkov. In bygone days Beketov, like Dostoevsky himself, had been an admirer of the French Utopian Socialists, and both had regarded such Socialist doctrines as a practical attempt to realize the ideals of Christ on earth. Dostoevsky praised Ozhighina's "kind, good, flattering, and in the highest degree precious" letter; and in sending his answer through Beketov, he also asked for more information about his correspondent.[8] The lady, Beketov informed him, was an extremely worthy, still-struggling, but now middle-aged survivor of the female liberation movement of the 1860s, who had tried to study medicine, taught in a female *gymnasium*, and even published a novel, *By My Own Road* (*Svoim Putyom*), in *Notes of the Fatherland*.

At the end of February 1878, he assured her that "you interest me, and I would be happy to get to know you." Her own letters have been lost, but some notion of their tenor may be gathered from Dostoevsky's response. "Do you think I'm the sort of person who saves hearts, soothes souls, drives away sorrow? Many people write me that—but I know *for certain* that I'm capable of sooner inspiring disappointment and disgust. I'm no good at singing lullabies, although I've sometimes tried. And really, all that lots of people need is to have lullabies sung to them." He well knew that in refusing to sing lullabies he was running a risk, and he cautiously thanks his correspondent "for your kind feelings toward me," hoping "that [such] feeling will not so soon change to hostility."[9]

Ozhighina continued to pour out her soul to him during March in installments of what she called "a letter diary," though not receiving any reply. In mid-April, however, an odd incident occurred in the Dostoevsky household, and there is good reason to believe that it involved this untiring correspondent. The family was sitting at dinner one day when the doorbell rang, and a woman's voice was heard inquiring of the maid whether Dostoevsky was still alive. When the supposed corpse went to inquire about this ghoulish question, he was told by "a middle-aged woman," overjoyed to find him still living, that a rumor had been making the rounds in Kharkov—that he had been deserted by his wife, had fallen seriously ill because of her unfaithfulness, and was lying helpless and abandoned. "And I came immediately to look after you," she said. "I'm here directly from the train station."[10]

The name of the lady is not given by Anna Dostoevsky, but she had arrived from Kharkov and, in all probability, was Lyudmilla Ozhighina, whose behavior would be consistent with the somewhat wayward determination of her character. To quiet Dostoevsky's furor, Anna advised him to write immediately to Beketov and obtain further information about the gossip circulating in that city. Outraged at the suggestion of having been abandoned by his wife, he attributed such a story to his "enemies," and certainly desired the unwelcome visitor to vanish from his doorstep, if not from the face of the earth. More considerately, Anna "had a talk with the strange woman, who turned out to be a school-teacher, a very kind person, but probably not very bright. She was doubtless fascinated by the idea of taking care of a famous writer who had been abandoned by his good-for-nothing wife, and probably also by the idea of seeing him off into the next world and then priding herself all the rest of her life that he had died in her arms." The good-hearted Anna invited the lady to stay for dinner, though Dostoevsky vanished at once after reluctantly agreeing. But the offer was refused, the lady left the premises, and she returned to Kharkov the very next morning.[11]

To a Leonid Grigoryev, who claimed to have known him in the 1840s and of whom he had no recollection, Dostoevsky replied with this confession: "This winter I read a novel of mine, *Crime and Punishment*, which I wrote ten years ago [actually twelve] and I read more than two-thirds as though it was something quite unfamiliar, as though it wasn't even I who had written it." From some details in Grigoryev's letter, he agrees "that you're nevertheless acquainted with me and know me." While touched by Grigoryev's "warm and friendly reminder about earlier Petersburg life," Dostoevsky nonetheless declares the present to be "a colossal time for Russia," and finds it "indisputable that new people are on the march (and will soon arrive), so that there is no reason to grieve and pine."[12]

Much less sympathetic is a letter to a schoolteacher, Nikolay Grishchenko, who had written to approve of Dostoevsky's anti-Semitism and to offer further information to support his charges. "You complain about the Jews in Chernigov province," he responds, "but in our literature here we already have a multitude of publications, newspapers, and journals, published with Yid money by Yids (of whom more and more are coming into literature), and it's just that the editors, hired by Yids, sign the newspaper or journal with Russian names—and that's all the Russian there is in them." He predicts that "the Yids will additionally seize a much larger influence in literature" and unabashedly declares that "the Yid and his *kahal* amount to the same thing as a plot against the Russians."[13]

Grishchenko had berated the new radical journal *Word* because it had published an article defending the right of Jews to live anywhere in Russia. For Dostoevsky, the editors of this journal are immediately transformed into "old gray-haired liberals who never loved Russia, who even hated it for its 'barbarism,' and who are convinced in their hearts that they love both Russia and the people." Such specimens "have long outlived their time," and they understand nothing of "the new current, and the future." Merely because it may have been "liberal and necessary" to defend the Jews in the eighteenth century, they continue to do so, even though "the Yids are now triumphant and oppressing the Russians." He accuses such friends of the Jews as in fact nourishing "a hatred of Christianity," though he offers no reasons for such a conclusion. But he sees those who are friendly toward the Jews as reacting against "a nationalistic revulsion and hatred for the Yids," which means reacting against the feelings of the Christian Russian people (though Dostoevsky had denied that they were anti-Semitic).[14]

4
------

Other letters help to throw light on the foundations of Dostoevsky's moral-religious convictions. A Nikolay Osmidov had written him in January 1878 both to deplore the cessation of the *Diary* and to express perplexity over his insistence that the only basis for human morality was the assumption of immortality. Without the *Diary*, he laments, "I will not be able to hear your thoughts about the necessity of the conception of the immortality of the soul for the progress of mankind. I have my own conception of the necessity of love for one's neighbor, and of progress based on other foundations and attributes of man." No issue was closer to Dostoevsky's heart, and he tries, as best he can, to cope with what he calls Osmidov's "fateful and eternal question," which can hardly be thrashed out "in a couple of lines in a letter." As a first step, he advises Osmidov "to read carefully all of the Apostle Paul's epistles," where "faith is actually spoken of a great deal . . . and it can't be said any better." He also counsels him "to read *the whole Bible*," for "that book makes an amazing impression as a whole." Whether one believes or not, "there is no other such book in all of humanity and there cannot be."[15]

He then remarks that "the immortality of the soul and God are all the same thing, one and the same idea." Without such a belief, there would be no motive for adhering to any sort of morality: "Tell me why I should then live well, and do good, if I'll die completely on earth." He also argues that "humanity as a whole is . . . an organism . . . that unquestionably has its own laws of existence," and these laws work for "its preservation and the nourishment of itself." But without belief in the immortality of the soul, the human organism as a whole would be living "only *for its own destruction,*" since social chaos would result from a world in which "God and the immortality of the soul did not exist." Humanity would thus be the great exception to the rule, established by science, that "every organism exists on earth so as to live, not to destroy itself."[16]

Another argument puts into conceptual form what had previously been so poignantly dramatized in "The Sentence." The human ego, the I, has risen above nature and thus stands "higher than all this, at least does not fit in just to this, but stands as though on the side, above all of this, judges and recognizes it." From which he infers that "the *I* not only is not subject to the earthly axiom, the earthly law, but goes beyond them and has a law higher than them." Such a law "is not on earth, where everything is finished and everything dies without a trace and without resurrection. Isn't there a hint [in the existence of the I] at the immortality of the soul?" Indeed, the very fact that his correspondent is troubled by the problem illustrates his point. "That means that you can't cope with your *I*: it does not fit into the earthly orbit but seeks something else besides the earth, to which it also belongs." He ends by wishing Osmidov well and urging him to "search, and perhaps you'll find."[17] Osmidov evidently followed Dostoevsky's advice to continue searching, and what he found was Tolstoy, of whom he later was a faithful disciple.

A letter from a student named Alexander Voevodin, who later became a journalist, directly challenged Dostoevsky's position on suicide. Voevodin wrote that every person has a right to commit suicide, even with "a belief in a future life [and] in God," and he enclosed two manuscripts, presumably fictional but obviously autobiographical, to illustrate his position. Dostoevsky replied somewhat impatiently that "even though I read more than half of your notebook, there is such disorder in it and it's written so intimately (that is, for you alone) that I confess it gave me a lot of work but few explanations." Voevodin had asked Dostoevsky to "give me a categorical reply: yes or no," and he answers that, if his correspondent is talking about suicide, "it's quite impossible to write letters on such topics, the more so as I do not know you personally and do not know your thoughts." He invites Voevodin to call on him, and, in a book published in 1901 containing later versions of his two manuscripts, Voevodin refers to such a visit of which nothing more is known.[18]

By far the most important letter on this subject came in the form of a manuscript by an unnamed writer now identified as the philosopher Nikolay F. Feodorov. He was a strange and enigmatic figure, the illegitimate son of a noble family and a librarian in the Rumyantsev Museum in Petersburg. He enjoyed a considerable underground reputation in his lifetime even though he never published anything under his own name, believing that all private property (in which category he included ideas) was sinful. Dostoevsky already had received an anonymous manuscript of his in 1876, a portion of which was quoted in the *Diary*. This citation argued that the absence of private organizations and associations in Russia (including labor unions) should not be judged a social deficiency. All such groups pit one part of society against another, while in Russia "there still lives, with a certain vigor, that feeling of unity without which human societies cannot exist. . . . Without this feeling of unity, of mutual affection, of intercourse between men, nothing great is conceivable, since society itself is inconceivable" (22: 82). The writer who had composed Raskolnikov's final dream in *Crime and Punishment*, where such social disintegration is depicted with terrifying vividness, found Feodorov's thoughts on this point a welcome confirmation of his own artistic vision.

This new letter dealt with the question of the resurrection of the dead and of the immortality of the soul. Feodorov's doctrines, which have been labeled "a mystical positivism," enjoyed an extraordinary vogue in the 1870s, attracting the admiration not only of Dostoevsky but also of Tolstoy and Vladimir Solovyev. At the heart of his speculations was the same eschatological hope that inspired Dostoevsky and Solovyev—the vision of a total transformation of earthly life into the Kingdom of God. He believed that Christ had appeared, not simply to promise resurrection and a triumph over death in some miraculously transformed world at the Second Coming, but rather to point the way for humanity to accomplish the work of resurrection itself. He asserted that this goal could be achieved through the application of humanity's collective will, determined to turn the Christian revelation into an empirical reality.

Feodorov's ideas are an odd blend of science fiction and what he called "supra-moralism." Like Charles Fourier, who had influenced him in his youth, he indulged in cosmological fantasies that would allow for the development of new organs and convert nature from a blind, hostile, oppressive force into a realization of human desire. The ultimate aim of this development was to be a state of "multiple unity," in which everything (including nature) would exist as part of one huge, living organism. Once this condition had been attained, the natural course of human life would be reversed; instead of producing children, humanity would begin to resurrect its ancestors by reassembling the atoms and molecules of which they had been composed and which still remained scattered throughout the universe. For him, humankind's reverence for its fathers is the root of that family feeling which, empirically, points the way to the future state of humanity as a universal organism, a future in which the source of all the evils in the world—egoism and individualism—would vanish because they would be deprived of the physical basis for their perpetuation.[19]

Dostoevsky responded to this document—sent by one of Feodorov's disciples, an ex-revolutionary named Peterson—with a long and excited letter of his own. "I must say that I am essentially in complete agreement with [Feodorov's] views," he declared. "Reading them, I felt I might have written them myself." So taken was he with Feodorov's ideas that he communicated them to Vladimir Solovyev at the first opportunity. "I read them today (anonymously) to V. S. Solovyev," he informs Peterson, "our young philosopher, who is now giving lectures on religion—lectures attended by an audience of nearly a thousand people. . . . He is in profound sympathy with your thinker and was intending to say almost exactly the same thing in his next lecture."[20]

In fact, Dostoevsky had written something very similar long ago in a notebook jotting while maintaining a vigil at the bier of his first wife. He too had seen the ultimate goal of humankind as the attainment of a state in which procreation would cease, the dead would be resurrected, and all humanity would literally be united in a new physical body with hitherto unknown qualities and attributes.[21] Dostoevsky, however, saw this final transformation of humankind as occurring only at the end of time, not in earthly life itself; nor did he envisage it being achieved empirically through human effort. Hence he expresses some concern over whether Feodorov's scientific fantasies had not led to a certain utopian secularism. "In your account of the ideas of this thinker the most essential thing, without any doubt, is the duty of resurrecting our forefathers who lived before us, a duty which, if it were carried out, would bring the birth of children to an end and establish what is called, in the Gospels and the Apocalypse, the first Resurrection. But in your account you do not give any indication of how you understand this resurrection of our forefathers, or in what form you represent it to yourself and believe in it."[22]

He was afraid that Feodorov might be conceiving of resurrection only in an "ideational or allegorical sense," similar to Ernest Renan's view that human cognition would develop to such a degree that all the past would be present and reincarnated in the enlarged consciousness of future human beings. "I warn you that we here," he affirms, "i.e., Solovyev and myself at least, believe in the real, literal, personal resurrection, and that it will come to pass on earth." For Dostoevsky and Solovyev, this meant that "the dead would be resurrected . . . actually, personally, really, in body"; but these bodies would not be "as they are now . . . but perhaps like Christ's body after his resurrection, before his ascension on Pentecost."[23] Solovyev later entered into correspondence with Feodorov, and the latter began a reply to Dostoevsky still unfinished at the novelist's death.

Dostoevsky's epistolary relations with Feodorov, which focus on the supreme metaphysical importance of the theme of fatherhood, occurred exactly at the moment when he was mulling over his first notes for *The Brothers Karamazov*. It would appear that he thought of introducing a discussion of Feodorov's ideas into the scene in Father Zosima's cell (Book 2, Chapter 5). An isolated jotting reads: "*The resurrection of (our) ancestors* depends on us" (15: 204). There is also the fragment of a conversation: "Ilinsky [Dimitry Karamazov] against his parents. . . . The landowner 'this (one) will not resurrect his parents'" (15: 203). This line is probably a remark about Dimitry made in the notes by the liberal landowner who is a relative of the Karamazovs by marriage. Another reflection of Feodorov may well be seen in the following entry: "The family will be enlarged: even nonkindred will enter into it, and a new organism will have been woven together" (15: 249). This last note appears among the plans for the conversations and exhortations of Father Zosima (Book 6, Chapter 3); and perhaps the most important influence may be located here. For even though Dostoevsky's works are suffused with a sense of the importance of mutual moral responsibility, nowhere is this theme stated more broadly than in *The Brothers Karamazov*, where each person is declared to be responsible for all. The bold conception of a future humankind that would literally be a huge, united, and interdependent organism—a humankind in which any separation between individuals would no longer even be physically conceivable—may well have guided Dostoevsky toward his epochal formulation.

5
———

Despite the worsening of his emphysema, his recurring epilepsy, and his intense absorption in constructing a scenario for his new novel, Dostoevsky regularly attended the "Wednesdays" of Prince Meshchersky, often went to K. P. Pobedonostsev's home on Saturday evenings, and frequented the salon of Elena Shtakenshneider. He attended Vladimir Solovyev's famous lecture series on Godmanhood, which ran through the winter and spring of 1878; and besides entertaining guests like Nikolay Strakhov at Sunday dinners, he exchanged visits with a large family circle. He also dined once a month at a dinner organized by the Society of Writers, which included all literary factions, and where, as Anna Dostoevsky notes, "Feodor Mikhailovich met and mingled with his sworn literary enemies."[24] No fund-raiser for the needy—especially for impoverished students—was organized without inviting him to read. Such invitations were rarely refused, because nothing was more important for him than to maintain his contact with the rising generation of Russian youth.

In November 1878 he was introduced, at her urgent request, to Countess Sofya Andreyevna Tolstaya by their mutual friend Vladimir Solovyev. The countess was the widow of the poet and playwright Aleksey K. Tolstoy and, if we are to believe Anna Dostoevsky, a woman "of great intellect, highly educated and well read," who enjoyed the company of writers and intellectuals and had established her own salon. According to his wife, Dostoevsky "never ceased to be amazed at her ability to understand and respond to the many subtleties of philosophic thinking scarcely accessible to any woman," and he visited her regularly. There he met not only other cultural luminaries but also ladies of the highest society, with whom he enjoyed conversing because their talk was not combative, like that of men, but always "delicate and restrained."[25]

The Russo-Turkish War, in which Dostoevsky had been so emotionally involved, also brought about a reunion with some of his old comrades from his days at the Academy of Military Engineers. Meeting with a former teacher, A. I. Savelyev, Dostoevsky expressed his admiration for a classmate, General F. F. Radetsky, one of the Russian heroes of the day, who had smashed the last Turkish resistance. Savelyev transmitted to him Dostoevsky's "ardent Russian greeting and a deep bow. . . . May the toiling and burdened great Slavic tribe be returned to life through the efforts of such people as you, through fulfilling the universal and great Russian cause."[26] In October, after the war had been concluded, a huge banquet in honor of Radetsky was organized by the Academy of Military Engineers in a fashionable Petersburg restaurant. One hundred and fifty places were set, and Dostoevsky offered the welcoming toast "to the good health of the Russian soldier," whose finest qualities were embodied in the famous general.

His ardent patriotism, so flamingly displayed in the *Diary*, also led to a rather comic contretemps that caused him a good deal of irritation. It began with a letter he wrote in March 1878 to the newspaper *Novoye Vremya* (*New Time*), wondering why the editors had not given more publicity to the efforts of a teacher of mechanics named Osip Livchak to exhibit a "fourth dimension." Livchak had succeeded in tying three knots in a rope that was secured at both ends, and this was taken by advocates of spiritualism as evidence for a mysterious force in nature accessible only to those with mediumistic powers (he later revealed this exploit to be only a skillful trick). Livchak was accordingly invited to exhibit his prowess at the home of D. I. Mendeleyev, and there he repeated his performance in the presence of such defenders of spiritualism as A. M. Butlerov, N. P. Wagner, and A. N. Aksakov, as well as

Dostoevsky. Obviously intrigued by this mysterious phenomenon, he wrote his enthusiastic letter decrying the failure to bring the fourth dimension to greater public attention.[27] But he soon had reason to regret his intervention.

A month and a half later he received a letter from the ingenious gentleman explaining that he was not interested in the fourth dimension at all. His real aim had been to pave the way for a new invention—a technical device that would guarantee Russian naval superiority over England in the inevitable future conflict. Dostoevsky was the only person he would entrust with this awesome secret, and he wrote that "I am quite certain that in the present instance you are very well suited for the role that *fate itself seems to thrust upon you.*" A package had been sent that only he should open, and after carefully studying its contents, he should think of how best to present it in the most accessible form. Then it was his destined task to lay it before Grand Duke Konstantin Nikolaevich, commander-in-chief of the Russian fleet. In other words, as Dostoevsky puts it, "I'm supposed to abandon my children, my work, forget about my health, don a dress coat, and seek an audience with His Highness at Kronstadt, at Sveaborg, petition, expound, report."[28]

Of course he understood very well why Livchak was persuaded that the hand of fate had chosen the writer for this momentous task. "Without doubt," he writes, "patriotism could move me, a weak, infirm person eternally burdened by disease and obligations, and could compel from me the readiness for such enormous labors." But how could he know for certain that "England will be defeated by it (and only by it)"? He could not possibly understand all the technical data, and hence he refused to take responsibility for something of which he was totally ignorant. If anything went wrong, he alone would have to bear the blame. The whole incident was so strange that he could not help but suspect the fine hand of a lady, Varvara Ivanovna Pribytkova, who enjoyed some reputation as a medium in Petersburg. She had spoken to him incomprehensibly, three days before Livchak's letter, of some package he would receive that only he was supposed to open, and which would make him the witness of something or other. He was certain that she had erroneously assured the inventor of his agreement in advance, but she "never told me anything about your affairs" and his acquaintance with her was of the slightest. "Many women," he remarks, "love to promise, offer patronage, petition"—and he was certain this was the case here, "*though I never promised her anything . . .* so that all this has fallen on me like a bolt from the blue."[29] Dostoevsky flatly refused this attempt to exploit his patriotic sentiments, and Livchak's invention, whatever it may have been, never came to the aid of the Russian Navy.

The Livchak episode was not the only occasion when Dostoevsky was called upon for help by complete strangers. In a letter to Mikhail Yazykov, whom he had known as a fellow member of the Belinsky circle in the 1840s, he complains: "Need I point out to you . . . as a characteristic trait of our present Russian way of life, the fact that since I began publishing the *Diary* I have begun receiving from all over Russia a great number of letters from people who are complete strangers to me, with requests to take up their business, errands (amazing in their diversity), but mainly to find a place of employment, service, and even state service for them. . . . Most characteristic of all is that they consider me to have ties to everyone on whom the dispensing of positions depends."[30]

The reason for this letter, however, turns out to be precisely a response to such a request for help. Yazykov was now head of a government department in Novgorod, and Dostoevsky inquires whether he could find a post for the husband of a friend of Anna Grigoryevna's. He was now stationed in Perm, but his spouse desired to move closer to the capital city. Yazykov replied that he had no vacancy at the moment, but urged the candidate to come and visit him. Dostoevsky also received a request from his sister Varvara M. Karepina to aid the career of his nephew, an army doctor serving at the front, by using his influence with General Radetsky to promote him to a higher rank and recommend him for a decoration. Whether he complied with this family entreaty is not known, but all these solicitations confirm the new stature he had acquired in Russian society.

## 6

The celebration in honor of General Radetsky in October 1878 testified to the strength and power of Russian arms and the Russian state. But Dostoevsky had also been present at an event earlier in the year, the trial of Vera Zasulich, that revealed the deep fissures splitting Russian society apart, and which surely filled him with gloomy forebodings.

Vera Zasulich was a determined young woman, twenty-eight years of age, who had moved in revolutionary student circles and been arrested in connection with the Nechaev affair in 1871. Nechaev had even proposed marriage to her at one point, though whether only to bind her further to his cause is not clear. She had, in any case, acted as one of his couriers after he went abroad, but she had no connection with the group that murdered Ivan Ivanov.

Kept imprisoned for two years, even though no charges were filed against her, she was declared innocent and emerged as a hardened revolutionary. On learning that General Feodor Trepov, the governor of St. Petersburg, had illegally ordered the flogging of a Populist political prisoner for refusing to remove his cap in the general's presence, she calmly walked into his office on the pretext of an official request and shot him, though wounding him only slightly. Her open trial, presided over by Dostoevsky's friend A. F. Koni, was conducted with scrupulous (and remarkable) impartiality, despite some pressure from official circles. Koni, whose later career suffered as a result, allowed the defense to introduce detailed testimony about the relentless flogging. The result was a triumphant acquittal of the defendant, to the wild applause of a courtroom packed with high government functionaries and notables from the most select Petersburg society. Admission to the courtroom was limited, but Dostoevsky was present with a card falsely declaring him to be a member of the legal profession.

During the course of the trial, other Populist prisoners, called as witnesses by the defense, unanimously testified to the constant indignities and brutalities they had been forced to endure; and these frightening glimpses into the reality of the prison world produced a shattering effect. Elizabeth Naryshkin-Kurakina, a lady-in-waiting to one of the grand duchesses (and an acquaintance of Dostoevsky's) was scarcely to be suspected of revolutionary sympathies. But she wrote in her *Memoirs*: "The appearance of a number of young political prisoners created quite a stir. They had been brought into the courtroom from the Peter-and-Paul Fortress merely as witnesses to the incident in the prison. Their pale faces, their voices trembling with tears and indignation, the details of their depositions—all these statements made me lower my eyes with shame."[31] G. K. Gradovsky, whom Dostoevsky had replaced in 1873 as editor of *The Citizen*, remembered feeling that, as the testimony of these youthful defense witnesses unrolled, not Vera Zasulich but he himself and all of Russian society stood accused and were standing trial.[32]

The tense drama of the Zasulich proceedings, which glaringly brought to light the rampant injustices of the entire Russian judicial and social system, took place before an audience of the most exclusive society and served as a model for the atmosphere that Dostoevsky would create two years later in the trial scenes of his novel. Also to be noted is the complexity of his attitude toward the crime itself, which he found it impossible purely and simply to condemn. During her testimony, Zasulich had said: "It is terrible to raise one's hand against a fellow man . . . but I decided that this is what I had to do." These words, expressing the clash between Zasulich's moral conscience and her social-political convictions, evidently made a deep impression on Dostoevsky. Two years later he recalled them in a notebook entry: "Zasulich: 'It is hard to raise a hand to shed blood'—this vacillation is more moral than the shedding of blood itself."[33]

Dostoevsky abhorred flogging and had raged against it vehemently in

*House of the Dead*; perhaps General Trepov's order reminded him of the savage brutalities of the sadistic Major Krivtsov of his prison camp years. Like so many others at the tribunal, he could not suppress a certain sympathy for the vengeful Zasulich; and he told others, once before the trial and then just before the acquittal, that to find Zasulich guilty would be a grave mistake. On the first occasion, he remarked that the jury should tell the prisoner: "You have sinned, you wished to kill a man, but you have already atoned for it. Go, and do not transgress again." On the second, he stated: "It's impossible to convict her, punishment is uncalled-for, superfluous; but say to her something like this: 'Go, but don't do it again.'" "But such a juridical formula," he added, "it would seem we do not possess, and worst of all, she will now be elevated into a heroine."[34] Whether he believed she would be convicted or acquitted, he felt that no formal legal judgment would be the best solution. If found guilty, she would become a martyr; if acquitted, her act would be given a legal sanction, and the authority of the Russian state would be undermined.

His prediction that Vera Zasulich would become a heroine was soon all too dramatically borne out. On emerging from the courthouse, she was carried on the shoulders of a celebrating crowd, and this militant rejoicing led to a demonstration that ended with a splattering of gunfire and one death. When the police tried to arrest Zasulich again, she vanished into the throng and was later smuggled out of the country. She continued a notable revolutionary career in Switzerland, eventually aligning herself with G. V. Plekhanov and the Mensheviks against Lenin and the Bolshevik revolution. Before crossing the frontier, however, she was given shelter in various homes, one of them, according to highly probable rumor, being that of Anna Pavlovna Filosofova. A number of letters to Anna from Dostoevsky precisely at this time reveal their collaboration in various charitable enterprises (one of which was finding a place in an old people's home for the aging nanny of the Dostoevsky children). Her close friendship with him, as well as his remarks about the trial, reveal the complexity of the social-political situation in which many Russians now found themselves, caught between an increasingly unbearable régime and the resort to armed resistance as a response.

The shot fired by Vera Zasulich echoed throughout Russia, and her example spurred on others for the first time to take up arms against Tsarist officials. Indeed, in the months following her trial a wave of terrorist attacks were carried out by her hitherto peaceful comrades, formerly devoted only to propaganda among the people. High officials of the régime were killed in Kiev and Odessa, and General Mezentsev, the head of the dreaded secret police, was struck down by a dagger in broad daylight in the very heart of St. Petersburg as revenge for the death of a

Populist prisoner. His assassin was S. M. Stepniak-Kravchinsky, a young Populist who had fought with the Serbs in their battle against the Turks and who, after the murder, escaped abroad. He became a noted writer, whose *Underground Russia* is still an indispensable source for the Populist movement, and while an exile in London helped Constance Garnett improve her Russian. He is often considered one of the prototypes of Razumov in Conrad's *Under Western Eyes*.

Dostoevsky comments on this event to Victor F. Putsykovich, an old journalist friend who had worked with him in the 1860s and then on *The Citizen*, and who was now attempting to publish a journal of the same name in Germany. "You write that Mezentsev's murderers have not been found and that it's probably a bunch of Nihilists. How could it be otherwise? That's surely how it is; but will we ever be cured of stagnation and of old routine methods—tell me that, please!" Putsykovich himself had received warning letters from "Odessa socialists," who threatened him with death if he did not stop printing articles against the Nihilists; and he had forwarded these to Mezentsev without ever receiving a reply.

Besides revealing the incompetence of the secret police, the reference to Odessa also occasions another display of Dostoevsky's anti-Semitic obsession. "Odessa, a city of Yids, turns out to be the center of our militant socialism. There's the same phenomenon in Europe: the Yids are terribly active in socialism, and I won't even mention the Lassalles and Karl Marxes. And it's understandable: for Yids the whole benefit is from any kind of radical shock or upheaval in the state, because they themselves are a *status in statu*, making up their own community that will never be shaken but will only gain from any kind of weakening of anything that is not the Yids."[35] In fact, very few of the Populists were of Jewish origin (Jewish youth would flock to the radical banner only later in the century), but Dostoevsky preferred not to accuse those purebred Russian lads whose desire for self-sacrifice he hoped to guide into other channels.

## CHAPTER 20

# Man in the Middle

The new eminence that Dostoevsky had attained through the *Diary of a Writer*, and the unique position he now occupied in Russian social-cultural life, is easily illustrated by two events. On the one hand, he was consulted as a moral guide by a collective letter from a group of "progressive" students; on the other, he was invited to become the unofficial tutor of several of the grand dukes of the realm, the sons of members of the royal family. No other individual in Russia had ever enjoyed such an extraordinary status.

However, his life was also overshadowed by a personal tragedy—the sudden and unexpected death of his three-year-old son Aleksey (Alyosha). A voyage to the famous monastery of Optina Pustyn helped to assuage the crippling effects of this blow, and also provided material for the monastic scenes of the early chapters of *The Brothers Karamazov*.

2

Among the tributes to Dostoevsky's *Diary of a Writer*, we have already cited the remark of Elena Shtakenshneider that the journal had made him "the teacher and idol of the youth"; and there is hardly a contemporary comment that does not reinforce this observation. Vsevolod Solovyev also referred to the *Diary* as "having such a strong effect on the young generation"; and a commentator in *Voice*, referring to the termination of the *Diary*, regretted its disappearance "particularly in relation to the young generation, among whom, as I can testify, it enjoyed a wide popularity, and to whom, doubtless, it could be of great benefit." The same writer remarked that Dostoevsky had not tried to ingratiate himself by flattery, "but the majority of the young, with their unspoiled intuition, were able to decipher his deep genuineness and sincerity and valued these very highly."[1] If there were any doubt about his exalted standing in this regard, and the oracular status he had now assumed, it can be easily dispelled by a letter sent to him on April 8, 1878, by a group of students at the University of Moscow.

"Dear Feodor Mikhailovich," the students wrote, "for two years now we have been accustomed to turn to your *Diary* for the solution, or for the proper posing, of the questions that loomed before us; we have been accustomed to use your decisions for the establishment of our own views, and to honor them even when we did not agree."[2] One of the six signatories was Pavel N. Milyukov, later a famous historian of Russian culture, leader of the Constitutional Democratic party in the Russian Duma after 1905, and then foreign minister in an interim government before the Bolshevik takeover. The immediate occasion for this joint missive was a manifestation of popular anger (to put it mildly) directed at the activities of the young dissidents from among the intelligentsia.

A number of Moscow students had gone to greet a convoy of other students from the University of Kiev, who had been arrested on minor charges and were being sent to the provinces in police custody. As they proceeded together peacefully through the streets, some butchers and shopkeepers from a local food market swarmed out and, to shouts of "Beat them," severely manhandled some of the young men. This physical attack was one of the first of its kind on such a scale, an eye-opening indication that the lower-class population did not approve of illegal behavior. This realization caused a crisis of self-questioning and consternation in the student ranks. "What is most important for us," they told Dostoevsky, "is to resolve the question: To what extent are we, the students, guilty, and what conclusions about us should be drawn by society, and by ourselves, from this occurrence?"

To the first part of this question, he gave an unequivocal reply: "Here is my answer: In my view you are not guilty at all. You are only children of that very same 'society' which you are now deserting, and which is 'a lie in every sense.'" Dostoevsky thus refuses bluntly to regard the discontent of the young generation in a negative light. Instead, he praises the youth in glowing and effusive terms: "Never have we had, in our Russian life, such an epoch, when youth (as if having a presentiment that all of Russia stands at some decisive point, tottering on the edge of an abyss) in its huge majority was more sincere than now, more pure-souled, more thirsting for truth and justice, more ready to sacrifice everything, even life itself, for truth and the word of truth. Truly, the great hope of Russia! I felt this long ago, and began to write about it long ago."[3]

As the children of a corrupt society, the young people could not help but reflect the continued influence of the false values they had absorbed. "This word of truth, for which youth is thirsting, it seeks God knows where, in surprising places (once again, in this way, coinciding with the rotting European-Russian society that bore it), and not in the people, in the land. The end result is that, up to now, neither youth nor society *knows the people.* Instead of going to the people so as to live their life, the young people, knowing nothing about it, on the contrary, simply despising its foundations, for example, religious faith, went not to learn from the people but to instruct it, to instruct it arrogantly, with contempt—a purely aristocratic, leisure-class pastime!"[4]

Dostoevsky then refers to the whole disillusioning experience of the "going to the people" movement, whose "unhappy and torturing facts" had now become evident. The students had wished "to lighten the sufferings of the people," but the people "refused to recognize their honest efforts." Nor was this a new phenomenon: he dates it from "as long ago as the 1860s," probably referring to the Petersburg fires at that time, when students were attacked in the streets as incendiaries. Another instance of this willful alienation from the people was the demonstration led by Plekhanov at the Church of Our Lady of Kazan in Petersburg. "You do not believe in God, but why do you insult the people by desecrating their temple?" He claims to have criticized "these Kazanskies . . . to their faces," but no record exists of such an encounter. The outlook for the future was thus very bleak if events continued along their present course. Although he deplores the beatings "because you never settle anything with fists," such violence was only to be expected; the people "are uncouth, they are *muzhiks*." Still, Dostoevsky concludes by reiterating that the students were not guilty: "never has youth been more honest and sincere. . . . But the trouble is that the youth bear the stamp of two centuries of our history." Even though the youth now believe in "the gospel of the revolver,"[5] they are only the misbegotten products of a society totally deformed by false European values against which they are in rightful revolt—though unfortunately still only in a European (that is, Socialist) manner totally alienating them from the people.

Despite the wave of assassinations during the spring and summer of 1878 that was causing panic in the country, Dostoevsky refused to lose heart, continuing to reaffirm his immovable belief that Russia was about to enter a glorious new era. In replying again to his long-lost acquaintance Leonid Grigoryev, he declares: "I am not at all a man of the '60s and not even of the '40s. It is rather the most recent years that I prefer because of what can clearly be seen to have been accomplished, instead of what was previously conjectural and idealistic." Nothing is easier, he continues, than for a Russian to fall into error about the state of his own country. "Time has passed since the liberation of the peasants—and what do you see: the hideousness of rural district administrations and morals, vast quantities of vodka, incipient pauperism and a kulak class, that is, a European proletariat and bourgeoisie, etc., etc." Dostoevsky thus had no illusions about the actual social situation; but if one stopped there—on the surface as it were—"you'll immediately lapse into error."[6]

What he saw (or certainly wished to see) to counterbalance this harsh and menacing reality was a new consciousness that had burgeoned among the people and been brought to light by the Russo-Turkish War:

"There has been established in them . . . a political consciousness, a precise understanding of Russia's meaning and mission." But to impute such a "precise" idea to the people was too much even for him, and so he adds (in parentheses) that this idea was at least *constantly becoming precise.* . . . In short, a higher idea has been established . . . and . . . as long as there are at least . . . the beginnings of higher ideas, then the rest will come." One must penetrate beneath the surface of the people to uncover the hidden reality; and the same is the case "with our youth of the intelligentsia," about whom one should not believe that "the hideous facts" reveal the essence of their ideals.[7]

At a recent banquet in honor of the memory of Timofey Granovsky (one of the originals of the immortal Stepan Trofimovich in *The Devils*), Nikolay Ketcher, a well-known figure of the 1840s, had called the young people "rotten"; but Dostoevsky most emphatically refuses to agree. "They are *seeking the truth*, with the boldness of the Russian heart and mind, and have only *lost their leaders.*"[8] He was unshakably convinced that the Populists' return to the moral ideals of a secular Christianity was only the first step in their eventual acceptance of the truth of a supernatural Christ; and he saw his mission as that of supplying the leadership in this direction that was still so woefully lacking.

3
———

During these very months, when Dostoevsky was consulted by students who, if they were not prowling the streets with revolvers themselves, unquestionably sympathized with those who were, he was also asked to meet regularly with some young men who might easily become their targets. Sometime in the first week of February 1878, he received a visit from D. S. Arsenyev, the tutor of the grand dukes Sergey and Paul, the younger sons of Alexander II. The purpose of the call, made in the name of the Tsar himself, was to invite him to become acquainted with Arsenyev's pupils, so that, to quote Anna Dostoevsky, "by his conversations Feodor Mikhailovich might have a beneficial influence on the youthful grand dukes." Even though he was just then beginning to sketch out the first notes for *The Brothers Karamazov*, such a royal request could not be refused. "[T]he wish of the Tsar-Liberator," to quote Anna again, "was of course law for him. He found it pleasant to know that it was in his power to carry out even a small desire of a personage he had always revered for the great achievement of emancipating the serfs, for realizing a dream dear to him in his youth, for which he himself had suffered so bitterly in his own day."[9]

What Dostoevsky must have felt at such a moment can well be imagined. He—who had been convicted of a crime against the state! He—

who had served a prison term at hard labor in Siberia and worn the shackles and striped garment of a convict for four painful years! He—who had sunk to the lowest depths of Russian society and shared the fate of the most hardened criminals! He—now invited to enter as an honored guest into the most exalted and exclusive court circles, and to serve as guide and counselor to those in whose hands the future of Russia would eventually be entrusted! His meetings with the grand dukes did not begin immediately, however, because Arsenyev felt that a certain period of preparation was necessary. "After my conversation with you," he wrote Dostoevsky on March 15, "I was surer than ever that it would be better to arrange things so that your acquaintance with the grand dukes would not appear to be contrived by parental advice or tutorial decree, but should result from their own wish." Arsenyev explains that such a wish had been encouraged "through (apparently) random conversations," which, having had the desired effect, led to the present dinner invitation.[10]

His first appearance at court was recorded in the diary of Grand Duke Konstantin Konstantinovich, a cousin of Sergey and Paul and the son of the commander of the Russian Navy.* "I dined at Sergey's," he wrote. "His guests were K. N. Bestuzhev-Ryumin and Feodor Mikhailovich Dostoevsky. I was very much interested in the latter, and had read his works. He is a slim person, who looks rather sickly, with a long, sparse beard and a particularly sad and thoughtful expression on his pale face. He speaks extremely well, as well as he writes."[11] This visit to his royal interlocutors was a success, and invitations to dine with them came regularly thereafter. Unfortunately, we have no information about the content of these seemingly social but in fact pedagogical conversations, though it may be assumed that the ideas and attitudes expressed in the *Diary* were also uttered at the dinner table.

He thus now found himself in the extraordinary position of being a cherished adviser, not only of the young radical generation, but also of the younger members of the reigning family. And if he felt that fate (or God) had entrusted him with a mission at this crucial moment of Russian history, he certainly had objective reasons for believing that such a momentous task should have fallen to his lot. Indeed, a quick glance at his career reveals with unmistakable clarity that, ever since returning from Siberia in 1860, he had endeavored to play precisely the role into

---

* Dostoevsky's relations with Grand Duke Konstantin Konstantinovich, who had serious literary interests, eventually became very cordial, and he told the royal scion, according to Anna Grigoryevna, that it was unfortunate he was destined for a naval career instead of devoting himself to literature. The grand duke later published poetry and plays under a pseudonym, and a number of his poems were set to music by Peter Tchaikovsky, with whom he also became friendly and who admired his talent.

which he had now been cast—that of arbitrator and conciliator between the dissident intelligentsia and Russian society as a whole.

His program of *pochvennichestvo*, or "return to the soil," called for the reunion of the intelligentsia with the Christian ideals of the Russian people, and hence with the Tsar whom the people revered as the earthly embodiment of God. In two of his great novels—*Crime and Punishment* and *The Devils*—he had portrayed the tragedy of those members of the intelligentsia who had become alienated from their Christian roots and hence from their people. But Dostoevsky did not confine himself solely to such literary efforts; at moments of acute social crisis he had attempted to intervene actively when he thought he might do some good. He had paid a personal visit to Nikolay G. Chernyshevsky in 1862, when St. Petersburg had been set ablaze by a series of mysterious fires attributed by the people to subversive students, and urged this noted radical spokesman to help in stopping such rumors. The same impulse prompted his courageous letter to his editor, the powerful Mikhail Katkov, just after the attempt on the Tsar's life by Dimitry Karakozov in 1866. Katkov had denounced this shocking deed as the result of a Polish conspiracy; but Dostoevsky, even though entirely dependent for subsistence on advances from Katkov while writing *Crime and Punishment*, asserted that the trouble lay in Russia itself. Only more freedom of speech and press could help alleviate the discontent of the intelligentsia.

Since then, the Populist ideology of the 1870s had given him a common ground on which to appeal to the moral instincts even of the most alienated and refractory. Never, indeed, could Dostoevsky have felt himself in a better position to influence public opinion than at this time. Had the *Diary of a Writer* not furnished ample proof of the power of his words to grip the minds and hearts of his readers? And never could he have felt it more essential to do so than in the late 1870s, when the earlier crises of Russian nineteenth-century society shrank into insignificance before the menace of the present. For a fraction of the Populists, driven to despair by the relentless persecutions of the government and the lack of any response to their peaceful propaganda among the peasantry, had launched a systematic campaign of terror against Tsarist officialdom and finally against the Tsar himself. Both the novel Dostoevsky was now beginning, *The Brothers Karamazov*, as well as his sensational speech at the ceremonies inaugurating a monument to Pushkin two years later, would mark his attempts to mediate the lethal conflict that was tearing Russian society apart.

4
———

Since returning in 1871 from his four-year sojourn in Europe, Dostoevsky had led a relatively peaceful and untroubled family life. The intelligent, efficient, and industrious Anna Grigoryevna looked after the household and the children (not to mention the family publishing business) with vigilant care. Life proceeded in the carefully organized routine that had enabled him to maintain the exacting schedule of his *Diary of a Writer*. The letters between the pair express their continually deepening bonds of mutual devotion and spiritual support, and in the case of Dostoevsky, his almost painfully anxious worry over his children. Earlier, some of his most agonizing letters had been sent from Geneva after the death of his first child, a six-week-old daughter christened Sofya. Such a memory may well account for the note of febrility that marks the overflowing love lavished on his later offspring, and the brooding disquietude he always expressed about their welfare.

His lingering premonitions, alas, proved to be only too well founded. On April 30, 1878, his three-year-old son Aleksey (Alyosha) suffered a first epileptic convulsion of four minutes that was taken only as a childish symptom. On May 16, however, he was overcome by a major epileptic fit lasting for twelve hours and forty minutes, ending with his death. In her *Reminiscences*, Anna explains that the first doctor assured them that the convulsive symptoms would pass away; by the time a specialist in nervous disorders arrived, it was too late. "My husband," she writes, "was crushed by this death. He had loved Alyosha somehow in a special way, with an almost morbid love. . . . What racked him particularly was the fact that the child had died of epilepsy—a disease inherited from him."[12] Anna Filosofova, who rushed to see the Dostoevskys on hearing the news, was struck by their isolation, prostration, and helplessness. She purchased a little coffin for them, and was told by Anna Grigoryevna, weeping inconsolably, that Dostoevsky had spent the entire previous night on his knees beside Alyosha's bed.[13]

The sudden and unexpected death of little Alyosha, who had been playing happily and prattling away on the very morning of the day he died, was a crushing blow for the family; and Anna Grigoryevna confirms the melancholy image of their state provided by Mme Filosofova. "As for me," she writes, "the death of our darling little boy was shattering. I so lost my bearings, mourned and cried so much, that I was unrecognizable. My customary cheerfulness vanished together with my normal flow of energy, which gave way to apathy." Her husband, after the first shock, "to outward appearance . . . was calm and bore with courage the blow that fell on us; but I very much feared that this suppression of his deep grief might react fatally upon his already shaky health."[14] His struggle to maintain his composure is evident in the laconicism of the funeral invitations he sent to his brother Nikolay and his stepson Pavel Isaev. But he did confess to his brother that "I'm sadder than I've ever been before."[15] Anna Grigoryevna soon rallied from her apathetic state, responding to his entreaties "to submit to God's will" and "to take pity on him and the children, to whom I had become, in his words, 'indifferent.'" Some of Anna's torments and even her very words were used "in the chapter of *The Brothers Karamazov* called 'Women of Faith,' in which a woman who has lost her child unburdens her grief to Father Zosima."[16]

Once having regained some stability, Anna thought it imperative to distract Dostoevsky from his own silent mourning by encouraging him to realize a long-cherished plan—that of visiting the famous monastery of Optina Pustyn. Vladimir Solovyev had called on them regularly during the period following Alyosha's death, and Anna persuaded him to convince her husband to undertake the quite arduous journey in his company. Dostoevsky had intended to travel to Moscow in mid-June and offer his new novel to Katkov for the *Russian Messenger*, and a trip to the monastery from there would be quite feasible. On June 10, he wrote Solovyev that he would be in Moscow on the twentieth and inquired whether the two could make the journey around that time.[17]

Arriving in Moscow after Alyosha's funeral, and despite having acquired a bad cough during the train trip, he immediately went to see Katkov, whose "face brightened" on hearing about the new novel. "But as soon as I mentioned 300 rubles a signature [sixteen pages] and an advance, he seemed to wince." Katkov explained that, because of his own failing health, he was not sure that he would continue to publish his monthly "thick" journal and could not commit himself to such an expenditure on the spot. After this first interview, Dostoevsky wrote Anna that "I'm sitting and thinking that tomorrow he *will undoubtedly refuse me.*"[18] Katkov, however, was too canny an editor to do anything of the sort, and a day later he accepted Dostoevsky's terms, offering an immediate advance and more to follow in a few months. "I'm on the best terms with Katkov that I've ever been," he relievedly informs Anna. "*He especially asked me to give you his best regards.*"[19] Besides visiting relatives and the Slavophil Ivan Aksakov, he also made a round of the booksellers to pick up the rather paltry proceeds from the sale of his works.

A day later he and Solovyev embarked on the voyage to Optina Pustyn, which proved to be far more adventurous than they had expected. They had been advised to take the train from Moscow to a station called Sergievo, and from there to proceed to Kozelsk; but they could not discover how far they would have to travel from Sergievo to reach their destination. "The main thing is that no one knows, so that it was impossible to find out ahead of time," he wrote to Anna in some surprise upon his return to Moscow. They finally set out on rut-filled country roads where they could not change carriage horses, "and it took us exactly two days to get to Kozelsk, that is, Optina Pustyn. We spent the nights in villages, and were jolted in a horrible carriage."[20]

Nonetheless, he by no means regretted having undertaken such a taxing pilgrimage. "My husband returned from Optina seemingly at peace
and much calmer," Anna writes, "and he told me a great deal about the
customs of the hermitage, where he had passed two days. He met with
the renowned elder [*starets*] Father Ambrose three times: once in the
presence of others and twice alone. These talks had a profound and
lasting effect on him."[21] Dostoevsky was very far from being the only
eminent Russian who found solace in the company of Father Ambrose.
Among many others, we can cite the words of Tolstoy, who had visited
Optina Pustyn a year earlier in the company of N. N. Strakhov. "This
Father Ambrose is a true saint," he wrote. "I had only to speak to him,
and my soul immediately felt relieved. It is when one speaks with men
like him that one feels the closeness of God."[22]

Father Ambrose was revered not only as a spiritual counselor but also
as a person of formidable knowledge and erudition, who directed the
work of translating and editing the texts of the Greek Fathers that had
given the Optina cloister its reputation as a center of theological learning. He was famed for possessing the same gift of moral-psychological
divination that will soon be attributed to Father Zosima; and the scene
in *The Brothers Karamazov* where Zosima receives and comforts the
peasant women who seek his aid is based on observations gathered during this Optina visit. Indeed, among the words that Zosima uses to assuage the grief of the peasant mother mourning her little son Aleksey
are those that Father Ambrose told Dostoevsky to convey to his wife.
They are probably the passage in which the elder tells the mother to
"weep and be not consoled, but weep. Only every time that you weep
be sure to remember that your little son is one of the angels of God,
that he looks down from there at you and sees you, and rejoices at your
tears, and points at them to the Lord God. . . . But [your weeping] will
turn in the end into a quiet joy, and your bitter tears will be only tears
of tender sorrow that purifies the heart and delivers it from sin" (14: 46).

Dostoevsky left no firsthand account of his meetings with Father Ambrose, but Solovyev reported that he was in "a very excited state all
through the visit." There is, however, an eyewitness account recently
unearthed, written by a close friend of N. N. Strakhov. He writes that
Dostoevsky, instead of "obediently and with fitting humility paying attention to the edifying discourses of the elder and monk, spoke more
than [Father Ambrose] did, became excited, heatedly raised objections,
developed and explained the meaning of the words pronounced by the
elder, and, without being aware of it, from someone desiring to listen
to an edifying discourse was transformed into a teacher."[23] However
that may be, there is no doubt that he drew a good deal of inspiration
for his next novel from this visit to the monastery. Indeed, Solovyev
wrote a few months later to Konstantin Leontiyev that Dostoevsky

"specifically went to Optina Pustyn ... for the first chapters of his novel,"[24] though this remark probably underestimates his need to overcome his grief.

Besides the possible use of Father Ambrose as a prototype for Father Zosima (though Dostoevsky never modeled a character on just one real-life figure), some of his information about the monastic institution of the elders (*starchestvo*) and the incidents connected with its history have been traced to a life of Father Leonid, the predecessor and teacher of Father Ambrose, published by the monastery press. The sketch of the revival of the institution of *starchestvo* that Dostoevsky provides is a recasting of a passage from that book, as is the story about the coffin of a saintly hermit, which is intended to illustrate the power that a *starets* exercises over his disciple. One such disciple, who disobeyed a command of his elder, could not be buried because his coffin was expelled three times from the church by some supernatural force; only when this command had been lifted could his remains lie in peace.

In the passage of her memoirs about the trip to Optina Pustyn, Anna writes that "I felt that Solovyev, even though he was a man 'not of this world,' would be able to look after Feodor Mikhailovich if he should have an epileptic seizure."[25] The odd expression employed about this immensely gifted young man—the most important Russian turn-of-the-century philosopher—indicates the sense of strangeness and immateriality that his personality conveyed—and by no means only to Anna Dostoevsky. His friendship with the novelist had once again become very close, and it was only to be expected that the Dostoevskys also faithfully attended the famous series of *Lectures on Godmanhood* that he gave in Petersburg all through the winter and early spring of 1878.

These lectures were a great public as well as cultural event, and the hall was filled not only with students normally adverse to anything smacking of the religious or theological, but also with the cream of Petersburg cultivated society. Nikolay Strakhov was there as well as the Dostoevskys, and on one occasion, instead of the usual conversation and exchange of pleasantries, they noticed a certain evasiveness in his behavior. Dostoevsky thought the cause might have been some unsuspected slight to the *amour-propre* of their touchy friend, but Strakhov later explained that his comportment in this instance "was a special case." "Count Leo Tolstoy came to the lecture with me. He asked me not to introduce him to anyone, and that was why I stayed away from all of you." Dostoevsky was surprised and disappointed that he had not at least been given the opportunity to scrutinize Tolstoy in the flesh: "But why didn't you whisper to me who was with you?" he asked Strakhov reproachfully. "I would have taken a look at him at least!" The two giants of Russian literature, who were for the only time in their lives in the same place at the same time, were thus deliberately kept apart. One wonders whether Strakhov pointed out Dostoevsky to Tolstoy, who would thus have been able to gather a personal impression. Anna notes that "in later years Feodor Mikhailovich more than once expressed his regret at never having met Tolstoy in person."[26]

Dostoevsky's regular attendance at Solovyev's lectures was much more than an encouraging gesture of politeness to a cherished young friend. It was, in addition, intimately linked with his own work and the ideas he was then mulling over for his next novel. No one reading the *Lectures on Godmanhood* can fail to be struck by the repeated echoes of Dostoevskian themes and preoccupations in Solovyev's text; whether Solovyev exercised any influence on him is a much more difficult question to answer. It is probable, however, that the trained philosophical mind of the young man both stimulated Dostoevsky and sharpened his awareness of some of the implications of his own convictions. (Strakhov, equally conversant with philosophical tradition, had performed much the same function in the 1860s.) One topic that preoccupied them both was the possibility of the establishment of the Kingdom of God on earth, a vision of Dostoevsky had always expressed through enraptured apocalyptic intimations. For him this notion presumably remained speculative and transcendent; it was only in a new and transfigured freshly garb that one could imagine such a glorious fulfillment. Solovyev, however, genuinely believed in the possibility of a free Christian theocracy, one in which the Christian law of love would entirely penetrate and spiritualize the workings of earthly life. His *Lectures* sketch the entrancing vision of a humanity gradually approaching such a blessed state of Godmanhood—a society in which, under the leadership of the Orthodox Christ and His Church, the divine and the human would fuse and follow the example of Christ the God-man Himself so far as this was possible. Indeed, Solovyev later wrote that, during their journey to Optina Pustyn, Dostoevsky had told him that "the Church as a positive social ideal must show itself to be the central idea of [his] new novel or new series of novels, of which only the first has been written—*The Brothers Karamazov*."[27]

There is an undoubted resemblance between Solovyev's utopia and Dostoevsky's hopes; but the notion of such a free Christian theocracy of love, under the exclusive hegemony of the Orthodox Church as both a social and a religious institution, is not taken with the same literality in both cases. It is Ivan Karamazov who expresses precisely such an idea, and argues for the validity of the view that "the Church ought to include the whole State, and not simply occupy a corner of it, and, if this is, for some reason, impossible at present, then it ought, in reality, to be set up as the direct and chief aim of the future development of

Christian society!" (14: 56–57). Ivan is wholeheartedly supported by the erudite Father Paissy, and he is accused by the Western liberal Miusov of advocating ultramontanism, that is, the Roman Catholic doctrine of the political subordination of the state to the church, which is not the same as the moral-spiritual transformation of the state into a church.

But Father Zosima, while agreeing that the aim of human society should be such a transformation, takes this goal out of history and places it in an eschatological perspective. Christian society, he says, though not now ready, "will continue still unshaken in expectation of its complete transformation from a society almost heathen in character into a single, universal, and all-powerful Church. So be it! So be it! Even though at the end of the ages, for it is ordained to come to pass!" (14: 61). Dostoevsky, of course, uses this argument over state and church to reveal the inner split in Ivan between his reason and his moral sensibility; but contemporaries immediately associated it with Solovyev. The noted historian Bestuzhev-Ryumin, often a dinner companion at the grand dukes', remarked in his diary: "Reading . . . *The Brothers Karamazov* (what a marvelous character is the elder! And what an agreement with Solovyev, Vl.). There's a mutual influence here."[28]

Another point of contact between the philosophies of the two men may be seen in the analysis of the three temptations of Christ, which appears both in the *Lectures on Godmanhood* and then, a year later, in the Legend of the Grand Inquisitor. For Solovyev, however, Christ's subjection to these temptations is part of the gradual cosmogonic process through which God actualizes Himself within the confines of time and earthly life, and affirms His willingness to accept human limitations on His divine powers. There is no hint of the intense pathos of freedom expressed in Dostoevsky's treatment of this same great theme, nothing similar to the sublimity of his emphasis on Christ's rejection of the temptations in order to safeguard the liberty of human conscience and preserve humankind from enslavement to external and material forces. Nor is there anyone like the Grand Inquisitor in Solovyev's version, that is, a former believer whose heart has been torn because of humankind's suffering and who is willing to use any means to allay its anguish.

To what extent the final shape of the Legend may have emerged from the intimate colloquies of the novelist and the philosopher can only remain a matter for conjecture; one should not forget the many anticipations of the Legend that had already appeared in the *Diary of a Writer*. Nonetheless, there is one passage in Solovyev so directly relevant that it must be cited. "Several years ago in Paris," he writes, "I heard a French Jesuit give the following reasoning: 'Of course, at present no one can believe the greater part of the Christian dogma, for example, the Divinity of Christ. But you will agree that civilized society cannot exist without a strong authority and a firmly organized hierarchy; only the Catholic Church possesses such an authority and such a hierarchy; therefore, every enlightened man who values the interest of mankind must side with the Catholic Church, that is to say, must be a Catholic."[29] Such a passage would not have taught Dostoevsky anything he had not long since believed and written about Roman Catholicism; but the frank affirmation of atheism from such a source, encountered exactly at this moment, may well have helped to shape the form in which the Legend finally was cast.

Dostoevsky was beginning to make notes for the first chapters of *The Brothers Karamazov* during the very months that Vladimir Solovyev was giving his lectures. It is thus time now to follow the creation of this great work as it came into being.

## CHAPTER 21

# A New Novel—and a Feuilleton

Dostoevsky set down the first notes for *The Brothers Karamazov* in mid-April 1878, but he had been thinking about this new novel all through the spring. The first two parts (designated as Books 1 and 2) were written quite rapidly, and he appears to have launched on this last and greatest of his works with much less trouble than his earlier ones. There is no evidence of the struggle to define the outlines of the action, to concretize the personality traits of the main characters, or to provide them with a biography and establish their relations to one another. There is no abrupt change of perspective or that sudden emergence of new characters which, in the past, had required extensive recasting and rewriting and sometimes even beginning again from scratch. At a later stage he added what is now Book 9, but this fitted neatly into the sequence of the action and required no major revision, though the work became lengthier than had been anticipated. In general, however, he would seem to have known where he was going from the very start.

Because an important aspect of *The Brothers Karamazov* is its relation to the literary tradition, his sources will be examined here more extensively than was necessary for earlier novels. A good deal of information is given by references in his notes as well as in his correspondence, much of which constitutes a running commentary on the novel.

2
---

From a letter in March 1878 to a schoolteacher named Vladimir Mikhailov, it is clear that Dostoevsky had been thinking about his book even earlier than the first dated notes. He asks Mikhailov, as someone deeply concerned about the problems of education in Russia, to provide him with information about children and share some of his observations about them. Dostoevsky had been much impressed "by the fact that you [Mikhailov] love children, have lived with children a lot, and that even now you spend time with them." As he explains, "I have conceived and will soon begin a long novel" in which "children will participate a lot."[1] But Mikhailov disappointingly replied in April that he was so terribly depressed, both for personal reasons and because of the condition of Russian society, that "he simply was unable to write."[2]

Dostoevsky thus failed to obtain any information from Mikhailov; and the same situation exists for us in relation to the early stages of his novel. It is one of the anomalies of the Dostoevsky canon that the notebooks for the lengthiest of his novels, *The Brothers Karamazov*, should be the scantiest of them all. To quote Edward Wasiolek, who edited all the notebooks for English translation: "The notes for *The Brothers Karamazov* are not those of germination, quest, and discovery. Dostoevsky knows what he is writing about; the subject is firm, the identities of the chief characters are fixed, and the basic dramatic situation is clear. Some of the scenes sketched in the notebooks are almost identical, even linguistically, with those of the final version. The differences between notes and novel are differences between schematic representation and dramatic embodiment, summary and amplification, between ideas and the dramatization of the idea."[3]

How is one to explain this marked difference between the notes for *The Brothers Karamazov* and those for earlier books? The extant notes resemble those that he usually had made at a relatively late stage in composition; and one possibility is that his notebooks containing the first groping searches for characters, plot intrigue, and underlying theme have simply disappeared. Anna Dostoevsky deposited a specially bound book for safekeeping in the Russian State Bank on June 14, 1899, and in her will stated that the book "contained material for the novel, *The Brothers Karamazov*." She withdrew this deposit from the bank and took it with her to Sochi and then to the Crimea in 1917, and its whereabouts since then have never been discovered.* Whatever this volume contained, however, it may not have included earlier notebooks. Anna also stated that the rough drafts of the manuscript and the galleys of *The Brothers Karamazov* "contain almost no variants with that of the printed text."[4]

There is also another possibility that must be taken into account. Perhaps it was not necessary for Dostoevsky, when he sat down to write *The Brothers Karamazov*, to go through the usual preliminary process of finding his subject, characters, and ideological leitmotifs. The note-

---

* Some effort was made in 1992 to trace the history of these manuscripts. According to documents and press accounts in 1920, they were found in the possession of a Lieutenant Vronsky, who was arrested when trying to get into Sochi without proper papers. They then turned up in the keeping of an I. A. Kandeli, but disappeared for another two years, when rumors surfaced that they were in Tiflis and available for sale. But then they vanished again. There are persistent suggestions that they came into the possession of Stefan Zweig, a notorious collector of Dostoevskiana, through his influential Russian friends such as Maksim Gorky; but no evidence for this possibility really exists. Zweig's library was scattered when he left Austria in 1934, and T. A. Ornatskaya suggests that efforts to trace it might prove useful. T. A. Ornatskaya, "K Istorii Utrati Rukopis Romana *Bratya Karamazovi*," *Dostoevskii: Materiali i Issledovaniya*, 10 (1992), 181–193.

books for *A Raw Youth* had already outlined certain essential elements of this future novel—the three brothers, one an atheist and egoist, another a socialist and fanatic, and the third representing the younger generation. As for the main plot action—the indictment and conviction of Dimitry Karamazov—it had already been outlined in the note "drama in Tobolsk," recalling Dostoevsky's innocent prison companion D. I. Ilinsky, falsely convicted of the murder of his father. This note also contains the love rivalry of two brothers for the same woman, anticipating that of Ivan and Dimitry for Katerina Ivanovna; and the rivalry over Katerina Akhmakova between father and son in *A Raw Youth* becomes that of Dimitry and Feodor Karamazov over Grushenka. The character of Ilinsky, the young officer who squandered his money on drink and debauchery without exhibiting any truly evil propensities, provided a schema for the creation of Dimitry Karamazov. As for Ivan, he is "the atheist and egoist" whose revolt against God's world Dostoevsky had first depicted in the tubercular Ippolit Terentyev of *The Idiot*, doomed by illness to an early death, and whose outrage had been sharpened and refined in the suicide letter of "The Sentence." It is thus entirely possible that he relied on such material, already contained in his notebooks or in earlier works, without feeling the need to make a completely fresh start.

Moreover, other essential components of what became *The Brothers Karamazov* had long existed. As he was completing *The Idiot* at the end of 1868, he informed Apollon Maikov of a plan for a major new novel, to be called *Atheism*. Its chief character would be a middle-aged Russian of respectable society who, after suddenly losing his faith in God, goes out to seek a substitute among the various competing groupings and sects (including Polish Catholic zealots and the Khlysty, the sect of the Flagellants) and finally "finds Christ and the Russian God." He speaks of this work in the most exalted terms as "his final novel," whose completion would allow him to die in peace.[5] A year later, at the outset of his work on *The Devils*, this plan evolved into a novel to be called *The Life of a Great Sinner*; and although this project was never undertaken as such, parts of it entered significantly into each of Dostoevsky's last three works.

The *Life* had been conceived as a work in several volumes, whose second book would be set in a monastery. The adolescent "great sinner" would come into contact there with a monk based on the historical figure of the mid-eighteenth-century Saint Tikhon Zadonsky, a character who, as Dostoevsky wrote Maikov, would at last allow him to provide "a majestic, positive, holy figure" to Russian literature.[6] Tikhon exercises a great spiritual influence on the maturing great sinner in a manner foreshadowing that of Father Zosima on his youthful acolyte, Alyosha

Karamazov: "The limpid stories of Tikhon about life and earthly joy. Of the family, fathers, brothers. Extremely naïve, and because of this touching, stories of Tikhon, of his sins toward those close to him, vanity, mockery ('how I should like to change all that now,' Tikhon says)" (9: 138). This note provides the core of what will later become the teachings of Father Zosima as recorded by Alyosha.

The narrative technique of *The Brothers Karamazov* also had been adumbrated in Dostoevsky's "great sinner" notes on a novel to be written in the form of a *zhitie*, that is, the hagiographic life of a saint: "N.B. Tone (the narrative is a *zhitie*, i.e., even though it comes from the author's pen, it is concise, not sparing with explanations, yet presented in scenic forms[)]." Many of these lives, such as that of Saint Tikhon Zadonsky himself, were written by disciples and attendants of the clergymen they revered, and the vita of Father Zosima, composed by Alyosha Karamazov, follows this traditional pattern. Moreover, Dostoevsky's remarks refer not just to Tikhon but to the great sinner as well, whose life should also be a *zhitie* without actually emerging as such. "Yet it is also important that the dominant idea of the vita be apparent, i.e., even though the whole dominant idea may never be explained in so many words. . . . The reader still ought to know at all times that the whole idea is a pious one. . . . The selection of the subject matter of the narrative should continuously convey a certain *something* . . . and the man of the future [which is exactly how Dostoevsky views Alyosha] is to be exhibited for everyone to see, and to be placed on a pedestal" (9: 132–133).

This tonality of an implicit saint's life is transposed from the great sinner to the career of Alyosha Karamazov and, indeed, to the style and attitude of the narrator of the book. In setting out to fulfill his long-cherished ambition to create a novel focused on the loss and recovery of religious faith, Dostoevsky could thus draw on what he had already sketched in a preliminary fashion and had thought about for many years.[7]

The notes for Books 1 and 2 of *The Brothers Karamazov* not only reveal a clear grasp of the actions and characters portrayed, but also refer to incidents and details that will occur much later. In the very first note, for example, Dostoevsky reminds himself "to find out whether it is possible to lie between the rails under a railway car when it passes over you at full speed." The schoolboy Kolya Krasotkin boasts of such a feat in Book 10, published two years later, and there is also a reference to "Philaret whose body began to stink," which anticipates the scandal caused by the malodorous putrefaction of Father Zosima's body in chapters also published considerably later (15: 199). Most of the notations are simply suggestive or shorthand reminders to Dostoevsky of what he will develop more fully in the text, but there are a few passages dealing with miracles, and with Alyosha's attitude toward them, that touch on major themes.

"He [Alyosha] understood that knowledge and faith are different and contradictory, that if there are other worlds and if it is true that man is immortal, that is, if man himself comes from other worlds, then there is a tie with these other worlds. There is such a thing as a miracle. And he thirsted for a miracle. But here the Elder [Zosima] and his saintliness, the holy relic" (15: 201). Father Zosima himself will later assert that humankind possesses "a precious mystic sense of our living bond with . . . the highest heavenly world" (14: 290), but this bond is no longer linked by him with the question of miracles. Indeed, since miracles provide, as it were, a material and tangible proof of the existence of the supernatural, Dostoevsky treats this "thirsting" for miracles as a sign that such faith is not yet pure and perfect. Without denying the possibility of miracles, which would have been inconsistent with faith, Dostoevsky as a writer is always very careful to remain within the conventions of realism. He either refers to miracles as having occurred in a time and place so remote as to obviate the question of verisimilitude, or he leaves open the possibility for a mundane explanation of what some might consider to be "miraculous."

### 3

These initial notes also document the strong influence of Friedrich Schiller on the conception of *The Brothers Karamazov*.[8] Schiller had produced an extremely powerful impression on Dostoevsky in his childhood and youth, and the German playwright, poet, and philosophical essayist had been equally important in Russia for Dostoevsky's entire generation. To be sure, the name of Schiller is often pronounced in Dostoevsky's works with an ironical or satirical edge, and the accusation of "Schillerism," or the use of a Schillerian phrase like "the sublime and the beautiful," became symbols for an impractical or purely abstract idealism, reflecting either genuine naïveté or some sort of moral self-deception or self-evasion. While these animadversions on "Schillerism" have sometimes been taken as expressing a loss of admiration for the writer himself, it is a mistake to interpret a literary device as an ideological rejection.

In 1861 Dostoevsky wrote that "the Russians ought to regard Schiller in a very special manner, for he was not only a great universal writer, but—above all—he was our national poet" (19: 17). Fifteen years later, he repeats that Schiller "soaked into the Russian soul, left an impression on it, and almost marked an epoch in the history of our development" (23: 31). This conviction helps to explain why he portrays the influence of Schiller as having unmistakably "soaked into" the souls of all the major characters of *The Brothers Karamazov*. Dimitry, Ivan, and even the lecherous old Feodor Pavlovich are all capable of citing Schiller by heart. Alyosha refers indirectly to Schiller's play theory of art, and a few lines of Schiller are woven into the speech of the defense attorney Fetyukovich. A Schillerian atmosphere envelops *The Brothers Karamazov* from the first page to the last, and contributes a good deal to the heightening of its poetic quality.

This Schillerian ambiance is indicated in the notes only by a laconic sentence, "Karl Moor, Franz Moor, Regierender Graf von Moor" (15: 209). These words link the novel with Schiller's sensational first play, *The Robbers* (*Die Räuber*), which Dostoevsky had been taken to see by his father at the age of ten. This first contact with Schiller, as Dostoevsky wrote in the very last year of his life, "affected my spiritual development very favorably."[9] In the early 1840s he had collaborated with his older brother Mikhail on a translation of *The Robbers* into Russian, and he thus possessed a very thorough knowledge of the text. Its importance for his novel is highlighted by a mocking sally of the old Karamazov. "That is my son," he says of Ivan, "flesh of my flesh, and most beloved of my flesh! He is my most respectful Karl Moor, so to say, while this one who has just come in, Dimitry Feodorovich, against whom I am seeking justice from you [Father Zosima], is the unrespectful Franz Moor—they are both out of Schiller's *The Robbers*, and so I am Regierender Graf von Moor. Judge us and save us!" (14: 66).

The ironic distortions contained in this speech illustrate the manner in which Dostoevsky plays his own variations on Schillerian themes. No one could be less like the tenderhearted, weak-willed, and abused Graf von Moor than the cynical, domineering, and rapacious Feodor Pavlovich; but they are structurally related as fathers involved in contentions with their sons. Karl Moor revolts against both the legal and the moral order because he believes (falsely) that his father denied him love and forgiveness; and although he resembles Ivan thematically because of his revolt against God's universe on behalf of a suffering humankind, his fiery, explosive temperament brings him much closer to Dimitry as a character type. The cold-blooded intellectual Ivan, unable to love humanity except in the abstract and from a distance, is similar to Franz Moor, Schiller's Machiavellian villain, whose rationalism causes him to doubt God and immortality and ruthlessly to order the murder of his father.

Not only does *The Robbers* depict the tragedy of a family split by deadly rivalry between father and sons, as well as between the sons themselves (Karl and Franz Moor both desire Amalia, just as Dimitry and Ivan are rivals for Katerina Ivanovna), it also poses the theme of parricide in even more lurid terms. For Schiller, as for Dostoevsky, the sacredness of family ties and family feeling is the temporal reflection of the eternal moral order of the universe. It models God's relation to his creation, and since the negation of the first involves the destruction of the second, it is the atheist and blasphemer Franz Moor who pours scorn on the belief that family ties create mutual obligations of love. "I've heard so much chatter about a so-called love based on blood ties that it's enough to make the head spin of any orderly man who looks after his affairs. But even more—it is your father! He gave you life, you are his flesh, his blood—so for you he must be holy!"[10]

Franz's rationalism, like that of Ivan, dissolves these primordial ties and obligations of family love in words that are echoed in the trial scene: "I must ask you, why did he create me? Surely not out of love for me, who first had to become an I?"[11] The remainder of this speech, and a later one along the same lines, are transposed by the defense attorney Fetyukovich into the argument that "such a father as the old Karamazov cannot be called a father and does not merit the name. Filial love for an unworthy father is an absurd and impossible thing." An unworthy father inevitably impels his son to ask the questions: "Did he really love me when he begat me? Did he beget me for my sake? He did not know me, nor did he know my sex at that moment, at the moment of passion, perhaps intensified by wine" (15: 171).

If *The Robbers* shows the morally disintegrating effects of such rationalism on the instinctive moral roots of human life, it also reveals, like *The Brothers Karamazov*, the strength of these roots in the human spirit and the inevitability of their triumph or revenge. Franz Moor's cynicism, at the last, gives way to a frenzied fear of eternal damnation for his manifold crimes; and he dies in a fit of terror, pleading for a prayer from his old servant. Karl Moor, appalled by the disastrously inhuman consequences of his revolt against the social iniquities of his time—a revolt that only unleashes the worst passions among his robber band, and includes the murder of a child—finally surrenders voluntarily as a sacrifice to the eternal moral order whose avenging instrument he had wished to become. Ivan, too, is appalled by the consequences of his own intellectual revolt as he sees his ideas put into practice by Smerdyakov; and like Franz Moor, he is tormented by the impossibility of resolving the inner conflict between his skeptical rationalism and the religious faith supporting a moral order. Dimitry follows Karl Moor in being led through suffering to a sense of pity and compassion for others, and an acceptance of the technical injustice of his conviction as a sacrifice for the temptation of parricide that he had willingly harbored in his breast.

*The Robbers* is not the only play of Schiller's that exercised an important influence on *The Brothers Karamazov*. We shall return later to speak of *Don Carlos*, also translated by Mikhail Dostoevsky with his brother's aid. Many references to Schiller's poetry are scattered throughout the text as well, and used to deepen and widen its thematic range. A cosmic and historical-philosophical dimension is provided for Dimitry's inner conflict between the ideal of the Madonna and that of Sodom by fragments of Schiller's "Das eleusische Fest" ("The Eleusinian Feast") and the famous "An die Freude" ("To Joy"), which also inspired Beethoven in his triumphant Ninth Symphony. Less overtly, Ivan's rebellion also moves within the orbit of the Schillerian lyric. When he hands back his "entrance ticket" to the promise of an ultimate eternal harmony of God's world because the price to be paid for it is too high in human suffering, Ivan repeats the gesture and uses the same terms as the protagonist of Schiller's poem "Resignation":

> Empfange meinen Vollmachtsbrief zum
>     Glücke!
> Ich bring' ihm unerbrochen dir zurucke;
> Ich weiss nichts von Glückseligkeit.*

Of even greater importance are the two lines from Schiller's "Sehnsucht" ("Longing"), which, placed at the beginning of his Legend of the Grand Inquisitor, condense an important aspect of the religious theme. The Russian version, by the poet V. A. Zhukovsky, is a free translation of Schiller that fits more closely into Dostoevsky's context than does the original. The literal sense of the Russian is:

> Believe what the heart tells you,
> Heaven does not make any pledges.

### 4

Dostoevsky's notes also contain additional traces of his reading. Anna Filosofova had loaned him two books in May, one by the radical publicist V. V. Bervi-Flerovsky, already mentioned in connection with the Dolgushintsy, and the other a copy of *L'Ancien Régime* by Hippolyte Taine, the first part of his multivolume *Les Origines de la France contemporaine*. "The idiot [Alyosha] explains to the children the position of mankind in the tenth century (Taine)." This notation was never used, nor was another interesting reference: "He [the idiot] explains the socialism which is rising, new people. Maxime du Camp, the negative, not the positive. Russia is the positive—Christians" (15: 202). Maxime du

---

* Translated literally, this reads: "Take back my permit to happiness! / I bring it back to you unopened / I know nothing of bliss."

Camp, now forgotten as a writer and best known as a friend of Flaubert's, had written a four-volume denunciation of the Paris Commune, *Les Convulsions de Paris*, with which Dostoevsky was apparently acquainted.

Aside from such literary references, two other works have plausibly been linked with the *The Brothers Karamazov*. Both are by George Sand, another writer, like Schiller, whom Dostoevsky adored in his youth and about whom he had recently written admiringly in the *Diary of a Writer*. He read a good bit of Sand again in the summer of 1876, along with his wife, who remarks that "I gradually read all of their novels [Balzac and Sand] as part of an impromptu course to acquaint [me] with French literature."[12] During their walks the couple discussed her reading, with Dostoevsky explaining the finer points. At this time he was also working at an article (now lost) on Belinsky and reviving his memories of the literary-cultural atmosphere of the early 1840s, when the novels of George Sand stood at the center of all the ideological discussions in intelligentsia circles.

The researches of V. L. Komarovich have brought out quite convincing resemblances between George Sand's novel *Mauprat* (1837) and the plot action of *The Brothers Karamazov*.[13] The novels are of course quite different in tonality—Sand combines a typically sentimental love story with Gothic trappings and various quaintly idyllic rustic characters—nor can there be any question of comparing their artistic stature; but notable similarities exist all the same. Both contain a crucial scene in which a young woman is on the point of being forced to sacrifice her honor, but at the last moment her presumptive ravisher renounces his villainous intentions; and this leads to an emotional entanglement between them in the future. In both, the young man is falsely accused of a murder, and tried and convicted on what seems unimpeachable circumstantial evidence. Sand's heroine, Edmée, like Katerina Ivanovna, reverses her testimony—but to exonerate rather than condemn. The surprise introduction of a letter written by the accused to the heroine, and prefiguring the crime, also plays a major role in the condemnation. A comparison of parallel passages from the trial scenes makes very clear that some of the plot elements of *Mauprat* had left ineradicable traces in Dostoevsky's memory.[14]

Another work of George Sand's, her quite unprecedented religious-philosophical novel *Spiridion* (1839), foreshadows *The Brothers Karamazov* on a deeper thematic level. *Spiridion* takes place entirely in a monastery and consists largely of conversations between a dying monk, Alexis—the inheritor of a semiheretical religious tradition handed down to him by his dead mentor, Spiridion—and a young novice named Angel. Alyosha Karamazov is also constantly called "angel," and his adoring relation to Father Zosima is very similar to that of Sand's young disciple to *his* saintly teacher, also regarded with great suspicion by monks of a more orthodox persuasion. Like Father Zosima, Alexis is on the point of death; and he conveys his dying words to Angel, whom he calls "the son of my intelligence," exactly as Zosima confides the story of his life and his teachings to Alyosha, whom he considers the reincarnation of his brother Markel. Of course Dostoevsky had long nourished the project of writing a work set in a monastery, and it could well be that *Spiridion*, which he had read on publication, encouraged such an intention at the very outset of his literary career.[15]

There is very little action in *Spiridion*, but at the novel's climax the monastery, located vaguely somewhere in Italy along the Mediterranean coast, is invaded by the armies of the French Revolution. Alexis is put to death, but he forgives the rampaging soldiers in his last words because he sees them acting "in the name of the *sans-culotte* Jesus," on whose behalf "they are desecrating the sanctuary of the Church." Jesus was thus for him a revolutionary figure, a *sans-culotte*, whose ideals of liberty, equality, and fraternity were being fulfilled in practice, though entirely unconsciously, by the marauding soldiers.[16] Here we have the Utopian Socialist Christ of Dostoevsky's own early manhood—the semi-secularized Christ whose social ideals he had never renounced, but whose aims, particularly in Russia, he had long ceased to believe could be attained through revolutionary violence.

On opening the tomb of Spiridion after Alexis's death, Angel finds buried with him the Gospel of Saint John (Dostoevsky's own favorite, from which he took the epigraph for *The Brothers Karamazov*), Jean de Parme's *Introduction to the Eternal Gospel* (a book written by a disciple of Joachim di Fiori, denounced as a heretic and burned in 1260), and Spiridion's own commentary on this latter text. He had interpreted it as a prophecy predicting the arrival of the reign of the Holy Ghost—the reign of the principles represented by the French soldiers, who were thus accomplishing God's will. His spiritual guide passes on this doctrine to Angel, who will take it into the world—just as Father Zosima passes on *his* teachings to Alyosha. Both mentors hold out the equally messianic hope (if only, for Father Zosima, at the end of time!) of a total transformation of earthly life into a realm of Christian felicity.

Aside from such similarities, it is impossible to read *Spiridion* without being struck by the concordance between some of Alexis's utterances and Dostoevsky's own most cherished convictions. No theme was more important for him in the 1870s than that of the first temptation of Christ, the turning of stones into bread. To yield to this temptation could only result in the surrender by humankind of its freedom of conscience; and Sand expressed the same thought forty years earlier. "This gigantic task of the French Revolution was not, it could not be," Alexis declares, "only a question of bread and shelter for the poor; it was something much loftier. . . . it had to, it still must . . . fully accomplish the task of giving freedom of conscience to the entire human race. This soul that torments me, *this thirst for the infinite* which devours me, will they be satisfied and appeased because the body is safe from want?"[17]

Nor was anything of greater moment for Dostoevsky than to emphasize the supreme significance for human life of the prospect of eternity, and to combat the atheistic confinement of existence to the limits of life on earth. Here too we find Alexis eloquently expressing the same longing, the same innate human need to transcend terrestrial boundaries. "And . . . when all the duties of men among themselves are established through a system of mutual interest, will this suffice for human happiness? . . . No matter how peaceful, how sweet one supposes life on earth to be, will it suffice for the desires of mankind, and will the world be vast enough to encompass human thought?" Alexis also proclaims one of Father Zosima's most sublime moral principles: the universal responsibility of each for all.[18] One can well understand why Dostoevsky felt no hesitation in stretching the literal, historical truth when, in his obituary of her in the *Diary*, he spoke of George Sand as "one of the most perfect confessors of Christ."

5
———

Even while engaged in writing the first chapters of *The Brothers Karamazov*, Dostoevsky found time to respond to a request from Victor Putsykovich for a contribution, however small, to *The Citizen*. What he sent was a feuilleton entitled "From the Summertime Strolls of Kuzma Prutkov and His Friend," his last attempt at a broad satire, based on an evidently fantastic incident, similar to what he had essayed in *The Crocodile* in 1864. Just as he had done there, he ridicules some of the intellectual fads of the moment; and one can view this unpretentious work as a lighthearted replay of one of his favorites themes—the inability of "science" and reason to cope with the mysteries of the universe and of human life.

The title refers to a comic character created by two other writers, Aleksey Tolstoy and Aleksey Zhemchuzhnikov. Kuzma Prutkov incarnates the essence of bureaucratic stupidity and mediocrity, and some of his majestically platitudinous utterances have become part of the Russian language. Dostoevsky shared a widespread appreciation of Kuzma Prutkov's embodiment of complacently blinkered officialdom, and he invoked the name to characterize "all the strolling public from high society" who witnessed an extraordinary occurrence on the evening of July 27.

As this public was peacefully sauntering around Elagin Island, a favorite haunt for Petersburgers wishing to enjoy some fresh, country air, the astonished pedestrians suddenly saw a Triton emerging from a pond (though no pond existed in that location). No matter! A Triton loomed up through the surface, "a Russian water sprite with moist green hair on his head and a beard." He gamboled about, dove up and down, uttered shrieks, laughed, splashed in the water, "and produced the usual impression on such occasions." The ladies rushed to feed him bonbons, but this "mythological character, remaining true to his antique nature," immediately indulged in such "body movements" that the ladies rushed away with shrill laughter, shielding their almost nubile daughters from the sight. At which the Triton shouted after them some "unceremonious expressions" that only increased their hilarity (21: 248).

Speculations aroused by the Triton's appearance and behavior immediately began to make the rounds (21: 248). One was the theory that the Triton was really that "great Yid" Disraeli, acting on behalf of British interests and trying by this playful attraction to lessen the warlike ardor of the Russians against the Turks. Lord Beaconsfield, however, was known to be in London, and it was really doing too much honor to the Russian bear to assume that the stately dignitary would disport himself in a Russian pond even for such a political purpose (21: 249). Another view is attributed to Mikhail Saltykov-Shchedrin, who was said to wish to include the incident in his monthly column for *Notes of the Fatherland.* He believed the Triton to be a police officer on special, undress duty, assigned to lurk in the pond "after our springtime disturbance in Petersburg" (a reference to the trial of Vera Zasulich) and report on any suspicious conversations.

The article ends with some pseudohistorical information on the Triton, parodying the work of a recent historian. The Triton actually came to Russia from Germany at the time of Peter the Great, along with pygmies and a famous court jester, and had been living in the pond ever since. Why he should have resurfaced on July 27 remained a mystery, and all the eminent Russian scientists who flocked to the pond to investigate—a list of their names is given—seeing nothing but circles in the water, refused to believe that the Triton had ever appeared. Efforts to coax him from the depths remained futile. However, the friend of Kuzma Prutkov who signs the article believes that the emergence of the Triton, short-lived and unique though it was, has at least enlivened public opinion, and this he considers in general to be a very good thing (21: 248–251).

Besides amusing himself in this fashion, Dostoevsky also found time in mid-July to visit a young adolescent in Staraya Russa, who has left a touching account of his one encounter with the famous novelist. Dostoevsky had heard about A. A. Alexandrov from no less a personage than

Mikhail Katkov, who, as he had told Anna in a letter from Moscow, patronized a lycée that "maintains orphans from the poorest classes and gives them an education."[19] Alexandrov, one of the students, had fallen ill and been sent to Staraya Russa for the curative baths there. He had been placed in charge of a doctor whom the Dostoevskys knew well, and Katkov had asked that they check on whether he was being looked after properly.

Alexandrov, later a noted journalist, recalls: "I was a completely unknown, ill, shy, unassuming boy, a passionate lover of literature and secretly writing poems. . . . I was already familiar with Dostoevsky as a writer, having had the time to read several of his novels and ardently admiring him." Dostoevsky immediately placed the embarrassed youngster at ease, and Alexandrov recalls that "at my first glance at him, at the first sound of his voice, there remained not a shred of my shyness and agitation. Within two minutes, it even seemed to me that he and I were old and good friends, even that we were very close." Unlike others, Alexandrov did not find his stare disturbing or upsetting. Even though he looked at a person very penetratingly, what his eyes conveyed "was not a stern judgment nor a mean, cold mockery, but something encouraging and affectionate, cordial and gentle, inspiring openness and trust."[20]

Dostoevsky began the conversation by blaming the tardiness of his visit on a recent epileptic attack from which he was still recovering. "Did I have any knowledge of the illness?" he asked. "Hearing that I knew a good deal about it from his own depiction in *The Idiot*, he shifted to literary activity and said that he was now very absorbed in *The Brothers Karamazov*, in which he wished to portray several new types; he did not as yet know whether he would succeed in doing them full justice. His conversation about this was quite brief and surprisingly unassuming and direct, without any shade of affectation, without any effort to place himself on a pedestal and display himself in full posture." He also questioned the young man about himself, and he "consoled and encouraged me greatly, predicting a quick recovery and good health in the future." Alexandrov never saw him again, but this single meeting exercised a formative influence on his life. It was one of those events, he writes, that "deeply penetrate the soul, taking full possession of it for the rest of one's days" and shaping one's worldview.[21]

## 6

On returning to Petersburg on October 3, the Dostoevskys moved into a new apartment for reasons that Anna Grigoryevna poignantly explains. "When we returned to Petersburg that autumn, we could not bring ourselves to go on living in that apartment, filled with memories of our dead child, and we moved to [the new one] where my husband was fated to die two and a half years later." Anna also dwells on the shadow that continued to hang over their lives because of Alyosha's death. "No matter how my husband and I strove to submit to God's will and not grieve, we could not forget our darling Alyosha. All that autumn and the following winter were darkened by desolate memories. Our loss had the effect on my husband (who had always been passionately attached to his children) of making him love them even more intensely and fear for them even more."[22] All this time Dostoevsky was working on *The Brothers Karamazov*, and the very problems raised in the impassioned declamations of Ivan—the unmerited suffering of little children and the difficulty of reconciling oneself to God's will because of their torments—thus lay at the very center of his own life and feelings. Whatever the literary and journalistic material on which he drew, the moving power of these pages certainly derives from his own inconsolable bereavement.

In the beginning of November 1878, with the first two books of *The Brothers Karamazov* completed, he traveled to Moscow to make the final arrangements for publication. Even though he had taken an advance from the *Russian Messenger*, he had been informed that the continued existence of the publication was in doubt and that nothing could be definitively settled at least until October. Indeed, when he received a proposition in the summer from another editor to publish his new novel, rumors of which were making the rounds in literary circles, he did not reject the possibility out of hand. The offer came from Sergey Yuriev, a well-known publicist and editor of Slavophil leanings and a friend of Vladimir Solovyev, who had been told by him (erroneously) that Dostoevsky's new novel was almost completed. Yuriev was planning to start his own periodical, and of course a novel of Dostoevsky's would be a very great asset. In reply, Dostoevsky explained that, while already committed to Katkov in principle, "he and I have not reached a final decision about my novel for reasons . . . which in essence consist of extraneous conditions that do not concern the literary essence of the novel." He promised to answer Yuriev one way or the other in the fall.[23]

On arrival, he rushed off to see Katkov and, not finding him at home, left a message that he would return at eight o'clock. In a reaction that calls to mind such characters as Devushkin in *Poor Folk* and particularly Mr. Golyadkin in *The Double*, who are continually frightened at what might be considered their effrontery, Dostoevsky then began to worry whether he had not committed a *faux pas*. "Since I'm the one who set the time and said I would come," he worriedly confides to Anna, "and he wasn't the one doing the inviting, I'm afraid he may refuse to see me. . . . That would be very humiliating for me, and at the present time

(6 P.M.) I'm in the most awful mood." But when he arrived punctually at eight, he was received "wonderfully and courteously," even though the editor "was obviously busy."[24]

The two men talked for an hour about the novel, whose first installment Katkov had not yet had time to read; but he assumed that Dostoevsky would surely "be here [in Moscow] five days or so or a week," and he promised to get in touch with him within that time. This assumption, however, confronted Dostoevsky with a dilemma. He had not planned to stay away from home for so protracted a period, but he decided it would be tactless and somewhat demeaning to attempt to accelerate matters. If he called on Katkov every day to inquire, he confided to Anna, "it would be as though I were rushing him and dying of impatience to know what he will say about my work." He thus resentfully resigned himself to waiting, though his sensibilities were somewhat soothed by the arrival of Katkov's family, who, though presumably having come to say good-night, "obviously wished to see me." On leaving, Dostoevsky suggested a further advance of two thousand rubles, but Katkov could provide him now with only one thousand; the remainder would come "in about three weeks."[25]

He still remained ruffled, however, by Katkov's failure to inquire about his own timetable, and also by the lack of a dinner invitation for the next day. The eighth of November was well known to be Katkov's name day, and Dostoevsky assumed it would be celebrated by a party for a large assemblage of guests. "Since he not only did not invite me, but himself mentioned the two or three days of waiting without concerning himself with what I would be doing in the meantime, I have decided definitely not to offer my congratulations today. That would mean simply fawning on him." Some of Dostoevsky's pique may be explained by another passage from the same letter. "In any event, I need to wait here fruitlessly . . . and I'm so terribly lonely, Anya, so lonely that I miss you all."[26]

Dostoevsky occupied himself with making the rounds of the booksellers who served as outlets for his publishing firm, picking up whatever proceeds had come in from sales. A conversation with one of these tradesmen fortunately prevented him from making a genuine *faux pas*. This middleman, described as "very courteous and in his usual way crafty and confused [presumably about sales figures]," asked Dostoevsky whether he had yet gone to pay his respects to Katkov. "And when I said no, he added: 'How can you not have gone? There was such a gathering there, a prayer service and so on.'" His words evidently caused Dostoevsky to think twice about his own incautious decision. Deciding to present himself after all, he was received with great civility as a guest of distinction and immediately taken in tow by Mme Katkova, who engaged him in a lengthy conversation before ushering him into her husband's study. And there, after a few moments, "in walked the governor-general himself, Prince Dolgoruky, wearing four stars and an emerald order of Saint Andrey."[27]

Dostoevsky was amused at the patriarchal style of the prince who, on being introduced to him, harrumphed exactly like a dignitary of the old régime: "'Of course, such a celebrity, hm, hm, hm,'—absolutely like forty years ago, in the good old days." Even though placed on a window seat behind Katkov, the editor was careful to include him in a conversation with the prince and thus "showed himself to be an extremely decent person." Katkov personally escorted Dostoevsky to the door on departure, and the latter noted with relief that the dining room table was set only for the family and their immediate relatives. That afternoon he also called on N. A. Lyubimov, an ex-professor of physics who was coeditor and would be in charge of publishing *The Brothers Karamazov*. Dostoevsky, again received very hospitably, was told by Lyubimov that he would try to "pester" Katkov into hastening his reading. Invited to stay for dinner, he was surprised by the sumptuousness of the meal. "If they eat that way every day," he remarks to Anna, "they must live well."[28]

To amuse himself, he went to the opening of a new play of Ostrovsky's, *The Girl without a Dowry* (*Bespridannitsa*). Otherwise, "in the evening I stay in my room and read the trials" (that is, the verdicts handed down in court proceedings involving crimes of greater or lesser gravity).[29] Such trials frequently served as sources for his inspiration; and in this instance one case probably furnished an important detail for *The Brothers Karamazov*. It involved a landowner who was accused of having, in the course of a quarrel, dragged his opponent out of a clubroom by his beard, an act considered particularly insulting and dishonoring. Dostoevsky used it for the altercation between Dimitry Karamazov and Captain Snegiryov, climaxed by the captain also being dragged out of a tavern by his wispy beard and humiliated before the eyes of his heartbroken son Ilyusha.

A day later, Dostoevsky heard from Lyubimov that Katkov had just leafed through his manuscript and turned it over to his coeditor, who had "read the first third and found it all very original." Impatient to obtain his advance and return home, he learned that the money could come only through the cashier, "who so orders everyone about that with regard to the paying out of money, even Katkov is entirely dependent on him." To make matters worse, Katkov had fallen ill and on the next day could not receive Dostoevsky at all. "He sent a man to tell me to come to see him in a couple of days." This meant further delay, and Dostoevsky assures Anna, who might be suspicious, that "of course he is not making excuses. He is really sick." He himself was suffering from constipation and censoriously declares that "everything is vile," including Ostrovsky's play. "I am terribly lonely here," he complains again, "unbearably so," and there has also been "the most rotten weather." Visits to his relatives provided the only bright spots in his unending catalogue of grievances, though even with them the talk turned on Alyosha's death (about which his Moscow family had remained ignorant). Nor was his temper improved by visits to the lawyers who were haggling over the details of the never-ending litigation concerning the Kumanina estate. Katkov's cashier, at long last, came to the hotel with the advance, and he was able to leave Moscow two days later after tidying up his other affairs.[30]

The strain of this trip probably took its toll on Dostoevsky's health. At the end of the month he felt it necessary to visit his physician, Dr. von Bretsall; and on some sheets of paper that also contain notes for Book 3 of *The Brothers Karamazov*, he scribbled a letter to a group of students at the Institute of Civil Engineering who had invited him to attend a musical-literary benefit evening. He rarely refused such invitations, but now felt forced to do so. "The doctor, as it turned out," he wrote them, "has advised me not to leave the house for several days. I ask you most earnestly also to convey my regrets to your comrades. . . . I would very much not wish them to doubt how highly I value their flattering attention."[31] This note was never sent because the newspaper *Voice* announced that the event had been canceled "for reasons that were not foreseen" (a euphemism very often used for some official interdiction). But the ingratiating tenor of Dostoevsky's apology indicates how highly he valued his reputation as someone who sympathized with the aspirations of the younger generation.

## CHAPTER 22

# The Great Debate

The first installment of *The Brothers Karamazov* was published on February 1, 1879. A few days later, the governor-general of Kharkov—a cousin of the anarchist-revolutionary Peter Kropotkin—was killed, and in March an unsuccessful attempt was made on the life of the new head of the secret police, the successor of General Mezentsev, as he was driving in his carriage through the center of Petersburg. In April, a revolutionary acting on his own, but with the knowledge of the Populist Zemlya i Volya, attempted to assassinate the Tsar as he was taking his morning walk in the Winter Palace grounds. The would-be assassin, Alexander Solovyev, was a bad shot, missed his mark, and was publicly hanged in May.

It was in this atmosphere of murder and mayhem that Dostoevsky's novel was being read. It was also the atmosphere in which he and Turgenev appeared together at benefit readings and banquets to represent the two extremes of the great debate that was taking place in the minds and hearts of all educated Russians—the debate between a despotic Tsarism, unwilling to yield an inch of its authority, and the longing for a liberal, Western-style constitution that would allow for greater participation of the public in government affairs.

2

The new year of 1879 was ushered in by the Dostoevskys with a family party. His younger brother Andrey, then in Petersburg, was invited, along with all four of Andrey's grown children and their families living in the capital. He did not forget either to send greetings to his youngest brother, Nikolay, along with the monthly stipend of seven rubles that he had begun to provide for him in 1878. Andrey wrote a friend that he often sees his brother, who "is greatly occupied with the publication in the *Russian Messenger* of his new novel."[1] The galleys of the first two chapters had just arrived, and he enlisted the help of Elena Shtakenshneider with the proofreading. She returned the proofs along with a request to send back a borrowed copy of Zola's *L'Assomoir*. Dostoevsky, as we know, was familiar with other Zola novels and evidently wished to keep up to date; *The Brothers Karamazov* contains ironic references to the physiologist Claude Bernard, the main source of Zola's theories about heredity and environment, and Dostoevsky was writing his own family novel, with its defense of the freedom of the human personality, in direct competition with Zola's deterministic Rougon-Macquart series.

Just how intensively he was working at this time may be judged from the dispatch of the next section of *The Brothers Karamazov* (Book 3, Chapters 6–11) on January 31, even before the first installment had been published. The extremely scanty notes for this part consist largely of a paragraph sketching the sophistical reasoning of Smerdyakov as he sneers at Foma Danilov and justifies a renunciation of Christian faith under torture by Muslim captors. In his letter to N. A. Lyubimov, Dostoevsky explains that this material concludes "the entire first part of the novel," which will consist of three books. The first two books of Part 1 had been printed in January, and he asked that the third appear "in the February issue . . . in its entirety, without a break, without running it over [into March]. . . . the harmony of artistic proportion will be quite destroyed" if it is split in two. He apologized for not being able to provide anything new for the March issue ("it's beyond me") but promised to send a new installment for April, which he requests should also be published as a whole.[2]

Dostoevsky rarely expressed satisfaction with what he had just written (usually he conveys a sense of disappointment), but in this instance he allows himself a moment of triumph. "I do not at all consider this third book, now being sent off, bad," he confides to Lyubimov. "On the contrary. I think it a success." As if surprised at his own reaction, he adds: "(Please forgive the slight boasting. Remember the Apostle Paul: 'People do not praise me, so I'll start praising myself')."[3] Readers can share some of Dostoevsky's satisfaction over chapters that contain Dimitry Karamazov's "Confessions of a Passionate Heart," in which the rowdy rake and regimental brawler suddenly reveals himself as a person of greater moral-spiritual sensibility than could possibly have been imagined. They also contain the splendid scene in which the dishonored but spirited temptress Grushenka turns the tables on her patronizing "benefactress" Katerina Ivanovna. *The Brothers Karamazov* will rise to greater heights as the book proceeds, but these pages are enough to explain his unusual sense of accomplishment.

3
———

Just about this time, in the winter of 1878–1879, a young woman named E. P. Letkova-Sultanova (who had aspirations to a literary career that would later be realized, but was still only a *kursistka* in the higher education courses for women) wrote in her diary about a meeting with Dostoevsky at one of the famous "Fridays" of the poet Yakov P. Polonsky. Polonsky had invited her to come that particular week and promised that "this time there will be something especially interesting." On arriving, she was surprised both by the overflow of overcoats and overshoes in the entrée and by the strange silence that prevailed despite such evidence of a considerable crowd. Advancing into the drawing room, she saw everyone, dignified gentlemen and smartly dressed ladies, clustered around one of the three windows and intently listening to someone talking. Suddenly she caught a glimpse of the speaker and realized that the voice was that of Dostoevsky, whom she recognized even though never having seen him before. Her first impression did not correspond at all to the dominating and imperious image she had formed in her mind; he was shriveled, rather short, and struck her as someone who looked *vinovatyi*, that is, as if he felt guilty about something. The window before which he stood gave onto Semenovsky Square, where in 1849 he and other members of the Petrashevsky circle had been brought to undergo the ordeal of a mock execution before being sentenced; and he was holding the other guests spellbound as he relived the past. It was Polonsky who had led him to the window and asked if he recognized what he saw. "Yes! . . . Yes! . . . Really! . . . How could I not recognize it," he had replied.[4]

Letkova then offers her recollections of Dostoevsky's words, which came tumbling out in a stream of spasmodic sentences. He evoked the freezing coldness of the morning as he and his fellows stood without outer garments, and the horror that overcame them as they heard the death sentence being pronounced. "That just could not be! *It could not be!* . . . It could not be that I, amidst all the thousands who were alive—in something like five to six minutes would no longer exist!" The appearance of a priest with a cross, which they all kissed (though refusing confession), convinced them that death was inevitable. "They could not joke even with the cross! . . . They could not stage such a tragicomedy!" Dostoevsky remembered that a feeling of numbness and torpor overcame him after a certain point: "Everything seemed insignificant compared to this last terrible minute of transition to somewhere, . . . to the unknown, to darkness"; and this numbness did not lift even after he learned that his life, and that of the others, had been spared. He began to speak of Nikolay Grigoryev, who had gone mad under the torture of these moments—and then he fell silent! Polonsky approached him to break the tension and said consolingly, "Well, all this is past and gone," inviting him to drink some tea with their hostess. "Is it really gone?" Dostoevsky asked mysteriously.[5] Letkova and Polonsky interpreted this question, uttered under his breath, as a reference to his epilepsy; but it can be given a wider sense. He may have been alluding to the indelible impact of this confrontation with death, which exercised such a decisive transformatory effect on the remainder of his days.

Letkova was deeply moved by Dostoevsky's words, uttered in breathless bursts that revealed all his inner agitation as one image after another came flooding back; and she describes him, when he finished, standing "as if a waxen figure: sallow and pale, eyes sunken, lips bloodless, smiling but with a look of suffering."[6] Her opinion of Dostoevsky up to that moment had been anything but favorable, and she tells of the heated discussions in her student group caused by each issue of the *Diary of a Writer*. It was generally agreed that his anti-Semitism was intolerable; nor could they endorse the warmongering chauvinism of his articles about the Russo-Turkish War, whose sacrifice in human lives now seemed so vain and futile. Letkova and her fellow students had unanimously detested *The Devils*, and they felt light-years removed from Dostoevsky's political tendency and ideas.

All this was forgotten, however, in the aftermath of what she had just heard. What now emerged before her mind's eye was "his entire sacrificial path: the torture of awaiting death, its replacement by prison camp [*katorga*], the 'House of the Dead' with all its horrors: the shackles never removed (even in the bathhouse), the filth and stench of the barracks, the relentless guards; and all this had been borne by this puny man, who suddenly appeared to me greater than everyone surrounding him." Everything else vanished into oblivion before this vision, and "a feeling of unbelievable happiness, the happiness one can only feel when young, took hold of me. And I wanted to throw myself on my knees and bow down to his sufferings."[7]

Letkova, to be sure, had just heard Dostoevsky himself reminisce about his past; but everyone had read *House of the Dead*, and the emotion she experienced was widely shared by all those who, at one public event or another, had listened to him read (usually from his own works). Her reaction thus helps to explain some of the astonishing responses called forth by Dostoevsky's presence on the platform before a mass audience—an audience that, in the majority and at a more sober moment, could well have been antagonistic to his politics. If it was true, as he untiringly maintained, that the Russian peasants particularly revered the suffering of their Christian saints who had endured martyrdom for their faith, then some of this reverence appears to have been transferred—by the new generation who once again accepted the value of suffering and self-sacrifice—to such a figure as Dostoevsky himself.

Shortly afterward, Letkova met Dostoevsky again at a celebration of the founding of the University of St. Petersburg. Many prominent writers took part, and Letkova was curious to ascertain how he would perform as a reader. What she heard surpassed all her expectations. "Before me," she wrote, "was again a great writer, suffering in his words not only for me, for us, but for everyone. When he read Pushkin's 'The Prophet,' it seemed that Pushkin had envisaged someone like him when he wrote: 'With my word, sear the hearts of men.'"[8] As the youthful sister-in-law of L. S. Makov, the minister of internal affairs, Letkova had met many well-known writers at his home, and on her way to the exit she ran into Ivan Goncharov and D. V. Grigorovich (the latter's role in Dostoevsky's life had become well known since the *Diary of a Writer*). P. I. Weinberg, always active in organizing such festivities, then approached the group and invited the young lady to come backstage, where the literary participants had gathered to partake of refreshments.

Among them was Dostoevsky, and she approached him timidly, wondering whether he would recall their earlier meeting. Rising from his chair, his first words, spoken "with a particular ironically amiable smile," were: "'I heard from Yakov Petrovich [Polonsky] that you write. . . . ' 'I'm getting ready to do so, Feodor Mikhailovich. . . . ' 'With fasting and prayers?' he said, still in the same ironical tone. 'Almost' [she replied]." He then somewhat unexpectedly continued to speak with seriousness: "'That's good. . . . That's what is necessary.'" At this point they were interrupted by Weinberg, who hurried up and, taking Dostoevsky's arm, said jovially: "Time to wet our whistles, Feodor Mikhailovich." The conversation backstage, where all the eminent guests were gathered, turned largely on the Balkan crisis, on the plight of the Slavic "brothers," and on the Russo-Turkish War. Most of the comments about the war were either hostile or disabused, but Dostoevsky said nothing. When Grigorovich, in what might be considered a direct jibe at Dostoevsky, asked loudly, with wrathful irony, "The Cross on Saint Sophia?" he simply rose and moved to the other side of the room.[9]

Everyone soon filed out to listen to a singer, but both Dostoevsky and Letkova put on their overcoats to leave; and as she approached him to say good-bye, he suddenly continued their conversation with this advice: "Never sell your soul. . . . Never work under constraint . . . because of an advance. . . . Believe me . . . I have suffered from this all my life, all my life I have written in haste. . . . And how much suffering this has cost me." He went on in this painfully confessional vein for some time, much to his listener's surprise, just as he had done with Vsevolod Solovyev some years earlier when comparing his own working conditions with those of Tolstoy. Letkova remarks that Dostoevsky was clearly in a very excitable state, probably caused both by the reading of Pushkin and by his distress at what he had just heard in the talk about the war. No doubt he must again have felt very isolated, just as when he had been exposed to the censure of his old friends; and this hostility released all of his pent-up emotions about the adverse economic conditions under which he alone, compared with all the others, had been forced to labor all his life. Letkova is quite right in perceiving that only an unusual state of inner agitation could explain why "he was able to speak so passionately and sincerely to a young girl completely unknown to him, and who came to him as a friend, a brother."[10]

4
———

Work on *The Brothers Karamazov* continued apace, and Dostoevsky was not only writing but also gathering information for future chapters. A letter from K. P. Pobedonostsev spoke of a visit from the Archimandrite Simeon (an archimandrite is the head of a monastery or a group of monasteries), who had brought information about the rituals of monastic burial to be passed along to Dostoevsky. This material would be used in Chapter 1 of Book 7, where a book of church ritual is quoted and the whole procedure of preparing the body is carefully described in all its details. He was always very meticulous about such matters, and felt it of first importance not to be caught in errors that would allow his critics to tax him with ignorance of the world he was depicting.

At the beginning of March, he was the victim of what Anna Dostoevsky called "an unpleasant experience."[11] Walking home one evening on his accustomed stroll and passing through a lower-class section of the city, he was approached by a person obviously the worse for drink, who asked for alms to relieve his hunger. Perhaps sunk in his own thoughts, Dostoevsky paid no attention—and was struck on the head by a blow that sent him sprawling into the street as the beggar shouted, "the well-fed do not believe the hungry." A policeman rushed to Dostoevsky's aid, and the culprit was collared a few blocks away as he tried to lose himself in the crowd. Refusing to press charges, a day or two later he attempted through K. P. Pobedonostsev to prevent the matter from coming before a court. But since a crime had been committed and a charge filed immediately, he was called to testify several weeks later. Claiming he could not identify the person who had struck him, he remarked that he could very well understand why a hungry man, whose appeal for help had been ignored, could become angry and strike someone who had remained totally indifferent to his plea. The judge, well known in the district for his sharp tongue, commented that if everybody behaved like Dostoevsky, "it would become impossible to take a stroll in Petersburg."[12]

Despite the disclaimer, the judge sentenced the prisoner to a month in jail, which, as Dostoevsky said, was a matter for the judge's conscience, and he left three rubles to be given to his aggressor on his release. Turning to the accused after the victim's departure, the judge shouted: "Do you know, you unhappy wretch, against whom you lifted your insolent fist? You struck down the greatest of Russian writers and the most kindhearted of the Russian people."[13]

A dinner invitation from Grand Duke Sergey for March 5, which arrived two days after the "unpleasant experience," could of course not be refused. Conveyed through D. S. Arsenyev, the letter informed him that by this time the grand duke had perused *House of the Dead, Crime and Punishment,* and the first part of *The Brothers Karamazov.* Hence he was even more eager, now being better prepared, to enjoy the benefits of Dostoevsky's conversation, of which he retained "a pleasant memory." At the table were also K. P. Pobedonostsev and Grand Duke Konstantin Konstantinovich, who made some comments about the evening in his diary: "Feodor Mikhailovich pleases me very much, not only because of his writings but simply because of himself. I questioned him about a passage in *The Idiot,* where he describes the feelings of someone condemned to death; I cannot understand how, not having experienced this—these terrible feelings could be so clearly and vividly portrayed. Dostoevsky himself was condemned, he was taken to the scaffold. . . . " Several days later, he again notes in his dairy: "I have obtained *The Idiot* of Dostoevsky. When you read his works, it's enough to drive you out of your mind."[14]

Even though invited to dine with younger members of the royal family for the purpose of broadening their minds and shaping their sensibilities, the anomalies of Russian society were such that Dostoevsky was still, as an ex-convict, under the surveillance of the secret police. To end this exasperating situation, he decided to use the considerable influence he could now muster. On March 10 he received a letter from Lieutenant-General A. A. Kireyev, an aide-de-camp of Grand Duke Konstantin Niko-laevich, the brother of the Tsar, obviously in response to efforts to acquaint some important personages with his plight. Kireyev informed Dostoevsky that he had spoken about his problem with L. S. Makov and that no obstacle existed to complying with his request; but it would be necessary to make the demand himself to the proper authorities. (It is amusing to note that he was also reminded not to forget to affix a sixty-kopek stamp.) The necessary document, written the same day, dispassionately outlines the facts of his promotion to officer in 1856 and the restoration of his civil rights. Dostoevsky concludes: "On hundreds of pages I have spoken, and still continue to speak, of my political and religious convictions. I hope that these convictions are such that they cannot give cause to suspect my political morality."[15] His name was thus finally stricken from the list of those on whom the Third Section was keeping a watchful eye, but he was, alas, destined to enjoy this freedom for only two more years.

Social obligations continued to pile up. On March 8 he received a visit from Anna Pavlovna Filosofova, ever busy with charitable endeavors and now arranging a reading for the Literary Fund. Turgenev, just returned to Russia, had been invited the day before, and she now solicited Dostoevsky's participation in the same event. The Literary Fund helped needy writers and artists, and Dostoevsky not only had enjoyed its largesse in the 1860s but also served as one of its officials. Such an event, which put him on display with numerous other literary and artistic celebrities, was likely to attract a considerable audience from the cultivated public (especially students), and of course he accepted.

Filosofova asked him to read the confessional monologue of Marmeladov from the early pages of *Crime and Punishment*, in which the abject drunkard painfully details all his iniquities but appeals, in a mosaic of citations from the Gospels, to the all-forgiving love of Christ for repentant sinners. But he "made a sly, sly face," and said: "'I'll read you something better.' 'What, what?' [Filosofova] asked him. 'I won't say.'" It was thus with "inexpressible impatience" that the impresario awaited the next evening's event, not only out of curiosity about Dostoevsky's choice but also because the reading would herald Turgenev's re-entry on the Russian public scene.[16]

Turgenev's return to Russia at this time developed into a major public event, which in effect amounted to a rehabilitation of his reputation among the radicals who had mercilessly repudiated him after *Fathers and Children*. His next novel, *Smoke*, had aroused even more hostility among all sections of the reading public because of the speeches of one character, who caustically denied that Russia had contributed anything of value to world culture except the samovar. *Virgin Soil*, his most recent work, presented a not unsympathetic yet disabused view of the Populist "going to the people" movement, and was generally considered a pathetic failure. Few champions had come forward to defend these later novels, as Dimitry Pisarev had done with *Fathers and Children*; and Turgenev's self-imposed exile, prompted in part by his desire to live near his beloved, the diva Pauline Garcia-Viardot, was also a means of escaping the implacable hostilities of Russian literary life. This absence from Russia had also injured his reputation. Even Anna Filosofova, surely more sympathetic to his reformist liberalism than to Dostoevsky's intransigent Tsarism, remarked: "I respect him less than Dostoevsky. Feodor Mikhailovich bears the traces of all the miseries of Russia on his skin, he has suffered through them and was tortured by all his convictions, while Ivan Sergeyevich became frightened and fled, and all his life he criticized us from the beautiful beyond."[17]

By the spring of 1879, however, the social-political situation in Russia had become intolerably tortuous because of the continuing assassinations. As a result, the return of the Europeanized liberal Turgenev, which led to public banquets and celebrations in his honor, assumed a special significance. The festivities in which he took part became symbols of the longing, which could not be expressed openly, for some concessions on the part of the iron-fisted, despotic government to the increasingly desperate radical youth. P. V. Annenkov, Turgenev's alter ego, commenting on the enthusiasm aroused by his appearance in Russia, wrote in April that a "complete rehabilitation has been occurring of the representatives of the 1840s, a public recognition of their services, and they are accorded a deep, classless, and typically Russian bow, even to the earth and to the point of prostration. It may be that the exploits of Nechaev, Tkachev, and tutti quanti have moved society to the side of the old development, beginning under the banner of art, philosophy, and morality; but however that may be—the present moment in Russia may be the most important of all that it has lived through these last twenty-five years."[18]

What Anna Filosofova tells us of Turgenev's reception by the audience at the reading for the Literary Fund amply confirms Annenkov's words. "The hall was filled to overflowing. The public awaited Turgenev. Everyone impatiently kept their eyes fixed on the entrance door [to the stage]. Suddenly Turgenev appeared. . . . It is remarkable what truly moved us all . . . everybody rose as one and bowed to the king of the [enlightened] mind. I recalled the episode of Victor Hugo when he returned from exile to Paris [at the end of the Franco-Prussian War] and the whole city poured into the streets to greet him."[19] Other writers also participated, but all eyes were fixed on Turgenev and Dostoevsky. Their juxtaposed presence on the stage brought together the opposing poles of Russian culture. As the writer B. M. Markevich put it: "What is there in common, I asked myself . . . between such an 'incurable Westernizer,' to use Turgenev's own words about himself, and that eternal seeker of the *genuine* Russian truth—whose name is Dostoevsky?"[20] Both were competing, on these nominally apolitical occasions, for the minds and hearts of the public on whom would depend the future; and everyone felt, like Annenkov, that their country was facing its greatest social-political crisis since the Crimean War.

## 5

Dostoevsky and Turgenev had long nurtured a personal hostility toward each other. If we are to believe one account of their meeting backstage at this charitable gathering—an account based only on hearsay and left by a partisan of Turgenev's—the latter preserved the proprieties. Always the urbane gentleman, he stretched out his hand to Dostoevsky—who refused to reciprocate and turned away. This snub might well have occurred (Dostoevsky could be unpardonably rude), but if the incident did occur, it took place out of sight of the audience.[21] Turgenev read early in the program, and chose a story, "The Bailiff," from his classic *A Sportsman's Sketches*. Dostoevsky always preferred to read in the second half, after the intermission, and he then produced the "something else" he had spoken of. What he read was the as yet unpublished "Confession of a Passionate Heart," which elicited a sensational response. As Anna Filosofova wrote, "He read that part where Katerina Ivanovna takes the money to Mitya Karamazov, to a beast who wishes to show his superiority to her and to dishonor her because of her pride. But then the beast calmed down and the human being triumphed. . . . Good God! How my heart beat . . . is it possible to convey the impression left by the reading of Feodor Mikhailovich? We all sobbed, everyone was filled to overflowing with some sort of moral ecstasy." And she continues: "For me, that evening, Turgenev somehow vanished, and I almost did not hear him."[22]

Also present in the audience was Varvara Timofeyeva, Dostoevsky's one-time assistant and confidante at the time he was editing *The Citizen*. She had not met him since, and in fact had come "in order only to see and hear Turgenev"; but she emerged from the hall "with the impression left only by Dostoevsky." Indeed, her account does not mention Turgenev's reading at all, though she describes Saltykov-Shchedrin's "bilious, lazily-snappish, and monotonous voice" as he read his satirical story. The appearance of Dostoevsky moved her deeply, and memories of the many hours they had spent together came surging back when she heard his voice again. "He read a chapter from *The Brothers Karamazov*," and for her—as well as, in her opinion, for many others—it was "something like the revelation of our destiny. . . . It was the anatomical dissection of our ailing, gangrenous corpse—a dissection of the abscesses and illnesses of our stultified conscience, our unhealthy, rotten, still serflike life."[23]

Not only Timofeyeva but the whole audience was stirred to its depths, and she depicts an unknown young man sitting next to her who "shivered and sighed" and "blushed and turned pale, convulsively shaking his head and clenching his fists, as if restraining himself with difficulty from breaking into applause." When the applause finally came, it was deafening, lasting for fifteen minutes and calling him back to the stage five times. The emotions that Dostoevsky had succeeded in communicating may be expressed in the words of Timofeyeva: "We suddenly felt that not only was it unnecessary 'to wait' [a reference to the story of Saltykov-Shchedrin], but that really it was impossible to hesitate for a single moment. . . . It was impossible because each moment brings us closer to eternal darkness or to eternal light—to the evangelical ideals or to bestiality."[24] Dostoevsky's apocalyptic sensibility could not have been better attuned to the tension-ridden mood of his audience, torn by conflicting emotions over the desperate duel between the ever-more oppressive régime of the Tsar-Liberator, now fighting for his life, and the revolutionaries who had begun by invoking the example of Christ and were now committing murder. No wonder Turgenev no longer held center stage alone. Nikolay Strakhov wrote to Tolstoy: "I was very pleased that the public greeted Dostoevsky with the same enthusiasm as Turgenev." To the poet A. A. Fet, he also wrote: "Dostoevsky for the first time received an ovation that made him equal with Turgenev. He was very happy."[25] When Dostoevsky visited Filosofova the next day, even before he could ask her, in a trembling voice, whether the evening "had gone well," she threw her arms around his neck and began to weep with deep feeling.[26]

## 6

Hostilities between the two writers came out into the open on March 13, at a banquet organized in Turgenev's honor by the group of Petersburg literati to which Dostoevsky belonged. Some of the speeches made in Turgenev's honor, which came to more than twelve, were embarrassingly fulsome. D. V. Grigorovich, for example, said that if one were to place Turgenev against a window, light would shine through him as through a piece of crystal, "so pure is he morally among us." The famous lawyer V. D. Spasovich, whom Dostoevsky had so severely castigated in the *Diary of a Writer*, hailed the guest of honor in equally complimentary terms; but he also spoke of "the midnight hour" of Russian social life in which they were all living. Turgenev, however, intervened with the remark that "there is no night where can be found Lev Tolstoy, Goncharov, Dostoevsky, Pisemsky."[27] Dostoevsky was also mentioned in another speech, in which the assemblage was asked to raise their glasses "in honor of all the notable creators of the 1840s."

At last Turgenev rose and greeted what he saw as the new reconciliation of the generations, whose separation he had once depicted in *Fathers and Children*. The moment had come, he affirmed, when the split could at last be healed because both generations now accepted "an ideal that is not remote and not unclear but well defined, one that can be realized, that perhaps is quite close, and in which they are unanimously united."[28] Such Aesopian language was of course necessary under the circumstances, but everybody knew that he was referring to the possibility of "crowning the edifice" (as the Russians liked to call it), that is, the granting of a Western-style constitution by Alexander II that would, by creating a representative democracy, complete the process begun with the liberation of the serfs.

This speech elicited a thunderous ovation, and when others flocked to congratulate the speaker, Dostoevsky chose this moment to precipitate a scandal enshrined in the annals of Russian literary history—a scandal that may well have been caused by his dismay at the news of the latest assassination attempt earlier that day. He too approached Turgenev, but, instead of some approving words, shot out the question: "Tell me now, what is your ideal? Speak!" Instead of replying, Turgenev merely lowered his head and waved his arms helplessly, but others present said loudly: "Don't speak! We know!" Some voices apparently supported the query, but they were drowned out by Turgenev's partisans. According to one account, he did not follow the advice of his admirers to keep silent but replied that "the issue concerned a constitution." Dostoevsky's unseemly behavior, which as one journal put it broke "the general tone of veneration accorded to Turgenev," was of course more than an outburst of ill humor or, perhaps, envy.[29] He was, and always had been, an unrelenting opponent of the notion of a Russian constitution, on the ground that it would benefit only the educated portion of the population rather than the peasantry. Mikhailovsky had advanced much the same view in his notable article on *The Devils*.

If Dostoevsky attempted to pin Turgenev against the wall by his inopportune question, he himself, on the same occasion, was confronted by a similar dilemma. Two young journalists from *Nedelya* (*Week*), a journal with pronounced Populist sympathies, took the occasion to ask Dostoevsky why his new novel was appearing in the journal of Mikhail Katkov, with whose repressive right-wing politics they simply assumed he could not be in accord. This conversation was overheard by another guest, L. E. Obolensky, as well as by Dostoevsky's old friend Apollon Maikov, who went home in a rage to write a letter that was never sent. But a draft has been preserved, and it allows us to understand why Dostoevsky's replies should have aroused such indignation in the breast of someone who, despite occasional friction, had proven to be a staunch friend.

In answer to the journalists' challenge, Obolensky reports, "Dostoevsky began heatedly to justify himself by explaining that he had to support and feed his family, and that other journals with a more sympathetic tendency would not print him."[30] What upset Maikov was that he appeared to be apologizing for publishing in Katkov's pages. With all the poetic eloquence at his command, Maikov begins his protest by expressing distress at the testimonials offered to Turgenev. "Falsity and untruths, self-preening and stupidity, one and the same topic, in a word, all the madhouse of the Petersburg press with Spasovich in the lead. . . . Turgenev's concluding words startled and frightened me . . . something like that, in my view, is the beginning of the end." (There is some possibility that Turgenev had spoken more openly of "crowning the edifice" in his speech, but then modified his words for the printed version quoted here.) But despite his indignation at the reigning mood of liberal reformism at the banquet, Maikov asserts that the greatest blow struck at him that day, which caused his heart to flinch, was delivered by no one other than Dostoevsky—a blow that struck "in the very holy of holies of my soul, [and] shook my faith in a person."[31]

Summarizing in three points what Dostoevsky had said to the journalists, Maikov gives a fuller account than Obolensky: (1) Katkov paid better than other journals and gave larger advances; (2) the official censorship was easier to cope with and almost nonexistent; (3) and no Petersburg journal would touch his work. "I quite expected a fourth part," Maikov wrote, "and was ready and eager to support you—but you evaded the issue."[32]

What Maikov had hoped for was that "you, as independent," would have proclaimed "your sympathy and respect for Katkov, even agreement on many important points, if only on those that were spoken about at the banquet—[but] you stepped aside, said nothing." Maikov felt betrayed because Dostoevsky, who had just created a public hubbub by posing a question to Turgenev that implied his own alignment with opponents of reform like Katkov, in private conversation with Populist sympathizers refused to acknowledge this allegiance. "What?" Maikov exclaimed. "Because of money you print with Katkov? Really, that's not serious, it's not so. What's this? Recantation? As Peter recanted? For what reason? For fear of the Jews? For popularity? Perhaps this showed me one example of how you acquire the trust of the young! Hiding the most important from them, toadying to them!"[33] Such accusatory words would have certainly put an end to the friendship; but they were never sent, and relations between the two men remained apparently unchanged.

Still, the questions raised require some answer. Was Dostoevsky concealing the truth of his convictions, as Maikov charges? In fact, Dostoevsky had never agreed with Katkov's advocacy of harshly repressive policies. He had told him so, though very diplomatically, as far back as the late 1860s after the attempt on the life of the Tsar by Dimitry Karakozov. Both Dostoevsky and Katkov were antiradicals and loyal supporters of Tsarism, but their opposition to the idea of revolution did not mean that they agreed politically on how it should be fought. The liberal reformism of Turgenev that had aroused Dostoevsky's ire was of course anathema to Katkov; but it was equally rejected, even if for different reasons, by the radical Populists. Like Dostoevsky, they were primarily concerned with the welfare of the peasantry, and his two questioners obviously felt that he was closer to them on this issue than to Katkov. Moreover, in refusing openly to ally himself completely with Katkov, who had advocated that the government take the harshest measures to suppress the radicals, he was simply remaining faithful to his own belief that such merciless policies supplied no answer to the agonizing problems facing Russian society. However, in refusing to acknowledge *any* agreement with Katkov there was unquestionably a certain evasiveness in his replies.

## 7

The evening on behalf of the Literary Fund had been such a huge success that Anna Filosofova decided to repeat it a week later, and she gained the consent of both writers to appear again. Just how important such events were for Dostoevsky in general, and at this moment in particular, may be judged from what occurred two days after the Turgenev banquet. On March 15 he received a dinner invitation from Grand Duke Konstantin Konstantinovich, who wrote graciously that "you will meet people you already know, and to whom, like myself, your presence will provide great satisfaction."[34] An invitation from the royal family was not easily to be refused; but Dostoevsky did not hesitate to inform the grand duke that he found it "absolutely impossible for me to fulfill your wish and take advantage of your so flattering invitation."[35] He explained that, because his name had appeared on the program of the benefit, his cancellation would oblige the organizers to refund the money to the public. Since Turgenev and other notables were also on the program, this excuse hardly holds water; but no offense was taken at his lack of deference.

The second benefit for the Literary Fund only continued the competition between the two writers. Dostoevsky had chosen to read "The Confession of a Passionate Heart" again; Turgenev selected another story, "The Wolf," but also appeared in a special event that terminated the program. He and the ravishing young actress M. G. Savina, for whom he had come to nourish a superannuated passion, were to perform scenes from his play *A Provincial Lady* (*Provintsialka*). Dostoevsky's reading was electrifying as always, and S. A. Vengerov has left an account of the effect he always produced. All the other writers, Vengerov remarks, read quite well (except for Saltykov-Shchedrin and Polonsky), and yet "the listeners did not lose their sense of their own ego; they reacted to what they heard in one way or another. . . . But when Dostoevsky read, the listener—just like the reader of his novels of nightmarish genius—lost his 'I' completely and fell utterly under the hypnotic power of this emaciated, unprepossessing, elderly man, with his piercing gaze fixed somewhere in the distance and burning with mystic fire: that same fire, perhaps, which once blazed in the eyes of the Archpriest Avvakum [the leader of the Old Believers, who was burned at the stake]."[36]

Thunderous applause greeted him at the close; he was called back twenty times by the enraptured public, and a bouquet of fresh roses was brought to the stage and presented by "a young beauty" (the daughter of Anna Filosofova). Marya Savina, who wrote about this event thirty years later, recalled that he seemed nervous with the tribute and did not know what to do with the flowers. Unaccustomed to being honored in this way, he juggled them nervously for a while and then deposited them behind the curtain. Turgenev, who also received a bouquet (but not, apparently, of fresh flowers), bowed gallantly to those presenting it, and seemed much more at ease. The climax of the evening occurred when, after the performance by Turgenev and his charming partner, the audience insisted that both Turgenev and Dostoevsky return to the stage. The two not only came forward but, to the roaring delight of the crowd, shook hands firmly. It was as if, in face of the menace hanging over the future of the country, the intelligentsia audience wished to see their own spiritual authorities united rather than divided. It was as if they wished to heal the rift made public at the banquet—which of course had quickly become common knowledge—and had succeeded in doing so at least externally. But the pact would break down the next year, when both men participated in the dedication of a monument to Pushkin in Moscow.

## 8

Turgenev left Russia shortly afterward, encouraged to do so by a request from the authorities, who had become upset over the social-political implications of the public demonstrations in his honor. He and Dostoevsky met again, however, just a day after the second Literary Fund evening, in the salon of Countess Sofya Tolstaya. Whether they exchanged anything more than a few perfunctory words is not known; but present also was Vicomte Eugène Melchior de Vogüé, an aspiring young French *homme de lettres* then in the diplomatic service and stationed in the French embassy in St. Petersburg. He had laboriously acquired a fluent command of Russian during his first two years there, married into the highly placed Annenkov family (his wife was a lady-in-waiting to the Tsarina), and moved assuredly in the cultivated circles of the capital. Having immersed himself in Russian literature, the vicomte was of course familiar with the works of Dostoevsky; and he has left some observations of their meetings, especially valuable because they come from a neutral foreign observer. Dostoevsky's face "was that of a Russian peasant, a true *muzhik* of Moscow: the flattened nose, small eyes blinking under the arched eyebrows, burning with a fire sometimes gloomy, sometimes gentle; a large brow, mottled with indentations and protuberances, the temples receding as if shaped by hammer blows; and all these features drawn, contorted, collapsed onto a painful mouth. Never have I seen on a human face such an expression of accumulated suffering. . . . His eyelids, his lips, all the fibers of his face trembled with nervous tics."[37]

Some of their conversations have been preserved for posterity by de Vogüé in his pathbreaking study, *Le Roman russe*, which introduced the great Russian writers to the Western world. "Literary discussions with Dostoevsky," he remarks with quiet irony, "ended very quickly; he stopped me with a word of prideful compassion: 'We possess the genius of all the peoples and also have our own; thus we can understand you and you cannot understand us.'" Much the same opinion, if less laconically, had been expressed in the *Diary of a Writer*. Following this reminiscence, the well-bred de Vogüé appealingly asks pardon of the deceased Dostoevsky's shade, because "I am trying today [in his book on Russian literature] to prove the contrary."[38] The worldly Frenchman was also entertained by his opinions about Western Europe, which he found to be "of an amusing naïveté." One evening he spoke of Paris "as Jonah must have spoken of Nineveh, with biblical fire." What he said was: "A prophet will appear one night in the Café Anglais and will write three flaming words on the wall; and that will be the signal of the end of the old world and Paris will collapse in blood and fire with everything of which it is proud, its theaters and its Café Anglais." De Vogüé could only raise his eyebrows at this tirade against the Café Anglais, "that inoffensive establishment," which Dostoevsky seemed to consider "the umbilical cord of Sodom."[39] Little did Dostoevsky know that the elegant French diplomat he was hectoring would, six years later, be primarily responsible for making his name familiar among cultivated European readers.

In a letter to Victor F. Putsykovich, who had recently quit his editorship of *The Citizen* and wished to become a foreign correspondent for Katkov's journal, Dostoevsky writes happily that "*The Brothers Karamazov* is producing a furor here—in the palace, among the reading public, and at public readings, which however you'll see from the newspapers."[40] A few days later, writing from Moscow, Putsykovich replied: "Your novel is creating the same furor here as in Petersburg." His letter, of which only an extract is available, also contains some reference to a criticism of the published chapters made by Katkov in conversation. "The observation of Katkov," he writes, "referred only to the extreme realism—two to three chapters. He does not at all deny the artistic importance of these chapters, but only said that you developed them needlessly in such a way that he must, because of them, hide from his daughters the entire second part."[41] In the past, Katkov had insisted that Dostoevsky rewrite the initial version of the chapter of *Crime and Punishment* in which Sonya reads to Raskolnikov the New Testament pages describing the raising of Lazarus; but no such editorial ukaze was handed down to the author who had now become such a dominating figure in Russian cultural life.

In mid-March, *Voice* contained an account of the trial of two foreigners, a couple named Brunst, who were accused of mistreating their five-year-old daughter in a monstrous fashion; and Dostoevsky used some of its details (the smearing of the child's face with excrement) in Ivan Karamazov's rebellious vituperation against God for creating a world in which such outrages were possible. Unfortunately, another trial at the time also attracted his attention, that of nine Georgian Jews accused of murdering a young girl in the Kutais district of that region. The girl had disappeared on the eve of Passover, and although the blood libel was not mentioned in the indictment, there had been much discussion in the Russian press, including *The Citizen*, as to whether in fact "fanatical [Jewish] sectarians" kidnapped and killed Christian children to obtain their blood for ritual purposes at this time of year. Everyone thus knew what the charge involved, and it says much for the reformed Russian judicial system that the Kutais Jews, against whom there was no evidence at all, were acquitted on March 17. An appeal to a higher court a year later met with no more success.

Unfortunately, simply judging from the newspaper accounts, Dostoevsky came to an opposite conclusion. Writing to Olga Novikova, whose contributions to the English press earned her the title of "the M. P. from Russia," he said: "How disgusting that the Kutais Jews are acquitted. They are beyond doubt guilty. I'm persuaded by the trial and by everything, including the vile defense by Alexandrov, who is here a remarkable scoundrel—'a lawyer is a hired conscience'"[42] P. A. Alexandrov had defended Vera Zasulich, of whose guilt there had been no question at all, and this may have influenced Dostoevsky's judgment. But it is shocking and unforgivable to see him accepting the possibility of the blood libel while totally disregarding the lack of evidence against the accused. This bit of news too, alas, becomes part of *The Brothers Karamazov*.

It is little wonder that *The Brothers Karamazov* was causing a furor among the Russian reading public. Not only was Dostoevsky's artistic mastery so triumphantly self-evident, but the thematic issue that the book posed—whether murder to destroy a monstrous evil could morally be justified—was placed before the same readers practically every time they opened their newspapers. One official after another fell victim to the revenge of the Populists, who had in effect declared war on the Tsarist régime; and on April 2, as noted earlier, an attempt was made on the life of the Tsar himself. In 1866, when Alexander had escaped assassination, there had been a huge outpouring of national support for the government and widespread rejoicing at the Tsar's good fortune. Nothing even remotely similar occurred this time. As a government commission noted two months later, "especially noteworthy of attention is the almost complete failure of the educated classes to support the government in its fight against a relatively small band of evildoers. . . . They [the educated classes] are to some extent waiting for the results of the battle."[43] Dostoevsky had been almost hysterical on hearing of the failed assassination in 1866, and we may presume that he was also upset this time as well; but there is no firsthand account of any reaction. However, one episode in the memoir literature has been plausibly linked to this event.

M. V. Kametskaya, the daughter of Anna Filosofova, recalls hearing the doorbell of their apartment ring one day, and when she went to greet the visitor, there was Dostoevsky, "embarrassed, apologetic, [who] suddenly understood that all this was not necessary. He stood before me, his face drained of color, wiping the perspiration from his brow and breathing heavily from having hurried up the stairs. 'Is Mama home? Well, God be praised!' Then he took my head in his hands and kissed me on the brow: 'Well, God be praised! I was just told that you had both been arrested!'"[44] A rumor had spread in the city that both mother and daughter had been taken into custody. Although Kametskaya does not specify the date of this visit, it has credibly been placed on the day of the assassination attempt.[45] Indeed, it would not be long before the authorities decided to put a stop altogether to the activities of Anna Filosofova. In November 1879 she was politely but firmly requested to go to Wiesbaden, where she often vacationed, and not to return. Alexander II told her husband that it was only in gratitude for his services that she had not been sent to a much less pleasant place of exile.

Work on *The Brothers Karamazov* of course continued without a pause, but Dostoevsky nonetheless accepted two new reading dates in early April. One, which gave him particular pleasure, came from the Froebel

Society, a group dedicated to advancing the educational theories of Friedrich Froebel, the German inventor of the kindergarten system. Because the audience was to consist mainly of children, he read his "Little Boy at Christ's Christmas Party," and Anna Grigoryevna also brought their own children along to listen to their father. The day was a great success, and as his wife later wrote, he "stayed to the end of the festive occasion, walking about the halls with his children, watching the games, and enjoying the children's delight at sights they had never seen before."[46]

A few days later, on April 5, he read again for a benefit on behalf of needy (female) students of the Bestuzhev Higher Education Courses for Women. Many others read as well, but as was now customary he attracted the most attention and appreciation. The event was reported in the newspaper *New Time*, which commented that "the usual cordiality and warmth with which the female youth in general receive writers and artists was transformed into a triumphant ovation when F. M. Dostoevsky came on the stage." He read from *The Brothers Karamazov*, this time what seems to have been Chapter 2 of Part 2, Book 4, in which Ilyusha Snegiryov is attacked by the other schoolboys and bites Alyosha Karamazov's finger. According to the newspaper account, the "chief character was a nine-year-old boy suffering deeply for his father, a retired staff captain, who had been gravely insulted by one of the Karamazovs. The deeply dramatic subject, the fine analysis of psychic pulsations, the highly artistic truth in general—all this, in the masterly reading of Feodor Mikhailovich, stood out with unusual relief." The public listened so attentively that no other sound could be heard except his voice; everyone strained to hear each word, "and when the reading was over, the walls of the hall simply shook with the deafening outburst of enthusiasm."[47] A large wreath, crowned with fresh flowers, was brought to the stage, and the journalist adds that this tribute was only a fleeting shadow of the wreath woven for Dostoevsky in the hearts of the studious female youth.

Twelve days later he left for his rustic retreat in Staraya Russa, where he would be able to continue writing in relative tranquillity. The immense success of what he had already published only convinced him even more strongly, if conviction were necessary, that his book was touching an extremely aching nerve in the public. It was not merely a literary event but an inspired response to the moral complexities of the crisis situation that all literate Russians were then living through. And if Dostoevsky had any doubts on this score, they would have been dissipated by a letter he received from the influential editor Sergey Yuriev, who had just received permission to launch his new journal, *Russkaya Mysl* (*Russian Thought*). In urging Dostoevsky once more to contribute a novel, he wrote that it would not only "embellish his pages" but also serve to drain "the moral abscess which is eating up our life."[48]

## CHAPTER 23

# Rebellion and the
# Grand Inquisitor

Dostoevsky quit St. Petersburg for Staraya Russa on April 17, where he was to remain until July 17 hard at work on the continuation of his novel. He was then writing Book 5 of Part 2, "Pro and Contra," which contains some of the most powerful portions of the work—Ivan's rebellion against God's world and the Legend of the Grand Inquisitor. His life during this period was spent entirely tied to his desk, turning out chapter after chapter of his final masterpiece.

To avoid misunderstandings that might lead to objections, and perhaps efforts at censorship, each section he sent was accompanied by a letter of explanation. These provide a running self-commentary on Dostoevsky's ideological and artistic aims that are extremely valuable and quite unique in the corpus of his work. Elsewhere we have notes and letters, but nothing that elucidates the finished text in this fashion.

2

Outlining his future plans to N. A. Lyubimov on April 30, he apologizes for not sending in his next chapters, as he had promised, in early May; but he guaranteed them for no later than the fifteenth. "The problem is," he explains, "that this is now the culminating point of the novel for me. I need to do a good job of it, and for that not to be in too much of a hurry." He adds that "everything that follows from now on will be in finished form for each book. That is, no matter how small or large the fragment, it will contain something whole and finished."[1] Each section dealing with a specific character or thematic motif would thus be complete in itself.

Dostoevsky also includes some remarks about his friend Victor Putsykovich, who had left Russia for Berlin to escape from debtor's prison. Putsykovich was trying to publish an edition of the journal in Germany, and Dostoevsky tried (unsuccessfully) to enlist Katkov's support for the project. A few days later, he makes a very tentative promise to Putsykovich of a future contribution to the proposed journal. He also writes: "I'll ask you most earnestly not to reply to *Voice* and others, with regard to the Karamazovs and so on, in the first issues. Because it seems indecent to me to have a piece by me and to belabor others in my defense in the same issue. I'll answer *Voice*, but not until the fall, when I find out exactly who wrote it. I very much need that for the character of the reply."[2]

Dostoevsky also offers some other advice that throws an indirect light on his novel. Encouraging Putsykovich to include a rubric entitled "From the Life of Russians Abroad," he assures him that readers would be interested to learn about such expatriates, their "apathetic attitude toward Russia, laziness, nihilism, indifference, and so on, and most important their private lives." But he urges also that "if you write about Russian Nihilists, then you shouldn't criticize them as much as you should their fathers. Develop that idea, because the root of Nihilism is not only in the fathers, but the fathers are even worse Nihilists than the children. Our underground villains have a sort of vile ardor, while the fathers have the same feelings, but cynicism and indifference, which is even more vile."[3] Such remarks jibe quite well with the fashion in which Ivan Karamazov and his father are portrayed.

Seven days later, Dostoevsky sent off the first half of Book 5, "Pro and Contra"—a title suggesting that he may have originally intended this section to include not only Ivan's impassioned rebellion against God's world but also its refutation by Father Zosima. An exchange in the notes between Ivan and Alyosha intimates that the presentation of Ivan's revolt might have been immediately followed by the response of Father Zosima. "Is your Pater Seraphicus alive?" Ivan asks his brother.* "He is alive, and has written down his last word," Alyosha answers—a reply suggesting that this "last word" would very soon be forthcoming (15: 230). But Dostoevsky decided to reserve a separate book for Father Zosima's preachments, which are given in the form of a traditional *zhitie* written by Alyosha. Consequently, the "Pro and Contra" refers only to the inner debate taking place in Ivan himself between his recognition of the moral sublimity of the Christian ideal and his outrage against a universe of pain and suffering. And on a world-historical scale, by his questioning of the moral foundations of both Christianity and Socialism in the Legend of the Grand Inquisitor.

Dostoevsky knew that the powerful indictment of Ivan Karamazov would offend not only the religious pieties of many of his readers but those of his editors as well. He thus thought it wise to accompany his chapters with some explanatory comment. Calling Book 5 "the culminating point of the novel" (a designation that he would also give to later sections), he describes his intention as "the portrayal of the uttermost

---

* Ivan ironically uses this appellation, taken from the final scene of the second part of Goethe's *Faust*, to designate Father Zosima.

blasphemy and the seed of the idea of destruction in our time in Russia among the young people uprooted from reality, and, along with the blasphemy and anarchy—the refutation of them, which is now being prepared by me in the last words of the dying elder Zosima, one of the characters in the novel." He characterizes these convictions of Ivan "as a synthesis of contemporary Russian anarchism. The rejection not of God, but of the meaning of His creation. All of Socialism has sprung from and began with the denial of the meaning of historical reality and ended in a program of destruction and anarchism."[4]

In the 1860s, the negation of the existence of God had gone hand in hand with a rejection of Christian morality itself; but the effort to establish human life on entirely altered moral-social foundations, derived from philosophy and science, had now been abandoned. The Populists had restored the morality of the Christian God (whatever their own opinions about divinity) and were now applying it to His own creation. Indeed, they were rejecting "the meaning of historical reality" that He had presumably established in order to correct His work in the light of the very Christian principles He had proclaimed. Ivan's protest against God's world is thus couched in terms of the Christian value of compassion—the very value that Dostoevsky himself (or Prince Myshkin in *The Idiot*) had once called "the chief and perhaps the only law of all human existence" (8: 192). "My heroes take up the theme," Dostoevsky continues, "*that I think* irrefutable—the senselessness of the suffering of children—and derive from it the absurdity of all historical reality."[5] Reason or rationality cannot cope with the senselessness of such suffering; and Father Zosima will respond to it only with a leap of faith in God's ultimate goodness and mercy.

Invoking the considerable authority of K. P. Pobedonostsev, Dostoevsky attempts to counter in advance the usual charges made against him. He informs Lyubimov that, while some of the characters in *The Devils* had been criticized as pathological fantasies, they "were all vindicated by reality and therefore had been discerned accurately. I have been told by [Pobedonostsev] about two or three cases of arrested anarchists who were amazingly similar to the ones depicted by me." To reinforce this claim to an impeccable "realism," despite the critical outcry, he adds that "everything my protagonist says in the text that has been sent to you is based on reality." All the tortures that Dostoevsky portrays through Ivan's feverish words were taken from newspaper accounts or from historical sources for which he was ready to give the exact reference. He also assures the editor that his pages do not contain "a single indecent word," but worries that some of his details might be softened. He "beg[s] and implore[s]" that the expression used in describing the punishment inflicted on a child—"the tormentors who are raising her *smear her with excrement* for not being able to ask to go to the bathroom at night"—be retained. "You mustn't soften it . . . that would be very, very sad! We are not writing for ten-year-old children." (The wording was not changed.) And then, turning to a larger issue, Dostoevsky reassures the editor that "my protagonist's blasphemy . . . will be solemnly refuted in the following (June) issue, on which I am now working with fear, trepidation, and reverence, since I consider my task (the rout of anarchism) a civic feat."[6]

There were ample precedents in Dostoevsky's work for his thematic focus on the problem of theodicy raised by Ivan—the problem of the existence of evil and suffering in a world presumably created by a God of love. No Judeo-Christian reader can help but think of the Book of Job in this connection, and Dostoevsky's creation is one of the few whose voice rings out with an equal eloquence and an equal anguish. Although there is no explicit reference to Job in the notes for these chapters, his name appears three times in other sections; and Father Zosima will narrate the story of Job, stressing its consolatory conclusion, in his departing words. In a letter to his wife already quoted but worth citing again, he had written in 1875 that "I am reading Job and it puts me into a state of painful ecstasy; I leave off reading and I walk about the room almost crying. . . . This book, dear Anna, it's strange, it was one of the first to impress me in my life. I was still practically an infant."[7] This recollection is then attributed to Father Zosima, who recalls hearing the Book of Job read aloud in church at the age of eight, "and I feel as I did then, awe and wonder and gladness. . . . Ever since then . . . I've never been able to read that sacred tale without tears" (14: 264–265). Nourished by Dostoevsky's own grief over the loss of his son Aleksey, this magnificent chapter drew as well on feelings that had been stirring within him throughout his life.*

* Russian scholarship has also located a more contemporary source that may have had some effect on Dostoevsky's text, though its influence remains only a possibility. It involves the figure of Belinsky, who played such an important role in Dostoevsky's life, and who, as we shall see, is also linked to the origins of the Legend of the Grand Inquisitor. A. N. Pypin published a biography of Belinsky in 1875 that included extensive extracts from his letters of the early 1840s. At this time Belinsky was breaking free from an erroneous interpretation of Hegel propagated by Bakunin, for the moment a zealous propagandist of right-wing Hegelianism. Bakunin insisted that Hegel was advocating "a reconciliation with reality" (the terrible reality of the Russia of Nicholas I!) because the philosopher had proclaimed that "the real is the rational." When Belinsky began to find this doctrine intolerable, he exploded in letters denouncing, very much as does Ivan, the apologia for evil contained in the notion that the immolation of some is necessary for the harmony of the whole. "Even if I attained to the actual top of the ladder of human development," he wrote, "I should at that point still have to ask [Hegel] to account for all the victims of life and history, all the victims of accident and superstition, of the Inquisition and Philip II, and so on and so forth; otherwise I will throw myself off head-downwards" (cited in *PSS*, 15: 470). One may assume that Dostoevsky would have read Pypin's book, and this letter was also

In mid-May, Dostoevsky provides K. P. Pobedonostsev with another explanation for producing such an extremely suspect and powerful condemnation of God. Repeating that Book 5 "in my novel is the culminating one," he defines "the point of the book" as being "blasphemy and the refutation of blasphemy." "The blasphemy I have taken as I myself sensed and realized it, in its strongest form, that is, precisely as it occurs among us now in Russia with the whole (almost) upper stratum, and primarily with the young people, that is, the scientific and philosophical rejection of God's existence has been abandoned now, today's practical socialists don't bother with it at all (as people did the whole last century and the first half of the present one). But on the other hand God's creation, God's world, and *its* meaning are *negated* as strongly as possible. That's the only thing that contemporary civilization finds nonsensical."[8]

Dostoevsky had always argued that characters like Stavrogin and Kirillov, who were hardly "realistic" in the sense of being recognizably typical, nonetheless revealed more of the essence of Russian life than their less "fantastic" literary counterparts; and he now maintains that his presentation of Ivan Karamazov is far from being only an artistic invention. "Thus I flatter myself," he insists, "that even in such an abstract theme [the rejection of God's world outlined above], I have not betrayed realism. The refutation of this (not direct, that is, not from one person to another) will appear in the last words of the dying elder. Many critics have reproached me for generally taking up in my novels themes that are allegedly wrong, unreal, and so forth. I, on the contrary, don't know anything more real than precisely these themes." His technique had always been to refute the ideas he was combating "indirectly," that is, not by explicit argument but by dramatizing their consequences on the fate of his characters. Indeed, he felt that any head-on confrontation might well be counterproductive. "Just recently I read in *New Time*," he remarks to his correspondent, "about a directive from the Ministry of Public Enlightenment ordering teachers to refute Socialism in their classes (and, therefore, squabble with their students). One can't even imagine what a dangerous idea that is."[9]

To illustrate the impotence of rationality in this domain, he refers to the recent execution of an officer named V. D. Dubrovin, whose regiment had been stationed in Staraya Russa and who was well known to the local population. Dubrovin had been in correspondence with a

quoted in an article by N. K. Mikhailovsky on "Proudhon and Belinsky" in the November 1875 issue of *Notes of the Fatherland*.

member of the underground organization Zemlya i Volya and had been condemned to death because he had offered armed resistance when arrested. Dostoevsky calls him "indisputably a madman," in whose ideas, if compared with the rest of his regiment, "you'll see such a difference, as if [they were] people from different planets, but meanwhile Dubrovin lived and acted in the firm belief that everyone and the whole regiment would become like him, and would reason like him in every particular." Such people "have their own logic, their teachings, their code of law, even their own god, and it's settled in so firmly that it couldn't be firmer." To dismiss Dubrovin's convictions only as "madness" is therefore totally beside the point; Dostoevsky attributes them to a much more deeply rooted cause. "We *lack culture* (which exists everywhere), dear Konstantin Petrovich, and we lack it because of the nihilist Peter the Great. It was torn out by the roots. And since man doesn't live by bread alone, our poor uncultured person can't help inventing something quite fantastic and absurd, so that it's not like anything seen before (because even though he has taken everything in its entirety from European socialism, he has redone even all that in such a way that it's like nothing ever seen before)."[10] In his portrait of Father Zosima and the monastery world in which he lived, one of Russia's age-old institutions, Dostoevsky surely was attempting to restore some of the continuity of Russian culture destroyed by Peter the Great.

Despite his premonitory pleas, he was forced to take editorial objections into account when working over the proofs of Ivan Karamazov's harangue. It would appear that the editor had spoken of the "distressing colors" displayed in the "whipping of the seven-year-old girl," and Dostoevsky answers that, while he "did not spare the coloring, I did not thicken it entirely because, in its pure form, this matter was unportrayable." He had simply repeated what he wrote about the Kroneberg case in the *Diary of a Writer*, "and if you knew from what personages, from what ladies, from what addresses I received a mass of gratefully enraptured letters, compliments, encouragements. . . . These 'distressing colors' did not then arouse repulsion for they were employed in a sacred cause." All the same, "so as not to contradict you," he writes conciliatorily, "I have toned it down."[11]

Dostoevsky also offers some pointed instructions on how properly to read his works, and indicates just how carefully he created the closely woven texture of his characters. In the *Diary*, he was writing in his own name and voice, while

now, here, in the novel *it is not I who am* speaking in distressing colors, exaggerations, and hyperboles (although there is no exaggeration concerning the reality), but a character of my novel, Ivan Karamazov. This is *his* language, his *style*, *his* pathos, and not mine. He is a gloomily irritable person who keeps silent about a good deal. He would not have spoken out for anything in the world if not for the accidental sympathy for his brother Aleksey that suddenly flares up. Besides, he is a very young man. How else could he speak out on what he had kept silent for so long without this particular transport of feeling, without foaming at the mouth. He had strained his heart to the utmost so as not to break forth. But I precisely wanted his character to stand out, and that the reader notice this particular passion, this leap, this literary, impulsively sudden behavior.[12]

Ivan's utterances, therefore, are carefully attuned to that aspect of his character which Dostoevsky especially wanted the reader to grasp. Lyubimov should not assume—as, we may add, is too often done by other interpreters as well—that the author here was speaking in his own voice.

Just how minutely Dostoevsky thought about his characters may be illustrated by the response to another criticism. The editor objected to one detail as being "a needless particularity," a euphemism concealing his true reason, namely, that he thought the detail indecent. The disputed phrase stated that the four-year-old child, whose face had been smeared with excrement, could hardly be expected to ask to be taken to the toilet at night. Dostoevsky agreed that "perhaps [this detail] could be superfluous if it came from me as author." But he insists that this observation of Ivan's is crucial for communicating the complexity he wishes to convey about Ivan's character; and his analysis reveals just how attentively he should be read if we are to appreciate all the nuances of his artistry.

"Oh, how many such details may seem superfluous!" he exclaims.

But those details, how necessary they are for the artistic task! Yes, simply the fact that a young, twenty-three-year-old man notices this already shows that he had thought and worried about it more seriously than many young people of his age. They usually are compassionate *in general*. No attention is paid to such minor details, and if a twenty-three-year-old notices, that means he took [them] to heart. It means that he turned them over in his mind, that he was an advocate of children, and no matter how heartless he is presented *there later* [in the book], compassion and the most sincere love of children remain in him still.

Ivan's remark discloses a deep-rooted trait of character and should influence the manner in which the reader regards him as the book proceeds. "This Ivan then obliquely commits a crime, but not out of calculation, not because he is greedy for the heritage, but, so to speak, out of principle, in the name of an idea, with which then he was not able to cope; and he gives himself up precisely because, it may be, that once, at some time, his heart, dwelling on the suffering of children, did not overlook such a seemingly insignificant circumstance." Dostoevsky then returns to what he knew had been bothering Lyubimov all along, assuring him that "such a detail is not *filthy* because everything that relates to children is pure, radiant, and *beautiful*. Even that."[13]

With reference to the episode in which a general unleashes a pack of dogs that tear a peasant boy apart before the eyes of his mother, Dostoevsky concedes that his first version was perhaps too generalized—"I related it to all generals"—and changes were obviously made to bring it in line with Lyubimov's demand for restraint. The episode of "the robbers killing children" was not, Dostoevsky also admits, "entirely clear," and he revised this scene as well. He repeats, however, that Lyubimov should remember in the future "in all doubtful cases (if such should occur) to pay attention to *what character is speaking*. For some character, because of his personality, sometimes could not speak in any other way."[14]

Despite these revisions, his friend K. P. Pobedonostsev still found the torments suffered by the children too strong for his taste. "I await now the appearance of the next issue of the *Russian Messenger*," he wrote him, "so as to know the conclusion of the conversation of the Karamazov brothers about faith. This is a very strong chapter—but why did you paint the torture of the children in this way?"[15]

### 4

In mid-June Dostoevsky sent off to Lyubimov another chapter of Book 5, "The Grand Inquisitor," accompanying it again with a commentary. "It finishes up," he explained, "*what the mouth speaking great things and blasphemies* says."* "A contemporary negator," Dostoevsky goes on,

> one of the most ardent, comes right out and declares himself in favor of what the devil advocates, and asserts this is truer for people's happiness than is Christ. To our Russian Socialism, which is so stupid (but also dangerous, because the young generation is with it), the lesson, it would seem, is very forceful—one's daily bread, the Tower of Babel (i.e., the future reign of Socialism), and the complete enslavement of freedom of conscience—that is the ultimate goal of this desperate denier and atheist!

* The italicized phrase is the King James translation of the passage in the Book of Revelation that Dostoevsky cites. The Russian version of the same text reads: "the mouth proud and blasphemous."

The difference is that our Socialists (and they are not just underground Nihilist scum—you know that) are conscious Jesuits and liars who do not admit that their idol consists of violence to man's conscience and the leveling of mankind to a herd of cattle, while my Socialist (Ivan Karamazov) is a sincere person who comes right out and admits that he agrees with the Inquisitor's view of humanity and that Christ's faith (allegedly) elevated man to a much higher level than where he actually stands. The question is stated in its boldest form: 'Do you despise humanity or admire it, its future saviors?' And all of this for them is allegedly in the name of love of humanity: Christ's law, they claim, is burdensome and abstract, and too heavy for weak people to bear—and instead of the law of Freedom and Enlightenment, they offer them the law of chains and enslavement through bread.[16]

Once more Dostoevsky does everything in his power to allay the fears that, as he certainly had good reason to believe, would arise in the breasts of his editors. "In the next book the elder Zosima's death and his deathbed conversations with his friends will occur. This is not preaching, but a kind of story, the story of his life. If I succeed, I'll have done a good thing. I'll have forced people to recognize that a pure, ideal Christian is not an abstract matter but one graphically real, possible, standing before our eyes, and that Christianity is the only refuge of the Russian land from its evils. I pray God I'll succeed; the piece will be moving, if only my inspiration holds out. And most important, it's the sort of theme that doesn't occur to any of our current writers and poets, and that means it's absolutely original. The whole novel is being written for its sake, but only let it succeed, that's what worries me now!"[17] He was quite justified in his conviction that both in the Grand Inquisitor and in Father Zosima's life story he would be creating something entirely unprecedented in the Russian novel.

Writing again to Putsykovich on the same day, Dostoevsky voices all his trepidation over the reception of his recent chapters. Urging him not to lose heart, and detailing his own sometimes carelessly offhand treatment at the hands of his editors, he remarks that "in my novel I've had to present several ideas and positions that, as I feared, would not be much to their liking, *since until the conclusion of the novel these ideas and positions really can be misinterpreted*; and now, just as I feared, it has happened; they're caviling at me; Lyubimov sends the proofs and makes notes and puts question marks in the margins. I've prevailed, with difficulty, so far, but I very much fear for yesterday's mailing for June [the Grand Inquisitor], that they'll rear up and tell me they can't print it" (italics added).[18]

The notes for Book 5 disappointingly deal largely with the earlier chapters of this section, those devoted to Alyosha and Liza Khokhlakova and to Smerdyakov's relation with the old woman and her daughter who live in the garden adjoining the Karamazov house. There are, however, some jottings concerning Ivan's disillusionment with life that contain passages stronger than those used in the text. For example, when the text refers to the possibility of living after the age of thirty, Ivan speaks of his father as "standing on a firm rock . . . he stands on his sensuality" (14: 210). In the notes, this passage refers to "beastly voluptuousness, with all its consequences, voluptuousness to the point of cruelty, crime, even to the point of the Marquis de Sade. . . . But in order to do this, one has to develop within oneself for one's whole life a fire in the blood, but even if you could, it's reptilian, that's why one has to kill oneself." In an exchange that follows this passage, Ivan presumably reflects: "Voluptuousness, but perhaps it will be impossible." And Alyosha answers: "—For you, *it will be impossible.* Voluptuousness. Steep yourself in bestial ecstasies, like my father" (15: 228–229).

The notes concerning the Grand Inquisitor also contain assertions much more provocative than those eventually used. The Inquisitor, for instance, asks Christ: "Why do we need the beyond? We are more human than thou. We love the earth—Schiller sings of joy, John of Damascus [a seventh-century theologian]." Another statement reads: "Inquisitor: *God as a merchant.* I love humanity more than *thee*" (15: 230). The reference remains unexplained, but may perhaps indicate that God picks and chooses those He will accept whereas the Grand Inquisitor accepts everyone. One of the bluntest challenges to Christ is the Inquisitor's charge: "I have only one word to say to thee, that thou hast been disgorged from Hell and art a heretic" (15: 232). Again, the Inquisitor predicts that "a mass of locusts will crawl out of the ground and will cry out that we are enslaving people, that we are despoiling virgins—but these unfortunate ones will submit" (15: 233). None of this imagery was ultimately kept, nor was the specific accusation, "They sing of thee [Christ] as Alone without Sin, but I say to thee that thou alone art guilty," though this accusation of Christ's guilt for humankind's turmoil is distinctly stated in the final text (15: 233). As Edward Wasiolek has written, these notes contain a much clearer assertion that "it is Christ who is guilty and cruel, and it is the Grand Inquisitor who is kind and innocent. It is Christ who demands that men suffer for Him, whereas the Grand Inquisitor suffers for men."[19] Anticipations of the Legend can also be found earlier in jottings made for the *Diary of a Writer*: "The Grand Inquisitor and Paul. The Grand Inquisitor with Christ. In Barcelona the devil was caught" (15: 407).

Even though Dostoevsky's notes contain no reference to sources for the Legend, this has not discouraged scholars (rather the contrary) from searching for them far and wide. Central of course are the New Testament accounts of the three temptations of Christ by the Devil, and we have seen these motifs—particularly the first and third temptations ("to command these stones to become loaves of bread"; to rule deceptively in the name of Christ with earthly, temporal power)—gradually crystallizing in Dostoevsky's imagination throughout the *Diary of a Writer*. As for the character of the Grand Inquisitor, the incarnation of spiritual despotism and tyranny over the conscience of mankind, his prototype can be found in another play of Schiller's, *Don Carlos*, translated by Mikhail Dostoevsky in the 1840s.

Dostoevsky's Grand Inquisitor, though, is humanized to a much greater degree than Schiller's. There is not a trace in the play of the compassion for humankind that imparts so much pathos to Dostoevsky's character; in Schiller it is not the Inquisitor but the enlightened aristocrat, the Marquis of Posa, who exhibits such emotions. The play, however, shares the same justification for the existence of evil in the world, the same answer to the problem of theodicy, that is at the heart of Dostoevsky's Legend—and indeed, at the heart of his religious worldview. This answer is given in the great scene in which the Marquis of Posa tries to persuade King Philip of Spain to grant freedom of conscience to his Protestant subjects in the Netherlands. Turning to the examples of nature and of the world for his argument, the marquis urges Philip to recognize that God Himself allows evil to exist rather than interfere with the moral-spiritual freedom of mankind—the freedom to choose between good and evil:

> . . . Look about you
> At the splendors of nature! On freedom
> Is it founded—and how rich it is
> Through Freedom—He, the great Creator—
> —He— . . . So as not to disturb the enchanting
> Appearance of Freedom—
> He leaves the dreadful army of evils
> To rage in his universe—He, the artist,
> Remains invisible, modestly He
> Hides himself in eternal laws.[20]

This is the fundamental idea that Dostoevsky had already expressed (in the letter cited in Chapter 15) when interpreting the first temptation, "turning stones into bread," and explaining why God had not provided mankind with *both* Beauty and Bread.

The motif of Christ's return, not to be confused with the Second

Coming, has also attracted much attention. The sporadic reappearance of Christ has been traced back to writings in the early years of Christianity, and similar texts continued to appear throughout the Middle Ages. They flourished with particular luxuriance during the period of the Thirty Years' War, when Protestants and Catholics were furiously slaughtering each other in His name. Such texts always arose as a protest against the deplorable adherence of the Church (in whatever period they were written) solely to the external trappings of a Christian faith that had come into possession of temporal power. In doing so, it lost sight of its original message of love, charity, and unlimited compassion for those who suffer. More recently, this motif had appeared in various compositions of Utopian Socialists of the 1840s, such as Theodore Dézamy and Etienne Cabet ("Christ before a Military Tribunal," and so on), and in poems like Victor Hugo's "Christ in the Vatican." The religious historian Ernst Benz has also pointed out that the leaders of Russian sects like the Khlysty and Skoptsy were considered to be genuine reincarnations of Christ who would suffer the same fate of persecution and crucifixion. The image of a returning Christ thus pervaded the spiritual world of the Russian sects that so fascinated Dostoevsky, who not only studied their doctrines but drew on them for some of the most hauntingly lyrical passages in his novels. Works of visual art are also included among some of the suggested sources of the Legend.[21]

Although there is no evidence that any of these works directly affected Dostoevsky's creation, it is generally accepted that one relevant text can hardly be placed in doubt. This is the article "Old People" ("Starye Liudi," discussed earlier in Chapter 4), in which Dostoevsky recorded one of the most crucial moments of his spiritual-ideological formation. Recounting a conversation about Christ with Belinsky, just then in transition between a religiously inspired Utopian Socialism and one based on atheism, he depicts the critic maintaining that existing conditions of society made it impossible to avoid "sin." Humankind cannot be "loaded down with obligations and with turning the other cheek," Dostoevsky quotes him as having said, "when society is set up in such a foul fashion that a man cannot help but do wrong." As the Grand Inquisitor would also maintain, humans are too weak to bear the burden of moral responsibility imposed on them by Christ. When the question arose of how Christ would behave, "were he born in our time," Belinsky first answered that "he would be utterly eclipsed by today's science, and by those forces that now advance humanity," but then he agreed with another interlocutor that, in the modern world, Christ "would certainly join the Socialists and follow them." All through this account, while reporting the words of Belinsky and the others present and commenting as narrator, Dostoevsky does not cite a single word of his own; like the

Christ in the Legend, he remains silent. Belinsky remarked, however, that each time he mentioned the name of Christ, the expression on Dostoevsky's face changed, "just as if he were going to cry" (21: 11).

The importance of this encounter for the Legend can be inferentially supported by some remarks made to Putsykovich in Berlin shortly after it had been written. With the composition of the Legend, Dostoevsky told the editor, "he had achieved the culminating height of his literary activity." When Putsykovich asked why he gave such importance to the Legend, rather than to the sensational success of his still-unfinished novel, Dostoevsky replied that "he had carried the theme of the Legend in his soul, so to speak, during the whole course of his life, and wished particularly now to place it in circulation since he did not know if he would ever again succeed in printing something important." He also explained the Legend as being directed "against Catholicism and the papacy, and particularly the most terrible period of Catholicism, that is, the period of the Inquisition, which had such awful effects on Christianity and on all of humanity."[22] Even though Dostoevsky said nothing about Socialism in these remarks, both Socialism and Catholicism had become identical for him as embodiments of both the first and third temptations of Christ, the betrayal of Christ's message of spiritual freedom in exchange for bread, and the aspiration toward earthly power.

Still another piece of evidence may be adduced to support Dostoevsky's claim that he had carried the Legend with him "all through his life." In the 1840s he had written a novella called *The Landlady*, abandoning the sentimental Naturalism of his Petersburg stories to try his hand, like Gogol, at a work in the Gothic folk-tale style influenced by German Romanticism. The experiment was not an artistic success, and Belinsky wrote caustically that the eyes of one of the characters, an imposing, mysterious, and grizzled old man Murin, contained "so much electricity, galvanism, and magnetism that he might have commanded a good price from a physiologist to supply the latter . . . with . . . lightning-charged crackling glances for scientific observation and experiments."[23] Although the story contributed to the decline of Dostoevsky's artistic reputation, Murin bears some physical resemblance to the later Grand Inquisitor, and we also find him uttering what is, at bottom, the essence of the Inquisitor's view of the human personality.

A key element of the story is the spiritual enslavement of the heroine, Katerina, to the power exercised over her by the psychic sorcery of Murin, who uses religious fear to hold her in thrall; and like the Grand Inquisitor, he generalizes the secret of his authority into a universal law. "Let me tell you, sir," he explains to the helpless hero of the story, "a weak man cannot stand alone. Give him everything, he will come of himself and return it all. . . . Give a weak man his freedom—he will bind it himself and give it back to you. To a foolish heart freedom is of no use!" (1: 317). Here in embryo, and still wrapped in the tinseled trappings of some of Gogol's Ukrainian tales, is the doctrine that the Grand Inquisitor will proclaim with such awesome majesty thirty years later.

## 5

Dostoevsky's schedule required him to send off a text on the tenth of each month, and he tried to snatch some time between installments to keep in touch with friends. On the fifteenth of June he wrote Elena Shtakenshneider that he was relaxing for a few days, but would have to get back to work immediately. The weather in Staraya Russa had been particularly inclement ("cold, high winds, and terrible rain"), and in addition the children were down with colds that might turn into whooping cough. His own health "is not at all satisfactory," and although he was contemplating a trip to Ems, no final decision had as yet been made. As usual, he was keeping a sharp eye on what he could glimpse through the newspapers of the current state of Russian society, and his remarks on two recent sensational events reveal his gnawing sense, so evident as well in the *Diary of a Writer*, of the ever-increasing disintegration of the social fabric. "And what will it be like when we meet this winter," he musingly asks his friend, "what will we talk about, what will the vital questions be? I sense that we will all be farther apart in our thinking than ever, some people going one way and some the other."[24]

One of the events that had captured Dostoevsky's attention was the theft of more than a million rubles from a bank in Kherson by a band of revolutionaries who tunneled into a vault. Another was the murder of an aged moneylender and her servant (*Crime and Punishment* once more!) by an officer and aristocrat, K. E. Landsberg, in order to repossess an IOU for five thousand rubles that was coming due. "Well," he comments, "just try to describe Landsberg, for instance, whose crime is considered so incredible that it is attributed to insanity—people will start yelling that it's incredible, slander, a morbid state. . . . Illness and a morbid state lie at the root of our society, and there's general outrage at those who are able to notice that and point it out."[25]

Dostoevsky was of course referring to the "outrage" directed against himself by his critics. Shtakenshneider had pointed out the difference between the "reading public," who eagerly awaited his every word, and the "writing public," who aimed to be "cleverer" than Dostoevsky and constantly took him to task. As an example, she instanced a serialized article by a critic named Evgeny Markov, whom she characterizes as "the darling of liberal Petersburg, its prophet and proclaimer of its truths." His article, entitled "Novelist-Psychiatrist," repeated the well-worn accusation against the so-called "pathological" nature of Dostoevsky's characters, in whose major novels of the last decade "the lives of people are represented as being far worse, far blacker, and more senseless than in reality."[26] The articles referred to were in fact lying on his desk, as yet unread, though he had some sense of their content if only from their title. "My very best reply," he maintains, "will be to do a decent job of finishing the novel [*The Brothers Karamazov*]; after completing the novel next year, I'll answer all the critics in one fell swoop. After a literary career of thirty-three years I need, finally, to explain myself."[27] Unfortunately, death prevented him from carrying out this intention to pen an *apologia pro vita sua*.

He then recalls his imprudent remark a year or so ago, when asked about the critic's capabilities, "that Evgeny Markov was an old chintz dress that had already been washed several times and long since faded." Word of this disobliging opinion had certainly gotten back to its object; and in addition, Markov was also a competitor as a fellow novelist. He "has been publishing a novel this year [*The Seashore* (*Bereg Morya*)], with a special claim to refute pessimists and find healthy people and healthy happiness in our society." The chief character settles on a small vineyard in the Crimea, cultivates it with his own labor, and leads an idyllic life while contemplating the majestic beauties of the nature by which he is surrounded and in which he finds contentment. "Well, let him," Dostoevsky exclaims. "The idea alone shows him to be a fool. It means you don't understand a thing in our society if you talk like that."[28]

Just at this time (June 21) he received the news that he had been elected, along with Tolstoy and Turgenev, a member of the Honorary Committee of the International Literary Alliance, which had recently held its congress in London (June 9–14). Victor Hugo had been its honorary president, and its purpose, as had been the case the year before, was to agitate for the legal protection of literary property. In his reply, written in French by Anna Jaclard (then vacationing in Staraya Russa with her family), Dostoevsky thanked the congress for the honor, adding: "How can one not be proud of taking a place among so many illustrious names, in the ranks of the most glorious notables of our contemporary literature!"[29] Aside from this letter, we know that Anna Jaclard was one of his favorite companions; his wife writes that "almost every day after his work my husband would go to have a talk with this fine, intelligent woman, who had been so important in his life."[30] Alas, we have no further information about the daily exchange of ideas between this seasoned revolutionary, ex-Communard, and intimate of Karl Marx, and the author who had just written the Legend of the Grand Inquisitor and was toiling at the chapters containing the teachings of Father Zosima.

A consoling letter to Anna Filosofova, not yet in exile, responds to her "bitter lines about human cruelty and the shamelessness of those very people on whom, truly loving them, you may have sacrificed your whole life and activity (that can be said for you)."[31] Some notes that have been published help to illustrate the truly agonizing situation in which she found herself. "I was," she wrote, "between two fires: on the one hand, my husband received proclamations from the nihilists that they would kill him, and that his name was on the list of their victims; on the other, the government sent my son into exile, and threatens me with the same." Her social-political views can be grasped from a letter to her husband in this very year: "You know very well that I hate our present government . . . that band of brigands, who are bringing Russia to ruin."[32]

Even while trying to raise her spirits, Dostoevsky's own letter is very far from being lighthearted—quite the contrary, he confesses that he is very "depressed" himself. "The main thing is that my health has gotten worse, the children have all been ill—the weather is horrible, impossible, it rains buckets from morning to night . . . it's cold, damp, likely to give one a cold. . . . In that state of mind . . . I was writing the whole time, working nights, listening to the high wind howling and breaking hundred-year-old trees." Filosofova was planning to take a cure in the Caucasus, and he humorously advises her "to choose an average doctor, a modest German" rather than a Russian of greater fame, adding that, while such advice may be inconsistent with his Slavophil convictions, he is firmly convinced of its soundness. In August she will be seeing her children, and this allows him to expatiate on the importance of offspring who "humanize existence in the highest sense. Children are a torment, but they are essential, without them there is no aim in life." He insists that even "splendid people" without children "always lack something, and (honest to God) in the higher problems and questions of life they seem to be weak."[33]

By this time, he had decided to travel to Bad Ems once again, and asks Filosofova to write to him there because "it's horrible that I'll have to endure so much tedium in my solitary treatment."[34] Dostoevsky also announced this decision to Lyubimov and requested that he be relieved of the obligation to supply a new installment of his novel for the July issue. "It's nearly ready," he assured his correspondent, "and with a certain effort I could send it to you even this month. But the important thing for me is that I consider the next book, Book 6 ('Pater Seraphicus,' 'The Elder's Death'), the novel's culminating point, and therefore I would like to polish it as well as possible, look through it, and clean it once more." He promised to send it from Ems for the August issue, and kept his word. He then outlined his plan for Book 7, which would appear in September and October and conclude the second part of the novel; Part 3, which Dostoevsky thought would not be as large as Part 2, then would follow.[35] In fact, the novel turned out to be longer than he had envisaged at this point, and it finally grew to contain a Part 4.

Even with this smaller, original plan, Dostoevsky told his editors that it was impossible for him, as he had initially intended, to complete the whole work in one year: "In undertaking the novel I didn't take into consideration the state of my health. In addition, I've begun to work much more slowly, and lastly, I view this work of mine more severely than any of the earlier ones. I want it to be finished off well, and there's an idea in it that I would like to put forth as clearly as possible. It contains the trial and punishment and presentation of one of the most important characters, Ivan Karamazov."[36] The trial and punishment of Ivan Karamazov are of course not legal like Dimitry's but moral-psychological; and Dostoevsky gives them so much importance because, through the depiction of Ivan's inner torments, he was attempting to undermine from within the intense humanitarian pathos of the Populist ethic.

He then proceeds to outline the tentative publication dates that he thought feasible at this juncture, though all would prove to be overoptimistic. Even so, he is already worried because the period of a year would be exceeded, and he asked to be allowed to print a public letter explaining the reason. He mentions the outcry that had arisen over *Anna Karenina*, also printed in the *Russian Messenger*, whose publication had dragged on from 1875 to 1877, with large lapses of time between chapters. Subscribers had complained, and critics had suggested that the reason for such inordinate delays was to sustain the faithfulness of the reading public. "But so that there not be any newspaper (satirical columnists) suggestions against the *Russian Messenger* . . . suggesting that the journal is purposely dragging the novel out for several years . . . in the October issue of this year . . . I will send you a letter of mine . . . in which I apologize for not having been able to finish the work this year because of ill health and saying that the only person to blame before the public is myself."[37] On July 17, Dostoevsky left Staraya Russa for Petersburg, Berlin, and Bad Ems.

## CHAPTER 24

# A Last Visit

Dostoevsky's final stay in Bad Ems was marked by the loneliness and isolation he had anticipated before departing, and his reaction to the environment of the fashionable spa, already quite atrabilious, reached a new pitch of irascibility. His anti-Semitism came into full play as well, though he exhibited a fine impartiality in scattering his abuse right and left. It is somewhat ironic that, concurrently, he was working to complete his chapters on the teachings of Father Zosima, whose message of love and universal reconciliation he hoped would answer the anathemas of Ivan Karamazov. One can hardly imagine a writer whose everyday feelings and emotions were more at odds with the sentiments he was pouring into his artistic work.

## 2

He arrived in Petersburg from Staraya Russa on July 18, after a grueling trip that left him, as he wrote to Anna, "collapsing from exhaustion . . . my head is spinning, and I can see spots before my eyes." Despite feeling that "I've grown as weak as a five-year-old child," he staunchly went about completing the necessary preparations for his journey. First collecting the money for the recent chapters of his novel, he then went off to the Blockhead embassy (as he called the Germans) to obtain a visa. Visiting the Dostoevsky apartment, he reported that everything was in good order—except that the tenants had complained about cockroaches (against which he had earlier waged a determined but clearly indecisive campaign). He remarks with some amusement that the insects had now vanished from his study—perhaps because he had been working on the Karamazovs, and once he left so had the black cockroaches (*kara* means black in the Tartar-Turkish language). His barber and others were surprised at his changed appearance for the worse (he had lost weight), and asked if he had been ill. "No, Anya, I'm in a bad way," he concludes, "and if Ems doesn't help, then I really don't know what's going to happen."[1]

The trip to Berlin was equally exhausting, and though he claims to have arrived "in fine fettle," he adds that "I have even gotten out of the habit of sleeping." Recalling the earlier Petersburg leg of his travels, he exclaims: "you wouldn't believe how sad it's been for me, especially in the evening, to think the whole way about the children and about you! ... We need to save up, Anya, we need to leave something for the children. That thought always torments me most of all when I personally draw near to a variety of people and see them in their selfishness, for instance, on the road."[2] He had uttered such thoughts before about his lack of savings, but his worsening illness gave them a new sense of urgency.

When his train crossed the Russian border and the passengers transferred to the German line, Dostoevsky writes, "a little Yid, a doctor from Petersburg, about fifty years old," who was on his way to Wiesbaden to treat his rheumatism, "introduced himself and kept me greatly amused on the trip and served as a translator for me with the Germans." There was also "an elderly German of gigantic size [who] especially looked after us, put me to bed, and saved me from the waiters' swindling at the stations." He was horrified not only at the swindling ("the swindlers are unimaginable," and every tradesman, Jewish or not, was a swindler) but also at the prices, which had "risen threefold since our time here eight years ago."[3]

The dust on the German railway had ruined his clothing, and it was necessary to order a new coat (which meant an extra day in the German capital). Nor did he particularly wish to see the awaiting Victor Putsykovich. "I'm terribly afraid of him: first, he'll attach himself and won't let go, will sit in front of me with his long (noble) nose and look out of the corner of his eye, and second, he'll want to borrow money, and I've become like a Yid: I terribly much want not to give any." When they met, Dostoevsky discovered that the supposedly impecunious editor had been receiving funds from Ivan Aksakov and Prince Golitsyn, as well as from his brother and from the sale of his belongings in Petersburg. "For all I know, there may even be some more people sending him money." Far from being down at heels, Putsykovich "is no longer living in the same place, is paying *at cut-rates*, has a good room, dinner, and *credit*."[4]

The two men went to visit the aquarium, the museum, and the Tiergarten, and Dostoevsky found himself, despite his prior determination, "paying for his beer, at the restaurant, the cabby, and so on." Moreover, "he borrowed forty-five marks from me for paper and stamps (postage) for the first issue, which will come out in a week." Dostoevsky's liberality, one assumes, was prompted by his willingness to support the worthy endeavor of establishing another version of *The Citizen* on German soil. The importunate Putsykovich urged Dostoevsky to commit himself to becoming a contributor to the new journal; but he refused to go beyond what had already been suggested from Staraya Russa. "For the first issue," he explains to Anna, "he's asking me not for a piece but just a letter stating that I'm *not opposed* to contributing sometime, although I'm busy with the Karamazovs. Well, that's not so much."[5]

Dostoevsky arrived at Ems on July 24 and took a room at the hotel Ville d'Alger. He immediately went to see Dr. Orth, and reported the diagnosis the next day. "He found that a part of my lung had moved from the spot and changed position, just as my *heart* also has changed from its former position and is now located in another one—all as a consequence of the emphysema, although he added by way of consolation [that] the heart is absolutely healthy, and all these changes don't mean very much either and are no special threat." Far from being reassured, he adds that "of course as a doctor he is obliged to say comforting things, but if the emphysema, still just at the outset, has already produced such effects, what's going to happen later?" A program of gargling and drinking the two types of curative waters (Kranchen and Kesselbrunnen) was prescribed, and he writes hopefully that "I'm relying on the waters greatly and began drinking them today."[6]

In reply to his request for a hundred extra rubles, Anna explained that she had not been able to obtain his last payment from the *Russian Messenger*, even though it had been sent to Staraya Russa; the money order had been made out in his name and thus could not be cashed by his wife. A letter to Lyubimov, written "politely but insistently," explained the problem and requested that it be rectified. He confided to Anna his suspicion that the editors "are acting like this on purpose, *so that I not forget myself*"—that is, Dostoevsky should take care to keep to his promised schedule for providing the installments of his novel, which he had not always done in the past.[7]

Unable to find any names that he knew in the guest register of the spa, he comments scornfully that "the majority of Russian names are rich Russian Yids." As bad luck would have it, Dostoevsky's neighbors in the hotel, a mother and her twenty-five-year-old son, were Jewish, and he complains about them to Anna as he had done in previous years about other neighbors in adjoining rooms. Accustomed to working in the total quiet of the late-night hours, he was constantly disturbed by the voices of other guests. Once more he groans that the Jewish mother and son "talk to each other from morning to night, loudly, at length, unceasingly, and keep me from reading and writing"; they talked "whole pages on end (in German and Yiddish) . . . [and] almost yell while they talk, as though they were alone in the hotel."[8]

After four days, "since it was already ten o'clock and time to sleep, I in fact yelled, *when getting into bed*: 'Oh, those damned Yids! When will they finally let a person sleep?'" Dostoevsky's neighbors protested to the landlady about his insulting language, and both parties threatened to move out; but neither did so, and Dostoevsky wrote that "it's bearable for me for the time being" because his neighbors, even if they continued to talk incessantly, now kept their voices down. He did, however, accept the landlady's proposal to move upstairs to a quieter room when it became available in a week's time.[9]

3

If Putsykovich had one virtue it was that of persistence, and he knew that Dostoevsky's name would provide a much-needed luster to his proposed journal. Reminding Dostoevsky of his promise, he received on July 28 the following letter for publication. "I'm glad for the resumption of *The Citizen.* You promise to speak in it with even greater firmness than before; so much the better. Your orientation, in any case, is sincere and incorruptible—even the enemies of your orientation are aware of that, and they have admitted as much themselves. In our days, in our sick and cynical days, what is more important and what is more impressive than sincere and incorruptible thought—most important, incorruptible, and not just with money." He continues by explaining that "all my energies and all my time" are swallowed up by "the novel I am now writing (*The Brothers Karamazov*)," and hence it is impossible for him to promise "a contribution at all significant or definite." But because "our time is such a fiery and such a stimulating one," if it happens that some new phenomenon strikes him forcefully "and about which I'll definitely want to say a few words without delay, I'll of course write something."[10]

This official letter was accompanied by a private one in which once again he gives rein to his dislike of "the polyglot crowd, almost half of them rich Yids from all over the globe." In this connection, he calls Putsykovich's attention to an article he had read in Katkov's newspaper, *Moskovski Vedomosti* (*Moscow News*), which summarized "a German tract that has just appeared: *Where Is the Jew Here?* Interestingly, it coincides with my own thought just as soon as I entered Germany: that the Germans will become completely Judaized and are losing their old national spirit."[11] The brochure mentioned in this article was a reply to another, from the pen of an ex-Socialist turned anti-Semite, which had attacked the growing Jewish influence on German life. As Dostoevsky wrote to K. P. Pobedonostsev, he took this controversy as confirmation of his own opinion that in Germany "there's the influence of the Jew everywhere."[12]

Putsykovich's new journal reached Dostoevsky a little over two weeks after the beginning of his sojourn, and he was far from entirely pleased with its contents. Although he thought "that the issue is quite good, and really would have attracted subscribers," he was quite appalled at the intemperance of its criticism of important Russian diplomats. "And how did you manage to make so many miscalculations?" Dostoevsky asks in astonishment. "I cannot imagine that the censorship could permit *personal insults* against well-known officials and mockery of them." After citing a few examples of such impermissible expressions, he advises the combative editor to "look at how our newspapers, under such censorship, manage to talk about this: in the *Moscow News* I read something ten times stronger than your exposé," but with none of the objectionable phrases that Putsykovich had permitted himself. "Don't be angry," Dostoevsky adds conciliatorily, "these are not admonitions—they're involuntary frustrations over the fact that a person is ruining his enterprise himself."[13]

Nine days later, he turned down another request for a contribution from the indefatigable Putsykovich and flatly refused to ask a wealthy lady, Yulia Zasetskaya, to provide the *Russian Citizen* with some financial assistance. A review of the first issue of the *Russian Citizen* had already appeared in *Voice*, and Dostoevsky comments on the highly critical reaction. "The article is stupid," he tells Putsykovich, but "everything it says about burning incense to Bismarck [on Putsykovich's part] is true. It made an unpleasant impression on me too. . . . If you even so much as once more publish an issue with such grovelings before Bismarck," he warns, "everyone in Russia will turn away from you." Dostoevsky was also afraid that if any further obeisance to the Iron Chancellor were printed, "I'll have put my foot in it with my letter about the incorruptibility of *The Citizen*'s orientation." He advised Putsykovich to retort to *Voice* "with noise and thunder" and "in an editorial, *not on the last page.*" He even gives the editor "a suggestion" of how to strike home. "There are two *precious phrases* there [in the hostile article]: '*The Citizen* is again attacking *everything* fine and noble that we have.' And all you did was write about nihilists and their fathers. So according to *Voice* the nihilists are noble."[14]

His reactions to the current social-cultural scene are also recorded in a letter to K. P. Pobedonostsev, in which he describes himself as "being sick and overanxious in my soul," partly, to be sure, because of "sitting here in the most complete and sorrowful isolation." But he also attributes his lamentable state of mind "to the depressing impression from observing what has been going on in the 'Madhouse' of the Russian press and [among] the intelligentsia too." Pobedonostsev had expressed objections to a recent article by A. D. Gradovsky, a professor at the University of Moscow, and Dostoevsky indicates his unqualified agreement with his friend's adverse reaction, commenting that "everyone now is afraid, even those who have something to say. What are they afraid of?

Definitely of a phantom. 'Pan-European' ideas of learning and enlight-enment stand despotically over everyone, and no one dares state his opinion." No one had the courage to take up the cudgels against Gra-dovsky, who "sees all the medicine for all the contemporary horrors of our disorder in that same Europe, in Europe alone." All these issues had worked up Dostoevsky to the point of "being tormented by the desire to continue the *Diary*, since I really do have things to say—and precisely as you would wish—without a fruitless, uncouth polemic, but instead with firm, fearless words."[15]

He then strikes off a passage accurately defining the unique place he had managed to carve out for himself amidst the deadly rivalries of Rus-sian social-cultural life—a position that allowed him alone to speak out "in firm, fearless words":

> I consider my literary position (I've never spoken to you about this) almost phenomenal: how has a person who writes at the same time against European principles, who has compromised himself forever with *The Devils*, that is, with reaction and obscurantism, how is it that this person, without the help of all their Europeanizing jour-nals, newspapers, and critics, has nonetheless been recognized by our young people, by those very same young Nihilists who have lost their moorings and so on? They have demonstrated this to me in many places, both in individual manifestations and in entire groups. They have announced to me that they await a sincere and sympathetic word from me *alone* and they consider me alone as a *guiding writer*. These declarations by the young are known to our literary leaders, brigands of the pen and swindlers of print, and they are all struck by that, otherwise they wouldn't allow me to write freely! They would eat me alive, like dogs, but they're afraid and watching in perplexity to see what happens next.[16]

If nothing else, such words reveal the burning sense of mission that inspired him, and led him to believe he could aid in saving his country from the catastrophe so clearly looming ahead. It was a catastrophe that could (and did) result, in his view, from the total alienation of the young generation from the traditions of their country and particularly its God.

4

---

Dostoevsky's letters are largely taken up with the details of his health and his cure, about whose effects he expresses various opinions at different times. "My spasmodic cough continues as before," he tells Anna, "but perhaps there will in fact be some help. I'm beginning to hope. My breathing seems easier, I can make more movements, the expectoration is good, although the coughing doesn't in fact stop."[17] But the doctor saw this as a promising sign; the waters were clearing the lungs and thus making them more irritable. "Who knows," Dostoevsky speculates dubiously, "perhaps there is in fact a drop of truth there, and, as dense a doctor as he may be, his incalculably long practice has given him some experience."[18] Just before ending his stay, he decided that "of myself I'll say that the treatment here seems not to have done me any good." "I cough exactly the same as when I arrived," though possibly, he concedes, the benefits of the cure might show up later.[19]

Laments over his terrible loneliness and isolation also abound. To his daughter Lyubov, he confides that "I don't have any friends here, so that I'm silent all the time and I'm afraid that I'll forget how to talk." One of his few diversions was to attend the local concerts, but "the music here, though good, is rarely Beethoven or Mozart. Instead, it's all Wagner (a very boring German rogue, despite all his fame), and all sorts of trash."[20] Anna did her best to relieve his solitude by offering detailed accounts of the activities of their group of intimates in Staraya Russa, among whom the Jaclard family took a prominent place. True to the reputation of all Frenchmen, Charles Jaclard was dangling after the wife of the local doctor, and Anna did not fail to inform Dostoevsky of this local tidbit.[21] When the pursuit of the lady was confirmed, with what success remains unknown, Dostoevsky comments semi-ironically: "How about Jaclard, huh! But what a fine fellow. That's how a person ought to be—plucking the flowers of pleasure, not like us downtrodden and frightened folk."[22] The Jaclards, in any case, were doing all they could to animate life in Staraya Russa, arranging a performance of Krylov's fables at their home in which the Dostoevsky children took part. Anna proudly sent him a poster announcing the performance, with the names of the cast prominently displayed.

He was always happy to receive news of his children, whom he missed terribly. "There are lots of children here," he writes Anna, "and I can't pass by them without a pain in my heart."[23] Quite concerned because his son Fedya did not yet know how to read, he tried to stimulate his desire to do so by example. "Try to learn how to read," he urges him. "There are lots of little boys here. They go to school. I even meet them every day. Some of them are only five years old, but already go to school."[24] To Anna, who had told him that Fedya had taken "to going off to be with the boys," he comments that the boy has now reached the age "when the crisis from the first childhood to conscious cognition occurs. . . . he'll soon begin seeking other and nastier consolations if he doesn't have a book."[25]

Dostoevsky also comments on the news of the death of his sister-in-law, the wife of his long-deceased and much-beloved older brother

Mikhail. "The news about Emilya Feodorovna saddened me very much. . . . True, things were headed in that direction. . . . But with her death, it's as though everything that was still left of my brother's memory on earth for me has come to an end." On the eve of the death (August 6), Dostoevsky had dreamed of his brother Mikhail "lying in bed, and on his neck an artery had been cut, and he was bleeding, and in horror I was thinking of running to the doctor's, and meanwhile I was stopped by the thought that after all he would bleed to death before the doctor got there." Believing in the prophetic power of dreams, he took this one as the prediction of a disaster—the demise of Emilya Feodorovna— occurring to his brother's family. Her passing evoked for him as well the responsibility he had always felt toward her, and which he considered that he owed to the memory of his dead brother. "I don't think I am guilty toward her: I helped her when I could, and gradually stopped helping her when there were already helpers very close to her, her sons and son-in-law. . . . Even my deceased brother could not reproach me from the other world."[26]

Even though Dostoevsky had no taste for philandering à la Charles Jaclard, his absence from home always inflamed his erotic passion for his much younger wife; and these letters express that passion with more fervor, ardency, and explicitness than in the past. Many years later, Anna Grigoryevna spent a good deal of time blacking out what she considered overly lubricious passages, in which her husband uninhibitedly expressed his desire for her caresses and how he would revel in their delights. When Anna wrote that he should contain himself, because their letters were being read by the censorship, he replied that he had no intention of doing so and that the censors would only be envious of his amatory infatuation with his wife.[27] When creating the intensity of Dimitry Karamazov's sensual intoxication with Grushenka, he did not have to *invent* such feelings at all; and now, for the first time in his work, he portrays the mutation of such tempestuous sensuality into the complex union of genuine love and self-sacrificial devotion that he celebrates in the happiness of his own marriage.

Anna had written of her intention to take a trip with the children to a nearby monastery, named after a sixteenth-century monk, Nil Stolobensky, adding that an acquaintance named Grushenka Menshova had stayed at the Dostoevskys' overnight. Since Miss Menshova came from a clerical family and, presumably, was quite familiar with the monastery in question, Dostoevsky remarks that "I consider Grushenka Menshova's visit a prelude to the Nilov monastery."[28] Other information (her given name was Agrippina, and she had been abandoned by a fiancé, a visiting lieutenant in the army) makes it likely that she provided some details for the Grushenka in the novel. The trip to the monastery never took place because Anna learned that the inheritors of the Kumanina estate had agreed to meet at the property near Ryazan to make the final dispositions.

Anna thus decided to travel with the children to this much more distant location, revealing her change of plan only when all the arrangements had been made. Dostoevsky was horrified at the news, and imagined the journey proceeding under the worst possible conditions. "Where will you stay, though? In a hut, where you'll probably be robbed and plundered? And where will the children stay while you and the others are looking in the woods?"[29] A week later, he is still envisaging disaster: "You're traveling in third class with small children. The Knaves of Hearts [a criminal gang recently much in the news] have such souls and such notions that your poor and humble appearance (in third class) should arouse their contempt for you. The Shers and Stavroskys [other inheritors] are all the same sort of people, swindlers, cheats, and robbers."[30] For all of his blustering, Anna went about the business with her usual calm and dispatch, and was happy to emerge with a better piece of land than they would otherwise have obtained.

## 5

What occupied Dostoevsky most during his stay in Bad Ems was of course his novel. At the beginning of August, he wrote Anna: "I've started writing, and it's going well for the time being."[31] Six days later, he remarks: "I finally sent Lyubimov a thick package, that is, the novel for August."[32] As usual, he accompanied his manuscript with an explanatory letter—a letter that already anticipated some of the criticism these chapters would receive. "I have entitled this book 'The Russian Monk'—a daring and provocative title, since all the critics who do not like us will scream: 'Is that what a Russian monk is like? How can you dare to put him on such a pedestal?' But so much the better if they scream, isn't it? (And I know they won't be able to restrain themselves.) I consider that I have not sinned against reality, however; it's correct, not only as an ideal but as an actuality too." Once again, as in the case of Ivan Karamazov, he asks the editor to remember that it is a character in the novel who is speaking, not the author himself. "It's obvious," he writes, "that many of the elder Zosima's teachings (or better to say, the manner of their expression) belong to his personage, that is, to the artistic depiction of it. Although I quite share the ideas that he expresses, if I personally were expressing them, *on my own behalf,* I would express them in a different form and a different language. He, however, could not have expressed himself in either a language or a *spirit* other than the one I gave him. Otherwise, an artistic personage wouldn't be created."[33]

Dostoevsky makes particular reference to "the elder's discussions about *what a monk is,* or *about servants and masters,* or *about whether one may be the judge of another person,* and so on. I took the character and figure from ancient Russian monks and saints: along with profound humility—boundless, naive hopes about the future of Russia, about her moral and even political mission. Didn't Saint Sergius and the metropolitans Pyotr and Aleksey always have Russia in mind in this sense?" He pleads with Lyubimov to assign a reliable proofreader to this text because the language is not ordinary Russian and he will be unable to correct the galleys himself. Of the chapter entitled "About the Holy Scriptures in the Life of Father Zosima," he writes: "That chapter is exalted and poetic: the prototype is taken from certain of Tikhon Zadonsky's teachings, and the naïveté of style from the monk Parfeny's book of wanderings. Look through them yourself, dear Nikolay Alekseyevich, be like a father!" To this plea, he adds a "grumbling *nota bene.*" In the last number of the journal, which contained "The Grand Inquisitor," he complains that "not only were my headings violated, but it was even printed all together, ten pages in a row, without even a shift *to another line* [presumably meaning no paragraph breaks]."[34]

Dostoevsky thus indicates the stylistic models he was imitating, which differ considerably from the tonal register of the remainder of the novel. V. L. Komarovich has given a helpful description of the style that Dostoevsky borrowed from *The Story of the Monk Parfeny about the Holy Mountain Athos, of His Pilgrimage and Voyages through Russia, Moldavia, Turkey and the Holy Land.*[35] This work, long a favorite of Dostoevsky's (it was one of the few books he took along on his European travels between 1866 and 1870), was also greatly appreciated by Westernizers such as Saltykov-Shchedrin and Turgenev for its touching images of Old Russian piety. The monk Parfeny had been born into a family of Old Believers and educated in their doctrines; but he had returned to the Orthodox Church after becoming dissatisfied with the intransigent fanaticism of the *raskolniki.* His own book is filled with such a moving spirit of kindness and benevolence, even toward those with whom he argued about questions of faith, that it attracted not only a reader like Dostoevsky but also many whose relation to Christianity was more cultural than religious.

In the stories and preachments of Father Zosima, as Komarovich notes, one finds "even in the arrangement of their parts, and the whole of their syntax, a rhythm entirely strange to Russian literary speech. It appears as a departure from all the norms of modern syntax, and at the same time imparts to the entire narration a special, emotional coloring of ceremonial and ideal tranquillity. The frequent repetition of the same words and even the same word combinations in successive sentences (a stylistic manner quite suitable to the inspiration and the emotion of the narrator); the alternation between long, rhythmically united sentences and introductory sentences in indirect speech; finally, the pleonasms, the tendency to pile up epithets that describe one and the same picture, as if words failed the narrator to attain the desired richness of expression—all this gives to the meaning of the teachings a certain shading of inexpressibility. The very title of Parfeny's book, even by itself, exhibits all the stylistic traits that we have noted in the teachings of Father Zosima."[36]

The influence of the monk Parfeny's book is not only stylistic but extends to many aspects of the depiction of monastic life as well. Dostoevsky had intended to use some details of this text for his never-written *Life of a Great Sinner*, and he wrote to Apollon Maikov that "in the monastery . . . there is also the monk Parfeny."[37] These earlier notes contain a reference to a "great, fasting ascetic and copious weeper of tears, the monk Ankitia," whose story had been detailed by Parfeny with considerable feeling. He was in fact an important Russian nobleman who had abandoned the world, become a monk on Mount Athos, and busied himself with restoring the Russian part of the monastery neglected by the Greeks and falling into ruins. In the notes for *The Devils*, there is also a reference to a monk who had "the gift of tears," and an unnamed character remarks, "I read [this] once in a book of the monk Parfeny about his voyage to Mount Athos." Many of these details from Parfeny are employed when Dostoevsky takes up the monastery locale again in *The Brothers Karamazov*. Father Zosima also weeps in moments of great emotion, when he is conveying what he considers to be the truth of God's word and the splendor and radiance of the universe that is His creation. Parfeny also has a number of references to falling to the earth and kissing it, and Father Zosima advises: "Love to throw yourself on the earth and kiss it. . . . Water the earth with the tears of your joy and love those tears" (15: 292).

## 6

The influence of Saint Tikhon Zadonsky, a mid-eighteenth-century Russian monk elevated to sainthood in 1860, goes back a long way in Dostoevsky's moral-spiritual evolution. He may well have came across Saint Tikhon's abundant literary legacy (fifteen volumes, strongly revealing the influence of German Pietism) in the early 1860s when he was editing *Time* and beginning to work out his own social-political ideal of *pochvennichestvo*. There are many reasons why he should have been attracted to the figure of Saint Tikhon, who was, as Father Georges Florovsky has pointed out in his great history of Russian theology, a writer of considerable power and eloquence; his literary merits alone might have attracted Dostoevsky's admiration. Florovsky also remarks that Saint Tikhon was one of the few Russian saints who underwent an intense inner struggle to attain his religious ideal—the conquest of "pride by humility, anger by gentleness and patience, hatred by love."[38] This aspect of his character is depicted in the memoirs left about him by those who served him in the monastery—just as Aleksey Karamazov gathers together all his recollections of Father Zosima in the *zhitie* given in the novel.

As Komarovich has suggested, Dostoevsky might well have seen a relation between his own personal character, his own struggle with his often difficult temperament, and that of Tikhon. "The bishop always displayed a tendency to nervous ailments and hypochondriacal onsets," wrote one of his cell servants. These episodes included accesses of anger and displeasure, and at the end of his life he "fell into a completely hypochondriacal state."[39] It was by no means easy for him to attain the state of self-mastery that would enable him to dominate his often hostile reactions to others. In addition, he was often the butt of mockery and derision in the monastery, and here again Dostoevsky might have felt some similarity with his own situation as a writer. Was he not also constantly ridiculed for creating psychologically unbalanced and pathological characters, and was not this aspect of his work often attributed to his well-known epileptic malady?

However that may be, there were other sides to Saint Tikhon that would have elicited Dostoevsky's profound admiration. One can find parallels in Tikhon to Father Zosima's adoration of the beauty of nature as a revelation of God's goodness and majesty. Tikhon also spoke of experiencing, during one "gentle, quiet, and luminous night," a vision that he took as a glimpse of heaven. "Suddenly," he told the memoirist, "the sky opened, and I saw within it such a flashing and sparkling that no human speech can convey it or human understanding grasp it."[40] On a more mundane level, the clergyman intervened, whenever he could, on behalf of peasants who were mistreated—and this during the darkest days of serfdom!—attempting to put into practice, on the level of social life, the ideas of Christian love that he was preaching. Several times he was struck by irate landowners, influenced by the prevalent antireligious Voltairianism then all the rage (and still reflected in the speeches of the totally unprincipled father of the Karamazov family). In each case, though not without an inner conflict, Tikhon finally begged the pardon of his assailants for having provoked them to rage; and such humility led to a complete change of heart on the part of his offenders. Dostoevsky probably saw in such episodes not only the clash of two opposing moral-religious principles—Old Russian piety and the new, destructive spirit of atheism—but also the power of humility to produce a moral transformation even in those who, under the influence of ratio-nalism, thought themselves immune to the effect of its redeeming force.

The issue of immortality, as we know, had become the foundation of Dostoevsky's own moral-religious convictions, and this Christian hope, including the Resurrection, was a recurrent preoccupation for Tikhon as well. "It is this churchly doctrine," writes Komarovich, "to which his spiritual ear is especially attuned, and like Dostoevsky, the saint attri-butes the spread of disbelief in his own day to the oblivion into which this conviction had fallen." Noteworthy, however, is that Saint Tikhon hardly ever mentions the Last Judgment when he evokes the Resurrec-tion (nor does Dostoevsky); this event was "never connected with the idea of retribution and punishment for sins, but always with the glory and ultimate bliss of 'God's children.' "[41] The Resurrection is also almost invariably linked by Tikhon with the image of the glory of "the Son of God," and he celebrates the eventuality of humankind attaining such glory in ecstatic words: "The flesh of our abasement will be trans-formed. . . . The chosen of God will be clothed in such exalted, wonder-ful glory that they will shine like the sun. . . . Since the Christians are children of God: in what glory will they be clothed, once they reveal themselves as such!"[42]

Dostoevsky would also have found in Tikhon's work rhapsodic de-pictions, very similar to those he would pen himself, of the Christian utopia of love that glimmered before his enraptured eyes as his ultimate earthly ideal. "Oh, how wonderful everything would be," Tikhon wrote, "if everyone would love one another! Then there would be no theft, no robbery, no deceit, no murder, no deception . . . the courts would not be overwhelmed with complaints, these avaricious people would not be roaming through the streets and town squares . . . the jails would not be overflowing with prisoners, locked up because of crimes, moneylending, failures to pay debts; there would finally be no poor and needy any longer, but all would be equal."[43] His own apoca-lyptic intimations of the earthly paradise could not have been expressed more vividly.

---

7

---

The name of Saint Tikhon as a literary character first appears in the notes for *The Life of a Great Sinner* in early 1870. Some of the jottings made at this time, as has already been noted, served Dostoevsky later for his portrait of Father Zosima. "The limpid stories of Tikhon about life and earthly joy. Of the family, father, brothers. Extremely naïve, and because of this touching, stories of Tikhon, of his sins toward those close to him, vanity, mockery (how I should like to change all this now,

Tikhon says)" (9: 138). The essence of Tikhon's teaching is condensed in a succinct sentence: "Tikhon. Of Humility (how powerful humility is). All on humility and free will" (ibid.). Tikhon had also taught—in what Dostoevsky may well have felt to constitute a response to Job—that humankind should be grateful for the existence of temptation, misfortune, and suffering because only through these could humans came to a knowledge of all the evil in their souls. Tikhon also declared, as Father Zosima would do, that "there is no kind of sin, and there cannot be any such on earth, that God would not pardon to someone who sincerely repents" (9: 511–514).

From a letter to Apollon Maikov, we know that Dostoevsky was seeking to create for Russian literature "a majestic, *positive*, holy figure," and that he believed he could do so by using Saint Tikhon as a prototype. He already presented such a "holy figure" in Prince Myshkin, but the prince could hardly be considered as either "majestic" or "positive" (in a worldly sense). Comparing his own conception with a whole range of pseudopositive types (as Dostoevsky saw them) in novels by Gogol, Goncharov, Turgenev, and Chernyshevsky, he explains that he wishes to stay as close as possible to the original: "True, I will not be creating anything; I will just portray the real Tikhon."[44] Parts of this "great sinner" project were eventually incorporated into *The Devils*. Tikhon appears as a character in the suppressed chapter containing Stavrogin's confession, depicted both as an eccentric personality afflicted with a nervous ailment and as a clairvoyant reader of souls. But this chapter was not published in Dostoevsky's lifetime, and the premonitory references to Tikhon were eliminated from the final text.

The ambition to represent Saint Tikhon appears to vanish in *A Raw Youth*, but in fact a new "positive image" is created—that of the Russian peasant pilgrim Makar Ivanovich, who inspires the young Arkady. This character may be seen as a transitional figure between the first attempt to portray Tikhon and the later Father Zosima, and the conversations between Makar and Arkady as preliminary versions of the discourses of Father Zosima set down by Alyosha.[45] The depiction of Makar, however, no longer bears any resemblance to the ailing, emotionally disturbed Tikhon of *The Devils*.[46] Instead, he is an imposing, broad-shouldered man with very blue and radiant eyes, whose tranquil serenity is accompanied by a warm and reassuring laugh; no conflict any longer exists between his inner moral-spiritual beauty and his outward appearance and behavior. Makar Ivanovich, as Komarovich has suggested, could well have served as a model for the Tikhon who finally became Father Zosima. In any case, Dostoevsky realized that "the real Tikhon" was hardly a fitting embodiment of the "majestic, positive" image he wished to create.

Just after mailing off these chapters, he wrote his wife: "I think I'm satisfied with what I sent off.... The result will be a very good thing ...that elder has been on my hands for a long time; I've been tormented by him since the beginning of the summer."[47] Dostoevsky is obviously speaking in the immediate context of the redaction of his novel, but we have seen that "the elder" (or at least his prototype) had been "on his hands" for a much longer period. In a letter to his confidant Pobedonostsev two days later, his satisfaction appears to have diminished. "I expect brickbats from the critics," he admits, "although I myself know that I didn't carry out a tenth of what I wanted to accomplish; please give this fragment your attention since I would very much like to have your opinion.... I wrote the book for *the few* and consider it the culminating point of my work."[48]

Dostoevsky was replying to a letter in which Pobedonostsev had remarked that "your 'Grand Inquisitor' produced a powerful impression on me. Rarely have I read anything so powerful. Only I have been waiting—from whence will come the repulse, the retort and elucidation—and so far it has not arrived."[49] For Dostoevsky, his Book 6, "A Russian Monk," had been conceived as the answer that Pobedonostsev (and perhaps a few others like him) had been awaiting. Later in the month, he replies more directly: "Your opinion of what you read of *The Kara-mazovs* flattered me very much (regarding the force and energy of what has been written), but right away you pose *a most essential question*: that I have not yet come up with replies to all these atheistic propositions, and they're needed." Dostoevsky tells him that the answer to this "*negative side*" of his work will come in Book 6, though at the same time he expresses all his trepidation over whether this will be "a *sufficient* reply."[50]

"The more so," he goes on, "as the reply, after all, is not a direct one, not to the previously stated propositions (in 'The Grand Inquisitor' and earlier), but only an indirect one. Here, something directly opposed to the above-stated worldview is offered, but again . . . in an artistic picture." He also worries because, while in effect composing a hagiographical portrait, he will be required by the demands of "realism" to enter into quotidian details usually banned from such elevated eulogies. "It has been necessary to present a modest and sublime figure, although his life is full of comicality and is sublime only in its inner sense, so that because of artistic requirements I was forced to touch on the most banal aspects of the biography of my monk so as not to violate artistic realism. Then there are a few of the monk's precepts in response to which people will absolutely yell that they're absurd in the everyday sense, but in another, inner sense I think they're right."[51] It is clear that as yet Pobedonostsev has no knowledge of Dostoevsky's still-unpublished text, and one can dismiss his boastful claim, made shortly after Dostoevsky's death, that the image of Father Zosima had been created in accordance with his "instructions."[52]

The notes for this section are quite scanty, mostly entries developed in the text, but a few remarks were eliminated in the final redaction. Highly critical references to parish priests (not the monastic clergy) repeat in much stronger terms observations that can also be found in the *Diary*. "None are so full of materialism as are the clergy. We have the mystery, we make the mystery. Children, atheism, and forthwith materialism (the priest in his vestments is respected, but without his vestments, he is a moneygrubber and a despoiler)" (15: 240). The same motif crops up a few pages later: "The clergy cry out that they do not earn enough. And others come and take possession of the flock. . . . You [the clergy] cry out that there's too little income: but you should have it worst, go on a fast and without shoes, and you will see how your love will increase and also your resources" (15: 253). Such reflections were no doubt considered inappropriate coming from Father Zosima, and would have clashed with the juxtaposition of Zosima and the benighted "asceticism" of Father Ferapont.

Over and over again Dostoevsky plays variations on his key motif: all are responsible for all, and "everyone is guilty before all and for everything, and *therefore* everyone is strong enough also to forgive everything for others, and all will then become the work of Christ, and He Himself will appear among them, and they will see Him and become united with Him." Indeed, he goes so far as to add: "And He will forgive also the grand priest Caliphe because he loved his people [loved them in his own way], and He will also forgive the clever Pilate who had reflected on the truth, because he did not know what he was creating. What is the Truth? It stood before him, Truth Itself" (15: 249). None of these reflections, which would hardly have been permitted by the censorship, can be found in the text. Nor do we find what can only be considered a reference to Chernyshevsky: "They dream of aluminum columns, the queen-woman prostituted" (15: 250)—a remark that, if it had appeared among Father Zosima's utterances, would have turned him implausibly into a reader of Vera Pavlovna's fourth dream in *What Is To Be Done?* There also seems to be a trace of Feodorov in one note: "The family becomes more encompassing: other than relatives enter into it, the beginnings of a new organism begins to develop" (15: 249).

After completing Book 6, Dostoevsky immediately began to work on the next installment, promised for the September issue. As he wrote to Anna: "I've gotten down to work on the novel, but I am writing little. *There's literally no time*, can you believe that! God grant that at the time of my arrival (the third or fourth of September) I bring a half for the

September issue, and I'll sit down to finish writing the other half the next day after my arrival, without taking a break. And meanwhile the work has to be neat, elegant, like a jewel cutter. These are the most important chapters, and they must establish the public opinion of the novel."[53]

Nine days later, he told Putsykovich that, required by mid-September to send the *Russian Messenger* "*everything* for the September issue . . . I don't even have *half of it* done." He also complains that "I've now started to write with such effort, so slowly, that getting three lines written is a torment for me."[54] This complaint can hardly be taken at face value considering the amount (and the quality) of the manuscript that Dostoevsky was turning out steadily; it may well have been meant only to fend off repeated requests for a contribution to *The Citizen*. But his departure from Ems on August 29/September 10, and the ensuing break of six days required for the journey, slowed down work on his next installment.

## CHAPTER 25

# An Impatient Reader

Most of Dostoevsky's time during the fall and winter of 1879 was spent attempting to maintain his self-imposed schedule for publication of *The Brothers Karamazov*. As we have seen, however, he realized he could not complete the book within a year. One reason was that Books 8 and 9 turned out to require much more development than anticipated, and the work was lengthened to include a Part 4. Another was that he interrupted his writing in the spring of 1880 to participate in the ceremonies attending the dedication of a monument to Pushkin in Moscow. His speech there created a sensation, and became an important cultural-historical event.

Despite the burden of his labors on the novel, he continued to accept invitations to read at charitable occasions, where, as he knew, the audience would be filled with the all-important student youth. Several of these readings were of extracts from his novel, including the Legend of the Grand Inquisitor. Evenings at the home of Elena Shtakenshneider, the "Fridays" of the hospitable poet Yakov P. Polonsky, and the salon of Countess Sofya A. Tolstaya also drew him out of his relative solitude.

## 2

Dostoevsky did not, as he had hoped, return to work the moment he arrived in Staraya Russa. The trip from Bad Ems had been so exhausting that it took him about a week to recover. He then informed Nikolay Lyubimov that he would be "*very* late" in dispatching the next installment, and worried that he might not be able to complete the whole section in time to make the deadline.[1] On September 16 he sent off the first three chapters of Book 7; the fourth, "Cana of Galilee," would be delayed because "an attack of epilepsy has forced me to postpone work for two days." Of this chapter, which marks a crucial phase in the spiritual development of Alyosha, he remarks that it "is the most vital one in the whole installment, and perhaps even in the novel."[2] Originally, Book 7 had been entitled "Grushenka," and would also have contained some of the episodes now involving Dimitry in Book 8. But the title was changed to "Alyosha" once he decided to terminate this section with the dream sequence in which his future hero conquers his own rebellion against God.

Anticipating possible objections, he as usual attempts to counter them in advance. Book 7, narrating the burial of Father Zosima and the scandal caused by the odor of corruption emanating from his corpse, contained one expression that Dostoevsky feared might give offense. "There's just one little word (about the body of a dead person): *started to stink* [*smerdit*]. But it's said by Father Ferapont, and he can't talk in any other way, and even if he could say *started to smell*, he wouldn't." There was also the mention of a laxative, "but that's written properly" (with, that is, no unduly coarse language), and the detail "is also vital, as an important accusation."[3] Most important of all, however, is what he includes in a postscript to these requests.

Because of the sanctity of Father Zosima's life, the community had anticipated that his remains would be much less subject than those of lesser mortals to the ordinary laws of earthly decay. Instead, his bodily decay had been unusually rapid, and the odor of his corpse thus caused a scandal. Dostoevsky was concerned lest his depiction be considered blasphemous, and he thus includes in his postscript "one small nota bene: please don't imagine that I would allow myself, in a work of mine, even the slightest doubt about the miraculous power of relics. The matter concerns only the relics of the deceased Father Zosima, and that is quite another thing. —A commotion like the one depicted by me in the monastery once occurred at Mount Athos, and is narrated in brief and with touching naïveté in *The Wanderings of the Monk Parfeny*." Dostoevsky also requests Lyubimov "to do a good job" of proofing the legend about the "onion," narrated by Grushenka and used as a symbol for the gratifying stirrings of kindness and compassion even amidst the more powerful drives of egoistic self-concern. "It's a gem," Dostoevsky declares. It was "written down by me from the words of a peasant woman, and, of course, *is recorded for the first time*."[4] Here he is mistaken. A Russian folklorist had printed a very similar legend in 1859; but this only illustrates the authenticity of his use of the moral-religious creations of the folk tradition.

The notes for Book 7 are mainly devoted to the visit of Alyosha, led by Rakitin, to Grushenka's home. As the change of title indicates, the original focus of this section had probably been on her intention to seduce Alyosha and on their mutual moral self-discovery. One note, however, exhibits Dostoevsky's anxiety to be accurate about the ceremony attending Father Zosima's burial. "Water, Oil. Holy cloth. Slippers. Cowl with a cross. On the wings of the cherubim, coat. Black cover, and the open cloak.— How much time in the cell before the taking of the body to the church? Who reads over the body? The priest-Monk. The Bible. The priest-Monks and the monk-deacons" (15: 254). There are also overt statements of crucial thematic issues: "When the cadaver began to smell, Alyosha began to doubt for the reasons that

Ivan had so clearly stated: 'The Elder is holy, but there isn't any God'"
(15: 255). Alyosha is also sexually troubled by Grushenka; even before
going to visit her, "*last night sensuous feelings* for Grushenka bit him."
Such stirrings are not mentioned in the text, though suggested when
she sits on his knees. In the notes she states bluntly to him, "I wanted
to corrupt you" (15: 254, 261).

On October 8, Dostoevsky informed Lyubimov that "I am again *forced
to be late*" with the next installment, but he would try to have it arrive
in a week or so.[5] The first four chapters contain the scene in which
Dimitry, lurking in his father's garden, gives the signal that brings the
old man to the window. His appearance fills Dimitry with an overpowering sense of personal repulsion, and he "suddenly pulled the brass
pestle out of his pocket," which he had snatched up a few pages back.
Dostoevsky stops the action at this point by inserting a line of dots,
leaving his readers in suspense; but the sentence immediately following
the hiatus was meant to suggest what had *not* occurred: "'God was
watching over me then,' Mitya himself said afterwards" (14: 355). The
scene continues with Dimitry's flight from the garden, interrupted by
the appearance of the servant Grigory, who attempts to stop him, and
whom he strikes on the head with his brass pestle. Just as in the case of
"The Sentence," however, Dostoevsky perhaps relied too much on the
perspicacity of his readers to decipher his meaning.

These chapters appeared on November 1, and on November 8 he replied to a letter received from a troubled reader unable to control her
impatience and wait for further clarification. It would appear that the
indirect one-sentence exculpation of Dimitry did not allay her doubts.
Dostoevsky replied to her categorically: "The old man Karamazov was
killed by his servant Smerdyakov. All the details will be clarified as the
novel progresses.... Ivan Karamazov participated in the murder only
obliquely and remotely, only by (intentionally) keeping from bringing
Smerdyakov to his senses during the conversation with him before his
departure for Moscow and stating to him clearly and categorically his repugnance for the crime conceived by him (which Ivan Feodorovich
clearly saw and had a premonition of) and thus *seemed to permit* Smerdyakov to commit the crime. The *permission* was essential for Smerdyakov.... Dimitry Feodorovich is completely innocent of the murder of
his father."[6]

Although many details of the novel had not yet been fully worked out,
Dostoevsky evidently had a clear grasp of his murder plot and its thematic significance. He also includes in his reply a little lesson on how
he should be read. "Not just the plot is important for the reader," he
tells her, "but in addition a certain knowledge of the human soul (psychology), which an author has the right to expect from a reader." He

then explains those elements in the text that should have served to reinforce the effect of Dimitry's reference to God. When Dimitry, instead of continuing his flight, leaps down from the fence to examine Grigory's wound and wipe the blood on his forehead, "he seemed to say to the reader already that he was *not* the parricide." His behavior shows compassion, not the cruelty of a murderer, and "if he had killed his father he wouldn't have stood over the servant's body with words of pity."[7] Razumikhin had argued much the same point in defense of Nikolay, the house painter suspected of murder in *Crime and Punishment*. He had been wrestling playfully with his work partner just about the time the murder had been committed: certain types of behavior are simply incompatible with killing another human being. Indeed, such a conviction is intimately linked with a real-life figure, Dostoevsky's erstwhile fellow convict D. I. Ilinsky, whose history initially served to generate the murder plot of the novel. It was difficult to believe the circumstantial evidence against him because of the carefree and lighthearted impression conveyed by his character.

3

October 30 was Dostoevsky's fifty-eighth birthday, and it was marked by a gift from his wife obtained with the help of Countess Tolstaya. He had long expressed admiration for Raphael's Sistine Madonna, a painting that had enthralled him during his visits to the Gemäldegalerie while residing in Dresden. The countess arranged for a large photographic reproduction to be made and presented to Anna by Vladimir Solovyev. When Dostoevsky went into his study that day, much to his surprise and delight he found the picture, framed in wood by Anna, hanging above the couch in his workroom. "How many times," Anna recalls, "[have] I found him in his study in front of that great picture in such deep contemplation that he did not hear me come in."[8] At such moments, she left him undisturbed.

His reverence for this painting is illustrated in an amusing anecdote also interesting from a literary point of view. It took place during an evening at the home of Sofya Kovalevskaya, formerly Korvin-Krukovskaya, whom Dostoevsky had known as an adolescent in the early 1860s while courting her older sister, now Anna Jaclard. Since then, Sofya had become the first woman in Europe to hold a chair in mathematics. The conversation turned on the contribution of various peoples to world art, and Dostoevsky insisted that the Italians were the greatest creators; in his eyes, the Germans had done nothing but copy. "The Greeks," he said, "expressed all the power of their representation of holiness as a beautiful human in the Venus de Milo, [but] the Italians represented the

14. The study in St. Petersburg where Dostoevsky worked on
*The Brothers Karamazov*

genuine Mother of God—the Sistine Madonna. What is the Madonna of
the best German painter, Holbein? A baker's wife! A petty bourgeois!
Nothing more!"[9]

Nor would he budge from this judgment when the talk turned to literature and it was remarked that, after all, Goethe's *Faust* was an original
creation, concentratedly expressing the deep creativity of the German
soul. Not at all, Dostoevsky retorted: "Goethe's *Faust*? It's only the experience of the Book of Job, read the Book of Job—and you will find there
what is important and valuable in *Faust*." Another guest, the well-
known artist Pavel Bryullov, took up this point to argue that the Sistine
Madonna was also "the experience of antiquity, the representation of
beauty in antiquity." Sharply objecting, Dostoevsky asked him to illustrate the point; and the unsuspecting artist replied, "in everything, in
the whole treatment, in every fold of the drapery." Whereupon Dostoevsky leaped up and ran around the room, clasping his head with his
hands and repeating in a voice of indignation and horror: "Drapery!
Drapery! Drapery!"[10] The startled artist told his son, who included the
anecdote in his memoirs, that he was afraid Dostoevsky would have an
epileptic fit; but he quieted down, took a seat, remained silent, and soon
left. The suggestion that such a technical detail could diminish the re-

464

splendent Christian majesty and originality of the Sistine Madonna was more than he could tolerate.

On November 16, he dispatched the remaining chapters of Book 8. In Chapter 3, "Gold Mines," he satirically depicts the flighty Mme Khokhlakova driving Dimitry into a frenzy by seeming at first to promise him the money he requires, but then urging him instead to obtain it (and even more!) by going off to the gold mines in Siberia. Babbling on in her giddy fashion, she suddenly, to exhibit her deep concern about current social issues, declares that "I am not at all opposed to the present movement. . . . The development of woman, and even the political emancipation of woman in the near future—that's my ideal!" Indeed, "I wrote a letter to the author, Shchedrin, on that subject" and signed it anonymously "a mother" rather than "contemporary mother" because "the word 'contemporary' might have reminded him of *The Contemporary*—a painful recollection owing to the present censorship" (15: 359).

By recalling here the suppression of the radical journal *The Contemporary* in 1866, Dostoevsky was reviving an old polemical quarrel with the satirist Mikhail Saltykov-Shchedrin. Not a man to be challenged lightly, Saltykov-Shchedrin immediately published a retort in a postscriptum to his regular column in *Notes of the Fatherland*. Calling Khokhlakova a *salopnitsa* (a gossipy vulgarian) and imitating Dostoevsky by intermingling fiction with fact, he declares that he never received such a letter and that the character must have invented it only to suggest that *The Contemporary* was still speaking through his voice. In a much lengthier broadside a month later, he displays all his satirical verve in characterizing her as a congenital liar, like all those society ladies first depicted by Gogol, and really so empty-headed that she confuses everything and had mistaken *The Contemporary* for *Time* and *Epoch* (Dostoevsky's own journals). Mr. Dostoevsky, he continues, with a mocking display of literary camaraderie, "forced her to mumble [about *The Contemporary*] totally in contradiction with the genuine artistic sensibility that constitutes the outstanding artistic quality of the productions of this most talented of the followers of Gogol."[11] On the other hand, he continues, Feodor Pavlovich Karamazov is a nasty, debauched, treacherous but by no means obtuse individual, capable of any betrayal. Such a remark coming from *him* would not have been offensive at all, and much more verisimilar. Dostoevsky, of course, had been accused of betrayal, both by the radicals since the mid-1860s and by his conservative friends because of the publication of *A Raw Youth* in Saltykov-Shchedrin's own journal. The thrust of this supposedly literary observation—which also implicitly identifies Dostoevsky with his most despicable character—would not have been lost on the satirist's Populist readers.

4

In the letter sent along with the second installment of Book 8, Dostoevsky announced to Lyubimov an important alteration of his initial plan. Book 8 had turned out to be longer than he had foreseen because "a great many completely new characters suddenly appeared . . . and each one had to be outlined as fully as possible, even though cursorily." The appearance and characterization of all those officials who come to take Dimitry into custody at Mokroe thus led to the addition of a new section. Dostoevsky had intended to stop publishing after the November installment of Book 8, and to resume only at the beginning of the new year; but now he declares, *"I'll send you an additional new book, a ninth, for the December issue*, so as thereby to finish up this part."[12] This decision was probably the result of conversations with A. A. Shtakenshneider, the brother of Elena, who had served as a public prosecutor, and with whom he consulted about "all those instances which concerned the judicial process" to make sure of their accuracy. In a letter to Elena he called her brother "my valued coworker."[13] This expert probably alerted Dostoevsky to the important changes that had occurred in Russian legal procedure, and which inspired an unforeseen addition to the novel.

"I originally wanted to limit myself just to *the judicial investigation* in court," he tells Lyubimov. "But in conferring with a prosecutor (someone with a lot of experience) I suddenly saw that an entire, extremely interesting, and extremely limping part of our criminal procedure (the sore spot in our criminal procedure) would thus disappear from my novel without a trace. That part of the procedure is called '*the preliminary investigation*,' with the old routine and the most modern abstract impersonality embodied in the young lawyers, judicial investigators, and so on."[14] All this material would constitute the new Book 9, promised for the December issue.

Aside from allowing him to dramatize once again, and on a larger scale, the shortcomings of the abstract notions of law imported from the West, whose human limitations he had already railed against through Razumikhin in *Crime and Punishment*, the preliminary investigation also gave Dostoevsky the possibility of enlarging his portrayal of Dimitry. In this new book, he informs Lyubimov, "I'll outline Mitya Karamazov's character even more strongly: he experiences a purification of his heart and conscience under the storm of misfortune and false accusation. *He accepts with his soul punishment not for what he did but for the fact that he was so hideous that he could and did want to commit the crime* of which he will be falsely accused through a judicial error [italics added]. It's a thoroughly Russian personality: if the thunder doesn't rumble, the peasant won't cross himself. His moral purification begins during the several hours of preliminary investigation to which I intend to devote this Book 9."[15]

He again repeats his intention to write an open letter taking all the blame for failure to finish the novel in one year and informing readers that the external structure of the novel had been extended from three parts to four. In addition, he asks Lyubimov to be especially careful about the proofreading of the chapters just submitted. "I have portrayed two Poles, who speak either in pure Polish or in a broken mixture of Russian and Polish. My purely Polish phrases are correct, but in the mixed speech the Polish words may have come out somewhat prepos- terously, but I think they're right too." He was also worried that the story about Podvysotsky in these chapters—"a legendary story of all Pol- ish cardsharps," which he claims to have heard three times with his own ears—might be taken badly by real-life individuals with the same family name; "but since *nothing offensive, shameful, or even funny* is actually said . . . I have left the real name." Nonetheless, he gives per- mission to change the spelling if Lyubimov thinks it preferable. He also informs the editor "that the [somewhat lewd] song sung by the chorus" of peasant girls at the Mokroe festivities "was recorded by me on the spot and in fact is a specimen of the latest peasant art."[16]

Dostoevsky found it impossible, however, to keep his promise to fin- ish Book 9 for the December issue. On December 8 he wrote Lyubimov that "I worked so hard that I fell ill, [and] the book's theme (the prelimi- nary investigation) has grown longer and more complicated." As with each successive section, he now feels that "this book turns out to be one of the most important for me in the novel," and "if I were to push myself and make a hash of it I would do harm to myself as a writer both now and forever." Aside from his own desire to produce as polished a work as possible, his novel, as he also stresses, has become an event that is galvanizing public opinion. "The novel is being read everywhere, people write me letters, it's being read by young people, it's being read in high society, it's being criticized or praised in the press, and never before, with regard to the impression produced all around, have I had such a success."[17] Dostoevsky assures Lyubimov that Book 9 will be sent for the January issue without fail, but he wishes to resume publication with Part 4 only in March.

His official letter to Katkov, absolving the journal from the charge of unduly prolonging publication of the novel, was printed in the Decem- ber issue. If the journal could be criticized for anything, he wrote, "then perhaps only for excessive consideration for me as a writer and for con- stant patient indulgence for my weakened health."[18] Writing personally to Lyubimov, he mentions having abandoned the idea of including in the published letter "a few explanations of the idea of the novel [and] an indirect response to certain critics without naming anyone." Dostoevsky had decided that such explanations could wait until the novel had been completed, but he asked the journal to reserve space in the future "for these explanations and answers which I may in fact write if I haven't changed my mind by then."[19] Such an article about the book in general was never written, although he set down a brief explanation of the Legend of the Grand Inquisitor at the end of December.

His strenuous labors on the novel did not prevent him from participating in literary evenings on behalf of charitable causes, and on December 14 he read for the benefit of the higher education courses established for women. He chose as his text the monologue of the twelve-year-old Nellie in *The Insulted and Injured*, who grows up in terrible destitution and whose fierce pride turns back on itself in a masochistic self-punishment labeled "the egoism of suffering." In his artistic gallery of characters, she is a first sketch for the outraged and vengeful self-debasement of Nastasya Filippovna in *The Idiot*. As usual, Dostoevsky held his audience spellbound, and the reporter covering the event for *New Time* wrote that "the authenticity, the directness, the naturalness of the speech, the degree of vivacity with which the very viewpoint of the child was given, caused many of those present to shed tears. One must give the author his due, he knew how to represent reality fully, and it was enough to close your eyes in order to believe that before you was prattling an adolescent girl."[20]

Two days later, he read "A Little Boy at Christ's Christmas Party" (it was, after all, the Christmas season) for the benefit of needy students at the Larinsky *gymnasium*. Among other notables participating were A. I. Palm and Aleksey Pleshcheev, both of whom had been members of the Petrashevsky circle in the mid-1840s. Dostoevsky had been particularly close to the latter, who as a very young man had published to some acclaim a volume of "civic" poetry. But he had not succeeded in sustaining his early success and, now on the staff of *Notes of the Fatherland*, had led an undistinguished journalistic career. It was probably this encounter, and perhaps some conversation, that reminded Dostoevsky of a long-standing debt to Pleshcheev, who had loaned him a thousand rubles in 1858 to make the trip from Siberia back to European Russia. A few days later Dostoevsky laboriously climbed the staircase to the Pleshcheev flat (they lived not too far apart) and left a portion of the repayment with his son, particularly asking the young man to tell his father that he had called in person. Dostoevsky also left a note, reading in part: "Here is an additional two hundred rubles in payment of my never-ending (to my shame) debt to you. . . . Please don't judge me too severely for this still partly unpaid debt. I'm ashamed of myself."[21] After Dostoevsky's death, the meticulous Anna Grigoryevna paid off the remaining amount.

He was also reminded of his past, though in a much more pleasant fashion, by a letter from the great actor Vasily Samoylov, whose talent he had enjoyed in the 1840s when Samoylov was beginning his career at the Alexandrinsky Theatre in St. Petersburg. His acting style, marked by intelligence and naturalness, was all the rage of the young generation and had been praised by Belinsky. The actor wrote to Dostoevsky that, in reading his works, he had been struck by the "precision" of the novelist's depiction of human character, "with its weaknesses and virtues," and regretted that he had never written anything for the stage. Dostoevsky replied gratefully that "your opinion is *dearer* to me than all the opinions and reviews of my works that I have managed to read." He praises Samoylov as "a great psychologist, who produced rapture in me already in my youth and adolescence . . . [and] *certainly* had a great influence on my heart and mind."[22] At the end of the month Dostoevsky took part in a benefit organized on behalf of the students at the University of St. Petersburg, and it was Samoylov on this occasion who read "A Little Boy at Christ's Christmas Party."

What he himself chose to read was the Legend of the Grand Inquisitor. A few days before the event, he informed the organizers that he had selected this text; and they thought it wise to submit the proposal to the theological authorities for permission. In reply, Archimandrite Iosif declared that certain passages could not be approved. These sections, referring to "certain monuments of religious literature and even to the lives of Orthodox saints," lacked "the respect [such references] deserved."[23] No further information is provided, but the archimandrite probably meant Ivan's introductory remarks, where he refers casually to Dante, the mystery plays in Victor Hugo's *Notre Dame de Paris*, and "similar plays . . . occasionally performed in Moscow, too, up to the time of Peter the Great. But besides the plays there were all sorts of legends and 'verses' scattered about the world, in which saints and angels and all the powers of Heaven took part when required" (14: 225). The pious clergyman could well have been upset by such offhand allusions to the use of sacred narrative and saintly lives for the purposes of worldly entertainment. Dostoevsky thus received permission to read the Legend, but presumably omitted the objectionable introductory section.

This clerical interdiction, however, probably motivated him to supply some prefatory remarks to replace what had been prohibited. In any event, he began the reading with his own explanation of the Legend:

An atheist, sick with disbelief, composes in a moment of torment a wild, fantastic poem in which he brings Christ into conversation with one of the most important priestly dignitaries of the Catholic Church—the Grand Inquisitor. The suffering of the creator of the poem has its immediate source in the fact that he, in the fantasy form of the Grand Inquisitor and his Catholic worldview, which is so far removed from the old apostolic orthodoxy, sees a truly existing servant of Christ. His Grand Inquisitor, however, is himself in substance an atheist. The fundamental thought is that if you distort the truth of Christ by identifying it with the aims of this world, you instantly lose the meaning of Christianity; your reason undoubtedly must fall prey to disbelief; instead of the true ideal of Christ, a new Tower of Babel is constructed. The sublime Christian view of mankind is reduced to regarding it [humankind] as if it were an animal herd, and under the guise of a social love of mankind there appears a scarcely masked contempt for it. The exposition is in the form of a conversation between two brothers. One brother, an atheist, narrates the subject of his poem to the other.[24]

Unfortunately, there is no journalistic account of the audience reaction on that evening, but it may be gathered indirectly from a letter Dostoevsky wrote a month and a half later in response to an invitation by the Literary Fund. Asked if he would agree to present the Legend of the Grand Inquisitor again, he replied regretfully that it was impossible. "The supervisor [of the St. Petersburg schools, Prince M. S. Volkonsky] allowed me to read 'The Grand Inquisitor' . . . at a literary reading. . . . The supervisor himself was present at the reading. But after the reading, he told me that, judging by the impression it had made, he would not allow me to read it from now on."[25] Evidently, it had affected the audience to such a degree that the wary prince thought it unwise to allow so much excitement to be stirred up once more. Perhaps the Grand Inquisitor, for all its historical distancing, could too easily be identified with the repressive Russian authorities, who just at this moment, even if they were not burning heretics at the stake, were attempting to stamp out the armed revolutionary unrest by summary executions.

Dostoevsky was always accompanied on such public appearances by Anna Grigoryevna, who certainly enjoyed "those tumultuous ovations" her husband was constantly receiving from "admiring Petersburg audiences." Moreover, she served as his "armor-bearer," carrying "the book my husband was to read from, his cough medicine (pastilles from Ems), an extra handkerchief in case he misplaced his, a plaid to wrap around his throat when he went into the cold, etc."[26] But such occasions were for her a source of irritation and exasperation as well, especially if one or another of the gentlemen present kissed her hand with what seemed, to the suspicious eye of her uncontrollably jealous husband, a little too much assiduity. Anna found such suspicions to be not only insulting but also ludicrous, since the supposedly potential seducers were invariably of such an advanced age that no sudden flare-up of passion could conceivably have occurred. Her account allows us an amusing glimpse of these readings from behind the scenes; but it also shows that, in describing the frantic jealousy of Dimitry Karamazov over Grushenka, Dostoevsky simply had to look into his own breast and write.

## 5

Several memoirs also enable us to observe Dostoevsky elsewhere than at his writing table toiling over *The Brothers Karamazov*. A young man named Evgeny Nikolaevich Opochinin, who worked in the library and museum of the Society for the Lovers of Old (Russian) Literature, was also an acquaintance of Dostoevsky's longtime friend Alexander P. Milyukov, and it was through him that the two met in 1879. Dostoevsky obviously took to the twenty-one-year-old, and their conversations are recorded in a notebook of Opochinin's first published in 1936. He describes the older man as follows: "An unimposing exterior; somewhat stooped; hair and beard reddish-brown; sickly face; a wart on the right cheek. Gloomy eyes, from time to time they gleam with suspicion and mistrust, but for the most part one sees some pensive thought and a hint of sorrow. In conversation occasionally his look catches fire, and sometimes becomes threatening (the conversation about Turgenev). 'All my life [Dostoevsky said] he bestowed on me his contemptuous condescension, and behind my back he gossiped, and spread slander and scandal.' "[27]

His lengthy tirade against Turgenev, obviously stemming from their recent hostile encounters, diagnoses the sociology of the landowning gentry class to which the rival novelist belonged by birth. "You know," he told Opochinin, "that is how it always was in those gentry circles: they were raised among the tale-telling of obsequious lackeys and sponging dependents, and they evaluated all those who did not resemble themselves hostilely and maliciously. It was enough for someone to be superior to the person judging him for a whole wall of calumny to collapse on him." Besides inheriting such traits, Turgenev allegedly was also terribly faint-hearted and wished to please everybody "so that everyone should extol and praise him—both at home and abroad. That's why he crawled before Flaubert and many others." Dostoevsky was quite scornful of this kowtowing to foreign celebrities, which served to enhance Turgenev's reputation at home: "'I am,' he says, 'a European writer, not like my other countrymen—I am a friend, you see, of Flaubert himself.'" He then goes on to pillory Turgenev as a "cosmopolitan" and a "citizen of the world," whose supposedly affectionate portrayal of Russian life was all pretense and falsity. "You feel that he does not at all love what he depicts in such a touching manner . . . with sighs, with tears." All those Russian peasants Turgenev treats so poetically were flogged by his mother, and Dostoevsky adds, quite viciously, that Turgenev "would not renounce this pleasure" if it had still been allowed.[28] Such a slanderous and totally unjustified remark shows Dostoevsky at his worst, at a moment when his rancor against Turgenev had become a source of gossip in Russian literary circles—to such an extent, indeed, that his old friend Polonsky was afraid to invite both notables to the same Friday gathering.

Walking through the streets with Opochinin on December 23, and passing the throngs of Christmas shoppers and children standing transfixed before the window displays of toy stores (much as in Dostoevsky's story, "A Little Boy at Christ's Christmas Party"), the novelist remarked to his companion how much he enjoyed such strolls at that time of year. "Christmas is essentially a children's holiday. That's how it should be. Children, even the youngest, ought to enjoy themselves in every way during these days: let them meet in joyfulness the Christ being born to the world." Turning his attention to some poorly dressed youngsters, emaciated and pale, engrossed at one of the windows, he exclaimed: "Just look at them. . . . What are they now thinking? What castles are they building? And if you ask them—they will say nothing! And your questions will be taken badly—that's why everything written about children is nonsense and lies."[29]

He then ridicules those who "lisp" over children with sentimental sweetness (the Russian is very onomatopoetic: *syusyukat*) and calls this *podlost* (which here probably means fakery or affectation). "There is a great depth in the souls of children; [they have] their own world, different from that of adults, with sometimes such tragedy in it that even a genius would lose his way." Dostoevsky will soon attempt to portray this children's world in his Book 10, and he seems here to be preparing himself inwardly for the task. And the spirit of Christmas may well have had its effect. When Opochinin attempted to turn the topic back to Turgenev, Dostoevsky closed the subject with a much more equable evaluation: "There are very few like [Turgenev]. . . . A brilliant and great talent. Too bad, really, that it's lodged in such a self-lover and dissembler; but after all, the sun is not without spots."[30]

Another conversation occurred when Dostoevsky was by no means in a receptive mood. Opochinin thought that his face showed "exhaustion and illness," and at first he hardly spoke at all. But suddenly he began to talk about a poem satirizing Russia, a poem written earlier in the century and published abroad because of its sacrilegious content. He quoted two lines and was much impressed when his interlocutor (who had come across the poem in one of his father's notebooks) recited the rest from memory. Two lines of the poem speak ironically of Russia: "Where God is only in images / Not in the convictions of men." Dostoevsky then began to inveigh against the poet, whose irony he attributes to not having "lived among the people and penetrated mentally into their souls. . . . How could he know that God must be in the soul and the heart (that is where he is among our people), that men must be united with him, and not only be convinced of the existence of God, for such a conviction is not faith. Nobody can *not* be convinced of the existence of God [italics added]. I think that even atheists preserve this conviction, even though they don't admit it, out of shame, perhaps?—I really don't know."[31] Uttered by the writer who will soon portray the moral-psychic breakdown of Ivan Karamazov, such words take on a considerable extra weight of meaning.

As for the line asserting that "God is only in images," Dostoevsky retorts that the poet "did not understand this, that if the people—note, the entire people—can revere the image of God, that is, feeble, sometimes even monstrous representations of God, Christ, and the Mother of God, how much more must they revere and love God himself! Among the people, God always takes first place. . . . They need sacred objects by their side, visible, as reflections of Godliness. . . . One must believe, aspire to the invisible God, but revere Him on earth with simple customs that are related [to Him]. You can tell me that such belief is blind and naïve, and I will reply that faith should be that way. We can't all be theologians."[32]

Such thoughts then led Dostoevsky into a lengthy diatribe against "seminarians," from whose ranks had come many of the most important Russian radicals, and whose presumed opportunism and unscrupulosity he was then caricaturing in his novel. The personage of Rakitin, a priestly novice preparing for a great career in radical journalism, was to be Dostoevsky's final effort to settle accounts with this prominent social-cultural type. Like Rakitin (though no such reference to this character is made in the conversation), the seminarians had read all the Church Fathers with an analogous result: "They produce the most vicious atheists, not to mention quite simply blasphemers. Nobody knows how to blaspheme so thoroughly and skillfully as a seminarian."[33]

Dostoevsky recalled conversations from the early 1860s with Nikolay Pomyalovsky, whose *Seminary Sketches* were an exposé, often compared with Dickens's *Nicholas Nickleby*, of the oppressive and tyrannical conditions existing in such educational establishments. Pomyalovsky told him such stories "that [my hair] stood on end," and "he knew every kind of blasphemous prayer, many exclamations, disgusting parodies of church services." Himself a radical, Pomyalovsky had narrated all these enormities so surprisingly well that Dostoevsky was startled at how little he had been offended. "One's repulsion simply slipped past, was forgotten as it were, so much was he inspired."[34] Art can thus deal with the most controversial material in such a way that what may be morally repellent is simply forgotten or overlooked. Perhaps Dostoevsky was hoping that the same would be true of the many passages in his own book which, if not blasphemous, certainly called into question the pieties of traditional Christian faith.

Toward the end of the 1870s, Dostoevsky regularly visited the salons of Elena Shtakenshneider, Polonsky (when Turgenev was not in Petersburg), and Countess Tolstaya. Well aware of his reputation as a somewhat misanthropic guest who could not always be counted on to observe the social niceties, he occasionally jested about himself in this regard. Once, after an exchange of civilities with Shtakenshneider, she wrote that "he brightened up once and for all. 'Here, just look at what worldly people we are,'" he said, referring to himself, "'and Polonsky is afraid to allow me in the same room with Turgenev.'"[35] Dostoevsky was by no means always bearish and forbidding in society, and was particularly responsive to younger people in whom he could detect a spark of sympathy. One young woman, also a guest at this salon, was Lidya Veselitskaya, who attracted his attention and about whom he spoke to Anna Grigoryevna.

"After two or three talks . . . ," she wrote, "he divined in her (notwithstanding her youth and understandable embarrassment) an uncommon young woman who held the promise of something higher: aspirations toward an ideal and, in all probability, a literary flair."[36] Writing under the pen name of V. Mikulich, she later produced a volume of short stories, *Mimochka*, which attracted attention because of their sharp criticism of the frivolity of the education given to upper-class girls. Veselitskaya also left her impressions of these Shtakenshneider "Tuesdays," including her view of Dostoevsky. "Involuntarily," she wrote, "I shifted my glance from the untroubled, innocent physiognomy of Strakhov to the spasmodically excitable, tortured face of Dostoevsky, with his burning eyes, and thought: 'How can they hold the same ideas? . . . One loves what is, the other what should be; one clings to what is and was, the other crucifies himself for what is coming, or at least should come. And if he awaits this, craves so much for what should come, does this not mean that he is hardly satisfied with what is?'"[37] These words express a generally felt attitude toward Dostoevsky that once again helps to explain why even those opposed to his particular social-political views were reluctant to place him in the camp of the diehard reactionaries.

## CHAPTER 26

# Terror and Martial Law

The new year of 1880 began auspiciously for the Dostoevskys. "Feodor Mikhailovich's health," wrote Anna Grigoryevna, "seemed much stronger after his trip to Ems of the previous year, and his epileptic attacks were a good deal less frequent. Our children were quite well. *The Brothers Kara-mazov* was undoubtedly a success, and Feodor Mikhailovich, always so severe with himself, was highly pleased with certain chapters."[1] For all this glowing report, it was clear that Dostoevsky's physical stamina was weakening in spite of temporary improvement; no one could say just how long he would be able to count on his full literary capacities. Nonetheless, he regularly produced new installments of the novel that was holding all of literate Russia transfixed, and he led a social and public life that would have proved taxing even for a much younger man.

Meanwhile, the social-political situation was going from bad to worse. An explosion occurred in the very precincts of the Winter Palace itself, just a few days before the official celebration of the twenty-fifth anniversary of the reign of Alexander II. The country was then placed under martial law. Writing on behalf of the Slavic Benevolent Society, Dostoevsky penned one of the ceremonial declarations of loyalty to the Tsar; but his text betrays all the inner uncertainty that Russia was experiencing at this frightening moment.

## 2

The Dostoevskys were now relatively well off, compared with their economic situation in the past, but they had been unable to amass any capital and were much concerned about the future of their children. The enterprising Anna Grigoryevna thus added a new business venture to the Dostoevsky publishing house already in operation, namely, the establishment of a book service for people in the provinces wishing to be supplied quickly and reliably with the latest publications. She counted on former subscribers to the *Diary of a Writer* and on admirers of Dostoevsky's work to respond to her announcement of the new service; and her expectations were not disappointed.

He himself was already laying plans for activities beyond the termination of his novel. He had been invited to be present at a Christmas party at a mental hospital some distance from the center of Petersburg, and he had tentatively accepted on December 22; but on the twenty-seventh he withdrew because of the lingering effects of an epileptic attack. "I have extremely distorted mental impressions . . . ," he wrote, "[and] I am afraid of increasing their number [the mental patients] with my own person." But he hopes that he can visit the hospital on some other occasion, explaining that "I may start up the *Diary of a Writer* again in the fall. A piece about visiting the patients . . . could turn out to be very interesting and suitable for my *Diary*."[2] Invitations during this holiday season came not only from the doctor in charge of the mental hospital but also from the highest circles of Russian society. In a letter to Sofya Khitrovo, the niece of Countess Sofya Tolstaya and the wife of an important diplomat with a literary salon of her own (as well as the great, unfulfilled passion of Vladimir Solovyev's life), Dostoevsky regretfully refused an invitation for dinner at the home of the countess for himself and Anna because she was ill.[3]

On January 8 he announced to Nikolay Lyubimov that Book 9 was entirely completed and would be sent in a few days. Anna's illness had delayed copying the text, and "this Book 9 has turned out to be incomparably longer than I had assumed." But he hastened to add that the unexpected bulk would not increase the length of the novel: "Part 4 will inevitably be shortened by just as much, since what was said in the 'Preliminary Investigation' naturally can now be communicated in Part 4 without details." The later trial scene could thus be (and was) abbreviated because so many of the facts at issue (though not, of course, their interpretation) would already be known. Dostoevsky had also been held up because "I need to read it all over to a former provincial public prosecutor [A. A. Shtakenshneider] so that there not be any important error or absurdity . . . even though I wrote it while consulting the whole time with this same public prosecutor."[4] Although he did not commit any "important" legal errors or absurdities, two minor mistakes have been located in his account of court procedures.

While in the midst of preparing his manuscript, he found the time to answer a letter from a completely unknown correspondent, a young *kursistka* enrolled in the Higher Education Courses for Women. The student began with profuse apologies for disturbing him and outlined the inner struggle she endured before being able to put pen to paper. But "I know that you, better than anyone else, can clarify for me all the questions touching the spiritual life of humankind"; and since she was on the point of losing her faith in God, she had now turned to him for spiritual succor. "People whose souls were eternally gloomy," she explains, "have taken away and destroyed my faith in Christ—as God." Instead, they have "offered something else—'the unattainable ideal of humankind.' But in this exalted abstraction of theirs—despite all desire—I have not the strength to believe." If she begins to talk with them about "Christ, about truth," they would respond, "a good meal, satisfied stomach, the satisfaction of all needs" "Here," she continues, "resounds a voice just as frightening as the one heard in the 'Grand Inquisitor.'"[5]

Expressing his regrets for not having replied sooner, Dostoevsky invites his correspondent to visit him, because such questions "*cannot be answered* in writing." Her own letter, he continues, "is passionate and sincere. You are really suffering and can't help suffering." He urges her not to lose heart: "You're not the first to have lost faith but later to save yourself." As for the people she speaks of, he advises her to ask who they really are—"not whether they're good or bad, but whether they know Christ, in essence." He assures her that they evidently do not, and are speaking in ignorance of what they deny. "They are all infected with a general unhealthy trait of all members of the Russian intelligentsia: that is, a frivolous attitude toward the subject, an extraordinary vanity surpassing what the greatest minds of Europe could think of, and a phenomenal ignorance of what they are judging." Encouraging her to keep up her spirits, he assures her that "I know many negators who at the end have gone over to Christ with all their being."[6]

Six days later he wrote to the persistent Victor Putsykovich, who had sent him several recent issues of the *Russian Citizen* without receiving any acknowledgment. "I haven't written you for a while," Dostoevsky admits, explaining: "In the last three months I've written and turned in nineteen signatures. I've wrecked my health, neglected everything: visits, calls, letters." But now he could enjoy "a week or even ten days of rest" before plunging into the next installment. Dostoevsky advises him to attempt to patch up things with Katkov, whose newspaper had praised the patriotic sentiments of the *Russian Citizen* in connection with the most recent attempt on the life of the Tsar.[7] The rumor that a new conservative weekly was on the point of being launched is greeted with mixed feelings ("that would be good if it were a success," he comments). There is also reference to a question directly related to Dostoevsky himself and the theme of *The Brothers Karamazov*.

A recent issue of the *Warsaw Diary* contained an editorial that, in Dostoevsky's view, "defends the abuse of children." The writer had poured scorn on the notion of founding a society for the protection of children, and, referring to the Kroneberg case, had objected to such matters being given so much publicity. "Nobody," the editorial declared, "informed society that such a public discussion of the issue between parents and children [the trial and, presumably, Dostoevsky's article in the *Diary*] destroys the foundation of the family. . . . The family

... is holy, and our law protects its inviolability." The already published chapter of his novel, "Rebellion," in which Ivan Karamazov so heart-breakingly details the torture of small children by parents, could very well be considered as included in this condemnation.[8]

"They mock the idea of a society for the protection of children," Dostoevsky heatedly exclaims to Putsykovich. "In their opinion, defending abused children means destroying the family. What absurdity! But the family where fathers smear a four-year-old daughter with shit, feed her shit, and lock her in a toilet on a freezing night—is that family a sacred thing, hasn't it already been destroyed? What an absurdity on their part!"[9] Dostoevsky's example, taken from the Brunst trial, is used by Ivan in his tirade against God; and the sacredness of a family in which the father is unworthy, willfully negligent, and intolerably tyrannical lies at the heart of Dostoevsky's novel.

## 3

On February 3, the members of the Slavic Benevolent Society selected Dostoevsky to write a congratulatory address to be presented to Alexander II on February 19, the twenty-fifth anniversary of his accession to the throne. He had been elected a member of this profoundly patriotic and Pan-Slavic organization in 1873, and just recently had become a member of its governing council. The text of this document, preferred to the Tsar on the appointed date, will be discussed below. But two weeks before the planned festivities, Russia was shaken by an event that cast a gloomy funereal pall over the prospective festivities.

On February 5, at twenty-two minutes past six in the early evening, a bomb exploded in the Winter Palace just under the dining room of the Tsar. A diplomatic dinner had been scheduled for that hour in honor of Prince Alexander von Battenburg, the newly elected ruler of Bulgaria, and the party was just about to enter the banquet chamber when the explosion occurred. Neither the Tsar nor his guests were injured, but the blast killed ten soldiers on guard duty and wounded fifty-six others. Responsible for the carnage was Narodnaya Volya (People's Will), a group of formerly Populist radicals who had decided that the assassination of Alexander II was an indispensable first step toward the hope of any social-economic improvement. One of their members, Stepan Khalturin, a skilled cabinetmaker and carpenter, had obtained employment in the palace under a pseudonym and lived in a room in the basement. He gradually smuggled in small quantities of dynamite, storing it at his bedside until he believed he had enough to accomplish his purpose; but the explosion, though powerful, had not been strong enough to collapse the dining room floor.

This was the fourth unsuccessful attempt by Narodnaya Volya to kill the Tsar—at long range, so to speak. Previously, they had made elaborate and carefully planned efforts to blow up the railroad carriage on which he traveled. But they were thwarted by a series of accidents, although in one case a baggage car, mistaken for the royal coach, was blown to smithereens. Despite this new failure, Khalturin's defiant invasion of the Tsar's own residence succeeded in creating an awesome image of the power of the hidden revolutionaries, who were apparently able to penetrate anywhere they pleased. The authorities were impotent to cope with their activities; and the terrified state of mind overwhelming the ruling circles can be caught in the diary of Dostoevsky's admirer, Grand Duke Konstantin Konstantinovich. "We are living through a time of terror," he wrote on February 7, "with this one difference. The Parisians during the revolution saw their enemies face-to-face, and we not only do not see them or know them, but have not the faintest idea of their number . . . general panic."[10]

There is no record of any immediate reaction on Dostoevsky's part to this frightening and sensational event, but some allusions to it can be found in his ceremonial address to the throne. He also spoke about it on February 20 to the journalist Aleksey S. Suvorin, who recorded the conversation in his diary. Before turning to these documents, however, the ominous atmosphere of these tension-filled and crisis-ridden days should be evoked in a little more detail. On February 7, Narodnaya Volya published a statement taking full responsibility for the explosion and expressing "deep distress" at the death of the soldiers, but declaring that such efforts would continue unless the Tsar handed over his powers to a constituent assembly. To gauge the state of public opinion, we may cite again the report of the commission appointed after the earlier assassination attempt by Alexander Solovyov, which had referred to "the almost complete failure of the educated classes to support the government in its fight against a relatively small band of evildoers . . . they are to some extent waiting for the outcome of the battle."[11] Historians agree that such public apathy was extremely widespread in the final years of Alexander's reign. There was, instead, a general sympathy for the young radicals of the "going to the people" movement, whose trials had unmasked the unconscionable mistreatment of these (at worst) peaceful propagandists. The sensational acquittal of Vera Zasulich, to the plaudits of a courtroom packed with society notables, had glaringly revealed this disaffection from the throne even among those who might have been expected to rally to its support.

In response to this new threat, erupting at the very moment when the Tsar's loyal subjects were scheduled to offer their expressions of fidelity and devotion, Alexander II decided that drastic measures had to be taken. Count Mikhail T. Loris-Melikov, an army officer of Armenian descent who had been ennobled in recognition of his heroism and victories in the Russo-Turkish War, had successfully suppressed terrorist radicals as governor-general of Kharkov while understanding the necessity of placating moderately liberal opinion. The Tsar now appointed him dictator in charge of the entire country, empowered "to make all dispositions and to take all measures" necessary to ensure public tranquillity not only in Petersburg but anywhere in the empire where this became necessary. The period of his rule, which began on February 12, has been called "the dictatorship of the heart" because of some slight easing of government controls. Dostoevsky reacted favorably to Loris-Melikov's assumption of power and queried Suvorin, who was close to the count's entourage, about his capabilities. "Is Loris surrounding himself with good people, is he sending good people to the provinces?" he inquired. "This is terribly important. —And there are good people, many to choose from."[12] One of Loris-Melikov's first moves was to issue two declarations appealing to Russian society (which of course meant its educated upper class) to cooperate in reestablishing a necessary basis for civic order. Dostoevsky, while certainly in agreement with the plea, complained that these appeals were "badly written." The memoirist also reports that he "heaped invective on Peter [the Great], who looked on all of Russia as his property."[13]

4
———

On February 14, Dostoevsky presented a draft of his jubilee address to the assembled members of the Slavic Benevolent Society, and, according to K. N. Bestuzhev-Ryumin, "he electrified the meeting in reading his confession of faith." Indeed, the document was much more a confession than a celebratory invocation.[14] The address was then submitted to the minister of the interior, L. S. Makov, who made some suggestions for changes that were accepted. The first paragraphs contain the obligatory conventional phrases expressing the devotion of the members of the Slavic Benevolent Society, along with all the Russian people (*narod*), to their beneficent and loving ruler; and Dostoevsky then eulogizes the reign of a Tsar who had, after all, liberated the serfs and instituted a far-reaching series of other quite praiseworthy reforms.[15] All the same, other passages transform this text into one of the most unusual documents ever written for such an occasion.

In accompaniment to its tribute, the document also informs the Tsar—as if he did not already know it full well!—that, among the vast majority of fervent and devoted servants of the fatherland, there had long since appeared, in "the cultured [*intelligentny*] stratum of society," people "not believing in either the Russian people or its truth, nor even in God." On the heels of such people came "impatient destroyers, ignorant even in their convictions . . . *sincere* evildoers, proclaiming the idea of total destruction and anarchy" but genuinely believing that whatever remained after destruction had done its work would be preferable to what exists. Now "the young Russian energies, alas, so *sincerely* deluding themselves, have at last fallen under the power of dark, underground forces, under the power of enemies of the Russian land and consequently of all Christendom" (italics added). These were the forces that, "with unexampled audacity," not long ago "committed unheard-of evil deeds in our country, which caused shudders of outrage in our upright and mighty people and in the entire world." (Whether it was diplomatic to have referred, even obliquely, to the Winter Palace explosion or to the earlier attempts on the Tsar's life may well be questioned.)

Nor does Dostoevsky denounce the perpetrators of these outrages with any of the strongly condemnatory epithets that might have been expected. For him they are "young Russian energies" whose motives, whatever their "evil deeds," could hardly be considered *entirely* criminal or wicked because they had been misguided in their *sincerity* and gone astray. In addition, the nefariousness of their actions begins to dissolve when these young people are viewed as the products of the entire course of Russian social-cultural development, the end result of what had begun with those who did not believe in the Russian people, in its truth, and in God (presumably the generation of the 1840s). Dostoevsky assures the Tsar that the Slavic Benevolent Society "stands, so far as their opinions are concerned, firmly opposed—both to the faintheartedness of so many fathers, and the wild madness of their children, *who believe in villainy and sincerely bow down before it.*" This repeated emphasis on the "sincerity" of the radicals was hardly the language that the Tsar was accustomed to hear about those attempting to destroy him and his régime.

Dostoevsky then highlights the contrasting convictions presumably held by the Slavic Benevolent Society—but of course voicing his own views—concerning the relations between the Tsar and his people. This relation is purely patriarchal and comes from "the ancient truth, which from time immemorial has penetrated into the soul of the Russian people: that their Tsar is also their father, and that children always will come to their father *without fear* so that he hears from them, with love, of their needs and wishes; that the children love their father and the father trusts their love; and that the relation of the Russian people to their Tsar-Father is lovingly free and *without fear*, not lifelessly formal and contractual" (italics added). This last phrase is a thrust at the idea of "crowning the edifice" by a Western-style constitution. Rumors had been widely circulating that, to celebrate the anniversary, the granting of such a constitution would be announced on that day.

Dostoevsky knew very well that this familial image of the relation between the Tsar and his people was much more a longed-for ideal than a reality. Whatever the people might feel about their Tsar-Father, their approach to him, if it took place at all, could occur only by means of a tightly controlled ritual and was hardly one of free and easy access. By twice emphasizing the importance of being able to appeal to the Tsar "without fear," he distinctly implies the absence of such a desirable state of affairs. Indeed, in a notebook entry made during the very last year of his life, he states his actual view of the situation: "I am a servant of the Tsar like Pushkin, because his children, the people, do not disdain to be servants of the Tsar. They would be his servants even more when he actually believes that the people are his children. *Something that, for a very long time, he has not believed*" (italics added).[16]

Like the radicals who had called for a constituent assembly, Dostoevsky was also admonishing the Tsar to allow himself to consult the people. Moreover, instead of emphasizing the immutability of the reign that he was presumably glorifying, he looks forward (though of course very discreetly) to its eventual modification in the public interest. For it is on the "unshakable" foundation of this father-child relation, he affirms, "that perhaps may be accomplished and completed the structure of every future transformation of our state, to the extent that these will be recognized as necessary." He too looked forward to a "crowning of the edifice," but not by the granting of a constitution; what he desired was the distribution of more land to the peasantry by the will of the Tsar.

This document, presented to the Tsar on February 19 by Minister of the Interior Makov, was read very carefully by its recipient, who perhaps understood its underlying drift more clearly than its official sponsors. For the Tsar remarked to his minister (his words were reported to Anna Grigoryevna after Dostoevsky death) that "I never suspected the Slavic Benevolent Society of solidarity with the Nihilists."[17] The Tsar could only have been speaking ironically, which means he had grasped those aspects of the address betraying not only a latent sympathy with the *sincere* radicals but also a desire that the Tsar allow the people to make their wishes known "without fear."

Dostoevsky visited Suvorin on the same day his address was given to the Tsar, and, in a two-hour conversation, the journalist found Dostoevsky in an extremely good mood, "very lively" and full of hope about a change for the better under Loris-Melikov. He was "happy about the pacification." (It had been suspected that the revolutionaries were planning something spectacular for the anniversary date, but nothing had occurred.) "You will see," he told Suvorin, "something new is beginning. I'm not a prophet, but you'll see. Now everything looks different."[18]

_____

On the day following the Tsar's anniversary celebration, an extraordinary conversation took place between Dostoevsky and Aleksey Suvorin. The former had just suffered another epileptic attack, and Suvorin found him, as was usual at such times, in a gloomy and depressed mood. The talk immediately turned to the wave of political crimes, and particularly to the explosion in the Winter Palace. "Deliberating on these events," Suvorin recalled, "Dostoevsky dwelt on the strange relation of society to these crimes. Society sympathized with them, as it were, or, closer to the truth, did not really know what to think about them." Then he invented a dramatic situation, as he had so often done for the characters in his novels, in which he himself would be confronted with having to choose a course of action that would define his moral attitude:

"Imagine that we both were standing at a window of [a store] and looking at some paintings. Near us stood a person, who was pretending to look. He was waiting for someone and kept looking around. Suddenly another person hastened to him and said: 'The Winter Palace will soon be blown up. I have placed the machine.' Imagine that we hear this, and that the men were so agitated that they did not take account of the circumstances or of their voices. Would we go to the Winter Palace to warn of the explosion, or would we turn to the police, or to a policeman on the beat to arrest them? Would you go?"
"No, [replied Suvorin], I would not go."
"Nor would I, [said Dostoevsky]. Why? But this is terrible. It's a crime. We perhaps could give a warning. I was thinking of this just before you came. I turned over all the reasons that would cause me to do it. Well-founded reasons, solid ones, and then considered all the reasons that would hold me back. These reasons are—simply insignificant. Simply the fear of being reputed to be an informer."[19]

In *A Raw Youth*, it may be recalled, the betrayal of the perfectly harmless Dergachev group to the authorities by the young Prince Sokolsky had been depicted as another symptom of his total moral collapse. And even though Narodnaya Volya had proved itself to be very far from harmless, Dostoevsky and Suvorin, both loyal Russian patriots and fervent nationalists, could not bring themselves to the point of deciding to betray the radicals to the authorities. One reason, certainly, was that these authorities had never been able to distinguish between peaceful propagandists like the Dergachev group and active terrorists. But nothing shows more glaringly the moral discredit into which the Tsarist régime had fallen by this time and the torturing moral-political dilemma that confronted all thinking Russians as they observed from the sidelines the attempts to kill the Tsar-Father. No wonder that every installment of *The Brothers Karamazov* was snapped up and read with such passionate intensity, as if the literate classes were hoping the novel would help them find some answer to their quandary.

Igor Volgin has perceptively compared Dostoevsky's imagined choice here to Ivan Karamazov's decisive one: he agrees to go to Chermashnaya at Smerdyakov's urging, then flees to Moscow, even though subliminally aware of the lackey's intention to clear the way for murder. One cannot help wondering if the later torments of Ivan's conscience, written after this conversation, do not reproduce some of Dostoevsky's own. There can be no doubt, in any case, that he felt the situation he and Suvorin were contemplating to have the most intimate connection with the thematics of his novel. For it was at the conclusion of this dialogue, and under its stimulation, that he outlined for his listener one of the possible continuations envisaged for his second volume (several others are mentioned in various memoirs). In this version, Alyosha Karamazov prepared himself "to pass through the monastery and become a revolutionary. He would commit a political crime. He would be executed. He would have searched for truth, and in these searches, naturally, he would have become a revolutionary."[20] While such words can only remain hypothetical, they surely indicate the close affinity between his morally positive hero Alyosha and the radicals. They also help us to understand why, despite all the "solid" reasons he could unquestionably muster for doing so, he flinched at the prospect of turning the terrorists over to the police.

On the very same day of this conversation, an attempt was made on the life of Count Loris-Melikov. A young Jewish radical, Ippolit Mlodetskii, apparently acting on his own and not as a deadly emissary of Narodnaya Volya, fired at the newly appointed plenipotentiary pointblank but missed. Mlodetskii was captured, tried by court-martial, and condemned to death. Soon afterward, Suvorin and Dostoevsky discussed this new act of violence, and the former writes that "the attempt on the life of Count Loris-Melikov agitated Dostoevsky, [who] was afraid of a reaction." "God forbid that we turn back to the old road," he is quoted as having said. In general, as Suvorin notes, "during the period of our political crimes he was in terrible fear of a massacre, a massacre of the educated class by the people, who would surge up as the avengers. 'You haven't seen what I saw,' he would say, 'you don't know what the people are capable of when they are enraged. I have seen terrible, terrible instances.'"[21] Dostoevsky thus feared both the reaction of the government, which would stifle the first, feeble flickerings of reform initiated by Loris-Melikov, and the rage of the people against the educated classes, whom they would confusedly identify with the revolutionary youth.

The public hanging of Mlodetskii took place on February 22, at the same Semenovsky Square where, thirty years before, Dostoevsky himself had stood as a condemned man. Now he took his place in the crowd of onlookers, which he estimated to be about fifty thousand. Volgin intriguingly suggests that perhaps he was present because he expected to witness what had occurred in his own case, and had been repeated in that of Nicholas Ishutin, implicated in Dimitry Karakozov's attempt to assassinate the Tsar in 1866, that is, a last-minute waiving of the death sentence. Could he have been anticipating a spectacular intervention by the Tsar, the courier arriving posthaste to save Mlodetskii's life? In the semihysterical state of public opinion, amidst the hopes already aroused by the few, insignificant liberal measures granted by Loris-Melikov, a speculation of this sort may well be accorded some credence. The young writer Vsevolod Garshin, well known for his brutally realistic stories about the Russo-Turkish War, had gone to plead with Loris-Melikov to spare Mlodetskii's life, and he had been received by the wily official for a private conversation. Whether or not Dostoevsky knew of this personal appeal, it well betrays the atmosphere of the time and the desperate longing for some token of clemency.

Alas, no such gesture was forthcoming. On the evening of the execution, Dostoevsky was present at one of Polonsky's Friday salons. Another guest noted that "Dostoevsky was not in good spirits . . . perhaps under the impression of something that had just occurred"—clearly the summary trial and its aftermath. When questioned about a rumor that another attempt on Loris-Melikov's life had been made at the site of the execution, he replied that, as an eyewitness, he could certify that such talk was idle gossip and that other, equally unreliable rumors were also circulating.[22]

He was still under the unhappy effect of this distressing event two days later when visited by Countess A. I. Tolstaya, who describes him in a letter to her daughter Ekaterina Yunge as "disturbed, sickly, terribly pale"; knowing him quite well, she attributes his condition to the Mlodetskii hanging.[23] To cheer him up, she asked Anna Grigoryevna to read a laudatory letter that Mme Yunge had written, which in fact contains some quite perceptive remarks about the published portions of *The Brothers Karamazov*. "Involuntarily," she tells her mother, "you compare Dostoevsky with European novelists—I pick only the best of them—the French: Zola, Goncourts, Daudet—they are all honorable, desire improvement; but, my God! how they paddle in shallow water! But he . . . [is] also a realist, such a realist as none of them are . . . and, along with this extreme realism, can you find anywhere else on earth such a poet and idealist!? . . . [someone] who [is] a realist, a precise investigator, a psychologist, an idealist, a philosopher."[24]

She also compared the effect produced by the "entire unrolling of the novel" to the gathering onrush of an expected storm. In conclusion, expressing a sentiment aroused in many others as well, she wrote that, after reading about the suffering of the children and then the Legend of the Grand Inquisitor, she was unable to continue and felt a desire "to make her confession before [Dostoevsky] and hear from him some sort of necessary, helpful . . . word."[25] As Dostoevsky listened to the young woman's encomium, his face gradually "lit up, acquired some living colors, his eyes sparkled with satisfaction, often with tears. . . . It seemed that he suddenly became younger." He told the countess that her daughter might become an author herself, judging from the letter, and he asked her to convey his thanks for such a comprehension of his novel, which "nobody has yet read so thoughtfully."[26]

Nor did Dostoevsky consider it inadmissible to discuss such nerve-shattering matters as the hanging on the social occasions when he mixed with members of the royal family. On February 23, he spent an evening in the Crimson Room of the Marble Palace in the company of Grand Duke Konstantin Konstantinovich, Countess Anna Komarovskaya (lady-in-waiting to the grand duke's mother), and other notables, including the singer and composer Yulia F. Abaza (the wife of the minister of finance, who had a reputation as a liberal). Part of the conversation dwelt on the Mlodetskii execution, and he expatiated on what he had observed of Mlodetskii's behavior on being led to the gallows, interpreting it in the light of his own emotions before his reprieve. To his elegant listeners, he described how Mlodetskii had "looked around from side to side and seemed to be indifferent," the reason being "that in these last minutes a person tries to chase away the image of death, he remembers most often consoling pictures, he transports himself to some sort of flourishing garden, full of springtime and sunlight." But the closer he comes to the end, the more ineluctable and tormenting becomes the image of unavoidable death. "The looming pain, the suffering just before death, is not frightening; what is terrifying is the transition to another, unknown form."[27] These words more or less reproduce the famous passage in *The Idiot* on the guillotining of a criminal observed by Prince Myshkin, but they acquire a very immediate resonance that may have given his eminent fellow guests some rather uneasy moments.

That Mlodetskii did not cease to preoccupy Dostoevsky is indicated by an entry in another diary, that of the novelist S. I. Smirnova-Sazonova, whose work he appreciated and with whom he had become friendly. On February 29 she jotted down, in her telegraphic style: "Dostoevsky came. He said that, at Mlodetskii's execution, the people jeered and shouted. . . . A great effect was produced by his kissing of the cross. On all sides, they began to say: 'He kissed it! He kissed the cross.'" The same evening, Smirnova went to some amateur theatricals at the home of Aleksey Suvorin, whose other guests included D. V. Grigorovich, Nikolay Leskov, and Dostoevsky. During supper, she heard him whisper to Suvorin "that he [Dostoevsky] was a Russian Socialist, and that this was wrongfully overlooked in the first part of *The Brothers Karamazov* where he had spoken out, explaining in what Russian Socialism consisted—the sharing of the state with the Church."[28] Dostoevsky here is alluding to the conversation in Book 2, Chapter 5, where the apocalyptic prospect of transforming the state *entirely* into the Church is broached and disputed. For Dostoevsky, "Russian Socialism" (a term first used by Herzen in an entirely secular, radical sense) meant the application of the Christian principle of love to the inequalities and injustices of social life.

The letter from Ekaterina Yunge to her mother, which had helped to lighten Dostoevsky's despondent mood, was followed by another from her addressed to him directly. A month later, he wrote a reply that reveals a good deal both about his own personality and about his work. He complains that he had wished to answer her perceptive missives sooner, but "honest to God, my life goes on at such a disorderly boil and even in such a bustle that I rarely belong to myself." Even now, Dostoevsky fears whether "I'll be able to write even a tiny fraction of what my heart would like to communicate to you"; and he generalizes this doubt into a sweeping statement about his own writings. "Can you imagine that at certain distressing moments of inner accounting I often recognize with pain that I have not expressed, literally, even a twentieth of what I would like to and perhaps even could express?" Just a few days earlier, he had attended the defense by Vladimir Solovyev of his doctoral dissertation, and he now cites a thought uttered during that learned disputation. "Humanity, according to my profound conviction," Solovyev had declared, "*knows much more* than it has succeeded in uttering in its science and its art thus far." Applying this idea to himself, Dostoevsky continues: "I sense that there is much more concealed in me than however much I have been able to express thus far."[29]

He thanks Mme Yunge for having written "such a subtle, such a profound evaluation of me as a writer," and he finds her words to be superior to most of the criticism published in the journals. Dostoevsky knew that she was a painter and (from her mother) that she was personally unhappy, "living in solitude and embittering [her] soul with recollections." He urges her to have recourse "to a single medicine: art and creative work." She had described for Dostoevsky the troubling "duality" that she felt in her personality, and his comments on this problem touch on one of the major leitmotifs of his own work. Such a personality trait, he tells her, "is peculiar to human nature in general," but not everyone suffers from it to the same degree as Mme Yunge—or himself. "That's precisely why you are so kindred to me, because that *split* in you is exactly the same as my own and has been so all my life. It's a great torment, but at the same time a great delight too. It's a powerful consciousness, a need for self-evaluation, and the presence in your nature of the need for moral obligation toward yourself and toward humanity. That's what that duality means."[30]

Such words offer a valuable insight into his own psyche, and also into the *moral* significance of all the so-called "schizophrenic" characters that he portrays. "If you were less developed in intellect," he writes, "if you were limited, you would be less conscience-stricken and there wouldn't be that duality. On the contrary, very great vanity would result. But the duality is nevertheless a great torment." The positive moral value assigned to "suffering" in Dostoevsky's work is always such an inner wrestling with the self; and the only source of comfort is to turn to Christ. As he advises Mme Yunge, "If you believe (or very much want to believe), then give yourself over to Him completely and the torment from that split will be greatly assuaged and you will receive an emotionally spiritual answer, and that's the main thing."[31] Accompanying this letter, at the urging of her mother Dostoevsky sent a set of proofs of Book 10 for the troubled Mme Yunge to read on her birthday as a token of his esteem.

## 6

Invitations to add his illustrious name to benefits for worthy causes continued to rain down, and he accepted as many as he could. On March 20 he read on behalf of an orphanage, choosing the episode from his novel in which Father Zosima speaks with the grief-stricken peasant woman seeking solace. The next evening he appeared on behalf of needy students of the Higher Pedagogical Courses for Women, this time choosing from *A Raw Youth* the monologue in which the mother of Olya describes why her daughter hanged herself out of despair. The only newspaper account of this evening criticized Dostoevsky's selection as inappropriate for such an audience. Was this the sort of example to place before the young women studying in the Higher Courses? Olya had been a star student in her *gymnasium*, obtaining a gold medal for excellence, but she then found it impossible to obtain work and was solicited to enter a house of prostitution. Many of Dostoevsky's listeners would be struggling to make their way in the world like Olya, and the journalist wondered why they had been presented with such a discouraging prospect.[32] Turgenev was also on the program that same evening and read his charming story "The Singers," from *A Sportsman's Sketches*. The two writers shook hands backstage but did not utter a single word. Turgenev sat in the audience and joined in the clamorous applause that greeted Dostoevsky's rendition; the latter was also in the audience for Turgenev, but whether he joined in the acclaim has not been recorded.

For reasons that remain unclear, perhaps because of the severely troubled political climate, Dostoevsky began to fear that the secret police might have renewed their surveillance of him as an ex-convict. In response to an inquiry made through A. A. Kireyev to the minister of the interior, the bureaucratic machinery began clanking again and the question was sent to the secret police, who replied that no such surveillance had been reinstituted. While these documents were being exchanged, he took part in another exclusive soirée on March 22 in the Crimson Room of the Marble Palace, where he met Princess Evgeniya Maximilianovna Oldenburgskaya, who, according to Grand Duke Konstantin, was particularly eager to make his acquaintance. The princess was a patroness of the orphanage for which Dostoevsky had read and may well have wished to express her gratitude personally in addition to the official thanks. The grand duke noted that "Evgeniya was very pleased with Dostoevsky, and conversed with him the entire evening."[33]

On this very same day, he received a letter that revealingly illustrates the extraordinary position he had managed to acquire in Russian society. It was written by a student in the Higher Courses on behalf of all her classmates in response to a letter from Dostoevsky. He had inquired whether they had not become angry because he had declined one of their invitations, and she answered: "We cannot wish that anything at all should disturb your tranquillity, or injure your health. We love you deeply and know how to cherish you in our hearts; we know that there is only one Feodor Mikhailovich—and there will never be another. . . . To separate you [from his work] never entered our heads. You belong to everyone. . . . Better that you never appear among us, and that you guard your strength, your health."[34] With such a letter on the one hand, and his visits with scions of the royal family and their friends on the other, Dostoevsky may well be forgiven the hubris of imagining that he could play a pacifying and reconciling role at this strife-torn juncture of Russian society.

Meanwhile, work on *The Brothers Karamazov* proceeded apace, and he sent Book 10 to Lyubimov sometime between the end of March and early April. Ever since *The Idiot*, Dostoevsky had wished to present the relationship between a group of children and an idealistic character like Prince Myshkin (or his various substitutes in later plans), who leads them toward the acceptance of a morality of love and self-sacrifice; and he was finally able to realize this long-cherished ambition in *The Brothers Karamazov*. The boys who appear in the novel are innocent enough, though his notes sketch out other serious and even abhorrent possibilities: the "torture of a four-year-old boy"; "the boys steal a trunk with money. Krasotkin: 'I detest that'"; "the suicide of a small boy" (15: 306). Happily, none of these suggestions are followed because they would have clashed too sharply with the tonality of childlike innocuousness that Dostoevsky wished to maintain.

Also, some ideological remarks made by the callow adolescent Kolya, who swaggeringly calls himself "a terrible Socialist," do not show up in the final text. "Under our zodiac," he says, "everything changes, consequently there is no such thing as good, wants to shoot himself" (ibid.). There is as well an unassigned note, probably said by Kolya to manifest his political derring-do: "And to establish a social commune on rational principles" (ibid.). Several notes refer to Kolya's statement, used in the text: "I'm not against Christ, he was a humane man [individuality] and if he lived in our times and had received a modern education, he would have immediately joined the revolutionaries. Look, that's clear" (15: 309). Kolya attributes this assertion to Belinsky, but when challenged ("Where did he say that?") cannot cite a source for the quotation by the great man himself. No wonder! This statement was only given currency by Dostoevsky in his 1873 reminiscences of Belinsky in the *Diary*.

His letter accompanying these chapters of Book 10 inquired about a circumstantial detail that he feared might have been overlooked. He was not sure if, at the period in which the novel was supposedly set (1863), boys of the age he was depicting were required to wear school uniforms; in the text they are attired in ordinary clothes. Lyubimov reassured him that boys of that age had not been obliged to wear uniforms, and also congratulated Dostoevsky on the excellence of these chapters, which he was sure would meet with great success. However, he found that Kolya Krasotkin was perhaps too precocious and suggested that a year be added to his age (fourteen instead of thirteen). Dostoevsky agreed, remarking that Anna Grigoryevna had raised the same objection.[35] (It was too late to make this change in the magazine text, and it was added only when the novel appeared as a separate volume.)

## 7

Whatever the stature Dostoevsky had now attained in Russian literary life, old social-cultural quarrels died very hard (if at all), and he was reminded of some of the embarrassments and discomfitures of his youthful literary début by a reference in the April issue of the liberal

Westernizing journal *Vestnik Evropi* (*European Messenger*). This influential publication had been running a series of reminiscences of the 1840s by Pavel V. Annenkov, later published as *A Remarkable Decade*—a book that takes its place just behind Herzen's *My Past and Thoughts* as the most penetrating and insightful portrait of the period. Many of Annenkov's pages are devoted to Belinsky, the central cultural figure of that day, and the critic's enthusiastic reception of Dostoevsky's first novel, *Poor Folk*, provides part of the story. But Annenkov, who was the closest Russian confidant of Turgenev and served as his literary factotum, could not resist paying back Dostoevsky for the deadly caricature of Turgenev in *The Devils* and for the more recent incident at the banquet. According to Annenkov's recollection, the young Dostoevsky became so inflated with his newly acquired fame that he imposed special conditions on how his first novel should be printed. He supposedly asked Nikolay A. Nekrasov, the editor of the *Petersburg Almanac*, "to separate it from all the other works by a special typographical sign, for example—borders. The novel was actually surrounded by such borders in the almanac."[36]

Incensed by this charge, Dostoevsky dashed off a letter to Suvorin, who a few days later printed a denial in *New Time*. "We have taken up the *Petersburg Almanac* for 1846" he wrote, "and saw . . . that *Poor Folk* was printed without any borders, in exactly the same type and format as all the other contributions to the almanac."[37] It is likely that Annenkov, failing to check this little tidbit, was simply relaying from memory, thirty-five years later, one of the many scoffing anecdotes about Dostoevsky that had circulated among the members of the Belinsky *pléiade* of young writers during 1845–1846. The success of *Poor Folk* had in fact gone to his head, as he admitted at the time in a letter to his brother Mikhail, and the inordinate vanity he exhibited, along with an exaggerated touchiness and sensitivity, had made him quite intolerable to others. A satirical poem about him, written jointly by Turgenev and Nekrasov, had passed around from hand to hand. It contains a jesting reference to a story of his that had been framed "with borders," and the anecdote resuscitated by Annenkov turns the jeering thrust into fact.[38]

After several other publicists joined in the fray, Dostoevsky ended the controversy by requesting Suvorin to print the following denial: "We have received a formal declaration from F. M. Dostoevsky that nothing similar to what was stated in the *European Messenger* ever happened, nor could it have."[39] But Dostoevsky "was so infuriated by Annenkov's slander," Anna Grigoryevna writes, "that he resolved not to recognize him if he met him at the Pushkin festivities, and if Annenkov should approach him he would refuse to shake hands."[40] We shall return to the Pushkin festivities in a moment, but let us follow the incident a bit further. Dostoevsky did not let the matter drop, at least in his own mind, and intended to reply personally and at length in his *Diary of a Writer* for 1881. The gossip about "borders" had cast doubt on his own account of his relations with Belinsky, and "I do not want any shadow of untruth to hang over my narrative. If I do not object, they would say that [Annenkov's version] was the correct one."[41]

At a benefit on April 27 for the Slavic Benevolent Society, he read from his latest chapters about the children with his usual tremendous success. His old typographer Mikhail A. Alexandrov, present in the audience, describes him as basking in the glowing warmth of his reception. "Amidst the numerous gathering of the public [the hall contained more than a thousand seats and had been sold out], he felt himself as comfortable, and behaved as unconstrainedly, as if among friends ... so that, as regards tone, the ovation accorded Feodor Mikhailovich by the public differed from the ovation accorded to whatever transient artistic celebrity in general happened to be passing through." Called back for an encore, he read the poem of Nekrasov, "Vlas," so often cited by him; and he prefaced his recital with the following words: "I will read the verses of a Russian poet—a true Russian poet, who unfortunately sometimes nurtured non-Russian thoughts, but when he spoke, always spoke truly as a Russian." The audience continued to ask for more, and, "strongly galvanized by the enthusiasm of the public," Dostoevsky also read the poem of Aleksey K. Tolstoy, *Ilya Muromets*.[42]

## 8

The Pushkin festivities mentioned by Anna Grigoryevna refer to the planned unveiling of a monument to Pushkin in Moscow and to a series of public receptions, speeches, and banquets celebrating Russia's national poet. The prestige of the Romantic and aristocratic Pushkin had been considerably damaged by the campaign carried on against him, and against art in general, by the radical publicists of the 1860s. Dimitry Pisarev in particular had lamented the amount of time and energy wasted on such trivial amusements when so many more pressing social problems remained. Dostoevsky had immediately taken a stand against this Utilitarian denigration of art, and his spokesman on this issue in *The Devils*, Stepan Trofimovich Verkhovensky, denounces "the shift of focus" that has occurred with the Nihilist generation, "the substitution of one beauty for another." "The whole misunderstanding lies only in this question: What is more beautiful, Shakespeare or boots, Raphael or petroleum?" (10: 372). The hostility against Pushkin and art had somewhat slackened by the 1870s, but Nikolay Mikhailovsky still disparaged literary works that did not directly address current social issues.

15. The Pushkin statue

Nonetheless, a large majority of educated Russians had read and admired Pushkin, whose poems formed part of the school curriculum, and
the idea of erecting a monument to him in Moscow had long been making the rounds. A desultory subscription to raise funds had been organized as far back as the 1860s, but the drive became serious only in 1871.
After several competitions, the sculptor A. M. Opekushin was chosen to
create the full-scale, standing statue, which he endowed with a Napoleonic pose: Pushkin's bent arm is placed in, and supported by, his jacket.
Its unveiling, along with the other planned events, was finally scheduled
for June 5–9, 1880. Dostoevsky had obviously been talking to friends
about the impending celebration, and he had even set down a few
thoughts for an article about Pushkin when, on April 5, he received a

letter from Sergey Yuriev, chairman of the Society of Lovers of Russian Literature (which was in charge of the preparations for the festivities). He was also editor of a new journal, *Russkaya Mysl* (*Russian Thought*), and had earlier asked Dostoevsky to contribute a new novel to his journal; this time he was approaching him for a contribution about Pushkin.

"I really have said here loudly," he replied on April 9, "that for the day of the dedication of the Pushkin monument a serious article about him (Pushkin) is needed in print. And I have even *dreamed*, if it were possible for me to go to Moscow for the day of the dedication, *of saying* a few words about him, but orally, in the form of a speech, since I assume that on the day of the dedication, speeches will certainly be made in Moscow." At present, however, "what with my unending work on the novel . . . I doubt whether I'll be able to find the time to write anything." But if he did so, Dostoevsky promised to keep *Russian Thought* in mind, because "I read your journal with great curiosity and sincerely wish you the greatest success."[43] It seems clear that he had as yet no specific intention of attending the festival, or of taking time to develop his notes into what became his famous Pushkin speech.

The month of April was so crowded with social engagements and obligations that he found it impossible to supply the *Russian Messenger* with a new installment. Vladimir Solovyev gave a brilliant defense of his doctoral dissertation, *A Critique of Abstract Principles* (*Kritika otvlechenniykh nachal*) on April 6, and both Dostoevsky and his wife were in the audience. (One of the philosopher's remarks was cited in the letter to Mme Yunge on April 11.) On April 14, Dostoevsky was elected vice president of the Slavic Benevolent Society, and he spent the evening of the twenty-fourth at "a literary reading" in the company of the grand dukes Konstantin and Sergey and Princess Oldenburgskaya and her sister.[44] On the twenty-seventh, as already mentioned, came the benefit for the Slavic Benevolent Society. Writing to Lyubimov on April 29, and apologizing for not having been able to furnish any copy for the May issue, he complains that "I am really prevented from writing here, and I need to flee Petersburg as soon as possible. *The Karamazovs* are again to blame for that. So many people come to see me every day apropos of them, so many people seek to make my acquaintance, invite me to their homes—that I'm absolutely at my wit's end and am now fleeing Petersburg!"[45]

Dostoevsky planned to leave for Staraya Russa "in a week, and in three weeks *I will have the whole novel finished*. Thus the continuation can begin (if you approve) with the June issue. Part 4 will end in the August issue, and then there will be a conclusion for the September issue . . . (a few words about the fate of the characters and a totally separate scene: the funeral of Ilyusha and Aleksey Karamazov's funeral oration to the boys, in which the meaning of the whole novel will be somewhat reflected)." As so often in the past, he was either genuinely overoptimistic in making such a forecast or perhaps exaggerating to placate the mistrust of his editors. The latter hypothesis is given some plausibility by his request that Lyubimov write him "about *whether you are angry with me or not.*" He also consoles the editor by remarking that the section on "The Children" is "so separate and episodic . . . [that] the reader won't be as upset as if it had broken off at the most incomplete spot and then read: Continuation to follow." Commenting on the success of his reading of that section at the benefit, he says that "the effect, I can say without exaggeration or boasting, was very powerful."[46] But his very success as a heart-stirring spellbinder on the platform prevented him from quitting the city and devoting himself to his novel as quickly as he desired.

Earlier on the very evening that he wrote to Lyubimov, Dostoevsky had read for the benefit of the Society of the Sisters of Mercy of St. George. He had chosen for them the scene between the peasant women and Father Zosima, particularly the lament, so close to Dostoevsky's own heart, of the mother who had lost her small son. The effect on the audience was shattering, and among his listeners happened to be the future empress of all the Russias, the Danish princess who had become the wife of Tsarevich Alexander. She was so moved that she expressed a desire to meet Dostoevsky, and a few days later, on May 4, he received an invitation from Grand Duke Konstantin for another evening in the Crimson Room on May 8. The Tsarevna, he was told, particularly wished to make his acquaintance and he already knew the other guests. "If you do not refuse to read something from your work, of course of your own choosing, we would be very grateful."[47] To gratify this royal request he postponed his departure.

His letter to Lyubimov makes clear that he had been working on Book 11 and that, although he was as yet unable to provide a finished text, the remainder of the novel was fully in his mind. If he had been able to work uninterruptedly in Staraya Russa, as he had hoped, he might have come closer to meeting the sanguine schedule he had outlined for his editor. On May 1, however, he received another letter from Yuriev, writing for himself and on behalf of the Society of Lovers of Russian Literature, inviting Dostoevsky to honor the society and the Pushkin festivities with his presence and his words. Yuriev was expressing the feeling "of all the Moscovites, from whom he [Yuriev] had very often heard the question: Will Dostoevsky . . . be speaking at our session?"[48]

An official invitation from the same body followed the next day, and Dostoevsky was asked "to honor the memory of the great poet" by speaking at one of the public sessions to take place after the unveiling of the monument. A private letter from Yuriev urged him to prefer the Moscow celebration to the one that would also take place in Petersburg (manifestations in honor of Pushkin were being organized simultaneously throughout Russia), and he lists the names of other participants who would be present: I. S. Aksakov, A. F. Pisemsky, A. N. Ostrovsky, I. S. Turgenev. Nor does he forget to request that Dostoevsky reserve whatever he writes about Pushkin for publication in his journal. On May 4, at a meeting of the Slavic Benevolent Society, the president, K. N. Bestuzhev-Ryumin heard from Dostoevsky that he had been invited to Moscow. "With the fervent agreement of all," he was appointed the society's representative to the Moscow festivities, and Dostoevsky accepted Yuriev's invitation the very next day.[49]

On May 8, he was again the guest of Grand Duke Konstantin and read fragments from *The Brothers Karamazov*, including, at the special request of his host, the confession of Father Zosima (it is not clear what this includes), which the grand duke considered one of the best pieces Dostoevsky had ever written. The Tsarevna, all through the evening, "listened very attentively and was in ecstasy"; one of the ladies present openly wept, and the eyes of the Tsarevna herself were filled with tears after he also read "A Little Boy at Christ's Christmas Party."[50]

Once this highly gratifying obligation had been fulfilled, the family left for Staraya Russa sometime between May 9 and 11. There Dostoevsky, to cite Anna Grigoryevna, was looking forward to being able "to think over and write, in tranquillity and freedom, his talk in honor of Pushkin, and then to work, setting everything else aside, on completing *The Brothers Karamazov*."[51]

# CHAPTER 27

# The Pushkin Festival

The Moscow Pushkin festival in the spring of 1880 has been remembered by posterity largely because of the sensation created by Dostoevsky's impassioned apotheosis of the great poet. At the time, however, the event assumed considerable importance for a number of other reasons. One was the tense and ominous social-political climate reigning in the country, which imparted a political coloring to any large manifestation of public opinion no matter how seemingly innocent. In this instance, the cream of the Russian intelligentsia gathered in the ancient capital (as well as in other major cities) to eulogize a poet who had incurred the displeasure of Nicholas I, had been sent into exile, and was known to have had close friends among the revolutionary Decembrists of 1825. Such a celebration was in itself something unprecedented and, indeed, was felt as an implicit demand for a liberty of expression still sadly lacking in Russian literature and society.

Even more, the initiative for this enterprise had come not from the government but from private individuals (a group of Pushkin's surviving classmates from the lycée in Tsarskoe Selo), and funds for the statue had been raised by private subscription. Eventually the project was approved and even patronized by the crown, and the Moscow Duma agreed to pay the expenses of all the invited guests; but participants did not feel they were taking part in any official function. Instead, as one observer put it, here "for the first time a social longing was displayed by us with such broad-ranging freedom. Those who attended felt themselves to be citizens enjoying a fullness of rights."[1]

Moreover, the official acceptance of this independent endeavor was hopefully seen as the augury of a new era in the relations between the Tsar and the intelligentsia, indeed, as a testimony to the influence that the educated class had begun to exercise. Count Loris-Melikov had appealed to them on taking office by relaxing censorship of the press slightly as a gesture of good will. Now he instructed the governor-general of Moscow not to require preliminary approval of the speeches to be given after the unveiling. An atmosphere of expectation was thus created; perhaps even more concessions by the government would be forthcoming. What seemed to be a purely cultural event thus took on—as was usually the case in Russia, where no unfettered political discussion of any kind was possible—an important social-political subtext.

On a more personal level, this subtext was dramatized by the culmination of the ideological duel that Turgenev and Dostoevsky had been carrying on ever since the mid-1860s.

2
___

In accepting Sergey Yuriev's invitation on May 5, Dostoevsky assured him that "even though I am very busy with my work . . . only some sudden illness or something of that sort will prevent me" from making the journey. He intended to arrive on May 25, and would then discuss with Yuriev the length of his address. He was afraid "of saying too little" in praise of the great poet; but would there be time for something longer after all the other scheduled speeches by eminent names? "Here in Petersburg, at the most innocent literary reading . . . every line, even one written twenty years ago, [has to be] submitted . . . for advance permission for reading. . . . Will they really [in Moscow] allow one to read something newly written without *someone's* advance censorship?"[2] If not, would there be time for his text to be submitted and approved? A few days later, he learned that the censorship requirements had been lifted and that his fear was unwarranted.

Aleksey Suvorin, unaware that Dostoevsky had received an invitation, offered to procure him a ticket on the special train from Petersburg chartered for the occasion; but, replying that he had been invited, he chose to depart directly from his rural retreat. He regretted that Suvorin was not coming himself, because "we Petersburg guests would have a better time if we were in a *large group*."[3] Five days later, Dostoevsky wrote to convey name day greetings to K. P. Pobedonostsev, and also to wish him "every wonderful success in your new labors" as head procurator of the Holy Synod, the council supervising the Russian Orthodox Church. Informing him of the impending trip to Moscow, Dostoevsky reveals some of the ideological dissensions that had immediately begun to surface in the preparations for the great event. As it happens, he writes, "I'll be going not for pleasure but perhaps even for downright unpleasantness. . . . I've already heard in passing even in Petersburg that there is a clique raging there in Moscow that is trying not to allow certain words at the dedication ceremony, and that they are afraid of certain *reactionary* words that could be spoken by *certain people* at the sessions of the Lovers of Russian Literature. . . . Even the newspapers have already published things about certain intrigues."[4]

Dostoevsky, however, firmly declares: "I have prepared my speech about Pushkin, and precisely in the most *extreme* spirit of my (that is *our*, I make bold to thus express myself) convictions, and therefore I expect, perhaps, a certain amount of abuse . . . but I'm not afraid, and one should serve one's cause, and I will speak without fear. The professors there are paying court to Turgenev, who is absolutely turning into a personal enemy of mine. (In the *European Messenger* he put forth a petty story about me regarding a certain incident thirty-five years ago that never happened.) But I can't praise Pushkin and preach 'Verochka.'"[5] This last remark refers to Vera Zasulich, who had been identified almost immediately as the prototype of the heroine Marianna in Turgenev's *Virgin Soil*; and Dostoevsky held Turgenev responsible for reviving the old canard about "borders."

In the background of these remarks is the attempt by the Society of Lovers of Russian Literature (henceforth referred to as SLRL) to ban Mikhail Katkov from speaking. The committee of the SLRL in charge of organizing the festivities was ideologically in league with the moderately liberal Westernizer orientation of influential professors at the University of Moscow, who felt reinforced by the presence of Turgenev. He had returned to Russia for the celebration and appointed an honorary member of the SLRL and of the committee. Turgenev and Katkov had long been enemies, and the latter had recently attacked the novelist for being in sympathy with the revolutionaries. In addition, Katkov had offended the intelligentsia as a whole by objecting to Loris-Melikov's appeal for their collaboration, which he regarded as a first step toward a weakening of the autocrat's power. "There is no need to seek support and aid from society," he had written after the explosion in the Winter Palace. "Only discipline in state ranks, which will make everyone in them fear deviating from their duty and deceiving the supreme power, and patriotism in the educated spheres of society—that's what's needed. . . . [I]t is necessary that we begin with discipline."[6] It was thus a simple matter for Turgenev to persuade the committee to blacklist Katkov, even though the latter was a member of the SLRL and had in fact defended the value of Pushkin's art against the attacks of the radical critics in the 1860s. An attempt was also made to blacklist Dostoevsky (there is no evidence that he ever became aware of it, though the possibility is not excluded) because of the incident at the dinner for Turgenev in March 1879; but Dostoevsky had too many admirers, including the chairman, Yuriev, for this effort to succeed. Rumors about the intention to exclude Katkov had begun to spread, and a story in *New Time* on May 17 had apprised Dostoevsky of what he may not have yet heard by word of mouth.

### 3

He left Staraya Russa on May 22, accompanied by Anna Grigoryevna, the children, and his mother-in-law. Anna had desired to travel to

Moscow herself with the children, but such an expenditure was beyond their means. "In later years," she wrote, "I regarded my inability to be present at the rare triumph vouchsafed my dear husband on the occasion of the Pushkin memorial festivities as the greatest deprivation of my life."[7] Worried about Dostoevsky's health, in view of the anticipated strain, Anna made him promise to write every day, and he faithfully kept his word—often writing not once but twice. A full, firsthand account thus exists of the swirling round of activities in which he became engulfed during a stay that was expected to be no more than a week, but in fact lasted twenty-two days.

One reason for this prolongation was the death of Tsarina Marya Alexandrovna, the estranged wife of Alexander II, on the very day of Dostoevsky's departure. He heard about it from fellow passengers, and his first thought, assuming that the festivities would be canceled, was to return home; but he decided to continue his trip nonetheless. Even if the public dedication of the monument were eliminated, some sort of purely literary consecration might still take place. On arriving in Moscow and learning that the Tsar had ordered a postponement of the dedication, he wrote Anna that he had come "without any purpose at all now."[8]

Planning to return on the twenty-eighth, he would use the interval to visit Lyubimov and Katkov "and talk over the most important thing" (the continuation of his novel). He would also make the rounds of booksellers to pick up the proceeds of sales and call on his relatives; perhaps, as well, "I'll finally find out the whole story about the literary intrigues." He was met at the train by his host Yuriev and the entire staff of *Russian Thought*, but he was too fatigued to accept an invitation for dinner. The cab driver who took him to a hotel, recommended as the best and most comfortable, at first refused any payment, "but I forced him to accept seventy kopeks." Dostoevsky had hoped to cover at least part of the expenses of the trip by the publication of his Pushkin speech, but writes: "I foresee that my piece won't be published for the time being because it would be strange to publish it now."[9]

The next day, he wasted his morning returning visits from various notables, including Ivan Aksakov, and then went to call on Yuriev. "An enthusiastic meeting with kisses," he reports with an edge of irony. He was not at all impressed with the editor, whom he compares with the scatterbrained character Repetilov in Griboyedov's classic comedy, *Woe from Wit*. "I couldn't get anything out of Yuriev about how things are going; he's a flibbertigibbet as a person, a Repetilov in a new form. He's clever, though. (There have indisputably been intrigues, however)." Yuriev failed to recall having pleaded to publish Dostoevsky's Pushkin piece, but suggested he would take it in the fall, "'and by then you'll have polished it carefully' (as though he knew for certain that it has not been carefully polished as of now)." This affront to Dostoevsky's literary conscientiousness was hardly adroit; and when that evening he went to see Lyubimov and Katkov, who received him very cordially, he mentioned the Pushkin piece to them. They were concerned primarily with his novel and wanted a new installment for June ("when I get home I'll have to work like the devil"), but were quite willing to accept the essay as well. "Furious with Yuriev, I *almost* promised. So that if *Russian Thought* wants the piece I'll charge a fortune; otherwise, it will go to Katkov."[10]

A dinner had been arranged in Dostoevsky's honor at the renowned hotel-restaurant "The Hermitage" at five o'clock on the twenty-fifth because "all the young Moscow writers are wildly anxious to meet me." Twenty-two guests attended, among them Ivan Aksakov and Nikolay Rubinshtein, founder and directory of the Moscow Conservatory, who had been placed in charge of the musical arrangements for the festival; there were also four unnamed professors of the university. Complaints were later made that many others had learned about the dinner only when it was too late for them to attend. He was impressed with the lavishness of the meal: "quail, amazing asparagus, ice cream, a river of fine wines and champagne. . . . [A]fter dinner, over coffee and liqueur, two hundred magnificent and expensive cigars appeared. They don't organize things the St. Petersburg way." Six laudatory speeches were given, and "mention was made of my 'great significance as an artist of worldwide sensitivity,' as a journalist, and as a Russian. . . . Everyone was in an enthusiastic state. . . . I replied to everyone with a quite successful speech that produced a great effect; moreover, I made Pushkin the topic of the speech."[11]

During the dinner, Dostoevsky announced that he was planning to leave on the twenty-seventh, and "an absolute din arose: 'We won't let you go.'" Earlier in the day, Prince Dolgoruky had told representatives of the SLRL that the festivities *would* take place sometime between June 1 and 5, and Dostoevsky was admonished: "All of Moscow will be grieved and indignant if you leave." When he pleaded that he had to work on *The Karamazovs*, it was instantly proposed that a deputation be sent to Katkov to demand a revision of the publication schedule. When he spoke of his family anxiously awaiting his return, there was talk of an explanatory telegram to Anna Grigoryevna and even a deputation to Staraya Russa. Under this pressure, he wavered and said he would come to a firm decision the next day. The same letter expresses his dilemma over where to publish the Pushkin piece; he had to choose between Yuriev and Katkov and did not wish to antagonize either. His anxieties were further increased because, since quitting Staraya Russa, he had so far not received a single letter from Anna.[12]

In a postscript, Dostoevsky then tells of a visit by Ivan Aksakov, who "came to see me to ask in the most insistent manner that I stay for the dedication, since it will occur, as everyone expects, around the fifth. He says that I can't leave, that I don't have the *right* to do that, that I have an influence in Moscow and most important on the students and young people in general, that [it will] be detrimental to the triumph of our convictions, that after hearing an outline of my speech yesterday at dinner he became convinced that I have to speak, etc." Also, he informed Dostoevsky that, as a representative of the Slavic Benevolent Society, he was officially obliged to remain and place a wreath on the statue of Pushkin. Dostoevsky thought this task could be handled by the other delegate, an official of the ministry of the interior named Zolotaryov, except that, alas, nobody knew the whereabouts of this worthy gentleman.[13]

Yuriev also arrived to make the same plea that he remain, and to appeal again for the Pushkin article: "He became terribly upset and distressed, apologized, asserted that I had misunderstood him." When Dostoevsky mentioned payment, Yuriev "yelled" that Lavrov (the publisher of *Russian Thought*, a wealthy merchant who was "[his] passionate, ecstatic admirer") would go as high as five hundred rubles. Katkov was paying only three hundred per signature for *The Brothers Karamazov*, and Dostoevsky was sorely tempted; the extra money from Yuriev "would pay for my delay here until the dedication of the monument." He also informs Anna that "Yuriev had a piece by Ivan Aksakov about Pushkin. That's why he was dodging me so the day before yesterday." But he had changed his mind after Dostoevsky's remarks about Pushkin at the dinner.[14]

On May 27, he learned that his expenses would be paid by the Moscow Duma. He had wondered about having been given a much better room at the hotel with no mention of any change in price (the window of his first, inexpensive room had looked out on a wall), and then he discovered that Yuriev had learned about his room change at the Moscow Duma. Surprised that the Duma took an interest in his lodging, he was then told that the assembly was covering the room and board of all the invited delegates. Far from being pleased, he objected strenuously but was told he would insult *all* of Moscow if he persisted in refusing. Why, even the surviving members of Pushkin's family, all residing in the same hotel, had accepted the hospitality of the Duma! In view of Dostoevsky's concern about expenses, one might think that his resistance was feigned; but there were good reasons why he should desire to pay his own way. A writer known to have accepted *any* kind of official support was assumed to have lost his independence; and Dostoevsky wished to avoid such an imputation at all costs. He thus tells Anna that he will "purposely go to restaurants for dinner so as to reduce as much as possible the bill that will be presented to the Duma by the hotel."[15] He did not want any gossip to spread that he was exploiting the situation unduly for his own advantage.

## 4

On the afternoon of May 26 it was learned that the ceremonies would definitely take place on June 5, and most of the deputations, which had come from all parts of Russia, decided to remain. "The liveliest animation reigns," Dostoevsky writes. "They absolutely won't let me go. I've decided now for certain that I think I'll stay." Both Yuriev and Dostoevsky's old friend D. V. Grigorovich had been assailing him with the dire consequences of an early departure. "People will say that I lacked sufficient civic feeling to neglect my own affairs for such a lofty goal, because in the restoration of Pushkin's significance throughout Russia everyone sees a means for a new turn of convictions, minds, directions." What continued to bother him was the need to provide a June install-ment of his novel; but this segment might not be necessary if B. M. Markevich, whose novel *The Turning Point* (*Perelom*) was alternating with *The Brothers Karamazov* in the *Russian Messenger*, sent in some chapters for June. Whether Markevich would meet *his* deadline still re-mained unknown, and Dostoevsky even thought (but quickly gave up the idea) of attempting to work on his novel in Moscow despite the social whirligig.[16]

Turgenev had been assigned the delicate, as well as unenviable, task of journeying to Yasnaya Polyana to persuade Tolstoy to attend the Pushkin celebration, even though Tolstoy by this time had renounced literature for reasons comparable to—though not identical with—those of the radical critics who had denounced Pushkin in the 1860s. Just what occurred during their meeting on May 2–3 is not known in detail, but Grigorovich, an inveterate gossip, told Dostoevsky "that Turgenev, who has come back from seeing Lev Tolstoy, is ill, while Tolstoy has nearly lost his mind, and has perhaps even quite lost it."[17] Writing to Nikolay Strakhov a day later, Tolstoy said: "I had many interesting conversations with Turgenev. Up to now, if you will forgive me for the presumption, it's always been my experience, fortunately, that people have said: 'What's Tolstoy doing, working away at some nonsense or other. He ought to be told to stop that nonsense.' And every time it's been the case that the people giving advice have become ashamed and fright-ened about themselves. I think it was the same with Turgenev too. I found it both painful and comforting to be with him. And we parted amicably." Another report, however, says that Turgenev was "hurt and offended" by the encounter.[18] In a succeeding letter, Dostoevsky writes:

"Katkov also confirmed about Lev Tolstoy that he has quite lost his mind. Yuriev has been trying to get me to see him. . . . But I won't go, even though it would be very interesting."[19]

On May 28, it was officially announced that the dedication of the monument would take place on June 4. Dostoevsky explained again to Anna that "*I should* stay . . . it's not just [the SLRL] who need me, but our whole party, our whole idea, for which we have been struggling thirty years now because the hostile party (Turgenev, Kovalevsky, and almost the entire university) definitely want to play down Pushkin's significance as a spokesman for the Russian national character, denying that very national character." Even though Ivan Aksakov would also speak, he "has gotten out of date and Moscow is sick of him"; as for Yuriev and company, "they don't carry any weight." "My voice will have weight and therefore our side will triumph too. I have fought for this my whole life and can't flee the field of battle now."[20] Moreover, as he had told the more practical Anna just the day before, "if my speech at the gala meeting is a success, then in Moscow (and therefore in Russia too) from then on I will be better known as a writer (that is, in the sense of the eminence already won by Turgenev and Tolstoy. Goncharov, for instance, who doesn't leave Petersburg [though in fact he had made a trip around the world with the Russian Navy] is known here, but from afar and coldly)."[21]

Amidst all these encounters and activities, a lady came to ask permission to publish a selection of his writings for children; but he denied her request because, as he told Anna, they themselves "should have carried out that idea long ago." Why make the enterprising editor "a gift of two thousand rubles"? Another female admirer, who "had come to express her infinite admiration, amazement, gratitude for everything that I had given her through my works," offered this appreciation to Yuriev and promptly left without even catching sight of her idol. Grigorovich clung to Dostoevsky all day, and in a restaurant they ran into the playwright Dimitry Averkiev and his wife, as well as two nephews of Pushkin, who asked if they could pay a call on Dostoevsky. Preparations for the great event were in full swing, and "the windows of the buildings surrounding the square are being rented out for fifty rubles a window." There would be a series of readings from Pushkin by well-known writers, and Dostoevsky had been assigned a monologue from his old favorite, *The Covetous Knight* (a speech of the miserly knight himself), the monologue of the monk Pimen from *Boris Godunov* (whom he would mention in his speech as the embodiment of the Russian folk spirit), and a poem on the death of Pushkin by Tyutchev.[22]

The next day he busied himself with inquiries about the practical details of his participation and was also told by P. S. Viskovatov, a visiting professor and admirer, that A. D. Saburov (the reputedly enlightened minister of education, newly appointed by Loris-Melikov), "had read certain passages of *The Karamazovs* while literally weeping with ecstasy." Of Viskovatov himself, he remarks, with a touch of sarcasm, that he "declared his love, asked why I didn't love him, and so on. Still and all, he was better than usual" (a characterization that can only be considered amusedly deprecating).* After dinner, they both went to call on Anna Nikolaevna Engelgardt, who had come to Moscow to visit a sick relative but was herself suffering from a leg ailment. A veteran of the woman's liberation movement of the 1860s, whose husband, a university professor, had been exiled from St. Petersburg for spreading "revolutionary" ideas among his students, the intrepid lady had herself spent half a month in the Peter-and-Paul Fortress. As a journalist and translator from the French (she had several novels of Zola to her credit), she also frequented the Shtakenshneider salon, where, as their hostess noted, Dostoevsky seemed to find her company very agreeable. Anna Nikolaevna had already retired when they arrived—it was ten o'clock— "but [she] was very glad to see us, and we stayed for an hour talking about the beautiful and sublime."[23] This gently ironic expression indicates his affection for the seasoned radical, and is another instance of his ability to overlook politics when personal sympathy prevailed.

On May 31, he finally received a letter from Anna Grigoryevna and was greatly relieved: "I'm very glad that you are all well, glad for the children, and an oppression seems to have lifted from my heart." To add to Anna's collection of autographs of important Russians, "Aksakov has promised me an autograph of Gogol's," but Dostoevsky was afraid he would have no time to pick it up. The provident Anna had also charged him with the task of inscribing the name of their son Feodor in the register of the nobility in Moscow; but after several reminders, he replied that "in the first place, even if it were possible, I don't have the time, and most important it needs to be done from Petersburg, *through people*." As a curiosity, he remarks that "a mathematician (I've forgotten his name), came to see me today and sat for a long time in the restaurant waiting for me to wake up. . . . He had dropped by to declare his profound admiration, amazement at my talent, devotion, gratitude. He stated all that *ardently* and left. A man with graying hair, a very nice

---

* It is worth noting this condescending attitude toward Viskovatov because, in the infamous letter that Nikolay Strakhov wrote to Tolstoy accusing Dostoevsky of having (like his character Stavrogin) seduced an adolescent girl, Strakhov cites Viskovatov as a firsthand source to whom Dostoevsky presumably made a "confession." It is intrinsically implausible that such a confession ever was made; and it is even more implausible that Dostoevsky should have made it to someone of whose pretensions to his intimacy he speaks so disrespectfully.

face."* Dostoevsky also mentions a young man assigned to guide him through the ceremonies: "to my pleasant surprise [I] found him to be an extremely bright, quite thoughtful, extremely decent person who also thoroughly shares my convictions."[24] This young man, L. M. Lopatin, later became a well-known Russian philosopher and professor at the University of Moscow.

A meeting had been held at Turgenev's lodgings on May 31 to make the final arrangements, and two days later Dostoevsky complains to Anna about having been excluded. To console him, Grigorovich attributed his presumed slight to chance; but Yuriev "let slip three days ago that they would be gathering at Turgenev's, Viskovatov came right out and told me he had received an invitation three days ago." On the morning of June 1, he thus learned that the monologue from *The Covetous Knight* had been reassigned to a well-known actor and that, instead of the poem by Tyutchev ("it was exactly that poem that I wanted to read"), he had been given Pushkin's "The Prophet," which of course he knew by heart. "I probably won't refuse 'The Prophet,' but how could they not notify me officially?" Then Lopatin arrived and, as a messenger from the committee, told Dostoevsky that he was scheduled to read along with the others at a dress rehearsal for *gymnasium* students. "Thus I'm being put in a very ticklish situation: it's been decided without me, no one asked for my consent to read the works *assigned* to me, and meanwhile I can't refuse to go to the rehearsal. . . . [P]eople will say that Dostoevsky didn't want to read for the young people."[25] This reading for students, however, was ultimately canceled.

Such offhand treatment was as nothing compared with the blow dealt to Katkov on the same day. Visiting him that evening, Dostoevsky met Lyubimov, who told him that Markevich "in fact promises to deliver an installment of the novel for June," and he thus no longer had to worry about the June installment of *his* novel. His relief at this good news, however, was blotted out by the shocking information that Yuriev, in the name of the SLRL, had *withdrawn* an invitation to Katkov as editor of the newspaper *Moskovskie Vedomosti* (*Moscow News*) on the ground that it had been sent through an error. Dostoevsky was outraged at this insulting display of ideological partisanship, even more so when he was told by the irrepressible tale-teller Grigorovich "that Yuriev was made to sign it, mainly by Kovalevsky but by Turgenev too" (there is evidence, however, that Yuriev was a willing participant in this affront). "It's vileness," Dostoevsky fumed, "and if I weren't so involved in these festiv-

---

* There has been speculation that this "mathematician" could have been N. V. Bugaev, professor of mathematics at the University of Moscow and father of the famous twentieth-century Russian novelist and poet Andrey Bely. The latter writes in his memoirs that his father had wide-ranging literary interests. See the commentary in *PSS*, 30/Bk. 1: 346–347.

ities, I would perhaps break off relations with them."[26] *Moscow News* printed a curt item referring to this incident, adding that the ticket sent to Katkov as publisher of the *Russian Messenger* (his monthly journal) had also been returned. A mystery still remains as to why the invitation to *Moscow News*, where Katkov's attacks on the intelligentsia had appeared, was sent without having been officially approved; but the chairman of the organizing committee, L. I. Polivanov, was known to be a strong supporter of the classical school curriculum instituted largely under Katkov's influence (and to which Kolya Krasotkin, though first in Latin, had already disdainfully referred in Book 10 of *The Brothers Karamazov*).

After calling on Katkov, Dostoevsky, Grigorovich, and Viskovatov dined at "The Hermitage" and then went to the theater that formed part of the amenities of this hotel-restaurant complex. They arrived during the second act of *Paul et Virginie*, an opera by Victor Massé, but left before the end. "The theater, orchestra, and singers were all decent," Dostoevsky reports. "It's just that the music is so bad (it had several hundred performances in Paris). There are lovely sets in the third act." He also informs Anna that he had paid a visit to "Bishop Aleksey and Nikolay [called Yaponskii, "the Japanese"]. I was very glad to make their acquaintance. . . . Both of them spoke very sincerely to me. They said that my visit did them a great honor and made them happy. They have read my works. They thus appreciate people who stand up for God. Aleksey blessed me with deep feeling. He gave me cut communion bread."[27]

Nikolay Yaponskii, the priestly appellation of I. D. Kasatkin, was a Russian clergyman who had headed a mission to Japan to convert the heathen. His presence in Moscow, where he was residing at the home of Bishop Aleksey, had aroused widespread interest and been reported in the newspapers. Dostoevsky's visit, in the midst of the social vortex, no doubt sprang from a genuine concern for the fortunes of the Russian Church abroad; but it was also an opportunity to gather material for the planned revival of the *Diary of a Writer*. An article on how Russian Orthodoxy had fared in Japan, as recounted by an eyewitness, could arouse a great deal of interest. This article was never written, but the meeting was recorded by Nikolay Yaponskii in his own unpublished diary, unearthed in 1990 by a Japanese Slavist. Dostoevsky exhibited a great deal of curiosity about Japan and the Japanese, particularly wishing to know if "there was anything special in their reception of Christianity." Nikolay also noted that "the well-known writer" spoke about "the Nihilists," assuring him that they "would soon become entirely transformed into religious people—and even now, it seems, they are emerging from the limits of their economic [orientation] onto a moral foundation." Of course, this was Dostoevsky's own fondest hope.[28]

On the morning of June 3, Grigorovich, Viskovatov, and Yuriev turned up. "We all attacked Yuriev fiercely for his letter to Katkov and gave him a terrible scolding." After dinner, Dostoevsky met the actor who would be performing the monologue from *The Covetous Knight* ("a little old man of sixty-four, who kept making speeches at me"), and they all went to a meeting of the executive committee of the SLRL, where—in spite of his previous suspicions—the final dispositions were made. "Everything was arranged to everyone's general satisfaction," he tells Anna contentedly. "Turgenev was rather nice to me, while Kovalevsky (a big fat hulk and enemy of our tendency) kept staring at me intently." He would read his Pushkin speech "on the eighth of June, on the second day of the morning meeting, and on the evening of the sixth I'm reading Pimen's scene from *Boris Godunov*. . . . At the second evening, on the eighth, I'll read three poems by Pushkin (two from *Songs of the Western Slavs*), and at the finale, for the *conclusion* of the celebrations, Pushkin's 'The Prophet.'" His public renditions of this poem had always created a sensation and become deservedly famous. "I was purposely put into the finale so as to produce an effect."[29]

On returning at ten o'clock, he found a card from Suvorin and hastened to the hotel where this Petersburg ally was staying with his wife. "I was terribly glad. Because of his articles he's in disgrace with the 'Lovers' [SLRL] just like Katkov." Suvorin had written several pieces attacking Yuriev's *Russian Thought*, and, though not defending Katkov directly, had assailed his enemies. These opinions had been enough for him to fall out of the good graces of the SLRL. "They didn't even give him a ticket for a morning meeting," but luckily an extra one was acquired from Dostoevsky's sister Varvara, who was unable to attend. Dostoevsky, Grigorovich, and Viskovatov planned to visit the Kremlin Museum of Antiquities the next day, and Suvorin begged that they "take him and his wife too," wishing to join them for dinner as well. "Poor fellow," Dostoevsky remarks, "he seems bored with his wife"—an attitude very far from his own sentiments. Replying to Anna's teasing accusation that "I don't love you," he confesses that "I keep having terrible dreams, nightmares every night, about your betraying me with others."[30] He also sets down his definitive timetable for departure: everything will be over by the eighth, he will make his visits on the ninth, take the train on the tenth, and be home on the eleventh.

5
———

The official opening ceremonies of "the Pushkin days" began on June 5. At two in the afternoon, all 106 delegations were received in the hall of the Duma by Prince Oldenburgsky, head of the commission for the Pushkin monument, and Governor-General Dolgoruky. "I can't describe the ceremony," Dostoevsky writes, "the fussing around, the chaos—it's impossible to describe." Each delegation advanced in turn to a stage covered with luxuriant greenery and dominated by a large bust of Pushkin, at the foot of which they deposited their wreaths. (Dostoevsky had been tormented by the problem of acquiring such a wreath and paying for it out of his own pocket.) The delegates then read speeches, and the press comments on the merits of these oratorical efforts were hardly complimentary. The Populist writer Gleb Uspensky, who covered the festival for *Notes of the Fatherland*—and to whose commentary we shall return—remarked that "there were speeches so strange that, even if one wanted to, one could not track down precisely where the main clause was located."[31] Dostoevsky says nothing about the oratory but mentions that he managed to speak to Pushkin's daughter while standing in line, and that "Turgenev ran up courteously," as did the playwright A. N. Ostrovsky, "the local Jupiter."[32]

For all the outward appearance of fraternal goodwill, Dostoevsky was very much aware of the latent hostilities in the background. "The other liberal parties, among them Pleshcheev and even the lame Yazykov [a functionary who had been part of the Belinsky circle in the 1840s], regard me with restraint and as though haughtily: 'You are a reactionary, while we are liberals.' . . . I'm afraid that because of the tendencies people may come to blows any one of these days. The story of Katkov's exclusion from the ceremonies terribly enrages many people." He had returned to his hotel early in the hope of finding a letter from Anna, to which he would reply "and then [look] over Pimen and my [Pushkin] piece." But his old friend Apollon Maikov suddenly arrived, along with the omnipresent Viskovatov. Dostoevsky chatted with them a bit but, determined to find some free time, showed them out very quickly. He was still worried about the publication of his Pushkin speech because "Yuriev is again being evasive for some reason," and Katkov might now want to wash his hands of anything linked with the festivities. Suvorin, at their first meeting in Moscow, had inquired about it for his *New Time* but had not mentioned it again, "and may not even repeat his wish. Then it will be bad."[33]

On June 7, he begins his letter to Anna with an account of the events of the day preceding, when the Pushkin monument had been unveiled and dedicated. His pen faltered, however, at depicting this epochal event. "What's the point of trying to describe it? You couldn't describe it even in twenty pages, and besides, I don't have even a moment's time. For three nights I've slept only five hours each, and tonight too."[34] As a prelude to the unveiling, a mass had been held at the Strastnoi Monastery just across the square from the monument, and Metropolitan Makarii—a member of the SLRL—solemnly wished "eternal

16. The unveiling of the Pushkin monument, June 6, 1880

memory" to Pushkin's shade. If we are to believe Suvorin's memoirs, Dostoevsky came to him and his wife during the service and asked Mme Suvorina to pray at his funeral as she had been praying for Pushkin. "I have been observing you all this time. Will you be there? Promise?"[35]

The initial plan had been for Makarii to lead a solemn procession from the church to the statue, which he would sprinkle with holy water; but the clergy remained within the church and the statue did not receive the expected blessing. Protests had been raised that such a blessing would be sacrilege, although all previous statues—including those of Russian generals belonging to the Lutheran faith—had received such a consecration. Thus, without benefit of clergy, the processions marched to the strains of "four orchestras and several choruses and groups of schoolchildren" led by Nikolay Rubinshtein. "Delegates wore badges and carried wreaths; some waved flags of red, white, and blue with their delegation's name stamped in gold." Other banners bore the names of Pushkin's poems, and one, reading "Robber Brothers," attracted a good deal of attention and some hilarity.[36]

The unveiling produced an explosion of joyful hysteria, and all accounts agree that "people were 'crazed with happiness'; many wept, and even the most hard-nosed of newspapermen admitted afterward to shedding a few tears." A columnist in *Voice* wrote of "how many good, warm, joyful thoughts were expressed in separate groups. . . . How many sincere handshakes, how many good, honest kisses people exchanged—often people who weren't even acquainted."[37] One should keep this generally ecstatic mood in mind in gauging what Dostoevsky tells us about the fervent testimonies of admiration lavished on him even before his speech. Once the unveiling had taken place, the delegations, marching to the music of Meyerbeer's "The Prophet," paraded to the monument and laid their wreaths at its foot. Not much remained of these wreaths once the ceremonies were finished; people pulled them to pieces because they wished to take home a branch or two as souvenirs.

That evening, a dinner held under the auspices of the Moscow Duma was to be followed by the first of the readings by the important authors present. Also, despite the maneuvers of the SLRL, Katkov had been invited to speak as a member of the Duma, and Dostoevsky mentions the talk briefly in his letter: "Yesterday at the Duma dinner Katkov took the risk of making a long speech, and nonetheless produced an effect, at least among part of the audience."[38] This laconic observation hardly reflects his agitation, noted by P. A. Gaideburov, editor of the semi-Populist *Week*, who called on him on the evening of the sixth, just before the dinner. "I drop by Dostoevsky's, and see that he is in a most horrible state; he is somehow twitching all over, in his eyes—anxiety, in his movements—irritation and alarm. I knew he was a highly nervous and impressionable person, who passionately gave himself up to every emotion, but I had never seen him in such a state before." Gaideburov asked what was wrong. "'Ah, what will happen, what will happen?' he exclaimed in answer with despair."[39] Gaideburov understood him as referring to the impending dinner and Katkov's speech. The pariah would now be able to speak his mind, and the result might be, as Dostoevsky had feared a day earlier, that people would come to blows.

When Katkov took the floor, after the speeches by various notables, his words were those of a reconciliation that he thought appropriate for the occasion. He spoke of the celebration as a "holiday of peace" and said that, "however we may differ on other matters, at this day, at this celebration, I hope we are of one mind, are all allies." His hope was also that "perhaps this passing rapprochement will serve us as a pledge for a more durable unity in the future that will lead to the dying out, or at least the mitigation, of hostilities." He concluded with the famous poetic toast of Pushkin: "Let the sun shine forth, let the darkness cease!" These pacifying words were generally well received and evoked some applause (just how much depended on what newspaper one read). Both Ivan Aksakov (as a Slavophil, a longtime ideological enemy of Katkov's emphasis on state power) and Gaideburov rose to congratulate the speaker; but when Katkov extended his arm to clink glasses with Turgenev, the latter turned away. The next day, to general indignation, *Voice* erroneously reported that *nobody* had responded favorably to Katkov's speech and that he had been unanimously ostracized. No mention of this episode is made by Dostoevsky; but according to M. M. Kovalevsky, Dostoevsky and Turgenev spoke about it later in the evening. Turgenev is cited as replying, presumably in answer to some regret expressed by Dostoevsky at the rebuff to Katkov: "Well, there are some things it is impossible to forget. How could I extend my hand to a person whom I consider a renegade?"[40]

During the dinner on June 6, which began at five o'clock in the afternoon, "two ladies," as he tells Anna, "brought me flowers" (he recognized them as the wife of P. M. Tretyakov, the founder of the famous gallery in Moscow where Dostoevsky's portrait was hanging, and Olga Golokhvastova, a writer and dramatist). But this tribute could not overcome his disappointment at what occurred that evening, when he read his assigned pieces, along with Pisemsky, Ostrovsky, Grigorovich, and, of course, the only other participant he cared about—Turgenev. "I read Pimen's scene," he writes Anna the next day. "Despite the difficulty of that choice (because Pimen can't yell so as to be heard in the whole room) and the fact that the reading was in the least resonant of the rooms, they say I read superbly, but they say they couldn't hear me very well." Although he "was greeted wonderfully" and called back three times, he still felt that he had been bested: "Turgenev, who read very badly, was called back more than I was."[41]

Turgenev had been greeted clamorously by the audience, and one of the poems he read, "Again in the Homeland," had a particular resonance because of his own self-exile. As he began to recite another poem from memory, it became obvious that he could not recall the text. "Helplessly throwing wide his arms," according to Dostoevsky's friend A. F. Koni, "he stopped. Then, from various parts [of the auditorium] the public began to prompt him louder and louder. He smiled, and recited the end of the poem in unison with the whole auditorium. This appealing episode only further warmed the general feeling toward him."[42] Dostoevsky, however, suspiciously persisted in believing that

Kovalevsky had planted a claque ("a hundred young people shouted in a frenzy when Turgenev came out") and that its purpose, besides applauding Turgenev, "was to humiliate us [the nonliberals] if we were to go against them." For all that, he could not complain of any lack of adulation on the part of the public. "The reception offered me yesterday was amazing. During the intermission I went through the hall, and a horde of people, young people, gray-haired people, and ladies, rushed up to me, saying: 'You are our prophet. You have made us better since we read *The Karamazovs.*' In short, I am convinced that *The Karamazovs* has colossal significance."[43] All this appreciation was only a foretaste of what would occur the very next day.

## CHAPTER 28

# Pushkin: Two Readings

The two most important literary figures at the Pushkin festival were Turgenev and Dostoevsky, and their barely concealed rivalry underlay all the solemn rituals of the occasion. On June 7 and 8, with Turgenev speaking on the first date and Dostoevsky on the second, this rivalry finally emerged into the light of day—not in any fashion that disturbed the gravity and decorum of the proceedings, but rather in the interpretations they offered of the importance and status of Pushkin.

Each gave entirely different readings of Pushkin—Turgenev viewing him in the context of European literature, Dostoevsky proclaiming his genius to be equal to, if not surpassing, anything that European genius had been capable of producing. Each presented not only a literary-critical view of Pushkin but also, implicitly, an evaluation of Russian achievement in relation to Europe. The argument, as the audience well understood, was thus only nominally about a literary figure; it was also a replay of the long-standing Westernizer-Slavophil debate carried on in Russian culture all through the nineteenth century. On this occasion, the historical record is perfectly clear: Dostoevsky emerged triumphant! Numerous testimonies have already been cited to his spellbinding power as a public speaker, but his success cannot be attributed solely to his oratorical gifts. He gave the public what it had been waiting to hear, and achieved a victory that astonished even himself.

## 2

June 7 marked the first session of the Pushkin festivities sponsored by the Society of Lovers of Russian Literature (SLRL), and the day opened with some words about Pushkin from the only foreign delegate to make the journey, the French Slavist Louis Léger. Telegrams were read from Victor Hugo, Berthold Auerbach, and Alfred Tennyson; but the main event, eagerly awaited by all—if for differing reasons—was Turgenev's speech. In composing it, Turgenev drew on two lectures he had given on Pushkin in the 1860s and on his famous article, "Recollections of Belinsky," which had paid tribute to the great critic who had first defined Pushkin's place in Russian literature. Indeed, much of what Turgenev says about Pushkin's historical position, compared with that of

Lermontov and Gogol, is derived from Belinsky's famous series of essays on the poet.

He begins by declaring Pushkin to be "the first Russian artist-poet," and praises him profusely as the founding father of modern Russian literature. Declaring art to be "the embodiment of the ideals lying at the foundation of a people's [*narodnoi*] life, [thus] defining its spiritual and moral physiognomy," he quickly moves on to some of the well-known facts of Pushkin's artistic career.[1] At first imitating foreign models (Voltaire and Byron are mentioned), Pushkin rapidly freed himself from such tutelage and found his own voice. But then, to an audience inflamed by patriotic fervor, Turgenev rather maladroitly equates Pushkin's rejection of foreign models in his poetry with an equal rejection of Russian folk poetry itself: "The independent genius of Pushkin quickly ... freed itself both from the imitation of foreign forms and from the temptation of the counterfeiting of a folk [*narodnoi*] tonality." When he yielded to this temptation, as in *Ruslan and Ludmilla* (1820), he produced "the weakest of all his works." In Russia "the simple people" (*prostoi narod*) do not read Pushkin any more than the German people read Goethe, the French Molière, or the English Shakespeare. For "every art is the elevating of life based on an ideal, [and] those remaining on the level of ordinary, everyday life remain lower than this ideal level."[2]

All the same, Goethe, Molière, and Shakespeare are *narodnoi* poets, poets of their people in the true sense of that word, which Turgenev defines in his own way. For him it means imparting to the values of one's own culture a national (*natsionalnie*) significance, thus attaining a level of universality that transcends mere class or regional boundaries. Such poets unquestionably represent their people, but they have so absorbed its values that they raise those values to the universal level of the ideal. To drive home this point, Turgenev disparages the slogan of "folk-character [*narodnost*] in art" as the sign of weak, inferior, and enslaved peoples struggling to preserve their existence and identity.[3] Russia, happily, is not such a country, and there is thus no reason for it to have recourse to such a palliative. At a moment when Populism (*Narodnichestvo*), in one form or another, was the dominating social-political, as well as artistic, ideal of the Russian intelligentsia both on the right and the left, Turgenev was completely at odds with the reigning mood of the vast majority of his audience.

He then raises the crucial question of whether Pushkin can be considered a "national" poet in this sense, equal to Shakespeare, Molière, and Goethe, and replies evasively: "For the moment we shall leave this open." There is no question, however, that Pushkin "gave us our poetic, our literary language, even though some argue that no such language exists even yet because it can only come from 'the simple people,' along with other tradition-preserving institutions" (a passing jab at the virtues attributed to the Russian peasant commune). Pushkin's language, all the same, expresses the best elements of the Russian character—its "virile charm, strength, and clarity, its straightforward truth, absence of deceit and pose, [its] simplicity, the openness and honesty of its feelings."[4] But then, to support such claims, Turgenev invokes remarks made to him by Victor Hugo and Prosper Merimée, as if his Russian audience were likely to be impressed by the approbation of such eminent foreign authorities.

Merimée, to be sure, at least knew Russian and had translated some Pushkin, even comparing "the equilibrium of form and content, of image and idea" in Pushkin's poetry with that of the ancient Greeks. But Merimée is also cited as favorably impressed by "the absence of any explanations and moral conclusions" in his poetry.[5] What Turgenev offered as artistic praise could well be seen by his audience as a denial that Pushkin's poetry had any moral significance whatever! Following Belinsky, Turgenev lauds Pushkin's capacity to enter poetically into the artistic forms and spirit of foreign cultures and peoples, but he immediately adds the disparaging observation that foreigners often speak disdainfully of this Russian capacity for "assimilation."[6] No qualification is made, however, of Pushkin's eminence in endowing Russian literature with a whole gamut of models and types, which were then developed by later writers.

For all his genius and his immense services to Russian literature, Pushkin did not escape the fate of other writers who also had been literary initiators. Even during his lifetime, his later works were greeted coldly, and "the following generations distanced themselves from him even more. . . . [I]t is only very recently that a return to his poetry has become visible."[7] As an illustration of Pushkin's disdainful reaction to his critics, Turgenev read in its entirety a sonnet expressing the poet's contempt for the "judgment of fools"; but he then goes on to justify such assaults as historically pardonable. Referring to the radical rejection of Pushkin in the 1860s, which merely developed the critique initiated by Belinsky in the late 1840s, he explains it as a result of "the historical development of society under conditions that gave birth to a new life, which stepped from a literary epoch into a political one." The adoration of art and Pushkin ceased, and he was replaced by the wrathful Lermontov, the satirical Gogol, and "the poet of revenge and sorrow" (Nekrasov). They won the adherence of succeeding generations and created a different kind of literature more responsive to the moral-social needs of the times.[8]

Turgenev thus refuses to condemn the assault on Pushkin by the radicals, which reflected the new realities of Russian life, but he rejoices that this period of artistic iconoclasm appears to be reaching its end. In

Pushkin's day, belles lettres had served as the unique expression of Russian society, but then a time came when the aims of art as such were entirely swept aside. "The previous sphere was too large; the second shrunk it to nothing; finding its natural limits, poetry will be firmly established forever." And then, perhaps, a poet will appear "who will fully deserve the title of a national-universal poet, which we cannot make up our mind to give to Pushkin, although we do not dare deprive him of it either."[9]

A concluding paragraph of panegyric follows, but the damage had been done. As Dostoevsky wrote to Anna immediately, Turgenev "had denigrated Pushkin by refusing him the title of national poet."[10] And this was the sentiment of a large part of the audience as well. Turgenev had finally balked, no matter how hesitantly and reluctantly, at placing the Russian among the very first rank of the European poets with whom he had been compared. The exhilaration of the ceremony was badly deflated by this embarrassing denial, which seemed to indicate the continued inferiority of Russian culture, supposedly being celebrated, vis-à-vis Europe.

Turgenev's talk left his audience with a general sense of disappointment, "dissatisfaction and indistinct vexation," to quote Nikolay Strakhov.[11] His subtly balanced considerations tried to unite a eulogy of Pushkin with an apologia for his rejection by the radical critics of the 1860s; and he had also expressed his own opposition, as a liberal Westernizer, to the Slavophil and Populist idolization of "the people." All these opinions were hardly in accord with the overheated emotional temperature of the moment, and he was quite well aware of his failure to stir his audience. A few days later, in sending a copy of his talk to the actress M. G. Savina, he wrote: "I don't know how much this will interest you (it did not produce a great impression on the public)."[12]

## 3

Delivered in the early afternoon, Turgenev's speech was followed by a dinner that evening. "The young people," Dostoevsky reports to Anna, "greeted me at my arrival, treated me, waited on me, made frenzied speeches to me—and that was still before dinner." Toasts were offered, one by the playwright A. N. Ostrovsky to Russian literature, and Dostoevsky was prevailed upon to speak. "I only said a few words—and there was a roar of enthusiasm—literally a roar." He proposed a toast to Pushkin as one of the greatest poets, "the purest, the most honorable, the most intelligent of all Russian men," thus giving a foretaste of what he would proclaim the following afternoon.[13] As the party broke up, he was surrounded by what one memoirist called "the Shakespeareans," a group of young people who had formed a society to study and stage Shakespeare's plays. In conversation with them, Dostoevsky complained about his illness, which prevented him from working; and then, pausing in silence for a moment, he continued: "'I will write my *Children* and die.' The novel *Children*, according to him, was the continuation of *The Brothers Karamazov*. In it, the *children* of the preceding novel would come forward as the main heroes."[14]

Speculation was of course rife about how he would continue the careers of his brothers Karamazov, and his conversation with Suvorin on this point has already been cited. Others were obviously discussing it as well, and on May 26 an item in the literary column of the *Novorossiskii Telegraf* (*New Russian Telegraph*) contained this further information: "From various rumors about the future content of the novel [*The Brothers Karamazov*], rumors that are widely spread in Petersburg literary circles, I may say . . . that Aleksey in the course of time will become a country schoolteacher, and under the influence of some peculiar psychic processes taking place in his soul, he even arrives at the idea of assassinating the Tsar."[15] Whether Aleksey was supposed to have attempted to carry out this idea is left unspecified.

Dostoevsky continues to describe the adulation he received on the night before his speech: "At 9:30 when I got up to go home, they [those guests remaining] raised a hurrah for me in which even people not in sympathy with me were forced to take part. Then this whole crowd rushed down the stairs with me, and without coats, without hats, followed me onto the street and put me in a cab. And then they suddenly started kissing my hands—and not one, but tens of people, and not just young people, but gray-haired old folks. No, Turgenev just has members of a claque, while mine have true enthusiasm." Turgenev, to be sure, also had devoted followers, who were far more than merely a claque; but Dostoevsky was not wrong in believing that the passion he aroused was totally genuine. "Tomorrow, the eighth, is my most fateful day," he goes on. "In the morning I read my piece." So far, the speech had not "been given the final going over," and it is probable that he took Turgenev's words into account while making his last revisions. Strangers had whispered to him that "at the morning reading, there's a whole lot of rot aimed at me and Aksakov," but so far nothing of the sort could be discerned. "Kovalevsky is on the surface very courteous to me" and had mentioned his name in a toast. "Turgenev did too. Annenkov tried to make up to me, but I turned away."[16]

4

The session of June 8 opened with some introductory remarks and a poem, "To the Memory of Pushkin," written and read by Dostoevsky's old companion in the Petrashevsky circle, Aleksey Pleshcheev. Then it was Dostoevsky's turn, and, to use the words of Marcus Levitt, he advanced to the podium "to hijack the festival."[17] Even though many accounts exist of what became an epochal event, not only in Dostoevsky's life but in that of Russian culture of the late nineteenth century, none takes us so directly to its heart as his own, written on the night of his astonishing triumph. "No, Anya, no," he writes, "you can never conceive of and imagine the effect it [his speech] produced! What are my Petersburg successes! Nothing, *zero*, compared to this! When I came out, the hall thundered with applause and it was a very long time before they let me read. I waved, made gestures, begging to be allowed to read— nothing helped: rapture, enthusiasm (all because of *The Karamazovs*). I finally began reading: I was stopped by thunderous applause on absolutely every page, and sometimes even at every sentence. I read loudly, with fire."[18]

From Gleb Uspensky, we obtain the view of an outside observer who, at the beginning of the session, noticed Dostoevsky sitting "as quietly as a mouse" (*smirnekhonko*) at the back of the stage as if in hiding, "scribbling something in a notebook."

> When his turn came, he *smirnekhonko* stepped up to the speaker's stand, and not five minutes had elapsed before everyone without exception present in the assemblage, all hearts, all thoughts, all souls, were in his power. He spoke to them simply, absolutely as if he were conversing with an acquaintance, not declaiming weighty phrases in a loud voice or tossing his head. Simply and distinctly, without the slightest digression or unnecessary embellishment, he told the public what he thought of Pushkin as someone who expressed the strivings, hopes, and wishes of that very public—the one listening to him at that moment, in that hall. He found it possible, so to speak, to bring Pushkin into that hall, and with his words clarify for all those gathered there something about their own present anxieties, their present anguish. Until Dostoevsky, no one had done that, and this was the major reason for the extraordinary success of his speech.[19]

How was Dostoevsky able to accomplish this remarkable feat? Just as Turgenev had drawn on his earlier lectures about Pushkin in the 1860s, so Dostoevsky drew on a lifetime of observations about Pushkin scattered through his work from the very beginning and continuing up through the *Diary of a Writer*. All of his major ideas can be found in previous writings, and these have been conscientiously noted in the scholarship.* More important is that, employing his most brilliant critical

---

* An excellent account is given in the commentary to the speech contained in *PSS*, 26: 445–451.

style, he unites these ideas as he had never done before into a powerful synthesis hailing Pushkin as the poetic herald of the glorious mission that Russia has been called upon to accomplish on behalf of humanity. Dostoevsky usually interprets literary works not in terms of the author's everyday personality or the concrete historical and social-cultural problems with which he/she may have been engaged, but always in the light of some larger issue. His criticism is thus an example of what Nietzsche called the "monumental" style of historical writing, in which the subject becomes a symbolic expression of some much greater theme, whether psychological, moral-metaphysical, or religious. In this instance, he turns Pushkin into a symbol of his own Russian messianism and his exalted conception of "the people," which now, as would not have been the case in the past, harmonized so perfectly with the emotions of the vast majority of his audience.

He begins by citing a sentence of Gogol, set down in 1835—"Pushkin is an extraordinary and, perhaps, unique manifestation of the Russian spirit"—a citation that wipes out at the very start Turgenev's reference to the replacement of the artistic Pushkin by the satirical Gogol. For Dostoevsky, Pushkin was not only "extraordinary" but above all "prophetic"; and it is the essence of this prophecy that he intends to illuminate. He divides Pushkin's work into three periods, though stressing that no hard-and-fast boundaries can be drawn because his creations, as a living organism, cannot be split into totally separate parts. "The accepted view is that during this first period of his work Pushkin imitated the European poets . . . particularly Byron." Such foreign inspiration is not denied; but again, contrary to Turgenev, Dostoevsky insists that "even [his imitations] expressed the extraordinary independence of his genius. Imitations never contain the kind of personal suffering and depth of self-consciousness that Pushkin displayed."

As an example, he takes Pushkin's early work, *The Gypsies* (1824), in which a Russian nobleman named Aleko leaves civilization to live with his gypsy mistress and joins her wandering tribe. Dostoevsky interprets this scenario as already emblematic of a fundamental Russian dilemma, which gave birth to a new character type. "In Aleko, Pushkin had already found and brilliantly rendered that unhappy wanderer in his native land, that historical, suffering Russian who appeared with such historical inevitability in our educated society after it had broken away from the people. This is a genuine and flawlessly conceived character, a type that has long become a permanent fixture in our Russian land" (26: 136–137).

As he enlarges on Pushkin's creation of this type, he manages, in Uspensky's words, to bring Pushkin into that very hall. The "Russian wanderer" has become "a permanent fixture" of the culture, and Dostoevsky now imagines his successors "running off to Socialism, which did not yet exist in Aleko's time."* Pushkin's "wanderer" thus becomes identical with the Socialist youth who were hanging from the rafters of the auditorium and drinking in Dostoevsky's every word—not to mention a Populist Socialist like Uspensky himself. And then, alluding to those who now "take this new faith in a different field and work it zealously" (those who "went to the people," in other words), Dostoevsky sees them as adding an additional trait to the character of the "Russian wanderer." What he needs is no longer something purely personal but something universal: he needs "the happiness of the whole world in order to find his own peace of mind" (26: 137).

Dostoevsky then steps back to glance at the historical roots of this character type, dating it from "just at the beginning of the second century after the great Petrine reforms"; it was then that educated Russian society became totally "detached from the people and the people's strength." Of course, an awareness of this detachment did not affect the vast majority of Russians, but "it is enough if it happens merely to 'the chosen few' . . . since through them the remaining vast majority will be deprived of their peace of mind." Aleko was seeking something but did not really know what ("there is a bit of Jean-Jacques Rousseau here"), but in fact he and those like him were seeking "for the truth which someone, somewhere had lost, and which he simply cannot find." Later Russian generations, instead of turning to nature, went to Europe's "stable historical order and well-established civic and social life" in search of this lost truth. This quest was a self-deception, however, because "the wanderer" must find the truth "first of all, within himself"; but how could he understand this necessity when he has become a stranger in his own native land, "no more than a blade of grass, torn from its stem and carried off by the wind. And he can sense that and suffer for it, and often suffer so painfully!" (26: 138). One cannot read such words without recalling Dostoevsky's own painful alienation when he found himself such a "stranger" among the peasant convicts in his prison camp, who unrelentingly hated him and those like him solely because they were educated and members of the upper class. "They [the peasant convicts] would have eaten us alive, given the chance," he had written his brother.[20]

---

* In an early variant of the Pushkin speech, Dostoevsky introduces a personal note that he later eliminated. Speaking of Aleko, he wrote: "If you had shown him then the system of Fourier, which was then still unknown, he would with joy have accepted it and rushed to work on its behalf. And if he had been sent somewhere because of this, he would have considered himself happy. . . . But there was no system of Fourier then." Dostoevsky, though not a Fourierist, had belonged to the Petrashevsky circle dominated by followers of Fourier, and he had certainly been sent "somewhere" for this reason (*PSS*, 26: 454).

Aleko was called "a disdainful man" by the gypsies, who finally drive him away after he commits a murder out of jealousy; and while Dostoevsky acknowledges this Romantic climax to be "far-fetched," he nonetheless accepts the characterization of Aleko as "real, and Pushkin's perception here [as] apt." Aleko is still a Russian nobleman who takes full advantage of his station and "angrily attacks his opponent and punishes him" when he is offended. But Dostoevsky also detects in the poem a suggestion of "the Russian solution" to Aleko's rage, a solution "in accordance with the people's faith and truth." This solution is: "Humble yourself, O haughty man; first curb thy pride; Humble yourself, O idle man; first labor on thy native soil!"* Here is Dostoevsky's statement of his positive ideal, which he identifies with the people's "truth." Urging "the Russian wanderer"—and all those like him in the audience—to accomplish such a self-conquest, Dostoevsky assures them "you will embark on a great task and make others free . . . you will find happiness . . . and you will at last understand your people and their sacred truth" (26: 138–139). No passage in the speech aroused more commentary, both positive and negative, than this call for humility and submission.

If "this solution . . . is already strongly suggested" in *The Gypsies*, Dostoevsky finds it even more clearly expressed in *Evgeny Onegin* (1833). The main figure is again a character who "wanders in anguish through his native land and through foreign parts" and is everywhere a stranger. "It's true that he loves his native land, but he has no faith in it" and looks down "with sad mockery" on those who do have such faith. Onegin kills Lensky "simply out of spleen," and such spleen "may have been caused by his longing for some universal ideal." He compares Onegin with Tatyana, whom he sees as the embodiment of the Russian ideal, and he regrets that the poet did not use her name for his title; it is she, after all, who is the positive protagonist of the work. "One might even say that a positive type of Russian woman of such beauty has almost never been repeated in our literature except, perhaps, in the character of Liza in Turgenev's *Nest of Gentlefolk*" (26: 140). This tribute to Turgenev was unexpected and much appreciated; he was sitting on the stage, and everyone could see that he blew a kiss in Dostoevsky's direction when the flattering reference was made.**

* Dostoevsky here is not so much citing Pushkin as rewriting him. In the poem, the elder of the Gypsy tribe simply says to Aleko after the murder. "*Ostav nas, gordi chelovek*" ("Leave us, proud man"). There is nothing about humbling oneself or toiling on thy native soil. A. S. Pushkin, *Polnoe Sobranie Sochinenii*, 6 vols. (Moscow, 1949), 2: 240.

** The reference to Liza was actually followed by one to Natasha Rostov of *War and Peace*. This addition is contained in the margin of one of the variants of the speech, and N. N. Strakhov mentions having heard the name pronounced; but it was

In comparing Onegin to Tatyana, Dostoevsky turns her into someone "who stands solidly on her own native soil" and is the incarnation of true Russian folk values (though in fact she is no more a member of "the people" than Onegin himself). Onegin's rejection of the love she offers him at the beginning of this novel in verse is transformed into an exemplum of his contempt for the treasures to be found in his native land. While Dostoevsky concedes that "he treated her honorably . . . Onegin's manner of looking down on people caused him to disregard Tatyana entirely when he met her for the first time, in a provincial backwater, and in the humble image of a pure, innocent girl so timid in his presence." He could not appreciate her sterling moral qualities because "he is a man of abstractions, he is a restless dreamer and has been so all his life." No doubt responding to Turgenev's invocation of Hugo and Merimée, Dostoevsky ironically imagines that if Childe Harold or "even Lord Byron himself" had come from England to point out "her shy, humble charm—oh, Onegin would at once have been amazed and astonished, for in these people afflicted with the sufferings of the world there is sometimes so much servility of spirit!" Onegin did not understand Tatyana, but, after the famous stanzas describing her visit to his room (Dostoevsky speaks of "their matchless beauty and profundity"), where she examines his foreign books and trinkets, she finally understands his essential hollowness: "*Uzh ne parodiya li?*" ("Is he not a parody?") (26: 140–141).

It is only later, when he meets her again as the queen of Petersburg society, "married to a worthy old general whom she cannot love because she loves Onegin," that he is suddenly overcome by her charms. But when he throws himself at her feet in adoration, she turns him away: "*No ya drugomu otdana / Ya budu vek emu verna*" ("But I have been given to another / And will be true to him for life"). Dostoevsky exalts this decision as Tatyana's "apotheosis"; here she speaks specifically "as a Russian woman" and as the embodiment of Russian moral values—at least as Dostoevsky understood them (26: 141). And here too, as everyone in the audience knew, he was taking issue with a famous passage of Belinsky's in which the critic, under the influence of French Utopian Socialism and George Sand, had refused to recognize any moral sublimity in Tatyana's conduct. She had allowed herself to be "given" in marriage (*otdana*) because of her mother's entreaties, not because she had made a free choice; and Belinsky considered her loyalty to a marriage bond not based on love as immoral rather than praiseworthy. Kolya Krasotkin, inspired by Belinsky, had very recently

---

drowned out by the storm of applause for Liza. Dostoevsky did not include it in the written text (*PSS*, 26: 496).

parroted this disparaging criticism of Tatyana as he paraded his adolescent braggadacio in the pages of *The Brothers Karamazov*.

For Dostoevsky, however, Tatyana's faithfulness stems from her deep-rootedness in the values of the Russian folk soul. He scornfully sweeps aside the notion that she refused Onegin because of "her standing as a society lady" (as had been suggested by Belinsky and more sharply by Pisarev) or because she lacked the boldness of "a southern woman or some Frenchwoman" (one memoirist took this as an allusion to Turgenev's long-standing relation with Pauline Garcia-Viardot). "No, the Russian woman will boldly follow one in whom she believes, and she has proved that." (Everyone remembered Dostoevsky's description of the Decembrist wives he had met in Siberia.) The real reason for Tatyana's decision is quite otherwise: she refused to evade the moral responsibility for her own earlier decision. She knew that the abandonment of her husband "would cast shame and disgrace upon him and would mean his death. And can one found happiness on the unhappiness of another?" Dostoevsky here speaks in the very accents of Ivan Karamazov as he poses the question of whether an "edifice" of happiness could be built "if its foundations rested on the suffering of, say, even one insignificant creature, but one who had been mercilessly and unjustly tortured?"* This query demonstrates the impossibility for Tatyana, as "a pure Russian soul," to have come to any other decision than to sacrifice *herself*, rather than to construct her own happiness on the destruction of her innocent husband. What surprises Dostoevsky "is that for such a long time we cast doubt on the moral solution to this question" (26: 142).

Carrying his analysis of this imbroglio one step further, he insists that Tatyana, even if she were free, would still have rejected Onegin and refused to link her life with his. She would have understood that his character had no substance, that he had become bedazzled by her position in society; his infatuation is no proof that he has come to any better understanding of the values of her soul, of "the Tatyana who was as humble as before." What he loves is "his fantasy; indeed, he himself is a fantasy." But she, on the other hand, "still has something solid and unshakable on which her soul can rely. These are her memories of childhood, her memories of her native home deep in the provinces where her humble, pure life began; it is 'the cross and the shade of

---

* In the manuscript version of the speech, this question is followed by a a summary of the conversation between Rastignac and Bianchon in Balzac's *Le Père Goriot*. Rastignac, it will be recalled, asks his friend if he could approve of the murder of an old mandarin in China that would ensure the happiness of someone he loved in France (*PSS*, 26: 288). For the influence of Balzac's novel on *Crime and Punishment*, see my *Dostoevsky: The Miraculous Years, 1865–1871* (Princeton, 1995), 73.

boughs o'er the grave of her poor nurse.'" All these evocations "represent contact with her native land, her native people and their sacred values." Onegin completely lacks any such sustenance: "he has no soil under his feet, this blade of grass borne by the wind," and even an "infinite compassion" for him would not allow her to "provide him . . . with an illusion of happiness, knowing full well that the very next day he would ridicule that happiness" (26: 143). Onegin at this point takes on some of the lineaments of Versilov in *A Raw Youth*, and Dostoevsky is obviously extrapolating from his own development of this Onegin type of "the wanderer."

He thus concludes that, with *Onegin*, Pushkin proved himself to be "a great national [*narodnyi*] writer" who had "identified the innermost essence of the upper class of our society that stood above the people" and also "identified the type of the Russian wanderer, who continues his wandering even in our days." But as well as depicting such negative images of Russian life, Pushkin also "showed us a whole series of positively beautiful Russian types he found among the Russian people." In addition to the example of Tatyana, Dostoevsky adduces "the type of Russian chronicler-monk" (Pimen in *Boris Godunov* [1831]) and somewhat later *The Tale of the Bear* and a peasant drinking song. Unlike other writers, who came from a different world and whose work "shows a wish to raise the people to their own level and make them happy by doing so," there was something in Pushkin "that *truly* makes him akin to the people, something that reaches the level of simple-hearted tenderness." From Pushkin, as a result, Russians derive "faith in our Russian individuality, our now conscious hope in the strength of our people, and with it our faith in our future independent mission in the family of European peoples" (26: 144).

The last part of the speech is devoted to "the third period" of Pushkin's work, a period in which "our poet stands forth as an almost miraculous and unprecedented phenomenon," with a universality surpassing even the greatest creators of European literature—Shakespeare, Cervantes, Schiller. In this period Pushkin began to write works that "reflect the poetic images of other nations and incarnate their genius." Dostoevsky briefly and expressively characterizes an array of such poems, but unlike Turgenev, who had praised such works rather halfheartedly, he gives them fundamental importance. He takes them not only as a tribute to Pushkin's versatility, but also as revealing examples of "the principal capacity of our individuality that he shares with our people, and it is this, above all, that marks him as a national poet." No other poet or writer in world literature has this capacity to enter into and reproduce the spirit of other cultures to the same degree because no other people except the Russian possess such universal empathy. "This we find only in Pushkin, and in this sense, I repeat, he is unprecedented and, in my view, prophetic." He was "prophetic" because this feature of his work, "his ability to infuse his spirit into the spirit of other nations," is precisely indicative of the great future mission of the Russian people (26: 145).

Dostoevsky equates this capacity of Pushkin with the reforms of Peter the Great, the adoption of "European clothing, custom, inventions, and European science" initiated during Peter's reign. Such absorption may have begun for "utilitarian" reasons (the usual explanation), but in fact "Peter undoubtedly followed a certain secret instinct that led him to work toward future goals that certainly were immensely broader than mere utilitarianism." These goals, also accepted by the Russian people, amounted to nothing less than to bring about "the universal brotherhood of peoples" that Russia was destined to accomplish in the future. Dostoevsky's messianism is here given a new power and resonance by being prefigured in Pushkin, and this linkage responded perfectly to the need for some uplifting vision felt by his agitatedly expectant audience. Russia's mission, Dostoevsky proclaimed, was "the general unification of all people of all the tribes of the great Aryan race." (This was the first time he had employed the word "Aryan," which reveals the influence of the anti-Semitic literature of the period, and it provoked a great deal of criticism.) He then declared that "all our Slavophilism and Westernizing" had been nothing but a great misunderstanding, because "to become a real Russian, to become completely Russian, perhaps, means just (in the final analysis—please bear that in mind) to become a brother to all peoples, a *pan-human*, if you like." Dostoevsky then repeats his assertion that Russian foreign policy, even in the past, had served Europe much more than Russia itself, and "not merely through the ineptness of our politicians" (26: 147).

Admitting that "my words may seem ecstatic, exaggerated, and fantastic," Dostoevsky is yet willing to let them stand as such. And at this point he makes his most masterly move by identifying Pushkin and Russia with the kenotic essence of Russian religious feeling, the reverence for the suffering and humiliated Christ. The claims he had made for Russia may, after all, seem merely pretentious; indeed, how could such "an impoverished, crude land" as Russia claim such an exalted destiny? "Can it be we who are ordained to utter a new word to humanity?" But he reminds his listeners that he is not making any claim to "economic prominence . . . the glory of the sword or science." Paraphrasing and quoting a beautiful poem of Tyutchev's, he intones: "'Our Land may be impoverished, but Christ Himself in slavish garb traversed this impoverished land and gave [it] His blessing!' Why may we not contain His ultimate word? Was He not born in a manger Himself?" After this climax,

Dostoevsky lowers the note and returns to Pushkin as evidence for his claims. "If my idea is a fantasy," he concedes, "then in Pushkin, at least, there is something on which this fantasy can be founded." But Pushkin died young, killed in a duel, "and unquestionably he took some great secret with him to the grave. And so we must puzzle out his secret without him"—a secret that, as Dostoevsky must have surely believed, his speech had already done a good deal to disclose (26: 148–149).

## 5

The effect of this speech on the audience was absolutely overwhelming, and the emotions it unleashed may be compared with the hysterical effusions typical of religious revival meetings. The memoirs of the period are full of its description, and we may begin with the image given by D. A. Lyubimov—the son of Dostoevsky's editor and then still a young student—of its finale. "Dostoevsky pronounced the last words of his speech in a sort of inspired whisper, lowered his head, and in a deathly silence, began rather hurriedly to leave the podium. The hall seemed to hold its breath, as if expecting something more. Suddenly from the back rows rang out a hysterical shriek, 'You have solved it!' [the secret of Pushkin], which was taken up by several feminine voices in chorus. The entire auditorium began to stir. You could hear the shrieks, 'You solved it! You solved it!' a storm of applause, some sort of rumbling, stamping, feminine screeches. I do not think that the walls of the Hall of the Moscow Nobility either before or since had ever resounded with such a tempest of ecstasy."[21]

Dostoevsky's own account to Anna of his spectacular success cannot be equaled in communicating the excitement of the moment:

Everything that I said about Tatyana was received with enthusiasm. (This is the great triumph of our idea over twenty-five years of delusions.) When I spoke at the end, however, of the *universal unity* of people, the hall was as though in hysteria. When I concluded—I won't tell you about the roar, the outcry of rapture, strangers among the audience wept, sobbed, embraced each other, and *swore to one another to be better, not to hate one another from now on, but instead to love one another.* The order of the meeting was violated; everyone rushed toward the platform to see me, highborn ladies, female students, state secretaries, students—they all hugged me and kissed me. All the members of our society [the SLRL] who were on the platform hugged me and kissed me. All of them, literally all of them wept from delight. The calls continued for half an hour; people waved handkerchiefs; suddenly, for instance, two old men whom I didn't know stopped me: "We had been enemies to one another for twenty years, hadn't spoken to one another, but now we have embraced and been reconciled. It's you who reconciled us, you, our saint, you, our prophet!" "Prophet, prophet" people in the crowd shouted.

Turgenev, for whom I put in a good word in my speech, rushed to embrace me with tears. Annenkov ran up to shake my hand and kiss my shoulder. "You're a genius, you're more than a genius!" they both told me. Aksakov (Ivan) ran up onto the platform and declared to the audience that my speech *was not just a speech, but a historic event!* A thundercloud had been covering the horizon, and now Dostoevsky's speech, like the sun coming out, had dissipated everything, illuminated everything. Beginning now, brotherhood had arrived and there would no longer be any perplexity. "Yes, yes!" everyone cried and again embraced and again there were tears. The meeting was broken up. I rushed to the wings to escape, but everyone from the hall burst in there, and mainly women. They kissed my hands, tormented me. Students came running in. One of them, in tears, fell to the floor before me in convulsions and lost consciousness. A complete, absolutely complete victory![22]

With the exception of the reconciliation of the two old enemies, every other detail of this account can be confirmed from independent sources. The young man who collapsed at his feet was the most conspicuous among those so overcome, but E. P. Letkova-Sultanova also refers to a female friend who lost consciousness at its conclusion.[23] As for Annenkov, in addition to embracing Dostoevsky, he buttonholed Nikolay Strakhov and said excitedly: "There, that's an example of a literary characterization made by a genius! It settles the affair in one stroke!"[24]

It took an entire hour for the session to resume again. Despite Aksakov's reluctance to take the floor, he was prevailed upon to do so by Dostoevsky himself and all the others. He did not, however, give his prepared talk but improvised some remarks, focusing in particular on the agreement with Dostoevsky's words manifested both by a representative of the Slavophils like himself and by the most important of the Westernizers, Turgenev. Henceforth all misunderstanding had been eliminated, and a new era of harmony in Russian culture was about to dawn. By this time, Dostoevsky "had grown weak and wished to leave, but was forcibly kept from going."[25]

During the hour that had elapsed after his speech, a large laurel wreath had been procured by a group of *kursistki*, who invaded the platform (Dostoevsky said they were more than a hundred) and crowned him with this weighty tribute. It bore the inscription in gold letters: "On behalf of Russian women, about whom you said so many good things." Again, "everyone wept, again there was enthusiasm." The head of the Moscow Duma thanked Dostoevsky on behalf of the city, and the session then came to an end. His letter was written at eight that evening, but for him the day was not yet finished. "In an hour," he tells Anna, "I'll go read at the second literary celebration. I'll read 'The Prophet.'"[26]

At this final session, he read from *Songs of the Western Slavs* and *The Tale of the Bear* in the first part of the program; in the second, he declaimed "The Prophet." Nikolay Strakhov recalled this latter performance as "the most remarkable" of the evening, which also included readings by Turgenev. "Dostoevsky recited it twice [he was called back by the audience], and each time with such intense passion that his listeners felt uncanny. . . . His right hand, tremblingly pointing out guilt, clearly refrained from any overwrought gestures; the voice was strained to an outcry." Strakhov thought that the effect "came out as too harsh, though the articulation of the verses was perfect."[27] Despite her hostility toward his speech, Dostoevsky's evening performance again profoundly impressed Letkova-Sultanova.[28] He always took great pains with his readings, and a copy of this poem was found in Anna Grigoryevna's notebooks with stresses marked on the words he wished to emphasize.

These events did not end the evening, which continued with a repetition of the public "apotheosis" of the bust of Pushkin that had begun the ceremonies. Wreaths were again placed there by all the writers present, and this time it was Dostoevsky, not Turgenev, who crowned Pushkin's head; Turgenev laid his tribute at the foot of the pedestal. This arrangement could well have been made at the very start so as to give the two most prominent writers these alternating roles; but it now seemed to be a symbolic gesture, objectifying what many in the audience had come to feel—that Dostoevsky had emerged victorious, and that it was he, not Turgenev, who had inherited the mantle of Pushkin. He was at last allowed to return to his hotel and obtain some much-needed rest, but was too excited and happy to remain quiet for very long. As Anna Grigoryevna tells it, "late at night he went to the Pushkin monument once again. The night was warm, but there was almost no one in the street. Arriving at Strastnaya Square, he lifted with difficulty an enormous laurel wreath which had been presented to him at the morning session after his speech, laid it at the foot of the monument to his 'great teacher,' and bowed down to the ground before it."[29]

## 6

Dostoevsky remained in Moscow for two more days, finding little respite from the busy round of activities in which he had been caught since his arrival. The success of the Pushkin speech made it all the more important for him to decide where it should be published. "I need to find a place for the piece," he tells Anna, "but whom to give it to—they're all snatching at it."[30] On the morning of the ninth, he sat for his portrait at the request of the best photographer in Moscow, M. M. Panov. At an "intimate" literary lunch, which included A. N. Ostrovsky, Grigorovich, and the Suvorins, Dostoevsky was obviously in an expansive mood. According to Mme Suvorina, he spoke enthusiastically of Dickens: "When I am very weary and feel out of sorts with myself, nothing calms and rejoices me more than that first-rate writer!"[31] By this time, he had already decided to give his Pushkin piece to Katkov, for publication not in his monthly journal but rather in his newspaper, the *Moscow News*, where it would appear more rapidly and reach a larger reading public.

Later in the afternoon, while he was making his round of obligatory visits before departing, he by chance ran into an acquaintance from Petersburg, Evgeny N. Opochinin, and the two strolled along until Dostoevsky became weary. Sitting down on a bench to continue their conversation, they suddenly heard "a cheerful voice" behind them hailing Dostoevsky—a voice that turned out to be Turgenev's. Joining the two men, Turgenev engaged Dostoevsky in a conversation to which, regrettably (though this is difficult to believe), Opochinin paid no attention. His own thoughts were interrupted when Dostoevsky suddenly rose from the bench, "his face pallid and with trembling lips." "'Moscow is very big,'" he angrily threw out at his interlocutor, "'but there is nowhere to hide in it from you!' And waving his arms, he strode away down the boulevard."[32]

Turgenev had become very upset at the accounts of Dostoevsky's speech in the newspapers, which had reported on his gracious gesture at the mention of Liza and his participation in the general enthusiasm. The words of Aksakov about the Westernizer-Slavophil reconciliation accomplished by Dostoevsky also troubled him deeply. And since he had said nothing at the moment to disrupt the rapturous jubilation, he feared his silence might be taken as agreement. On June 11 he wrote to M. M. Stasyulevich, editor of the *European Messenger*, requesting that he include in an article about the Pushkin celebration a denial that "he [Turgenev] had been completely subjugated" by Dostoevsky's speech and accepted it completely. "No, that's not so," Turgenev insisted. "It was a very clever, brilliant, and cunningly skillful speech, [and] while full of passion, its foundation was entirely false. But it was a falseness that was extremely appealing to Russian self-love."[33]

On the evening of the ninth, he was packing for his trip home when he was suddenly visited by Marya A. Polivanova, the wife of L. A. Polivanov, the chairman of the festival committee of the SLRL and an active participant in the preparations for the festival. Polivanova was a well-known pedagogue, the author of numerous textbooks dealing with Russian language and literature, and the founder and director of a *gymnasium* for male students in Moscow. Vladimir Solovyev, one of her former students, wrote admiringly about her "unceasing vibrations of mind and heart."[34] These vibrations were obviously quivering when she learned that Dostoevsky was leaving the next day, and she decided to visit him despite the unseemly lateness of the hour. Her reason, as she explains in a notebook entry made at that time, was that after all the noise and excitement, "after the powerful waves of his marvelous speech . . . I was drawn to look at him again, hear his voice, listen to his words."[35]

Dostoevsky was wearing felt slippers, some sort of old topcoat, and a nightshirt when he opened the door. Despite his surprise, he greeted the unexpected intruder, with whom he was already acquainted, with considerable friendliness and courtesy. Her pretense for coming was that she wished to make a copy of his speech before he left, and she asked if she could borrow the manuscript. He replied that this was impossible: he had already given it to the editors of the *Moscow News*. She told him, after he had poured some tea, of the purifying and reconciling effect created by his speech, and of the happy results she was sure it would have on many people. Of course he was very pleased, and repeated for her benefit the story of the two old enemies reconciled under its influence.

Just then, there was another knock on the door, and in marched Yuriev, who had come to claim the speech that had been promised for his journal. Denying that any explicit promise had ever been made, Dostoevsky strove to lighten the atmosphere by chiding him amiably about his flowery response to the French delegate, who had awarded him one of the numerous decorations provided by the French government for such occasions. "The French behave appropriately toward a great Russian poet, and we are surprised at this, make a fuss about it, and almost turn the French deputy into the hero of the day." The conversation then shifted to Pushkin himself, and Dostoevsky exclaimed: "We are pygmies compared to Pushkin, there is no such genius among us!" He had just recently re-read *The Queen of Spades* and was lost in admiration: "That's fantasy! I would like myself to write a fantastic story. My characters are all ready. I just have to finish *The Brothers Karamazov*."[36] Yuriev leaped at these words and made him promise that, *if* he wrote such a story, it would be reserved for *Russian Thought*. Dostoevsky agreed, but insisted that his promise was very conditional; only the future could tell whether he would have time to accomplish his wish.

Dostoevsky then returned to *The Queen of Spades* because, on saying good-bye, Yuriev once more mentioned "the fantastic story" and Dostoevsky's tentative commitment. "Then Dostoevsky flared up again," writes Polivanova. "Exactly as if he were in a fever, with a glitter in his eyes, he began to speak of *The Queen of Spades*. With subtlety he followed all the movements of Hermann's soul, all his torments, all his hopes, and finally, his awful, sudden defeat, as if he were Hermann himself." Turning to her, he asked if she had read the story. When she confessed not since the age of seventeen, he told her to go home, read it immediately, and send her impressions to him at Staraya Russa.[37] Dostoevsky's interest in "the fantastic" was nothing new (aside from his masterly novella, *The Double* [1846], he had written a brilliant article comparing Edgar Allan Poe and E.T.A. Hoffmann in 1861); but his focus on it in 1880 was hardly accidental. He was preparing to write, and had certainly already begun to think about, Book 11 of *The Brothers Karamazov*, in which Ivan's dialogue with the devil reached heights of "the fantastic" that have never been surpassed.

The next morning, while waiting for his train at the railroad station, Dostoevsky wrote the *Moscow News* requesting that his speech be printed "*as soon as possible*" and that the editors not make "any editorial corrections (that is, in sense and content)."[38] With that, he departed from Moscow for home, *The Brothers Karamazov*, and the special issue of the *Diary of a Writer*, which, as might have been expected, became much bulkier than he had planned.

## CHAPTER 29

# The Diary of a Writer,
## 1880

Dostoevsky returned from his trip to Moscow filled with the exuberance and excitement engendered by his great triumph. He genuinely believed that he had initiated what might become a new era in Russian social-cultural life—an era in which the old ideological rivalries would cease to exist (had he not furnished a basis for their reconciliation?) and in which the youth, who so much longed to identify themselves with "the people," would abandon the foreign ideologies by which they were being misled.

Soon realizing that such hopes were illusory, he nonetheless continued to remain buoyed by the enthusiasm and the reverence he had personally encountered from the adoring crowds at the festival. Their living testimony to his influence persuaded him that, whatever the opposition his ideas might (and soon did) encounter—largely from the liberal and radical intelligentsia, but not from them alone—his effect on the public would only increase in importance. In the next few months, the last remaining in his life, he thus threw himself with renewed vigor into completing *The Brothers Karamazov* and then into reviving his *Diary of a Writer.*

## 2

His first preoccupation concerned the disposition of his Pushkin speech. He had asked the *Moscow News* to send the proofs to Staraya Russa, but they were not there when he arrived. Instead, he received a wire informing him that, if he wished for the speediest publication, the text would have to be printed without any corrections. He dashed off a letter to go ahead, but regretted that he could not give the article a final polish. "Much as I corrected the piece at home, when I started to read it [during the railroad journey], I saw that two or three sentences turned out to be just unnecessary repetitions of things already said earlier. There are also major rough spots . . . in one passage, in some six lines, the word 'doubtless' . . . is used three or four times." Dostoevsky asked that the pages of his manuscript, "even if they've been cut in half by the compositors," be sent to him along with the newspaper in which it was printed.[1] He had scheduled an issue of the *Diary* for late July, and these would help in its production.

Meanwhile, he dispatched a letter the next day to Countess Sofya Tolstaya, who, along with Yulia Abaza and Vladimir Solovyev, had signed a collective telegram congratulating him on his Pushkin success. He repeats in brief much of what we already know—the stories of the two lifelong enemies reconciled, and of the student "who fell to the floor before me in a swoon from rapture." He also includes the glowing responses of Turgenev and Annenkov ("the latter absolutely an *enemy* to me"), and adds an extra detail. "'I'm not saying that because you praised my Liza,' Turgenev told me." Apologizing for "talking so much about myself," Dostoevsky insists, "I swear it isn't vanity: one lives for such moments, it's for them that you in fact come into this world. My heart is full—how can I help telling my friends. I'm still stunned."[2]

As a veteran campaigner in the Russian social-cultural wars, Dostoevsky was under no illusions that he would emerge unscathed or that battle would not rapidly be joined. "Don't worry—I'll soon hear 'the laughter of the crowd'" (a citation from Pushkin), he assures the countess. "I won't be forgiven this in various literary dark alleys and tendencies." From the summaries of his speech in the newspapers, he already saw that two of his main points were being overlooked. One is Pushkin's "universal responsiveness," which "none of the greatest world poets had yet ever had," and which "comes completely from our national spirit." Hence Pushkin "is in fact our most national poet," though Turgenev had denied him such a title. Dostoevsky also claimed, quite inaccurately, that "until now *absolutely* no one" had stressed this aspect of Pushkin's genius, although it is true that no one had given it such epochal importance. The second point was that "I gave a formula, a word of reconciliation for all our parties, and showed the way out to a new era. That's what everyone in fact felt, but the newspaper correspondents either didn't understand that or refused to."[3] He was convinced that he had been understood by the public, regardless of what the newspapers were saying or what the monthly journals would print in their next issues.

He promises to send the countess a copy of his speech when it is republished in his *Diary* "without cuts and with stringent proofreading. That's when I'll send it to you, dear Sofya Andreyevna, for your severe and subtle criticism, which I do not fear and which *I always love*, even if it's unfavorable to me." Conveying his regards to Yulia Abaza, who had been visiting her, he adds that "I kiss Vladimir Sergeevich ardently." "I got three photographs of him in Moscow," he says jestingly, "in his early years, his youth, and the last one in old age" (Solovyev was then thirty years old). He also asks if she knew "a new acquaintance" he had made in Moscow, Vera Mikhailovna Tretyakova, the wife of the owner of the Tretyakov Gallery.[4]

Dostoevsky had met her at the dinner of the Duma on June 6 at which Katkov had spoken, and the two took to each other immediately. He wrote Tretyakova on the same day as the countess, apologizing for not having called on her before leaving. He assures her of "how much I value the acquaintance and kind concern for me of such a wonderful person as yourself."[5] A day later he wrote her husband a similar letter, expressing his belief again that the Pushkin days, "with their general uplift of spirit and imminent expectation of something better in the future . . . had (and will still have) the most noble influence on our yearning society, and the seed sown will not perish, but will grow."[6] A month later, Tretyakova set down her recollections of the meeting with Dostoevsky, whose works (and particularly the installments of *The Brothers Karamazov*) had made a great impression on both herself and her husband.

She had complimented Dostoevsky for the morally elevating influence of his work; and "he believed me," she wrote, "because I had a kindly face and eyes, and [he said] that whatever I was telling him was always precious to hear from a woman." He then invited Tretyakova to join him at the table, but because "I already had an assigned cavalier, Turgenev, he peevishly distanced himself and for quite a while could not calm down because of this failure." Wishing to console Dostoevsky, at the end of the session Tretyakova brought him a bouquet of lilies, lilies of the valley, and laurel, "which would remind him of me—an admirer of those pure ideas that he advances in his works and that aid people to become better." The bouquet "gladdened him because I had thought of him during the banquet while sitting side by side with his literary enemy—Turgenev." On leaving, Dostoevsky hesitated to kiss her hand because, he explained, such a gesture was not suitable in a large gathering. But he did so anyway, "with gratitude," not only for the flowers but also for her assurance that his works had provided moral inspiration for her family.[7]

On June 15 Dostoevsky wrote to Yulia Abaza. He was responding not so much to the congratulatory telegram as to a letter of about six months earlier (according to his reckoning), which included a story on which she had asked him to comment. Not content with being a singer and composer, Abaza had also ventured into literature, and Dostoevsky's criticism of her effort, which apparently contained an element of the supernatural or fantastic (the text has been lost), leads him into reflections on *The Queen of Spades* that develop those already expressed in Moscow. Regrettably, it also furnishes him an occasion to release the anti-Semitic animus that now more and more dominated his thoughts.

The idea of Abaza's story, as Dostoevsky defines it, is "that races of people who have received their original idea from their founders, and *who subordinate themselves* to it exclusively over the course of several generations, subsequently must necessarily degenerate into something separate from humanity as a whole, and even, in the best conditions, into something inimical to humanity *as a whole*—that idea is true and profound." Whether Abaza explicitly presented this idea as being embodied in the Jewish people is not clear (her main character is a monk), but Dostoevsky interprets Jewish history as an instance of this general law. "Such, for instance, are the Jews [*evrei*] beginning with Abraham, and continuing to the present when they have turned into Yids [*zhidi*]. Christ (besides the rest of his significance) was the correction of this idea, expanding it into pan-humanness [*vsechelovechnost*—a key term in the Pushkin speech]. But the Jews refused the correction and remained in all their former narrowness and inflexibility, and therefore instead of pan-humanness have turned into the enemies of humanity, denying everyone except themselves, and now really remain the bearers of the anti-Christ and, of course, will be triumphant for a while."[8]

Only two years earlier, Dostoevsky had claimed that neither he nor the Russian people nurtured any hostility toward the Jewish religion; but his previous identification of "Yiddism" with the materialism of the modern world had now hardened into dogma and gained the upper hand over the human reality he had been capable of intuiting through the story of Dr. Hindenburg. The Jews had become the agents of the anti-Christ who would dominate the world for a time—as predicted in Dostoevsky's favorite Book of Revelation—before the world would be redeemed by the Russian Christ and the *vsechelovechnost* of the Russian people. But meanwhile, the reign of darkness was at hand, and the Jews "are coming, they have filled all of Europe, everything selfish, everything inimical to humanity, all of mankind's evil passions are for them—how could they not triumph, to the world's ruination!"[9] Such a passage shows him at the very worst of his anti-Semitic animosity.

Continuing his analysis, he finds that Abaza has "the same idea" (the one he has already defined), "but your descendant of horrible and sinful stock is depicted *impossibly*." Apparently, the central character of her story is an ascetic monk who lacks a heart, not metaphorically but physically; this organ has been replaced by a block of ice. Dostoevsky finds this detail totally implausible: "How can a person live without a physical organ? Even if it is a fantastic fairy tale, the fantastic in art has its limits and rules. The fantastic must come so close to the real that you are obliged to *almost* believe it." In *The Queen of Spades*, "the summit of fantastic art . . . you believe that Hermann really had a vision, and one precisely in conformity with his worldview, but meanwhile, at the end of the story . . . you don't know . . . whether the vision was a result of

Hermann's nature, or whether he is really one of those people who have come into contact with another world, one of evil spirits inimical to humanity (N.B. spiritualism and its teachings)."[10]

Because Abaza's character lacks a heart, she fails to endow him with what Dostoevsky considers essential: "You should just have given him moral suffering, consciousness, and be done with it, having made him someone in the image of Aleksey the Man of God or Maria the Egyptian [both saints mentioned in *The Brothers Karamazov*], who triumphed over her own blood and lineage through unheard-of suffering. But you, on the contrary, make up something crudely physical, a block of ice instead of a heart." All the same, he advised the lady not to abandon her "wonderful (and useful) idea" but to rewrite it from start to finish. "Give him spiritual suffering, give him the comprehension of his sin as that of an entire generation, be sure to set a woman before him, even if he is an ascetic monk—and make him consciously accept suffering for all his ancestors, and for everyone and everything, so as to atone for man's sins."[11] Dostoevsky here is obviously thinking more of Ivan and Dimitry Karamazov than of Abaza's ascetic monk, or rather, he is advising her to re-create him in the image of his own characters. He was just about to portray the oscillations of Ivan's anguished sensibility, and the acceptance by Dimitry of his guilt for "everyone and everything" (his first notes for this section were set down a day after writing this letter).

As of June 20, he had not received either the manuscript of his speech or a copy of the *Moscow News*, and he was furious at this tardiness. The sheets of his manuscript, he irately wrote the editor, contained passages "that were not printed in the *Moscow News*. Remember that this is literary property and must not get lost. . . . I can't understand how I have come to deserve such negligence." Unless he receives the sheets by the twenty-fourth, "it will be too late to publish the *Diary*, and impossible besides, because of my work for the *Russian Messenger*, and you will have done me significant harm."[12] A letter to Katkov, more temperate in tone but still quite firm, outlines the situation again and adds: "I am very painfully distressed by this."[13]

On July 6, a letter to Lyubimov accompanied the first five chapters of Book 11 of *The Brothers Karamazov*, the completion being promised for the August issue. By this time, Dostoevsky felt that he had the remainder of the novel well in hand and could furnish a schedule for its termination. "The final twelfth book" would be published in September, and then, "for the October issue there will follow (and *definitely* without a break either) a short 'Epilogue' . . . with which the whole novel would conclude." He reports that "I'm working rather easily, because everything has long since been jotted down and I have only to reconstruct it." Meanwhile, however, he has "been held up a bit by the publication of the *Diary*," which now, besides his speech, will include "a rather long foreword and, I think, an afterword, in which I want to say a few words in reply to my dear critics. I don't think I'll be held up for more than five days."[14]

## 3

Dostoevsky provides more information about the 1880 *Diary* in writing to Elena Shtakenshneider. After sending off a new installment of his novel, he explains, "I undertook to read everything written about me and my Moscow speech in the newspapers . . . and I decided to reply to Gradovsky, that is, not so much to Gradovsky as to write *our* whole *profession de foi* [profession of faith] for all of Russia." A. D. Gradovsky, a professor of civil law at the University of Moscow, had published a respectful but highly critical article on Dostoevsky's speech, entitled "Dreams and Reality," in *Voice* on June 25. The Russian press was filled with commentaries on the subject, as well as reprints of the speech in whole or in part; and Dostoevsky probably chose Gradovsky's article as the target of his reply because it was such a cogent and well-reasoned statement of the liberal Westernizer position, free from the acerbities of critics more influenced by radical ideas. He felt it essential to take up the polemical cudgels because, as he told his correspondent, "the portentous and wonderful *absolutely new* moment in the life of our educated society that manifested itself in Moscow at the Pushkin Festival has been sullied and destroyed with ill intention."[15]

Dostoevsky was thus still inspired by the afflatus of his Moscow experience, and remained persuaded that he had initiated an important social groundswell. What the response to his speech had meant, he insisted, was that "society doesn't want just laughing up one's sleeve at Russia and just abuse aimed at her, as has been the case until now." But this emergence of a more positive attitude toward Russia had disturbed the Petersburg press and thus "has to be sullied, destroyed, distorted, and everyone has to be dissuaded: ultimately nothing new happened, they say, it was just the good humor of kindly hearts after Moscow dinners." But something new *had* happened, in Dostoevsky's view, and he considered the task of asserting it so important that he wrote his afterword about Gradovsky on his son's birthday. "Guests came, and I sat to the side and finished up the work."[16]

His irate words hardly do justice to the temperate tone of Gradovsky's article, which begins with a considerable compliment: "No one has succeeded in penetrating so deeply into the essence of Pushkin's poetry as F. M. Dostoevsky." But while praising Dostoevsky's comprehension of Pushkin as a poet, Gradovsky refuses to accept the social-historical implications that he draws from Pushkin's work. Dostoevsky had not given any adequate explanation, for example, for the appearance in Russia of "the wanderers" whom he had described so well and who had become uprooted from their native soil. "Why did the enlightened part of Russian society feel *negatively* about the phenomena of Russian life, and as a result create for themselves the negative type of 'the wanderer?'" For a Russian reader, trained to decipher the Aesopian language of social-political discussion, the answer was self-evident: serfdom and political despotism. But because such an argument could not be printed, Gradovsky uses literature, as was customary, to make his points. "Pushkin, of course, depicted the first Russian wanderers, but by the very nature of his talent did not reflect that dismal world which they negated. It was Gogol who did so, [and who portrayed] the reverse, seamy side of Russian life." Gradovsky cites the names of various Gogolian characters who were moral monsters and from whose world the successors of Aleko, the "superfluous people" created by Herzen and Turgenev, had been trying to escape.[17]

Nor would Gradovsky accept that "the wanderers" had separated themselves "from the very essence of the Russian people, and thus had ceased to be Russians. . . . Even less accurate was it to call them 'prideful' people and to locate their alienation from the Russian people in this Satanic sin. . . . No answer is given [by Dostoevsky] to the question of what constitutes the 'pride' of 'the wanderers,' and still another [question] remains unanswered—before what are they supposed to 'humble themselves'?"[18] Gradovsky thus strikes unerringly at the social-political implications of Dostoevsky's speech, which had played so skillfully on both the patriotic and the Populist reverence for "the people," but had left so alluringly vague what it meant in concrete terms to accept their ideals.

More generally, Gradovsky underlines the fundamental weakness of Dostoevsky's exclusive appeal to personal morality as a remedy for large-scale social evils. "The betterment of people in a social sense," he writes, "cannot be done only through work 'on oneself' and through 'humbling oneself.' One can work on oneself and curb one's passions in a wilderness or on an uninhabited island. But as *social* creatures, people improve in working *alongside one another, and with one another*. That's why people's social betterment depends in such a large measure on the betterment of *social institutions* that develop, if not their Christian, then their civic virtues." And he illustrates this point by choosing an example from Russian history very close to Dostoevsky's own biography. No doubt, he says, there were many excellent Christians among Russian landowners under serfdom, "yet serfdom remained an abomination in the eyes of the Lord, and the Russian Tsar-Liberator came as one who expressed the demands not only of a *personal* but also of a *social* morality, the latter being a thing of which there were no proper conceptions in times of old, despite the fact that there were no fewer 'good people' then, perhaps, than there are now." Further, Gradovsky points out that "in demanding humility before the truth of the people, and their ideals, [Dostoevsky] accepts the 'truth' and these ideals as something given, unshakable, and eternal"; but in fact, "the social ideals of our people are still in a process of *formation and development*." Taking the very opposite view from Dostoevsky, he also states bluntly that "every Russian person who wishes to enlighten himself *necessarily* acquires his enlightenment from a West European source, owing to the complete absence of any Russian sources."[19]

Driven to a fury by such words, Dostoevsky counterattacked with all the considerable rhetorical resources at his command.

## 4

Written as an afterword to an explanatory introduction and the reprinting of his speech, Dostoevsky's answer is in fact a *profession de foi*, a declaration of principles rather than an attempt to reason with his opponent so as to convince him to alter his ideas. "You and I will never come to an agreement," he rightly says, "and so I have no intention whatsoever of trying to persuade or dissuade you." Indeed, Dostoevsky asserts that he is not addressing himself to Gradovsky at all but rather to his own readers. "I hear, I sense, I even see the rise of new elements who are longing for a new word, who have grown weary of the old liberal snickering over any word of hope for Russia" (26: 149). His article contains a summary of his beliefs and convictions as they had already been expressed in the *Diary of a Writer*, but these ideas had previously been set down with reference to one or another topical subject. Here they are stated boldly and unequivocally, asserted in their own right, and often supported by the same autobiographical anecdotes already used to illustrate the personal roots of his convictions.

He first deals with the charge that, if Russians wished to "enlighten" themselves, they must draw such "enlightenment" from Western European sources. But what does Gradovsky mean, Dostoevsky inquires, when he speaks of enlightenment? Does he mean "the sciences of the West, practical knowledge, trade, or spiritual enlightenment"? If the first, then all such ideas could come from Europe, "and we truly have no way to escape them, and no reason to try." But if he means "spiritual enlightenment that illuminates the soul, enlightens the heart, guides the mind, and shows it a path in life," then Russians have no need to appeal to Western European sources for *such* guidance. "I maintain that our people were enlightened long ago, when they took Christ and His teachings as their very essence." He then sketches, in vivid images, the endless sufferings endured by the Russian people throughout their history—years during which they had nothing but Christ to cling to as consolation. But he knows very well that "my words will seem childish babble" to those of Gradovsky's persuasion, indeed, "almost indecent" (26: 150–151).

Foreseeing the objection "that the whole range of enlightenment is by no means confined only to Christianity and the worship of Christ," Dostoevsky admits the truth of this contention. But he turns on his critics for refusing to concede "that the Christianity of the people is, *and always must remain,* the principal and vital foundation of their enlightenment." To those who accuse him of overlooking "the transgressions" of the supposedly Christ-loving Russian people, thus implying that he is ignorant of their true nature, he lashes back with a reference to his past. "I lived with them for some years, shared meals with them, slept alongside them, and was myself 'numbered among the transgressors'; I worked with them at real, backbreaking labor and at a time when others ... were playing at liberalism and snickering about the people. ... So don't tell me that I don't know the people! I know them: it was from them I accepted Christ into my soul again, Christ, whom I had known while still a child in my parents' home and whom I was about to lose when I, in my turn, transformed myself into a 'European liberal'" (26: 151–152). This is hardly an accurate account of Dostoevsky's quite complex moral-spiritual and ideological evolution, but it stresses fairly enough the crucial role played by his four years in the Siberian prison camp.*

Dostoevsky had always openly acknowledged the many glaring defects of the Russian people, but he pours scorn on the liberals who compare them unfavorably with the lower classes of Western nations. "Do you think that in the West ... there is less drunkenness and thievery, there is not the same brutality—and real cruelty with it (which is not the case among our people)—and genuine, honest-to-God ignorance?" But he had also always insisted that the Russian people "never accept, never will accept, and have no wish to accept their sin as truth! They will commit sins, but will always say, sooner or later, 'I have done wrong.'" In the West, on the other hand, there is "such a lawlessness that people there no longer think of it as sin but have begun to accept it as truth." Even the Russo-Turkish War, he argues, was "seized upon [by the people] as an expiatory sacrifice for their sins and unjust ways; they sent their

---

* For more information, see my *Dostoevsky: The Years of Ordeal, 1850–1859* (Princeton, 1983), 69–162.

sons to die for a sacred cause and did not shout that the ruble was falling and that the price of beef had gone up" (26: 152–153).

This denunciation of the West, with all its "enlightenment," reduces the entire social-political situation there to an illustration of the two slogans that presumably define the European moral horizon: *Chacun pour soi et Dieu pour tous* (Everyone for himself, and God for all), and *Après moi, le déluge!* (After me, the flood!). These are the slogans of the most arrant and egoistic individualism, and they rule all of Western social-political life. Similar slogans can also be found in the Russian language, but in Dostoevsky's hardly unprejudiced view they are not taken seriously and used only in jest. But in the West, "would you dare claim that 'Chacun pour soi et Dieu pour tous' is only a saying and not a social motto . . . that *everyone* there serves and believes in? At least all those who stand above the people, who keep them in check, who own the land and the proletariat, and who stand on guard for 'European enlightenment.' Why do we need that kind of enlightenment? We will find another sort here at home." To his eyes, "in the West there truly is no Christianity . . . although there are still many Christians." Catholicism is only "idolatry," and "Protestantism is taking giant steps toward atheism and toward inconstant, fashionable, changeable (and not eternal) morality" (26: 151–153).

The Russian "wanderers," Gradovsky had argued, were fleeing from the intolerable realities of Russian social life as represented by the characters of Gogol. "They are the background," he had written, "without which [Pushkin's "wanderers" and their descendants] cannot be understood. Yet these Gogolian characters were Russian—and, oh, what real Russians they were!" The Russian people thus do not contain *only* the exalted attributes that Dostoevsky discerns in them, and which guarantee their glorious future destiny. Dostoevsky picks up the challenge by arguing that such Gogolian types, even though seemingly rooted in Russian life, had really become as alienated from the people as "the wanderers." They knew the life of the people on a daily basis, but "they did not even suspect the existence of the people's soul, the things the people longed for and prayed for; they did not even suspect it because they had a terrible disdain for the people" (26: 155).

Once again he invokes the epiphanic incident in his adolescence when he saw a government courier "wearing a uniform tailcoat and three-cornered hat [the attire of an alien Western "civilization"] . . . brutally smashing his fist down on the back of his peasant driver, while the driver furiously slashed the steaming horses of the troika galloping at full speed." This scene had become a symbolic image for him, constantly invoked, of the relation between the Russian upper class and the people; the superficial gloss of Europeanism did not prevent this upper class from treating the peasants as the courier had treated his driver—

with a blow of the fist and a kick of "his polished Petersburg boots."
"The son of such a courier," he writes with sarcastic relish, "may be
a professor, perhaps—a patented European." Not until the rise of the
Slavophils, who emulated Pushkin in their understanding of the people,
did such attitudes begin to change; and even then, "everyone looked at
[the Slavophils] as if they were epileptics and idiots whose ideal was
'eating radishes and writing denunciations'" (a quotation from a poem
of Turgenev's, published in 1846) (26: 155–156). But then he arrives at
what he considers the main point: Gradovsky's defense of "the wanderers" as having been justified in running away from the repellent realities
of Russian life.

In truth, Dostoevsky charges, Aleko, Onegin, and others like them
"were Derzhimordas [a policeman in Gogol's *Inspector-General*] in their
own way, and in some respects even worse." Although he claims to be
"making no accusations against ["the wanderers"] at all," and to be
"completely admitting the tragic nature of their fates," he refuses to
make any distinction between their behavior toward the people and
that of Gogol's characters. The "wanderers" too were the products of
a European education, and "their relation to the people was that of a
master to a serf." As far back as the early 1860s, Dostoevsky had be-
labored educated Russians who fled their country with the excuse that
they could find nothing useful to do there. Could they not, he asked
tauntingly, at least teach just one peasant child to read? Picking up the
same refrain, he maintains the charge of "haughtiness" that he had
made against them in his speech, and which Gradovsky had refused to
accept.

If they had not been so haughty, according to Dostoevsky, if they had
not begun "to marvel at their own nobility and superiority," they might
"have seen that they themselves were also Derzhimordas . . . [and] they
might then have found a path toward reconciliation." He was especially
incensed that Gradovsky had neglected the larger aspect of the views
expressed in his speech, particularly his statement that "'the wanderers'
are the products of the historical process of our society." It is not true,
he complains, that "I am accusing Aleko only of personal failings and
overlooking the root of the matter," that is, precisely "the historical process" in question (26: 156–157). But while Dostoevsky implicitly acknowledges the social-historical genesis that produced "the wanderers" as a
Russian type (that is, the reforms of Peter the Great, which had also
resulted in the establishment of serfdom), the only *solution* he offers,
as Gradovsky rightly sees, is couched in purely personal terms—or
rather, in terms whose tacit social dimension was a submission to the
existing social order, with vaguely hopeful intimations of some impending Tsarist benevolence.

Finally Gradovsky is attacked for what Dostoevsky calls the "whole implicit content of your article, which, it seems, you wished to conceal." For Gradovsky regarded "the wanderers" as "normal and admirable, admirable by the very fact that they fled from the Derzhimordas." Indeed, Gradovsky had praised them "for their hatred of the slavery that oppressed the people," adding that "they loved the people in their own way, 'in a European way,' if you like. But who, if not they, prepared our society for the abolition of serfdom?" Dostoevsky refuses such a claim outright, retorting that those who fled from Russia in "civic sorrow" did not hate serfdom "for the sake of the Russian peasant who worked for them and fed them and who, accordingly, was oppressed by them, as well as by the others." Why, if "the wanderers" were "so overcome by civic sorrow that they had to run off to the gypsies or the barricades of Paris" (an allusion to Turgenev's Rudin, a character based on Bakunin), had they not "simply liberated their serfs with land"? Of course they would have had no income, and "one still needs money to live in 'gay Paree'" (26: 157–158).

With an allusion to Herzen that all his readers would understand, Dostoevsky speaks of those who "mortgaged, sold, or exchanged (is there any difference?) their peasants and, taking the money thus raised, went off to Paris to support the publication of radical French newspapers and magazines for the salvation of humanity, not merely the Russian peasant." (Herzen had helped Proudhon finance the publication of his newspaper.) Dostoevsky accuses "the wanderers," in an unworthy taunt, of having such a low opinion of the Russian peasantry that they thought flogging them was still necessary; and he refers to all the scabrous anecdotes circulating about peasant family life among "those whose own family lives were frequently houses of ill repute," and who accepted "the latest European ideas in the fashion of Lucrezia Floriani" (26: 159). (Lucrezia Floriani, a famous operatic diva, is the main character in a novel by George Sand, and bears a number of illegitimate children to various lovers while searching for an ideal mate.) This gibe is again aimed at Herzen, who had written about the affair of his own wife with the radical German poet Georg Herwegh, and who himself fathered several children with the wife of his best friend Nikolay Ogarev.

To illustrate the contempt with which such "enlightened" Russians looked down upon the people, he then, without naming the source, recounts an incident recently made public in Annenkov's *A Remarkable Decade*. After dinner "at a lovely Moscow dacha" in 1845, a party of "most humane professors, celebrated lovers and connoisseurs of the arts, . . . renowned democrats who subsequently became prominent figures of worldwide importance, critics, writers, and charmingly learned ladies" all went for a stroll in the surrounding countryside. There they caught sight of a group of peasants, men and women, who had been working all day gathering the harvest and who were dressed in what Annenkov calls an "almost primitive costume." Dostoevsky alters the text slightly, referring only to a woman working in a nearby rye field and believing herself unobserved. Her state of undress, caused by the discomfort of laboring all day in the burning sunlight, led one wag to remark that "the Russian woman is the only one in the world who feels no shame in front of anyone!" Another added that "it is only the Russian [woman] before whom no one feels ashamed about anything!" Others objected, and a controversy broke out; but Dostoevsky was convinced that even those who refused to accept such contemptuous remarks would not have seen the main point. "Why, it was for you, the universal wanderers, that she was working; it was her labor that let you eat your fill!" (26: 159–160).

Once again, quite unjustifiably, Dostoevsky declines to accord "the wanderers" any credit for having helped to prepare the way for the abolition of serfdom, "though naturally, all this entered into the overall total and was of use." Of far more weight, in his opinion, was the work of someone like the Slavophil Yury Samarin, who took an active part in the preparation of the reform and was a member of the commission that wrote the final statutes. Gradovsky, he notes, makes no reference at all to such people, "who were utterly unlike the wanderers." These latter became "quickly bored ... and once more they began to sulk squeamishly." On receiving the "redemption" payments for their former serfs, "they began selling their lands and forests to merchants and kulaks to be cut down and destroyed; the wanderers settled abroad, beginning our practice of absenteeism." As a result, Dostoevsky "simply cannot consent to accept this image, so dear to you [Gradovsky], of the superior and liberal person as the ideal of the real, normal Russian" (26: 160–161).

Extremely effective as a polemicist when drawing on such concrete examples of Russian life, Dostoevsky is much less so when forced to cope with more general ideas, such as, for example, Gradovsky's argument that "personal betterment in the spirit of Christian love" is not sufficient to bring about a fundamental moral improvement in society. Even if such landowners as Korobochka and Sobakevich in *Dead Souls* had been "perfect Christians," their faith, according to Gradovsky, would not have abolished serfdom. Dostoevsky cleverly seizes on this notion of "perfection" to advance his own case, for "had Korobochka only become, or could she have become, *a genuine*, perfect Christian, then serfdom on her estate would have disappeared altogether, so that there would be nothing to worry about, despite the fact that all the deeds and bills would have remained in the trunk as before." Indeed, "the erstwhile mistress and erstwhile slave would have vanished like mist before the sun, and entirely new people would have appeared and entirely new and unprecedented relationships among them." In other words, the transformation of moral feeling brought about by a *perfect* Christianity would triumph over the egoism of ordinary social relationships. Dostoevsky admits that this is "a fantastic proposition . . . [and] an amazing fantasy," but he insists that he is merely following Gradovsky's own logic to its end (26: 162–163). In fact, he is describing his own ideal world of Christian love, the ideal that lies at the root of all his own presumably social-political speculations and prophecies.

Although recognizing that Christianity at the time of Saint Paul had not abolished slavery, he argues that the reason "was simply because the churches that had arisen at the time were not yet *perfect* (something that is evident from Paul's epistles)." But those who criticize Christianity for "its alleged enshrinement of slavery . . . misunderstand the essence of the matter." No genuine, perfect Christian could possibly own slaves, even though there will continue to be masters and servants; and Dostoevsky cites Paul's epistles to his servant Timothy (whom the apostle calls his "son in faith") to prove that with perfect Christian love "there will no longer be masters, nor will servants be slaves." Father Zosima had already preached this inner Christian transformation of the master-servant relationship from one of dominance to that of mutual affection, and Dostoevsky now holds up the image of "a future perfect society" in which people like Kepler, Kant, and Shakespeare would be freely served by persons recognizing their importance for humanity. By serving such geniuses voluntarily, the person doing so would demonstrate that "I am in no way beneath thee in moral worth and that, *as a person*, I am equal to thee" (26: 163–164). One of the first touchingly naïve glimpses in Dostoevsky's work of such a voluntary and self-respecting acceptance of superior worth can be found in *House of the Dead*, when the peasant convicts in his prison camp ushered him into a front-row seat at the Christmas theatricals because he possessed a greater knowledge of the stage (4: 121–122).

Dostoevsky realizes, of course, that all such visionary beliefs will be scoffed at, and that people will ask: what good is such an ideal "when it seems that genuine Christianity doesn't exist on earth, or exists in small measure?" He ripostes by asking: "How many genuine citizens are needed to keep the ideal of civic virtue alive?" (As if being a good citizen and becoming a perfect Christian required the same degree of moral self-discipline!) But perhaps aware of the fragility of this reasoning, he then asserts his belief in the Christian ideal as an act of faith. "If I believe that the truth is here, in those very things in which I put my faith, then what does it matter to me if the whole world rejects my faith, mocks me, and travels a different road?" Here speaks the voice of his "ridiculous man," whose dream of the ideal cannot be shaken by the skepticism and incredulity of those who laugh at his preachments. The value of such an ideal cannot "be measured in terms of immediate benefit, but is directed toward the future, toward eternal ends and absolute joy" (26: 164). This is the vision that Dostoevsky upholds as the Russian answer to Western "enlightenment."

## CHAPTER 30

# Controversies and Conclusions

The single issue of the *Diary of a Writer* for 1880 was published on August 1, and both the Pushkin speech and Dostoevsky's article evoked a new flood of commentary. The reaction of the liberal and radical journals was of course unrelentingly hostile, and the article of Gradovsky was a relatively restrained example of their response; the outrightly radical press was much harsher in tone. Still another article, written by K. D. Kavelin, also aroused Dostoevsky's interest, and many entries in his notebook respond to this criticism; but death prevented a more developed rebuttal. (Kavelin was another noted academic, famous for his anti-Slavophil studies of Russian history, who had been tutored by Belinsky.)

Turgenev continued to remain extremely upset at the whole affair. V. V. Stasov, who met him in Paris in mid-July, reports him referring to the Pushkin speech as "abhorrent," even though "almost the whole intelligentsia, and thousands of people, had gone out of their minds about it." He "found unbearable all the lies and falsifications of [Dostoevsky's] preachment," his "mystical verbiage" about "the Russian all-man," the Russian "all-woman Tatyana," and he was "terribly vexed, terribly angry."[1]

It was not only the Westernizers, however, who found much to object to in Dostoevsky's irresistible oratory; even some of his admirers and friends were unable to accept the full implications of his views. And the same was true of those who, even if not supporters, could still be considered political allies. Writing to O. F. Miller, then composing an article on the festival for *Russian Thought*, Sergey Yuriev remarked ironically that "it is necessary to cancel out all questions about political freedom because [Father] Zosima feels free in chains." Miller's article, which defended Dostoevsky in general, nonetheless concedes gingerly that "to quarrel with Dostoevsky, and even with some success, is of course quite possible if one does so on particular points; his strength is not in these, but in . . . his thought *as a whole*. As particular points I would list the characterizations of Tatyana, Onegin, Aleko."[2] The most penetrating critique of this kind, which raised fundamental questions about his social-religious ideas, came from the intransigent reactionary pen of Konstantin Leontiyev.

2
———

In mid-July Dostoevsky wrote to his old friend Victor Putsykovich in Berlin, who by now had abandoned the *Russian Citizen* for lack of funds and was planning to open a reading room containing foreign, and particularly Russian, publications. He assures Putsykovich that the lack of response to earlier letters only underlined the burden of his work on his novel and the reply to Gradovsky. The latter had been necessary not because of personal vanity but for the sake of "an idea." "A new unexpected moment manifested itself in our educated society at the Pushkin celebration, and they rushed *to bespatter* and sully it, frightened at the new word in society, one reactionary to the extreme, in their opinion . . . and I wrote such a fierce piece, one that so breaks off all ties with them that everyone will now curse me." So hard had he worked in the last month, he complains, "that I am now exhausted and almost ill"; but despite his failing health, he will not be "going to Ems" this year and announces firmly that "I'll surely resume the *Diary* next year."[3]

A letter about the Kumanina property shows that all the details of the settlement still had not been agreed upon, and this unpleasant legal wrangle continued up to the eve of Dostoevsky's death; it may well have played a part in aggravating his final illness. He also answered an inquiry from K. P. Pobedonostsev, who as the secular head of the Orthodox Church had questioned him about a priest then living in Staraya Russa at the home of Father Rumyantsev. The clergyman had requested permission to leave the priesthood because of illness, and Dostoevsky confirmed that he was genuinely ailing, though "his illness is a strange one." Dostoevsky testifies to the reality of this condition because "I suffered from the same illness in '47, '48, and '49. I also have a brother who is afflicted with exactly the same illness." One result of this malady is that "in certain temperaments the attacks of this illness lead to psychic, mental derangement. A person becomes infected with boundless anxiety and toward the end imagines himself afflicted with every disease and continually takes treatment from a doctor and treats himself."[4] Dostoevsky was convinced that his years in the prison camp, though responsible for his epilepsy, had freed him from this earlier sickness.

He asks his friend to read the *Diary* and offer his reactions, complimenting him in turn on a "marvelous" speech Pobedonostsev had recently made to graduating students of a school for the daughters of clergymen. When Dostoevsky complains about his embattled situation—"I think everyone will throw stones at me"—his confidant consoles him in a curiously ambiguous manner. "How happy I am," Pobedonostsev replies, "at the news you give me about the imminent appearance of the *Diary*. If only your thought is anchored in yourself clearly and firmly, *in faith*, and not in vacillation—there is then no need to pay attention to how it is reflected in broken mirrors—such as are our journals and newspapers."[5] Such an insidious remark suggests that, at least in the eyes of Pobedonostsev, perhaps Dostoevsky's *own* faith manifested too much "vacillation" to make it unshakably reliable. What Pobedonostsev means here by "faith" is not quite clear; he may be referring to Dostoevsky's faith in his own convictions; but more likely he is alluding to religious "faith," with the particular moral-social connotations given such belief by Dostoevsky.

A reading of this kind finds indirect support in Pobedonostsev's next letter, ten days later, thanking Dostoevsky for having sent the *Diary*. "I am grateful to you," he says, "for having uttered the Russian truth."[6] At the same time, asking whether his correspondent has seen the article about the Pushkin speech published by Konstantin Leontiyev in three issues of the *Warsaw Diary*, he sends them along for perusal. Dostoevsky replied with gratitude for the approval of his *Diary* and for the receipt of the articles; but their dispatch would certainly have raised some questions in his mind. For Leontiyev deals critically, and quite discerningly, with the social-religious questions raised by the Pushkin speech, contrasting its equivocations with the firmness expressed by Pobedonostsev himself in the very graduation address that Dostoevsky had praised. Why should Pobedonostsev have called attention to Leontiyev's article if not to indicate what he too found suspect in Dostoevsky's convictions?

Leontiyev's article, "On Universal Brotherhood," contains a probing analysis of the wider implications of Dostoevsky's views as well as of his literary work as a whole. Often called the Russian Nietzsche, Leontiyev occupies a unique place in the social-cultural spectrum of his homeland. Educated as a doctor, and serving as a military surgeon during the Crimean War, he was a novelist as well as a brilliant, slashing, highly original essayist, writing from an archreactionary position. He hated bourgeois Western civilization in all its aspects, much preferring that of the Ottoman Empire, where he had served as a diplomat; and he advocated a reign of tyranny and despotism in Russia as a defense against the infiltration of Western ideals of progress and universal human betterment. During his later years, he underwent an intense religious phase, spending a year (1871) in the severely ascetic ambience of the Greek Orthodox monastery on Mount Athos. Later, he lived in the Optina Pustyn sanctuary and took monastic vows shortly before his death. Leontiyev thus wrote from a point of view that was hostile not only to Gradovsky's liberalism but also to Dostoevsky's inconsistency—at least so he charged—in offering essentially Western ideals as the fulfillment of those of Orthodox Christianity.[7]

Leontiyev well understood why those who had listened to Dostoevsky's impassioned declamation at the Pushkin festival should have been swept away by his eloquence. Reading his words in print, however, and at a remove allowing for sober consideration, he finds them incompatible with Christianity as he understands it. True, he recognizes Dostoevsky to be one of the few Russian writers who has "not lost faith in man himself," since he continues to attribute moral responsibility to the individual rather than shifting it to society. In this respect, he has remained faithful to a truly Christian demand on the personality. Nonetheless, Christianity does not believe "unconditionally . . . either in a better autonomous personal morality, or in the wisdom of humankind as a whole, which must sooner or later create an earthly paradise." It is this latter hope, so central to Dostoevsky's sensibility, that Leontiyev rejects as contrary to Orthodox Christianity; he equates it, rather, with "the doctrines of antinational eudaemonism in which there is nothing new so far as Europe is concerned. All these hopes of earthly love and earthly peace can be found in the verses of Béranger, and even more in George Sand and many others."[8] Leontiyev here discerns quite accurately the continuing influence of the Utopian Socialist Christianity of Dostoevsky's youth—the Christianity that defined itself as the application of the love-ethic of Christ to earthly social life.

Leontiyev's own position, on the contrary, is that of a "Christian pessimism," which confronts the "irremediable tragedy of earthly life" with an unflinching realism. "Suffering, loss, the disillusionment of injustice *must be*," he wrote. "They are even useful to us for our repentance and the salvation of our souls beyond the grave." He identifies his own position with that of Pobedonostsev's speech, which had not advocated any unconditional love for humanity at all. The most important love, the procurator had proclaimed, was love for the Orthodox Church and a strict, unswerving adherence to its dogmas. "Christ," as Leontiyev declared, "is not known otherwise than through the Church," but in Dostoevsky's speech the Saviour "is to such an extent available to all of us outside the Church [that] we allow ourselves the right to ascribe to him a promise he never uttered" (that is, the earthly paradise).[9]

Dostoevsky's immediate response to Pobedonostsev was to remark that "in the final analysis Leontiyev is a bit of a heretic . . . [though] there is much of interest in his opinions."[10] But since Pobedonostsev, as the official head of the Orthodox Church, clearly approved of Leontiyev's article (which cited his own words), Dostoevsky was in effect imputing a bit of "heresy" to him as well. Acutely conscious of having been accused of possible infidelity to his own principles, Dostoevsky replied: "It's not that I don't believe in what I myself have written, but I'm always tormented by the question of how it will be received, whether people will choose to understand the essence of the matter, and whether the result won't more likely be bad than good from my having *published* my cherished convictions."[11] One wonders what the procurator of the Holy Synod might have thought of the entry that Dostoevsky made in his notebook for a future (but never written) reply to his critic. "*Leontiyev (it is not worth doing good in the world, for it is said, it will be destroyed)*. There's something foolhardy and dishonest in this idea. Most of all, it's a very convenient idea for ordinary behavior: since everything is doomed, why exert oneself, why love to do good? Live for your paunch . . ." (27: 51–52). He thus refused, on moral-social grounds, to adopt the extremely fatalistic, exclusively otherworldly perspective of his critic, who saw the existence of evil as necessary for salvation and thus hardly to be combated or opposed. For Dostoevsky, though, humanity was endowed with the freedom to struggle against evil; and Christian love would ultimately triumph. It is never clear, however, whether in his apocalyptic predictions of a future transformation of mankind and human life, this will occur on the earth we know or is reserved for some miraculous heavenly upheaval.

## 3

On August 10, Dostoevsky sent off the concluding chapters (6–10) of Book 11, and told Lyubimov that he was satisfied with Chapters 6, 7, and 8. These depict Ivan's three visits to Smerdyakov, and he felt that they had "turned out well." "But I don't know," he adds, "how you'll view Chapter 9." Dostoevsky was concerned that the masterly depiction of Ivan's hallucination and encounter with the devil might not be accepted as written, and he assures Lyubimov that its details had been "checked with the opinion of doctors (and more than one) long since. They maintain that not only similar nightmares, but even hallucinations are possible just before 'brain fever.' My hero, of course, sees hallucinations too but confuses them with his nightmares." In other words, Ivan confuses his "nightmares," purely the product of his own psyche and recognized as such, with "hallucinations," which he accepts, at least momentarily, as actually existing in the world. Dostoevsky goes on to explain that "it's not just a physical (diseased) trait here, when a person begins at times to lose the distinction between the real and the unreal (which has happened to almost every person at least once in his life), but a spiritual trait as well, which coincides with the hero's character: in denying the reality of the phantom, he defends its reality when the phantom disappears. *Tormented by lack of faith, he (unconsciously) wishes at the same time that the phantom were not imaginary, but something real.*"[12]

Surely with Dante and Milton in mind, Dostoevsky humorously apologizes for having portrayed the devil in such an inglorious guise—"he's only a devil, a petty devil, and not Satan 'with scorched wings.'" He also asks that the phrase "the cherubim's hysterical shrieks" be left unchanged, no doubt fearing that it might strike his editors as too irreverent for inhabitants of the angelic realm. "I implore you to let that pass that way: after all, it's the *Devil* speaking and he can't speak any other way. If that's absolutely impossible, then instead of *hysterical shrieks* put *joyous shouts*." But this alternative "would really be very prosaic and off-key." Luckily, no such substitution was made in the text. Other questionable elements, such as the references to incidents occurring in Catholic confessionals, "are frivolous, but don't seem at all obscene." "Doesn't Mephistopheles," he asks, "sometimes talk rubbish in both parts of *Faust*?"[13] Judged by the standard of Goethe's Walpurgis-Nacht, Dostoevsky's few allusive passages are innocent indeed, and no change in them was required.

The notes made for Book 11 also clarify certain aspects of the final text. Ivan's unexpected amorous interest in Liza Khokhlakova was introduced to link this most intellectual of the brothers with the Karamazovian *plotoyadnost* (lustfulness or sensuality) that unites them all as a family trait. It also supports Smerdyakov's statement that, of the three, it was Ivan who resembled his father most of all. A note reads: "'I like that girl,'" [Ivan says]. "'Are you talking about Liza?' asks Alyosha staring at him. Without answering: 'I'm afraid that I am walking directly in Feodor Pavlovich's footsteps. In a certain respect at least' (he laughs)" (15: 324). The notes also contain several rearrangements of the sequence of chapters, especially those involving Ivan's three visits to Smerdyakov. In an early plan, the first and second visits were separated from the third by a series of events. Also, several notes indicate that Smerdyakov, after the second visit, would summon Ivan for the third; but this scenario would have undermined the unified movement of Ivan's dawning sense of guilt. Dostoevsky finally narrated all these visits retrospectively so as to obtain a continuous progression of Ivan's growing consciousness of his moral responsibility. A number of notes mention "Bernard," obviously the famous French physiologist and psychologist Claude Bernard, whose ideas Dimitry caricatures in a lengthy tirade. Bernard had died in 1878, and the spate of obituaries in the Russian press may have led Dostoevsky to choose him as a representative of "science." But he had long been familiar with Bernard's ideas. His major work, *Introduction à l'étude de la médecine expérimentale* (1865), had been translated by Nikolay Strakhov; and the literary prominence given by Zola to Bernard's deterministic theories of human character, as already remarked, imparted to his selection a literary as well as an ideological significance.

For imaginative brilliance and artistic mastery, the scene between Ivan and the devil indisputably rivals other set pieces in the book; but Dostoevsky remained uncertain whether he would write it until the very last moment. As he told Lyubimov: "Even though I myself think that this chapter *didn't have to be, I enjoyed* writing it, and I don't disavow it in the least."[14] We have seen that he had been thinking much about the problem of presenting "the fantastic"; and another reason for undertaking this challenge may have been a desire to compensate for what, in the *Diary of a Writer*, he had recently admitted to have been the failure of *The Double*. This work had left him unsatisfied, perhaps because, while containing a masterly depiction of a character driven into schizophrenia by an inner conflict, the double is sometimes treated as a purely psychological, subjective apparition, and sometimes as existing objectively and seen by other characters. This uncertainty about the status of the double, which is sometimes used for purely comic effect, undermines the seriousness of the social-psychological conflict embodied by the double's appearance. Dostoevsky himself had said, in a passage already quoted, that while nothing he had ever written was more serious than the artistic idea embodied in *The Double*, the "form" he had given this idea had been faulty and its execution botched. The "enjoyment" he felt in depicting Ivan's devil may well have sprung from being able at last to rectify his literary failure as a debutant.

For Dostoevsky, "the fantastic" was created by the oscillation between the real and the supernatural and the difficulty of deciding between the two. In his notes for Ivan's encounter with the devil, he thus reminds himself several times to depict the rather grubby materiality of Ivan's supernatural visitor. "Satan enters and sits down (a gray old man, warty)" (15: 320). A bit later, Dostoevsky records the French phrase used about him in the text (*qui frisait la cinquantaine* [who was touching fifty]), and another image is given: "Satan would cough from time to time (realism, wart)" (15: 334). Satan is also greatly concerned about his health, fearing that he has caught a bad cold on his journey to earth from the heavenly spheres through the glacial realms of interstellar space; and there are several references to "Hoffmann's Malt Extract" as a remedy, as well as to "honey and salt" (15: 336). All these anchor Satan firmly in the quotidian reality of ordinary existence, while he remains a supernatural Satan at the same time. In one note, however, the otherworldly powers of the devil appear to be manifest: "Ivan beats him [the devil], but he turns up on various chairs," each time thus presumably evading Ivan's blows (15: 321). But this demonstration of the devil's magical capacities, which would have undercut his materialization, was not included in the text.

Dostoevsky's stroke of genius was to provide this thematic *topos* with a religious-philosophical dimension by transforming Ivan's doubts about the reality of the devil into the question of whether or not he believes in the existence of a supernatural realm, and hence of God. He wishes to believe in order to convince himself, on the purely psychological level, that he is not losing his mind; but he also wishes Satan to be only a hallucination so as to preserve his conviction that God does not exist. "Satan to Ivan: 'Yet you believe that I am.' Ivan: 'Not for a minute (I would like you to exist).' Satan: 'Hey!'" (15: 320). Ivan's reason speaks in the first part of this second sentence; his subconscious desire to believe in the parenthetical phrase. Thus, the oscillation of "the fantastic" here receives perhaps its greatest literary expression as Dostoevsky turns its ambiguities into a probing of the question of religious faith.

## 4

In mid-August, Anna Grigoryevna traveled to St. Petersburg to look after the distribution of the 1880 *Diary of a Writer*, which was now in great demand. "You've placed a lot of copies [with distributors], but how will they sell?" Dostoevsky writes his spouse somewhat skeptically.[15] He had been left in charge of the children, with of course a nanny, and was greatly aided by Father Rumyantsev and his family. His report from home was very reassuring ("the children are behaving well and *want* to behave"), but he was irritated by the lack of notice accorded the appearance of the *Diary*. "If Goncharov hiccuped, all the newspapers would immediately start crying: 'Our venerable novelist has hiccuped'—while they ignore me, as if they have given their word to do so."[16] On August 16, though, he tells Pobedonostsev that "some three thousand copies were bought up in Petersburg alone. . . . I think I'll have to put out a second edition." He asks his friend also to read the September issue of the *Russian Messenger*, "where the fourth and final part of *The Karamazovs* will conclude. In that September issue there will be *the trial*—our public prosecutors and attorneys—this will all be shown in a somewhat special light."[17]

During the same weeks in August when these chapters were being written, Dostoevsky corresponded with Marya Polivanova, who had turned to him for guidance in a personal crisis. Her relations with her husband were very strained, and she had asked Dostoevsky whether such a situation could continue indefinitely without any resolution. He replied: "You ask me a question that is very hard to resolve and that, unfortunately, is so universal. Is there a human being in our time who isn't plagued by such a question? A person can be *split in two* forever, and will of course suffer as a result." He advises as a remedy "some new, outside activity, one capable of giving the spirit food, quenching its thirst"; but he describes himself as being the last person to ask for this kind of advice. The reason is that "I have for myself the always ready activity of writing, to which I devote myself with enthusiasm, into which I put all my efforts, all my joys and hopes. . . . I'll always find spiritual activity that at once takes me away from distressing reality into another world." His vocation as a writer thus always served him as a safeguard, but he realizes "how hard it is for people who don't have such a resolution, such a *ready* activity" to rescue themselves from "the desperate questions" that assail them.[18]

Another correspondent who had written him previously, Nikolay Ozmidov, now asks what type of reading might be suitable for the proper education of his young daughter. He had so far kept her away from literary works because her imagination might become unhealthily over-developed; but Dostoevsky warned against continuing this deprivation, which might lead to the very result he feared. "The imagination," he explained, "is an inborn force in a person, and the more so in any child, in whom it is developed, from the earliest years above all the other capacities, and requires satisfying." Care should thus be taken not to stifle a child's imagination but to cultivate it with "impressions of the beautiful . . . [which] are specifically needed in childhood." Moreover, some of the inspiration for his most recent novel, as already noted, came from Dostoevsky's own childhood encounter with Schiller on the stage. "At the age of ten," he writes, "I saw a performance of Schiller's *The Robbers* with Mochalov, and I assure you that the very powerful impression I came away with then affected my spiritual side very fruitfully. At the age of twelve . . . I read all of Walter Scott, and though I developed imagination and sensitivity in myself . . . I took . . . into life so many beautiful and lofty impressions from that reading that, of course, they formed in my soul a great force for the struggle with seductive, passionate, and corrupting impressions." Walter Scott had long since fallen out of literary fashion, but Dostoevsky still calls him "a great writer" who "has a lofty educational significance."[19]

He goes on to list other novelists and novels he would recommend— all of Dickens, *Don Quixote, Gil Blas*, and, among the Russians, all of Pushkin, Gogol, Turgenev, and Goncharov. As for his own works, "I don't think they would all be suitable for her"; but "Lev Tolstoy should be read in his entirety," and Shakespeare, Schiller, and Goethe were all available in Russian. Several historians are listed, the best-known being Karamzin and the American William Prescott, whose books on the conquest of Mexico and Peru are often mentioned as among his favorites. "Newspaper literature should be eliminated as much as possible," he warns, adding though that he is speaking quite personally, and by no means pretending to be an authority on the reading to be provided to children.[20] When Dostoevsky, around this time, read *The Robbers* to his own children, the exercise, alas, was far from successful.

Otherwise, he was totally absorbed in writing the final chapters of *The Brothers Karamazov*. Orest Miller, on behalf of the Slavic Benevolent Society, invited him at the end of August to read at a gala organized in celebration of the 500th anniversary of the Battle of Kulikovo, where Russians for the first time defeated a Mongol army. Dostoevsky felt forced to refuse because "there is no chance of [my] returning to Petersburg by the eighth of September!" He hoped to finish his novel by the end of that month in the relative calm of Staraya Russa, though he regretted having to make this decision because the celebration was "a wonderful idea." "We need to revive the impression of great events in our intelligentsia society, which has forgotten and spat upon our history." One Russian hero of that battle, Dimitry Donskoy, had been portrayed in an unfavorable light by an important historian with whom Dostoevsky had long disagreed, and he is pleased at the news that K. N. Bestuzhev-Ryumin planned to re-gild Donskoy's reputation. "We need loftily to restore this wonderful image and rub out the myriad vile ideas that have been put forth about our history over the last twenty-five years." As for himself, "you see how I've caught it everywhere from our press . . . for my speech. It's as though I had committed embezzlement or forgery in a bank." Not even a recent notorious swindler "had mud thrown at him the way it has been at me."[21]

In late August he replied to Ivan Aksakov, who had made some criticisms of his attack on Gradovsky. Totally in sympathy with Dostoevsky's point of view, Aksakov nonetheless felt that Dostoevsky tended to obscure or lose his main point because (just as was the case with Tolstoy), as an artist rather than a publicist, he could not resist wandering off the main subject onto tempting bypaths. He also objected to a certain dissonance caused by the intemperance of Dostoevsky's *tone*, which constantly appealed to the figure of Christ while adopting a deliberately insulting manner of polemicizing with his opponent. Also, the stylistic verve with which Dostoevsky castigated the excesses of Western immorality created the impression that he rather enjoyed writing about them himself. Dostoevsky did not bristle at such criticism because he was convinced of Aksakov's sympathy and goodwill. He even thanked him for his remarks since he was thinking about the future reissue of his *Diary* and "precisely about how to speak, what tone to speak in, and what not to speak about at all." To discuss these issues with Aksakov, however, would require a much lengthier letter than he now had time to write. "I am finishing *The Karamazovs*; consequently I am summing up a work which I at least value, because much of what is me has gone into it. . . . I've been working altogether nervously, with torment and concern. When I work hard I fall ill, even physically." Despite the accumulation of notes jotted down over three years, "would you believe that . . . I sometimes write one chapter or another, throw it away, write it anew and anew. Only the inspired passages come out at once, at one go, while all the rest is very hard work." Profusely apologizing to Aksakov for not being able to answer more in detail, he promises to do so in mid-September, "when I'm free."[22]

5

Despite such firm intentions, Dostoevsky confesses to Lyubimov on September 8 that he simply cannot complete the novel as yet. "Hard as I have tried to finish and send off the whole *twelfth* and final book of the Karamazovs, so as to have it printed all together, I have finally come to see that it's impossible for me." Instead, he sent off the first five chapters of Book 12, which end just before the prosecutor and the defense attorney make their final speeches. These five chapters formed a unit by themselves ("the story really can represent something integral"), and in any case "the action has been interrupted by me for a while"—that is, by the two lengthy speeches planned for the concluding chapters. "And here [on the speeches] it's necessary to do as good a job as possible . . . the more so as the defense attorney and the prosecutor in my presentation are partly representative types from our contemporary justice system (although they are not copies of anyone personally), with their mores, liberalism, and view of their role."[23] The remainder of Part 4, as well as an Epilogue, was promised for the October issue.

By September 30, Dostoevsky had completed Chapters 6–14 of Book 12, which terminates with the conviction of Dimitry Karamazov for the murder of his father. Work on these chapters had been interrupted on September 2 by "a terrible epileptic attack" that incapacitated him for eight days; but on the eleventh he resumed work, and these pages were sent to Lyubimov on October 6, the same day that the Dostoevsky family returned to Petersburg from Staraya Russa. Only the Epilogue, containing the funeral of little Ilyusha and Alyosha's graveside speech to the assembled boys, remained to be written.

Meanwhile, on October 15, he penned a long letter to Pelagaya Guseva, a lady hitherto unknown in the annals of his life, whom he had met in Bad Ems in 1875. Guseva was a novelist and translator, and she had reprimanded him in several letters for not replying to her missives, which asked him not only to retrieve a manuscript of hers from a journal called *Ogonka* (*Light*) but also to aid her in placing it elsewhere. Dostoevsky acceded to her request, even though "I wouldn't lift a finger for anyone else," because "this is for you, in memory of Ems; I remember you *too well*."[24] Some light on such intriguing words may be cast by one of Guseva's letters, in which she confesses that, while not "indifferent" to Dostoevsky in Bad Ems, she had "heroically concealed" from him "her sinful feelings." Possibly she had not succeeded as well as she imagined, and it was for this reason that Dostoevsky still felt a certain obligation to a lady who had found him so powerfully attractive.

Before acceding to her request, however, he details all the woes by which he is presently afflicted. He has worked so intensively at finishing his novel that, "if there is a person at hard labor, it's me. I was at hard labor in Siberia, for four years, but the work and life there were more bearable than the present one." He has no time at all to read a single book, or even to talk to his children ("and I don't"). His emphysema is so bad that "my days are numbered. Because of my hard work my epilepsy also has gotten worse." Moreover, he is assailed by people asking him for answers to all their personal problems; and unless "I resolve some insoluble 'cursed' question," the petitioner says he will "be driven to shoot himself. (And I'm seeing him for the first time.)" Overwhelmed by invitations to participate in every benefit reading, Dostoevsky wails, "When am I to think, when am I to work, when am I to read, when am I to live?"[25]

Four days later, he felt free enough to attend one of the regular Tuesday salons at the home of Elena Shtakenshneider. The gathering lasted until three in the morning, much later than customary, and the evening was so unusually animated that it led Elena to write an especially lengthy entry in her diary. Poems were read, songs were sung by talented guests accompanied at the piano by accomplished musicians, and "no one noticed how time was passing." Dostoevsky read "The Prophet" again (since the Pushkin festival it had more and more become identified with his own personality), as well as some other poems from Pushkin, Dante, and one from John Bunyan's *Pilgrim's Progress*. As usual, he produced a stunning effect with "The Prophet"—except on the playwright Dimitry Averkiev, who for some reason "railed against everything Dostoevskian." As for herself, Elena writes: "What a fantastic and devious old man! [Dostoevsky] is himself a magical tale, with its miracles, unexpected surprises, transformations, with its enormous terrors and its trifles."[26]

To illustrate her characterization, she describes him as often sitting in her living room morose and silent, brooding over some imagined slight, his eyes sunken, his head hanging, his lower lip twisted in a crooked half-smile. At such moments he spoke to no one, or if he did so, only in abrupt outbursts; but if he managed to say something "with a drop of malice," then his ill mood vanished, "as if a spell had been lifted," and he would smile and join in the general conversation. "To those who knew him," Elena adds, "he is very kind, genuinely kind, despite all his malice; he may give way to the wretched disposition of his soul, but then he repents and wishes to compensate with amiability."[27] Dostoevsky had written apologetically about this aspect of his character thirty-three years earlier to his older brother Mikhail, who had reproached him. "But I have such an awful, repulsive character. . . . I am ready to give my life for you and yours, but sometimes, when my heart is full of love, you can't get a kind word out of me. . . . I am ridiculous and disgusting, and I always suffer from the unjust conclusions drawn about me."[28]

Another guest that evening spoke of N. Ya. Danilevsky's new but as yet unpublished book on Darwinism, which had begun to circulate among the cognoscenti. This ex-Fourierist, whom Dostoevsky had known in the Petrashevsky circle during the 1840s, had maintained in 1869 that Russia would create an independent Slavic civilization initiating the next phase of world history; and Dostoevsky had used some of Danilevsky's ideas for the character of Shatov in *The Devils*.[29] By profession, however, Danilevsky was a naturalist, and the thesis of his new anti-Darwinian work (as expounded that evening) was that "all of creation possesses the gift of consciousness, not only humans but also animals and plants. A pine tree, for example, also says: 'I am!' But the pine tree cannot speak at any time, every hour and every minute, as we people do, but only through the course of a century, a hundred years." Dostoevsky then intervened, without disagreeing, to remark that "to be conscious of one's existence, the power to say 'I am!'—is a great gift, but to say 'I am not,' to destroy oneself for others, to have that force, if you like, is even higher." At this, Averkiev leaped from his seat and declared: "Of course that's a great gift, but it does not and has never existed with one exception, and that is God." Dostoevsky objected, others joined in, but Averkiev heatedly and vociferously insisted "that except for Christ, nobody destroyed themselves for others" (a notion that comes close to the heresy of denying the humanity of Christ). Realizing that her husband had gone too far, the extremely attractive Mme Averkieva then approached Dostoevsky and asked him to read; but he sulkily refused. Another guest finally broke the tension by playing the piano.[30]

The kindness in Dostoevsky that Elena Shtakenshneider was capable of discerning is illustrated by a letter to a Vladimir Kachenovsky, a former fellow student with him at Chermak's boarding school in Moscow during 1834–1839. He had painted a gloomy picture of this establishment in *A Raw Youth*, but his references to it in the letter suggest that his literary usage had perhaps been more determined by his theme (the sufferings of his narrator, the abandoned and illegitimate Arkady Dolgoruky) than by his actual experiences. "When I am in Moscow," he tells Kachenovsky, "I always ride past the building on Basmannaya Street with emotion. I remember you very well. You were the short little boy with wonderful big dark eyes." Indeed, he remarks sadly that "there are not many of us Chermakovites left," and lists the names of some whom he had been happy to encounter in later years.[31] Kachenovsky had fallen on hard times, and Dostoevsky personally intervened with the Literary Fund to grant him a pension.

A more intimately personal illustration of this aspect of Dostoevsky's character is contained in another entry in Elena Shtakenshneider's diary. Dostoevsky was scheduled to read at an afternoon benefit for the Literary Fund devoted to the works of Pushkin, and Anna Grigoryevna and the children visited the Shtakenshneiders earlier in the day. "Really, her husband is a curious fellow, judging from her words," Elena writes. "He does not sleep at night, thinking over ways to provide for his children, works like a convict, denies himself everything, never even taking a carriage to go anywhere, and he, without saying a word about it, supports his brother and stepson [somewhat an exaggeration] . . . [and] still concerns himself with the first person he meets if this is requested." Anna Grigoryevna went on in this vein with examples of his charities, complaining that he could not go anywhere, for a walk or a journey, without an open pocketbook, ready to scatter largesse to all who appealed to his kindness. "That's how we live," she concluded. "And if something happens, where do we turn? How will we live? We are poor! No pension will be coming our way."[32] (In fact, a pension was granted to the family after his death by Alexander II.)

His reading for the Literary Fund, which included "The Prophet," was once more an enormous success. Even though the audience, as Elena notes, was not made up of students, the applause was enthusiastic and sustained. This reading took place in a hall so large that it was often difficult to hear those who recited there, leading Elena to marvel that Dostoevsky, "ill, with a sickly chest and emphysema," could be heard so clearly everywhere. He seemed "to grow in size and become healthier" as he read. In ordinary conversation he coughed continually, but his cough vanished when he declaimed, "as if it did not dare" to manifest itself.[33]

Such triumphs on the platform no doubt gave him immense pleasure and served to reassure him about the "prophetic" mission he had assumed, but it is very likely that nothing at this time brought him greater satisfaction than a few lines in a letter that Tolstoy wrote to his faithful correspondent Nikolay Strakhov on September 26: "Just recently I was feeling unwell and read *House of the Dead*. I had forgotten a good bit, read it over again, and I do not know a better book in all our new literature, including Pushkin. It's not the *tone* but the wonderful point of view—genuine, natural, and Christian. A splendid, instructive book. I enjoyed myself the whole day as I have not done for a long time. If you see Dostoevsky, tell him that I love him."[34] Dostoevsky was then living in Staraya Russa, and it was only on November 2 or thereabouts that Strakhov conveyed Tolstoy's praise to him. His intense gratification at such words of appreciation is easy to imagine.

"I saw Dostoevsky," Strakhov informs the recluse of Yasnaya Polyana, "and transmitted to him your praise and love. He was greatly overjoyed, and I had to leave with him the page of your letter containing such precious words. He was a little annoyed at your derogation of Pushkin which is expressed there. . . . 'How including [Pushkin]?' he asked. I said that you had been even earlier, and now had particularly become, a hardened freethinker."[35] What is both amusing and striking about this incident is Dostoevsky's defense of Pushkin, even at the expense of his own work; and equally, Tolstoy's admiration for the least typical of all of Dostoevsky's major books, the one that, in its detailed, objective depiction of milieu, is closest to his own literary manner.

Since Dostoevsky was planning to resume his *Diary of a Writer*, he was happy to renew contact with the typesetter Mikhail A. Alexandrov, who had devotedly supervised the earlier production of that publication. A post of head typesetter had become vacant in the press of the left-wing journal *Delo* (*Deed*), edited by G. E. Blagosvetlov, a die-hard radical publicist of the 1860s, and Alexandrov visited Dostoevsky to ask for his recommendation. Quickly becoming aware that his ex-patron "had a strong antipathy to the literary camp in which G. E. Blagosvetlov belonged," he was told that an endorsement by him might not really help; nor did Dostoevsky wish to write a personal note to Blagosvetlov. Desiring to help Alexandrov all the same, he dictated a few lines without addressing them to anyone in particular but praising "the diligence, reliability, and, I can say boldly, talent" of his ex-collaborator, who "was himself a writer." The board of editors chose Alexandrov over a host of other applicants, "primarily, of course," he was convinced, "as a result of the written recommendation of Feodor Mikhailovich."[36] The result, however, was that Dostoevsky found it impossible to engage Alexandrov for his renewed *Diary of a Writer* because he refused to have his name associated with the printing plant of the radical journal.

5
———

Dostoevsky finally succeeded in replying to Ivan Aksakov at the beginning of November. Commenting on the published announcement of Aksakov's new weekly, *Rus*, he finds it "superb"; but there are "people here . . . (and just imagine—people who in many things share our way of thought), who find that your announcement is insolent, vague, and *impudent.*" As for the question of his own polemical tone, he says: "I can't get out of my head your argument to me about the tone of talking about sacred things in society, that is, without frenzy and abusiveness. Abusiveness isn't necessary, of course, but may one not be oneself, not sincere? Accept me such as I am, that's how I would have my readers look at me. To drape yourself in clouds of magnificence (Gogol's tone, for instance, in *A Correspondence with Friends*) is insincerity, and even the most inexperienced reader senses insincerity. It's the first thing that gives you away."[37] Father Zosima's preachments had been immediately compared with those of Gogol in the ill-famed work just mentioned; and if Dostoevsky had been careful to avoid any trace of pomposity in the tone of his *starets*, it was because he was so aware of the opposition aroused by Gogol's failure to do so. He had good reason to remember Gogol's text, which had stirred Belinsky to write a furious response that Dostoevsky read aloud at meetings of the Petrashevsky circle; and these readings of the incendiary article constituted one of the charges that had sent him to Siberia.

On the very same day that he wrote to Aksakov, Dostoevsky jotted down some remarks in his notebook about the execution of two radicals, members of Narodnaya Volya, who had been arrested in a recent roundup. No doubt he intended to use the notes for a future issue of his *Diary*, but his comments also echo Father Zosima's apocalyptic vision of a time when society will be ruled exclusively by the law of love embodied in the (Orthodox) Church. He writes: "The execution of Kvyatkovsky and Presnyakov and the pardon of the rest [they were condemned to life imprisonment]. NB! How the government—it could not pardon them (except the will of the monarch). What is execution?—In government—sacrifice for an idea. But if the Church—there is no execution. The Church and government, the two must not be confused." Dostoevsky then adds that "if the two are confused [it] is a good sign," presumably because "it means that it [the government] bows to the Church." Ordinarily so harsh in his criticism of the West, he remarks that "in England and France they would not even think of hanging—Church and monarch at the head" (27: 31). These elliptical notes seem to reflect the general revulsion of Russian society, also noted by Elena Shtakenshneider, against these most recent hangings. Even *New Time*, a generally conservative journal, wrote that, "God willing, let this be the last execution, God willing, let the very weapon of execution retreat into being a thing of the past."[38]

On November 7, Dostoevsky completed work on *The Brothers Karamazov* and sent the final section to Lyubimov. "Well, and so the novel is finished," he wrote elegiacally. "I have worked on it for three years, spent two publishing it—this is a significant moment for me. . . . Allow me not to say farewell to you. After all, I intend to live and write for another twenty years."[39] As we see, Dostoevsky's relation to the prospect of his own longevity could swing from gloom to exuberant optimism. The completion of the manuscript of his greatest work had no doubt filled him with a happy sense of renewed vigor, which overshadowed his earlier comments about the dangerous state of his health. Alas, the more pessimistic prediction in so many of his letters turned out to be all too justified. But before continuing with the last three months of his life, let us turn to a more detailed examination of the great novel he had just completed.

# PART IV

# The Brothers Karamazov

## CHAPTER 31

# The Brothers Karamazov:
# Books 1–2

With *The Brothers Karamazov*, Dostoevsky fully recouped his artistic powers and reasserted the mastery kept in check in *A Raw Youth*. Indeed, this work towers even over his earlier masterpieces, and succeeds in achieving a classic expression of the great theme that had preoccupied him since *Notes from Underground*: the conflict between reason and Christian faith. Never before had Dostoevsky expressed this clash with such poetic power, such symbolic elevation, and in terms of so broad a depiction of Russian social types and Russian life. No previous work gives the reader such an impression of controlled and measured grandeur, a grandeur that spontaneously evokes comparison with the greatest creations of Western literature. *The Divine Comedy, Paradise Lost, King Lear, Faust*—these are the titles that naturally come to mind as one tries to measure the stature of *The Brothers Karamazov*. For these too grapple with the never-ending and never-to-be ended argument aroused by the "accursèd questions" of mankind's destiny.

## 2

By its proportions alone, which aim for some of the amplitude of *War and Peace, The Brothers Karamazov* clearly aspired to greatness; but Dostoevsky was wise enough not to attempt to compete with Tolstoy in any other fashion. He retains his usual focus on an action that presents a crisis situation at its highest point of strain and intensity; his usual sparsity of description and expository narration; his usual presentation of characters through dramatic monologue as self-revealing and self-reflecting consciousnesses. By considerably enlarging the scale of his habitual poetics of subjectivity and dramatic conflict, Dostoevsky imparts a monumental power of self-expression to his characters which rivals that of Dante's sinners and saints, Shakespeare's titanic heroes and villains, and Milton's gods and archangels. Dostoevsky's personages seem to dwarf their surroundings with the same superhuman majesty as the figures of Michelangelo's Sistine Chapel; and this monumentality probably accounts for the often-repeated assertion (erroneous if taken literally) that his characters are placed in some disembodied locale scarcely depicted at all.

If the characters of *The Brothers Karamazov* take their place in such exalted company, however, the reason is not simply the greater amplitude of their dimensions. There is, in addition, the deployment of a stylistic feature that appears sporadically in earlier works but here is used more consistently and purposefully than in the past. When Raskolnikov compares himself with the figure of Napoleon in his frenzied cogitations, his petty and sordid crime suddenly takes on a symbolic dimension far exceeding its naturalistic importance; but Dostoevsky's aim was precisely to bring out the *incongruity* between this Napoleonic ambition and his character's actual circumstances. In *The Brothers Karamazov*, each of the major characters is given a similar symbolic dimension but one appropriate to his or her situation and personality. They are all thus not only private individuals, not only contemporary social types, but are linked with vast, age-old cultural-historical forces and moral-spiritual conflicts.

The internal struggle in Ivan Karamazov's psyche, for example, is expressed through the legends and mystery plays of the Middle Ages in Europe (imitated somewhat later in Russia), the autos-da-fé of the Spanish Inquisition, the eschatological myth of the returning Christ, and the New Testament narrative of Christ's temptations by Satan. Dimitry is surrounded with the atmosphere of Schiller's Hellenism and the struggle between the Olympian gods and the dark, bestial forces that had subjugated humankind before their coming. Father Zosima is the direct inheritor of the thousand-year-old rituals and traditions of the Eastern Church and a representative of the recently revived institution of *starchestvo*, both of which are evoked so solemnly in the early chapters. Alyosha is situated in this same religious context, and his crisis of doubt, which, like those of King Lear and Hamlet, calls into question the entire order of the universe, is resolved only by a cosmic intuition of the secret harmony linking the earth with the starry heavens and other worlds.

Feodor Pavlovich's anecdotes about Diderot and Catherine the Great, as well as his quotations from Voltaire, tinge his grossness and cynicism with a distinct eighteenth-century flavor. He is also placed much farther back in time when he takes pride in possessing "the countenance of an ancient Roman patrician of the decadent period" (14: 22). Dostoevsky always associated these later years of the declining Roman Empire with rampant licentiousness and moral breakdown, and in 1861 he wrote that this period, symbolized for him by Cleopatra, was the world "to which our divine redeemer descended. And you [his readers] understand much more clearly the meaning of the word redeemer" (19: 137). Nor should one forget the rich network of biblical and literary allusions and parallels that interweave with the action throughout the book (details of which, regrettably, we shall only be able to glance at in passing).[1] This symbolic amplification thickens and enriches the texture of the work, and gives its conflicts the range and resonance we are accustomed to finding in poetic tragedy rather than in the more quotidian precincts of the novel. As E. M. Forster has so strikingly written, in Dostoevsky, and particularly in *The Brothers Karamazov*, "the characters and situations always stand for more than themselves; infinity attends them; though yes, they remain individuals, they expand to embrace it and summon it to embrace them."[2]

*The Brothers Karamazov* also differs from Dostoevsky's other novels, and particularly from its immediate predecessor, by the clarity and simplicity of its construction. There is not one central figure in *The Brothers Karamazov* but five; it is the story of a family and a community, not primarily of an individual. This structure allowed Dostoevsky to narrate events with a relative lack of intrigue, in contrast with his usual reliance on a plot full of surprises and coincidences. Here he simply alternates the stories of his main figures in successive sections, sometimes with an overlap of time from one to the other that creates suspense without the need for intrigue. All are loosely but naturally knit together by the quarrel between Dimitry and his father over money and Grushenka, and by the events culminating in the murder and the trial.

Not only is the construction of *The Brothers Karamazov* less strained and convoluted than other Dostoevsky novels, but its tonality is also relatively less harsh and dissonant. The world it evokes is still racked by all the human passions at their extremest stretch; but the book does not end in tragedy to the same degree as, for example, *The Idiot* or *The Devils*. There is also, for the first time, the extensive presentation of another world of true faith, love, and hope in the monastery, as well as in the evolution of the relations between Dimitry and Grushenka and among the children. Acute social misery is also brushed in; but while the lot of the Snegiryovs is hardly enviable, it does not match the hopeless wretchedness of the Marmeladovs in *Crime and Punishment*. Although there is both a murder and a suicide, they take place offstage and are not depicted with the grisly detail of Raskolnikov's murderous deed or the terrifying demise of Kirillov. The worst moments, perhaps, are those contained in Ivan's account of the tortures suffered by innocent children; but these are softened by the pity and anguish of their chronicler. The comparative absence of characters treated purely as satirical grotesques (the single exception, Maximov, is handled quite gently) further contributes to the muting of the sharply clashing tonal contrasts hitherto associated with Dostoevsky's art. There are, to be sure, parody aplenty and brilliant satire in Ivan's conversation with the devil; but these do not stand out too sharply and are carefully assimilated into the main plot line.

All these reasons contribute to the impression of classic grandeur made by the book, but most important of all is the weight and dignity of its theme. With *The Brothers Karamazov,* Dostoevsky takes up the subject of the breakdown of the Russian family that had begun to preoccupy him in the early 1870s and had furnished the starting point for *A Raw Youth.* But if that novel had shown him anything, it was that he could not do himself justice as an artist if he confined this subject to a social-psychological level. For Dostoevsky, the breakdown of the family was only the symptom of a deeper, underlying malaise: the loss of firmly rooted moral values among educated Russians stemming from their loss of faith in Christ and God. This loss of faith had long been the subject of his major novels; but earlier he had presented it through exploring all the disastrous psychological and social consequences arising from the abandonment of Christian moral values. Now these values had once again become accepted—but not their linkage to the supernatural presuppositions of the Christian faith, which for Dostoevsky offered their only secure support.

The conflict between reason and faith—faith now being understood very sharply as the irrational core of the Christian commitment—was thus, as Dostoevsky saw it, posed much more centrally in current Russian culture than had been the case in the 1860s. And its new prominence gave him his long-cherished opportunity to place this problem, grasped at its highest moral-philosophical level, at the center of a major work. In this last novel, he thus brought all the resources of his sensibility, his intelligence, his culture, and his art to cope with this new version of radical ideas—just as he had done earlier with Chernyshevsky's materialism and Utilitarianism in *Notes from Underground,* with Pisarev's Nihilism in *Crime and Punishment,* and with the revolutionary amorality of the Bakunin-Nechaev ideology in *The Devils.*

This opposition is dramatized with incomparable force and sublimity in the famous ideological center of *The Brothers Karamazov* (Books 5 and 6 of Part 2). It contains Ivan's revolt against a Judeo-Christian God in the name of an anguished pity for a suffering humanity, and the indictment of Christ Himself in the Legend of the Grand Inquisitor for having imposed a burden of free will on humankind too heavy for it to bear. In reply, there is Father Zosima's preachment of the necessity for a faith in God and immortality as the sole guarantee for the active love for one's fellow man demanded by Christ. Here this conflict is expressed in overt religious terms and in relation to the age-old problem of theodicy, which, ever since the Book of Job, has furnished the inspiration for so much of the religious problematic in the Western tradition. But if we are to do justice to Dostoevsky's great masterpiece, it is not enough to focus attention solely on these magnificent set pieces. For the same theme of reason and faith appears in all the multiplicity of action in the book, and its specifically religious form serves as a symbolic center from which it radiates analogically through all the situations in which the major characters are involved.

Dostoevsky, as we have seen, rather incautiously spoke of the utterances of Father Zosima in Book 6 as having been designed specifically to answer the accusations of Ivan against God; but he did so partly to pacify the fears of K. P. Pobedonostsev that the reply would not be as powerful as the attack. Later, however, in an entry in his notebook set down *after* the work had been completed, he wrote that "the whole book" was a reply to the Legend of the Grand Inquisitor (27: 48). This remark indicates much more accurately the linkages that exist among its various parts and levels—a linkage based on the analogy between the human situation reflected in Ivan's poem and the conflicts of all but the most accessory and secondary characters. For an intellectual like Ivan, his anguish at the sufferings of humankind opposes any surrender to the Christian hope—a hope justified by nothing but what Kierkegaard called a "leap of faith" in the radiant image of Christ the God-man. Similarly, all the other major characters are confronted with the same necessity to make a leap of faith in something or someone beyond themselves, to transcend the bounds of personal egoism in an act of spiritual self-surrender. For these characters, this conflict is not presented in terms of a specific religious choice but rather in relation to their own dominating drives and impulses, their own particular forms of egoism. They too are called upon to accomplish an act of self-transcendence, an act "irrational" in the sense that it denies or overcomes immediate ego-centered self-interest. The identification between "reason" (which on the moral level amounted to Utilitarianism) and egocentrism was deeply rooted in the radical Russian thought of the period; and this convergence enables Dostoevsky to present all these conflicts as part of one pervasive and interweaving pattern. Indeed, the continuing power of the novel derives from its superb depiction of the moral-psychological struggle of each of the main characters to heed the voice of his or her own conscience, a struggle that will always remain humanly valid and artistically persuasive whether or not one accepts the theological premises without which, as Dostoevsky believed, moral conscience would simply cease to exist.

Such a pattern, indeed, may be found not only in the thematic involvements of the book but even in the organization of the plot action. The central plot is carefully constructed so as to lead, with irresistible logic, to the conclusion of Dimitry's guilt; the accumulated mass of circumstantial evidence pointing to him as the murderer is literally overwhelming. The fact remains, however, that he is technically innocent of the crime (though implicated in it by his parricidal impulses), and the reader is thus constantly confronted with the discrepancy between what reason might conclude and the intangible mystery of the human personality, capable even at the very last instant of conquering the drives of hatred and loathing. The entire arrangement of the plot action thus compels the reader to participate in the experience of discovering the limitations of reason. Moreover, only those among the characters who are willing to believe *against* all the evidence—only those whose love for Dimitry and whose faith, deriving from this love, are stronger than the concatenation of facts—only they are able to pierce through to the reality of moral-spiritual, as well as legal, truth in its most literal sense. The importance given by Dimitry himself to such declarations of faith in his innocence only accentuates the importance of this motif, and illustrates why Dostoevsky could legitimately maintain that "the whole book" is a reply to the "Euclidian understanding" that created the Legend of the Grand Inquisitor.

3
---

*The Brothers Karamazov* begins with a preface labeled "From the Author" ("Ot Avtora"), and some question has arisen as to whether this "author" is Dostoevsky himself or the fictional narrator of his story. This question raises the more general issue of his fictional narrator as such, who determines the perspective from which a good deal of the novel will be read. The qualification "a good deal" is necessary because, in fact, two narrators are provided. There is one who comes to the foreground and is indirectly characterized in various ways; there is another who allows the characters to express themselves in lengthy monologues or in dramatic confrontations with hardly any commentary at all. Dostoevsky, as we know, was well aware of this problem of narrative perspective, and the solution he adopts here is similar to his earlier choice for *The Devils*. There we find the same two types of narration, one expository and the other dramatic; but while the expository narrator in that novel participated, even if minimally, in the dramatic action, in *The Brothers Karamazov* he is totally detached from the events. Since these took place in the past, he serves only as a historian or chronicler, but one who indicates some personal acquaintance with the events at the time they occurred. Although he may disappear as a presence in the dramatic scenes, he is nonetheless quite important otherwise and exhibits a distinct physiognomy. To characterize him, we shall follow the lead of the Russian scholar-critic V. E. Vetlovskaya, whose careful book on the poetics of *The Brothers Karamazov* contains an illuminating study of its fictional narrator.[3]

Vetlovskaya writes that Dostoevsky deliberately blurred the lines between himself as author and his fictional narrator because this indistinction allowed him to express his own opinions in a veiled and seemingly naïve and innocent fashion. He was writing what she calls (rightly, in my view) a "philosophical-publicistic" work, which advanced a definite tendency and advocated a specific moral-religious point of view—and one to which, as he well knew, many of his readers would be opposed. He thus tried to defuse negative reactions by creating a figure who evokes a "modernized" version of the tone and attitude typical of the pious narrators of the hagiographical lives of Russian saints. His language constantly plays on associations that would recall such saints' lives to the reader; and many other attributes of the narrator's style, such as syntactical inversions that would be felt as archaisms, can also be traced to such an intent. (Many of these stylistic devices are of course lost in translation.) The fumbling, tentative quality of his assertions, his uncertainty about details, his moralistic judgments and evaluations, his emotional involvement in the lives of the characters (especially Alyosha), his relative lack of literary sophistication, and the heavy-handedness of his expository technique—all can be seen as an up-to-date version of the pious, reverent, hesitant, hagiographical style of the Russian religious tradition. Such a narrator would be apt to produce a sense of trust in the reader by his very awkwardness and simplicity; and his constant appeal to the opinion of the community also imparts a choruslike quality to the testimony that he offers. Dostoevsky thus uses him to insinuate his own point of view without arousing an instantly hostile response.[4]

The style of the preface does not differ notably from that of the obtrusive fictional narrator and is presumably distinct from that of Dostoevsky the author; but these pages also contain remarks about Russian criticism and critics that would come more naturally from the pen of a professional writer than from the obscure, amateur provincial chronicler of the history of the Karamazov family. Moreover, it is more the author than the chronicler who explains that from the outset he wished to focus attention on Alyosha, even though he is still "a vague and undefined protagonist" (14: 5). The narrator explains that this character will become more important in a second volume (which, regrettably, Dostoevsky never lived even to begin). The book thus recounts events that supposedly occurred thirteen years earlier, although no attempt is made to preserve a strict historical coloring (as can be seen from the reference to Foma Danilov, whom Dostoevsky wrote about in the 1877

*Diary*). But because he also wished to indicate the future importance of Alyosha, he felt it necessary to say a few words about him outside the framework of this first story.

Just as with his choice of a fictional narrator, Dostoevsky sets out immediately to counter the prejudices that he knew would be stirred by Alyosha's Christian commitment and the other peculiarities of his character. Alyosha, he writes, is "an original" (*chudak*), but this singularity does not mean that his strangeness and eccentricity have nothing to teach to others. "For not only is an eccentric 'not always' a particularity and a separate element, but on the contrary, it happens sometimes that such a person . . . carries within himself the heart of the whole, and the rest of the men of his epoch have for some reason been temporarily torn from it, as if by a gust of wind." Alyosha and his teacher, Father Zosima, were certainly the heart of the Russian "whole" for Dostoevsky; and one aim of the book was to drive this point home to those who rejected the divinity of Christ while revering the values of the Russian people who came to adore Him through the person of Father Zosima.

Dostoevsky also well knew that his insistence on placing the world of Alyosha and Father Zosima at the "center" of Russian life would encounter a great deal of hostility; and he responded in advance by the ironically feigned apology for his decision to write two novels about such an "insignificant" protagonist. Alyosha's unimportance could provide an excuse for readers to neglect the planned second novel, or even to put down the first—"the book can be abandoned at the second page of the first tale, never to be opened again." But of course, as he proclaims with tongue in cheek, all Russian critics "absolutely must read to the end, so as not to be mistaken in their impartial judgments"; and his heart feels lighter because his words about Alyosha will give them "a perfectly legitimate pretext to abandon the tale at the novel's first episode" (14: 6). Since Dostoevsky felt that nothing had been less impartial than the judgments usually passed on his works, he was in effect challenging his critics, if they continued to read, to exhibit some of the impartiality they pretended to exemplify.

## 4

The book opens with a series of short background chapters devoted to the history of the Karamazov family—as it were, an overture to the work in its entirety. Although the fictional narrator never presents himself directly, he is evidently a local resident of the town (whose unattractive name, Skotoprigonyevsk, meaning cattle pen, he reluctantly mentions only in the very last pages), and he writes as someone personally acquainted with the Karamazov story and an eyewitness at Dimitry's trial.

In these early chapters, Dostoevsky touches in a brief and condensed form on all the main characters and thematic motifs that he will develop so luxuriantly later. A similar technique of suggestive foreshadowing had been employed for such characters as Stavrogin in *The Devils* and Versilov in *A Raw Youth*, but now he uses the same device for all the major figures.

These characters will of course develop as the novel proceeds, but they do so in a manner quite different from those of Tolstoy or George Eliot, who evolve and change over a long period of time. Dostoevsky's characters, always portrayed in a relatively brief time span, obviously cannot undergo such a process of maturation. Instead, they rather appear to grow in size and stature. His technique causes each to expand vertically, as it were, like a Japanese paper blossom, which, when moistened, metamorphoses from a tiny ball into a full-fledged flower; even if a change occurs, it is accomplished through developing latent aspects of the personality already present from the very start. The essential core of Dostoevsky's characters thus remains the same, but becomes enlarged as their dimensions continue to grow; and this is probably why, as the characters visibly amplify before our eyes, the reader receives so strong an impression of their monumentality.

All of the four central characters are introduced in this opening section, and so is the august figure of Father Zosima. Feodor Pavlovich, the randy progenitor of the Karamazov brood, is a familiar Dostoevskian type—the vengeful buffoon, like Foma Fomich Opiskin in *The Village of Stepanchikovo*, who begins life as a nauseating toady and sycophant and, after attaining wealth and power, revenges himself unmercifully on others for his humiliations. To this type is now added an uncontrollable sensuality, as well as an unscrupulous rapaciousness in business affairs that places him firmly in the group of those who, in the opinion of both the Populists and Dostoevsky, were ravaging and destroying the traditional life of the Russian countryside. Anti-Semitism also comes into play as the narrator speaks of Feodor Pavlovich having spent several years in Odessa, where "he made the acquaintance at first, in his own words, 'of a lot of low Jews, Jewesses, and Jewkins.' . . . It may be presumed that at this period he developed a peculiar faculty for making and hoarding money." On his return to the town, "he opened a great number of new taverns in the district," and "many of the inhabitants of the town and district were soon in his debt" (14: 21).

The elder Karamazov thus incarnates the very epitome of personal and social viciousness, totally neglecting his three children by his two wives, who grow up as members of the kind of "accidental family" that Dostoevsky increasingly felt to be typical of educated Russian society. His presumed bastard, Smerdyakov (though this paternity is never

575

confirmed), is treated with somewhat more concern, but with a contempt that only increases his resentment and hidden rage. Feodor Pavlovich, however, is not simply a monster of wickedness existing solely on the level of his insatiable appetites; he is clever and cynical, educated enough to sprinkle his talk with French phrases, to be familiar with Schiller's *The Robbers*, and he is shown to have strange velleities that suggest some concealed modicum of inner life. On receiving the news of the death of his domineering first wife—the mother of Dimitry, who has inherited her stormy spirit—he both shouts with joy and weeps at the same time. Years later, though drinking furiously and continuing to abuse the monks, he donates a thousand rubles to the monastery to pay for requiems for her soul. This leitmotif of the "broad" Russian nature, swinging between competing moral-psychological extremes, characterizes both Feodor Pavlovich and his eldest son; and its symbolic significance will be highlighted toward the end of the book.

Dimitry Karamazov and his brother Ivan are characterized much more briefly than either their father or their younger brother, Alyosha. At first sight, Dimitry appears to be little more than the typical young regimental brawler so familiar in Russian fiction. He has inherited both the combative proclivities of his mother, who is said to have beaten Feodor Pavlovich rather than the other way round, and the tempestuous sensuality of the Karamazovs. The narrator sketches his recklessly dissipated army career and his expectation that he would inherit money from his mother on coming of age. In fact, however, his father had so entangled the estate that Dimitry was now destitute. No glimpse into his thoughts and feelings is given until Book 3, when the full "breadth" of his character begins to be developed.

Ivan possesses the familiar traits of Dostoevsky's young intellectuals: the reserved and somewhat morose nature thrown back on itself and brooding over its grievances as well as over the injustices of the world. Such characters are those most susceptible to "progressive" ideas, and Ivan is no exception, but the ideas that absorb him now express the core of the Populist problematic as Dostoevsky saw it. Is it possible to transform the world into a realization of the Christian ideal without a belief in Christ? Ivan's inner conflict is immediately suggested by the ambiguity surrounding his article on the ecclesiastical courts, which had been applauded both by the Church party and the secularists. The issue at stake was whether such courts should be subordinate to the state (and hence secular) authorities, or whether, on the contrary, state courts should ultimately be absorbed by ecclesiastical ones, whose decisions would be made according to the law of Christ. Ivan had presented both extreme positions with equal force, and each party thought it could claim him as an advocate. In reality, his apparent refusal to choose between one or the other already presents the inner conflict that will ultimately lead to his mental breakdown. The dominant features of his personality are indicated in the narrator's speculations about his attitude toward his father: "It must be noted that he did not even attempt to communicate with his father, perhaps from pride, from contempt for him, or perhaps from his cool common sense which told him that from such a father he would get no real assistance" (14: 15). One type of motive stems from his emotions (pride, contempt), the other from his intellect; and although the two coincide here, we shall see him struggling desperately to bring his feelings and his reason into some sort of unity when they later diverge.

It is to Alyosha that, after Feodor Pavlovich, the narrator devotes the most attention, and Dostoevsky endeavors to persuade the reader that, unlike the previous incarnation of his moral ideal in Prince Myshkin, such a figure is not "pathological" or abnormal in any obvious sense. He was not "a fanatic . . . and not even a mystic" (14: 17); on the contrary, he was "a well-grown, red-cheeked, clear-eyed lad of nineteen, radiant with health" (14: 24). He is immediately associated with Christian values by his earliest memory, that of his mother, partially deranged by her suffering at the hands of Feodor Pavlovich, who prays with and for him before the image of the Mother of God. "He remembered one still summer evening, an open window, the slanting rays of the setting sun . . . and on her knees before the image his mother, sobbing hysterically with cries and shrieks, snatching him up in both arms, squeezing him close till it hurt, and . . . holding him out from her embrace to the image with both arms as though to put him under the Mother's protection" (14: 18). Dostoevsky had often spoken of the importance of such childhood recollections for the later development of character; and Alyosha's moral sensibility is thus shaped by the all-forgiving love traditionally associated with the Mother of God in Russian Orthodoxy. "There was something about [Alyosha] which made one feel at once (and it was so all his life afterward) that he did not care to be a judge of others—that he would never take it upon himself to criticize and would never condemn anyone for anything" (ibid.).

The depiction of Alyosha's character and behavior, which the narrator makes no attempt to explain psychologically, conforms closely to the hagiographical pattern; the moral purity of his nature, and the love that he inspires in everyone despite his "eccentricity," are traditional saintly attributes. The forces that move him, which are left deliberately vague so as to suggest a possibly otherworldly inspiration, come from the childhood impressions just mentioned, and from the nature of the religious vocation they have inspired. It is no accident, of course, that his namesake, Saint Aleksey, the Man of God, is mentioned very early in Book 2. Alyosha was thus instinctively religious and instinctively devout. Until his faith is tested later in the book, he has had no doubts about God or immortality, or even about the truth of the miraculous legends connected with the institution of elders (*startsy*), the special class of monks to which Father Zosima belonged. The narrator briefly sketches the revival of this institution in certain Russian monasteries and the opposition it encountered, which anticipates the rivalry between Father Ferapont and Father Zosima. Novices who chose to entrust themselves to an elder voluntarily committed their will entirely to his guidance in "the hope of self-conquest, of self-mastery," and Alyosha had decided to submit himself to Father Zosima in this way. He fully shared the Russian peasantry's adoration of the ideals of holiness and righteousness embodied in the saintly monk, whom he also believed to possess the gift of a spiritual force—the force of Christian love—capable of redeeming the world. The narrator remarks that "the monks used to say that [Father Zosima] was more drawn to those who were more sinful, and the greater the sinner, the more he loved him" (14: 28).

This submission to Father Zosima does not mean, however, that Alyosha is detached from the questions posed by the modern world. Indeed, Dostoevsky brings Alyosha's character into immediate relation with the social-political situation by describing him as "an early lover of humanity," as "a youth of our last epoch" passionately seeking truth and justice and ready to sacrifice himself for these ideals on the spot (14: 17). These phrases unmistakably associate Alyosha with the discontent and moral idealism of the generation of the 1870s; and he is clearly intended, at least in this initial volume, to offer an alternative form of "action" and "sacrifice" to that prevalent among the radical youth. For if Alyosha, we are told, "had decided that God and immortality did not exist, he would at once have become an atheist and Socialist (for Socialism is not merely the labor question or that of the fourth estate, it is the question of atheism in its contemporary incarnation, the question of the Tower of Babel built without God, not to mount to Heaven from earth but to bring down Heaven on earth)" (14: 25). The same ideals and feelings that had led Alyosha to Zosima might have led him to atheism and Socialism since both offer divergent paths leading to the same goal of the transformation of earthly life into a society closer to the Kingdom of God; but the first would be guided by Christ, while the second is deprived of the moral compass that He provides.

It is also in relation to Alyosha that the main theme of the novel—the conflict between reason and faith—receives its first exemplification. When the narrator touches on Alyosha's belief in miracles, he immediately explains that this did not prevent him from being "more of a realist than anyone" (14: 24). Alyosha's "realism" does not counteract his faith because the latter is defined as an inner state or disposition anterior to (or at least independent of) anything external, visible, tangible, empirical. Alyosha's faith thus colors and conditions all his apprehension of the empirical world; it is not the evidence from that world which inspires or discourages faith. An unbeliever "would rather disbelieve his own senses" than admit a miracle; or, if he cannot deny the evidence, he interprets the miracle as a hitherto unknown fact of nature (Father Zosima usually leaves the choice hanging in the air). But if "the realist once believes, then he is bound by his very realism to admit the miraculous also." The doubting Apostle Thomas said he would not believe until he saw the transfigured and resurrected Christ. "Was it the miracle forced him to believe? Most likely not, but he believed solely because he desired to believe and possibly he fully believed in his secret heart even when he said, 'I do not believe until I see'" (14: 24–25). This passage anticipates Alyosha's spiritual crisis caused by the decay of Father Zosima's body, a crisis that is only one instance of Dostoevsky's major theme—that true faith must be detached from anything external, any search for, or reliance on, a confirmation or justification of what should be a pure inner affirmation of the emotive will.

Dostoevsky plays endless variations on this irreconcilable opposition between faith on the one hand, and the empirical and rational on the other—an opposition first dramatized in a brief dialogue between Alyosha and his father. Feodor Pavlovich's jeering words foreshadow Ivan's soaring speculations, and they link the two in more than merely a father-son relation; but what will be noble and elevated in Ivan becomes vulgarly and cheaply cynical in the corrupt old scoundrel. Agreeing to let Alyosha enter the monastery, the half-drunken Feodor Pavlovich explains the reason: "You'll pray for us sinners; we have sinned too much here. I've always been thinking who would pray for me, and whether there's anyone in the world to do it." But this implicit admission of moral awareness and of a faith in an afterlife is immediately canceled by a scoffing inability to imagine the physical paraphernalia of Hell. If there are hooks in Hell that will drag Feodor Pavlovich down, where did they come from? Were they attached to a ceiling? "If there's no ceiling there can be no hooks, and if there are no hooks it all breaks down, which is unlikely again, for then there would be none to drag me down to Hell, and if they don't drag me down what justice is there in the world? *Il faudrait les inventer*, those hooks, on purpose for me alone" (14: 23–24). This is the debased and niggling form of "realism"— a parody of Russian Voltairianism—in which Ivan's "Euclidian understanding" becomes manifest in his father, in Mme Khokhlakova, in Smerdyakov, and, finally, in the hallucinatory devil, whom Ivan will accuse of representing "the nastiest and stupidest" of his blasphemous thoughts and feelings.

5
———

The action of the novel per se begins in Book 2, after the prefatory exposition of Book 1, with the gathering of the Karamazov clan in the monastery to discuss the dispute between Dimitry and his father, presumably on their best behavior in the presence of Father Zosima. No indication has been given earlier that this quarrel involves anything except the question of Dimitry's inheritance from his mother; but both have become inflamed by the alluring temptress Grushenka, and the question of money is now intertwined with the rivalry for her favors. Indeed, all the threads of the main plot and subplots are skillfully exposed as the father and son shout furious insults at each other, which bring to light Dimitry's tortuous relations with his fiancée Katerina Ivanovna, Grushenka's equivocal status as the concubine of the merchant Samsonov, and the assault committed on the hapless Captain Snegiryov by an enraged Dimitry, who had pulled him out of a tavern by his beard before the horrified eyes of his son Ilyusha and the latter's classmates.

This section also serves to bring the reader into the secluded world of the monastery, which Dostoevsky had never depicted before, and to contrast the dignity and serenity of its inhabitants (at least those in the entourage of Father Zosima) with the various types of egoistic self-concern exhibited by the secular characters. Feodor Pavlovich plays his role of buffoon to the hilt, often with amusingly inventive erudition, and responds to the implicit contempt that he inwardly fears from his interlocutors with a fireworks of scabrous observations on monastic life and sacrilegious anecdotes aimed to embarrass and discomfit his listeners. Most upset of all, though, is not Father Zosima but the dignified Westerner and liberal Miusov, a distant relative of Dimitry through his mother, whose depiction would undoubtedly have recalled Alexander Herzen to a reader of the time. Miusov finds Feodor Pavlovich's presence intolerable precisely because his scandalous utterances and outrageous behavior do not really differ in essence from Miusov's own enlightened and self-righteous antagonism to "the clericals." Well aware of this distaste, Feodor Pavlovich gleefully persecutes Miusov by displaying his "advanced" and "progressive" ideas in their shoddiest and shabbiest form. The relation between the two is a comically exaggerated version of that between Feodor Pavlovich and Ivan, except that the pompously self-inflated Miusov entirely lacks the dimension of spiritual self-awareness that makes Ivan such a tragically impressive figure. The minor character Maximov, a pitiful and pathetic example of the buffoon type, "doubles" for Feodor Pavlovich in certain scenes; and when, at the end of Book 2, Ivan viciously kicks Maximov out of the carriage, his action dramatizes all the pent-up hatred for this father that Ivan does not allow himself to express directly.

The grouping and succession of chapters is an important part of Dostoevsky's technique of conveying thematic motifs without direct authorial intervention, and we can see it operating quite clearly in Book 2. After "the old buffoon" (the title of Chapter 2) has begun his offensive and sacrilegious antics in the cell of Father Zosima, the narrative shifts to the profoundly moving faith of the peasants assembled to receive the elder's spiritual counsel and blessing. Father Zosima heals a "possessed" woman by touching her with his stole, and the narrator explains the effect of his gesture "by the expectation of the miracle of healing and the implicit belief that it would come to pass; and it did come to pass, though only for a moment" (14: 44). What seems to be a miracle thus can occur if faith is strong enough to believe it will happen; it is the belief that accomplishes the miracle, not the presumably wonder-working power of the priestly garment.

The second episode, one of the most poignant in the book, is linked with the recent death of Dostoevsky's three-year-old son. A peasant woman grieves for the death of her own three-year-old named Aleksey, the last of her four children. At first, Father Zosima attempts to comfort her with the thought that her dead child would, according to widespread belief, be among the angels in Heaven and closest to God; but this conventional consolation offers no relief. The grieving mother has heard the same words from her husband, and they provided no real solace. The image of her vanished little boy, whose voice and pattering footsteps she wishes to hear for one last time, continues to fill her with unappeasable grief. Father Zosima then advises his suppliant, in some of the words that Father Ambrose of Optina Pustyn asked Dostoevsky to convey to Anna Grigoryevna: "Be not comforted. Consolation is not what you need. Weep and be not consoled." But still remember "that your little son is one of the angels of God." Her grief will never vanish and she will continue to weep: "But [your weeping] will turn in the end into a quiet joy, and your bitter tears will be only tears of tender sorrow that purifies the heart and delivers it from sin" (14: 46). He advises her to return home and comfort her husband, who has taken to drink, and to turn her love toward him while always remembering that her little boy "is living, for the soul lives forever, and though he is not in the house, he is near you, unseen" (14: 47). Father Zosima's words about grief turning into quiet joy will soon be parodied by Ivan in a totally different situation; and the suffering of innocent children in God's world will provide the main reason for his rejection of the "entrance ticket" to an "eternal harmony" in which such suffering would be forgiven.

The "glowing eyes" of another peasant woman attract Father Zosima's attention, and her painfully reluctant words intimate that she probably killed a much older, cruelly sadistic husband, or at least hastened his end when he became ill. The sin, occurring three years earlier, had begun to haunt her. "I am afraid to die," she laments, even though she had already confessed twice and had been admitted to communion. Her torments of conscience plainly foreshadow those of Father Zosima's "mysterious stranger," and later of Ivan and Smerdyakov as well. Father Zosima urges her "to fear nothing" and assures her that "if only your repentance fail not, God will forgive all. . . . Man cannot commit a sin so great as to exhaust the infinite love of God." He repeats the passage from Saint Luke declaring that there is more joy in Heaven over one repentant sinner than over ten righteous men (14: 48).

Another of Father Zosima's petitioners had been advised to pray for her son as if he were dead, on the theory that this would trouble his soul and impel him to write a letter. (Such an idea had actually been suggested to the nanny looking after Dostoevsky's children, and he had warned her against it.) Father Zosima rebukes the woman for having contemplated this "great sin, akin to sorcery," that is, attempting to manipulate the supernatural to obtain a specific, practical end; but he predicts that her son will soon come back or that a letter will arrive. When this occurs a day later, it is considered a "miracle," though its status as such is left ambiguous (14: 47). Finally, there is a "healthy peasant woman" who had walked four miles carrying her baby daughter because she had heard that Father Zosima was ill and she wished to look upon him one last time. After observing Father Zosima ministering to his flock, she cheerfully (but mistakenly) concludes that he is not gravely ill and leaves sixty kopeks to distribute to those poorer than herself. The chapter thus ends on this comforting note of Christian love and solidarity operating among the Russian people on the most mundane level.

This tonality of reverential seriousness is now replaced by amusingly satirical comedy. Father Zosima turns from the suffering peasantry to the spoiled and wealthy Mme Khokhlakova and her crippled daughter Liza, waiting for his attention in a special antechamber of his cell. This giddy and flirtatious lady is Dostoevsky's diverting portrait of an idle and affluent society matron with intellectual pretensions, who swings like a weather vane in response to every fashionable ideological gust. Such a type had previously been depicted, with much sharper satirical strokes, in Yulia von Lembke, the wife of the governor-general in *The Devils*; but Mme Khokhlakova, perhaps because she is in no position to cause any actual harm, is treated with affectionate condescension rather than lashing scorn. The tone is given by Father Zosima's reply when she protests her overflowing "love for humanity" and her occasional dreams of becoming a sister of mercy. "Sometimes, unawares," he observes, "you may do a good deed in reality" (14: 52). The self-indulgent lucubrations of Mme Khokhlakova not only provide an obvious antithesis to the peasants, but the exchange between Zosima and the burbling lady also prefigures one of the book's deepest motifs.

For the chatterings of Mme Khokhlakova anticipate, in a seriocomic version, Ivan Karamazov's doubts and hesitations concerning God and immortality, and Father Zosima's response condenses the essence of what will soon be dramatized much more seriously and powerfully. Mme Khokhlakova has picked up at second hand some of the fashionable atheism of the period, and wonders whether faith does not simply come from terror. What if, she asks with charming illogic, she discovers when she dies that "there's nothing but the burdocks growing on my grave" (as Turgenev had written at the end of *Fathers and Children*)? "How, how," she asks despairingly, "is one to prove it?" To which Father Zosima replies that no proof is possible, but that one could become convinced "by the experience of active love. . . . If you attain to perfect self-forgetfulness in the love of your neighbor, then you will believe without doubts and no doubt can possibly enter your soul" (14: 52). The difference between such Christian love and a "rational love for humanity," which leaves the emotive roots of egoism untouched, is stressed in Father Zosima's story of the doctor who confessed—as Ivan will do very soon—that "the more I detest men individually, the more ardent becomes my love for humanity" (14: 53).

<hr />

6

<hr />

No other novelist can rival Dostoevsky's ability to develop his themes, and reveal the moral-psychological sensibility of his characters, through discussions of seemingly abstract ideas. His mastery in this domain is illustrated when Father Zosima returns to the fractious Karamazov assemblage gathered in his cell. An important place is given here to the discussion arising out of Ivan's article on Church jurisdiction, which enlarges on the hints already given about his character. Ivan had argued that the Christian Church should aspire to transform and absorb the State into itself, and should not be satisfied with a limited area of power; but this does not mean that the Church should assume the prerogatives of a state. Roman Catholicism, according to Slavophil theology, had betrayed Christianity a thousand years ago when it became a pagan empire under Constantine, claiming temporal power over humanity. Rather, the law of Christian love that rules in the Church should penetrate every area of secular and social existence, and the principles governing the relations among people would then be based, not on external force and constraint, but on the free and voluntary operation of the Christian moral conscience. Such a world would truly be the establishment of the Kingdom of God on earth, the total triumph of religious faith over secular reason; and Ivan's eloquent exposition of this goal indicates how deeply he responds to this Christian ideal in its loftiest form.

When Father Zosima joins this discussion in support of Ivan's apocalyptic vision of such a future, the elder remarks with a smile that although "Christian society now is not ready" for such a transformation, "it will continue still unshaken in its expectation" because the kingdom will surely come, "even though at the end of the ages"—which yet may be closer at hand than anyone anticipates. "So it will be! So it will be!" he proclaims (14: 61). The Europeanized liberal Miusov interjects that such a vision was even "beyond the dreams of Pope Gregory VII" (who claimed secular authority over earthly kingdoms in the eleventh century), but the learned Father Paissy rebukes him for confusing the Russian Orthodox ideal with that of Catholicism. The claim of Pope Gregory "is the third temptation of the devil," he declares severely, anticipating Ivan's poem of the Grand Inquisitor (14: 62). And when Miusov, in what may appear an irrelevant anecdote, relates his story of the French police official who told him that "the Socialist who is a Christian is more to be dreaded than a Socialist who is an atheist," Father Paissy asks him bluntly whether "you apply [such words] to us, and look upon us as Socialists" (ibid.). No answer is given because Dimitry then suddenly appears; but Dostoevsky once again, as with Alyosha, wishes to bring Christianity and Socialism into juxtaposition as alternate paths to the same goal of applying Christian ideals to earthly society.

Ivan's emotive receptivity to this Orthodox-Slavophil Christian ideal is only one aspect of his character; another—equally absolute, rigorous, and uncompromising—is exhibited by the conversation on which Miusov maliciously reports. Ivan had publicly declared that the Christian law of love could not be detached from the Christian faith, and that, without a belief in God and immortality, "the moral law of nature must immediately be changed into the exact contrary of the former religious law, and that egoism, even extending unto crime, must become not only lawful but recognized as the inevitable, the most rational, even honorable outcome of [this] position" (14: 64–65). Only Christian faith supports the application of the law of love in the world; otherwise, there is nothing to oppose selfishness and the depredations of vainglory. Ivan refuses to stop at any halfway house here, anymore than he had done on the issue of Church and State; and his own inner conflict is mirrored

by the absolute incompatibility between these alternatives. His rationalism prevents him from believing in Christ and immortality, but his
moral sensibility will make it impossible for him to accept the terrible
consequences that logically flow from such a lack of faith.

Father Zosima, the experienced reader of souls, straightway sees
through to the anguish of Ivan's spiritual condition; and the dialogue
between them highlights both the genuineness and the agonizing uncertainty of Ivan's plight. When Zosima accuses him of believing neither
in immortality nor in what he had written in defense of the supremacy
of the Church, Ivan acknowledges the accusation of dilettantism. But,
jolted out of his detached security, he adds: "I wasn't altogether joking."
Zosima again pierces to the quick by telling Ivan that he is playing with
the martyrdom of his own indecision and despair. Completely discom-
fited, Ivan fully exposes himself by asking Zosima "strangely, looking at
the elder with [an] inexplicable smile," whether the question of God
"can be answered by him in the affirmative." Father Zosima's response
here may be taken as an expression of Dostoevsky's own attitude toward the whole generation of young Russians whom Ivan was meant to
represent:

> If it can't be decided in the affirmative, it will never be decided in
> the negative. You know that is the peculiarity of your heart, and all
> its suffering is due to it. But thank the Creator who has given you a
> lofty heart capable of such suffering, "of thinking and seeking
> higher things, for our dwelling is in the heavens." God grant that
> your heart will attain the answer on earth, and may God bless your
> path.

Ivan had only bowed formally to Zosima on first entering his cell; now
he goes to the elder to receive his blessing and reverently kisses his
hand (14: 65–66).

The presentation of Dimitry in Book 2 is much less directly revelatory,
but the outlines of his character come through quite clearly nonetheless. His physical description already indicates his future oscillations:
"His rather large, prominent dark eyes had an expression of firm determination, and yet there was a vague look in them, too . . . his eyes
somehow did not follow his mood, but betrayed something else, sometimes quite incongruous with what was passing" (14: 63). These details
suggest the instability of his temperament, which, on the level of social
behavior, corresponds to Ivan's religious-philosophical fluctuations.
"People who saw something pensive and sullen in his eyes," we are told,
"were startled by his sudden laugh, which bore witness to mirthful and
lighthearted thoughts at the very same time when his eyes were
gloomy" (ibid.). For all his rowdiness and dissipation, there is a longing

in Dimitry for "seemliness," already suggested in Book 1 by the narrator's observation that Dimitry had agreed to the family gathering in Father Zosima's cell because "he secretly blamed himself for his outbursts of temper with his father on several occasions" (14: 30). He is the only "educated" character who kisses Father Zosima's hand as a matter of course, and he is capable, even in the midst of the furious altercation with his father, of sincerely acknowledging guilt. "Father, I don't justify my action," he says of his assault on Captain Snegiryov. "Yes, I confess it publicly, I behaved like a brute to the captain, and I regret it now, and I'm disgusted with myself for that brutal rage" (14: 67). Whipped up, however, by his father's falsely pathetic taunts and reproaches about Katerina Ivanovna and Grushenka, Dimitry's rage becomes uncontrollable. "Tell me," he thunders to the assembled audience, "can [Feodor Pavlovich] be allowed to go on defiling the earth?" (14: 69). It is immediately after this suggestion of parricide that Father Zosima—having noted both the terrible violence of Dimitry's nature and his occasional displays of conscience—bows down at his feet.

Alyosha is scarcely developed at all in this section and, after the opening pages, remains in the background until a later stage in the book. As Robin Feuer Miller has remarked, he functions more or less as what Henry James called a *ficelle*, that is, a string tying together the action of the other characters as he goes from one to the other.[5] All the same, we learn here about his blossoming tenderness for Liza Khokhlakova, whom he had known as a child, and it is here too that he receives the command of Father Zosima to quit the monastery after the Father's demise and serve the cause of truth in the world. Both of these motifs probably point toward the second volume of the work, and for this reason are left relatively undeveloped. The crippled Liza is a character who recalls Ippolit Terentyev in *The Idiot*; like him, she combines a youthfully touching innocence and precocity with an egoistic ferocity nurtured by illness (Ippolit was dying from tuberculosis). Both may be seen as instances of the pathetic-demonic, though Liza is far and away the most pathological specimen of this type that Dostoevsky ever created. He uses her as an example of the emotional perversity engendered even in the pure and unsophisticated by a life of total self-indulgence and an atmosphere of moral emptiness and futility.

These chapters are thematically rounded out by the one devoted to Alyosha and his negative counterpart, the envious and self-serving Rakitin, a young novice in the monastery who has secretly and painlessly converted to atheism, science, and positivism. Rakitin is "a young man bent on a career," ready to sell his soul—in which he does not believe—for material success and social advancement (14: 71). If Ivan represents the aspect of Populist youth that Dostoevsky saw as genuinely inspired by Christian ideals, Rakitin indicates how easily these ideals, when divorced from even a modicum of feeling for their original source, can be converted into a mask for meanness and mendacity. Rakitin is a total cynic, who believes that Father Zosima's bow to Dimitry was "only the usual holy mummery." Dimitry's rage and explosive temperament had shown him that a murder was very likely in the offing, and so the Father had "tapped the ground to be ready for what turned up" and to furbish his reputation as a prophet (14: 73). Rakitin also provides a coolly disillusioned analysis of the Karamazov family situation that helps to clarify the plot action, especially the situation between Ivan and Katerina Ivanovna. It includes as well a denunciation of Ivan's "stupid theory" that "if there's no immortality of the soul, then there's no virtue and everything is lawful" (14: 76).

Setting himself up as Ivan's intellectual opponent, Rakitin declares that "humanity will find in itself the power to live for virtue even without believing in immortality. It will find it in love for freedom, for equality, for fraternity." But Rakitin is incapable of imagining that anyone can truly "live for virtue" or act except from the most shamelessly selfish motives (ibid.). Ivan predicts the path that Rakitin will follow to success as the owner of a journal "on the liberal and atheistic side, with a Socialistic tinge, with a tiny gloss of Socialism," and with "a great house in Petersburg" whose upper stories would be let to lodgers (14: 77). Such words may well indicate a plausible schema for the development of Rakitin in the anticipated second volume. Here, however, Dostoevsky uses Rakitin's disabused perspective as a foil to contrast the gross and vulgar materialism of his "progressive" point of view with the actual human and moral complexity of the situation in which his characters have become embroiled.

## CHAPTER 32

# The Brothers Karamazov:
# Books 3–4

With the end of Book 2, Dostoevsky has completed his introduction, brought the reader into contact with all the major characters except Smerdyakov, and begun all the plot actions that will interweave in the remainder of the text. The next two books consist externally of a round of visits that Alyosha makes to various personages. This device allows Dostoevsky to develop more fully such characters as Grushenka, Katerina Ivanovna, and Captain Snegiryov, who have been seen so far only in the distorted and partial images provided by the furious exchanges between Dimitry and his father. Also, by using Alyosha as the pivot of these sections, Dostoevsky frames the multiplicity of events, with their abundant displays of human folly, passion, and suffering, within the overarching shadow of the monastery and the impending death of Father Zosima.

## 2

Before this sequence of scenes, however, we are briefly introduced to the history of Smerdyakov, who may, according to widespread rumor in the community, be the illegitimate son of Feodor Pavlovich. His mother was a village idiot, "stinking Lizaveta," who roamed though the town as a sort of "holy fool" and was always treated very kindly in accordance with Russian religious tradition. She gave birth to Smerdyakov in the garden of the Karamazov dwelling, into which she had climbed that night, and her choice of this locale was taken as an indirect suggestion of Feodor Pavlovich's paternity. (When Feodor Pavlovich boasts to Alyosha that "I never thought a woman ugly in my life—that's my rule," he seems to make an implicit admission [14: 125].) In any case, as the narrator comments, "How, in her condition, she managed to climb over the high, strong fence remained a mystery. Some maintained that she must have been 'lifted over' by somebody, others hinted at something more uncanny" (14: 92).

This question of how Lizaveta climbed over the fence is referred to twice in the crucial scene on the night of the murder; and although it is

17. A page from the manuscript of *The Brothers Karamazov*

shrugged off by the narrator, who prefers a simple explanation ("Liza-veta [was] accustomed to clambering over hurdles to sleep in gardens"), the suggestion of an "uncanny" dimension nonetheless imparts a symbolic overtone to this detail. (It so struck Marcel Proust that he read the whole book as a classic revenge tragedy of crime, vengeance, and expiation. The murder of Feodor Pavlovich was a punishment for having violated a sacred innocent, a revenge inflicted by the illegitimate son who was the fruit of this transgression; and it was then expiated by the suffering of the innocent Dimitry.[1]) In addition to these passages about Smerdyakov, we are also informed about the old man's living arrangements, described as if in passing. But Dostoevsky rarely introduces naturalistic detail simply for its own sake, and here the topography of the Karamazov dwelling is explored because it will later play an important part in Dimitry's trial.

Moreover, this description accompanies the presentation of Feodor Pavlovich's relation with his faithful servant Grigory; and this attachment offers the first dramatic analogue for the central thematic conflict between reason and faith. Dostoevsky's aim is to suggest the moral-psychological difficulty of a totally amoral reason to sustain itself, not

589

only on the level of Ivan's sophisticated ratiocinations, but even on the lowest and most primitive plane of the subconscious psyche. "Corrupt and often cruel in his lust, like some noxious insect, Feodor Pavlovich was sometimes, in moments of drunkenness, overcome by superstitious terror and a moral convulsion which almost, so to speak, physically shook his soul." In such moments, "he could not have explained the extraordinary craving for someone faithful and devoted, which sometimes unaccountably came upon him all in a moment" (14: 86). For succor at such instants he turned to Grigory, stubborn and taciturn, intensely religious in a fanatic and semiliterate peasant fashion, slavishly faithful to his master while deeply disapproving of his outrageous violations of the laws of God and man. The mere presence of Grigory, whom Feodor Pavlovich sometimes woke at night on the most trivial of pretexts and called to his room, was enough to quiet his fears. The pacifying effect of Grigory's sullen solicitude is compared with that of Alyosha on his father, and this similarity indicates its Christian significance. The old scoundrel, relying on the solace of Grigory's presence, makes an irrational leap of faith in his loyalty and devotion. The relation between the two mimics, in a semiparodistic fashion, the challenge that all the characters are called upon to confront.

### 3

These chapters on Smerdyakov's dubious origins are followed by Alyosha's accidental encounter with his brother Dimitry, who has been lurking in the back gardens near his father's house to waylay Grushenka if she were to try and slip in there at night. And this meeting is the occasion for Dimitry's "Confession of a Passionate Heart"—three memorable chapters of feverish monologue, stimulated partly by cognac and partly by the excitement of Dimitry's decision to break with Katerina Ivanovna once and for all. Here Dimitry suddenly reveals an unexpected depth and impressiveness; the rowdy young officer and boisterous brawler metamorphoses into a figure of a new dimension, whose every word vibrates with turbulent and impassioned poetry. It is this type of transformation that accounts for the already-mentioned sudden enlargement of stature in the main figures.

Dimitry has so far been seen as a character who combines an unbridled, tempestuous nature and dissolute life with a lurking sense of guilt at having given free rein to his sensuality and his uncontrollable rages. Dostoevsky now poetically elevates both these sides of his personality to a mythical stature. The snatches of poetry that he quotes from Nekrasov, Goethe, and Schiller interweave with his feverish narrative and constantly expand and amplify its range. The irresistible drive of his passions, as well as the deep disgust at his own degradation, now rise above the purely private and the personal; they become the struggle of humankind from the earliest ages to sublimate and purify its animal lusts and instincts. Dimitry sees himself in the guise of "the naked troglodyte" of Schiller's "Das eleusische Fest" ("The Eleusinian Festival"), who appears, in the eyes of the Olympian goddess Ceres, as living in a state of hideous savagery:

> From the fields and from the vineyards
> Came no fruit to deck the feasts,
> Only flesh of blood-stained victims
> Smoldered in the altar-fires,
> And wher'er the grieving goddess
> Turns her melancholy gaze,
> Sunk in vilest degradation
> Man his loathsomeness displays. (14: 98)

The forces at work in Dimitry are those of natural man, who can all too easily become a slave to his instincts and his passions. But Dimitry has an obscure sense of nature as God's handiwork, which cannot be totally evil and unredeemable, and he feels in his own uncontrollable exuberance some of the overflowing joy that Schiller called "the soul of all creation." Dimitry is incapable of curbing and suppressing the elemental sensuality that makes him what he is. Unlike his shameless father, however, who glories in his depravity, Dimitry longs for some alteration *within* his own nature that will enable him to attain self-respect. His longing and his dilemma are summed up by Schiller again:

> Would he purge his soul from vileness
> And attain to light and worth,
> He must turn and cling forever
> To his ancient mother Earth.

"But the difficulty is," Dimitry exclaims piteously, "how am I to cling forever to Mother Earth. I don't kiss her. I don't cleave to her bosom. . . . I go on and I don't know whether I'm going to shame or to light and joy." Varying the imagery as the passage continues, and turning from Schiller's Hellenism to Christianity and the Bible, Dimitry rises to heights of inspired eloquence in the famous and much-quoted passage on humankind's disquieting capacity to harbor both the ideal of the Madonna and the ideal of Sodom in its breast. "Beauty is a terrible thing. . . . Here all the boundaries meet and all contradictions exist side by side. . . . The awful thing is that beauty is mysterious as well as terrible. God and the devil are fighting there and the battlefield is the heart of man" (14: 100).

It is against this vast cultural-historical background, and the eternal struggle of humankind with the contradictions of its own nature, that the story of Dimitry's involvement with Katerina Ivanovna unfolds. Only when he is seen as this sort of Antaeus, irrevocably bound to the earth, can the calamity of their engagement be rightly understood. Dimitry had set out to seduce Katerina solely out of pique and wounded vanity at her contemptuous indifference, not because she appealed to his senses. The very means he chose to bend her to his will, offering to save her father from disgrace as the price of her surrender, was a profound insult; his refusal to take advantage of her when she complied was an even deadlier blow to her pride and gave him the psychological advantage in their relations. Katerina's only weapon in this struggle of wills was a magnanimity that, in constantly reminding Dimitry of his moral inferiority, would allow her to maintain the upper hand. Life has thus become intolerable for Dimitry under the burden of Katerina's "gratitude," which at the same time deprives him of any cause for grievance. The sensuous and tantalizing Grushenka appeals not to his pride or vanity but to his most deeply rooted passions; and for the moment, he thinks of this fatal infatuation only as a return to the degradation from which he had been trying to escape.

4

Attention then shifts to Smerdyakov in the next four chapters, which focus on this haunting and enigmatic character who inspires pity and repulsion at the same time. Twenty years earlier, in *The Village of Stepanchikovo*, Dostoevsky had sketched the outline of a similar type, a peasant valet laboriously trying to ape the Frenchified elegance and polish of the upper class. At that time, this type was primarily comic, but it now takes on more complicated overtones. There is something ludicrous about Smerdyakov's affectation of a pseudo gentility, but the effect he conveys is more sinister and menacing as well. Among Dostoevsky's notes, we find a citation in French from Hugo's *Ruy Blas*: "*L'âme d'un conspirateur et l'âme d'un laquais* [the soul of a conspirator, and the soul of a lackey]" (15: 205). Although this description is not attached to any character, it fits the cold, somber, and outwardly servile Smerdyakov to the life.

Smerdyakov is depicted as someone who had been mean, sadistic, and blasphemously scornful of religion even in childhood, someone completely devoid of any natural feeling of gratitude or obligation. These personal traits are ideologically transposed in the discussion that he carries on with Feodor Pavlovich, Ivan, and Grigory. Here he is revealed as another of the "rationalists" like Feodor Pavlovich who people the book; and like the latter's obscene jests and scoffing sacrileges, Smerdyakov's "rationalism" is another caricature, in the form of crafty logical sophistry, of Ivan's tortured moral ratiocinations. Debating the heroism of Foma Danilov, the Russian soldier who had been tortured and put to death by Muslim enemies for refusing to renounce his Christian faith, Smerdyakov argues that the heroic martyr had really been a fool. The mere thought of renouncing Christianity to save his life would have immediately separated him from God and Christ, and he would thus not have committed any sin as a Christian. Weakness of faith is in any case the most ordinary and venial kind of sin, because nobody any longer can command nature to perform such miracles as moving mountains—except perhaps, as he concedes, much to the delight of Feodor Pavlovich, one or two hermits in the desert. And do not the Scriptures, Smerdyakov asks triumphantly, promise such powers to *all* those who have faith?

Such arguments are those of a petty and calculating nature, which seeks to rationalize and justify its own inclinations for treachery and betrayal, and uses "reason" to undermine and dissolve any firm moral commitment. At the same time, though, Smerdyakov is enough of a Russian peasant to believe in the wonder-working powers of one or two hermits in the desert. The importance of this point is stressed when Feodor Pavlovich asks Alyosha, "That's the Russian faith all over, isn't it?" and Alyosha agrees, "that's purely Russian" (14: 120–121). Smerdyakov's casuistry cannot entirely destroy his belief in the sanctity of those two hermits.

His function in the book is to serve as Ivan's alter ego in the same fashion as Svidrigailov had done for Raskolnikov; he carries Ivan's theories to their logical and repugnant extreme, and exhibits their distorted and dangerous refraction in a more uncouth and less high-minded nature. But Smerdyakov is also meant to convey more than mere thematic extrapolation. For he is a definite and well-marked social type—the peasant who has been uprooted from his community and his group values, who has acquired a smattering of urban culture and manners, and who feels immeasurably superior to his benighted fellow peasants and resentful at his inferior social status. It is among such peasants, Dostoevsky is suggesting, that the destruction of the Christian faith by the "rationalism" of the Ivans is most likely to be greeted with awe and admiration and to have the most explosive consequences.

Indeed, he evokes such possibilities in Aesopian imagery when his fictional narrator compares Smerdyakov with a type of peasant "contemplative" depicted in a painting by I. N. Kramskoy. "There is a forest in winter, and on a roadway through the forest, in absolute solitude, stands a wandering peasant in a torn caftan and bark shoes." He is not thinking but brooding inwardly, "contemplating." If asked about what was passing through his mind, he would not be able to reply; but "probably he had hidden within himself the impression which had dominated him during the period of contemplation." And then he "may suddenly . . . abandon everything and go off to Jerusalem on a pilgrimage for his soul's salvation, or perhaps he will suddenly set fire to his native village, and perhaps do both" (another instance of the "broad" Russian nature) (14: 116–117).

Every contemporary reader would know that such a "contemplative" contained a threat of revolution, or at least of a *jacquerie*; and this suggestion is reinforced a few pages later in the conversation about Smerdyakov between Feodor Pavlovich and Ivan. Noting that the lackey is enthralled by Ivan, his father asks: "What have you done to fascinate him?" Ivan answers, "Nothing whatever," but then adds: "He's a lackey and a mean soul. A prime candidate, however, when the time comes."* From the context, it is understood that this means "a prime candidate" for some sort of uprising, though Ivan also adds: "There will be others and better ones. . . . His kind comes first, and better ones after." But it is also possible, he continues, that "the rocket will go off and fizzle out, perhaps. The peasants are not very fond of listening to these soup makers, so far" (14: 22). (Smerdyakov had been sent to Petersburg to learn cooking, and his specialty was soup.) Elsewhere, Ivan directly calls Smerdyakov "raw material for revolution"; and the relation between them thus contains a distinct social-political subtext.

Just as Smerdyakov, in ridiculing Danilov, is shown as advocating a betrayal of moral principle, so we see Ivan in the next scene also justifying such a betrayal, though with much less complacency. The discussion with Smerdyakov ends when Dimitry, frantically in search of Grushenka and believing her with his father, suddenly invades the room in which the three have been talking. Flinging his father to the floor, he "kick[s] him two or three times with his heel in the face." Ivan wrestles Dimitry away, helped by Alyosha, and later remarks that "if I hadn't pulled him away, perhaps he'd have murdered him." This leads Alyosha to exclaim: "God forbid!" To which Ivan replies, "with a malignant grimace: 'One viper will devour the other. And serves both of them right, too.'" As the conversation continues, Ivan declares that, although he would always act as he had just done to defend the father he hates, "in

* The "prime candidate" here (Garnett-Matlaw translation) renders *peredovoe miaso* in the Russian text, which Victor Terras translates literally as "progressive flesh" in his indispensable, almost line-by-line commentary on *The Brothers Karamazov*. Terras also offers "cannonfodder of progress" as an alternative. Pevear and Volkhonsky translate the phrase as "prime cannon fodder." The adjective *peredovoe* (progressive) is what gives the phrase a specific social-political meaning. See Victor Terras, *A Karamazov Companion* (Madison, 1984), 181.

my wishes I reserve myself full latitude in this case" (14: 128, 129, 132). He instinctively behaved according to the accepted moral code, but nothing in his thoughts ("wishes") would cause him to oppose such a murder; his moral sensibility and his convictions are thus totally at odds. This scission in his personality will deepen and intensify as the book proceeds, and his statement about "the vipers" will come back to haunt him.

5

The figures of Katerina Ivanovna and Grushenka are developed in the next chapter, and the scene between them in some respects echoes Katerina's relations with Dimitry. Just as with him, she tries to gain control over Grushenka with her condescending "magnanimity." Katerina believes she has impressed and won over Grushenka by her patronizing acceptance and superior sympathy, but then she is herself humiliated in the presence of Alyosha by Grushenka's refusal to be dominated. Grushenka's turning of the tables nakedly reveals the egoistic roots of Katerina's "kindness" and "generosity"; these are merely the means she uses to attain moral-psychological mastery over others. As for Grushenka, her sexual seductiveness is very strongly stressed, and even Alyosha is subliminally affected by the suggestiveness of her walk—"that softness, that voluptuousness of her bodily movements, that catlike noiselessness" (14: 136). We see her character here as willful, capricious, treacherous, and defiantly independent; so far she seems nothing but a headstrong temptress, though we learn through Katerina about Grushenka's earlier history of betrayal by the Polish officer. It is only later that she will appear in a different and more sympathetic light.

The scene between the two women is followed by the sudden and unexpected encounter, at the end of Book 3, between Dimitry and Alyosha, when the former suddenly appears in the darkness as Alyosha is returning to the monastery. During their conversation about Katerina and Grushenka, in which Dimitry denounces himself as "a thorough scoundrel" because of his treatment of the former, there is a passage of great importance for the plot action—but one that Dostoevsky deliberately leaves imprecise. Dimitry asks Alyosha to "look at me well" and then declares: "You see here, here, there's a terrible disgrace in store for me." And as he spoke, "Dimitry Feodorovich struck his chest with his fist with a strange air, as though the dishonor lay precisely on his chest, in some spot, in a pocket perhaps, or hanging around his neck" (14: 143–144). Dimitry in fact does have something hanging around his neck, a small pouch in which he has placed half the money given him by Katerina, supposedly to mail to relatives; the other half has been squandered on attempting to seduce Grushenka. And this gesture, which Alyosha will recall suddenly at the trial, is the sole shred of "evidence," entirely hearsay, against the charge that Dimitry had obtained a large sum of money suddenly by murdering and robbing his father.

In Book 4, Dostoevsky keeps the spotlight focused on Katerina Ivanovna and devotes another chapter to her—"Laceration in the Drawing-Room"—in which Ivan, who had been deeply infatuated with her in the past, breaks with Katerina as decisively as Dimitry had done a bit earlier. The supremely intelligent Ivan analyzes her behavior with exemplary acuity, and explains why she is incapable of any but a "lacerated" love. "You need [Dimitry] so as to contemplate continually your heroic fidelity and to reproach him for infidelity. And it all comes from your pride. Oh, there's a great deal of humiliation and self-abasement about it, but it all comes from pride" (14: 175). Ivan's peroration here has unquestionably been sharpened by the intensity of his own frustrated passion; but his insight also springs from a deeper and more thematically relevant source. It is not simply that Ivan and Katerina resemble each other in education, taste, and sensibility, and that, as Mme Khokhlakova keeps insisting, it would be much more suitable for Katerina to be Ivan's bride than Dimitry's. More profoundly, the character traits of both are fundamentally the same: Ivan has only to look into himself to understand the motives of his tormentress.

The parallels between the two, indeed, are an excellent example of Dostoevsky's carefully wrought thematic texture. All the attitudes exhibited by Katerina vis-à-vis the other characters are the exact replica, on the moral-psychological level, of Ivan's ideological dilemma. Katerina thus expands and rounds out the human qualities of Ivan's character, presented mainly in the transposed form of theological argument and poetic symbol. Ivan's intellectual arrogance and spiritual egoism will prevent him from surrendering to the mystery of faith and the reality of God's love; and Katerina's inability to love anyone but herself exhibits the same qualities in terms that are social and personal. Just as Katerina needs Dimitry's betrayals to reinforce her own virtue, so Ivan tortures himself with the horrors of the sufferings of the innocent to nourish the pride of his own rejection of God's world and its inhabitants. Katerina's distant and detached charity toward the Snegiryovs—she enlists Alyosha as her agent, and visits their hovel only at the very end of the book—may be taken as a foretaste of Ivan's approval of the compassionate program of the Grand Inquisitor to aid a weak and erring humanity. Moreover, when Katerina hysterically cries in a frenzy, "I will be a god to whom [Dimitry] can pray" (14: 172), she reveals the deepest symbolic meaning of Ivan's Legend.

One should also note in relation to Katerina, the inversion of Father

Zosima's advice to the peasant woman who had lost her little boy. He had told her to grieve and not be consoled, that her grief "will turn in the end into a quiet joy . . . that purifies the heart and delivers it from sin." When Katerina declares that she will devote her entire life to Dimitry and thus sacrifice herself despite his rejection, Ivan predicts that "your life, Katerina Ivanovna, will henceforth be spent in painful brooding over your own feelings, your own heroism, and your own suffering, but in the end that suffering will be softened and will pass into sweet contemplation of the fulfillment of a proud and personal design" (14: 173). Unlike the heartsick grief of the peasant mother, who returns home to comfort her despairing husband, Katerina's "painful brooding" will only serve to reinforce and strengthen the rampant egoism concealed under the elegant surface of her civilized manners.

## 6

Two other thematic motifs in Book 4 also require some comment. One is the chapter devoted to the fanatical old ascetic Father Ferapont, which forms part of a bridge sequence linking Books 3 and 4. Alyosha returns to the monastery in the last chapter of Book 3 and, before setting out again in the second chapter of Book 4, visits the dying Father Zosima. This chapter allows Dostoevsky to frame the action of these two books within the moral perspective provided by the impending death of the saintly monk and also to direct attention to Zosima's enemy, Father Ferapont. Various passing references had been made earlier to the opposition against Zosima and against the whole institution of elders. Indeed, the cunning Feodor Pavlovich had mouthed some of these arguments during the paroxysm of the scandal scene in the quarters of the Father Superior. Dostoevsky's depiction of this internecine monastic conflict was based both on the enmity encountered by Saint Tikhon in his lifetime and on contemporary tensions within Russian monastic life, which he used for his own purposes.

One such purpose was to guard against the accusation of advocating a backward and obscurantist position by portraying a Russian monk not only as the major positive figure among all his characters but presumably as an inspiration for all of Russian life. Father Ferapont's unbalanced fanaticism allowed Dostoevsky to dissociate himself from the harsher and more repellent forms of Russian asceticism, and to stress, on the contrary, the humane and enlightened features of Zosima's Christianity, which did not fear to open itself to the influences of the modern world. Dostoevsky prepares the way for Ferapont's appearance by emphasizing the all-embracing nature of Zosima's Christian love, which will form such a sharp contrast, a page or two later, with

Ferapont's half-crazed insistence on rigidly dogmatic observances. "Hate not those who reject you," Alyosha quotes Zosima as saying, "who insult you, who abuse and slander you. Hate not the atheists, the teachers of evil, the materialists—and I mean not only the good ones— for there are many good ones among them, especially in our day—hate not even the wicked ones" (14: 149). This acknowledgment that atheists and materialists could also be "good," and "especially in our day," was certainly intended for the Populist-influenced readers whom Dostoevsky sought to win over.

Ferapont, however, is much more than a caricatural figure intended to bring Zosima's virtues into higher relief; he also takes on a symbolic importance as part of the great theme of reason and faith. For the ascetic and visionary Ferapont, in his own fashion, is also a literalist of the supernatural like Feodor Pavlovich. There is a concealed "rationalism" in his reduction of spiritual life to the observance of external rules about fasting and in the naïvely materialistic fashion in which, concretizing the mysteries of faith, he claims to see devils with his own eyes and to have killed one by catching its tail in a door. For both the cynically Voltairian Feodor Pavlovich and the superstitiously pious Father Ferapont, religious faith depends on such physical evidence of its reality; and they are thus thematically united in this manner despite their evident divergences otherwise. Nor should one overlook Father Ferapont's fierce pride—he is convinced that Christ will come to carry him away like the Prophet Elijah—a claim that again is counterpointed against Zosima's profound meekness and humility. The treatment of Father Ferapont illustrates the subtlety and delicacy of Dostoevsky's handling of his theme of faith and the profundity of his intuition, rivaling that of Kierkegaard, of its total irrationality and subjectivity.

## 7

Two chapters of Book 4 are devoted to the Snegiryovs, a family that, after the disappearance of the monastery world from the novel upon the death of Father Zosima, will provide Dostoevsky with his major contrast to the world of the Karamazovs. The Snegiryov family is familiar to all readers of Dostoevsky. They are the equivalent of the Marmeladovs in *Crime and Punishment* and of all the insulted and injured he had depicted since the beginning of his literary career. In this case, the Snegiryovs are carefully conceived to counterbalance the self-destructive hatreds of the "accidental" Karamazov family. Captain Snegiryov is a buffoon type like Feodor Pavlovich, but one whose masochistic ironies conceal a deeply wounded sensibility that has not turned resentful or revengeful. Far from having neglected his family, the cashiered captain has done his best, under impossible conditions, to provide them with both love and care. His little son Ilyusha, who bites Alyosha's finger to revenge his father's public humiliation by Dimitry, also sturdily defends his father against the insults of his jeering classmates; and even Ilyusha's sister Varvara—a "progressive" student with "rational" ideas, home from her Petersburg studies—sacrifices herself unselfishly, if resentfully, to care for her hapless kinfolk. The captain's beautiful monologue about Ilyusha's unhappiness over his father's degradation and about the son's schoolboyish dreams of revenge and escape ranks high among other touching and moving "philanthropic" passages from Dostoevsky's pen.

All the same, it seems a bit excessive to have saddled the luckless captain not only with a crippled wife, who is mentally in her second childhood, but also with a hunchback, crippled daughter. The latter, who bears her painful suffering uncomplainingly and with heroic self-abnegation (Dostoevsky was perhaps thinking here of his friend Elena Shtakenshneider), is clearly the obverse of the similarly crippled but spoiled and ferociously egotistical Liza Khokhlakova. The mentally deficient mother may have been meant as an oblique comment on the scarcely less absurd vagaries and caprices of Mme Khokhlakova. He wisely leaves these two in the background, however, and concentrates on the adolescent Ilyusha, who will later, along with his classmates, allow Dostoevsky to fulfill his long-cherished desire to depict the relation between a charismatic Christian figure and a group of children. The scene in which Alyosha visits the miserable hovel of the Snegiryovs, entitled "Laceration in a Cottage," is placed immediately after Katerina Ivanovna's "Laceration in the Drawing-Room." Dostoevsky obtains the same effect of contrast here as in the shift from Father Zosima and the peasants to Mme Khokhlakova. The laceration in the drawing room is the result of self-will and pride, which perverts suffering into an instrument of domination; the laceration in the cottage, when the captain hysterically tramples on the badly needed money offered by Alyosha, is a pathetic effort to maintain a last, remaining shred of self-respect and to justify Ilyusha's desperate faith in his father's honor and dignity.

By the time he completed Book 4, Dostoevsky had presented all his characters, clearly indicated the future course of the main plot action, and raised his primary ideological issue of reason and faith in a fascinating variety of scenes and characters. In Books 5, 6, and 7, this theme comes to the foreground and is treated directly in some of the greatest pages in the history of the novel.

## CHAPTER 33

# The Brothers Karamazov:
# Book 5

The two set pieces of Book 5, Ivan's "rebellion" and the Legend of the Grand Inquisitor, reach heights that have rarely been equaled, and certainly never surpassed. Indeed, few other novels rise to such ideological altitudes, and in the nineteenth century one can think only perhaps of Balzac's *Seraphita* and *Louis Lambert*, George Sand's *Spiridion*, or possibly Flaubert's *La Tentation de Saint Antoine* (more a prose-poem than a novel). These inspired pages also take their place in a Western literary tradition that begins with Aeschylus's *Prometheus Bound* and the Book of Job (which Dostoevsky will soon invoke through Father Zosima). They also continue the Romantic titanism of the first half of the nineteenth century, represented by such writers as Goethe, Leopardi, Byron, and Shelley. The Czech critic Vaclav Cerny, in a penetrating and too-little-known book, saw Dostoevsky (along with Nietzsche) as the culmination of this Romantic tradition of protest against God on behalf of a suffering humanity.[1]

## 2

Book 5 opens with a touching scene in which Alyosha, having been commanded by Father Zosima to subject himself to the temptations of the world, plights his troth with Liza, who alternates between teasing mockery and tenderly admiring affection. Alyosha also observes the situation of his own family with increasing gloom. "My brothers are destroying themselves," he says, and cites Father Paissy's remark about "the primitive force of the Karamazovs . . . a crude, unbridled earthly force." Even more, he wonders whether "the spirit of God move[s] above that force," which he also feels stirring within himself: "I only know that I, too, am a Karamazov." Such words indicate all the uneasiness and self-doubt he has begun to feel even *before* being subjected to Ivan's "rebellion"—doubts that suddenly come to a head when he blurts out to Liza: "And perhaps I don't even believe in God" (14: 201). The narrator comments that "there was something too mysterious, too subjective in these last words of his, perhaps obscure to himself, but yet torturing him" (ibid.). This unexpected doubt may be linked to the impending death of Father Zosima, which looms over Alyosha and will precipitate his own timid and muted "rebellion."

The focus then shifts to Smerdyakov, flirting with the neighbor's daughter in a parody of the courtship of Alyosha and Liza. While the latter couple intermingle their shy endearments with conversation about the unhappy situation of the Snegiryov family, the second have no thoughts for any but themselves. Smerdyakov serenades his lady-love with a guitar, ludicrously aping a Romantic troubadour, while she— a former lady's maid in an aristocratic household, another peasant corrupted by upper-class European attitudes—imagines with delectation young officers dueling to the death over some coveted beauty. Smerdyakov here is openly and self-consciously anti-Russian, even asserting that "it would have been a good thing if [Napoleon and the French] had conquered us," and he makes no bones about expressing a bitterly smoldering resentment against the disgrace of his birth and inferior status (14: 205). Ivan's denunciatory diatribe, which soon follows, is a much more lofty assimilation of European culture than Smerdyakov's half-baked pretentiousness. But in both instances—whether on the level of the satirically ludicrous, or of the serious and morally elevated—such influence is understood to have poisoned and split the Russian moral psyche.

Formally, the three chapters devoted to Ivan are similar to Dimitry's "Confession of a Passionate Heart." Here too we encounter that sudden vertical expansion of a character which so greatly enlarges his symbolic status and poetic power. To be sure, this change of scale is less unexpected in the intellectual Ivan than in the relatively rough-hewn Dimitry, but it begins by revealing a hitherto unsuspected aspect of Ivan's personality. Just as the passionate and tempestuous Dimitry, who seemed to exist solely on the level of instinct, was shown to have moral-spiritual aspirations, so now the coldly conceptual and distant Ivan is shown to be consumed by the same passionate thirst for life as his older brother. Indeed, as Alyosha tells him affectionately at the beginning of their conversation in the tavern, "You are just as young as other young men of twenty-three . . . you are just a young and fresh nice boy, green in fact!" (14: 209).

Ivan "good-humoredly" confirms Alyosha's judgment and confesses to such a purely instinctive love of life. "It's a feature of the Karamazovs, it's true," he says, "that thirst for life regardless of everything, you have it no doubt too, but why is it base?" Of course it can become so, as in old Feodor Pavlovich or Dimitry's escapades, but it can be a life-sustaining force as well. As Ivan acknowledges, "even if I didn't believe in life, if I lost faith in the order of things, were convinced in fact that everything is a disorderly, damnable and perhaps devil-ridden chaos, if I were struck by every horror of man's disillusionment—still I would want to live, and, having once tasted of the cup, I would not turn away from it till I had drained it" (ibid.). This loss of faith is exactly what torments Ivan, but his primordial love for life is powerful enough to counteract the dispiriting conclusions of his reason: "I have a longing for life, and I go on living in spite of logic."

Enumerating all the endearments that still link him to life, he lists not only nature ("I love the sticky little leaves as they open in spring. I love the blue sky") but also "the precious graveyard" of European civilization, filled with the glories of the past, before which he "shall fall to the ground and kiss those stones and weep over them." Such thoughts and actions may be totally irrational, but "it's not a matter of intellect or logic, it's loving with one's inside, with one's guts." This capacity for an irrational love, whether of nature or the monuments of culture, is the first step toward an understanding of the meaning of life; for such understanding is possible only when the ego is taken beyond itself. To Ivan's question whether we should "love life more than the meaning of it," Alyosha replies: "Certainly, love it regardless of logic as you say, it must be regardless of logic, and it's only then one can understand the meaning of it." But because Ivan's "logic" has already concluded that life has no meaning, he declares that when "I am thirty . . . I shall begin to turn aside from the cup, even if I have not emptied it and then turn away—where, I don't know" (14: 209–210). Such words raise the specter of a suicide out of despair; but the emphasis on Ivan's youthfulness and his "longing for life" hold out the hope of other possibilities.

This friendly encounter of the two brothers, who for the first time come to know each other a little more intimately, is placed in the foreground of Chapter 3; but the shadow of an archetypal murder lurks in the background and has already been suggested. Questioned about Dimitry's whereabouts, Smerdyakov answered "superciliously": "How am I to know. . . . It's not as if I were his keeper." A few pages later, after learning about Ivan's imminent departure, Alyosha anxiously asks about the quarrel between Dimitry and their father: "How will it end?" And Ivan irritably snaps back: "What have I to do with it? Am I my brother Dimitry's keeper?" Then he suddenly smiles "bitterly": "Cain's answer to God about his murdered brother—wasn't it. Perhaps that's what you're thinking at this moment?" (14: 206, 211). Both Ivan and Smerdyakov, who echo each other's thoughts, are thus linked with the murder motif by this biblical reference, which also intimates their subterranean connection.

The conversation between the two brothers continues in a "stinking tavern," Dostoevsky's usual venue for dialogues that explore the furthest moral-philosophical implications of his characters' beliefs and values. The same pattern is maintained here as Ivan challenges, with unexampled vehemence and moral pathos, Alyosha's devotion to Father Zosima's world of all-embracing forgiveness and overflowing, selfless love. The encounter between the two brothers is more complex than before, because such sinister figures as Prince Valkovsky (in *The Insulted and Injured*) and Svidrigailov (in *Crime and Punishment*) had been either totally or largely negative. Ivan, however, is struggling inwardly against his own yearning to accept the very worldview he is attacking with such passion. Indeed, he half admits to himself, "quite like a little gentle child," that he does not "want to corrupt you [Alyosha], or to turn you from your stronghold, perhaps I want to be healed by you." Alyosha "had never seen such a smile on his face before," but this moment of reassuring tenderness is soon swept away (14: 215).

The social-political overtones of the ensuing conversation are immediately suggested by Ivan's remark about the propensity of "Russian boys," when they come together in a tavern, "to talk of nothing but the eternal questions." What they talk about is "the existence of God and immortality. And those who do not believe in God talk of socialism or anarchism, of the transformation of all humanity on a new pattern, so that it all comes to the same, they're the same questions turned inside out" (14: 213). Alyosha and Ivan are shown to share the view that contemporary radicalism is a secularized form of the Christian faith and its morality of love; but the younger brother has chosen to return to the original religious source, while the elder refuses to go beyond its modern avatar. Ivan then introduces his famous distinction between "Euclidian" (earthly) and "non-Euclidian" (supernatural) understanding, insisting that, although he is perfectly willing to accept the existence of this non-Euclidian world (and hence of God), his Euclidian understanding refuses to reconcile itself to all the moral horrors of the world created by such a divinity.

Since Ivan does not believe in God as more than a possible hypothesis, his opinion on this point reflects the same ambiguity that marked his article on church jurisdiction. "As for me," he says, refusing to decide for or against Feuerbach, "I've long resolved not to think whether man created God or God man." Such a question is "utterly inappropriate for a mind created with an idea of only three dimensions" (and hence Euclidian). Ivan remains neutral on this issue, though perfectly willing to accept all the sublime consequences that flow from postulating the existence of God. Paraphrasing the Gospel of Saint John, he declares, both with deep feeling and a touch of irony: "I believe in the underlying order and the meaning of life; I believe in the eternal harmony in which they say we shall one day be blended. I believe in the

Word to Which the entire universe is striving, and Which Itself was 'with God,' and Which Itself is God, and so on, and so on, to infinity" (14: 214). But truly to profess these beliefs as more than hypotheses would mean possessing a faith that transcends reason—a faith that Ivan is not only unable but also morally unwilling to muster even if he could manage to do so. What he desires is that such ecstatic expectations should justify themselves before the bar of his Euclidian understanding, of his earthly reason—and this, obviously, they cannot do.

Ivan refuses to make the leap of faith that would allow him to believe that the actual earthly world could ever be transformed into one that fully realizes the ideals of Christ. Moreover, even if "at the moment of eternal harmony, something so precious will come to pass that it will suffice for all hearts, for the comforting of all resentments, for the atonement of all the crimes of humanity . . . [even then], though all that may come to pass, I don't accept it, I won't accept it" (14: 215). Ivan now finds himself in the same position as those unbelievers, mentioned earlier by the narrator, who would not accept miracles even if they were accomplished before their very eyes. As the conflict between the Euclidian and the non-Euclidian is thus playing itself out in Ivan's mind and heart, he conveys all the anguish of this indecision to Alyosha as well.

## 3

The dialogue between Ivan and Alyosha serves as a prelude to the chapter entitled "Rebellion" (Book 5, Chapter 6), an attack on God and the world He created so powerful that many critics have doubted whether the book as a whole succeeds in overcoming its subversive and disrupting impact. Dostoevsky made some effort, however, to moderate the disquieting effects of his deeply moving jeremiad even before composing what he hoped would be its "refutation" in Book 6. For Ivan begins by exhibiting his emotional incapacity to experience the fundamental act of Christian fellow-feeling, that of loving one's neighbor. "I could never understand," he says, "how one could love one's neighbors . . . though one might love them at a distance." Citing an extreme and rather repulsive example of self-sacrificial Christian love from Flaubert's *Legende de St. Julien l'Hospitalier* (the embrace by the saint of a frozen beggar with some loathsome disease), Ivan sees it only as "a love imposed by duty, as a penance," similar to Katerina Ivanovna's "love" for Dimitry. It is an act accomplished "from the laceration of falsity" rather than from a sincerely spontaneous response to human suffering. For Ivan, the precepts of Christianity thus become transformed into a duty and obligation contrary to human nature. Alyosha, on the other hand, insists that "there's a great deal of love in mankind, an almost Christ-like love" (14: 215–216). Ivan's feverishly overstrained compassion for humanity that follows is thus undermined by the suspicion that he may also be experiencing only a "laceration of falsity."

The details of Ivan's searing indictment of God unroll a catalogue of atrocities that Dostoevsky drew from many sources—the court cases he had covered, some of the barbarities reported about the Russo-Turkish War, a pamphlet distributed by an aristocratic Christian sect describing the edifying conversion of a criminal in Geneva just before his execution, which did not for a moment stop his being put to death. Ivan dwells particularly on the torture deliberately inflicted on helpless and innocent children, and does so with a morbid delectation that makes Alyosha distinctly uneasy; there are definite indications that Ivan's fascination with human evil has begun to unbalance his mental equilibrium (he speaks "as though in delirium"). Humanity has become for Ivan nothing but a creature of destruction and darkness, an image not of God but of the devil. "I think if the devil doesn't exist," he tells Alyosha, "and therefore was created by man, he has created him in his own image and likeness." When Alyosha ripostes, "Just as he did God then?" Ivan smilingly comments, quoting Polonius in *Hamlet*, that his little brother knows how to turn words around.

It is the existence of all this suffering and misery in the world that Ivan finds emotionally unendurable and intellectually incomprehensible. The suffering of adults may be terrible, but they have eaten of the tree of the knowledge of good and evil; they have sinned, and thus can be held accountable and made to pay a price. But how is one to accept the idea of original sin—the idea that children must suffer for the sins of their fathers (a doctrine much less important in Eastern Orthodoxy, where Saint Augustine has had little or no influence, than in Western Christianity)? For Ivan, "such a truth is not of this world and is incomprehensible for the heart of man here on earth. The innocent must not suffer for another's sins, and especially such innocents!" Dostoevsky even allows Ivan to reject in advance the position from which he will be opposed. "Do you understand why this infamy must be permitted?" he shouts at Alyosha. "Without it, I am told, man could not have existed on earth for he could not have known good and evil. Why should he have known that diabolical good and evil when it costs so much?" (14: 215–220). The force of Ivan's argument is adroitly countered by the adjective "diabolical," which reveals the implicitly Manichean premise of his indignation, his conviction that humans can use freedom *only* to accomplish evil.

Ivan's tortured cogitations reject the very idea of "a universal harmony" in the future as something monstrous and unjust. With bitter irony, he declares that he can well envisage how glorious it would be "when the mother embraces the fiend who threw her child to the dogs, and all three cry aloud with tears, 'Thou art just, O Lord.'" He can understand this sublime apotheosis, but he cannot accept it: "It's not worth the tears of that one tortured child who beat itself on the breast with its little fist and prayed in the stinking outhouse, with its unexpiated tears, to 'dear, kind God!'" The tears of the little child tear at Ivan's heart, and nobody, he argues, has the right to forgive her torturer. "Is there in the whole world a being who would have the right to forgive and could forgive?" he cries. "I don't want harmony. From love for humanity, I don't want it. I would rather be left with unavenged suffering ... *even if I were wrong*" (14: 223). The intensity of Ivan's inner conflict—the conflict between his desire for "rational" retributive justice on the one hand, and the sublimity of universal forgiveness on the other—is revealed by Dostoevsky's underlining. Nonetheless, he is unyielding in his refusal, which culminates in his famous declaration: "And so I hasten to give back my entrance ticket, and if I am an honest man I must give it back as soon as possible. . . . It's not God that I don't accept, Alyosha, only I most respectfully return Him my ticket" (the ticket to a world of non-Euclidian eternal harmony that would redeem all suffering in the Euclidean realm).

Independently of this issue, Ivan at this point has set out to unsettle Alyosha's non-Euclidian faith, and he succeeds momentarily. When he asks Alyosha whether a general who had unleashed his dogs on a peasant boy should be shot "for the satisfaction of our moral feelings," Alyosha cannot help replying: "'To be shot!' lifting his eyes to Ivan with a pale, twisted smile: 'Yes, shot!'" Delighted at this reply, Ivan exclaims: "Bravo! . . . so there is a little devil sitting in your heart, Alyoshka Karamazov!" (which confirms that to agree with Ivan is to surrender to the temptation of the devil) (14: 221). Ivan then challenges Alyosha to answer whether he would consent to found the fabric of human destiny—"the fabric that would bring future happiness to mankind"—on the unavenged torture of an innocent child. Alyosha again replies in the negative, both for himself and for humanity; both would refuse "to accept their happiness on the foundation of the unexpiated blood of a little victim." But then, recovering himself, Alyosha recalls that the fabric of human destiny (at least in their moral universe) is founded on another principle—that of *self*-sacrificial Christian love. In response to Ivan's other question—whether there is "in the whole world a being who would have the right to forgive and could forgive" the terrible tapestry of human suffering he has just unrolled—Alyosha replies with a passionate affirmation. "But there is a Being and He can forgive everything, all *and for all*, because He gave His innocent blood for all and everything.

You have forgotten Him, and on Him is built the edifice, and it is to Him they cry aloud, 'Thou art just, O Lord, for Thy ways are revealed!'" (14: 223–224).

These pages are among the most justly famous in all of Dostoevsky's work, and they reveal once again his admirable boldness in giving the most powerful expression to the very attitudes he was attempting to combat. Aside from Alyosha's final invocation of Christ, there has been no attempt up to this point to counter Ivan's implacable attack on God's world. Nor would any such effort have been consistent with Dostoevsky's artistic strategy. The ideas he opposed are invariably combated by portraying their effects on the lives of his characters, not by attempting to demonstrate their lack of theoretical persuasiveness or rational coherence. Ivan's sense of despair and inner desolation, his disabused cynicism about his own youthful love of life, the contempt for mankind that has corrupted his feelings despite all his supposed "love for humanity"—all these are meant to illuminate indirectly the hopelessly self-destructive nature of his convictions. Nor should one underestimate the force of Alyosha's sudden appeal to the image of the God-man who had shed His innocent blood for *all*, an image that lights up in a flash the narrowness and vindictiveness of Ivan's "love of humanity." His insistence on justice—and hence on punishment and retribution—glaringly contrasts with Christ's gospel of all-reconciling and all-forgiving love and the hope of infinite mercy for the sinner who repents.

Numerous commentators have quite understandably stressed the moving pathos of Ivan's humanitarianism and the irresistible force of his tirade; it has even been suggested, as Blake said of Milton, that Dostoevsky was really of the Devil's party and could not suppress his emotional agreement with Ivan. There is no question that the Dostoevsky who wrote these pages poured into them all his own anguish, both personal and social, over the abominations he was recording. But it would be a serious underestimation of the integrity of his talent and of the depth and daring of his Christian irrationalism to assume that he endowed Ivan's voice with such overpowering resonance only through lack of artistic control. Ivan represents, on the highest level of intellectual and moral sensibility, the supreme and most poignant dramatization of the conflict between reason and faith at the heart of the book, and it would have been inconsistent with his thematic aim to have softened or weakened his utterances. Faith, as Dostoevsky wishes it to be felt in *The Brothers Karamazov*, must be totally pure, a commitment supported by nothing except a devotion to the image and example of Christ; and the arguments of reason against it must thus be given at their fullest strength.

4
---

What provides Ivan's overwhelming monologue with its still-undiminished power is the relentless rejection of God's world in the name of the very morality of love and compassion that Christ Himself had brought to it. Ivan is here expressing what Dostoevsky saw as the deepest challenge of the Populist mentality to a genuine acceptance of the Christian faith of the Russian people. To combat this challenge, Alyosha had called the image of Christ to his aid, the image of the true source of Ivan's own morality. He accuses his brother of having "forgotten" Christ, and in reply Ivan narrates a prose-poem of his own composition, never written down but still fresh in his memory. This is the justly renowned Legend of the Grand inquisitor (though the word "Legend" does not appear in the text). An extremely complex narrative creation, it encompasses three levels: that of Dostoevsky the author, that of the fictional narrator of his novel, and that of Ivan himself, the presumed creator, whose moral-social psychology it symbolically dramatizes in all the tangle of its oppositions. Of most importance for its interpretation are the first and third levels; the fictional narrator vanishes during Ivan's majestic monologue.

As a preface, the erudite Ivan indulges in a brief survey of the universal popularity of similar poems and plays in the past, when "it was customary . . . to bring down heavenly powers on earth." He refers to Dante, to the mystery and morality plays of the Middle Ages, to the imitation of this genre in the Russian theater up to Peter the Great, to Victor Hugo (who presented such a play as part of his *Notre Dame de Paris*), and, most important of all, to a Byzantine apocryphal tale from the twelfth century, "The Wanderings of Our Lady in Hell," which Ivan finds "as bold as Dante." It depicts the Mother of God being led through Hell by the archangel Michael. Horrified by the suffering of the damned, "shocked and weeping," she falls before God "and begs for mercy for all in Hell—for all she has seen there, indiscriminately." God points to the crucified Christ and asks how "His tormentors" can be forgiven; but He relents when Our Lady summons "all the saints, all the martyrs, all the angels and archangels" to join her in pleading for mercy. When God finally agrees to "a respite of suffering" for those in Hell every year from Good Friday until Trinity Day (eight weeks after Easter), the sinners "raise a cry of thankfulness" and chant, "Thou art just, O Lord, in this judgment" (14: 224–225).

Ivan's evident admiration for this tale, standing in such sharp contrast to his own outraged cry for retribution, reveals all the contradictions of the inner struggle between his reason and the Christian hope symbolized by the Mother of God. Other aspects of his prelude, in which Ivan cites lines from Schiller, Tyutchev, and the less-well-known A. I. Polezhaev, are also of importance. The stanza from Feodor Tyutchev, among Dostoevsky's favorites, once again proclaims the sanctity of the Russian land, through whose poor *izba*s the heavenly king, Christ Himself, laden with the burden of the cross, had once wandered in the guise of a lowly peasant-slave. "And that certainly was so, I assure you," Ivan tells Alyosha, affirming the truth of *this* return of Christ and His sanctification of the Russian soil. Ivan's own poem is placed in a totally different setting, sixteenth-century Spain, where Christ appears again. "Fifteen centuries have passed since He promised to come in His glory," and humankind awaited Him with "greater faith" than ever because "it is fifteen centuries since man had ceased to see signs from Heaven." And then Ivan cites the two lines from Schiller that anticipate the gist of what follows: "Have faith in the heart's prompting / For the heavens give no pledge." By this time, according to Ivan, "there was nothing left but faith in what the heart prompts." A new heresy had begun in the north of Europe, the German Reformation, "which began blasphemously denying miracles. But those who remained faithful were all the more ardent in their faith," which came from "the heart" and needed no justification. It is into a world filled with such yearning and such faith that Ivan imagines Christ returning—not to Germany but southern Spain, in the darkest days of the Inquisition.

Ivan then paints the scene in a few suggestive strokes, calling to his aid both poetry and, more extensively, the New Testament (which Dostoevsky both cites, sometimes in altered form, and draws on for certain details). The reader is taken to Seville the day after a hundred heretics have been burned in a magnificent auto-da-fé "in the presence of the king, the court, the knights, the cardinals, the most charming ladies of the court, and the whole teeming population of Seville." At this juncture, "Christ suddenly appears softly, unobserved, and yet, strange to say, everyone recognized Him. . . . He moves silently in their midst with a gentle smile of infinite compassion. The sun of love burns in His heart. Light, Enlightenment, and Power shine from His eyes, and their radiance, shed on the people, stirs their hearts with responsive love." Out of the fullness of His overflowing love, He brings back the sight of a blind man and raises a little girl from the dead on the steps of the cathedral; "the crowd weeps and kisses the earth . . . there are cries, sobs, confusion among the people."

Just at that moment the Grand Inquisitor happens to be passing, and these miracles, prompted by "the responsive love" between Christ and His adoring people, arouse his hostile attention because they threaten the basis of his own authority (14: 226–227). "He is an old man, almost ninety, tall and erect with a withered face and sunken eyes, in which there was still a gleam of light, like a fiery spark." No longer dressed "in his gorgeous cardinal's robes," he is wearing his "coarse, old monk's cassock. He knits his thick gray brows and his eyes gleam with a sinister fire." He orders the guards to arrest Christ, and the terrified crowd shrinks back as the God-man is led "to the close, gloomy, vaulted prison in the ancient palace of the Holy Inquisition." The day comes to an end and night falls, a "dark, heavy, breathless night" when "the air is fragrant with laurel and lemon" (a citation from Pushkin). "In the pitch darkness the iron door of the prison is suddenly opened, and the Grand Inquisitor himself comes in with a light in his hand" (14: 227–228). This whole scene, particularly the arrest and the nocturnal visit, is reminiscent of those Gothic novels that Dostoevsky had loved as a boy, and whose early exemplars, written by English Anglican authors, had also been ferociously anti–Roman Catholic.

The Grand Inquisitor and Christ now confront each other face-to-face. Christ does not utter a word; but His silence, with eyes fixed on His jailer, is more effective and pregnant with meaning than any speech. For His mute presence serves as a goad to the conscience of the Grand Inquisitor, who, while pretending to carry out Christ's wishes on earth, is well aware that he is doing quite the opposite. The monologue of the Inquisitor, swinging between his accusations against Christ and self-exculpation, betrays all the uneasiness and disquietude lurking behind the awesome façade of his power. This tension is gnawing at his conscience, a conscience which has led him, out of pity for the sufferings of a weak and unhappy humanity, to decide to "correct" Christ's work by relieving humankind of the primary source of its misery: the burden of free will. Ivan had refused to accept God's world in the previous chapter, and now he indicates how he would reconstruct it according to more "humane" specifications.

His narrative is a free variation on the Gospel version of the temptations of Christ included in Saints Mark, Matthew, and Luke. According to the sacred text, Christ spent forty days in the desert being tempted by the Devil before embarking on his mission to humanity. Like Milton in *Paradise Regained*, though in much briefer form, Ivan elaborates this account into a magnificent historiosophical panorama of the future course of human history, which he sees as prefigured in this temptation episode of the New Testament. Indeed, the Grand Inquisitor is certainly speaking for Dostoevsky when he rapturously praises the three questions put to Christ in the desert by "the wise and dread spirit, the spirit of self-destruction and nonexistence." He is certain that these questions must be the product not of "the fleeting human intelligence . . . but [of] the absolute and eternal," because the mind of man could not possibly have invented by itself the grandeur of this prophetic vision (14: 229–230).

Why, Christ is asked by the Grand Inquisitor, had He come to man "with empty hands, with some promise of freedom," when He could have performed the miracle of turning "these stones in this parched and barren wilderness" into bread? "Turn them into bread," the Devil had advised in the first temptation, "and mankind will run after Thee like a flock, grateful and obedient, though forever trembling, lest Thee withdraw Thy hand and deny them Thy bread." Christ refused because "Thou would not deprive man of freedom . . . thinking, what is that freedom worth if obedience is bought with bread?" (14: 230). Faith in Christ should arise as the free choice of love, not in exchange for the means of subsistence. But the Grand Inquisitor, prophesying the victory of what, from the terminology, can only be Socialism, foresees that "ages will pass, and humanity will proclaim by the lips of their sages that there is no crime, and no sin, there is only hunger." And then, "for the sake of that earthly bread the spirit of the earth will rise up against Thee and will strive with Thee and overcome Thee, and all will follow him, crying: 'Who can compare with that beast? He has given us fire from heaven!'" (a citation that combines the Book of Revelation with the myth of Prometheus) (14: 230).

As we know from the *Diary of a Writer*, Dostoevsky believed in the possibility of Roman Catholicism joining forces with the Socialists to lead the impending revolution that would destroy the West. Both, in his eyes, had surrendered to the first temptation of Christ by subordinating His message—freedom of conscience—to earthly aims and ambitions, and were thus united in his imagination. Incorporating this vision into the Legend, he also presents the two, more plausibly, as ultimately competing to gain mastery over humanity as a whole. "The spirit of the earth" will thus achieve a temporary victory because Christ chose to preserve humanity's freedom to decide between good and evil rather than transforming stones into bread. This decision had led to a thousand years of suffering for the human race, which had been plunged into the chaos that ultimately led to atheism and Socialism. "Where Thy temple stood will rise a new building, the terrible Tower of Babel will be built again, and though, like the one of old, it will not be finished, Thou mightest have prevented the new tower and have cut short the sufferings of men for a thousand years" (14: 230).

During this period of atheistic Socialism, the Grand Inquisitor and his minions would once again be "hidden underground in the catacombs, for we shall again be persecuted and tortured"; but humanity will finally come to lay its disastrous freedom at their feet. For "no science will give them [humankind] bread so long as they remain free . . . [because] freedom and bread enough for all are inconceivable together, for never, never, will they be able to share between them" (14: 230–231). The moral principle of "sharing" cannot originate from any source other than the true Christ, who calls for the free sacrifice for others out of love; and humankind will finally be forced to return to Him as the sole fount of morality. In this instance, however, it will return to a false Christ, the Roman Catholic one of the Grand Inquisitor, who believes that "nothing has ever been more insupportable for a man and human society than freedom," and that humanity "can never be free," for it is "weak, vicious, worthless, and rebellious" (14: 231).

Despite this disparaging view of human nature, Ivan's Grand Inquisitor makes the same appeal to pity that has already been heard in the chapter on "Rebellion." He acknowledges that although the doctrine of "the bread of Heaven," the freedom of the human conscience, may appeal to "thousands and tens of thousands [who] shall follow Thee," millions more "will not have the strength to forgo the earthly bread for the heavenly"; and it is for these millions, "who are weak, but love," that the Grand Inquisitor is speaking. "No, we care for the weak too. They are sinful and rebellious, but in the end they too will become obedient" (14: 231). This "care," however, will not be accepted unless concealed by falsity and deception, unless offered in the name of the *true* Christ preaching freedom and love while His ideal is being distorted and betrayed. Peter Verkhovensky in *The Devils* had wished to set up Stavrogin as Ivan the Tsarevich, the hitherto concealed inheritor to the throne of the Tsars, thus implicitly appealing to the devotion of the people to their God-anointed Tsar as a revolutionary weapon for destroying his rule. Similarly, the Grand Inquisitor is forced to speak in the name of the true Christ in order to falsify *His* message and subvert and destroy His influence. "But we shall tell them that we are Thy servants and rule them in Thy name. We shall deceive them again, for we will not let Thee come to us again. That deception will be our suffering, for we shall be forced to lie" (ibid.).

An important shift now occurs as the Grand Inquisitor turns from the first temptation, that of "earthly bread," to the more properly religious issue of whether humanity possesses the moral strength to support the freedom proclaimed by Christ. For the Grand Inquisitor is willing to agree with Christ—the only time he does so!—"that if someone gains possession of [humankind's] conscience—Oh! then [it] will cast away Thy bread and follow after him who has ensnared [its] conscience. In that Thou wast right. For the secret of man's being is not only to live but to have something to live for." In other words, man does not live by bread alone; but Christ refused to take command over the conscience of humanity, thus denying it the tranquillity of certitude and obedience. "Didst Thou forget that man prefers peace, and even death, to freedom of choice in the knowledge of good and evil?" (14: 232).

Far from providing a new and immutable guide for human conscience, Christ, the Grand Inquisitor charges, only increased its plight. "Nothing is more seductive for man than his freedom of conscience, but nothing is a greater source of suffering." Christ came to give His life for humanity out of love, but in refusing "to take possession of man's freedom, Thou didst increase [his freedom] and burdened the spiritual kingdom of mankind with its sufferings forever. . . . In place of the rigid ancient law, man must hereafter with free heart decide for himself what is good and what evil, having only Thy image before him as a guide" (ibid.).

To guarantee such freedom, Christ had rejected the second temptation, that of offering proof of His divinity. He refused to leap from the pinnacle of the Temple, secure in the knowledge that, as the Son of God, He would be supported by angels. Nor had He descended from the Cross when "they shouted at Thee, mocking, and reviling Thee: 'Come down from the Cross and we will believe that Thou art He.'" "Thou wouldst not enslave man by a miracle and didst crave faith given freely, not based on a miracle." And finally, he had turned away from the third temptation offered Him by the Devil, that of assuming power over "all the kingdoms of the earth," not wishing like the Grand Inquisitor to enforce faith with the temporal power symbolized by the auto-da-fé. Christ had thus repudiated what the Grand Inquisitor declares to be "the three powers . . . able to conquer and to hold captive forever the conscience of the impotent rebels for their own happiness—these forces are miracle, mystery, and authority" (14: 232). A page or so later, the Grand Inquisitor repeats the same charge with even greater emphasis: "We have corrected Thy work and have founded it upon *miracle, mystery, and authority*" (14: 234).

No segment of the Legend poses a knottier problem, or is more difficult to unravel, than this charge leveled against Christ. Interpreters of the stature of Nikolay Berdyaev have taken it as Dostoevsky's own definitive declaration—made *a contrario* through Ivan—that mankind's freedom of conscience, the freedom defended by Christ in the Legend, is totally imcompatible with magic, mystery, and authority. Such a reading, however, can hardly be reconciled with the description earlier given of the reappearance of Christ. What is this reincarnation except a divine mystery? Does He not perform miracles in restoring sight to the blind and resurrecting the dead? Does He not instantly command authority over the surrounding crowd who experience the radiance of His love? As Roger Cox has pointed out, when the Grand Inquisitor accuses Christ of having abandoned miracle, mystery, and authority, "the Inquisitor's most characteristic language and imagery come directly from the Book of Revelation, where it is associated with the 'false prophet.'"[2] To what extent Dostoevsky expected his readers to catch such an allusion cannot be known; but surely we should not neglect this earlier image in endeavoring to grasp Dostoevsky's thematic aim.

Earlier in the novel, when Alyosha had submitted himself to the *starets* Father Zosima, the narrator premonitorily warns "that this instrument . . . may be a two-edged weapon . . . it may lead some not to humility and complete self-control but to the most Satanic pride, that is, to bondage and not freedom" (14: 27). The forces of legitimate miracle, mystery, and authority are thus open to perversion, as we see in the case of the Grand Inquisitor, but the text clearly indicates that they are far from having been repudiated by Christ in their authentic manifestation. For Him, however, they derive their legitimate power only from a genuinely unconditional faith, only in that interpenetration of the earthly and the heavenly proclaimed by Father Zosima. When the Grand Inquisitor berates Christ for having abandoned such powerful instruments of control, the imperious prelate is speaking of them only as a means of coercion and domination. But they can exercise their influence by means of "responsive love," and Dostoevsky hardly desired them to be viewed only through the distorted lens that the Grand Inquisitor provides. As Cox cogently puts it, the Grand Inquisitor has debased the authentic forms of miracle, mystery, and authority into magic, mystification, and tyranny.

5
———

The remainder of the Legend elaborates on the motifs already established. Once again the Grand Inquisitor asserts his own love of humanity, a love that "so meekly acknowledg[es] their feebleness, lovingly lighten[s] their burden, and permit[s] their weak nature even sin with our sanction." Referring to the "first resurrection" prophesied in the Apocalypse, the resurrection of all those who "had borne Thy cross . . . [and] endured scores of years in the barren, hungry wilderness, living upon locusts and roots," the Inquisitor remarks: "They were only some thousands, and gods at that; and what of the rest? . . . Canst Thou really have come only to the elect and for the elect?" And he rebukes Christ again: "Why hast Thou now come to hinder us?" But even though Christ continues to remain mute, His immovable gaze clearly troubles His accuser. "And why dost Thou look silently and searchingly at me with Thy mild eyes?" he asks. "Be angry, I don't want Thy love, for I love Thee not." Under the challenge of this gaze, the Inquisitor finally confesses the secret he has not yet openly declared, even though he had exalted the wisdom of "the wise and dread spirit, the spirit of self-destruction and nonexistence." Now he defies Christ with this admission: "We are not with Thee, but with *him*—that is our mystery. It's long—eight centuries since we have been on *his* side and not on Thine" (14: 234).*

* The dating comes from the year 756, when Pepin the Short granted sovereignty over Ravenna to Pope Stephen III, thus recognizing the right of the pope to assume temporal power.

Christ had refused the third temptation of the Devil—power over all the kingdoms of the earth—but the Roman Church had treacherously accepted it in Christ's name. In so doing, the Grand Inquisitor now explains, it had "accomplished all that man seeks on earth—that is, someone to worship, someone to keep his conscience, and some means of uniting all in one unanimous and harmonious ant-heap" (14: 234–235). (The word "ant-heap" is frequently used by Dostoevsky to characterize a social order where no free will exists.) Having taken up the sword of the Caesars, the Inquisitor is certain that "we [the Roman Church] shall triumph and be Caesars, and then we shall plan the universal happiness of man." But this ultimate state will not be achieved before the interregnum, mentioned earlier, of "the ages . . . yet to come of the confusion of free thought, of their science and cannibalism," when humans will try to construct the Tower of Babel solely on the basis of reason and science and will end in devouring each other in a Darwinian struggle for life. Only then, the Inquisitor foresees, in imagery again drawn from the Book of Revelation, "the beast will crawl to us and lick our feet and spatter them with tears of blood. . . . And we shall sit upon the beast and raise the cup, and on it will be written: 'Mystery'" (14: 235).

It is then that the Grand Inquisitor and his henchmen will seize the opportunity to deceive humankind entirely. For by this time, even those who had initially served the true Christ ("the elect") will have "grown weary of waiting for Thee," and "they will transfer the powers of their spirit and the warmth of their heart to the other camp, and end by raising their *free* banner against Thee." The very banner of Christ Himself now will be transformed into its delusory opposite. "Oh, we shall persuade them that they will become free only when they renounce their freedom to us and submit to us." Humankind will then be reduced to the level of children and will be given "the quiet humble happiness of weak creatures such as they are by nature." Like children, "they will tremble impotently before our wrath," but will be just as "ready at a sign from us to pass to laughter and rejoicing, to happy mirth and childish song." Even sin will be allowed to these will-less creatures, "because we love them, and the punishment for these sins we take upon ourselves." Every detail of their existence, including the most intimate sexual and family matters, "the most powerful secrets of their conscience," will be under the Grand Inquisitor's control.* Here is the earthly

---

* No part of the Legend has been more influential and important than this prediction of what is, in effect, the world of twentieth-century totalitarianism, whether Communist or Fascist. Dostoevsky's nightmare vision of the surrender of inner freedom for untroubled security was also a predecessor of the literary genre of dystopia, represented by such works as Eugene Zamiatin's *We*, Aldous Huxley's *Brave New World*, and George Orwell's *1984*. The motif of deception—the Grand Inquisitor's pretense to speak in the name of the true Christ—is closer to the Communist model.

paradise of the Grand Inquisitor, presumably arising from the freedom proclaimed by Christ but in fact its fraudulent facsimile. "Peacefully they will die, peacefully they will expire in Thy name, but beyond the grave they will find nothing but death." Immortality does not exist, but "for their happiness we shall entice them with the reward of heaven and eternity" (14: 235–236).

The Legend, we should not forget, is Ivan's creation, and is therefore meant to objectify dramatically the struggle in his own consciousness between reason and faith. This struggle suddenly comes to the fore when the Grand Inquisitor reveals himself to be someone who has only reluctantly abandoned the true Christ, and who still feels the lofty beauty of the Christian faith and its image of humanity as free and morally responsible. Until this point, the Inquisitor has been shown primarily as the unrelenting embodiment of the power that he represents; but now he confesses to Christ that he too had once been a genuine believer. "I too have been in the wilderness, I too lived on roots and locusts, I too prized the freedom with which Thou hast blessed us, I too was striving to stand among Thy elect, among the strong and powerful. . . . But I awakened and would not serve madness." If Christ were to return again one day, he defiantly asserts, not quietly and almost secretly as in Seville but in the thunderclap and tremendous upheaval of the Second Coming, then the Grand Inquisitor and his fellows could say, "pointing out to Thee the thousand millions of happy children who have known no sin . . . 'Judge us if Thou canst and darest.'" Even more, he concludes his harangue by declaring that he will order Christ to be burned at the stake as a heretic the following day "for coming to hinder us. For if anyone ever deserved our fires, it is Thou . . . *Dixi*" (14: 236–237).

At this point, Alyosha interjects: "Your poem is in praise of Jesus, not in blame of Him—as you meant it to be." And surely Alyosha's interpretation may be taken as Dostoevsky's own. To rebuke Christ for proclaiming humankind's freedom of will, for insisting on humanity's right to choose between good and evil solely according to the dictates of their hearts, was in effect to praise Him for protecting the very foundation of man's humanity as Dostoevsky conceived it. Ivan does not reply to this first exclamation of Alyosha's, but he responds at length when charged with having endowed the Grand Inquisitor with more moral dignity than he deserves. For Alyosha heatedly affirms that the Grand Inquisitor and his Romish army of Jesuits represent "a simple lust for power, for filthy earthly gain, for domination—something like a universal serfdom with them as masters" (14: 237–239).

Refusing to accept such a reductive accusation, Ivan enlarges on the image of the Grand Inquisitor as a disillusioned believer who turned to atheism and joined "the clever people" (a symbolic designation) when he became convinced that humans "had been created as a mockery, [and] that they will never be capable of using their freedom." Ivan thus portrays the Grand Inquisitor as a tragic figure, genuinely suffering because he "has wasted his whole life in the desert and yet could not shake off his incurable love for humanity." And his tragedy is deepened because he is obligated to "lead men consciously to death and destruction and yet deceive them all the way . . . in the name of Him in whose ideal the old man had so fervently believed all his life long" (14: 237–239). Ivan refuses Alyosha's derogatory view of the Grand Inquisitor, who is a grandiose extrapolation of his own inner conflict; and the tragic nature of the Inquisitor's dilemma—the tragedy of having accepted the morality of Christ the Son and of acting in His name while no longer believing in God the Father—is also a preparation for the dénouement of the Legend.

When Alyosha inquires of his brother whether his narrative is finished, Ivan proposes the following conclusion. The Prisoner, who had been "looking gently" into the Grand Inquisitor's face all this time, continued to remain silent, and this unbroken muteness "weighed down" on his jailer. "The old man longed for Him to say something, however bitter and terrible. But He suddenly approached the old man in silence and softly kissed him on his bloodless, aged lips." The Grand Inquisitor shuddered and, reversing his previous sentence of death, opened the cell door. "'Go,' he said, 'and come no more—come not at all, never, never.' And he let Him out into the dark squares of the town." As for the now solitary Grand Inquisitor, Ivan says that "the kiss glows in his heart, but the old man adheres to his idea." Alyosha immediately recognizes this last sentence to be applicable to Ivan himself, torn between his sensitivity to the Christian ideal and his "idea" that "everything is lawful" once faith in God and immortality has been lost. To Alyosha's anguished question: "How will you live? . . . With such a hell in your heart and your head, how can you?" Ivan reasserts his former "rebellious" declaration: the "Karamazov baseness" will see him through until age thirty, and then he will dash the cup to the ground. He promises, however, to come and visit Alyosha before doing so (perhaps another anticipation of the second volume) (14: 240).

Ivan's character oscillates in these two chapters between the lonely young man gropingly expressing a yearning for friendship and intimacy, and the haughty young intellectual attempting to break down Alyosha's naïvely trusting faith. At the end of their conversation, when Alyosha looks at him in silence, Ivan expresses, "with unexpected feeling," a certain sadness because "now I see that there is no place for me in your heart, my dear hermit." This sentiment motivates the touching gesture of Alyosha kissing Ivan on the lips and being jokingly accused of "plagiarism" by an Ivan "highly delighted" at this symbol-laden reenactment.

Presented here in his most humanly appealing side, Ivan is shown as fully aware of the grief gnawing at his brother's heart at this moment. He says to Alyosha, "Go now to your *Pater Seraphicus* [Father Zosima, in a term taken from Goethe's *Faust*], he is dying. If he dies without you, you will be angry with me for having kept you" (14: 241).

Dostoevsky, however, did not wish to end on such an entirely sympathetic image of Ivan, who had succeeded in provoking Alyosha to approve of an act of revenge. And so the narrator introduces a subtly discordant note in the final paragraphs as Ivan walks away after directing his brother, "and now you go to the right and I to the left." Alyosha "suddenly noticed that Ivan swayed as he walked and that the right shoulder looked lower than the left." Whether this is an optical illusion remains uncertain; but, traditionally, the Devil is associated with the left side,[3] and because he limps when he walks, the left shoulder seems higher than the right (14: 241). The narrator thus uses folk beliefs to associate Ivan with the dread spirit the latter had just evoked so approvingly in his Legend; and as Alyosha enters the hermitage copse in which "the ancient pines murmured gloomily about him," Ivan's influence is shown to have been harmful even on the level of the plot action. Alyosha had been entrusted by Father Zosima with the task of seeking out Dimitry and staying by his side to prevent any catastrophe from occurring; and he had resolved to do so even if it meant not returning to the monastery. But "several times afterward he wondered how he could, on leaving Ivan, so completely forget his brother Dimitry" as he hastened back to the bedside of Father Zosima (ibid.).

## 6

The chapters containing Ivan's rebellion and his Legend are framed between his two encounters with Smerdyakov. Upon parting with Alyosha, Ivan returns home to encounter the obsequiously insinuating but also vaguely sinister presence of his father's cook and manservant. The subconscious expectation of meeting Smerdyakov plunges him, though he is not fully aware of this reason himself, into a state of intense depression. The relation between the two—only hinted at previously—is now developed more fully.

Ivan had initially "taken an interest in Smerdyakov, and had even thought him very original." They discussed questions such as the literal accuracy and truthfulness of some of the statements in the Old Testament, and Smerdyakov had begun to see himself as Ivan's disciple. Indeed, when Smerdyakov was ridiculing the heroism of Foma Danilov in refusing to renounce his faith, Feodor Pavlovich had said to Ivan: "He's got this all up for your benefit. He wants you to praise him" (14: 118).

Ivan and Smerdyakov had also discussed all the "scandals" arising from his brother Dimitry's behavior, "but though Smerdyakov always talked of that with great excitement, it was impossible to discover what he desired to come of it." Why the lackey Smerdyakov should have had any "desire" at all in this regard is not explained; but such a mysterious interest hints that he will not remain a mere passive onlooker.

Ivan soon comes to feel an "aversion" to Smerdyakov that replaces his earlier interest; the lackey "began to betray a boundless vanity, and a wounded vanity," that Ivan finds intolerable. The irony of this observation is obvious: Smerdyakov's "vanity" is a parody of his admired model, who in the person of the Grand Inquisitor had imagined himself capable of "correcting" the work of God. Worst of all, from Ivan's point of view, is that Smerdyakov now acts as if they "had some kind of compact, some secret between them," unknown to everyone else, which created a bond (14: 242–243). Such a bond exists whether Ivan desired it or not because Smerdyakov has become indoctrinated with the amoral nihilism of Ivan's ideas, which had now begun to ferment within a mind and heart quite lacking his own sensitivity to human suffering. The dialogue that now ensues is portrayed on two levels—the actual exchange of words between them, accompanied by the dialogue of Ivan with himself. In this second dialogue, the loathing Ivan has come to feel for Smerdyakov is dominated by his subconscious sense that both are linked by a secret, subliminal compact—one that he resents but cannot resist or shake off. Ivan's clash of feelings about Smerdyakov dramatizes, on the moral-psychological level, the same conflict between reason and faith (the source of moral conscience for Dostoevsky) that forms the basis of Ivan's character.

Even though, as he approaches the house, Ivan does not wish to speak to Smerdyakov at all, asking himself silently, "What have I to do with you, fool!" he finds himself involuntarily addressing Smerdyakov in a tone inviting conversation. Indeed, Ivan behaves under a compulsion, almost a fascination, that can only arise from the tormenting paralysis resulting from his inner conflict. In the course of their exchange, Smerdyakov insinuates in veiled terms all the events that will leave the way clear, if Ivan goes to Chermashnaya, for Dimitry to invade the house again and carry out the threat to kill his father. As he listens, Ivan becomes incensed by Smerdyakov's allusive words, which seemingly provide purposeless information but in fact hint at the likelihood of murder. Almost throwing himself upon the servant in a sudden paroxysm of rage, he then quietly announces instead that he will leave for Moscow the next day. Ivan's contradictory behavior has been foreshadowed by his words to Alyosha, after they both pulled Dimitry away from their bloodied father. "One viper will devour the other," he had said. "And serves both of them right, too." Nonetheless, while insisting to Alyosha that he would always defend his father, Ivan had also added: "But in my wishes I reserve myself full latitude in this case."

Ivan's "wishes" prove stronger than his asserted obedience to the moral code, and he decides to leave even after becoming aware that his absence might bring on the crime. That night he could not sleep, and was filled with feelings and impulses he could not understand—"he felt himself that he had lost his bearings." The narrator, however, self-consciously refuses to enter into any extended analysis: "This is not the place to look into that soul—its time will come." Instead, he reports objectively on the turmoil in Ivan's spirit, "fretted by all sorts of strange and almost surprising desires," such as wishing to go to the lodge and beat Smerdyakov. He could not have explained why, "except perhaps that he loathed the lackey as one who had insulted him more gravely than anyone in the world" (14: 251). Smerdyakov's "insult," consisted in his perfectly justified assumption that Ivan had no deeply rooted objection to the murder of his loathsome father, though he himself refused to face up to this truth. During that night, hearing his father stirring downstairs while waiting in hope for Grushenka's arrival, Ivan went out on the staircase and listened for five minutes "with a sort of strange curiosity, holding his breath while his heart throbbed." And he never forgot the memory of that brief span of time. "That 'action,' all his life afterward he called 'infamous,' and at the bottom of his heart, he thought of it as the basest action of his life" (ibid.). It was the moment when he decided to let the two vipers devour each other—or so he believed.

Ivan tells his father the next morning that he will go to Chermashnaya, as the old man had requested, to sell a copse for him. Feodor Pavlovich is delighted, "because you are a clever man," but Ivan avoids kissing him on departure (14: 253). Smerdyakov jumps on the carriage to wrap Ivan in his rug and says to him privately, "It's always worthwhile speaking to a clever man" (14: 254). This repeated designation echoes Ivan's remark to Alyosha that the Grand Inquisitor, after losing his faith in Christ, had joined "the clever people." As Ivan rolls through the countryside, he at first feels a sense of relief, but then recalls the lackey's parting words, whose implications he pretends not to understand. "'What did he mean by that?' The thought seemed suddenly to clutch at his breathing." Changing his plans, Ivan travels to Moscow, "to a new life, new places, and no looking back!" But his gloom and anguish do not vanish, and on arriving in Moscow he has a moment of truth: "'I am a scoundrel,' he said to himself" (14: 255). It is only much later, however, that he will experience the full implications of such a recognition.

## CHAPTER 34

# The Brothers Karamazov:
# Book 6

The "reply" to Ivan Karamazov that Dostoevsky had promised to K. P. Pobedonostsev is contained in Book 6, "The Russian Monk." These pages, which offer an account of Father Zosima's life and teachings, are perhaps the most artistically daring section of the work—daring in the sense that it is almost unprecedented to include in a novel, except perhaps for purposes of parody, an extended example of a text imitative of a purely religious genre. There may be other instances that could be adduced—the only one that comes to mind is Father Mapple's sermon in *Moby Dick* on Jonah and the whale—but Melville's masterpiece is written in such a richly rhetorical style that the sermon does not clash too dissonantly with its novelistic context. This is not the case with Dostoevsky's Book 6, cast in the form of a *zhitie*, that is, the hagiographical biography of the life of a saint as composed by his disciple, Aleksey Karamazov.

This section displays a stylistic register in sharp contrast with the remainder of the work. While *The Brothers Karamazov* is filled with violent movement, strong passions, and intense psychological dramatics, the *zhitie* lacks (quite intentionally) the powerful vehemence to which it is meant to respond. Most modern readers have considered it disappointingly ineffectual in countering the brunt of Ivan's unbridled assault. However that may be, there is no doubt that Father Zosima conveys the essence of Dostoevsky's own moral-social views, expressed in a form and manner appropriate to his fictional spokesman. These chapters have sometimes been criticized as a rather tedious excrescence, justified if at all only by the loosest links with the course of the developing action. In fact, however, the account of Father Zosima's life plays a more important part in the structure of the novel than has generally been appreciated.

Dostoevsky was trying to present here an alternative attitude toward life, and toward the problem of human suffering, than had been displayed in Ivan's fiery denunciations. It was an attitude of serene (if not necessarily passive) acceptance of human destiny, with all its sufferings and misfortunes—an acceptance deriving from an unalterable conviction in the all-forgiving mercy of a loving and compassionate God. To present a character imbued with such a point of view creates a special artistic problem; it is well known that figures embodying states of virtuous beatitude are much more difficult to make interesting and convincing (especially in the novel, but not only there) than those struggling with themselves or with others to confront the problems of human existence. As Chateaubriand once remarked, "[A] heaven in which limitless happiness reigns is too far above the human condition for the soul to be greatly touched by the happiness of the chosen . . . that is why the poets have been more successful in the descriptions of hell . . . where the torments of the guilty remind us of the sorrows of our life."[1]

Nonetheless, Dostoevsky took the risk of couching the response to Ivan in a genre usually reserved for the lives of saints. He had often urged the readers of his *Diary of a Writer* to acquaint themselves with such texts, and he deplored the educated public's ignorance of this important part of their cultural heritage. Accordingly, he may well have decided to take matters into his own hands by presenting his version of a *zhitie* to those who might not have come into contact with such compositions since childhood. Whatever the reason, we have here a text in a highly poetic style full of Church Slavonic expressions and the pious language of Saint Tikhon Zadonsky's eighteenth-century clerical sentimentalism.

Such a saint's life was "a sort of dramatic sermon, the most popular genre in Old Russian literature," and it was "usually idealized with standardized and selected details to make the moral lesson as striking as possible."[2] Since no attempt is made to ground such a narrative in realistic particularities or verisimilar psychological analyses, it is totally opposed to the novel form as such. Events occur according to the laws of the moral lesson to be illustrated, not by the causality of mundane existence. There is a timeless quality about such narratives precisely because they are related to the real world only in an ancillary fashion, and the moral they exemplify remains valuable for any time and any place. They may thus be seen as the literary equivalent of "a precious, hallowed, old-church icon,"[3] and, quite suggestively, Father Zosima's cell contains such an icon hanging on the wall (one dating from before the *raskol*, the split over the reforms of the church in the seventeenth century).

Moreover, the presumed insufficiency of Book 6 tends to stand out very sharply in critical opinion because, as already noted, it is viewed primarily as a direct answer to the Legend of the Grand Inquisitor. Commentators have not paid sufficient attention to Dostoevsky's remark that "*the whole novel* is an answer" to Ivan and his Legend. Even if, for unsympathetic readers, this shift of focus does nothing to strengthen the persuasiveness of Father Zosima's preachments *in themselves*, it makes us aware that Dostoevsky was not depending *only* on these stories and utterances to accomplish his artistic task. This will be achieved through the interweaving of Father Zosima's experiences with the remainder of the plot-action. Such interaction will reveal the salutary effect of his own life, and of the values he proclaimed and practiced, on that of others, and will illustrate as well that the image delineated by the Grand Inquisitor of a weak, debased humanity, incapable of fulfilling Christ's law of love, is delusory and pernicious.

## 2

Opening with Alyosha's return to the bedside of the dying elder, Book 6 consists largely of the monk's last words to his assembled friends and disciples, his departing recollections and reflections as set down by Aleksey Feodorovich Karamazov (the narrator uses Alyosha's full name to mark the solemnity of the document). The narrator raises the issue of whether it includes the conversations of Zosima on other occasions as well, finally concluding: "I must repeat, Alyosha took a great deal from previous conversations and added them to it [the one recorded at Zosima's bedside]" (14: 260). Such a consideration indicates his conscientiousness in establishing the facts, but also copes with a problem of verisimilitude. Father Zosima's story is presented "without interruption, as though he told his life to his friends in the form of a story," even though he was so weak that "he was sometimes gasping for breath" and was forced to lie down and rest (ibid.). A reader could well question whether he was physically capable of relating such a lengthy narrative, even though we learn that "after his deep sleep in the day he seemed suddenly to have found new strength, which kept him up through a long conversation" (ibid.). Wrestling with the question presented by Alyosha's text, the narrator finally decides that, even though Zosima was making "a last effort of love, which gave him incredible energy" during these last moments (ibid.), the "Notes of the Life in God of the Deceased Priest and Monk, the Elder Zosima, Taken from His Own Words" is a composite of utterances made at different times during Alyosha's discipleship.

The first part consists of three narratives dealing with Father Zosima's early life; the second contains more general reflections in the form of brief sermons. The stories are narrated, as in a *zhitie*, in a style intended to awaken pious and reverential responses, and to communicate a sense of serenity opposed to the agitations and passions depicted elsewhere. It begins with the brief life of Zosima's elder brother Markel, eight years older than himself, who left an ineffaceable impression on him as a child—one that ultimately led to his priestly vocation. Alyosha's face reminded his mentor of Markel, not so much in appearance as in spiritual character, and he could not help favoring him over the other novice also in his service. This resemblance of Alyosha to Markel, which to worldly eyes may appear only a coincidence, for Zosima suggests a reincarnation, something "mysterious . . . come back to me at the end of my pilgrimage as a reminder and an inspiration" (14: 259).

Markel was a young man with a "hasty, irritable temperament," withdrawn and unsociable, who died at seventeen of tuberculosis. A learned freethinker had converted him to atheism, and he shocked everyone, not only by refusing to fast at Lent, but also by superciliously explaining that all talk of God was only "silly twaddle." But then, taken seriously ill, he realized that death was near, and "a marvelous change passed over him, his spirit was transformed" (14: 261). The imminence of death does not frighten Markel but awakens him to the beauty and value of life, and he attempts to stanch his mother's flow of tears by telling her that "life is paradise, and we are all in paradise, but we won't see it; if we would, we should have heaven on earth the next day" (14: 262).

Prince Myshkin in *The Idiot* had once advised the tubercular Ippolit, embittered because his young life would soon be cut short, to "pass by and forgive us [the others who were still healthy] our happiness" (8: 433). Ippolit was unable to do so, but Markel accomplishes this feat of self-transcendence. He feels unworthy of the love lavished on him by his friends, and desires to change places with the servants "so I will be the servant of my servants, the same as they are to me." And he tells his mother that "every one of us has sinned against all men, and I more than any." Like Saint Francis, he asks pardon from the birds and from nature because "there was such a glory of God all about me, birds, trees, meadows, sky, only I lived in shame and dishonored it all and did not notice the beauty and glory" (14: 263).

The family doctor, a man of science, reacts to such talk by declaring that Markel's "disease is affecting his brain" (14: 262), but the afflicted young man is only rejoicing in that ecstatic apprehension of life as an ultimate good that even Ivan had experienced—and that Dostoevsky himself had once voiced in the shadow of death. Just after returning to prison from his mock execution, and still under its impact, he had written to his brother Mikhail, "Life is a gift, life is happiness, every minute can be an eternity of happiness," and he had wished "to love and embrace just someone from among those I knew." Markel obviously embodies this crucial epiphanic sentiment, which is passed on through him to Father Zosima and then to Alyosha.[4]

Father Zosima also confides some further details of his own early years that help to fill out the picture of his spiritual formation; and here again Dostoevsky draws on particularities from his own life. The Father speaks of having learned to read from a German Pietist religious primer "with excellent pictures," and he remembers the deep impression made on him by the Book of Job during a pre-Easter mass, as "the incense rose from the censer and softly floated upward and, overhead in the cupola, mingled in rising waves with the sunlight that streamed in at the little window" (14: 264). The Book of Job, the ancient biblical cry of anguish against a presumably merciful God who submits His faithful servitor to the worst torments in order to test his loyalty, bears the closest connection with Dostoevsky's thematics, and Father Zosima is still deeply moved by it: "Yesterday I took it up—I've never been able to read that sacred book without tears." Some have been incited by it to speak of God "with words of mockery and blame" because of the terrible fate so unjustly meted out to the righteous Job, whom God delivers into the power of Satan; but the greatness of the work "lies just in the fact that it is a mystery—that the passing earthly scene and the eternal verity are brought together in it" (14: 265). To be sure, Father Zosima says nothing about Job's own anguished outcries, lamentations, and accusations. The "mystery" of the tale for the Father is that, despite his "earthly" sufferings, Job still proclaims his faith in God and in the goodness of God's creation. Using a citation from Saint Tikhon, Father Zosima also declares that Job eventually will come to love his new children as much as the ones he had lost because "it's the great mystery of human life that old grief gradually passes into tender joy" (ibid.).

The remainder of this section consists of a plea to village priests to spread the Gospel among the people rather than confining themselves to the performance of their routine clerical duties. Taking up a theme that Dostoevsky had already broached in the *Diary of a Writer*, Father Zosima urges the priests to set up classes in their homes where the Bible would be read. The stories of Abraham and Sarah, Isaac and Rebecca, Joseph and his brothers—all these narratives and others will move the peasant heart and plant a seed that "will live in his soul all his life . . . hidden in the midst of his distress, in the midst of the foulness of his sin, like a bright spot, like a great reminder" (14: 266). Father Zosima also advises reading the legendary lives of saints especially revered in Russia, such as Aleksey, the man of God, and Saint Mary of Egypt, who abandoned a life of sin to live in the desert.

In conclusion, he recounts an incident from his own days as a wandering priest in which the lyrically tender Franciscan note is struck again. He and a young peasant lad talk together as night falls on the bank of a river, and the Father elaborates on his brother Markel's rapturous vision of nature, in which "every blade of grass, every insect, ant, and golden bee . . . all . . . bear witness to the majesty of God and continually accomplish it themselves." The young peasant was a bird catcher who knew all their calls, and he was especially moved by the legend of Saint Sergey of Radonezh, who offered a piece of bread to a savage bear, which then walked away peacefully. "Christ be with you," the saint had said, and these words had tamed the wildness of the animal (14: 267–268).*

If Father Zosima's first narrative is associatively linked to Alyosha, then the second, dealing with his life as a young man, is related to Dimitry. Sent by his mother to a school for military cadets in Petersburg, Zinovy (his secular name) had, by the time he graduated, been "transformed into a cruel, absurd, almost savage creature." He and the other cadets looked on the "soldiers in their service as cattle," and what they prided themselves on most was "drunkenness, debauchery, and deviltry." Not that these young fellows were bad by nature, but "they behaved badly, and I most of all" (14: 268). Nonetheless, Zinovy was fond of reading and carried around a Bible, though without ever opening its pages. What Father Zosima reveals about himself here is a mirror image of Dimitry, to whom, it now becomes clear, he had bowed down because his own past had enabled him to understand Dimitry's nature and the danger by which he was threatened.

Not yet Father Zosima, Zinovy forms an attachment to a fine young girl who appears to welcome his suit; but he hesitates to abandon his licentious life and delays asking for her hand. On returning from a two-month absence, he finds the girl married to a much more suitable husband, and discovers that she had been engaged to this suitor all along. Furious at this blow to his vanity and pride, he provokes the husband into a duel; but the day before it was to take place, "in a savage and brutal humor," he strikes his orderly Afanasy very hard and bloodies his face. On waking, the beauty of the morning sun fills him with shame ("the leaves were rejoicing and sparkling, the birds were trilling the praise of God"), and, implicitly, the lessons of Markel begin to work in his soul (14: 270). Consumed with remorse, he bows down to Afanasy and asks forgiveness, an action that causes the astonished soldier to break into tears. Inwardly transformed by this self-conquest, he allows his opponent a first shot that goes wide, refuses to fire himself, and then apologizes for his insulting words. This action caused a scandal in the regiment; but because he had faced his opponent's shot, there could

---

* This reverential relation to nature goes back a long way in Dostoevsky's sensibility. A story entitled *A Little Hero*, written between 1849 and 1850 while he was imprisoned in the Peter-and-Paul Fortress, contains the following passage: "The neverending concert of those who 'sow not, neither do they reap' and are as free as the air they cleave with their sportive wings was all about us. It seemed as though at the moment every flower, every last blade of grass, exhaling its sacrificial aroma, was saying to its creator, 'Father! I am blessed and happy!'" (2: 292–293).

be no imputation of cowardice. And when he resigned his commission, announcing that he was entering a monastery, all was forgiven. Here there is a foreshadowing of Dimitry's future self-discovery and moral transformation.

## 3

The third of Father Zosima's stories, "The Mysterious Visitor," is clearly connected with Ivan. A respected citizen of the community, middle-aged and the father of a family, well known for his charitable activities, unexpectedly comes to visit the iconoclastic young officer. Zinovy has become known because of his courage in confronting the opprobrium of society and acting in accordance with *his* moral conscience rather than submitting to the totally non-Christian code of his position and rank. The older man wishes to inquire about the motives that had led the younger to come to such a painful decision. His own interest was inspired not by idle curiosity but because he had "a secret motive of my own, which I may perhaps explain to you later on" (14: 274). The secret turns out to be that he himself is a murderer. As a young man, out of jealousy, he had killed a girl who had refused his suit. The crime had been committed skillfully, despite the tempest of his emotions, and he had been self-possessed enough to make it appear a robbery. No one suspected him, and a discontented serf who had uttered threats against the lady while drunk was arrested and died in prison, thus closing the case. At first, the murderer was not troubled, took part in philanthropic enterprises, and finally married. He had hoped that family life would help him escape brooding over his past; but the presence of his wife and children only made the memory of his crime more oppressively painful, and he became haunted by the idea of ending his torments with a full confession. This is why he had come to visit the young man who had been bold enough to follow the dictates of conscience rather than risk committing a socially tolerated murder.

Moreover, the visitor was concerned not only with his personal problems but also, like Ivan, with the general moral situation of society and human life. He agrees with Zinovy's declaration, which had made everyone else laugh indulgently, "that life is a paradise," and he adds that "paradise is hidden in all of us." If people only realize that "all men are responsible to all for all, apart from our sins . . . the Kingdom of Heaven will be for them not a dream but a reality" (14: 275). The visitor also reiterates one of the favorite ideas expressed again and again in the *Diary*, namely, that the modern world is living through a period of "isolation" in which the solidarity of humans with each other has been replaced by separation and division. Change for the better can come only through "a spiritual, psychological process. . . . Until you have become really, in actual fact, a brother to everyone, brotherhood will not come to pass. No sort of scientific teaching, no kind of common interest, will ever teach us to share property and privileges with equal consideration for all." But eventually, "this terrible individualism must indubitably have an end. . . . And then the sign of the Son of Man will be seen in the heavens," the sign presumably announcing the Second Coming of Christ (ibid.).

The struggle of "the mysterious visitor" with himself is resolved when, despite all the torments that he knows will ensue for himself and those he loves, he follows Zinovy's advice to confess. Nobody believes the confession of this model citizen, who has led such an exemplary life (any more than Ivan will be believed in the courtroom scene later). And when the "visitor," producing evidence of his crime, is declared insane, the parallel with Ivan could not be clearer. A few days later the penitent murderer is taken ill and dies; before his death he admits to Zinovy that, on his last visit, he had come back to kill him. But "the Lord vanquished the devil in my heart" and stayed his hand (exactly as will occur with Dimitry) (14: 283). All three stories are what French critics call a *mise en abyme*, that is, a relatively subordinate narrative element either reproducing *in nuce* the main theme of the work, or presenting it as here in a form somewhat altered but still recognizable. Father Zosima's *zhitie* is thus not his alone but that of the three Karamazov brothers as well. Each story indicates the paths that all (including Ivan) will take in the remainder of the book to refute his Legend of the Grand Inquisitor.

4

Father Zosima's narratives are followed by a chapter of his "conversations and exhortations," in which Dostoevsky, without concern for their didacticism, allows himself to develop some of his own most cherished ideas. Monasticism and the Russian monks are defended against their numerous critics, among them Feodor Pavlovich, who had given abusive voice to the charge, widespread among the impious, that monks are "sluggards" and "gluttons," not to mention anything more odious. Father Zosima replies in terms of Dostoevsky's religious messianism: it is the Russian monks who "keep the image of Christ pure and undefiled. . . . And when the time comes, they will show it to the tottering creeds of the world. That is a great thought. That star will rise out of the East" (14: 284). By contrast, those worldly people who criticize the monks "have science; but in science there is nothing but what is the object of sense. The spiritual world, the higher part of man's being is rejected altogether, dismissed with a sort of triumph, even hatred" (ibid.). The modern world has proclaimed "the reign of freedom" and "the multiplication of desires," but such an unregulated existence can only lead among the rich to "*isolation* and spiritual suicide; in the poor, [to] envy and murder; for they have been given rights, but have not been shown the means of satisfying their wants" (ibid.).

Father Zosima continues to play variations on this contrast between the life of the worldly, who sacrifice everything to their ever-increasing desires (sometimes committing suicide if they cannot satisfy them), and the régime of the monks, which consists of "obedience, fasting, and prayer." For Dostoevsky, "freedom" meant mastery and suppression of one's desires, not liberation from all constraints on their satisfaction; such a life of self-control was for him the only "way to real, true freedom." Later, Father Zosima returns to the charge that the monks are concerned solely with their own salvation, and replies that in the past, "leaders of the people came from among us, and why should they not again?" (The reference is to the Time of Troubles in the early seventeenth century, when monks took an important part in the resistance against Polish invaders.) Just as they had worked to save Russia in the past, "the same meek and humble ascetics" will do so in the future because "the salvation of Russia came from the people. . . . And the Russian monk has always been on the side of the people. . . . The people believe as we do, and an unbelieving reformer will never do anything in Russia, even if he is sincere in heart and a genius" (14: 284–285). This was unquestionably true in Dostoevsky's lifetime, but Zosima's hope that "the people will meet the atheist and overcome him" did not prove equally perspicacious.

But even the Russian people were not immune to the new forces of disintegration undermining society, and Father Zosima utters a horrified castigation of "the fire of corruption" spreading through the peasantry itself, here coming closest of all to touching on the actual problems of Russian society. Like the Populists, Father Zosima observes with dismay that "the spirit of isolation is coming upon the people too. Moneylenders and devourers of the commune are rising up." Worst of all, "the peasants are rotting in drunkenness and cannot shake off the habit. And what cruelty to their wives, their children even!" The mention of children leads to a bitter denunciation of child labor: "I've seen myself in the factories children of ten, frail, rickety, bent and already depraved. . . . There must be no more of this, monks, no more torturing of children, rise up and preach that, make haste, make haste!" (14: 286). But what will ultimately save the Russians, Father Zosima affirms, is the consciousness of their iniquity—one of the extremely dubious linchpins of Dostoevsky's ideology ever since the early 1860s.

Father Zosima then launches into an encomium of the Russian

peasantry, who "in spite of their degraded sins and poverty-stricken appearance are not servile, and even after two centuries of serfdom, they are free in manner and bearing, yet without insolence and not revengeful and envious." And he dreams of a halcyon social future, one that "will come to pass when even the most corrupt of our rich will end by being ashamed of his riches before the poor, and the poor, seeing his humility, will understand and give way before him, and will respond joyfully and kindly to his honorable shame" (14: 286). Here, unquestionably, is Dostoevsky's own dream-world of the Russian future, expressed with all the naïveté suitable for Father Zosima.

Master and servants no longer exist in this ideal Christian world of the future because they become "brothers in spirit," and Zosima illustrates such a possibility by an incident from his own life. He recalls an accidental meeting with his old orderly Afanasy during his days as a wandering monk, when their situations had become completely reversed. Afanasy invites his ex-superior into his house for a meal, pressing a small contribution for the monastery into his hand as he takes his leave. No longer master and servant, "a human bond" has been created between them, and Father Zosima asks whether "it is so inconceivable that that good and simple-hearted unity might in due time become universal among the Russian people?" Never doubt it, affirms the Father, who believes "that it will come to pass and that the time is at hand."

Of course all these ingenuous expectations will be met with scorn and mockery, but Father Zosima thinks that those who rely on reason alone to reach the same goal of a world of unity and solidarity (that is, the Socialists) "have more fantastic dreams than we. They aim at justice, but, denying Christ, they will end flooding the earth with blood." Indeed, "were it not for Christ's covenant, they would slaughter one another down to the last two men on earth," and even these two would kill each other "in their pride." To relieve this grim vision, as well as to counter the skepticism of his critics, Dostoevsky has Father Zosima end on a more humorous note, recalling that people had asked him, while still an officer, whether they should invite their servants to tea. "Why not, sometimes at least," he had replied, though admitting that his "answer was not clear . . . [yet] the thought in it was to some extent right" (14: 287–288).

The most overtly theological preachment of all appears to speak directly to Alyosha (the words are addressed to a "young man"), but Father Zosima later shifts to "brothers." He tells them "not to be forgetful of prayer," and to pray every day for all those whose souls were appearing before God at that moment. Many had no one to plead for them, and such a prayer is only one expression of the universality of love that is the leitmotif of Father Zosima's admonitions. "For all is like an ocean, all is flowing and blending; a touch in one place sets up movement at the other end of the earth." He also insists that it is necessary "to love a man even in his sin, for that is the semblance of the Divine love and is the highest love on earth." And one should love not only man in his sin but "all God's creation, the whole and every grain of sand in it. Love every leaf, every ray of God's light, love the animals, love the plants, love everything." A special mention is made again of children, whose abuse had so enraged Ivan: "Love children especially, for they too are sinless like the angels, they live to soften and purify our hearts and as it were to guide us. Woe to him who offends a child!" Alyosha had agreed with Ivan that the cruelly sadistic general who had set his dogs on the peasant boy should be shot; but Father Zosima, asking whether the "force of humble love" should be a response to man's sins, answers: "Always decide to use humble love." According to him, "loving humility is marvelously strong, the strongest of all things, and there is nothing like it" (14: 288–289).

Many of Dostoevsky's contemporary critics refused to accept such a response as sufficient, and while such skepticism could have been expected among his Westernizer opponents, they were not the only ones to find it unsatisfactory. Even among those who sympathized with him, we find Sergey Yuriev writing to Orest Miller that "the Christian ideal— the ideal of Father Zosima . . . is terribly one-sided, and should be filled out with the advocacy of an *active love* . . . leading to the remaking of all the national and social life that surrounds us."[5]

Father Zosima also urges his listeners "to pray to God for gladness" and not to let "the sin of men . . . confound you in your work." Because sin is omnipresent, a good deal of effort is required to achieve the state of mind that he recommends. As a remedy, "there is only one means of salvation": "Take yourself and make yourself responsible for all men's sins . . . for as soon as you sincerely make yourself responsible for everything and for all men, you will see at once that it is really so, and that you are to blame for everyone and for all things" (14: 290). To take on oneself the burden of universal guilt thus becomes the only antidote to despair at the existence of evil (though one should remember that Father Zosima was addressing fellow priests, who *did* take upon themselves the sins of all those who came to them for confession). In any event, only by taking responsibility for *all* sin could they avoid "sharing the pride of Satan and murmuring against God" (as Ivan had of course done, though his rebellion was much more strident than merely a "murmur") (ibid.).

All these injunctions are very difficult for human reason to understand, as Dostoevsky well knew, and as a last resort Father Zosima falls back on the mystery of all human life itself. Indeed, "the pride of Satan" is precisely such a mystery: "It is hard for us on earth to comprehend it, and therefore it is easy to fall into error and to share it, even imagining that we are doing something good and fine" (another thrust at Ivan and his Legend). Much is concealed in the earthly life of humankind, and "many of the strongest feelings and movements of our nature we cannot comprehend. . . . On earth, indeed, we are as it were astray, and if it were not for the precious image of Christ before us, we should be undone and altogether lost, as was the human race before the flood." Here Dostoevsky sets down Father Zosima's often-quoted words of the link between earthly life and other worlds: "God took seeds from different worlds and sowed them on the earth, and His garden grew and everything came up that could come up, but what grows lives and is alive only through the feeling of its contact with other mysterious worlds." Once "such contact is lost, then you will be indifferent to life and even grow to hate it" (14: 290–291).

## 5

In a world in which all are guilty for all, how is it possible, Father Zosima asks, for anyone to pass judgment on another for committing a crime? The answer is that one should avoid doing so: "If you can take upon yourself the crime of the criminal your heart is judging, take it at once, suffer for him yourself, and let him go without reproach." The Father admits that although this behavior "may sound absurd, it is true." Even a judge appointed by law should "act in the same spirit so far as possible, for [the criminal] will go away and condemn himself more bitterly than you have done" (14: 291). Such would be the ideal situation, already mentioned by Father Zosima in discussing Ivan's article, when the State would be transformed into a Church and the punishment of a criminal would be exclusively the work of his own moral conscience. If the criminal should go away unredeemed, however, "mocking at you," his or her self-chastisement will eventually occur, if not at that moment then in another. Nothing that actually happens can thus infirm such a faith. "Believe that," the Father exhorts his listeners, "believe that without doubt; for in that lies all the hope and faith of the saints" (ibid.).

Faith does not require confirmation by miracles, nor should failure in combating evil lead to discouragement. Father Zosima urges his listeners to subdue any "desire for vengeance on the evildoers" by seeking suffering and blaming only themselves. "If you had been a light, you would have lighted the path for others too. . . . And even though your light was shining, yet you see men were not saved by it, hold firm and doubt not the power of the heavenly light. . . . The righteous man departs, but the light remains. Men are always saved after the death of the deliverer" (14: 292). This later redemption is what occurred in the case of Christ, and we will soon see it repeated after Father Zosima's death as well. The Father then returns to the Franciscan note of cosmic mysticism in affirming the beauty and goodness of all God's creation: "Love to throw yourself on the earth and kiss it. Kiss the earth and love it with an unceasing, consuming love. Love all men, love everything. . . . Water the earth with the tears of your joy and love those tears" (ibid.).

After such an ecstatic summation, Father Zosima returns once more to the problem of the human condition in the last section of his exhortations: "Of Hell and Hellfire, A Mystic Reflection." Hell contains no scenario of hooks and grappling irons, à la Feodor Pavlovich, and Father Zosima embarks instead upon a meditation on the creation of humanity. "Once in infinite existence, inconceivable in time and space, a spiritual creature was given, on his coming to earth, the power of saying: 'I am and I love.'" The primary attribute of human existence is not the power of thought (a reference to Descartes) but that of love: "Once, only once, there was given him a moment of active *living* love, and for that earthly life was given him." But "that happy creature rejected the priceless gift, prized it and loved it not, and remained callous." It is only in the afterlife of eternity that this spiritual creature realizes, with unrelievable anguish, just how precious this gift had been, and that it is impossible "to cool the fiery thirst of spiritual love which burns in me now, though I despised it on earth." Hell, according to Father Zosima, is this eternal torment, "the suffering of no longer being able to love." So far as "hellfire in the material sense" is concerned, he declares "that I don't go into that mystery and I shun it" (14: 292–293). Hell is purely a spiritual torment, not to be depicted, *pace* Dante and Milton, in physical imagery at all. Dostoevsky thus remains faithful to his poetics of subjectivity by transforming even Hell into an attribute of the human psyche. Milton had preceded him when Satan says in *Paradise Lost,* "The mind is its own place, and in itself / Can make a Heaven of Hell, a Hell of Heaven," but this is not accompanied by a rejection of the traditional imagery.[6]

It is typical of Dostoevsky as well that hope of consolation is not lost altogether even for those in Hell. Although "their spiritual agony cannot be taken from them, for their suffering is not external but within them," some alleviation of their condition is still possible. If "the righteous in Paradise should forgive them . . . and called them up to heaven in their infinite love," their anguish would at first only be increased, because the forgiveness and the call would arouse "in them still more keenly a flaming thirst for a responsive, active, and grateful love which is now impossible." But Father Zosima imagines that by eventually accepting their condition with submissiveness and humility, they might attain to "a certain semblance of that active love which they scorned in life." Father Zosima also prays for suicides, even though the official Church "tells us that it is a sin to pray for them." Only those who "remain proud and fierce even in Hell, in spite of their certain knowledge and contemplation of the absolute spirit," those "who have given themselves over to Satan and his proud spirit entirely," will be doomed to unalleviated suffering forever. "They will yearn for death and annihilation. . . . But they will not attain to death" (14: 293). Ivan has clearly entered on this dangerous path, but he will not continue to "remain proud and fierce."

So ends Alyosha's rendition of Father Zosima's *zhitie*, and the thread of the story is then taken up again by the narrator. We return to the cell where Zosima was speaking to his intimates, "so cheerful and talkative" that he seemed to have undergone a temporary recovery; but he dies on this very day. "He seemed suddenly to feel an acute pain in his chest, he turned pale and pressed his hand to his heart. But though suffering, he still looked at them with a smile, sank slowly from his chair on his knees, then bowed to the ground, stretched out his arms and as though in joyful ecstasy, praying and kissing the earth (as he taught), quietly and joyfully gave up his soul to God" (14: 294). The peacefully solemn demise of Father Zosima is fully in accord with the sanctity of his life since becoming a priest, and with the teachings that Alyosha had recorded. But the narrator informs us also that his tranquil death soon gave rise to "something . . . so unexpected, so strange, upsetting, and bewildering" that its effect vividly remained in the memory of the monks and the townspeople even after many years (14: 295). This upsetting, unforgettable event will be discussed in the next chapter.

## 6

This *zhitie* of Father Zosima, and Dostoevsky's whole depiction of the monastic milieu met with a mixed reception. Several clerical journals printed favorable articles, gratified at the positive aspects of his portrayal, but it was subjected to severe censure by Konstantin Leontiyev, who also reported that it had displeased the community of Optyna Pustin. He acknowledged that Dostoevsky "relates to [the Russian monks] with great respect," but objected to their characterization in terms familiar from his criticisms of the Pushkin speech. He found that "*a genuine mystical* sentiment was . . . even expressed rather weakly, but the sentiment of *humanitarian idealization* even in the speeches of the monks was expressed very ardently and at length." Dostoevsky's monks never engaged in such customary monastic activities as church services, prayers, or works of penance, and he also objected that Father Ferapont, "a hermit and a strict ascetic," was portrayed so "unfavorably and grotesquely."[7] A similar and much more detailed assessment has been more recently made by Sergei Hackel, who has carefully examined the travels of Parfeny, the writings of Saint Tikhon Zadonsky, and the discourses of Saint Isaac of Syria (mentioned in the novel), among others. Dostoevsky draws on all this material, but, as Hackel has shown, he invariably does so in a manner consistent with "his humanitarian and humanistic train of thought" (this particular remark concerns Father Zosima's totally psychological conception of Hell).[8]

It is not my aim, nor does it fall within my competence, to decide whether Dostoevsky's religious views remain within the boundaries of the tenets of Orthodox theology, which in any case, for lack of a central dogmatic authority, possess a very wide latitude. Two points made by Hackel, however, require some further consideration. One is a comment on the assertion, first made by Markel and then by "the mysterious visitor," that the secret of transforming life into an earthly paradise is hidden in all of us, that it is entirely within man's will to make paradise come true. Nothing is said about any cooperation of man with God in effectuating such a transmutation, and it thus appears to be an entirely secular and worldly event, only requiring, as the Utopian Socialists had once preached, the unconditional application of the Christian law of love to earthly life (though Hackel does not make this comparison himself). Nor, it may be added, does the cosmic mysticism indigenous to Eastern Orthodoxy, as Father Zosima expresses it, require any supernatural grace to be experienced.

Hackel also points out that Dostoevsky's Russian messianism, which so closely associates the conception of God with the Russian people as "God-bearing," comes dangerously close to reducing God, as Stavrogin had once accused Shatov of doing, to "an attribute of nationality." Dostoevsky had carefully distinguished between religion and nationality in *The Devils*, but Father Zosima seems much less cautious when he declares that "whoever does not believe in God is not going to believe in God's people." Does this mean that whoever does not believe in God's people does not (or cannot) believe in God? From Hackel we also learn that an Eastern Orthodox Church council in 1872 had denounced as heretical "a teaching whereby nationalistic concepts distort and challenge the Church's universal mission."[9] It is quite possible that the passions aroused by the Russo-Turkish War had now inclined Dostoevsky more in this direction than had been the case in the past.

## CHAPTER 35

# The Brothers Karamazov:
# Book 7

With the completion of Book 6, Dostoevsky has laid down the framework for the remainder of the novel. Ivan's Legend and Father Zosima's *zhitie* have established the polarities of the conflict between reason and faith, and each of the main characters will be confronted by a crisis that requires choosing between them. Faith of some kind will prevail in all of these climactic moments—not necessarily faith in a specifically moral-religious form, as will occur with Alyosha, but a faith that incarnates some aspect of the morality of love and the self-transcendence of egoism represented and preached by Father Zosima.

On the level of plot action, the oedipal clash of Dimitry and his father over Grushenka has been depicted, as well as the secret complicity of Ivan and Smerdyakov—but as yet only in relation to the possibility of a murder by Dimitry. The moral physiognomy of Ivan, torn between moral-intellectual nihilism and a conscience he cannot suppress, has also been sharply delineated. Alyosha appears to be the least conflict-ridden of the three brothers, though the scene with Liza has momentarily opened up hidden depths. He is also, however, the first of the three brothers whose life experiences have been foreshadowed by those of Father Zosima, and there is a structural parallel between the unrolling of the crisis situations and the order of the linkage of the brothers with Zosima's life. It is thus with Alyosha that the first conflict between reason and faith is posed and resolved.

## 2

Alyosha's disaccord occurs, as is only suitable for the devotee and disciple of Father Zosima, on the moral-religious level they both embody. It arises as a result of Father Zosima's death and the accompanying expectation nourished throughout the entire community that God would provide some external reward for the sanctity of his life. Some of the townspeople immediately brought sick family members, and especially ailing children, to the monastery, believing, "in accordance with their faith," that Father Zosima's remains would effectuate some miraculous

636

cure. But it was not only the common people who anticipated such a wondrous event; the monks were also filled with excitement and expectation—to such a degree that the learned Father Paissy, versed in Church doctrine and history, considered it "unseemly" and "an evil temptation." And so it was: a version of the second temptation of Christ, who had refused to demonstrate His immunity to the laws of nature by leaping unharmed from the pinnacle of the temple. Yet Father Paissy himself, reproving as he was of others, "secretly, at the bottom of his heart, cherished almost the same hopes and could not but be aware of it" (14: 296).

Father Zosima's body was carefully prepared for burial according to the rites that the narrator describes in detail, and then placed back in his cell for one day before interment. It was felt to be almost sacrilegious to think of opening the windows, even though it was late August, because the sanctity of Zosima's life seemed to guarantee a respite from the normal laws of earthly decay. But "the odor of corruption" emitted by the corpse soon assailed everyone, and caused an even greater scandal because of the stirrings aroused by the hope of some manifestation of God's grace. These events lead to a lengthy intervention by the narrator, who expresses shock at all the agitation caused by such a natural process, especially because the same had occurred in the past to "monks of very holy life . . . God-fearing old men whose saintliness was acknowledged by all" (14: 298).

Other reports, however, claimed that "there had been, in former times, saints in the monastery whose memory was carefully preserved, and whose relics, *according to tradition*, showed no sign of corruption" (14: 298; italics added). Such reports were thus traditions, which might or might not be accepted, and they were "taken by the monks as touching and miraculous, and as a promise of God's grace." The narrator also conveys the remarks of the "gentle" librarian Father Iosif about a competing tradition. The monks of Mount Athos, it would seem, did not consider the corruptibility of the body as very important; God's favor or displeasure was indicated by the color of the bones after the body had been interred for several years. But the narrator notes that even Father Iosif was troubled, and "had not been entirely convinced of the veracity of his own opinion." Although relating these beliefs with great respect, as was appropriate and necessary, he carefully avoids expressing any judgment as to whether they should be taken as more than devout legends.

Instead of dwelling on such ticklish issues, he attributes what next occurred to the much more human and comprehensible opposition already existing in the monastery against the institution of *starchestvo* in general and Father Zosima in particular. For "the odor of corruption" was immediately seized on by those unfriendly to him as a sign of heavenly disapproval, and a malevolent chorus of criticism was unleashed. "'[Father Zosima's] teaching was false, he taught that life is a great joy and not a vale of tears,' said some of the most unreasonable" of his opponents. (The view that "life is a great joy" will take on a good deal of significance in Book 7.) Objections were also made that Father Zosima "followed the fashionable belief, he did not recognize material fire in hell" (perfectly true); still others concluded that Father Ferapont had been quite justified in his opposition to Zosima's all-embracing tolerance for sin (14: 301).

It is at this moment that Ferapont, followed by the usual curious crowd of sensation-seekers, creates one of Dostoevsky's typical scandal scenes by bursting into the cell where the Gospel was being read at Zosima's bier. He noisily casts out the devils, as was his wont, and when rebuked by Father Paissy for creating disorder, he shouts, "like a holy fool," that Zosima did not believe in devils. As proof, he exclaims that Zosima had once advised a priest, haunted by visions of evil spirits, to take a purgative in addition to his "continual prayer and rigid fastings." He also repeats some of the charges that the profane Feodor Pavlovich had gleefully thrown at the monks in the opening chapters. Father Zosima "did not keep the fasts according to the rules and the sign has come.... He was seduced by sweets, ladies brought them to him in their pockets, he sipped tea, he worshiped his belly, filling it with sweet things and his mind with haughty thoughts.... And for this he was put to shame" (14: 302–303). Whether profane or sacred, these two literalists of the supernatural are again linked by such an echoing of motifs; and Dostoevsky's narrator leaves us in no doubt about *his* opinion of Ferapont, characterizing him as "a fanatic carried away by a zeal that outstripped his reason" (ibid.).

Father Ferapont finally retreats, but not before disclosing the purely personal jealousy that lies behind his charges of heresy. As both a priest and a monk, Zosima is entitled to the singing of a particular canticle during the burial ceremony; but Ferapont, only a monk, will receive a lesser honor, only "a little canticle," as he says, "suddenly leaning his cheek on his hand despondently ... [and] looking at the coffin of the elder." Ferapont also falls to the ground like Zosima, but there is nothing Franciscan in this presumed gesture of adoration. "'My God has conquered! Christ has conquered as the sun is setting!' he shout[ed] frantically, stretching out his hands to the sun, and, falling face downward on the ground, he sobbed like a little child, shaken by his tears and spreading out his arms on the ground" (14: 303–304). Unlike Zosima, he is not watering the earth with tears of joy and forgiveness for all; rather, he is giving vent to his resentment and rage, and the narrator uses strong language ("the frantic outcries of bigots") to describe what Father Paissy felt about Ferapont's disruption of the funeral service and his denunciation of the corpse.

The attitude of the narrator himself is much the same. "I feel it almost repulsive to recall that event," and he would not have done so "if it had not exerted a very strong influence on the heart and soul of the chief, though *future*, hero of my story" (14: 297). Indeed, the death of Zosima and the "odor of corruption" present a turning point not only in the life of Alyosha but in that of Grushenka as well. Unlike them, many who had officially devoted their lives to the service of God reveal little of the true spirit of Christian love, exhibiting rather the pettiness of their natures and the obscurantism of their convictions. Ironically, it is the inexperienced novice Alyosha and the repentant sinner Grushenka who display the truth of Zosima's words that "men are always saved after the death of the deliverer."

3

Book 7 portrays the temptation of Alyosha, begun in Book 5 during his conversation with Ivan in the tavern. Since then, Ivan's powerful attack on God for having created a world of suffering and injustice had continued to undermine Alyosha's formerly untroubled and unquestioning faith; and the death of Father Zosima, coupled with his seeming disgrace, had dealt a staggering blow to the tranquil stability of his convictions. But his faith will reemerge strengthened from the trial; and this reaffirmation is already foreshadowed by the encounter with Grushenka. Two of the four chapters deal with the Grushenka-Alyosha meeting and the similarity in their situations. Grushenka is struggling between feelings of resentment and rage against the Polish officer who had seduced and abandoned her as a young girl, and a desire to forgive in the hope of beginning a new, honorable life. Alyosha is struggling between his initial, naïve faith in a loving God and a hitherto unknown resentment against Him for having exposed His faithful servitor, Father Zosima, to posthumous humiliation.

Father Zosima's death had plunged Alyosha into the profoundest grief. When Father Paissy observes him slinking away from the monastery rather than assisting at evening prayer and asks, "Can you be with those of little faith?" he receives no reply, only "a wry smile" and "a strange, a very strange look" (14: 305). Alyosha's evasive behavior causes the narrator to enter into an unusually detailed account of his state of mind. In fact, Dostoevsky as author was faced with a particular problem here because he wished to avoid equating Alyosha's reaction with that displayed by the monks hostile to Zosima. Still, Alyosha had found it impossible to maintain the equilibrium of Father Paissy or Father Iosif, who, even if troubled, either refuse to give the odor of corruption any oracular significance or invoke other traditions to establish sanctity. On the surface Alyosha thus joins the hostile monks, although he is dismayed rather than gratified (as so many of them were) by the seeming repudiation of his revered mentor; and the narrator thus feels it necessary to distinguish his response from theirs.

"Reasonable people," he agrees, could regard the commotion over Zosima as "superstition"—surely a significant admission by Dostoevsky that his readers might at best smile tolerantly at such benighted monkish beliefs! And so he raises the question of whether a young man like Alyosha, so strongly affected by such beliefs, should be treated as the future hero of a narrative set in the modern world. The narrator insists that he does not wish to "apologize" for Alyosha, but he in fact does so by stressing his youth and by explaining that his reaction had sprung not from any "frivolous and impatient expectation of miracles" (presumably like that of many of the monks), or because he desired "the triumph of some preconceived idea" (presumably that the sanctity of Father Zosima would receive a heavenly reward). No, his dismay was caused solely by his overwhelming love for Father Zosima; and the narrator argues that "it is really more creditable to be carried away by an emotion, *however unreasonable*, which springs from a great love, than to be unmoved" (14: 305–306; italics added).

It was this "great love" for Father Zosima that had caused Alyosha to question Providence and to ask why God had hidden His face. Why had He disgraced, by the indignity of premature decay, "the holiest of holy men . . . as though involuntarily submitting to the blind, dumb, pitiless laws of nature"? The narrator insists that "it was not miracles [Alyosha] needed but only 'the higher justice' which had been in his belief outraged by the blow that had so suddenly and so cruelly wounded his heart." Because such "higher justice" presumably would have meant displaying a certain immunity to "the pitiless laws of nature," Alyosha was hoping for confirmation of his belief in the holiness of Father Zosima. All the narrator's apologetic efforts cannot conceal that, even if inspired by the greatness of his love, Alyosha has yielded like the others to the second temptation of the Devil. And at this moment, quite appropriately, Alyosha also recalls the "vague but tormenting impression left by his conversation with Ivan the day before," who had also found intolerable this lack of any "higher justice" in a creation that allowed the suffering of innocent children (14: 306–307).

Most likely this is why, for the first and only time, the narrator allows himself to criticize the character he had taken under his wing: "All the love that lay concealed in his pure young heart for 'everyone and everything' had, for the past year, been concentrated—*and perhaps wrongly so*—primarily . . . on his beloved elder, now dead" (14: 306; italics added). As a result, the shock of the event led him to neglect his obligations to "everyone and everything"—for example, to his brother Dimitry, whom he had been told to watch over, and to the Snegiryov family, for whom he had been entrusted with two hundred rubles by Katerina Ivanovna. Alyosha's situation is similar, though of lesser magnitude, to that of Ivan, whose "rebellion" allowed him to stifle any resistance to a possible murder. The parallel is clearly drawn in his conversation with the cynical and disabused Rakitin. Observing Alyosha's disillusionment, the latter scoffs at his dismay "because your old man had begun to stink," amusedly accusing him of "being in a temper with your God, you are rebelling against him." Alyosha's reply—"I am not rebelling against my God; I simply 'don't accept his world'"—quotes Ivan's very words (14: 308).

## 4

A characteristic of Dostoevsky's mature technique is to refract a thematic motif through a succession of characters, each of whom expresses a different aspect or level of its meaning. The totally unprincipled Rakitin is thus another version of Ivan, completely lacking those moral-religious yearnings that Father Zosima had instantly detected in the young, controversial publicist. The narrator exhibits no mercy whatever toward Rakitin, who is now shown as wishing to tempt the weakened Alyosha on another level. At first, he merely inquires whether Alyosha will break the dietary rules of the monastery; and when the latter unexpectedly agrees to this minor infraction, his pretended friend decides to lead the innocent to the home of Grushenka. In the past, she had urged Rakitin to bring Alyosha for a visit, believing that, as the purest of the pure, he looked down on her with contempt; and she wished to obtain revenge by seducing her presumed despiser. However, this aim had now been replaced by a worthier emotion, for at this critical moment of her life she was awaiting the summons from her Polish ex-lover to come and join him. Her mood had thus entirely changed, and Alyosha, who had only seen her previously in the act of humiliating Katerina Ivanovna, observed that "her eyes glowed, her lips laughed, but it was a good-natured, merry laugh. Alyosha had not expected to see such a kind expression on her face" (14: 314).

All the same, urged on by Rakitin, she sits on Alyosha's knees, "like a nestling kitten," though "the great grief in his heart swallowed up every sensation that might have been aroused" (14: 315). But when she hears of Father Zosima's death, she "instantly slipped off his knees," crossed herself, and apologized to Alyosha for her frivolity at such a time. The genuine piety of her reaction moves him deeply, "and a light seemed to dawn in his face." He tells Rakitin that "I've found a true sister, I have found a treasure—a loving heart. She had pity on me just now" (14: 318). Alyosha's words stir a similar response in Grushenka, who expresses remorse over her evil intention to "get [Alyosha] in her clutches" as she had done with Dimitry and their father; and she confesses to having offered Rakitin twenty-five rubles, which she pays on the spot, to bring him to her house (the symbolism of Judas is obvious). But now everything is transformed, and memories of her unsullied childhood resurface as she retells the folktale of the onion, heard long ago from a peasant woman still in her employ.

This tale embodies that condemnation of a totally self-centered egoism which, according to Dostoevsky, was typical of the morality of the Russian folk character, and it is narrated by Grushenka in a style imitative of folk poetry. A wicked old woman, submerged in the fiery lake of Hell, had once given an onion to a beggarwoman, and her guardian angel endeavors to save her because of this one good deed. The angel lowers an onion to pull her up; but when other sinners cling to her as she rises, she cries back at them, "It's my onion, not yours." At this expression of selfishness the stem snaps, she falls back into Hell, and the angel sadly departs (14: 319).

This childhood recollection provokes an even stronger crisis of conscience in Grushenka, and the full story of her unhappy past comes tumbling forth as she accuses herself of being "a violent, vindictive creature" whose behavior had been inspired by revengefulness. Alyosha is so moved by her confession and repentance, as well as the strength of her desire to forgive her Polish betrayer, that he tells Rakitin: "She is more loving than we" (14: 321). When the disgruntled cynic asks what Alyosha has said that stirs Grushenka so profoundly, she falls on her knees before her "cherub" and answers: "I've been waiting all my life for someone like you. I knew that someone like you would come and forgive me . . . would really love me, not only with a shameful love" (14: 323). The scene recalls the first meeting between Prince Myshkin and Nastasya Philippovna in *The Idiot*, when the prince recognizes the purity of her spirit despite her past degradation.

Just as in *The Idiot* again, where Nastasya asks Prince Myshkin to decide whether she should marry, Grushenka asks Alyosha to make the fateful decision whether she should now forgive her seducer. Alyosha replies: "You have forgiven him already" (14: 322). Although she appears to agree, Grushenka a moment later, "with a sort of menace in her voice," wonders if his words are true; and all her outrage erupts again as she imagines taking revenge by tempting her ex-seducer with her mature beauty and then discarding him the next moment. On the point of departure, she shouts out a message for Alyosha to give to Dimitry: "Grushenka has fallen to a scoundrel, and not to you, noble heart," and to add that she had loved Dimitry "only one hour" but that he should "remember that hour all his life" (14: 324). This message foreshadows their future union, and the symbolic meaning of this scene is brought out by the comment of the disappointed Rakitin. Having hoped to debauch Alyosha, he spitefully refers instead to his intended victim as having "turned the Magdalene onto the true path." The sarcasm of his embittered words nonetheless reluctantly recognizes the truth: "So you see that the miracles you were looking for just now have come to pass" (ibid.). Genuine miracles occur when faith succeeds in aiding the morality of love to conquer egoistic resentment, hatred, and revenge.

## 5

Alyosha's second encounter with Grushenka thus restores him to himself, and reveals the depths of unselfish love hidden in the human conscience. Men and women are not as weak and selfish as Ivan's Grand Inquisitor had claimed; they are quite capable of putting into practice the morality of love stemming from a faith in Christ. The meeting thus serves as a transition to the resolution of Alyosha's crisis. This begins when he reenters the cell where Father Paissy, holding a vigil beside Father Zosima's corpse, is reading aloud from the Gospel of Saint John. The agitations of the day have taken their toll, and Alyosha is exhausted; but unlike the other novice sleeping on the floor with "the deep sound sleep of youth," he falls on his knees and begins to pray. His state of mind had entirely changed, and "the odor of corruption . . . no longer made him feel miserable and indignant." Instead, "there was a sweetness in his heart . . . and joy, joy was glowing in his mind and in his heart" (14: 325).

Such joy, a leitmotif of this chapter, indicates the first effect of his meeting with Grushenka, and it continues to dominate his subconscious. After dozing off, his thoughts mingle with what he hears being read—the account of the wedding feast in "Cana of Galilee." Dostoevsky's narrator here employs a stream-of-consciousness technique that fuses the external and the internal. Thoughts about Grushenka ("there is happiness for her too") and Rakitin ("he will always go off to the back alley") blend with the Gospel narrative. The passage from Saint John is one that Alyosha has always loved—"it's Cana of Galilee," he tells himself, "the first miracle"—the miracle in which Christ changed water into wine at the wedding feast of a poor, humble couple.

The thought that "He worked His first miracle to help man's joy" passes through Alyosha's mind, and he also recalls that Father Zosima had said, "He who loves men loves their joy too." The Mother of Christ was present at the feast, and Alyosha muses that she "knew that He had come not only to make His great, terrible sacrifice" but also to bring joy to humankind. By now asleep and dreaming, Alyosha suddenly sees Father Zosima, no longer lying in his coffin but moving among the guests, approaching his adoring young disciple. Raising Alyosha from his knees, Zosima invites him to join the feast, explaining his presence at the joyous occasion by saying, "I gave an onion to a beggar. And many here have given only an onion each—only one little onion . . . " Alyosha too had "known how to give an onion to a famished woman today"; and the Father tells him, "Begin your work, dear one, begin it, gentle one," in effect instructing Alyosha to continue the "work" he had instinctively begun with Grushenka. Christ, also among the guests, is not named but referred to as "our Sun"; and when Alyosha is too overcome even to cast a glance in His direction, Zosima urges him to do so. "He is terrible in His greatness, awful in His sublimity, but infinitely merciful"; He "had made Himself like unto us from love and rejoices with us." The opponents of Father Zosima had thus been right in charging that *his* Christ did not view earthly life only as "a vale of tears"; unlike them, the saintly monk sees it rather as the venue for the happiness and joy of mutual love and forgiveness. With this resurrected image of Father Zosima still before his mind's eye, and as "tears of rapture rose from his soul," Alyosha "uttered a cry and woke up" (14: 325–327).

Alyosha's awakening is the prelude to the great scene in which, symbollically, the spirit of Father Zosima becomes reembodied in the young novice. After gazing at the corpse lying in state, whose voice he had just heard in his dream, Alyosha walks out into the night, where "the vault of heaven, full of soft, shining stars stretched vast and fathomless above him." Dostoevsky exerts all his poetic powers to evoke the beauty of the spectacle, and to infuse it with a sense of religious awe. "The white towers and golden domes of the cathedral gleamed out against the sapphire sky," and Alyosha, invaded by a feeling that "the mystery of the earth was one with the mystery of the stars," throws himself down, following the injunctions of his teacher, to embrace the earth and water it with his tears. "There seemed to be threads from all those innumerable worlds of God, linking his soul to them, and it was trembling all over 'in contact with other worlds.' He longed to forgive everyone and for everything, and to beg forgiveness" (14: 328).

The climax of this scene is a famous and oft-quoted passage:

With every instant, [Alyosha] felt clearly and, as it were, palpably, that something firm and unshakable as that vault of heaven had entered into his soul. It was as though some idea had seized the sovereignty of his mind—and it was for all his life forever and ever. He had fallen to earth a weak youth, but he rose up a resolute champion. . . . "Someone visited my soul in that moment," he used to say afterward, with firm belief in his words. (Ibid.)

What Dostoevsky conveys here—the confluence of the earthly and the heavenly that Father Zosima had proclaimed—cannot be mistaken, and it is reinforced by Alyosha's decision to leave the monastery three days later, obeying Father Zosima's command to "sojourn in the world." Nonetheless, some commentators have remarked on the imprecision and vagueness of the language used—"something firm and unshakable"; "someone visited my soul"—and have wondered whether what Alyosha felt might not be considered more an instance of nature-mysticism than "the foundation of a Christian Orthodox commitment."[1] The question has thus arisen as to why no specific mention of Christ is made in this crucial passage.

One should keep in mind that Dostoevsky knew he was writing for a skeptical audience (recall the narrator's comments about Alyosha), and may reasonably have thought that a religious reverence inspired by nature—which Father Zosima had already expressed, and to which his readers would offer little internal resistance—would be enough, combined with the monastic setting, to communicate the Christian import of this scene. In effect, the unnamed Christ is awesomely present and triply praised in Alyosha's dream. Moreover, the sublime meaning of the Incarnation had been expressed: "He had made Himself like unto us from love." Modern commentators too often forget that Dostoevsky was writing under a triple censorship—of his editors, of the government, and of the religious authorities. He had by no means forgotten Katkov's objection to his first version of Sonya's reading of the raising of Lazarus in *Crime and Punishment*, when he had been required to rewrite the entire chapter. Even earlier, he had complained in a letter to his brother about the official censors who had mutilated Part I of *Notes from Underground* by eliminating the passages "where I concluded with the need for faith and Christ."[2] In this instance, he may well have decided not to take any risks, and preferred to rely on the Christ-image evoked earlier, strengthened by the cosmic mysticism that is also an important element of Orthodox theology.

## CHAPTER 36

# The Brothers Karamazov:
# Books 8–9

From Alyosha, Dostoevsky shifts to Dimitry in Book 8, and there is a change in tonality as well as in character focus. These chapters contain much more external action, and the horizon widens to include more than the monastery world and the immediately surrounding town. This broader perspective provides an opportunity to delineate new figures: Grushenka's aged protector, the wealthy merchant Kuzma Samsonov living in antiquated opulence; the charitably tolerant peasant coachman Andrey; and the dishonest innkeeper Trifon Borisovich, a kulak who despises and exploits the peasantry. At least one contemporary review praised the novel for providing such a wide-ranging image of Russian society. Books 7 and 8 also overlap chronologically, since the death of Father Zosima, as the narrator has reminded us, caused Alyosha to lose sight of his brother Dimitry, and Book 8 returns to depict Dimitry in this same time interval. During these hours, Alyosha recovered not so much a faith in God that he had never lost as a faith in the ultimate beauty and goodness of God's universe. Dimitry, on the other hand, was frantically watching to see whether Grushenka would visit his father, and searching desperately for the means of obtaining the money that might allow him to begin a new life with her.

## 2

The narrator takes great pains to explain all the twist and turns of Dimitry's agitated emotions, which had become concentrated on the rivalry with his father rather than on Grushenka's Polish ex-lover. Dimitry had heard vaguely about the latter's possible arrival but did not believe him any immediate threat; it was his father whose competition he feared. Nor was he seeking for money in order to bid against the old sensualist for Grushenka's favors. Mingled with his sexual passion was also the hope of some sort of moral regeneration, though the narrator treats this longing with a touch of irony: "Oh, then [if he obtained the money] he would bear her away at once . . . to the furthest end of Russia, if not of the earth . . . then he would marry her *incognito* . . . then, oh then, a new life would begin at once! Of this different, reformed, and 'virtuous' life ('it must be, it must be virtuous') he dreamed feverishly at every moment" (14: 330). Despite the narrator's skepticism, Dimitry's yearning for a reformed and virtuous life already prepares the way for the resolution of *his* inner crisis.

All sorts of frantic thoughts race through his mind, but care is taken to specify that Dimitry's thoughts for the future were a complete blank. "Mitya did not know what would happen [if Grushenka were not to choose him]. That must be said to his credit. He had no definite intentions, he had planned no crime" (ibid.). So as not to slacken the suspense already aroused, the narrator also quotes Dimitry as saying that "it would be better to murder and rob someone than fail to pay my debt to Katya," that is, the money confided to him by Katerina Ivanovna and which he had presumably squandered on Grushenka at Mokroe (14: 331). The action of the first three chapters of Book 8 thus focuses on Dimitry's futile and hopeless quest for financial succor. This search allows Dostoevsky to slow down the tempo of his plot action, to indulge in a bit of local-color realism and satirical comedy, and to emphasize the importance to Dimitry of his sense of honor—he *must* repay his debt—as well as to illustrate his good-natured simplicity.

He first attempts to obtain the money from Grushenka's aged protector, Kuzma Samsonov, offering him in exchange a dubious deed on a property owned by Feodor Pavlovich to which Dimitry believed he had a legal right. Poor Dimitry imagined that he might obtain some help because the feeble old man, close to death, perhaps felt some remorse over his relations with Grushenka; but this expectation merely testifies to distress over his own past and makes clear that, "in spite of all his vices, he was a very simple-hearted man" (14: 332). The reader is both ironically and pityingly amused as Dimitry is bamboozled by the tight-fisted merchant, who earlier had advised Grushenka not to have anything to do with Dimitry but to marry his rich father.

Dostoevsky had previously portrayed a merchant household in *The Idiot*, but there he had wished to communicate an atmosphere of doom-laden Gothic gloom; here he combines an empty, decrepit grandeur with the tyrannical and capricious power familiar from the playwright Alexander Ostrovsky's depiction of the same milieu. Samsonov refuses Dimitry's offer, but cannot resist sadistically taking advantage of his simplicity by sending him off on a wild-goose chase for a possible purchaser. The pathos of the episode is enhanced by Dimitry's overflowing gratitude as he offers his thanks for this treacherous advice: "It's a Russian who says that, Kuzma Samsonov, a R-r-russian!" (14: 336). Dashing off to seek the presumed buyer, who turns out to be dead drunk in a forest hut in the middle of the night, Dimitry saves him from suffocation by charcoal fumes but cannot get a sensible word from the drink-sodden, wily, and suspicious peasant.

These semicomic episodes are climaxed by a visit to Mme Khokhlakova, when Dimitry suddenly recalls that she had always opposed his engagement to Katerina Ivanovna. The scene between them, in Dostoevsky's best vein of satirical mockery, is the most unalloyedly comic of these chapters. The scatterbrained dowager initially arouses Dimitry's highest hopes. "You ask for a certain sum, for three thousand, but I can give you more, immeasurably more, I will save you," she assures him (14: 348). The overjoyed Dimitry can hardly believe his ears; but then he realizes that all she has to offer is the advice to go to the Siberian gold mines, where she is certain he will make a fortune. Ready to fluctuate like a weather vane to every change in the ideological climate, the formerly devout admirer of Father Zosima now maintains that, "after all the business with Father Zosima, which has so upset me, from this very day I'm a realist and I want to devote myself to practical usefulness. I'm cured. 'Enough!' as Turgenev says" (14: 348). (Whether questioning Father Zosima about immortality or now rallying to the banner of "realism," the loquacious lady always ends with a citation from Turgenev.) On the very next page, however, she puts a necklace with the picture of a wonder-working saint from Kiev around Dimitry's neck. At last understanding that he will not obtain a kopek, Dimitry becomes so enraged that he frightens her to death; but when he reaches the street, he "burst out crying like a little child" (14: 351).

## 3

Temporal continuity is then skillfully restored when Dimitry learns of events already familiar to the reader. Believing that Grushenka has gone to Feodor Pavlovich's and that his worst fears have come true, he rushes to his father's house and leaps over the fence at the very spot "where, according to tradition, he knew that Stinking Lizaveta had once climbed over it" to give birth to Smerdyakov (14: 353). Once inside the garden, he cannot see Grushenka in the room where Feodor Pavlovich is feverishly awaiting her; to make certain, and since the door of the house opening onto the garden is closed, he taps on the window frame with the signal (learned from Smerdyakov) that would announce her arrival. His father approaches the window, and the narrator describes Dimitry's feelings at the sight: "The old man's profile that he loathed so, his pendant Adam's apple, his hooked nose, his lips that smiled in greedy expectation, were all brightly lit by the slanting lamplight. A terrible fury of hatred suddenly surged up in Mitya's heart." And Dimitry himself recalls having told Alyosha that he might kill his father in an excess of rage, because "I'm afraid he'll suddenly be so loathsome to me *at that moment,* with that face of his." The fateful moment seems to have arrived: "Mitya was beside himself. He suddenly pulled out the brass pestle" (this instrument had been snatched up in passing)—and then the action stops! (14: 354–355).

A line of dots marks the mysterious hiatus left by the narrator at this point, and the reader remains in the dark about Dimitry's next move. The narrative resumes again with the statement: " 'God,' as Mitya himself later said, 'watched over me then' " (ibid.). This sentence, interrupted by a semicolon in the Russian, then continues with a shift to the servant Grigory, who awakens and tries to stop Dimitry as he is running to climb back over the fence. Victor Terras, in his very valuable commentary on the novel, writes that this half-sentence "make[s] it quite clear that Dimitry did not kill his father."[1] But the letter to Dostoevsky from the troubled reader (discussed in Chapter 25) reveals a continuing uncertainty over whether Dimitry was or was not the murderer. It would seem that Dostoevsky had built up his character's motivation so strongly that the half-sentence, combined with the gap in the narrative, had been insufficient to clarify the matter for her (and perhaps for others as well). One reason for the blank, and Dostoevsky's laconicism, was no doubt to avoid, so far as possible, weakening the chain of events designating Dimitry as the murderer. Another is also, perhaps, to suggest that not everything occurring in this location on that fateful night has been told. It is only much later, during Ivan's last interview with Smerdyakov (Book 11, Chapter 8), that the reader discovers what has been earlier omitted.

Although Dimitry did not attack his father, he does beat off Grigory, striking the old man with the brass pestle he still holds and then leaping back into the garden to ascertain whether he has killed him. Dimitry's hands and clothes become covered with the blood streaming from the old man's skull, and he fears him to be dead. Dimitry then rushes to Grushenka's house, terrorizing the servants with his bloodstained appearance and his fury, only to discover that she has left to meet her Polish officer. Suddenly, Dimitry realizes his error in considering his father to be his most important rival. A complete change then takes place in his mood as the oedipal antagonism vanishes, now replaced by a surge of tenderness for Grushenka, gone to meet a first, never forgotten, love. Dimitry is a man of honor (or wishes to consider himself so), and he instantly feels he has no right to attempt to oppose Grushenka's chance for happiness and respectability.

Earlier, Dimitry had declared that the ideal of the Madonna and the ideal of Sodom were battling in the heart of man, and his own character is an embodiment of this conflict. Despite his tumultuous passions, the ideal of the Madonna had gained the upper hand when he had refrained from violating Katerina Ivanovna; and the ideal of the Madonna, the all-merciful Mother of God, had just exerted her power again in staying his hand against his father. It is this same ideal that now affects his feelings for Grushenka when, speaking to the terrified servants "as gently and quietly as a gentle and affectionate child," he learns of the tender parting words that Grushenka had shouted to Alyosha—that Dimitry should "remember forever that she had loved him for an hour." When asked about his bloodstained appearance, he replies: "That is human blood, and, my God! Why was it shed?"

Believing that he has killed Grigory, who had been a substitute father to him, and that he no longer has any right to pursue Grushenka, he decides on a high-Romantic, Wertherian suicide consistent with his Schillerian citations. The fence he had just vaulted now becomes emblematic of his life, and he declaims to the bewildered servants, though actually addressing the image of Grushenka in his heart: "At dawn tomorrow, when the sun rises, Mitya will leap over that fence. . . . I'll step aside, I know how to step aside. . . . Live, my love, you loved me for an hour, remember Mityenka Karamazov so forever" (14: 357–358). Such words are the prelude to the burgeoning of a genuinely passionate and "normal" love relation with Grushenka that brings out the finest feelings in both—the only instance in Dostoevsky's novels of such a reciprocated relation treated on so extensive a scale. The love between Dunya Raskolnikov and Razumikhin in *Crime and Punishment* is kept largely in the background and lacks the element of sensual attraction maturing into wholehearted devotion that Dostoevsky now portrays.

With suicide in mind, Dimitry goes to retrieve the set of dueling pistols he had pawned with the very proper and conscientious young official Dimitry Ilyich Perkhotin; but the previously penniless Dimitry is now awkwardly brandishing a wad of bills, as if surprised himself by their appearance in his hands. Overwrought and distraught, he alternates between bewilderment and exaltation; and on the spur of the moment, accidentally hearing the name of the most luxurious grocery shop in town, decides to repeat the turbulent festivities of his first visit with Grushenka to Mokroe—the night when she had loved him for an hour. Surprised at Dimitry's sudden affluence, Perkhotin cannot resist asking if he had found "a gold mine," provoking a roar of laughter and the advice to visit Mme Khokhlakova, "who'll stump up three thousand for you if only you'll go" (14: 362). Dimitry thus leaves the impression, without actually saying so, that she had been the source of his money.

All through this conversation, Dimitry alternates between suggestions of his intended suicide and ecstatic invocations to his love of life. When loading one of his pistols, he examines the bullet very carefully, explaining to his curious companion: "It's going into my brain, so it's interesting to look and see what it's like" (14: 363, 367). Swinging from one extreme to the other, he answers an "uneasy" inquiry of his companion: "I was fooling about the bullet. I want to live. I love life. . . . I love golden-haired Phoebus and his warm light" (14: 367). His resolution to "step aside" has also led Dimitry, in what he believes to be these final hours, to take stock of his life; and the remorse he had expressed earlier about his behavior now reaches its apogee. When Dimitry remarks that "I have never liked all this disorder," Perkhotin thinks he is referring to the bustle of the store (they have both gone to the grocer's). "That's not what I mean," Dimitry says. "I'm talking of a higher order. There is no order in me, no higher order. My whole life has been a disorder, and one must set it in order" (14: 366). The events of that night have thus determined Dimitry to end his life both with a final orgy and a moral self-condemnation. "Let's drink to life, dear boy," he invites the disconcerted Perkhotin. "I propose the toast. I'm ready to bless God and His creation directly, but . . . I must kill one noxious insect for fear it should crawl and spoil life for others" (ibid.).

His departure for Mokroe leaves unanswered all the questions that had arisen in the mind of the judicious Pyotr Ilyich, who at first dismisses them as merely another product of Dimitry's well-known and ill-famed reputation for brawling, drunkenness, and incoherent threats. But when he mentions Dimitry's mysterious wealth to others while playing billiards in a tavern, "the story of Mme Khokhlakova's present was received with some skepticism," and someone asks: "Hasn't he robbed the old father, that's the question?" (14: 369). All these suggestions disturb the already troubled young official, who keeps silent in public about the blood he had helped Dimitry wash off his face and hands. A sudden impulse causes him, though he is terribly annoyed with himself for doing so, to walk toward Grushenka's house to question her servant Fenya. She had appeared just as the carriage was leaving for Mokroe and had begged Dimitry, in Perkhotin's presence, not to harm her mistress. Chapter 5 ends with Perkhotin knocking at the door and, obtaining no response, knocking even harder. At this point the narrator leaves him frozen like a character in *Tristram Shandy*; not until three chapters later will his knock be answered.

4

The three chapters devoted to Dimitry's trip to Mokroe and to the events following on his arrival provide Dostoevsky with another opportunity to diversify his narrative with some local-color realism. As Dimitry gallops off to his last rendezvous (or so he believes) with the woman now forever beyond his grasp, he feels inspired by a "new and unknown feeling, surprising even to himself, a feeling tender to devoutness, to self-effacement before her" (14: 370). On the way, his peasant driver Andrey, having heard Fenya's tearful plea that Dimitry not harm Grushenka, worries about taking him to commit an evil deed; but Dimitry replies, in terms that Andrey can understand, that "a driver must not run over people" and that he has no intention of doing so. Andrey then responds in a manner illustrating Father Zosima's loftiest words about the beliefs of the Russian people. "You're quite right, one mustn't crush or torment a man, or any kind of creature, for every creature is created by God" (14: 311). Dimitry further asks "Andrey, simple soul," whether "Dimitry Feodorovich Karamazov will go to Hell." Andrey replies with a variant of Ivan's legend about the harrowing of Hell by the Mother of God. "When the Son of God was nailed on the Cross and died, He went straight down to Hell from the Cross, and set free all sinners that were in agony." The Devil groaned because he feared that Hell would remain unpopulated, but God reassured him that it would be filled to overflowing with the rich and the mighty of the earth, all "the rulers, the chief judges," until He came again. As for the judgment of the people about Dimitry, they think that "you're like a child . . . that's how we look upon you . . . and though you're hasty-tempered, sir, yet God will forgive you for your kind heart" (14: 372).

Greeting Dimitry on his arrival at the inn is Trifon Borisovich, a successful Smerdyakov devoid of religiously diabolic overtones. He is a peasant who has risen above his lowly origins and become a kulak, "forever dreaming of improving his position." "More than half of the peasants were in his clutches, every one in the neighborhood was in debt to him," and he speaks of them with the utmost contempt (14: 373). When Dimitry orders an expensive feast with music and dancing, the innkeeper thinks such prodigality a terrible waste. "To spend a sum like that on such coarseness and rudeness! What's the good of giving a peasant a cigar to smoke, the stinking ruffian! And the girls are all lousy" (14: 374). Trifon is also, as the narrator specifies, "very fond of emptying the pockets of a drunken guest," and, to the tune of two or three hundred rubles, he had done just that a month earlier with Dimitry (14: 373).

Among the guests at the tavern are two Poles come to meet Grushenka. With the single exception of his Polish fellow prisoners in *House of the Dead*, written before the Polish uprising of 1863–1865 against Russian rule, Dostoevsky's portrayal of Polish characters is invariably caricatural. In *The Gambler*, the obsequious Polish scroungers haunting the tables are all petty crooks; and in *The Idiot*, Aglaya Epanchina marries a glamorous and presumably patriotic Polish count, professing the highest ideals, who turns out be a complete impostor. The Polish characters in *The Brothers Karamazov* do not fare any better. Dostoevsky remains true to his xenophobic form, and the two Poles assume an air of unassailable dignity and nobility to compensate for the obvious inferiority of their social status.

Dimitry had resolved to behave in a decorous manner during his final hours, though he breaks down and cries on catching sight of Grushenka; but he quickly recovers and calls for champagne, trying as best he can to exhibit his willingness to "step aside" for the sake of her presumed happiness. The pathetically comic buffoon Maximov, who has turned up at the inn by chance, raises the hackles of the Poles by his off-color anecdotes about "Polish ladies"; and they insult Dimitry by refusing to drink a toast to Russia (except as "she was before 1772," that is, before the first partition of Poland). To ease the situation Dimitry proposes a card game, in which he suffers considerable losses until the pompous Poles are exposed as cheats.

From the very beginning of these scenes, it is clear that Grushenka has become totally disillusioned with the Polish object of her girlish infatuation, who had returned, she now realizes, purely for mercenary reasons. "I've been a fool, a fool," she declares, "to have been miserable these five years. And it wasn't for his sake, it was my anger made me miserable. . . . And this isn't he. . . . It might be his father" (14: 388). After the Poles are evicted from the main room in disgrace, a genuine party begins as the village girls arrive to dance and sing, accompanied by a Jewish band. Both Dimitry and Grushenka become drunk, and she finally confesses that she has loved him ever since their first night at Mokroe. She begs Dimitry "to kiss me, kiss me hard. . . . I'll be your slave now, your slave for the rest of my life" (15: 395–396). Nonetheless, she discerns that he is troubled for reasons she cannot understand. Dimitry himself has now reached the acme of his desires, but is anguished at the thought that he probably murdered Grigory and will have to pay the price. Citing Christ in the Gospels, he silently implores God to "restore to life the man I knocked down at the fence! Let this fearful cup pass from me!" (14: 394). Forgetting this torment in Grushenka's arms, his too-ardent caresses are repulsed as she tells him to await the proper moment; but the background action brings out the passionate eroticism of their encounter. The pantomime and songs of the peasant girls make the pure young man Kalganov, a paler version of Alyosha, feel as if he were "besmirched with dirt," and the antics of Maximov, who hopes to obtain some sexual favors from one or another of the girls, parody the unquenchable lust of Feodor Pavlovich (14: 392).

In the midst of her happiness, the moral transformation that Grushenka has already undergone with Alyosha continues to exercise its influence. Recalling Alyosha's inspiring words to her, she instructs

Dimitry to provide some money for the gyrating Maximov ("Give him a present, he's poor you know"). Unconstrained revelry was the order of the day, but the flush of joy inspires the new Grushenka to declare that God would not look unkindly on their merrymaking: "God will forgive us, if I were God, I'd forgive everyone: 'My dear sinners, from this day forth I forgive you'" (14: 397). Here again, as with the coachman Andrey, the voice of the Russian people speaks in accents that echo Father Zosima. Grushenka now forgives her Polish ex-lover, as Alyosha had predicted, and tells Dimitry to invite him and his companion to watch her dance; but she is too overcome with drink to do so. Dimitry carries the collapsing Grushenka to an adjoining bedroom while the festivities continue and they doze off together, but not before we see again the metamorphosis that has lifted their mutual love above sensuality to a level that Kierkegaard would have called "ethical." "It must be honorable. . . . It shall be honorable for the future," Grushenka says, and Dimitry fervently agrees. Then she adds a Populist peasant-rooted nuance to their decision to start a new life together: "But we'd better go and work the land. I want to dig the earth with my own hands" (14: 398–399).

Using a masterful stream-of-consciousness technique again, the narrator evokes the images flitting through Grushenka's somnolence. Haunted by guilt over Grigory, Dimitry had said, "I'll love you in Siberia," and Grushenka weaves this declaration together with her own thoughts and the sounds filtering into her sensibility. "Why Siberia . . . there's snow in Siberia . . . I love driving in the snow . . . and must have bells. . . . Do you hear a bell ringing? Where is the bell ringing? There are people coming. . . . Now it's stopped" (14: 399). The bells intruding into her reveries were those of the carriage bringing a party from the city—the police captain, the deputy prosecutor, the district attorney, the inspector of police—come to arrest Dimitry. On catching sight of them, Dimitry cries aloud: "The old man! . . . The old man and his blood! . . . I understand." His words of course refer to Grigory, but are taken to mean Feodor Pavlovich, and the older police captain roars: "Your father's blood cries out against you!" (14: 400). It is only this old-fashioned official who expresses any moral outrage, thereby shocking the younger representatives of the new legal system, who behave with cold and controlled formality, by this breach of legal decorum.

5

Once again a time overlap in the narrative is used to create the shock effect of the sudden appearance of the legal authorities. As already noted, Dostoevsky had not intended to include a chapter dealing with the preliminary investigation that takes place at Mokroe. Once having decided to do so, however, he immediately saw that it could be used to great advantage for two purposes. One was to portray what he considered "a sore spot" in the criminal trial procedure of the new legal system established in the mid-1860s. It was then that the "preliminary investigation" had been instituted, combining, as Dostoevsky saw it, "with the old routine . . . the most abstract impersonality embodied in the young lawyers, judicial investigators, and so on." Another was to develop the moral growth and stature of Dimitry, a process that had already begun with his self-sacrificing decision "to step aside" and with the blossoming of his genuine love for Grushenka. Dimitry too undergoes a decisive moral transformation, and his "spiritual purification" is completed during the several hours of the examination to which Book 9 is devoted.

Filling in what had occurred simultaneously with the Mokroe chapters, the narrator returns to the troubled Perkhotin knocking at the door of Grushenka's house and finally arousing the frightened Fenya, who tells him about Dimitry's earlier visit, his snatching of the brass pestle, and his return with "the blood simply flowing, dripping from him, dripping!" "This horrible detail," the narrator remarks critically, anticipating many such gross exaggerations in the future, "was simply the product of her disordered imagination" (14: 401). Poor Pyotr Ilyich again is in a quandary, not wishing to go to Feodor Pavlovich's house but overcome by "a haunting uneasiness . . . growing more and more painful and driving him against his will." Because Dimitry had spoken of Mme Khokhlakova, Perkhotin decides to visit her to find out the truth about the money. The scene between them again provides comic relief as the lady is first understandably indignant at being awakened, and then becomes convinced that only a "miracle" had saved her from being murdered by Dimitry, to whom no money had been given. By the time the interview is over, the impressionable widow is quite taken by the good sense and efficiency of "the rather good-looking young man"; and he finds the wealthy lady in her fetching negligee "by no means so elderly." The meeting, indeed, "turned out to be the foundation of the whole career of that practical and precise young man" (14: 402, 406). The deepening passion of Dimitry and Grushenka is thus juxtaposed with this hint of the beginning of another amorous relation—one to which, as the narrator tantalizingly suggests, he may return after finishing the history of the Karamazovs.

Attention then shifts to the police captain, Mikhail Makarovich, to whom Pyotr Ilyich rushes with his information and whose home he finds filled with guests. The narrator spends some time describing two members of this assemblage—those who will conduct the preliminary investigation—and in so doing highlights all the petty personal attributes that will affect the questioning of the suspect. The public prosecutor Ippolit Kirillovich preferred to be addressed by a title above his real rank, and was "vain and irritable, though he had a good intellect"; he also has "artistic leanings," which gave him a special interest in "psychology . . . a special study of the human heart, a special knowledge of the criminal and his crime." (One might recall that the "psychologists" who examined Raskolnikov found it impossible to understand why, since his aim was to obtain money, he had never even looked at the loot he had stolen.) The district attorney, who "was short and weak and delicate looking," wore "a number of big, glittering rings on his fingers," and liked to tease the ladies by claiming to know all their "secrets." However, he "became extraordinarily grave" when performing his official duties, "realizing his position and the sanctity of the obligation laid upon him," obviously deriving a sense of self-importance from his legal status (14: 408). The "psychology" of the one, and the need for self-assertion of the other, give them little incentive for attempting to unravel the complexity of Dimitry's behavior.

Pyotr Ilyich, to his surprise, found the assembled company already talking of the murder of Feodor Pavlovich. A scream of Smerdyakov's, presumably in the throes of an epileptic fit, had awakened Grigory's wife, who then heard her husband's groans in the garden. There she found him still lying prostrate and muttering, "he has murdered . . . his father murdered" (14: 409). (What flashes through her mind is the recollection of similar sounds coming from the garden many years before, when Lizaveta had given birth to Smerdyakov, thus evoking once more this viciously immoral and implicitly sacrilegious crime attributed to Feodor Pavlovich.) Looking into the window of the house, she saw the old man's bloodied corpse lying on the floor, and on returning to the lodge she found Smerdyakov "writhing in convulsions, his eyes fixed in a squint, and . . . foam . . . flowing from his lips" (14: 410). The door leading from the house into the garden was wide open, and Grigory told her to go to the police captain. The news had arrived just five minutes before Pyotr Ilyich, and the local authorities immediately sprang into action by arranging for a trip to Mokroe to apprehend Dimitry, unquestionably guilty in the eyes of all concerned.

The titles of the chapters (3, 4, and 5 of Book 9) devoted to the questioning of Dimitry are "A Soul's Journey through Torments," and three such torments (*mitarstva*) are enumerated. A Russian reader would recognize this structure as an allusion to the Orthodox belief that the soul after death, as it ascends from earth to heaven, is subject to trials by various evil spirits. In a notebook entry of 1877 already cited, Dostoevsky mentions wishing to write about the *sorokovina* (a memorial service held on the fortieth day after death) in the form of "a book of pilgrimages" that would describe the trials of such a soul. This idea is now secularized and applied to the "torments" that Dimitry experiences as, in effect, he bares his soul under the pressure of the pitiless questioning. But the ordeal leads him to a much more severe self-examination than he had ever known before, and culminates not only in an overwhelming feeling of pity for human suffering as a whole, but also a desire to suffer himself for all his past misdeeds.

The preliminary investigation exposes what Dostoevsky saw as the deficiencies of the new legal system, in which a personal motive, such as the vanity attributed to Ippolit Kirillovich, might prevent a prosecutor from searching for the truth impartially. He was highly critical of the "abstraction" encouraged by the adoption of Western norms, which consisted largely in the accumulation of material evidence. In the case of Dimitry, exclusive reliance on such evidence prevented discernment of the truth, which could have been revealed by a more direct perception of human character. Dimitry had never concealed his true feelings about anything, even about his hatred and loathing for his father, but his word is given no credence whatever when he denies the murder. The investigators, who simply assume his guilt, are much more concerned with establishing a sequence of facts that points to his motivation, which they assume establishes his guilt. One may see in these chapters a reduced legal replication of the novel's main theme of the conflict between reason and faith. The "rational" presuppositions of the investigators eliminate any possibility of even considering giving any weight to Dimitry's word as "a man of honor."

At the moment of his arrest, Dimitry believes that he has killed the servant Grigory and is being apprehended for this reason. Learning that Grigory is still alive, he is of course overjoyed; and because he knows he did not kill his father, he assumes at first that the whole matter can easily be settled. Time and again, though, he candidly acknowledges all the overpowering impulses that might have led him to commit such a murder and, under the calculated questioning of the investigators, unwittingly builds the case against himself. For their part, they disregard completely his desire to obtain information about the crime, as well as his reaction on being informed of the details. "'That's horrible!' Mitya shuddered, and putting his elbows on the table, hid his face in his right hand" (14: 416). And even while reiterating all the reasons for hating his father, to the great satisfaction of his questioners, he adds, "But now that he's dead, I feel differently. . . . I wish I hadn't hated him so" (14: 417). Dimitry has now begun that process of self-scrutiny and self-judgment that will lead to his moral metamorphosis. "I'm not very beautiful," he says, "so that I had no right to consider him repulsive" (ibid.). None of these responses is taken into account, any more than his statement that he is "a man who has done a lot of nasty things, but has always been, and still is, honorable at bottom, in his inner being" (14: 416).

The only official who treats Dimitry humanely is the police captain Mikhail Makarovich, who represents the old-fashioned Russian responsiveness to immediate human distress that Dostoevsky believed was being stifled by the new legal reforms. When the police captain is told to escort the tempestuous Grushenka downstairs, he comes to understand the love between the couple that has been transformed into genuine devotion. Returning to reassure Dimitry, "there was a look of warm, almost fatherly feeling for the luckless prisoner on his face." Her message to Dimitry is that he should remain calm so that he can better clear himself and not worry about her. The worthy official reassures Dimitry that she is being cared for by the landlord's daughters, and the narrator comments, with a subdued thrust: "The good-natured police captain said *a great deal that was irregular,* but Grushenka's suffering, a fellow creature's suffering, touched his good-natured heart and tears stood in his eyes" (14: 418; italics added).

As the investigators weave the web of incriminating circumstances in which Dimitry is becoming entangled, much of what the reader already knows is presented again; but what has been seen previously from the perspective of Mitya's agitated and unpremeditated frenzy of jealousy and rage is now depicted—anticipating many such multiperspectival effects in the modern novel—through the determinedly prejudicial eyes of the investigators. Indeed, the narrator himself points out the difference when Dimitry describes having leaped off the fence to examine the prostrate Grigory. "Alas, it never entered Mitya's head," he comments, "to tell them, though he remembered it, that he had jumped back from pity, and standing over the prostrate figure had even uttered some words of regret." The prosecutor, on the other hand, "could only draw one conclusion: that the man had jumped back 'at such a moment and in such excitement' simply with the object of ascertaining whether the only witness of the crime were dead" (14: 430). Even though familiar events are replayed, Dostoevsky never allows the reader's interest to flag because the narrator, except for the comment already quoted, now presents them exclusively from the prosecutorial point of view.

Only two new "facts" are introduced, and one is not a fact at all but an obstinate delusion. When the question arises as to where Dimitry obtained the money for his second night of carousing with Grushenka at Mokroe (the investigators assume that it was the three thousand rubles acquired by the murder of his father), he explains, to their disbelieving ears, that it was the second half of the amount entrusted to him earlier by Katerina Ivanovna, which he had carried in a small pouch around his neck all this time. A hint of the existence of such a pouch had been given in Dimitry's conversation with Alyosha earlier, but so vaguely that it now comes as new information. The other detail, which the reader knows to be an error, is that the door leading from the house to the garden had been open. Grigory affirmed having seen the door open when he emerged from his house to run after Dimitry, and thus seemed to confirm that Dimitry had gone into the house, committed the murder, and then fled through the open door.

As the circumstantial evidence piles up against Dimitry, and the rashness and intemperance of his earlier statements and actions are thrown back in his face, his mood becomes darker and darker. He sees himself at last through the eyes of those he calls "blind moles and scoffers," and struggles to define himself against the image they have been constructing. "If I were guilty," he tells them, "I swear I wouldn't have waited for your coming, or for the sunrise as I meant to at first, but would have destroyed myself before this, without waiting for the dawn. I know that about myself now. I couldn't have learned so much in twenty years as I've found out in this accursed night" (14: 437–438). Dimitry has now discovered that, at the core of his character are concern and anguish over others—over Grushenka, to be sure, but also a terrible sense of remorse over Grigory. It is this realization that now pierces through, even as he flares up against his questioners and displays all the storminess and irascibility of his temperament. That Dostoevsky manages to make him credible on both levels is another testimony to his genius for complex moral-psychological portraiture.

## 6

The climax of this development comes after Dimitry has been further humiliated by being ordered to strip completely (some ill-fitting clothes are furnished by the kindly Kalganov) and after all the witnesses have confirmed much of the evidence against him. By this time, he has been reduced to despair and is at the end of his considerable physical tether: "His eyes were closing with fatigue." He had declared publicly to Grushenka once more that he was innocent, and she had accepted his word after crossing herself before the icon. Turning to his questioners, she affirms that "he'll never deceive you against his conscience. He's telling the whole truth, you may believe it" (14: 455). But such utterances of faith are futile, and Dimitry finally sinks into a deep sleep on a chest in the room. Like Alyosha, he then dreams a dream crystallizing the moral conversion that has taken place within him as a result of all his "torments."

Dimitry's dream, "utterly out of keeping with the place and time," visualizes him driving somewhere in the steppes during an early winter snowstorm. In the distance he could see the ruins of a burned-down village, and as his carriage approaches he meets a line of women standing along the road, "all thin and wan," and especially one, "a tall, bony woman" looking much older than her years and carrying a crying baby. "Her breasts must have been so dry that there was not a drop of milk in them." Dimitry asks his driver why the baby was crying, and the peasant assumes he is referring to the immediate situation: "They're poor people burned out. They have no bread." But Dimitry is really asking the same question that had been posed so vehemently by Ivan and led to his attack on God. "Why are people poor?" Dimitry queries. "Why is the babe poor? Why is the steppe barren? . . . Why don't they sing songs of joy? Why are they dark from black misery? Why don't they feed the babe?" (14: 455–456).

No answer is given to *these* questions, which Dimitry himself felt "were unreasonable and senseless," but his response is a sudden upsurge of emotion that marks the completion of his moral-spiritual transformation. "And he felt that a passion of pity, such as he had never known before, was rising in his heart, and he wanted to cry that he wanted to do something for them all . . . that no one should shed tears from that moment, and he wanted to do it at once, regardless of all obstacles, with all the Karamazov recklessness." Quite appropriately, he also hears "the voice of Grushenka," full of emotion, saying, "I won't leave you now for the rest of your life." On waking, he finds that someone had put a pillow under his head, and he is moved "with a sort of ecstatic gratitude" by this little gesture of concern (14: 456–457).

Dimitry's dream objectifies the transformation that has taken place in his consciousness as a result of his own suffering, bringing on a new awareness of the wretchedness of others. Such human distress, though of a different nature, had led to Ivan's upsurge of rebellion against God, but with Dimitry it leads to a passionate desire to throw himself into alleviating the world's miseries instead of, as in the past, increasing their number by giving free rein to all his impulses and appetites. Just before departing under escort back to the town, he describes the new realization to which he has come. In the past, "I've sworn to amend every day of my life, beating my breast, and every day I've done the same filthy things." But now, under the blows of fate, he has undergone a decisive change: "I accept the torment of accusation, and my public shame, and I want to suffer and by suffering I shall be purified." Once more he declares himself not guilty of his father's blood, but adds: "I accept my punishment, not because I killed him, but because I meant to kill him and perhaps I really might have killed him" (14: 458).

After embracing Grushenka and asking pardon "for ruining you, too, with my love," he offers his hand to the district attorney, once a boon companion, who now refuses to take it. The thieving innkeeper also sternly fails to return his farewell salute. Only the pure-hearted young Kalganov runs out to press his hand, and then breaks down in tears. Part 3 thus ends with Dimitry acknowledging his moral guilt but insisting, so far as legal guilt is concerned, that "I'll fight it out with you to the end, and then God will decide" (ibid.). Both Alyosha and Dimitry have chosen to follow Father Zosima's path of love and Christian faith, each in their own way. It will be the turn of Ivan to follow the same route, but one which, in his case, leads to a tormenting, brilliantly depicted, much more severe inner struggle and total mental breakdown.

## CHAPTER 37

# The Brothers Karamazov:
# Books 10–11

One might imagine, after all the incomparable high points already reached in *The Brothers Karamazov*—Dimitry's "confessions," Ivan's "rebellion," the Legend of the Grand Inquisitor, Father Zosima's "odor of corruption" and its aftermath, the night on which Dimitry *almost* commits the murder—that the remainder of the novel would contain little to equal their stature. But Dostoevsky was now writing at the top of his form, buoyed by the enthusiasm of the public and stimulated rather than discouraged by the press reaction. Even hostile critics, who savaged the novel's ideological implications, could not refuse to recognize the power of his talent. The public awaited the novel's dénouement with eager impatience, and he was determined not to disappoint their expectations.

## 2

Book 10, entitled "Boys," is set two months after the action of the previous sections. Dostoevsky thus interrupts the narrative course of Dimitry's fate after his arrest and shifts instead to a thematic motif introduced much earlier. In doing so, he realizes one of his long-held literary ambitions—to present, on a larger canvas than in *The Idiot*, the interaction between an idealistic Christian character and a group of children. Alyosha here becomes the spiritual guide of the bunch of boys introduced in Book 4, Chapter 2, as the classmates of Ilyusha Snegiryov and who had become his enemies when he fought with them in defense of his father.

Now Ilyusha is lying gravely ill with tuberculosis, perhaps aggravated by the stone that had struck him in the chest during the schoolboy fracas. Alyosha, dressed in secular garb—he has quit the monastery, following the command of Father Zosima—has led the way for all the boys to make peace with their dying schoolmate. Ilyusha has been tormented by a sadistic prank taught him by Smerdyakov, the inciter to evil—that of putting a pin into a piece of bread and throwing it to hungry dogs. He had done just that to a dog called Zhuchka, which had run off and disappeared, and the poor boy was haunted by the possibility that the dog might be dead. As Ilyusha tells his father, "It's because I killed Zhuchka, Dad, that I am ill now. God is punishing me for it" (14: 482). All the boys, and Alyosha as well, had been searching for Zhuchka in the hope of easing Ilyusha's torments of guilt.

The chapters of Book 10 center on the relations of Ilyusha, Alyosha, and the group of boys—particularly one named Nikolay (Kolya) Krasotkin. Kolya is the most daring and independent of the lot, obviously a future leader, who in the past had taken Ilyusha under his wing. The ailing boy had looked up to him as a friend and protector, and when Kolya had failed to rally to his side in the fight over his father, the embattled Ilyusha had stabbed him with a penknife. Kolya, however, understood his sense of betrayal and had long forgiven this incident. Nonetheless, while the other boys had been flocking around Ilyusha's bedside for some time, Kolya had remained aloof until the morning on which the action of Book 10 begins.

Kolya is portrayed as a prideful youth, haughtily insisting on his independence from the others, intelligent and self-assured, ready to take unusual risks to prove his superiority—he lies between the railroad tracks while a train passes over him—and scornful of any sort of "sheepish sentimentality." His poor, widowed mother, who slavishly devotes her life to him, would tearfully "reproach him with his coldness"; but he was not really cold-hearted, only resistant to displays of emotion that might suggest any sort of weakness, any loss of self-control (14: 463). Despite this assumed façade of youthful egoism, he breaks down when his mother goes into hysterics on learning of the train episode, and he "sobbed like a boy of six" (14: 465). In the delightful chapter "Children," Kolya affectionately and tenderly takes care of "the kids," a girl of eight and a boy of seven who have a wonderfully solemn conversation about what they have heard from their peasant nurses about how babies arrive.

The youthful and still relatively harmless egoism of Kolya, who has had access to the library left by his father and "read some things unsuitable for his age," is exhibited in various ways (14: 463). One is the condescending tone of superiority that he takes with peasants, while insisting that he is "always glad to do them justice" (14: 474). At the same time, as he tells his admiring disciple, the slightly younger Smurov, "I like to stir up fools in every class of society" (14: 477), and he behaves with the peasants as if they were all such fools. Rakitin has also been busy among the schoolchildren, in competition with Alyosha, and he is cited by Kolya as an authority who has converted him into being a "Socialist." He has become convinced by Rakitin that "the social relations of men" are more ridiculous than those of dogs, and that "everything is

habit with men, everything even in their social and political relations"
(14: 474).

Critics have long recognized Kolya as an embryonic Ivan, through
whom Dostoevsky brilliantly transposes some of the dominating motifs
of his book into an adolescent register. Kolya, for example, tells Alyosha
that "God is only a hypothesis" (exactly Ivan's position) and that "it's
possible for one who doesn't believe in God to love mankind" (as does,
in his perversely pitying fashion, Ivan's Grand Inquisitor) (14: 499–500).
Dostoevsky amuses himself when Kolya repeats what he has picked up
from Rakitin: "I am not opposed to Christ . . . ," Kolya declares magnanimously. "He was a most humane person, and if He were alive today,
He would be found in the ranks of the revolutionaries, and would perhaps play a conspicuous part" (14: 500). When asked for the source of
this claim, presumably the opinion of Belinsky, Kolya can only reply
that "they say he said it"—and of course it was Dostoevsky himself who
had made public this utterance of Belinsky's in the *Diary of a Writer*.

Kolya knows that he has acquired all these opinions at second hand
and is terribly worried that Alyosha, whom he wishes to impress, will
think him ridiculously boastful and pretentious. Dostoevsky uses Kolya,
moreover, not only to parody the already familiar image of Ivan but also
to anticipate the drama soon to be played out. One of Kolya's escapades, which had led to trouble with the authorities, was to induce "a
stupid, round-mugged fellow of twenty" to see what would occur if a
cart was moved just as a goose was nibbling at a bag of oats with its
neck under a wheel. A slight displacement of the cart then breaks the
neck of the goose (14: 495). When the two are hauled into court by the
infuriated owner of the goose, "the errand boy" blubbered that Kolya
had egged him on. But "I answered," he explains to Alyosha, "with the
utmost composure that I hadn't egged him on, that I simply stated the
general proposition, had spoken hypothetically" (14: 495–496). Ivan had
assumed exactly the same role with Smerdyakov, stating the general
proposition that "everything was permitted" and, at least for the moment, refusing like Kolya to accept any responsibility for what might
occur as a result. The justice of the peace, amused by Kolya's sophistry,
lets him off with only a warning; but Ivan's conscience will not allow
him to escape so lightly.

Kolya harmed no one except the goose in this particular exhibition of
egoistic playfulness, but the same is not the case with his treatment of
poor, suffering Ilyusha. Even though Kolya knew that Ilyusha wished to
see him most of all, he failed to join the other boys in visiting the bedside of their stricken comrade. One reason was that his pride would not
tolerate his seeming to act under the influence of Alyosha; another was
that he had found Zhuchka, alive and well, whom he had renamed

Perezvon ("the chiming of bells"). Kolya had spent some time teaching the dog all sorts of tricks, and delayed producing it until the training period was completed. Ilyusha is overcome with surprise and rapture as Kolya puts the animal through its paces, his "great eyes almost popping out of his head." But the narrator remarks sadly that "if Krasotkin, who had no suspicion of it, had known what a disastrous and fatal effect such a moment might have on the sick child's health, nothing would have induced him to play such a trick on him" (14: 491). "With an involuntary reproach in his voice," Alyosha asks: "'Can you really have put off coming all this time simply to train the dog?'" (14: 492).

Kolya's need to dominate others, and to control every situation in which he becomes involved, mimics the aim of Ivan's creation, the Grand Inquisitor, to relieve humankind of the burden of freedom. Indeed, Kolya's relation to Ilyusha in the past may well be seen as a callow facsimile of Ivan's poetic invention. Ilyusha "was proud," Kolya tells Alyosha, "but he was slavishly devoted to me, and yet all at once his eyes would flash, and he'd refuse to agree with me, fly into a rage." Ilyusha seemed to be developing, as Kolya puts it, "a little free spirit of his own." The reason was that "I was cold in responding to his endearments," and "the tenderer he became, the colder I became" (14: 480, 482). Kolya's aversion to "sheepish sentimentality" excludes any reciprocity of feeling, just as Ivan's rationalism excludes (or represses) any emotions stemming from his moral conscience. But when Kolya comes face-to-face with the wasted, fever-ridden visage of the dying Ilyusha, "his voice failed him . . . his face suddenly twitched and the corners of his mouth quivered" (14: 488). As had happened with his mother, Kolya's posture of commanding self-control breaks down, and he gives way to his feelings of pity and compassion.

### 3

Dostoevsky uses the long-suffering Snegiryov family, and the poignant love that exists between Ilyusha and his father, as a foil to set off the rankling hatreds of the Karamazovs. The family's condition has improved because the captain has accepted the charity of Katerina Ivanovna. But nothing can relieve his wrenching agony as he watches his doomed son expire before his eyes. (Matters are made even worse by the visit of a heartless medical luminary from Moscow, paid for by Katerina, who cruelly holds out a feeble hope of improvement if the family should travel to foreign climes—a possibility completely out of their reach.) Kolya had scornfully called the captain "a mountebank, a buffoon," but Alyosha's analysis presents Dostoevsky's own understanding of this particular character-type. "These are people of deep feeling," Alyosha says, "who have been somehow crushed. Buffoonery in them is a sort of resentful irony against those to whom they daren't speak the truth, from having been for years humiliated and intimidated by them. Believe me, Krasotkin, that sort of buffoonery is sometimes tragic in the extreme" (14: 483). By such observations, Alyosha succeeds in bringing the boy to an awareness of how badly his pride had misled him in his treatment of Ilyusha and his contempt for the captain.

Father Zosima had sent Alyosha into the world to do his work there, and the scene with Kolya and the boys is the first illustration of how such work might be accomplished. Alyosha listens patiently to all of Kolya's prattle about "Socialism" and the various other "subversive" notions that he has picked up from Rakitin about Voltaire, God, and so on, all of which ape Ivan. Alyosha answers him "quietly, gently, and quite naturally, as though he were talking to someone of his own age, or even older." Kolya was particularly struck by Alyosha's apparent diffidence about his opinion of Voltaire. "He seemed to be leaving the question for him, little Kolya, to settle" (14: 500). Ready to bridle at any challenge, but shown as still inwardly insecure and fearful of being ridiculed, Kolya now relaxes his guard completely and gives vent to all the emotions carefully kept bottled up until that moment.

He thus undergoes a miniature conversion experience, similar to that of Alyosha and Dimitry, and confesses that "I am profoundly unhappy, I sometimes fancy all sorts of things, that everyone is laughing at me, the whole world, and that I feel ready to overturn the whole order of things." He realizes now that "what kept me from coming [to see Ilyusha earlier] was my conceit, my egoistic vanity, and the beastly willfulness which I can never get rid of, though I have been struggling with it all my life." After this avowal, he asks Alyosha if he does not find him "ridiculous"; and Alyosha admonishes him to overcome any fear of confessing his faults and failures. Indeed, such vanity is now "almost a sort of insanity," Alyosha declares. "The devil has taken the form of that vanity and entered into a whole generation." " 'It's simply the devil,' added Alyosha, without a trace of the smile that Kolya, staring at him, expected to see" (14: 503). Alyosha takes the devil seriously, refusing amusedly to dismiss such an antiquated superstition. Ivan will soon find himself oscillating between Kolya's incredulity and Alyosha's gravity as he struggles to determine whether the devil he sees is (or is not) a hallucination.

Book 10 ends with a variation on the Job motif that runs throughout the novel, and Dostoevsky now makes no effort to soften or mollify its emotionally devastating impact. The captain gives way to abject despair when the doctor from the capital fails to hold out any hope, and Ilyusha embraces both his father and Kolya, "uniting them in one embrace, and hugging them as tightly as he could." "The captain suddenly began to shake with sobs," and Kolya also bursts into tears as he says good-bye and promises to come again. "Oh, how I could curse myself for not having come before," he mutters. Ilyusha poignantly tells his father to "get a good boy" when he dies and "love him instead of me." But the grief-stricken father, on leaving the room, tells Kolya and Alyosha "in a wild whisper": "I don't want a good boy, I don't want another boy. . . . 'If I forget thee, Jerusalem, may my tongue . . .'"—a biblical allusion that Kolya does not understand and asks Alyosha to explain (14: 507). Such a scene could well have been maudlin, but from Dostoevsky's pen it conveys an overpowering purity and intensity of emotion. The death of his son Aleksey just two years before certainly contributed its share to the moving pathos of these pages. And he himself had written an anguished letter in 1868 on the death of his two-month-old daughter, Sofya, expressing the same inconsolable grief as the captain's. "And now they tell me in consolation that I will have other children. But where is Sofya? Where is that little individual for whom, I dare to say, I would have accepted crucifixion so that she might live?"[1]

4
———

Even though there are important thematic correspondences between Book 10 and the remainder of the novel, these chapters contain only one fleeting mention of the main plot line—the remark of Kolya to Smurov that he finds it hard to understand Alyosha. "His brother is going to be tried tomorrow or next day for such a crime, and yet he has so much time to spend on sentimentality with boys" (14: 472). In Book 11 the focus returns to the main characters and events in the two-month interval since Dimitry's arrest.

When Alyosha goes to visit Grushenka, who had been taken severely ill after Dimitry's imprisonment, he observes the decisive change in her character. "A look of firmness and intelligent purpose had developed in her face. There were signs of a spiritual transformation in her, and a steadfast, fine, and humble determination that nothing could shake could be discerned in her" (15: 5). She has given shelter to the pitiable Maximov, and even sends food and a few rubles to the two destitute Poles in spite of their "arrogant dignity" and pomposity. She and Dimitry quarrel fiercely, while continuing to love each other deeply, because he is jealous of her kindness to her Polish ex-lover and she fears his gratitude toward Katerina, who had brought a doctor from Moscow to testify for Dimitry and contributed, along with Ivan and Alyosha, to hire a famous defense attorney on his behalf. The murder, for some unexplained reason, is said to have become famous all over Russia, and the

eminent defense lawyer Fetyukovich has agreed to come to the provinces for a nominal fee—"more for the glory of the thing" than for any
other purpose (15: 10). Grushenka reports to Alyosha that Ivan has also
been to see Dimitry secretly in prison, and the two appear to be involved in some private plan. The mystery of Ivan's behavior and motivation thus begins to move into the foreground.

Dostoevsky, as we know, often introduces a serious theme by first
giving it a comic or scandalous form. As Alyosha goes from Grushenka
to visit Liza Khokhlakova, he is, as usual, waylaid by her garrulous
mother, who, ever since "the young official, Perkhotin, had become a
regular visitor at her house," has begun to dress more alluringly (15: 13).
She rambles on about the impending trial and the fact that there were
allusions to her in a story about the case in a new newspaper called
*Gossip*. As he had done in *The Idiot*, Dostoevsky then parodies what he
considered the exaggerations, distortions, and outright slanders of the
radical press. In one version, spread by the resentful and disappointed
suitor Rakitin, now replaced by Perkhotin, Mme Khokhlakova was said
to have offered three thousand rubles to Dimitry if he would elope with
her to the gold mines, but he preferred to murder his father instead.

The satire becomes more serious as the loquacious lady chatters on
about the possibility of a plea of temporary insanity, which Dimitry had
insisted he would not accept because it implied his guilt. But Mme
Khokhlakova is enchanted by the notion that the crime could be just an
"aberration" for which Dimitry was not really responsible. "They found
out about aberrations," she tells Alyosha happily, "as soon as the law
courts were reformed." When Alyosha interrupts her "rather sharply"
to insist that his brother is not the murderer, she immediately shifts to
Grigory, who had also suffered an "aberration" because of the blow to
his head. Indeed, for her no one can be guilty of anything, because
"who isn't suffering from aberration nowadays?—you, I, all are in a state
of aberration and there are ever so many examples of it" (15: 18–19). This
universal malady thus becomes a parodistic reversal of Father Zosima's
universal guilt, in which all are responsible for all. Mme Khokhlakova's
mindless volubility also brings into view the motif of mental instability
and madness that will soon be illustrated by Ivan.

Mental imbalance, specifically linked with the devil, appears both
frighteningly and pathetically in the next chapter. On visiting Liza, who
is now able to walk again, Alyosha notices a change for the worse rather
than the better in her mental state. "There was not a trace of humor or
jesting in her face now, though, in the old days, fun and gaiety never
deserted her even at her most 'earnest' moments" (15: 22). Instead of
gaiety, she has begun to revel in sadomasochistic fantasies of destroying
both others and herself—and hence has become "the little demon" of

the chapter's title. "Yes, I want disorder," she tells Alyosha, affirming her desire that "everything might be destroyed." Alyosha admonishes her that "you take evil for good," though he cannot simply negate one of her provocative taunts: "Listen, your brother is being tried now for murdering his father, and everyone loves his having killed his father." Then she tells him of a dream in which devils assailing her withdraw when she crosses herself; but they return when she begins to revile God out loud. "'It's awful fun,' she says, 'it takes your breath away'" (15: 22–23). Alyosha, quite unexpectedly, confesses to having experienced the exact same dream—thus admitting that he too, in his subconscious, had been playing with faith. It is possible to take such words as an effort to calm and reassure Liza; but they may perhaps prefigure undeveloped aspects of his character that were to emerge in the unwritten continuation of his life story. Indeed, the entire relation of Alyosha and Liza remains embryonic and points toward the future, as do other unresolved situations arising in these concluding pages.

Liza has also been visited by Ivan, and he had encouraged her worst proclivities. Instead of attempting, like Alyosha, to counter her sadomasochistic inclinations, he had reinforced them by his complicity. When she tells him of how "nice" it would be to eat pineapple compote (an extreme luxury in Russia at that time) while watching the prolonged agonies of a crucified child, "he laughed and said it really was nice" (15: 24). Ivan, as we shall soon learn, is now being visited by a devil himself, and the implication is that he has brought his own illness with him to aggravate Liza's. But she is not yet completely possessed by the evil spirit, and she appeals to Alyosha as her only rescuer. "'Alyosha save me!' she suddenly jumped from the couch, rushed to him and seized him with her hands. 'Save me!' she almost groaned" (15: 25). Liza still struggles against her worst impulses, and at the conclusion of this scene she puts her finger in the crack of the doorjamb, slams the door shut, and mutilates herself as punishment. "I am a wretch, a wretch, wretch, wretch!" she whispers (ibid.), duplicating Ivan's self-castigation as "a scoundrel" after he had departed on the day of the murder.

There is another aspect of this scene that (alas!) cannot be overlooked. Liza's fantasy about a crucified child comes from a book she has read about the trial of a Jew accused of such a crime, and she asks Alyosha: "Is it true that at Easter Jews steal a [Christian] child and kill it?" The monstrosity in question is the widespread blood libel against the Jews, to which, as we have seen, Dostoevsky had given credence in a letter. And the response of Alyosha—the exemplar of Christian virtue, the inheritor of Father Zosima's doctrine of all-forgiving love—is limited to a confession of ignorance: "I don't know." It may be argued that such a reply is verisimilar, given the intellectual limitations of his background; and the fact that Alyosha does not simply affirm the truth of this charge may be considered a small concession to decency. But that Dostoevsky should have introduced such material at all, no matter how topical it may have been, leaves a permanent stain on his reputation that nothing can efface (15: 25). The inner seesaw of his emotions about the Jews, still perceptible in his article on "The Jewish Question," seems to have vanished entirely. *Now*, he gives the widest possible circulation to this age-old vilification, first used in classical antiquity against the early Christians themselves.

## 5

The revelatory effect of Dimitry's dream about the burned-out village and the crying baby has permanently altered his own character and sense of values. Grushenka tells Alyosha, in some bewilderment, that he is always talking "about some child," declaring that "it's for that babe I am going to Siberia now. I am not a murderer, but I must go to Siberia" (15: 10). When Alyosha visits him in prison, he finds his brother very upset because Rakitin has been attempting to undermine his faith in God. The future journalist intended to write an article about the crime "to prove some theory," namely, that Dimitry "couldn't help murdering his father, he was corrupted by his environment, etc." (15: 28). Like Mme Khokhlakova's "aberration," the doctrine of "environment" eliminates moral responsibility, and Dostoevsky had satirized it earlier in *Crime and Punishment.* His target is now the ideas of Claude Bernard, the French physiologist, whose deterministic doctrines had exercised a considerable influence on the popular and influential Zola.

In a seriocomic recitation about what he has learned from Rakitin, Dimitry expresses his dismay. "I'm sorry to lose God," he says. God has been replaced by "sorts of little tails, the little tails of those nerves, and as soon as they begin quivering—then an image appears. . . . That's why I see and think, because of those tails, and not at all because I've got a soul and that I am some sort of image and likeness" (that is, of God) (15: 28). When Dimitry had objected to this explanation, paraphrasing Ivan's thesis that "without God and immortal life all things are lawful," Rakitin laughingly agreed that "a clever man can do what he likes" (15: 29). This reiteration of Ivan's doctrine by the unscrupulous Rakitin lays the groundwork for the upcoming depiction of Ivan's struggle with *his* conscience in the chapters that immediately follow. All the same, as Dostoevsky makes clear, the despicable Rakitin and the tormented Ivan are not comparable. Although Dimitry as yet cannot fathom Ivan because of his silence, he nonetheless states explicitly: "Brother Ivan is not Rakitin. There is an idea in him."

The first part of the chapter title here, "A Hymn and a Secret," refers to the hymn that Dimitry sings to the "new man" he has now become, whose faith remains unshaken by Rakitin's scornful sallies. Innocent though he knows himself to be, Dimitry is ready to go to Siberia "for all the babes . . . [and] because we are all responsible for all," echoing again the doctrine of Father Zosima and implying the analogy with Christ ("I go for all") (15: 10). Dostoevsky then probably draws on memories of his own imprisonment when Dimitry exclaims: "One cannot exist in prison without God, it's even more impossible than out of prison. And then we men underground will sing from the bowels of the earth a tragic hymn to God, with Whom is joy. Hail to God and His joy! I love Him!" Dimitry's rapturous affirmations rise to a climax when he declares: "I think I could stand any suffering, only to be able to say and to repeat to myself every moment: 'I exist'" (15: 31).

Dimitry's ecstatic exaltation, however, is tempered by "the secret" that he and Ivan have been sharing. This is a plan for Dimitry to escape after, as now seems certain, he is found guilty. With the necessary amount of money, it could easily be arranged for him and Grushenka to flee to America. A new conflict thus arises between Dimitry's need for atonement and his redeeming love for Grushenka, from whom he would be separated if sent to Siberia. Alyosha advises him to postpone any decision until his trial is over, and Dimitry suddenly blurts out a question that has been torturing him all along: Does *Alyosha* believe him guilty? His face lights up with bliss when Alyosha replies: "I've never for an instant believed that you were the murderer!" (15: 36). How the innocent Dimitry will decide the question of escape, if legally condemned, remains unresolved to the end.

## 6

The five remaining chapters of Book 11 all focus on Ivan. He has been constantly alluded to in the preceding four, whether indirectly (through the parallel with Kolya) or more explicitly as the action advances. He finally appears in person when Alyosha goes to visit Katerina Ivanovna. As Ivan departs, Katerina implores Alyosha to follow him because "he's mad . . . he's in a fever, a nervous fever. The doctor told me so" (15: 38). Ivan himself is aware of his increasing mental instability, oscillating as he does between states of lucidity and what he fears to be hallucinations (such as being visited by the devil). His state of mind is revealed when he asks Alyosha if it is possible to know that one is going mad.

On the surface, Ivan refuses to accept "the myth about that crazy idiot, the epileptic Smerdyakov" (15: 39), having committed the murder. Indeed, Katerina had shown him a letter written by Dimitry that seems to confirm the latter's guilt. Nonetheless, Alyosha possesses Father Zosima's intuitive gift of moral-psychological penetration, and realizes that Ivan has been brooding these last two months over his own possible responsibility. When Ivan calls Dimitry a "murderer" and a "monster," Alyosha objects; and when challenged to name someone else, he replies: "I know only one thing . . . *it wasn't you* who killed father." Alyosha feels that he is speaking now "not out of himself, not of his own will, but obeying some irresistible command"; and Ivan is so taken aback by this reply, touching on all his own hidden fears, that he thinks Alyosha must know of his conversations with the devil (or with his hallucination) on the same subject (15: 40). The haughty Ivan is so infuriated by this divination of his concealed moral turmoil that he breaks off all relations with his brother "from this moment and probably forever" (15: 40–41). But then Ivan suddenly decides to visit Smerdyakov—not for the first but the third time, the two earlier encounters having already led to the demented condition in which we find him at this point.

The narrator then goes back in time, not only to describe Ivan's visits but also to summarize his feelings about his brother Dimitry in general. "He positively disliked him, at most, felt sometimes a compassion for him, and even that was mixed with great contempt, even repugnance." Ivan also loved Katerina Ivanovna, whose devotion to Dimitry, stemming from pride and vanity rather than love, filled him with "indignation." All the same, he had gone to visit his brother in prison five days after the murder—and emerged convinced of his guilt. Dimitry had accused Smerdyakov but also continued to rail against his father. Everything he said was "fearfully muddled. . . . He hardly seemed to wish to defend himself to Ivan or to anyone else." Moreover, he insulted Ivan to the quick by "telling him sharply that it was not for people who declared that 'everything was lawful' to suspect and question him" (15: 42).

It is in this state of mind that Ivan first goes to visit Smerdyakov, then still in the hospital and quite weak and sickly from prolonged epileptic fits. What bothers Ivan is the recollection of their conversation on the eve of the murder. When he brings it up, Smerdyakov insists, with the dialectical ingenuity he has already displayed, that when he urged Ivan to go to Chermashnaya and thus remain in the neighborhood rather than depart for distant Moscow, he was in fact telling him to stay because of what might occur at home owing to Dimitry's fury. Despite his uneasiness, Ivan is persuaded by Smerdyakov's argument that, if he had been planning some crime himself, he would hardly have told Ivan that he could sham an epileptic fit, thus "giving evidence against myself beforehand" (15: 47). This rational consideration ends the discussion, though it is based on a premise that Ivan subconsciously knows to be false, namely, that Ivan would have been opposed to a crime against

Feodor Pavlovich. But he is only too happy to seize on Smerdyakov's rationalization as a means of exculpating both of them from any suspicion of guilt.

After leaving the bedside, Ivan still felt there was something "insulting" about the agreement to keep their earlier conversation concealed. But he was determined to believe in Smerdyakov's innocence, which meant his own as well, and so "he did not want to analyze the reason for this feeling, and even felt a positive repugnance at prying into his sensation" (15: 47). As time passes, Ivan learns about the overwhelming weight of circumstantial evidence against Dimitry and becomes even more certain of his brother's guilt. He is unable, however, to brush off Alyosha's quiet insistence that Dimitry is innocent, which leaves Smerdyakov as the only possible suspect. Also, he is haunted by recollections—of what he had felt during Dimitry's attack on Feodor Pavlovich ("one viper will devour the other"), of creeping out on the staircase to listen to his father stirring below, of having said, on arriving in Moscow, "I am a scoundrel!" When he now asks Alyosha if the latter had thought that he wanted Dimitry to kill the old man, and that "I myself was even prepared to help bring that about," Alyosha replies: "Forgive me, I did think that, too, at the time" (15: 49). This accusatory admission so shakes Ivan's relative composure that it compels him to visit Smerdyakov for the second time.

Smerdyakov has now recovered his health and wears "a motley, padded dressing gown, rather dirty and frayed, however." His attitude also is different, as if he resented the intrusion over a matter that he considered settled; Ivan noticed the "positively malicious, churlish, and haughty" look in his eyes (15: 50). This time Smerdyakov makes no bones about speaking bluntly, telling Ivan that "you probably too were very desirous of your father's death" (15: 51). He now explains his conversation with Ivan before his departure as a means of finding out "whether you wanted your father to be murdered or not"; but when Ivan accuses him of the murder, he replies ambiguously that "it wasn't I who murdered him. And I should have thought there was no need to speak of it again to a clever man" (51: 52). This gibe both upholds the accusation against Dimitry but also feeds Ivan's fears that there is much more to be said.

Smerdyakov thus rips away the last shreds of Ivan's self-deception and reveals the true significance of his behavior. Indeed, he adds insult to injury by attributing Ivan's motivation to a sordid matter of money—a desire to prevent Feodor Pavlovich from marrying Grushenka and disinheriting his sons. Now almost entirely convinced that Smerdyakov is the murderer, Ivan sees himself as a participant in the crime. Rushing off to Katerina, whom he tells about this encounter, he declares: "If it's not

Dimitry, but Smerdyakov who's the murderer, I share his guilt. . . . If he is the murderer . . . I am the murderer too" (15: 54). It is then that Katerina again produces the letter that appears to prove Dimitry's guilt. Writing in a tavern when he was drunk, at the very beginning of the events two months earlier, Dimitry had declared: "Tomorrow I shall try and get it [the money owing to Katerina] from everyone, and if I can't borrow it, I give you my word of honor I shall go to my father and break his skull and take the money from under his pillow, if only Ivan has gone" (15: 55). Nothing would seem to be clearer than that Dimitry had carried out this threat, and that Ivan's presumed influence on Smerdyakov was not the cause of the crime.

Although the narrator now states that "Ivan was completely reassured" and "resolved to dismiss [Smerdyakov] with contempt and forget him" (15: 56), there are ample indications that Ivan's resolution cannot be carried out. He falls ill and goes to consult the visiting doctor from Moscow, who had warned Katerina Ivanovna that Ivan is suffering from "a nervous fever" and is really "mad." It is during this period that Ivan proposes his escape plan to Dimitry, even though "he hated Mitya more and more every day." But he offered to finance the escape because Smerdyakov had pointed out that, if Dimitry were convicted, Ivan's share of the estate would be increased; and he recoils at the idea of benefiting financially from the murder. He also wonders whether he is eager to aid Dimitry's escape "because I am as much a murderer at heart?" (15: 56). All these vacillations indicate that Ivan's doubts about Smerdyakov are far from having been allayed, and they are renewed both by Alyosha's words and by Katerina, who a bit later tells Ivan that "I've been at Smerdyakov's myself!" (15: 57). Her visit could only mean that she too, despite the letter, had some doubts about Dimitry's guilt and was seeking to learn the truth. This is the immediate cause of Ivan's return to confront Smerdyakov for the third and last time.

Dostoevsky now adjusts nature to accord with the turmoil of Ivan's agitated emotions, and the episode is also set within a frame narrative dramatically portraying the moral-spiritual consequences of this final dialogue. A violent snowstorm begins as Ivan makes his way through the unlit streets on his way to Smerdyakov's cottage, and he stumbles into a drunken peasant singing the first two lines of a popular ditty: "Ach, Vanka's gone to Petersburg / I won't wait till he comes back." This song recalls to Ivan his own departure for Moscow, and what had occurred before *he* returned; and although such a connection is not made explicitly, no doubt this is why "Ivan felt an intense hatred for [the peasant] before he had thought about him at all" (15: 57). When the peasant lurches against him, Ivan knocks him down and leaves him lying in the snow, apparently unconscious. As he continues uninterruptedly on his way, the thought crosses his mind that "he will freeze."

Smerdyakov, as Ivan had learned earlier through town gossip, had become ill again, and each immediately remarks on how sickly the other looks; both are being undermined by the same moral-psychic anguish. In the past, Ivan had been the superior because of his social status and intellect, but now it is Smerdyakov who has the upper hand. As he has come to understand, Ivan is fearful that his implicit consent to the crime would be exposed, and the lackey tells his erstwhile master, "not simply with contempt, but almost with revulsion," that he has nothing to fear (15: 59). But then, disgusted by Ivan's unwillingness to face the truth, Smerdyakov admits his own guilt while refusing to assume it alone. "You murdered him," he tells Ivan, "you are the real murderer, I was only your instrument, your faithful servant . . . and it was following your words that I did it" (ibid.). Smerdyakov then continues, under Ivan's persistent questioning—he is avid to learn all the details—to explain exactly how the crime had been committed just after Dimitry had struck Grigory and leaped over the fence. Hearing the noise, Smerdyakov awakened, saw that Dimitry had not broken in, and "determined on the spot to make an end of it" (15: 64). When Feodor Pavlovich opened the door in response to Smerdyakov's signal, the latter seized an iron paperweight, struck him on the skull, and hid the money he took from behind the icons. Returning to his room, he "began groaning with suspense and impatience, to wake Martha Ignatyevna as soon as possible" (15: 65).

There is another aspect of this dialogue, however, that should not be overlooked. Just after Smerdyakov has made his confession, and his interlocutor has "shuddered all over with a cold shiver," Ivan mutters that "I'm afraid you're a dream, a phantom sitting there before me." Smerdyakov replies that there "are only us two and one other," immediately adding: "No doubt that he is here, that third, between us." This reference to "a third" terrifies Ivan, who takes it as a mention of the devil and looks around, with "his eyes hastily searching for someone in all the corners." Smerdyakov, however, explains "that this third one is God, sir, Providence itself, sir, it's right here with us now, sir, only don't look for it, you won't find it" (15: 60). While the devil has been appearing to Ivan's tormented and demented consciousness, Smerdyakov apparently has been returning to the sources of his own faith since losing his respect for Ivan's ideas. That he has been seeking moral comfort in such a return is indicated by a small detail: he covers the money he obtained from the murder, and which he now displays to Ivan, with a copy of *The Sayings of the Holy Father Isaac the Syrian*, a collection of popular religious texts by a sixth-century ascetic. Father Isaac has replaced the

French grammar Smerdyakov had been studying at the time of the second visit; and we may recall that, even at the height of his fascination with Ivan and his ideas, he had still accepted the existence of the two or three hermits in the desert who could move mountains.

Smerdyakov is filled with contempt for Ivan's dismay at the recognition of his own share of guilt, and his struggle to diminish it as much as possible. " 'God sees,' Ivan raised his hand, 'perhaps I, too, was guilty, perhaps I really had a secret desire for my father's . . . death, but I swear I was not as guilty as you think and I didn't urge you on at all' " (15: 66–67). Nonetheless, he tells Smerdyakov that he will disclose the truth at the trial tomorrow, including his own share of responsibility; but Smerdyakov refuses to believe that he will have the courage to perform what would, in any case, be only a futile gesture. Smerdyakov would simply deny Ivan's testimony and argue that he was trying to help his brother by "sacrificing yourself to save him and . . . invent[ing] it all against me" (15: 67). Most wounding of all, he taunts Ivan with the inconsistency between his sentiments and his ideas: "You used to say yourself that everything is lawful, so now why are you so upset, too? You even want to go and give evidence against yourself." Smerdyakov, however, is caught in a similar inner conflict: denying that he again believes in God, he no longer has any faith in what had replaced God for him, namely, Ivan's ideas. His peasant conscience has made him ill, just as Ivan's educated sense of guilt has been undermining *him*; and the suicide of Smerdyakov will coincide exactly with Ivan's mental breakdown in the next chapter.

The scene ends with Ivan, as he walks out into the snowstorm, firmly deciding to meet Smerdyakov's challenge. "He was conscious of unbounded resolution; he would make an end to the wavering that had so tortured him of late." Stumbling against the inert body of the peasant, "still lying senseless and motionless," Ivan now brings him to a police station, arranges for a doctor, and saves his life (15: 68–69). This is the first effect of his new resoluteness, which overcomes all the contempt for erring and sinful humankind that he had previously exhibited, and which perhaps foreshadows his role in the envisaged second volume. In any case, although he is now capable of such a spontaneous gesture of personal human solidarity, it is a different matter when he thinks of going to the prosecutor at once to denounce Smerdyakov as the murderer and reveal his own share of responsibility. Choosing to put off this ordeal until morning, his determination to act decisively thus wavers; once again he is caught in the toils of his moral-psychological dilemma—the dilemma of intending to follow the dictates of a conscience whose precepts his reason cannot justify. On entering his room, "he felt something like a touch of ice in his heart" and, trying to keep from falling asleep, he "got up uneasily and walked across the room to shake off his drowsiness" (15: 69). This last phrase, conveying Ivan's own awareness, turns out to be entirely illusory; he is now in fact asleep and only dreaming that he walked across the room. "I have dreams now . . . ," Ivan tells Alyosha in the next chapter, "yet they are no dreams but reality. I walk about, talk, and see" (15: 86). Ivan has thus become incapable of distinguishing between his dreams and the objective world; and when he looks uneasily at a sofa in his room, he observes someone sitting there "who had not been in the room when Ivan Feodorovich came into it, on his return from Smerdyakov" (15: 70).

7

*The Brothers Karamazov* is filled with remarkable scenes, but none testifies so abundantly to the brilliance and bite of Dostoevsky's satirical talent as the chapter devoted to Ivan's dialogue with the devil. It is customary to allude to the inspiration of Goethe's *Faust*, and several references to it are contained in this scene as well as elsewhere in the text; but the relation between Ivan (who has been called "the Russian Faust") and his devil is quite different from that of Faust and Mephistopheles. There is no question in Goethe about the reality of Mephistopheles's existence or of the supernatural world from which he sprang. This is precisely the issue, however, that is posed to Ivan by the obsequiously ingratiating patter of his amiable visitor. Nowhere is Dostoevsky's theme—the antagonism between reason and faith—dramatized with more subtlety and finesse than in these mocking pages, which illustrate Dostoevsky's extraordinary ability to play with his own most deeply held convictions.

The portrait of the devil, as Victor Terras has remarked, contains more descriptive detail than that of any other character.[2] Dostoevsky thus takes great pains to present him in entirely earthly terms as a Russian social type. Because Ivan keeps insisting that the devil is just a figment of his imagination, Dostoevsky ironically gives him a very solid embodiment. He shows up as a rather down-at-heels member of the landed gentry, a gentleman no longer able to support himself because the income from his estate has vanished since the abolition of serfdom; but he still exhibits all the social graces of his former position, such as (like Feodor Pavlovich) embroidering his conversation with French phrases. His clothes were good, but now somewhat out of fashion: "in brief, there was every appearance of gentility on straitened means" (15: 70). He lives as what the Russians call a *prizhivalchik*, a sponger on more affluent relatives and friends, who continue to offer him hospitality because he is, after all, a gentleman; his manners are good, he can be presented in society, and he is agreeable, accommodating, and sometimes even amusing. Terras has suggested that such an image derives from Ivan having felt himself to be a hanger-on in other people's houses as a young boy; but there is certainly a wider symbolic meaning here as well.[3] Religion itself, from Dostoevsky's point of view, was now a hanger-on in Russian educated society, accepted as a respectable relic of the past but hardly exercising its old power and influence. As the devil remarks himself, "it's an axiom generally accepted in society that I am a fallen angel. . . . if I ever was, it must have been so long ago that there's no harm in forgetting it" (15: 73).

Ivan's dialogue with the devil plays on the continual fluctuation between the stirrings of his conscience and the amorally nihilistic conclusions that he has drawn from his refusal to accept God and immortality. The devil had first appeared to Ivan once he began to brood over his possible part in the murder, and in this sense the devil represents paradoxically (unlike any other treatment of this *topos* known to me) the voice of Ivan's conscience revolting against his reason. Dostoevsky's devil, however, does not preach moral sermons but ridicules the inconsistency between Ivan's pangs of conscience and the ideas he has accepted and expounded. "Everything is permitted" for those who do not believe in God and immortality, and Ivan has rejected both. Why, then, should he be tormented by feelings of moral guilt that derive from such principles? The devil arrives to personify Ivan's self-mockery of his own moral-psychic contradictions, which have driven him into what Dostoevsky called brain fever and we now diagnose as schizophrenia. Ivan will finally break down completely—but not before the devil has exhibited both Ivan's longing for faith and the difficulty of attaining it for someone who refuses to accept any non-Euclidian world.

The involutions of Ivan's conversation with the devil are so intricate that it is impossible to give in brief any adequate account of their complexities. Essentially, however, its aim is to dramatize the antinomies in which Ivan is trapped once his conscience comes into clashing opposition with those rational convictions that gave rise to his rebellion against God and Christ. The supreme irony, of course, is that it should be the devil who apparently leads him along the path to faith; and Ivan (who is of course speaking to himself *through* the devil) realizes all the incongruity of such a situation. As the devil remarks, "if you come to that, does proving there is a devil prove that there is a God?" (15: 71–72). Ivan keeps insisting all through the dialogue that the devil is only his hallucination and has no independent reality. "'You are a lie, you are my illness, you are a phantom . . . you are my hallucination,'" he cries out "with a sort of fury" (15: 72). So long as Ivan believes this, he does not have to accept that the devil emanates from some non-Euclidian, irrational world of Christian faith; but the upsurge of moral conscience from which he has begun to suffer makes it impossible for him to dismiss such a possibility entirely.

The devil himself both asserts his ontological reality, which Ivan vehemently denies, and then helps Ivan to reinforce such a denial. When Ivan accuses the devil of lying (!), the latter obligingly agrees: "Just so. But hesitation, suspense, conflict between belief and disbelief—is sometimes such torture to a conscientious man, such as you are, that it's better to hang oneself at once." For Ivan's benefit, the devil explains, he is using a "new method," no longer the old one in which belief and disbelief were presented as polar opposites; now he is employing homeopathic medicine, in which small doses of a drug that augment the disease can result in a cure. "I lead you to belief and disbelief by turns . . . ," the devil says; "as soon as you disbelieve in me completely, you'll begin assuring me to my face that I cannot be a dream but a reality." Reason may prevent Ivan from believing; but the moment he refuses, his moral conscience will drive him to the opposite pole despite all the conclusions of his logic. By this method, the devil will sow in Ivan "only a tiny grain of faith and it will grow into an oak tree—and such an oak tree that, sitting on it, you will try to enter into the ranks of 'the hermit monks and chaste women' [a quote from Pushkin] for that is what you are secretly longing for. You'll dine on locusts, you'll wander in the wilderness to save your soul" (15: 80). Ivan's devil knows him very well: this is precisely the path the Grand Inquisitor had followed before he lost his faith.

The devil lives up to his reputation as an amiable and entertaining interlocutor, and several of his amusingly debonair anecdotes are even sexually titillating (being aimed, naturally, at the Catholic confessional). Others, though equally diverting, are more serious in purpose and contain that combination of a scoffing skepticism with a yearning desire for faith that typify Ivan, though he is enraged at being confronted with himself in this guise through the devil's repartee. Many of the devil's sallies include parodies of one or another idea expressed by Ivan earlier, either in the chapter "Rebellion" or in his Legend of the Grand Inquisitor; and they are written with a satirical brio for which it would be hard to find any equal since Swift. Indeed, Dostoevsky hardly does himself justice when Ivan says to the devil: "All my stupid ideas—outgrown, thrashed out long ago, and flung aside like a dead carcass—you present to me as something new!" This may be true for Ivan as a character, but such deprecatory terms do not apply to Dostoevsky as a satirist.

One of the most expressive of these parodies manifestly takes off from Ivan's having indignantly refused to join in the "hosannahs" of the universal harmony, of the final reconciliation ("when everything in heaven and earth blends in one hymn of praise" to the Lord). It is contained in a legend that the devil recounts even though it is now out of date in *his* world (which he does not want Ivan to confuse with the earthly one, though he then immediately adds that there is no difference at all between the two). This legend could not be more explicit in depicting Ivan's quandary, and its resolution ends on an ironic note that can be taken as a self-reflexive allusion to Dostoevsky himself. It involves "a thinker and philosopher" who on earth "rejected everything, 'laws, conscience, faith' [a citation from Griboyedov] and, above all, the future life." Indignant at finding himself living such a future life after his death, he protested and was punished by being told he would have to walk a quadrillion kilometers before reaching the gates of heaven and being forgiven.

Combining "the soul of an enlightened Russian atheist . . . with the soul of the prophet Jonah, who sulked for three days and nights in the belly of the whale," he lay there for a thousand years; but he finally picked himself up and went on. Ivan then interjects that the philosopher behaved stupidly by agreeing to move at all because, by Euclidian reckoning, it would take him a billion years to reach his goal. But in fact, as the devil explains, "he got there long ago," because all such mathematical reckonings refer to the present earth, and "our present earth may have been repeated a billion times . . . [d]isintegrat[ing] into its elements, again 'the water above the firmament' [a quotation from Genesis in Church Slavonic], then again a comet," and so on. Dostoevsky here appeals to the same idea of eternal recurrence, a commonplace in classical antiquity, that Nietzsche would employ for his own purposes; and like his German counterpart, Ivan also finds this prospect "insufferably tedious." The lexical admixture of the scientific terminology of the period with biblical references is typical of the devil's narrative style and conveys the quandary in which Ivan is trapped.

Reaching his goal at last, the philosopher had not been there for two seconds (though the devil doubts that he still had a watch) when "he cried out that those two seconds were worth walking not a quadrillion kilometers but a quadrillion of quadrillions, raised to the quadrillionth power." In fact, he was so carried away that "he sang 'hosannah' and overdid it so that some persons there of lofty ideas wouldn't shake hands with him at first—he'd become too rapidly reactionary, they said" (15: 78–79). Is this not Dostoevsky sarcastically referring to the criticisms he so often encountered of being a turncoat? And although Ivan then recalls having written this anecdote to ridicule religion when he was seventeen and still a schoolboy, it also reveals, underneath the jesting, his subliminal longing for faith, a longing equally expressed in the devil's desire to leave the realm of non-Euclidian "indeterminate equations" and become incarnate "once for all and irrevocably in the form of some merchant's wife, weighing two hundred fifty pounds and . . . believing all she believes" (15: 73–74). This yearning is disclosed directly by Ivan when, after asserting that "not for a minute" did he believe in the reality of the devil, he adds "strangely": "But I should like to believe in you" (15: 19).

The full implications of Ivan's ideas become clear when the devil reminds him of one of his earlier compositions—not the "Grand Inquisitor," whose mention causes Ivan to become "crimson with shame"—but a work called "The Geological Cataclysm" (15: 83). This title refers to a future when men will have lost all notion of God, and human life will be as much transformed as if the earth had undergone a geological mutation. Dostoevsky here employs his familiar symbolism of the Golden Age, when "men will unite to take from life all it can give, but only for joy and happiness in the present world." This would again be a Feuerbachian universe, where "love will be sufficient only for a moment of life, but the very consciousness of its momentariness will intensify its fire, which now is dissipated in dreams of an eternal love beyond the grave . . . and so on and so on in the same style." This would be a world in which "man will be lifted up with a spirit of divine titanic pride and the man-god would appear." And by "extending his conquest of nature infinitely by his will and his science, man will feel such lofty joy . . . that it will make up for all his old dreams of the joys of heaven" (15: 83).

Such had been Ivan's vision, which draws on imagery recalling Kirillov in *The Devils* (who believed that his suicide would initiate the reign of the man-god), as well as that of the Golden Age. But because of "man's inherent stupidity," of which Ivan is only too well aware, the devil understands that it may take a thousand years or more before such a world can come into being; and perhaps it may never be born at all. Ivan and those who share his ideas will therefore become impatient, like those "elect" who finally joined the Grand Inquisitor, and decide that "everyone who recognizes the truth even now may legitimately order his life as he pleases, on the new principles. In that sense 'all things are lawful for him' . . . and since there is no God and no immortality anyway, the new man may well become the man-god . . . who may lightheartedly overstep all the barriers of the old morality of the old slave-man, if necessary." (The proto-Nietzschean term "slave-man," *rab-chelovek*, is quite literal.) As the devil cynically comments, all this theorizing "is very charming, but if you want to swindle why do you want a moral sanction for doing it?" (15: 83–84). Idealistic dreams of a transformed humanity can lead not only to swindling but also, as Ivan has now become aware, to a justification for murder. It is impossible here not to think again of Dostoevsky's actual social-political situation, in which those whom he was willing to accept as misguided "idealists" were bent on murdering the Tsar-Father.

All through this dialogue, the violence of Ivan's reactions to the devil's words is turned back against himself. For if the devil is nothing but his hallucination, why respond so furiously? When Ivan threatens to kick the devil in anger, the latter responds: "I won't be altogether sorry, for then my object will be attained. If you kick me, you must believe in my reality, for people don't kick ghosts" (15: 73). At the climax of the scene, as the devil runs on about "The Geological Cataclysm," Ivan "suddenly snatched a glass from the table and flung it at the orator," who leaps up, brushes off the drops of tea, and comments: "He remembers Luther's inkstand [which Luther had flung at the devil]! He takes me for a dream and throws glasses at a dream!" (15: 84). The devil has thus succeeded in convincing Ivan that he is "real," though the latter continues to insist that the visitation is still only part of himself. But Ivan can no longer refuse to understand what he has been telling himself through the devil—that reason cannot eradicate the torments of his moral conscience.

At this point, the outside world begins to intrude on the sleeping Ivan, and he hears "a loud, persistent knocking . . . at the window." This knocking is still incorporated in his dream because the devil urges him to respond: "it's your brother Alyosha with the most interesting and surprising news" (ibid.). Dream and reality here intermingle, and they finally separate only when Ivan at last struggles up from sleep. On waking, he finds that the physical events he had dreamed of had never taken place. He had put no wet towel to his feverish brow, no glass of tea had moved from its place on the table, nor was there any nagging visitor sitting on the sofa facing him. Ivan's first reaction is then to affirm the "reality" of what he had earlier insisted had been only an apparition. "It was not a dream! No, I swear it was not a dream, it all happened just now!" he cried out to himself, thus trying to preserve the safeguard of his sanity. When he opens the window, Alyosha informs him that "an hour ago Smerdyakov had hanged himself" (15: 85).

Alyosha is greatly upset by Ivan's distraught appearance and confused mental state, especially when Ivan insists that "I knew Smerdyakov hanged himself," affirming that "*he* [the devil] had told me so just now." This is not literally true, but the devil had indeed warned Ivan that the conflict between belief and disbelief was such torture that "it could be enough to make you hang yourself" (15: 80). And in Ivan's disordered frame of mind, such words applied to himself could well have been shifted to Smerdyakov, similarly tormented by the same uncertainties. Alyosha's arrival causes the devil to vanish from Ivan's psyche, if not as a recollection then as a presence, and Ivan's inner debate with himself continues. Completely bewildered, he insists that the devil had been in his rooms, but then acknowledgeds that "*he* is myself . . . All that's base in me, all that's mean and contemptible." Still, Ivan admits that "he told me a good deal that was true about myself. . . . I would never have owned it to myself" (15: 87). Most of all, the devil understood the source of Ivan's mortification: "You are going to perform an act of heroic virtue," he had told Ivan, "and you don't believe in virtue; that's what tortures you and makes you angry, that's why you are so vindictive" (ibid.). Now that Smerdyakov is dead, any hope of saving Dimitry has vanished, and yet, the devil sneers, Ivan will go anyway. "And it would be all right if you believed in virtue. . . . But you are a little pig like Feodor Pavlovich and what do you want with virtue?" (15: 88).

Alyosha attempts to calm his brother, who echoes Dimitry in calling him "a cherub." The use of this word, with its heavenly overtones, evokes a series of stream-of-consciousness associations in Ivan—such as the devil's irreverent reference to "the thunderous howl of the seraphim," along with the idea that the seraphim may be only an astronomical formation ("perhaps a whole constellation"), or the notion that "perhaps that constellation is only a chemical molecule" (15: 85–86). The whirligig of Ivan's mind is thus once again displayed, but the devil had had no doubt about how he would act: "No matter if they disbelieve you [now that Smerdyakov is dead], you are going for the sake of principle. . . . Oh, you'd give a great deal to know yourself why you go? And can you have made up your mind?" Not at all, but "you'll go because you won't dare not to go," though why this should be so "is a riddle for you" (15: 88). But it is not a riddle for Alyosha, who finally puts Ivan to bed when he collapses and loses consciousness.

Alyosha "began to understand Ivan's illness. The anguish of a proud determination. A deep conscience! God, in Whom he disbelieved, and His Truth were gaining mastery in his heart." Alyosha naturally imagines that "God will conquer," and we shall soon see that Ivan will indeed obey the voice of his conscience. But Alyosha's fears also leave open the possibility, not resolved by the time the novel ends, that Ivan will "perish in hate, revenging himself on himself and on everyone for having served the cause he does not believe in" (15: 89).

## CHAPTER 38

# The Brothers Karamazov:
# Book 12

The final section of *The Brothers Karamazov* deals with Dimitry's trial, followed by a brief, concluding epilogue. This section differs from all the others because the narrator is no longer a detached observer or commentator whose viewpoint is retrospective and all-inclusive. He now steps forward to become an eyewitness of events, apologetically explaining that he will confine himself only "to what struck me personally, and what I especially remembered" (15: 89). One reason for such a limited perspective is self evident. Dostoevsky will be recapitulating a good deal of what the reader already knows, and he wished to foreshorten his account. Also, his depiction of the courtroom atmosphere draws on impressions he had personally gathered during the trial of Vera Zasulich; and this experience may well have influenced his choice of a narrative stance.

These chapters also contain the extensive speeches of both the prosecuting attorney and the defense; and while such speeches are more customary in novels than the hagiographic life of a saint, they have rarely been presented elsewhere so lengthily. Dostoevsky uses them not only to provide the proper climax to the plot action involving both Dimitry and Ivan, but also as a means of internal commentary on the novel itself. The two lawyers argue about a particular case of murder, but their orations also illuminate the larger moral-spiritual (and hence implicitly social and political) problems that the novel has presented with such majestic amplitude.

## 2

Since the Karamazov case has attracted nationwide attention, visitors swarmed into the little provincial community from "the chief town of our province [and] . . . from Moscow and Petersburg. . . . Among them were lawyers, ladies, and even several distinguished personages as well" (15: 89–90). The lawyers, looking forward to an oratorical duel between the local prosecutor, Ippolit Kirillovich, and the famous defense attorney Fetyukovich, were so numerous that a special section of the courtroom had been set aside where they could stand. The narrator comments acidly that, while everyone else was concerned with the verdict, the lawyers "were more interested in the legal than in the moral aspect of the case" (15: 91). In Dostoevsky's eyes, the new breed of lawyers were so preoccupied with legal issues and tactics that they completely lost sight of the "moral" aspects of the causes they were debating.

Opinions in the courtroom were divided along lines of gender, but again, neither sex is shown as especially concerned with moral questions. The ladies believe that Dimitry is guilty but should be acquitted, as the narrator puts it ironically, "perhaps chiefly because of his reputation as a conqueror of female hearts" (15: 90). Moreover, they awaited in eager anticipation the spectacle of the testimony of his two conquests—the haughty, aristocratic beauty Katerina Ivanovna, and "the hetaera" Grushenka, although they could not understand how both father and son should have been enthralled by such "a common, ordinary Russian woman" (15: 90). The men disliked the turbulent and quarrelsome Dimitry, and were "bitterly prejudiced against him"; there were even heated family quarrels over this difference of opinion (ibid.). The jury, a nondescript lot of peasants and low-level officials, was considered, especially by the ladies, to be incapable of dealing with "such a delicate, complex, and psychological case," and the narrator agrees with them: "One might well wonder, *as I did as soon as I looked at them*, what men like that could possibly make of such a case" (15: 93; italics added). Dostoevsky, so far as is known, was not an opponent of the jury system in principle, but he had criticized specific jury decisions as far back as 1873. Indeed, if we assume that his ideal of justice was expressed by Father Zosima, it is difficult to see how any secular system of justice could live up to such aspirations.

During the examination of witnesses, Fetyukovich succeeds in undermining the credibility of all but one of those testifying for the prosecution. In the case of Rakitin, who makes a rousing, denunciatory speech filled with "progressive" clichés, the attorney calls attention to a fulsome pamphlet he had written celebrating Father Zosima and published by the church press, whose ideas hardly accorded with those he expressed so eloquently in court. But Fetyukovich can do nothing with Grigory, who not only remains unshaken and sticks to his story about the open door, but also defends his dignity by protesting against the defense lawyer's public ridicule of a social inferior. Some comic relief is provided by the medical testimony, which discloses a conflict between the specialist from Moscow and the local medical official, Dr. Varvinsky. The first declares Dimitry insane because he used words like "ethics" and "Bernard"; Dr. Varvinsky finds Dimitry to be perfectly sane, though "in a nervous and exceedingly excited state before his arrest" (15: 104,

105). The most important medical testimony is that of the aged and kindly German practitioner Dr. Herzenstube, who, while also persuaded that Dimitry's mental faculties were in an abnormal state, recalls an incident that for the first time places the accused in a more favorable light.

Once taking pity on the young Dimitry, a totally neglected little boy running around in torn, ragged clothes, the warmhearted Herzenstube had bought him a pound of nuts and taught him the words for the Holy Trinity in German. Just recently, twenty-three years later, Dimitry had thanked him for the gift and repeated the religious formula; the two had embraced and wept together, though Dimitry was also laughing during this encounter. The anecdote illustrates both Dimitry's enduring gratitude for a small act of kindness and his total abandonment by his father—a point to which Fetyukovich will eloquently return in his speech for the defense. The incident also exemplifies a leitmotif echoing throughout the book: the importance of sacred and morally radiant childhood memories for the shaping of character and later conduct. This leitmotif will emerge, in the final epilogue, as the means of laying the groundwork for a more hopeful future.

The testimony of the doctors is followed by that of Alyosha, who suddenly recalls the conversation in which Dimitry had spoken of the "dishonor" he was carrying with him and "struck his chest with his fist with a strange air, as though the dishonor lay precisely on his chest, in some spot, in a pocket perhaps, or hanging around his neck." This recollection confirms Dimitry's claim that he was carrying half the sum entrusted to him by Katerina Ivanovna in a little pouch around his neck, and that the money spent during his second visit to Mokroe was not obtained by the murder of his father. Alyosha also continues to insist that Dimitry is innocent, even though his brother had hated Feodor Pavlovich. He names Smerdyakov as the killer, though he can furnish "no proof whatever [except his] brother's word and the expression of his face" (15: 108).

The appearance of Katerina Ivanovna created a considerable stir; "the ladies stretched their lorgnettes and opera glasses," and "some men stood up to get better views." Looking particularly handsome, she was quiet and controlled, "but there was a resolute gleam in her dark and gloomy eyes" (15: 112). She spoke composedly of her betrothal to Dimitry and, putting his behavior toward her in the best possible light, made no effort to protect her own reputation. Deliberately concealing that it was Dimitry who had suggested their first meeting, she depicts his honorable course of conduct at that time in a respectful tone that could only redound to his favor. The narrator marvels at the courage of her self-exposure, and confesses that "it was something tremendous! I turned cold and trembled as I listened." As Katerina recounted her appearance in Dimitry's quarters with complete disregard for her own reputation, "I had a painful misgiving at heart!" the narrator comments. "I felt that calumny might come of it later (and it did, in fact it did!)" (15: 112).

When her turn came, Grushenka found it impossible to imitate the composure of Katerina, and the ladies interpreted her expression as "concentrated and spiteful." The narrator defends her against such impressions, though she was "irritated and painfully suspicious of the contemptuous and inquisitorial eyes of the scandal-loving public" (15: 113). Blaming herself for the rivalry between Dimitry and his father ("I brought both of them to this"), she too asserts that Smerdyakov was the murderer, but again only on the basis of what Dimitry himself had said. Rakitin here is given a final coup de grâce when Grushenka explains that she supplied him with funds because he was her cousin (though he had asked her to keep their relation secret because "he is so dreadfully ashamed of me"). "All of Mr. Rakitin's earlier speech, all its nobility, all its outbursts against serfdom, against the civil disorder of Russia—all of it was now scrapped and destroyed in the general opinion" (15: 115).

Sharp shifts of perspective are a standard feature of Dostoevsky's novelistic technique; and just as the public and the jury begin to look on Dimitry in a somewhat more approving light, "a sudden catastrophe" seals his doom. This catastrophe occurs when Ivan, although excused because of illness, appears in the courtroom and insists on testifying. "He was irreproachably dressed," the narrator reports, "but his face made a painful impression, on me at least; there was a look in it of something, as it were, touched by the earth, the look of a dying man." Behaving in a distracted manner, laughing abruptly at the instructions addressed to him by the president of the court, his comportment gives everyone "a feeling of something strange." At first he answered questions quite rationally, though "with a sort of disgust which grew more and more marked." Complaining of feeling ill at one point, he began to walk out of the courtroom; but then returned, producing the money given him by Smerdyakov. "He [Smerdyakov] murdered him and I incited him to do it. Who doesn't desire his father's death?" (15: 115–117).

All of Ivan's contempt for humanity—the contempt underlying the Legend of the Grand Inquisitor, despite its humanitarian pathos—now comes to the fore as he turns on the judges and all the spectators at the trial. When the startled president asks if Ivan is in his right mind, he replies: "I should think I am in my right mind . . . in the same nasty mind as you . . . and all those . . . ugly faces." Humankind now becomes identified with himself: "They all desire the death of their fathers. One reptile devours another." Alyosha cries out that Ivan has "brain fever," but Ivan continues: "I am not mad, I am only a murderer." When asked for proof of his accusation against Smerdyakov, he replies that he has no witnesses—except possibly the devil—and then rambles on, as if confiding a secret, in a stream-of-consciousness monologue composed of fragments taken from earlier scenes. "I told him I don't want to keep quiet and he talked about the geological cataclysm . . . idiocy! Come . . . release the monster [Dimitry] . . . he's been singing a hymn. . . . That's because his heart is light. . . . It's like a drunken man in the street howling how 'Vanka went to Petersburg,' and I would give a quadrillion quadrillions for two seconds of joy" (15: 117–118). The poignancy of these last words requires no comment, though perhaps the reference to the dream anecdote points to the future. But now Ivan reacts violently when seized by the bailiff, who forcibly removes him as he "yelled and screamed something incoherent" (ibid.).

Ivan's madness is more than Katerina Ivanovna can bear, and, sobbing and shrieking herself, she hysterically asks to be heard by the court. Producing the letter from Dimitry in which his alleged commission of the crime is anticipated, she discredits her previous testimony. Both of them had understood that she gave the money to Dimitry to test whether he would dishonor himself by spending it on Grushenka; and Dimitry confirms her words: "Despise me as a scoundrel," he shouts. Katerina, speaking "like a madwoman," now also admits the distorted basis of her presumed "love" for Dimitry, actually founded on wounded pride. "He has always despised me, he has despised me from the very moment that I bowed down to him for that money" (15: 119–121). The narrator indicates her misconception: "she had been firmly convinced, perhaps since that bow, that the simple-hearted Mitya, who even then adored her, was laughing at her and despising her. She had loved him with a near hysterical, lacerated love . . . that . . . was not like love but more like revenge." After Katerina's outburst, Grushenka wails, quite rightly, "Mitya . . . your serpent has destroyed you," and both she and Dimitry are removed from the courtroom as they struggle to reach each other (15: 121–122). The narrator comments caustically that "the ladies who came to see the spectacle must have been satisfied" (ibid.).

3
-----

The two summing-up speeches of the attorneys allow Dostoevsky not only to exhibit his mastery of the legal rhetoric of the period, but also to provide some clues as to how he wished the book to be interpreted. The narrator begins by stressing that Ippolit Kirillovich, despite his passion for "psychology," "unexpectedly revealed that at least some feeling for the public welfare and 'the eternal questions' lay concealed in him. He genuinely believed in the defendant's guilt . . . and in calling for ven-

geance, he quivered with a genuine passion for 'the security of society'"
(15: 123). Such comments were surely meant to guide the reader toward
taking very seriously what Ippolit Kirillovich initially has to say about
the larger meaning of the case. It is only in the latter half of his peroration, when he comes to analyze Dimitry's behavior more specifically,
that his insistence on a purely "psychological" interpretation of motive
leads him astray.

Beginning with a broad moral-social generalization, Ippolit Kirillovich
argues that Russians are no longer horrified by the crime of murder (in
this instance parricidal), and he raises the question of "the causes of
our indifference, our lukewarm attitude to such deeds, to such signs of
the times, ominous of an unenviable future." The resonance of such
words, amidst all the acts of terrorism and attempts on the life of the
Tsar, can hardly be overestimated. Without attempting to answer his
own question, the prosecutor details examples of the frequency of such
murders committed by members of the upper class; and then, in a reference that Dostoevsky's readers might certainly apply not only to Ivan
but to themselves as well, he adds: "Another man will not commit the
murder, but will feel and think just like [the murderer], and is just as
dishonorable as he in soul. In silence, alone with his conscience, he
asks himself perhaps: 'What is honor, and isn't the condemnation of
bloodshed a prejudice?'" (15: 123–124). In the context of the time, this
indictment would certainly have been read as a condemnation of those
who, if not in sympathy with terrorism, then at least remained neutrally
indifferent to its ravages. And perhaps, recalling Dostoevsky's conversation with Suvorin, it may be taken as a self-castigation as well.

Ippolit Kirillovich then dwells on the epidemic of suicides among the
youth, repeating what Dostoevsky had written about this problem in
the *Diary of a Writer*. Young people no longer display any concern with
"Hamlet's question"; and this is why, like the courtroom audience depicted with raillery by the narrator, "we really gloat over the spectacle
[of murder], and love strong and eccentric sensations which tickle our
cynical, pampered idleness" (15: 125). Reference is then made to the famous passage in Gogol's *Dead Souls*, where Russia is compared with a
troika, furiously galloping to some distant destination and before which
all the other nations give way. But if, the orator goes on, the troika were
being pulled by the main characters of Gogol's novel—an unscrupulous
and unworthy lot—then the glorification of Russia contained in this
image was a "childish and naïve optimism." "And these were the heroes
of an older generation," he declares. "Ours are worse specimens still"
(ibid.).

The Karamazov family, he maintains, presents in symbolic miniature
"certain fundamental features of our educated class today." In a draft

of the unfinished article intended for the *Russian Messenger* and meant to furnish a riposte to his critics, Dostoevsky had stated the same idea: "Place all these four characters together [Feodor Pavlovich, Alyosha, Ivan, and Dimitry], and you obtain, though reduced by a thousand degrees, a picture of our contemporary reality, our contemporary educated Russia."[1] What Ippolit Kirillovich says about Feodor Pavlovich certainly corresponds with Dostoevsky's own conception. He was an "unhappy, vicious, unbridled old man" who "saw nothing in life but sensual pleasure." Even though the head of a family, "he had no feeling for his duty as a father" and in fact "ridiculed these duties. . . . He was an example of everything that is opposed to civic duty, of the most complete and malignant individualism." On a broader level, he could be regarded as "one of the typical fathers of the day," because "many modern fathers only differ in not openly professing such cynicism as his, for they are better educated, more cultured, but their philosophy is essentially the same" (15: 125–126). Feodor Pavlovich thus represents—in the extreme, symbolically expressive form that only Dostoevsky knew how to create—the older generation of Russians among whom stable moral-social standards had entirely disappeared.

Ippolit Kirillovich's description of Ivan also concurs with the author's point of view. Ivan "is one of those modern young men of brilliant education and vigorous intellect who have, however, lost faith in everything" and as a result conclude that "everything in the world is lawful . . . and nothing must be forbidden in the future." This citation is taken from Smerdyakov's testimony under questioning, and the prosecutor charges: "I believe that idiot [Smerdyakov] was driven out of his mind by this theory" (15: 126–127). Although not literally accurate, this conclusion is nonetheless true symbolically and expresses an important social-political motif—the possibility that the intelligentsia's atheism will undermine the still-devout Russian people. But Ivan's appearance in court, however distressing it may have been, still indicated "that the direct force of truth lives in his young heart, that family-feeling has not been destroyed in him by lack of faith and cynicism" (15: 127). But Ippolit Kirillovich is incapable of appreciating the deepest source of Ivan's mental collapse, and speaks of his moral nihilism somewhat apologetically as having "come to him more by inheritance than by the genuine effort of independent thought" (ibid). Still, if the image of Feodor Pavlovich has led to "pessimism" about the "fathers," that of Ivan, without undue optimism, suggests that all hope has not been lost for the "sons."

The prosecutor's remarks about Alyosha offer an excellent example of Dostoevsky's ability to place himself at a point of view antithetical to his own and give it a powerful and convincing expression. As a Westernizer, Ippolit Kirillovich can only speak condescendingly of the religious novice Alyosha, who had almost become a monk. Alyosha is "an excellent and gifted young man," one who "seeks to cling to the 'ideas of the people,' or what goes by that clever name in some theoretical circles." Fearful of "cynicism and its corrupting influences," young men like Alyosha "mistakenly attribute all the mischief to European enlightenment" and flee to a monastery or wish to return to their "'native soil' . . . like frightened children" (ibid.).

The allusion to "native soil" refers to Dostoevsky's own program of *pochvennichestvo*, here treated from a patronizing, if not completely hostile, Westernizer point of view. All the same, Ippolit Kirillovich wishes this "gifted young man every success"; but he hopes that Alyosha's "youthful idealism may never degenerate, as often happens, on the moral side into gloomy mysticism, and on the political into blind chauvinism" (ibid.). Both these charges had been leveled against Dostoevsky after the Pushkin speech, and were renewed from the first moment that chapters of the novel had appeared. In allowing the prosecutor to characterize Alyosha's religious orientation as backwardness and obscurantism, Dostoevsky was giving his opponents their just due; and the whole purpose of his novel was to persuade readers that such judgments were mistaken and misguided.

The bulk of the prosecutor's speech is devoted to Dimitry, of whom he paints a portrait very close to Dostoevsky's own—but with a crucial difference. In contrast to Ivan's embrace of "Europeanism" and Alyosha's supposedly frightened retreat to the monastery and "the principles of the people," Dimitry is seen as a symbol of Russia itself. He "represents Russia directly. . . . Yes, here she is, our Mother Russia, the very scent and smell of her. Oh, we are spontaneous, we are a marvelous mingling of good and bad, we are lovers of culture and Schiller, yet we brawl in taverns and pluck the beards of our boon companions" (15: 128). Dostoevsky certainly intended Dimitry to be apprehended as a representative of the "broad" Russian character; and at least one journalistic critic immediately recognized him as a new type in Russian literature as well as in Dostoevsky's work.

But Ippolit Kirillovich then adds, quite erroneously from everything that has been shown to the reader, "Oh, we too can be good and noble, *but only when all goes well with us*" (ibid.; italics added). When the prosecutor raises the question of which version of Katerina Ivanovna's story should be accepted by the jury—the image of the noble Dimitry given in the first, or of the ignoble, conscienceless debauchee and murderer portrayed in the second—he decides that no choice is necessary because both are true. Both are part of the Karamazov character, which is "capable of containing the most incongruous contradictions and simultaneously contemplating both abysses, the abyss above, the abyss of the highest ideals, and the abyss below us, the abyss of the lowest and foulest degradations" (15: 129). These words echo Dimitry's about the ceaseless conflict between the ideal of Sodom and that of the Madonna; but the entire book has shown his struggle to wrench himself free from the temptations of Sodom and commit himself to the Mother of God. Ippolit Kirillovich denies that Dimitry is capable of any such struggle, citing Rakitin in support: "the sense of their own degradation," he had said, "is as essential to these reckless, unbridled natures [the Karamazovs] as the sense of their lofty generosity" (ibid.). That the prosecutor has allied himself with Rakitin surely indicates that such an image of Dimitry is totally erroneous.

Ippolit Kirillovich then launches into a detailed "psychological" analysis of Dimitry based on these assumptions. "Psychology" for Dostoevsky meant not merely a study of the flow of inner life but an approach to human character based on certain extremely limited and simplistic "rational" assumptions about motivation. No room was left in so-called "scientific psychology" for the fluctuations of emotion or the influence of ideas and values on how such emotions lead (or in the case of Dimitry do not lead) to action; no room was left for the possibility of moral choice or decision: The existence of such an entity as free will never appears in Ippolit Kirillovich's indictment of the luckless Dimitry, presented as predestined by his "reckless and unbridled" Karamazov nature to commit a premeditated murder; no other possibility is taken into account as the course of his behavior is minutely analyzed.

In conclusion, the prosecutor returns again to the image of the Russian troika, which he now uses to instruct the jury in the importance of their task. The jurors represent, he tells them, all "of our holy Russia, . . . her principles, her family, everything that she holds sacred!" The whole country awaits their verdict, as "our fatal troika dashes on in headlong flight, perhaps to destruction, and for a long time past men have stretched out imploring hands and called a halt to its furious, reckless course." Other nations stand aside, "not from respect . . . but simply from horror," and he warns that some day they may "form a firm wall confronting the hurrying apparition . . . for the sake of their own safety, enlightenment, and civilization." The jury, Ippolit Kirillovich warns, must not increase "their growing hatred by a sentence justifying the murder of a father by his son" (15: 150).

4
———

The famous defense attorney Fetyukovich, the star of the Petersburg bar, now makes his plea, and he does so with such effectiveness and insight that, at least to my mind, his speech raises some intriguing questions. Dostoevsky had denied being an opponent of the new court system, and there is no evidence that he wished to see it abolished or desired any return to the abuses of the administrative fiat of the past. Still, his articles in the *Diary of a Writer* had expressed a highly critical view of the new breed of defense lawyers, of whom Fetyukovich was an example. Dostoevsky denied selecting any individual as a prototype, but the assumption is that a primary model was V. D. Spasovich.

Fetyukovich is not described at any length, though his name has pejorative connotations;* but the narrator fixes on one of his physical mannerisms that, like the description of Peter Verkhovensky in *The Devils*, seems to suggest a reptile. "He kept bending forward, especially at the beginning of his speech, not exactly bowing, but as though he were about to dart at his listeners, bending his long back in half, as though there were a spring in the middle of that long and narrow back that enabled him to bend at right angles" (15: 153). But he spoke quite unpretentiously, "made no attempt at eloquence, at pathos, or emotional phrases" (in contrast to Ippolit Kirillovich), and "there was something genuine and simple" in the sound of his voice (ibid.). No further effort is made to caricature him in any hostile fashion; even more, Fetyukovich offers a masterly defense of Dimitry in terms that the reader recognizes as accurate. His defense not only discredits the psychological inferences drawn by Ippolit Kirillovich, but he also understands, or at least is willing to accept, that Dimitry could act under the influence of love, honor, and pity as well as by the rage and jealousy considered his sole motivations by the prosecutor. If Dostoevsky had wished to discredit defense attorneys, he could hardly have chosen a less effective means of doing so. His main criticism, however, had been that defense lawyers, carried away by their task, often lost sight of the larger moral implications of their arguments; and this is exactly what occurs here. Fetyukovich goes too far, swept beyond the bounds of the morally legitimate by the desire to defend his client (who in this case at least was innocent).

Fetyukovich's chief aim is to destroy the psychological foundations of Ippolit Kirillovich's argument. He does so by demonstrating that, as he says in one of Dostoevsky's most often-quoted phrases: "psychology . . . [is] a knife that cuts both ways" (15: 154). The defense lawyer, even though a stranger in the community, has learned that Dimitry is "a man of turbulent and violent temper" who "has insulted perhaps hundreds

---

* The lawyer's name is derived from *fetyuk*, "jerk, drip, sourpuss," a slang expression Dostoevsky may have learned from Gogol's *Dead Souls*, chap. 4, where Gogol's footnote defines it: "*Fetyuk*, a word insulting to a man, comes from the letter theta [in the Russian alphabet], considered by some to be an obscene letter." Victor Terras, *A Karamazov Companion* (Madison, 1981), 357.

of persons in this town," thus predetermining the case against him. In fact, although there is "an overwhelming chain of evidence against the defendant," Fetyukovich argues that "not one fact will stand criticism" if looked at in itself rather than as part of a pattern interpreted according to the condemnatory assumptions of the prosecutor. For example, Dimitry's leap from the fence to examine Grigory after striking him had been characterized as a cold-blooded effort to check whether a witness to his crime was dead. Yet the prosecution had also depicted Dimitry as having been so agitated a few moments earlier, just after presumably committing the murder, that he had carelessly left the envelope containing the money lying on the floor. At one moment, he is "as blood-thirsty and keen-sighted as a Caucasian eagle, while the next [he is] as timid and blind as a mole" (15: 153–155). The prosecutor never considered that Dimitry may have gone back and wiped away the blood from Grigory out of a feeling of remorse; such a motive would be inconsistent with his "psychology."

Dimitry, it has been assumed, had killed in order to rob, but the money presumably stolen had not been produced in evidence. Moreover, on his second trip to Mokroe, Dimitry had spent only half of the three thousand rubles supposedly stolen from Feodor Pavlovich on the night of the murder; the remainder of the money, not having been found, was assumed to have been hidden somewhere in Mokroe. "Why not in the dungeons of the castle of Udolpho?" Fetyukovich asks mockingly, referring to the famous Gothic novel of Anne Radcliffe that had delighted Dostoevsky's youth (15: 158). Alyosha's testimony had not been accepted because someone of Dimitry's character, the prosecutor had argued, could not have exercised such self-control. The "broad Karamazov nature" swings between extremes; but in this instance, as Fetyukovich points out, on the side of the Madonna there now was love, "the new love that had flared up in his heart" (15: 159–160). The letter he wrote, taken as proof that he planned the crime in advance, was that "of a drunken man," whose words prove nothing except intoxication. Time and again in the *Diary of a Writer* Dostoevsky had insisted that the intention to commit a crime does not necessarily mean it would be carried out; a margin of freedom always exists which, as in the case of Dimitry, could lead to a change of heart. Fetyukovich then applies his own "psychology" to Katerina Ivanovna, in whose reversal of testimony "we heard only cries of resentment and revenge, cries of long-concealed hatred" (15: 159). All the other circumstantial evidence is examined in the same fashion and called into question. Fetyukovich also offers a much more accurate estimate of Smerdyakov's character, concluding that, under "a mask of naïveté," he was "a distinctly spiteful creature, excessively ambitious, vindictive, and intensely envious" (15: 164).

Up to this point, Fetyukovich's performance cannot be faulted. But he treads on dangerous ground when he raises the question of whether the murder of such a reprehensible and irresponsible father as Feodor Pavlovich could really be condemned. While continuing to insist that Dimitry is innocent, he nonetheless argues that such a murder could well be justified, driving home the point with examples taken from a tirade of the villainous Karl Moor in Schiller's *The Robbers*. The indignant narrator now labels him "an adulterer of thought" (the chapter's title); and it is here that the defense plea intersects with the novel's deepest moral-philosophical motifs. "Filial love for an unworthy father," Fetyukovich insists, "is an absurdity, an impossibility. Love cannot be created from nothing: only God can create something from nothing" (15: 169). If fathers wish to be loved by their children, they should earn such love by their deeds. Love for a father should rest not "on mystical prejudice, but on a rational, responsible, and strictly humanitarian basis"; it should not derive from a "mystical meaning which I cannot comprehend with my intellect, but only accept by faith, or better, *on faith*, like many other things which I do not understand, but which religion leads me to believe" (15: 170). The courtroom audience, as the narrator notes sarcastically, went wild over this denunciation of a filial love based solely on faith. "Even persons of high position, old men with stars on their breasts, sitting on specially reserved seats behind the judges, applauded the orator and waved their handkerchiefs" (15: 171). The bitter irony of this comment is certainly reminiscent of what had occurred in the Zasulich courtroom, when high government officials had frenziedly applauded her acquittal.

Fetyukovich is here making the same argument against unconditional filial love, based only on faith, that Ivan had made against a God-Father who incomprehensibly permits the undeserved suffering of His children. But the lawyer goes still further when he suggests that, even if Dimitry had entered the house—which of course he denied having done—with no intent to kill, he might have struck Feodor Pavlovich precisely *because* he was his father, "not an ordinary enemy. . . . The mere sight of the father who had hated him from his childhood, had been his enemy, his persecutor, and now his unnatural rival, was enough" (15: 172). His feeling of hatred would have become so strong that he might have dealt him a blow, "not knowing that he would kill him" and not intending at all to do so. But if he *had* killed him, "the murder of such a father," Fetyukovich insists, "cannot be considered parricide . . . [and] can only be reckoned a parricide by prejudice" (ibid.).

In stretching Dimitry's defense to the point of justifying a possible parricide, Fetyukovich undermined his own case by raising doubts as to whether he himself believed in the innocence of his client. Moreover, the terms of Fetyukovich's argument recall those that Ivan had made against the God-Father. But in asking the reader to accept Ivan's attack on God and Dimitry's hatred of Feodor Pavlovich as equally inadmissible and impious assaults on the sacrosanct principle of fatherhood, Dostoevsky was taking a considerable artistic-ideological risk. "Grotesque as the analogy might seem," W. J. Leatherbarrow has aptly written, "both Feodor Pavlovich and God serve to illustrate [the] rejection of an unlovable father."[2] Indeed, if there is some question among interpreters as to whether Dostoevsky ever truly succeeded in blunting the force of Ivan's rebellion, an even stronger doubt arises over his effort to merge the levels of this same thematic motif. God, after all, bestowed on man the immense gift of freedom, however badly this gift may have been abused and misused; and while He can be held implicitly responsible for all the horrors that have ensued, they occurred, as even Ivan conceded in his Legend, because He refused to enslave the dignity of the human conscience.

It is entirely different, however, to substitute Feodor Pavlovich for God, and to ask readers to accept a refusal to love *him* unconditionally as an equivalent violation of the sacred principle of fatherhood. The stark realism with which his cynicism and debauchery are displayed, and his complete lack of any redeeming features, undermine the parallel that Dostoevsky was trying to establish. Readers, in this case, are likely to ally themselves with Fetyukovich's insistence that mundane filial-paternal love should involve reciprocity and mutual responsibility. Nonetheless, just as Dostoevsky had not softened the asperities of Ivan's attack on the shortcomings of both God and Christ, so here too he dares to proffer the protection of the sacrosanct principle of fatherhood, unassailable by reason and justified by faith alone, even to so hateful and irresponsible a specimen as Feodor Pavlovich. One cannot help wondering whether the extremity of this effort was not a forlorn response to the nerve-racking situation that all of Russia was then living through, as one attempt after another was made on the life of the Tsar-Father.

After appealing to reason to defend a crime that Dimitry had not committed, Fetyukovich then concludes by evoking a totally opposite principle—that of Christian mercy. He does so, however, in a manner totally inappropriate to Dimitry's social position and status. For he speaks as if Dimitry were a common, lower-class criminal who, if convicted, would hate society because "these people have done nothing for my bringing up, for my education, nothing to improve my lot, nothing to make me better, nothing to make me a man." None of this is relevant to Dimitry, who had been educated in a military academy, was an officer in the Russian Army, and had lived the reckless, spendthrift life traditional for his class? And, in asking for mercy, Fetyukovich continues to create the impression that Dimitry is probably guilty, though from time to time his innocence is reasserted. On the one hand, the counsel cites Peter the Great (without mentioning his name), who had said that it is "better to acquit ten guilty men than to punish one innocent man." On the other, he reminds the jury that "the Russian court does not exist for punishment only, but also for the salvation of the fallen man." But if Dimitry is innocent, why should the jury be concerned about his salvation? As he goes on, Fetyukovich's eloquent words continue to ask for mercy in a manner implying Dimitry's guilt. "Let other nations think of retribution and the letter of the law, we will cling to the spirit and the meaning—the salvation and reformation of the lost" (15: 172–173). The argument is thus a tissue of contradictions, more an apologia for the crime than a clear-cut defense of Dimitry's innocence.

These concluding words excited a demonstration from the audience that was like "an irresistible storm." Everyone wept, and even "two important personages shed tears" at this combination of rationalism and an appeal to a sentimental humanitarianism deriving from Christian principles. When Ippolit Kirillovich rose to protest, "shaking with emotion . . . people positively looked at him with hatred." In his articles, Dostoevsky had often criticized the use or what he considered the abuse of the Gospels by defense lawyers, and Ippolit Kirillovich charges Fetyukovich with such malpractice by his reference to Christ as "the crucified lover of humanity . . . in opposition to all of orthodox Russia, which calls to Him, 'for thou art our God.'" He also rejects the use of the truncated citation, "What measure ye mete so shall it be meted unto you," as expressing the teachings of Christ. "Religion and the Gospels," Ippolit Kirillovich cries, "are corrected—that's all mysticism, we are told, and ours is the only true Christianity which has been subjected to the analysis of reason and common sense." Replying to this assault "lightly and ironically," Fetyukovich only became serious when he countered that his "reputation as a citizen and loyal subject had been impugned by the charge that he had uttered 'unorthodox opinions'" (15: 173–175). The president of the court had already stopped Ippolit Kirillovich from pursuing this dangerous accusation, and he now checks Fetyukovich as well.

Dimitry, allowed to make a statement, rose to deny once again that he had killed his father, adding that Fetyukovich "needn't have supposed so." He asks for mercy as well, but not at all in the same terms as his counsel, who had depicted him as a victim of society. He indicates rather his repentance and remorse for the sins of his past life. "I erred," he admits, "but I loved what was good. Every instant I strove to reform, but I lived like a wild beast." If spared, "I will become a better man, I give you my word before God that I will." If convicted, "I know myself, I shall rebel." Dimitry's tempestuous character is thus not likely to change, even though he now speaks "in a weak voice," in which "there was a new note of humility, defeat, and submission" (15: 175–176).

The jury then retires, and while the courtroom waits for its decision, the narrator sets down some snatches of conversation among the public. Everyone, it seems, was convinced of an acquittal despite the weight of the evidence. The ladies saw the whole matter as a crime of passion, perfectly pardonable under the circumstances; others believed he would get off because, as one official said, "suppose he did murder him—there are fathers and fathers! . . . If I'd been in Fetyukovich's place, I would have simply said straight out: 'He murdered him, but he is not guilty, what the hell!'" (15: 177). These choral voices seem to justify Ippolit Kirillovich's opening statement that murder is now taken as a matter of course in Russia. Like the public, Fetyukovich too was convinced that he had won the case; but after an hour's deliberation the jury returned to find Dimitry guilty on all counts and, even worse, made no recommendation for mercy. This decision created an indescribable hubbub in the courtroom, during which Dimitry shouted, "Katya, I forgive you," and asked everyone "to have pity on the other woman." His voice then "broke into a terrible, sobbing wail," while Grushenka uttered "a piercing shriek." The narrator leaves in the midst of this pandemonium and before the session is officially ended, but he recalls one exclamation heard as he was descending the steps: "Well, our peasants have stood firm" (15: 178).

The culmination of this central plot action thus creates a mixed impression—one both negative and positive at the same time. An obvious "miscarriage of justice" (the title of the entire Book 12) has occurred on the legal level, though Dimitry has inwardly accepted the justice of suffering for his parricidal impulses. But "the peasants have stood firm" against justifying the murder of a father for *any* reason, thus upholding the "mystic" sanctity of the moral-religious law that Dimitry had violated in thought if not in deed.

## 5

The epilogue is composed of two episodes, one detailing the relations between Ivan, Katerina, and Dimitry, the other between Alyosha and the group of boys who had clustered around the bedside of the ailing Ilyusha. Katerina, once again flouting convention, is now nursing Ivan in her apartment, where he is lying "unconscious in a high fever," his life hanging in the balance; the doctors "could not yet give [any] positive hopes of recovery" (15: 179). Ivan's future thus remains unknown, and this uncertainty was no doubt intended to sustain interest for the next volume. Still, his moral conscience has triumphed over the resistance of his reason, thus providing a more or less satisfactory resolution to (presumably) this first stage of his life. Dimitry, also fallen ill with "a nervous fever," is waiting to be sent to Siberia; whether he will escape along the way is left in doubt. Ivan had entrusted the instructions for this escape to Katerina, even providing the money necessary for it to be accomplished, and she had agreed to carry it out in case Ivan himself was unable to do so (foreseeing the possibility of his illness). The greatest obstacle to the plan was Alyosha: "It's you he [Dimitry] is most afraid of," she tells him. "He is afraid you won't approve of his escape on moral grounds" (15: 181).

Katerina is shown here in all the complexity of her prideful vanity. She had quarreled with Ivan, the man she loves wholeheartedly, because her hatred of Grushenka had led to an expression of resentment at the escape plan, which if successful would allow Grushenka and Dimitry to be reunited. Katerina's animosity had led Ivan to suspect that she really loved Dimitry, and this suspicion had so wounded her that it became impossible to express her love for Ivan directly. She feared, as she confesses to Alyosha, that Ivan would regard any declaration of love simply as gratitude for his aid to Dimitry, and "I was so exasperated over the possibility of such an unjust thought on his part that I . . . flew into a fury again! . . . It's my character, my awful, unhappy character! Oh, you will see, I shall end by driving him, too, to abandon me for another with whom he can get on better, like Dimitry" (ibid.). Such an unprecedented confession from Katerina, Alyosha suspects, was really inspired by her "treachery at the trial," which "her conscience was compelling her to confess . . . with tears and cries and hysterical writhings on the floor"—which luckily did not occur (ibid.). But her indirect repentance makes it easier to deliver the message that Dimitry had asked him to convey. Simply, Dimitry wishes her to pay him a visit in his cell, and she finally consents under the pressure of Alyosha's insistence that "for the sake of his infinite suffering in the future, visit him now" (15: 82).

Dimitry himself "had become terribly preoccupied since the trial"; silent and self-absorbed, "he looked sometimes with a face of suffering at his brother" (15: 184). He is tormented not only by his desire to make peace with Katerina but also from anguish over the problem of his possible escape. He realizes, as he had said at the trial, that he would prove incapable of submitting to any brutal treatment: "If they beat me on the way or *there* . . . I will kill someone and will be shot for it" (15: 185). He has thus concluded, as the narrator had anticipated, that he is too weak to bear the burden which, in a moment of rapture, he had believed he could assume: "I am not able to resign myself. I wanted to sing a 'hymn'; but if a guard speaks to me, I haven't the strength to bear it." With Grushenka at his side, however, "I would bear anything . . . anything except blows. . . . But she won't be allowed to come *there*" (ibid.). Such words solicit Alyosha's approval of the escape plan, although in fact Dimitry has already made up his mind to carry it out.

Alyosha agrees that "you are not ready, and such a cross is not for you," that is, the cross of an *imitatio Christi*, the acceptance of punishment by an innocent as expiation for the sins and injustices of others. "If you had murdered our father," Alyosha continues, "it would grieve me that you should reject your cross. But you are innocent, and such a cross is too much for you." Dimitry had wished to make himself "another man by suffering" and had in fact gone a long way toward becoming that "other man" spiritually. Alyosha assures him that if "you only remember that other man always, all your life and wherever you escape to . . . that will be enough for you" (ibid.). No one would be punished for allowing Dimitry to escape; and although bribery was dishonest under any circumstances, Alyosha admits that in this instance he might do it himself. The disciple of Father Zosima is prepared to break the letter of the law so as to avert an obvious injustice and a human tragedy. This scene, quite possibly, could be a preparation for a more serious violation of the law in the future (as suggested by the various rumors already cited about the novel's continuation).[3] Both brothers agree that they are reasoning like "Jesuits," and when Alyosha says that he will not "condemn" Dimitry, the latter replies: "But I shall condemn myself, and I will pray for my sins forever" (15: 186).

Dimitry then imagines his life after the escape; and curiously, we find him duplicating some of the details of Chernyshevsky's novel *What Is To Be Done?*, one of the major sources of Russian radicalism since the 1860s. Dimitry plans to flee to America with Grushenka, as one of the radical heroes of Chernyshevsky's novel had done, though such an exile would be "as bad, perhaps, as Siberia," thus allowing him to assuage his conscience. Life in America would be terrible indeed (Dostoevsky had previously referred to it as such in *The Devils*): "I hate that America already. And though they might be wonderful at machines . . . they are not my people, they are not of my soul. I love Russia, Alyosha, I love the Russian God." Dimitry thus plans to go with Grushenka somewhere "in the country of *The Last of the Mohicans*," where they would be isolated ("I'm told there are still Redskins there"), work, and study grammar; after three years they would return to Russia as American citizens to live in some remote corner of the Russian provinces. Dimitry will change his appearance, through surgery if necessary, and if caught, then "let them send us to Siberia—I don't care" (ibid.). Chernyshevsky's character had done exactly the same—returning to Russia with an altered appearance and an American passport, marrying, and settling down to await the revolution that was certain to break out at any moment. Dostoevsky, perhaps, may have wished to offer an alternative image of what would inspire such a desire for repatriation.

The climactic scene of this chapter provides its title: "For a Moment the Lie Becomes Truth." When Katerina finally appears, the one-time "love" between her and Dimitry flares up again momentarily in impassioned words. "You love another woman and I love another man," Katerina says, "and yet I shall love you forever, and you will love me, do you know that?" Alyosha can hardly believe what he is hearing and seeing, and stands "speechless and confused" as Katerina declares: "But now let what might have been come true for a minute" (15: 187–188). Katerina confesses to Dimitry that, even when testifying against him, she had not believed him to be guilty. "When I was giving evidence I persuaded myself and believed it, but when I finished speaking I stopped believing it at once" (15: 188). Grushenka then unexpectedly arrives, and Katerina, in a supreme act of humiliation, asks for her forgiveness, "turn[ing] white as chalk." But Grushenka knows that "we are both full of hatred, my girl, you and I," and no forgiveness between them is possible. She adds, however: "Save him, and I'll forgive you everything" (ibid.). Dimitry reproaches her for refusing to forgive, but Alyosha rebukes *him* as having no right to do so. Grushenka wants no part in the lie becoming truth: "'Her proud lips spoke, not her heart,' she brought out in a tone of disgust." These words are confirmed a moment later when Katerina speaks to Alyosha in the street. "'She [Grushenka] would not forgive me. . . . I like her for that!' she added, in an unnatural voice, and her eyes flashed with fierce anger" (15: 189).

The book ends not on this note of enmity but with the funeral of little Ilyusha. No one but Dickens can rival Dostoevsky's well-known "philanthropic" manner here, as he depicts the anguish and despair of the desolate Captain Snegiryov and his afflicted family. Twelve of Ilyusha's schoolmates, gathered round his bier, were soon joined by Alyosha; and this symbolic number provides a Christological aura to the pathos of the scene. Kolya Krasotkin, foremost among the boys as usual, asks Alyosha whether Dimitry was really guilty and, when assured he was not, exclaims: "So he will perish an innocent victim for the truth—though ruined he is happy!" Astonished at this reaction, Alyosha objects, "but not in such a cause, and with such disgrace and such horror." Kolya agrees, but then continues: "I would like to die for all humanity, and as for disgrace, I don't care about that. . . . I respect your brother!" (15: 190). Dostoevsky had emphasized this desire to "die for humanity," to sacrifice oneself for "the truth," as typical of the new generation of the 1870s; and perhaps we catch a glimpse here of what he intended the future to hold for both Kolya and Alyosha.

Ilyusha's casket lies in the middle of the Snegiryovs' hovel, covered with flowers sent by Liza Khokhlakova and Katerina; "strange to say," the narrator comments laconically, "there was practically no smell from the corpse" (15: 190). The captain's behavior is pathetically distraught, and he runs "fussing and distracted" after the coffin as it is carried by the boys to its final resting place (15: 191). Readers of Dostoevsky will recall a similar scene in his very first novel, *Poor Folk*, where a touching buffoon character also runs pitifully after the coffin of his stepson. The Franciscan echo resounds once more when the captain pulls a crust of bread from his pocket, explaining that Ilyusha had wished him to crumble it on his grave so that the birds will come to feed there. After the church service, the semiconscious father almost falls into the open grave, and "he did not seem to understand fully what was happening" (15: 192). Overcome with grief on his return home, where the crazed mother and the crippled daughter are weeping, he convulsively snatches up and kisses Ilyusha's little boots. This image of family despair is so heartrending that the boys and Alyosha leave temporarily, though agreeing to come back for the traditional funeral dinner with pancakes (*blinis*) later in the evening. "It's all so strange, Karamazov," remarks Kolya, "such sorrow and then pancakes after it, it all seems so unnatural in our religion" (15: 194).

The group of boys then passes the stone under which Ilyusha had wished to be buried, and where he and his father had often come to console each other and dream of a happier future. The memory of Dimitry's humiliation of the captain and Ilyusha's heartbreak at his father's degradation suddenly sweeps over Alyosha, and he calls the boys together to make a little speech. Addressing them as "gentlemen" to stress the solemnity of his words, but then shifting to "my dear, dear children," he explains that he will soon part from them, "perhaps for a long time." But he asks them to make a pact then and there never to forget Ilyusha or one another, "whatever happens to us later in life." He urges them to recall the boy at whom they had once thrown stones, "and afterwards we grew so fond of him," and to remember "how good it was once here when we were all together united by a good and kind feeling." Alyosha then proclaims that "there is nothing higher and stronger and more wholesome and good for life in the future than some good memory, especially a memory of childhood and home" (15: 195). A "good and sacred memory" of this kind is the best protection against the evil that may arrive, and will remain so no matter how badly some among them may go astray.

Alyosha's words grip the hearts of his young listeners, all of whom are moved and inspired by his injunction to remember Ilyusha, "his face and clothes, his poor little boots, and his unhappy, sinful father, and how boldly he stood up for him alone against the whole school." And when the boys promise to remember, shouting at the same time, "Karamazov, we love you," Alyosha adds: "And may the dear boy's memory live eternally!" The mention of eternity impels Kolya to ask whether "it is true what's taught us in religion," that a bodily resurrection will occur and we "shall live and see each other again, all, Ilyushechka too?" Alyosha answers, "half laughing, half ecstatic": "Certainly we shall all arise again, certainly we shall all see each other." And then "hand in hand" they all go to the funeral dinner to eat pancakes. "It's a very old custom," Alyosha explains, "and there's something nice in that." Kolya once more shouts, "Hurrah for Karamazov," and "once more all the boys chimed in."

The tragedy of the Snegiryovs thus vanishes into "a sacred memory" that will guard against evil in the future; and death is overcome by the Christian hope of resurrection—when, as Alyosha promises, "we shall tell each other with joy and gladness all that has happened" (15: 196–197). The book ends on this boyish note of innocence and optimism, providing a welcome relief, similar to the epilogues of eighteenth-century plays or operas, to all the tragic tensions that have gone before. And just as those earlier examples pointed to the moral of the story, so Dostoevsky reaffirms, in a naïvely acceptable and touching form, the basic beliefs and moral-religious convictions he has sought to champion so peerlessly all through his greatest novel.

# PART V

# Death and Transfiguration

## CHAPTER 39

# Notes for a Phantom Future

After the intense pressure under which he had been laboring for the past three years, Dostoevsky might well have felt a need to relax, rest, and recoup his strength. But now that the first volume of *The Brothers Karamazov* had been completed, he threw himself, with his usual assiduity, into the task of gathering material for his revived *Diary of a Writer*. Well aware of the severe demands this renewal would make on his gradually deteriorating health, he was driven by economic need—other sources of income were quite insufficient—and also by the mission he had assumed to speak out against the forces disintegrating the fabric of Russian society.

## 2

On November 21, 1880, he joined other writers in a reading on behalf of the Literary Fund. Present was V. A. Posse, later a prominent journalist, editor, and publisher who became a friend and admirer of Maksim Gorky. The account he left testifies once again to the hypnotic power of Dostoevsky's elocution, but also affords a glimpse into the variety of responses to his most recent novel. Posse himself expresses an intense dislike of Katkov's journal, obviously too reactionary for his tastes; but since it had been serializing Dostoevsky's novel, he confesses to having awaited each issue "with a pleasurably uneasy excitement." One of his friends, having been strengthened by the novel in his "Christianity, Orthodoxy, and [respect for] monasticism," had gone to visit Dostoevsky and spoken with him at length. "In me," Posse writes, "it strengthened atheism, and gave birth to anarchism."[1]

Dostoevsky's read a famous poem of Nekrasov's on this occasion, "When from the darkness of delusion." Written in the 1840s, it is a notable expression of the social-humanitarian ideology of that period long since abandoned by Dostoevsky ("Nekrasov belonged to a camp hostile to Dostoevsky," as Posse notes). The poem is a monologue, addressed by a member of the intelligentsia to a young woman whom he has redeemed from her former life as a prostitute ("the darkness of delusion"), and he urges her to forget this shameful past as his wife. It had become a classic, along with Dostoevsky's own first novel *Poor Folk*, of the "philanthropic" literature of the 1840s. More than twenty years later, in *Notes from Underground*, Dostoevsky used a fragment of the poem ironically to highlight the egoistic vanity of the speaker rather than his presumed benevolence. At the climax, the prostitute Liza is shown to be morally superior to the underground man, who has taken the place of Nekrasov's protagonist.

Now, however, Dostoevsky threw himself into reading the same verses with such fervent sympathy that Posse could write: "Such a reading I have never heard again. In the nervous play of his pallid face there was suffering and exaltation, the voice was soft, slightly sing-song. Tender, prayerful words emerged from the depths of the soul, from the depths of the heart. The public no longer existed. He appealed directly to the suffering soul . . . to the soul of the woman, fallen but at the same time sacred."[2] Dostoevsky could thus easily re-create the "philanthropic" mode of his youth, which indeed he had never ceased to employ as a subordinate thematic topos all through the intervening years. It had recently been refurbished once again for the Snegiryov family.

In a letter accompanying the epilogue to his novel, he had requested N. A. Lyubimov to send him two copies of the proofs in preparation for a public reading at the end of November. "I've read through all of my things," he explained, "but this is something new, and I'll read the last chapter: Ilyushechka's funeral and Alyosha's speech to the boys. I know from experience that such passages in a reading produce a certain impression."[3] His experience was an excellent barometer, and when he read on November 30, Anna Grigoryevna recalled being surrounded by "depressed and weeping countenances, and not only among the women."[4] A newspaper story described his delivery: "Now groans and howls, now tears of joy, now terrible hatred and Christian humility, now, finally, sincere remorse sounded in the voice of the reader, who knew how to communicate, in an inimitable fashion, all the psychological movements of the human soul."[5]

Just a few days previously, on November 27, *New Time* and other journals had carried an announcement of the reappearance of the *Diary of a Writer*. A day later Dostoevsky wrote to his younger brother Andrey, with whom he was on the best of terms, to congratulate him on his name day and thank him for similar congratulations to himself a month earlier. Despite his exuberant promise to Lyubimov that he would continue writing for another twenty years, his mood, in response to his brother's best wishes for continued health and longevity, is now much more somber. "I doubt that I'll live long," he replies sadly, "it's very hard for me, with my emphysema, to get through the Petersburg winter." He is envious of his brother's happiness in being able to see his children fully grown and perpetuating a "kind, wonderful, loving family." He fears that "I'll be leaving my children still teenagers, and that thought is sometimes very depressing for me." Urging his brother to look after his health, Dostoevsky adds: "As for me, it's impossible for me to watch out for it here . . . work is nearly too much for me." What worries him about the *Diary of a Writer* "is that the issues *come out on fixed days.* With my health, that's very difficult. But . . . if you don't publish, there won't be any money either." He hopes to be able to hold out until spring and then go to Ems—"the treatment there always revives me."[6]

Two memoirists portray Dostoevsky at this time as quite aged, feeble, and sickly. One was I. I. Popov, then a student at the Pedagogical Institute in Petersburg and later a member of Narodnaya Volya. He lived quite close to the Dostoevsky residence and often saw the writer sitting in the park of the nearby church, watching the children at play. "I sometimes went to the park and always bowed to him. Hunched up, emaciated, with a yellowish-colored face, hollow cheeks, sunken eyes. . . . He gave the impression of a person seriously ill."[7] Popov once saw him walking with his old friend and fellow author D. V. Grigorovich, dragging himself along and leaning heavily on an umbrella; the thought came to the onlooker that Grigorovich would surely outlive his companion (which he did).

A similar image is given by E. P. Letkova-Sultanova, the young woman whose memories of Dostoevsky have already been cited several times. She saw him again at the home of the marquis Paulucci, where he took part in a benefit evening along with other literary and artistic notables (he may have read from the later sections of *The Brothers Karamazov*). When she came across him in the stately and brilliantly lit reception room, filled with elegant, fashionably dressed society, he was attired in an ill-fitting formal evening suit too large for his frame and appeared quite out of place. He seemed to her "even more shrunken, more emaciated, more pallid than ever," and she was struck by "his look of suffering."[8]

## 3

While busily preparing to publish a two-volume edition of *The Brothers Karamazov*, Dostoevsky was also accumulating notes for the *Diary of a Writer*. One of these dealt with the recent refusal of the Russian Academy of Sciences to elect the world-famous chemist D. I. Mendeleyev among its members. An indignant article in *New Time* about this scandalous affront compared it with voting down Shakespeare and Pushkin in academies of drama or poetry. "As regards the rejection of Mendeleyev," Dostoevsky comments, "why not establish for our own scholars a Free Russian Academy of Sciences?" The existing academy membership was made up largely of Germans, and Dostoevsky echoes the nationalistic slant of the newspaper's headline: "The Germans Have Triumphed!" (27: 54, 336).

Another note (December 2) dwells on a sensational incident reported from Paris, which took place during the performance of a play about Garibaldi. "Telegram from Paris that at the *Théâtre des Nations,* socialists in the galleries [———ed] on the audience. As if to say, we are poor, and you are rich, so take that! The point is not that only 2,000 people listen to Rochefort and Felix Pyat [prominent radical journalists], but that the mood of the nation's fourth estate is against the rich. . . . That is the element from which everything will emerge" (27: 55). Such an item confirmed his long-entrenched conviction that European society and civilization would be destroyed by a relentless class war. Russia, with its supposedly contented peasantry, would be happily spared such a disastrous fate. "The peasants did not massacre you [the upper class] at emancipation," he continues, "and now they are getting along with you, but in France the poor people s[——]t onto the rich from the loge."

Many entries in the notebooks rebut K. D. Kavelin, an important liberal Westernizer and university professor who had been tutored by Belinsky as a young student. Kavelin had taken issue with the Pushkin speech by denying that the Russian people possessed those unique national characteristics attributed to them by Dostoevsky, and declared by him to be their predestined birthright. The supposed responsiveness and receptivity of Russians to foreign ideas and values, and their capacity to assimilate such ideas as their own, could also be found in the childhood of any "especially gifted and intelligent people" and were far from being unique Russian endowments. To which he retorts: "All people in their youth are like that—how thoughtless, stupid. This means that you [Kavelin] do not even understand what you are talking about. All the elements are identical, but the distribution is different. From that comes different things, objects, personalities" (27: 55). His exasperation can be felt in the following remark: "*To Kavelin.* But when will they finally stop, these lords of the people (from above). You yourself say this is an old story [the Westernizer-Slavophil debate about the Russian people] . . . and . . . you start in again on the same old story, i.e., you deny the spiritual nature of the Russian people" (ibid.). For Dostoevsky, the attitude of the Westernizers was a relic of serfdom: "The scornful attitude toward the people in our liberals (in all of them), and the extolling of the intelligentsia layer—is a consequence of, and the remains of, serfdom (in Kavelin, for example), even among those who did not have serfs" (27: 59).

Another note refers to Kavelin's comparison of Russian Orthodoxy with Western Christianity, much to the detriment of the former. For the

Western Christians, Kavelin had written, "Christianity was called on to improve, perfect, and renew not only hermits, but people living in the world and in the midst of quotidian unpleasantnesses and temptations." The emphasis of Eastern Christianity, however, was ascetic and otherworldly, and he deplores the practical effects of this tendency. "The renunciation of the world, the mortification of the flesh, spiritual contemplation as the highest good and highest perfection"—these were viewed as the only remedy for "misfortune, disaster, and the troubles of earthly life" (27: 339). Dostoevsky had reacted against the excesses of this very inclination in his caricature of Father Ferapont, and his reply on this point is rather feeble. "The saintly separated themselves from the world, not from loathing but for the sake of achieving moral perfection. In fact, the ancient hermits lived in the public square. The monk Parfeny" (27: 55). Parfeny was a wandering monk who had not withdrawn physically from the world, just as Father Zosima had been such a monk at one stage of his life; but this one example hardly meets the general issue that had been posed.

A number of other entries are more successful in countering criticisms of the Pushkin speech and Dostoevsky's reply to A. D. Gradovsky. Kavelin attacks Dostoevsky's belief that personal moral betterment could provide the basis for an improved (indeed, for an "ideal") society. Much like Gradovsky, he drew a distinction between morality—a purely private, internal sense of right and wrong—and the externally imposed rules and obligations necessary for a society to be constituted and to function. Society could be changed for the better only by social-political action, not by that Christian self-perfecting of individuals advocated by Dostoevsky as an infallible remedy for Russia's social ills. By defining morality as a purely *personal* sense of right and wrong, however, Kavelin provided an opening that was immediately exploited.

"Conscience without God is a horror," Dostoevsky writes warningly, "it can deviate to the most immoral things. It is not enough to define morality as being true to one's convictions. One must also constantly raise the question: Are my convictions true? There is only one way to test them—Christ. That is not philosophy but faith, and faith is the red flower." He develops this observation by asking whether "being in harmony with internal convictions" can be seen as morality at all. "This is only *honesty* (the Russian language is rich), but not morality. For me, there is only one moral model and ideal, Christ. I ask: Would He have burned heretics—no. So that means that the burning of heretics is an immoral act." He then offers an illustration calculated to place Kavelin's position in the worst possible light: "Conscience—the conscience of the marquis de Sade—that is absurd." He also turns to his own Legend of the Grand Inquisitor: "The Inquisitor is so singularly immoral that in his heart, in his conscience, the idea of the necessity of burning people could be accommodated" (27: 56).

As he elaborates on the distinction between honesty and morality, Dostoevsky clarifies not only his objections to Kavelin but also, incidentally, his portrayal of figures like Dimitry and Ivan Karamazov (particularly the latter). "What is *moral* is not completely decided by the simple concept of consistency with one's convictions, and the convinced personality himself, keeping his own convictions intact, stops because of some feeling and does not complete the act. He curses himself and feels contempt in his own mind, but in his feeling, which means his conscience, he cannot complete it and he stops . . . he recognized that stopping and not following his conviction was an act more moral than if he had followed it." He illustrates the point by citing some words of Vera Zasulich, who had said at her trial that "it is hard to raise a hand to shed blood." Such evidence of the existence of a moral conscience in the diehard radical prompted Dostoevsky to remark that "her vacillation was more moral than the shedding of blood could have been" (27: 57).

These notes also reaffirm, in the very last month of his life, one of the basic beliefs that had sustained him ever since emerging from the Siberian prison camp in 1854. At that time, he had written the famous letter declaring that, "if someone proved to me that Christ is outside the truth, and that *in reality*, the truth were outside of Christ, then I would prefer to remain with Christ rather than with the truth."[9] The same type of choice is posited more than twenty years later with reference to the Christian commandment of selfless love: "Turn the other cheek, love more than yourself, not because it is useful, but because it is pleasing, to the point of a burning feeling, to the point of passion. Christ made mistakes—it has been proven! This burning feeling says: It is better for me to stay with a mistake, with Christ, rather than with you" (27: 57). Christ is thus no longer placed in opposition to "the truth," but rather, He has made "mistakes." These remain unspecified, but we may assume they correspond to the charges made in Ivan's Legend of the Grand Inquisitor.

Another passage recalls an earlier notebook entry written while Dostoevsky had been maintaining an all-night vigil at the bier of his first wife. Then too he had stressed the *extreme* nature of the demands made by Christ on the human personality: "Christ alone could love man as himself, but Christ was a perpetual eternal ideal to which man strives and, according to the law of nature, should strive" (20: 172). He now recasts this idea, and stresses its opposition to Utilitarian reasoning. "Good is what is useful, evil is what is not useful." "No, [good is] what we love," he writes. "All of Christ's ideas can be debated by the human mind and *seem impossible to fulfill*. To turn the other cheek, to love more than yourself. For goodness sake, now why should that be? I am

here for an instant, there is no immortality, I will live in my [obscenity]"
(27: 56; italics added).

Despite his conviction that "science" offered no answers to the "ac-cursèd questions" of human existence, Dostoevsky saw no reason why these matters should be entirely excluded from scientific purview. "The tremendous fact of the appearance on earth of Jesus, and all that came after that, in my opinion demand scientific elaboration. But at the same time, science cannot reject the meaning that religion does have for hu-manity, if only as a historical fact that is staggering in its continuity and tenacity. The conviction that humanity has about *coming in contact with another world* is also very significant and cannot be resolved with one stroke of the pen the way you [Kavelin] resolved the question about Russia, i.e., all infantile peoples have . . . and so forth" (27: 85).

Kavelin's tone of lofty professorial self-assurance also provoked Dos-toevsky to an extremely rare outburst of self-praise. "The Inquisitor and the chapter about children," he confides to his notebook. "In view of these chapters, you [Kavelin] could regard me from a scientific point of view, but not so arrogantly when it concerns philosophy, although philosophy is not my specialty. Even in Europe, such a force of atheistic *expression* does not exist, *nor did it ever*. Therefore, it is not like a child that I believe in Christ and profess faith in him, but rather, my *hosanna* has come through the great *crucible of doubt*, as the devil says in that same novel of mine. Now, perhaps you have not read 'Karamazov'—that is another matter entirely, and in that case I beg your pardon" (27: 86). Kavelin's criticisms prompted Dostoevsky to probe and clarify his own convictions very carefully, and it is unfortunate that his response re-mains only fragmentary.

Another note is so closely related that it may be cited in this context. "The scoundrels [his critics] provoke me with *an ignorant* and retro-grade faith in God. These asses could not even dream of such a powerful negation of God as is depicted in the Inquisitor and the preceding chap-ter, *to which the entire novel serves as an answer*. It is not like a fool or a fanatic that I believe in God. And they want to teach me, and sneer at my backwardness. Yes, their stupidity could not dream of as strong a negation as I went through. They teach me! . . . Ivan Feodorovich is pro-found, not one of the contemporary atheists, who demonstrate in their disbelief only the paltriest narrowness of their stupid abilities" (27: 48; italics added).

## 4

On December 3, Dostoevsky finally replied to a letter that Ivan Aksakov had sent a month earlier "The main reason for the delay," he writes, "has been petty, silly things to take care of, such as public readings and the like which can't be avoided, but most of all my very bad health . . . my emphysema has worsened, there's a shortness of breath, and because of this a decline in strength."[10] Still, Dostoevsky had been scrutinizing the daily press with the same care and intensity as in the past, including the three issues of the new weekly journal, *Rus*. As an experienced editor, he finds both good and bad in the new Slavophil publication, with whose orientation he of course sympathized. Praising Aksakov's own leading articles, he notes worriedly that "your journal's personnel is weak. Besides you, who is there?" He hopes his friend will enjoy a long life so that he can carry on the battle. One piece on which he comments favorably is a conversation between three people, interspersed with extracts from a newspaper whose contents were being ridiculed. But he finds, all the same, that this contribution contains too little "*sting*" and explains that he does not mean "abusive criticism . . . a sting is just the wit of profound feeling, and therefore you should definitely introduce it."[11] Aksakov, it will be recalled, had criticized Dostoevsky's reply to Gradovsky for the stridency of its polemical manner, and he here ripostes diplomatically that a little more stridency might benefit Aksakov's own publication.

The bulk of the letter is devoted to the cultural-ideological issues that were in the forefront for both Dostoevsky and his correspondent. The demand of the Westernizers for a constitution on the European model, as we know, was spoken of euphemistically as "a crowning of the edifice" (a phrase taken from the French), and much of the polemic surrounding this issue was thus cast in architectural metaphors. Aksakov had ridiculed the phrase because, he maintained, one could not "crown an edifice" that did not exist; it was first necessary to build one from the ground up. He suggested that reformers begin with the local *zemstvo*s, the largely self-governing provincial councils elected democratically, which could serve as the foundation on which an edifice could be constructed. A. D. Gradovsky once again charged into the fray with an article entitled "Not Architecture, But Life." The real issue, he insisted, was not whether the edifice was built from the top or the bottom but whether a form of social life could be organized for living people (another Aesopian allusion to a constitution). Dostoevsky, who had read citations from Gradovsky's piece in the newspapers, tells Aksakov that "you state an idea about the *zemstvo*s that is extremely clear and as comprehensible as two times two," and he assumes that "you will continue elucidating your idea in the following issues too." He warns him, however, not to expect any success; acclaim will certainly go to Gradovsky, rather than to a Slavophil point of view, and he paraphrases what he is sure the public reaction will be: "He [Gradovsky] has a solution, he points out the way, and you're just a paradoxicalist."[12]

A striking feature of this letter is Dostoevsky's unqualified hostility to the historical legacy of Peter the Great. The Slavophils had always looked on Peter very critically, but Dostoevsky had never fully shared their total rejection. Now, however, he finds that Aksakov, having written that Peter "moved us into Europe and gave us European civilization," had not sufficiently stressed the unhappy consequences of this presumably beneficial feat. Peter's reforms, Dostoevsky insists, had divided Russian society into layers—"the authorities, the enserfed masses, and the city dwellers, with fourteen classes among them. That's Peter's work. Liberate the people [as had been done] and it would seem that Peter's work was undone. But the belt, the zone between the authorities and the masses won't retreat for anything and won't give up its privilege of ruling the broad masses." The social transformation, begun with the liberation of the serfs, had ground to a halt, and Aksakov should have made clear that as a result of the "pseudo-likeness" of European civilization imported by Peter, "what in fact lies between the authorities and the people like a fatal belt [is] made up of the 'best people' from the fourteen classes."[13] In the only issue of the *Diary* that Dostoevsky was able to complete before his death, he proposes that this "fatal belt" be swept away entirely.

In closing, he expresses his gratitude for an editorial note appended to a review of *The Brothers Karamazov* published in *Rus*. A critic named I. Pavlov had made the usual charge, which came both from the right and the left, that Dostoevsky was too preoccupied with "pathological phenomena," adding that "virtue is not shown as a need of human nature, not as a general, natural law . . . but attained only at the cost of self-castigation and an arduous struggle." Aksakov had thought it wise to temper such criticism by writing that the novel required a much more exhaustive study, both artistic and psychological, than had been supplied by Pavlov. It merited an analysis that took more adequate account of "the richness, importance, and depth of the questions it poses, [of] the vividness of its artistic merits and shortcomings, [of] the unprecedented strength of the talent appearing here with greater brilliance than in all the earlier works of Dostoevsky." His journal, he told his readers, hoped to provide such a study in the future, and Dostoevsky was thus reassured that the publication to which he probably felt closest did not take a negative view of his latest creation. "I can only thank you," he writes, "for your editorial note and for the promise to say something more. Do so."[14]

The notes' being set down at this time echoes the same antagonism to Peter the Great that we find in this letter. All of Russian educated society, he believed, had been corrupted by the European social-cultural pattern so forcibly imposed by Peter, and by the ideas that accompanied the imitation of such European institutions. One note reads:

"Nihilism appeared in our country because we are *all nihilists*. What frightened us was only the new, original [Russian] form of its manifestation. (All are Feodor Pavloviches right down to the last man.)" Dostoevsky ridicules "the wise men" who wonder where the Nihilists came from and replies: "They were all among us, within us, and part of us (*The Devils*). No, how can it be, the wise men reason, we are not Nihilists, we simply want to save Russia by rejecting her (i.e., form *a layer* of aristocrats above the people, raising the people up to our own nothingness)" (27: 54). In earlier issues of the *Diary of a Writer*, he had found it difficult to specify what the people might learn from the European-educated upper class; now he had come to see the "enlightenment" of that class as entirely deleterious. It could only poison the people; and the only solution for the current state of Russian disarray was for the upper class to accept the people's religious faith.

Another note states the problem with great explicitness: "The Russian people are entirely within Orthodoxy and its idea. There is nothing else in them or for them—and in fact they need nothing else because Orthodoxy is everything. —Orthodoxy is the Church, and the Church is the crowning touch and is forever." Only those who understand Orthodoxy, he continues, can understand the people; anyone who does not "cannot love the Russian people, but would love them only as he would want them to be." Moreover, the people will not "accept such a person as their own . . . if you do not love what I love, do not believe in what I believe in, and do not honor what I hold sacred, then I do not honor you as being one of us." But "our intelligentsia from the Finnish bogs [St. Petersburg]" do not understand this, and "they get angry when they are told that they do not know the people." Unfortunately, Dostoevsky adds, even "the Church is in a sort of paralysis, and has been for some time"; hence he sees no way out of the present impasse except "to call them [the people] together, ask them directly," and hope for some miraculous solution (27: 64–65). This is precisely the course he will advocate in the *Diary*.

5

By December 9, the two-volume edition of *The Brothers Karamazov* was ready. Half of the three thousand copies sold out in a few days, as Anna Grigoryevna proudly remarked, and it was necessary to print a thousand more immediately. Dostoevsky began to distribute gift copies among his friends and family, and one was sent to K. P. Pobedonostsev, who advised him to present the book in person to Tsarevich Alexander. The heir to the throne was extremely eager to receive a copy, Dostoevsky was told, because he did not like to read by bits and pieces and so had awaited the completion of the entire work. Dostoevsky replied immediately that he could not come to the Anichkov Palace on any of the days that Pobedonostsev proposed because he was having a volume specially bound for the occasion. Another date was set a week later, and he was then received by the Tsarevich and his consort, Marya Feodorovna. The only account of this presentation was left by Lyubov Dostoevskaya, then still a child, who probably relays what her mother had been told by Pobedonostsev. Her father is described as behaving in the presence of royalty exactly "as he was accustomed to behave in the salons of his friends. He spoke first, rose when he found that the conversation had gone on sufficiently long, and, taking leave of the Tsarevich and his wife, quitted the room as he had always done, turning his back" to his hosts. The Tsarevich reportedly "was not offended by this, and later spoke of my father with esteem."[15]

Dostoevsky's correspondence at this time contains numerous letters from enthusiastic readers regarding one aspect or another of his last novel; but he could no longer reply, as he explains to an unidentified correspondent, as generously as he had done in the past. "The publication [of the *Diary of a Writer*] is such a burden, and I have so little health and strength, that if I answer all the letters and inquiries . . . I'll have absolutely no time for writing and taking care of my own business." Nonetheless, the correspondent in this case had inquired about what reading to give to his son, and because Dostoevsky faced the same problem as a father (not to mention that the books would certainly be ordered from the Dostoevsky bookstore), he picked up his pen to offer some advice. "I'll just say in general: select and give him only what produces *beautiful impressions and gives birth to lofty thoughts.*" Not knowing the age of the son, Dostoevsky suggests that, if he were sixteen or older, he be supplied with European classics in translation (Schiller, Goethe, Shakespeare), as well as a large selection of Russian poets and novelists, "especially Tolstoy . . . all of Gogol . . . in short, the Russian classics." "You may give him Belinsky," he adds. "But wait with the other critics" (presumably those of the 1860s). If he were younger than sixteen, "Dickens and Walter Scott can be given to thirteen-year-old children." But he recommends "above all, of course, the Gospel, the New Testament in translation," though "if he can read it in . . . Church Slavonic, that would be best of all."[16]

On the same day, he replied to a Dr. Alexander Blagonravov, whose letter touched on ideological and artistic matters with which he was greatly concerned. He was certainly pleased to hear from the doctor that, even in so backward a province as his own, young people who had been nurtured on frivolous novels were beginning to read *The Brothers Karamazov* under the guidance of those (presumably older) who were capable of comprehending it. More important, though, the doctor displayed a penetrating knowledge of Dostoevsky's social-religious position. He had written that, whereas Aksakov saw the root of the evils of contemporary society in the negation of *narodnost* (a belief in the virtues and ideals of the people), Dostoevsky traced them to a loss of religious faith. Convinced that the latter diagnosis went deeper, the doctor agreed all the same that "those who negate *narodnost* also negate faith."[17]

"You conclude correctly," Dostoevsky replies, "that I see the cause of evil in unbelief, but that a person who disclaims national roots [*narodnost*] disclaims faith as well . . . because with us all our national roots are founded in Christianity." Declaring that "the most important question now is to make our intelligentsia agree with this," he dispiritedly adds: "Just try to start talking about that. You'll either be eaten alive, or considered a traitor." Indeed, he appears to have given up on the educated class entirely, "because only from [the people] can one expect anything, not from the Russian intelligentsia." Hopefully, though, he foresees "a new intelligentsia . . . on the march, and it wants to be with the people."[18] The acclaim accorded his novel, and the reverential homage that greeted him whenever he appeared in public, could well have led him to nourish such expectations.

Dr. Blagonravov's letter also testified to the artistic accuracy of Ivan Karamazov's visitation by the devil. As a medical man, the doctor felt a special competence in speaking of mental illness, and he praised the novelist for having "depicted the form of mental illness called hallucinations by science so naturally and so artistically that scarcely any of our array of psychiatrists could match it." Dostoevsky delightedly replies that "for the chapter of *The Karamazovs* (about the hallucinations) that you, a doctor, are so satisfied with, they've already tried to call me a reactionary and fanatic who has started writing about 'the devil knows what!'" He thanks the doctor for confirming the exactitude of his portrait—"an expert opinion will support me"—and explains that "I want to elucidate that chapter later on in a future *Diary*."[19]

The endless negotiations over the Kumanina estate continued to drag on, and a letter from his younger brother Nikolay indicates how far matters were from being settled. Dostoevsky's sister Alexandra had filed a suit against her brothers over the projected agreement, and Nikolay wished to sell some of his share of the estate to pay off a debt to Alexandra. The Dostoevskys agreed in principle, but only if their share (a portion of forest called Shiryaev Woods) were guaranteed by all the other heirs with a written contract; but nothing had been definitively concluded at the time of Dostoevsky's death.

On December 22, he took part in yet another reading, along with old friends such as Apollon Maikov and Ya. P. Polonsky, on behalf of a shelter for the homeless patronized by Countess A. F. Megden. This occasion was marked by a very special event: at the intermission he was conducted to an interior room of the countess's mansion, and found awaiting him there no less a personage than Grand Duchess Marya Feodorovna, who "wished to engage him in private conversation, and spoke to him at great length."[20] Unfortunately, what was said during this tête-à-tête remains unknown. More informative is an account left by Lidya I. Veselitskaya, a young woman with literary ambitions (her pen name was Vera S. Mikulich), of an evening spent at the Shtakenshneiders' sometime during the Christmas season in late December.

In her book of memoirs, she speaks of having ventured to question Dostoevsky about his opinions of other writers, both Russian and European. On learning that she had not read *Le Père Goriot*, he refused to speak about Balzac any further until she had done so; but when asked whether he would place Balzac higher or lower than himself, he replied: "Each of us is valuable only to the extent that he brings something of his own into literature, something original. That's most important of all. And I am not able to make a comparison between us. I think that in each of us there is our own merit." When Veselitskaya, with girlish hero-worship, expressed regret that Gogol had not lived to read *The Brothers Karamazov*, which he would have enjoyed as a splendid continuation of his own work, her remark was greeted quite coolly. "It seems that this did not please Feodor Mikhailovich very much, and he said: 'Really, do you think so?'" Perhaps he was tired of this exhausted comparison; or perhaps his interlocutress had forgotten that Gogol was the author not only of *Dead Souls* but also of *Correspondence with Friends*. Dostoevsky had always disliked this latter book, both for its pompous tone and because its author had found nothing at all to criticize in serfdom. Moreover, hostile critics had recently, much to Dostoevsky's displeasure, found resemblances between the preachments of Father Zosima and those contained in Gogol's piously obsequious letters. About Turgenev, he said not a word, but declared of Tolstoy: "Yes, Tolstoy, he is a—force. And a remarkable talent. He has not yet said everything."[21] He also spoke proudly to the young woman about Tolstoy's letter to Strakhov praising *House of the Dead*.

The youthful Lydia Veselitskaya was not the only young writer who recalled having met Dostoevsky at this time. In the case of the fifteen-year-old Dimitry Merezhkovsky, later to become one of the most important Russian novelists and critics of the twentieth century (his two-volume study, *Tolstoy and Dostoevsky*, did much to shape later critical opinion about both writers), it was his father who took the initiative after meeting Dostoevsky by pure chance in the salon of Countess Sofya

Tolstaya. The young Dimitry had begun to write poetry, and his father seized the opportunity to obtain a professional opinion about his son's adolescent scribblings. "I remember," Merezhkovsky wrote in an auto-biographical fragment, "the diminutive apartment in Kuznechny alley with its low ceiling and cramped living room, piled with copies of *The Brothers Karamazov*, and the study, almost as narrow, in which Feodor Mikhailovich sat over galleys. Blushing, turning pale, and stuttering, I read my childish, paltry verses. He listened silently, with impatient annoyance. We must have been disturbing him. 'Weak, bad, worth nothing,' he said at last. 'In order to write well, one must suffer, suffer!' 'No,' said my father, 'let him not write any better, only let him not suffer.' I recall the pellucid and penetrating look of the pale blue eyes when Dostoevsky shook my hand. I never saw him again, and then very shortly learned that he had died."[22]

On December 27, Dostoevsky wrote a note to Countess Anna Komarovskaya, accepting her invitation to come to the Winter Palace at five on the afternoon of December 30. This titled lady was a member of the intimate court circle with which he had become acquainted, and at her request he read from his works for the guests she had assembled. Among them was Countess Alexandra Andreyevna Tolstaya, a distant relative of the novelist, who had spent her life as lady-in-waiting to one or another grand duchess but whose cultivation and intelligence were valued so highly by Tolstoy that she became one of his epistolary confidantes. Dostoevsky was extremely eager to meet and speak with her about the enigmatic sage of Yasnaya Polyana; and she, on whom *Crime and Punishment* had produced an ineffaceable impression ("no other novel had ever stirred me so strongly"), had looked forward impatiently to making his acquaintance. Once the introduction was over, he immediately posed a question about Tolstoy, in whom, his interlocutress notes, he took "a passionate interest." "Can you explain his new tendency?" he asked. "I see in this something special, and to me as yet unknown." The countess admitted that it was "mysterious" to her as well, but she promised to produce Tolstoy's most recent letter to her, where he spoke about all this—only on the condition, however, that he come to visit her for its transmission.[23]

He set January 11 as the date, and we shall abandon chronology a bit to round out this episode. "This enchanting and unique evening has remained fixed in my memory forever," the countess continues. "I heard Dostoevsky with reverence: he spoke, like a true Christian, about the fate of Russia and the whole world; his eyes burned, and I felt in him a prophet." The countess, a devout Christian, had broken into tears when her cousin Lev had announced to her in 1878 that he no longer accepted the divinity of Christ or regarded Him as the Saviour; and the letter she read to Dostoevsky contained many of the same sentiments. "I can see Dostoevsky before me now, as he clutched his head and in a despairing voice repeated: 'Not that! Not that!' He did not sympathize with a single thought of Lev Nikolaevich; despite which he gathered up all the writing lying on the table: the original and the copy of Lev's letter. From some of his words I concluded that the desire was stirring within him to dispute the false ideas of Lev Nikolaevich."[23] Countess Tolstaya's intuition was quite accurate, and although he did not live to carry out this intention, his last notebook contains the entry: "To what extent man has *worshiped* himself (Lev Tolstoy)" (27: 43).

## CHAPTER 40

# A National Symbol

The new year of 1881 found Dostoevsky in a relatively buoyant mood, despite the occasionally gloomy predictions in his letters and conversations. To D. V. Grigorovich, sometime in the early part of January, he said that he doubted whether he would live out the winter months,[1] but Anna wrote that "in the first half of January Feodor Mikhailovich was in excellent spirits. He frequented his friends, and even agreed to take part in some private theatrics which the Countess S. A. Tolstaya intended to stage at the beginning of the next month. He wished to play the part of the ascetic recluse in the play, *The Death of Ivan the Terrible* by A. K. Tolstoy, the countess's deceased husband."[2] His emotions probably wavered constantly, depending on his mood; and since he understood so well the importance of hope in resisting despair, he would have struggled against the occasional onslaughts of dejection brought on by his increasing physical debility.

## 2

On January 1, he and Anna were in the audience of the Alexandrinsky Theatre, where they saw a mediocre comedy by their occasionally quarrelsome acquaintance D. V. Averkiev, *The Sidorenko Affair*. It was saved, according to the critics, by the brilliant performance of the leading lady, Marya Savina, already mentioned as Turgenev's partner in *A Provincial Lady*. An affectionate letter from Dostoevsky's sister Varvara conveyed New Year's greetings and brought him up to date on family news. A curious item at this time, included in the announcement of the appearance of a new journal, *Semeinie Vechera* (*Family Evenings*), has caused some speculation. Among the future works promised to appear in its pages was "a story by F. M. Dostoevsky," of which nothing else is known. It is possible that he had spoken of one of his ideas to the editors of this children's journal, who were among his close friends, and that they capitalized on a vague promise to provide them with something in the future.

One catches a glimpse of Dostoevsky in the memoirs of his former proofreader, Varvara V. Timofeyeva, on which we have already drawn so extensively. When she happened to pass him in the street at the beginning of 1881, he failed to recognize her, and she was too timid to approach him; but her words indicate the change of sentiment about him on the part of her generation. "I so much wished to go to him, hear his voice again, tell him *how* deeply I now understood him, and how much that was good he had brought to me. . . . I felt myself to be his disciple, indebted to him for my moral world, my spiritual freedom. . . . But shyness and pride served to shackle me. And I passed by him not saying a word."[3]

Such sentiments were not the result only of personal acquaintance, as can be seen from an anecdote contained in the memoirs of a writer now fallen into oblivion, A. V. Kruglov. "I was walking along the Nevsky Prospect with a medical student," he recalled. "Dostoevsky happened to come past us in a carriage. The medical student quickly, before I could do so myself, raised his hat. 'Do you perhaps know Dostoevsky?' I asked. 'No, but what does that matter? I did not *bow* to him, but bared my head as I did in Moscow when I walked past the statue of Pushkin.' "[4]

He had now become a revered, symbolic figure who stood above the merciless battle of ideologies. Even though his works encompassed all the burning issues of the day, he had raised them far beyond the limits of a narrow partisanship. Indeed, contemporaries found it puzzling that he should have attained so remarkable a status, and his friend Orest Miller raised this very question in the January issue of the Populist-Slavophil journal *The Week*. While Dostoevsky was being pilloried by the liberal and radical press, the presumably left-wing students were receiving him with open arms; and the reason, Miller wrote, was that he always spoke "openly and boldly in all directions, not worrying what would be said about him. The youth welcome, with the discernment of the heart, everything straightforward and unservile, and contemptuously avoid everything evasive and mealymouthed."[5] One might add what Miller could not have said openly: that for all his support of the existing political status quo, he always held out hope that radical social change could be brought about, as everything else in Russia always had been, by the will of the Tsar.

On January 6, Dostoevsky took note of an article in *New Time* that reported on a speech given in Berlin by a German professor dealing with the relations between church and state. This problem had provided an important motif for *The Brothers Karamazov*, and it was an issue that continued to preoccupy him on the practical level as well. The speaker, a progressive, had advocated a liberal state in which the differing religious beliefs of its inhabitants would not affect their rights or status in any way. Dreaming of a state that would become a church according to *his* conception of Christianity, Dostoevsky noted his objections. "Our difference from Europe," he writes. "The government is primarily a Christian society striving to become a church. *It's the opposite of Europe.*" Dostoevsky understands, however, what the European scholar feared: "If the Christians take over, they will immediately begin to massacre the non-Christians. On the contrary, complete freedom of faith and freedom of conscience is the soul of true Christianity. *Believe freely*—that is our formula. The Lord did not step down from the cross to inculcate belief *by force* of external miracle, but precisely wished for freedom of conscience. That is the soul of our people and of Christianity" (27: 80–81). Nothing better than such a passage illustrates the baffling mixture in Dostoevsky of an advocacy of the most reactionary social structures in the name of the most liberal principles.

While he was organizing the notes for the January issue of his *Diary*, others for February and March continued to pile up. Some deal with the obligatory classical curriculum in the *gymnasiums*, which had become a bone of contention and to which Kolya Krasotkin had contemptuously referred. "Latin and Greek," he had proclaimed, parroting radical opinion, "were introduced because they are a bore and because they stupefy the intellect" (14: 498). In fact, their study had been promulgated as a means to counteract the subversive influence of scientific rationalism. Dostoevsky had been in favor of this reform, though it was widely unpopular, on the ground that a liberal education would be of benefit even to those who later became scientists; but he thought that the classical languages should have been introduced more gradually and not "by the cudgel." Also, a serious mistake had been the importing of Czech teachers, who were "cold, indifferent, hostile to the youth, ignorant of the Russian language and looking down on it" (27: 67).

The notes indicate as well that he intended to continue one of the most popular and appealing features of his *Diary*, the literary reminiscences that had always given this publication such a personal, intimate, and historically significant character. Just ten days before his death, he told his friend Aleksey Suvorin that he wished "to begin writing his literary memoirs," and he may well have planned to run them as a series in future issues.[6] For the moment, he wanted to answer personally the anecdote about "borders" that P. V. Annenkov had once again placed in circulation. "All this," he wrote in the draft of a reply, "may be nonsense, I repeat, and of course is not worth bothering with. But I have written about Belinsky myself and of my meeting with him. And I do not wish the shadow of a lie to hang over my account. If I do not reply, it will be said that [Annenkov's version] is true" (27: 198). It is quite likely that he intended to add new touches to the portrait of Belinsky already given: "Belinsky. Unusual striving for the assimilation of new ideas with an unusual desire, each time, along with the assimilation of the new, to trample on everything old with hatred, vilification, contempt. As though a thirst for vengeance against the old—'and I burn everything to which I used to bow'" (27: 50).

In the same draft article, we find another reference to a personal attack on Dostoevsky whose source is not identified, but whose implications he also wished to rebut. "I do not want it to be said," he writes, "that I boast of my prison years. It sickens me that my good friends (and I have some), or later my children, now still small, should suspect it to be true that I boasted, glorified myself; because *il en reste, il en reste* [something remains]." He feared such a charge being made, and three disconnected sentences perhaps indicate how he meant to answer. "Yes, if I had wished to glorify myself. I invented another character in *House of the Dead*. [He] killed his wife" (20: 197). Dostoevsky is here referring to the fictional narrator of his prison memoirs, the wife-murderer Goryanchikov, who conceals the author's own identity as a prisoner.

Other writers—Tolstoy, Saltykov-Shchedrin, Goncharov—would also have been discussed in the renewed *Diary*. Polemics with Shchedrin had already begun apropos of Mme Khokhlakova, and Dostoevsky intended to cross swords again with this old antagonist, who had inflicted some still-smarting wounds in the 1860s. Calling him "the satirical elder," Dostoevsky writes: "No one would dare to go against him: a liberal, they would say . . . liberal through and through. . . . No, you are playing at being liberal, *when it is not advantageous*—that is when I should take a look at you" (27: 46).

Shchedrin was then publishing a series of travel sketches, *Across the Border* (*Za Rubezhom*), one of which satirized the zealousness of the German police. Dostoevsky thinks that the real target of his satire should be the laxness of the Russian constabulary. "Insult to a woman at Palkin's [a fashionable restaurant]. Theft and personal insult, shooting at Loris-Melikov, but they just simply salute— Once, forty years ago, they took Shchedrin off to the police station and so he became frightened. But that was to a prosecutor's post." (Shchedrin had been exiled, but served in such a post during that time.) "He almost wrote 'Prison and Exile,'" Dostoevsky jeers, certainly thinking of his own prison years (27: 48–49).

Another writer singled out for sarcastic needling is Ivan Goncharov. Dostoevsky's relations with him were externally friendly but he had never liked him personally (though he admired *Oblomov*). The press paid Goncharov so much attention that it annoyed and irritated his fellow novelist; and when Goncharov published a letter regretting that, despite the importance of Pushkin for his own work, he had been unable to attend the Pushkin festival, Dostoevsky took this as a piece of self-advertisement. Everyone, he jotted down, felt that everything had already been said about Pushkin at the festival; "still, they had forgotten one virtue, nearly the most important, that he was the teacher of our Goncharov. . . . And if Ivan Alexandrovich had not reminded us of this in his letter, we would not have remembered this virtue of Pushkin" (27: 55).

Goncharov had also republished an essay on Griboyedov's classic comedy *Woe from Wit*, in which he heaped praise on the main character Chatsky, a Westernizer who returns to Moscow from Europe and finds the atmosphere in his homeland stiflingly intolerable. Goncharov had declared Chatsky superior even to such sacrosanct figures as Onegin and Pechorin; but Dostoevsky had expressed reservations about Chatsky's pro-Westernism as far back as his *Winter Notes* (1863), and also used him as one of the prototypes for the inwardly torn Versilov in *A Raw Youth*. Suvorin had praised Goncharov's interpretation as superior to any that he knew, and this estimation probably stimulated Dostoevsky to offer his own competing and much less flattering opinion. Citing a line of Chatsky's concluding monologue, in which he says, "I will go to seek in the world . . . ," Dostoevsky asks: "But where? For him there is only the world that he sees through his window, that of the best Moscow society, he is not going to the people. And since the Moscovites rejected him, this means that 'the world' designates Europe. He wants to flee across the border" (27: 87). In his account of their conversation, Suvorin writes: "He [Dostoevsky] did not find Chatsky sympathetic. He was too haughty, too much an egoist. He lacked kindness."[7]

## 3

An important source of information about these final days are several articles written by Aleksey Suvorin shortly after Dostoevsky's decease. The latter had spoken very freely to this perspicacious interlocutor, and what Suvorin recorded offers a valuable glimpse into Dostoevsky's thoughts and what the future *Diary of a Writer* might have contained. One comment reveals the astonishing paradox, already noted, of Dostoevsky's social-political position—the dream of an ideal Russia coming to birth in a state embodying the very opposite of what such a dream was striving to attain. "In his opinion," Suvorin writes, "it is possible for us to attain complete freedom, a freedom existing nowhere else, and all this without any revolution, any restrictions, any controls. Complete freedom of conscience, press, assembly, and he added: 'Complete. A law for the press—can this be freedom of the press? This is still its humiliation. . . . Let it say anything it wishes. We need freedom more than all others . . . because we have more work to do; we need complete sincerity, so that nothing remains unuttered.'"[9]

Such thoughts were confided not only to friends like Suvorin, a journalist and editor, but also to people who occupied important government posts. Sometime after publishing an obituary of Dostoevsky that contains the above reflections about freedom of the press, Suvorin wrote another article with additional information: "Just a few days before Dostoevsky's death, he told the writer of these lines that 'I spoke of all this to some highly placed people. They were in agreement with much that I said, but they could not understand an unlimited freedom of the press. And without understanding this, it's impossible to understand anything.'"[10] Such a reaction apparently did not discourage him from continuing to hope that progress along these lines might someday be possible. On January 10 he made a fiery speech before the Slavic Benevolent Society advocating the establishment of a journal by that organization to propagate "the Russian idea," promising to dedicate his own *Diary of a Writer* to the same cause.

The *Diary*, however, was not the only subject discussed with Suvorin. When asked why, since his novels are so full of monologues and intense dramatic scenes, he had never written for the theater, he replied: "I have a certain prejudice as regards the drama." And then he referred to a remark of Belinsky's "that a true dramatist should begin to write at the age of twenty. That remained in my head. I just didn't dare. However, this summer I thought of turning one episode of the 'Karamazovs' into a play."[11] Presumably Dostoevsky spoke to others of this intention as well. A journalist named Petersen mentions it as being a well-known fact that Dostoevsky wished "to dramatize the crime of the unknown person who visits Father Zosima while he was still an officer."[12]

In a conversation about the continuation of *The Brothers Karamazov*, Suvorin summarizes what he heard from the author. "Alyosha Karamazov would emerge as the hero of the novel's continuation, a hero from whom [Dostoevsky] wished to create a type of Russian Socialist, not the usual type that we know and which sprouted entirely out of European soil." Grand Duke Alexander Mikhailovich recalls Suvorin as having also quoted these words: "It seems to you that in my last novel, *The Brothers Karamazov*, there was much that was prophetic. But wait for the continuation. In it Alyosha will leave the monastery and become an anarchist. And my pure Alyosha will kill the Tsar."[13] Dostoevsky spoke to Suvorin a month or so *before* Alexander II was assassinated, which leads the commentator to assume that the grand duke meant to speak of *an attempt* on the Tsar's life; but Dostoevsky could well have envisaged its accomplishment. If there is any mistake in the testimony of the grand duke, it would be in characterizing Alyosha as an "anarchist" rather than as the much more plausible "Russian Socialist," a term that receives some support from the *Diary*.

Orest Miller, who visited Dostoevsky on January 17, found him so immersed in writing the *Diary* that he flatly refused an invitation to participate in a Pushkin evening on January 29. All he wished to talk about was his fear that the censorship would not accept "several of the sentences, whose substance he felt called upon to develop in future issues of the *Diary*."[14] He and Anna attended a concert that evening by the French pianist Louis Brassena, and their presence was noted by a gossip columnist with the pseudonym Amicus (P. A. Monteverdi). Two days after Dostoevsky's death he wrote that the novelist "appeared livelier and healthier than usual, and spoke abundantly and with fire about the *Diary of a Writer* and his plans and projects, expressing the solid hope that quite soon [we] will be able to speak more straightforwardly and freely about 'everything that moves our soul.'"[15] Such words reflect the inordinate expectations aroused by the minor concessions of Loris-Melikov relaxing supervision of the press.

On January 20, Dostoevsky himself went to the office of the censorship bureau and asked that the censor assigned to his *Diary* be changed, though why is not known. The newly appointed head of the censorship, N. S. Abaza (no relation to the minister of finance), offered to remove the preliminary censorship entirely from his distinguished suppliant; but Dostoevsky replied: "No . . . you know . . . it's much better, more peaceful" to have a censor's reading in advance.[16] The obliging official offered to read the manuscript himself, and returned it unchanged the next day with a note apologizing for the delay. On the twentieth as well Dostoevsky changed his mind about the Pushkin evening, evidently feeling some remorse about his abrupt dismissal of a devoted friend. "Here, perhaps, I have lost another person," he said to his wife, instructing Anna to tell Miller that he would agree to read from the later chapters of *Evgeny Onegin*.[17] A letter from D. V. Grigorovich on the same date asks for permission, which was granted, for a sculptor named L. Bernshtam to visit and to work on a bust.

Two days later, Anna Dostoevsky records in her notebook that, in speaking of their plans for the summer, they had discussed a long-cherished ambition to purchase a country estate. "In the evening," she writes, "we talked about where to go, and he spoke of his dreams."[18] With the money still owed him by the *Russian Messenger*, and the subscriptions continuing to pour in for the new *Diary*, he thought it possible to make this dream come true. On the twenty-fourth, he was a dinner guest of Countess Tolstaya and borrowed a copy of her late husband's play about Ivan the Terrible to prepare for the theatrics. Apparently on this day as well he made the final corrections to the *Diary*. The next day, January 25, he went personally to the printing plant with these pages and asked that galleys be sent the day following. He also wrote to Countess Komarovskaya, accepting her invitation to the Winter Palace on the first day he thought he would be free, January 29.

## 4

The final issue of the *Diary of a Writer* (January 1881) was completed on the last day of Dostoevsky's working life, and published just as his remains were being taken to the grave. These are accidental events, the result of chance, but one cannot help assigning to them a certain larger and inherently meaningful significance. It is as if circumstances themselves were conspiring to ensure that Dostoevsky's voice would continue to speak to the world from beyond the grave; and his voice has continued to do so up to our own day. Unfortunately, what Dostoevsky has to say here cannot be counted among his most impressive and appealing utterances. But his last printed words should be read with the background of his great creative achievements always in mind—the masterpieces that far outweigh and overshadow his social-political illusions and self-deceptions.

The first article in the *Diary*, entitled "Finances," expresses the author's own astonishment at engaging with such a subject: "Good Lord! Can it be that after three years of silence I now resume my *Diary* with an article on economics?" The answer, as so often in Dostoevsky, is both yes and no. Beginning with such a topic, he immediately digresses to bring the question round to his own concerns. "The fall of the ruble! The deficit!" These calamities were on everyone's mind, but individuals troubled by such fiscal problems are probably the same people who had opposed the Russo-Turkish War on economic grounds: "Cold cash was better than noble deeds." These people had quite evidently overlooked the great "upsurge of popular feeling" that, in Dostoevsky's view, had justified both the war and his belief in the growth of the people's national self-consciousness (27: 5).

Opponents of the war had refused to believe that the people were anything but "some inert, deaf-and-dumb mass organized to pay taxes and support the intelligentsia, a mass which, if it did contribute pennies through the church [for the war], did so because the priest and the authorities commanded them to do so." He replies, as he so often does, with a personal anecdote about a peasant woman who ran a small inn "in a remote area of the provinces." She had asked him, at the time of the Berlin Congress after the war (at which Russia had been deprived of most of the fruits of its victory), "Can you tell me, good sir, how they decided our case over there in Europe?" (27: 6). He promises to write more in the future about this burgeoning of patriotic awareness among the people.

True, the Russian economy is running a huge deficit, but for Dostoevsky the real question is why Russia is always being compared unfavorably with Europe. "In Europe the taler is strong everywhere, while our ruble is low. So why aren't we Europe?" (ibid.). He now attempts to answer *this* question, and to transform Russian idiosyncrasy into something positive rather than negative. His social-political implications become clear when, in the now-familiar Aesopian imagery, he writes that "everyone started shouting about 'crowning our edifice'" as a solution, or rather, not everyone but "only a few white waistcoats." If any such crowning is to be done at all, he goes on, "it would be much better to begin from below, from the peasant's coat and bast shoes, not from the white waistcoats" (ibid.).

Playing with the architectural metaphor, he agrees that "crowning the edifice from below" seems absurd, but he decides that because "everything in Russia is distinctive, utterly unlike Europe," this image may well describe the Russian situation, "to the amazement and indignation of our Russian European thinkers." In fact, there is already an existing structure in Russia composed of the peasantry, "solid and unshakable, erected over centuries . . . though still not fully developed," and it is this foundation that will someday become "our future and architecturally complete edifice" (ibid.). It is only the "herd mentality" of the Russian Europeans which leads them to imagine that a "mechanically soothing," imitatively Western-style constitution is the answer to Russia's problems (ibid.).

But Dostoevsky had no illusions about the condition of the countryside, whose economy had been expected to flourish after the liberation of the serfs. Instead, "the peasants sank to the very minimum of what the land was capable of producing," and "the whole former system of land tenure by the nobility has broken down" (27: 9–10). At this point, he comes dangerously close not only to criticizing government policy but also to impugning its very basis." I believe as a matter of economics," he writes in a passage that could well be considered subversive, "that the land is *possessed*, not by railway magnates, not by the industrialists, not by the millionaires, not by the banks, and not by the Yids, but only by those who cultivate it . . . the tillers of the soil are themselves the state, its nucleus, its vital core." But the financing of railways, which were built at a speed much greater than in Europe, was done "at the cost of destroying our agriculture": "The railways attracted all the capital at the very time when the land was most in need of it" (27: 10).

Obviously, he cannot enlarge on this subject without attacking government policy even more openly and directly. (No wonder he was so concerned about getting this issue of the *Diary* through the censorship!) It was impossible for him to expatiate any further on the question of "possession" without implying that the peasants should not be required to buy back their own land from those who had no right to its ownership. Passages such as these preserved Dostoevsky's good name among the largely radicalized students, however much they might differ with him on more strictly political questions. He concludes by wondering, not at the absence of a sound European economic system in Russia, but at the fact that "we have managed to keep on our feet at all." Only "the steadfast, unifying strength of the people" has kept Russia financially afloat (ibid.).

Nevertheless, the results of Russia's peculiar history have been disastrous. "There has been no proper culture for a century and a half—no culture at all, perhaps," leading to a total lack of "spiritual serenity." Dostoevsky then paints a picture of the upper class as so many replicas of Captain Kopeikin, a character in an inset story of Gogol's *Dead Souls*, a wounded war veteran who tried to obtain some compensation for his injuries. When he failed to receive any just payment, he turned to highway robbery. Now, "a new breed" of Kopeikins has appeared, and "of course they'll all be quickly transformed, if not into highway robbers like the real Captain Kopeikin, then into industrial pickpockets." And there are also those whom Dostoevsky calls the "Kopeikin-liberals," presumably in favor of reform but with an eye on the main chance. "Who hasn't seen them?—the cosmopolitan liberal, the cheap atheist who flaunts his five-kopeck education before the people!" (27: 12). Ivan Karamazov had done just that with Smerdyakov, but his torments of conscience no doubt distinguished him in Dostoevsky's eyes from the run-of-the-mill variety.

Offering his own recommendations for a possible remedy to the widely acknowledged ills of Russian society, Dostoevsky declares that the best way "to establish sound finances in a state that has experienced certain upheavals" is—just not to think about finances at all, or at least as little as possible. Of much greater importance is "to think only of restoring the roots" (27: 12–13). The peasants, of course, are the "roots" of Russia, and one should think primarily about *them*, not about the economic and monetary issues that occupy everyone else. Naturally, the government had always been concerned with the peasants; numerous commissions had been appointed over the years to study their "economic health" and every aspect of their way of life. Just recently, the minister of finance had "abolished the salt tax," and "still more reforms are expected—extraordinary, fundamental, 'radical' ones" (27: 13). Heightened expectations had indeed been stirred by Loris-Melikov, leading to all sorts of rumors, such as the impending grant of a constitution (as desired by the educated class) and/or a redistribution of land (as desired by the peasantry).

All this concern about immediate and pressing issues is of course important, and although Dostoevsky advises forgetting about them, he confesses: "I thought that if I began with an absurdity I might make myself clearer" (a rhetorical technique that should be kept in mind before taking Dostoevsky *too* literally) (27: 14). But he continues to maintain, at least in principle, that there is no good reason to pay so much attention to practical affairs if only because they would be looked after in any case. Far more important is to focus on "making the roots healthy." This process could begin if the bureaucracy realized that "Petersburg is not Russia at all." Indeed, "with each generation that passes, our Petersburg intelligentsia understands Russia less and less, simply because it is isolated from Russia in its Finnish swamp." The intelligentsia has no real comprehension of "the broad ocean" of Russian life that constitutes the remainder of the country, and views this broad ocean in terms appropriate only for "the microscopic dimensions of Karlsruhe" (a slap at Turgenev, who lived there) (27: 14–15). Dostoevsky knows full well that he will be told, "All this is only worn-out Slavophil ravings," and that, far from saying anything substantial, "it's something spiritual even." Agreeing that something "spiritual *is* involved," he sets out to explain what he means by "making the roots healthy" (27: 15–16).

5

For Dostoevsky, the real problem facing Russia is not a practical but a moral-spiritual one. While paying proper tribute to everything that the present régime has done for the peasantry, "beginning with the liberation," he insists that this enormous class is nonetheless "spiritually sick," though fortunately not to the death. "[A] sea of drunkenness [has] washed over Russia," but nonetheless, "what the people are continually seeking is the truth, some outlet to it, but they cannot find it." This truth can only be a religious one since the sole basis of their life is Orthodoxy. And in a passage unquestionably stemming from his own past, he writes: "I am convinced that if Nihilist propaganda has not yet managed to make inroads among the people, it is entirely due to the lack of ability, stupidity, and lack of preparation among the propagandists, who do not even know how to approach the people" (27: 16–17). (The propaganda planned by the underground group to which Dostoevsky had belonged in 1849 preached a Christian egalitarianism rather than modern social notions, and was written in a Church Slavonic whose vocabulary would evoke religious associations.)

Citing a passage from Saint Matthew in which Christ warns against accepting the word of false prophets, Dostoevsky then refers to "the various strange rumors of partitions of land and land allotments . . . and of some new golden charters" (27: 17). Talk of "golden charters," by which the Tsar supposedly gave more land to the peasants than the local authorities had conceded, already had circulated in the period of the liberation and was mentioned ironically in *The Devils.* So persistent had these reports now become that a statement denouncing them had been read in the churches in 1879; but this denial had only strengthened peasant convictions that some such reallotment was imminent. Dostoevsky retails an anecdote, perhaps invented for the occasion, of peasants who had refused to make a profitable purchase of land on the assumption that the parcel would soon be theirs gratis; and this incident illustrated the peasants' total distrust of anything they heard from "the authorities." The people have become totally alienated from all the social institutions of Russia because the *zemstvo*s and the courts are all under the control of the bureaucracy. Even the *obshchina*, that bastion of Russian peasant democracy, "seems to be moving toward becoming a kind of authority" because its elections are now overseen by "some government official or other" (ibid.).

Indeed, the more the authorities try to aid the people, the worse the situation becomes. "There are now nearly twenty government officials standing over [the people], protecting and looking after them. . . . The peasant has about as much freedom of movement as a fly caught in a plate of molasses" (ibid.). To make matters even worse, these authorities have no understanding of the people at all, much less any sympathy with their ideas or values (27: 18). Their total misunderstanding derives from a failure to grasp the importance of Orthodoxy, which in fact constitutes the very essence of the people's being. Once again Dostoevsky admits, as he has so often done, that the Russian people are capable of committing acts "that are foul, vile, criminal, barbarous, and sinful." But once again he insists that "the criminal and the barbarian . . . still pray to God, in the higher moments of their spiritual life, that their sins and abominations may cease and that everything may derive from their beloved 'idea' once more." This "idea" lying at the core of Russian peasant life is nothing less than that "salvation is ultimately to be found in *worldwide union in the name of Christ.*"

In a startling passage, Dostoevsky goes on: "I am speaking now not about church buildings and not about sermons; I am speaking about our *Russian socialism* (and . . . I am taking this word, which is quite the opposite of all that the church represents, to explain my idea)" (italics added). In daring to apply the phrase "Russian socialism" to his own messianic hope, he employs a term first coined by Herzen. The latter had used it to predict that the peasant-based cooperative social institutions of Russia, such as the *obshchina* and the *artel*, would take the lead over Europe in creating the Socialist world of the future. Dostoevsky thus stresses, as he had already done with Alyosha Karamazov, the simi-larity between his own ultimate aims and those of the Russian radicals. But for him, this aim had now become identified with "the establish-ment of the universal church on earth, insofar as the earth is capable of containing it"; and he believed that such an aim was shared, even if only inchoately and unconsciously, by the vast multitude of the Russian peasantry (27: 18–19).

The people trust only in God and the Tsar, and for Dostoevsky the first step toward relieving their malaise is to sweep away everything that stands between them and their revered ruler. "Summon the gray peas-ant coats," he admonishes, "and ask them what they lack and what they need and they will tell the truth, and all of us, for the first time perhaps, will hear the real truth!" (27: 21). Today we can hardly imagine just how daring such a Populist suggestion was in a totally despotic state, all of whose policy and decisions were determined in secrecy by the Tsar and his advisers, and in which the democratic notion of consulting the peo-ple was considered nothing less than lèse-majesté. Nor was Dostoevsky suggesting what the Russians call a *zemskii sobor*, an assembly of all classes in the land, which had been convoked during the Time of Trou-bles and established the Romanov family as the ruling house. No, only the peasantry, should be consulted. "[A]nd we, 'the people's intelligen-tsia,' shall stand meekly aside for the moment and at first merely look on while they speak and we listen" (27: 24). Since it is only from the peasants that the intelligentsia can learn the truth, Dostoevsky explains that he is asking the latter to step aside not for "political" but for peda-gogical reasons. This image of the people is so ennobling and sublime that one understands why it was either scornfully dismissed, or more charitably regarded as just another flight of Dostoevsky's artistic-poetic imagination.

As for more practical matters, he preferred to leave to those in power the organization of this consultation. The people could be questioned in their villages and *izba*s, and even one by one; because "they are one" in spirit, there would be no discrepancy between individual and group opinion. Indeed, even "the *kulak* and the bloodsucker" should be con-sulted, because, as peasants themselves, they would inevitably speak the truth (27: 21). (Can this be the same man who created the innkeeper Trifon Borisovich?) What leads Dostoevsky to such extravagance is his long-cherished assumption that a truly patriarchal relation existed be-tween the peasantry and the Tsar. ("[W]ho has not seen them around the Tsar, near the Tsar, in his presence?") For them, "the Tsar was not an external power," a conqueror like the French kings, but "the incarna-tion of themselves," from whom they had expected (and recently re-ceived, "in a monumental fashion") "deliverance from the land of

Egypt" (ibid). Such a notion is already familiar from the document presented to the Tsar; but if this was the feeling of the people, Dostoevsky well knew, in a passage already cited, that the Tsar "for a long time . . . has not very much believed" that the people were his children (27: 86).

In conclusion, Dostoevsky devotes several rapturous pages to describing the wonders that would ensue if such "a spiritual bonding of our entire educated class" and the people should actually take place. For one thing, the haughty intelligentsia could learn from "the people's humility, their businesslike approach, the seriousness and down-to-earth nature of their world." With this revelation, only a few "old believers and doctrinaires of the forties and fifties, old, incorrigible children," would fail to be converted. Moreover, once the period of "pseudo-Europeanism" had ended, "civic liberty could be established in Russia on a most extensive scale, more extensive than anywhere else in the world"; and this liberty would be based not "on some writing on a piece of paper" (a constitution), but "exclusively on the childlike love of the people for the Tsar their father." Once again Dostoevsky looks forward to the establishment of a progressively liberal society while relying on the most primitive and archaic form of social rule for its attainment (27: 22–24).

One of the greatest obstacles to such a happy outcome was the centuries-old entrenched Russian bureaucracy; and Dostoevsky introduces "a witty bureaucrat" to speak on its behalf. This gentleman is a typical Dostoevskian creation, someone who provocatively takes ideas to their uttermost extreme. "For almost two hundred years now," he declares, "since the time of Peter the Great himself, we, the bureaucrats, have constituted *everything* within the state; in essence, it is we who are the state and are *everything*—the rest is merely excess baggage." He compares the bureaucracy to "the skeleton of a living organism. . . . if the skeleton is taken apart . . . the living body will perish as well" (27: 28–29). In truth, the bureaucracy holds up not only the state, as it were, but everything else—even "all the self-governments and *zemstvo*s of yours" (his presumably liberal interlocutors)—for they all eventually come to reproduce the dominating traits of the bureaucracy, "taking over our spirit and image and copying everything from us."

Nor is this dominance the result of any special effort of the bureaucracy to perpetuate its own features; it just happens naturally because "it's difficult to drop centuries-old habits." Of course, the clever bureaucrat realizes that he and his fellows really "aren't *everything*, in fact"; another world exists outside the "Finnish swamps" where they flourish. There is, after all, "the broad ocean" of the people; but do they really represent a new and different principle that can support a state? Like Dostoevsky's critics, the witty bureaucrat is very dubious and thinks that reform is just "a mirage," just "a bird in the bush" that should not be exchanged for the bird in hand—himself and his fellows. Even those who seemingly oppose the bureaucracy, such as the liberal Russian Europeans, are really its unsuspecting allies because the bureaucracy is "the incarnation of the entire formula of Russian Europeanism." Hence both the bureaucrats and the liberals are united in their opposition to "the *zemstvo*s and, indeed, all those new things set up in the spirit of populism." The liberals speak in favor of such innovations, but in fact, as Russian Europeans, they really play into the hands of the bureaucrats and should be given medals "for their Europeanism." They merge perfectly well with the bureaucracy, "though they abuse us—only a case of kith not recognizing kin" (27: 29–30).

After thus identifying his liberal critics with the much-hated bureaucracy, Dostoevsky then comments on his ironic creation. He admits that "there really did seem to be 'something' in [the bureaucrat's] words, a kind of melancholy truth that actually exists." To be sure, he consoles himself with the thought that "it is only people on their way out who speak in such a tone," but "the melancholy" lingers all the same and is never really dissolved. He ends by quoting a Krylov fable about a boar digging up acorns among the roots of an ancient oak tree, not realizing that he could destroy the roots while doing so. It is the oak itself that tells the greedy animal: "If you could only raise your head / Above the ground you'd see / That acorns only grow on oaks like me" (27: 31).

## 6

The enigmatic words "Geok Tepe" appear in the title of the next and final section of the *Diary*, along with the question: "What Does Asia Mean to Us?" Dostoevsky concludes this issue with some reflections on Russian foreign policy, prompted by the advance of a Russian expeditionary force into Central Asia. One Russian attempt to take the oasis of Geok Tepe had been repelled in 1879, and another had been launched in 1880. Nothing about these campaigns appeared directly in the Russian press, but reports from the correspondent of the London *Daily News* had been printed. Finally, on January 1, Russian newspapers were allowed to write about the siege, which ended with the storming and capture of the oasis on January 12. The liberal St. Petersburg journals were highly critical of this imperialist adventure and raised serious doubts about its justification, particularly in view of the financial difficulties with which the country was struggling. Dostoevsky took up the cudgels, not only to praise the victorious General Skobelev and his troops, but also to expound again the thematic leitmotif of this first issue of his revived *Diary*—namely, that Russia was not Europe, and hence should not determine its foreign policy with European interests and concerns in mind.

For Dostoevsky, Russian Asia (which includes Siberia) was of first importance because "it is Asia, perhaps, that provide[s] the main outlet for our future destiny." The spread of Russian power in Central Asia will shake the prestige of England and convince all the peoples "up to the very borders of India . . . of the invincibility of the white Tsar and the omnipotence of his sword." Of course he anticipates the indignation that will be aroused by "this reactionary proposition of mine," but he shrugs it off as part of the Russian inferiority complex vis-à-vis Europe. In fact, "this mistake of ours has cost us dear," and he then repeats his often-uttered refrain that Russian foreign policy has continually sacrificed its own interests to those of the European powers. Why, after driving Napoleon out of Russia, had the Russians not allowed the emperor a free hand in Europe in return for one in the Near East and Asia? (There is some historical basis for Dostoevsky's assertion that such an idea had at least been discussed.) But Russia believed it was obliged to save Europe, and now "every group and every tribe over there has long been secretly nursing malice against us, ready to bring it into the open at the first conflict." Continuing in this vein, Dostoevsky adduces more and more examples of how Europe "will not acknowledge us as her own, secretly despises us, and openly considers us as a people beneath her." This is why "Asia might truly serve as an outlet for our future—this is what I shout out once more!" (27: 32–36).

The article then becomes a dialogue, with voices that raise objections and, as usually happens, cause him to qualify the stridency of his assertions. Russia, of course, "will not turn away from Europe forever," only "temporarily"; Europe after all is "the land of holy miracles" (a phrase from a poem by the Slavophil Aleksey Khomyakov, used long before in *Winter Notes*). Dostoevsky now speaks of Europe as "a second mother" to Russian culture, to whom "we don't mean to be ungrateful." Referring to his own Pushkin speech, in which he had spoken of Russia's predestined, universal Christian mission of reconciling all national antagonisms, he remarks that "everyone heaped mud and abuse on me, even some of those who embraced me at the time because of what I said" (27: 36). Turgenev and Annenkov were far from having been forgotten (or forgiven).

But even though Europe will ultimately be included in the glorious world of the future, to be inaugurated under Russian auspices, the time is now ripe for Russia to think of Asia, which could play the same role for it as the discovery of America had done for Europe. All of Russia would be rejuvenated by this acquisition, the country would free itself from its inertia and sense of dependence on Europe, and a brave new world would come to birth. "In Europe we were hangers-on and slaves, while in Asia we shall be the masters." Like other advocates of imperialism, Dostoevsky argues that Russia will perform "a civilizing mission" in Asia, but he is perhaps more straightforward in pointing to all the riches that could be exploited—"the metals, the minerals, the countless coal fields." And Asiatic expansion would not only "civilize" the foreign peoples but revitalize the Russians themselves. "Our mission will elevate our spirits, it will help give us dignity and self-awareness—and these are things we lack altogether now, or at least have in very small quantity" (27: 36–37). One cannot read such words without recalling Conrad's *Heart of Darkness*, with its terrifying images of the frightful human reality to which such grandiose and self-serving notions are likely to lead.

Dostoevsky had always relished predicting the downfall of European civilization, whose glory lay in the past, and he now adds some new touches to the usual evocation of merciless class warfare. "Let people understand that when Europe, because of overcrowding alone, establishes the inevitable and humiliating communism, which she herself will loathe, when whole crowds of people will have to press around a single hearth and, little by little, individual households will be destroyed and families will abandon their own homes and start living collectively in communes, when children (three-quarters of them foundlings) are raised in institutions, then—then we shall still have broad expanses, fields, and forests, and our children will grow up with their own fathers, not in cramped stone prisons, but amid orchards and cultivated fields, seeing the pure, blue sky above them" (27: 38). Presumably, Asiatic expansion will drain off enough of the Russian population to avoid the "overcrowding" that will stifle Europe.

He returns to "finances" again by suggesting that, if economies must be made, perhaps Russia should reduce its expenses in Europe by ceasing to support "so many embassies . . . with all their costly glitter, their subtle wit and banquets, the superb but costly staffs" (ibid.). He believes that this belt-tightening would win the respect of the Europeans themselves as an assertion of Russian independence. European politics, in any event, is caught in interminable local struggles, and he thinks the conflicts will become much more aggravated with time, especially if Russia refuses its aid to one side or another. "And it now appears that European Socialism has not only not died, it continues to be a very serious threat" (27: 39). Russia should refrain from meddling in European affairs, but take advantage of any crisis to advance its own interests and protect the Western Slavs who had recently been annexed by Austria-Hungary with the support of Bismarck. As for Constantinople, no one thinks any longer that it should become Russian immediately;

the issue can wait for the far-distant future. England is now Russia's main opponent in Central Asia, and "if you're afraid of England," Dostoevsky writes, "then don't leave home." And so he concludes: "Long live Skobelev and his good lads, and eternal memory to the heroes who were 'struck off the rolls'" (27: 40). Three days after inditing this celebratory elegy, Dostoevsky's name itself vanished from the rolls of the living.

\*   \*   \*

It is regrettable that the last words from his pen should be this glorification of imperial conquest, and perhaps we can alleviate their dispiriting effect by citing some others, written at approximately the same time, that provide a more adequate picture of the full scope of his complex and self-conflicted personality. In his last notebooks, he wrote: "*With total realism, to find the man in mankind.* This is primarily a Russian trait, and in this sense I am really in the last analysis of the people [*naroden*] (for my tendency flows from the depths of the Christian soul of the people)—although I am unknown to the Russian people at present, I will be known [to them] in the future" (italics added). On the same page, we find another attempt at self-definition: "They call me a psychologist: it's not true, I am a realist in a higher sense, that is, I depict all the depths of the human soul" (27: 65). This is the Dostoevsky who has become an important part of the patrimony of world culture, not the misguided patriot waving the banner of imperial domination, though it is part of the mystery of the human personality with which he struggled that both could coexist in his breast.

## CHAPTER 41

# Finale

If life had imposed severe hardships on Dostoevsky, then it may be said that death treated him more kindly and magnanimously. He died within three days of the onset of his final illness on January 28, 1881, gently, peacefully, suffering no pain or prolonged death agony, almost as if he had passed away in his sleep. He maintained full consciousness all through this time, with occasional temporary relapses from loss of blood; and perhaps, almost to the very end, he hoped against hope, relying on reassurances from his doctors that a recovery was still possible.

From the very first, however, he made preparations to die like a good Christian—which he did. Should his apparent calmness and serenity be interpreted as evidence of a rooted religious faith and a belief in immortality? No proper answer can be given to this question; but when he had been faced with execution thirty years earlier, he was quoted as having said: "We shall be with Christ."[1] Moreover, he was no stranger to the prospect of an imminent death, constantly fearing for most of his life that it would result from his unpredictably recurring epileptic attacks.

What he could not have foreseen was that his death would provide him with his greatest triumph. Although he had enjoyed unrivaled public acclaim during his lifetime, nothing equaled the immense public outpouring of grief produced by his end. Once the news became known, a massive and unprecedented funeral procession, composed of every branch of the educated Russian public, organized itself spontaneously in St. Petersburg to accompany his remains to their last resting place.

2

On the twenty-fifth of January, Dostoevsky was busily engaged in the activities occupying his attention at that time. The letter to Countess Komarovskaya accepting her invitation to the Winter Palace has already been mentioned, and early in the afternoon he was visited by two of his oldest friends, Apollon Maikov and Nikolay Strakhov. Conversation turned on the January issue of the *Diary* as well as his plans for the February number, and Strakhov was very curious about the letter that Tolstoy had sent to his cousin, the countess. Dostoevsky passed on the copy he had obtained from her for the perusal of his longtime literary ally, also one of Tolstoy's faithful correspondents, and then Orest Miller arrived.

Miller had his own business to transact about the arrangements for the Pushkin evening. Posters for the event, listing Dostoevsky as having agreed to read from Pushkin's masterpiece, had been printed and were already on display. There is some dispute, however, about whether, as Anna wrote, Miller now asked her husband to read something else, or whether, as Miller recalled, Dostoevsky decided against his first choice and wished to read some of Pushkin's shorter poems. Because Anna Dostoevsky was never averse to altering the historical record in order to place her husband in the best possible light, Miller's version may be considered the more trustworthy. Nor is it difficult to understand his considerable exasperation over Dostoevsky's change of mind. Aside from the problem of the posters, it could lead to endless bother with the censorship and the other authorities whose consent would be required for any alteration.

Anna writes that "Feodor Mikhailovich became somewhat irritated" and flatly declared that he would read the shorter poems or nothing. Miller also became quite exasperated and "imprudently" accused Dostoevsky of treating him rather highhandedly. At such words, Dostoevsky's annoyance changed to genuine anger, and he replied: "And is it not a sin to say something like that, after all the times that I read for students at your request?"[2] Matters were finally settled when Miller agreed to the change; but there is no doubt that, on the late afternoon of January 25, Dostoevsky had been seriously upset and subjected to severe nervous and physical strain.

After this unfortunate disaccord, he departed for the printing plant to hand in the final corrections for the last pages of the *Diary*. Returning home at 7:30, the usual time for the family dinner, he joined Anna and the children, who had been to the theater and seen a play taken from *The Pickwick Papers*. "And all through the dinner," Anna writes, "we spoke of the Pickwick club, recalling every particularity, telling him about them, and then I asked who that actor was [meaning a character]. 'Mr. Jingle,' answered Feodor Mikhailovich."[3] There is something extremely touching about this image of Dostoevsky, on one of the last days of his life, talking lightheartedly with his wife and children about Dickens, an author whom he loved both for his gaiety and for his Christian compassion—a compassion so much less tortured and tormented than his own.

Once dinner was over, he went to his desk to write the last letter that came from his hand. It was to his editor at the *Russian Messenger*, N. A. Lyubimov, and asked if it were possible for the journal to pay immediately for the final chapters of his novel, a sum which he estimated would come to four thousand rubles. He apologizes for not waiting for the journal's own timetable of payments and explains that "I happen to be undertaking a certain expenditure and am terribly in need of money, otherwise the matter will get away from me."[4] This is presumably a reference to the country estate that the Dostoevskys had in mind, and about which Anna had also spoken to Elena Shtakenshneider. Another phrase in the letter, which refers to it as "perhaps [my] last request," has sometimes been taken as an intimation of his own demise. But Anna remarked jokingly, as it was being written, "Look, you will write the 'Karamazovs' again, and again will ask for an advance," thus indicating that it was a reference only to editorial affairs.[5] Dostoevsky then went for a brief stroll before settling down to work.

3

---

On the night of January 25–26, Dostoevsky suffered a slight nosebleed, to which he paid no attention, but which was the first symptom of a fatal rupture of a pulmonary artery. On awaking in the late morning, he presumably told Anna about the events of the night, explaining, according to her account, that a small stand on his writing table containing his pens and the material for rolling his cigarettes had fallen off and slid under a bookcase. To retrieve it, he had moved the heavy piece of furniture, and this exertion had brought on the insignificant flow of blood, which had stopped almost immediately. Beginning his usual routine, he went though the morning mail and set down in his notebook the figures for the number of subscribers to the *Diary*—so far, 909 in all—as well as for the recent sales of his novels. Despite his reassuring account of the nosebleed, Anna was quite frightened and secretly sent for the family physician, Dr. von Bretzell; but he was occupied with other patients and could not come until five. Meanwhile, Dostoevsky was completely calm, spoke and joked with the children, and began to read the newspaper, *New Time*.

What occurred in the course of that afternoon became known only much later, with the publication of a letter from Anna and, in 1922, the memoirs of Dostoevsky's daughter Lyubov—a work that must be read with a great deal of caution, but in this instance appears reliable. According to Anna, at three o'clock a visitor (unnamed) appeared, an old and good friend, very sympathetic, but who unfortunately had one flaw of character—he loved to argue, and "always disputed violently." He and Dostoevsky became engaged in just such an argument, despite the worried Anna's attempts to pacify them, and their guest left at five. The family was then preparing to dine when Dostoevsky suddenly collapsed on his couch and Anna saw with horror that his chin was covered with blood; a thin stream was also flowing into his beard. Nothing, however, was said about this disputatious guest in the first biography of Dostoevsky published in 1883, and for a very good reason—he did not exist!

In a letter written in 1883 to Nikolay Strakhov, who shared with Orest Miller the task of putting together this first biography, Anna abandons the fictitious "guest" and tells the truth. "During the day," she wrote, "it happened that [Dostoevsky] had an angry exchange and almost a quarrel with his sister Vera Mikhailovna, who had arrived from Moscow (of course this should not be mentioned in print)." The quarrel, whose details we learn from Lyubov Dostoevsky, concerned the Kumanina estate and took place at the dinner table; but it did not begin all at once. He was on very good terms with this sister, and the conversation at first consisted of affectionate reminiscences of their childhood and youthful games. But then the issue of the estate arose, and the fact that, despite having renounced his claims to a share in 1844, he had succeeded in being reinstated and now owed money to his sisters. Vera Mikhailovna, speaking for the others as well, thought his reinstatement had been very unfair. Tempers rose as these matters came to the fore, with Vera finally breaking into tears. "Dostoevsky lost patience," his daughter writes, "and in order to cut short these painful recriminations, rose from the table before the meal was finished. At the same time as my mother tried to detain her sister-in-law, continuing to weep and preparing to return home as quickly as possible, my father shut himself in his room." Emerging after this bitter quarrel and sitting down at his writing table, he passed his hand over his mouth and moustaches, and then withdrew it in fright—it was covered with blood! There are some discrepancies of detail in these two versions ("during the day"; at dinner), but the main facts are clear enough, and Lyubov's account is much more extensive.[6]

At six that evening Anna sent an imploring letter to Dr. von Bretzell, who finally arrived. After he had auscultated the patient, a strong new flow of blood began that caused Dostoevsky to lose consciousness for a brief time. Dr. von Bretzell thought it wise to send for a noted specialist, Professor Koshlakov, who did not disturb the patient with another examination. Since the flow of blood had diminished, he speculated that perhaps a "clot" had developed and that "the case was going in the direction of recovery." After recommending that Dostoevsky speak and move as little as possible, the specialist left; but von Bretzell was less sanguine and advised Anna to send for a priest. One came from the nearby Vladimirsky church to administer communion to Dostoevsky and listen to his confession.

4
———

At this point, we shall diverge for a moment to a different topic but one not unrelated to the subject at hand. Anna Dostoevsky, as we have seen, concealed Dostoevsky's quarrel with his sister to avoid disclosing an embarrassing family dispute. Are there other parts of her account that might be called into question? The issue arises because, on the night of the twenty-fifth—the night his nosebleed occurred—other events were taking place in the very building where the Dostoevskys occupied apartment 10. Apartment 11 was actually a small rooming house where individuals could rent single accommodations. Sometime before midnight on the twenty-fifth, the police entered that apartment and carried out a thorough search of one of the rooms in the presence of witnesses. Its inhabitant had been arrested elsewhere earlier that day, and, although he carried a false passport, there was a well-founded suspicion that he was a member of the executive committee of the terrorist Narodnaya Volya. His name was Alexander Ivanovich Barannikov, and he enjoyed a considerable reputation in the eyes of the police as one of the most dangerous and daring of their opponents. Handsome, swarthy (his mother was Georgian), always carefully and correctly dressed, possessed of undaunted courage and unusual physical strength—though a member of the minor nobility and educated in a military academy, he had worked as a blacksmith—Barannikov had been involved in all the attempts so far made to assassinate Alexander II. He was best known as the accomplice of Kravchinsky in the murder of General Mezentsev, having distracted attention from the assassination by firing a shot and then driving the carriage in which both men escaped. That Dostoevsky had been living side by side, for two and a half months, with one of the most sought-after terrorists in his country was noticed by Victor Shklovsky, who made their neighborliness the subject of a short story in 1933. He embellished the facts by depicting Barannikov as living in Dostoevsky's flat, and he also discussed the incident in his short book on Dostoevsky years later.[7] The topic has been more recently investigated by Igor Volgin, who has examined all the circumstances surrounding this intriguing issue much more thoroughly.

The name of Dostoevsky is not mentioned in any of the police reports, but there is a suggestive remark in the memoirs of another revolutionary, M. F. Frolenko, one of Barannikov's comrades. He remembers Barannikov's surprising calm in face of the possibility of capture, and attributes this both to the quietness of the neighborhood in which he resided and to the fact that he lived in "the apartment" of Dostoevsky (presumably meaning "apartment house").[8] The writer's presence was thus far from being unknown to his neighbor; and he felt it to be an additional protection against suspicion and discovery. Whether Dostoevsky, who liked to chat with people in the street, and especially with young men, ever exchanged a word with the well-mannered Barannikov can only remain a matter for conjecture.

Aside from its interest as a sensational tidbit of information, the story of the police search next door also raises a question about Anna's account of Dostoevsky's behavior on the night of the twenty-fifth. As we know from the unpleasant incidents at Bad Ems, he needed absolute silence while engaged in writing, and would not hesitate to attempt to end any disturbing commotion. Is it possible that he was upset by the disruptive noises next door and, on going out to inquire, became terribly upset when he discovered what was taking place? Or might the police, still trying to establish the identity of their prisoner, have come to his flat and questioned him about his next-door neighbor? None of these speculations is beyond the realm of possibility; but in the absence of any further evidence, we can be certain of only one thing: if any such incident *had* occurred, the Anna Dostoevsky who had invented a story to conceal a family quarrel would not have hesitated a moment to concoct another tale to cover up a police search. To have Dostoevsky's name associated with someone like Barannikov, a notorious terrorist, might lead to all sorts of compromising rumors that would have to be prevented at all costs.

Is there any reason, then, to cast doubt on her version of the events on that night? Nothing definitive can be established, but some suggestive facts emerge from Volgin's inspection of the original notebook draft of Anna's *Reminiscences*. The first reference to that night's incident mentions Dostoevsky's having *lifted* "a heavy chair" and rupturing an artery; nothing is said about having lost any object from his desk. The next version is closer to the final one (he "moves a heavy bookcase"), but still there is no reference to attempting to retrieve a fallen object. The notation "his pen rolled behind," then "rolled behind the bookcase," is written above a sentence where other words are crossed out, and the detail about the cigarettes was added only in the final version to provide additional motivation. It is obvious that Anna did not begin with a clear picture of what had occurred, though she pretends only to be reporting what she had been told by her husband; and although none of these alterations allows any firm conclusions, we cannot help but wonder why all these discrepancies should exist.[9]

## 5

On the evening of January 26, Dostoevsky had taken confession and communion from the priest of the nearby church. At two in the morning of January 27, Anna wrote a note to Orest Miller, explaining that her husband had become "seriously ill" the night before and could not fulfill his obligation to read on the Pushkin evening. She requested that his name be removed from the posters because the doctor "had strongly insisted that F. M. should not move or speak for at least a week." Anna also wrote to Countess Komarovskaya, whom she told, in much the same words, that he could not keep his promise to accept her invitation to the Marble Palace on January 29.[10]

On the morning of the twenty-seventh, after sleeping soundly, Dostoevsky awoke feeling "cheerful and healthy." The flow of blood had ceased, no new onset recurred throughout the day, and hope thus revived that the worst was over. A. S. Suvorin describes him as being "jovial and calm, joking, speaking of the future, of his work, of his children, soothing those around him. 'Why are you reading my funeral service? I will outlive all of you.'"[11] Miller and Elena Shtakenshneider came to call, and letters and telegrams began to pile up as friends and acquaintances passed on the word of his illness. In response to "one kind letter" (unidentified), Dostoevsky decided to dictate a "bulletin" about his health to Anna. Although this document has been lost, a draft of a similar one, addressed to Countess Elizaveta Geyden, appears as the last letter in his correspondence.

It is written in the third person, as if coming from Anna, but the copy among her papers specifies that it was a dictation, in which Dostoevsky impassively describes what has occurred and the temporary betterment of his condition. "But since the burst vein has not healed, a hemorrhage may start again. And then, of course, death is likely. Now, however, he is fully conscious and vigorous, but afraid that the artery will again burst."[12] He was indeed "fully conscious," and when the typesetter arrived with the galleys of the *Diary* for final approval, he was able to participate in a necessary correction. There were seven lines too many for the format, and Anna suggested shortening some earlier sentences to solve the problem; but this was not done until he had given his consent.

Professor Koshlakov, returning about seven in the evening, found the patient much improved, predicting that he would be up and about in a week. Vera Mikhailovna and Dostoevsky's stepson, Pavel Isaev, also showed up, though Anna, who had nourished a solid and by no means unjustified dislike of him for many years, hardly welcomed his presence. Dostoevsky slept quite soundly through most of the night, but when Anna awoke at seven and looked over at him, she found his eyes staring at her fixedly. Speaking in a half-whisper, he said: "You know, Anna, I have not been sleeping for three hours now, and have been thinking all that time; and only now have I clearly realized that I shall die today."

Sweeping aside whatever she may have hastily uttered in reply, he continued: "Light a candle, Anna, and hand me the New Testament." This was the volume given to him by the Decembrist wives in Siberia, with ten rubles concealed in the binding. He had read this copy of the

New Testament again and again in the prison camp, and throughout his life it had never left his possession. Opening its pages at random, as he had often done in the past to divine what the future might hold, he asked Anna to read the first passage he had come across. This was from Saint Matthew, chapter 13, verses 14–15, in which Jesus asks John the Baptist to baptize him and John replies: "I have need to be baptized of thee, and comest thou to me?" The King James version then reads: "And Jesus answering said unto him: 'Suffer *it to be* so now for thus it becometh to fulfill all righteousness.'" The Russian text, translated literally, reads: "And Jesus said to him: 'Delay not, for thus it becomes us to fulfill the great truth.'" As Anna was reciting this passage in a trembling voice, and with tears in her eyes, he said: "You hear—delay not—that means I will die."[13]

Anna never forgot the next few hours during which her husband tried to console her, "uttering tender and affectionate words, thanking me for the happy life that he had spent with me. He entrusted the children to my care, said that he believed in me, and hoped I would always love and protect them." One utterance above all was cherished, which, as she writes, not many other husbands could proffer to their wives after fourteen years of marriage: "Remember, Anya, I have always loved you passionately, and never betrayed you once, not even in thought."[14] Clutching her hand, he fell asleep about ten o'clock, but woke suddenly at eleven, sank back on the pillow, and blood began to flow again. If we are to believe Suvorin, Dostoevsky had felt so well that morning that he had insisted on trying to put on his shoes, and this untimely effort could well have brought on the new spasm. He recovered somewhat from this attack, but when Anna tried to console him, "he only sadly shook his head, as if fully convinced that the prediction of his death today would not be gainsaid."[15]

He remained fully alert, however, and even gave instructions to Anna—repeating the injunction several times—that, in case of death, subscribers to the *Diary* should be reimbursed. Page proofs had arrived during the morning, and when he was unable to sign the necessary approval, Anna told the messenger: "Come tomorrow; he'll be better and will sign." It appears that he summoned enough strength to sign later in the day. *New Time* published the first announcement of Dostoevsky's illness on January 28, and a flood of visitors immediately began to besiege the grief-stricken Anna. E. A. Rikacheva, the daughter of his younger brother Andrey, was at the Dostoevskys at two o'clock that afternoon and wrote her father: "Uncle is peaceful, and nobody was admitted to see him; but he was told about all who came to visit—he certainly wanted to know who they were."[16] Only Apollon Maikov, at Dostoevsky's special request, was allowed to come to his bedside, though it is not known whether they spoke or obeyed the doctor's order of silence.

The newspaper story announced that his name would not appear on the new posters for the Pushkin evening because "he had fallen seriously ill on January 26 and [was] lying in bed." It then went on, in a mixture of sarcasm and eulogy: "Those people who, not long since, reproached him for too often seeking ovations at public readings, may now quiet down: the public will not listen to him again very soon. If only the precious life be preserved for the Russian people of the most profound of our contemporary writers, the direct inheritor of our literary geniuses!"[17] When this passage was read to Dostoevsky, who was curious ("What are they saying about me?"), he asked Anna to read it again. In his very last hours he thus had the satisfaction of hearing his enemies mocked, and his own genius celebrated as the continuator of the great Russian literary tradition. It is possible that he took communion and confession again; and at five o'clock he dictated the bulletin to Countess Geyden already mentioned.

According to Anna's notebooks, our chief source of information, Pavel Isaev remained true to form and asked that a notary be summoned so that his stepfather could make a final disposition of his estate. Dostoevsky had made a will in 1873, clearly leaving everything to his wife, and Pasha's words thus went unheeded. Anna depicts Dostoevsky, when Pasha approached, withdrawing his hand as his stepson bent to kiss it. He then asked that the children be summoned, and they kissed him on the cheek while he gave them his final blessing, enjoining them always to love and obey their mother. He requested that his copy of the New Testament be given to his son Fedya and that the parable of the Prodigal Son be read to the children. Lyubov later recalled him telling them that, if they should ever commit a crime (*prestuplenie*, which has a wider meaning than a merely legal offense) to trust God as their Father, plead with Him for forgiveness, and be certain that He would rejoice in their repentance, just as the father had done on the return of the Prodigal Son. It was this parable of transgression, repentance, and forgiveness that he wished to leave as a last heritage to his children, and it may well be seen as his own ultimate understanding of the meaning of his life and the message of his work.

There was again a copious flow of blood at about 6:30, and he fell into a coma from which he never awoke. During the final death throes, which lasted for approximately two hours, he was mercifully unconscious. Anna and the children were "kneeling and crying" all the while, but trying to choke back their sobs because they had been told that the auditory sense was the last to go and that any sound might prolong the suffering of the dying. "I held the hand of my husband in my own,"

Anna writes, "and felt the pulse becoming feebler and feebler."[18] Apollon Maikov had sent for another doctor, and when the writer Boleslav Markevich came to the door (he had been dispatched by Countess Tolstaya to inquire after Dostoevsky's condition), he was mistaken for this personage. With a "heartrending shriek," the eleven-year-old Lyubov rushed to meet him, shouting: "Doctor, Doctor, for God's sake, save my father [*papashy*], he is wheezing."[19] This was the last death rattle, and when the doctor arrived a few moments later, he could do nothing but certify the decease. Markevich, who was known for his melodramatic effects, pictures Anna and Lyubov in hysterics, with Anna exclaiming, "Oh, whom have I lost! Whom have I lost!" as she sank into a chair. "'Whom has Russia lost' involuntarily, and at the same time, broke out of Maikov and myself."[20] This final sentence could not have more feelingly expressed the sentiment of all of literate Russia.

6
———

Anna's brother arrived that evening, two hours after Dostoevsky's death, and "thanks to [him], I was relieved of all practical problems, and was spared much that was difficult and unpleasant in these sorrowful days."[21] The next morning, the twenty-ninth, Suvorin was in the apartment early and, in an article the next day, described with a shudder how the corpse had been washed and prepared for burial. He dashed off a note to the artist I. N. Kramskoy, informing him of the death and asking him to come round immediately because Anna had spoken of "photographs and masks" being made. "You could do his portrait," he said, "even if it would be sketchy."[22] Kramskoy did produce a famous drawing of the dead Dostoevsky, with his head lying on a pillow and with what seems to be the beginning of a faint half-smile on his face. No other portrait or photograph shows any similar expression, but it cannot be attributed to the invention of the artist. All of the many memoirists confirm that Kramskoy had caught the unusual expression they had seen themselves. The photographer K. A. Shapiro also arrived and attempted to take some photographs, but because of the bad lighting in the cramped room none were successful. The sculptor L. Bernshtam, instead of beginning on the planned bust of Dostoevsky, took a plaster cast for a death mask.

Dostoevsky's friends in high places also began to do what they could on behalf of the family. Konstantin Pobedonostsev informed Count Loris-Melikov of the death and requested that he inform Alexander II. He also wrote the Tsarevich to enlist his aid in obtaining some financial help for the family, urging him to to speak to Loris-Melikov as well. An official of the Ministry of Internal Affairs soon arrived to inform Anna

18. Dostoevsky on his bier, by I. N. Kramskoy

that the expenses of the funeral would be borne by the government; but Anna claimed to have proudly refused: "I considered it my moral obligation to bury my husband with the money he had earned."[23] No such refusal is mentioned in the official report, and she is described as having expressed gratitude for the aid.

The first service for the dead (*panikhida*) began at one o'clock in the afternoon. It had been announced in the newspapers, and Anna observed that "known and unknown [visitors] arrived to pray at his coffin, and there were so many that very quickly all the five rooms were filled with a dense crowd, and when the office for the dead was recited the children and I had a hard time pushing through the crowd to stand near the coffin."[24] Pobedonostsev wrote to Katkov the same day, requesting that the money owed Dostoevsky be sent to Anna as speedily as possible, along with the authority to collect it in her name. "Today was the first *panikhida*," he added. "He seems as if still alive, with a face of total quietude, as in the best moments of his life."[25] Anna's brother then went to the Novodeichy monastery, where, at the time of Nekrasov's funeral, Dostoevsky had expressed a desire to be buried. But the price demanded for a grave site seemed so exorbitant that it was decided to seek elsewhere. Anna suggested the Okhtinsky monastery, which contained the graves of their son Alyosha and of Anna's father, and they planned to go there the next morning to buy a plot.

Meanwhile, however, others had heard of the Dostoevskys' difficulties, and an important editor and publisher, prompted by the wife of a general, approached Metropolitan Isidor of the Alexander Nevsky *lavra* (a religious compound containing a cemetery) to suggest that it would be fitting for Dostoevsky to be buried there free of charge. Their request was met with a flat refusal: the worthy as well as learned metropolitan said that he was nothing but "a simple novelist, who never wrote anything serious," and that in addition his funeral might cause a "disorder undesirable within the walls of the *lavra*."[26] When Pobedonostsev, now the highest secular official in charge of the Russian Church, heard of this retort at the evening *panikhida*, he responded, "We will allocate the money for the burial of Dostoevsky." Metropolitan Isidor was no doubt read a thorough lesson in private, and the next day the newspapers announced that the place of burial would be the Alexander Nevsky *lavra*.

At the evening *panikhida*, the by no means spacious apartment of the Dostoevskys was even more filled to overflowing; a newspaper correspondent wrote that those arriving at eight could not reach the coffin until at least ten. Dostoevsky's niece told her father that the apartment was "literally packed with people, mostly young, and only at eleven did the crowd thin out."[27] Saltykov-Shchedrin was there, and so was Countess Komarovskaya, accompanied by Baroness Feleisen. In a letter to Grand Duke Konstantin Konstantinovich, the countess described how the two titled ladies were unable to approach the coffin all through the service—no doubt a new experience for those before whom everyone made way. When the countess finally saw Dostoevsky, she too was struck by the expression of his countenance: "As if alive, a bright, peaceful face . . . like a man who has done his duty, borne everything, not at all embittered." The children were busy around the coffin, lighting candles that had been snuffed out by the lack of air and "asking visitors not to kiss the forehead [of the corpse] but the icon."[28]

Ever since his return from Siberia in 1860, Dostoevsky had dreamed of uniting Russian society into one harmonious whole linked by faith and love. The closest this sublime chimera ever came to being realized was during the days when his body lay in its bier. All—literally *all*—of those who made up the cultural-political life of St. Petersburg, the nerve center of the Russian Empire, came to pay him homage. Saltykov-Shchedrin rubbed elbows with Countess Komarovskaya; N. K. Mikhailovsky, who had just begun to write under a pseudonym for the underground newspaper of Narodnaya Volya, found himself in the same rooms with K. P. Pobedonostsev and Grand Duke Dimitry Konstantinovich, who was there accompanied by his tutor. Contemporaries themselves could not help marveling at the unanimity of grief and of reverence suddenly exhibited by all sections of a society otherwise torn apart by unceasing conflict—a conflict that, just a month later, would culminate in the assassination of Alexander II. Anna Dostoevsky later remarked that, if her husband had not died on January 28, he would have had only a month longer to live—the news about Alexander would certainly have brought on an arterial rupture.

It is not surprising that those who had known him personally, or had taken part either for or against him in the literary polemics of the day, should have felt it obligatory to participate in the funeral ceremonies. More remarkable is the astonishingly widespread response that the news of his death aroused in the community at large, especially (though not exclusively) among the student youth. A. F. Koni recalls one of his young lawyers, whom he had asked to read a legal brief aloud, hesitating and stumbling while doing so. When asked if he were ill, he blurted out the news (which Koni had not yet heard) that Dostoevsky was dead, and then dissolved into tears.[29] As the word spread in the *gymnasiums* and the schools of higher learning in the capital, groups immediately began to organize, to assign delegates to attend the *panikhida*, and to collect funds to buy wreaths so that they could participate en masse in the burial ceremonies.

Dostoevsky's appeal to the student youth was never more apparent than on this final occasion. I. I. Popov—the young man studying at the Pedagogical Institute, who had observed him in the church park—explains that this appeal had grown considerably in the last year or two. Those like the left-leaning Popov had never forgiven him for *The Devils*, nor could they accept the injunction of the Pushkin speech: "Humble thyself, O haughty man!" But the speech nonetheless, he admits, had given all of them "rich material for controversy" over their evening tea; and then, "drawn by the general movement," they began to find in the *Diary* ideas that were not only acceptable but even attractive. Dostoevsky's remarks about "coarsely garbed Russia" (the peasants), which should be recognized as containing the possibility of creating a better world, "we regarded as a Populist, democratic tendency. He won the sympathy of most of us, and we greeted him enthusiastically when he appeared at literary evenings. This alteration in the relation of the youth to Dostoevsky appeared in the last year of his life."[30]

A similar observation can be found in the journals of I. F. Tyumenev, a student at the Academy of Fine Arts, who left a classic account of the funeral and the procession in which he and his comrades took part. He remarked that if Turgenev, Goncharov, or Ostrovsky had died, their loss would not have been as "painful" as that of Dostoevsky, "who had just begun to attract the attention of society, just begun to interest everyone with his 'Karamazovs,' and [was] just getting ready to continue narrating the fate of Alyosha, this (according to his intention) new Russian evangelical socialist."[31] Tyumenev is obviously in sympathy with what he quite accurately calls Alyosha's "evangelical socialism," and he also speaks as if his work had just come to public attention and gained a widespread readership. Although far from being true, this error helps us to understand why a new generation had become so receptive to his influence; they had grown up absorbing Populist (not Nihilist) ideas, and thus would not turn away from the Christian implications of Dostoevsky's moral ideal. The remainder of this entry describes the instantaneous decision of the students in the academy to collect funds. When those assigned to the task were met occasionally by the question, "And who is this Dostoevsky?" no answer was given; some of the collectors even spat to show their contempt for such ignorance.

On the afternoon of January 30, the head of the censorship, N. S. Abaza, who had been so obliging about the *Diary*, presented Anna with a letter from the Ministry of Finance informing her that the Tsar had deigned to grant her a lifetime pension of two thousand rubles a year "because of [her husband's] services to Russian literature."[32] This was, apparently, the first pension of its kind ever awarded in Russia to a writer as such. (Those given to Pushkin and Karamzin, who had occupied official government positions more or less as sinecures, were for their services to the state.) Two vacancies, one in the prestigious Corp of Pages and the other in the Smolny Institute (a school for daughters of the nobility), also were to be reserved for the Dostoevsky children; and while Anna accepted all these offers gratefully, she later sent both children to other educational institutions.

Meanwhile, on the evening of the same day, D. V. Grigorovich thought it wise to organize the funeral procession. He made a list of all the groups who had indicated a desire to march (there turned out to be many more than he put down) and established an order of the places where the various delegations should assemble to avoid becoming a milling mob. The student representatives were told to help in maintaining order, and they took this responsibility very seriously; older Dostoevsky friends were also appointed to oversee various groupings. The procession would begin at 10:30 the next morning (actually it started at 11) and proceed from the apartment to the Alexander Nevsky *lavra* along the Nevsky Prospect.

## 7

January 31, a Saturday, dawned bright and clear. As already mentioned, the *Diary of a Writer* appeared on that very day; and an article by O. F. Miller in *New Time* urged subscribers to forgo the reimbursement on which Dostoevsky had insisted and instead contribute the money to a fund for the publication of a complete edition of his works. A number-less crowd had gathered around the apartment at Kuznechny alley by nine o'clock that morning, all bearing wreaths and banners inscribed with the names of their institutions and societies, including journals and newspapers. A count made of the line of march came to sixty-seven such groups, though the number was later estimated at seventy-four, with fifteen choirs accompanying the cortège. The opera was fully represented, along with all the other dramatic arts, and the famed baritone of the Mariinsky Theater received a reprimand from the management because, by risking a cold in this way, he could have endangered the repertory.

The words with which I. F. Tyumenev described the moment when the coffin emerged from the house and appeared to the crowd are particularly expressive. "From the belfry of the Vladimirsky church sounded the bell, and just right after the first impact a solemn 'Holy God' rang out. . . . At the first sound of the prayer all heads were bared . . . and to many of us, sobs rose in our throats. At that moment everyone, whether believer or not, felt something like the breath of godliness."[33] The procession wound its way through the streets, the coffin being carried by alternating bearers; among the first were Dostoevsky's surviving fellow Petrashevtsy, A. I. Palm and A. N. Pleshcheev. They were followed by mourners stretching for almost a mile, with banners and wreaths, some bearing only his name, others those of his works (though there was none for *The Devils*), still others with a phrase or a sentence characterizing some aspect of his life or thought. Their number was estimated to be thirty thousand. "The funeral of Dostoevsky," wrote Nikolay Strakhov, "represented a manifestation that struck everybody. . . . It can boldly be said that, up until then, there had never before been such a funeral in Russia."[34]

Considering the size of the crowd, observers were struck by its good behavior and orderliness. The police kept their distance, except for one episode not reported in the newspapers but appearing in two private memoirs. One delegation of women students, instead of a wreath, displayed a pair of the convict shackles that Dostoevsky had worn and about which he had written in *House of the Dead*. When the police came to appropriate them, there was a slight scuffle; but they were soon surrendered peacefully so as not to disturb the solemnity of the occasion. Dostoevsky's prison past was one of his badges of honor, and when an elderly passer-by asked a member of the delegation of dramatic artists who was receiving such a majestic funeral, the answer came back: "A *katorzhnik*" (an exiled convict). The mass of the population assumed that such an imposing cortège must be that of some important general or other because only such personages had ever been considered distinguished enough to receive so grandiose a tribute.

It took two hours for the coffin to reach the portals of the Alexander Nevsky *lavra*, where it was met at the gateway by the students of the Theological School and Seminary and the clergy in their ceremonial robes, led by the head of the *lavra*, Archimandrite Simeon, and the rector of the Theological Seminary, Father Yanishev. He was an old friend of Dostoevsky's from Wiesbaden days, a distinguished theologian whose conception of Christianity exercised some influence on Dostoevsky's views and whose intellect and character he had admired.[35] After the coffin was carried into the Church of the Holy Spirit within the *lavra*, the doors of the entry were closed and only delegations with wreaths were admitted. The crowd was told that the church could hold at most fifteen hundred mourners, and the procession began to disperse until about four the next day, when the burial would take place. At eight o'clock that evening the night service for the dead began, attended by Anna and the children (Lyubov had almost been crushed in the crowd around the gates earlier in the day). "The church," Anna wrote, "was filled with those in prayer; many were young people, students of various higher educational institutions, the Theological Academy and *kursistok* [female students]. The majority of them stayed in the church the entire night, relaying each other in reading the psalms over Dostoevsky's coffin."[36]

On February 1, the day of the burial, a second edition of the *Diary of a Writer* was published, its first page rimmed with a black border. At ten o'clock, a Mass was performed in the church in the presence of K. P. Pobedonostsev and other high officials of the government; and this was followed by the *otpevanie*, the service for the dead. Father Yanishev then spoke a few solemnly penetrating words about his friend, all of whose work as a novelist, he said quite acutely, was an echo of Christ's Sermon on the Mount. The coffin, which remained closed on Pobedonostsev's order so as to spare Anna and the children, was then carried to a plot in the cemetery adjoining the grave of the poet V. A. Zhukovsky. Lyubov gave a heartrending cry, which moved all those present to their depths when she exclaimed: "Good-bye [*proshchai*, which can also mean forgive], dear, kind, good papa, good-bye."[37] Various people spoke at the grave, and I. I. Popov, who climbed a tree to get a better view above the crowd, recalled "the apostolic figure of V. S. Solovyev [with his] curls falling on his forehead," and "who spoke with great pathos and expressiveness."[38]

Let us end with some of Solovyev's words, ones not spoken at the grave site but a few days earlier (January 30) in the lectures he was giving both at the University of St. Petersburg and at the Bestuzhev Higher Courses for Women, whose students were among Dostoevsky's most fervent admirers. To the first, he said that "last year, at the Pushkin festival, Dostoevsky called Pushkin a prophet, but Dostoevsky himself deserves this title to an even greater degree." To the female students, he declared: "Just as the highest worldly power somehow or other becomes concentrated in one person, who represents a state, similarly the highest spiritual power in each epoch usually belongs in every people to one man, who more clearly than all grasps the spiritual ideals of mankind, more consciously than all strives to attain them, more strongly than all affects others by his preachments. Such a spiritual leader of the Russian people in recent times was Dostoevsky."[39]

# NOTES

## ABBREVIATIONS

*DVS*   *F. M. Dostoevsky v Vospominaniakh Sovremennikov*, ed. K. Tyunkin, 2 vols. (Moscow, 1990).

*PSS*   F. M. Dostoevsky, *Polnoe Sobranie Sochinenii*, ed. and annotated by G. M. Fridlender et al., 30 vols. (Leningrad, 1972–1990). This definitive edition of Dostoevsky's writings, which is now complete, contains his correspondence and provides an extensive and reliable scholarly apparatus.

## CHAPTER 2

1. *PSS*, 29/Bk. 1: 218; July 18, 1871.
2. Ibid.
3. Ibid. This is the first indication of what would become Dostoevsky's growing anti-Semitism.
4. Anna Dostoevsky, *Reminiscences*, trans. and ed. Beatrice Stillman (New York, 1973), 175.
5. Ibid., 173.
6. Ibid., 176.
7. Ibid., 178–179.
8. V. P. Meshchersky, *Moi Vospominaniya*, 3 vols. (St. Petersburg, 1898), 2: 159.
9. *PSS*, 29/Bk. 1: 224; January 24, 1872.
10. Ibid., 224.
11. Ibid.
12. Ibid., 226; February 4, 1872.
13. Ibid., 226; February 4, 1872.
14. Ibid., 229; February 4, 1872.
15. Cited in *PSS*, 12: 259.
16. Ibid., 258.
17. *PSS*, 29/Bk. 1: 208; April/May 1871.
18. Ibid., 225; also 484.
19. Ibid., 225.
20. Anna Dostoevsky, *Reminiscences*, 189.
21. Ibid., 169.
22. Cited in *Istoria Russkogo Iskusstva*, 2 vols. (Moscow, 1957–1960), 2: 41.
23. *PSS*, 29/Bk. 1: 229; February 4, 1872.
24. Ibid., 227; February 4, 1872.
25. Ibid., 235; April 20, 1872.
26. Anna Dostoevsky, *Reminiscences*, 191.
27. Ibid., 194.
28. Ibid., 199.
29. *PSS*, 29/Bk. 1: 237; May 27, 1872.
30. Ibid., 240; May 28, 1872.
31. Ibid., 242–243; June 3, 1872.
32. Ibid., 245; June 5, 1872.
33. Ibid., 240; May 30, 1872.
34. Ibid., 249; June 12, 1872.
35. Ibid., 250; June 14, 1872.
36. Anna Dostoevsky, *Reminiscences*, 205.
37. Ibid., 378–379.
38. *PSS*, 29/Bk. 1: 226–227.
39. Ibid., 232; March/April 1872.
40. Ibid., 487.
41. Ibid., 254; October 9, 1872.
42. Anna Dostoevsky, *Reminiscences*, 206.
43. Ibid., 209–210.
44. Ibid., 214, 220.
45. *PSS*, 21: 362.

## CHAPTER 3

1. V. P. Meshchersky, *Moi Vospominaniya*, 3 vols. (St. Petersburg), 2: 179.
2. *DVS*, 2: 512.
3. Ibid., 139.
4. Ibid., 141.
5. Ibid., 256.
6. Ibid., 257.
7. Ibid., 140.
8. Ibid., 142. The question was whether a comma should always be placed before

the relative pronoun "that" (*chto*), which Dostoevsky sometimes omitted.

9. Ibid., 143.

10. Ibid., 142.

11. Ibid., 163–164.

12. Ibid., 264.

13. Ibid., 144.

14. Ibid.

15. Ibid., 145.

16. Ibid., 146.

17. Ibid., 150.

18. Ibid., 179.

19. Ibid., 151.

20. Andrzej Walicki, *A History of Russian Thought from the Enlightenment to Marxism*, trans. Hilda Andrews-Rusiecka (Stanford, 1979), 133.

21. *DVS*, 2: 160–161.

22. Ibid., 156.

23. Ibid., 184–185.

24. Ibid., 179–180.

25. Ibid., 180–181.

26. Ibid., 161–162.

27. *Pisma*, ed. A. S. Dolinin, 4 vols. (Moscow-Leningrad, 1928–1959), 3: 229.

28. Cited in *Literaturnoe Nasledtsvo*, 83 (Moscow, 1971), 331.

29. V. V. Zenkovsky, *A History of Russian Philosophy*, trans. G. L. Kline, 2 vols. (London and New York, 1953), 2: 473.

30. Anna Dostoevsky, *Reminiscences*, trans. and ed. Beatrice Stillman (New York, 1973), 223.

31. *PSS*, 29/Bk. 1: 258–259; January 31, 1873.

32. Ibid., 262; February 26, 1873.

33. Ibid.

34. Ibid., 273–274; July 5, 1873.

35. Ibid., 280; July 20, 1873.

36. F. I. Tyutchev, *Polnoe Sobranie Stikhotvorenie* (Leningrad, 1987), 223.

37. *PSS*, 21: 286.

38. *PSS*, 29/Bk. 1: 284; July 26, 1873.

39. Ibid., 285–286; July 29, 1873.

40. Ibid., 281–282; July 23, 1873.

41. Ibid., 273, 282; July 26, 1873.

42. Ibid., 293; August 19, 1873.

43. Ibid., 284; July 26, 1873.

44. Ibid., 260–261; February 10, 1873.

45. Cited in A. V. Arkhipov, "Dostoevskii i Kishenskii," in *Dostoevskii: Materiali i Issledovania* (Leningrad, 1976), 2: 205.

46. *PSS*, 11: 303.

47. *PSS*, 29/Bk. 1: 307; November 12, 1873.

48. Ibid., 519.

49. Ibid., 311–312; January 4, 1874.

50. Ibid., 522.

51. Anna Dostoevsky, *Reminiscences*, 227.

52. *DVS*, 2: 211–213.

53. Ibid.

54. Ibid., 213.

55. *Literaturnoe Nasledtsvo*, 86 (Moscow, 1973), 426.

56. Anna Dostoevsky, *Reminiscences*, 226.

57. *PSS*, 29/Bk. 1: 308; November 12, 1873.

58. Ibid., 314–315; November 3–4, 1873.

59. Ibid., 262; February 26, 1873.

60. *DVS*, 2: 209.

61. Ibid.

62. Ibid., 2: 186. In a letter, Dostoevsky attributed a similar statement to Apollon Grigoriev. See *PSS*, 29/Bk. 1: 32; March 18/30, 1869.

## CHAPTER 4

1. Cited in B. S. Itenberg, *Dvizhenie Revolyutsionnogo Narodnichestvo* (Moscow, 1965), 134.

2. Ibid., 136.

3. Ibid., 136–137.

4. Peter Kropotkin, *Memoirs of a Revolutionist* (Garden City, N.Y., 1962), 201.

5. Cited in E. Lampert, *Sons Against Fathers* (Oxford, 1965), 325.

6. Franco Venturi, *Roots of Revolution*, trans. Francis Haskell (New York, 1966), 449.

7. P. L. Lavrov, "The Cost of Progress," in *Russian Philosophy*, ed. J. M. Edie, J. P. Scanlan, and M. B. Zeldin, 3 vols. (Chicago, 1964), 2: 141.

8. Cited in Itenberg, *Dvizhenie Revolyutsionnogo Narodnichestvo*, 83.

9. N. G. Chernyshevsky, *Selected Philosophical Essays* (Moscow, 1953), 94.

10. Cited in V. V. Zenkovsky, *A History of Russian Philosophy*, trans. G. L. Kline, 2 vols. (London and New York, 1953), 1: 354.

11. Ibid., 369.

12. N. K. Mikhailovsky, *Polnoe Sobra-*

*nie Sochinenii,* 10 vols. (St. Petersburg, 1909), 4: 38–39.

13. Quoted in James H. Billington, *Mikhailovsky and Russian Populism* (Oxford, 1958), 131–132.

14. D. N. Ovsyaniko-Kulikovsky, "Istoria Russkoi Intelligentsii," in *Sobranie Sochinenii,* 10 vols. (St. Petersburg, 1910–1911), vol. 8, part 2, 197.

15. Cited in Billington, *Mikhailovsky,* 131.

16. Quoted in ibid., 132.

17. *PSS,* 28/Bk. 2: 154; April 25, 1866.

18. Cited in Billington, *Mikhailovsky,* 67–68.

19. Ibid., 67.

20. Ibid., 66.

21. Kropotkin, *Memoirs of a Revolutionist,* 199.

22. Quoted in V. Bogucharskii, *Aktiv-*

*noe Narodnichestvo Semidesyatikh Godov* (Moscow, 1912), 179.

23. *Sochinenia N. K. Mikhailovskogo,* 7 vols. (St. Petersburg, 1888), 2: 272–273.

24. Cited in *PSS,* 21: 468.

25. *Sochinenia N. K. Mikhailovskogo,* 2: 273.

26. Ibid., 274–275.

27. Ibid., 277.

28. Ibid., 284, 307.

29. Ibid., 304.

30. Ibid., 306–307.

31. Ibid.

32. See *Literaturnoe Nasledstvo,* 83 (Moscow, 1971), 290.

33. Ibid.

34. Quoted in Itenberg, *Dvizhenie Revolyutsionnogo Narodnichestvo,* 346.

## Chapter 5

1. Mikhail Bakhtin, *Problems of Dostoevsky's Poetics,* trans. and ed. Caryl Emerson (Minneapolis, 1984), 93.

2. *PSS,* 29/Bk. 1: 215; May 18/30, 1871.

3. Ernest Renan, *Vie de Jésus* (Paris, 1863), 457–469; see also *PSS,* 21: 381.

4. *PSS,* 28/Bk. 2: 260; February 18/March 1, 1868.

5. Sir Donald Mackenzie Wallace, *Russia on the Eve of War and Revolution,* ed. Cyril R. Black (New York, 1961), 83–91.

6. L. M. Rosenblyum, *Tvorcheskie Dnevniki Dostoevskogo* (Moscow, 1981), 123–124.

## Chapter 6

1. See the commentary to "Vlas" in *PSS,* 21: 396–401.

2. *Literaturnoe Nasledtsvo,* vol. 83 (Moscow, 1971), 294.

3. Ivan Goncharov, *Sobranie Sochinenii,* 8 vols. (Moscow, 1955), 8: 457.

4. Ibid., 459.

5. For Bakhtin's analysis, see his *Problems of Dostoevsky's Poetics,* trans. and ed. Caryl Emerson (Minneapolis, 1984), 137–141.

6. See the commentary to *Bobok* in *PSS,* 21: 402.

## Chapter 7

1. Anna Dostoevsky, *Reminiscences,* trans. and ed. Beatrice Stillman (New York, 1973), 228.

2. *PSS,* 29/Bk. 1: 319; May 5, 1874.

3. *PSS,* 29/Bk. 1: 321; June 6, 1874.

4. See ibid., 531.

5. Ibid., 322; June 6, 1874.

6. Ibid., 323–324.

7. Ibid., 325; June 12/24, 1874.

8. Ibid., 326.

9. Ibid., 327.

10. Ibid., 328.

11. Ibid., 331; June 16/28, 1874.

12. Ibid., 329; June 12/24, 1874.

13. Ibid., 331; June 16/28, 1874.

14. Ibid., 332.

15. Ibid.

16. Ibid., 336; June 23/July 5, 1874.

17. Ibid., 337.
18. Ibid., 340; June 28/July 10, 1874.
19. Ibid., 331; June 16/28, 1874.
20. Ibid., 346; July 5/17, 1874.
21. Ibid., 344.
22. Ibid., 333; June 16/24, 1874.
23. Ibid., 338; June 23/July 5, 1874.
24. Ibid.
25. The text of Strakhov's remarks is given in *PSS*, 29/Bk. 1: 471nn. 14 and 15.

26. Ibid., 338; June 23/July 5, 1874.
27. Ibid., 354; July 14/26, 1874.
28. Ibid., 352.
29. Ibid., 353.
30. Ibid., 360.
31. Anna Dostoevsky, *Reminiscences*, 233–234.

## Chapter 8

1. Anna Dostoevsky, *Reminiscences*, trans. and ed. Beatrice Stillman (New York, 1973), 235.
2. Ibid., 236.
3. *PSS*, 29/Bk. 1: 361; July 20/August 1, 1874.
4. Andrzej Walicki, *A History of Russian Thought from the Enlightenment to Marxism*, trans. Hilda Andrews-Rusiecka (Stanford, 1979), 224.
5. See A. S. Dolinin, *Poslednie Romani Dostoevskogo* (Moscow-Leningrad, 1967), 89–90.
6. *PSS*, 17: 302.
7. *PSS*, 29/Bk. 1: 364; November 4, 1874.
8. Ibid., 366–367; December 11, 1874.
9. Ibid., 370–371; December 20, 1874.
10. Ibid., 368; December 17, 1874.
11. Ibid., 368–369; December 18, 1874.
12. Ibid., 370; December 30, 1874.
13. Ibid.
14. *PSS*, 29/Bk. 2: 8; February 6, 1875. See also ibid., 194.
15. Ibid., 9; February 4, 1875.
16. Ibid., 12; February 8, 1875.
17. Ibid., 11; February 1, 1875
18. Ibid., 13; February 9, 1875.
19. Ibid., 15–16; February 11, 1875.
20. Ibid., 16–17; February 12, 1875.
21. Orest Miller and N. N. Strakhov, *Biografia, Pisma, iz Zapisnoi Knizhki* (St. Petersburg, 1883), 247.
22. Cited in *PSS*, 17: 345.
23. *DVS*, 2: 214–215.
24. *Literaturnoe Nasledtsvo*, 83 (Moscow, 1971), 619–620.

25. *PSS*, 29/Bk. 2: 18; February 12, 1875.
26. Anna Dostoevsky, *Reminiscences*, 247.
27. Cited in *PSS*, 17: 346.
28. Ibid.
29. Dolinin, *Poslednie Romani Dostoevskogo*, 94.
30. *PSS*, 29/Bk. 2: 10; February 7, 1875.
31. Ibid.
32. Ibid., 20; February 14, 1875.
33. Ibid., 18; February 12, 1875.
34. Anna Dostoevsky, *Reminiscences*, 241.
35. Ibid., 242.
36. Ibid., 244.
37. Ibid., 245–246.
38. *PSS*, 29/Bk. 2: 25–26; April 6, 1875.
39. Ibid., 27–28; May 13, 1875.
40. Ibid., 29–30; May 24, 1875.
41. Ibid., 30; May 27/June 8, 1875.
42. Ibid., 31; May 29/June 10, 1875.
43. Ibid., 36; June 4/16, 1875.
44. Ibid., 43; June 10/22, 1875.
45. Ibid., 40; June 7/19, 1875.
46. Ibid., 36; June 4/16, 1875.
47. Ibid., 55–56; June 21/July 3, 1875.
48. Ibid., 43; June 10/22, 1875.
49. *PSS*, 29/Bk. 2: 49; June 15/27, 1875.
50. Ibid., 46–47; June 13/25, 1875.
51. Ibid., 37–39; June 5/17, 1875. See also ibid., 212.
52. Ibid., 57; June 23/July 5, 1875; Anna Dostoevsky, *Reminiscences*, 251.
53. *PSS*, 29/Bk. 2: 58; June 23/July 5, 1875.
54. Ibid., 63; July 6, 1875.

## Chapter 9

1. For more information on this projected work, see my *Dostoevsky: The Miraculous Years, 1865–1871* (Princeton, 1995), Chap. 19.

2. See E. I Kiiko, "Russkii Tip 'vsemir-nogo boleniya za vsex,' v *Podrostok*," *Russkaya Literatura*, 1 (1975), 155–161.

3. For more information about the influence of Chaadaev on the novel, see A. S. Dolinin, *Poslednie Romani Dostoev-*

*skogo* (Moscow-Leningrad, 1967), 104–125.

4. *PSS*, 29/Bk. 1: 315; March 1, 1874.

5. Ibid., 216; May 18/30, 1871.

6. Cited in *PSS*, 17: 347.

## Chapter 10

1. Horst-Jurgen Gerigk, *Versuch uber Dostoevskij's "Jungling"* (Munich, 1965).

2. A. S. Dolinin, *Poslednie Romani*

*Dostoevskogo* (Moscow-Leningrad, 1967), 182–184.

## Chapter 11

1. Anna Dostoevsky, *Reminiscences*, trans. and ed. Beatrice Stillman (New York, 1973), 253.

2. Ibid., 213.

3. *PSS*, 21: 371–372.

4. Ibid., 28/Bk. 2: 141; November 8, 1865.

5. Ibid., 29/Bk. 1: February 26/March 10, 1869.

6. Cited in *DVS*, 2: 364–365.

7. *PSS*, 22: 136.

8. *DVS*, 2: 275–277.

9. Ibid., 278.

10. Ibid., 277–279.

11. *PSS*, 29/Bk. 2: 82–83; May 29, 1876.

12. Ibid.

13. *DVS*, 2: 286.

14. Ibid., 282–283.

15. Ibid., 284.

16. Ibid.

17. Ibid., 285.

18. *PSS*, 29/Bk. 2: 66–67; November 10, 1875.

19. Ibid., 71–72; January 7, 1876.

20. Ibid., 75–76; March 10, 1876.

21. Ibid., 124–125; September 6, 1876.

22. *PSS*, 28/Bk. 1: 164; December 23, 1849.

23. *PSS*, 29/Bk. 2: 78; April 9, 1876.

24. Ibid.

25. *DVS*, 2: 242–243.

26. Ibid.

27. *PSS*, 29/Bk. 2: 130; November 5, 1876.

28. Cited in the commentary to the letter of Maslannikov, the lawyer who offered his help, in *Dostoevsky i Ego Vremya* (Leningrad, 1971), 277.

29. *PSS*, 29/Bk. 2: 65; December 4, 1875.

30. Ibid., 68; December 21, 1875.

31. Ibid.

32. Ibid., 71; January 7, 1876; also Wagner's letter, cited in the commentary, 231.

33. *PSS*, 24: 199.

34. Ibid., 462. Leskov's article is cited in the commentary to Dostoevsky's notebooks.

35. *PSS*, 24: 199.

36. *PSS*, 22: 127.

37. Ibid., 335. Solovyev's letter is cited in the commentary.

38. *PSS*, 24: 158–159.

## Chapter 12

1. *DVS*, 2: 235.

2. *PSS*, 29/Bk. 2: 79; April 9, 1876.

3. Ibid.

4. *DVS*, 2: 333.

5. Ibid., 334.

6. Ibid., 335.

7. Ibid.

8. Ibid., 337.

9. Ibid., 336.

10. Ibid., 228.

11. Ibid., 138.

12. Ibid.

13. Ibid., 340.

14. Ibid., 343.

15. Ibid., 344.

16. Ibid., 345.

17. For a very well-informed discussion of suicide in Russia, see Irina Pa-

perno, *Suicide as a Cultural Institution in Dostoevsky's Russia* (Ithaca, 1997).

18. *DVS*, 2: 345.

19. *PSS*, 29/Bk. 2: 81; April 16, 1876.

20. Ibid., 89–92; July 7/19, 1876.

21. Ibid., 93; July 9/21, 1876.

22. Ibid.

23. Ibid., 95–98; July 13/25, 1876.

24. Ibid.

25. Anna Dostoevsky, *Reminiscences*, trans. and ed. Beatrice Stillman (New York, 1973), 264.

26. *PSS*, 29/Bk. 2: 105; July 18/30.

27. See the discussion of Eliseev in James H. Billington, *Mikhailovsky and Russian Populism* (Oxford, 1958), 46–49 and passim.

28. *PSS*, 29/Bk. 2: 104; July 21/August 2, 1876.

29. Ibid., 117; July 30/August 11, 1876.

30. Ibid., 119–120; August 2/14, 1876.

31. Ibid., 99–100; July 15/27, 1876.

32. Ibid., 104, 106; July 18/30, 1876.

33. Ibid., 101–103; July 16/28, 1876.

34. Ibid.

35. Ibid., 103.

36. Ibid., 114; July 24/August 5, 1876.

37. Ibid., 118; August 2/14, 1876.

38. *DVS*, 2: 346.

39. *PSS*, 29/Bk. 2: 271; November 13, 1876.

40. Ibid., 132–133; November 16, 1876.

## CHAPTER 13

1. Cited in *Letopis Zhizni i Tvorchestvo F. M. Dostoevskyskogo*, ed. N. F. Budanova and G. M. Fridlender, 3 vols. (St. Petersburg, 1995), 3: 187.

2. For more details, see my *Dostoevsky: The Seeds of Revolt, 1821–1849* (Princeton, 1976), 137–139.

3. *Literaturnoe Nasledstvo*, vol. 83 (Moscow, 1971), 409.

4. *PSS*, 29/Bk. 2: 80; April 15, 1876.

5. Ibid., 29/Bk. 2: 135; January 13, 1877.

6. *PSS*, 27: 120–121.

7. Ibid.

8. *PSS*, 29/Bk. 2: 143–145; March 7, 1877.

9. *DVS*, 2: 377.

10. Ibid.

11. *PSS*, 29/Bk. 2: 153–154; April 21, 1877.

12. Ibid., 156–157; May 19, 1877.

13. Ibid., 152–153; April 20, 1877.

14. Anna Dostoevsky, *Reminiscences*, trans. and ed. Beatrice Stillman (New York, 1973), 282.

15. *PSS*, 29/Bk. 2: 155–156; May 15, 1877.

16. Ibid.; see also ibid., 291.

17. Anna Dostoevsky, *Reminiscences*, 283.

18. *PSS*, 29/Bk. 2: 161–162; July 7, 1877.

19. Ibid., 163.

20. Ibid.

21. Ibid., 170–173; July 17, 1877.

22. Ibid., 171.

23. Anna Dostoevsky, *Reminiscences*, 284.

24. *PSS*, 29/Bk. 2: 176; November 28, 1877.

25. Ibid., 176–177; December 7, 1877.

26. Ibid., 178–179; December 17, 1877.

27. Ibid.

28. Ibid., 175; November 18, 1877.

29. Anna Dostoevsky, *Reminiscences*, 287–288.

30. Ibid., 288.

31. *PSS*, 26: 416.

32. Ibid.

33. See Franco Venturi, *The Roots of Revolution*, trans. Francis Haskell (New York, 1966), 586.

34. Quoted in ibid.

35. D. N. Ovsyaniko-Kulikovsky, "Istoria Russkoi Intelligentsia," in *Sobranie Sochinenii*, 10 vols. (St. Petersburg, 1910–1911), vol. 8, part 2: 193–194.

36. Quoted in V. Bogucharskii, *Aktivnoe Narodnichestvo Semidesyatikh Godov* (Moscow, 1912), 298.

37. Ibid., 301.

## CHAPTER 14

1. *PSS*, 22: 279–280.

2. Quoted in I. L. Volgin, *Dostoevskii Zhurnalist* (Moscow, 1982), 45–46.

3. Ibid., 17.

4. D. N. Ovsyaniko-Kulikovsky, "Istoria Russkoi Intelligentsia," in *Sobranie Sochinenii*, 10 vols. (St. Petersburg, 1910–1911), vol. 8, Part 2: 205.

5. Josef Bohatec, *Der Imperialism-usgedanke und die Lebensphilosophis Dostojewskijs* (Graz, 1951).

6. Fyodor Dostoevsky, *A Writer's Diary*, trans. Kenneth Lantz (Evanston, Ill., 1993), 31. The quotation is taken from

Gary Saul Morson's penetrating introduction, a small treatise in itself.

7. *PSS*, 29/Bk. 1: 137–138; August 17/29, 1870.

8. *PSS*, 28/Bk. 2: 281; March 21–22/April 2–3, 1868.

## CHAPTER 15

1. *PSS*, 29/Bk. 2: 84–86; June 7, 1876.

2. Ibid.

## CHAPTER 16

1. N. V. Gogol, *Polnoe Sobranie Sochinenii*, 14 vols. (Moscow, 1940–1952), 2: 130.

2. David Goldstein, *Dostoevsky and the Jews* (Austin, 1981), 21.

3. Felix Philipp Ingold, *Dostojewski und das Judentum* (Frankfurt am Main, 1982), 57.

4. See Goldstein, *Dostoevsky and the Jews*, 39–40; also V. S. Nechaeva, *Zhurnal M. M. i F. M. Dostoevskikh, "Vremya," 1861–1863* (Moscow, 1973), 29.

5. See the analysis of Lyamshin in Goldstein, *Dostoyevsky and the Jews*, 67–85.

6. *PSS*, 29/Bk. 2: 139; February 14, 1877.

7. Leonid Grossman, *Confession of a Jew*, trans. Roanne Moab (New York, 1975), 76. This is the English version of the main work devoted to Arkady Kovner: Leonid Grossman, *Ispoved odnogo evreya* (Moscow-Leningrad, 1924). For a more recent discussion of Kovner, see Irina Paperno, *Suicide as a Cultural Institution in Dostoevsky's Russia* (Ithaca, 1997), chap. 5.

8. Grossman, *Confession of a Jew*, 76.

9. Ibid., 59.

10. *PSS*, 29/Bk. 2: 139; February 14, 1877.

11. Grossman, *Confession of a Jew*, 81.

12. *PSS*, 29/Bk. 2: 139; February 14, 1877.

13. Ibid., 140.

14. Ibid., 139.

15. Grossman, *Confession of a Jew*, 78.

16. *PSS*, 29/Bk. 2: 139; February 14, 1877.

17. Grossman, *Confession of a Jew*, 85.

18. *PSS*, 29/Bk. 2: 279–280. The second letter of Kovner is published in the commentary to Dostoevsky's reply in *PSS*.

19. Grossman, *Confession of a Jew*, 82.

20. Ibid.

21. Ibid. 84.

22. *PSS*, 29/Bk. 2: 140; February 14, 1877.

23. Simon Dubnow, *History of the Jews in Russia and Poland*, 3 vols. (Philadelphia, 1918), 3: 188.

24. Goldstein, *Dostoevsky and the Jews*, 96–97.

25. *PSS*, 29/Bk. 2: 140; February 14, 1877.

26. Ibid., 280; January 28, 1877.

27. *PSS*, 28/Bk. 1: 176; January–February 20, 1854.

28. *PSS*, 29/Bk. 2: 141; February 14, 1877.

29. Leonid Grossman, *Beichte eines Juden*, ed. René Fulop-Miller and Friedrich Eckstein (Munich, 1927), 122–132. I cite the German translation of Grossman's book because it contains letters not in the original edition.

30. Ibid.

31. *PSS*, 29/Bk. 2: 147; March 11, 1877.

32. Goldstein, *Dostoevsky and the Jews*, 139–140.

33. Grossman, *Beichte eines Juden*, 161–162.

## CHAPTER 17

1. I. S. Turgenev, *Sobranie Sochinenii*, 12 vols. (Moscow, 1954–1958), 4: 393.

2. Mikhail Bakhtin, *Problems of Dostoevsky's Poetics*, trans. Caryl Emerson (Minneapolis, 1984), 238.

3. Cited in James H. Billington, *Mikhailovsky and Russian Populism* (Oxford, 1958), 70.

## Chapter 18

1. *PSS*, 24: 390.
2. Ibid., 29/Bk. 2: 72; January, 11, 1876.
3. G. M. Fridlender, *Realizm Dostoevskogo* (Moscow-Leningrad, 1964), 290–308.
4. For more on this point, see my *Dostoevsky: The Years of Ordeal, 1850–1859* (Princeton, 1983), chaps. 6–11.

5. Ibid., 58.
6. See N. I. Prutskov, "Utopia ili anti-utopia," in *Dostoevskii i Ego Vremya* (Leningrad, 1971), 352. This is an excellent essay on the question raised in the title.

## Chapter 19

1. *Letopis Zhizhni i Tvorchestvo F. M. Dostoevskogo*, ed. N. F. Budanova and G. M. Fridlender, 3 vols. (St. Petersburg, 1995), 3: 250.
2. Anna Dostoevsky, *Reminiscences*, trans. and ed. Beatrice Stillman (New York, 1973), 296.
3. Ibid., 297.
4. *PSS*, 30/Bk. 1: 26–27; April 2/14, 1878.
5. For more information, see my *Dostoevsky: The Miraculous Years, 1865–1871* (Princeton, 1995), 13–24.
6. I. S. Knizhnik-Vetrov, *Russkie Deyatelnitsi Pervogo Internatsionala i Parizhkoi Kommuni* (Leningrad, 1964), 185–190.
7. *PSS*, 30/Bk. 1: 11; March 16, 1878.
8. Ibid., 29/Bk. 2: 177; December 17, 1877.
9. Ibid., 30/Bk. 1: 9–10; February 28, 1878.
10. Anna Dostoevsky, *Reminiscences*, 301–302.
11. Ibid.
12. *PSS*, 30/Bk. 1: 16–18; March 27, 1878.
13. Ibid., 19; March 27, 1878. See also ibid., 270.
14. *PSS*, 30/Bk. 1: 8–9; February 28, 1878.
15. Ibid.
16. Ibid., 10–11; February 1878.
17. Ibid.
18. Ibid. 25–26; April 24, 1878. The letter and information about Voevodin comes

from N. I. Galitskii, *Na beregakh Nevi* (St. Petersburg, 1901).
19. An introduction to Feodorov's thought can be found in George M. Young Jr., *Nikolai Feodorov* (Belmont, Mass., 1979).
20. *PSS*, 30/Bk. 1: 13–15; March 24, 1878.
21. See my *Dostoevsky: The Stir of Liberation, 1860–1865* (Princeton, 1986), chap. 20.
22. *PSS*, 30/Bk. 1: 13–15; March 24, 1878.
23. Ibid.
24. Anna Dostoevsky, *Reminiscences*, 297.
25. Ibid., 325.
26. *PSS*, 30/Bk. 1: 20; April 16, 1878. See also ibid., 271.
27. Ibid., 16; March 27, 1878.
28. Ibid., 28–30; May 6, 1878.
29. Ibid.
30. Ibid., 38–40; July 14, 1878.
31. Quoted in Samuel Kucherov, *Courts, Lawyers, and Trials under the Last Three Tsars* (New York, 1953), 217.
32. G. K. Gradovsky, *Itogi, 1862–1907* (Kiev, 1908).
33. *Literaturnoe Nasledtsvo*, 83 (Moscow, 1971), 676.
34. See *Letopis*, 3: 262; also *PSS*, 27: 341.
35. *PSS*, 30/Bk. 1: 42–44; August 29, 1878.

## Chapter 20

1. *Letopis Zhizhni i Tvorchestvo F. M. Dostoevskogo*, ed. N. F. Budanova and G. M. Fridlender, 3 vols. (St. Petersburg, 1995), 3: 243, 247.
2. *PSS*, 30/Bk. 1: 21–25; April 18, 1878.
3. Ibid.
4. Ibid.

5. Ibid.
6. Ibid., 40–41; July 21, 1878.
7. Ibid.
8. Ibid.
9. Anna Dostoevsky, *Reminiscences*, trans. and ed. Beatrice Stillman (New York, 1973), 297–298.

10. Quoted in ibid., 298.

11. *Literaturnoe Nasledtsvo*, 86 (Moscow, 1973), 135.

12. Anna Dostoevsky, *Reminiscences*, 292.

13. *Letopis*, 3: 273.

14. Anna Dostoevsky, *Reminiscences*, 292.

15. *PSS*, 30/Bk. 1: 31; May 16, 1878.

16. Anna Dostoevsky, *Reminiscences*, 293.

17. *Letopis*, 3: 275–276.

18. *PSS*, 30/Bk. 1: 32; June 20, 1878.

19. Ibid., 34–35; June 22, 1878.

20. Ibid., 35–36; June 29, 1878.

21. Anna Dostoevsky, *Reminiscences*, 294.

22. Cited in John B. Dunlop, *Staretz Amvrosy* (Belmont, Mass., 1972), 60–61.

23. *Letopis*, 3: 279.

24. Ibid.

25. Anna Dostoevsky, *Reminiscences*, 293.

26. Ibid., 291–292.

27. V. S. Solovyev, *Sobranie Sochinenii*, 10 vols. (St. Petersburg, 1911–1914), 3: 197.

28. *Letopis*, 3: 301.

29. See Vladimir Solovyev, *Chtenia o Bogochelovechestve* (St. Petersburg, 1994), 195–196.

## CHAPTER 21

1. *PSS*, 30/Bk. 1: 11–12; March 16, 1878.

2. Ibid.

3. *The Notebooks for "The Brothers Karamazov,"* ed. and trans. Edward Wasiolek (Chicago, 1971), 12–13.

4. *PSS*, 15: 605.

5. *PSS*, 28/Bk. 2: 329; December 11/23, 1868.

6. *PSS*, 29/Bk. 1: 118; March 25/April 6, 1870. For more about Saint Tikhon, see my *Dostoevsky: The Miraculous Years, 1865–1871* (Princeton, 1995), 376–381; also, Nadejda Gorodetzky, *St. Tikhon Zadonsky* (London, 1951).

7. Commentators have noticed many other anticipations and parallels from earlier works integrated into *The Brothers Karamazov*, as well as motifs from the *Diary of a Writer*. For more details, see the commentary in *PSS*, 15: 401–410.

8. For a classic study of the influence of Schiller, particularly on *The Brothers Karamazov*, see Dimitry Tschizhevskii, "Schiller und *Die Bruder Karamazov*," *Zeitschrift für slavische Philologie*, 4 (1929), 1–42.

9. *PSS*, 30/Bk. 1: 212; August 18, 1880.

10. Friedrich Schiller, *Samtliche Werke*, 16 vols. (Stuttgart and Berlin, n.d.), 3: 15.

11. Ibid., 16.

12. Anna Dostoevsky, *Reminiscences*, trans. and ed. Beatrice Stillman (New York, 1973), 135.

13. V. L. Komarovich, "Dostojewski und George Sand," in *Die Urgestalt des Bruder Karamasoff* (Munich, 1928), 167–235. Incidentally, Freud's famous article on "Dostoevsky and Parricide" was written as an introduction to this volume.

14. Ibid., 214–219.

15. See the excellent book of Isabelle Hoog Naginski, *George Sand* (New Brunswick, 1991), 260. An appreciative discussion of the little-known *Spiridion* is contained in chap. 6.

16. Ibid., 146.

17. Quoted in ibid., 149–150.

18. Ibid., 150, 143.

19. *PSS*, 30/Bk. 1: 35; April 22, 1878.

20. *F. M. Dostoevskii v zabitikh i neizvestnikh vospominaniyakh sovremennikov*, ed. S. V. Belov (St. Petersburg, 1993), 241–242. This is a very useful collection of lesser-known memoir literature about Dostoevsky.

21. Ibid., 243, 241.

22. Anna Dostoevsky, *Reminiscences*, 294.

23. *PSS*, 30/Bk. 1: 28; July 11, 1878.

24. Ibid., 45–46; November 7, 1878.

25. Ibid., 46–47; November 8, 1878.

26. Ibid.

27. Ibid., 48–49; November 9, 1878.

28. Ibid.

29. Ibid.

30. Ibid., 51–52; November 11, 1878.

31. Ibid., 52; November 26, 1878.

## CHAPTER 22

1. *Letopis Zhizhni i Tvorchestvo F. M. Dostoevskogo*, ed. N. F. Budanova and G. M. Fridlender, 3 vols. (St. Petersburg, 1995), 3: 299.

2. *PSS*, 30/Bk. 1: 54–55; January 30, 1879.
3. Ibid.
4. *DVS*, 2: 444–445.
5. Ibid.
6. Ibid., 445.
7. Ibid., 446.
8. Ibid., 448.
9. Ibid.
10. Ibid.
11. Anna Dostoevsky, *Reminiscences*, trans. and ed. Beatrice Stillman (New York, 1973), 303.
12. This incident is described in a little-known memoir published in *F.M. Dostoevskii v zabitikh i neizvestnikh vospominaniyakh sovremennikov*, ed. S. V. Belov (St. Petersburg, 1993), 236–238.
13. Ibid.
14. *Letopis*, 3: 303–305, 306.
15. *PSS*, 30/Bk. 1: 247.
16. *DVS*, 2: 378.
17. Ibid., 377.
18. Ibid., 553.
19. Ibid., 377–378.
20. *Letopis*, 3: 306.
21. I. Volgin, *Poslednie God Dostoevskogo* (Moscow, 1986), 67.
22. *DVS*, 2: 178.
23. Ibid., 192–193.
24. Ibid., 193.
25. Cited in Volgin, *Poslednie God*, 72.

26. *DVS*, 2: 378.
27. Cited in Volgin, *Poslednie God*, 74–75.
28. *PSS*, 25: 60.
29. Reports of this incident come from Volgin, *Poslednie God*, 75–76; also, *Letopis*, 3: 308.
30. Volgin, *Poslednie God*, 242.
31. Ibid., 243–244.
32. Ibid.
33. Ibid.
34. *PSS*, 30/Bk. 1: 289.
35. Ibid., 57; March 15, 1879.
36. Vengerov is quoted in *Literaturnoe Nasledtsvo*, 86 (Moscow, 1973), 478.
37. E. M. de Vogüé, *Le Roman russe* (Paris, 1910), 269.
38. Ibid., 270.
39. Ibid., 270–271.
40. *PSS*, 30/Bk. 1: 57; March 12, 1879.
41. *Letopis*, 3: 309.
42. *PSS*, 30/Bk. 1: 59; March 28, 1879.
43. Franco Venturi, *Roots of Revolution*, trans. Francis Haskell (New York, 1966), 633.
44. *DVS*, 2: 380.
45. *Letopis*, 3: 312.
46. Anna Dostoevsky, *Reminiscences*, 304.
47. *Letopis*, 3: 313–314.
48. Ibid., 314.

## CHAPTER 23

1. *PSS*, 30/Bk. 1: 60; April 30, 1879.
2. Ibid., 61–62; May 3, 1879.
3. Ibid.
4. Ibid., 63; May 10, 1879.
5. Ibid.
6. Ibid., 64.
7. *PSS*, 29/Bk. 2: 43; June 10/22, 1875.
8. *PSS*, 30/Bk. 1: 66; May 19, 1879.
9. Ibid., 67.
10. Ibid.
11. This hitherto unknown letter, first published in 1990, is included in the volumes of the Academy of Sciences edition of the correspodence only as an addendum. See *PSS*, 30/Bk. 2: 45–46.
12. Ibid.
13. Ibid.
14. Ibid.
15. *Literaturnoe Nasledstvo*, 15 (Moscow, 1934), 138.
16. *PSS*, 30/Bk. 1: 68; June 11, 1879.
17. Ibid.

18. Ibid., 70; June 11, 1879.
19. *The Notebooks for "The Brothers Karamazov*,*"* ed. and trans. Edward Wasiolek (Chicago, 1971), 63.
20. Friedrich Schiller, *Samtliche Werke*, 16 vols. (Stuttgart and Berlin, n.d.), 4: 161.
21. For a survery of the scholarship on this motif, see *PSS*, 15: 463–465; also Ernst Benz, "Der wiederkehrende Christus," *Zeitschrift für Religions und Geistesgeschichte* 6 (1954), 305–323.
22. *Letopis Zhizhni i Tvorchestvo F. M. Dostoevskogo*, ed. N. F. Budanova and G. M. Fridlender, 3 vols. (St. Petersburg, 1995), 3: 332.
23. V. G. Belinsky, *Selected Philosophical Works* (Moscow, 1948), 478.
24. *PSS*, 30/Bk. 1: 72; June 15, 1879.
25. Ibid.
26. Ibid., 198, 297–299.
27. Ibid., 72; June 15, 1879.
28. Ibid., 72–73.

29. Ibid, 74–75; beginning of July 1879.
30. Anna Dostoevsky, *Reminiscences,* trans. and ed. Beatrice Stillman (New York, 1973), 305.
31. *PSS,* 30/Bk. 1: 77–79; July 11, 1879.
32. Ibid., 301.
33. Ibid., 77–79; July 11, 1879.
34. Ibid.
35. Ibid., 75–77; July 8, 1879.
36. Ibid.
37. Ibid.

## Chapter 24

1. *PSS,* 30/Bk. 1: 79–80; July 19, 1879.
2. Ibid., 81; July 22/August 3, 1879.
3. Ibid.
4. Ibid., 83–84; July 24/August 5, 1879.
5. Ibid.
6. Ibid., 85–87; July 25/August 6, 1879.
7. Ibid.
8. Ibid., 89; July 28/August 9, 1879.
9. Ibid., 93; July 30/August 11, 1879.
10. Ibid., 91; July 28/August 9, 1879.
11. Ibid., 90–91; July 28/August 9, 1879.
12. Ibid., 104–105; August 9/21, 1879.
13. Ibid., 112–113; August 14/26, 1879.
14. Ibid., 117–119; August 23/September 1, 1879.
15. Ibid., 120–122; August 24/September 5, 1879.
16. Ibid.
17. Ibid., 92; July 30/August 11, 1879.
18. Ibid., 97; August 4/16, 1879.
19. Ibid., 124; August 27[25]/September 6, 1879.
20. Ibid., 101, 100; August 7/19, 1879.
21. Ibid., 96–98; August 4/16, 1879.
22. Ibid., 114–115; August 16/28, 1879.
23. Ibid., 86; July 25/August 6, 1879.
24. Ibid., 101–102; August 7/19, 1879.
25. Ibid., 110; August 13/25, 1879.
26. Ibid., 109.
27. Ibid., 94; August 1/13, 1879.
28. Ibid., 87; July 25/August 6, 1879.
29. Ibid., 116; August 19/31, 1879.
30. Ibid., 120; August 24/September 5, 1879.
31. Ibid., 95; August 1/13, 1879.
32. Ibid., 99; August 7/19, 1879.
33. Ibid., 102–103; August 7/19, 1879.
34. Ibid.
35. *Die Urgestalt der Bruder Karamasoff,* ed. V. L. Komarovich (Munich, 1928), 127–128.
36. Ibid.
37. *PSS,* 29/Bk. 1: 118; March 25/April 6, 1870.
38. Georgii Florovsky, *Puti Russkogo Bogosloviya* (Paris, 1983), 123–125.
39. Quoted in Komarovich, *Die Urgestalt,* 78.
40. Quoted in ibid., 111.
41. Ibid., 107.
42. Quoted in ibid., 108.
43. Quoted in ibid., 114.
44. *PSS,* 29/Bk. 1: 118; March 25/April 6, 1870.
45. Komarovich, *Die Urgestalt,* 93–95.
46. Ibid., 91.
47. *PSS,* 30/Bk. 1: 100; August 7/19, 1879.
48. Ibid., 105; August 9/21, 1879.
49. *Literaturnoe Nasledtsvo,* 15 (Moscow, 1934), 139.
50. *PSS,* 30/Bk. 1: 121–122; August 24/September 5, 1879.
51. Ibid.
52. See the commentary to note 6 in *PSS,* 30/Bk. 1: 315.
53. Ibid., 114; August 14/26, 1879.
54. Ibid., 117; August 23/September 4, 1879.

## Chapter 25

1. *PSS,* 30/Bk. 1: 125; September 8, 1879.
2. Ibid., 125–126; September 16, 1879.
3. Ibid.
4. Ibid.
5. Ibid., 127; October 8, 1879.
6. Ibid., 129; November 8, 1879.
7. Ibid.
8. Anna Dostoevsky, *Reminiscences,* trans. and ed. Beatrice Stillman (New York, 1973), 326.
9. From *F. M. Dostoevskii v zabitikh i neizvestnikh vospominaniyakh sovremennikov,* ed. S. V. Belov (St. Petersburg, 1993), 250–251.
10. Ibid.
11. M. E. Saltykov-Shchedrin, *Sobranie*

*Sochinenii*, 20 vols. (Moscow, 1972), 13: 774, 779.

12. *PSS*, 30/Bk. 1: 130; November 16, 1879.

13. Anna Dostoevsky, *Reminiscences*, 325; *PSS*, 30/Bk. 1: 199; July 17, 1880.

14. *PSS*, 30/Bk. 1: 130; November 16, 1879.

15. Ibid.

16. Ibid., 131–132.

17. Ibid., 132; December 8, 1879.

18. Ibid., 134; December 12, 1879.

19. Ibid., 135; December 12, 1879.

20. *Letopis Zhizhni i Tvorchestvo F. M. Dostoevskogo*, ed. N. F. Budanova and G. M. Fridlender, 3 vols. (St. Petersburg, 1995), 3: 357.

21. *PSS*, 30/Bk. 1: 136; December 21, 1879.

22. Ibid., 135–136; December 17, 1879.

See the commentary to this letter for Samoylov's note.

23. *Letopis*, 3: 360.

24. *PSS*, 15: 198.

25. *PSS*, 30/Bk. 1: 143; March 21, 1880.

26. Anna Dostoevsky, *Reminiscences*, 311–312.

27. *DVS*, 2: 381–382.

28. Ibid.

29. Ibid., 383–384.

30. Ibid.

31. Ibid., 387.

32. Ibid.

33. Ibid., 387–388.

34. Ibid.

35. Ibid., 359.

36. Anna Dostoevsky, *Reminiscences*, 324.

37. *Letopis*, 3: 363.

## CHAPTER 26

1. Anna Dostoevsky, *Reminiscences*, trans. and ed. Beatrice Stillman (New York, 1973), 321.

2. *PSS*, 30/Bk. 1: 137; December 27, 1879.

3. Ibid., 139; January 9, 1880.

4. Ibid., 138–139; January 8, 1880.

5. Quoted in Igor Volgin, *Poslednie God Dostoevskogo* (Moscow, 1986), 108.

6. *PSS*, 30/Bk. 1: 139–140; January 15, 1880.

7. Ibid., 141; January 21, 1880.

8. Ibid. See also ibid., 323.

9. Ibid., 141.

10. Quoted in P. Zaionchkovskii, *Krisis Samoderzhaviya na rubezhe 1870–1880-x godov* (Moscow, 1964), 148.

11. Quoted in Franco Venturi, *Roots of Revolution*, trans. Francis Haskell (New York, 1966), 633.

12. *Letopis Zhizhni i Tvorchestvo F. M. Dostoevskogo*, ed. N. F. Budanova and G. M. Fridlender, 3 vols. (St. Petersburg, 1995), 3: 378.

13. Ibid., 379.

14. Ibid.

15. The text of this address can be found in *PSS*, 30/Bk. 2: 47–48.

16. Orest Miller and N. N. Strakhov, *Biografia, Pisma, iz Zapisnoi Knizhki* (St. Petersburg, 1883), 366; cited in Volgin, *Poslednie God*, 84.

17. *Letopis*, 3: 381.

18. Ibid.

19. Ibid., 3: 381–382.

20. Ibid.

21. Cited from the *Diary* of A. S. Suvorin in Volgin, *Poslednie God*, 141.

22. *Letopis*, 3: 383.

23. Ibid., 384.

24. *Literaturnoe Nasledtsvo*, 86 (Moscow, 1973), 496.

25. Ibid.

26. *Letopis*, 3: 384.

27. Ibid., 384–385.

28. Ibid., 385–386.

29. *PSS*, 30/Bk. 1: 147–149; April 11, 1880.

30. Ibid.

31. Ibid.

32. *Literaturnoe Nasledtsvo*, 86 (Moscow, 1973), 318.

33. *Letopis*, 3: 393.

34. Ibid.

35. *PSS*, 30/Bk. 1: 146–147, 149–150; April 9 and 13, 1880.

36. *PSS*, 30/Bk. 1: 335.

37. Ibid.

38. See my *Dostoevsky: The Seeds of Revolt, 1821–1849* (Princeton, 1976), chap. 12.

39. *PSS*, 30/Bk. 1: 155; May 14, 1880.

40. Anna Dostoevsky, *Reminiscences*, 330.

41. *PSS*, 27: 198.

42. *DVS*, 2: 309.

43. *PSS*, 30/Bk. 1: 147; April 9, 1880.

44. *Letopis*, 3: 402.

45. *PSS*, 30/Bk. 1: 151–152; April 29, 1880.

46. Ibid.

47. *Letopis*, 2: 409.

48. *Literaturnoe Nasledtsvo*, 86 (Moscow, 1973), 509.

49. *PSS*, 30/Bk. 1: 153–154; May 5, 1880.

50. *Literaturnoe Nasledtsvo*, 86 (Moscow, 1973), 137.

51. Cited in *Letopis*, 3: 411.

## CHAPTER 27

1. *PSS*, 26: 442.

2. Ibid., 30/Bk. 1: 153–154; May 5, 1880.

3. Ibid., 155; May 14, 1880.

4. Ibid., 155–156; May 19, 1880.

5. Ibid.

6. Cited in Marcus C. Levitt, *Russian Literary Politics and the Pushkin Celebration of 1880* (Ithaca, 1989), 62. My account of the Pushkin celebration is greatly indebted to this excellent book.

7. Anna Dostoevsky, *Reminiscences*, trans. and ed. Beatrice Stillman (New York, 1973), 329.

8. *PSS*, 30/Bk. 1: 157–158; May 23/24, 1880.

9. Ibid.

10. Ibid., 158–159; May 25, 1880.

11. Ibid., 160–161; May 26, 1880.

12. Ibid.

13. Ibid., 163; May 25, 1880.

14. Ibid.

15. Ibid., 165; May 27, 1880.

16. Ibid., 168; May 27/28, 1880.

17. Ibid., 165; May 27, 1880.

18. The quotations are from Levitt, *Russian Literary Politics*, 101.

19. *PSS*, 30/Bk. 1: 168; May 27/28, 1880.

20. Ibid., 169; May 28/29, 1880.

21. Ibid., 168; May 27/28, 1880.

22. Ibid., 169–171; May 28/29, 1880.

23. Ibid., 171; May 30/31, 1880.

24. Ibid., 173–174; May 31, 1880.

25. Ibid., 175–176; June 2/3, 1880.

26. Ibid., 179; June 3/4, 1880.

27. Ibid., 177.

28. *Letopis Zhizhni i Tvorchestvo F. M. Dostoevskogo*, ed. N. F. Budanova and G. M. Fridlender, 3 vols. (St. Petersburg, 1995), 3: 423.

29. *PSS*, 30/Bk. 1: 177–179; June 3/4, 1880.

30. Ibid.

31. *DVS*, 2: 396.

32. *PSS*, 30/Bk. 1: 180; June 5, 1880.

33. Ibid., 181.

34. Ibid., 182; June 7, 1880.

35. *Letopis*, 2: 428.

36. Levitt, *Russian Literary Politics*, 83–85.

37. Ibid., 85.

38. *PSS*, 30/Bk. 1: 183; June 7, 1880.

39. Cited in Levitt, *Russian Literary Politics*, 86.

40. *Letopis*, 2: 429.

41. *PSS*, 30/Bk. 1: 182; June 7, 1880.

42. Ibid., 354.

43. Ibid., 182; June 7, 1880.

## CHAPTER 28

1. I. S. Turgenev, *Polnoe Sobranie Sochinenii i Pisem*, 28 vols. (Moscow-Leningrad, 1968), 15: 66.

2. Ibid., 68.

3. Ibid., 69.

4. Ibid., 69–70.

5. Ibid., 70.

6. Ibid., 71.

7. Ibid., 72.

8. Ibid., 73–74.

9. Ibid.

10. *PSS*, 30/Bk. 1: 182; June 7, 1880.

11. Quoted in Turgenev, *Polnoe Sobranie Sochinenii i Pisem*, 15: 827.

12. Ibid.

13. *PSS*, 30/Bk. 1: 183; June 7, 1880. See also ibid., 354.

14. *Letopis Zhizhni i Tvorchestvo F. M. Dostoevskogo*, ed. N. F. Budanova and G. M. Fridlender, 3 vols. (St. Petersburg, 1995), 3: 430.

15. Ibid. The author of this column, published under the pseudonym "Z," has never been identified. One can assume from the date of its publication that the writer was one of the correspondents covering the Pushkin festival.

16. *PSS*, 30/Bk. 1: 183; June 7, 1880.

17. Marcus C. Levitt, *Russian Literary Politics and the Pushkin Celebration of 1880* (Ithaca, 1989), 122.

18. *PSS*, 30/Bk. 1: 184; June 8, 1880.

19. *DVS*, 2: 398.

20. *PSS*, 28/Bk. 1: 169; January 30/February 22, 1854.

21. *DVS*, 2: 418.

22. *PSS*, 30/Bk. 1: 184–185; June 8, 1880.
23. *DVS*, 2: 453.
24. *PSS*, 26: 461.
25. *PSS*, 30/Bk. 1: 185; June 8, 1880.
26. Ibid.
27. Ibid., 358.
28. Ibid.
29. Anna Dostoevsky, *Reminiscences*, trans. and ed. Beatrice Stillman (New York, 1973), 235.
30. *PSS*, 30/Bk. 1: 185; June 8, 1880.

31. *Letopis*, 3: 433.
32. Quoted in Igor Volgin, *Posledni God Dostoevskogo* (Moscow, 1986), 300–301.
33. Turgenev, *Polnoe Sobranie Sochinenii i Pisem*, 12/Bk. 2: 272.
34. *DVS*, 2: 569.
35. Ibid., 433.
36. Ibid., 436–437.
37. Ibid., 437–438.
38. *PSS*, 30/Bk. 1: 186; June 10, 1880.

CHAPTER 29

1. *PSS*, 30/Bk. 1: 186–187; June 12, 1880.
2. Ibid., 187–188; June 13, 1880.
3. Ibid.
4. Ibid., 188–189.
5. Ibid., 189–190; June 13, 1880.
6. Ibid., 190–191; June 14, 1880.
7. The memoir of Tretyakova is cited in the commentary to Dostoevsky's letter to her, ibid., 190–191; June 14, 1880. See also ibid., 360.
8. Ibid., 191; June 15, 1880.
9. Ibid., 192.

10. Ibid.
11. Ibid.
12. Ibid., 194–195; June 20, 1880.
13. Ibid., 195–196; June 20, 1880.
14. Ibid., 196–197; July 6, 1880.
15. Ibid., 197–198; July 17, 1880.
16. Ibid.
17. The citations from Gradovsky's article are taken from the commentary in *PSS*, 26: 476–478.
18. Ibid.
19. Ibid.

CHAPTER 30

1. *Letopis Zhizhni i Tvorchestvo F. M. Dostoevskogo*, ed. N. F. Budanova and G. M. Fridlender, 3 vols. (St. Petersburg, 1995), 2: 449.
2. *PSS*, 26: 487.
3. Ibid., 30/Bk. 1: 199–200; July 18, 1880.
4. Ibid., 202–203; July 25, 1880.
5. *Literaturnoe Nasledtsvo*, 15 (Moscow, 1934), 145.
6. Ibid., 146.
7. For a brief but cogent introduction to Leontiyev's ideas, see Andrzej Walicki, *A History of Russian Thought from the Enlightenment to Marxism*, trans. Hilda Andrews-Rusiecka (Stanford, 1979), 300–308.
8. Konstantin Leontiyev, *Sobranie Sochinenii*, 9 vols. (St. Petersburg, 1912), 8: 188–189, 199.
9. Ibid., 203, 207.
10. *PSS*, 30/Bk. 1: 210; August 16, 1880.
11. Ibid., 209.
12. Ibid., 205; August 10, 1880.
13. Ibid.
14. Ibid., 205; August 10, 1880.

15. Ibid., 207; August 12, 1880.
16. Ibid., 206–207; August 11, 1880.
17. Ibid., 209–210; August 16, 1880.
18. Ibid., 210–211; August 16, 1880.
19. Ibid., 211–212; August 18, 1880.
20. Ibid.
21. Ibid., 213; August 26, 1880.
22. Ibid., 213–214; August 28, 1880.
23. Ibid., 215; September 8, 1880.
24. Ibid., 216–218; October 15, 1880.
25. Ibid.
26. *DVS*, 2: 360.
27. Ibid.
28. *PSS*, 28/Bk. 1: 139; January/February 1847.
29. See my *Dostoevsky: The Miraculous Years, 1865–1871* (Princeton, 1995), 354–355.
30. *DVS*, 2: 361.
31. *PSS*, 30/Bk. 1: 218–219; October 16, 1880.
32. *DVS*, 2: 363.
33. Ibid.
34. *Letopis*, 3: 478.
35. Ibid., 493.

36. *DVS*, 2: 378.

37. *PSS*, 30/Bk. 1: 225–227; November 4, 1880.

38. *Letopis*, 3: 495.

39. *PSS*, 30/Bk. 1: 227–228; November 8, 1880.

## CHAPTER 31

1. For an impressive "poetic" reading of the novel, which tries to do justice to this dense web of references, parallels, and figural anticipations, see Diane O. Thompson, *The Brothers Karamazov and the Poetics of Memory* (Cambridge, 1991).

2. E. M. Forster, *Aspects of the Novel* (New York, 1954), 192.

3. V. E. Vetlovskaya, *Poetika Romana "Bratya Karamazovi"* (Leningrad, 1977), chap. 1.

4. Ibid.

5. Robin Feuer Miller, *The Brothers Kzaramazov* (New York, 1992), 23.

## CHAPTER 32

1. See Victor Terras, *A Karamazov Companion* (Madison, 1981), 119–120.

## CHAPTER 33

1. Vaclav Cerny, *Essai sur le titanisme dans la poésie romantique occidentale entre 1815 et 1850* (Prague, 1935).

2. Roger L. Cox, *Between Earth and Heaven* (New York, 1969), 194.

3. Victor Terras, *A Karamazov Companion* (Madison, 1981), 239.

## CHAPTER 34

1. Cited from Sven Linnér, *Starets Zosima in "The Brothers Karamazov"* (Stockholm, 1975), 120.

2. Nathan Rosen, "Style and Structure in *The Brothers Karamazov*," in the Norton Criticial Edition of *The Brothers Karamazov* (New York, 1976), 845. This is an excellent essay, which properly calls attention to Dostoevsky's important statement that the whole novel is a refutation of the Legend.

3. Ibid., 849.

4. *PSS*, 28/Bk. 1: 164; December 22, 1849.

5. Cited in *PSS*, 15: 500.

6. John Milton, *Paradise Lost*, ed. Merritt Y. Hughes (New York, 1935), 235. I am indebted to my friend and colleague Theodore Weiss for having located this passage for me.

7. Cited in *PSS*, 15: 497.

8. Sergei Hackel, "The Religious Dimension: Vision or Evasion?" in *New Essays on Dostoevsky*, ed. Malcolm V. Jones and Garth M. Terry (Cambridge, 1983), 154–156.

9. Ibid., 156–158.

## CHAPTER 35

1. Again, see Sergei Hackel, "The Religious Dimension: Vision or Evasion?" in *New Essays on Dostoevsky*, ed. Malcolm V. Jones and Garth M. Terry (Cambridge, 1983), 162–164. Hackel's essay also contains an illuminating comparison be-

tween Father Zosima and Victor Hugo's Monseigneur Bienvenu in *Les Misérables*.

2. See my *Dostoevsky: The Stir of Liberation, 1860–1865* (Princeton, 1986), 294.

## CHAPTER 36

1. Victor Terras, *A Karamazov Companion* (Madison, 1981), 290.

## CHAPTER 37

1. *PSS*, 28/Bk. 2: 297; May 18/30, 1868. See my *Dostoevsky: The Miraculous Years, 1865–1871* (Princeton, 1995), 293.

2. Victor Terras, *A Karamazov Companion* (Madison, 1981), 385.
3. Ibid., 387.

## CHAPTER 38

1. See the citation of this text in *PSS*, 15: 435.
2. W. J. Leatherbarrow, *The Brothers Karamazov* (Cambridge, 1992), 35.
3. In a carefully reasoned article, D. D. Blagoi makes a powerful case for accepting Suvorin's testimony that Alyosha might later engage in revolutionary activity. See Blagoi, "Put Alyeshi Karamazova," *Seriya Literaturi i Yazhika (Izvestiya Akademii Nauk SSSR)*, 33, no. 1 (January–February 1974), 8–26.

## CHAPTER 39

1. *DVS*, 2: 439.
2. Ibid., 441.
3. *PSS*, 30/Bk. 1: 227; November 8, 1880.
4. Cited in ibid., 384.
5. *Letopis Zhizhni i Tvorchestvo F. M. Dostoevskogo*, ed. N. F. Budanova and G. M. Fridlender, 3 vols. (St. Petersburg, 1995), 3: 502.
6. *PSS*, 30/Bk. 1: 229–230; November 28, 1880.
7. *DVS*, 2: 475.
8. *Letopis*, 3: 503.
9. *PSS*, 28/Bk. 1: 176; February 20, 1854.
10. Ibid., 30/Bk. 1: 232; December 3, 1880.
11. Ibid., 233–234.
12. Ibid., 232.

13. Ibid., 233.
14. Ibid., 234. See also ibid., 388.
15. *Letopis*, 3: 513.
16. *PSS*, 30/Bk. 1: 237–238; December 19, 1880.
17. Ibid., 390.
18. Ibid., 236–237; December 19, 1880.
19. Ibid.
20. *Letopis*, 3: 516.
21. Ibid., 519; also I. Volgin, *Poslednie God Dostoevskogo* (Moscow, 1986), 374–375.
22. The passage is cited in G. M. Fridlender, "D. S. Merezhkovii i Dostoevskii," in *Dostoevskii, Materiali i Issledovania*, vol. 10 (St. Petersburg, 1992), 4.
23. *DVS*, 2: 363–364.
23. Ibid.

## CHAPTER 40

1. *Letopis Zhizhni i Tvorchestvo F. M. Dostoevskogo*, ed. N. F. Budanova and G. M. Fridlender, 3 vols. (St. Petersburg, 1995), 3: 529.

2. Anna Dostoevsky, *Reminiscences,* trans. and ed. Beatrice Stillman (New York, 1973), 341.

3. *DVS,* 2: 195.

4. Cited in I. Volgin, *Poslednie God Dostoevskogo* (Moscow, 1986), 387.

5. *Letopis,* 3: 526–527.

6. *DVS,* 2: 469.

7. Ibid.

8. Ibid.

9. Ibid., 469–470.

10. *Letopis,* 3: 535.

11. *DVS,* 2: 469.

12. *Letopis,* 3: 536.

13. Ibid., 3: 535–536; *DVS,* 2: 473.

14. *Letopis,* 3: 534.

15. Cited in Volgin, *Poslednie God,* 395.

16. *Letopis,* 3: 537.

17. Cited in Volgin, *Poslednie God,* 412.

18. *Letopis,* 3: 539.

## CHAPTER 41

1. See my *Dostoevsky: The Years of Ordeal, 1850–1859* (Princeton, 1983), 58.

2. I. Volgin, *Poslednie God Dostoevskogo* (Moscow, 1986), 413. My chapter on Dostoevsky's last days is greatly indebted to Volgin's book.

3. Ibid., 414.

4. *PSS,* 30/Bk. 1: 241; January 26, 1881.

5. *Letopis Zhizhni i Tvorchestvo F. M. Dostoevskogo,* ed. N. F. Budanova and G. M. Fridlender, 3 vols. (St. Petersburg, 1995), 3: 541–542.

6. Volgin, *Poslednie God,* 416–418.

7. See Victor Shklovsky, *Za I Protiv* (Moscow, 1957), 254–255. Even though the official documents give the number of Barannikov's apartment as 11, Shklovsky continues to maintain that it was Dostoevsky's apartment (No. 10) that was searched and that the number was changed in the official documents. He offers no evidence to support this assertion.

8. Volgin, *Poslednie God,* 436.

9. Ibid., 444. Volgin went back to examine the manuscript of Anna's memoirs.

10. *Letopis,* 3: 543.

11. See the citations in Volgin, *Poslednie God,* 420.

12. *PSS,* 30/Bk. 1: 242–243; January 28, 1881.

13. Anna Dostoevsky, *Reminiscences,* trans. and ed. Beatrice Stillman (New York, 1973), 345–346.

14. Ibid., 346.

15. Volgin, *Poslednie God,* 422.

16. Ibid.

17. *Letopis,* 3: 545–546.

18. Anna Dostoevsky, *Reminiscences,* 348.

19. Volgin, *Poslednie God,* 429–430.

20. Ibid., 430.

21. Anna Dostoevsky, *Reminiscences,* 351.

22. *Letopis,* 3: 547–548.

23. Anna Dostoevsky, *Reminiscences,* 352.

24. Ibid.

25. *Letopis,* 3: 550.

26. Ibid., 551.

27. Ibid.

28. Ibid.

29. *DVS,* 2: 246.

30. Ibid., 2: 474.

31. Ibid., 2: 479.

32. *Letopis,* 3: 554.

33. *DVS,* 2: 480.

34. Cited in Volgin, *Poslednie God,* 495.

35. See my *Dostoevsky: The Miraculous Years, 1865–1871* (Princeton, 1995), 37–38.

36. Anna Dostoevsky, *Reminiscences,* 359.

37. *Letopis,* 3: 561.

38. *DVS,* 2: 478.

39. *Letopis,* 3: 548, 553.